Perspectives on American Government

Perspectives on American Government

A Comprehensive Reader

WILLIAM LASSER

Clemson University

D. C. HEATH AND COMPANY
Lexington, Massachusetts   Toronto

Address editorial correspondence to:

D. C. Heath
125 Spring Street
Lexington, MA 02173

Design: Margaret Ong Tsao

Cover Design: Dustin Graphics

Cover Photo: *Washington Monument* Peter Gridley/FPG International

Published simultaneously in Canada.

Printed in the United States of America.

International Standard Book Number: 0-669-21875-8.

Library of Congress Catalog Number: 91-73465.

10 9 8 7 6 5 4 3 2

To Susan J. S. Lasser, with love

Preface

"I attach a few preliminary words to the LIFE AND ADVENTURES OF MARTIN CHUZZLEWIT: more because I am unwilling to depart from any custom which has become endeared to me by having prevailed between myself and my readers on former occasions of the same kind, than because I have anything particular to say."

—Charles Dickens
Martin Chuzzlewit, Preface to the First Edition

The editor of a collection of readings can perhaps be excused if he grows accustomed to relying on other people's writings and loses the habit of writing anything by himself. So it is tempting simply to print someone else's preface (perhaps the one in *Martin Chuzzlewit*) and be done with it.

Unlike Dickens, however, I do have one or two things in particular to say, both about the nature of this book and about those who helped to make it possible.

THE PURPOSE OF THIS BOOK

Why compile a new American government reader? What have I set out to accomplish that makes this book different—and I hope better—than others of the same type?

My goal was to create a reader that would be more than just a collection of writings on or about American politics. That is, I wanted to develop a collection that would be clearly organized and fully coherent; that could be easily integrated into an American government course and actually help in teaching the course; and that would hold the students' (and professor's) attention by presenting a wide variety of viewpoints, writing styles, and approaches. Most important, I wanted to create a book that showed students just why I—and all other professors of American government—find this subject so meaningful and enjoyable.

I quickly discovered that the challenge in compiling a reader is to maintain structure and coherence without sacrificing the extraordinary eclecticism that marks the enormous body of writings about American government. The solution was to begin each chapter with certain key questions in mind and then to present a set of readings designed to provide various perspectives on those questions. All of the readings, however diverse they might be, would revolve around the central chapter questions and thus maintain a clear and cohesive relationship with each other.

I devised category designations for each selection to make these relationships explicit. They show at a glance whether an individual selection is theoretical or practical, historical or contemporary, comparative or institutional. They make it easy to identify "issue and debate" topics or "insider" points of view. (A complete discussion of these categories appears below.)

Another goal was to produce a reader that professor and students alike would find easy to use. The 18 chapters of this book correspond to the most frequently assigned chapters of most American government textbooks, so they should fit neatly into any standard syllabus. Introductory material and questions for individual selections help to orient students and provide key background information.

Instructors will find it easy to integrate this book into their courses. Many of the chapter questions, for example, can serve as excellent essay assignments, and "issue and debate" selections can be used as a starting point for class discussions of controversial issues. The readings in this book should help students develop critical thinking skills along with providing a deeper and clearer appreciation for the complexities of American politics.

Finally, I wanted this reader to be fun. For over 200 years, politics has been a source of amusement to Americans; it ought to be a federal offense to make it a dry and humorless subject. Here and there I have presented readings whose main purpose is to be enjoyed, and political cartoons are sprinkled throughout the text. On several occasions, my editors even permitted me an outright joke, though most of these were rejected by my wife and friends.

THE CATEGORIES

All of the readings are grouped into categories. No chapter contains a selection from every category, although most of the chapters follow a loose pattern, beginning with classic or theoretical works; progressing through historical, comparative, and institutional approaches; and ending with various contemporary accounts, insiders' views, and topics of debate.

The categories highlight the key perspectives used to organize this reader. The most fundamental perspectives are the theoretical, constitutional, institutional, historical, and comparative. The complete list follows.

- *The Classic Texts.* Readings from classic works in or relating to American politics, such as de Tocqueville's *Democracy in America* or classic works of contemporary political science.

- *The Constitutional Context.* Court decisions and other works discussing the constitutional basis of American politics. Some articles from the *Federalist Papers* fit here instead of in *The Classic Texts.*

- *The Perspective of History.* Articles providing historical background or comparing American politics today with the past, usually taking a long-term view.

- *Trends.* Articles underscoring recent trends in American politics, especially since the 1960s and 1970s.

- *Interconnections.* Articles highlighting the relationships among different branches of the government, between the state and federal governments, or between topic areas covered in the book (an article on media coverage of campaigns, for example, might fit into this category).

- *The International Context.* Selections placing American politics in a comparative context or discussing the international implications of issues in American politics.

- *The Unwritten Constitution.* Readings highlighting the role of institutions and practices that form an essential part of the American political system but were not contemplated by the authors of the Constitution, for example, the role of congressional staff.

- *View from the Inside.* First-person (or, more rarely, third-person) accounts of the inner workings of American political institutions, for example, excerpts from Jimmy Carter's autobiography.

- *Focus.* Selections zeroing in on a particular issue or aspect of the material for a detailed look.

- *Issue and Debate.* Articles presenting two or more points of view on a controversial issue, designed to facilitate class discussion and student issue papers or other assignments.

Certain categories naturally lend themselves to particular chapters; others are regular features of nearly every chapter. Never (well, hardly ever) did I try to force material into these categories.

SOME TECHNICAL NOTES

I have used several standard conventions throughout the text. The omission of large amounts of material is indicated by centered bullets (• • •); smaller omissions are indicated by ellipses (. . .). In general I have not corrected antique spellings, nor have I modified older styles of punctuation or capitalization. I have eliminated virtually all footnotes; readers who are interested in source notes and other references should go directly to the originals. Where necessary, I have inserted explanatory or additional matter in italics, within brackets. For the sake of clarity, I have frequently shortened selection titles, and in some cases (particularly issue and debate selections) I have modified them substantially.

Within the limitations imposed by space considerations, I have tried to leave large sections of the original material intact. Classic works like the *Federalist Papers* are presented either whole or in very large blocks.

INSTRUCTOR'S EDITION

The instructor's edition contains a brief commentary on each chapter and provides discussions of why particular readings were selected and suggestions for using the readings in an introductory course. It also contains recommendations on additional sources, options for omitting some of the readings when necessary, and a few idiosyncratic comments I thought might be useful.

AN APOLOGY, MORE OR LESS

No anthology can contain everything. When in doubt, I have tried to provide more rather than less, but undoubtedly there will still be those who are shocked or scandalized at the omission of a favorite article, case, or essay. Still other articles might discomfit or even offend. If you have criticisms, compliments, or suggestions, please let me know.

ACKNOWLEDGMENTS

I am grateful for the advice and assistance of many colleagues and friends. My colleagues at Clemson—particularly Chuck Dunn, Marty Slann, and Dave Woodard—gave much helpful advice, did not mind when I forgot to return their books after six or seven months, and were patient when my own patience had run out. James Q. Wilson's advice and encouragement were, as always, greatly appreciated. A number of others read and critiqued various parts of this manuscript or otherwise gave helpful suggestions: Alice Fleetwood Bartee, Southwest Missouri State University; David T. Cannon, Duke University; James L. Carter, Sam Houston State University; David Louis Cingranelli, State University of New York at Binghamton; Eliot A. Cohen, Johns Hopkins University; William F. Connelly, Washington and Lee University; Morris P. Fiorina, Harvard University; Stanley B. Klein, Long Island University—C.W. Post Campus; David McLaughlin, Northwest Missouri State University; R. Shep Melnick, Brandeis University; Dean A. Minix, University of Houston; Linda L. Norman, California State University—San Bernardino; Larry W. O'Connell, University of New Hampshire; Howard L. Reiter, The University of Connecticut; Robert Y. Shapiro, Columbia University; Joseph K. Unekis, Kansas State University; Robert Vipond, University of Toronto. Wendy Blackwood was of inestimable help in keeping the project organized and on schedule, and Sharon Fletcher, Kathlyn Harbin, and Kate Myrick provided cheerful assistance.

It was a pleasure to work with the editorial staff at D. C. Heath and Company. Paul Smith's enthusiasm for this project from inception to publication never waivered; I only hope that some day his Red Sox will finally win the World Series. I also enjoyed working with, and appreciate the contributions of, Shira Eisenman and Renée Mary.

Finally, I thank my wife, Susan J. S. Lasser, who served as editorial consultant, sounding board, and critic *par excellence*. More than that, her love and unfailing enthusiasm are a constant inspiration.

Contents

CHAPTER 4 AMERICAN POLITICAL CULTURE _____109

Part Two / Opinion, Interests, and Organizations

Part One

The American System

Chapter 1

Introduction

_A_merican government and politics is a study in paradox. One of the most technologically advanced nations in the world is governed by the oldest national constitution in existence. The most powerful nation in the world exists in a form designed for an isolated, relatively weak country whose greatest desire was to avoid entangling alliances abroad. A political system that prizes democracy and popular government nonetheless takes great care at every turn to restrain and limit the direct power of the people to govern. A national government designed to limit power by dividing it among three branches has evolved a variety of mechanisms to deal with domestic and international crises.

Resolving—or at least clarifying—these issues is the purpose of this book. Presenting a few examples is the purpose of this introductory chapter. The issues raised here will be addressed in much more detail in later chapters through a variety of readings. For now, it is enough to raise them and to recognize their significance.

Chapter Questions

1. Consider—in a preliminary way—the meaning and implications of the following ideas: equality, democracy, liberty, constitutional government. Do the arguments presented in this chapter suggest that these concepts can conflict with one another? How have the different authors represented in this chapter coped with such conflicts?

2. The Framers, as we will see in Chapter 2, sought a form of government that would be strong enough to perform its essential functions yet not so powerful that it would be unable to control itself or be controlled by the people. What do the readings in this chapter suggest about their success in achieving this delicate balancing act?

I THE CONSTITUTIONAL CONTEXT

The Federalist Papers *are among the most important documents in American political history. Originally a series of newspaper articles written in 1787–1788 during the debate in New York State over the ratification of the Constitution, the eighty-five essays comprising the* Federalist Papers *explain, defend, and elaborate on the proposed Constitution. The essays were written by three prominent proponents of the Constitution: John Jay, Alexander Hamilton, and James Madison. Following the style of the day, they were signed by a pseudonym, Publius, by which the authors perhaps sought to imply that their views represented the public interest.*

Federalist No. 1, by Hamilton, serves as an introduction to the series. This brief essay clearly reflects the Framers' belief that the American Republic was a grand experiment in rational self-government and that the success or failure of that experiment would have implications far beyond the immediate future of the thirteen American states.

Note in particular Hamilton's key question, expressed in the first paragraph: "whether societies of men are really capable or not of establishing good government from reflection and choice, or whether they are destined to depend for their political constitutions on accident and force."

Questions

1. Do the style, approach, and tone of this essay reflect the model of "reflection and choice," or does it make a subtle but clear appeal to interest and passion?
2. How would you answer Hamilton's central question? Are humans capable of establishing good government from reflection and choice? Consider not only the experiences of the United States but those of other countries as well.

1.1 Federalist *No. 1*

Alexander Hamilton

After an unequivocal experience of the inefficacy of the subsisting federal government, you are called upon to deliberate on a new Constitution for the United States of America. The subject speaks its own importance; comprehending in its consequences nothing less than the existence of the UNION, the safety and welfare of the parts of which it is composed, the fate of an empire in many respects the most interesting in the world. It has been frequently remarked that it seems to have been reserved to the people of this country, by their conduct and example, to decide the important question, whether societies of men are really capable or not of establishing good government from reflection and choice, or whether they are forever destined to depend for their political constitutions on accident and force. If there be any truth in the remark, the crisis at which we are arrived may with propriety be regarded as the era in which that decision is to be made; and a wrong election of the part we shall act may, in this view, deserve to be considered as the general misfortune of mankind.

This idea will add the inducements of philanthropy to those of patriotism, to heighten the solicitude which all considerate and good men must feel for the event. Happy will it be if our choice should be directed by a judicious estimate of our true interests, unperplexed and unbiased by considerations not connected with the public good. But this is a thing more ardently to be wished than seriously to be expected. The plan offered to our deliberations affects too many particular interests, innovates upon too many local institutions, not to involve in its discussion a variety of objects foreign to its merits, and of views, passions, and prejudices little favorable to the discovery of truth.

Among the most formidable of the obstacles which the new Constitution will have to encounter may readily be distinguished the obvious interest of a certain class of men in every State to resist all changes which may hazard a diminution of the power, emolument, and consequence of the offices they hold under the State establishments; and the perverted ambition of another class of men, who will either hope to aggrandize themselves by the confusions of their country, or will flatter themselves with fairer prospects of elevation from the subdivision of the empire into several partial confederacies than from its union under one government.

It is not, however, my design to dwell upon observations of this nature. I am well aware that it would be disingenuous to resolve indiscriminately the opposition of any set of men (merely because their situations might subject them to suspicion) into interested or ambitious views.

Candor will oblige us to admit that even such men may be actuated by upright intentions; and it cannot be doubted that much of the opposition which has made its appearance, or may hereafter make its appearance, will spring from sources, blameless at least if not respectable— the honest errors of minds led astray by preconceived jealousies and fears. So numerous indeed and so powerful are the causes which serve to give a false bias to the judgment, that we, upon many occasions, see wise and good men on the wrong as well as on the right side of questions of the first magnitude to society. This circumstance, if duly attended to, would furnish a lesson of moderation to those who are ever so thoroughly persuaded of their being in the right in any controversy. And a further reason for caution, in this respect, might be drawn from the reflection that we are not always sure that those who advocate the truth are influenced by purer principles than their antagonists. Ambition, avarice, personal animosity, party opposition, and many other motives not more laudable than these, are apt to operate as well upon those who support as those who oppose the right side of a question. Were there not even these inducements to moderation, nothing could be more ill-judged than that intolerant spirit which has at all times characterized political parties. For in politics, as in religion, it is equally absurd to aim at making proselytes by fire and sword. Heresies in either can rarely be cured by persecution.

And yet, however just these sentiments will be allowed to be, we have already sufficient indications that it will happen in this as in all former cases of great national discussion. A torrent of angry and malignant passions will be let loose. To judge from the conduct of the opposite parties, we shall be led to conclude that they will mutually hope to evince the justness of their opinions, and to increase the number of their converts by the loudness of their declamations and by the bitterness of their invectives. An enlightened zeal for the energy and efficiency of government will be stigmatized as the offspring of a temper fond of despotic power and hostile to the principles of liberty. An over-scrupulous jealousy of danger to the rights of the people, which is more commonly the fault of the head than of the heart, will be represented as mere pretense and artifice, the stale bait for popularity at the expense of public good. It will be forgotten, on the one hand, that jealousy is the usual concomitant of violent love, and that the noble enthusiasm of liberty is too apt to be infected with a spirit of narrow and illiberal distrust. On the other hand, it will be equally forgotten that the vigor of government is essential to the security of liberty; that, in the contemplation of a sound and well-informed judgment, their interests can never be separated; and that a dangerous ambition more often lurks behind the specious mask of zeal for the rights of the people than under the forbidding appearance of zeal for the firmness and efficiency of government. History will teach us that the former has been found a much more certain road to the introduction of despotism than the latter, and that of those men who have overturned the liberties of republics, the greatest number have begun their career by paying an obsequious court to the people, commencing demagogues and ending tyrants.

In the course of the preceding observations, I have had an eye, my fellow-citizens, to putting you upon your guard against all attempts, from whatever quarter, to influence your decision in a matter of the utmost moment to your welfare by any impressions other than those which may result from the evidence of truth. You will, no doubt, at the same time have collected from the general scope of them that they proceed from a source not unfriendly to the new Constitution. Yes, my countrymen, I own to you that after having given it an attentive consideration, I am clearly of opinion it is your interest to adopt it. I am convinced that this is the safest course for your liberty, your dignity, and your happiness. I affect not reserves which I do not feel. I will not amuse you with an appearance of deliberation when I have decided. I frankly acknowledge to you my convictions, and I will freely

lay before you the reasons on which they are founded. The consciousness of good intentions disdains ambiguity. I shall not, however, multiply professions on this head. My motives must remain in the depository of my own breast. My arguments will be open to all and may be judged of by all. They shall at least be offered in a spirit which will not disgrace the cause of truth.

I propose, in a series of papers, to discuss the following interesting particulars:—*The utility of the UNION to your political prosperity*—*The insufficiency of the present Confederation to preserve that Union*—*The necessity of a government at least equally energetic with the one proposed, to the attainment of this object*—*The conformity of the proposed Constitution to the true principles of republican government*—*Its analogy to your own State constitution*—and lastly, *The additional security which its adoption will afford to the preservation of that species of government, to liberty, and to property.*

In the progress of this discussion I shall endeavor to give a satisfactory answer to all the objections which shall have made their appearance, that may seem to have any claim to your attention.

It may perhaps be thought superfluous to offer arguments to prove the utility of the UNION, a point, no doubt, deeply engraved on the hearts of the great body of the people in every State, and one which, it may be imagined, has no adversaries. But the fact is that we already hear it whispered in the private circles of those who oppose the new Constitution, that the thirteen States are of too great extent for any general system, and that we must of necessity resort to separate confederacies of distinct portions of the whole. This doctrine will, in all probability, be gradually propagated, till it has votaries enough to countenance an open avowal of it. For nothing can be more evident to those who are able to take an enlarged view of the subject than the alternative of an adoption of the new Constitution or a dismemberment of the Union.

•••

II   THE CLASSIC TEXTS

The Declaration of Independence is perhaps the most famous political document in American history. With extraordinary compactness, it sets out a theoretical defense of the right of revolution, along with the specific reasons justifying the Americans' case. The document was written by Thomas Jefferson, edited by a committee, and adopted by the Continental Congress in July 1776. Its essential political philosophy derives, in part at least, from the work of the English philosopher John Locke; its lawyerlike bill of particulars derives from the colonists' experiences over the preceding decade and a half. Its words are so familiar that they are rarely studied in detail, but they more than merit careful analysis.

Questions

1. What does the Declaration say about equality? What precisely does Jefferson mean by the phrase, "all men are created equal"? Are Americans today bound by the eighteenth-century meaning of these words?

2. What is the connection between the Declaration's theory of equality and the idea of democracy? Does this document explicitly or implicitly endorse a democratic form of government?

3. Examine the Constitution of the United States (appendix A). How many of the specific charges against King George III enumerated in the Declaration of Independence are reflected in particular provisions of the Constitution or the Bill of Rights?

1.2 *The Declaration of Independence*

In Congress, July 4, 1776,

The Unanimous Declaration of the Thirteen United States of America,

When in the Course of human events, it becomes necessary for one people to dissolve the political bands which have connected them with another, and to assume among the Powers of the earth, the separate and equal station to which the Laws of Nature and of Nature's God entitle them, a decent respect of the opinions of mankind requires that they should declare the causes which impel them to the separation.

We hold these truths to be self-evident, that all men are created equal, that they are endowed by their Creator with certain unalienable Rights, that among these are Life, Liberty and the pursuit of Happiness. That to secure these rights, Governments are instituted among Men, deriving their just powers from the consent of the governed, That whenever any Form of Gov-

I Have a Dream

For many Americans—African-Americans, women, and others—the Declaration's promise of equality was more a dream than a reality for centuries. America did not even begin to provide equality under the law for these groups until the successes of the civil rights movement in the 1950s and 1960s.

A high point of the civil rights movement came on August 28, 1963, when nearly 250,000 Americans marched on Washington, D.C., to demonstrate for equality. The most important speech was delivered by the Reverend Martin Luther King, Jr., who declared his version of the American dream— an America that, as he put it, would redeem the promissory note of the Declaration of Independence. An excerpt follows.

I am happy to join with you today in what will go down in history as the greatest demonstration for freedom in the history of our nation.

Five score years ago, a great American, in whose symbolic shadow we stand today, signed the Emancipation Proclamation. This momentous decree came as a great beacon light of hope to millions of Negro slaves, who had been seared in the flames of withering injustice. It came as a joyous daybreak to end the long night of their captivity.

But one hundred years later, the Negro still is not free. One hundred years later, the life of the Negro is still sadly crippled by the manacles of segregation and the chains of discrimination. One hundred years later, the Negro lives on a lonely island of poverty in the midst of a vast ocean of material prosperity. One hundred years later, the Negro is still languished in the corners of American society and finds himself an exile in his own land.

So we've come here today to dramatize a shameful condition. In a sense we've come to our nation's capital to cash a check. When the architects of our Republic wrote the magnificent words of the Constitution and the Declaration of Independence, they were signing a promissory note to which every American was to fall heir. This note was a promise that all men—yes, black men as well as white men—would be guaranteed the unalienable rights of life, liberty, and the pursuit of happiness.

It is obvious today that America has defaulted on this promissory note insofar as her citizens of color are concerned. Instead of honoring this sacred obligation, America has given the Negro people a bad check, a check which has come back marked "insufficient funds." But we refuse to believe that the bank of justice is bankrupt. We refuse to believe that there are insufficient funds in the great vaults of opportunity of this nation. So we've come to cash this check—a check that will give us upon demand the riches of freedom and the security of justice.

We have also come to this hallowed spot to remind America of the fierce urgency of now. This is no time to engage in the luxury of cooling off or to take the tranquilizing drug of gradualism. . . . There will be neither rest nor tranquility in America until the Negro is granted his citizenship rights. The whirlwinds of revolt will continue to shake the foundations of our nation until the bright day of justice emerges.

But that is something that I must say to my people who stand on the warm threshold which leads into the palace of justice. In the process of gaining our rightful place we must not be guilty of wrongful deeds. Let us not seek to satisfy our

---

ernment becomes destructive of these ends, it is the Right of the People to alter or to abolish it, and to institute new Government, laying its foundation on such principles and organizing its powers in such form, as to them shall seem most likely to effect their Safety and Happiness. Prudence, indeed, will dictate that Govern-

ments long established should not be changed for light and transient causes; and accordingly all experience hath shown, that mankind are more disposed to suffer, while evils are sufferable, than to right themselves by abolishing the forms to which they are accustomed. But when a long train of abuses and usurpations, pursu-

thirst for freedom by drinking from the cup of bitterness and hatred.

We must forever conduct our struggle on the high plane of dignity and discipline. We must not allow our creative protest to degenerate into physical violence. . . .

I say to you today, my friends, so even though we face the difficulties of today and tomorrow, I still have a dream. It is a dream deeply rooted in the American dream.

I have a dream that one day this nation will rise up and live out the true meaning of its creed: "We hold these truths to be self-evident; that all men are created equal."

I have a dream that one day on the red hills of Georgia the sons of former slaves and the sons of former slaveowners will be able to sit down together at the table of brotherhood.

I have a dream that one day even the state of Mississippi, a state sweltering with the heat of injustice, sweltering with the heat of oppression, will be transformed into an oasis of freedom and justice.

I have a dream that my four little children will one day live in a nation where they will not be judged by the color of their skin but by the content of their character.

I have a dream today.

I have a dream that one day, down in Alabama, with its vicious racists, with its governor having his lips dripping with the words of interposition and nullification, one day right there in Alabama little black boys and black girls will be able to join hands with little white boys and white girls as sisters and brothers.

I have a dream today.

I have a dream that one day every valley shall be exalted, every hill and mountain shall be made low, the rough places will be made plain and the crooked places will be made straight, and the glory of the Lord shall be revealed, and all flesh shall see it together. . . .

So let freedom ring. From the prodigious hilltops of New Hampshire, let freedom ring. From the mighty mountains of New York, let freedom ring, from the heightening Alleghenies to Pennsylvania!

Let freedom ring from the snowcapped Rockies of Colorado!

Let freedom ring from the curvaceous slopes of California!

But not only that.

Let freedom ring from Stone Mountain of Georgia!

Let freedom ring from Lookout Mountain of Tennessee!

Let freedom ring from every hill and mole hill of Mississippi.

From every mountainside, let freedom ring, and when this happens . . . when we allow freedom [to] ring, when we let it ring from every village and every hamlet, from every state and every city, we will be able to speed up that day when all God's children, black men and white men, Jews and Gentiles, Protestants and Catholics, will be able to join hands and sing in the words of the old Negro spiritual, "Free at last! Free at last! Thank God Almighty, we are free at last!"

—*Martin Luther King, Jr.*

ing invariably the same Object evinces a design to reduce them under absolute Despotism, it is their right, it is their duty, to throw off such Government, and to provide new Guards for their future security.—Such has been the patient sufferance of these Colonies; and such is now the necessity which constrains them to al-

ter their former Systems of Government. The history of the present King of Great Britain is a history of repeated injuries and usurpations, all having in direct object the establishment of an absolute Tyranny over these States. To prove this, let Facts be submitted to a candid world.

He has refused his Assent to Laws, the most wholesome and necessary for the public good.

He has forbidden his Governors to pass Laws of immediate and pressing importance, unless suspended in their operation till his Assent should be obtained; and when so suspended, he has utterly neglected to attend to them.

He has refused to pass other Laws for the accommodation of large districts of people, unless those people would relinquish the right of Representation in the Legislature, a right inestimable to them and formidable to tyrants only.

He has called together legislative bodies at places unusual, uncomfortable, and distant from the depository of their Public Records, for the sole purpose of fatiguing them into compliance with his measures.

He has dissolved Representative Houses repeatedly, for opposing with manly firmness his invasions on the rights of the people.

He has refused for a long time, after such dissolutions, to cause others to be elected; whereby the Legislative Powers, incapable of Annihilation, have returned to the People at large for their exercise; the State remaining in the mean time exposed to all the dangers of invasion from without, and convulsions within.

He has endeavoured to prevent the population of these States; for that purpose obstructing the Laws of Naturalization of Foreigners; refusing to pass others to encourage their migration hither, and raising the conditions of new Appropriations of Lands.

He has obstructed the Administration of Justice, by refusing his Assent to Laws for establishing Judiciary Powers.

He has made Judges dependent on his Will alone, for the tenure of their offices, and the amount of payment of their salaries.

He has erected a multitude of New Offices, and sent hither swarms of Officers to harass our People, and eat out their substance.

He has kept among us, in times of peace, Standing Armies without the Consent of our legislature.

He has affected to render the Military independent of and superior to the Civil Power.

He has combined with others to subject us to a jurisdiction foreign to our constitution, and unacknowledged by our laws; giving his Assent to their acts of pretended legislation:

For quartering large bodies of armed troops among us:

For protecting them, by a mock Trial, from Punishment for any Murders which they should commit on the Inhabitants of these States:

For cutting off our Trade with all parts of the world:

For imposing taxes on us without our Consent:

For depriving us in many cases, of the benefits of Trial by Jury:

For transporting us beyond Seas to be tried for pretended offences:

For abolishing the free System of English Laws in a neighbouring Province, establishing therein an Arbitrary government, and enlarging its Boundaries so as to render it at once an example and fit instrument for introducing the same absolute rule into these Colonies:

For taking way our Charters, abolishing our most valuable Laws, and altering fundamentally the Forms of our Governments:

For suspending our own Legislature, and declaring themselves invested with Power to legislate for us in all cases whatsoever.

He has abdicated Government here, by declaring us out of his Protection and waging War against us.

He has plundered our seas, ravaged our Coasts, burnt our towns, and destroyed the lives of our people.

He is at this time transporting large armies of foreign mercenaries to compleat the works of death, desolation and tyranny, already begun with circumstances of Cruelty & perfidy scarcely parallelled in the most barbarous ages, and totally unworthy the Head of a civilized nation.

He has constrained our fellow Citizens taken Captive on the high Seas to bear Arms against their Country, to become the execution-ers of their friends and Brethren, or to fall themselves by their Hands.

He has excited domestic insurrections amongst us, and has endeavoured to bring on the inhabitants of our frontiers, the merciless Indian Savages, whose known rule of warfare, is an undistinguished destruction of all ages, sexes and conditions.

In every stage of these Oppressions We have Petitioned for Redress in the most humble terms: Our repeated Petitions have been answered only by repeated injury. A Prince, whose character is thus marked by every act which may define a Tyrant, is unfit to be the ruler of a free People.

Nor have We been wanting in attention to our Brittish brethren. We have warned them from time to time of attempts by their legislature to extend an unwarrantable jurisdiction over us. We have reminded them of the circumstances of our emigration and settlement here. We have appealed to their native justice and magnanimity, and we have conjured them by the ties of our common kindred to disavow these usurpations, which, would inevitably interrupt our connections and correspondence. They too have been deaf to the voice of justice and of consanguinity. We must, therefore, acquiesce in the necessity, which denounces our Separation, and hold them, as we hold the rest of mankind, Enemies in War, in Peace Friends.

We, therefore, the Representatives of the united States of America, in General Congress, Assembled, appealing to the Supreme Judge of the world for the rectitude of our intentions, do, in the Name, and by Authority of the good People of these Colonies, solemnly publish and declare, That these United Colonies are, and of Right ought to be Free and Independent States; that they are Absolved from all Allegiance to the British Crown, and that all political connection between them and the State of Great Britain, is and ought to be totally dissolved; and that as Free and Independent States, they have full Power to levy War, conclude Peace, contract Alliances, establish Commerce, and to do all other Acts and Things which Independent States may of right do. And for the support of this Declaration, with a firm reliance on the Protection of Divine Providence, we mutually pledge to each other our lives, our Fortunes and our sacred Honor.

John Hancock
[and fifty-five others]

III  INTERCONNECTIONS

Three months after the Civil War began, President Abraham Lincoln called Congress into special session to deal with the crisis. Before Congress met, however, he took steps to cope with the outbreak of war: without specific congressional approval, he called up the militia and issued a call for volunteers; instituted a naval blockade; and suspended the writ of habeas corpus so that suspected rebels could be held without trial. Lincoln used his message to Congress to defend these actions, which were of dubious constitutionality, and to request that Congress retroactively approve the extraordinary measures he had taken. Eventually Congress complied.

Lincoln's message, delivered on July 4, 1861, remains the premier statement in American history of the president's extraordinary responsibilities and powers in times of crisis. Lincoln's claim—that the president's highest responsibility is to the safety of the Union and of the people—has served as a model for many of his successors.

Questions

1. What clauses of the Constitution (see appendix A) does Lincoln use to justify his extraordinary actions? Do his arguments seem persuasive?

2. When the Civil War broke out, Congress was not in session. Nevertheless, later presidents have assumed extraordinary powers even when Congress was in session. How might such presidents justify their actions under these circumstances?

1.3 *Message to Congress of July 4, 1861*

Abraham Lincoln

Fellow-citizens of the Senate and
House of Representatives:

Having been convened on an extraordinary occasion, as authorized by the Constitution, your attention is not called to any ordinary subject of legislation.

At the beginning of the present Presidential term, four months ago, the functions of the Federal Government were found to be generally suspended within the several States of South Carolina, Georgia, Alabama, Mississippi, Louisiana, and Florida, excepting only those of the Post Office Department.

• • •

The Forts remaining in the possession of the Federal government, in, and near, these States, were either besieged or menaced by warlike preparations; and especially Fort Sumter was nearly surrounded by well-protected hostile batteries, with guns equal in quality to the best of its own, and outnumbering the latter as perhaps ten to one.

• • •

The government [therefore] . . . commenced preparing an expedition . . . to relieve Fort Sumter . . . and it was resolved to send it forward. As had been intended, in this contingency, it was also resolved to notify the Governor of South Carolina, that he might expect an attempt would be made to provision the Fort; and that, if the attempt should not be resisted, there would be no effort to throw in men, arms, or ammunition, without further notice, or in case of an attack upon the Fort. This notice was accordingly given; whereupon the Fort was attacked, and bombarded to its fall, without even awaiting the arrival of the provisioning expedition.

It is thus seen that the assault upon, and reduction of, Fort Sumter, was, in no sense, a matter of self defence on the part of the assailants. They well knew that the garrison in the Fort could, by no possibility, commit aggression upon them. They knew—they were expressly notified—that the giving of bread to the few brave and hungry men of the garrison, was all which would on that occasion be attempted, unless themselves, by resisting so much, should provoke more. They knew that this Government desired to keep the garrison in the Fort, not to assail them, but merely to maintain visible possession, and thus to preserve the Union from actual, and immediate dissolution—trusting, as herein-before stated, to time, discussion, and the ballot-box, for final adjustment; and they assailed, and reduced the Fort, for precisely the reverse object—to drive out the visible authority of the Federal Union, and thus force it to immediate dissolution.

That this was their object, the Executive well understood; and having said to them in the inaugural address, "You can have no conflict without being yourselves the aggressors," he

FOUR SCORE AND SEVEN YEARS AGO---

Drawing by O. Soglow; © 1959 The New Yorker Magazine, Inc.

took pains, not only to keep this declaration good, but also to keep the case so free from the power of ingenious sophistry, as that the world should not be able to misunderstand it. By the affair at Fort Sumter, with its surrounding circumstances, that point was reached. Then, and thereby, the assailants of the Government, began the conflict of arms, without a gun in sight, or in expectancy, to return their fire, save only the few in the Fort, sent to that harbor, years before, for their own protection, and still ready to give that protection, in whatever was lawful. In this act, discarding all else, they have forced upon the country, the distinct issue: "Immediate dissolution, or blood."

And this issue embraces more than the fate of these United States. It presents to the whole family of man, the question, whether a constitutional republic, or a democracy—a government of the people, by the same people—can, or cannot, maintain its territorial integrity, against its own domestic foes. It presents the question, whether discontented individuals, too few in numbers to control administration, according to organic law, in any case, can always, upon the pretences made in this case, or on any other pretences, or arbitrarily, without any pretence, break up their Government, and thus practically put an end to free government upon the earth. It forces us to ask: "Is there, in all republics, this inherent, and fatal weakness?" "Must a government, of necessity, be too *strong*

for the liberties of it own people, or too *weak* to maintain its own existence?"

So viewing the issue, no choice was left but to call out the war power of the Government; and so to resist force, employed for its destruction, by force, for its preservation.

• • •

Recurring to the action of the government, it may be stated that, at first, a call was made for seventy-five thousand militia; and rapidly following this, a proclamation was issued for closing the ports of the insurrectionary districts by proceedings in the nature of Blockade. So far all was believed to be strictly legal. At this point the insurrectionists announced their purpose to enter upon the practice of privateering.

Other calls were made for volunteers, to serve three years, unless sooner discharged; and also for large additions to the regular Army and Navy. These measures, whether strictly legal or not, were ventured upon, under what appeared to be a popular demand, and a public necessity; trusting, then as now, that Congress would readily ratify them. It is believed that nothing has been done beyond the constitutional competency of Congress.

Soon after the first call for militia, it was considered a duty to authorize the Commanding General, in proper cases, according to his discretion, to suspend the privilege of the writ of habeas corpus; or, in other words, to arrest, and detain, without resort to the ordinary processes and forms of law, such individuals as he might deem dangerous to the public safety. This authority has purposely been exercised but very sparingly. Nevertheless, the legality and propriety of what has been done under it, are questioned; and the attention of the country has been called to the proposition that one who is sworn to "take care that the laws be faithfully executed," should not himself violate them. Of course some consideration was given to the questions of power, and propriety, before this matter was acted upon. The whole of the laws which were required to be faithfully executed, were being resisted, and failing of execution, in nearly one-third of the States. Must they be allowed to finally fail of execution, even had it been perfectly clear, that by the use of the means necessary to their execution, some single law, made in such extreme tenderness of the citizen's liberty, that practically, it relieves more of the guilty, than of the innocent, should, to a very limited extent, be violated? To state the question more directly, are all the laws, *but one*, to go unexecuted, and the government itself go to pieces, lest that one be violated? Even in such a case, would not the official oath be broken, if the government should be overthrown, when it was believed that disregarding the single law, would tend to preserve it? But it was not believed that this question was presented. It was not believed that any law was violated. The provision of the Constitution that "The privilege of the writ of habeas corpus, shall not be suspended unless when, in cases of rebellion or invasion, the public safety may require it," is equivalent to a provision—is a provision—that such privilege may be suspended when, in cases of rebellion, or invasion, the public safety *does* require it. It was decided that we have a case of rebellion, and that the public safety does require the qualified suspension of the privilege of the writ which was authorized to be made. Now it is insisted that Congress, and not the Executive, is vested with this power. But the Constitution itself, is silent as to which, or who, is to exercise the power; and as the provision

was plainly made for a dangerous emergency, it cannot be believed the framers of the instrument intended, that in every case, the danger should run its course, until Congress could be called together; the very assembling of which might be prevented, as was intended in this case, by the rebellion.

No more extended argument is now offered; as an opinion, at some length, will probably be presented by the Attorney General. Whether there shall be any legislation upon the subject, and if any, what, is submitted entirely to the better judgment of Congress.

The forbearance of this government had been so extraordinary, and so long continued, as to lead some foreign nations to shape their action as if they supposed the early destruction of our national Union was probable. While this, on discovery, gave the Executive some concern, he is now happy to say that the sovereignty, and rights of the United States, are now everywhere practically respected by foreign powers; and a general sympathy with the country is manifested throughout the world.

The reports of the Secretaries of the Treasury, War, and the Navy, will give the information in detail deemed necessary, and convenient for your deliberation, and action; while the Executive, and all the Departments, will stand ready to supply omissions, or to communicate new facts, considered important for you to know.

It is now recommended that you give the legal means for making this contest a short, and a decisive one; that you place at the control of the government, for the work, at least four hundred thousand men, and four hundred millions of dollars. That number of men is about one tenth of those of proper ages within the regions where, apparently, *all* are willing to engage; and the sum is less than a twentythird part of the money value owned by the men who seem ready to devote the whole. A debt of six hundred millions of dollars *now*, is a less sum per head, than was the debt of our revolution, when we came out of that struggle; and the money value in the country now, bears even a greater proportion to what it was *then*, than does the population. Surely each man has as strong a motive *now*, to *preserve* our liberties, as each had *then*, to *establish* them.

• • •

It might seem, at first thought, to be of little difference whether the present movement at the South be called "secession" or "rebellion." The movers, however, well understand the difference. At the beginning, they knew they could never raise their treason to any respectable magnitude, by any name which implies *violation* of law. They knew their people possessed as much of moral sense, as much of devotion to law and order, and as much pride in, and reverence for, the history, and government of their common country, as any other civilized, and patriotic people. They knew they could make no advancement directly in the teeth of these strong and noble sentiments. Accordingly they commenced by an insidious debauching of the public mind. They invented an ingenious sophism, which, if conceded, was followed by perfectly logical steps, through all the incidents, to the complete destruction of the Union. The sophism itself is, that any state of the Union may, *consistently* with the national Constitution, and therefore *lawfully*, and *peacefully*, withdraw from the Union, without the consent of the Union, or of any other state. . . .

This sophism derives much—perhaps the whole—of its currency, from the assumption, that there is some omnipotent, and sacred supremacy, pertaining to a *State*—to each State of our Federal Union. Our States have neither more, nor less power, than that reserved to them, in the Union, by the Constitution—no one of them having been a State *out* of the Union. The original ones passed into the Union even *before* they cast off their British colonial dependence; and the new ones each came into the Union directly from a condition of dependence, excepting Texas. And even Texas, in its temporary independence, was never designated a State. The new ones only took the des-

ignation of States, on coming into the Union, while that name was first adopted for the old ones, in, and by, the Declaration of Independence. Therein the "United Colonies" were declared to be "Free and Independent States"; but, even then, the object plainly was not to declare their independence of *one another*, or of the *Union*; but directly the contrary, as their mutual pledge, and their mutual action, before, at the time, and afterwards, abundantly show. The express plighting of faith, by each and all of the original thirteen, in the Articles of Confederation, two years later, that the Union shall be perpetual, is most conclusive. Having never been States, either in substance, or in name, *outside* of the Union, whence this magical omnipotence of "State rights," asserting a claim of power to lawfully destroy the Union itself? Much is said about the "sovereignty" of the States; but the word, even, is not in the national Constitution; nor, as is believed, in any of the State constitutions. What is a "sovereignty," in the political sense of the term? Would it be far wrong to define it "A political community, without a political superior"? Tested by this, no one of our States, except Texas, ever was a sovereignty. And even Texas gave up the character on coming into the Union; by which act, she acknowledged the Constitution of the United States, and the laws and treaties of the United States made in pursuance of the Constitution, to be, for her, the supreme law of the land. The States have their *status* IN the Union, and they have no other *legal status*. If they break from this, they can only do so against law, and by revolution. The Union, and not themselves separately, procured their independence, and their liberty. By conquest, or purchase, the Union gave each of them, whatever of independence, and liberty, it has. The Union is older than any of the States; and, in fact, it created them as States. Originally, some dependent colonies made the Union, and, in turn, the Union threw off their old dependence, for them, and made them States, such as they are. Not one of them ever had a State constitution, independent of the Union. Of course, it is not forgotten that all the new States framed their constitutions, before they entered the Union; nevertheless, dependent upon, and preparatory to, coming into the Union.

Unquestionably the States have the powers, and rights, reserved to them in, and by the National Constitution; but among these, surely, are not included all conceivable powers, however mischievous, or destructive; but, at most, such only, as were known in the world, at the time, as governmental powers; and certainly, a power to destroy the government itself, had never been known as a governmental—as a merely administrative power. This relative matter of National power, and State rights, as a principle, is no other than the principle of *generality*, and *locality*. Whatever concerns the whole, should be confided to the whole—to the general government; while, whatever concerns *only* the State, should be left exclusively, to the State. This is all there is of original principle about it. Whether the National Constitution, in defining boundaries between the two, has applied the principle with exact accuracy, is not to be questioned. We are all bound by that defining, without question.

What is now combatted, is the position that secession is *consistent* with the Constitution—is *lawful*, and *peaceful*. It is not contended that there is any express law for it; and nothing should ever be implied as law, which leads to unjust, or absurd consequences.

• • •

The seceders insist that our Constitution admits of secession. They have assumed to make a National Constitution of their own, in which, of necessity, they have either *discarded*, or *retained*, the right of secession, as they insist, it exists in ours. If they have discarded it, they thereby admit that, on principle, it ought not to be in ours. If they have retained it, by their own construction of ours they show that to be consistent they must secede from one another, whenever they shall find it the easiest way of settling their debts, or effecting any other selfish, or unjust object. The principle itself is one of disintegration, and upon which no government can possibly endure.

• • •

Our popular government has often been called an experiment. Two points in it, our people have already settled—the successful *establishing*, and the successful *administering* of it. One still remains—its successful *maintenance* against a formidable [internal] attempt to overthrow it. It is now for them to demonstrate to the world, that those who can fairly carry an election, can also suppress a rebellion—that ballots are the rightful, and peaceful, successors of bullets; and that when ballots have fairly, and constitutionally, decided, there can be no successful appeal, back to bullets; that there can be no successful appeal, except to ballots themselves, at succeeding elections. Such will be a great lesson of peace; teaching men that what they cannot take by an election, neither can they take it by a war—teaching all, the folly of being the beginners of a war.

• • •

IV  THE INTERNATIONAL CONTEXT

On January 6, 1941, nearly a year before the Japanese attack on Pearl Harbor, President Franklin D. Roosevelt addressed the U.S. Congress and the American people in his annual message on the State of the Union. It was a critical time in world history: only Great Britain stood between Nazi Germany and the complete conquest of Europe, and there was reason to fear for the security of even the United States. Yet for years, Americans had been reluctant to come to Europe's defense.

Under these conditions, Roosevelt laid out his rationale for U.S. involvement in Europe. American intervention in the affairs of foreign nations was justified not only by the direct threat to the United States, he argued, but also by the obligation of the United States to "regain and maintain a free world." American foreign policy was intended to secure a world based on "four essential human freedoms": freedom of speech, freedom of religion, freedom from want, and freedom from fear.

The essential rationale of FDR's "Four Freedoms" speech remains a focal point of U.S. foreign policy even today. American policymakers have justified U.S. involvement in many foreign conflicts by suggesting that the purpose of U.S. action was to defend freedom. This argument has been advanced most recently by President George Bush in his address to the nation at the beginning of the Persian Gulf War in 1991.

Questions

1. Do you think that Americans have an obligation to "maintain a free world"? If so, why does such an obligation fall specifically on the United States?

2. Has the United States consistently followed a rights-based foreign policy? Or has its defense of world freedoms been selective or even arbitrary?

1.4 Four Freedoms Speech _____

Franklin D. Roosevelt

• • •

Just as our national policy in internal affairs has been based upon a decent respect for the rights and the dignity of all our fellow men within our gates, so our national policy in foreign affairs has been based on a decent respect for the rights and dignity of all nations, large and small. And the justice of morality must and will win in the end.

Our national policy is this:

First, by an impressive expression of the public will and without regard to partisanship, we are committed to all-inclusive national defense.

Second, by an impressive expression of the public will and without regard to partisanship, we are committed to full support of all those resolute peoples, everywhere, who are resisting aggression and are thereby keeping war away from our Hemisphere. By this support, we express our determination that the democratic cause shall prevail; and we strengthen the defense and the security of our own nation.

Third, by an impressive expression of the public will and without regard to partisanship, we are committed to the proposition that principles of morality and considerations for our own security will never permit us to acquiesce in a peace dictated by aggressors and sponsored by appeasers. We know that enduring peace cannot be bought at the cost of other people's freedom.

In the recent national election there was no substantial difference between the two great parties in respect to that national policy. No issue was fought out on this line before the American electorate. Today it is abundantly evident that American citizens everywhere are demanding and supporting speedy and complete action in recognition of obvious danger.

Therefore, the immediate need is a swift and driving increase in our armament production.

Leaders of industry and labor have responded to our summons. Goals of speed have been set. In some cases these goals are being reached ahead of time; in some cases we are on schedule; in other cases there are slight but not serious delays; and in some cases—and I am sorry to say very important cases—we are all concerned by the slowness of the accomplishment of our plans.

The Army and Navy, however, have made substantial progress during the past year. Actual experience is improving and speeding up our methods of production with every passing day. And today's best is not good enough for tomorrow.

I am not satisfied with the progress thus far made. The men in charge of the program represent the best in training, in ability, and in patriotism. They are not satisfied with the progress thus far made. None of us will be satisfied until the job is done.

No matter whether the original goal was set too high or too low, our objective is quicker and better results.

To give you two illustrations:

We are behind schedule in turning out finished airplanes; we are working day and night to solve the innumerable problems and to catch up.

We are ahead of schedule in building warships but we are working to get even further ahead of that schedule.

To change a whole nation from a basis of peacetime production of implements of peace to a basis of wartime production of implements of war is no small task. And the greatest difficulty comes at the beginning of the program, when new tools, new plant facilities, new assembly lines, and new ship ways must first be constructed before the actual matériel begins to flow steadily and speedily from them.

The Congress, of course, must rightly keep itself informed at all times of the progress of the program. However, there is certain information, as the Congress itself will readily recognize, which, in the interests of our own security and those of the nations that we are supporting, must of needs be kept in confidence.

New circumstances are constantly begetting new needs for our safety. I shall ask this Congress for greatly increased new appropriations and authorizations to carry on what we have begun.

I also ask this Congress for authority and for funds sufficient to manufacture additional munitions and war supplies of many kinds, to be turned over to those nations which are now in actual war with aggressor nations.

Our most useful and immediate role is to act as an arsenal for them as well as for ourselves. They do not need man power, but they do need billions of dollars worth of the weapons of defense.

The time is near when they will not be able to pay for them all in ready cash. We cannot, and we will not, tell them that they must surrender, merely because of present inability to pay for the weapons which we know they must have.

I do not recommend that we make them a loan of dollars with which to pay for these weapons—a loan to be repaid in dollars.

I recommend that we make it possible for those nations to continue to obtain war materials in the United States, fitting their orders into our own program. Nearly all their matériel would, if the time ever came, be useful for our own defense.

Taking counsel of expert military and naval authorities, considering what is best for our own security, we are free to decide how much should be kept here and how much should be sent abroad to our friends who by their determined and heroic resistance are giving us time in which to make ready our own defense.

For what we send abroad, we shall be repaid within a reasonable time following the close of hostilities, in similar materials, or, at our option, in other goods of many kinds, which they can produce and which we need.

Let us say to the democracies: "We Americans are vitally concerned in your defense of freedom. We are putting forth our energies, our resources and our organizing powers to give you the strength to regain and maintain a free world. We shall send you, in ever-increasing numbers, ships, planes, tanks, guns. This is our purpose and our pledge."

In fulfillment of this purpose we will not be intimidated by the threats of dictators that they will regard as a breach of international law or as an act of war our aid to the democracies which dare to resist their aggression. Such aid is not an act of war, even if a dictator should unilaterally proclaim it so to be.

When the dictators, if the dictators, are ready to make war upon us, they will not wait for an act of war on our part. They did not wait for Norway or Belgium or the Netherlands to commit an act of war.

Their only interest is in a new one-way international law, which lacks mutuality in its observance, and, therefore, becomes an instrument of oppression.

The happiness of future generations of Americans may well depend upon how effective and how immediate we can make our aid felt. No one can tell the exact character of the emergency situations that we may be called upon to meet. The Nation's hands must not be tied when the Nation's life is in danger.

We must all prepare to make the sacrifices that the emergency—almost as serious as war itself—demands. Whatever stands in the way of speed and efficiency in defense preparations must give way to the national need.

A free nation has the right to expect full cooperation from all groups. A free nation has the right to look to the leaders of business, of labor, and of agriculture to take the lead in stimulating effort, not among other groups but within their own groups.

The best way of dealing with the few slackers or trouble makers in our midst is, first, to shame them by patriotic example, and, if that fails, to use the sovereignty of Government to save Government.

As men do not live by bread alone, they do not fight by armaments alone. Those who man our defenses, and those behind them who build our defenses, must have the stamina and the courage which come from unshakable belief in the manner of life which they are defending. The mighty action that we are calling for cannot be based on a disregard of all things worth fighting for.

The Nation takes great satisfaction and much strength from the things which have been done to make its people conscious of their individual stake in the preservation of democratic life in America. Those things have toughened the fibre of our people, have renewed their faith and strengthened their devotion to the institutions we make ready to protect.

Certainly this is no time for any of us to stop thinking about the social and economic problems which are the root cause of the social revolution which is today a supreme factor in the world.

For there is nothing mysterious about the foundations of a healthy and strong democracy. The basic things expected by our people of their political and economic systems are simple. They are:

Equality of opportunity for youth and for others.

Jobs for those who can work.

Security for those who need it.

The ending of special privilege for the few.

The preservation of civil liberties for all.

The enjoyment of the fruits of scientific progress in a wider and constantly rising standard of living.

These are the simple, basic things that must never be lost sight of in the turmoil and unbelievable complexity of our modern world. The inner and abiding strength of our economic and political systems is dependent upon the degree to which they fulfill these expectations.

Many subjects connected with our social economy call for immediate improvement.

As examples:

We should bring more citizens under the coverage of old-age pensions and unemployment insurance.

We should widen the opportunities for adequate medical care.

We should plan a better system by which persons deserving or needing gainful employment may obtain it.

I have called for personal sacrifice. I am assured of the willingness of almost all Americans to respond to that call.

A part of the sacrifice means the payment of more money in taxes. In my Budget Message I shall recommend that a greater portion of this great defense program be paid for from taxation than we are paying today. No person should try, or be allowed, to get rich out of this program; and the principle of tax payments in accordance with ability to pay should be constantly before our eyes to guide our legislation.

If the Congress maintains these principles, the voters, putting patriotism ahead of pocketbooks, will give you their applause.

In the future days, which we seek to make secure, we look forward to a world founded upon four essential human freedoms.

The first is freedom of speech and expression—everywhere in the world.

The second is freedom of every person to worship God in his own way—everywhere in the world.

The third is freedom from want—which, translated into world terms, means economic understandings which will secure to every nation a healthy peacetime life for its inhabitants—everywhere in the world.

The fourth is freedom from fear—which, translated into world terms, means a worldwide reduction of armaments to such a point and in such a thorough fashion that no nation will be in a position to commit an act of physical aggression against any neighbor—anywhere in the world.

That is no vision of a distant millennium. It is a definite basis for a kind of world attainable in our own time and generation. That kind of world is the very antithesis of the so-called new order of tyranny which the dictators seek to create with the crash of a bomb.

To that new order we oppose the greater conception—the moral order. A good society is able to face schemes of world domination and foreign revolutions alike without fear.

Since the beginning of our American history, we have been engaged in change—in a perpetual peaceful revolution—a revolution which goes on steadily, quietly adjusting itself to changing conditions—without the concentration camp or the quick-lime in the ditch. The world order which we seek is the cooperation of free countries, working together in a friendly, civilized society.

This nation has placed its destiny in the hands and heads and hearts of its millions of free men and women; and its faith in freedom under the guidance of God. Freedom means the supremacy of human rights everywhere. Our support goes to those who struggle to gain those rights or keep them. Our strength is our unity of purpose.

To that high concept there can be no end save victory.

Chapter 2

The Constitution

_T_he U.S. Constitution forms the basis of the American political system. Despite extraordinary changes in the American economy and in the nation's role and responsibilities in the world, the Constitution remains essentially the same document as written in Philadelphia in the summer of 1787. Over the years, several amendments have made it more inclusive and extended the "blessings of liberty" to previously excluded groups, including blacks and women. At the same time countless decisions of the U.S. Supreme Court have altered the nuances and interpretations of the original text. Still, the original document, and the political philosophy that lies behind it, are well worth studying.

The political philosophy of the Constitution is largely that of the Federalists, its primary supporters. The Federalists were less than a political party; they were a loosely organized group of individuals who shared a commitment to the proposed Constitution and to the ideas it represented. Because they won and because they counted among their number such leading figures as Alexander Hamilton and James Madison, the Federalists are far better known than their opponents, who went by the unfortunately negative-sounding name "Antifederalists." To understand the Federalists and their political philosophy, however, it is essential to understand the views and opinions of the opposition.

This chapter reviews the background of the original struggle over the Constitution and the ideas that emerged. It begins with a presentation of the major ideas of the Federalists and the Antifederalists (selections 2.1 through 2.6). Next it considers the persistent controversy between those who would emphasize the Founders' ideas and those who would instead focus on them as individuals and politicians (selections 2.7 and 2.8). It concludes with an article (selection 2.9) by Gordon S. Wood that analyzes the social and intellectual divisions between the Federalists and Antifederalists. Addi-

tional information on the two groups, especially with respect to their views on the power of the states versus the national government, can be found in chapter 3.

Chapter Questions

1. In what senses are the Federalists properly described as "aristocrats" and the Antifederalists as "democrats"? Consider both the social standing of the two groups and their ideas about politics.

2. Did the Federalists believe in democracy? What evidence is there that they did? that they did not? How can these two views be reconciled?

3. Were the Antifederalists correct in at least some of their charges against the Constitution? Which of their complaints look more reasonable after 200 years? Which look less so?

I THE CLASSIC TEXTS

There is no better way to understand the political philosophy of the Federalists than to read the Federalist Papers. *Originally a selection of newspaper columns written during the debate over the ratification of the Constitution in New York State, the* Federalist Papers *are a compendium of eighty-five essays explaining, defending, and elaborating on the proposed Constitution. The* Federalist, *as it is known, is widely regarded as the definitive statement of the Federalists' views on the Constitution and thus is a frequent reference point for those (like federal judges) who seek to know the intent of the Constitution. The essays that make up the* Federalist *were written by three prominent proponents of the Constitution: John Jay, Alexander Hamilton, and James Madison. Following the style of the day, the articles were signed by the pseudonym Publius, a name that perhaps sought to imply that the authors spoke for the public interest.*

Federalist No. 10, written by James Madison, is concerned with the problem of factions. Frequently it appears in a textbook chapter on interest groups, and it might profitably be reread along with the selections in chapter 9. Its real importance, however, lies in Publius's discussion of human nature and representative government. Publius believes that in a free society, there will soon arise factions, or groups of individuals motivated by a common interest or passion adverse to the interests of other citizens or to the public interest. These factions arise because individuals are free to think for themselves about "religion . . . government, and many other points" and because they have different abilities for acquiring property. Once factions arise, it is in the nature of human beings that they will attempt to use the government to advance their own interests, even at the expense of others. In a pure democracy, the majority faction will pursue its own interest at the expense of the minority, with the result that rational government is impossible. The solution is to construct a representative gov-

ernment covering a large area, so that each representative will represent many diverse interests, and no one faction will be able to dominate.

Notice the consequences of Publius's theory: representative government is not merely a means of approximating a direct democracy but an improvement on it, and representatives are expected not merely to echo the interests of their constituents but to refine and filter those interests and balance them against the interest of others and against the public interest.

In Federalist Nos. 47–51, James Madison lays out his theory of the separation of powers. Contrary to the assumption of most other Americans, Madison did not believe that legislative, executive, and judicial power should be rigidly constrained each to its own branch of government. In fact, Federalist No. 47 was written explicitly to challenge the assumption that the separation of powers means that the three departments of government "ought to have no partial agency in, or no control over, the acts of each other." Quite the opposite is true, in Madison's opinion: each branch should be given a share of the others' powers. It is only if "the whole power of one department is exercised by the same hands which possess the whole power of another department" that liberty is threatened.

Having demonstrated that the separation of powers does not demand a strict separation of functions, Madison then lays out the psychological basis for the separation of powers. Put simply, human beings are not angels; they are and will always be ambitious and power hungry. The only security against such individuals (and what human being is not such a person?) is to make sure that ambition checks ambition. By dividing power among ambitious men and then making them compete for power among themselves, liberty is protected.

All of this may be a sad commentary on human nature, as Madison suggests, but "what is government itself but the greatest of all reflections on human nature?" Madison's political theory here tracks the Scottish economist Adam Smith's theory of capitalism: we rely for bread not on the assumption that the baker will want to feed his fellow human beings but on his personal desire for money. Similarly, Madison relies for the protection of liberty not on politicians' love of the people but on their desire to protect their own power.

Also included here are selections from the Antifederalists, who opposed the Constitution. That they lost their battle does not mean that their arguments were without merit. The Antifederalists were in general educated and intelligent men, whose ideas on politics presented a viable alternative to that presented by the Federalists. In fact, the Antifederalists' views typically represented the conventional eighteenth-century wisdom as compared to the much more innovative—and therefore controversial—ideas of the Federalists.

The Antifederalists produced no such book as the Federalist Papers. Their writings were diverse, uncoordinated, and of uneven quality. Two examples are given below. The first is the report of the minority of the Pennsylvania ratifying convention of 1787; it presents one of the most systematic statements of the Antifederalists' arguments. Notice in particular the minority's fearful and suspicious tone—justifiable, considering the way they were treated by the majority—along with their objections to a large republic; the mixing of legislative, executive, and judicial power; the lack of limits to federal authority over the states; and the absence of a Bill of Rights.

Following is an excerpt from the essays of Brutus, an anonymous Antifederalist who, some scholars believe, may have been Robert Yates of New York. Brutus was particularly concerned about the new federal judiciary, which he feared would assume limitless and arbitrary power.

Other selections from the Federalist Papers *are contained in chapters 1, 3, 11, 12, 14, and 16.*

Questions

1. What is a faction? Why are majority factions more dangerous than minority factions, according to Madison?

2. According to Madison, what advantages does a large republic have over a smaller one? How might the Antifederalists respond to Madison's position?

3. How does Madison respond to the Antifederalists' charge that the Constitution impermissibly blends executive, legislative, and judicial power? Why, in Madison's view, is it necessary to blend the three types of power?

4. Compare and contrast the Federalists' and Antifederalists' views on human nature. Pay particular attention to Madison's argument in *Federalist* No. 51.

2.1 Federalist *No. 10*

James Madison

Among the numerous advantages promised by a well-constructed Union, none deserves to be more accurately developed than its tendency to break and control the violence of faction. The friend of popular governments never finds himself so much alarmed for their character and fate as when he contemplates their propensity to this dangerous vice. He will not fail, therefore, to set a due value on any plan which, without violating the principles to which he is attached, provides a proper cure for it. The instability, injustice, and confusion introduced into the public councils have, in truth, been the mortal diseases under which popular governments have everywhere perished, as they continue to be the favorite and fruitful topics from which the adversaries to liberty derive their most specious declamations. The valuable improvements made by the American constitutions on the popular models, both ancient and modern, cannot certainly be too much admired; but it would be an unwarrantable partiality to contend that they have as effectually obviated the danger on this side, as was wished and expected. Complaints are everywhere heard from our most considerate and virtuous citizens, equally the friends of public and private faith and of public and personal liberty, that our governments are too unstable, that the public good is disregarded in the conflicts of rival parties, and that measures are too often decided, not according to the rules of justice and the rights of the minor party, but by the superior force of an interested and overbearing majority. However anxiously we may wish that these complaints had no foundation, the evidence of known facts will not permit us to deny that they are in some degree true. It will be found, indeed, on a candid review of our situation, that some of the distresses under which we labor have been erroneously charged on the operation of our governments; but it will be found, at the same time, that other causes will not alone account for many of our heaviest misfortunes; and, particularly, for that prevailing and increasing distrust of public engagements and alarm for private rights which are echoed from one end of the continent to the other. These must be chiefly, if not wholly, effects of the unsteadiness and injustice with which a factious spirit has tainted our public administration.

By a faction I understand a number of citizens, whether amounting to a majority or minority of the whole, who are united and actuated by some common impulse of passion, or of interest, adverse to the rights of other citizens, or to the permanent and aggregate interests of the community.

There are two methods of curing the mischiefs of faction: the one, by removing its causes; the other, by controlling its effects.

There are again two methods of removing the causes of faction: the one, by destroying the liberty which is essential to its existence; the other, by giving to every citizen the same opinions, the same passions, and the same interests.

It could never be more truly said than of the first remedy that it was worse than the disease. Liberty is to faction what air is to fire, an aliment without which it instantly expires. But it could not be a less folly to abolish liberty, which is essential to political life, because it nourishes faction than it would be to wish the annihilation of air, which is essential to animal life, because it imparts to fire its destructive agency.

The second expedient is as impracticable as the first would be unwise. As long as the reason of man continues fallible, and he is at liberty to exercise it, different opinions will be formed. As long as the connection subsists between his reason and his self-love, his opinions and his passions will have a reciprocal influence on each other; and the former will be objects to which the latter will attach themselves. The diversity in the faculties of men, from which the rights of property originate, is not less an insuperable obstacle to a uniformity of interests. The protection of these faculties is the first object of government. From the protection of different and unequal faculties of acquiring property, the possession of different degrees and kinds of property immediately results; and from the influence of these on the sentiments and views of the respective proprietors ensues a division of the society into different interests and parties.

The latent causes of faction are thus sown in the nature of man; and we see them everywhere brought into different degrees of activity, according to the different circumstances of civil society. A zeal for different opinions concerning religion, concerning government, and many other points, as well of speculation as of practice; an attachment to different leaders ambitiously contending for pre-eminence and power; or to persons of other descriptions whose fortunes have been interesting to the human passions, have, in turn, divided mankind into parties, inflamed them with mutual animosity, and rendered them much more disposed to vex and oppress each other than to cooperate for their common good. So strong is this propensity of mankind to fall into mutual animosities that where no substantial occasion presents itself the most frivolous and fanciful distinctions have been sufficient to kindle their unfriendly passions and excite their most violent conflicts. But the most common and durable source of factions has been the various and unequal distribution of property. Those who hold and those who are without property have ever formed distinct interests in society. Those who are creditors, and those who are debtors, fall under a like discrimination. A landed interest, a manufacturing interest, a mercantile interest, a moneyed interest, with many lesser interests, grow up of necessity in civilized nations, and divide them into different classes, actuated by different sentiments and views. The regulation of these various and interfering interests forms the principal task of modern legislation and involves the spirit of party and faction in the necessary and ordinary operations of government.

No man is allowed to be a judge in his own cause, because his interest would certainly bias his judgment, and, not improbably, corrupt his integrity. With equal, nay with greater reason, a body of men are unfit to be both judges and parties at the same time; yet what are many of the most important acts of legislation but so many judicial determinations, not indeed concerning the rights of single persons, but concerning the rights of large bodies of citizens? And what are the different classes of legislators but advocates and parties to the causes which they determine? Is a law proposed concerning private debts? It is a question to which the creditors are parties on one side and the debtors on the other. Justice ought to hold the balance between them. Yet the parties are, and must be, themselves the judges; and the most numerous party, or in other words, the most powerful faction must be expected to prevail. Shall domestic manufacturers be encouraged, and in what degree, by restrictions on foreign manufacturers? are questions which would be differently decided by the landed and the manufacturing classes, and probably by neither with a sole regard to justice and the public good. The apportionment of taxes on the various descriptions of property is an act which seems to require the most exact impartiality; yet there is, perhaps, no legislative act in which greater opportunity and temptation are given to a predominant party to trample on the rules of justice. Every shilling with which they overburden the inferior number is a shilling saved to their own pockets.

It is in vain to say that enlightened statesmen will be able to adjust these clashing interests and render them all subservient to the public good. Enlightened statesmen will not always be at the helm. Nor, in many cases, can such an adjustment be made at all without taking into view indirect and remote considerations, which will rarely prevail over the immediate interest which one party may find in disregarding the rights of another or the good of the whole.

The inference to which we are brought is that the *causes* of faction cannot be removed and that relief is only to be sought in the means of controlling its *effects*.

If a faction consists of less than a majority, relief is supplied by the republican principle, which enables the majority to defeat its sinister views by regular vote. It may clog the administration, it may convulse the society; but it will be unable to execute and mask its violence under the forms of the Constitution. When a majority is included in a faction, the form of popular government, on the other hand, enables it to sacrifice to its ruling passion or interest both the public good and the rights of other citizens. "To secure the public good and private rights against the danger of such a faction, and at the same time to preserve the spirit and the form of popular government, is then the great object to which our inquiries are directed." Let me add that it is the great desideratum by which alone this form of government can be rescued from the opprobrium under which it has so long labored and be recommended to the esteem and adoption of mankind.

By what means is this object attainable? Evidently by one of two only. Either the existence of the same passion or interest in a majority at the same time must be prevented, or the majority, having such coexistent passion or interest, must be rendered, by their number and local situation, unable to concert and carry into effect schemes of oppression. If the impulse and the opportunity be suffered to coincide, we well know that neither moral nor religious motives can be relied on as an adequate control. They are not found to be such on the injustice and violence of individuals, and lose their efficacy in proportion to the number combined together, that is, in proportion as their efficacy becomes needful.

From this view of the subject it may be concluded that a pure democracy, by which I mean a society consisting of a small number of citizens, who assemble and administer the government in person, can admit of no cure for the mischiefs of faction. A common passion or interest will, in almost every case, be felt by a majority of the whole; a communication and concert results from the form of government itself; and there is nothing to check the inducements to sacrifice the weaker party or an obnoxious individual. Hence it is that such democracies have ever been spectacles of turbulence and contention; have ever been found incompatible with personal security or the rights of property; and have in general been as short in their lives as they have been violent in their deaths. Theoretic politicians, who have patronized this species of government, have erroneously supposed that by reducing mankind to a perfect equality in their political rights, they would at the same time be perfectly equalized and assimilated in their possessions, their opinions, and their passions.

A republic, by which I mean a government in which the scheme of representation takes place, opens a different prospect and promises the cure for which we are seeking. Let us examine the points in which it varies from pure democracy, and we shall comprehend both the nature of the cure and the efficacy which it must derive from the Union.

The two great points of difference between a democracy and a republic are: first, the delegation of the government, in the latter, to a small number of citizens elected by the rest; secondly, the greater number of citizens and greater sphere of country over which the latter may be extended.

The effect of the first difference is, on the one hand, to refine and enlarge the public views by passing them through the medium of a chosen body of citizens, whose wisdom may best discern the true interest of their country and whose patriotism and love of justice will be least likely to sacrifice it to temporary or partial considerations. Under such a regulation it may well happen that the public voice, pronounced by the representatives of the people, will be more consonant to the public good than if pro-

nounced by the people themselves, convened for the purpose. On the other hand, the effect may be inverted. Men of factious tempers, of local prejudices, or of sinister designs, may, by intrigue, by corruption, or by other means, first obtain the suffrages, and then betray the interests of the people. The question resulting is, whether small or extensive republics are most favorable to the election of proper guardians of the public weal; and it is clearly decided in favor of the latter by two obvious considerations.

In the first place it is to be remarked that however small the republic may be the representatives must be raised to a certain number in order to guard against the cabals of a few; and that however large it may be they must be limited to a certain number in order to guard against the confusion of a multitude. Hence, the number of representatives in the two cases not being in proportion to that of the constituents, and being proportionally greatest in the small republic, it follows that if the proportion of fit characters be not less in the large than in the small republic, the former will present a greater option, and consequently a greater probability of a fit choice.

In the next place, as each representative will be chosen by a greater number of citizens in the large than in the small republic, it will be more difficult for unworthy candidates to practise with success the vicious arts by which elections are too often carried; and the suffrages of the people being more free, will be more likely to center on men who possess the most attractive merit and the most diffusive and established characters.

It must be confessed that in this, as in most other cases, there is a mean, on both sides of which inconveniencies will be found to lie. By enlarging too much the number of electors, you render the representative too little acquainted with all their local circumstances and lesser interests; as by reducing it too much, you render him unduly attached to these, and too little fit to comprehend and pursue great and national objects. The federal Constitution forms a happy combination in this respect; the great and aggregate interests being referred to the national, the local and particular to the State legislatures.

The other point of difference is the greater number of citizens and extent of territory which may be brought within the compass of republican than of democratic government; and it is this circumstance principally which renders factious combinations less to be dreaded in the former than in the latter. The smaller the society, the fewer probably will be the distinct parties and interests composing it; the fewer the distinct parties and interests, the more frequently will a majority be found of the same party; and the smaller the number of individuals composing a majority, and the smaller the compass within which they are placed, the more easily will they concert and execute their plans of oppression. Extend the sphere and you take in a greater variety of parties and interests; you make it less probable that a majority of the whole will have a common motive to invade the rights of other citizens; or if such a common motive exists, it will be more difficult for all who feel it to discover their own strength and to act in unison with each other. Besides other impediments, it may be remarked that, where there is a consciousness of unjust or dishonorable purposes, communication is always checked by distrust in proportion to the number whose concurrence is necessary.

Hence, it clearly appears that the same advantage which a republic has over a democracy in controlling the effects of faction is enjoyed by a large over a small republic—is enjoyed by the Union over the States composing it. Does this advantage consist in the substitution of representatives whose enlightened views and virtuous sentiments render them superior to local prejudices and to schemes of injustice? It will not be denied that the representation of the Union will be most likely to possess these requisite endowments. Does it consist in the greater security afforded by a greater variety of parties, against the event of any one party being able to outnumber and oppress the rest? In an equal degree does the increased variety of parties comprised within the Union increase this security. Does it, in fine, consist in the greater obstacles opposed to the concert and accomplishment of the secret wishes of an unjust and interested majority? Here again the extent of the Union gives it the most palpable advantage.

The influence of factious leaders may kindle a flame within their particular States but will be unable to spread a general conflagration through the other States. A religious sect may degenerate into a political faction in a part of the Confederacy; but the variety of sects dispersed over the entire face of it must secure the national councils against any danger from that source. A rage for paper money, for an abolition of debts, for an equal division of property, or for any other improper or wicked project, will be less apt to pervade the whole body of the Union than a particular member of it, in the same proportion as such a malady is more likely to taint a particular county or district than an entire State.

In the extent and proper structure of the Union, therefore, we behold a republican remedy for the diseases most incident to republican government. And according to the degree of pleasure and pride we feel in being republicans ought to be our zeal in cherishing the spirit and supporting the character of federalists.

2.2 Federalist No. 47

James Madison

. . . One of the principal objections inculcated by the more respectable adversaries to the Constitution is its supposed violation of the political maxim that the legislative, executive, and judiciary departments ought to be separate and distinct. In the structure of the federal government no regard, it is said, seems to have been paid to this essential precaution in favor of liberty. The several departments of power are distributed and blended in such a manner as at once to destroy all symmetry and beauty of form, and to expose some of the essential parts of the edifice to the danger of being crushed by the disproportionate weight of other parts.

No political truth is certainly of greater intrinsic value, or is stamped with the authority of more enlightened patrons of liberty than that on which the objection is founded. The accumulation of all powers, legislative, executive, and judiciary, in the same hands, whether of one, a few, or many, and whether hereditary, self-appointed, or elective, may justly be pronounced the very definition of tyranny. Were the federal Constitution, therefore, really chargeable with this accumulation of power, or with a mixture of powers, having a dangerous tendency to such an accumulation, no further arguments would be necessary to inspire a universal reprobation of the system. I persuade myself, however, that it will be made apparent to everyone that the charge cannot be supported, and that the maxim on which it relies has been totally misconceived and misapplied. In order to form correct ideas on this important subject it will be proper to investigate the sense in which the preservation of liberty requires that the three great departments of power should be separate and distinct.

The oracle who is always consulted and cited on this subject is the celebrated Montesquieu. If he be not the author of this invaluable precept in the science of politics, he has the merit at least of displaying and recommending it most effectually to the attention of mankind. Let us endeavor, in the first place, to ascertain his meaning on this point.

The British Constitution was to Montesquieu what Homer has been to the didactic writers on epic poetry. As the latter have considered the work of the immortal bard as the perfect model from which the principles and rules of the epic art were to be drawn, and by which all similar works were to be judged, so this great political critic appears to have viewed the Constitution of England as the standard, or to use his own expression, as the mirror of political liberty; and to have delivered, in the form of elementary truths, the several characteristic principles of that particular system. That we may be sure, then, not to mistake his meaning in this case, let us recur to the source from which the maxim was drawn.

On the slightest view of the British Constitution, we must perceive that the legislative, executive, and judiciary departments are by no means totally separate and distinct from each other. The executive magistrate forms an integral part of the legislative authority. He alone has the prerogative of making treaties with foreign sovereigns which, when made, have, under certain limitations, the force of legislative acts. All the members of the judiciary department are appointed by him, can be removed by him on the address of the two Houses of Parliament, and form, when he pleases to consult them, one of his constitutional councils. One branch of the legislative department forms also a great constitutional council to the executive chief, as, on another hand, it is the sole depository of judicial power in cases of impeachment, and is invested with the supreme appellate jurisdiction in all other cases. The judges, again, are so far connected with the legislative department as often to attend and participate in its deliberations, though not admitted to a legislative vote.

From these facts, by which Montesquieu was guided, it may clearly be inferred that in saying "There can be no liberty where the legislative and executive powers are united in the same person, or body of magistrates," or, "if the power of judging be not separated from the legislative and executive powers," he did not mean that these departments ought to have no *partial agency* in, or no *control* over, the acts of each other. His meaning, as his own words import, and still more conclusively as illustrated by the example in his eye, can amount to no more than this, that where the *whole* power of one department is exercised by the same hands which possess the *whole* power of another department, the fundamental principles of a free constitution are subverted. This would have been the case in the constitution examined by him, if the king, who is the sole executive magistrate, had possessed also the complete legislative power, or the supreme administration of justice; or if the entire legislative body had possessed the supreme judiciary, or the supreme executive authority. This, however, is not among the vices of that constitution. The magistrate in whom the whole executive power resides cannot of himself make a law, though he can put a negative on every law; nor administer justice in person, though he has the appointment of those who do administer it. The judges can exercise no executive prerogative, though they are shoots from the executive stock; nor any legislative function, though they may be advised by the legislative councils. The entire legislature can perform no judiciary act, though by the joint act of two of its branches the judges may be removed from their offices, and though one of its branches is possessed of the judicial power in the last resort. The entire legislature, again, can exercise no executive prerogative, though one of its branches constitutes the supreme executive magistracy, and another, on the impeachment of a third, can try and condemn all the subordinate officers in the executive department.

The reasons on which Montesquieu grounds his maxim are a further demonstration of his meaning. "When the legislative and executive powers are united in the same person or body," says he, "there can be no liberty, because apprehensions may arise lest *the same* monarch or senate should *enact* tyrannical laws to *execute* them in a tyrannical manner." Again: "Were the power of judging joined with the legislative, the life and liberty of the subject would be exposed to arbitrary control, for *the judge* would then be *the legislator.* Were it joined to the executive power, *the judge* might behave with all the violence of *an oppressor.*" Some of these reasons are more fully explained in other passages; but briefly stated as they are here they sufficiently establish the meaning which we have put on this celebrated maxim of this celebrated author.

If we look into the constitutions of the several States we find that, notwithstanding the emphatical and, in some instances, the unqualified terms in which this axiom has been laid down, there is not a single instance in which the several departments of power have been kept absolutely separate and distinct. New Hampshire, whose constitution was the last formed, seems to have been fully aware of the impossibility and inexpediency of avoiding any mixture whatever of these departments, and has qualified the doctrine by declaring "that the legislative, executive, and judiciary powers ought to be kept as separate from, and independent of, each other *as the nature of a free government will admit; or as is consistent with that chain of connection that binds the whole fabric of the constitution in one indissoluble bond of unity and amity.*" Her constitution accordingly mixes these departments in several respects. The Senate, which is a branch of the legislative department, is also a judicial tribunal for the trial of impeachments. The President, who is the head of the executive department, is the presiding member also of the Senate; and, besides an equal vote in all cases, has a casting vote in case of a tie. The executive head is himself eventually elective every year by the legislative department, and his council is every year chosen by and from the members of the same department. Several of the officers of state are also appointed by the legislature. And the members of the judiciary department are appointed by the executive department.

The constitution of Massachusetts has observed a sufficient though less pointed caution in expressing this fundamental article of liberty. It declares "that the legislative department shall never exercise the executive and judicial powers, or either of them; the executive shall never exercise the legislative and judicial powers, or either of them; the judicial shall never exercise the legislative and executive powers, or either of them." This declaration corresponds precisely with the doctrine of Montesquieu, as it has been explained, and is not in a single point violated by the plan of the convention. It goes no farther than to prohibit any one of the entire departments from exercising the powers of another department. In the very Constitution to which it is prefixed, a partial mixture of powers has been admitted. The executive magistrate has a qualified negative on the legislative body, and the Senate, which is a part of the legislature, is a court of impeachment for members both of the executive and judiciary departments. The members of the judiciary department, again, are appointable by the executive department, and removable by the same authority on the address of the two legislative branches. Lastly, a number of the officers of government are annually appointed by the legislative department. As the appointment to offices, particularly executive offices, is in its nature an executive function, the compilers of the Constitution have, in this last point at least, violated the rule established by themselves. . . . [*Publius next reviews other state constitutions.*]

In citing these cases, in which the legislative, executive, and judiciary departments have not been kept totally separate and distinct, I wish not to be regarded as an advocate for the particular organizations of the several State governments. I am fully aware that among the many excellent principles which they exemplify they carry strong marks of the haste, and still stronger of the inexperience, under which they were framed. It is but too obvious that in some instances the fundamental principle under consideration has been violated by too great a mixture, and even an actual consolidation of the different powers; and that in no instance has a competent provision been made for maintaining in practice the separation delineated on paper. What I have wished to evince is that the charge brought against the proposed Constitution of violating the sacred maxim of free government is warranted neither by the real meaning annexed to that maxim by its author, nor by the sense in which it has hitherto been understood in America. This interesting subject will be resumed in the ensuing paper.

2.3 Federalist No. 48

James Madison

It was shown in the last paper that the political apothegm there examined does not require that the legislative, executive, and judiciary departments should be wholly unconnected with each other. I shall undertake, in the next place, to show that unless these departments be so far connected and blended as to give to each a constitutional control over the others, the degree of separation which the maxim requires, as essential to a free government, can never in practice be duly maintained.

It is agreed on all sides that the powers properly belonging to one of the departments ought not to be directly and completely administered by either of the other departments. It is equally evident that none of them ought to possess, directly or indirectly, an overruling influence over the others in the administration of their respective powers. It will not be denied that power is of an encroaching nature and that it ought to be effectually restrained from passing the limits assigned to it. After discriminating, therefore, in theory, the several classes of power, as they may in their nature be legislative, executive, or judiciary, the next and most difficult task is to provide some practical security for each, against the invasion of the others. What this security ought to be is the great problem to be solved.

Will it be sufficient to mark, with precision, the boundaries of these departments in the constitution of the government, and to trust to these parchment barriers against the encroaching spirit of power? This is the security which appears to have been principally relied on by the compilers of most of the American constitutions. But experience assures us that the efficacy of the provision has been greatly overrated; and that some more adequate defense is indispensably necessary for the more feeble against the more powerful members of the government. The legislative department is everywhere extending the sphere of its activity and drawing all power into its impetuous vortex.

The founders of our republics have so much merit for the wisdom which they have displayed that no task can be less pleasing than that of pointing out the errors into which they have fallen. A respect for truth, however, obliges us to remark that they seem never for a moment to have turned their eyes from the danger, to liberty, from the overgrown and all-grasping prerogative of an hereditary magistrate, supported and fortified by an hereditary branch of the legislative authority. They seem never to have recollected the danger from legislative usurpations, which, by assembling all power in the same hands, must lead to the same tyranny as is threatened by executive usurpations.

In a government where numerous and extensive prerogatives are placed in the hands of an hereditary monarch, the executive department is very justly regarded as the source of danger, and watched with all the jealousy which a zeal for liberty ought to inspire. In a democracy, where a multitude of people exercise in person the legislative functions and are continually exposed, by their incapacity for regular deliberation and concerted measures, to the ambitious intrigues of their executive magistrates, tyranny may well be apprehended, on some favorable emergency, to start up in the same quarter. But in a representative republic where the executive magistracy is carefully limited, both in the extent and the duration of its power; and where the legislative power is exercised by an assembly, which is inspired by a supposed influence over the people with an intrepid confidence in its own strength; which is sufficiently numerous to feel all the passions which actuate a multitude, yet not so numerous as to be incapable of pursuing the objects of its passions by means which reason prescribes; it is against the enterprising ambition of this department that the people ought to indulge all their jealousy and exhaust all their precautions.

The legislative department derives a superiority in our governments from other circumstances. Its constitutional powers being at once more extensive, and less susceptible of precise limits, it can, with the greater facility, mask, under complicated and indirect measures, the encroachments which it makes on the co-ordinate departments. It is not unfrequently a question of real nicety in legislative bodies whether the operation of a particular measure will, or will not, extend beyond the legislative sphere. On the other side, the executive power being restrained within a narrower compass and being more simple in its nature, and the judiciary being described by landmarks still less uncertain, projects of usurpation by either of these departments would immediately betray and defeat themselves. Nor is this all: as the legislative department alone has access to the pockets of the people, and has in some constitutions full discretion, and in all a prevailing influence, over the pecuniary rewards of those who fill the other departments, a dependence is thus created in the latter, which gives still greater facility to encroachments of the former.

• • •

The conclusion which I am warranted in drawing from these observations is that a mere demarcation on parchment of the constitutional limits of the several departments is not a sufficient guard against those encroachments which lead to a tyrannical concentration of all the powers of government in the same hands.

2.4 Federalist No. 51

James Madison

To what expedient, then, shall we finally resort, for maintaining in practice the necessary partition of power among the several departments as laid down in the Constitution? The only answer that can be given is that as all these exterior provisions are found to be inadequate the defect must be supplied, by so contriving the interior structure of the government as that its several constituent parts may, by their mutual relations, be the means of keeping each other in their proper places. Without presuming to undertake a full development of this important idea I will hazard a few general observations which may perhaps place it in a clearer light, and enable us to form a more correct judgment of the principles and structure of the government planned by the convention.

In order to lay a due foundation for that separate and distinct exercise of the different powers of government, which to a certain extent is admitted on all hands to be essential to the preservation of liberty, it is evident that each department should have a will of its own; and consequently should be so constituted that the members of each should have as little agency as possible in the appointment of the members of the others. Were this principle rigorously adhered to, it would require that all the appointments for the supreme executive, legislative, and judiciary magistracies should be drawn from the same fountain of authority, the people, through channels having no communication whatever with one another. Perhaps such a plan of constructing the several departments would be less difficult in practice than it may in contemplation appear. Some difficulties, however, and some additional expense would attend the execution of it. Some deviations, therefore, from the principle must be admitted. In the constitution of the judiciary department in particular, it might be inexpedient to insist rigorously on the principle: first, because peculiar qualifications being essential in the members, the primary consideration ought to be to select that mode of choice which best secures these qualifications; second, because the permanent tenure by which the appointments are held in that department must soon destroy all sense of dependence on the authority conferring them.

It is equally evident that the members of each department should be as little dependent as possible on those of the others for the emoluments annexed to their offices. Were the executive magistrate, or the judges, not independent of the legislature in this particular, their independence in every other would be merely nominal.

But the great security against a gradual concentration of the several powers in the same department consists in giving to those who administer each department the necessary constitutional means and personal motives to resist encroachments of the others. The provision for defense must in this, as in all other cases, be made commensurate to the danger of attack. Ambition must be made to counteract ambition. The interest of the man must be connected with the constitutional rights of the place. It may be a reflection on human nature that such devices should be necessary to control the abuses of government. But what is government itself but the greatest of all reflections on human nature? If men were angels, no government would be necessary. If angels were to govern men, neither external nor internal controls on government would be necessary. In framing a government which is to be administered by men over men, the great difficulty lies in this: you must first enable the government to control the governed; and in the next place oblige it to control itself. A dependence on the people is, no doubt, the primary control on the government; but experience has taught mankind the necessity of auxiliary precautions.

This policy of supplying, by opposite and rival interests, the defect of better motives, might be traced through the whole system of human affairs, private as well as public. We see it particularly displayed in all the subordinate distributions of power, where the constant aim is to divide and arrange the several offices in such a manner as that each may be a check on the other—that the private interest of every individual may be a sentinel over the public rights. These inventions of prudence cannot be less requisite in the distribution of the supreme powers of the State.

But it is not possible to give to each department an equal power of self-defense. In republican government, the legislative authority necessarily predominates. The remedy for this inconveniency is to divide the legislature into different branches; and to render them, by different modes of election and different principles of action, as little connected with each other as the nature of their common functions and their common dependence on the society will admit. It may even be necessary to guard against dangerous encroachments by still further precautions. As the weight of the legislative authority requires that it should be thus divided, the

weakness of the executive may require, on the other hand, that it should be fortified. An absolute negative on the legislature appears, at first view, to be the natural defense with which the executive magistrate should be armed. But perhaps it would be neither altogether safe nor alone sufficient. On ordinary occasions it might not be exerted with the requisite firmness, and on extraordinary occasions it might be perfidiously abused. May not this defect of an absolute negative be supplied by some qualified connection between this weaker department and the weaker branch of the stronger department, by which the latter may be led to support the constitutional rights of the former, without being too much detached from the rights of its own department?

If the principles on which these observations are founded be just, as I persuade myself they are, and they be applied as a criterion to the several State constitutions, and to the federal Constitution, it will be found that if the latter does not perfectly correspond with them, the former are infinitely less able to bear such a test.

There are, moreover, two considerations particularly applicable to the federal system of America, which place that system in a very interesting point of view.

First. In a single republic, all the power surrendered by the people is submitted to the administration of a single government; and the usurpations are guarded against by a division of the government into distinct and separate departments. In the compound republic of America, the power surrendered by the people is first divided between two distinct governments, and then the portion allotted to each subdivided among distinct and separate departments. Hence a double security arises to the rights of the people. The different governments will control each other, at the same time that each will be controlled by itself.

Second. It is of great importance in a republic not only to guard the society against the oppression of its rulers, but to guard one part of the society against the injustice of the other part.

Different interests necessarily exist in different classes of citizens. If a majority be united by a common interest, the rights of the minority will be insecure. There are but two methods of providing against this evil: the one by creating a will in the community independent of the majority—that is, of the society itself; the other, by comprehending in the society so many separate descriptions of citizens as will render an unjust combination of a majority of the whole very improbable, if not impracticable. The first method prevails in all governments possessing an hereditary or self-appointed authority. This, at best, is but a precarious security; because a power independent of the society may as well espouse the unjust views of the major as the rightful interests of the minor party, and may possibly be turned against both parties. The second method will be exemplified in the federal republic of the United States. Whilst all authority in it will be derived from and dependent on the society, the society itself will be broken into so many parts, interests and classes of citizens, that the rights of individuals, or of the minority, will be in little danger from interested combinations of the majority. In a free government the security for civil rights must be the same as that for religious rights. It consists in the one case in the multiplicity of interests, and in the other in the multiplicity of sects. The degree of security in both cases will depend on the number of interests and sects; and this may be presumed to depend on the extent of country and number of people comprehended under the same government. This view of the subject must particularly recommend a proper federal system to all the sincere and considerate friends of republican government, since it shows that in exact proportion as the territory of the Union may be formed into more circumscribed Confederacies, or States, oppressive combinations of a majority will be facilitated; the best security, under the republican forms, for the rights of every class of citizen, will be diminished; and consequently the stability and independence of some member of the government, the only other security, must be proportionally increased. Justice is the end of government. It is the end of civil society. It ever has been and ever will be pursued until it be obtained, or until liberty be lost in the pursuit. In a society under the forms of which the stronger faction can readily unite and oppress the weaker, anarchy may as truly be said to reign as in a state of nature, where the weaker individual is not secured against the violence of the stronger; and as, in the latter state, even the stronger individuals are prompted, by the uncertainty of their condition, to submit to a government which may protect the weak as well as themselves; so, in the former state, will the more powerful factions or parties be gradually induced, by a like motive, to wish for a government which will protect all parties, the weaker as well as the more powerful. It can be little doubted that if the State of Rhode Island was separated from the Confederacy and left to itself, the insecurity of rights under the popular form of government within such narrow limits would be displayed by such reiterated oppressions of factious majorities that some power altogether independent of the people would soon be called for by the voice of the very factions whose misrule had proved the necessity of it. In the extended republic of the United States, and among the great variety of interests, parties, and sects which it embraces, a coalition of a majority of the whole society could seldom take place on any other principles than those of justice and the general good; whilst there being thus less danger to a minor from the will of a major party, there must be less pretext, also, to provide for the security of the former, by introducing into the government a will not dependent on the latter, or, in other words, a will independent of the society itself. It is no less certain than it is important, notwithstanding the contrary opinions which have been entertained, that the larger the society, provided it lie within a practicable sphere, the more duly capable it will be of self-government. And happily for the *republican cause*, the practicable sphere may be carried to a very great extent by a judicious modification and mixture of the *federal principle.*

2.5 The Address and Reasons of Dissent of the Minority of the Convention of Pennsylvania to Their Constituents

It was not until after the termination of the late glorious contest, which made the people of the United States, an independent nation, that any defect was discovered in the present confederation. It was formed by some of the ablest patriots in America. It carried us successfully through the war; and the virtue and patriotism of the people, with their disposition to promote the common cause, supplied the want of power in Congress.

The requisition of Congress for the five *per cent* impost was made before the peace, so early as the first of February, 1781, but was prevented taking effect by the refusal of one state; yet it is probable every state in the union would have agreed to this measure at that period, had it not been for the extravagant terms in which it was demanded. The requisition was new moulded in the year 1783, and accompanied with an additional demand of certain supplementary funds for 25 years. Peace had now taken place, and the United States found themselves labouring under a considerable foreign and domestic debt, incurred during the war. The requisition of 1783 was commensurate with the interest of the debt, as it was then calculated; but it has been more accurately ascertained since that time. The domestic debt has been found to fall several millions of dollars short of the calculation, and it has lately been considerably diminished by large sales of the western lands. The states have been called on by Congress annually for supplies until the general system of finance proposed in 1783 should take place.

It was at this time that the want of an efficient federal government was first complained of, and that the powers vested in Congress were found to be inadequate to the procuring of the benefits that should result from the union. The impost was granted by most of the states, but many refused the supplementary funds; the annual requisitions were set at nought by some of the states, while others complied with them by legislative acts, but were tardy in their payments, and Congress found themselves incapable of complying with their engagements, and supporting the federal government. It was found that our national character was sinking in the opinion of foreign nations. The Congress could make treaties of commerce, but could not enforce the observance of them. We were suffering from the restrictions of foreign nations, who had shackled our commerce, while we were unable to retaliate: and all now agreed that it would be advantageous to the union to enlarge the powers of Congress; that they should be enabled in the amplest manner to regulate commerce, and to lay and collect duties on the imports throughout the United States. With this view a convention was first proposed by Virginia, and finally recommended by Congress for the different states to appoint deputies to meet in convention, "for the purposes of revising and amending the present articles of confederation, so as to make them adequate to the exigencies of the union." This recommendation the legislatures of twelve states complied with so hastily as not to consult their constituents on the subject; and though the different legislatures had no authority from their constituents for the purpose, they probably apprehended the necessity would justify the measure; and none of them extended their ideas at that time further than "revising and amending the present articles of confederation." Pennsylvania by the act appointing deputies expressly confined their powers to this object; and though it is probable that some of the members of the assembly of this state had at that time in contemplation to annihilate the present confederation, as well as the constitution of Pennsylvania, yet the plan was not sufficiently matured to communicate it to the public.

The majority of the legislature of this commonwealth, were at that time under the influence of the members from the city of Philadelphia. They agreed that the deputies sent by them to convention should have no compensation for their services, which determination was calculated to prevent the election of any member who resided at a distance from the city. It was in vain for the minority to attempt electing delegates to the convention, who understood the circumstances, and the feelings of the people, and had a common interest with them. They found a disposition in the leaders of the majority of the house to chuse themselves and some of their dependants. The minority attempted to prevent this by agreeing to vote for some of the leading members, who they knew had influence enough to be appointed at any rate, in hopes of carrying with them some respectable citizens of Philadelphia, in whose principles and integrity they could have more confidence; but even in this they were disappointed, except in one member: the eighth member was added at a subsequent session of the assembly.

The Continental convention met in the city of Philadelphia at the time appointed. It was composed of some men of excellent characters; of others who were more remarkable for their ambition and cunning, than their patriotism; and of some who had been opponents to the independence of the United States. The delegates from Pennsylvania were, six of them, uniform and decided opponents to the constitution of this commonwealth. The convention sat upwards of four months. The doors were kept shut, and the members brought under the most solemn engagements of secrecy. Some of those who opposed their going so far beyond their powers, retired, hopeless, from the convention, others had the firmness to refuse signing the plan altogether; and many who did sign it, did it not as a system they wholly approved, but as

the best that could be then obtained, and notwithstanding the time spent on this subject, it is agreed on all hands to be a work of haste and accommodation.

Whilst the gilded chains were forging in the secret conclave, the meaner instruments of despotism without, were busily employed in alarming the fears of the people with dangers which did not exist, and exciting their hopes of greater advantages from the expected plan than even the best government on earth could produce.

The proposed plan had not many hours issued forth from the womb of suspicious secrecy, until such as were prepared for the purpose, were carrying about petitions for people to sign, signifying their approbation of the system, and requesting the legislature to call a convention. While every measure was taken to intimidate the people against opposing it, the public papers teemed with the most violent threats against those who should dare to think for themselves, and *tar and feathers* were liberally promised to all those who would not immediately join in supporting the proposed government be it what it would. Under such circumstances petitions in favour of calling a convention were signed by great numbers in and about the city, before they had leisure to read and examine the system, many of whom, now they are better acquainted with it, and have had time to investigate its principles, are heartily opposed to it. The petitions were speedily handed into the legislature.

Affairs were in this situation when on the 28th of September last a resolution was proposed to the assembly by a member of the house who had been also a member of the federal convention, for calling a state convention, to be elected within *ten* days for the purpose of examining and adopting the proposed constitution of the United States, though at this time the house had not received it from Congress. This attempt was opposed by a minority, who after offering every argument in their power to prevent the precipitate measure, without effect, absented themselves from the house as the only alternative left them, to prevent the measure taking place previous to their constituents being acquainted with the business—That violence and outrage which had been so often threatened was not practised; some of the members were seized the next day by a mob collected for the purpose, and forcibly dragged to the house, and there detained by force whilst the quorum of the legislature, *so formed,* compleated their resolution. We shall dwell no longer on this subject, the people of Pennsylvania have been already acquainted therewith. We would only further observe that every member of the legislature, previously to taking his seat, by solemn oath or affirmation, declares, "that he will not do or consent to any act or thing whatever that shall have a tendency to lessen or abridge their rights and privileges, as declared in the constitution of this state." And that constitution which they are so solemnly sworn to support cannot legally be altered but by a recommendation of a council of censors, who alone are authorised to propose alterations and amendments, and even these must be published at least *six months,* for the consideration of the people.—The proposed system of government for the United States, if adopted, will alter and may annihilate the constitution of Pennsylvania; and therefore the legislature had no authority whatever to recommend the calling a convention for that purpose. This proceeding could not be considered as binding on the people of this commonwealth. The house was formed by violence, some of the members composing it were detained there by force, which alone would have vitiated any proceedings, to which they were otherwise competent; but had the legislature been legally formed, this business was absolutely without their power.

In this situation of affairs were the subscribers elected members of the convention of Pennsylvania. A convention called by a legislature in direct violation of their duty, and composed in part of members, who were compelled to attend for that purpose, to consider of a constitution proposed by a convention of the United States, who were not appointed for the purpose of framing a new form of government, but whose powers were expressly confined to altering and amending the present articles of confederation.—Therefore the members of the continental convention in proposing the plan acted as individuals, and not as deputies from Pennsylvania. The assembly who called the state convention acted as individuals, and not as the legislature of Pennsylvania; nor could they or the convention chosen on their recommendation have authority to do any act or thing, that can alter or annihilate the constitution of Pennsylvania (both of which will be done by the new constitution) nor are their proceedings in our opinion, at all binding on the people.

The election for members of the convention was held at so early a period and the want of information was so great, that some of us did not know of it until after it was over, and we have reason to believe that great numbers of the people of Pennsylvania have not yet had an opportunity of sufficiently examining the proposed constitution.—We apprehend that no change can take place that will affect the internal government or constitution of this commonwealth, unless a majority of the people should evidence a wish for such a change; but on examining the number of votes given for members of the present state convention, we find that of upwards of *seventy thousand* freemen who are intitled to vote in Pennsylvania, the whole convention has been elected by about *thirteen thousand* voters, and though *two thirds* of the members of the convention have thought proper to ratify the proposed constitution, yet those *two thirds* were elected by the votes of only *six thousand and eight hundred* freemen.

In the city of Philadelphia and some of the eastern counties, the junto that took the lead in the business agreed to vote for none but such as would solemnly promise to adopt the system in *toto,* without exercising their judgment. In many of the counties the people did not attend the elections as they had not an opportunity of judging of the plan. Others did not consider themselves bound by the call of a set of men who assembled at the statehouse in Philadelphia, and assumed the name of the legislature of Pennsylvania; and some were prevented from voting by the violence of the party who were determined at all events to force down the measure. To such lengths did the tools of despotism carry their outrage, that in the night of the election for members of convention, in the city of Philadelphia, several of the subscribers (being then in the city to transact your business) were grossly abused, ill-treated and insulted while they were quiet in their lodgings, though they did not interfere, nor had any thing to do with the said election, but as they apprehend, because they were supposed to be adverse to the proposed constitution, and would not tamely surrender those sacred rights, which you had committed to their charge.

The convention met, and the same disposition was soon manifested in considering the proposed constitution, that had been exhibited in every other stage of the business. We were prohibited by an express vote of the convention, from taking any question on the separate articles of the plan, and reduced to the necessity of adopting or rejecting *in toto.*—'Tis true the majority permitted us to debate on each article, but restrained us from proposing amendments.—They also determined not to permit us to enter on the minutes our reasons of dissent against any of the articles, nor even on the final question our reasons of dissent against the whole. Thus situated we entered on the examination of the proposed system of government, and found it to be such as we could not adopt, without, as we conceived, surrendering up your dearest rights. We offered our objections to the convention, and opposed those parts of the plan, which, in our opinion, would be injurious to you, in the best manner we were able; and closed our arguments by offering the following propositions to the convention.

1. The right of conscience shall be held inviolable; and neither the legislative, executive nor judicial powers of the United States shall have authority to alter, abrogate, or infringe any part of the constitution of the several states, which provide for the preservation of liberty in matters of religion.

2. That in controversies respecting property, and in suits between man and man, trial by jury shall remain as heretofore, as well in the federal courts, as in those of the several states.

3. That in all capital and criminal prosecutions, a man has a right to demand the cause and nature of his accusation, as well in the federal courts, as in those of the several states; to be heard by himself and his counsel; to be confronted with the accusers and witnesses; to call for evidence in his favor, and a speedy trial by an impartial jury of his vicinage, without whose unanimous consent, he cannot be found guilty, nor can he be compelled to give evidence against himself; and that no man be deprived of his liberty, except by the law of the land or the judgment of his peers.

4. That excessive bail ought not to be required, nor excessive fines imposed, nor cruel nor unusual punishments inflicted.

5. That warrants unsupported by evidence, whereby any officer or messenger may be commanded or required to search suspected places, or to seize any person or persons, his or their property, not particularly described, are grievous and oppressive, and shall not be granted either by the magistrates of the federal government or others.

6. That the people have a right to the freedom of speech, of writing and publishing their sentiments, therefore, the freedom of the press shall not be restrained by any law of the United States.

7. That the people have a right to bear arms for the defence of themselves and their own state, or the United States, or for the purpose of killing game; and no law shall be passed for disarming the people or any of them, unless for crimes committed, or real danger of public injury from individuals; and as standing armies in the time of peace are dangerous to liberty, they ought not to be kept up; and that the military shall be kept under strict subordination to and be governed by the civil powers.

8. The inhabitants of the several states shall have liberty to fowl and hunt in seasonable times, on the lands they hold, and on all other lands in the United States not inclosed, and in like manner to fish in all navigable waters, and others not private property, without being restrained therein by any laws to be passed by the legislature of the United States.

9. That no law shall be passed to restrain the legislatures of the several states from enacting laws for imposing taxes, except imposts and duties on goods imported or exported, and that no taxes, except imposts and duties upon goods imported and exported, and postage on letters shall be levied by the authority of Congress.

10. That the house of representatives be properly increased in number; that elections shall remain free; that the several states shall have power to regulate the elections for senators and representatives, without being controuled either directly or indirectly by any interference on the part of the Congress; and that elections of representatives be annual.

11. That the power of organizing, arming and disciplining the militia (the manner of disciplining the militia to be prescribed by Congress) remain with the individual states, and that Congress shall not have authority to call or march any of the militia out of their own state, without the consent of such state, and for such length of time only as such state shall agree.

That the sovereignty, freedom and independency of the several states shall be retained, and every power, jurisdiction and right which is not by this constitution expressly delegated to the United States in Congress assembled.

12. That the legislative, executive, and judicial powers be kept separate; and to this end that a constitutional council be appointed, to advise and assist the president, who shall be responsible for the advice they give, hereby the senators would be relieved from almost constant attendance; and also that the judges be made completely independent.

13. That no treaty which shall be directly opposed to the existing laws of the United States in Congress assembled, shall be valid until such laws shall be repealed, or made conformable to such treaty; neither shall any treaties be valid which are in contradiction to the constitution of the United States, or the constitutions of the several states.

14. That the judiciary power of the United States shall be confined to cases affecting ambassadors, other public ministers and consuls; to cases of admiralty and maritime jurisdiction; to controversies to which the United States shall be a party; to controversies between two or more states—between a state and citizens of different states—between citizens claiming lands under grants of different states; and between a state or the citizen thereof and foreign states, and in criminal cases, to such only as are expressly enumerated in the constitution, and that the United States in Congress assembled, shall not have power to enact laws, which shall alter the laws of descents and distribution of the effects of deceased persons, the titles of lands or goods, or the regulation of contracts in the individual states.

After reading these propositions, we declared our willingness to agree to the plan, provided it was so amended as to meet these propositions, or something similar to them; and finally moved the convention to adjourn, to give the people of Pennsylvania time to consider the subject, and determine for themselves; but these were all rejected, and the final vote was taken, when our duty to you induced us to vote against the proposed plan, and to decline signing the ratification of the same.

During the discussion we met with many insults, and some personal abuse; we were not even treated with decency, during the sitting of the convention, by the persons in the gallery of the house; however, we flatter ourselves that in contending for the preservation of those invaluable rights you have thought proper to commit to our charge, we acted with a spirit becoming freemen, and being desirous that you might know the principles which actuated our conduct, and being prohibited from inserting our reasons of dissent on the minutes of the convention, we have subjoined them for your consideration, as to you alone we are accountable. It remains with you whether you will think those inestimable privileges, which you have so ably contended for, should be sacrificed at the shrine of despotism, or whether you mean to contend for them with the same spirit that has so often baffled the attempts of an aristocratic faction, to rivet the shackles of slavery on you and your unborn posterity.

Our objections are comprised under three general heads of dissent, viz.

We dissent, first, because it is the opinion of the most celebrated writers on government, and confirmed by uniform experience, that a very extensive territory cannot be governed on the principles of freedom, otherwise than by a confederation of republics, possessing all the powers of internal government; but united in the management of their general, and foreign concerns.

• • •

We dissent, secondly, because the powers vested in Congress by this constitution, must necessarily annihilate and absorb the legislative, executive, and judicial powers of the several states, and produce from their ruins one consolidated government, which from the nature of things will be *an iron handed despotism*, as nothing short of the supremacy of despotic sway could connect and govern these United States under one government.

• • •

3. We dissent, Thirdly, Because if it were practicable to govern so extensive a territory as these United States includes, on the plan of a consolidated government, consistent with the principles of liberty and the happiness of the people, yet the construction of this constitution is not calculated to attain the object, for independent of the nature of the case, it would of itself, necessarily, produce a despotism, and that not by the usual gradations, but with the celerity that

has hitherto only attended revolutions effected by the sword.

To establish the truth of this position, a cursory investigation of the principles and form of this constitution will suffice.

The first consideration that this review suggests, is the omission of a BILL of RIGHTS, ascertaining and fundamentally establishing those unalienable and personal rights of men, without the full, free, and secure enjoyment of which there can be no liberty, and over which it is not necessary for a good government to have the controul. The principal of which are the rights of conscience, personal liberty by the clear and unequivocal establishment of the writ of *habeas corpus*, jury trial in criminal and civil cases, by an impartial jury of the vicinage or county, with the common-law proceedings, for the safety of the accused in criminal prosecutions; and the liberty of the press, that scourge of tyrants, and the grand bulwark of every other liberty and privilege; the stipulations heretofore made in favor of them in the state constitutions, are entirely superceded by this constitution.

• • •

We will now bring the legislature under this constitution to the test of the foregoing principles, which will demonstrate, that it is deficient in every essential quality of a just and safe representation.

The house of representatives is to consist of 65 members; that is one for about every 50,000 inhabitants, to be chosen every two years. Thirty-three members will form a quorum for doing business; and 17 of these, being the majority, determine the sense of the house.

The senate, the other constituent branch of the legislature, consists of 26 members being *two* from each state, appointed by their legislatures every six years—fourteen senators make a quorum; the majority of whom, eight, determines the sense of that body; except in judging on impeachments, or in making treaties, or in expelling a member, when two thirds of the senators present, must concur.

The president is to have the controul over the enacting of laws, so far as to make the concurrence of *two* thirds of the representatives and senators present necessary, if he should object to the laws.

Thus it appears that the liberties, happiness, interests, and great concerns of the whole United States, may be dependent upon the integrity, virtue, wisdom, and knowledge of 25 or 26 men—How unadequate and unsafe a representation! Inadequate, because the sense and views of 3 or 4 millions of people diffused over so extensive a territory comprising such various climates, products, habits, interests, and opinions, cannot be collected in so small a body; and besides, it is not a fair and equal representation of the people even in proportion to its number, for the smallest state has as much weight in the senate as the largest, and from the smallness of the number to be chosen for both branches of the legislature; and from the mode of election and appointment, which is under the controul of Congress; and from the nature of the thing, men of the most elevated rank in life, will alone be chosen. The other orders in the society, such as farmers, traders, and mechanics, who all ought to have a competent number of their best informed men in the legislature, will be totally unrepresented.

The representation is unsafe, because in the exercise of such great powers and trusts, it is so exposed to corruption and undue influence, by the gift of the numerous places of honor and emoluments at the disposal of the executive; by the arts and address of the great and designing; and by direct bribery.

The representation is moreover inadequate and unsafe, because of the long terms for which it is appointed, and the mode of its appointment, by which Congress may not only controul the choice of the people, but may so manage as to divest the people of this fundamental right, and become self-elected.

The number of members in the house of representatives *may* be increased to one for every 30,000 inhabitants. But when we consider, that this cannot be done without the consent of the senate, who from their share in the legislative, in the executive, and judicial departments, and permanency of appointment, will be the great efficient body in this government, and whose weight and predominancy would be abridged by an increase of the representatives, we are persuaded that this is a circumstance that cannot be expected. On the contrary, the number of representatives will probably be continued at 65, although the population of the country may swell to treble what it now is; unless a revolution should effect a change.

• • •

The next consideration that the constitution presents, is the undue and dangerous mixture of the powers of government; the same body possessing legislative, executive, and judicial powers. The senate is a constituent branch of the legislature, it has judicial power in judging on impeachments, and in this case unites in some measure the characters of judge and party, as all the principal officers are appointed by the president-general, with the concurrence of the senate and therefore they derive their offices in part from the senate. This may biass the judgments of the senators and tend to screen great delinquents from punishment. And the senate has, moreover, various and great executive powers, viz. in concurrence with the president-general, they form treaties with foreign nations, that may controul and abrogate the constitutions and laws of the several states. Indeed, there is no power, privilege or liberty of the state governments, or of the people, but what may be affected by virtue of this power. For all treaties, made by them, are to be the "supreme law of the land, any thing in the constitution or laws of any state, to the contrary notwithstanding."

And this great power may be exercised by the president and 10 senators (being two-thirds of 14, which is a quorum of that body). What an inducement would this offer to the ministers of foreign powers to compass by bribery *such concessions* as could not otherwise be obtained. It is the unvaried usage of all free states, whenever treaties interfere with the positive laws of the land, to make the intervention of the legislature necessary to give them operation. This became necessary, and was afforded by the parliament of Great-Britain. In consequence of the late commercial treaty between that kingdom and France—As the senate judges on impeachments, who is to try the members of the senate for the abuse of this power! And none of the great appointments to office can be made without the consent of the senate.

Such various, extensive, and important powers combined in one body of men, are inconsistent with all freedom; the celebrated Montesquieu tells us, that "when the legislative and executive powers are united in the same person, or in the same body of magistrates, there can be no liberty, because apprehensions may arise, lest the same monarch or *senate* should enact tyrannical laws, to execute them in a tyrannical manner."

"Again, there is no liberty, if the power of judging be not separated from the legislative and executive powers. Were it joined with the legislative, the life and liberty of the subject would be exposed to arbitrary controul; for the judge would then be legislator. Were it joined to the executive power, the judge might behave with all the violence of an oppressor. There would be an end of every thing, were the same man, or the same body of the nobles, or of the people, to exercise those three powers; that of enacting laws; that of executing the public resolutions; and that of judging the crimes or differences of individuals."

The president general is dangerously connected with the senate; his coincidence with the views of the ruling junto in that body, is made essential to his weight and importance in the government, which will destroy all independency and purity in the executive department, and having the power of pardoning without the concurrence of a council, he may skreen from punishment the most treasonable attempts that may be made on the liberties of the people, when instigated by his coadjutors in the senate. Instead of this dangerous and improper mixture of the executive with the legislative and judicial, the supreme executive powers ought to have been placed in the president, with a small independent council, made personally responsible for every appointment to office or other act, by having their opinions recorded; and that without the concurrence of the majority of the quorum of this council, the president should not be capable of taking any step.

• • •

From the foregoing investigation, it appears that the Congress under this constitution will not possess the confidence of the people, which is an essential requisite in a good government; for unless the laws command the confidence and respect of the great body of the people, so as to induce them to support them, when called on by the civil magistrate, they must be executed by the aid of a numerous standing army, which would be inconsistent with every idea of liberty; for the same force that may be employed to compel obedience to good laws, might and probably would be used to wrest from the people their constitutional liberties. The framers of this constitution appear to have been aware of this great deficiency; to have been sensible that no dependence could be placed on the people for their support; but on the contrary, that the government must be executed by force. They have therefore made a provision for this purpose in a permanent STANDING ARMY, and a MILITIA that may be subjected to as strict discipline and government.

• • •

As this government will not enjoy the confidence of the people, but be executed by force, it will be a very expensive and burthensome government. The standing army must be numerous, and as a further support, it will be the policy of this government to multiply officers in every department: judges, collectors, tax gatherers, excisemen and the whole host of revenue officers will swarm over the land, devouring the hard earnings of the industrious. Like the locusts of old, impoverishing and desolating all before them.

We have not noticed the smaller, nor many of the considerable blemishes, but have confined our objections to the great and essential defects; the main pillars of the constitution; which we have shewn to be inconsistent with the liberty and happiness of the people, as its establishment will annihilate the state governments, and produce one consolidated government that will eventually and speedily issue in the supremacy of despotism.

2.6 Essays on the Nature and Extent of the Judicial Power of the United States

Brutus [Robert Yates?]

The nature and extent of the judicial power of the United States, proposed to be granted by this constitution, claims our particular attention.

Much has been said and written upon the subject of this new system on both sides, but I have not met with any writer, who has discussed the judicial powers with any degree of accuracy. And yet it is obvious, that we can form but very imperfect ideas of the manner in which this government will work, or the effect it will have in changing the internal police and mode of distributing justice at present subsisting in the respective states, without a thorough investigation of the powers of the judiciary and of the manner in which they will operate. This government is a complete system, not only for making, but for executing laws. And the courts of law, which will be constituted by it, are not only to decide upon the constitution and the laws made in pursuance of it, but by officers subordinate to them to execute all their decisions. The real effect of this system of government, will therefore be brought home to the feelings of the people, through the medium of the judicial power. It is, moreover, of great importance, to examine with care the nature and extent of the judicial power, because those who are to be vested with it, are to be placed in a situation altogether unprecedented in a free country. They are to be rendered totally independent, both of the people and the legislature, both with respect to their offices and salaries. No errors they may commit can be corrected by any power above them, if any such power there be, nor can they be removed from office for making ever so many erroneous adjudications.

The only causes for which they can be displaced, is, conviction of treason, bribery, and high crimes and misdemeanors.

This part of the plan is so modelled, as to authorise the courts, not only to carry into execution the powers expressly given, but where these are wanting or ambiguously expressed, to supply what is wanting by their own decisions.

That we may be enabled to form a just opinion on this subject, I shall, in considering it,

1st. Examine the nature and extent of the judicial powers—and

2d. Enquire, whether the courts who are to exercise them, are so constituted as to afford reasonable ground of confidence, that they will exercise them for the general good.

With a regard to the nature and extent of the judicial powers, I have to regret my want of capacity to give that full and minute explanation of them that the subject merits. To be able to do this, a man should be possessed of a degree of law knowledge far beyond what I pretend to. A number of hard words and technical phrases are used in this part of the system, about the meaning of which gentlemen learned in the law differ.

Its advocates know how to avail themselves of these phrases. In a number of instances, where objections are made to the powers given to the judicial, they give such an explanation to the technical terms as to avoid them.

Though I am not competent to give a perfect explanation of the powers granted to this department of the government, I shall yet attempt to trace some of the leading features of it, from which I presume it will appear, that they will operate to a total subversion of the state judiciaries, if not, to the legislative authority of the states.

In article 3d, sect. 2d, it is said, "The judicial power shall extend to all cases in law and equity arising under this constitution, the laws of the United States, and treaties made, or which shall be made, under their authority, &c."

The first article to which this power extends, is, all cases in law and equity arising under this constitution.

What latitude of construction this clause should receive, it is not easy to say. At first view, one would suppose, that it meant no more than this, that the courts under the general government should exercise, not only the powers of courts of law, but also that of courts of equity, in the manner in which those powers are usually exercised in the different states. But this cannot be the meaning, because the next clause authorises the courts to take cognizance of all cases in law and equity arising under the laws of the United States; this last article, I conceive, conveys as much power to the general judicial as any of the state courts possess.

The cases arising under the constitution must be different from those arising under the laws, or else the two clauses mean exactly the same thing.

The cases arising under the constitution must include such, as bring into question its meaning, and will require an explanation of the nature and extent of the powers of the different departments under it.

This article, therefore, vests the judicial with a power to resolve all questions that may arise on any case on the construction of the constitution, either in law or in equity.

1st. They are authorised to determine all questions that may arise upon the meaning of the constitution in law. This article vests the courts with authority to give the constitution a legal construction, or to explain it according to the rules laid down for construing a law.— These rules give a certain degree of latitude of explanation. According to this mode of construction, the courts are to give such meaning to the constitution as comports best with the common, and generally received acceptation of the words in which it is expressed, regarding their ordinary and popular use, rather than their grammatical propriety. Where words are dubious, they will be explained by the context. The end of the clause will be attended to, and the words will be understood, as having a view to it; and the words will not be so understood as to bear no meaning or a very absurd one.

2d. The judicial are not only to decide questions arising upon the meaning of the constitution in law, but also in equity.

By this they are empowered, to explain the constitution according to the reasoning spirit of it, without being confined to the words or letter.

"From this method of interpreting laws (says Blackstone) by the reason of them, arises what we call equity;" which is thus defined by Grotius, "the correction of that, wherein the law, by reason of its universality, is deficient[");] for since in laws all cases cannot be foreseen, or expressed, it is necessary, that when the decrees of the law cannot be applied to particular cases, there should some where be a power vested of defining those circumstances, which had they been foreseen the legislator would have expressed; and these are the cases, which according to Grotius, ["]lex non exacte definit, sed arbitrio boni viri permittet."

The same learned author observes, "That equity, thus depending essentially upon each individual case, there can be no established rules and fixed principles of equity laid down, without destroying its very essence, and reducing it to a positive law."

The Articles of Confederation and the Constitution of the United States: A Comparison

Selected from the Articles of Confederation

To all to whom these Presents shall come, we the undersigned Delegates of the States affixed to our Names send greeting. Whereas the Delegates of the United States of America in Congress assembled did on the fifteenth day of November in the Year of our Lord One Thousand Seven Hundred and Seventy seven, and in the Second Year of the Independence of America agree to certain articles of Confederation and perpetual Union between the States . . .

No state shall be represented in Congress by less than two, nor by more than seven Members; and no person shall be capable of being a delegate for more than three years in any term of six years; nor shall any person, being a delegate, be capable of holding any office under the united states, for which he, or another for his benefit receives any salary, fees or emolument of any kind.

Each state shall maintain its own delegates in a meeting of the states, and while they act as members of the committee of the states.

In determining questions in the united states, in Congress assembled, each state shall have one vote.

Selected from the Constitution

We the people of the United States, in Order to form a more perfect Union, establish Justice, insure domestic Tranquility, provide for the common defence, promote the general Welfare, and secure the Blessings of Liberty to ourselves and our Posterity, do ordain and establish this Constitution for the United States of America.

Representatives and direct Taxes shall be apportioned among the several States which may be included within this Union, according to their respective Numbers, which shall be determined by adding to the whole Number of free Persons, including those bound to Service for a Term of Years, and excluding Indians not taxed, three fifths of all other Persons.

The Senate of the United States shall be composed of two Senators from each State, chosen by the Legislature thereof, for six Years; and each Senator shall have one Vote.

From these remarks, the authority and business of the courts of law, under this clause, may be understood.

They will give the sense of every article of the constitution, that may from time to time come before them. And in their decisions they will not confine themselves to any fixed or established rules, but will determine, according to what appears to them, the reason and spirit of the constitution. The opinions of the supreme court, whatever they may be, will have the force of law; because there is no power provided in the constitution, that can correct their errors, or controul their adjudications. From this court there is no appeal. And I conceive the legislature themselves, cannot set aside a judgment of this court, because they are authorised by the constitution to decide in the last resort. The

Selected from
the Articles of Confederation

All charges of war, and all other expences that shall be incurred for the common defence or general welfare, and allowed by the united states in congress assembled, shall be defrayed out of a common treasury, which shall be supplied by the several states, in proportion to the value of all land within each state . . .

The united states in congress assembled shall also have the sole and exclusive right and power of regulating the alloy and value of coin struck by their own authority, or by that of the respective states—fixing the standard of weights and measures throughout the united states.—regulating the trade and managing all affairs with the Indians, not members of any of the states, provided that the legislative right of any state within its own limits be not infringed or violated—

[No executive branch]

[No judicial branch]

Selected from
the Constitution

The Congress shall have Power To lay and collect
Taxes, Duties, Imposts and Excises, to pay the Debts and provide for the common Defence and general Welfare of the United States: but all Duties, Imposts and Excises shall be uniform throughout the United States.

The Congress shall have Power:
. . . To regular Commerce with foreign Nations, and among the several States, and with the Indian Tribes;
. . . To coin Money, regulate the Value thereof, and of foreign Coin, and fix the Standard of Weights and Measures.

The executive Power shall be vested in a President of the United States of America.

The judicial Power of the United States, shall be vested in one supreme Court, and in such inferior Courts as the Congress may from time to time ordain and establish.

---

legislature must be controuled by the constitution, and not the constitution by them. They have therefore no more right to set aside any judgment pronounced upon the construction of the constitution, than they have to take from the president, the chief command of the army and navy, and commit it to some other person. The reason is plain; the judicial and executive derive their authority from the same source, that the legislature do theirs; and therefore in all cases, where the constitution does not make the one responsible to, or controulable by the other, they are altogether independent of each other.

The judicial power will operate to effect, in the most certain, but yet silent and imperceptible manner, what is evidently the tendency of the constitution:—I mean, an entire subversion of the legislative, executive and judicial powers of the individual states. Every adjudication of the supreme court, on any question that may arise upon the nature and extent of the general government, will affect the limits of the state jurisdiction. In proportion as the former enlarge the exercise of their powers, will that of the latter be restricted.

That the judicial power of the United States, will lean strongly in favour of the general government, and will give such an explanation to the constitution, as will favour an extension of its jurisdiction, is very evident from a variety of considerations.

1st. The constitution itself strongly countenances such a mode of construction. Most of the articles in this system, which convey powers of any considerable importance, are conceived in general and indefinite terms, which are either equivocal, ambiguous, or which require long definitions to unfold the extent of their meaning. The two most important powers committed to any government, those of raising money, and of raising and keeping up troops, have already been considered, and shewn to be unlimitted by any thing but the discretion of the legislature. The clause which vests the power to pass all laws which are proper and necessary, to carry the powers given into execution, it has been shewn, leaves the legislature at liberty, to do every thing, which in their judgment is best. It is said, I know, that this clause confers no power on the legislature, which they would not have had without it—though I believe this is not the fact, yet, admitting it to be, it implies that the constitution is not to receive an explanation strictly, according to its letter; but more power is implied than is expressed. And this clause, if it is to be considered, as explanatory of the extent of the powers given, rather than giving a new power, is to be understood as declaring, that in construing any of the articles conveying power, the spirit, intent and design of the clause, should be attended to, as well as the words in their common acceptation.

This constitution gives sufficient colour for adopting an equitable construction, if we consider the great end and design it professedly has in view—these appear from its preamble to be, "to form a more perfect union, establish justice, insure domestic tranquility, provide for the common defence, promote the general welfare, and secure the blessings of liberty to ourselves and posterity." The design of this system is here expressed, and it is proper to give such a meaning to the various parts, as will best promote the accomplishment of the end; this idea suggests itself naturally upon reading the preamble, and will countenance the court in giving the several articles such a sense, as will the most effectually promote the ends the constitution had in view—how this manner of explaining the constitution will operate in practice, shall be the subject of future enquiry.

2d. Not only will the constitution justify the courts in inclining to this mode of explaining it, but they will be interested in using this latitude of interpretation. Every body of men invested with office are tenacious of power; they feel interested, and hence it has become a kind of maxim, to hand down their offices, with all its rights and privileges, unimpaired to their successors; the same principle will influence them to extend their power, and increase their rights; this of itself will operate strongly upon the courts to give such a meaning to the constitution in all cases where it can possibly be done, as will enlarge the sphere of their own authority. Every extension of the power of the general legislature, as well as of the judicial powers, will increase the powers of the courts; and the dignity and importance of the judges, will be in proportion to the extent and magnitude of the powers they exercise. I add, it is highly probable the emolument of the judges will be increased, with the increase of the business they will have to transact and its importance. From these considerations the judges will be interested to extend the powers of the courts, and to construe the constitution as much as possible, in such a way as to favour it; and that they will do it, appears probable.

3d. Because they will have precedent to plead, to justify them in it. It is well known, that the courts in England, have by their own authority, extended their jurisdiction far beyond the limits set them in their original institution, and by the laws of the land.

The court of exchequer is a remarkable instance of this. It was originally intended principally to recover the king's debts, and to order the revenues of the crown. It had a common law jurisdiction, which was established merely for the benefit of the king's accomptants. We learn from Blackstone, that the proceedings in this court are grounded on a writ called quo minus, in which the plaintiff suggests, that he is the king's farmer or debtor, and that the defendant hath done him the damage complained of, by which he is less able to pay the king. These suits, by the statute of Rutland, are expressly directed to be confined to such matters as specially concern the king, or his ministers

in the exchequer. And by the articuli super cartas, it is enacted, that no common pleas be thenceforth held in the exchequer contrary to the form of the greater charter; but now any person may sue in the exchequer. The surmise of being debtor to the king being matter of form, and mere words of course; and the court is open to all the nation.

When the courts will have a precedent before them of a court which extended its jurisdiction in opposition to an act of the legislature, is it not to be expected that they will extend theirs, especially when there is nothing in the constitution expressly against it? and they are authorised to construe its meaning, and are not under any controul?

This power in the judicial, will enable them to mould the government, into almost any shape they please. . . .

II THE PERSPECTIVE OF HISTORY

It is all too easy to view the participants in the constitutional debate as detached philosophers crafting a new system of government in a political vacuum—or, conversely, as nothing more than self-interested politicians with little regard for the public or for posterity. Neither view is completely correct; to understand the Framers and the Constitution they wrote, it is necessary to steer a middle course. The Framers were propelled by a variety of motivations, some noble, some base. They were constrained by the political realities of their day, but they also thought seriously about political philosophy and the public interest.

The two following selections present two diverse approaches to the study of the Federalists. To the political scientist John P. Roche, the men who met in Philadelphia in 1787 were democratic politicians operating within very real political constraints. In Roche's view, much of the elegant political philosophy that emerged from the debate, especially the Federalist Papers, *originated as simple matters of political compromise. Roche's position on the Framers as politicians is probably overstated, but it offers a welcome perspective on the constitutional debate. The political scientist Martin Diamond, by contrast, emphasizes the ideas of the Federalists and argues that they were strongly committed to the ideal of democracy.*

Questions

1. Madison, Roche suggests, was originally in favor of a "unitary central government" but compromised over the course of the convention. What fac-

tors created the necessity for such a compromise? What were the essential outlines of the compromise?

2. Review the Declaration of Independence (selection 1.2) and the selections from the *Federalist Papers* in this chapter. Is Diamond correct in criticizing those who would argue that "the Constitution was a falling back from the fuller democracy of the Declaration"?

3. Recent debate on the role of the Supreme Court in constitutional decision making (see selections 14.9 and 14.10) has centered on the justices' attempt to discern the Framers' original intent on various provisions of the Constitution. What do Roche and Diamond suggest about the validity or desirability of such an approach?

2.7 The Founding Fathers: A Reform Caucus in Action

John P. Roche

• • •

Standard treatments of the [Constitutional] Convention divide the delegates into "nationalists" and "states'-righters" with various improvised shadings ("moderate nationalists," etc.), but these are *a posteriori* categories which obfuscate more than they clarify. What is striking to one who analyzes the Convention as a case-study in democratic politics is the lack of clear-cut ideological divisions in the Convention. Indeed, I submit that the evidence—Madison's *Notes*, the correspondence of the delegates, and debates on ratification—indicates that this was a remarkably homogeneous body on the ideological level. Yates and Lansing, Clinton's two chaperones for Hamilton, left in disgust on July 10. (Is there anything more tedious than sitting through endless disputes on matters one deems fundamentally misconceived? It takes an iron will to spend a hot summer as an ideological *agent provocateur*.) Luther Martin, Maryland's bibulous narcissist, left on September 4 in a huff when he discovered that others did not share his self-esteem; others went home for personal reasons. But the hard

core of delegates accepted a grinding regimen throughout the attrition of a Philadelphia summer precisely because they shared the Constitutionalist goal.

Basic differences of opinion emerged, of course, but these were not ideological; they were *structural*. If the so-called "states'-rights" group had not accepted the fundamental purposes of the Convention, they could simply have pulled out and by doing so have aborted the whole enterprise. Instead of bolting, they returned day after day to argue and to compromise. An interesting symbol of this basic homogeneity was the initial agreement on secrecy: these professional politicians did not want to become prisoners of publicity; they wanted to retain that freedom of maneuver which is only possible when men are not forced to take public stands in the preliminary stages of negotiation. There was no legal means of binding the tongues of the delegates: at any stage in the game a delegate with basic principled objections to the emerging project could have taken the stump (as Luther Martin did after his exit) and denounced the convention to the skies. Yet

Madison did not even inform Thomas Jefferson in Paris of the course of the deliberations and available correspondence indicates that the delegates generally observed the injunction. Secrecy is certainly uncharacteristic of any assembly marked by strong ideological polarization. This was noted at the time: the *New York Daily Advertiser*, August 14, 1787, commented that the ". . . profound secrecy hitherto observed by the Convention [we consider] a happy omen, as it demonstrates that the spirit of party on any great and essential point cannot have arisen to any height."

Commentators on the Constitution who have read *The Federalist* in lieu of reading the actual debates have credited the Fathers with the invention of a sublime concept called "Federalism." Unfortunately *The Federalist* is probative evidence for only one proposition: that Hamilton and Madison were inspired propagandists with a genius for retrospective symmetry. Federalism, as the theory is generally defined, was an improvisation which was later promoted into a political theory. Experts on "federalism" should take to heart the advice of David Hume, who warned in his *Of the Rise and Progress of the Arts and Sciences* that ". . . there is no subject in which we must proceed with more caution than in [history], lest we assign causes which never existed and reduce what is merely contingent to stable and universal principles." In any event, the final balance in the Constitution between the states and the nation must have come as a great disappointment to Madison, while Hamilton's unitary views are too well known to need elucidation.

It is indeed astonishing how those who have glibly designated James Madison the "father" of Federalism have overlooked the solid body of fact which indicates that he shared Hamilton's quest for a unitary central government. To be specific, they have avoided examining the clear import of the Madison-Virginia Plan, and have disregarded Madison's dogged inch-by-inch retreat from the bastions of centralization. The Virginia Plan envisioned a unitary national government effectively freed from and dominant over the states. The lower house of the national legislature was to be elected directly by the people of the states with membership proportional to population. The upper house was to be selected by the lower and the two chambers would elect the executive and choose the judges. The national government would be thus cut completely loose from the states.

The structure of the general government was freed from state control in a truly radical fashion, but the scope of the authority of the national sovereign as Madison initially formulated it was breathtaking—it was a formulation worthy of the Sage of Malmesbury himself. The national legislature was to be empowered to disallow the acts of state legislatures, and the central government was vested, in addition to the powers of the nation under the Articles of Confederation, with plenary authority wherever ". . . the separate States are incompetent or in which the harmony of the United States may be interrupted by the exercise of individual legislation." Finally, just to lock the door against state intrusion, the national Congress was to be given the power to use military force on recalcitrant states. This was Madison's "model" of an ideal national government, though it later received little publicity in *The Federalist*.

The interesting thing was the reaction of the Convention to this militant program for a strong autonomous central government. Some delegates were startled, some obviously leery of so comprehensive a project of reform, but nobody set off any fireworks and nobody walked out. Moreover, in the two weeks that followed, the Virginia Plan received substantial endorsement *en principe;* the initial temper of the gathering can be deduced from the approval "without debate or dissent," on May 31, of the Sixth Resolution which granted Congress the authority to disallow state legislation ". . . contravening *in its opinion* the Articles of Union." Indeed, an amendment was included to bar states from contravening national treaties.

The Virginia Plan may therefore be considered, in ideological terms, as the delegates' Uto-

pia, but as the discussions continued and became more specific, many of those present began to have second thoughts. After all, they were not residents of Utopia or guardians in Plato's Republic who could simply impose a philosophical ideal on subordinate strata of the population. They were practical politicians in a democratic society, and no matter what their private dreams might be, they had to take home an acceptable package and defend it—and their own political futures—against predictable attack. On June 14 the breaking point between dream and reality took place. Apparently realizing that under the Virginia Plan, Massachusetts, Virginia and Pennsylvania could virtually dominate the national government—and probably appreciating that to sell this program to "the folks back home" would be impossible—the delegates from the small states dug in their heels and demanded time for a consideration of alternatives. One gets a graphic sense of the inner politics from John Dickinson's reproach to

Madison: "You see the consequences of pushing things too far. Some of the members from the small States wish for two branches in the General Legislature and are friends to a good National Government; but we would sooner submit to a foreign power than . . . be deprived of an equality of suffrage in both branches of the Legislature, and thereby be thrown under the domination of the large States."

The bare outline of the *Journal* entry for Tuesday, June 14, is suggestive to anyone with extensive experience in deliberative bodies. "It was moved by Mr. Patterson [*sic,* Paterson's name was one of those consistently misspelled by Madison and everybody else] seconded by Mr. Randolph that the further consideration of the report from the Committee of the whole House [endorsing the Virginia Plan] be postponed til tomorrow, and before the question for postponement was taken. It was moved by Mr. Randolph seconded by Mr. Patterson that the House adjourn." The House adjourned by obvious prearrangement of the two principals: since the preceding Saturday when Brearley and Paterson of New Jersey had announced their fundamental discontent with the representational features of the Virginia Plan, the informal pressure had certainly been building up to slow down the steamroller. Doubtless there were extended arguments . . . between Madison and Paterson, the latter insisting that events were moving rapidly towards a probably disastrous conclusion, towards a political suicide pact. Now the process of accommodation was put into action smoothly—and wisely, given the character and strength of the doubters. Madison had the votes, but this was one of those situations where the enforcement of mechanical majoritarianism could easily have destroyed the objectives of the majority: the Constitutionalists were in quest of a qualitative as well as a quantitative consensus. This was hardly from deference to local Quaker custom; it was a political imperative if they were to attain ratification.

[I]

According to the standard script, at this point the "states'-rights" group intervened in force behind the New Jersey Plan, which has been characteristically portrayed as a reversion to the *status quo* under the Articles of Confederation with but minor modifications. A careful examination of the evidence indicates that only in a marginal sense is this an accurate description. It is true that the New Jersey Plan put the states back into the institutional picture, but one could argue that to do so was a recognition of political reality rather than an affirmation of states'-rights. A serious case can be made for the advocates of the New Jersey Plan, far from being ideological addicts of states'-rights, intended to substitute for the Virginia Plan a system which would both retain strong national power and have a chance of adoption in the states. The leading spokesman for the project asserted quite clearly that his views were based more on counsels of expediency than on principle; said Paterson on June 16: "I came here not to speak my own sentiments, but the sentiments of those who sent me. Our object is not such a Governmt. as may be best in itself, but such a one as our Constituents have authorized us to prepare, and as they will approve." This is Madison's version; in Yates' transcription, there is a crucial sentence following the remarks above: "I believe that a little practical virtue is to be preferred to the finest theoretical principles, which cannot be carried into effect." In his preliminary speech on June 9, Paterson had stated ". . . to the public mind we must accommodate ourselves," and in his notes for this and his later effort as well, the emphasis is the same. The *structure* of government under the Articles should be retained:

> 2. Because it accords with the Sentiments of the People
>
>   [Proof:] 1. Coms. [Commissions from state legislatures defining the jurisdiction of the delegates]
>   2. News-papers—Political Barometer. Jersey never would have sent Delegates under the first [Virginia] Plan—

Not here to sport Opinions of my own. Wt. [What] can be done. A little practicable Virtue preferrable to Theory.

This was a defense of political acumen, not of states'-rights. In fact, Paterson's notes of his speech can easily be construed as an argument for attaining the substantive objectives of the Virginia Plan by a sound political route, *i.e.*, pouring the new wine in the old bottles. With a shrewd eye, Paterson queried:

> Will the Operation and Force of the [central] Govt. depend upon the mode of Representn.— No—it will depend upon the Quantum of Power lodged in the leg. ex. and judy. Departments—Give [the existing] Congress the same Powers that you intend to give the two Branches, [under the Virginia Plan] and I apprehend they will act with as much Propriety and more Energy . . .

In other words, the advocates of the New Jersey Plan concentrated their fire on what they held to be the *political liabilities* of the Virginia Plan— which were matters of institutional structure— rather than on the proposed scope of national authority. Indeed, the Supremacy Clause of the Constitution first saw the light of day in Paterson's Sixth Resolution; the New Jersey Plan contemplated the use of military force to secure compliance with national law; and finally Paterson made clear his view that under either the Virginia or the New Jersey systems, the general government would ". . . act on individuals and not on states." From the states'-rights viewpoint, this was heresy: the fundament of that doctrine was the proposition that any central government had as its constituents the states, not the people, and could only reach the people through the agency of the state government.

Paterson then reopened the agenda of the Convention, but he did so within a distinctly nationalist framework. Paterson's position was one of favoring a strong central government in principle, but opposing one which in fact *put the big states in the saddle.* (The Virginia Plan, for all its abstract merits, did very well by Virginia.) As evidence for this speculation, there is a curious and intriguing proposal among Paterson's preliminary drafts of the New Jersey Plan:

> Whereas it is necessary in Order to form the People of the U.S. of America in to a Nation, that the States should be consolidated, by which means all the Citizens thereof will become equally intitled to and will equally participate in the same Privileges and Rights . . . it is therefore resolved, that all the Lands contained within the Limits of each state individually, and of the U.S. generally be considered as constituting one Body or Mass, and be divided into thirteen or more integral parts.
>
> Resolved, That such Divisions or integral Parts shall be styled Districts.

This makes it sound as though Paterson was prepared to accept a strong unified central government along the lines of the Virginia Plan if the existing states were eliminated. He may have gotten the idea from his New Jersey colleague Judge David Brearley, who on June 9 had commented that the only remedy to the dilemma over representation was ". . . that a map of the U. S. be spread out, that all the existing boundaries be erased, and that a new partition of the whole be made into 13 equal parts." According to Yates, Brearley added at this point, ". . . then a government on the present [Virginia Plan] system will be just."

This proposition was never pushed—it was patently unrealistic—but one can appreciate its purpose: it would have separated the men from the boys in the large-state delegations. How attached would the Virginians have been to their reform principles if Virginia were to disappear as a component geographical unit (the largest) for representational purposes? Up to this point, the Virginians had been in the happy position of supporting high ideals with that inner confidence born of knowledge that the "public interest" they endorsed would nourish their private interest. Worse, they had shown little willingness to compromise. Now the delegates from the small states announced that they were unprepared to be offered up as sacrificial victims to a "national interest" which reflected Virginia's parochial ambition. Caustic Charles Pinckney was not far off when he remarked sardonically that ". . . the whole [conflict] comes to this": "Give N. Jersey an equal vote, and she will dismiss her scruples, and concur in the Natil. system." What he rather unfairly did not add was that the Jersey delegates were not free agents who could adhere to their private convictions; they had to take back, sponsor and risk their reputations on the reforms approved by the Convention—and in New Jersey, not in Virginia.

Paterson spoke on Saturday, and one can surmise that over the weekend there was a good deal of consultation, argument, and caucusing among the delegates. One member at least prepared a full length address: on Monday Alexander Hamilton, previously mute, rose and delivered a six-hour oration. It was a remarkably apolitical speech; the gist of his position was that *both* the Virginia and New Jersey Plans were inadequately centralist, and he detailed a reform program which was reminiscent of the Protectorate under the Cromwellian *Instrument of Government* of 1653. It has been suggested that Hamilton did this in the best political tradition to emphasize the moderate character of the Virginia Plan, to give the cautious delegates something *really* to worry about; but this interpretation seems somehow too clever. Particularly since the sentiments Hamilton expressed happened to be completely consistent with those he privately—and sometimes publicly—expressed throughout his life. He wanted, to take a striking phrase from a letter to George Washington, a "strong well mounted government"; in essence, the Hamilton Plan contemplated an elected life monarch, virtually free of public control, on the Hobbesian ground that only in this fashion could strength and stability be achieved. The other alternatives, he argued, would put policy-making at the mercy of the passions of the mob; only if the sovereign was beyond the reach of selfish influence would it be possible to have government in the interests of the whole community.

From all accounts, this was a masterful and compelling speech, but (aside from furnishing John Lansing and Luther Martin with ammunition for later use against the Constitution) it made little impact. Hamilton was simply transmitting on a different wave-length from the rest of the delegates; the latter adjourned after his great effort, admired his rhetoric, and then returned to business. It was rather as if they had taken a day off to attend the opera. Hamilton, never a particularly patient man or much of a negotiator, stayed for another ten days and then left, in considerable disgust, for New York. Although he came back to Philadelphia sporadically and attended the last two weeks of the Convention, Hamilton played no part in the laborious task of hammering out the Constitution. His day came later when he led the New York Constitutionalists into the savage imbroglio over ratification—an arena in which his unmatched talent for dirty political infighting may well have won the day. For instance, in the New York Ratifying Convention, Lansing threw back into Hamilton's teeth the sentiments the latter had expressed in his June 18 oration in the Convention. However, having since retreated to the fine defensive positions immortalized in *The Federalist*, the Colonel flatly denied that he had ever been an enemy of the states, or had believed that conflict between states and nation was inexorable! As Madison's authoritative *Notes* did not appear until 1840, and there had been no press coverage, there was no way to verify his assertions, so in the words of the reporter, ". . . a warm personal altercation between [Lansing and Hamilton] engrossed the remainder of the day [June 28, 1788]."

[II]

On Tuesday morning, June 19, the vacation was over. James Madison led off with a long, carefully reasoned speech analyzing the New Jersey Plan which, while intellectually vigorous in its criticisms, was quite conciliatory in mood. "The great difficulty," he observed, "lies in the affair of Representation; and if this could be adjusted, all others would be surmountable." (As events were to demonstrate, this diagnosis was correct.) When he finished, a vote was taken on whether to continue with the Virginia Plan as the nucleus for a new constitution: seven states voted "Yes"; New York, New Jersey, and Delaware voted "No"; and Maryland, whose position often depended on which delegates happened to be on the floor, divided. Paterson, it seems, lost decisively; yet in a fundamental sense he and his allies had achieved their purpose: from that day onward, it could never be forgotten that the state governments loomed ominously in the background and that no verbal incantations could exorcise their power. Moreover, nobody bolted the convention: Paterson and his colleagues took their defeat in stride and set to work to modify the Virginia Plan, particularly with respect to its provisions on representation in the national legislature. Indeed, they won an immediate rhetorical bonus; when Oliver Ellsworth of Connecticut rose to move that the word "national" be expunged from the Third Virginia Resolution ("Resolved that a *national* Government ought to be established consisting of a *supreme* Legislative, Executive and Judiciary"), Randolph agreed and the motion passed unanimously. The process of compromise had begun.

For the next two weeks, the delegates circled around the problem of legislative representation. The Connecticut delegation appears to have evolved a possible compromise quite early in the debates, but the Virginians and particularly Madison (unaware that he would later be acclaimed as the prophet of "federalism") fought obdurately against providing for equal representation of states in the second chamber. There was a good deal of acrimony and at one point Benjamin Franklin—of all people—proposed the institution of a daily prayer; practical politicians in the gathering, however, were mediating more on the merits of a good committee than on the utility of Divine intervention. On July 2, the ice began to break when through a number of fortuitous events—and one that seems deliberate—the majority against equality of representation was converted into a dead tie. The Convention had reached the stage where it was "ripe" for a solution (presumably all the therapeutic speeches had been made), and the South Carolinians proposed a committee. Madison and James Wilson wanted none of it, but with only Pennsylvania dissenting, the body voted to establish a working party on the problem of representation.

The members of this committee, one from each state, were elected by the delegates—and

a very interesting committee it was. Despite the fact that the Virginia Plan had held majority support up to that date, neither Madison nor Randolph was selected (Mason was the Virginian) and Baldwin of Georgia, whose shift in position had resulted in the tie, was chosen. From the composition, it was clear that this was not to be a "fighting" committee; the emphasis in membership was on what might be described as "second-level political entrepreneurs." On the basis of the discussions up to that time, only Luther Martin of Maryland could be described as a "bitter-ender." Admittedly, some divination enters into this sort of analysis, but one does get a sense of the mood of the delegates from these choices—including the interesting selection of Benjamin Franklin, despite his age and intellectual wobbliness, over the brilliant and incisive Wilson or the sharp, polemical Gouverneur Morris, to represent Pennsylvania. His passion for conciliation was more valuable at this juncture than Wilson's logical genius, or Morris' acerbic wit.

There is a common rumor that the Framers divided their time between philosophical discussions of government and reading the classics in political theory. Perhaps this is as good a time as any to note that their concerns were highly practical, that they spent little time canvassing abstractions. A number of them had some acquaintance with the history of political theory (probably gained from reading John Adams' monumental compilation *A Defense of the Constitutions of Government*, the first volume of which appeared in 1786), and it was a poor rhetorician indeed who could not cite Locke, Montesquieu, or Harrington *in support* of a desired goal. Yet up to this point in the deliberations, no one had expounded a defense of states'-rights or the "separation of powers" on anything resembling a theoretical basis. It should be reiterated that the Madison model had no room either for the states or for the "separation of powers": effectively *all* governmental power was vested in the national legislature. The merits of Montesquieu did not turn up until *The Federalist;* and although a perverse argument could be made that Madison's ideal was truly in the tradition of John Locke's *Second Treatise of Government*, the Locke whom the American rebels treated as an honorary president was a pluralistic defender of vested rights, not of parliamentary supremacy.

It would be tedious to continue a blow-by-blow analysis of the work of the delegates; the critical fight was over representation of the states and once the Connecticut Compromise was adopted on July 17, the Convention was over the hump. Madison, James Wilson, and Gouverneur Morris of New York (who was there representing Pennsylvania!) fought the compromise all the way in a last-ditch effort to get a unitary state with parliamentary supremacy. But their allies deserted them and they demonstrated after their defeat the essentially opportunist character of their objections—using "opportunist" here in a non-pejorative sense, to indicate a willingness to swallow their objections and get on with the business. Moreover, once the compromise had carried (by five states to four, with one state divided), its advocates threw themselves vigorously into the job of strengthening the general government's substantive powers—as might have been predicted, indeed, from Paterson's early statements. It nourishes an increased respect for Madison's devotion to the art of politics, to realize that this dogged fighter could sit down six months later and prepare essays for *The Federalist* in contradiction to his basic convictions about the true course the Convention should have taken.

[III]

Two tricky issues will serve to illustrate the later process of accommodation. The first was the institutional position of the Executive. Madison argued for an executive chosen by the National Legislature and on May 29 this had been adopted with a provision that after his seven-year term was concluded, the chief magistrate should not be eligible for reelection. In late July this was reopened and for a week the matter was argued from several different points of view. A good deal of desultory speech-making ensued, but the gist of the problem was the opposition from two sources to election by the

legislature. One group felt that the states should have a hand in the process; another small but influential circle urged direct election by the people. There were a number of proposals: election by the people, election by state governors, by electors chosen by state legislatures, by the National Legislature (James Wilson, perhaps ironically, proposed at one point that an Electoral College be chosen by lot from the National Legislature!), and there was some resemblance to three-dimensional chess in the dispute because of the presence of two other variables, length of tenure and reeligibility. Finally, after opening, reopening, and re-reopening the debate, the thorny problem was consigned to a committee for resolution.

The Brearley Committee on Postponed Matters was a superb aggregation of talent and its compromise on the Executive was a masterpiece of political improvisation. (The Electoral College, its creation, however, had little in its favor as an *institution*—as the delegates well appreciated.) The point of departure for all discussion about the presidency in the Convention was that in immediate terms, the problem was non-existent; in other words, everybody present knew that under any system devised, George Washington would be President. Thus they were dealing in the future tense and to a body of working politicians the merits of the Brearley proposal were obvious: everybody got a piece of cake. (Or to put it more academically, each viewpoint could leave the Convention and argue to its constituents that it had *really* won the day.) First, the state legislatures had the right to determine the mode of selection of the electors; second, the small states received a bonus in the Electoral College in the form of a guaranteed minimum of three votes while the big states got acceptance of the principle of proportional power; third, if the state legislatures agreed (as six did in the first presidential election), the people could be involved directly in the choice of electors; and finally, if no candidate received a majority in the College, the right of decision passed to the National Legislature with each state exercising equal strength. (In the Brearley recommendation, the election went to the Senate, but a motion from the floor substituted the House; this was accepted on the ground that the Senate already had enough authority over the executive in its treaty and appointment powers.)

This compromise was almost too good to be true, and the Framers snapped it up with little debate or controversy. No one seemed to think well of the College as an *institution;* indeed, what evidence there is suggests that there was an assumption that once Washington had finished his tenure as President, the electors would cease to produce majorities and the chief executive would usually be chosen in the House. George Mason observed casually that the selection would be made in the House nineteen times in twenty and no one seriously disputed this point. The vital aspect of the Electoral College was that it got the Convention over the hurdle and protected everybody's interests. The future was left to cope with the problem of what to do with this Rube Goldberg mechanism.

In short, the Framers did not in their wisdom endow the United States with a College of Cardinals—the Electoral College was neither an exercise in applied Platonism nor an experiment in indirect government based on elitist distrust of the masses. It was merely a jerry-rigged improvisation which has subsequently been endowed with a high theoretical content. When an elector from Oklahoma in 1960 refused to cast his vote for Nixon (naming Byrd and Goldwater instead) on the ground that the Founding Fathers intended him to exercise his great independent wisdom, he was indulging in historical fantasy. If one were to indulge in counterfantasy, he would be tempted to suggest that the Fathers would be startled to find the College still in operation—and perhaps even dismayed at their descendants' lack of judgment or inventiveness.

The second issue on which some substantial practical bargaining took place was slavery. The morality of slavery was, by design, not at issue; but in its other concrete aspects, slavery colored the arguments over taxation, commerce, and representation. The "Three-Fifths Compro-

mise," that three-fifths of the slaves would be counted both for representation and for purposes of direct taxation (which was drawn from the past—it was a formula of Madison's utilized by Congress in 1783 to establish the basis of state contributions to the Confederation treasury) had allayed some Northern fears about Southern over-representation (no one then foresaw the trivial role that direct taxation would play in later federal financial policy), but doubts still remained. The Southerners, on the other hand, were afraid that Congressional control over commerce would lead to the exclusion of slaves or to their excessive taxation as imports. Moreover, the Southerners were disturbed over "navigation acts," *i.e.,* tariffs, or special legislation providing, for example, that exports be carried only in American ships; as a section depending upon exports, they wanted protection from the potential voracity of their commercial brethren of the Eastern states. To achieve this end, Mason and others urged that the Constitution include a proviso that navigation and commercial laws should require a two-thirds vote in Congress.

These problems came to a head in late August and, as usual, were handed to a committee in the hope that, in Gouverneur Morris' words, ". . . these things may form a bargain among the Northern and Southern states." The Committee reported its measures of reconciliation on August 25, and on August 29 the package was wrapped up and delivered. What occurred can best be described in George Mason's dour version (he anticipated Calhoun in his conviction that permitting navigation acts to pass by majority vote would put the South in economic bondage to the North—it was mainly on this ground that he refused to sign the Constitution):

> The Constitution as agreed to till a fortnight before the Convention rose was such a one as he would have set his hand and heart to. . . . [Until that time] The 3 New England States were constantly with us in all questions . . . so that it was these three States with the 5 Southern ones against Pennsylvania, Jersey and Del-

aware. With respect to the importation of slaves, [decision-making] was left to Congress. This disturbed the two Southernmost States who knew that Congress would immediately suppress the importation of slaves. Those two States therefore struck up a bargain with the three New England States. If they would join to admit slaves for some years, the two Southern-most States would join in changing the clause which required the ⅔ of the Legislature in any vote [on navigation acts]. It was done.

On the floor of the Convention there was a virtual love-feast on this happy occasion. Charles Pinckney of South Carolina attempted to overturn the committee's decision, when the compromise was reported to the Convention, by insisting that the South needed protection from the imperialism of the Northern states. But his Southern colleagues were not prepared to rock the boat and General C. C. Pinckney arose to spread oil on the suddenly ruffled waters; he admitted that:

> It was in the true interest of the S[outhern] States to have no regulation of commerce; but considering the loss brought on the commerce of the Eastern States by the Revolution, their liberal conduct towards the views of South Carolina [on the regulation of the slave trade] and the interests the weak Southn. States had in being united with the strong Eastern states, he thought it proper that no fetters should be imposed on the power of making commercial regulations: *and that his constituents, though prejudiced against the Eastern States, would be reconciled to this liberality.* He had himself prejudices agst the Eastern States before he came here, but would acknowledge that he had found them as liberal and candid as any men whatever. (Italics added)

Pierce Butler took the same tack, essentially arguing that he was not too happy about the possible consequences, but that a deal was a deal. Many Southern leaders were later—in the wake of the "Tariff of Abominations"—to rue this day of reconciliation; Calhoun's *Disquisition on Government* was little more than an extension of the argument in the Convention against permitting a congressional majority to enact navigation acts.

[IV]

Drawing on their vast collective political experience, utilizing every weapon in the politician's arsenal, looking constantly over their shoulders at their constituents, the delegates put together a Constitution. It was a makeshift affair; some sticky issues (for example, the qualification of voters) they ducked entirely; others they mastered with that ancient instrument of political sagacity, studied ambiguity (for example, citizenship), and some they just overlooked. In this last category, I suspect, fell the matter of the power of the federal courts to determine the constitutionality of acts of Congress. When the judicial article was formulated (Article III of the Constitution), deliberations were still in the stage where the legislature was endowed with broad power under the Randolph formulation, authority which by its own terms was scarcely amenable to judicial review. In essence, courts could hardly determine when ". . . the separate States are incompetent or . . . the harmony of the United States may be interrupted"; the National Legislature, as critics pointed out, was free to define its own jurisdiction. Later the definition of legislative authority was changed into the form we know, a series of stipulated powers, *but the delegates never seriously reexamined the jurisdiction of the judiciary under this new limited formulation.* All arguments on the intention of the Framers in this matter are thus deductive and *a posteriori*, though some obviously make more sense than others.

The Framers were busy and distinguished men, anxious to get back to their families, their positions, and their constituents, not members of the French Academy devoting a lifetime to a dictionary. They were trying to do an important job, and do it in such a fashion that their handiwork would be acceptable to very diverse constituencies. No one was rhapsodic about the final document, but it was a beginning, a move in the right direction, and one they had reason to believe the people would endorse. In addition, since they had modified the impossible amendment provisions of the Articles (the requirement of unanimity which could always be frustrated by "Rogues Island") to one demanding approval by only three-quarters of the states, they seemed confident that gaps in the fabric which experience would reveal could be rewoven without undue difficulty.

• • •

2.8 *Democracy and* The Federalist: *A Reconsideration of the Framers' Intent*_____

Martin Diamond

• • •

Our major political problems today are problems of democracy; and, as much as anything else, the *Federalist* papers are a teaching about democracy. The conclusion of one of the most important of these papers states what is also the most important theme in the entire work: the necessity for "a republican remedy for the diseases most incident to republican government." The theme is clearly repeated in a passage where Thomas Jefferson is praised for displaying equally "a fervent attachment to republican government and an enlightened view of the dangerous propensities against which it ought to be guarded." *The Federalist*, thus, stresses its commitment to republican or popular government, but, of course, insists that this must be an enlightened commitment.

But *The Federalist* and the Founding Fathers generally have not been taken at their word. Predominantly, they are understood as being only quasi- or even anti-democrats. Modern American historical writing, at least until very recently, has generally seen the Constitution as some sort of apostasy from, or reaction to, the radically democratic implications of the Declaration of Independence—a reaction that was undone by the great "democratic breakthroughs" of Jeffersonianism, Jacksonianism, etc. This view, I believe, involves a false understanding of the crucial political issues involved in the founding of the American Republic. Further, it is based implicitly upon a questionable modern approach to democracy and has tended to have the effect, moreover, of relegating the political teaching of the Founding Fathers to the pre-democratic past and thus of making it of no vital concern to moderns. The Founding Fathers themselves repeatedly stressed that their Constitution was wholly consistent with the true principles of republican or popular government. The prevailing modern opinion, in varying degrees and in different ways, rejects that claim. It thus becomes important to understand what was the relation of the Founding Fathers to popular government or democracy.

I have deliberately used interchangeably their terms, "popular government" and "democracy." The Founding Fathers, of course, did not use the terms entirely synonymously and the idea that they were less than "democrats" has been fortified by the fact that they sometimes defined "democracy" invidiously in comparison with "republic." But this fact does not really justify the opinion. For their basic view was that *popular government was the genus, and democracy and republic were two species* of that genus of government. What distinguished popular government from other genera of government was that in it, political authority is "derived from the great body of the society, not from . . . [any] favoured class of it." With respect to this decisive question, of where political authority is lodged, democracy and republic—

as *The Federalist* uses the terms—differ not in the least. Republics, equally with democracies, may claim to be wholly a form of popular government. This is neither to deny the difference between the two, nor to depreciate the importance *The Federalist* attached to the difference; but in *The Federalist's* view, the difference does not relate to the essential principle of popular government. Democracy means in *The Federalist* that form of popular government where the citizens "assemble and administer the government in person." Republics differ in that the people rule through representatives and, of course, in the consequences of that difference. The crucial point is that republics and democracies are equally forms of popular government, but that the one form is vastly preferable to the other because of the substantive consequences of the difference in form. Those historians who consider the Founding Fathers as less than "democrats," miss or reject the Founders' central contention that, while being perfectly faithful to the *principle* of popular government, they had solved the *problem* of popular government.

In what way is the Constitution ordinarily thought to be less democratic than the Declaration? The argument is usually that the former is characterized by fear of the people, by preoccupation with minority interests and rights, and by measures therefore taken against the power of majorities. The Declaration, it is true, does not display these features, but this is no proof of a fundamental difference of principle between the two. Is it not obviously possible that the difference is due only to a difference in the tasks to which the two documents were addressed? And is it not further possible that the democratic principles of the Declaration are not only compatible with the prophylactic measures of the Constitution, but actually imply them?

The Declaration of Independence formulates two criteria for judging whether any government is good, or indeed legitimate. Good government must rest, procedurally, upon the consent of the governed. Good government, substantively, must do only certain things, *e.g.*, secure certain rights. This may be stated another way by borrowing a phrase from Locke, appropriate enough when discussing the Declaration. That "the people shall be judge" is of the essence of democracy, is its peculiar form or method of proceeding. That the people shall judge rightly is the substantive problem of democracy. But whether the procedure will bring about the substance is problematic. Between the Declaration's two criteria, then, a tension exists: consent can be given or obtained for governmental actions which are not right—at least as the men of 1776 saw the right. (To give an obvious example from their point of view: the people may freely but wrongly vote away the protection due to property.) Thus the Declaration clearly contained, although it did not resolve, a fundamental problem. Solving the problem was not its task; that was the task for the framers of the Constitution. But the man who wrote the Declaration of Independence and the leading men who supported it were perfectly aware of the difficulty, and of the necessity for a "republican remedy."

What the text of the Declaration, taken alone, tells of its meaning may easily be substantiated by the testimony of its author and supporters. Consider only that Jefferson, with no known change of heart at all, said of *The Federalist* that it was "the best commentary on the principles of government which was ever written." Jefferson, it must be remembered, came firmly to recommend the adoption of the Constitution, his criticisms of it having come down only to a proposal for rotation in the Presidency and for the subsequent adoption of a bill of rights. I do not, of course, deny the peculiar character of "Jeffersonianism" nor the importance to many things of its proper understanding. I only state here that it is certain that Jefferson, unlike later historians, did not view the Constitution as a retrogression from democracy. Or further, consider that John Adams, now celebrated as America's great conservative, was so enthusiastic about Jefferson's draft of the Declaration as to wish on his own account that hardly a word be changed. And this same Adams, also without any change of heart and without complaint, accepted the Constitution as embodying many of his own views on government.

The idea that the Constitution was a falling back from the fuller democracy of the Declaration thus rests in part upon a false reading of the Declaration as free from the concerns regarding democracy that the framers of the Constitution felt. Perhaps only those would so read it who take for granted a perfect, self-subsisting harmony between consent (equality) and the proper aim of government (justice), or between consent and individual rights (liberty). This assumption was utterly foreign to the leading men of the Declaration.

[I]

The Declaration has wrongly been converted into, as it were, a super-democratic document; has the Constitution wrongly been converted in the modern view into an insufficiently democratic document? The only basis for depreciating the democratic character of the Constitution lies in its framers' apprehensive diagnosis of the "diseases," "defects" or "evil propensities" of democracy, and in their remedies. But if what the Founders considered to be defects *are* genuine defects, and if the remedies, without violating the principles of popular government, *are* genuine remedies, then it would be unreasonable to call the Founders anti- or quasi-democrats. Rather, they would be the wise partisans of democracy; a man is not a better democrat but only a foolish democrat if he ignores real defects inherent in popular government. Thus, the question becomes: are there natural defects to democracy and, if there are, what are the best remedies?

In part, the Founding Fathers answered this question by employing a traditional mode of political analysis. They believed there were several basic possible regimes, each having several possible forms. Of these possible regimes they believed the best, or at least the best for America, to be popular government, but only if purged of its defects. At any rate, an unpurged popular government they believed to be inde-

fensible. They believed there were several forms of popular government, crucial among these direct democracy and republican—or representative—government (the latter perhaps divisible into two distinct forms, large and small republics). Their constitution and their defense of it constitute an argument for that form of popular government (large republic) in which the "evil propensities" would be weakest or most susceptible of remedy.

The whole of the thought of the Founding Fathers is intelligible and, especially, the evaluation of their claim to be wise partisans of popular government is possible, only if the words *"disease," "defect,"* and *"evil propensity"* are allowed their full force. Unlike modern "value-free" social scientists, the Founding Fathers believed that true knowledge of the good and bad in human conduct was possible, and that they themselves possessed sufficient knowledge to discern the really grave defects of popular government and their proper remedies. The modern relativistic or positivistic theories, implicitly employed by most commentators on the Founding Fathers, deny the possibility of such true knowledge and therefore deny that the Founding Fathers *could* have been actuated by knowledge of the good rather than by passion or interest. (I deliberately employ the language of *Federalist* No. 10. Madison defined faction, in part, as a group "united and actuated by . . . passion, or . . . interest." That is, factions are groups *not*—as presumably the authors of *The Federalist* were—actuated by reason.) How this modern view of the value problem supports the conception of the Constitution as less democratic than the Declaration is clear. The Founding Fathers did in fact seek to prejudice the outcome of democracy; they sought to alter, by certain restraints, the likelihood that the majority would decide certain political issues in bad ways. These restraints the Founders justified as mitigating the natural defects of democracy. But, say the moderns, there are no "bad" political decisions, wrong-in-themselves, from reaching which the majority ought to be restrained. Therefore, ultimately, nothing other than the specific interests of the Founders can explain their zeal in restraining democracy. And inasmuch as the restraints were typically placed on the many in the interest of the propertied, the departure of the Constitution is "anti-democratic" or "thermidorean." In short, according to this view, there cannot be what the Founders claimed to possess, "an *enlightened* view of the dangerous propensities against which [popular government] . . . ought to be guarded," the substantive goodness or badness of such propensities being a matter of opinion or taste on which reason can shed no light.

What are some of the arrangements which have been considered signs of "undemocratic" features of the Constitution? The process by which the Constitution may be amended is often cited in evidence. Everyone is familiar with the arithmetic which shows that a remarkably small minority could prevent passage of a constitutional amendment supported by an overwhelming majority of the people. That is, bare majorities in the thirteen least populous states could prevent passage of an amendment desired by overwhelming majorities in the thirty-six most populous states. But let us, for a reason to be made clear in a moment, turn that arithmetic around. Bare majorities in the thirty-seven least populous states can pass amendments against the opposition of overwhelming majorities in the twelve most populous states. And this would mean in actual votes today (and would have meant for the thirteen original states) constitutional amendment by a minority against the opposition of a majority of citizens. My point is simply that, while the amending procedure does involve qualified majorities, the qualification is not the kind that requires an especially large numerical majority for action.

I suggest that the real aim and practical effect of the complicated amending procedure was not at all to give power to minorities, but to ensure that passage of an amendment would require a *nationally* distributed majority, though one that legally could consist of a bare numerical majority. It was only adventitious that the procedure has the theoretical possibility of a minority blocking (or passing) an amendment. The aim of requiring nationally distributed majorities was, I think, to ensure that no amendment could be passed simply with the support of the few states or sections sufficiently numerous to provide a bare majority. No doubt it was also believed that it would be difficult for such a national majority to form or become effective save for the decent purposes that could command national agreement, and this difficulty was surely deemed a great virtue of the amending process. This is what I think *The Federalist* really means when it praises the amending process and says that "it guards equally against that extreme facility, which would render the Constitution too mutable; and that extreme difficulty, which might perpetuate its discovered faults." All I wish to emphasize here is that the actual method adopted, with respect to the numerical size of majorities, is meant to leave all legal power in the hands of ordinary majorities so long as they are national majorities. The departure from simple majoritarianism is, at least, not in an oligarchic or aristocratic direction. In this crucial respect, the amending procedure does conform strictly to the principles of republican (popular) government.

Consider next the suffrage question. It has long been assumed as proof of an anti-democratic element in the Constitution that the Founding Fathers depended for the working of their Constitution upon a substantially limited franchise. Just as the Constitution allegedly was ratified by a highly qualified electorate, so too, it is held, was the new government to be based upon a suffrage subject to substantial property qualifications. This view has only recently been seriously challenged, especially by Robert E. Brown, whose detailed researches convince him that the property qualifications in nearly all the original states were probably so small as to exclude never more than twenty-five per cent, and in most cases as little as only five to ten per cent, of the adult white male population. That is, the property qualifications were not designed to exclude the mass of the poor but only the small proportion which lacked a concrete—however small—stake in society, *i.e.*, primarily the transients or "idlers."

The Constitution, of course, left the suffrage question to the decision of the individual states. What is the implication of that fact for deciding what sort of suffrage the Framers had in mind? The immediately popular branch of the national legislature was to be elected by voters who "shall have the qualifications requisite for electors of the most numerous branch of the State Legislature." The mode of election to the electoral college for the Presidency and to the Senate is also left to "be prescribed in each State by the legislature thereof." At a minimum, it may be stated that the Framers did not themselves attempt to reduce, or prevent the expansion of, the suffrage; that question was left wholly to the states—and these were, ironically, the very hotbeds of post-revolutionary democracy from the rule of which it is familiarly alleged that the Founders sought to escape.

In general, the conclusion seems inescapable that the states had a far broader suffrage than is ordinarily thought, and nothing in the actions of the Framers suggests any expectation or prospect of the reduction of the suffrage. Again, as in the question of the amending process, I suggest that the Constitution represented no departure whatsoever from the democratic standards of the Revolutionary period, or from any democratic standards then generally recognized.

What of the Senate? The organization of the Senate, its term of office and its staggered mode of replacement, its election by state legislatures rather than directly by the people, among other things, have been used to demonstrate the undemocratic character of the Senate as intended by the Framers. Was this not a device to represent property and not people, and was it not intended therefore to be a non-popular element in the government? I suggest, on the contrary, that the really important thing is that the Framers thought they had found a way to protect property *without* representing it. That the Founders intended the Senate to be one of the crucial devices for remedying the defects of democracy is certainly true. But *The Federalist* argues that the Senate, as actually proposed in the Constitution, was calculated to be such a device as would operate only in a way that "will consist . . . with the genuine principles of republican government." I believe that the claim is just.

Rather than viewing the Senate from the perspective of modern experience and opinions, consider how radically democratic the Senate appears when viewed from a pre-modern perspective. The model of a divided legislature that the Founders had most in mind was probably the English Parliament. There the House of Lords was thought to provide some of the beneficial checks upon the popular Commons which it was hoped the Senate would supply in the American Constitution. But the American Senate was to possess none of the qualities which permitted the House of Lords to fulfill its role; *i.e.*, its hereditary basis, or membership upon election by the Crown, or any of its other aristocratic characteristics. Yet the Founding Fathers knew that the advantages of having both a Senate and a House would "be in proportion to the dissimilarity in the genius of the two bodies." What is remarkable is that, in seeking to secure this dissimilarity, they did not in any respect go beyond the limits permitted by the "genuine principles of republican government."

Not only is this dramatically demonstrated in comparison with the English House of Lords, but also in comparison with all earlier theory regarding the division of the legislative power. The aim of such a division in earlier thought is to secure a balance between the aristocratic and democratic elements of a polity. This is connected with the pre-modern preference for a *mixed* republic, which was rejected by the Founders in favor of a *democratic* republic. And the traditional way to secure this balance or mixture was to give one house or office to the suffrages of the few and one to the suffrages of the many. Nothing of the kind is involved in the American Senate. Indeed, on this issue, so often cited as evidence of the Founders' undemocratic predilections, the very opposite is the case. The Senate is a constitutional device which *par excellence* reveals the strategy of the Founders. They wanted something like the advantages earlier thinkers had seen in a mixed legislative power, but they thought this was possible (and perhaps preferable) without any introduction whatsoever of aristocratic power into their system. What pre-modern thought had seen in an aristocratic senate—wisdom, nobility, manners, religion, etc.—the Founding Fathers converted into stability, enlightened self-interest, a "temperate and respectable body of citizens." The qualities of a senate having thus been altered (involving perhaps comparable changes in the notion of the ends of government), it became possible to secure these advantages through a Senate based wholly upon popular principles. Or so I would characterize a Senate whose membership required no property qualification and which was appointed (or elected in the manner prescribed) by State legislatures which, in their own turn, were elected annually or biennially by a nearly universal manhood suffrage.

The great claim of *The Federalist* is that the Constitution represents the fulfillment of a truly novel experiment, of "a revolution which has no parallel in the annals of society," and which is decisive for the happiness of "the whole human race." And the novelty, I argue, consisted in solving the problems of popular government by means which yet maintain the government "wholly popular." In defending that claim against the idea of the Constitution as a retreat from democracy I have dealt thus far only with the easier task: the demonstration that the constitutional devices and arrangements do not derogate from the legal power of majorities to rule. What remains is to examine the claim that the Constitution did in fact remedy the natural defects of democracy. Before any effort is made

in this direction, it may be useful to summarize some of the implications and possible utility of the analysis thus far.

Above all, the merit of the suggestions I have made, if they are accurate in describing the intention and action of the Founders, is that it makes the Founders available to us for the study of modern problems. I have tried to restore to them their *bona fides* as partisans of democracy. This done, we may take seriously the question whether they were, as they claimed to be, wise partisans of democracy or popular government. If they were partisans of democracy and if the regime they created was decisively democratic, then they speak to us not merely about bygone problems, not from a viewpoint—in this regard—radically different from our own, but as men addressing themselves to problems identical in principle with our own. They are a source from within our own heritage which teaches us the way to put the question to democracy, a way which is rejected by certain prevailing modern ideas. But we cannot avail ourselves of their assistance if we consider American history to be a succession of democratizations which overcame the Founding Fathers's intentions. On that view it is easy to regard them as simply outmoded. If I am right regarding the extent of democracy in their thought and regime, then they are not outmoded by modern events but rather are tested by them. American history, on this view, is not primarily the replacement of a pre-democratic regime by a democratic regime, but is rather a continuing testimony to how the Founding Fathers' democratic regime has worked out in modern circumstances. The whole of our national experience thus becomes a way of judging the Founders' principles, of judging democracy itself, or of pondering the flaws of democracy and the means to its improvement.

• • •

III  FOCUS: FEDERALISTS AND ANTIFEDERALISTS

The Federalists were the supporters of the new Constitution; the Antifederalists were opponents. That much is clear. That the two groups had different ideas about politics is also clear (see selections 2.1 through 2.6). But what factors—social, economic, or otherwise—made an individual more or less likely to cast his lot with one side or the other?

The answer is not obvious. There were northern and southern Federalists and northern and southern Antifederalists. Farmers, lawyers, and merchants lined up on both sides. The two sides were not clearly divided by age or education. And although it is popular to argue that the Federalists were rich and the Antifederalists poor (the so-called Beard thesis, after the early twentieth-century historian Charles Beard), recent research has debunked this distinction as greatly overdrawn.

Yet there was a clear distinction between the two groups, and understanding that difference is critical to understanding their disagreements over the Constitution. As the historian Gordon S. Wood suggests, the difference between the Federalists and the Antifederalists is best viewed as one of social class. The Federalists, in Wood's view, viewed themselves and were seen as aristocrats; the Antifederalists, in contrast, were democrats. This difference was partly one of economic wealth, but it was deeper and more fundamental. The Federalists, as John Jay, himself a Federalist, put it, were "the better sort of people . . . who are orderly and industrious, who are content with their situations and not uneasy in the circumstances." The Antifederalists, by contrast, "lacked those attributes of social distinction and dignity that went beyond mere wealth." The Federalists were urbane and cosmopolitan; the Antifederalists were more parochial.

The key to Wood's argument is that wealth alone was not the issue. The Antifederalists stood for the proposition that those who governed should be like the people themselves; the Federalists held to the idea that the leaders of a community should be the "natural aristocracy," the best men, to whom the rest of the people could look for wisdom, experience, and guidance.

Questions

1. What precisely does Wood mean by "aristocracy" and "democracy" as social concepts? In what sense did the Federalists view themselves as the "better sort of people"?

2. What did the Federalists mean by the term *natural aristocracy*? How does a natural aristocracy differ from a traditional aristocracy, as in England?

3. What were the implications of the Federalists' aristocratic philosophy on their ideas about government? Consider this question in the light of the previous selections in this chapter.

2.9 The Worthy against the Licentious

Gordon S. Wood

The division over the Constitution in 1787–88 is not easily analyzed. It is difficult, as historians have recently demonstrated, to equate the supporters or opponents of the Constitution with particular economic groupings. The Antifederalist politicians in the ratifying conventions often possessed wealth, including public securities, equal to that of the Federalists. While the relative youth of the Federalist leaders, compared to the ages of the prominent Antifederalists, was important, especially in accounting for the Federalists' ability to think freshly and creatively about politics, it can hardly be used to explain the division throughout the country. . . . There were many diverse reasons in each state why men supported or opposed the Constitution that cut through any sort of class division. The Constitution was a single issue in a complicated situation, and its acceptance or rejection in many states was often dictated by peculiar circumstances—the prevalence of Indians, the desire for western lands, the special interests of commerce—that defy generalization. Nevertheless, despite all of this confusion and complexity, the struggle over the Constitution, as the debate if nothing else makes clear, can best be understood as a social one. Whatever the particular constituency of the antagonists may have been, men in 1787–88 talked as if they were representing distinct and opposing social elements. Both the proponents and opponents of the Constitution focused throughout the debates on an essential point of political sociology that ultimately must be used to distinguish a Federalist from an Antifederalist. The quarrel was fundamentally one between aristocracy and democracy.

Because of its essentially social base, this quarrel, as George Minot of Massachusetts said, was "extremely unequal." . . .

The Antifederalists were not simply poorer politicians than the Federalists; they were ac-tually different kinds of politicians. Too many of them were state-centered men with local interests and loyalties only, politicians without influence and connections, and ultimately politicians without social and intellectual confidence. In South Carolina the up-country opponents of the Constitution shied from debate and when they did occasionally rise to speak apologized effusively for their inability to say what they felt had to be said, thus leaving most of the opposition to the Constitution to be voiced by Rawlins Lowndes, a low-country planter who scarcely represented their interests and soon retired from the struggle. Elsewhere, in New Hampshire, Connecticut, Massachusetts, Pennsylvania, and North Carolina, the situation was similar: the Federalists had the bulk of talent and influence on their side "together with all the Speakers in the State great and small." In convention after convention the Antifederalists, as in Connecticut, tried to speak, but "they were browbeaten by many of those Cicero'es as they think themselves and others of Superior rank." "The presses are in a great measure secured to *their* side," the Antifederalists complained with justice: out of a hundred or more newspapers printed in the late eighties only a dozen supported the Antifederalists, as editors, "afraid to offend the great men, or Merchants, who could work their ruin," closed their columns to the opposition. The Antifederalists were not so much beaten as overawed. . . .

Because the many "new men" of the 1780's, men like Melancthon Smith and Abraham Yates of New York or John Smilie and William Findley of Pennsylvania, had bypassed the social hierarchy in their rise to political leadership, they lacked those attributes of social distinction and dignity that went beyond mere wealth. Since these kinds of men were never assimilated to the gentlemanly cast of the Livingstons or the

Morrises, they, like Americans earlier in confrontation with the British court, tended to view with suspicion and hostility the high-flying world of style and connections that they were barred by their language and tastes, if by nothing else, from sharing in. In the minds of these socially inferior politicians the movement for the strengthening of the central government could only be a "conspiracy" "planned and set to work" by a few aristocrats, who were at first, said Abraham Yates, no larger in number in any one state than the cabal which sought to undermine English liberty at the beginning of the eighteenth century. Since men like Yates could not quite comprehend what they were sure were the inner maneuverings of the elite, they were convinced that in the aristocrats' program, "what was their view in the beginning" or how "far it was Intended to be carried Must be Collected from facts that Afterwards have happened." Like American Whigs in the sixties and seventies forced to delve into the dark and complicated workings of English court politics, they could judge motives and plans "but by the Event." And they could only conclude that the events of the eighties, "the treasury, the Cincinnati, and other public creditors, with all their concomitants," were "somehow or other, . . . inseparably connected," were all parts of a grand design "concerted by a few *tyrants*" to undo the Revolution and to establish an aristocracy in order "to lord it over the rest of their fellow citizens, to trample the poorer part of the people under their feet, that they may be rendered their servants and slaves." . . .

Nothing was more characteristic of Antifederalist thinking than this obsession with aristocracy. Although to a European, American society may have appeared remarkably egalitarian, to many Americans, especially to those who aspired to places of consequence but were made to feel their inferiority in innumerable, often subtle, ways, American society was distinguished by its inequality. "It is true," said Melancthon Smith in the New York Ratifying Convention, "it is our singular felicity that we have no legal or hereditary distinctions . . . ; but still there are real differences." "Every society naturally divides itself into classes. . . . Birth, education, talents, and wealth, create distinctions among men as visible, and of as much influence, as titles, stars, and garters." Everyone knew those "whom nature hath destined to rule," declared one sardonic Antifederalist pamphlet. Their "qualifications of authority" were obvious: "such as the dictatorial air, the magisterial voice, the imperious tone, the haughty countenance, the lofty look, the majestic mien." In all communities, "even in those of the most democratic kind," wrote George Clinton (whose "family and connections" in the minds of those like Philip Schuyler did not "entitle him to so distinguished a predominance" as the governorship of New York), there were pressures—"superior talents, fortunes and public employments"—demarcating an aristocracy whose influence was difficult to resist.

Such influence was difficult to resist because, to the continual annoyance of the Antifederalists, the great body of the people willingly submitted to it. The "authority of names" and "the influence of the great" among ordinary people were too evident to be denied. "Will any one say that there does not exist in this country the pride of family, of wealth, of talents, and that they do not command influence and respect among the common people?" "The people are too apt to yield an implicit assent to the opinions of those characters whose abilities are held in the highest esteem, and to those in whose integrity and patriotism they can confide; not considering that the love of domination is generally in proportion to talents, abilities and superior requirements." Because of this habit of deference in the people, it was "in the power of the enlightened and aspiring few, if they should combine, at any time to destroy the best establishments, and even make the people the instruments of their own subjugation." Hence, the Antifederalist-minded declared, the people must be awakened to the consequences of their self-ensnarement; they must be warned

"Founding Fathers! How come no Founding Mothers?"

Drawing by Dana Fradon © 1972 The New Yorker Magazine, Inc.

over and over by popular tribunes, by "those who are competent to the task of developing the principles of government," of the dangers involved in paying obeisance to those who they thought were their superiors. The people must "not be permitted to consider themselves as a grovelling, distinct species, uninterested in the general welfare."

Such constant admonitions to the people of the perils flowing from their too easy deference to the *natural aristocracy*" were necessary because the Antifederalists were convinced that these "men that had been delicately bred, and who were in affluent circumstances," these "men of the most exalted rank in life," were by their very conspicuousness irreparably cut off from the great body of the people and hence could never share in its concerns nor look after its interests. It was not that these "certain men exalted above the rest" were necessarily "des-

titute of morality or virtue" or that they were inherently different from other men. "The same passions and prejudices govern all men." It was only that circumstances in their particular environment had made them different. There was "a charm in politicks"; men in high office become habituated with power, "grow fond of it, and are loath to resign it"; "they feel themselves flattered and elevated," enthralled by the attractions of high living, and thus they easily forget the interests of the common people, from which many of them once sprang. By dwelling so vividly on the allurements of prestige and power, by emphasizing again and again how the "human soul is affected by wealth, in all its faculties, . . . by its present interest, by its expectations, and by its fears," these ambitious Antifederalist politicians may have revealed as much about themselves as they did about the "aristocratic" elite they sought to displace. Yet at the same time by such language they contributed to a new appreciation of the nature of society.

In these repeated attacks on deference and the capacity of a conspicuous few to speak for the whole society—which was to become in time the distinguishing feature of American democratic politics—the Antifederalists struck at the roots of the traditional conception of political society. If the natural elite, whether its distinctions were ascribed or acquired, was not in any organic way connected to the "feelings, circumstances, and interests" of the people and was incapable of feeling "sympathetically the wants of the people," then it followed that only ordinary men, men not distinguished by the characteristics of aristocratic wealth and taste, men "in middling circumstances" untempted by the attractions of a cosmopolitan world and thus "more temperate, of better morals, and less ambitious, than the great," could be trusted to speak for the great body of the people, for those who were coming more and more to be referred to as "the middling and lower classes of people." The differentiating influence of the environment was such that men in various ranks and classes now seemed to be broken apart from one another, separated by their peculiar circumstances into distinct, unconnected, and often incompatible interests. With their indictment of aristocracy the Antifederalists were saying, whether they realized it or not, that the people of America even in their several states were not homogeneous entities each with a basic similarity of interest for which an empathic elite could speak. Society was not an organic hierarchy composed of ranks and degrees indissolubly linked one to another; rather it was a heterogeneous mixture of "many different classes or orders of people, Merchants, Farmers, Planter Mechanics and Gentry or wealthy Men." In such a society men from one class or group, however educated and respectable they may have been, could never be acquainted with the "*Situation* and Wants" of those of another class or group. Lawyers and planters could never be "adequate judges of

tradesmens concerns." If men were truly to represent the people in government, it was not enough for them to be for the people; they had to be actually of the people. "Farmers, traders and mechanics . . . all ought to have a competent number of their best informed members in the legislature." . . .

At first the Federalists tried to belittle the talk of an aristocracy; they even denied that they knew the meaning of the word. "Why bring into the debate the whims of writers—introducing the distinction of *well-born* from others?" asked Edmund Pendleton in the Virginia Ratifying Convention. In the Federalist view every man was "*well-born* who comes into the world with an intelligent mind, and with all his parts perfect." Was even natural talent to be suspect? Was learning to be encouraged, the Federalists asked in exasperation, only "to set up those who attained its benefits as butts of invidious distinction?" No American, the Federalists said, could justifiably oppose a man "commencing in life without any other stock but industry and economy," and "by the mere efforts of these" rising "to opulence and wealth." If social mobility were to be meaningful then some sorts of distinctions were necessary. If government by a natural aristocracy, said Wilson, meant "nothing more or less than a government of the best men in the community," then who could object to it? Could the Antifederalists actually intend to mark out those "most noted for their virtue and talents . . . as the most improper persons for the public confidence?" No, the Federalists exclaimed in disbelief, the Antifederalists could never have intended such a socially destructive conclusion. It was clear, said Hamilton, that the Antifederalists' arguments only proved "that there are men who are rich, men who are poor, some who are wise, and others who are not; that indeed, every distinguished man is an aristocrat."

But the Antifederalist intention and implication were too conspicuous to be avoided: all distinctions, whether naturally based or not, were being challenged. Robert Livingston in the New York Convention saw as clearly as anyone what he thought the Antifederalists were really after, and he minced no words in replying to Smith's attack on the natural aristocracy. Since Smith had classified as aristocrats not only "the rich and the great" but also "the wise, the learned, and those eminent for their talents or great virtues," aristocrats to the Antifederalists had in substance become all men of merit. Such men, such aristocrats, were not to be chosen for public office, questioned Livingston in rising disbelief in the implications of the Antifederalist argument, "because the people will not have confidence in them; that is, the people will not have confidence in those who best deserve and most possess their confidence?" The logic of Smith's reasoning, said Livingston, would lead to a government by the dregs of society, a monstrous government where all "the unjust, the selfish, the unsocial feelings," where all "the vices, the infirmities, the passions of the people" would be represented. . . .

In the Federalist mind therefore the struggle over the Constitution was not one between kinds of wealth or property, or one between commercial or noncommercial elements of the population, but rather represented a broad social division between those who believed in the right of a natural aristocracy to speak for the people and those who did not.

Against this threat from the licentious the Federalists pictured themselves as the defenders of the worthy, of those whom they called "the better sort of people," those, said John Jay, "who are orderly and industrious, who are content with their situations and not uneasy in their circumstances." Because the Federalists were fearful that republican equality was becoming "that *perfect equality* which deadens the motives of industry, and places Demerit on a Footing with Virtue," they were obsessed with the need to insure that the proper amount of inequality and natural distinctions be recognized. "Although there are no nobles in America," observed the French minister to America, Louis Otto, in 1786, "there is a class of men denominated 'gentlemen,' who, by reason of their wealth, their talents, their education, their families, or the offices they hold, aspire to a preeminence which the people refuse to grant them." "How idle . . . all disputes about a technical aristocracy" would be, if only the people would "pay strict attention to the natural aristocracy, which is the institution of heaven. . . . This aristocracy is derived from merit and that influence, which a character for superiour wisdom, and known services to the commonwealth, has to produce veneration, confidence and esteem, among a people, who have felt the benefits. . . ." Robert Morris, for example, was convinced there were social differences—even in Pennsylvania. "What!" he exclaimed in scornful amazement at John Smilie's argument that a republic admitted of no social superiorities. "Is it insisted that there is no distinction of character?" Respectability, said Morris with conviction, was not confined to property. "Surely persons possessed of knowledge, judgment, information, integrity, and having extensive connections, are not to be classed with persons void of reputation or character."

In refuting the Antifederalists' contention "that all classes of citizens should have some of their own number in the representative body, in order that their feelings and interests may be the better understood and attended to," Hamilton in *The Federalist*, Number 35, put into words the Federalists' often unspoken and vaguely held assumption about the organic and the hierarchical nature of society. Such explicit class or occupational representation as the Antifederalists advocated, wrote Hamilton, "was not only impractical but unnecessary, since the society was not as fragmented or heterogeneous as the Antifederalists implied. The various groups in the landed interest, for example, were perfectly united, from the wealthiest landlord down to the poorest tenant," and this "common interest may always be reckoned upon as the surest bond of sympathy" linking the landed representative, however rich, to his constituents. In a like way, the members of the commercial community were "immediately connected" and most naturally represented by the merchants. "Mechanics and manufacturers will always be inclined, with few exceptions, to give their votes to merchants, in preference to persons of their own professions or trades. . . . They know that the merchant is their natural patron and friend; and . . . they are sensible that their habits in life have not been such as to give them those acquired endowments, without which in a deliberative assembly, the greatest natural abilities, are for the most part useless." However much many Federalists may have doubted the substance of Hamilton's analysis of American society, they could not doubt the truth of his conclusion. That the people were represented better by one of the natural aristocracy "whose situation leads to extensive inquiry and information" than by one "whose observation does not travel beyond the circle of his neighbors and acquaintances" was the defining element of the Federalist philosophy.

It was not simply the number of public securities, or credit outstanding, or the number of ships, or the amount of money possessed that made a man think of himself as one of the natural elite. It was much more subtle than the mere possession of wealth: it was a deeper social feeling, a sense of being socially established, of possessing attributes—family, education, and refinement—that others lacked; above all, of being accepted by and being able to move easily among those who considered themselves to be the respectable and cultivated. It is perhaps anachronistic to describe this social sense as a class interest, for it often transcended immediate political or economic concerns, and, as Hamilton's argument indicates, was designed to cut through narrow occupational categories. The Republicans of Philadelphia, for example, repeatedly denied that they represented an aristocracy with a united class interest. "We are of different occupations; of different sects of religion; and have different views of life. No factions or private system can comprehend us all." Yet with all their assertions of diversified interests the Republicans were not without a social consciousness in their quarrel with the supporters of the Pennsylvania Constitution. If there were any of us ambitious for power, their apology continued, then there would be no need to change the Constitution, for we surely could attain power under the present Constitution. "We have already seen how easy the task is for *any character* to rise into power and consequence under it. And there are some of us, who think not so meanly of ourselves, as to dread any rivalship from those who are now in office."

In 1787 this kind of elitist social consciousness was brought into play as perhaps never before in eighteenth-century America, as gentlemen up and down the continent submerged their sectional and economic differences in the face of what seemed to be a threat to the very foundations of society. . . . The fear of social disruption that had run through much of the writing of the eighties was brought to a head to eclipse all other fears. Although state politics in the eighties remains to be analyzed, the evidence from Federalist correspondence indicates clearly a belief that never had there occurred "so great a change in the opinion of the best people" as was occurring in the last few years of the decade. The Federalists were astonished at the outpouring in 1787 of influential and respectable people who had earlier remained quiescent. Too many of "the better sort of people," it was repeatedly said, had withdrawn at the end of the war "from the theatre of public action, to scenes of retirement and ease," and thus "demagogues of desperate fortunes, mere adventurers in fraud, were left to act unopposed." After all, it was explained, "when the wicked rise, men hide themselves." Even the problems of Massachusetts in 1786, noted General Benjamin Lincoln, the repressor of the Shaysites, were not caused by the rebels, but by the laxity of "the good people of the state." But the lesson of this laxity was rapidly being learned. Everywhere, it seemed, men of virtue, good sense, and property, "almost the whole body of our enlighten'd and leading characters in every state," were awakened in support of stronger government. "The scum which was thrown upon the surface by the fermentation of the war is daily sinking," Benjamin Rush told

Richard Price in 1786, "while a pure spirit is occupying its place." "Men are brought into action who had consigned themselves to an eve of rest," Edward Carrington wrote to Jefferson in June 1787, "and the Convention, as a Beacon, is rousing the attention of the Empire." The Antifederalists could only stand amazed at this "weight of talents" being gathered in support of the Constitution. "What must the individual be who could thus oppose them united?"

Still, in the face of this preponderance of wealth and respectability in support of the Constitution, what remains extraordinary about 1787–88 is not the weakness and disunity but the political strength of Antifederalism. That large numbers of Americans could actually reject a plan of government created by a body "composed of the first characters in the Continent" and backed by Washington and nearly the whole of the natural aristocracy of the country said more about the changing character of American politics and society in the eighties than did the Constitution's eventual acceptance. It was indeed a portent of what was to come.

_____Chapter 3

Federalism

$\mathcal{T}$he idea of dividing political power between a central government and its component parts while preserving both elements was one of the great innovations of American political thought. In the eighteenth century, the accepted wisdom was that sovereignty—that is, the ultimate political power in a community—could not be divided. In
a confederation, either the states would have to retain sovereignty, authorizing the
national government to take on only certain specific tasks with the approval of all the
states, or the states would lose their power and identity and be swallowed up into one
great whole. There was, according to this line of thought, no middle ground.

Throughout the constitutional debate of the 1780s, the Antifederalists clung to
this traditional point of view. The Articles of Confederation, after all, was just that: a
confederation of fully sovereign states that came together in a league, much like a
modern alliance, for certain limited purposes. The Articles began, in fact, "We the
. . . Delegates of the States." The Antifederalists conceded that the Articles needed
modification, but they resisted attempts to strengthen the national government too
much, fearing that it would become a threat to the sovereignty of the states.

The Federalists' great innovation was the creation of dual federalism or, commonly, federalism. Under this theory, ultimate sovereignty rested in the people; they
delegated some of their sovereignty to the national government, some to the states, and
retained some for themselves. (Read the Tenth Amendment to the Constitution, for an
example.) Within their respective spheres of authority, both the states and the national
government were supreme.

The Antifederalists' charge that such a system could not work was dismissed out
of hand by the Federalists. Nevertheless, in the more than two hundred years since the
ratification of the Constitution, power has definitely shifted from the states to the
national government. The idea of federalism and the validity of the Antifederalists'
charge that the national government would eventually swallow up the states form the

main themes of this chapter. A more practical treatment of the working relationship between the states and Washington is discussed in selection 3.6.

There are many reasons that power has gravitated to the national government over time: the complexities of the modern economy, the growing role of the United States in world affairs, and the growth of technology, especially in communications and transportation. Another factor has been the ongoing conflict over race relations. The issue of slavery nearly broke up the Union and forced the national government to fight a war over the principle of a strong national government. Conflicts over race relations once again pitted the states against the national government in the mid-twentieth century (see chapter 17).

Throughout the centuries, a major player in the struggle between the federal government and the states has been the U.S. Supreme Court. Early on, the Court made a series of critical decisions—the most important of which was McCulloch v. Maryland (see selection 3.4)—establishing itself as the key arbiter between the national government and the states and laying the foundation for a broad expansion of federal power. More recently, the Court has been a key actor in applying to the states federal standards on civil rights and civil liberties. Given that the Court is and always has been a component part of the national government, is it any surprise that the national government seems to have emerged triumphant from its power struggles with the states?

Chapter Questions

1. What is the meaning of "dual federalism"? How does the theory of dual federalism differ from traditional understandings of the nature of sovereignty?

2. To what extent can it be said that federalism in America is dead? If it is dead, what factors led to its demise?

3. How does federalism in practice differ from federalism in theory? Is there a difference between the national government's theoretical power over the states and the relationship, in practice, between the national government and the states?

I THE CONSTITUTIONAL CONTEXT

One of the principal differences of opinion between the Federalists and the Antifederalists was, as their names imply, over the question of federalism—how much power the states should have as compared to the national government. The Antifederalists, as Herbert Storing explains in the following reading, objected to the Constitution above all because they feared it would concentrate power in the national government at the expense of the states. Instead of throwing away the Articles of Confederation and starting over with the Constitution, the Antifederalists suggested merely modifying and updating the Articles, leaving sovereignty in the states.

One of the problems the Antifederalists encountered was that, despite their name, they were strong believers in federalism—which, by its conventional definition, meant a government of sovereign states joined together in a loose confederation. But as Storing points out, the word federalism had already developed an ambiguous meaning that made it possible for the Federalists to adopt that name and make it stick.

Often the Antifederalists are dismissed as inconsequential, narrow-minded politicians who lacked the vision and the insights of the Federalists. Perhaps, however, that point of view is unfair. As you read Storing's account, try to remember that the Antifederalists were not merely "against" the Constitution; they had strong beliefs and political principles and a coherent way of looking at politics.

Questions

1. How did the Antifederalists define federalism?
2. What did they view as the major threat posed by the new "federalism" of the U.S. Constitution?

3.1 *What the Antifederalists Were For*

Herbert Storing

Far from straying from the principles of the American Revolution, as some of the Federalists accused them of doing, the Anti-Federalists saw themselves as the true defenders of those principles. "I am fearful," said Patrick Henry, "I have lived long enough to become an old fashioned fellow: Perhaps an invincible attachment to the dearest rights of man, may, in these refined enlightened days, be deemed *old fashioned*: If so, I am contented to be so: I say, the time has been, when every pore of my heart beat for American liberty, and which, I believe, had a counterpart in the breast of every true American." The Anti-Federalists argued, as some historians have argued since, that the Articles of Confederation were the constitutional embodiment of the principles on which the Revolution was based:

> Sir, I venerate the spirit with which every thing was done at the trying time in which the Confederation was formed. America had then a sufficiency of this virtue to resolve to resist perhaps the first nation in the universe, even unto bloodshed. What was her aim? Equal liberty and safety. What ideas had she of this equal liberty? Read them in her Articles of Confederation.

The innovators were impatient to change this "most excellent constitution," which was "sent like a blessing from heaven," for a constitution "essentially differing from the principles of the revolution, and from freedom," and thus destructive of the whole basis of the American community. "Instead of repairing the old and venerable fabrick, which sheltered the United States, from the dreadful and cruel storms of a tyrannical British ministry, they built a stately palace after their own fancies. . . ."

The principal characteristic of that "venerable fabrick" was its federalism: the Articles of Confederation established a league of sovereign and independent states whose representatives met in congress to deal with a limited range of common concerns in a system that relied heavily on voluntary cooperation. Federalism means that the states are primary, that they are equal, and that they possess the main weight of political power. The defense of the federal character of the American union was the most prominent article of Anti-Federalist conservative doctrine. While some of the other concerns were intrinsically more fundamental, the question of federalism was central and thus merits fuller discussion here, as it did in that debate.

To begin with an apparently small terminological problem, if the Constitution was opposed because it was anti-federal how did the opponents come to be called Anti-Federalists? They usually denied, in fact, that the name was either apt or just, and seldom used it themselves. They were, they often claimed, the true federalists. Some of them seemed to think that their proper name had been filched, while their backs were turned, as it were, by the pro-Constitution party, which refused to give it back; and versions of this explanation have been repeated by historians. Unquestionably the Federalists saw the advantage of a label that would suggest that those who opposed the Constitution also opposed such a manifestly good thing as federalism. But what has not been sufficiently understood is that the term "federal" had acquired a specific ambiguity that enabled the Federalists not merely to take but to keep the name.

One of the perennial issues under the Articles of Confederation involved the degree to which the general government—or the instrumentality of the federation per se—was to be supported or its capacity to act strengthened. In this context one was "federal" or "anti-federal" according to his willingness or unwillingness to strengthen or support the institutions of the federation. This was James Wilson's meaning when he spoke of the "fœderal disposition and character" of Pennsylvania. It was Patrick Henry's meaning when he said that, in rejecting the Constitution, New Hampshire and Rhode Island "have refused to become federal." It was the meaning of the New York Assembly when in responding coolly to the recommendations of the Annapolis Convention it nevertheless insisted on its "truly federal" disposition. This usage had thoroughly penetrated political discussion in the United States. In the straightforward explanation of Anti-Federalist George Bryan, "The name of Federalists, or Federal men, grew up at New York and in the eastern states, some time before the calling of the Convention, to denominate such as were attached to the general support of the United States, in opposition to those who preferred local and particular advantages. . . ." Later, according to Bryan, "this name was taken possession of by those who were in favor of the new federal government, as they called it, and opposers were called Anti-Federalists." Recognizing the pre-1787 usage, Jackson Turner Main tries, like Bryan, to preserve the spirit of Federalist larceny by suggesting that during the several years before 1787 "the men who wanted a strong national government, who might more properly be called 'nationalists,' began to appropriate the term 'federal' for themselves" and to apply the term "antifederal" to those hostile to the measures of Congress and thus presumably unpatriotic. But there was nothing exceptional or improper in the use of the term "federal" in this way; the shift in meaning was less an "appropriation" than a natural extension of the language, which the Federalists fully exploited.

The point of substance is that the Federalists had a legitimate *claim* to their name and therefore to their name for their opponents. Whether they had a better claim than their opponents cannot be answered on the basis of mere linguistic usage but only by considering the arguments. When, during the years of the Confederation, one was called a "federal man," his attachment to the principles of federalism was not at issue; that was taken for granted, and the point was that he was a man who (given this federal system) favored strengthening the "federal" or general authority. The ambiguity arose because strengthening the federal *authority* could be carried so far as to undermine the federal *principle*; and that was precisely what the Anti-Federalists claimed their opponents were doing. Thus The Impartial Examiner argued that, despite the "sound of names" on which the advocates of the Constitution "build their fame," it is the opponents who act "on the broader scale of true *fœderal principles.*" They desire "a continuance of each distinct sovereignty—and are anxious for such a degree of energy in the general government, as will cement the union in the strongest manner." It was possible (or so the Anti-Federalists believed) to be a federalist in the sense of favoring a strong agency of the federation and, at the same time, to be a federalist in the sense of adhering to the principle of a league of independent states. In the name of federalism in the former sense, it was claimed, the proponents of the Constitution had abandoned federalism in the latter (and fundamental) sense.

The Anti-Federalists stood, then, for federalism in opposition to what they called the consolidating tendency and intention of the Constitution—the tendency to establish one complete national government, which would destroy or undermine the states. They feared the implications of language like Washington's reference, in transmitting the Constitution to Congress, to the need for "the consolidation of our Union." They saw ominous intentions in Publius' opinion that "a NATION, without a NATIONAL GOVERNMENT, is, in my view, an awful spectacle." They resented and denied suggestions that "we must forget our local habits and attachments" and "be reduced to one faith and one government." They saw in the new Constitution a government with authority extending "to every case that is of the least importance" and capable of acting (preeminently in the crucial case of taxation) at discretion and independently of any agency but its own. Instead of thus destroying the federal character of the Union, "the leading feature of every amendment" of the Articles of Confederation ought to be, as Yates and Lansing expressed it, "the preservation of the individual states, in their uncontrouled constitutional rights, and . . . in reserving these, a mode might have been devised of granting to the confederacy, the monies arising from a general system of revenue; the power of regulating commerce, and enforcing the observance of foreign treaties, and other necessary matters of less moment."

A few of the Anti-Federalists were not sure, it is true, that consolidation would be so bad, if it were really feasible. James Monroe went so far as to say that "to collect the citizens of America, who have fought and bled together, by whose joint and common efforts they have been raised to the comparatively happy and exalted theatre on which they now stand; to lay aside all those jarring interests and discordant principles, which state legislatures if they do not create, certainly foment and increase, arrange them under one government and make them one people, is an idea not only elevated and sublime, but equally benevolent and humane." And, on the other hand, most of the Federalists agreed or professed to agree that consolidation was undesirable. Fisher Ames, defending the Constitution in Massachusetts, spoke the language of many Federalists when he insisted that "too much provision cannot be made against a consolidation. The state governments represent the wishes, and feelings, and local interests of the people. They are the safeguard and ornament of the Constitution; they will protract the period of our liberties; they will afford a shelter against the abuse of power, and will be the natural avengers of our violated rights." Indeed, expressions of rather strict federal principles were not uncommon on the Federalist side, although they were often perfunctory or shallow.

Perhaps the most conciliatory Federalist defense of federalism, and not accidentally one of the least satisfactory in principle, was contained in a line of argument put forward by James Wilson and some others to the effect that, just as individuals have to give up some of their natural rights to civil government to secure peaceful enjoyment of civil rights, so states must give up some of theirs to federal government in order to secure peaceful enjoyment of federal liberties. But the analogy of civil liberty and federal liberty concedes the basic Anti-Federal contentions, and Wilson did not consistently adhere to it. As each individual has one vote in civil society, for example, so each state ought, on this analogy, to have one vote in federal society. As the preservation of the rights of individuals is the object of civil society, so the preservation of the rights of states (not individuals) ought to be the object of federal society. But these are Anti-Federal conclusions. Thus, when Agrippa assessed the proposed Constitution from the point of view of the interests of Massachusetts, he did so on *principled* ground, the same ground that properly leads any man to consider the civil society of which he is or may become a member, not exclusively but first and last, from the point of view of his interest in his life, liberty, and property. Wilson, on the other hand, argued for the priority of the general interest of the Union over the particular interests of the states. And this position is not defensible—as Wilson's own argument sufficiently demonstrates—on the basis of the federal liberty–civil liberty analogy.

The more characteristic Federalist position was to deny that the choice lay between confederation and consolidation and to contend that in fact the Constitution provided a new form, partly national and partly federal. This was Publius' argument in *The Federalist*, no. 39. It was Madison's argument in the Virginia ratifying convention. And it was the usual argument of James Wilson himself, who emphasized the strictly limited powers of the general government and the essential part to be played in it by the states. The Anti-Federalists objected that all such arguments foundered on the impossibility of dual sovereignty. "It is a solecism in politics for two coordinate sovereignties to exist together. . . ." A mixture may exist for a time, but it will inevitably tend in one direction or the other, subjecting the country in the meantime to "all the horrors of a divided sovereignty." Luther Martin agreed with Madison that the new Constitution presented a novel mixture of federal and national elements; but he found it "just so much federal in appearance as to give its advocates in some measure, an opportunity of passing it as such upon the unsuspecting multitude, before they had time and opportunity to examine it, and yet so predominantly national as to put it in the power of its

movers, whenever the machine shall be set agoing, to strike out every part that has the appearance of being federal, and to render it wholly and entirely a national government."

The first words of the preamble sufficiently declare the anti-federal (in the strict sense) character of the Constitution, Patrick Henry thought; and his objection thundered over the Virginia convention sitting in Richmond:

> [W]hat right had they to say, *We, the People*? My political curiosity, exclusive of my anxious solicitude for the public welfare, leads me to ask, who authorised them to speak the language of, *We, the People*, instead of *We, the States*? States are the characteristics, and the soul of a confederation. If the States be not the agents of this compact, it must be one great consolidated National Government of the people of all the States.

The clearest minds among the Federalists agreed that states are the soul of a confederacy. That is what is wrong with confederacies: "The fundamental principle of the old Confederation is defective; we must totally eradicate and discard this principle before we can expect an efficient government."

Here lies the main significance of the mode of ratification in the proposed Constitution. The new procedure—ratification by special state conventions rather than by Congress and the state legislatures and provision that the Constitution shall be established on ratification of nine states (as between them), rather than all thirteen states as required under the Articles of Confederation—was not merely illegal; it struck at the heart of the old Confederation. It denied, as Federalists like Hamilton openly admitted, the very basis of legality under the Articles of Confederation. The requirement in the Articles of Confederation for unanimous consent of the states to constitutional changes rested on the assumption that the states are the basic political entities, permanently associated indeed, but associated entirely at the will and in the interest of each of the several states. Even if it were granted that government under the Articles had

"Splendid, sir! It gives you that Founding Father look!"

Drawing by Ed Fisher; © 1983 The New Yorker Magazine, Inc.

collapsed (which most Anti-Federalists did not grant), there was no justification for abandoning the principles of state equality and unanimous consent to fundamental constitutional change. As William Paterson had put it in the Philadelphia Convention,

> If we argue the matter on the supposition that no Confederacy at present exists, it cannot be denied that all the States stand on the footing of equal sovereignty. All therefore must concur before any can be bound. . . . If we argue on the fact that a federal compact actually exists, and consult the articles of it we still find an equal Sovereignty to be the basis of it.

Whether in the Articles of Confederation or outside, the essential principle of American union was the equality of the states. As Luther Martin had argued in Philadelphia, "the separation from G. B. placed the 13 States in a state of nature towards each other; [and] they would

have remained in that state till this time, but for the confederation. . . ."

The provision for ratifying the Constitution rested, in the main, on the contrary assumption that the American states are not several political wholes, associated together according to their several wills and for the sake of their several interests, but are, and always were from the moment of their separation from the King of England, parts of one whole. Thus constitutional change is the business of the people, not of the state legislatures, though the people act in (or through) their states. As one nation divided into several states, moreover, constitutional change is to be decided, not by unanimous consent of separate and equal entities, but by the major part of a single whole—an extraordinary majority because of the importance of the question. The Federalists contended that the colonies declared their independence not individually but unitedly, and that they had never been independent of one another. And the implication of this view is that the foundation of government in the United States is the interest of the nation and not the interests of the states. "The Union is essential to our being as a nation. The pillars that prop it are crumbling to powder," said Fisher Ames, staggering through a metaphorical forest. "The Union is the vital sap that nourishes the tree." The Articles of Confederation, in this view, were a defective instrument of a preexisting union. The congressional resolution calling for the Philadelphia Convention had described a means—"for the sole and express purpose of revising the Articles of Confederation"—and an end—to "render the federal constitution adequate to the exigencies of Government & the preservation of the Union." If there was any conflict, the means ought to be sacrificed to the end. The duty of the Philadelphia Convention and the members of the ratifying conventions was to take their bearings, not from the defective means, but from the great end, the preservation and well-being of the Union.

II THE CLASSIC TEXTS

The question of federalism, not surprisingly, runs throughout the Federalist Papers, *a series of articles published in New York newspapers during the debate over ratification of the Constitution. The Federalists favored a strong national government and criticized the Articles of Confederation for establishing a weak central government. Many of the eighty-five papers defend the powers granted to the national government under the Constitution, especially its powers to regulate commerce, levy taxes, and maintain foreign and domestic peace. Others urge a broad and generous interpretation of the powers of the national government.*

In The Federalist Nos. 39 and 45, *James Madison, (author of the* Federalist Papers *with John Jay and Alexander Hamilton) makes general arguments in favor of the new system of government. In No. 39, he defends the Constitution against charges that it would be anti-Republican and that it would allow the states to be swallowed up by the national government. In No. 45, he again makes the argument that the national government will never threaten the sovereignty or authority of the states. Just beneath the surface, however, his tilt toward a strong national government becomes clear. All prior confederacies have perished because the central government was too weak, he writes in No. 45; moreover, "as far as the sovereignty of the States cannot be reconciled to the happiness of the people," he declares, "Let the former be sacrificed to the latter."*

Madison's argument that the "powers delegated by the proposed Constitution to the federal government are few and defined," while "those which are to remain in the State governments are numerous and indefinite" is still formally true. All actions of the national government must be justified with reference to a specific provision of the Constitution granting that power (see the Constitution, Article I, section 8). By contrast, the states possess police powers—that is, powers to regulate the public health, safety, welfare, and morals.

The powers of the national government may be limited in theory, but in practice the Supreme Court has interpreted the Constitution's grants of power in broad terms. The key case was McCulloch v. Maryland *(1819), which held that the Constitution* gave Congress sweeping powers and broad discretion to choose how to carry out those powers. Although the Court on occasion has deviated from this principle, in general it has followed the logic of McCulloch and refused to interfere with congressional attempts to assert national authority.

Thus Madison's argument in Federalist No. 45 that "the State governments will have the advantage of the federal government . . . [in] the disposition and faculty of resisting and frustrating the measures of the other" has been disproved by history. Certainly since the Civil War, there has been no successful threat to federal supremacy. In any event, Madison's emphasis in No. 45 on the importance of a strong national government makes one wonder whether the argument was made seriously in the first place.

Questions

1. What are the reasons Madison gives for his argument that the states will be able to resist the encroachments of the national government—just as the members of earlier confederations were able to do so? How does the Court's decision in McCulloch affect this argument?

2. Why do you think that threats to the supremacy of the federal government have been unsuccessful?

3.2 Federalist No. 39

James Madison

The last paper having concluded the observations which were meant to introduce a candid survey of the plan of government reported by the convention, we now proceed to the execution of that part of our undertaking.

The first question that offers itself is whether the general form and aspect of the government be strictly republican. It is evident that no other form would be reconcilable with the genius of the people of America; with the fundamental principles of the Revolution; or with that honorable determination which animates every votary of freedom to rest all our political experiments on the capacity of mankind for self-government. If the plan of the convention, therefore, be found to depart from the republican character, its advocates must abandon it as no longer defensible.

What, then, are the distinctive characters of the republican form? Were an answer to this question to be sought, not by recurring to principles but in the application of the term by political writers to the constitutions of different States, no satisfactory one would ever be found. Holland, in which no particle of the supreme authority is derived from the people, has passed almost universally under the denomination of a republic. The same title has been bestowed on Venice, where absolute power over the great body of the people is exercised in the most absolute manner by a small body of hereditary nobles. Poland, which is a mixture of aristocracy and of monarchy in their worst forms, has been dignified with the same appellation. The government of England, which has one republican branch only, combined with an hereditary aristocracy and monarchy, has with equal impropriety been frequently placed on the list of republics. These examples, which are nearly as dissimilar to each other as to a genuine republic, show the extreme inaccuracy with which the term has been used in political disquisitions.

If we resort for a criterion to the different principles on which different forms of government are established, we may define a republic to be, or at least may bestow that name on, a government which derives all its powers directly or indirectly from the great body of the people, and is administered by persons holding their offices during pleasure for a limited period, or during good behavior. It is *essential* to such a government that it be derived from the great body of the society, not from an inconsiderable proportion or a favored class of it; otherwise a handful of tyrannical nobles, exercising their oppressions by a delegation of their powers, might aspire to the rank of republicans and claim for their government the honorable title of republic. It is *sufficient* for such a government that the persons administering it be appointed, either directly or indirectly, by the people; and that they hold their appointments by either of the tenures just specified; otherwise every government in the United States, as well as every other popular government that has been or can be well organized or well executed, would be degraded from the republican character. According to the constitution of every State in the Union, some or other of the officers of government are appointed indirectly only by the people. According to most of them, the chief magistrate himself is so appointed. And according to one, this mode of appointment is extended to one of the co-ordinate branches of the legislature. According to all the constitutions, also, the tenure of the highest offices is extended to a definite period, and in many instances, both within the legislative and executive departments, to a period of years. According to the provisions of most of the constitutions, again, as well as according to the most respectable and received opinions on the subject, the members

of the judiciary department are to retain their offices by the firm tenure of good behavior.

On comparing the Constitution planned by the convention with the standard here fixed, we perceived at once that it is, in the most rigid sense, conformable to it. The House of Representatives, like that of one branch at least of all the State legislatures, is elected immediately by the great body of the people. The Senate, like the present Congress and the Senate of Maryland, derives its appointment indirectly from the people. The President is indirectly derived from the choice of the people, according to the example in most of the States. Even the judges, with all other officers of the Union, will, as in the several States, be the choice, though a remote choice, of the people themselves. The duration of the appointments is equally conformable to the republican standard and to the model of State constitutions. The House of Representatives is periodically elective, as in all the States; and for the period of two years, as in the State of South Carolina. The Senate is elective for the period of six years, which is but one year more than the period of the Senate of Maryland, and but two more than that of the Senates of New York and Virginia. The President is to continue in office for the period of four years; as in New York and Delaware the chief magistrate is elected for three years, and in South Carolina for two years. In the other States the election is annual. In several of the States, however, no explicit provision is made for the impeachment of the chief magistrate. And in Delaware and Virginia he is not impeachable till out of office. The President of the United States is impeachable at any time during his continuance in office. The tenure by which the judges are to hold their places is, as it unquestionably ought to be, that of good behavior. The tenure of the ministerial offices generally will be a subject of legal regulation, conformably to the reason of the case and the example of the State constitutions.

Could any further proof be required of the republican complexion of this system, the most decisive one might be found in its absolute prohibition of titles of nobility, both under the federal and the State governments; and in its express guaranty of the republican form to each of the latter.

"But it was not sufficient," say the adversaries of the proposed Constitution, "for the convention to adhere to the republican form. They ought with equal care to have preserved the *federal* form, which regards the Union as a *Confederacy* of sovereign states; instead of which they have framed a *national* government, which regards the Union as a *consolidation* of the States." And it is asked by what authority this bold and radical innovation was undertaken? The handle which has been made of this objection requires that it should be examined with some precision.

Without inquiring into the accuracy of the distinction on which the objection is founded, it will be necessary to a just estimate of its force, first, to ascertain the real character of the government in question; secondly, to inquire how far the convention were authorized to propose such a government; and thirdly, how far the duty they owed to their country could supply any defect of regular authority.

First.—In order to ascertain the real character of the government, it may be considered in relation to the foundation on which it is to be established; to the sources from which its ordinary powers are to be drawn; to the operation of those powers; to the extent of them; and to the authority by which future changes in the government are to be introduced.

On examining the first relation, it appears, on one hand, that the Constitution is to be founded on the assent and ratification of the people of America, given by deputies elected for the special purpose; but, on the other, that this assent and ratification is to be given by the people, not as individuals composing one entire nation, but as composing the distinct and independent States to which they respectively belong. It is to be the assent and ratification of the several States, derived from the supreme authority in each State—the authority of the people themselves. The act, therefore, establishing

the Constitution will not be a *national* but a *federal* act.

That it will be a federal and not a national act, as these terms are understood by the objectors—the act of the people, as forming so many independent States, not as forming one aggregate nation—is obvious from this single consideration: that it is to result neither from the decision of a *majority* of the people of the Union, nor from that of a *majority* of the States. It must result from the *unanimous* assent of the several States that are parties to it differing no otherwise from their ordinary assent than in its being expressed, not by the legislative authority, but by that of the people themselves. Were the people regarded in this transaction as forming one nation, the will of the majority of the whole people of the United States would bind the minority, in the same manner as the majority in each State must bind the minority; and the will of the majority must be determined either by a comparison of the individual votes, or by considering the will of the majority of the States as evidence of the will of a majority of the people of the United States. Neither of these rules has been adopted. Each State, in ratifying the Constitution, is considered as a sovereign body independent of all others, and only to be bound by its own voluntary act. In this relation, then, the new Constitution will, if established, be a *federal* and not a *national* constitution.

The next relation is to the sources from which the ordinary powers of government are to be derived. The House of Representatives will derive its powers from the people of America; and the people will be represented in the same proportion and on the same principle as they are in the legislature of a particular State. So far the government is *national,* not *federal.* The Senate, on the other hand, will derive its powers from the States as political and coequal societies; and these will be represented on the principle of equality in the Senate, as they now are in the existing Congress. So far the government is *federal,* not *national.* The executive power will be derived from a very compound source. The immediate election of the President is to be made by the States in their political characters. The votes allotted to them are in a compound ratio, which considers them partly as distinct and coequal societies, partly as unequal members of the same society. The eventual election, again, is to be made by that branch of the legislature which consists of the national representatives; but in this particular act they are to be thrown into the form of individual delegations from so many distinct and coequal bodies politic. From this aspect of the government it appears to be of a mixed character, presenting at least as many *federal* as *national* features.

The difference between a federal and national government, as it relates to the *operation of the government*, is by the adversaries of the plan of the convention supposed to consist in this, that in the former the powers operate on the political bodies composing the Confederacy in their political capacities; in the latter, on the individual citizens composing the nation in their individual capacities. On trying the Constitution by this criterion, it falls under the *national* not the *federal* character; though perhaps not so completely as has been understood. In several cases, and particularly in the trial of controversies to which States may be parties, they must be viewed and proceeded against in their collective and political capacities only. But the operation of the government on the people in their individual capacities, in its ordinary and most essential proceedings, will, in the sense of its opponents, on the whole, designate it, in this relation, a *national* government.

But if the government be national with regard to the *operation* of its powers, it changes its aspect again when we contemplate it in relation to the extent of its powers. The idea of a national government involves in it not only an authority over the individual citizens, but an indefinite supremacy over all persons and things, so far as they are objects of lawful government. Among a people consolidated into one nation, this supremacy is completely vested in the national legislature. Among communities united for particular purposes, it is vested partly in the general and partly in the municipal legislatures. In the former case, all local authorities are subordinate to the supreme; and may be controlled, directed, or abolished by it at pleasure. In the latter, the local or municipal authorities form distinct and independent portions of the supremacy, no more subject, within their respective spheres, to the general authority than the general authority is subject to them, within its own sphere. In this relation, then, the proposed government cannot be deemed a *national* one; since its jurisdiction extends to certain enumerated objects only, and leaves to the several States a residuary and inviolable sovereignty over all other objects. It is true that in controversies relating to the boundary between the two jurisdictions, the tribunal which is ultimately to decide is to be established under the general government. But this does not change the principle of the case. The decision is to be impartially made, according to the rules of the Constitution; and all the usual and most effectual precautions are taken to secure this impartiality. Some such tribunal is clearly essential to prevent an appeal to the sword and a dissolution of the compact; and that it ought to be established under the general rather than under the local governments, or, to speak more properly, that it could be safely established under the first alone, is a position not likely to be combated.

If we try the Constitution by its last relation to the authority by which amendments are to be made, we find it neither wholly *national* nor wholly *federal*. Were it wholly national, the supreme and ultimate authority would reside in the *majority* of the people of the Union; and this authority would be competent at all times, like that of a majority of every national society to alter or abolish its established government. Were it wholly federal, on the other hand, the concurrence of each State in the Union would be essential to every alteration that would be binding on all. The mode provided by the plan of the convention is not founded on either of these principles. In requiring more than a majority, and particularly in computing the proportion by *States*, not by *citizens*, it departs from the national and advances towards the *federal* character; in rendering the concurrence of less than the whole number of States sufficient, it loses again the *federal* and partakes of the *national* character.

The proposed Constitution, therefore, even when tested by the rules laid down by its antagonists, is, in strictness, neither a national nor a federal Constitution, but a composition of both. In its foundation it is federal, not national; in the sources from which the ordinary powers of the government are drawn, it is partly federal and partly national; in the operation of these powers, it is national, not federal; in the extent of them, again, it is federal, not national; and, finally in the authoritative mode of introducing amendments, it is neither wholly federal nor wholly national.

3.3 Federalist *No. 45*

James Madison

• • •

The adversaries to the plan of the convention, instead of considering in the first place what degree of power was absolutely necessary for the purposes of the federal government, have exhausted themselves in a secondary inquiry into the possible consequences of the proposed degree of power to the governments of the particular States. But if the Union, as has been shown, be essential to the security of the people of America against foreign danger; if it be essential to their security against contentions and wars among the different States; if it be essential to guard them against those violent and oppressive factions which embitter the blessings of liberty and against those military establishments which must gradually poison its very fountain; if, in a word, the Union be essential to the happiness of the people of America, is it not preposterous to urge as an objection to a government, without which the objects of the Union cannot be attained, that such a government may derogate from the importance of the governments of the individual States? Was, then, the American Revolution effected, was the American Confederacy formed, was the precious blood of thousands spilt, and the hard-earned substance of millions lavished, not that the people of America should enjoy peace, liberty, and safety, but that the governments of the individual States, that particular municipal establishments, might enjoy a certain extent of power and be arrayed with certain dignities and attributes of sovereignty? We have heard of the impious doctrine in the old world, that the people were made for kings, not kings for the people. Is the same doctrine to be revived in the new, in another shape—that the solid happiness of the people is to be sacrificed to the views of political institutions of a different form? It is too early for politicians to presume on our forgetting that the public good, the real welfare of the great body of the people, is the supreme object to be pursued; and that no form of government whatever has any other value than as it may be fitted for the attainment of this object. Were the plan of the convention adverse to the public happiness, my voice would be, Reject the plan. Were the Union itself inconsistent with the public happiness, it would be, Abolish the Union. In like manner, as far as the sovereignty of the States cannot be reconciled to the happiness of the people, the voice of every good citizen must be, Let the former be sacrificed to the latter. How far the sacrifice is necessary has been shown. How far the unsacrificed residue will be endangered is the question before us.

Several important considerations have been touched in the course of these papers, which discountenance the supposition that the operation of the federal government will by degrees prove fatal to the State governments. The more I revolve the subject, the more fully I am persuaded that the balance is much more likely to be disturbed by the preponderancy of the last than of the first scale.

We have seen, in all the examples of ancient and modern confederacies, the strongest tendency continually betraying itself in the members to despoil the general government of its authorities, with a very ineffectual capacity in the latter to defend itself against the encroachments. Although, in most of these examples, the system has been so dissimilar from that under consideration as greatly to weaken any inference concerning the latter from the fate of the former, yet, as the States will retain under the proposed Constitution a very extensive portion of active sovereignty, the inference ought not to be wholly disregarded. In the Achæan league it is probable that the federal head had a degree and species of power which gave it a considerable likeness to the government framed by the convention. The Lycian Confederacy, as far as its principles and form are transmitted, must have borne a still greater analogy to it. Yet history does not inform us that either of them ever degenerated, or tended to degenerate, into one consolidated government. On the contrary, we know that the ruin of one of them proceeded from the incapacity of the federal authority to prevent the dissensions, and finally the disunion, of the subordinate authorities. These cases are the more worthy of our attention as the external causes by which the component parts were pressed together were much more numerous and powerful than in our case; and consequently less powerful ligaments within would be sufficient to bind the members to the head and to each other.

In the feudal system, we have seen a similar propensity exemplified. Notwithstanding the want of proper sympathy in every instance between the local sovereigns and the people, and the sympathy in some instances between the general sovereign and the latter, it usually happened that the local sovereigns prevailed in the rivalship for encroachments. Had no external dangers enforced internal harmony and subordination, and particularly, had the local sovereigns possessed the affections of the people, the great kingdoms in Europe would at this time consist of as many independent princes as there were formerly feudatory barons.

The State governments will have the advantage of the federal government, whether we compare them in respect to the immediate dependence of the one on the other; to the weight of personal influence which each side will possess; to the powers respectively vested in them; to the predilection and probable support of the people; to the disposition and faculty of resisting and frustrating the measures of each other.

The State governments may be regarded as constituent and essential parts of the federal government; whilst the latter is nowise essential to the operation or organization of the former. Without the intervention of the State legislatures, the President of the United States cannot be elected at all. They must in all cases have a great share in his appointment, and will, perhaps, in most cases, of themselves determine it. The Senate will be elected absolutely and exclusively by the State legislatures. Even the House of Representatives, though drawn immediately from the people, will be chosen very much under the influence of that class of men whose influence over the people obtains for themselves an election into the State legislatures. Thus, each of the principal branches of the federal government will owe its existence more or less to the favor of the State governments, and must consequently feel a dependence, which is much more likely to beget a disposition too obsequious than too overbearing towards them. On the other side, the component parts of the State governments will in no instance be indebted for their appointment to the direct agency of the federal government, and very little, if at all, to the local influence of its members.

The number of individuals employed under the Constitution of the United States will be much smaller than the number employed under the particular States. There will consequently be less of personal influence on the side of the former than of the latter. The members of the legislative, executive, and judiciary departments of thirteen and more States, the justices of peace, officers of militia, ministerial officers of justice, with all the county, corporation, and town officers, for three millions and more of people, intermixed and having particular acquaintance with every class and circle of people must exceed, beyond all proportion, both in number and influence, those of every description who will be employed in the administration of the federal system. Compare the members of the three great departments of the thirteen States, excluding from the judiciary department the justices of peace, with the members of the corresponding departments of the single government of the Union; compare the militia officers of three millions of people with the military and marine officers of any establishment which is within the compass of probability, or, I may add, of possibility, and in this view alone, we may pronounce the advantage of the States to be decisive. If the federal government is to have collectors of revenue, the State governments will have theirs also. And as those of the former will be principally on the seacoast, and not very numerous, whilst those of the latter will be spread over the face of the country, and will be very numerous, the advantage in this view also lies on the same side. It is true that the Confederacy is to possess, and may exercise, the power of collecting internal as well as external taxes throughout the States; but it is probable that this power will not be resorted to, except for supplemental purposes of revenue; that an option will then be given to the States to supply their quotas by previous collections of their own; and that the eventual collection, under the immediate authority of the Union, will generally be made by the officers, and according to the rules, appointed by the several States. Indeed it is extremely probable that in other instances, particularly in the organization of the judicial power, the officers of the States will be clothed with the correspondent authority of the Union. Should it happen, however, that separate collectors of internal revenue should be appointed under the federal government, the influence of the whole number would not bear a comparison with that of the multitude of State officers in the opposite scale. Within every district to which a federal collector would be allotted, there would not be less than thirty or forty, or even more, officers of different descriptions, and many of them persons of character and weight whose influence would lie on the side of the State.

The powers delegated by the proposed Constitution to the federal government are few and defined. Those which are to remain in the State governments are numerous and indefinite. The former will be exercised principally on external objects, as war, peace, negotiation, and foreign commerce; with which last the power of taxation will, for the most part, be connected. The powers reserved to the several States will extend to all the objects which, in the ordinary course of affairs, concern the lives, liberties, and properties of the people, and the internal order, improvement, and prosperity of the State.

The operations of the federal government will be most extensive and important in times of war and danger; those of the State governments in times of peace and security. As the former periods will probably bear a small proportion of the latter, the State governments will here enjoy another advantage over the federal government. The more adequate, indeed, the federal powers may be rendered to the national defense, the less frequent will be those scenes of danger which might favor their ascendancy over the governments of the particular States.

If the new Constitution be examined with accuracy and candor, it will be found that the change which it proposes consists much less in the addition of NEW POWERS to the Union than in the invigoration of its ORIGINAL POWERS. The regulation of commerce, it is true, is a new power; but that seems to be an addition which few oppose and from which no apprehensions are entertained. The powers relating to war and peace, armies and fleets, treaties and finance, with the other more considerable powers, are all vested in the existing Congress by the Articles of Confederation. The proposed change does not enlarge these powers; it only substitutes a more effectual mode of administering them. The change relating to taxation may be regarded as the most important; and yet the present Congress have as complete authority to REQUIRE of the States indefinite supplies of money for the common defense and general welfare as the future Congress will have to require them of individual citizens; and the latter will be no more bound than the States themselves have been to pay the quotas respectively taxed on them. Had the States complied punctually with the Articles of Confederation, or could their compliance have been enforced by as peaceable means as may be used with success towards single persons, our past experience is very far from countenancing an opinion that the State governments would have lost their constitutional powers, and have gradually undergone an entire consolidation. To maintain that such an event would have ensued would be to say at once that the existence of the State governments is incompatible with any system whatever that accomplishes the essential purposes of the Union.

3.4 McCulloch *v.* Maryland

[In 1816 Congress authorized the creation of a Bank of the United States to act as a depository for U.S. funds and perform other financial functions. The new bank replaced the first Bank of the United States, which had been created in 1791 but expired in 1811. The second bank was highly controversial and prompted much opposition, largely from those who viewed it as an unwarranted extension of national power. Several states sought to interfere with the bank's functions by prohibiting it from operating branches or by levying taxes against it. McCulloch v. Maryland arose when the Baltimore branch of the bank refused to pay such a tax. The case went to the U.S. Supreme Court, which held that it was unconstitutional for a state to tax an "instrument employed by the government of the Union to carry its powers into execution." First, however, the Court had to decide whether Congress itself possessed the power to create a national bank. Chief Justice John Marshall's affirmative answer to that question laid the foundation for a broad interpretation of national power under the Constitution. A portion of his opinion follows.]

The first question made in the cause is, has Congress power to incorporate a bank?

• • •

If any one proposition could command the universal assent of mankind, we might expect it would be this—that the government of the Union, though limited in its powers, is supreme within its sphere of action. This would seem to result necessarily from its nature. It is the government of all; its powers are delegated by all; it represents all, and acts for all. Though any one State may be willing to control its operations, no State is willing to allow others to control them. The nation, on those subjects on which it can act, must necessarily bind its component parts. But this question is not left to mere reason: the people have, in express terms, decided it, by saying, "this constitution, and the laws of the United States, which shall be made in pursuance thereof," "shall be the supreme law of the land," and by requiring that the members of the State legislatures, and the officers of the executive and judicial departments of the States, shall take the oath of fidelity to it.

The government of the United States, then, though limited in its powers, is supreme; and its laws, when made in pursuance of the constitution, form the supreme law of the land, "any thing in the constitution or laws of any State to the contrary notwithstanding."

Among the enumerated powers, we do not find that of establishing a bank or creating a corporation. But there is no phrase in the instrument which, like the articles of confederation, excludes incidental or implied powers; and which requires that every thing granted shall be expressly and minutely described. Even the 10th amendment, which was framed for the purpose of quieting the excessive jealousies which had been excited, omits the word "expressly," and declares only that the powers "not delegated to the United States, nor prohibited to the States, are reserved to the States or to the people;" thus leaving the question, whether the particular power which may become the subject of contest has been delegated to the one government, or prohibited to the other, to depend on a fair construction of the whole instrument. The men who drew and adopted this amendment had experienced the embarrassments resulting from the insertion of this word in the articles of confederation, and probably omitted it to avoid those embarrassments. A constitution, to contain an accurate detail of all the subdivisions of which its great powers will admit, and of all the means by which they may be carried into execution, would partake of the prolixity of a legal code, and could scarcely be embraced by the human mind. It would probably never be understood by the public. Its nature, therefore, requires, that only its great outlines should be marked, its important objects designated, and the minor ingredients which compose those objects be deduced from the nature of the objects themselves. . . . In considering this question, then, we must never forget, that it is *a constitution* we are expounding.

Although, among the enumerated powers of government, we do not find the word "bank" or "incorporation," we find the great powers to lay and collect taxes; to borrow money; to regulate commerce; to declare and conduct a war; and to raise and support armies and navies. The sword and the purse, all the external relations, and no inconsiderable portion of the industry of the nation, are entrusted to its government. It can never be pretended that these vast powers draw after them others of inferior importance, merely because they are inferior. Such an idea can never be advanced. But it may with great reason be contended, that a government, entrusted with such ample powers, on the due execution of which the happiness and prosperity of the nation so vitally depends, must also be entrusted with ample means for their execution. The power being given, it is the interest of the nation to facilitate its execution. It can never be their interest, and cannot be presumed to have been their intention, to clog and embarrass its execution by withholding the most appropriate means. Throughout this vast republic, from the St. Croix to the Gulph of Mexico, from the Atlantic to the Pacific, revenue is to be collected and expended, armies are to be marched and supported. The exigencies of the nation may require that the treasure raised in the north should be transported to the south, *that* raised in the east conveyed to the west, or that this order should be reversed. Is that construction of the constitution to be preferred which would render these operations difficult, hazardous, and expensive? Can we adopt that construction, (unless the words imperiously require it,) which would impute to the framers of that instrument, when granting these powers for the public good, the intention of impeding their exercise by withholding a choice of means? If, indeed, such be the mandate of the constitution, we have only to obey; but that instrument does not profess to enumerate the means by which the powers it confers may be executed; nor does it prohibit the creation of a corporation, if the existence of such a being be essential to the beneficial exercise of those powers. It is, then, the subject of fair inquiry, how far such means may be employed.

It is not denied, that the powers given to the government imply the ordinary means of execution. That, for example, of raising revenue, and applying it to national purposes, is admitted to imply the power of conveying money from place to place, as the exigencies of the nation may require, and of employing the usual means of conveyance. But it is denied that the government has its choice of means; or, that it may employ the most convenient means, if, to employ them, it be necessary to erect a corporation.

On what foundation does this argument rest? On this alone: The power of creating a corporation, is one appertaining to sovereignty, and is not expressly conferred on Congress. This is true. But all legislative powers appertain to sovereignty. The original power of giving the law on any subject whatever, is a sovereign power; and if the government of the Union is restrained from creating a corporation, as a means for performing its functions, on the single reason that the creation of a corporation is an act of sovereignty; if the sufficiency of this reason be acknowledged, there would be some difficulty in sustaining the authority of Congress to pass other laws for the accomplishment of the same objects.

The government which has a right to do an act, and has imposed on it the duty of performing that act, must, according to the dictates of reason, be allowed to select the means; and those who contend that it may not select any appropriate means, that one particular mode of effecting the object is excepted, take upon themselves the burden of establishing that exception.

• • •

But the constitution of the United States has not left the right of Congress to employ the necessary means, for the execution of the powers conferred on the government, to general reasoning. To its enumeration of powers is added that of making "all laws which shall be necessary and proper, for carrying into execution the foregoing powers, and all other powers vested by this constitution, in the government of the United States, or in any department thereof."

• • •

The argument on which most reliance is placed, is drawn from the peculiar language of this clause. Congress is not empowered by it to make all laws, which may have relation to the powers conferred on the government, but such only as may be *"necessary and proper"* for carrying them into execution. The word *"necessary,"* is considered as controlling the whole sentence, and as limiting the right to pass laws for the execution of the granted powers, to such as are indispensable, and without which the power would be nugatory. That it excludes the choice of means, and leaves to Congress, in each case, that only which is most direct and simple.

Is it true, that this is the sense in which the word "necessary" is always used? Does it always import an absolute physical necessity, so strong, that one thing, to which another may be termed necessary, cannot exist without that other? We think it does not. If reference be had to its use, in the common affairs of the world, or in approved authors, we find that it frequently imports no more than that one thing is convenient, or useful, or essential to another. To employ the means necessary to an end, is generally understood as employing any means calculated to produce the end, and not as being confined to those single means, without which the end would be entirely unattainable. Such is the character of human language, that no word conveys to the mind, in all situations, one single definite idea; and nothing is more common than to use words in a figurative sense. Almost all compositions contain words, which, taken in their rigorous sense, would convey a meaning different from that which is obviously intended. It is essential to just construction, that many words which import something excessive, should be understood in a more mitigated sense—in that sense which common usage justifies. The word "necessary" is of this description. It has not a fixed character peculiar to itself. It admits of all degrees of comparison; and is often connected with other words, which increase or diminish the impression the mind receives of the urgency it imports. A thing may be necessary, very necessary, absolutely or indispensably necessary. To no mind would the same idea be conveyed, by these several phrases.

• • •

This word, then, like others, is used in various senses; and, in its construction, the subject, the context, the intention of the person using them, are all to be taken into view.

Let this be done in the case under consideration. The subject is the execution of those great powers on which the welfare of a nation essentially depends. It must have been the intention of those who gave these powers, to insure, as far as human prudence could insure, their beneficial execution. This could not be done by confiding the choice of means to such narrow limits as not to leave it in the power of Congress to adopt any which might be appropriate, and which were conducive to the end. This provision is made in a constitution intended to endure for ages to come, and, consequently, to be adapted to the various *crises* of human affairs. To have prescribed the means by which government should, in all future time, execute its powers, would have been to change, entirely, the character of the instrument, and give it the properties of a legal code. It would

have been an unwise attempt to provide, by immutable rules, for exigencies which, if foreseen at all, must have been seen dimly, and which can be best provided for as they occur.

• • •

We admit, as all must admit, that the powers of the government are limited, and that its limits are not to be transcended. But we think the sound construction of the constitution must allow to the national legislature that discretion, with respect to the means by which the powers it confers are to be carried into execution, which will enable that body to perform the high duties assigned to it, in the manner most beneficial to the people. Let the end be legitimate, let it be within the scope of the constitution, and all means which are appropriate, which are plainly adapted to that end, which are not prohibited, but consist with the letter and spirit of the constitution, are constitutional.

• • •

III  THE PERSPECTIVE OF HISTORY

The Antifederalists' key charge against the new Constitution was that the national government would eventually come to dominate the states. Historians Forrest McDonald and Ellen Shapiro McDonald argue that the Antifederalists were right in the long run.

Questions

1. The McDonalds place much of the blame for the demise of federalism at the steps of the U.S. Supreme Court. The Court, they suggest, eroded federalism in two stages. Identify these two stages and the significant decisions made during each.

2. The states, the McDonalds write, sold their birthright for "a very large mess" of pottage. What do the authors mean?

3. As you read the following selection after this one (3.6), consider whether the McDonalds overstate the case when they write that federalism "no longer exists on its native soil."

3.5 Federalism in America: An Obituary

Forrest McDonald and Ellen Shapiro McDonald

A central feature of the new order that was created in Philadelphia in 1787—perhaps the central feature—was federalism, which in America has historically had three distinct dimensions. The first is the representation of the states as states in the national government: what James Madison had in mind when he wrote in *Federalist* number 39 that the Constitution established a system that was partly national and partly federal. The second involves the source of sovereignty in America and the nature of the constitutional union. The third, and ultimately the most important, has to do with the division of the powers of sovereignty between national and state governments.

In each of these dimensions federalism has a separate history, but the end result has been the same. For many years, the system served as a protector of liberty and a preserver of local autonomy, as the authors of the Constitution intended. Over the course of time, however, federalism in each of its aspects has been undermined, eroded, or destroyed.

Under the Articles of Confederation the Congress had been a purely federal body. Its members were elected by the state legislatures, the states had one vote apiece, and Congress could act only through the agency of the state governments. The Constitution wrought a fundamental change by vesting the national government with power to act directly upon individuals in certain limited and specified areas, but it retained the federal principle in three of the four branches of the government it established. The Senate continued the old system, its members being elected directly by the state legislatures, and the states continued to be equally represented in it, though with two votes apiece instead of one. The president was to be elected by electors, who were to be chosen in such manner as the several state legislatures should determine; in the early elections the legislatures themselves often chose the electors and thus indirectly elected the president. Judges, being appointed by the president with the approval of the Senate, were likewise indirectly the creatures of the state legislatures, though at yet another stage of remove.

These arrangements were undone by the growth of democracy. The popular election of presidential electors was a matter of evolution: one by one the states changed their election laws until, by 1836, only the legislature of South Carolina continued to choose the electors. The popular election of senators was slower in coming: it was adopted by a number of states late in the nineteenth century and early in the twentieth, and it became a part of the Constitution upon the ratification of the Seventeenth Amendment in 1913.

The second dimension of federalism—that relating to the source of sovereignty and the nature of the union—was considerably more complex. At the time of the Revolution, there had been some disagreement as to where sovereignty devolved upon the severance of America's ties with Britain, but the matter was resolved by the way in which the Constitution was established. The Articles of Confederation had been ratified by the state legislatures, but as Madison pointed out during the Federal Convention, a constitution ratified by the legislatures could be construed as being a treaty "among the Governments of Independent States," and thus it could be held that "a breach of any one article, by any of the parties, absolved the other parties" from any further obligation.

To avoid that construction, Madison continued, it was necessary to submit the Constitution to "the supreme authority of the people themselves." Yet it could not be submitted to the people of the United States as a whole, because

States' Rights

The terms federalism *and* states' rights *are often confused. Although both refer to the division of power between the states and the national government, the two phrases have very different connotations.* Federalism *is the more neutral word; it refers to the constitutional principle under which power is divided between the central government and the component states while each retains independence and supremacy within its respective share.* States' rights *is more of a political slogan, used throughout history by opponents of certain national policies, especially those concerning the rights of black Americans. (Advocates of states' rights, by the way, always capitalize* States' *to show the priority they place on the states over the national government.)*

Thus, "states' rights," and by implication federalism itself, is tainted with the ideology of slavery and, later, of opposition to desegregation (see Selections 17.1 through 17.3). That identification has had an unfortunate impact, at times, on legitimate arguments for the power of the states.

The following excerpt gives a brief survey of the history of the States' rights movement.

"*S*tates' rights" is better understood not as a term of art denoting a constitutional principle but as a slogan with tactical value in political controversy. The slogan of states' rights has been raised at one time or another by advocates from every region of the country and by partisans of every political persuasion. The phrase emphasizes one element of federalism, but it is a serious error to equate federalism with states' rights. . . .

In the nineteenth century the growing sectional rivalry between the commercial, and increasingly industrial, North and the agrarian South was reflected in competing theories of the Union. The states' rights position came to be identified in public discourse with the interest of the slave power. It found its champion in John C. Calhoun, who, in the South Carolina Exposition and Protest (1828–1829), announced the doctrine of nullification as a logical consequence of the state compact theory. Nullification, of course, was an empty threat unless it was backed up by the possibility of secession.

One attempt was made to implement Calhoun's doctrine, the South Carolina Ordinance of Nullification directed against the Tariff Act of 1828, and that was a failure. In 1861, when the election of Abraham Lincoln as President clearly signaled that slavery had been belatedly set upon its course of ultimate extinction, eleven southern

the Constitution amended each of the state constitutions in various ways, and if it were adopted by majority vote of the whole people, the people in some states would be altering the constitutions of other states. This, in the nature of things, they could not have the authority to do. Accordingly, the Constitution was submitted for ratification by conventions in each of the states, delegates to which were elected by the people of the several states in their capacities as people of the several states. Madison put it thus in *Federalist* number 39: "Ratification is to be given by the people, not as individuals composing one entire nation, but as composing the distinct and independent States to which they respectively belong. It is to be the assent and ratification of the several States, derived from the supreme authority in each State,—the authority of the people themselves." This procedure unmistakably implied that the source of sovereignty was the people of the states, severally, and that the residue of sovereignty which was not committed by them to either the national government or the state governments remained in them—an implication that was subsequently made explicit by the Tenth Amendment. The process of ratification also indicated that the Union was a compact among political societies, which is to say among the people of Virginia with the people of Massachusetts with the people of Georgia, and so on.

Now, though the nature of the compact was

states withdrew from the Union. Lincoln denied not only the legitimacy but also the very possibility of secession, and the victory of the Union in the Civil War vindicated his position for all practical purposes. Whatever rights the states have they have as members of the Union.

The Fourteenth Amendment, adopted after the Civil War, proved an obstacle to state regulation of economic activity begun under the influence of the Populist and Progressive movements. Because the Bill of Rights applied only to the federal government, individuals whose rights were infringed by actions of the state governments (unless they were the victims of bills of attainder, ex post facto laws, or laws impairing the obligation of contracts) previously had been able to rely only on the state constitution, political system, or courts for redress. In the late nineteenth and early twentieth centuries, however, the Supreme Court held the substantive guarantees (life, liberty, and property) of the Fourteenth Amendment's due process clause to be effective limitations on state legislative power. In the rhetoric of the reformers, the federal government (or at least its judicial branch) had infringed on the states' right to regulate their internal affairs.

In the 1920s the cry of "states' rights" was raised both by those who opposed federal intrusions into areas of state legislative concern and by those states that were frustrated in the attempt to expand state regulatory power. It is instructive that states' rights claims were raised in both Massachusetts v. Mellon (1923) and Pierce v. Society of Sisters (1925), the first in the interest of less and the second in the interest of more governmental regulation.

Between the late 1940s and the late 1960s, the cause of states' rights became virtually identified with the cause of southern opposition to civil rights legislation. The national commitment to abolishing racial segregation, first in publicly owned facilities and then in private establishments dealing with the public, aroused fierce opposition among those who were destined to lose their privileged position. Despite its long history of service to every shade of political opinion, the slogan of "states' rights" may have been permanently tarnished by its association with state-sponsored racial discrimination.

—*Encyclopedia of the American Constitution*

perfectly understood at the time, it was both subtle and unprecedented; and it is scarcely a source of wonderment that alternative formulations of what had happened were soon forthcoming. Nor is it surprising that those alternative formulations had profoundly different implications.

One of the formulations was the juristic, which was first suggested by Chief Justice John Jay but given its fullest expression by John Marshall, both as historian (in his five-volume, highly partisan biography of Washington) and as chief justice in his decision in *M'Culloch* v. *Maryland* (1819). The juristic view was that the Constitution had been created by the people as a whole, that the process of ratification by states had been resorted to only as a matter of convenience, and thus that any claims to state sovereignty or states' rights were unfounded.

The opposite view was formulated by James Madison in 1798 and was adopted by the legislature of Virginia in protest against the Alien and Sedition Acts. Conveniently forgetting what he had said earlier, Madison wrote that the federal government had resulted "from the compact to which the states are parties." From that premise it followed that when Congress enacts statutes that exceed its constitutional authority, the state governments "have the right and are in duty bound to interpose" their own authority between their citizens and the federal government, to prevent the unconstitutional enactments from being enforced. Thomas Jefferson, in the counterpart Kentucky Resolutions, referred to the federal compact as being among "sovereign and independent states."

The Virginia and Kentucky Resolutions met with a cold reception when they were proclaimed, but soon their doctrines—both about the nature of the constitutional compact and about interposition—came into widespread acceptance. It is commonly supposed that interposition was largely a southern doctrine, and the supposition is given credence by the frequency with which Virginia, Maryland, South Carolina, Kentucky, Georgia, Alabama, and other southern states defied the authority of the president, acts of Congress, treaties, and Supreme Court rulings. But it must be remembered that the legislatures of Connecticut and Massachusetts explicitly endorsed interposition in 1808; that the Hartford Convention of 1814 did likewise; that in 1840 Vermont made it a crime to aid in the capture of a runaway slave, despite the federal fugitive slave act; that in 1846 the House of Representatives of Massachusetts declared the Mexican War unconstitutional; that a decade later Wisconsin asserted the supremacy of its supreme court over the United States Supreme Court; that the official motto of Illinois was "State Sovereignty and Union." In sum, interposition was common currency throughout the country during the ante-bellum period; whether it was invoked depended, as in the adage, upon whose ox was being gored.

Meanwhile, the original, compact-among-peoples understanding was not entirely forgotten, but it was rarely appealed to because its implications were so radical. It was brought up in New England in 1805 and again in 1814, amidst talk of and as a justification for secession—a justification that no less ardent a nationalist than Gouverneur Morris declared to be sound. It arose again during the nullification controversy of 1832/33, with more ominous portents.

That controversy is remembered as a conflict between South Carolina and the national government and between John C. Calhoun and Andrew Jackson; the procedures that were followed, though of crucial importance, are often forgotten. Late in 1832 Governor James Hamilton called the state legislature into special session, and the legislature passed a law calling for a popularly elected state convention. The maneuver was carefully chosen. As the Constitution had been ratified in South Carolina by a popularly elected convention, the state was now returning to such a convention as the ultimate source of sovereignty. The convention met and adopted ordinances declaring the tariff acts of 1828 and 1832 null and void, forbidding appeal to the Supreme Court in cases arising under the ordinances, and asserting that the state would have just cause for seceding from the Union if the national government should attempt to use force to collect the tariff.

The outcome of the confrontation was indecisive. Congress backed down, passing Henry Clay's compromise tariff; but it also enacted Jackson's Force Bill, which authorized the president to use the army against South Carolina if it continued to defy the law. The state, for its part, rescinded its nullification ordinances, but it also formally nullified the Force Bill.

South Carolina's position was what in the eighteenth century was called a "return to first principles," and when it was adopted, it could be refuted only by the sword. And it was adopted during the winter of 1860/61: each of the eleven seceding states left the Union the way the original thirteen states had entered into it, by means of conventions elected by the people for the purpose. The defeat of the Confederacy in the Civil War resolved the issue for all time, though not immediately. Radicals in Congress first insisted that the southern states had committed political suicide by seceding and that they were therefore to be treated as "conquered provinces." Subsequently, however, the Radicals realized that the votes of the southern states would probably be necessary to ensure the ratification of the Fourteenth Amendment. Accordingly, they reversed themselves and—on condition that the amendment be ratified—now held that the states had never left the Union. The Supreme Court confirmed that interpretation in the case of *Texas* v. *White* (1869). Disregarding the fact that Virginia had been dismembered, in palpable violation of the Constitution, by the creation of West Virginia in 1863, the Court ruled that the Constitution "looks to an indestructible Union, composed of indestructible states."

Unintentionally, however, in rendering that decision the Court reconfirmed the Madisonian-Jeffersonian interpretation of the Constitution as a compact among state governments and thereby left the door open for a revival of the doctrine of interposition. Despite the Fourteenth Amendment, the southern states were able, late in the nineteenth century and early in the twentieth, to deprive their black citizens of most of their civil rights; and when the Court began trying to restore those rights during the 1950s and 1960s, interposition barred the way. None of the southern states officially embraced the doctrine, though a number of people urged them to do so; but as a practical matter the southern governors and legislatures resisted desegregation by doing precisely what Madison had called for in 1798. Their efforts succeeded only in discrediting what, in other and more morally defensible contexts, was a valid and valuable protection against the encroachments of the national government—even as South Carolina's position had been discredited in defense of slavery a century earlier.

The third dimension of federalism arose from the fact that the Framers of the Constitution did something that political theorists since ancient times had insisted could not be done, which is to say, divide sovereignty. In the eighteenth century, sovereignty was defined as the supreme law-making power; as Blackstone said, "Sovereignty and legislature are indeed convertible terms." Having two sovereignties in the same territory was obviously impossible. The

Framers worked their way around that stumbling block by attacking the problem in an ingenious way. Conceiving of sovereignty, not as a single power, but as an aggregate of many specific powers, they could allocate those specific powers among different governments and among different branches of the same government. Each government or branch of government had, in Hamilton's words, "sovereign power as to *certain things,* and not as to *other things.*"

The Constitution bestowed sovereign powers upon the national government only in regard to a handful of general objects. All other powers, except those that were forbidden to both national and state governments, remained in the hands of the states. As Madison explained in *Federalist* number 45: "The powers delegated by the . . . Constitution to the federal government are few and defined. Those which are to remain in the State governments are numerous and indefinite. The former will be exercised principally on external objects, as war, peace, negotiation, and foreign commerce; with which last the power of taxation will, for the most part, be connected. The powers reserved to the several States will extend to all the objects which, in the ordinary course of affairs, concern the lives, liberties, and properties of the people, and the internal order, improvement, and prosperity of the State." These state powers were commonly referred to as the power of "internal police," or simply the police power, which included the definition and punishment of crimes, the administration of justice, the governance of property rights and relationships, and the regulation of all matters concerning the health, manners, morals, safety, and welfare of the citizenry. The national government had no police power, and such powers as it did have were further curtailed by the adoption of the Bill of Rights—which imposed limitations on the national government but not on the state governments.

Despite Article VI, which declares the Constitution and congressional enactments passed in pursuance thereof to be the supreme law of the land, the preponderance of powers thus lay with the states, and most states insisted from the outset that all disputes about which governments could do what should be decided in favor of the states. As early as 1790, Virginia was challenging what it saw as congressional usurpation of powers reserved to the states, provoking Alexander Hamilton to declare that this was "the first symptom of a spirit which must either be killed or will kill the constitution." The very first decision in which the Supreme Court ruled against a state—that in *Chisholm* v. *Georgia* (1793)—resulted in a constitutional amendment curtailing the Court's jurisdiction and protecting the sovereignty of the states against suits by foreigners or citizens of other states. Repeatedly during Marshall's tenure (1801–35) the Court ruled that the states could not constitutionally do one thing or another, and the states did them anyway. Under Chief Justice Roger Brooke Taney (1836–64) the Court erected a virtual wall of separation around the states. The adoption of the Fourteenth Amendment in 1868 provided features that might have been employed to curtail state power, but apart from the relatively minor restrictions imposed under the doctrine of substantive due process, the states continued to be the principal units of government until well into the twentieth century. A rough indication of the relative importance of the levels of government can be expressed statistically: as late as 1929, state and local governments had nearly five times as many employees as the national government had (nearly ten times as many if post-office personnel are excluded) and spent three times as much money.

The process by which the balance of federal and state powers was overturned was long and involved, but the major phases can be described under three broad headings. First came the evolution of a national police power. The police power had resided exclusively in the states, and it had been consistently upheld by the Court even when there were conflicts with other constitutional provisions, as there were, for example, in *Stone* v. *Mississippi* (1880) and *Holden* v. *Hardy* (1898). But just after the turn of the century, Congress passed an act prohibiting the interstate transportation of lottery tickets and an act imposing a tax on oleomargarine, the latter on the pretext that margarine was dangerous to the health. In upholding these acts in 1903 and 1904, the Supreme Court ruled for the first time that the national government does in fact have a police power. The passage of the Pure Food and Drug Act and the Meat Inspection Act soon followed. Other such legislation steadily accumulated, and between 1937 and 1957—during which period the Court declared only one act of Congress unconstitutional—the whole range of police-power legislation was invaded by Congress.

A second group of developments was fiscal. The adoption of the Sixteenth Amendment, authorizing taxes on incomes; the passage of the Glass-Steagall Act of 1932, basing federal-reserve note currency upon governmental debt; and the abandonment of the gold standard; all these combined to make possible virtually unlimited and uncontrollable spending by the national government. Closely related to that development and in part growing out of it was the emergence of revenue sharing in one form and another—the subsidization of state and local governments by the national government and the ever-increasing dependence of the first two upon the last. It is to be observed that southerners, despite their traditional adherence to federalism and states' rights, did not resist this turn of events and were indeed in the vanguard of bringing it about. As the Bible puts it, they proved willing to sell their birthright for a mess of pottage. (A very large mess, but a mess nonetheless.)

The final blows were wielded by the Supreme Court, largely through the doctrine of incorporation, which runs roughly as follows. The Bill of Rights, as originally passed and as interpreted by the courts for 134 years, restricted the federal government but did not apply to the state governments. Then in 1925 the Court declared, in its decision in the case of *Gitlow* v. *New York,* that the Fourteenth Amendment's protection of liberty against state interference extended some of the fundamental liberties guaranteed by the Bill of Rights to apply to the states. For a time, the consequences of that declaration were minimal; the Court was loath to determine just what was a "fundamental" liberty. The conviction of Gitlow for publishing Communist propaganda in violation of a New York law, for instance, was upheld on the ground that freedom of speech is not an absolute right. A number of other cases were settled in similar fashion during the next dozen years; they culminated in a case in which the Court ruled that the Fifth Amendment's protection against double jeopardy was not a fundamental liberty. The Court continued to be cautious about applying the doctrine of incorporation throughout the 1940s and the 1950s. Indeed, it was not until 1961 that incorporation began to be applied on a grand scale, but since that time the Court has manufactured "fundamental rights" with reckless abandon. The result has been that control over matters of local concern has been transferred from local and state governments to the national government in Washington.

Constitutional traditionalists, especially in the South, have been incensed by most of this, and much of the relevant litigation has arisen in the South. The rights of accused criminals were established in suits originating in Arizona and Illinois; but both pioneering abortion cases,

many of the landmark cases concerning school prayer, some of the most important affirmative-action cases, and all of the major legislative-reapportionment cases were southern in origin.

There are some ironies in all this. Among the foremost apostles of the doctrine of incorporation, especially in regard to First Amendment rights, was the next-to-the-last southerner to sit on the Supreme Court, Hugo Black of Alabama. But Black, toward the end of his long and distinguished career, at last came to recognize the dangers inherent in carrying the principle too far. In a dissenting opinion in 1968 he pointed out that the nation had always understood "that it could be more tranquil and orderly if it functioned on the principle that the local communities should control their own peculiar affairs under their own particular rules." In 1970, the year before he died, he warned that if the Court did not exercise restraint, it would destroy the federal system created by the Constitution by reducing the state governments to "impotent figureheads."

The larger irony is this. Political scientists and historians are in agreement that federalism is the greatest contribution of the Founding Fathers to the science of government. It is also the only feature of the Constitution that has been successfully exported, that can be employed to protect liberty elsewhere in the world. Yet what we invented, and others imitate, no longer exists on its native shores.

IV  TRENDS

Since the 1970s, several forces have combined to reduce the federal government's role across a variety of social policy areas. These forces include the rising federal budget deficit and a succession of Republican administrations in Washington whose predilections have been in favor of a smaller role for the federal government. In many cases, this curbing of Washington's power has provided an opportunity for the states—an "entrepreneurial" opportunity, according to Carl E. Van Horn—to become more active in social policymaking.

As in any other entrepreneurial situation, not all states are equally willing or able to take up the slack. Some are reluctant to push forward active social agendas. Others lack a progressive tradition or are concentrating on building up their economic, political, or educational infrastructures. Still others are reluctant to take risks and would rather let other states take the lead.

Van Horn examines this new phenomenon and assesses its implications for state politics and government.

Questions

1. What does Van Horn mean when he describes the states as "entrepreneurs"? In what particular policy areas have the states been active?

2. What has happened to the structure of state governments as they have adopted the entrepreneurial approach? Why has entrepreneurship generated distrust, power struggles, and a decrease in "institutional accountability"?

3. How do developments in your own state fit into the trend Van Horn describes? How would you rate your state on a scale of entrepreneurship?

3.6 The Entrepreneurial States

Carl E. Van Horn

State government political institutions are infused with an entrepreneurial spirit. No longer passive partners in the federal system, the states are a driving force in American politics. They raise and spend vast sums of money; manage vexing public problems; and seek to conquer new policy frontiers. States aggressively set policy agendas for the nation and fashion innovative solutions for stimulating the growth of high technology firms, treating the medically indigent, curbing drunken driving, reforming the schools, and other important matters.

The foundation of the entrepreneurial states may be found in the changes in representation, governmental organization, and professionalization that appeared in the 1960s. Demands and expectations for a greater state government activism rose during the 1980s. A burgeoning federal budget deficit, cutbacks in domestic spending, and a popular president who sought a

larger state role convinced citizens and interest groups to turn their attention away from Washington, D.C. Repeating a pattern that has occurred before in American history, the states were thrust forward as the federal government withdrew.

Governmental activism has been stimulated and reinforced by institutional and individual entrepreneurship. Reforms ostensibly designed to strengthen the competence of state governments to perform their duties simultaneously made it possible for individualism to flourish. State government institutions are not only better equipped to assume leadership but also politically motivated to expand the scope of their endeavors. Governors, legislators, judges, and bureaucrats are moving boldly to assert power in the high stakes politics of state government.

Entrepreneurship creates a new set of problems for state government institutions, how-

ever. State politics are now more competitive and conflict-ridden. Power is fragmented. Policy makers generally agree that they want their government to tackle the state's tough problems, but they often have trouble endorsing a specific plan of action or budget request. As distrust deepens, governors, judges, legislators, and administrators jealously guard their personal and institutional prerogatives and plot to curb the power of each other. Frequently, conflicts have escalated into battles for control of the institutions and the policy agendas of state government.

Active, fragmented, and conflictual policy making decreases institutional accountability. Individuals have succeeded in gaining more power, but in the process clear lines of responsibility are blurred. Positive developments that created more democratic and responsive state governments also created some troubling problems.

Modernization

The states trailed the federal government in recognizing and responding to the challenges of the post-war era. But, contemporary state governments are capable and resourceful; they are strong participants in the design and implementation of public programs. Constitutions have been amended, political institutions have been restructured and strengthened, and professional expertise has been assembled.

The first step in modernizing state government were changes that improved the representativeness of political institutions. The policy-making circles of state governments—in legislatures, courts, bureaucracies, and governors' mansions—have gradually expanded beyond the upper-middle class, white males that dominated politics throughout most of American political history. Stimulated by landmark reapportionment decisions, legislatures were transformed from unrepresentative, homogeneous institutions to modern, representative bodies.

First, in *Baker* v. *Carr*, and then in *Reynolds* v. *Sims*, the U.S. Supreme Court removed barriers to direct representation of voters and reapportioned legislatures according to the principle of one person, one vote. The Voting Rights Act of 1965 provided for full participation by black Americans in the politics of their communities and states. Black registration in the seven states of the deep South covered by the law increased by more than one million between 1964 and 1972, a jump from 29 percent to 57 percent of eligible voters. Paralleling legal mandates were remarkable improvements in the participation of minorities and women in all aspects of American society. Eventually, the new attitudes and behavior of millions of Americans were reflected in state government institutions.

Women and minorities still occupy far fewer seats than their numbers in the population would assume. However, today's legislatures and state government agencies have greatly increased their representativeness from twenty years ago. Women holding legislative office, for example, increased from 4 percent in 1969 to 16 percent in 1988. In some states—New Hampshire, Maine, Colorado, Vermont, and Washington—women hold more than 25 percent of the seats in the legislature. Women have been less successful in obtaining statewide offices. In 1988, three women were serving as governors. Only nine women have been elected governor and two women elected attorney general in American history. Women's participation in state government positions has risen, however, at the appointive policy-making levels.

Minority participation in elected and appointed policy-making positions in state government has also increased significantly during the last twenty years. Blacks held 396 state legislative positions in 1988 versus 168 in 1970. Hispanics have also increased their share of elected positions in states where they make up a significant part of the population—California, New Mexico, Arizona, and Colorado. Nationwide, there are now 120 state legislators of Hispanic origin.

The election of individuals from heretofore unrepresented or underrepresented groups has ushered in new policy perspectives. Many of the newly empowered groups support government intervention as the preferred strategy for ameliorating social and economic problems and favor more benefits for disadvantaged groups or communities. These new state legislators reflect their life experiences and professional training. The substantial increase in teachers, working women, and others has injected new concerns about education and child care into the legislative process.

The prevailing attitude about the responsibilities of a state representative also has changed. Late-1980s legislators are likely to act as delegates of their constituency's interests, rather than as free agents exercising their best judgment. Modern representatives aggressively pursue political self-interest, which usually translates into advancing the interests of their district and their political career. Political leaders, such as county chairs, governors, and legislative leaders, no longer command those in their own party. With antennae tuned to the voters back home and campaign contributors, the legislators often ignore the appeals of their political leaders.

Citizen participation in policy making has also grown enormously in the past two decades. State government agencies afford citizens an opportunity to voice their concerns through such devices as public boards and commissions, ombudsmen and public advocates, and public hearings about policy decisions. Environmentalists, consumer advocates, and senior citizen activists have increased in number and clout. They raise money and contribute to candidates, advertise in the mass media, and frequently exert considerable influence over governors and legislatures.

Citizens and interest groups have also relied upon the initiative process, whereby public officials are petitioned to place issues on the ballot for approval or disapproval without waiting for the governor or state legislature to act. The number of ballot initiatives doubled between 1976 and 1986. Each election year more than fifty public propositions appear on state ballots. Voters are asked to establish regulations governing pornography, set limits on personal injury claims, and restructure state tax systems. In 1988, for example, voters considered state policy on auto insurance rates in California, gun control registration rules in Maryland, and the right to an abortion in Michigan.

Along with the growth in democratic participation and representation, state governments have equipped themselves with the modern tools of governing—larger and more professional staffs, computer equipment, and consultant expertise. Like the changes that occurred in representation, the professionalization of state government came about gradually. But the cumulative effects were dramatic. State governments now plan and execute ambitious public policy initiatives. Decision-making authority was seized by the states or delegated to them by the federal officials; state governments acquired a new cadre of government professionals to do the job.

The size and competence of state government institutions have grown enormously. Governors have increased their staff in nearly all the states. Legislators now meet regularly—in some cases year round. Many pay salaries that allow members to concentrate entirely on their legislative career. And legislatures have more and better trained staff. The number of full-time employees serving state legislatures has grown from approximately five thousand in the mid-1960s to fifteen thousand in the mid-1980s.

In accord with entrepreneurship, institutions have often enlarged their staffs to remain competitive with the other players in state government. Governors expanded staffs overseeing the bureaucracy, monitoring developments in the nation's capital, and shepherding the flock of legislative proposals in the statehouse. Legislatures bolstered staffs to keep a watchful eye on the executive branch and to provide more effective service to the folks in their districts. Courts added judges, law clerks, and administrative officers to cope with rising demands for court review of policy and administrative cases.

The Entrepreneurial States

The politics of activism, growth, and innovation has become a central defining characteristic of state politics and public policy. State government political institutions and political professionals are delivering new programs, launching far-reaching initiatives, and building a record of accomplishment. The rise of the entrepreneurial states was made possible by changes in the economy and federalism. It was reinforced by greater democratization, representation, and professionalization in state government.

State governments are imperialistic, pragmatic, and nonideological. Governors and legislators clamor for new ideas that will permit them to expand government spending and regulation, but they are not excited by the topic of government management and coordination. States are leading the nation with ambitious efforts to improve public schools; reform public welfare programs; protect the environment; restructure the housing industry; and rebuild roads, bridges, and sewers. A trend, no matter how powerful, does not sweep all fifty states at once or always appear in the same form. But entrepreneurship has been under way for some time and is manifest throughout the nation in large and small states and in every region.

The strong desire to follow an entrepreneurial public policy course has blurred ideological and partisan distinctions. State political parties and elected leaders have undergone policy convergence. For instance, the policy differences that have traditionally distinguished Republican and Democratic governors are far fewer than they were twenty-five years ago. Republicans elected to statewide office are typically more centrist or even liberal than national-level Republicans. The policies of Republican governors Tom Kean of New Jersey, Jim Thompson of Illinois, and Lamar Alexander of Tennessee reflected pragmatic, progovernment positions long advocated by Democrats.

State government policies and priorities have been nationalized in education, civil rights, economic development, and health care. State leaders are seldom ideologues for long. The pragmatic orientation of the states' principal policy-making institutions helps explain why the conservative policies of Ronald Reagan never took hold in state capitals. When states deal with AIDS, homelessness, uncompensated health care, or economic development, they usually adopt solutions that involve a heavy dose of government involvement and higher spending. For example, Democratic and Republican governors developed similar strategies for reforming public assistance and implemented them in their states. Federal welfare reform legislation incorporating principles advocated by a bipartisan group of governors was eventually adopted, but not without considerable partisan wrangling in Washington, D.C.

The buzzwords of the 1970s—zero-based budgeting, executive reorganization, and cutback management—have been replaced by a new doctrine. State politicians have quickly moved away from the tax-cutting mood spurred by California's Proposition 13 and the fear of a taxpayer revolt. The love affair with the idea of curbing government growth turned out to be a brief flirtation.

Ironically, the spurt in government spending has its roots in the economic crisis of 1982–1983. Faced with the prospects of greater social welfare spending and reduced tax collections, twenty-eight states raised their income taxes, and thirty states raised sales taxes. Even without additional tax increases these actions would have yielded a fiscal bonanza. Nineteen states boosted either their income or sales taxes again in 1984 and 1985. In addition, the 1986 federal tax reform law brought millions of additional dollars rolling into state treasuries.

Significant differences remain on fiscal policy. Republicans, as compared with Democrats, are less likely to raise taxes, usually opposing higher personal income or business taxes. Even so, traditional liberal/conservative distinctions are clouded because Republicans and Democrats alike have been raising taxes and expanding their budgets in the 1980s.

The engine of economic recovery—sustained, low-inflation growth—reduced government outlays for such costly entitlement programs as unemployment insurance and welfare, and pulled in more revenues. As state treasuries bulged, most state-level policy makers chose to spend the additional revenues rather than return them to taxpayers. Several states established so-called rainy day funds to cushion the shock of another recession, but typically new state revenues were quickly committed to new or expanded programs.

In New Jersey, for example, both sales and income taxes went up in 1982 so that the state could balance its budget. Since then, the state budget has more than doubled, and the state enjoys a $500 million surplus. At no point during this period did any major political leader propose rolling back any major tax hikes.

This rosy fiscal picture could turn sour when the economic growth ebbs, especially if the next recession is long lasting. The federal government is not going to prime the state government pump with substantial increases in expenditures because the federal government now suffers from a large budget deficit. Responsibility has shifted to the states. If the experience of the 1982–1983 recession is any guide, most states will respond to the next fiscal crisis by raising revenues rather than cutting state programs. Because states cannot borrow huge sums of money to satisfy their fiscal appetites, state officials may regard tax increases as the policy of first resort.

Activism by state legislatures and governors is matched by activism in the state courts. The courts have taken aggressive action on several public policy fronts. For example, the courts set forth strong liberal positions in the field of civil rights. They have expanded the rights of women, minorities, and criminal defendants, often relying upon state constitutions to establish rights that the U.S. Supreme Court has not found in the U.S. Constitution. They have also expanded the rights of individuals to recover for personal injuries and imposed strict liability rules for faulty products. Once regarded as the obstacles to civil liberties, the state courts have become the champions of change.

Power Struggles

Power within state government institutions has been fragmented and decentralized. Reforms undertaken in the name of modernization carved up institutional power into bits and pieces and undermined the ability of any one institution or political leader to dominate. Power struggles are a common feature of state political life. Individualism was encouraged at the expense of institutional responsibility.

Competitive, conflict-ridden politics promotes entrepreneurship and policy convergence. Legislators, governors, and agency executives are eager to discover new policy approaches and distribute benefits to constituencies. This creates unrelenting pressure to boost government spending and an unceasing need to expand the pool of available resources. Because there is more to win and more to lose in the governance of states, everyone has a greater incentive to seek power and control.

Democratization within political institutions has engendered fierce battles for the control of policy agendas and outcomes. Greater competition and conflict are apparent in all phases of state political life from elections to state budget decisions. More legislators, judges, bureaucrats, and interest groups have sufficient clout to engage in the struggle, but few have enough power to rule for long.

The desire to hold onto power strongly shapes the political process within institutions, especially in legislatures where electoral considerations are paramount. The quest for power is hardly a new phenomenon in American politics, but entrepreneurial, careerist politics have made power struggles more intense.

Because legislators are obsessed with keeping their jobs, they must constantly deliver benefits, claim credit for accomplishments, and attack opponents in the executive branch or elsewhere. They are also emboldened to seek out new territory for legislative involvement, through oversight of administrative rules and regulations, closer scrutiny of the state budget, and investigations into the performance of government agencies. Clearly, these strategies serve their intended purpose: incumbents rarely lose.

Strategies mounted to protect incumbents are equaled by rigorous competition during elections. The costs of elections are rising because people are willing and able to spend huge sums of money to gain elective office. The staples of modern campaigns—media consultants, pollsters, and television advertising—are ex-

pensive. The sudden jump in campaign costs has driven some people away from the arena and attracted others. Statewide candidates must collect considerable amounts of money or have a large fortune to spend on getting elected. Even legislative candidates are now required to assemble substantial resources, except in the smaller states.

The practices of statewide interest groups buttress entrepreneurship. Educators, dentists, senior citizens, builders, and others are sophisticated and effective advocates for their interests. These groups often supply the campaign funds that keep incumbent politicians around to serve them another day. Groups and individuals who cannot afford to participate in this costly process are less likely to be heard and thus special interest politics usually triumphs.

State politics appears to be locked in a spiraling institutional arms race. Seeking more control over the direction of state government, governors, legislators, and bureaucrats are acquiring new techniques and strategies—new weapons and technology, larger troops—to carry out their mission. Governors have asserted greater control over the bureaucracy. Legislatures have stepped up efforts to challenge governors and oversee government agencies. Interest groups compete with elected officials by resorting to the initiative. State courts are adjudicating disputes between legislators and governors and making policy independently.

There is nothing wrong with conflict per se. Representative government and deliberation are often well served by sharp clashes of strongly held views. Few observers of American politics are nostalgic for a return to an era when only a handful of party bosses and top-ranking elected officials called the shots. But many of the conflicts in state government revolve around ambiguous authority, not disputed policy goals. And, in some cases, these conflicts between institutions have escalated so far that they have disrupted the policy process.

Governors and legislatures, the states' principal policy making entities, regularly engage in battles over the state budget, the interpretation of administrative rules, executive orders, political appointments, and the execution of policy. For example, it is now more common for governors to exercise the line item veto as a tool of institutional and partisan power rather than as a means to control expenditures. Institutional conflicts are exacerbated by divided party control of the two branches—a trend that the electorate increasingly supports through a remarkable increase in split-ticket voting. Dual control of legislatures has also increased from four states in 1961 to twelve states in 1987.

As battles for power multiply, others are drawn into the fray. When legislators and governors fail to reach clear decisions, they often delegate hard choices to the bureaucracy. Combative institutions may "resolve" their differences by creating new administrative entities. Thus, there has been a proliferation of commissions, "independent authorities," and other organizations made up of legislative and gubernatorial appointments, so that both institutions can influence outcomes.

State courts are frequently asked to mediate between the executive and legislative branches. In recent years they have ruled on such diverse subjects as the authority of governors to exercise their line-item veto power and their powers of appointment and removal. By entering into these disputes, the court "allocates and exerts political power." Such court interventions generate more controversy from those who regard themselves as the losers.

Clashes over institutional authority have encouraged courts to become active policy makers. The courts' liberal activism in civil rights and other fields reflects the fragmentation of state politics and the rise of conservatism in the U.S. Supreme Court. When courts extend government policy against the will of majoritarian institutions, legislators, governors, and voters may reassert control through initiatives, legislative decisions, or judicial elections. The courts become a battleground for both sides in an ideological struggle.

In recent years, interest groups, legislators, and governors have tried to overturn or amend court decisions. The courts have been able to fend off objections to their authority in the interpretation of constitutional law. But their power to interpret common law has been challenged. For example, state legislatures have narrowed the rights of injured parties, but they have been less successful in curbing the state courts' support for the civil liberties of criminal defendants and the rights of women in sex discrimination cases.

Judicial confirmation elections have become the stage on which objections to the liberalism of judges and efforts to rein in the courts have been played out. Decisions on controversial issues, such as support for the death penalty, are frequently central issues in campaigns to oust judges. Spending on judicial elections and the number of direct challenges have risen substantially. Ballot initiatives have overturned liberal court decisions affecting criminal defendant rights. While the defeat of incumbent judges and anticourt initiatives are still rare, the fear of defeat may curb the courts' liberal leanings.

As with the courts, bureaucracies are embroiled in disputes over their activities, purposes, and performance. Legislatures have increased their oversight of agency decisions through such mechanisms as sunset laws and reviews of administrative rules and regulations. Governors have exerted greater control through executive reorganizations—reducing the number of boards and commissions; centralizing budgeting techniques; and issuing executive orders that mandate direct accountability to the governor.

The federal bureaucracy and federal courts have also asserted greater control over the states. For example, federal judges have ordered sweeping changes in state actions regarding the mentally ill and state prisoners. The courts have argued that the federal constitution gives them the right to guarantee due process of law—asserting constitutional control over states. Governors and the federal government have gotten into battles over interpretations of federal statutes, such as environmental laws.

Governance

The rise of governmental, institutional, and individual entrepreneurship has important implications for the ability of state governments to cope with the problems they will face in the 1990s. The accountability of political institutions for their actions has been replaced by individual accountability. In many states, incumbent governors and legislators have successfully separated themselves from responsibility for the actions of their own government or institutions. They have inoculated themselves from corporate responsibility. Unfortunately, when everyone is responsible, no one is responsible.

Legislators have tried to insulate themselves from executive domination, party leaders, and legislative leaders. Governors increasingly portray themselves as the clarion of the people, not the head of state government. They play to the press and go over the heads of party and legislative leaders. Political parties have been nudged aside by candidate-centered politics, in which the actions of the incumbent, not the party, are open for judgment. Partisanship is on the rise, but responsible party governance may be on the decline. Even judges are now more wary of voter and interest group reaction to their decisions.

When political officials become independent contractors in the political system, leadership becomes problematic. Leaders serve at the pleasure of their members so they are more likely to wield influence by distributing campaign funds than by threats or the art of persuasion. Legislators and governors used to be primarily concerned with governing. They are now displacing local party organizations and taking over electoral functions through leadership caucuses and political action committees.

The dramatic increase in the cost of elections and the desire to remain in office means that elected officials are more accountable to campaign contributors and special interest groups and less accountable to the public at large. The emphasis on fund raising diverts time from governing responsibilities and lowers ethical standards. It is, for example, quite common for legislators and governors to hold large fund-raising events while important policy issues are under consideration. Elected officials regularly solicit and receive campaign contributions from companies that either have contracts with the state or want to do business in the future. Partisan staff in the executive and legislative branches are routinely deployed to work on election activities.

Institutional warfare between the legislature and governor has also increased the power of the bureaucracy and courts and thus reduced accountability to the public. Because it is more difficult to reach agreement and compromise, more decisions are delegated from democratic institutions to the bureaucracy. While administrative agencies appear to be more accountable than before, the custody battles between governors and legislatures and between courts and the bureaucracy may make it more difficult to establish who is in charge. Ultimately these conflicts may generate more contradictions, delay, rigidity, and uncertainty. As an increasing number of decisions are made by the courts, the "judicialization of state administration" may result.

Of greatest concern are the possible effects of the new state politics on the shape of public policy. The entrepreneurial politics of the 1980s has boosted the power of narrow, special interests over the public interest. Policy makers favor policies that guarantee their political survival. This undermines their willingness to look ahead and to make difficult choices. It also encourages policy gridlock and delegation to the bureaucracy.

Governors and legislators are more reactive and responsive to their own short-run political needs, but less deliberative and responsible about the long-run interests of the state as a whole. If electoral expediency crowds out other values, state officials will practice the art of easy money, saying yes when they should say no. In the future it may be harder to exercise fiscal restraint. When everyone fights for a piece of the action, the compromise is to do a little of everything. Unlike the federal government, which has indulged in this practice for decades, the states cannot borrow their way out. State policy makers will have either to raise taxes or cut programs. In the current climate, government leaders will probably be able to slow the growth of spending, but not eliminate government programs.

The reliance on statewide initiatives to resolve public policy disputes represents a troubling development. In some of the nation's more populous states, such as California, state elected officials have ceded the responsibility for making many controversial decisions to political campaigns. These "issue elections" are seldom grass-roots citizen petitions of the government. Instead, they are dominated by interest groups that spend lavishly on television advertising, direct mail, and tracking polls. For example, the insurance industry spent $60 million attempting to defeat a proposal to cut insurance premiums in California. The consumer activists succeeded, in part, because they were able to raise $20 million. Not surprisingly, the issue is now so confused that it has landed in the lap of the California Supreme Court.

The decline of institutional responsibility raises serious implications for the ability of political institutions to cope with public policy problems. Expansion, distribution, and innovation are popular, but power struggles within and across institutions reduce the possibilities for reaching consensus on matters involving difficult trade-offs. State governments have vastly increased their capacity and power to help citizens and respond to the needs of their states. The entrepreneurial state politics of the 1980s have brought many positive changes in the performance of state government. Unfortunately, they have also unleashed forces that may undermine the practice of wise governance.

_____Chapter 4

American
Political Culture

$\mathcal{B}$ecause we are immersed in our own political culture, we have difficulty seeing
that Americans have an identifiable and common set of beliefs in government and
politics. We are so accustomed to focusing on what divides us (Republican versus
Democrat, liberal versus conservative) that we often lose sight of what unites us.
Exactly what makes us American in a cultural sense is difficult to define, but that
there is an American political culture seems clear.

Perhaps the best way to understand American political culture is to see ourselves
through the eyes of people from other cultures. Because they view the United States
against the backdrop of their own political cultures, foreign observers often provide
keen insights into the nature of American political life. They allow us to see ourselves,
as Robert Burns put it, as others see us.

The most noteworthy foreign observer of American politics in our history undoubtedly was Alexis de Tocqueville (see selection 4.1). Tocqueville visited the United
States in the 1830s and, like many other observers of the American scene, was struck
by the American commitment to equality, liberty, participation in politics, and religion. To this day, visitors to the United States often remark on the informal, easy
manner in which Americans relate to one another, at our deep-seated religiosity, and—
at least until recently—at our passion for politics. We are, in a word, a democratic
society—not only in politics but in our attitudes toward public and private life. Our
underlying belief in democracy and all it connotes forms an essential part of the American polity.

Americans' attitudes toward politics, moreover, are in some ways a subset of our
attitudes toward life in general. Political culture is reflected in and affected by our
attitudes toward religion, family, and social relationships. Even our tastes in movies
and television, as selection 4.3 suggests, reveal something about our views on politics.

The effort to define a distinctive American political culture creates a tendency toward overgeneralizations or even stereotypes. But the United States is a country of many different regional, ethnic, and social subcultures and what may be true of most Americans will certainly not be true of all. In addition, as the readings in this chapter make clear, American political culture is hardly static; it changes year by year and decade by decade. As you read the following selections, compare the authors' comments to your own knowledge and experience and make your own judgments as to the validity of their claims regarding the existence of a definitive and distinctive American political culture.

Chapter Questions

1. What attitudes and assumptions about politics are distinctively "American"—that is, seem to be held by most Americans, no matter what their political beliefs may be? How do these attitudes and assumptions differ from those of other nations?

2. How has American political culture changed since Tocqueville visited 150 years ago? since the 1960s? since Ronald Reagan was elected in 1980? Are these changes permanent and fundamental, or fleeting and insignificant?

3. How does American political culture relate to American culture in general? Are our attitudes toward politics related to our attitudes toward life in general?

I THE CLASSIC TEXTS

Alexis de Tocqueville, a French nobleman, traveled to the United States in 1831 to study and report back to the French government on the American prison system. As a result of his nine-month trip, he produced not only a report on the prison system but also Democracy in America, *which, published in 1835, was immediately hailed as a masterpiece of political and social commentary. It remains one of the most important books ever written about American political life. (Tocqueville, incidentally, was accompanied on his trip by his friend Gustave de Beaumont, who also wrote a book on America. It was a novel about a slave woman in Baltimore, titled* Marie, or Slavery in the United States.)

Although he wrote more than 150 years ago, Tocqueville's keen observations of life in the United States offer insights into American political culture that are still valid. The following excerpts highlight three of the themes that struck Tocqueville as keys to understanding American politics, especially as compared to politics in his own country. The three themes are equality, religion, and political participation.

1. To what extent is American politics today still based on the idea of equality? Consider not only questions of legal or political equality but also social equality. (See the boxed material on p. 112.)
2. How does Tocqueville reconcile the importance of religion in America with the separation of church and state?

4.1 Democracy in America

Alexis de Tocqueville

Social State of the Anglo-Americans

The social state is commonly the result of circumstances, sometimes of laws, but most often of a combination of the two. But once it has come into being, it may itself be considered as the prime cause of most of the laws, customs, and ideas which control the nation's behavior; it modifies even those things which it does not cause.

Therefore one must first study their social state if one wants to understand a people's laws and mores.

The Striking Feature in the Social Condition of the Anglo-Americans Is That It Is Essentially Democratic

There are many important things to be said about the social condition of the Anglo-Americans, but one feature dominates all the others.

The social state of the Americans is eminently democratic. It has been like that ever since the birth of the colonies but is even more so now.

. . . A high degree of equality prevailed among the immigrants who first settled on the coast of New England. In that part of the states even the seeds of aristocracy were never planted. There only intellectual power could command influence, and the people came to respect certain names as symbols of enlightenment and virtue. The views of some citizens carried such weight that if it had invariably passed from father to son, their influence might reasonably have been called aristocratic.

That was the case to the east of the Hudson. To the southwest of that river and right down to the Floridas things were different.

Great English landowners had come to settle in most of the states southwest of the Hudson. They brought with them aristocratic principles, including the English law of inheritance. I have explained the reasons that made it impossible ever to establish a powerful aristocracy in America. Those reasons applied southwest of the Hudson too, but with less force than to the east thereof. In the South one man and his slaves could cultivate a wide extent of land. So there were rich landowners in that part of the country. But their influence was not exactly aristocratic, in the sense in which that word is used in Europe, for they had no privileges, and the use of slaves meant that they had no tenants and consequently no patronage. However, the great landowners south of the Hudson did form an upper class, with its own ideas and tastes, and in general it did concentrate political activity in its hands. It was a sort of aristocracy not very different from the bulk of the people whose passions and interests it easily embraced, arousing neither love nor hate. It was, to conclude, weak and unlikely to last. That was the class which, in the South, put itself at the head of the rebellion; it provided the best leaders of the American Revolution.

At that time society was shaken to the core. The people, in whose name the war had been fought, became a power and wanted to act on their own; democratic instincts awoke; the English yoke had been broken, and a taste for every form of independence grew; little by little the influence of individuals ceased to carry weight; customs and laws began to march in step toward the same goal.

The first generation passed away; land began to be divided. As time passed, the change grew faster and faster. Now, hardly sixty years later, the aspect of society is already hard to recognize; the families of the great landowners have almost mingled with the common mass. In the state of New York, where formerly there were many, only two still keep their heads above the waters which are ready to swallow them too. The sons of these wealthy citizens are now merchants, lawyers, or doctors. Most of them have fallen into the most complete obscurity. The last trace of hereditary ranks and distinctions has been destroyed; the law of inheritance has everywhere imposed its dead level.

It is not that in the United States, as everywhere, there are no rich; indeed I know no other country where love of money has such a grip on men's hearts or where stronger scorn is expressed for the theory of permanent equality of property. But wealth circulates there with incredible rapidity, and experience shows that two successive generations seldom enjoy its favors.

This picture, which some may think overdrawn, would give only a very imperfect

---

☆   ☆   ☆

Why I Love America

Tocqueville is not the only foreign observer of American politics to notice the informal equality that marks American society. Henry Fairlie, a British-born immigrant to America who wrote on politics for the New Republic *magazine until his death in 1990, recalls his first exposure to equality, American style.*

*O*ne spring day shortly after my arrival, I was walking down the long, broad street of a suburb, with its sweeping front lawns (all that space), its tall trees (all that sky), and its clumps of azaleas (all that color). The only other person on the street was a small boy on a tricycle. As I passed him, he said "Hi!"—just like that. No four-year-old boy had ever addressed me without an introduction before. Yet there was this one, with his cheerful "Hi!". Recovering from the culture shock, I tried to look down stonily at his flaxen head, but instead, involuntarily, I found myself saying in return: "Well—hi!" He pedaled off, apparently satisfied. He had begun my Americanization.

"Hi!" As I often say—for Americans do not realize it—the word is a democracy. (I come from a country where one can tell someone's class by how they say "Hallo!" or "Hello!" or "Hullo," or whether they say it at all.) But anyone can say "Hi!". Anyone does. Shortly after my encounter with the boy, I called on the then Suffragan Bishop of Washington. Did he greet me as the Archbishop of Canterbury would have done? No. He said, "Hi, Henry!". I put it down to an aberration, an excess of Episcopalian latudinarianism. But what about my first meeting with Lyndon B. Johnson, the President of the United States, the Emperor of the Free World, before whom, like a Burgher of Calais, a halter round my neck, I would have sunk to my knees, pleading for a loan for my country? He held out the largest hand in Christendom, and said, "Hi, Henry!".

—*Henry Fairlie*

---

impression of what goes on in the new states of the West and Southwest.

At the end of the last century a few bold adventurers began to penetrate into the Mississippi valley. It was like a new discovery of America; soon most of those who were immigrating went there; previously unheard of communities suddenly sprang up in the wilderness. States that had not even been names a few years before took their places in the American Union. It is in the West that one can see democracy in its most extreme form. In these states, in some sense improvisations of fortune, the inhabitants have arrived only yesterday in the land where they dwell. They hardly know one another, and each man is ignorant of his nearest neighbor's history. So in that part of the American continent the population escapes the influence not only of great names and great wealth but also of the natural aristocracy of education and probity. No man there enjoys the influence and respect due to a whole life spent publicly in doing good. There are inhabitants already in the new states of the West, but not as yet a society.

But it is not only fortunes that are equal in America; equality to some extent affects their mental endowments too.

I think there is no other country in the world where, proportionately to population, there are so few ignorant and so few learned individuals as in America.

Primary education is within reach of all; higher education is hardly available to anybody.

That is easily understood and is indeed the necessary consequence of what has been said before.

Almost all Americans enjoy easy circumstances and can so easily acquire the basic elements of human knowledge.

There are few rich men in America; hence almost all Americans have to take up some profession. Now, every profession requires an apprenticeship. Therefore the American can devote only the first years of life to general education; at fifteen they start on a career, so their education generally ends at the age when ours begins. If it is continued beyond that point, it aims only at some specialized and profitable objective; science is studied in the same spirit as one takes up a trade; and only matters of immediate and recognized practical application receive attention.

In America most rich men began by being poor; almost all men of leisure were busy in their youth; as a result, at the age when one might have a taste for study, one has not the time; and when time is available, the taste has gone.

So there is no class in America in which a taste for intellectual pleasures is transmitted with hereditary wealth and leisure and which holds the labors of the mind in esteem.

Both the will and the power to engage in such work are lacking.

A middling standard has been established in America for all human knowledge. All minds come near to it, some by raising and some by lowering their standards.

As a result one finds a vast multitude of people with roughly the same ideas about religion, history, science, political economy, legislation, and government.

Intellectual inequalities come directly from God, and man cannot prevent them existing always.

But it results from what we have just been explaining, that, though mental endowments remain unequal as the Creator intended, the means of exercising them are equal.

Therefore, in America now the aristocratic element, which was from the beginning weak, has been, if not destroyed, at least made feebler still, so that one can hardly attribute to it any influence over the course of things.

On the other hand, time, circumstances, and laws have made the democratic element not merely preponderant but, one might say, exclusive.

One cannot trace any family or corporate influence; it is often hard even to discover any durable individual influence.

So the social state of America is the very strange phenomenon. Men there are nearer equality in wealth and mental endowments, or, in other words, more nearly equally powerful, than in any other country of the world or in any other age of recorded history.

Political Consequences of the Social State of the Anglo-Americans

It is easy to deduce the political consequences of such a social state.

By no possibility could equality ultimately fail to penetrate into the sphere of politics as everywhere else. One cannot imagine that men should remain perpetually unequal in just one respect though equal in all others; within a certain time they are bound to become equal in all respects.

Now, I know of only two ways of making equality prevail in the political sphere; rights must be given either to every citizen or to nobody.

So, for a people who have reached the Anglo-Americans' social state, it is hard to see any middle course between the sovereignty of all and the absolute power of one man.

One must not disguise it from oneself that the social state I have just described may lead as easily to the one as to the other of those results.

There is indeed a manly and legitimate passion for equality which rouses in all men a desire to be strong and respected. This passion tends to elevate the little man to the rank of the great. But the human heart also nourishes a debased taste for equality, which leads the weak to want to drag the strong down to their level and which induces men to prefer equality in servitude to inequality in freedom. It is not that peoples with a democratic social state naturally scorn freedom; on the contrary, they have an instinctive taste for it. But freedom is not the chief and continual object of their desires; it is equality for which they feel an eternal love; they rush on freedom with quick and sudden impulses, but if they miss their mark they resign themselves to their disappointment; but nothing will satisfy them without equality, and they would rather die than lose it.

On the other hand, when the citizens are all more or less equal, it becomes difficult to defend their freedom from the encroachments of power. No one among them being any longer strong enough to struggle alone with success, only the combination of the forces of all is able to guarantee liberty. But such a combination is not always forthcoming.

So, nations can derive either of two great political consequences from the same social state; these consequences differ vastly from each other, but both originate from the same fact.

The Anglo-Americans who were the first to be faced with the above-mentioned alternatives were lucky enough to escape absolute power. Circumstances, origin, education, and above all mores allowed them to establish and maintain the sovereignty of the people.

• • •

Political Association in the United States

Better use has been made of association and this powerful instrument of action has been applied to more varied aims in America than anywhere else in the world.

Apart from permanent associations such as townships, cities, and counties created by law, there are a quantity of others whose existence and growth are solely due to the initiative of individuals.

The inhabitant of the United States learns from birth that he must rely on himself to combat the ills and trials of life; he is restless and defiant in his outlook toward the authority of society and appeals to its power only when he cannot do without it. The beginnings of this attitude first appear at school, where the children, even in their games, submit to rules settled by themselves and punish offenses which they have defined themselves. The same attitude turns up again in all the affairs of social life. If some obstacle blocks the public road halting the circulation of traffic, the neighbors at once form a deliberative body; this improvised assembly produces an executive authority which remedies the trouble before anyone has thought of the possibility of some previously constituted authority beyond that of those concerned. Where enjoyment is concerned, people associate to make festivities grander and more orderly. Finally, associations are formed to combat exclusively moral troubles: intemperance is fought in common. Public security, trade and industry, and morals and religion all provide the aims for associations in the United States. There is no end which the human will despairs of attaining by the free action of the collective power of individuals.

Later I shall have occasion to speak of the effects of association on civil life. For the moment I must stick to the world of politics.

The right of association being recognized, citizens can use it in different ways. An association simply consists in the public and formal support of specific doctrines by a certain number of individuals who have undertaken to cooperate in a stated way in order to make these doctrines prevail. Thus the right of association can almost be identified with freedom to write, but already associations are more powerful than the press. When some view is represented by an association, it must take clearer and more precise shape. It counts its supporters and involves them in its cause; these supporters get to know one another, and numbers increase zeal. An association unites the energies of divergent minds and vigorously directs them toward a clearly indicated goal.

Freedom of assembly marks the second stage in the use made of the right of association. When a political association is allowed to form centers of action at certain important places in the country, its activity becomes greater and its influence more widespread. There men meet, active measures are planned, and opinions are expressed with that strength and warmth which the written word can never attain.

But the final stage is the use of association in the sphere of politics. The supporters of an agreed view may meet in electoral colleges and appoint mandatories to represent them in a central assembly. That is, properly speaking, the application of the representative system to one party.

So, in the first of these cases, men sharing one opinion are held together by a purely intellectual tie; in the second case, they meet together in small assemblies representing only a fraction of the party; finally, in the third case, they form something like a separate nation within the nation and a government within the government. Their mandatories, like those of the majority, represent by themselves all the collective power of their supporters, and, like them in this too, they appear as national representatives with all the moral prestige derived therefrom. It is true that, unlike the others, they have no right to make laws, but they do have the power to attack existing laws and to formulate, by anticipation, laws which should take the place of the present ones.

Imagine some people not perfectly accustomed to the use of freedom, or one in which profound political passions are seething. Suppose that, besides the majority that makes the laws, there is a minority which only deliberates and which gets laws ready for adoption; I cannot help but think that then public order would be exposed to great risks.

There is certainly a great gap between proving that one law is in itself better than another and establishing that it ought to be substituted for it. But where trained minds may still see a wide gap, the hasty imagination of the crowd may be unaware of this. Moreover, there are times when the nation is divided into two almost equal parties, each claiming to represent the majority. If, besides the ruling power, another power is established with almost equal moral authority, can one suppose that in the long run it will just talk and not act?

Will it always stop short in front of the metaphysical consideration that the object of associations is to direct opinions and not to constrain them, and to give advice about the law but not to make it?

The more I observe the main effects of a free press, the more convinced am I that, in the modern world, freedom of the press is the principal and, so to say, the constitutive element in freedom. A nation bent on remaining free is therefore right to insist, at whatever cost, on respect for this freedom. But *unlimited* freedom of association must not be entirely identified with freedom to write. The former is both less necessary and more dangerous than the latter. A nation may set limits there without ceasing to be its own master; indeed, in order to remain its own master, it is sometimes necessary to do so.

In America there is no limit to freedom of association for political ends.

One example will show better than anything I could say just how far it is tolerated.

One remembers how excited the Americans were by the free-trade-tariff controversy. Not opinions only, but very powerful material interests stood to gain or lose by a tariff. The North thought that some of its prosperity was due thereto, while the South blamed it for almost all its woes. One may say that over a long period the tariff question gave rise to the only political passions disturbing the Union.

In 1831, when the quarrel was most envenomed, an obscure citizen of Massachusetts thought of suggesting through the newspapers that all opponents of the tariff should send deputies to Philadelphia to concert together measures to make trade free. Thanks to the invention of printing, this suggestion passed in but a few days from Maine to New Orleans. The opponents of the tariff took it up ardently. They assembled from all sides and appointed deputies. Most of the latter were known men, and some of them had risen to celebrity. South Carolina, which was later to take up arms in this cause, sent sixty-three people as its delegates. On October 1, 1831, the assembly, which in American fashion styled itself a convention, was constituted at Philadelphia; it counted more than two hundred members. The discussions were public, and from the very first day it took on an altogether legislative character; discussion covered the extent of the powers of Congress, theories of free trade, and finally the various provisions of the tariff. After ten days the assembly broke up, having issued an address to the American people. In that address it declared first that Congress had not the right to impose a tariff and that the existing tariff was unconstitutional, and second that it was against the interest of any people, in particular the American people, that trade should not be free.

It must be admitted that unlimited freedom of association in the political sphere has not yet produced in America the fatal results that one might anticipate from it elsewhere. The right of association is of English origin and always existed in America. Use of this right is now an accepted part of customs and of mores.

In our own day freedom of association has become a necessary guarantee against the tyranny of the majority. In the United States, once a party has become predominant, all public power passes into its hands; its close supporters occupy all offices and have control of all organized forces. The most distinguished men of the opposite party, unable to cross the barrier keeping them from power, must be able to establish themselves outside it; the minority must use the whole of its moral authority to oppose the physical power oppressing it. Thus the one danger has to be balanced against a more formidable one.

The omnipotence of the majority seems to me such a danger to the American republics that the dangerous expedient used to curb it is actually something good.

Here I would repeat something which I have put in other words when speaking of municipal freedom: no countries need associations more—to prevent either despotism of parties or the arbitrary rule of a prince—than those with a democratic social state. In aristocratic nations secondary bodies form natural associations which hold abuses of power in check. In countries where such associations do not exist, if private people did not artificially and temporarily create something like them, I see no other dike to hold back tyranny of whatever sort, and a great nation might with impunity be oppressed by some tiny faction or by a single man.

The meeting of the great political convention (for conventions are of all kinds), though it may often be a necessary measure, is always, even in America, a serious event and one that good patriots cannot envisage without alarm.

That came out clearly during the convention of 1831, when all the men of distinction taking part therein tried to moderate its language and limit its objective. Probably the convention of 1831 did greatly influence the attitude of the malcontents and prepared them for the open revolt of 1832 against the commercial laws of the Union.

One must not shut one's eyes to the fact that unlimited freedom of association for political ends is, of all forms of liberty, the last that a nation can sustain. While it may not actually lead it into anarchy, it does constantly bring it to the verge thereof. But this form of freedom, howsoever dangerous, does provide guarantees in one direction; in countries where associations are free, secret societies are unknown. There are factions in America, but no conspirators.

• • •

The Main Causes Tending to Maintain a Democratic Republic in the United States

Indirect Influence of Religious Beliefs upon Political Society in the United States

. . . The direct action of religion on politics in the United States [is great]. Its indirect action seems to me much greater still, and it is just when it is not speaking of freedom at all that it best teaches the Americans the art of being free.

There is an innumerable multitude of sects in the United States. They are all different in the worship they offer to the Creator, but all agree concerning the duties of men to one another. Each sect worships God in its own fashion, but all preach the same morality in the name of God. Though it is very important for man as an individual that his religion should be true, that is not the case for society. Society has nothing to fear or hope from another life; what is most important for it is not that all citizens should profess the true religion but that they should profess religion. Moreover, all the sects in the United States belong to the great unity of Christendom, and Christian morality is everywhere the same.

One may suppose that a certain number of Americans, in the worship they offer to God, are following their habits rather than their convictions. Besides, in the United States the sovereign authority is religious, and consequently hypocrisy should be common. Nonetheless, America is still the place where the Christian religion has kept the greatest real power over men's souls; and nothing better demonstrates how useful and natural it is to man, since the country where it now has widest sway is both the most enlightened and the freest.

I have said that American priests proclaim themselves in general terms in favor of civil liberties without excepting even those who do not admit religious freedom; but none of them lend their support to any particular political system. They are at pains to keep out of affairs and not mix in the combinations of parties. One cannot therefore say that in the United States religion influences the laws or political opinions in detail, but it does direct mores, and by regulating domestic life it helps to regulate the state.

I do not doubt for an instant that the great severity of mores which one notices in the United States has its primary origin in beliefs. There religion is often powerless to restrain men in the midst of innumerable temptations which fortune offers. It cannot moderate their eagerness to enrich themselves, which everything contributes to arouse, but it reigns supreme in the souls of the women, and it is women who shape mores. Certainly of all countries in the world America is the one in which the marriage tie is most respected and where the highest and truest conception of conjugal happiness has been conceived.

In Europe almost all the disorders of society are born around the domestic hearth and not far from the nuptial bed. It is there that men come to feel scorn for natural ties and legitimate pleasures and develop a taste for disorder, restlessness of spirit, and instability of desires. Shaken by the tumultuous passions which have often troubled his own house, the European finds it hard to submit to the authority of the state's legislators. When the American returns from the turmoil of politics to the bosom of the family, he immediately finds a perfect picture of order and peace. There all his pleasures are simple and natural and his joys innocent and quiet, and as the regularity of life brings him happiness, he easily forms the habit of regulating his opinions as well as his tastes.

Whereas the European tries to escape his sorrows at home by troubling society, the American derives from his home that love of order which he carries over into affairs of state.

In the United States it is not only mores that are controlled by religion, but its sway extends even over reason.

Among the Anglo-Americans there are some who profess Christian dogmas because they believe them and others who do so because they are afraid to look as though they did not believe in them. So Christianity reigns without obstacles, by universal consent; consequently, as I have said elsewhere, everything in the moral field is certain and fixed, although the world of politics seems given over to argument and experiment. So the human spirit never sees an unlimited field before itself; however bold it is, from time to time it feels that it must halt before insurmountable barriers. Before innovating, it is forced to accept certain primary assumptions and to submit its boldest conceptions to certain formalities which retard and check it.

The imagination of the Americans, therefore, even in its greatest aberrations, is circumspect and hesitant; it is embarrassed from the start and leaves its work unfinished. These habits of restraint are found again in political society and singularly favor the tranquillity of the people as well as the durability of the institutions they have adopted. Nature and circumstances have made the inhabitant of the United States a bold man, as is sufficiently attested by the enterprising spirit with which he seeks his fortune. If the spirit of the Americans were free of all impediment, one would soon find among them the boldest innovators and the most implacable logicians in the world. But American revolutionaries are obliged ostensibly to profess a certain respect for Christian morality and equity, and that does not allow them easily to break the laws when those are opposed to the executions of their designs; nor would they find it easy to surmount the scruples of their partisans even if they were able to get over their own. Up till now no one in the United States has dared to profess the maxim that everything is allowed in the interests of society, an impious maxim apparently invented in an age of freedom in order to legitimatize every future tyrant.

Thus, while the law allows the American people to do everything, there are things which religion prevents them from imagining and forbids them to dare.

Religion, which never intervenes directly in the government of American society, should therefore be considered as the first of their political institutions, for although it did not give them the taste for liberty, it singularly facilitates their use thereof.

The inhabitants of the United States themselves consider religious beliefs from this angle. I do not know if all Americans have faith in their religion—for who can read the secrets of the heart?—but I am sure that they think it necessary to the maintenance of republican institutions. That is not the view of one class or party among the citizens, but of the whole nation; it is found in all ranks.

In the United States, if a politician attacks a sect, that is no reason why the supporters of that very sect should not support him; but if he attacks all sects together, everyone shuns him, and he remains alone.

While I was in America, a witness called at assizes of the county of Chester (state of New York) declared that he did not believe in the existence of God and the immortality of the soul. The judge refused to allow him to be sworn in, on the ground that the witness had destroyed beforehand all possible confidence in his testimony. Newspapers reported the fact without comment.

For the Americans the ideas of Christianity and liberty are so completely mingled that it is almost impossible to get them to conceive of the one without the other; it is not a question with them of sterile beliefs bequeathed by the past and vegetating rather than living in the depths of the soul.

I have known Americans to form associations to send priests out into the new states of the West and establish schools and churches there; they fear that religion might be lost in the depths of the forest and that the people growing up there might be less fitted for freedom than those from whom they sprang. I have met rich New Englanders who left their native land in order to establish the fundamentals of Christianity and of liberty by the banks of the Missouri or on the prairies of Illinois. In this way, in the United States, patriotism continually adds fuel to the fires of religious zeal. You will be mistaken if you think that such men are guided only by thoughts of the future life; eternity is only one of the things that concern them. If you talk to these missionaries of Christian civilization you will be surprised to hear them so often speaking of the goods of this world and to meet a politician where you expected to find a priest. "There is a solidarity between all the American republics," they will tell you; "if the republics of the West were to fall into anarchy or to be mastered by a despot, the republican institutions now flourishing on the Atlantic coast would be in great danger; we therefore have an interest in seeing that the new states are religious so that they may allow us to remain free."

That is what the Americans think, but our pedants find it an obvious mistake; constantly they prove to me that all is fine in America except just that religious spirit which I admire; I am informed that on the other side of the ocean freedom and human happiness lack nothing but Spinoza's belief in the eternity of the world and Cabanis' contention that thought is a secretion of the brain. To that I have really no answer to give, except that those who talk like that have never been in America and have never seen either religious peoples or free ones. So I shall wait till they come back from a visit to America.

There are people in France who look on republican institutions as a temporary expedient for their own aggrandizement. They mentally measure the immense gap separating their vices and their poverty from power and wealth, and they would like to fill this abyss with ruins in an attempt to bridge it. Such people stand toward liberty much as the medieval *condottieri* stood toward the kings; they make war on their own account, no matter whose colors they wear: the republic, they calculate, will at least last long enough to lift them from their present degradation. It is not to such as they that I speak, but there are others who look forward to a republican form of government as a permanent and tranquil state and as the required aim to which ideas and mores are constantly steering modern societies. Such men sincerely wish to prepare mankind for liberty. When such as these attack religious beliefs, they obey the dictates of their passions, not their interests. Despotism may be able to do without faith, but freedom cannot. Religion is much more needed in the republic they advocate than in the monarchy they attack, and in democratic republics most of all. How could society escape destruction if, when political ties are relaxed, moral ties are not tightened? And what can be done with a people master of itself if it is not subject to God?

The Main Causes That Make Religion Powerful in America

• • •

Eighteenth-century philosophers had a very simple explanation for the gradual weakening of beliefs. Religious zeal, they said, was bound to die down as enlightenment and freedom spread. It is tiresome that the facts do not fit this theory at all.

There are sections of the population in Europe where unbelief goes hand in hand with brutishness and ignorance, whereas in America the most free and enlightened people in the world zealously perform all the external duties of religion.

The religious atmosphere of the country was the first thing that struck me on arrival in the United States. The longer I stayed in the country, the more conscious I became of the important political consequences resulting from this novel situation.

In France I had seen the spirits of religion and of freedom almost always marching in opposite directions. In America I found them intimately linked together in joint reign over the same land.

My longing to understand the reason for this phenomenon increased daily.

To find this out, I questioned the faithful of all communions; I particularly sought the society of clergymen, who are the depositaries of the various creeds and have a personal interest in their survival. As a practicing Catholic I was particularly close to the Catholic priests, with some of whom I soon established a certain intimacy. I expressed my astonishment and revealed my doubts to each of them; I found that they all agreed with each other except about details; all thought that the main reason for the quiet sway of religion over their country was the complete separation of church and state. I have no hesitation in stating that throughout my stay in America I met nobody, lay or cleric, who did not agree about that.

• • •

In several states the law, and in all the rest public opinion, excludes them from a career in politics.

When I finally came to inquire into the attitudes of the clergy themselves, I found that most of them seemed voluntarily to steer clear of power and to take a sort of professional pride in claiming that it was no concern of theirs.

I heard them pronouncing anathemas against ambition and bad faith, under whatsoever political opinions those were at pains to hide. But I learned from their discourses that men are not guilty in the sight of God because of these very opinions, provided they are sincere, and that it is no more a sin to make a mistake in some question of government than it is a sin to go wrong in building one's house or plowing one's field.

I saw that they were careful to keep clear of all parties, shunning contact with them with all the anxiety attendant upon personal interest.

These facts convinced me that I had been told the truth. I then wished to trace the facts down to their causes. I wondered how it could come about that by diminishing the apparent power of religion one increased its real strength, and I thought it not impossible to discover the reason.

The short space of sixty years can never shut in the whole of man's imagination; the incomplete joys of this world will never satisfy his heart. Alone among all created beings, man shows a natural disgust for existence and an immense longing to exist; he scorns life and fears annihilation. These different instincts constantly drive his soul toward contemplation of the next world, and it is religion that leads him thither. Religion, therefore, is only one particular form of hope, and it is as natural to the human heart as hope itself. It is by a sort of intellectual aberration, and in a way, by doing moral violence to their own nature, that men detach themselves from religious beliefs; an invincible inclination draws them back. Incredulity is an accident; faith is the only permanent state of mankind.

Considering religions from a purely human point of view, one can then say that all religions derive an element of strength which will never fail from man himself, because it is attached to one of the constituent principles of human nature.

I know that, apart from influence proper to itself, religion can at times rely on the artificial strength of laws and the support of the material powers that direct society. There have been religions intimately linked to earthly governments, dominating men's souls both by terror and by faith; but when a religion makes such an alliance, I am not afraid to say that it makes the same mistake as any man might; it sacrifices the future for the present, and by gaining a power to which it has no claim, it risks its legitimate authority.

When a religion seeks to found its sway only on the longing for immortality equally tormenting every human heart, it can aspire to universality; but when it comes to uniting itself with a government, it must adopt maxims which apply only to certain nations. Therefore, by allying itself with any political power, religion increases its strength over some but forfeits the hope of reigning over all.

Why Democratic Nations Show a More Ardent and Enduring Love for Equality Than for Liberty

The first and liveliest of the passions inspired by equality is, I need not say, love of that equality itself. My readers will therefore not be surprised if I speak of that before all the others.

Everybody has noticed that in our age, and especially in France, this passion for equality is daily acquiring a greater hold over the human heart. It has been said a hundred times that our contemporaries love equality much more ardently and tenaciously than liberty. But I do not think that anyone has yet adequately explained the reason for this fact. I will try to do so.

It is possible to imagine an extreme point at which freedom and equality would meet and blend.

Let us suppose that all the citizens take a part in the government and that each of them has an equal right to do so.

Then, no man is different from his fellows, and nobody can wield tyrannical power; men will be perfectly free because they are entirely equal, and they will be perfectly equal because they are entirely free. Democratic peoples are tending toward that ideal.

That is the completest possible form for equality on this earth. But there are a thousand other forms which, though less perfect, are no less cherished by those nations.

There can be established equality in civil society, though there is none in the world of politics. One can have the right to enjoy the same pleasures, to engage in the same professions, and to meet in the same places—in a word, to live in the same manner and seek wealth by the same means—without all taking the same part in the government.

There can even be a sort of equality in the world of politics without any political freedom. A man may be the equal of all his fellows save one, who is the master of all without distinction and chooses the agents of his power equally from among all.

One can easily invent several other hypotheses in which a great deal of equality is easily combined with institutions more or less free, or even not free at all.

Although men cannot be absolutely equal without being entirely free, and consequently equality, in its most extreme form must merge with freedom, there is good reason to distinguish one from the other.

So men's taste for freedom and their taste for equality are in fact distinct, and, I have no hesitation in adding, among democracies they are two unequal elements.

On close inspection one finds in every age some peculiar and predominating element which controls all the rest. This element almost always engenders some seminal thought or ruling passion which in the end drags all other feelings and ideas along in its course. It is like a great river which seems to make all surrounding rivulets flow toward it.

Freedom is found at different times and in different forms; it is not exclusively dependent on one social state, and one finds it elsewhere than in democracies. It cannot therefore be taken as the distinctive characteristic of democratic ages.

The particular and predominating fact peculiar to those ages is equality of conditions, and the chief passion which stirs men at such times is the love of this same equality.

Do not ask what singular charm the men of democratic ages find in living as equals or what special reason they may have for clinging so tenaciously to equality rather than the other advantages society offers. Equality forms the distinctive characteristic of the age in which they live. That is enough to explain why they prefer it to all the rest.

But apart from that reason there are several others which at all times lead men to prefer equality to liberty.

If a people could ever succeed in destroying or even diminishing the equality prevailing in its body social, it could only do so by long and laborious efforts. They would have to modify their social condition, repeal their laws, supersede their opinions, change their habits, and alter their mores. But political liberty is easily lost; neglect to hold it fast, and it is gone.

Men therefore hold on to equality not only because it is precious to them; they are also attached to it because they think it will last forever.

Nobody is so limited and superficial as not to realize that political liberty can, if carried to excess, endanger the peace, property, and lives of individuals. But only perceptive and clear-sighted men see the dangers with which equality threatens us, and they generally avoid pointing them out. They see that the troubles they fear are distant and console themselves that they will only fall on future generations, for which the present generation hardly cares. The ills which liberty brings may be immediate; all can see them and all, more or less, feel them. The ills produced by extreme equality only become apparent little by little; they gradually insinuate themselves into the body social; they are only occasionally noticed, and when they do become most excessive, habit has already made them pass unfelt.

The good things that freedom brings are seen only as time passes, and it is always easy to mistake the cause that brought them about.

The advantages of equality are felt immediately, and it is daily apparent where they come from.

Political liberty occasionally gives sublime pleasure to a few.

Equality daily gives each man in the crowd a host of small enjoyments. The charms of equality are felt the whole time and are within the reach of all; the noblest spirits appreciate them and the commonest minds exult in them. The passion engendered by equality is therefore both strong and general.

Men cannot enjoy political liberty without some sacrifice, and they have never won it without great effort. But equality offers its pleasures free; each little incident in life occasions them, and to taste them one needs but to live.

Democratic peoples always like equality, but there are times when their passion for it turns to delirium. This happens when the old social hierarchy, long menaced, finally collapses after a severe internal struggle and the barriers of rank are at length thrown down. At such times men pounce on equality as their booty and cling to it as a precious treasure they fear to have snatched away. The passion for equality seeps into every corner of the human heart, expands, and fills the whole. It is no use telling them that by this blind surrender to an exclusive passion they are compromising their dearest interests; they are deaf. It is no use pointing out that freedom is slipping from their grasp while they look the other way; they are blind, or rather they can see but one thing to covet in the whole world.

The foregoing applies to all democratic nations, what follows only to the French.

Among most modern nations, especially those of Europe, the taste for freedom and the conception of it only began to take shape and grow at the time when social conditions were tending toward equality, and it was a consequence of that very equality. It was the absolute monarchs who worked hardest to level down ranks among their subjects. For the peoples equality had come before liberty, so equality was an established fact when freedom was still a novelty; the one had already shaped customs, opinions, and laws to its use when the other was first stepping lonely forward into broad daylight. Thus the latter was still only a matter of opinion and preference, whereas the former had already insinuated itself into popular habits, shaped mores, and given a particular twist to the slightest actions of life. Why, then, should we be surprised that our contemporaries prefer the one to the other?

I think democratic peoples have a natural taste for liberty; left to themselves, they will seek it, cherish it, and be sad if it is taken from them. But their passion for equality is ardent, insatiable, eternal, and invincible. They want equality in freedom, and if they cannot have that, they still want equality in slavery. They will put up with poverty, servitude, and barbarism, but they will not endure aristocracy.

This is true at all times, but especially in our own. All men and all powers who try to stand up against this irresistible passion will be overthrown and destroyed by it. In our day freedom cannot be established without it, and despotism itself cannot reign without its support.

Of Individualism in Democracies

I have shown how, in ages of equality, every man finds his beliefs within himself, and I shall now go on to show that all his feelings are turned in on himself.

"Individualism" is a word recently coined to express a new idea. Our fathers only knew about egoism.

Egoism is a passionate and exaggerated love of self which leads a man to think of all things in terms of himself and to prefer himself to all.

Individualism is a calm and considered feeling which disposes each citizen to isolate himself from the mass of his fellows and withdraw into the circle of family and friends; with this little society formed to his taste, he gladly leaves the greater society to look after itself.

Egoism springs from a blind instinct; individualism is based on misguided judgment rather than depraved feeling. It is due more to inadequate understanding than to perversity of heart.

Egoism sterilizes the seeds of every virtue; individualism at first only dams the spring of public virtues, but in the long run it attacks and destroys all the others too and finally merges in egoism.

Egoism is a vice as old as the world. It is not peculiar to one form of society more than another.

Individualism is of democratic origin and threatens to grow as conditions get more equal.

Among aristocratic nations families maintain the same station for centuries and often live in the same place. So there is a sense in which all the generations are contemporaneous. A man almost always knows about his ancestors and respects them; his imagination extends to his great-grandchildren, and he loves them. He freely does his duty by both ancestors and descendants and often sacrifices personal pleasures for the sake of beings who are no longer alive or are not yet born.

Moreover, aristocratic institutions have the effect of linking each man closely with several of his fellows.

Each class in an aristocratic society, being clearly and permanently limited, forms, in a sense, a little fatherland for all its members, to which they are attached by more obvious and more precious ties than those linking them to the fatherland itself.

Each citizen of an aristocratic society has his fixed station, one above another, so that there is always someone above him whose protection he needs and someone below him whose help he may require.

So people living in an aristocratic age are almost always closely involved with something outside themselves, and they are often inclined to forget about themselves. It is true that in these ages the general conception of *human fellowship* is dim and that men hardly ever think of devoting themselves to the cause of humanity, but men do often make sacrifices for the sake of certain other men.

In democratic ages, on the contrary, the duties of each to all are much clearer but devoted service to any individual much rarer. The bonds of human affection are wider but more relaxed.

Among democratic peoples new families continually rise from nothing while others fall, and nobody's position is quite stable. The woof of time is ever being broken and the track of past generations lost. Those who have gone before are easily forgotten, and no one gives a thought to those who will follow. All a man's interests are limited to those near himself.

As each class catches up with the next and gets mixed with it, its members do not care about one another and treat one another as strangers. Aristocracy links everybody, from peasant to king, in one long chain. Democracy breaks the chain and frees each link.

As social equality spreads there are more and more people who, though neither rich nor powerful enough to have much hold over others, have gained or kept enough wealth and enough understanding to look after their own needs. Such folk owe no man anything and hardly expect anything from anybody. They form the habit of thinking of themselves in isolation and imagine that their whole destiny is in their own hands.

Thus, not only does democracy make men forget their ancestors, but also clouds their view of their descendants and isolates them from their contemporaries. Each man is forever thrown back on himself alone, and there is danger that he may be shut up in the solitude of his own heart.

How Individualism Is More Pronounced at the End of a Democratic Revolution Than at Any Other Time

It is just at the moment when a democratic society is establishing itself on the ruins of an aristocracy that this isolation of each man from the rest and the egoism resulting therefrom stand out clearest.

Not only are there many independent people in such a society, but their number is constantly increasing with more and more of those who have just attained independence and are drunk with their new power. These latter have a presumptuous confidence in their strength, and never imagining that they could ever need another's help again, they have no inhibition about showing that they care for nobody but themselves.

There is usually a prolonged struggle before an aristocracy gives way, and in the course of that struggle implacable hatreds have been engendered between the classes. Such passions last after victory, and one can see traces of them in the ensuing democratic confusion.

Those who once held the highest ranks in the subverted hierarchy cannot forget their ancient greatness at once and for a long time feel themselves strangers in the new society. They regard all those whom society now makes their equals as oppressors whose fate could not concern them; they have lost sight of their former equals and no longer feel tied by common interests to their lot; each of them, in his separate retreat, feels reduced to taking care of himself alone. But those formerly at the bottom of the social scale and now brought up to the common level by a sudden revolution cannot enjoy their new-found independence without some secret uneasiness: there is a look of fear mixed with triumph in their eyes if they do meet one of their former superiors, and they avoid them.

Therefore it is usually at the time when democratic societies are taking root that men are most disposed to isolate themselves.

There is a tendency in democracy not to draw men together, but democratic revolutions make them run away from each other and perpetuate, in the midst of equality, hatreds originating in inequality.

The Americans have this great advantage, that they attained democracy without the sufferings of a democratic revolution and that they were born equal instead of becoming so.

How the Americans Combat the Effects of Individualism by Free Institutions

Despotism, by its very nature suspicious, sees the isolation of men as the best guarantee of its own permanence. So it usually does all it can to isolate them. Of all the vices of the human heart egoism is that which suits it best. A despot will lightly forgive his subjects for not loving him, provided they do not love one another. He does not ask them to help him guide the state;

it is enough if they do not claim to manage it themselves. He calls those who try to unite their efforts to create a general prosperity "turbulent and restless spirits," and twisting the natural meaning of words, he calls those "good citizens" who care for none but themselves.

Thus vices originating in despotism are precisely those favored by equality. The two opposites fatally complete and support each other.

Equality puts men side by side without a common link to hold them firm. Despotism raises barriers to keep them apart. It disposes them not to think of their fellows and turns indifference into a sort of public virtue.

Despotism, dangerous at all times, is therefore particularly to be feared in ages of democracy.

It is easy to see that in such ages men have a peculiar need for freedom.

Citizens who are bound to take part in public affairs must turn from the private interests and occasionally take a look at something other than themselves.

As soon as common affairs are treated in common, each man notices that he is not as independent of his fellows as he used to suppose and that to get their help he must often offer his aid to them.

When the public governs, all men feel the value of public goodwill and all try to win it by gaining the esteem and affection of those among whom they must live.

Those frigid passions that keep hearts asunder must then retreat and hide at the back of consciousness. Pride must be disguised; contempt must not be seen. Egoism is afraid of itself.

Under a free government most public officials are elected, so men whose great gifts and aspirations are too closely circumscribed in private life daily feel that they cannot do without the people around them.

It thus happens that ambition makes a man care for his fellows, and, in a sense, he often finds his self-interest in forgetting about himself. I know that one can point to all the intrigues caused by an election, the dishonorable means often used by candidates, and the calumnies spread by their enemies. These do give rise to feelings of hatred, and the more frequent the elections, the worse they are.

Those are great ills, no doubt but passing ones, whereas the benefits that attend them remain.

Eagerness to be elected may, for the moment, make particular men fight each other, but in the long run this same aspiration induces mutual helpfulness on the part of all; and while it may happen that the accident of an election estranges two friends, the electoral system forges permanent links between a great number of citizens who might otherwise have remained forever strangers to one another. Liberty engenders particular hatreds, but despotism is responsible for general indifference.

The Americans have used liberty to combat the individualism born of equality, and they have won.

The lawgivers of America did not suppose that a general representation of the whole nation would suffice to ward off a disorder at once so natural to the body social of a democracy and so fatal. They thought it also right to give each part of the land its own political life so that there should be an infinite number of occasions for the citizens to act together and so that every day they should feel that they depended on one another.

That was wise conduct.

The general business of a country keeps only the leading citizens occupied. It is only occasionally that they come together in the same places, and since they often lose sight of one another, no lasting bonds form between them. But when the people who live there have to look after the particular affairs of a district, the same people are always meeting, and they are forced, in a manner, to know and adapt themselves to one another.

It is difficult to force a man out of himself and get him to take an interest in the affairs of the whole state, for he has little understanding of the way in which the fate of the state can influence his own lot. But if it is a question of taking a road past his property, he sees at once that this small public matter has a bearing on his greatest private interests, and there is no need to point out to him the close connection between his private profit and the general interest.

Thus, far more may be done by entrusting citizens with the management of minor affairs than by handing over control of great matters, toward interesting them in the public welfare and convincing them that they constantly stand in need of one another in order to provide for it.

Some brilliant achievement may win a people's favor at one stroke. But to gain the affection and respect of your immediate neighbors, a long succession of little services rendered and of obscure good deeds, a constant habit of kindness and an established reputation for disinterestedness, are required.

Local liberties, then, which induce a great number of citizens to value the affection of their kindred and neighbors, bring men constantly into contact, despite the instincts which separate them, and force them to help one another.

In the United States the most opulent citizens are at pains not to get isolated from the people. On the contrary, they keep in constant contact, gladly listen and themselves talk any and every day. They know that the rich in democracies always need the poor and that good manners will draw them to them more than benefits conferred. For benefits by their very greatness spotlight the difference in conditions and arouse a secret annoyance in those who profit from them. But the charm of simple good manners is almost irresistible. Their affability carries men away, and even their vulgarity is not always unpleasant.

The rich do not immediately appreciate this truth. They generally stand out against it as long as a democratic revolution is in progress and do not admit it at once even after the revolution is accomplished. They will gladly do good to the people, but they still want carefully to keep their distance from them. They think

that that is enough, but they are wrong. They could ruin themselves in that fashion without warming their neighbors' hearts. What is wanted is not the sacrifice of their money but of their pride.

It would seem as if in the United States every man's power of invention was on the stretch to find new ways of increasing the wealth and satisfying the needs of the public. The best brains in every neighborhood are constantly employed in searching for new secrets to increase the general prosperity, and any that they find are at once at the service of the crowd.

If one takes a close look at the weaknesses and vices of many of those who bear sway in America, one is surprised at the growing prosperity of the people, but it is a mistake to be surprised. It is certainly not the elected magistrate who makes the American democracy prosper, but the fact that the magistrates are elected.

It would not be fair to assume that American patriotism and the universal zeal for the common good have no solid basis. Though private interest, in the United States as elsewhere, is the driving force behind most of men's actions, it does not regulate them all.

I have often seen Americans make really great sacrifices for the common good, and I have noticed a hundred cases in which, when help was needed, they hardly ever failed to give each other trusty support.

The free institutions of the United States and the political rights enjoyed there provide a thousand continual reminders to every citizen that he lives in society. At every moment they bring his mind back to this idea, that it is the duty as well as the interest of men to be useful to their fellows. Having no particular reason to hate others, since he is neither their slave nor their master, the American's heart easily inclines toward benevolence. At first it is of necessity that men attend to the public interest, afterward by choice. What had been calculation becomes instinct. By dint of working for the good of his fellow citizens, he in the end acquires a habit and taste for serving them.

There are many men in France who regard equality of conditions as the first of evils and political liberty as the second. When forced to submit to the former, they strive at least to escape the latter. But for my part, I maintain that there is only one effective remedy against the evils which equality may cause, and that is political liberty.

II ‖ THE PERSPECTIVE OF HISTORY

Political analysts have long recognized the existence of an American creed, that is, a core set of ideas and ideals that lies at the heart of Americans' conceptions of life and politics. Drawn ultimately but not exclusively from the writings of the political philosopher John Locke, the American creed stresses such values as liberty, equality, democracy, and justice. These ideals can broadly be called liberal in the classic sense and are shared widely by Americans.

Recognizing the existence of an American creed does not, of course, imply that all Americans share such values or that America has always lived up to these ideals. In fact, a major part of Samuel Huntington's study on American politics, from which the following selection is drawn, argues that the gap between these ideals and reality represents a key dynamic in understanding American history. Furthermore, although Americans seem to agree on the broad outlines of this creed, they disagree sharply over its precise meaning. Opponents and proponents of affirmative action programs, for example, both justify their positions in terms of a commitment to the principle of equality. And at times in American history, allegiance to this creed (or, more specifically, a particular version of it) has been unjustly made a litmus test for loyalty to the United States itself. Nevertheless, to anyone familiar with American politics, Huntington's description of the American creed resonates clearly.

Questions

1. What does Huntington mean when he suggests that the American creed is "unsystematic and unideological"? Does the creed provide clear answers to specific problems in American political life?

2. In what senses do the various elements of the creed conflict with one another? Give specific examples. How are such conflicts resolved? Have they been resolved?

4.2 American Politics: The Promise of Disharmony

Samuel P. Huntington

What are the values of the American Creed? Innumerable studies have itemized them in various ways, but the same core political values appear in virtually all analyses: liberty, equality, individualism, democracy, and the rule of law under a constitution. These are different and yet related political ideas; they stemmed from several different sources and yet came together so as to reinforce one another in the American mind in the late eighteenth and early nineteenth centuries.

These core ideas are set forth succinctly in the Declaration of Independence. More broadly, they can be thought of as involving several major elements. The oldest is the constitutional strand, with its roots in medieval ideas of fundamental law as a restraint on human behavior. Law, in this sense, was conceived of as something that was beyond human control but not beyond human knowledge. Man discovered law, he did not make it, and this law, whether viewed as divine law, natural law, or customary law, provided the norms for human behavior. In Europe in the seventeenth century, these traditional ideas of law began to be supplanted by new ideas of absolute sovereignty and the power of men—be they absolute monarchs or members of supreme parliaments—to make law as they saw fit. In that same century, however, the older ideas of fundamental law as a restraint on human action were exported to and took root on the American continent.

A second major source of the ideas of the American Creed is seventeenth-century Protestantism, which contributed elements of moralism, millennialism, and individualism to the American political outlook. More particularly, Protestantism stressed the primacy of the individual conscience, the close connection between the spirit of liberty and the spirit of religion, the role of the congregation as a voluntary association, the importance of democracy within the church and its implications for the polity ("no bishop, no king"), and, in due course, the abandonment of religious establishments. The United States is the only country in the world in which a majority of the population has belonged to dissenting Protestant sects. Protestant values reinforced republican and democratic tendencies in the eighteenth century and provided the underlying ethical and moral basis for American ideas on politics and society.

To these strands, the eighteenth century added Lockean and Enlightenment ideas of natural rights, liberty, the social contract, the limited role of government, and the dependence of government upon society. Finally, the idea of equality—set forth boldly in the Declaration of Independence as the basis for organizing society—challenged accepted ideas of the legitimacy of distinctions based on rank, status, and inherited privilege. If all men are created equal, then all must count equally politically, and hence all must have an equal right to vote for their governing officials. The basis was laid for popular sovereignty and the democratization of government in the nineteenth century. The idea of equality, one aspect of the Protestant strand in the American Creed, was thus reinforced by the democratic and revolutionary currents at the end of the eighteenth century.

Ideas of constitutionalism, individualism, liberalism, democracy, and egalitarianism are no monopoly of Americans. In some societies, some people subscribe to many of these ideas and in other societies many people subscribe to some of these ideas. In no other society, however, are all of these ideas so widely adhered to by so many people as they are in the United States.

"I hate *everybody*, regardless of race, creed, or place of national origin!"

Drawing by Peter Arno; © 1952, 9 1980 The New Yorker Magazine, Inc.

People sometimes speak of an American "ideology." But in the American mind, these ideas do not take the form of a carefully articulated, systematic ideology in the sense in which this term is used to refer to European belief systems such as traditional conservatism, liberalism, Marxism, social democracy, and Christian democracy. They constitute a complex and amorphous amalgam of goals and values, rather than a scheme for establishing priorities among values and for elaborating ways to realize values. They do not have the key characteristics that distinguish an ideology from other sets of political ideas. They are, for instance, far more diffuse, incoherent, and undeveloped intellectually than Marxism. Some have described these ideas in terms of the "liberal tradition" in America. If one had to apply one adjective to them, "liberal" would be it, but even this term does not convey the full richness and complexity of the amalgam. It thus seems more accurate and appropriate to speak of American political ideas or beliefs in the plural, and in the singular to follow Gunnar Myrdal and others and simply speak of the American Creed.

The unsystematic and unideological character of this Creed is reflected in the fact that no theory exists for ordering these values in relation to one another and for resolving on a theoretical level the conflicts that inherently exist among them. Conflicts easily materialize when any one value is taken to an extreme: majority rule versus minority rights; higher law versus popular sovereignty; liberty versus equality; individualism versus democracy. In other societies, ideologies give priority to one value or the other, but in American society all these values coexist together in theory, even as they may conflict with each other when applied in practice. They coexist, indeed, not only within American society, but also within individual citizens. Though every American may have his own view of the proper balance among these conflicting values, few Americans would unhesitatingly give absolute priority to one value over another. However much one values majority rule, at some point its application is limited by the need to recognize minority rights. However much one believes in individual liberty, at some point individual aggrandizement cannot be permitted to make a mockery of political and moral equality. The checks and balances that exist among the institutions of American politics are paralleled by the checks and balances that exist among the ideas of the American Creed. This political "ideology," as Robert McCloskey noted, is not "a consistent body of dogmas tending in the same direction, but a conglomerate of ideas which may be and often are logically inconsistent." It is "characteristic of the American mind . . . to hold contradictory ideas simultaneously without bothering to resolve the potential conflict between them."

Nowhere is this better illustrated than in the relation between liberty and equality in the American Creed. In Europe these two values are commonly thought to be inherently opposed to each other. From Plato on, political theorists saw the extension of equality as ultimately involving the destruction of liberty, as society becomes homogenized and leveled, paving the way for the rise of the despot. In the eighteenth century, liberty was the aristocratic value and equality the bourgeois democratic value; in the nineteenth century, liberty became the bourgeois value and equality the proletarian value. The expansion of equality thus involved in the eighteenth century the suppression of the rights, liberties, and privileges of estates, orders, and corporations, and in the nineteenth century the restriction of rights of contract and private property. Tocqueville's view of equality in America reflected this European experience. Few Americans have shared his fear that the expansion of equality would signal the death-knell of liberty. The American approach is instead well summed up by Michael Walzer's argument that "liberty and equality are the two chief virtues of social institutions, and they stand best when they stand together." In the United States they did historically move hand-in-hand. They developed in conjunction with, not in opposition to, each other, representing not so much the political values of opposing social classes as the opposing political values of a single middle class. The eighteenth-century value of liberty was quickly joined by the nineteenth-century value of equality. Americans generally give liberty precedence over equality, but different groups assign different weights to each, and virtually all groups give high levels of support to both values. A continuing theme of American political discourse has been the effort to reconcile one with the other, most notably in the economic sphere, where ideas of equality of opportunity coexist with ideas of liberty of achievement. Those who have been concerned with the promotion of one have generally also been concerned with the promotion of the other. "In the United States," Daniel Bell observed, "the tension between liberty and equality, which framed the great philosophical debates in Europe, was dissolved by an individualism which encompassed both." As Herbert Croly put it, "the Land of Freedom became in the course of time also the Land of Equality."

How broad has been the agreement on these ideas? The Americans, said Tocqueville in one of his most quoted remarks, "are unanimous upon the general principles that ought to rule human society." Some foreign and native observers before him and countless numbers after him have reiterated this point. "Americans," Gunnar Myrdal argued, echoing Tocqueville's language one hundred years later, "of all national origins, classes, regions, creeds, and colors, have something in common: a social *ethos*, a political creed." In the mid-twentieth century, the validity of these impressionistic observations was underscored by the overwhelming evidence provided by public opinion poll data. Such data indicated that the key values of the American liberal-democratic Creed commanded the support of well over 75 percent of the population. When the key values and principles of the American Creed are expressed in highly general terms, support of liberty, democracy, majority rule, minority rights, freedom of speech and religion, and, less clearly, equality approaches unanimity from virtually all groups in the American public. As the formulation of values is made more specific and related to concrete applications of these values to particular situations, support drops off considerably and cleavage may become more pronounced than consensus. In such circumstances, those who have more education, who are more active in politics, or who occupy leadership positions in community organizations are more likely to support the values of the Creed. The consensus on the values of the system, in short, is broadest among those most active in the system and who benefit the most from it. Those with higher socioeconomic status also are less likely than those of lower status to perceive major differences between the values of the system and the reality of the system. In terms of overall preferences, however, there would appear to be little doubt that, as one comprehensive analysis in the early 1970s concluded, "the United States has had a high degree of consensus on fundamental political values at the community and regime levels."

The broad agreement that has existed throughout American history on these values is reflected in the fate of potential alternative political value systems. Such systems could only develop where there was some social and economic base to nurture political beliefs different from those that generally prevailed. Three such bases—regional, class and ethnic—conceivably have existed at one time or another in American history.

The most significant effort to develop an alternative set of political values was that which occurred in the prebellum South. A society based on slavery clearly contradicted virtually all the core values of the American Creed. As a result, as the slave system came under increasing attack after 1830, Southern writers and thinkers developed a highly articulate and systematic conservative defense of the society built on that foundation. Resorting to classic conservative ideas and arguments which historically had been used to defend many other types of societies, they strove to develop an ideological alternative, and the writings of the "Reactionary Enlightenment," to use Hartz's term, constitute an outpouring of political theorizing unique in American history. Conservative ideas were, for them, a weapon to be used to defend their society against the growing economic and demographic preponderance of the North and the intensifying ideological assault of the abolitionists. Their substantive theory, however, remained ambivalent. Wishing to retain what they could of their Jeffersonian heritage, they wavered uncertainly between the philosophies of John Locke and Sir Robert Filmer. In the end, when their society was destroyed in the Civil War, their efforts at alternative political theory died too and were quickly forgotten.

The rapid industrialization that followed the Civil War necessarily involved the creation of an industrial proletariat which, presumably, created the socioeconomic base for a socialist movement comparable to those that were simultaneously emerging in Europe. The failure of such a movement to develop mass political appeal is perhaps the most dramatic evidence of the preponderance of liberal-democratic values in America. The issue of "Why no socialism in the United States?" has been explored at length by a variety of social scientists beginning with Marx and Engels, and various causes have been assigned a variety of weights. The absence of feudalism permitted the unchallenged spread of liberal, bourgeois values and this, in turn, prevented socialism from developing significant appeal: in effect, "no feudalism, no socialism." In addition, the nature of the original settlers (particularly those of the dissenting and separatist religious sects), the abundance of free land, and the opportunities of horizontal and then vertical mobility all promoted the dominance of the middle class. In an agricultural society the basic form of wealth is land, and in most agricultural societies the amount of land is always limited and usually fixed. The population is permanently divided between those who own land and those who do not or between those who own more land and those who own less. In America, however, no such division of the people could last. The opportunities for land ownership were too real. The resulting failure (outside the plantation South) to develop a system of agricultural classes and the pervasiveness of a "free-farmer society" set the pattern of relative abundance and relative mobility which survived industrialization and urbanization and ensured the widespread adoption of middle-class values and standards.

Although the first working-class parties in the modern world were formed in the United States in the 1830s, industrialization failed to produce a class-conscious working-class movement committed to Marxism or some other form of socialism. This was a result of the prior achievement of universal while male suffrage, the general openness of political institutions, the continuing opportunities for vertical and horizontal mobility, the ethnic diversity and geographic dispersion of the working class, and the preexisting prevalence of the liberal-democratic norms of the American Creed. In some measure, the latter, with their stress on equality and mobility, served indeed as a surrogate form of socialism.

A third possible social base for an alternative to liberal democracy was furnished by the massive influx of poor immigrants with peasant backgrounds from southern and eastern Europe at the end of the nineteenth and beginning of the twentieth centuries. These immigrants, Hofstadter argued, brought with them an outlook that contrasted dramatically with the prevailing values and moralistic emphases based "upon the indigenous Yankee-Protestant political traditions, and upon middle-class life." This other system,

> founded upon the European backgrounds of the immigrants, upon their unfamiliarity with independent political action, their familiarity with hierarchy and authority, and upon the urgent needs that so often grew out of their migration, took for granted that the political life of the individual would arise out of family needs, interpreted political and civic relations chiefly in terms of personal obligations, and placed strong personal loyalties above allegiance to abstract codes of law or morals. It was chiefly upon this system of values that the political life of the immigrant, the boss, and the urban machine was based.

The interaction between the immigrant ethic and the indigenous ethic provides one way of looking at changes in American politics during the first half of the twentieth century.

The immigrant ethic left its mark upon American political organization and practice, particularly during the New Deal years. But by the early 1960s, the most important development in urban politics was precisely the extent to which the immigrants and their children were replacing their own traditional ethos with that which had been traditional in the United States. "The immigrant lower class has been and is still being absorbed into the middle class at a rapid rate. This has profoundly affected the outlook of the electorate, for the middle class has always held to the Anglo-Saxon Protestant political ideal and those who have joined it have accepted this ideal along with others. . . . Increasingly the 'new immigrant' has come to demand candidates who, whatever their origins, have the community-serving ethos and the public virtues that have long been associated with the Protestant elite." The subsequent political events of the 1960s and 1970s confirmed the perspicacity of this analysis. The enhanced significance of ethnic power in American politics was paralleled by the withering of the ethnic ethic in American politics.

No lasting and significant alternatives to the liberal-democratic value system have emerged in the United States. In this respect, the basic proposition of the consensus paradigm is valid. There is, however, still the possibility that the content of the consensus, the mix of values in the liberal-democratic amalgam, may have changed over time. Are the predominant American political values of the late twentieth century basically the same as those of the late eighteenth century? By and large, the classic (that is, Tocquevillian) answer to this question has stressed the continuity in American values: "Two things are surprising in the United States: the mutability of the greater part of human actions, and the singular stability of certain principles. Men are in constant motion; the mind of man appears almost unmoved. When once an opinion has spread over the country and struck root there, it would seem that no power on earth is strong enough to eradicate it. . . . Cogent reasons . . . prevent any great change from being easily effected in the principles of a democratic people."

Well over a century later, the judgments of mid-twentieth-century social scientists generally confirmed Tocqueville's conclusion. "Though there were shadings through time," argued Clyde Kluckhohn in 1958, "the central and distinctive aspects of the American value system were remarkably stable from the eighteenth century until the [nineteen] thirties and, in spite of some changes that have occurred and are in process, the characteristic American values remain highly influential in the life of the United States." Five years later Seymour Martin Lipset concluded that "there is more continuity than change with respect to the main elements in the national value system." In 1967 Lloyd Free and Hadley Cantril argued that the Mayflower Compact, John Locke, and the Declaration of Independence "reflect the basic political values that have shaped the American political system for nearly three hundred and fifty years. . . . The underlying personal political credos of the majority of Americans have remained substantially intact at the ideological level." An exhaustive survey in 1972 led Donald Devine to affirm in similar language that "the values of Locke, Madison, and the other liberals of the seventeenth and eighteenth centuries represent essentially the same values which comprise the American political culture at the present. Although it has changed, the remarkable phenomenon is that American political culture has survived so unchanged under substantial environmental pressure."

The relative lack of change in American political values is also reflected in the way in which three distinguished European observers summarized the prevailing values at three different points in American history. From Maine to the Floridas, Tocqueville argued,

> and from the Missouri to the Atlantic Ocean, the people are held to be the source of all legitimate power. The same notions are entertained respecting liberty and equality, the liberty of the press, the right of association, the jury, and the responsibility of the agents of government.
> . . . The Anglo-Americans acknowledge the moral authority of the reason of the community as they acknowledge the political authority of the mass of citizens; and they hold that public opinion is the surest arbiter of what is lawful or forbidden, true or false. The majority of them believe that a man by following his own interest, rightly understood, will be led to do what is just and good. They hold that every man is born in possession of the right of self-government, and that no one has the right of constraining his fellow creatures to be happy. They have all a lively faith in the perfectibility of man.

A half-century after Tocqueville, James Bryce summed up the principal elements of the Creed in strikingly similar fashion: (1) the individual has sacred rights; (2) the source of political power is the people; (3) all governments are limited by law and the people; (4) local government is to be preferred to national government; (5) the majority is wiser than the minority; (6) the less government the better. A half-century after Bryce, Gunnar Myrdal argued that Americans had in common a creed of "humanistic liberalism," which developed out of the Enlightenment and which embodied the "ideals of the essential dignity of the individual human being, of the fundamental equality of all men, and of inalienable rights to freedom, justice, and a fair opportunity."

All this suggests little change in basic American political values. In the 1950s, however, the thesis was advanced that fundamental changes were taking place in both American national character and American values. The "inner-directed" person was giving way to the "other-directed" person; the group was replacing the individual; the traditional, Puritan, moralistic style and its associated values were being supplanted by a more tolerant, more relativistic, more socially oriented and less achievement-directed style and set of values. If this thesis was valid, it would suggest that substantial changes were under way in the content of the American consensus and that, at least for a time, the consensus would be disrupted along generational and perhaps class lines.

The change thesis was, however, dubious for three reasons. First, a persuasive case was made that the attitudes and values presented by the change thesis as new developments on the American scene had actually figured prominently in descriptions of America by foreign observers since the early nineteenth century. What the change thesis argued was new was, in fact, actually old. Second, the 1960s saw a recrudescence of individualism and moral passion in American politics, as intense as any in American history. What the change thesis argued was passé, in fact turned out to be present a decade later. Finally, the evidence is mixed concerning the extent to which the change thesis holds valid for personal values. Looking at children's reading texts, for example, inner-directed achievement imagery increased during the nineteenth century, then decreased in the twentieth at the same time that other-directed affiliation imagery increased. Surveys of children's ideals (that is, whom they would most like to resemble) during the first six decades of the twentieth century, however, do not show any significant shift away from achievement motivation or any change in aspiration levels. With respect to political values, the evidence overwhelmingly suggests a high level of continuity. Writings purporting to identify peculiarly American traits or values in four different periods of American history (pre–Civil War, 1865–1917, 1918–1933, 1933–1940) showed "no important difference between the traits mentioned by modern observers and those writing in the earlier periods of American history." Traits such as democracy, equality, and freedom were mentioned in all four periods. The verbal symbols in Presidential inaugural addresses also changed little during the first one hundred fifty years of American history. While clearly ideals such as liberty and equality acquire different meanings through their application in new contexts, the core meaning of the value remains. It is, indeed, reaffirmed by being continually reapplied.

III  TRENDS

If, as de Tocqueville suggests, American political culture pervades all areas of life in the United States, we can learn a good deal about American politics from looking at other areas of popular culture. In the following excerpt from a book that seeks to explain Ronald Reagan's appeal to the American electorate, John Kenneth White sur-

veys American cinema and television to gain some insights into the values on which Reagan's popularity rested.

White suggests that Reagan's appeal—like that of many recent television shows and movies—reflects a nostalgic desire to return to traditional values and a more traditional way of life. This nostalgia for the 1940s and 1950s reflects, perhaps, the same trends in American political culture noted in the preceding essays by de Tocqueville and Huntington.

Questions

1. How have politicians attempted in recent years to capitalize on the nostalgia for traditional values that White illustrates in the following selection?

2. What is the connection between these traditional values and religion in America?

4.3 The New Politics of Old Values

John Kenneth White

In 1968 Joe McGinniss wrote an expose of the Nixon campaign's advertising strategy titled *The Selling of the President 1968*. Should there be a sequel, *The Selling of the President 1988* would have to account for a revolution in the economic and political marketplaces. Consider: Nearly twenty years ago Beatle John Lennon was singing a tune called "Revolution." Student demonstrators in Paris were successfully ousting Charles de Gaulle from power, while in the United States protestors against the Vietnam War were marching in the streets. Now the song is used as a jingle on television commercials for Nike athletic sneakers. Company spokesman Kevin Brown says the ad "wouldn't have worked" a decade ago, but " 'Revolution can be interpreted differently today"—meaning the overthrow not of an unpopular government, but a revolution in public attitudes toward physical fitness.

Another sign of the times is the changing patterns in circulation of men's magazines. Two decades ago more American boys came of age than at any other time in history. Subscribers to *Playboy* in 1972 totaled seven million; circulation

now is slightly more than three million. Other indicators tell of the bunny's slowed hop: corporate profits fell from $19.3 million in 1981 to $2.5 million just six years later. Advertising pages shrank 17 percent in the same period. *Playboy,* it seemed, was undergoing a mid-life crisis.

Changing demographic patterns accounted for only a portion of *Playboy*'s woes. Attacks on the magazine came from several quarters, including the attorney general's office. Edwin Meese fought to have it removed from drugstore racks, where it was often within easy reach of children. A commission appointed by the nation's chief law enforcement officer gave warning of action unless stores voluntarily removed *Playboy* and other similar publications such as *Penthouse, Hustler,* and *Playgirl* from their shelves. Many complied—including the 7-Eleven chain—prompting *Playboy* to feature a "Girls from 7-Eleven" layout in one issue.

Fundamentalists applauded the Reagan administration's actions, but the political threat *Playboy* and the other "skin magazines" faced came not so much from Meese or the born-again

Reprinted by permission of Steve Artley.

Christians as from the altered values of Americans generally. Similarly, the wives of U.S. Senator Albert Gore and Treasury Secretary James Baker launched a campaign to expunge sexual innuendo from rock music lyrics.

The Meese-Gore-Baker efforts were not hatched in a smoke-filled room. Instead, they reflected the celebration of family values that began in the early 1980s. Karlyn Keen, managing editor of *Public Opinion*, observed that the celebration of the family has become the norm on television. "The Diors have married and have had a child. Charlie, the independent Revlon woman, is rumored to be getting engaged."

Sex, particularly promiscuous sex, is no longer condoned. Female rock singer Madonna sings about keeping her out-of-wedlock baby and marrying her boyfriend in "Papa, Don't Preach." Male vocalist Huey Lewis proclaims it is "Hip To Be Square." The AIDS epidemic encouraged this move toward monogamy, but the trend was in place long before the virus left central Africa. Beginning with its June 1987 issue, *Playboy* featured fewer nudes and more articles on issues and ideas along with advice on fashion, cooking, driving, and vacationing.

Clearly, presidents do not make the times, they reflect them. When some members of Congress began to talk of a tax increase, Reagan promised a veto using Clint Eastwood's famous movie line: "Go ahead. Make my day!" On another occasion when discussing the military budget, Reagan likened the uniforms to "Pentagon wardrobe."

Presidents, especially Reagan, do more than lift an occasional phrase from a movie. They mirror a national mood that is often captured in film or on record. During World War II, American culture reflected the preoccupation with the war effort. The most popular songs in 1942 were "Praise the Lord and Pass the Ammunition," "The Fuehrer's Face," and "You're a Sap, Mr. Jap." Theatre marquees boasted titles such as *Wake Island, Atlantic Convoy, One of Our Aircraft Is Missing, Torpedo Boat, Remember Pearl Harbor,* and *Flying Tigers.* Even advertisements signaled the nation's war mentality. Munsingwear's advertisements of undergarments for women pictured a WAC saying, "Don't tell me bulges are patriotic." Sergeant's Flea Powder showed "Old Sarge" exclaiming, "Sighted flea—killed same." Best-sellers included John Scott's *Duel for Europe,* Ethel Vance's *Reprisal,* and Herbert Agar's *A Time for Greatness.*

The premise of these works was that the United States was the most blessed land on earth, and its people were exceptional. In his last inaugural address Franklin Roosevelt declared that God had given the American people "stout hearts and strong arms with which to strike mighty blows for freedom and truth." Roosevelt added that the nation was possessed with a "faith which has become the hopes of all peoples in an anguished world."

By 1979 America had become part of an "anguished world." Jimmy Carter gave his malaise speech; in it he said he felt the nation's "pain"—mirroring the national funk. During the last two years of his administration, the most popular movies were *Coming Home* and *The Deerhunter,* each a bitter denunciation of the Vietnam War and the government that prosecuted it. In the bookstores Bob Woodward and Carl Bernstein's *The Final Days,* an unflattering account of the Nixon presidency, was a bestseller. Other books emulated Carter's predilection for self-examination, particularly Gail Sheehy's *Passages* and Alex Haley's *Roots.* Still others were filled with foreboding about the future; foremost among these was Howard J. Ruff's 1979 best-seller, *How to Prosper During the Coming Bad Years.*

Today the marketplace echoes the mood of another time—the 1950s. In the summer of 1987 Annette Funicello, aged forty-four, and Frankie Avalon, aged forty-six, headlined theatre marquees in *Back to the Beach,* a sequel to the "beach-blanket" movies they made decades before. The cast of "The Andy Griffith Show" was reunited in a made-for-television movie, as were the surviving actors of the "Perry Mason" series. And the stranded passengers on "Gilligan's Island" were finally rescued in a highly rated sequel.

No one is more sensitive to the power of film than Reagan. ABC News anchor Peter Jennings says that Reagan has always "brought his past forward, forward, forward with him." The themes of heroism, faith, and patriotism liberally season the presidential rhetoric. There are equally heavy doses of these in the movies Reagan made when he was an actor. In the touchstone 1940 film *Knute Rockne—All American,* Reagan as George Gipp says of his coach, "He's given us something they don't teach in schools.

Something clean and strong inside. Not just courage, but a right way of living none of us will ever forget." A year later in *King's Row*—a title derived from a fictional village that was "a good place to live"—Reagan took the part of a playboy who found himself penniless when his fortune vanished with an absconding bank officer. At the film's conclusion Reagan's legs are amputated by a self-righteous surgeon who disapproved of the playboy's life-style. Upon awakening Reagan delivers his famous line, "Where's the rest of me?" *King's Row* reflects the values espoused by the New Deal. The "common man" is shown in combat with the conniving "economic royalists" whom Roosevelt denounced—a plethora of bad guys taking away their money and political power.

For more than a decade Reagan's movies continued to evoke New Deal–like themes. The 1951 film *Bedtime for Bonzo* features Reagan as a psychology professor who was engaged to marry the dean's daughter, that is, until the dean learns that the professor's father was a hardened criminal. Says Reagan, "Given a decent start in life, my father would have gone as far in the right direction as he went in the wrong one." To prove it, he adopts a chimpanzee and tries to rear him as a human child. Bonzo, the chimp, often makes Reagan look every bit as crooked as his jailbird father, but in the final scenes Bonzo shows the very altruism Reagan has been trying to instill—proving Reagan innocent and the New Deal triumphant.

Reagan's subsequent films reflected his growing conservatism. In *Hellcats of the Navy,* the only movie he made with his wife Nancy, Reagan shows no remorse at killing enemy and friendly soldiers alike. In one scene he leaves a crewman for dead, supposedly to ensure the safety of all. The dead sailor, however, had been a rival for Nancy's love.

The themes of heroism, patriotism, and family that form so many of Reagan's movie and political lines have become a ubiquitous hallmark. Heroism, especially the depiction of ordinary men and women succeeding against the odds, is the order of the day. *Indiana Jones and the Temple of Doom* depicts a pistol-toting Harrison Ford overcoming the odds against an evil empire. The *Star Wars* films show an embattled Luke Skywalker and his companions (including Ford, again) waging war against Darth Vader. The advertisement for *Ghostbusters* reads, "They're here to save the world." Clint Eastwood pummels ne'er-do-wells of every sort in his *Dirty Harry* movies.

Optimism is also regnant. In *Back to the Future* Michael J. Fox, a.k.a. Marty McFly, returns to the year 1955. The film is filled with delicious irony. In one scene Marty is asked by his mentor, Doc Brown, who the president of the United States is in 1985. When Marty answers, "Ronald Reagan," Brown retorts, "And I suppose Jerry Lewis is Vice-President?" Before travelling three decades backward in time, McFly's parents are the antithesis of the American dream. Lorraine is an alcoholic, and George is a none-too-successful, white-collar employee whose supervisor is his former high school tormentor, Biff. When Marty returns to 1985—after having made some changes in the past—his parents are living the dream fulfilled. Lorraine is a more wholesome character, and George is a very successful science fiction writer. Their surroundings are beautiful, and their healthy financial picture is depicted in their leisurely return from a Saturday morning at the golf course.

Marty literally falls down at the sight, particularly in one scene where his father gives his nettlesome high school friend, Biff, orders to wash the car (Biff has been demoted to car washer). Three times—in the past, present, and future—the characters remind one another of the adage: "If you put your mind to it, you can accomplish anything." As to the future, old Doc Brown, the inventor of the time machine, says: "Where we're going, we don't need roads." (Reagan quoted this line in his 1986 State of the Union Address.)

The man who best exemplifies the new mood is not Reagan—although he comes close—but auto magnate Lee Iacocca. To borrow a slogan from the army's television advertisements, he is a good illustration of the "be-all-you-can-be" American. In 1985 Iacocca received more than eleven million dollars as chairman of the board of the Chrysler Corporation—number thirteen on the "Fortune 500" list. Often called the country's "first corporate folk hero," this son of Italian immigrants began life in humble Allentown, Pennsylvania. He did not attend college—no money for that sort of luxury—but started a career as a car salesman. Iacocca's ability to sell was so great that he attracted the attention of Henry Ford II, who had him transferred to company headquarters in Detroit. There Iacocca was involved in designing Ford's most successful car, the Mustang. From that triumph he went on to become president of the company, but was later fired by Ford and demoted to an insignificant office that he described as "little more than a small cubicle with a desk and telephone." Iacocca's motto, given to him by his wife, was "Don't get mad; get even." Adhering to that adage, the ex-Ford president moved to more spacious quarters at the Chrysler Corporation, where he was installed as its chief executive.

Iacocca came to Chrysler at a time when, due to poor management and the popularity of Japanese imported cars, the company was floundering on the edge of bankruptcy. It took a controversial loan guarantee from the federal government—an action supported by the Carter administration and opposed by Reagan—to keep creditors away from the door. But it was Iacocca who ultimately saved the company from foreclosure. He went on television pitching Chrysler's new line of cars. Like Reagan, Iacocca could sell just about anything to anybody.

Iacocca's commercials gained him new visibility, and from that platform he wrote an autobiography, with William Novak, appropriately titled *Iacocca*. It became the largest-selling nonfiction book ever, remaining on the *New York Times* list for nearly two years. More than five million copies are in print. In the book Iacocca detailed his rise to the top. Robert Lacey, author of *Ford: The Men and the Machine*, writes that Iacocca's account of his departure from Ford was a far more complex tale than the one Iacocca tells. Lacey quotes one of Iacocca's colleagues at Ford as saying, "He had grown lazy, self-indulgent."

The public persona of Lee Iacocca, however, is far different from the private one described by Lacey. Separating fact from fiction mattered little, as Lacey points out when explaining the auto magnate's ascent into mythology:

> It was only right that he should become a folk hero. His cars were not always that good, but people bought them because he told them to. You could trust him. A lot of ordinary men and women felt they could identify with his blunt, no-nonsense ways. . . . He became a national personality. Highly paid aides helped craft his columns for the newspapers, and when a ghostwriter helped the hero produce what passed for the truth about his life, mixed in with his thoughts on the state of the nation and some simplistic nostrums about how readers could duplicate his business success, it naturally produced a runaway best-seller. It was small wonder people started talking about him for the presidency.

As for the dingy office that Iacocca said propelled him to Chrysler, it was a good three hundred square feet of floor space (not counting the outer office used by his secretary), complete with a large teak desk, a three-cushion sofa and chair, and a long, low table graced by a stylish brass lamp with cream shade. Actually, the office had been previously used by the retired chairman of the board of the Ford Motor Company, Ernest R. Breech. But, as in the case of George Gipp, what passes for reality is unimportant.

Lee Iacocca, the myth, and Lee Iacocca, the reality, are one in the public's mind—in much the same way that "the Gipper" and Ronald Reagan were once inseparable. According to Gallup polls taken in 1985, Iacocca was the man most respected in the United States after Reagan and Pope John Paul II. Ordinary folks still write him at the rate of five hundred letters a day. Many relate their personal stories of how they, like him, are making the American dream a reality.

Iacocca's success has spawned a series of life stories, each of which depicts its hero-subject's overcoming nearly impossible obstacles to live the American dream. Air Force General Chuck Yeager overcomes death-defying odds in his best-selling *Yeager;* Frank Sinatra defies everyone in Kitty Kelley's *His Way;* Armand Hammer chronicles his rise to the top in the business world in *Hammer;* Betty Davis tells her tale in *This n' That.*

Some of the "I-can-do-it" feeling engendered by Iacocca has been carried to excess—starting with the Chrysler board chairman himself. Iacocca launched his company's 1987 advertising campaign by leasing Texas Stadium where "America's team," the Dallas Cowboys, play. In the presence of the Cowboys and their cheerleaders, he introduced Chrysler's new models. The emphasis on glitz is duplicated by pop singer Madonna. At concerts as she warbles the tune "Material Girl," she pulls wads of fake banknotes from the top of her dress and tosses them to the audience. Tina Turner, another rock star, has made a comeback with a song entitled "What's Love Got To Do With It?" Ben Stein writes that on television's "Miami Vice" mankind is often mocked, and materialism is glorified: "In the world of Crocket and Tubbs [the two principal characters], man's spirit cannot be trusted, but a black Ferrari can. The camera worships it, lovingly laves it with its lens, bathes it in adoration." "Miami Vice," however, remains something of an exception. With the 1980s has come the glorification of the family on television, led by the most popular program in the medium's short history, "The Cosby Show."

"The Cosby Show": Father (and Mother) Knows Best

Since its inception in the fall of 1984, "The Cosby Show" has had a firm grip on first place in television's A.C. Nielsen ratings. When Heathcliff and Clair Huxtable (Bill Cosby and

Phylicia Rashad) take to the airwaves, some sixty-three million Americans are watching. What they see are a very successful husband and wife—he's an obstetrician; she's a lawyer—and their five well-behaved, highly motivated children. The cast embodies much of the American dream. Heathcliff and Clair attend art auctions, making regular purchases, but they emphasize something more than materialism. They have the certitude that they are living better than their parents (who don't seem to be doing too badly, either), and that their children's lives will be even more comfortable than their own. In an interview, Cosby claimed, "My point is that this is an American family—an *American* family—and if you want to live like they do, and you're willing to work, the opportunity is there."

Richard Zoglin writes, "Like Ronald Reagan, another entertainer with a warm, fatherly image who peaked relatively late in life, Cosby purveys a message of optimism and traditional family values." Each episode of "The Cosby Show" uses the trivia of everyday family life to reaffirm folk values. In one, Heathcliff Huxtable purchases a used car for his oldest daughter; in another, one of the Huxtable children tries to explain away a bad grade. The Huxtable children espouse their parents' values, sometimes ad nauseam. In one episode, for example, a friend of thirteen-year-old Vanessa lights a cigarette in the Huxtable home, violating a parental rule. Each child chastised the girl, with eight-year-old Rudy sounding "like an ad for the American Cancer Society."

Even the decor on the program is used to convey a subtle message. According to Cosby, he and the show's producers carefully selected the paintings that adorn the set. Most are portraits of black Americans by black Americans. Says Cosby: "When you look at the art work, there is a positive feeling, an up feeling. You don't see down-trodden, negative I-can't-do-I-won't-do. You see people with heads up. That's the symbolism. That's the strength."

Americans, of course, realize that the Huxtables are an idealized version of family life in the United States. Today the family is beset by many troubling issues: drugs, divorce, premarital sex, and teenage pregnancy are just a few of these. According to Anne Roiphe, co-author of *Your Child's Mind*, these problems make for loyal viewers: "'The [Cosby] Show' demonstrates what Americans wish the world was like. This is what is missing in our lives—the strong support of a family."

Cosby echoes the American longing for traditional family values in real life. His book, *Fatherhood*, sold more than 2.6 million copies and spent more than a year on the best-seller list. A second book, *Time Flies*, has advance orders of 1.75 million copies. What gives a comedian, who received a Ph.D. in education from the University of Massachusetts, much expertise in parenting or aging is a mystery. But the character of Heathcliff Huxtable lends authenticity to Cosby's pronouncements—as, once again, man and myth merge.

So many other programs have emulated "The Cosby Show" that the industry has concocted the term *warmedies*—signifying warm, family comedies—to describe them. One of the warmedies is "Family Ties." Like "The Cosby Show," it projects a close-knit family, much like those of the 1950s pictured in "Father Knows Best," "Leave it to Beaver," and "The Adventures of Ozzie and Harriet." While the show reflects the values of its precursors, there is one difference: Alex P. Keaton, the oldest boy, played by Michael J. Fox, is an ardent Republican. . . . In one episode he is shown as a child carrying his school lunchbox with a picture of Richard Nixon on its cover. Alex always defends Reagan and castigates government, much to the annoyance of his parents, who are " '60s Democrats."

Another program that emphasizes family values but uses a different format is "Wheel of Fortune." The game show, a variation of the children's game "hangman," usually has three happily married contestants. Host Pat Sajak often allows each one a wave to his or her children or to some other relative. Something of a sensation is hostess Vanna White. This lovely young woman projects an image of wholesomeness, despite the fact that she has been featured nearly nude in *Playboy.* The public, however, continues to view her and Sajak as "one of us." "Wheel of Fortune" wins its time slot in nearly every market and has earned millions for creator Merv Griffin.

"Gus Witherspoon," the salt-of-the-earth grandfather on the NBC warmedie "Our House," says, "Family may be an old-fashioned word. Well, I'm a little old-fashioned myself." Most would agree. American Enterprise Institute scholar Michael Novak tells of how his children once obliged him to watch in sequence "The Cosby Show," "Family Ties," and "Cheers":

> These were episodes with a remarkable treatment of classic family values. The humor is directed against the sorts of values that were common in the 1960s and 1970s. In fact, that was the explicit theme of one of the episodes— a friend of the family from the Berkeley days drops in on the family. The humor was delicious, understanding, and sympathetic. Those with traditional values could get the feeling—at least temporarily—of being in on the jokes rather than being the butt of them.

Other programs, not usually thought of as keepers of traditional values, are cleaning up their acts. In the police drama "Cagney and Lacey," Cagney's former lovers have included David, a civil liberties lawyer; Lars, a ski bum; Ted, a paraplegic; Dory, a fellow police officer; and Ross, a journalist. Currently, Cagney has become a one-man woman, partly because of the AIDS epidemic but also as a consequence of the return to the more conservative values regarding fidelity and commitment. According to the show's creator, it is "no longer credible to write plots that include a lot of casual sex." On "Dynasty," a homosexual character was made heterosexual and celibate. "Dallas" has tracked the pitfalls of the Ewing clan, including the "resurrection" and remarriage of Bobby and Pam. George Dessart, the head of television programming at CBS, says of the altered plots,

"For a lot of reasons marriage is back in style. It's partly because of AIDS and herpes, but it also reflects some thinking about the nature of commitment and traditional values." Terry Louise Fisher, one of the originators of "L.A. Law," agrees: "I think the sexual revolution is over. We may be heading for a new repression, a new 'Father Knows Best' era."

Concurrent with the ascendancy of family values is the different treatment accorded authority figures on television. The Huxtable children on "The Cosby Show" disobey their parents from time to time, but they never question parental discipline or ridicule their parents. This is a monumental change from the 1970s, when authority figures were mocked on television. "All in the Family" established the pattern. Michael Stivik, Archie Bunker's son-in-law, ridiculed Archie, the government, religion, and every other vestige of authority. Archie would retort by calling Michael a "meathead." Archie, meanwhile, was filled with his own dislikes. His political hero, "Richard E. Nixon," was to be admired because he was the antithesis of the establishment created by Franklin Roosevelt. Bunker, in fact, opened the show by singing, "Mister we could use a man like Herbert Hoover again." Wife Edith was also ridiculed each time she tried to exert authority, and Archie stuck her with the moniker "dingbat."

"M*A*S*H" also derided authority, at least in its early years. Lieutenant Colonel Henry Blake, the commander of the surgical hospital, was a compassionate buffoon. Major Frank Burns was a buffoon without compassion. Another major, Margaret Houlihan, went by the nickname "Hot Lips." Meanwhile, that pervasive symbol of authority, the army, could do nothing right. Each of its representatives was either drunk, or incompetent, or both. The characters provided the perfect foils for the aptly named "Hawkeye Pierce," "Trapper-John McIntyre," and "B. J. Honeycutt."

In its later episodes, however, attitudes toward authority changed. Henry Blake died, and his successor, Colonel Sherman Potter, commanded respect. Frank Burns was replaced by

Charles Emerson Winchester III, who argued with Hawkeye, and even got the better of him sometimes—all the while receiving the respect accorded his rank of major. Margaret Houlihan did not leave the cast; instead, her character was transformed from a caricature of promiscuity into a mature women cooperating with, and earning the admiration of, the nursing staff. And Corporal Maxwell Klinger exchanged his women's dresses for army fatigues and became the unit's company clerk.

The Reagan Presidency and American Culture

The resurrection of the authoritative hero, suggests polltaker Wirthlin, is one reason for young voters' preference for Reagan in 1984: "When we examined the importance of authority figures—that is, the need to hold someone in a position of freely given authority—young voters ranked very high. They viewed Reagan as an authoritative figure, not as an authoritarian figure." Respect for authority seems to be so great that even a popular cartoonist like Garry Trudeau, whose "Doonesbury" strip has taken readers on a tour of a void called "Reagan's Brain" among other irreverences, finds his material relegated to the editorial page.

The new mind-set regarding authority figures in television and in politics has produced its own kind of historical revisionism. *New York Times* theater critic Vincent Canby writes that the Vietnam War and the violent public aversion to it "now appears to have been so effectively rewritten—at least by hugely popular movies like *Rambo* and *Missing in Action*—that a defeat has been turned into a victory." In *Hamburger Hill*, a 1987 film about the 101st Airborne Division's struggle to take Hill 937 in Vietnam's Ashau Valley, a soldier received a letter from his stateside girlfriend saying that their relationship was over because the war that he is fighting is "immoral." The movie also shows a television news reporter informing the soldiers that "Senator Kennedy says you don't have a chance." The Vietnam War certainly has not been forgotten, Canby notes, but it has been "accommodated as an unpleasantness with a happy ending."

In such a manner, Ronald Reagan's use of American values both reflects and designs American popular culture. Family, work, neighborhood, and authority are rediscovered themes in entertainment, from "Leave It to Beaver" (which has returned for yet another run) to "The Cosby Show." In all of this, Reagan is as much a creator of the climate in which these shows work so successfully as are any of their producers, performers, or network scheduling czars. From bookstore to playhouse, the values Reagan has so repeatedly espoused seem firmly ensconced, for now, in the nation's culture.

Part Two

Opinion, Interests, and Organizations

_____Chapter 5

Public Opinion

$\mathcal{B}$ecause a democratic government must in some way represent the will of the people, public opinion is vital. There must be some way to measure it and then ensure that politicians and government officials are responsive to changes in it. On the other hand, as James Madison pointed out in the Federalist No. 10, a government that follows public opinion too slavishly creates its own share of dangers. The very purpose of a Republic, in Madison's view, was to "refine and enlarge the public views, by passing them through the medium of a chosen body of citizens, whose wisdom may best discern the true interest of their country, and whose patriotism and love of justice, will be least likely to sacrifice it to temporary or partial considerations" (see selection 2.1). If politicians constantly took the public pulse and adapted their every action to short-term swings in public opinion, Madison's scheme would be quickly subverted.

The selections in this chapter serve several purposes. The first, by political scientist V. O. Key, explores the concept of public opinion, which is surprisingly difficult to understand in a theoretically satisfactory way. The second, by Russell J. Dalton, compares public opinion in the United States to that in several Western European democracies, providing a touch point for understanding public attitudes in the United States. The third selection examines how politicians try to cope with an issue that divides and inflames public opinion. The last two readings examine the appropriate role of public opinion polling in American politics and government.

Chapter Questions

1. What is public opinion? How can it be measured and tracked? How has public opinion changed in the United States over the past several decades?
2. How closely should politicians seek to follow public opinion? How much can they—or should they—try to lead or influence public opinion? Is it dangerous for politicians to ignore public opinion? to follow it too closely?

I THE CLASSIC TEXTS

It is tempting to say about public opinion what Supreme Court justice Potter Stewart said about obscenity: we may not be able to define it, but we surely know it when we see it. On the one hand, public opinion might refer simply to the views of the American people as expressed most typically through public opinion poll results. Often, however, we use the term public opinion *in a broader sense—as a representation of the public consciousness or the public will. When we say, for example, that the president was forced to do this or that by public opinion, we are expressing an idea that, although imprecise, nonetheless contains a certain germ of meaning. The question is whether such a conception of public opinion has any practical validity to scholars or practitioners of politics and, if so, how much. In the following selection, political scientist V. O. Key surveys the idea of public opinion, providing a theoretical backdrop for the other readings in this chapter.*

Questions

1. Why does Key suggest that "more is lost than is gained in understanding by the organismic view of the public"? What does he suggest in its stead?

2. "Not all opinions are public, even when widely held within the population," Key writes. Explain what he means.

5.1 *Public Opinion and American Democracy*

V. O. Key

Among philosophers, publicists, and spare-time commentators on public affairs, the discussion of public opinion is conducted with style. Aphorisms, epigrams, axioms, and figures embellish the verbal display. One can, with Pascal, christen public opinion the "Queen of the World." One can observe, with the authors of *The Federalist*, that "all government rests on opinion" or with Hume, that it is "on opinion only that government is founded." One can assert that governments derive their powers from the "consent of the governed" or can picture public opinion as "a giant who is fickle and

ignorant yet still has a giant's strength, and may use it with frightful effect."

Such metaphors serve principally to ornament prose rather than to enlighten the reader about the nature of public opinion. Yet the discussion of public opinion becomes murky when meticulous scholars try to define their conceptions and to form distinctions that enable them to make statements that seem to fit the observable realities of the interaction of public opinion and government. This murkiness by no means flows solely from the incomprehensibility of men of learning. To speak with precision of public opinion is a task not unlike coming to grips with the Holy Ghost. Public opinion, Leiserson notes, "has come to refer to a sort of secular idol, and is a 'god-term' to which citizens, scientists, and office-holders alike pay allegiance, partly as an act of faith, partly as a matter of observation, partly as a condition of sanity." Nevertheless, a brief review of some of the conceptions and distinctions that have been developed by scholars in their discussions of the topic should be of value as an aid in orientation.

Public as Organic Entity

Some speculators on public opinion have imagined the public to be a semiorganized entity that in some way or another could move through stages of initiation and debate and reach a recognizable collective decision on an issue. The images of the city-state and of the New England town meeting often color such attempts to form a conception of the reality of public opinion in the modern state. The intricate structure of the nation-state cannot easily be grasped, and some students seek in the processes of opinion formation the equivalent of the citizenry gathered in the town hall or in the market place to discuss, debate, and settle public issues. In its simplest form this analogous thinking personifies the public: "The public expects"; "The public demands"; "Public opinion swept away all opposition." Perhaps a comparable conception is concealed in the assertion that public opinion "is a deeply persuasive organic force," which "articulates and formulates not only the deliberative judgments of the rational elements within the collectivity but the evanescent common will, which somehow integrates and momentarily crystallizes the sporadic sentiments and loyalties of the masses of the population."

Some observers, in their search for a conception to encompass the public opinion process as a whole, produce statements more complex than the town-meeting analogy but not fundamentally different in kind. An image emerges of a rudimentary organism consisting of individuals and groups linked together by mass communications, which centers its attention on an issue, discusses and deliberates, and in some mysterious way proceeds to a decision. A public becomes a social entity, different from a mob and not the same as a mass. Thus, Young

"I WAS SICK AND TIRED OF THE CONNIVING, INCOMPETENT INCUMBENT, SO I VOTED FOR THE CONNIVING, INCOMPETENT CHALLENGER . . . !"

Drawing by Bob Gorrell. Reprinted with permission of Copley News Service.

notes that "in terms of stability and degree of institutionalization, . . . a public is a transitory, amorphous, and relatively unstructured association of individuals with certain interests in common." From the conception of the "public" as a social entity it is but a short step to the attempt to identify some pattern of actions or behavior through which the entity travels to reach decision or to form public opinion on an issue. Analysis in such terms is called the study of the dynamics of opinion formation, in contrast with the study of opinion as static (or at a moment in time). On occasion the process is likened to individual action in response to a problem. "Public opinion then becomes a form of group thinking, and the process bears more than an analogous relation to the individual's complete act of thought." Or a sequence of steps is suggested as a standard pattern through which the public moves in the formation of opinion—for example, the rise of an issue, discussion and deliberation, and arrival at a decision.

More is lost than is gained in understanding by the organismic view of the public. Occasionally, in relatively small communities, citizen concern and involvement over an issue may be widespread and community consideration may move in close articulation with the mechanisms of authority to a decision that can realistically be said to be a decision by public opinion. At far rarer intervals great national populations may be swept by a common concern about a momentous issue with a similar result. Yet ordinarily a decision is made not by the public but by officials after greater or a lesser consideration of the opinion of the public or parts of the public.

Special Publics and the General Public

While the organismic conceptions of the public and of the opinion process may be of more poetic than practical utility, other distinctions developed by students of public opinion serve as handy aids to thought on the subject. There is, for example, the distinction between special

publics and the general public. At one time it was the custom to speak of "the public." In due course it became evident that on only a few questions did the entire citizenry have an opinion. The notion of special publics was contrived to describe those segments of the public with views about particular issues, problems, or other questions of public concern. In actual politics one issue engages the attention of one subdivision of the population, while another arouses the interest of another group, and a third question involves still another special public. This distinction between general and special publics, does, of course, do violence to the basic idea that "the" public shall prevail; it also warps the meaning of the term "public." Yet the usage mirrors the facts of political life and, incidentally, creates a problem for the public opinion theorist. He sometimes copes with the difficulty by the assertion that when the concern of a small special public prevails, it does so with the tacit consent of the general public.

Blumer deals in a different way with the problem created by the existence of special publics. He remarks that public opinion may be "different from the opinion of any of the groups in the public. It can be thought of, perhaps, as composite opinion formed out of the several opinions that are held in the public; or better, as the central tendency set by the striving of these separate opinions and, consequently, as being shaped by the relative strength and play of opposition among them." Blumer thus brings together the opinions of the special publics into something of a weighted average that takes into account both the numbers holding different kinds of opinions (or no opinion) and the strength of the holders of opinion. Whether this notion has validity, the question of who has what kind of opinion is of basic significance in a consideration of interactions between public and government.

Public and Private Opinion

There are opinions and opinions; their number is as numerous as the kinds of objects about which men have preferences and beliefs. On what range of topics may opinion be considered to be public? Not all opinions of the public, even when widely held within the population, are to be properly regarded as public opinion. It may be assumed that opinions about the desirability of tailfins on Chevrolets are not public opinions, or that preferences for striped or solid white toothpaste fall outside the concern of the student of public opinion. On the other hand, opinion about the length of automobile tailfins may become public opinion if the question becomes one of whether the length of nonfunctional automobile ornamentation has become a public nuisance by its pressure on the available parking acreage. Goldhamer suggests that an opinion is public "if it attaches to an object of public concern." The content of the phrase, "object of public concern," may vary from time to time with the changing scope of governmental action, or it may differ from society to society.

Many American students of public opinion have limited themselves to a narrow range of public opinion; they have tended to regard public opinion as concerned with substantive issues of public policy. That focus results from the basic tenet that public opinion should determine public policy, but it excludes a range of opinions of undoubted political relevance. Opinions about candidates, views about political parties, attitudes about the performance of governments, basic assumptions about what is right and proper in public affairs, and general beliefs and expectations about the place of government in society are also opinions of political relevance, as would be such opinions or states of mind as are embraced by the term "national morale."

Characteristics of Public Opinion

The differentiation between opinions about public objects and about private objects crudely defines the outer limits of the opinion sphere that may be regarded as public. It leaves untouched the question of the characteristics of public opinion. In recent decades considerable scholarly effort has been devoted, principally by social psychologists, to ascertaining the characteristics of public opinion. In an earlier day the practice was to treat the direction of opinion in simple pro and con categories. The majority could be described as for or against, as voting yes or no. The psychometricians have made it clear that a pro-and-con categorization of opinion often conceals wide gradations in opinion. They have contrived scales to measure opinion in its dimension of direction. For example, a division of people who support and oppose government ownership of industry does not provide a useful indication of the nature of public opinion on the question of government policy toward economic activity. Views on economic policy may be arranged along a scale from the extreme left to the extreme right. The opinion of an individual may be located at any one of many points along such a scale. One person may favor governmental ownership of all the means of production; another may be satisfied with a large dose of governmental regulation; still another may prefer only the most limited control of the economy; and others may wish to abolish whatever controls exist. The determination of the distribution of the population along such scales measuring the direction of opinion makes possible a more informed estimate of the nature of public opinion, in its dimension of direction, than did earlier and cruder conceptions.

Closely related to the conception of direction of opinion are ideas about the qualities or properties of opinion. Intensity of opinion is one of these qualities. A person may be an extreme conservative or radical on the scale of direction of opinion, but he may care a great deal, a little, or scarcely at all about that opinion; that is, opinions may vary in the intensity with which they are held. Obviously the incidence of opinion intensity within the electorate about an issue or problem is of basic importance for politics. An issue that arouses only opinion of low intensity may receive only the slightest attention, while one that stirs opinions of high intensity among even relatively small numbers of people may be placed high on the governmental agenda. Another quality of opinion of some importance is its stability. An individual, for example, may have a view, expressed on the basis of little or no information, which may readily be changed. On the other hand, an opinion may be so firmly held that it is not easily altered. Issues that relate to opinions of high stability widely held within the population present radically different problems for government than do those matters on which opinion is unstable.

Students of public opinion often differentiate between opinion and custom. Utilizing this distinction, public opinion concerns those issues whose solution is not more or less automatically provided by custom or by the expectations shared predominantly by members of the group. Public opinion, then, concerns live issues. Park said that public opinion emerges when action is in process; it is opinion "before it has been capitalized and, so to speak, funded in the form of dogma, doctrine, or law." The exclusion from public opinion of the settled attitudes of the community unduly narrows the meaning of the term. Governments must pay heed to the mores, the customs, the "funded" or the "standing" opinions quite as much as to the effervescence of today's popular discussion. The distinction between opinion and custom really amounts to a differentiation between qualities of opinions.

Prerequisites for the Existence of Public Opinion

Students of public opinion have also sought to identify those broad conditions under which public opinion could sensibly be said to exist as a force in government. Democratic theorists that they were, they specified democratic conditions as a prerequisite for even the existence of public opinion. Freedom of speech and discussion, for example, are said to be prerequisites, since it is by public discussion that opinion is formed. Closely associated with this condition is that of the free availability of information about public issues and public questions; those problems handled by government in secrecy can scarcely be a subject of informed public debate.

Opinion theorists almost uniformly place emphasis on the importance of the existence of a consensus on fundamentals as a basis for the settlement of the differences involved in the development of a prevailing opinion on transient issues. Otherwise, government cannot be founded upon public opinion. "There is," says MacIver, "no public opinion unless an area of common ground lies underneath and supports the differences of opinion, finding expression in the traditions and conventions and behavior patterns characteristic of the folk." Similarly, Park argued that there needs to be within the public "a general understanding and a community of interest among all parties sufficient to make discussion possible."

In keeping with this general vein of thought, Lowell sharply restricted the content of the term "public opinion." In his system the views of people generally on public questions of all sorts did not constitute public opinion. For a "real" public opinion to exist, it had to be a community opinion. Thus, when two highwaymen meet a traveler on a dark road and propose to relieve him of his wallet, it would be incorrect to say that a public opinion existed favorable to a redistribution of property. Public opinion, Lowell thought, need not be a unanimous opinion, but it should create an "obligation moral or political on the part of the minority," an obligation, at least under certain conditions, to submit. He laid great stress on the grounds of consensus as a basis for public opinion. "A body of men are politically capable of a public opinion only so far as they are agreed upon the ends and aims of government and upon the principles by which those ends shall be attained." No public opinion could exist in nations with large minorities unwilling to abide by majority decision. Moreover, public opinion could exist only when "the bulk of the people are in a position to determine of their own knowledge or by weighing a substantial part of the facts required for a rational decision," or when the question involves an issue of "apparent harmony or contradiction with settled convictions."

It seems clear that consensus does not have to prevail for opinions to exist to which governments must accord weight. Yet the emphasis on consensus identifies special problems in governments that accord deference to public opinion. If the public is to project its opinions into public policy, some sectors of the public must be prepared to accept actions distasteful to them. The limits of the general consensus may fix the limits within which widespread participation in public affairs may lead to decisions distasteful yet acceptable to those whose opinions do not prevail.

II THE INTERNATIONAL CONTEXT

Comparisons between the United States and Europe are usually made to highlight the differences between the Old and New Worlds, and for the most part such comparisons are useful and illuminating. It is also worthwhile to take note of the similarities between the United States and Europe, however, especially as the information revolution continues and the distance across the Atlantic continues to shrink.

The democracies of Western Europe and the United States, writes Russell J. Dalton, share a common trend in the development of public values across a wide range of social and political issues. The dominant trend, according to Dalton, is a movement away from the "material goals" orientation of older citizens toward a "postmaterial" view that stresses self-expression and participation in politics and encompasses such diverse movements as environmentalism, disarmament, and social equality.

The value change thesis, as it is called, is not universally accepted by social scientists. One reason is that, although the shifts found in the surveys cited by Dalton are real, postmaterialists still make up only a small percentage of the population on both sides of the Atlantic. Another is that some social scientists question whether the shifts Dalton notes are permanent, long-term shifts or merely fleeting changes.

Whatever the validity of Dalton's thesis may be, it nevertheless challenges us to examine the long-term drift of American public opinion at the deepest level and to place such changes in the increasingly important worldwide context.

Questions

1. What is meant by "materialist" and "postmaterialist" views? Would you characterize yourself as materialist or postmaterialist? Neither? Both?
2. Do college students today seem to fit Dalton's claim for increased postmaterialism?

5.2 Citizen Politics in Western Democracies ——————

Russell J. Dalton

The values of the mass public define the essence of democratic politics. Value priorities identify what are important to citizens—what are, or should be, the goals of society and the political system. The clash between alternative value systems underlies much of the political conflict and competition in Western democracies. Broad value orientations often are a strong influence on the more explicitly political attitudes and behaviors of the mass public.

Another element in the new style of citizen politics involves a fundamental change in the value priorities of many individuals. Even the most casual comparison of contemporary societies to those of a generation ago would uncover substantial evidence of changing social norms. Hierarchical relationships and deference toward authority are giving way to decentralization, quality circles, and participatory decision making. Citizens demand more control over the decisions affecting their lives. . . . The new values are affecting attitudes toward work, life styles, and the individual's role in society.

The definition of societal goals and the meaning of "success" are also changing. Until fairly recently, the mark of success for many Americans was measured almost solely in economic terms: a large house, two cars in the garage, and other signs of affluence. In Europe the threshold for economic success might have been lower, but material concerns were equally important. Once affluence became widespread, many people realized that bigger is not necessarily better, and that small is beautiful. The consensus in favor of economic growth was also tempered by a strong concern for environmental quality. Attention to the quality of life in advanced industrial societies is now as important as the quantity of life.

Social relations and acceptance of diversity are another example of values in change. Progress on racial, sexual, ethnic, and religious equality are transforming American and European societies. Moreover, social norms involving sex, social relations, and the choice of life styles have changed dramatically in a few short decades. Evidence of value change is all around us, if we look.

We think in the present, and so the magnitude of these changes is not always appreciated. But compare, if you will, the diversity of contemporary American life styles to the images of American life depicted on vintage TV reruns from the 1950s. Series such as "Ozzie and Harriet," "Father Knows Best," and "Leave It to Beaver" reflect many values of a bygone era. How well would the Nelsons or the Cleavers adjust to a world with women's liberation, the new morality, racial desegregation, punk rock, and alternative life styles?

A similar process of value change is affecting Western Europe. The clearest evidence of these changes can be seen in the attitudes and behaviors of the young. Student movements proliferated throughout Europe in the late 1960s. What often began as criticisms of specific government policies frequently led to deeper questions about the basic goals and procedures of the social and political systems. These views contributed to . . . protests and citizen action groups. . . . An alternative cultural movement gradually developed from these new value orientations. Many large European cities contain distinct counterculture districts where natural food stores, cooperative businesses, child-care centers, and youth-oriented restaurants and cafes offer a life style attuned to the new values. These communities place less emphasis on profit and stress self-management and social service. The influence of these alternative centers is gradually spreading into the rest of society. Many older Europeans view these developments with shock or dismay, especially when they equate the alternative scene only with punk hairdos, heavy metal, and unconventional life styles. But clearly the rivers of change run much deeper (and broader) than fashions and fads. Basic value priorities are being transformed in America and Western Europe.

• • •

The Distribution of Values

Most individuals attach a positive worth to both material and postmaterial goals. The average individual prefers both economic growth and a clean environment, social stability and individual freedom. Politics, however, often involves a conflict between these valued goals. To understand fully the process of value change, it is important to identify which goals take priority in the public's mind.

The public's value priorities were assessed by asking survey respondents to rank the most important goals from a list of alternatives. Table 1 (p. 154) presents the top priorities of Americans and West Europeans across a set of twelve social goals. . . .

Most citizens on both sides of the Atlantic still place material goals at the top of their value hierarchy. Americans give top priority to a stable economy, crime prevention, and a strong defense. Europeans most often stress the need for stable prices, law and order, and economic growth. Despite this emphasis on material goals, Europeans and Americans also give high rankings to the postmaterial goals of participating in job-related and political decision making. A significant proportion of these publics, albeit a small number, stress the other postmaterial goals.

A subset of the above items has been used to construct a single measure of material/postmaterial values. Survey respondents are asked the question:

> There is a lot of talk these days about what the aims of the country should be for the next ten years. On this card are listed some of the goals which different people would give as top priority. Would you please say which of these you consider the most important? And which would be the next most important?

- Maintaining order in the nation
- Giving people more say in important government decisions
- Fighting rising prices
- Protecting freedom of speech

Individuals are classified into one of three value-priority groups on the basis of the choices made among these four items. Materialists select the first and third items, displaying an emphasis on personal and economic security. Postmaterialists choose the other two items, indicating their emphasis on self-expression and participation. Survey respondents who select one material and one postmaterial item are classified as having mixed value priorities. This four-item index is a very crude measure of the complex and extensive value systems we wish to study. Still, the simplicity of the index has led to its adoption in surveys of more than twenty nations.

The distribution of value groups is presented in tables 2 and 3 (p. 155). In all four nations the number of materialists exceeds the number of postmaterialists by a sizable margin. In the most recent French survey, for example, 36 percent of the public selected both material goals, while only 12 percent chose both postmaterial goals. This is not surprising; the conditions fostering value change should take several generations to accumulate, and in historical perspective the development of advanced industrialism is a relatively recent phenomenon. At the same time, these data provide important support for the value-change thesis. Already less than half of these populations focus exclusively on material concerns. Even the relatively small number of "pure" postmaterialists—8 to 15 percent—should not be discounted. Other studies find that postmaterialists are disproportionately represented among political elites and those actively involved in politics.

Many critics of the value-change thesis maintain that these are transitory beliefs, nurtured by the affluence and domestic tranquillity of the 1950s and early 1960s. At the first sign of socioeconomic difficulties, it is argued, the public's priorities will revert to material goals. The

TABLE 1
The Distribution of Values (in Percent)

Value	United States	Great Britain	West Germany	France
Fighting rising prices (M)	29	25	25	33
Fighting crime (M)	43	32	23	22
Economic growth (M)	18	29	26	13
Maintaining a stable economy (M)	51	23	33	11
Maintaining order in the nation (M)	27	18	23	15
A friendlier, less impersonal society (PM)	6	9	11	31
Protecting freedom of speech (PM)	14	16	12	18
Giving people more say to work and in their community (PM)	25	12	8	21
Giving people more say in important government decisions (PM)	27	10	7	11
Maintaining strong defense forces (M)	39	11	5	3
A society where ideas count more than money (PM)	13	4	3	11
More beautiful cities	4	3	7	6

Sources: *United States*, Political Action Study, 1981; *other nations*, Eurobarometer 10.

Notes: Table entries are the percentages ranking each goal as most important or second in importance from a list of twelve goals; in the United States the top three rankings are combined. Material goals are denoted by (M), postmaterial goals by (PM).

data in these tables undermine this criticism. In the face of major economic recessions and domestic disorders during the last decade, the distribution of value priorities has held fairly constant. Once value priorities are socialized, they appear to be relatively resistant to subsequent changes in social conditions. There certainly has not been a resurgence of material values; if anything, these data describe a continuing decline in the percentage of materialists. Indeed, the most recent American time point displays a significant shift away from material concerns, and a similar trend is evident in Britain, West Germany, and most other Western democracies.

If data for a longer time period were available, we would expect to find a very substantial decline in material values over the past several generations. This is because the process of value change has been closely tied to generational change within Western democracies. Older generations, reared in the years before World War II, grew up in a period of widespread uncertainty. These individuals suffered through the Great Depression in the 1930s, endured two world wars and the social and economic traumas that accompanied these events. Social conditions were especially severe in Germany; older generations had successively experienced World War 1, economic collapse in the 1920s, the Great Depression in the 1930s, the consolidation of the authoritarian Nazi state, and then the massive destruction of World War II. Given these circumstances, it is understandable that older generations in all four nations became concerned with material goals: economic growth, economic security, domestic order, and social and military security.

TABLE 2
The Trend in Material/Postmaterial Values in Europe (in Percent)

Country	1970	1973	1976	1979	1982	1984
Great Britain						
Material	36	32	36	25	25	24
Mixed	56	60	56	63	61	59
Postmaterial	8	8	8	11	14	17
	100	100	100	100	100	100
PDI[a]	28	24	28	15	11	17
West Germany						
Material	46	42	42	37	32	23
Mixed	44	50	47	52	54	58
Postmaterial	11	8	11	11	13	20
	100	100	100	100	100	100
PDI[a]	35	34	31	26	19	3
France						
Material	38	35	41	36	34	36
Mixed	51	53	47	49	55	51
Postmaterial	11	12	12	15	11	12
	100	100	100	100	100	100
PDI[a]	27	23	29	21	23	24

Sources: European Community Studies, 1970, 1973; Eurobarometers 6, 12, 18 and 20.
a. PDI (Percentage Difference Index) is the difference between the percent with material values and the percent with postmaterial values.

TABLE 3
The Trend in Material/Postmaterial Values in the United States (in Percent)

	1972	1976	1980	1984
Material	35	31	34	21
Mixed	55	59	56	63
Postmaterial	10	10	10	16
	100	100	100	100
PDI[a]	25	21	24	5

Source: CPS Election Studies.
a. PDI (Percentage Difference Index) is the difference between the percent with material values and the percent with postmaterial values.

In contrast, younger generations in Europe and North America were raised in a period of unprecedented affluence and security. Present-day living standards are often two or more times higher than most Western nations ever experienced before World War II. The rapid growth of the welfare state now protects most citizens from even major economic problems. Postwar generations also have a broader world view, reflecting their higher educational levels, greater exposure to political information, and more diverse cultural experiences. Furthermore, the past four decades are one of the longest periods of international peace in modern European history. Under these conditions, the material concerns that preoccupied prewar generations have diminished in urgency. Growing up in a period when material and security needs seem assured, postwar generations are apparently shifting their attention toward postmaterial goals.

The changing values of the young were most clearly evident in the 1960s and 1970s, when the clash between generations occasionally spilled over into the streets. In recent years, the popular media has emphasized a seemingly different trend among the young: The growth of the Yuppie phenomenon and patterns of conspicuous consumption by some young people. In fact, the Yuppies are an example of the social changes we are discussing; young, highly educated professionals now earn salaries in excess of their basic needs. The use of this disposable income necessarily creates a materialist image. The value-change thesis maintains, however, that wealth cannot always be equated with materialism. While some young people measure success by the standards of the Ewings, such traditional values are not as widespread as they once were. As one counterexample to the Yuppie image, in 1985 the director of the Peace Corps went on a TV talk show asking for 600 volunteers to work on African relief projects (at a salary of $250 a month). By the weekend, the Peace Corps headquarters was overwhelmed with over 10,000 inquiries. Clearly many young people are not preoccupied with their careers and buying a BMW. Events such as Band-Aid, Live-Aid, Farm-Aid, Sport-Aid, and Hands Across America tap the activism and social concern that exists among the young. With scientific survey evidence we can determine how far the process of generational change has actually progressed.

A sense of the generational pattern in value priorities can be gained by examining age differences in value orientations. Since values tend to be enduring beliefs, different age groups should retain the mark of their formative generational experiences.

Figure 1 displays the age differences in value priorities within each nation. Values are measured by the Percentage Difference Index (PDI), which is simply the percentage of materialists in each age group minus the percentage of postmaterialists. Positive numbers thus indicate a preponderance of materialists. Generally speaking, the younger cohorts socialized during affluent postwar years display greater attachment to postmaterial values, while the older cohorts reared in less affluent and secure periods retain a higher priority for material values.

The value difference between young and old also presents a cross-national pattern consistent with national historical conditions. Germany, for example, experienced tremendous socioeconomic change during the past few generations. Consequently, the value differences between the youngest (PDI = 1) and oldest West German cohorts (PDI = 38) are larger than for any other nation. In contrast, Britain's economic condition was already at a relatively high level early in this century and increased only gradually over the past fifty years. Thus, British cohorts display much smaller generational differences (youngest PDI = 5, oldest PDI = 18). In short, these data are quite consistent with a generational model of value change.

These age differences can, of course, also reflect life-cycle differences in value orientations. That is, it is possible that younger individuals show a greater preference for postmaterial values because they have, as yet, not experienced the demands of careers, mortgages, and other family responsibilities. Youth is a time when one is free to espouse new ideas and aesthetic values relatively unencumbered by practical economic realities. The life-cycle thesis holds that as these younger cohorts age, their value priorities should come to resemble those which older cohorts now display. Everyone knows of examples where radical young people became more conventional with age. Is

FIGURE 1   Age Differences in Value Priorities

Sources: *United States*, 1980 CPS American Election Study; *other nations*, Eurobarometer 18. The Percentage Difference Index shows the difference between the percentage with material value and the percentage with postmaterial values.

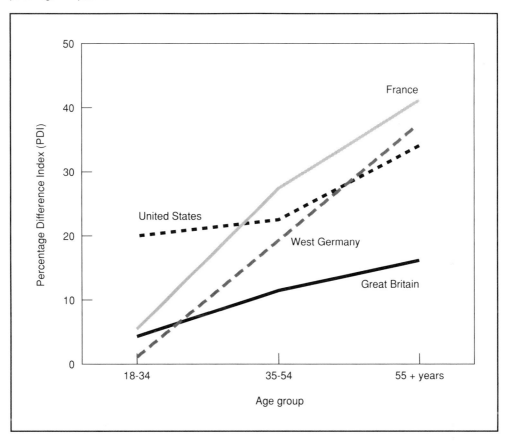

this effect sufficient to explain all the age-group differences in figure 1?

The debate over the generational versus life-cycle interpretation of age differences in value priorities has been pursued at great length. There is evidence to support both the generational and life-cycle theories; both processes are apparently influencing the public's value priorities to some extent. The weight of the evidence, however, suggests that generational change is the major explanation for the present value differences between young and old. This can be seen in figure 2 (p. 158), which tracks the value priorities of several European generations from 1970 until 1982. The oldest cohort, age 65 to 85 in 1970, is clearly oriented toward material goals. The youngest cohort, age 15 to 24 in 1970, is almost evenly balanced between material and postmaterial values. More important, the broad generational differences in value orientations remain fairly constant over time, even though all cohorts are moving through the life cycle. The youngest cohort, for example, is approaching middle age by the end of the survey series, and yet its postmaterial value orientations do not lessen significantly. Life-cycle experiences can modify, but do not replace, the early learning of value priorities.

FIGURE 2 Longitudinal Cohort Differences in Value Priorities

Sources: European Community Studies, Eurobarometers; results are based on the combined samples of France, West Germany, Italy, Belgium, the Netherlands, and Luxembourg.

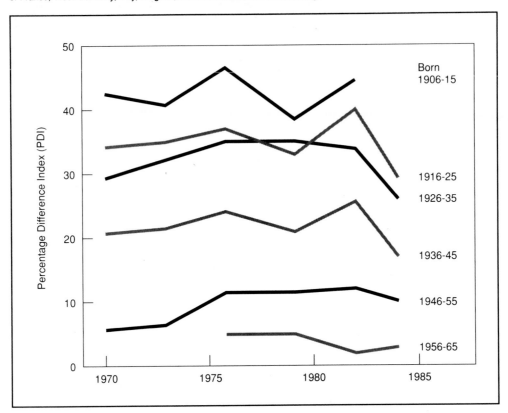

Another factor affecting value priorities is educational level. Obviously, the effects of education overlap with those of generation; the young are more likely to be better educated than the old. Educational level also is an indirect indicator of an individual's economic circumstances during adolescence, when value priorities were being formed. Educational level in the class-stratified European educational systems reflects the family's social status during an individual's youth. Education also may affect value priorities because of the content of instruction. Higher education generally places more stress on the values of participation, self-expression, intellectual understanding, and other postmaterial goals. Moreover, the diversity of the modern university milieu may encourage a broadening of social perspectives.

Differences in material/postmaterial values (PDI scores) by educational level are presented in figure 3. In every nation, individuals with only a primary education are oriented predominantly toward material goals. In France, for instance, this educational group was 50 percent materialist and only 3 percent postmaterialist, yielding a PDI score of 47. The proportion of materialists decreases fairly steadily with educational level. Among citizens with some college, postmaterialists actually outnumber materialists in all three European nations.

FIGURE 3 Education Differences in Value Priorities
Sources: *United States*, 1980 CPS American Study; *other nations*, Eurobarometer 18.

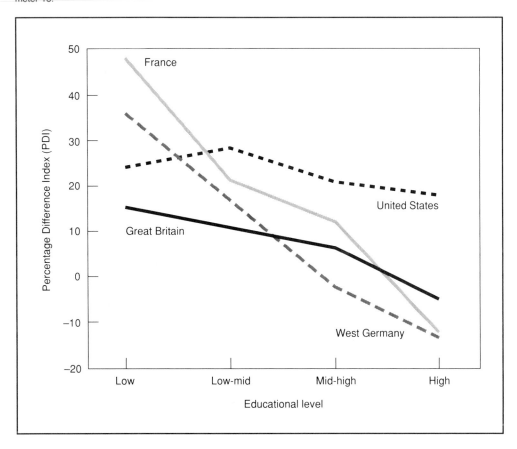

The concentration of these new values among the young and better educated gives added significance to these value orientations. If [the value change] theory is correct, the percentage of postmaterialists should gradually increase over time, as older materialist cohorts are replaced by younger, more postmaterialist generations. Similarly, if expanding educational opportunities continue to increase the public's educational level, support for postmaterial values should also grow. Value change has the appearance of an ongoing process.

The Consequences of Value Change

Even though postmaterialists now constitute only a small minority in most Western democracies, the impact of these values is already apparent, extending beyond politics to all aspects of society. At the workplace, for example, these new value orientations are fueling demands for a more flexible and individually oriented work environment. Rigid, hierarchical, assembly-line systems of production are being challenged by worker participation (codetermination), quality circles, and flexible working hours. Postmaterial values are linked to a shift from extrinsic occupational goals (security and a good salary) to intrinsic goals (a feeling of accomplishment and sense of responsibility). Many business analysts bemoan the decline of the work ethic, but it is more accurate to say that the work ethic is becoming motivated by a new set of goals.

In more general terms, social relations are also changing in reaction to the public's new value orientations. Deference to authority of all forms is generally declining, as individuals are more willing to challenge elites. Bosses, army officers, university professors, and political leaders all decry the decline in deference to their authority. But the postmaterial credo is that authority is earned by an individual, not bestowed by a position. Similarly, many citizens are placing less reliance on social norms—from class, religion, or community—as a guide for behavior. The public's behavior in all aspects of social and political life is becoming more self-directed. This shows in the declining brand-name loyalty among consumers, and the decline of political party loyalty among voters. In short, contemporary life styles reflect a demand for greater freedom and individuality, which appears in fashions, consumer tastes, social behavior, and interpersonal relations. Two recent bestsellers, Alvin Toffler's *The Third Wave* (1980) and John Naisbitt's *Megatrends* (1982), discuss these and related phenomena in fascinating detail.

If we focus our attention on the realm of politics, postmaterial values have been linked to several elements of the new style of citizen politics. Postmaterialists have, for example, championed a new set of political issues—environmental quality, nuclear energy, women's rights, and consumerism—that often were overlooked by the political establishment. Debates in Washington about acid rain, toxic waste, and the safety of nuclear plants have close parallels in the capitals of Europe; and the proponents of these issues have similar characteristics. Many other issues—disarmament, codetermination, and social equality—have been revived by postmaterial groups and reinterpreted in terms of new value perspectives. No longer are these transient "sunshine" issues, since the public's concern for these issues has persisted and grown through the 1970s and early 1980s. This new set of issues has been added to the political agenda of contemporary democracies.

Value change also affects the patterns of political participation. . . . Postmaterial values stimulate direct participation in the decisions affecting one's life—whether at school, the workplace, or in the political process. Figure 4 documents the relationship between value priorities and general interest in politics. Postmaterialists are consistently more involved in politics than are materialists. The process of value change increases demands for greater citizen input. In addition, because postmaterialists are more active in politics, their political influence is greater than their small numbers imply. Indeed, among the group of future elites—university educated youth—postmaterial values predominate. As these individuals succeed into positions of economic, social, and political leadership, the impact of changing values should strengthen.

So far, at least, the participatory orientation of postmaterialists has not affected all participation modes equally. Postmaterial values are not related to electoral participation, and in some instances voting turnout is actually lower among postmaterialists. This is partially because the establishment parties have been hesitant to respond to new issue demands. In addition, postmaterialists are generally skeptical of established hierarchical organizations, such as most political parties. Instead, postmaterial values have stimulated participation in citizen initiatives, protests, and other forms of unconventional political activity. In the 1981 European Values Survey, for instance, postmaterialists are more than twice as likely as materialists to participate in protests (figure 5, p. 162). These nonpartisan participation opportunities provide postmaterialists with a more direct influence on politics, which matches their value orientations.

FIGURE 4 Political Interest by Value Priorities

Source: *United States*, Political Action Study, 1974; *other nations*, 1981 European Values Study.

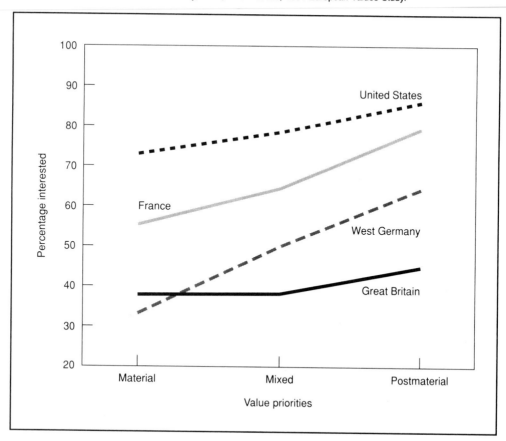

Most postmaterialists also possess the political skills to carry out these more demanding forms of political action. . . . Along with increasing levels of citizen involvement has come a change in the form of political participation.

Value Change and Value Stability

This [selection] has emphasized the changing values of Western publics, but a more accurate description would stress the increasing diversity of value priorities. Most people still give primary attention to material goals and the socioeconomic issues deriving from these values will continue to dominate political debate for decades to come. The persistence of traditional

values should not be overlooked. At the same time, a new type of postmaterial values is spreading within Western publics. For nearly every example of the persistence of traditional material value patterns, there is now a counterexample reflecting postmaterial values. For every Yuppie driving a BMW, someone is conscientiously volunteering time to work on some issue (often it is the same person). The diversity of values marks a major change in the nature of citizen politics.

The consequences of value change can be seen in the issues of contemporary political debate. Concerns for environmental protection, individual freedom, social equality, participation, and the quality of life have been *added* to

FIGURE 5 Protest Participation by Value Priorities

Sources: *United States,* Political Action Study, 1974; *other nations,* 1981 European Values Survey.

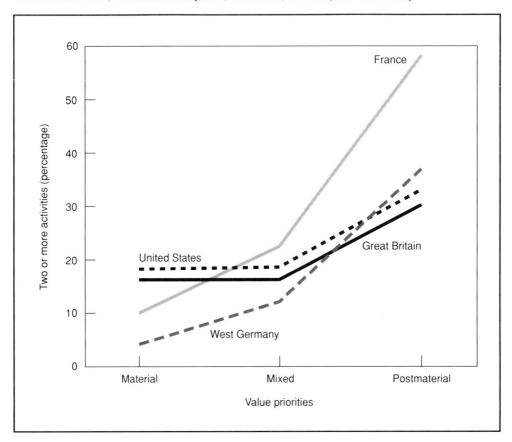

the traditional political agenda of economic and security issues. For now, and the foreseeable future, democratic politics will be marked by a mix of material and postmaterial issues.

Inevitably, changes in the public's basic value priorities should carry over to the structures of the political process. Already there are signs of institutional change to accommodate these new political demands. For example, there has been a general increase in the use of referendums in Western democracies, at least partially in reaction to demands for more participatory democracy. Even in West Germany, where Hitler's plebiscites in the 1930s discredited direct democracy methods, environmental and other postmaterial groups are calling for a

revival of the referendum and initiative. Similarly, bureaucracies in most systems are being pressured to open the policy process to citizen advisory panels and planning groups.

Another question involves the impact of these new values on the political parties and citizen voting behavior. Most of the established political parties are still oriented to traditional social divisions, and if anything, they have resisted attempts to incorporate postmaterial issues into a partisan framework. Nevertheless, . . . postmaterial values and issue concerns are injecting new volatility into Western party systems, often leading to the fragmentation of the established parties or the creation of new parties.

Only a few skeptics still doubt that value priorities are changing among Western publics; the evidence of change is obvious. It is more difficult to anticipate all of the consequences of this process of value change. By monitoring these trends, however, we may get a preview of the future nature of citizen politics in advanced industrial democracies.

III  INTERCONNECTIONS

Nothing makes life more difficult for a politician than when the public is deeply divided on an important question of public policy. Under such circumstances, the politician can hardly win; anything he or she does is guaranteed to anger a significant percentage of the electorate. Politicians in such cases have three choices: do nothing, hoping that someone else (the courts, for example) will take the heat; try to split the difference with a compromise; or take some type of symbolic action that might appease some of the people on one side but not upset those on the other too badly.

Probably the most controversial and divisive issue in the United States today is the abortion question, and politicians have tried all three of these strategies at one time or another. For a while, they were let off the hook by the Supreme Court, which took the issue out of their hands in the famous case of Roe v. Wade *(1973). More recently, however, in* Webster v. Reproductive Health Services *(1989), the Court has indicated that it would tolerate increased regulation of abortion by the states.* Webster *put state and local politicians back in the abortion quagmire. (See selections 16.3 and 16.5.)*

In the following selection, Rob Gurwitt looks at how politicians cope when public opinion is deeply—and bitterly—divided.

Question

1. Suppose you are an adviser to a state legislator, and he or she asks you to discuss possible options for dealing with the abortion issue. Suppose further that your state and district are deeply divided over the abortion question. Consider your response from the point of view of (a) a conservative Republican who is strongly opposed to abortion; (b) a liberal Democrat who strongly supports a woman's right to choose; and (c) a middle-of-the-roader with no strong views on the abortion question but with a strong desire to be reelected.

5.3 Abortion: The Issue Politicians Wish Would Just Go Away

Rob Gurwitt

When abortion opponents rallied one warm July morning on the south side of the county courthouse in Lafayette, Indiana, Sheila Klinker was there. And when, a half-hour later, abortion-rights supporters mustered on the north side of the courthouse, Sheila Klinker was there, too.

Klinker was engaged in a bit of shuttle politicking. For one crowd, she recounted her support for restrictions on abortions. For the other, she reaffirmed her belief that in limited circumstances women should be free to choose an abortion. She pledged to both that, as a Democratic member of the Indiana House, she would listen carefully to their concerns, and she called for a statewide referendum to see just what Hoosiers thought about the whole matter.

As Klinker saw it, her twin appearances reflected her own divided thinking, as well as her constituents'. Raised a Roman Catholic, the product of parochial schools, she believes both "religiously and personally" that abortion is wrong. "But I also feel there are extenuating circumstances, such as incest, rape, the life of the mother being in danger," she says. "I represent a lot of people out there, and I don't feel all my religious beliefs have to be shared by others."

To those who watched the entire performance, and to many who didn't, it seemed a classic display of light-toed political footwork. Newspapers around the state chided Klinker for playing to both sides of the issue; a letter to her home-town newspaper from a local minister warned, "People who walk the middle of the road are liable to be hit by a car from either side. . . . Representative Klinker's appearance at both rallies is the worst kind of politics." Even among her colleagues at the statehouse, the episode gained a small measure of notoriety.

"It wasn't lots of fun," she now admits. "I knew I wouldn't make either side happy, and I didn't."

Klinker's approach may have lacked subtlety, but she is hardly alone among legislators across the country in looking for a politically comfortable response to the abortion debate. The rallies that straddled the Tippecanoe County courthouse came five days after the U.S. Supreme Court's [1989] ruling . . . upholding a Missouri law imposing some strict limitations on the availability of abortions. That decision, in *Webster v. Reproductive Health Services,* was widely seen as opening the door to greater state legislative activism to restrict abortion rights. Since then, legislators across the country have been facing ever more concerted pressure to line up on one side or the other.

On the one hand, abortion-rights advocates have been jarred from a decade and a half of thinking that the court's 1973 *Roe v. Wade* decision legalizing abortion had settled the matter, and are stretching unaccustomed political muscles in preparation for the battles to come. Abortion foes, worried by a series of setbacks in the months following the July 3 ruling, have been girding for this year's legislative sessions with equal intensity. Caught in the middle, sensitive to their constituents' desires and, often, genuinely equivocal on the issue are many of the country's state legislators.

It is true that in a handful of places, lawmakers responded quickly to the *Webster* ruling. In Florida, Republican Governor Bob Martinez tried to add new restrictions on abortion, only to watch legislators defeat every one of his proposals. In Pennsylvania, by contrast, legislators extended their role as one of the leaders of the states' anti-abortion effort by banning abortions after 24 weeks of gestation and requiring mar-

Copyright, 1990, Boston Globe. Distributed by Los Angeles Times Syndicate. Reprinted with permission.

ried women to notify their husbands before aborting a fetus.

In the main, however, most legislators around the country would just as soon decline the honor handed them by the Supreme Court. Few are comfortable upholding immovable convictions or embracing moral absolutes. "We are so used to dealing in shades of gray," says Dick Dellinger, the Republican floor leader in the Indiana House, "that we don't like it when we have to see in black and white."

So while newly mobilized activists on both sides are looking to this year's legislative sessions to continue their struggle over the lives of unborn children and the women who carry them, most legislators are worrying about the 1990 elections and trying to keep the matter from tying up their institutions. For the most part, they will be unable to keep the seething public debate over abortion from spilling into their cool marble halls, but they are determined to contain it once it does.

To understand just how the abortion debate is faring in the post-*Webster* world, it helps to spend some time in a place like Indiana.

For one thing, it is an undeniably conservative state, a place stitched through with rural and small-town values that exalt family life, the work ethic and the glories of small business and the free market. "The pollsters say that if you take any national results, subtract 5 percent from the liberal side and add 5 percent to the conservative side, you've got Indiana," says Bill Schreiber, the chief assistant to Democratic House Speaker Mike Phillips. "I suspect that's not far off the truth."

Despite its conservatism, Indiana has never shown much interest in joining the first rank of anti-abortion states—a distinction belonging chiefly to Illinois, Minnesota and Missouri, in addition to Pennsylvania. Unlike Missouri, for example, Indiana does not require doctors to test for fetal viability before performing an abortion, nor does it prohibit abortions in publicly funded health facilities. But it has still followed a fairly restrictive line, prohibiting public funding for abortions, requiring parental notification by minors seeking abortions and making it state policy that "childbirth is preferred, encouraged and supported over abortion."

At first blush, then, it might seem entirely in character for new restrictions on abortion to have an easy time of it this year in Indiana. In fact, their future is anything but assured.

The biggest reason is politics. Long a Republican preserve in both national and state politics, Indiana has begun showing a decided bent for unpredictability. In 1988, it handed the governorship to the Democrats for the first time in two decades, electing Evan Bayh. That same year, Democrats won exactly half the seats in the House, giving them a measure of control over the body's agenda for the first time since 1976. They also picked up enough seats in the Senate to bring them within two votes of the Republicans.

The legislative split in the House led to an agreement between the two parties that the House would be run by two speakers, Phillips and Republican Paul Mannweiler—"stereo speakers," as they are known around the statehouse. It also guaranteed one of the stiffest battles in the country in the 1990 legislative elections, since a shift of one seat will give control of the House to the winner's party. The stakes are enormous, because redistricting is on the horizon next year, and both parties are in essence playing for the decade to come.

It should come as no surprise, then, that Republican and Democratic leaders in the Indiana legislature are unlikely to view the debate over abortion solely on its merits. "Going into those primaries and fall campaigns, they're not going to be thinking about 'abortion, pro or con,' " says Bob Margraf, the chief lobbyist for the Indiana State Teachers Association. "They're thinking about who's going to control the legislature for 10 long years."

The problem is, no one is certain how the issue will affect the elections. The notion that upholding abortion rights is politically risky was knocked to the ground by November's gubernatorial elections in New Jersey and Virginia, in which Democratic candidates won after turning their opponents' anti-abortion records against them. But while those results have caused urgent rethinking of the GOP's anti-abortion platform and nudged a number of politicians in both parties away from a strong anti-abortion stance, few have wholeheartedly embraced the cause of abortion rights.

That may be because it's not entirely clear where voters will come down. In Indiana, a survey done last fall by a private polling firm showed, basically, that they're as confused as the people who represent them. A full 87 percent of Indianians opposed outlawing all abortions, while some 72 percent agreed with the notion that abortion is a decision that government should have no role in. At the same time, a majority also favored some restrictions, especially parental notification by minors seeking abortions and limiting public hospitals to performing an abortion only when necessary to save the life of the mother. "Those people today are all in a quandary," says Mark Lubbers, executive vice president of the Hudson Institute, an Indianapolis-based think tank. "They understand both sides, and they say, 'Don't make me think about it, leave it like it is.' "

All of this leaves party leaders with an intense wish that the issue would just go away. Once abortion becomes an electoral issue, they fear they will have very little control over it. That is especially worrisome for the GOP, which is still bruised from its 1988 losses. "Republicans know what they have lost. They don't know how abortion will affect the elections, but they don't want to take a chance on it knocking them out," says Mannweiler's top aide, Roger Schmelzer. He is echoed on the Democratic side by Stan Jones, his party's floor leader in the House. "We think our candidates have other strengths," he says. "We don't want them to get hurt on this."

The uncertainty about abortion's impact is compounded by the fact that in Indiana, as in a good number of other states, the issue doesn't break down strictly on party lines. Phillips, the Democratic speaker, is from conservative southern Indiana and has generally lined up with anti-abortion forces in the past; one of the most vocal abortion opponents in the legislature is another Democrat, Frank Newkirk. At the same time, the Republicans are all over the map: Mannweiler, although he has voted for some restrictions in the past, has played his cards fairly close to the vest; the Republican floor leader, Dick Dellinger, has been an anti-abortion leader; Mannweiler's closest friend and running mate in his three-member Indianapolis district, John Keeler, is a dedicated supporter of abortion rights.

While circumstances in Indiana may make legislative leaders especially chary of handling the abortion issue this year, they are far from alone in facing a rank and file that does not want to deal with the matter. "There is more nervousness about addressing this issue than there has ever been," says Kathryn Kolbert, who works on the issue nationally for the American Civil Liberties Union. Says Jones, "When *Webster* first hit, a few legislators were enthusiastic about the opportunity to have this back in the legislature. Now, the large number of legislators are saying, 'This is an opportunity we're not sure we want handed to us.' "

Under these circumstances, the temptation may be strong to follow Sheila Klinker's example and appeal to both sides. But there is apprehension, in Indiana and elsewhere, that the rules of the game have changed. "This could be that rare case where the middle ground is not the safe place to be," says Jones. "It will be a rare legislator who can stand in the middle and take shots from both sides."

Certainly, both national parties and local party leaders have urged their members to take a position—any position—and then stick with it. [The late] Republican National Chairman Lee Atwater delivered that message when he came through Indiana last year, and it has been echoed since in both caucuses. "The thing we've told our members is, it's important to be consistent, if only for the sake of not being embarrassed," says Schmelzer.

But many members are clearly having a hard time settling into a comfortable position. Some simply don't know how. Ray Richardson, for example, is a 12-term Republican from Greenfield, a large town that sits just outside Indianapolis' orbit. He came within a few hundred votes of losing his seat in 1988 and is widely considered one of the legislature's most vulnerable incumbents this time around. "I have maintained a low profile on this issue, and I really want to continue to do that," he says. "I don't know the right thing to do, is all. I don't have an innate feeling one way or the other. I watch other people that do know and say to myself, 'Gee, that must be nice.'"

Others are comfortable with where they stand but worry that they may be open to fire from both sides. Mike Dvorak, a Democrat from the blue-collar and Roman Catholic environs of South Bend, favors heavy restrictions—up to a point. "I cannot personally support abortion, and my legislative response will be that I don't want to do anything that promotes abortion. But I don't think I would support an out-and-out ban on abortion," he says.

The problem, Dvorak and others contend, lies in explaining the intricacies of their positions to their constituents. "I'm just not sure whether I or other legislators will be able to get the ear of constituents to explain that complexity," Dvorak says.

Not surprisingly, the leadership's approach so far has been extremely cautious, aimed largely at keeping a lid on the issue. Speakers Mannweiler and Phillips in the House, and President Pro Tem Robert Garton and Democratic leader Dennis Neary in the Senate, have all signaled that they want to deal as quickly as they can with abortion and then move on to other issues. This year's session, which begins January 3, will last only 30 legislative days; legislators also have to deal with drug enforcement and state prison overcrowding, how to handle the state's $900 million budget surplus and whether to offset a decision to foot a smaller percentage of the cost of state employees' health-care benefits by improving other fringe benefits.

In some states, party leaders hoping to bypass the abortion controversy may be able to convince loyal members to hold off on introducing any new legislation—arguing, perhaps, that it's better to wait for the Supreme Court's expected ruling later this year on several other abortion cases. That probably won't work in Indiana, in large part because of Frank Newkirk.

One of the most outspokenly anti-abortion members of the House, Newkirk is also, at 32, one of its youngest and most independent-minded. On several key votes in the past, he has shown no hesitation about bolting Democratic caucus positions—"skating," in Indiana statehouse parlance. "I come from a district where I was lucky to be elected, and didn't know whether I could come back for another term," he says. "So I look at every session as *the* session to accomplish my goals."

Newkirk comes from Salem, a small town in the southern half of the state. Like virtually all southern Indiana Democrats, he is conservative, in keeping with the area's rural, German Catholic character. He traces his views on abortion in part to his own origins: He was born to a high school teenager whose minister and doctor had counseled her to bear her child and put him up for adoption. "Now, if it had been 1977 or 1987, instead of 1957, would that have happened?" he asks. "You'll never be able to convince me, with that background, that this is just a women's issue. I've been given the opportunity to speak for other unwanted children."

Although several other legislators plan to introduce anti-abortion bills, Newkirk's is likely to be the one that gets the most attention. It would bring Indiana into line with the Missouri statutes, putting it on record as believing that life begins at conception, prohibiting abortions in any publicly funded facilities and preventing doctors from aborting a fetus older than 20 weeks if they determine that it would be viable outside the womb. Newkirk also wants to require that anyone considering an abortion be told in detail what will happen to the fetus during the procedure, so that she can make "an informed choice."

Although there are committed partisans on the other side who are determined to block Newkirk's legislation, it may be possible to keep the issue from tying the legislature in knots. For one thing, individual committee chairmen may be able to prevent the matter from reaching the floor. But even if it does, the *Webster* ruling is at its heart fairly limited; it does not open the question of the legality of abortion itself but only allows states to add a few more restrictions to the circumstances under which it can legally be performed. If party leaders can cast the matter as a pair of limited votes on whether to require viability testing and whether public health facilities, which tend to serve the poor, should be allowed to perform abortions, they may escape without much controversy.

Then again, they may not. It's possible that the activists massing on the issue will force legislators to escalate their deliberations. "Both sides are ready to fight over the essence of abortion," says Ray Richardson. "It's true, they thought they would be fighting over the elephant, and the Supreme Court has only allowed them to fight over peanuts. But once having

built up their energies, it's not going to be easy for either side to wind them down." What happens in Indiana and in other states may well turn on how legislators respond to the disjuncture between the passions raging outside statehouse walls and the limited debate they are trying to carve out within.

Even a cursory glance at the forces that are gathering around the statehouse makes it clear that ignoring the partisans will be difficult. Over the last decade, in Indiana as in other states, those favoring abortion rights have had very little political presence. *Webster* has changed that.

In the last few months, a group of women calling themselves the Indiana Women's Network for Political Action has established a political action committee to donate money to pro-choice candidates. What sent ripples through Indiana's political community—and among abortion-rights activists nationally—was not so much the group's founding, but the speed with which it garnered $100,000 worth of pledges. "None of us in our wildest imagination thought the money would come in so fast," says Sheila Kennedy, a Republican lawyer who is one of the group's leaders.

The network's aim is not only to fund sympathetic candidates but also to pressure legislators to oppose any new restrictions on abortion. "Our goal is to be sure that nothing happens to Indiana abortion law," says Kennedy. The group is counting on the political connections of its members, most of them financially well-off and politically articulate, to get the point across. "Our membership is executives and lawyers and CPAs who are well situated politically and economically to have an impact on their friends in the political process," says Marilyn Schultz, a former state legislator who is now director of the Indiana Mental Health Association. Kennedy has already begun that process, telling Republican candidates for whom she has helped raise money in the past that they can count on nothing from her or her friends unless they side with her on abortion. "By and large, pro-choice people have not been single-issue voters. But for the foreseeable future, that is what we will be," she predicts.

On the other side is a collection of organizations—the state Roman Catholic conference, right-to-life groups and others—that have been working the field for well over a decade. One of its most prominent figures is Eric Miller, an Indianapolis lawyer whose conservative Christian group, Citizens Concerned for the Constitution, has in past years carved out a prominent place for itself in the statehouse. "There are legislators who are very scared of Eric Miller and the people he can bring out," says one statehouse aide. Miller has already pledged to bring his members to the statehouse every Tuesday during the session.

Miller leaves no doubt about what he expects of legislators. "We believe legislators are going to be presented with reasonable laws, and in our opinion, there's no half way. If a legislator votes against viability testing, and for the use of government money [to perform abortions], then that legislator doesn't begin to be pro-life or pro-family," he says.

With Miller's forces ready to insist that legislators take a stand, and Kennedy and her allies pulling from the opposite direction, keeping the legislative debate from getting out of hand and spilling over into the elections will be tricky. According to Schreiber, Democratic Speaker Phillips' aide, the key will be for the leadership to be seen as having treated the matter head-on and without playing favorites. "The overriding interest for both Phillips and Mannweiler is to protect themselves from the charge that they dealt with this unfairly," he says. That will give them the leverage, Schreiber suggests, to keep the debate as dispassionate as possible.

Whether they opt for that route or pursue a strategy that keeps new restrictions on abortion from reaching the floor, though, it is clear that the *Webster* ruling has handed the legislative future of abortion to people for whom the arguments on both sides of the issue must take a back seat to practical political concerns.

"It has to be more a matter of tactics than of persuasion this year," says Stan Jones, the House Democratic floor leader. "This will be a session for the process people, not for the persuasion people." The question is whether they can keep it that way.

IV ◎ FOCUS: PUBLIC OPINION POLLS

Public opinion polls are not simply neutral devices used to measure American public opinion. They have become tools of the trade for politicians and presidents, especially in recent years. Pollsters play a key role in helping candidates to shape their campaigns and in helping political leaders govern.

The use of pollsters by presidents and other politicians has become the source of some controversy. Critics point out that the overuse of public opinion polls tends to turn leaders into followers and also encourages politicians to tell the public only what they want to hear—a practice that can lead to erratic public policy, a dangerous short-term point of view, and a loss of critically needed perspective. Paradoxically, critics suggest, politicians who rely too much on public opinion polls may end up losing touch with the people; they would be better off relying instead on their own political instincts and leadership abilities.

In selection 5.4, political commentator Michael Barone recounts the history of pollsters in the White House and assesses the appropriate role of the presidential poll-

ster in modern American government. Then, in selection 5.5, Peverill Squire examines the most famous—or infamous—poll in American political history.

Questions

1. Would you advise an incoming president to hire a full-time White House pollster? What advantages would such an adviser bring to the president? What dangers might he or she present? Consider the experiences of the Carter White House in answering.

2. Consider the role of the political pollster in American governance in the light of the arguments concerning democracy presented by James Madison in *Federalist* No. 10 (selection 2.1). Do public opinion polls increase the possibility that majority factions will exert an overpowering influence at the national level?

5.4 *The Power of the Presidents' Pollsters*

Michael Barone

As the president-elect was preparing to enter office, he received some advice form his pollster. Patrick Caddell told Jimmy Carter that, although the president was about to undertake new responsibilities, he should continue "campaigning." He should use fireside chats and town hall meetings, he should eschew the accoutrements of high office and shun the luxuries of the rich. The advice evidently was heeded. In his first act after taking the oath, Carter stepped out of the presidential limousine and walked down Pennsylvania Avenue to the White House. Within weeks he appeared on television before a fire, wearing a sweater and talking unpretentiously to the American people.

Over the next four years, the advice changed, and the president did not always follow it. But Patrick Caddell, seldom seen in Washington in the Carter years without his White House pass dangling from his breast pocket, achieved a level of influence greater than that of any pollster before or since.

It was a precedent not entirely congenial to the polling profession. Political pollsters, after all, earn their fees by helping politicians win elections; Caddell's client saw a big lead wind up as a narrow victory in 1976 and was soundly defeated in 1980. An argument can be made—and I would make it—that Carter did entirely too much "campaigning" in his four years in office and not enough governing, that he spent too much time emphasizing the outsider themes that had worked for him as an unknown challenger and not enough time establishing himself as an insider who knew how to lead.

Even so, the Carter-Caddell experience did not result in the banishment of pollsters from the White House. Ronald Reagan's pollster, Dr. Richard Wirthlin, has been conducting frequent surveys during the Reagan years (paid for by the national Republican party, as Caddell's were by the national Democratic party, even when Carter had a primary opponent). Wirthlin has been less influential than Caddell, but his work has made an imprint on the Reagan presidency. This year [1988] Robert Teeter for George Bush and Irwin "Tubby" Harrison for Michael Dukakis are wearing the "pollsters general" mantle. Pollsters are with us in presidential politics and presidential governing, and they are likely to remain so. All this raises interesting questions: How did they get there? How should they be used now that they're there?

Humble Beginnings

The answer is that pollsters got to the White House even before Dr. George Gallup published his first public opinion survey in October 1935. That was a month after the murder of Huey Long, and so Gallup was not able to give us any results on one of the tantalizing might-have-beens of political history: how much damage would Long have done as a third-party candidate against Franklin Roosevelt in 1936? But Roosevelt himself had already received a report on that, at dinner in June 1935 with James Farley, Joseph Kennedy, and Will Hays, the 1920s Republican national chairman and 1930s movie czar—how one would like to have been a fly on that wall!—plus a statistician named Emil Hurja. Hurja presented results from a poll that showed "the president weaker that [sic] at any time since his inauguration" and "showed that [Roosevelt] would carry without difficulty all of the western states with the possible exception of Colorado, including Wisconsin and Minnesota, of course. It showed that in the eastern states he had lost some ground, which, of course, does not worry us because that condition can be corrected in due course." From the results—I have not been able to track down any written version—Farley predicted that Roosevelt would be elected by a five-million-vote plurality, and that Long would win three to four million votes and run uniformly throughout the country. Translated into percentage terms, this comes to something like a 51–39 percent Roosevelt lead over the Republicans, with 10 percent for Long, a drop from Roosevelt's 57–40 percent win over Herbert Hoover in 1932; it would have cost him Massachusetts, New Jersey, and Ohio, and have made New York and Michigan unsure.

Hurja's poll may have done something to inspire Roosevelt's shift to the left in May and June 1935, even though it seems that move started three weeks before, after NRA [the National Recovery Administration] was declared unconstitutional May 27. Roosevelt had other reasons to believe that Long was a threat. The most sophisticated of the day's polls, Elmo Roper's quarterly surveys that began appearing in *Fortune* in July 1935, had made it clear that most voters were wary of the economic redistributionist politics of some New Dealers and were hostile to the militant new CIO [Congress of Industrial Organizations] unions. But while this was true of the traditional base each party had held since the Civil War—the Republican northern farmlands and the Democratic Deep South—these policies were popular among the electoral groups that were not firmly attached to either party—the Jews of New York City and the German- and Scandinavian-American Progressives of Wisconsin, Minnesota, and the old Northwest. Roosevelt seems to have understood this without polls, for this was the coalition he had been thinking about assembling since the 1920s. But polls helped convince liberal Republicans to appeal to the swing groups.

Wendell Willkie was surely aware of the *Fortune* polls, since *Fortune* managing editor Russell Davenport was his campaign organizer. Willkie made a point of saying blunt and supposedly impolitic things, which any reader of the *Fortune* polls would have known were widely popular. As Davenport himself wrote in the April 1940 issue, "The fascinating characteristic of Mr. Willkie's position is that most people will agree with it."

The always well-organized and professionally advised Thomas E. Dewey also consulted polls closely. He studied the national polls and even polls in supposedly one-party states such as Florida. "Through Ben Duffey of the New York advertising agency Batten, Barton, Durstine and Osborne," writes Dewey's definitive biographer Richard Norton Smith, "daily telephone conversations were arranged with pollster Archibald Crossley. Both Gallup and Roper offered to make known their findings to Duffey in advance of publication. Gallup did have one question. Why, he asked Duffey, did the Republican campaign want to spend money on polling? The results, after all, were a 'foregone conclusion.' "

So both candidates in 1948 may have appreciated the limits of polling better than the pollsters. Dewey because he didn't seem to trust them (Gallup's last poll was taken October 15–25 and showed Truman with a gain that would certainly prompt any of today's pollsters to stay in the field), Truman because he, like most other Democrats of the times, paid little attention to polls.

Polls Taking Root

Gallup and other pollsters for years had suggested that polls predicted election results, rather than make the more modest but more accurate claim (accurate probably even in 1948) that they showed opinion at a particular time; and by comparing their final polls to election results, calculated to even tenths of a percentage, they suggested that polls have a greater precision than they can ever realistically claim. Pollsters paid for these sins after 1948, when their final surveys all showed Dewey well ahead.

In the 1952 campaign neither side (even the Eisenhower campaign with its advertising agents) seems to have relied much on pollsters or paid much attention to them. Eisenhower himself overrode the professionals and insisted on campaigning in the South, where he believed correctly that he could carry several states. Among Taft conservatives it had become dogma that there was a huge reservoir of conservative votes among nonvoters—a dogma that surely would not have been supported by polls. Adlai Stevenson's backers quickly developed a distaste for "selling a candidate like soap" and for the survey research associated with such efforts. Most published polls during the campaign showed the race closer than in 1948, with the result that the final 56–44 percent Eisenhower margin came as a great surprise.

When in 1960 the pollster finally became a fixture of a major presidential campaign, the scene was not some high-tech office but a "pink-and-white children's bedroom on the second floor" of one of the Kennedy Hyannis Port houses. It

> had been cleared that evening as a data-analysis section, the beds removed, the baby chairs thrust to the side, a long table set up with mounds of voting statistics; there public opinion analyst Lou Harris was codifying reports received from the communications center downstairs and from the four teletypewriters of the wire agencies installed in the adjacent bedroom.

Back before the networks established reliable voter analysis models—their projections seesawed from a Kennedy landslide to a Nixon landslide on election night—Harris was doing most of this not very useful work himself, for except perhaps in Chicago the votes had already been cast. Harris, however, had done other work in the campaign, sampling opinion nationally, testing responses to issues, looking at poll results in a particular state. This was important in a campaign that was always tightly contested and in which at least the Kennedys (if not the television networks) were aware that past patterns would not obtain. Reactions to new issues and—even more important—the ties of ancestral religion would make all the difference.

The Kennedy's reliance on Lou Harris in the 1960 campaign was the first of several instances in which the Democrats, once so scornful of poll takers, seem to have used them at least as assiduously as the usually better-heeled Republicans. In 1964 Lyndon Johnson was endlessly fascinated with the polls that showed him so popular, and he hired Oliver Quayle as his pollster (Harris having gone out of the candidate polling business in 1963); Barry Goldwater, painfully aware that his was a losing cause, was more interested in being faithful to his principles and his followers than in following any advice that might be suggested by the polls. In

1968 Richard Nixon clearly ran a more organized and deliberate campaign than Hubert Humphrey, whose campaign consultant Joseph Napolitan was typing out his fall campaign plan as Humphrey was being nominated in Chicago in the last week of August. Yet neither campaign, in my view, fully appreciated the insights that sophisticated polling could have provided in that confusing and turbulent year. Humphrey, for example, was clearly out of sync with opinion when he championed, a month after Martin Luther King was murdered, "the politics of joy." Nixon, who saw Humphrey's support rise while his remained stagnant around the 43 percent level, was not much better.

The Players in Presidential Polling

Around this time the pollsters who have dominated presidential polling in most of the years since had begun to emerge. Robert Teeter, of Detroit's Market Opinion Research, is a quiet, calm, thoughtful, ideologically tolerant Republican from the ancestral Republican territory of outstate Michigan, who has played some role in every Republican presidential campaign since 1968. He was the lead pollster in Gerald Ford's very nearly successful attempt to overcome a 62–29 deficit in 1976—a campaign that sounded the themes of national pride and accomplishment that proved so resonant for Ronald Reagan in the 1980s—and he was the lead pollster for George Bush in 1980 and 1988. The other major Republican pollster has been Richard Wirthlin, a Mormon academic from Utah who bridled at supporting Barry Goldwater in 1964 but who has been Ronald Reagan's pollster since 1970. Wirthlin has calmly provided the president with figures and recommended strategies that, over the years, have sometimes pleased and sometimes enraged Reagan's ideological supporters.

On the Democratic side the dominant figure from 1972 until sometime in 1984 was Patrick Caddell. Only twenty-two years old in 1972, a Harvard undergraduate from a career military family in the redneck city of Jacksonville, Florida, he managed to attach himself to George McGovern's longshot campaign. Caddell's great contribution there was the idea, common in academia, of alienation: it was he who counseled McGovern to appeal to supporters of George Wallace on the grounds that they all wanted a change and a removal of the people in power in Washington.

Caddell's problem was that he became a kind of johnny-one-note. A similar alienation theme worked well for Jimmy Carter, as he campaigned in the wake of Watergate in 1975 and 1976 as a candidate who was not from Washington, was not a lawyer, who carried his own suitbag, and who would never lie to you. As late as July 1979, Caddell wrote Carter a memorandum describing a national "malaise" and helped to put together the domestic summit in which Carter ludicrously summoned government officials and national notables up to his mountaintop—as if he were not in charge of the government himself.

Caddell's and Carter's strategy was still to run against Washington and against government—an approach that became unsustainable when Carter was in Washington and headed the government. In contrast, Ronald Reagan once in office used his 1940s movie experience— the best popular culture since Dickens—and identified himself and his political cause with the heart of the country and the concerns that most citizens have at heart.

Caddell's approach was adolescent, always complaining about the grownups in power. Reagan's approach was adult, celebrating the success of those who have worked hard over the years and inviting the next generation to join them. For a moment in the 1970s, when Americans' confidence in their government and their country was low, Caddell's adolescent approach struck a chord. But over the longer haul, as the success of our own country and the weaknesses of our adversaries became harder to hide, Reagan's adult approach summed up the national mood better.

What Polls Can't Do

Do pollsters manipulate politicians who will manipulate voters in turn? These have been the fears of intellectuals ever since the polling profession was born. Actually, the fears go back further. Politicians have always been eager to understand public opinion in any way they can, if only by sampling the opinion of their neighbors and relatives as every American family does at the Thanksgiving dinner table. The fear is that the pollster, being in possession of information so much more reliable and so much more capable of producing political results than anyone else, can become a kind of Svengali.

The history I have recounted does not, I think, substantiate such fears. A Caddell can influence one candidate's campaign, but that influence is still limited in time and place. Politicians are increasingly sophisticated about using pollsters, having learned with the public to understand the limitations of the polling instrument and having observed that following slavishly the implications of any poll at one moment does not guarantee a favorable result in the long run. The ultimate limit is that voters want officeholders who not only campaign effectively but who also govern effectively. And the instincts, the policies, the strategies that produce effective governance are no more discoverable by pollsters than they are by anyone else.

Polling is a tool, not magic; and political pollsters at their best are inspired mechanics, like the guys who without saying an articulate word in English, can get your old Ford Mustang or your old musty refrigerator working again. They are not—certainly they are not yet—our masters.

5.5 *Why the 1936* Literary Digest *Poll Failed*

Peverill Squire

[*Probably the most infamous public opinion poll ever taken was that conducted in 1936 by the news magazine the* Literary Digest. *The poll's infamy derives from a classic combination of factors: high public expectations concerning the reliability of the poll as a predictor of the presidential election and the poll's spectacular failure to predict Franklin D. Roosevelt's massive landslide victory. Ever since, this poll has stood as a chastening reminder to overly optimistic or boastful poll takers.*

The public's high expectations for the accuracy of the 1936 poll were due to the poll's great success in the 1932 presidential election (within 1 percent of the actual vote) and the vastness of the enterprise: the Literary Digest *polled over 2 million Americans, an extraordinary technical and practical accomplishment. More than that, the poll captured the depression-era public's imagination and its predilection for the new scientific age they saw on the horizon.*

Given the historical significance of the Literary Digest *poll, Peverill Squire's analysis of its embarrassing failure is of interest in its own right. The issues of sampling error (those who received ballots did not represent a random cross-sample of the electorate) and response bias (those who actually sent back their ballots were not part of a representative sample) are no longer serious ones in modern polls that are conducted by reputable pollsters. They remain serious concerns, however, in many local polls and in many polls conducted by nonneutral parties, such as interest groups or political candidates. The 1936 experience reminds us not to rely too completely on any single poll result.*

The fact that the Literary Digest *poll succeeded in 1932 but failed in 1936 has been cited by some scholars as evidence of the increased importance of economic class in the second Roosevelt election as compared to the first. Although both polls presumably were based on a response population biased toward the rich, only the 1936 poll suffered in accuracy as a result. The explanation, some argue, is that rich and poor tended to vote alike in 1932 but diverged in their voting habits in 1936.*]

The 1936 [presidential] campaign concluded with the *Literary Digest* publishing survey results forecasting a landslide victory for the Republican presidential candidate, Alf Landon. The actual election was, of course, won by the incumbent, Franklin Roosevelt, by a large margin. Thus the *Literary Digest* poll gained an infamous place in the history of survey research.

Almost every book on presidential elections or survey methodology contains some scathing reference to the poll and gives reasons why it failed to forecast the correct results. Some claim the error resulted from a biased sample. A few assert that the sample was acceptable but that the low response rate produced the incorrect forecast. Many others state that a combination of these problems was responsible. Surprisingly, these claims are mere speculation; no analysis has been conducted to determine why the *Literary Digest* poll was wrong. Consequently, we have some ideas—really competing hypotheses—as to why the poll failed but no empirical research by which to determine the source of the error.

In this article I present evidence on why the *Literary Digest* poll failed, using data from a 1937 Gallup Poll which asked about participation in the magazine's survey. Examining who was asked to participate in the poll and who actually did so allows us to determine where the poll went wrong.

The 1936 *Literary Digest* Poll

The 1936 poll was not the *Literary Digest*'s first survey. The magazine had run a poll on every presidential election since 1920 and had correctly forecast the winner in each. Indeed, they called Roosevelt's victory in 1932 within one percentage point of the actual result. The poll had gained credibility among the public and politicians. According to Katz and Cantril:

> During the 1936 campaign, for example, the *New York Herald Tribune* devoted as much space to the *Literary Digest* results as to those of the American Institute of Public Opinion for which

it was paying. The Hearst papers had their own poll (Crossley's Survey) deep in the back pages while featuring . . . the *Digest*'s.

The magazine was fond of quoting Democratic party chairman James A. Farley saying, "The *Literary Digest* poll is an achievement of no little magnitude. It is a Poll fairly and correctly conducted." There are indications that the 1936 poll's favorable results encouraged the Landon campaign.

There were some skeptics. Academics and the pioneering professional pollsters were less enamored of the *Literary Digest* survey and its methods. A study of straw polls by a Columbia University sociologist discussed eight sources of potential error, including class and participation biases. By 1936 George Gallup, Archibald Crossley, and Elmo Roper were conducting competing surveys based on more scientific sampling procedures.

How did the *Literary Digest* conduct its 1936 poll? The magazine sent out more than *10 million* straw vote ballots. The sample was drawn primarily from automobile registration lists and telephone books. Coverage in certain locales was astonishing. The *Literary Digest* claimed to have polled every third registered voter in Chicago, every other registered voter in Scranton, Pennsylvania, and every registered voter in Allentown, Pennsylvania. The ballots were mailed in late summer and the returns were published each week from 6 September to 31 October as they were tabulated. The magazine stated the ballots were not "weighted, adjusted, nor interpreted." Over 2.3 million ballots were returned, an impressive number but representing less than a 25% participation rate.

The magazine's final count before the election gave Landon 1,293,669 votes (55%), Roosevelt 972,897 (41%), and Lemke 83,610 (4%). The actual results on election day gave the president 61% of the vote and his Republican challenger only 37%. This huge and apparently inclusive survey produced a most embarrassing prediction and is considered a major cause of the magazine's demise in 1938.

Explanations of What Went Wrong

The week following the election the *Literary Digest* tried to discern what went wrong. They dismissed the notion that their sample was flawed because it systematically excluded the poor:

> Well, in the first place, the "have nots" did not reelect Mr. Roosevelt. That they contributed to his astonishing plurality no one can doubt. But the fact remains that a majority of farmers, doctors, grocers and candlestick-makers *also* voted for the President. . . . Besides—We *did* reach these so-called "have not" strata.

The *Literary Digest* saw some problems in the response rate to their mail survey, although they had no explanation for it. Referring to their 1928 straw vote the magazine observed: "We wondered then, as we had wondered before and have wondered since, why we were getting better cooperation in what we have always regarded as a public service from Republicans than we were getting from Democrats. Do Republicans live nearer mail-boxes?"

The first wave of comments by professional pollsters and academics pointed to response bias as the primary culprit. . . . In any event, competitor surveys headed by Gallup, Roper, and Crossley predicted the 1936 election with reasonable accuracy, sounding the death knell for the *Literary Digest* polling methodology.

Explanations for the poll's failure, however, have continued for 50 years past the event. They break down into three categories. First are those who place the blame on the sample and its failure to include the supposed core of Roosevelt's support, the poor. The main assumption of this view is that many of the president's supporters were excluded from the survey by virtue of not owning autos or telephones. [One analyst] . . . claimed that the survey "greatly overweighted the well-to-do, and voters less well-to-do, not able to have telephones, were for Mr. Roosevelt." Others have advanced some variant of this explanation.

Another, less-popular perspective is that the full sample was not the problem but that the response rate produced the error. [In other words, this explanation suggests that Landon voters were not overrepresented in the sample but were instead more likely to return the questionnaire than were Roosevelt voters.] The major proponent of this explanation is Maurice C. Bryson, a statistician, who, without supporting data, reasoned that the full *Literary Digest* sample was not particularly biased and should still have supported Roosevelt because the ownership of cars and telephones in 1936 was too widespread to account for the poll's forecast. Instead, Bryson placed blame on the response rate. . . .

Finally, many commentators cite both the sample and the response rate as being flawed. This position was advanced by Charles Smith and George Gallup in the decade following the poll and has been carried into the present [by others]. . . . These writers assert that the initial bias toward overrepresentation of Republicans in the sample was exacerbated by the fact that better-educated and wealthy people who tended to be Landon supporters were more likely to respond to the survey.

Data for Testing These Hypotheses

As noted above, none of these explanations has been subjected to empirical scrutiny. One data source available for testing these ideas has never, to my knowledge, been exploited. Between 19 and 24 May 1937, Gallup asked a series of questions regarding the *Literary Digest* poll:

1. Did you receive a *Literary Digest* straw vote ballot in the Presidential campaign last fall?

2. Did you send it in?

3. Did you change your mind regarding the candidate between the time you sent it in and the election?

The survey also asked who the respondent had voted for in the 1936 election and, as part of the standard demographic series, whether the respondent had a car or a telephone.

This survey is the best available tool for determining why the *Literary Digest* poll failed. It must be noted, however, that Gallup's own quota sampling procedure did have significant flaws. Moreover, like almost all postelection surveys, it overestimates the vote for the winning candidate—in this case by 5 percentage points. The poll also overrepresents the percentage of people who had a telephone or car, and the number of people who received a *Literary Digest* ballot and returned it. These shortcomings necessarily leave the evidence to be presented below less than perfect. Nonetheless, the data do permit reasonable estimation of the relative contributions of sampling error and nonresponse bias to the poll's failure. There is no reason to suppose that error in the Gallup data systematically biases such estimates from one side or the other.

Testing the Hypotheses

The *Literary Digest* poll was a failure because its estimate of the actual vote was wildly incorrect, and it even predicted the wrong winner. Commentary on the poll reveals two hypotheses to explain why it failed. They could both be wrong, either could be correct, or jointly they could be right. I will examine the hypotheses one at a time.

The Literary Digest *poll failed simply because the sample was biased.* For this to be the sole source of the problem the Gallup data should reveal that owners of cars and telephones gave most of their support to Landon, as should the majority of those who received *Literary Digest* straw vote ballots. Tables 1 and 2 (p. 178) reveal

that these expectations are off the mark. Owners of only an automobile or a telephone were less supportive of Roosevelt than those who did not have either, but they were still strongly for him. Even respondents who had both a car and a telephone were for the president.

More importantly, those who claimed to have received a *Literary Digest* ballot went for Roosevelt by 55% to 44%. Employing the rough 5% overestimate of the president's vote—and the 4% underestimate of Landon's share—still leaves Roosevelt the winner, although by very little. The margin for Roosevelt is considerably wider among those who did not participate in the magazine's survey. But if everyone who received a ballot had returned it the results would have, at least, correctly predicted Roosevelt a winner. The projected vote percentages, however, would have greatly underestimated the president's margin of victory.

This suggests that *the response rate was an important source of error.* Evidence supporting this claim is presented in Table 3 (p. 178). Among those who responded—correcting for those who remembered changing their mind before the election—a slight majority favored Landon. While the Gallup survey numbers do not reach the same level of support for the Republican reported in the *Literary Digest* poll, they are in the same direction. The well-known tendency for survey respondents to incorrectly remember having voted for the winning candidate may inflate Roosevelt's numbers in the Gallup survey.

The percentage of those who claim to have returned their straw vote ballot is too high, ob-

TABLE 1
1936 Presidential Vote by Car and Telephone Ownership (in Percent)

Presidential Vote	Car & Phone	Car, No Phone	Phone, No Car	Neither
Roosevelt	55	68	69	79
Landon	45	30	30	19
Other	1	2	0	2
Total N	946	447	236	657

Source: American Institute of Public Opinion, 28 May 1937.

TABLE 2
Presidential Vote by Receiving *Literary Digest* Straw Vote Ballot or Not (in Percent)

Presidential Vote	Recieved Poll	Not Receive Poll	Do Not Know
Roosevelt	55	71	73
Landon	44	27	25
Other	1	1	3
Total N	780	1339	149

Source: American Institute of Public Opinion, 28 May 1937.

TABLE 3
Presidential Vote by Returning or Not Returning Straw Vote Ballot (in Percent)

Presidential Vote	Did Return	Did Not Return	Do Not Know
Roosevelt	48	69	56
Landon	51	30	40
Other	1	1	4
Total N	493	288	48

Source: American Institute of Public Opinion, 28 May 1937.

viously inflated by many respondents claiming incorrectly that they participated. But if anything, this overreporting would seem likely to overestimate the support for the president. It does not seem probable that Roosevelt supporters would claim to have returned a ballot marked for the Republican challenger. On balance, then, it seems reasonable to conclude from this evidence that a low response rate together with a nonresponse bias contributed greatly to the failure of the *Literary Digest* poll to correctly call the winner.

But, more importantly, the initial sample was flawed; when compounded with the response bias it produced the wildly erroneous forecast of the vote percentages. As noted earlier, the Gallup poll produces an estimated vote of 66% for Roosevelt, 5% above the figure he actually received in the election. Thus, a rough calculation of the bias produced by the sample is around 11%, with another 7% accounted for by problems with the responses.

Conclusion

The evidence presented here strongly supports the conclusion that the 1936 *Literary Digest* poll failed to project the correct vote percentages or even the right winner not simply because of its initial sample, but also because of a low response rate combined with a nonresponse bias. Those who reported receiving straw vote ballots were supportive of the president. But a slight majority of those who claimed to have returned their ballot favored Landon.

This conclusion does have some relevance today. We are, of course, subjected to nonrandom sample surveys daily. Most deal with trivial matters like determining who is the public's favorite television or movie star. A few concern important issues: who "won" a presidential debate or whether baseball should keep the designated hitter rule. We are all aware of the flaws inherent in such surveys and why their results should rarely be believed.

The analysis here should also call our attention to the other potential problem with any survey: nonresponse bias. Those who conduct the most reliable surveys are concerned with this problem, and much effort is expended devising ways to cope with it. Failure to properly handle participation problems can damage the results produced by any poll, but many surveys do not report or discuss their response rates. Consumers of public opinion surveys, as well as practitioners, must be reminded of this potential problem in order to avoid a future disaster like the *Literary Digest* poll of 1936.

Chapter 6

Political Participation

_P_olitical participation can be thought of as all the activities of private citizens _"aimed at influencing the selection of government personnel and/or the actions they take."*_ Such activities include voting, contributing to political candidates, working for a political campaign, and running for political office. It also encompasses such activities as writing to a congressional representative, watching a presidential press conference, or even staying up late to follow the election returns.

Measuring political participation is not difficult. The percentage of citizens who vote—voter turnout—is easy to calculate. Political polls and surveys can gauge citizens' interest in politics and the extent of their politically oriented activities. These figures can be compared over time, across different regions or socioeconomic groups, or among different countries.

Determining the significance of these numbers is a far more difficult task. Is a drop in participation a sign of political health or disease? Is nonvoting an act of laziness and irresponsibility, or is it a rational response to a political system that presents few real choices? Can we really say that one country's democratic system is stronger because more people vote, or that another's is weaker because citizens seem to care little about politics?

At one time, questions about political participation were easy to answer. Voting was a civic duty; a citizen who did not keep up with political news and events was derelict (consider, for example, the ideas of Miss E., in selection 6.2). More participation was good; less participation was bad. Only a nation with active, involved citizens could sustain democracy.

* Sidney Verba and Norman H. Nie, _Participation in America: Political Democracy and Social Democracy_ (New York: Harper & Row, 1972), p. 2.

In the 1990s, however, as we have gradually become used to extraordinarily low turnout rates—only 50 percent in the presidential campaign of 1988 and less in non-presidential years—the impact of such low participation rates has become unclear. Some even suggest that nonvoting is itself a form of political participation—a silent but eloquent statement that voting is not worth the bother.

Several of the readings in this chapter focus on voter turnout, the easiest and most direct method of participating in democratic politics. Citizens who do not vote may be less likely to participate in other ways; citizens who vote but do nothing else can nonetheless be counted as participants in the political life of the nation.

Chapter Questions

1. Who votes and who doesn't? Why (or why not)? Does it matter? Why is voter turnout in the United States lower than in other countries? Why is it lower than it once was? Do these trends bode well or ill for the American political system?

2. Americans, most scholars and commentators believe, are less active in politics and more apathetic than they were two or three decades ago. What evidence supports this trend? Would you characterize most Americans today as active participants in politics? most students today?

I THE INTERNATIONAL CONTEXT

One way to assess the level and degree of political participation in the United states is to compare it with that of other democracies. Are Americans more likely to vote than their counterparts in Europe or Australia? Is the average American more involved in politics than, say, the average German, Belgian, or Swede? Such questions are not easy to answer because of differences in culture and in the rules of the political game, but they do cast light on issues that, in a vacuum, are vague and unclear.

In the following reading, David Glass, Peverill Squire, and Raymond Wolfinger argue that the low turnout in American elections is not a function of political culture but of the obstacles that must be overcome in order to vote. Specifically, they charge, American voter registration requirements are responsible for much of the difference in turnout levels between Americans and Europeans.

Questions

1. What evidence do the authors present to suggest that low turnout levels in the United States are not the result of Americans' dissatisfaction with or alienation from government?

2. What is the difference between turnout as conventionally defined in the United States and the alternative statistic proposed by the authors of this

selection: the percentage of registered voters who actually vote? Why do the authors place so much emphasis on this statistic?

6.1 Voter Turnout: An International Comparison

David Glass, Peverill Squire, and Raymond Wolfinger

Everyone knows that Americans vote less than citizens of other democratic countries. There are several explanations offered for this disparity. One theory is that low American turnout reflects alienation or mistrust that can discourage voting. We have concluded that this is not true. Another possibility is that calculating turnout percentages on different bases affects comparisons of the United States and other democracies. We conclude that this is indeed the case; when the base used is people who are registered, American turnout measures up very well against other countries.

Some election specialists recognize that the United States computes turnout differently from other countries: the percentage of the American *voting-age population* who vote is contrasted with the turnout rate of *registered persons* elsewhere. The latter figure includes only those people who are legally qualified to vote in the current election. The voting-age population includes a great many people who could not possibly vote: millions of aliens, who are categorically ineligible to vote; over a million citizens who are ineligible in most states—ex-felons and inmates of prisons and mental hospitals; and, most numerous, citizens who would be eligible if they had taken the step of establishing that eligibility by registering. This apples-and-oranges international comparison inevitably casts American voting performance in the most unfavorable light. To the best of our knowledge, no one has compared turnout in the United States and in other countries on both percentage bases: as a percentage of the voting-age popu-

Drawing by Locher. Reprinted with permission of Tribune Media Services.

lation and as a percentage of registered voters. How would American turnout stack up if the same yardstick were used for all countries?

Table 1 compares turnout in the most recent national election in the United States and a number of other countries for which we could obtain data. The left column in table 1 presents the data in the customary way, with American turnout as a percentage of the voting-age population and other countries' turnout as a percentage of registered voters. This produces the familiar picture: at 52.6 percent, the United States places twenty-third among the two dozen nations. Only Switzerland (48.3 percent) has lower turnout. At the top of the list, five countries have voting rates above 90 percent (see table 1).

The right column in table 1 provides a common base for all countries: the number of votes cast divided by the voting-age population. This is a fairer comparison, but it does not make the United States look any more like a nation of voters. Of the twenty-one nations for which we could obtain data, the United States ranked twentieth, with Switzerland again the only country lagging behind. The gap between the United States and the top-ranked country is the same as in the first column. In short, ranking turnout by the American standard does little to dispute the traditional finding that fewer Americans vote than do the citizens of any other democratic country (except, of course, Switzerland). Now that we have established that Americans do indeed vote less, our task is to explain why.

Alienation's Not the Answer

One plausible—and certainly popular—hypothesis about low American turnout is that it is caused by alienation from the political system. Commentaries deploring the state of American politics often link low turnout to public disaffection. Yet, repeated cross-sectional analyses have shown that the relationship between alienation and turnout is weak or non-existent. Our concern, though, is with levels of alienation in the United States compared with those in other countries. Data on this point are scarce. None of the handful of comparative studies includes

TABLE 1
Ranking of Countries by Turnout in Their Most Recent National Election[a]

Traditional Measure of Turnout[b]		Vote as a Percentage of Voting-Age Population	
1. Belgium	94.6	1. Italy	94.0
2. Australia	94.5	2. Austria	89.3
3. Austria	91.6	3. Belgium	88.7
4. Sweden	90.7	4. Sweden	86.8
5. Italy	90.4	5. Portugal	85.9
6. Iceland	89.3	6. Greece	84.9
7. New Zealand	89.0	7. Netherlands	84.7
8. Luxembourg	88.9	8. Australia	83.1
9. Germany	88.6	9. Denmark	82.1
10. Netherlands	87.0	10. Norway	81.8
11. France	85.9	11. Germany	81.1
12. Portugal	84.2	12. New Zealand	78.5
13. Denmark	83.2	13. France	78.0
14. Norway	82.0	14. United Kingdom	76.0
15. Greece	78.6	15. Japan	74.4
16. Israel	78.5	16. Spain	73.0
17. United Kingdom	76.3	17. Canada	67.4
18. Japan	74.5	18. Finland	63.0
19. Canada	69.3	19. Ireland	62.3
20. Spain	68.1	20. United States	52.6
21. Finland	64.3	21. Switzerland	39.4
22. Ireland	62.2		
23. United States	52.6		
24. Switzerland	48.3		

[a] Most recent as of 1981.

[b] In the "Traditional Measure of Turnout," U.S. turnout is calculated as the percentage of the voting-age population, while turnout elsewhere is calculated as the percentage of registered voters.

most of the countries in which we are interested, but together they give some clues about relationships between alienation and turnout across national boundaries.

We begin with a 1959 survey, which asked respondents in the United States and three European democracies about aspects of their countries in which they took pride. Fully 85 percent of the Americans said they were proud of their political institutions, compared to 46 percent of the Britons, 7 percent of the West Germans, and 3 percent of the Italians. The question about pride seems not to have been asked in Europe since 1959. At that time, when the turnout gap was only slightly smaller than at present, Americans clearly were far prouder of their political institutions than were Europeans.

More recent European data are available on a closely related topic, citizens' satisfaction with their political system. *Euro-Barometre* regularly asks Europeans, "On the whole, are you very satisfied, fairly satisfied, not very satisfied, or not at all satisfied with the way democracy works in [your country]?" The 1980 National Election Study asked Americans "how good a job you feel [the federal government] is doing for the country as a whole" on a scale from zero ("very poor job") to 8 ("very good job"). These two questions are not identical. The European question asks respondents to judge "democracy" as part of their assessment of their government's performance. The NES item has no such cosmic implications and seems more likely to evoke partisan answers. Thus, the NES question invites more critical responses than does the European one. Fifty-nine percent of American respondents gave answers ranging from "fair job" to "very good job"; the mean for ten European countries was 51 percent. Respondents in Luxemborg (77 percent), West Germany (73 percent), and Denmark (60 percent) were more satisfied than Americans; people were less satisfied in Belgium, France, Greece, Ireland, Italy, Holland, and Great Britain.

Americans may vote less than citizens in other democracies, but they also seem less alienated. Ireland and Switzerland, the two countries that resemble the United States in their anemic turnout, also exhibit high levels of confidence and support for the system. In 1973, the only year for which we could find data about Switzerland, the Swiss ranked first (67 percent) in satisfaction with how democracy worked in their country, and the Irish were in third place. Residents of the two countries with highest turnout, Belgium and Italy, ranked second (62 percent) and last (27 percent), respectively.

Finally, we have the results of an eleven-nation survey conducted by the Gallup Organization in 1981, reported in *The Confidence Gap* by Seymour Martin Lipset and William Schneider. Gallup asked about the respondents' degree of confidence in

> the armed forces, the legal system, the educational system, the churches or organized religion, the press, labor unions, major companies, the civil service, and the parliament or Congress. . . . The overall level of confidence turned out to be higher in the United States than in any other country surveyed except Ireland. After Ireland and the United States came Britain, Denmark, Spain, West Germany, Belgium, Holland, France, Japan, and Italy, in that order.

Whatever the reasons for Americans' lower turnout, dissatisfaction with their political system is not one of them.

Americans also surpass Europeans in other attitudes that seem conducive to voting, such as a belief in their ability to influence political developments. In 1982 *Euro-Barometre* asked respondents in ten nations, "Do you think that if things are not going well [in this country] people like yourself can help to bring about a change for the better or not?" The 1980 National Election Study solicited agreement or disagreement with this statement: "People like me don't have any say about what the government does." Fifty-nine percent of the American respondents disagreed with this statement; that is, they expressed feelings of political efficacy. An efficacious response to the *Euro-Barometre* question was given by 62 percent of Greeks and

56 percent of Danes. Luxemburg and Great Britain followed at 42 percent; all other countries had even fewer citizens who expressed efficacious feelings.

Americans are also more likely to engage in all forms of political participation other than voting. A mid-1970s comparative survey asked Americans and Europeans about their participation in both conventional activities like discussing politics, attending political rallies, and the like, *and* unconventional or protest behavior, such as signing petitions and going to lawful demonstrations. The levels of participation were higher in the United States than in Austria, the Netherlands, West Germany, and Great Britain.

Using the European Denominator

If activity, optimism, and self-confidence about political participation determined turnout, Americans would lead the world. But there are some important steps between impulse and action, when the action is voting. Enthusiasm is not enough; in order to vote in this country, one's name must appear on a register of those whose qualifications have been established. What happens if American, as well as foreign, turnout is measured as a percentage of these registered voters who go to the polls?

The decentralization of election administration in the United States makes it difficult to tell exactly how many people register, and how many of those vote. No one source is completely satisfactory. Of those available, we have most confidence in the Vote Validation Study conducted as part of the Michigan 1980 National Election Study, in which interviewers inspected voting records to establish whether each of their survey respondents had registered and voted. The major drawback of this source is the somewhat upscale character of the Michigan sample, which underrepresents some underprivileged elements of society, particularly uneducated young men. Doubtless this is why the vote-validated Michigan sample shows a 1980 turnout rate of 60 percent. While this surely exaggerates turnout, it should be noted that the Census Bureau's 52.6 percent figure understates it.

Eighty-seven percent of the registered respondents in the Michigan sample voted in 1980. The 1980 Voter Supplement of the Census Bureau's Current Population Survey, based on unverified responses from a sample of more than 90,000, yields an estimate that 88.6 percent of those registered voted. Both figures are very respectable rates in the international rankings of turnout. *If the basis of comparison with other countries uses the American denominator—the percentage of the voting-age population who vote—the United States looks bad. If the yardstick is the measure used elsewhere in the world—the percentage of those registered who vote—then the United States looks pretty good, as table 2 (p. 186) shows.* Using this European denominator, the United States ranks eleventh among the twenty-four countries, more than 38 percentage points ahead of last place Switzerland, and at least ten percentage points higher than Greece, Israel, Great Britain, Japan, Canada, Spain, Finland, and Ireland. Moreover, the gap between the United States and top-ranked Belgium is not very wide—only eight points in table 2 instead of the 42 percentage points in table 1. By this measure the United States looks better than most countries and nearly as good as any country.

The Impediments

Two aspects of the election laws in different countries seem to be particularly important in explaining international variations in turnout. One of these is "compulsory voting" (actually penalties for nonvoting) present in five countries: Belgium, Australia, Italy, Spain, and Greece. Political scientist G. Bingham Powell's analysis revealed that such provisions are associated with about a 10 percent increase in turnout. The rather substantial impact of these laws seems to be achieved through moral suasion rather than actual sanctions. British political scientist Ivor Crewe confirms that "both convictions and sanctions against nonvoters appear to be negligible. . . ." Nevertheless, their impact is substantial; mean turnout in the Netherlands

TABLE 2
Turnout of Those Who Are Registered

Vote as a Percentage of Registered Voters		Compulsion Penalties	Automatic Registration
1. Belgium	94.6	Yes	Yes
2. Australia	94.5	Yes	No
3. Austria	91.6	No (some)[a]	Yes
4. Sweden	90.7	No	Yes
5. Italy	90.4	Yes	Yes
6. Iceland	89.3	n.a.	n.a.
7. New Zealand	89.0	No (some)[a]	No
8. Luxembourg	88.9	n.a.	n.a.
9. W. Germany	88.6	No	Yes
10. Netherlands	87.0	No	Yes
11. United States	86.8	No	No
12. France	85.9	No (some)[a]	No
13. Portugal	84.2	n.a.	n.a.
14. Denmark	83.2	No	Yes
15. Norway	82.0	No	Yes
16. Greece	78.6	Yes	Yes
17. Israel	78.5	No	Yes
18. United Kingdom	76.3	No	Yes
19. Japan	74.5	No	Yes
20. Canada	69.3	No	Yes
21. Spain	68.1	Yes	Yes
22. Finland	64.3	No	Yes
23. Ireland	62.2	No	Yes
24. Switzerland	48.3	No (some)[a]	Yes

[a] Penalties apply only to small portions of the country or certain types of elections.

dropped 11 percentage points after that country abandoned compulsory voting. The most formidable sanctions may be in Italy, which does not formally require its citizens to vote, but whose constitution declares that voting is a duty; Italians who fail to vote have "DID NOT VOTE" stamped on their identification papers. What prudent Italian would risk blighting his chances of favorable consideration by a government official?

The second source of variation in turnout, and one that is much more important for the United States, is the location of responsibility for registration. In most countries, voter registration is automatic, a by-product of government-maintained records of every citizen's name and location. In a few countries, voter registration is a separate step, but one that the government initiates through a systematic canvass, either by public officials or payments to party workers. Great Britain and Canada, which register by canvass, have lower turnout than continental nations that make use of more automatic procedures. *The United States is the only country where the entire burden of registration falls on the individual rather than the government.*

Registration requirements make voting in the United States more troublesome than in any other country. The need to register—and the difficulty of doing so—impedes Americans' relatively strong impulse to participate, helping to produce a relatively low rate of voting. In most American states, registration is separated from voting by both time and geography. Registration usually does not provide the emotional gratification that voting does. Election day is the climax to a widely publicized and hotly contested competition. In contrast, the deadline for registration is as obscure as the registration requirements and procedures themselves. What is more, almost anyone who moves must register all over again; and in any given year one-sixth of the population moves.

The deterrent effect of American registration procedures can be tested by examining turnout in those states whose registration laws pose the smallest obstacles to voters. The most important legal provision in this respect is the closing date for registration; all other factors held constant, the closer to election day one can register, the greater the likelihood of voting. Four states permit election-day registration (Maine, Minnesota, Oregon, and Wisconsin), and one requires no registration (North Dakota). How does turnout in these five states compare with that in other countries?

Table 3 shows that the five states allowing election-day registration or requiring no registration had considerably higher turnout than did the United States as a whole. The national percentage of the voting-age population who voted was 52.6 percent; for the five states, it ranges from a low of 61.5 percent (Oregon) to 70.1 percent (Minnesota). By comparing tables 3 and 1, we see that even our most permissive states do not match most other countries in turnout, although they come close to a few. All but Oregon exceed Finland and Ireland. Minnesota does better than Canada as well.

If the difficulty of registration accounts for much of the poor American turnout, why is there still such a gap between the permissive states and Europe? One reason is that the measures of turnout are still not equal. The numerator of the turnout percentage, the "number of votes cast," is some millions less than the number of all voters in the United States, because it excludes spoiled ballots, people who go to the polls but do not vote for a presidential candidate, and those whose write-in votes are not counted. According to Ivor Crewe, turnout elsewhere "includes invalid and blank votes (a more than negligible proportion in a few countries). . . ." These differences account for one to two percentage points of the turnout gap.

A second explanation is that election-day registration as practiced in some states is not equivalent to automatic registration. In Maine and Oregon, the voter must make two trips—one to register and one to vote. Oregon voters must first register with the county clerk, which may mean quite a trek for people in small towns

TABLE 3
Turnout in States with Election-Day Registration (1980)

State	Percent of the Voting-age Population Who Voted	Where to Register
Minnesota	70.1%	At polls on election day, City Hall, City Clerk, County Auditor
Wisconsin	67.2	Election day at polls with identification, Municipal Clerk or Board of Election Commissioners in counties where registration is required
North Dakota	64.8	No registration
Maine	64.6	Registrar of Voters, Board of Registration, Justice of Peace, Notary Public
Oregon	61.5	County Clerk
All U.S.	52.6	

David Glass, Peverill Squire, and Raymond Wolfinger **187**

and on farms. Another impediment may be that people are unaware how easy it is to vote. One-third of the nonvoting respondents in North Dakota—the best example, since it has no registration requirement—said they could not vote because they had not registered.

Finally, the sheer number of elections that confront Americans in a year may result in low turnout figures. The only evidence on this point is fragmentary but fascinating. Richard Boyd found that the number of residents in a Connecticut town who voted *at some time* during the year was considerably higher than the number who participated in any single election. In short, voters may simply grow weary of voting.

One explanation that we have found unsatisfactory is that the political choices in this country are not defined sharply enough to mobilize people to vote. There is no left-wing party, for example, to represent the workers' interests. Clearly, this notion cannot account for most of the gap between turnout in the United States and, say, France. Turnout in France is 15 percentage points higher than in the United States, but only three to five points higher than in Wisconsin or Minnesota. Since it is difficult to believe that either the class basis of the political parties or the character of partisan competition in these high-turnout states is different from that in states with average turnout (say California or Colorado), this line of thought has its limitations as an explanation of American turnout.

The Registration Obstacle

Analyses of group differences in turnout usually emphasize that impediments to voting are greater for some than for others. In fact, this applies to registration far more than it does to actual voting. Tables 4 and 5 provide strong confirmation for our hypothesis that registration is the critical hurdle. Table 4, for example, contrasts the relative difficulty for those of different ages and at different levels of education. Only 51 percent of people with a grammar school education managed to vote in the 1980 election, compared to 84 percent of those with

a college degree or more—a gap of 33 percentage points. This is a familiar story. The gap, however, narrows to 17 percentage points when the comparison shifts to *registered respondents*. In other words, the less educated act much more like the better educated once they have crossed the crucial barrier of registration.

The same pattern also appears among age groups and those with different levels of political interest. The gap in turnout between the young and old, and between the least and most interested, narrows significantly when the comparison is among those who have registered. It is especially striking among different age groups. Young Americans are notoriously light voters. Only 42 percent of those aged 18 to 24 made it to the polls in 1980, far behind the 69 percent turnout rate of those 65 and older. Yet, among young people who managed to register, 86 percent voted, compared to 90 percent of those aged 35 to 64. The gap between various age groups all but disappears among those who registered; the young vote at the same rate as the old once they pass the registration hurdle.

Even those least likely to vote—the uneducated, young, and politically uninterested—vote at fairly impressive rates if they are registered. Seventy-nine percent of people with only a grammar school education who were registered, for example, managed to vote. Comparing this with the data in table 2, we see that this group would rank sixteenth; higher than Greece, Israel, and Great Britain, and just below Norway and Denmark. The youngest group in table 4, with an 86 percent turnout, would rank much higher. Even people who were "hardly at all interested" in politics turned out at a rate of 74 percent (see table 5).

Remedies

Once we understand that the basic cause of our low voting rate is the registration requirement, we can see where major efforts to raise turnout should be directed. If we were to institute the European model of automatic registration, turnout would increase dramatically. This would be the surest method, but it goes strongly against

TABLE 4
Turnout and Registration (1980), by Age and Education

	Percent of All Respondents Who Voted	Percent of Respondents Registered to Vote	Percent of Registered Respondents Who Voted
By age:			
18–24 years	42%	49%	86%
25–34	57	65	88
35–64	69	77	90
65 and over	69	82	85
By education:			
0–8 years	51	65	79
9–12	53	64	84
1–4 college	68	75	90
5 or more college	84	87	96
All U.S.	60	69	87

TABLE 5
Interest in Politics, Turnout, and Registration in 1980

Follow Politics	Percent of All Respondents Who Voted	Percent of Respondents Registered to Vote	Percent of Registered Respondents Who Voted
Hardly at all	38%	51%	74%
Only now and then	54	64	84
Some of the time	70	76	92
Most of the time	75	83	91

the grain of American political culture. Far more than people elsewhere, Americans seem possessed by a desire to guard individual privacy from governmental intrusion. In fact, there are no records of all inhabitants in any American locality, and Americans have shown a genuine aversion to establishing them in the past.

Short of making it automatic, what might be done to ease the burden of registration? One impediment to voting is a closing date far in advance of election day. The closer the deadline to the election, the more people will vote. Many states could shorten their 30-day closing dates to a week or two before the election, without any apparent sacrifice of convenience or procedural safeguards. Potent interest groups oppose this step. County election officials often plead their need for a full month to consolidate records and then distribute them to precincts in time, although those states with shorter deadlines seem to get the job done in less time. Another interesting source of opposition to shorter closing dates is candidates for office, many of whom spend most of their campaign budgets on direct mailings in the last two or three weeks before the election; an early closing date permits them to use an up-to-date set of addresses. With a deadline just before the election, candidates would have to use lists from the primary election, which would be missing recent immigrants to their district and also would include people who had moved away. In addition to these procedural opponents, shorter closing dates, like other reforms, are often opposed by conservatives who believe that they would strengthen liberals; the evidence shows that more permissive registration procedures would increase the number of voters but not change their political character.

Election-day registration carries to a logical extreme the goal of shortening closing dates. While this provision unquestionably increases turnout, it has some potential for serious voting fraud. The brief experience in Minnesota and Wisconsin has not produced any scandals, but this may reflect the clean politics culture of those states more than the presence of adequate safeguards. One study of the two states concluded that election-day registration was an "honor system" without adequate procedural protection. Moreover, this seems to be an idea whose time has come and gone; Congress easily defeated President Carter's proposal for a nationwide system in 1977, and since then the provision has made very little progress.

Two more modest proposals occur to us. One concerns the possibility that some Americans refrain from registering because they fear that doing so will make them liable to jury duty. Voter registration lists are used almost everywhere as a basis (sometimes the only one) for selecting jury panels, and serving on juries is a form of civic participation that many Americans wish to avoid. There is no hard evidence on this point, but there is a wealth of anecdotes from precinct workers and local election officials. If states were to use other sources in addition to registration rolls for selecting juries, such as lists of people who have registered their cars or obtained drivers' licenses, and then publicized the policy, people might be less motivated to avoid jury duty by refusing to register to vote.

The burden of registration is most likely to deter two kinds of people: those whose interest or clerical skill is insufficient to get them over this threshold, and people who, having moved, need to re-register. Movers do eventually get around to registering, but their registration rate takes approximately five years to catch up with those who have stayed put. Movers take their time about registering, but they cannot be so casual about telephone service, electric power connections, and similar arrangements that are made on arriving at a new home. Concerted efforts to include registration by mail forms with the paperwork required by utility companies might boost registration in those states that permit it (some 60 percent of the population). Some of these organizations are accustomed to including civic-minded material in their monthly mailings.

Post office change-of-address notices are an even more interesting possibility. If these were filled out in duplicate, the second copy could be mailed to the relevant secretary of state. In the case of intra-state moves by those who are already registered (83 percent of moves are within the same state), the secretary of state might be able to transfer the registration to the new address. Mail registration forms could be sent to the unregistered. Pilot programs to try these suggestions in limited areas are feasible, and would be appropriate subjects for financial support by foundations or a federal grant program.

If almost everyone who is registered votes, measures such as holding elections on Sunday, making election day a holiday, or extending the hours that polls are open would do little to improve turnout. All these are designed to encourage those who are already very likely to vote. Money, energy, and political capital should be reserved for actions that have more potential—getting people to register, on the amply documented assumption that once people register, they vote.

II TRENDS

In an influential book published in 1963, political scientists Gabriel A. Almond and Sidney Verba studied the political culture in five democracies. They found Americans to be very involved in politics—so much so that they described the United States as a "participant civic culture." Almond and Verba's observations would probably have been no surprise to de Tocqueville, who found Americans very active in politics even in the 1830s (see selection 4.1). Nearly thirty years later, the American political system seems completely different. Voter turnout has dropped, interest in politics has waned, and Americans are much more likely to be described as apathetic than as involved.

The following two selections demonstrate the dramatic change in American attitudes toward political participation over the past three decades. In the excerpt from their book, Almond and Verba describe two "typical" Americans—both deeply involved in politics. In the second selection, published in 1990, everything is different.

Questions

1. What are the causes in the decline of citizen involvement over the past thirty years?
2. Would you describe your own involvement in politics as more like the participant or the apathy model?

6.2 The Civil Culture

Gabriel A. Almond and Sidney Verba

[Americans] . . . are very frequently exposed to politics. They report political discussion and involvement in political affairs, a sense of obligation to take an active part in the community, and a sense of competence to influence the government. They are frequently active members of voluntary associations. Furthermore, . . . they report emotional involvement during political campaigns, and they have a high degree of pride in the political system. And their attachment to the political system includes both [satisfaction with the system as a whole] . . . as well as satisfaction with specific governmental performance.

• • •

[Here are two examples:]

An American Stenographer: An Allegiant Participant. Miss E. illustrates that civic norms may be fairly well developed by the time an individual first enters an adult political role.

Miss E. is an eighteen-year-old American girl, living in a small country town in the South. She lives at home and is engaged to be married. She had a short working experience as a stenographer in a lawyer's office, but found the legal terminology difficult. She adds: "I just don't like working in an office. I'd rather be a plain housewife, and that's what I'm planning to be." She does remember her employer quite fondly: "He was just as nice as he could be, not hard-boiled. I guess I was pretty dumb, but he always joked with me and put up with whatever I did."

Miss E. is one of four children. She is used to having her father have the final word in family decisions, but feels free to state her views. She thinks that perhaps young people do not have quite enough voice in family decisions, but then adds: "Oh, I guess they do, really! It's just that sometimes we think we don't."

Miss E.'s main outside interest is her Baptist church. She attends services and meetings about three times a week and is a member of two church organizations as well as the YWCA. Of religion she says: "I think it should be very important. I believe our leaders should be good men and look to God for help, but I think it's wrong to say that they should belong to one church or can't belong to another. I think it's all right for a Catholic to be President, because one of the things that we were always taught was that this country was founded for the religious freedom, and even if our preacher says we shouldn't have a Catholic I don't see why not." [Miss E. here reflects the controversy over the election of the first Catholic president, John F. Kennedy, in 1960.]

Miss E.'s neighbors are mostly rural working class. The majority, including her father, are employed at a large local paper mill, but there are still some full-time farmers and farm laborers in the area. The neighborhood is stable and friendly. Miss E. says: "When there's sickness in the family or a death, all the neighbors come in and help. The family below us had a fire, and the people for miles around brought clothes and furniture, money too, to help them get started over." Miss E.'s childhood is still too recent for her to have much perspective on it. She knows that they have become a little more prosperous of late and were able to build a new five-room house a few years ago. She describes her father as the stricter parent: "He was the one we all minded. We kind of jumped when he told us to do something. He was good to us though, and he was a lot of fun. He was pretty

strict, but not any stricter than we needed. Mama was the one who always took our part, and she'd listen to us more." The children were permitted some participation in the family decisions that concerned their future, but they had little to say in matters such as family purchases. Miss E. was fairly content, though. She says: "I never thought much about it. I just knew we always got along fine. We never thought they were too hard on us, or almost never. Maybe, they wouldn't let us do everything we thought we ought to, but they were probably right."

Miss E. has happy memories of her elementary and high school days. She says of her teachers: "They were very sweet. They helped you all they could. They seemed to be able to make the children mind without being too hard on them." Miss E. remembers that there was "a student council. There was a student from every homeroom on it, and they took any problems the students had to the council, where the council voted on the problems." The school was quite active in the areas of government and civics. Miss E. says: "They taught us a lot! Especially in my last year, we studied current events and we had an awfully good course in American history, and at the end of the year we took up the study of the government—what the different branches are, what each one does, and what the different duties are. We were taught to understand our government and respect it. In elementary school, especially, we had patriotic programs—about Washington, Lincoln, and great men in the South."

The subject of politics is very much on the family's mind at the moment. Miss E. says: "It's the main subject around here this year. Our most recent discussion was yesterday. It was whether a Catholic should be elected President. There was a crowd around here, including two preachers, and we discussed it pretty strong. . . . We all speak our minds. Mama is interested and reads a lot, and of course Daddy has always liked it." The family disagrees at times, and Miss E. recalls: "In the Democratic primary for governor, Daddy was for one man, and Mama and I were for another. Mama and Daddy both voted the way they pleased for different candidates."

Miss E. finds that she is beginning to be very interested in politics at this time, as it is an election year. She says: "I guess it's because Mama and Daddy talk about it a lot. Then there's a lot on TV and in the papers about it now. I think it's sort of exciting." She finds that the people who care about politics are the ones "who are well informed, people who read, and people who have been brought up in families where their parents talk about it." Of the kind of people who are not interested in politics Miss E. says: "They are mainly people who aren't educated, but sometimes education isn't the main thing, for lots of people with education are just careless or indifferent or something. They just don't take any interest in politics, but I think everybody should. Well, if you're really interested in your country, you ought to be interested in electing good people."

Miss E. considers herself a Democrat, although she is still too young to vote. She says: "I guess it's because my family are Democrats. I've always thought it stands for the little people. . . . But I feel that when I have children they can make up their own minds. If they felt like being Republicans, I'd feel they had good reasons." Miss E. feels particularly strongly about religion as an issue in the coming election. She says: "It don't seem fair to me to hold anyone's religion against them. If they believe in God, I don't see why Jesus wouldn't save a Catholic too, and our country is supposed to have religious freedom, and it just makes me mad what they are telling about Catholics. Of course, I don't know much about Catholics, but I just don't believe what they are saying is all so, that they worship idols and that they are worse than Communists."

Miss E. is well informed on the uses of tax funds and is on the whole satisfied with the ways in which tax money is being used. She has had some routine official contacts, at the local Social Security Office for instance, and she found the officials "in every way as nice as could be." She remembers her father's writing

to the governor about some state problem and receiving a pleasant and courteous reply. She feels that she would always be treated with friendliness and consideration by any government official.

Miss E. thinks that a good citizen should vote and should take part in community, church, and school affairs. He "should be loyal and obey the laws. He should be patriotic, be proud of his country, and do whatever he can to keep it free." If she disapproved of some ordinance of her local government, Miss E. would "talk to them, go to see them, and tell them I didn't approve of it. I could get up a petition if they would let me—if I was old enough." On the national level she would write to her congressman. Miss E. takes pride in her country, and says: "We have freedom. It's a democracy. We can worship as we feel we want to. We have a good government, and we are one of the great powers in the world. We can elect the people we want to to run the government."

A Retired Civil Engineer: An Allegiant Participant. Mr. C. is politically aware and has a relatively well developed sense of competence. He is generally allegiant to the system, but his strong views lead to some serious reservation and to a fairly high level of hostility to political opponents.

Mr. C. is a retired civil engineer living in a small town. He is married and has three grown sons. Mr. C. finds that life has changed considerably since he was young: "It's been the general changes in the economy and system of government, and other things: they're all different. When we were young we didn't buy unless we had enough money to pay for it. Nowadays, you buy and then pay if and when you can. This country is up to its neck in credit. . . ."

In talking about family problems in general, Mr. C. feels that today "kids have too much rope" and should be brought up more strictly. They should be permitted to voice their opinions at home in matters concerning their education or their future, but nowadays they "just do as they please and the parents let them."

Mr. C. is a Protestant and considers himself to be a religious person. He has strong and varied feelings about the general role of religion. He says: "It should occupy a prominent place in the life of the country. I don't believe in prohibiting the reading of the Bible in schools. . . . I believe in the separation of church and state, yet I believe that some part of religion should be recognized by the government, and those who don't like it should get the hell out. I believe that Jews and other non-Christians should be tolerated, but they should not dictate to the government what religious policies should be. The principle is: this country is Christian. I don't believe in public support of Catholic schools."

Mr. C. grew up in the same town in which he lives now. He knows most of the people in it, considers many of them his friends, but does little actual visiting. He trusts people but finds most of them quite selfish. His father was a small storekeeper who, though his income was limited, managed to support his wife and son. Mr. C. remembers that "father was a good person. He got along very well with other people. He was a good businessman. I admire him for being a good worker. He was well trusted by those in town. My mother was strict as far as the family was concerned. She and father were religious and were both active in religious work." Mr. C. found that he could talk freely to both parents and was allowed a voice in personal matters, such as clothing or school decisions. Mr. C. remembers that people were more helpful in those days. "Now they want to know what they can get out of it, maybe because of changes in employer-employee relationships. Before unions there was cooperation."

Mr. C. admired his teachers at school: "They were well prepared and well trained scholastically, and they had discipline. They didn't spare the rod. Of course, it's not the teachers' fault today. The parents will have them in jail if they dare touch their child. . . . There was one teacher who was able to teach me more than the others. He was a very strict disciplinarian." At college Mr. C. was a member of a politics club. He remembers: "We talked politics, and one thing that I noticed is that action is too slow in a democratic form of government. I don't know what can be done about it."

Mr. C. has a wide range of political memories: "I was a Republican because my father was. I don't know today—the parties are different from when I was a boy. Parties should have different names, maybe Conservative and Liberal, something like that. I have always been concerned with the outcome of all the socialist principles that you hear nowadays—Social Security and things like that. I am wondering what the end result will be." Mr. C. remembers all specific political events clearly and with firm convictions. He finds that the First World War was a Democratic device to get the country out of economic trouble, and that the Depression was a natural consequence and unconnected with politics. He opposed the New Deal: "I felt the New Deal came from underneath the deck. . . . Because of it, I made up my mind never to work for a Democrat." The Second World War " . . . was probably unavoidable, but again it was a Democratic administration" and " . . . we should have let Hitler and Stalin knock each other off." Of the Korean War Mr. C. says: "I thought it was a mistake of President Truman to get rid of MacArthur"; and of the desegregation decision: "I'm in favor of the Negro having just as good schools as the white, but I'm not in favor of mixing them up. The good Lord didn't make white and black with the idea of mixing them up so you can't tell the difference."

Mr. C. is vitally interested in politics, and the family has lively political discussions. Mr. C. recalls the last Fourth of July, when the whole family was together and everyone discussed Cuba, Communism, and the presidential campaign, with special reference to the religion of the candidates. Everyone talked; parents, sons, and daughters-in-law. Opinions varied, but the discussion was amiable. He gives as his reason for political interest: "It's everybody's duty. Whatever is done has an effect on everybody, individually and collectively." He finds that all alert and public-spirited people care, but he has contempt for what he calls "professional politicians." He supports the Republican party, as he considers himself "by nature a conservative"; and he criticizes the Democratic party for "all those socialistic principles: social security, fixing of minimum wages, the support of unions. . . . I can't understand why a working man should tell an employer what he's going to do, what he's going to pay." He would not like to see his children join the Democratic party.

Mr. C. never misses an election. He has had some routine contacts with tax officials and with a state senator and in both cases found the officials cordial and quite helpful. Mr. C. finds that a good citizen "should take office if called upon and should be active in social and charitable affairs in his community. He should support the country morally and financially and should support those elected officials who are trying to enforce the laws." If you disapprove of some local ordinance, Mr. C. says that you should "fight against it in your conversations and get your ideas across to other people." In a national matter he would write to his congressman or try to have a political candidate commit himself before election. The things he admires most in his country are "its freedom of speech and religion, its freedom in general."

6.3 A National Morale Problem

Paul Taylor

What if they held an election and nobody came? This fall [1990] an estimated 110 million to 120 million Americans, nearly two-thirds of the electorate, will not vote—the largest group of nonvoters in U.S. history.

What if they took a census and nobody stood up to be counted? This spring, 33 million American households have not sent back their forms. The 63 percent mail-back rate is a dozen points lower than government officials had expected. A preliminary review suggests that most of the problem is not in poor communities, where the Census Bureau had conducted an intensive promotional campaign, but in middle-class communities, where it had not thought promotion was necessary.

What if they sent out tax forms and nobody paid? This year, for every $5 in federal taxes owed, $1 is being evaded—mostly by sole proprietors and small businesses. The annual tax gap is expected to exceed $100 billion for the first time ever, according to the Internal Revenue Service.

The voting booth, the census form and the tax return are among the few civic venues where the federal government asks its citizens to take part in the ongoing enterprise of public life. And now, more than ever, Americans are declining the invitation. At a time when democracy is flourishing around the globe, it is losing market share here.

"I get so embarrassed when I see elections in Central America where you can get shot by either the left or the right for voting, and yet they vote at twice the rate we do in this country," says Republican Rep. Bill Frenzel of Minnesota. "I think that as a society we're going through a scattering of what used to be called national purpose. At one time this country had a manifest destiny. Nowadays, everyone is chasing a different butterfly."

"Clearly we have something of great interest going on here, and it sounds to me like what we've got is a collective national morale problem," says Walter Dean Burnham, a professor of government at the University of Texas.

Reprinted with special permission of North America Syndicate, Inc.

"For a lot of Americans, there is no longer a moral distinction between those who choose to be involved and those who don't," says Geoffrey Garin, a Democratic pollster who has done extensive research on citizenship. "People don't feel any sense of ownership over the federal government. It isn't them, and it isn't theirs."

As these varied observations suggest, explanations for the decline in civil participation cut a wide swath across the realms of ideology, sociology and history. Among them:

- It is a byproduct of a long season in which anti-government populism has been the reigning political idea. This is a favorite theory of liberals, and it implicates former president Ronald Reagan as the villain. Democratic Sen. Edward M. Kennedy of Massachusetts says Reagan used the Oval Office to issue a "summons to selfishness" and Garin says his message was that "you can love your country but hate your government."

    Liberals also blame Reagan's laissez-faire economic policies for making the poor

poorer and less tethered to the civic order. They note that the drop-off in voting over the last three decades has occurred disproportionately among these least well-off Americans. "I would think there is something to the proposition that we have had this enormous pig-out atmosphere in the past decade and it has created a morale problem for everyone not invited to the barbecue," says Burnham.

- It is the result of the long-term weakening of the political parties. In virtually every other democracy around the world, political parties still play a vital role in delivering political information and mobilizing citizen participation. "In this country, our parties can no longer punch their way out of a paper sack," says Frenzel, who will retire next year after 20 years in Congress. "When I was first elected, the most powerful political forces in my state were the Democrats and the Republicans. Now, they are the Minnesotans for Life, the AFL-CIO and the National Education Association. They have legitimate claims on the process, but all of them operate under a much smaller umbrella than the parties."

- It is the result of wholesale failures of government for the past quarter-century. The list is familiar: Vietnam, Watergate, inflation, standard-of-living stagnation, gas lines, budget and trade deficits. These setbacks have been magnified by media that are both more adversarial and, as a result of television, more pervasive than ever before. "If the message [people] get is that politics is all about tactics and corruption and hypocrisy, it should be no surprise that they are going to develop a 'voting-just-encourages-'em' sort of cynicism," says Garry Orren, a professor of public policy at Harvard's Kennedy School of Government.

- It is the result of the atomization of the popular culture—the segmenting of the population by forces of modern marketing and technology into demographic ghettos, each with its own cable channel, prime-time television show, shopping mall and consumer magazine, and none with a felt need to connect up to the broader community.

- It is a result of Americans' loss of faith in the future. Nations turn inward when they lose their self-confidence. Our economic position, relative to the rest of the world's, has been declining for a generation. Our political structure seems ossified, in hock to special interests and unable to balance a budget, much less confront the larger problems. Burnham calls it a "revolution of declining expectations"—the less people demand from their government, the less they get, the more they drop out.

- It is the result of happy apathy, and it is a far healthier development than the naysayers suggest. This is a favorite theory of conservatives, who note that while participation may have atrophied at the federal level, it is vibrant and growing at the local level, where volunteerism, charitable giving and neighborhood associations are on the rise. "It's only people inside the Beltway who think government and politics is the most important way to participate in America," says Burton Yale Pines, executive vice president of the Heritage Foundation, a conservative think tank. "I see it as an inverse indicator. When they're not upset, they drop out to a degree. As a conservative, I'm much more interested in parents going to PTA meetings. That's citizenship."

None of these theories is without flaws. Just as the liberal critique fails to account for the degree to which Reagan was a creature, rather than a creator, of the anti-government era, the conservative explanation fails to account for polling data that show nonvoters are among the *least* content members of the electorate.

There is a strong—and growing—class dimension to nonvoting. People in the highest 20 percent of income are almost twice as likely to vote as people in the lowest 20 percent. Poor people tend to be most cynical about, and least connected to, "the system." Roy Teixeira, a leading authority on nonvoting, cites the decline in what he calls "political efficacy" as the chief cause of the drop in voter turnout in presidential campaigns from a modern high of 63 percent in 1960 to a 64-year low of 50.2 percent in 1988. Turnout rates in off-year elections are even lower; in 1986, it was 37.6 percent, the lowest since 1942.

Garin marvels at how profound this feeling of disconnection can be. "In focus-group discussions, when we bring up the cost of the savings and loan bailout, we often hear people say, 'Why do the taxpayers have to come up with the money? Why can't the government?' "

Disconnection can easily sour into hostility. The low return rate on census forms and the high incidence of tax evasion both seem, in part, to be expressions of anger at government. "A lot of people who don't pay their taxes feel like all they are doing is getting even," Garin says. "They feel like the system is rigged—that somebody else has been getting all the breaks and that they're the victim."

There is another explanation for the growth in tax evasion: The federal government has slashed funding for the IRS to the level that fewer than one percent of all returns were audited last year, a modern low. When Michael S. Dukakis tried to make an issue of this in 1988, George Bush ridiculed him for advocating "an IRS agent in every kitchen."

In general, though, President Bush has paid much more attention to the idea of civic participation than did his predecessor. His inaugural address was an elegant exhortation to Americans [to] turn away from material self-interest. "From now on in America, any definition of a successful life must include serving others," he said last year as he set up a "points of light" initiative that encourages volunteerism at the local level.

But Bush's critics think this is the equivalent of "cheap grace," in the phase of New York Democratic Gov. Mario M. Cuomo.

"It creates a very peculiar dynamic when the leaders we elect to perform the public tasks that are too large for us to do by ourselves tell us that these tasks are worthy but that we should accomplish them by our own altruism," says Benjamin Barber, a professor of political science at Rutgers University. "Altruism isn't enough when the problems are structural and will only respond to structural solutions. Altruism isn't citizenship, and there is some harm when we confuse the two."

In the long run, Barber adds, the danger is that as the ties that bind a big and pluralistic nation corrode, we will lack the sense of common purpose to respond to great challenges.

"One of the things we've found from our research is that young people, in particular, have an impoverished notion of citizenship," says Sanford Horwitt, director of a citizen participation project at People for the American Way. "Basically, they think it's not breaking the law, and that's all. I don't think they have been well-served by the adult world. Unless these values are passed along, they disappear. And a democracy that does not value citizenship is not a very healthy place."

III INTERCONNECTIONS

Voting is not the only way Americans can participate in politics. They can, for example, join a political party, work in a campaign, take part in a demonstration, or write a letter to any elected official, including the president.

Increasingly Americans are turning to organized groups to advance their political interests. Such groups, which are examined in detail in chapter 9, take the lead in organizing various forms of activity designed to influence governmental policy. In recent years, as the following selection demonstrates, such groups have turned to the courts to advance their interests or redress their grievances—often with great success.

Question

1. Why does litigation as a strategy appeal to groups such as women's rights groups? Why are traditional forms of political participation less effective?

6.4 Beyond Legislative Lobbying: Women's Rights Groups and the Supreme Court

Karen O'Connor and Lee Epstein

While women's rights groups have been able to attain some of their goals in the legislative sphere, their inability to secure ratification of highly visible objectives including the Equal Rights Amendment and other important "rights" legislation through conventional lobbying, allows them to be classified as "disadvantaged." According to Richard C. Cortner, "disadvantaged" groups are wise to pursue their goals through judicial lobbying. The National Association for the Advancement of Colored People (NAACP), for example, initially used the courts to achieve its objectives. In contrast, women's rights groups generally have relied heavily on legislative as opposed to judicial lobbying to achieve their goals, even though the Burger Court is receptive to claims of gender-based discrimination.

To assess whether litigation may provide an additional political strategy, this article examines the results of gender-based discrimination cases brought by women's rights groups in the 1970s. More specifically, we examine all 63 gender-based cases decided during the 1969 to 1980 terms of the United States Supreme Court and the groups that participated in those cases.

Disadvantaged Groups and the Court

Writing in 1968, Cortner claimed there were numerous disadvantaged groups that:

> are highly dependent upon the judicial process as a means of pursuing their policy interests, usually because they are temporarily, or even permanently, disadvantaged in terms of their abilities to attain successfully their goals in the electoral process, within the elected political institutions or in the bureaucracy. If they are to succeed at all in the pursuit of their goals they are almost compelled to resort to litigation.

Notable and well studied examples of disadvantaged groups that have relied on litigation include the NAACP and the independent NAACP Legal Defense Fund (LDF), the Jehovah's Witnesses and the American Jewish Congress.

Additionally, while many scholars have agreed on the utility of litigation, they have also offered similar reasons for the success of these groups. For example, control over the course of litigation, generally in the form of group sponsorship of test cases—facilitated by the presence of only one major organization—often has been noted as critical to the NAACP LDF's victories in several issue areas.

Support from and cooperation with other groups is another factor offered for the success of disadvantaged litigators. This kind of assistance, generally in the form of "compatible" amicus curiae briefs, is welcomed by most disadvantaged groups. . . .

Another factor that played a role in the successes of disadvantaged groups including the NAACP LDF and the Jehovah's Witnesses was the relative absence of organized opposition. While individual and loosely organized groups opposed their various efforts, no major interest groups appeared to challenge their respective arguments in Court.

Thus, for most disadvantaged groups, control of litigation, cooperation with other groups and absence of organized opposition played a major role in their successes. Most important, however, was their initial recognition of the utility of litigation as a political mechanism.

Women's Groups and Litigation

As has been noted, however, women's rights organizations did not initially rely heavily on litigation. While most groups recognized the potential importance of litigation, initial efforts to lobby the courts in a systematic fashion were fraught with internal organizational problems and intergroup conflicts. For example, although the National Organization for Women (NOW), the first major women's rights organization, tried to model itself after the NAACP as early as 1966, it was unable to create a working legal defense fund until 1977.

NOW's initial litigation efforts were hampered by several factors: first, internal dissension over the conduct of employment discrimination cases led some NOW attorneys to found their own group, Human Rights for Women (HRW). This defection left NOW without experienced litigators. Second, NOW's leadership was divided as to the form a legal defense fund should take. Third, the battle for the ERA and other types of antidiscrimination legislation led NOW to concentrate its efforts in those areas—to the detriment of litigation. Finally, by 1972, other groups, particularly the American Civil Liberties Union (ACLU), were beginning to attack gender-based discrimination through litigation.

In 1972, the ACLU created a Women's Rights Project (WRP) to fill the void it perceived in gender-based litigation. By this time, the Women's Equity Action League (WEAL) had also begun negotiations with the Ford Foundation to secure funding for its own legal defense fund. Thus, during the early 1970s, numerous other groups interested in litigation allowed NOW to concentrate its efforts in the legislative forum.

In the wake of the recent defeat of the ERA, many women's rights groups now are reevaluating their strategies, and many are considering increased resort to litigation. Given the kinds of problems that have traditionally hampered women's rights groups in the legislative sphere, litigation may, in fact, provide a more expedient political mechanism for the expansion of women's rights as it has also done for other disadvantaged groups.

Women's Groups and the Court

To assess how litigation may be used by women's rights groups in the future, we examine their past performance in the U.S. Supreme Court. More specifically, we address the following questions:

- Which groups have been involved;
- What strategies have they employed;
- What kind of external opposition have they faced; and,
- How successful have women's rights groups been.

To address these questions, we identified 63 cases that the Supreme Court decided between its 1969 to 1980 terms, which involved gender-based discrimination. Gender-based cases were defined as those that had ramifications on women's rights including those where reproductive freedom issues were at stake. A women's rights issue, however, did not have to be the primary issue presented to the Court to be included in this analysis.

Only full opinion cases were considered because accurate information concerning group participation in those cases is available on microfiche. Group participation was identified by reading briefs of direct sponsors and amicus curiae in all 63 cases. Women's rights groups participated in 73 per cent of these case.

Participation

. . . Several women's rights groups participated in Supreme Court litigation. The ACLU, however, clearly emerged as "the" representative of women before the Court, with NOW, WEAL, and the Women's Legal Defense Fund (WLDF), entering more than 20 per cent of the cases in which at least one women's group participated. Additionally, the Center for Constitutional Rights (CCR), a New York–based radical public interest law firm, whose female attorneys are specifically interested in women's rights, participated in nine cases.

The ACLU's early commitment to gender-based discrimination litigation increased throughout the decade. . . . Over the 12 term period, it participated in 66 per cent of the 63 gender-based discrimination cases decided by the Supreme Court. In fact, it was involved in all but four of the cases in which at least one women's rights organization was present. It is interesting to note that even though the remarkably linear trend of the ACLU was somewhat disturbed when the other groups became more active, the aggregated level of its activity still increased.

Its continued commitment to litigation can be attributed to several factors: first, the Women's Rights Project (WRP) and later the Reproductive Freedom Project (RFP) were established at a time when ACLU leaders recognized that the Court was willing to expand interpretations of the Constitution. Thus, the ACLU acted quickly to take full advantage of a favorable judicial climate. Second, establishment of the projects allowed lawyers to specialize in gender-based discrimination litigation and to develop their expertise. Third, while funds for women's rights litigation were scarce, the ACLU could draw upon its own resources and its own experience in seeking outside funding. By the mid-1970s, then, most groups were willing to defer to the expertise of the ACLU. Consequently, the ACLU's prominence in this area has gone unchallenged.

While the ACLU's dominance cannot be disputed, other groups, particularly since the late 1970s, also have litigated for expanded rights. . . . NOW, WEAL, and WLDF have played increasingly important roles in gender-based discrimination litigation. Although NOW participated in seven cases during the 1969 to 1977 terms, its participation was largely reactive, and not part of a planned strategy. . . . Beginning in 1977, however, NOW began to turn to the courts in a more systematic fashion. At that time, funds finally were allocated for a lawyer, whose addition to the staff allowed NOW belatedly to initiate litigation, or at least to be sufficiently informed to file important amicus curiae briefs.

WEAL also began participating before the Supreme Court with greater frequency in the late 1970s. While it created a legal defense fund in 1972, funding problems hampered its own litigation activities. Additionally, in 1974 the Center for Law and Social Policy's Women's

Rights Project began to handle cases on WEAL's behalf.

In contrast to NOW and WEAL, which created special funds to litigate, WLDF initially was created in 1971 to "provide *pro bono* legal assistance to women," particularly to those who had suffered employment discrimination. Since 1978, WLDF has played an increasingly visible role in gender-based discrimination litigation, often soliciting the participation of, or representing, other women's rights groups before the U.S. Supreme Court.

While other groups have participated in gender-based discrimination litigation, these four organizations—ACLU, NOW, WEAL, WLDF—have been the major women's rights participants in this area. Collectively, they have been involved in 73 per cent of the 63 cases.

Strategies

Interest group participation in U.S. Supreme Court litigation can take several forms, with direct sponsorship or submission of amicus curiae briefs among the most common. . . . Only one women's rights group has regularly sponsored litigation at the Supreme Court level. The ACLU sponsored 25.4 per cent of the 63 gender-based cases. Its greatest concentration, however, occurred in cases involving challenges to facially discriminatory governmental programs or laws. For example, . . . the ACLU represented parties claiming that gender-based discrimination violated constitutional principles of equal protection or due process. During the 1970s, the ACLU also sponsored test cases dealing with expanded abortion rights and jury discrimination. Thus, like other disadvantaged groups, ACLU attorneys saw the utility in controlling litigation, particularly when constitutional issues were involved.

In contrast, NOW, WEAL, WLDF and CCR have generally limited their participation to that of amicus curiae. . . . While NOW and CCR each sponsored one case, women's groups' limited resources and deference to the ACLU have led them to opt for the amicus curiae strategy.

The amicus curiae can be a particularly effective strategy when used in cooperation with direct sponsors or with other amicus curiae. . . . Several women's groups regularly supported each other's efforts. For example, NOW regularly supported the ACLU. In 78.9 per cent of the cases in which NOW participated, it either filed an amicus curiae brief with or in support of the ACLU. Most women's rights groups, in fact, revealed very high support for the ACLU.

The support that most groups lent to the ACLU, however, was not uniformly revealed in their support of other women's rights groups. For example, CCR, the most radical of these groups and WEAL, generally regarded as somewhat traditional in nature have little in common. Not surprisingly, therefore, they were not supportive of each other's litigation activities.

In general, though, women's groups' litigation efforts reveal a high degree of intergroup support. The average support score between any two groups was .483. More specifically, most groups support the ACLU through submission of amicus curiae briefs.

External Opposition

When women's rights groups lobby state or national legislatures they face opposition from several sources including other women's groups, business interests, and conservative organizations. While women's rights groups' legislative lobbying efforts generally have attracted opposition across issue areas, their judicial lobbying efforts have not met consistent opposition. In general, women's rights groups faced organized third party opposition in 58.6 per cent of their cases. Similar to the opposition faced in the legislative arena, opposition in Court came from women's groups, business interest, and conservative organizations. Yet, the intensity, the scope and the sources of this opposition varied considerably by the nature of the issue(s) at stake.

For example, women's rights groups faced substantial opposition when discriminatory employment practices were alleged. In the 13 employment discrimination cases in which a women's rights group participated, they faced third party opposition in 69.2 per cent with conservative groups and business interests accounting

for 100 per cent. Yet, no women's group challenged the claims of women's rights organizations seeking expanded employment rights. This finding is not surprising given the near unanimous agreement among women about the importance of equal job opportunity. Thus, women's rights groups have faced vigorous opposition from business interests, but those interests have an economic stake in the outcome of the cases and are not necessarily opposed to expanded women's rights *per se*.

Opposition to women's rights claims also was evident in cases involving reproductive freedom. In the 12 reproductive freedom cases in which women's rights groups participated, they faced opposition from organized anti-abortion or religious groups in 75 per cent. Like groups involved in employment discrimination cases, organizations including Americans United for Life and the United States Catholic Conference opposed expanded abortion rights based on moral grounds and *not* upon general opposition to equality for women. In contrast to cases involving employment discrimination, however, some women's groups opposed expanded abortion rights. In three cases, women's groups, including Feminists for Life and Women for the Unborn, filed amicus curiae briefs urging the Court to uphold the constitutionality of restrictive state abortion or consent laws. Thus, similar to legislatures, the Court has been the target of competing women's groups. But, the intensity of this opposition has been far less emotional and extensive than women's rights groups encountered in the legislative sphere.

In contrast to litigation involving abortion or employment discrimination, cases alleging discrimination in the distribution of or qualifications for government benefits generated minimal opposition to women's rights groups' claims. In only one case, . . . involving a divorced woman's claim to a share of her former husband's military pension, did any organized group oppose her claims.

The absence of opposition from other organized interests, especially from conservative women, is exceptionally interesting given the nature of the cases in this area. Many involved challenges to traditional assumptions about women's roles in society. When the same kinds of changes are proposed in the legislative sphere—alimony, child support or custody, for example—conservative women's groups turn out in large numbers to lobby against any proposed changes in the traditional family relationship. When these same issues are addressed through litigation, no conservative women's groups appeared. Litigation in this area then may be particularly attractive and amenable to the purposes of women's rights groups because of the absence of opposition.

Thus, unlike the situation in the legislative sphere, conservative women's groups generally *do not* oppose expanded rights for women before the U.S. Supreme Court. Almost all the opposition that women's rights groups have faced has come from pro-business interests that have an economic stake in the outcome of the litigation or from anti-abortion groups that are morally opposed to expanded abortion rights. Therefore, particularly in cases involving the distribution of benefits, the absence of opposition makes the Court an attractive forum for women's rights groups to use to attain expanded rights.

Success

Whether participating as direct sponsors or as amicus curiae, women's rights organizations were successful. They won 63 per cent of their 46 cases. A major reason for this high success rate has been the consistent efforts of the ACLU. In fact, the ACLU's presence in a case increased the chances of success for a gender-based claim by 16 per cent.

Even when the ACLU's participation met with only mixed results, its presence before the Court tended to minimize losses—which can be considered another facet of success. For example, in *Dothard v. Rawlinson* its amicus curiae brief provided the Court with a fall back position if the Court was to uphold Alabama's refusal to hire women as prison guards. In noting that the state's prisons were among the worst in the nation, the ACLU gave the Court the

"out" to construe narrowly the bona fide occupational qualification exception to Title VII.

While the ACLU is a very successful litigator, its initial efforts might have been even more successful if it had been supported by other women's groups. For example, *Kahn v. Shevin*, a case sponsored by the ACLU, resulted in a major doctrinal loss when a majority of the Court upheld the constitutionality of benign discrimination. In *Kahn*, no women's rights groups filed amicus curiae briefs in support of the ACLU; amicus curiae briefs could have shown the Court that women were uniformly opposed to such benign forms of discrimination. Thus, the absence of support in this and other cases, may have made crucial differences in the outcome of litigation.

In recent years, then, the increased interest of women's rights groups in litigation . . . has undoubtedly aided the cause of equal rights. For example, in *County of Washington v. Gunther*, a case that few commentators predicted would result in such a resounding victory for women's rights forces, the Court adopted the position advocated by 16 women's rights groups. This was particularly significant given the tremendous business opposition to the concept of equal pay for comparable work and the potential ramifications of *Gunther*. Thus, while women's rights groups generally have been successful, greater cooperation and participation could have a positive impact on the Court's disposition of future cases.

Conclusion

Women's rights groups have been unable to secure all or even most of their goals in the legislative forum. To assess whether women's rights groups, like other disadvantaged groups, would be better served by increased reliance on litigation, we examined their efforts in the Supreme Court during the 1970s. More specifically, we analyzed four aspects of that activity. First, we found that the ACLU was a major participant. Other women's rights groups have only recently begun to use litigation in a systematic fashion. Second, we discovered that while the ACLU prefers the direct sponsorship tactic, other women's rights groups often appear as amicus curiae. Most of those amicus curiae efforts, however, have been in support of ACLU arguments. Third, we discovered that both the intensity and the sources of opposition to women's rights groups' claims differed from those in the legislative forum. In general, groups opposed women's rights groups claims on economic or moral grounds and not because they opposed the expansion of women's rights, *per se.* Finally, we found that women's rights groups have been very successful before the United States Supreme Court.

Thus, we conclude that women's rights groups, like other disadvantaged groups, may continue to find that the Court is receptive to their arguments because thus far, unlike the legislative forum, women have faced relatively minimal opposition in Court. And, the nature of this opposition, given the constraints of the judicial forum, is less emotional and less highly charged than the opposition in the legislative forum. Perhaps more important, however, the ACLU's emergence as "the" spokesperson of women's interests has influenced the Court, particularly when its efforts have been supported by other groups.

Thus, while women's groups' efforts often have been frustrated in legislative forums, the Supreme Court has served as a source of expanded women's rights. Women's rights groups have used this forum effectively in the past. Based on this study, continued efforts in this forum would appear likely to result in further success.

[*Although this article was written in 1983, its conclusions generally remain true. On the issue of abortion, however, women's rights groups are finding the courts less friendly than in years past. In 1989, in the case of* Webster v. Reproductive Health Services, *the Supreme Court pulled away from its 1973 decision proclaiming that a woman's right to terminate a pregancy is protected by the Constitution. See selections 5.3, 16.3, 16.4, and 16.5 for related articles.*]

IV ISSUE AND DEBATE: DOES LOW VOTER TURNOUT MATTER?

Should we be concerned that turnout in American elections is so low? Robert Kuttner suggests in the first of the following readings that it would be "very salutory for American democracy" if more Americans voted. Charles Krauthammer takes the opposite view in the second selection; nonvoting, he suggests, is a logical and rational act. No matter what the League of Women Voters might say, Krauthammer concludes, a low turnout may be just what the doctor ordered.

6.5 Why Americans Don't Vote— and Why They Should

Robert Kuttner

The universal vote is both the essence of political democracy and its most jarringly radical aspect. When people from all economic walks of life have an equal say in governance, ordinary power relationships are transformed. Some people, by dint of wealth, education, or position, normally enjoy more influence than others. Yet in the electoral realm, these deep economic and social inequalities are supposedly neutralized by the egalitarian logic of one person-one vote.

Not surprisingly, modern democracies experience a tension between these two sets of logic—the economic and the political. The tension is evident whenever campaign contributions buy votes, whenever family fortunes win elections, whenever the political power of have-nots takes something of economic value from the haves, or whenever wide differences in voting participation exist between different races or social classes. The tension is especially acute in the United States, which is both the most durably democratic of nations and the most fiercely capitalist of the democracies. Ours is also the democracy where the fewest citizens bother to vote. In the 1986 election, voting turnout as a fraction of the adult population, about 38 percent, was the lowest since the wartime election of 1942. In states outside the South, it was the lowest since 1798.

One of the most consistent findings of voting research in America is that when voting participation falls off, it is the poorer, less educated people who stop voting, and that the inclination of low-status people to stay home has much to do with their greater cynicism about whether civic participation can make much difference in their lives. Among the wealthiest fifth of citizens, about 75 percent of eligible voters turned out in recent presidential elections. Among the poorest fifth, less than 40 percent voted. In effect, upper-middle-class and well-educated Americans still turn out to vote at near-European levels. The decay in our civic culture has been mainly at the bottom.

As a matter of practice, most politicians do not care very much about the general level of political participation. They care about getting their own likely supporters to the polls. And most well-educated and affluent Americans seem to harbor an intuitive belief that if poorly educated, lower-class people (who are probably not well informed on the issues anyway) do not bother to vote, that is a kind of natural purgative. "Voting ought to be a little bit difficult" is an axiomatic rejoinder to those who call for easier registration and more nearly universal voting. People with the purest of democratic souls catch themselves saying words to the effect of: voting is a privilege, not a right.

In a democracy, of course, voting is a right—even for the unwashed, the ill-informed, and the mean-spirited. Though it may seem counterintuitive, it is the political participation of all social classes that helps build political community and social cohesion. But the narrowing of the franchise makes it easier for the inegalitarian market to coexist with the egalitarian polity, because it reduces the political influence of the less well-off. This phenomenon is especially vivid in the United States, despite our deeply democratic origins as a nation of scant class differences and our liberty-loving spirit.

The Founding Fathers, after all, gave us a Republic. A republic is generally defined as an indirect and qualified democracy. The early Fed-

Voter Registration and Turnout

Who votes? Who doesn't? Do Americans vote more or less now than in the past? The answers lie in statistics measuring voter turnout by race or ethnicity, sex, region, age, socioeconomic status, and educational level and measuring voter turnout over time. The graph and table in this box present such data.

It is well worth examining this material in some detail. The graph, which charts voter turnout over time, makes it clear that turnout levels are far lower today than they were in the late nineteenth century and significantly lower now than they were even in 1960. Congressional election turnout, once on a par or even above presidential election turnout, is now well below.

The table presents, by category, the percentage of Americans who registered, the percentage who voted, and the percentage of registered voters who actually voted in the 1988 presidential election. Note the relatively large differences by category in the percentage of Americans registered to vote and in the overall percentage voting, compared to the relatively small differences in the percentages of those registered who actually vote.

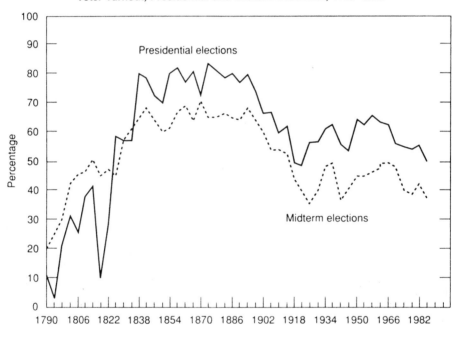

Voter Turnout, Presidential and Midterm Elections, 1790–1988

eralists worried as much about the tyranny of majorities as the tyranny of elites, putting all kinds of constraints into their Constitution, including the well-known checks and balances, as well as the indirect election of presidents and senators. Most of the fathers of the federal Republic also presumed a fairly limited franchise. Though states determined the eligibility of vot-

ers, property qualifications were then the norm. In elections of the late 18th century, less than five percent of adults constituted the typical electorate.

It was only in the populist Jacksonian era that the somewhat patrician Republic began evolving into a more universalist and raucous Democracy. Gradually property qualifications

Citizens Registered and Voting, 1988 Presidential Election

	Percentage Registered	Percentage Voting	Percent of Those Registered Who Actually Voted
Race/Ethnicity			
White	68	59	87
Black	65	52	80
Hispanic	36	29	81
Sex			
Male	65	56	86
Female	68	58	85
Region			
Northeast	65	57	88
Midwest	73	63	86
South	67	55	82
West	63	56	89
Age			
18–20	45	33	73
21–24	51	38	75
25–34	58	48	83
35–44	69	61	88
45–64	76	68	89
65+	78	69	88
Employment			
Employed	67	58	87
Unemployed	50	39	78
Not in Labor Force	67	57	85
Education			
8 years or less	48	37	77
1–3 years high school	53	41	77
4 years high school	65	55	85
1–3 years college	74	65	88
4+ years college	83	78	94
Total	67	57	85

Note: Figures reflect persons who reported registering and voting, not those who actually registered and voted. 57 percent of Americans said they voted, but only 50 percent actually did so. The other 7 percent, apparently, lied.

fell, and "universal manhood suffrage" was the cry of the early populists. According to Walter Dean Burnham of MIT, the leading student of voting participation and social class, voting participation began rising dramatically in the 1820s. By the 1830s it was already higher than it is in most states today. Between 1848 and 1896, roughly 75 percent of eligible voters voted.

But as participation increased, so did epic voting fraud, especially in large cities. As the rabble was drawn into partisan politics, electoral abuse became flagrant. According to the historian Joseph P. Harris, in a charming 1929 volume recapitulating earlier histories of voting, "Hoodlums were rounded up and lodged for a night or so in various lodging houses or cheap hotels and then registered from all of them. On the day of the election, gangs of 'repeaters' were hauled from precinct to precinct and voted under different names. Sometimes the same persons would vote several times at each precinct, changing coats and hats between times."

The system responded with a variety of restraints, such as literacy requirements and voter registration systems. Some of these had only the most purely civic intentions. Often, however, the evident purpose was not only to eliminate fraud but to restore the narrower franchise of the earlier Republic. By the 1880s most states had some form of voter registration. The Civil War gave Southern states one more good reason to erect barriers to voting. Complex "literacy" requirements, poll taxes, grandfather clauses, and the like became normal in much of the South, to restrict the Negro vote. Elsewhere there were tighter residency restrictions and repeated re-registration requirements, with periodic "purges" to rid the rolls of dead people (and also people who had moved, or had failed to vote in the last election). In this cumbersome and politically unique legacy, civic purpose and patrician purpose are hard to disentangle. But by the turn of the 20th century, populist America paradoxically had erected a series of subtle and overt barriers that gradually reduced the voting participation of society's lower classes.

Restoring broader voting participation, as a civic goal or even as a partisan one, strikes many citizens as a ho-hum, League of Women Voters sort of issue. Jimmy Carter's proposal for easier voter registration roused little support. The last time voter registration pervaded the national consciousness was during the civil rights struggles of the 1960s, and then only as a racial equity issue. By 1984 black and white voting turnout rates were very nearly equal, while participation among poorer people of both races continued to decline.

In recent years a number of liberal and social reform groups have perceived a connection between low voting turnout of lower-class voters and the current conservative tilt of recent American politics. But among most politicians enthusiasm for broader voter registration efforts has remained lukewarm, even among partisan and liberal Democrats. Linda Davidoff, the director of one such voter-mobilization group called Human-SERVE (Human Service Employee's Voter Registration and Education), says, "The [national] Democratic Party wants the working class to vote, but not necessarily in this election in my district. A lot of elected officials cannot stand the idea of people being allowed to register on election day, for example, because that means a whole bunch of new voters coming out of the woodwork. And if people up in Harlem vote, then you have to go up there and campaign at them, on their issues. If they don't vote, you can stay in more familiar territory."

Human-SERVE was formed in 1983, the brainchild of two activist-scholars, Frances Fox Piven and Richard Cloward, who have spent two decades working on welfare rights movements and similar efforts to increase the political organization and participation of the poor. They arrived, finally, at the most fundamental political act of all: voting. Their initial plan was that the voting participation of the poor might be increased dramatically if workers at human service agencies, such as welfare and food stamp offices, were put in the business of voter registration. The idea was unveiled before the 1984 election, endorsed by 30 organizations of human-service professionals, as well as the National League of Cities, representing mayors. A few venturesome governors—in Texas, Ohio, New York, and New Mexico, among others—issued orders permitting registration at welfare offices, but did so reluctantly. For the plan seemed to confirm the most lurid conservative stereotypes of a symbiosis between the welfare state and its dependent clients. Welfare workers, in this view, were the modern counterpart of Professor Harris's corrupt ward heelers. Welfare recipients were the modern "hoodlums," being "voted" by those with a partisan interest in electing tax-and-spend liberals. Even worse, the whole scheme reinforced the awkward image of the Democratic Party as an alliance between professional do-gooders and the undeserving, dependent poor.

The 1984 voter registration drive, by Human-SERVE and by several groups sponsored by liberal foundations, was a modest success, registering millions of new voters, mostly minority and poor. After 1984 Human-SERVE moved to a higher and more sophisticated ground, operating as a national lobby to reduce systematically barriers to voting, and leaving mobilization and direct organizing to others. The group promotes a shrewd concept, pioneered more than a decade ago in Michigan, dubbed "Motor-Voter." The idea is that you should get certified as a voter at the same time that you get certified to drive a car. This nicely takes the pro-welfare sting out of the project; and in fact driving as a function of social class is slightly skewed away from the urban poor, though far less skewed than current voting proclivities. "What could be more American than driving a car?" asks Davidoff.

Well, voting could be. Motor-Voter has recently been adopted by Arizona, Iowa, Minnesota, Nevada, and Colorado. Under the Nevada and the Colorado versions, which took effect in 1985, it is not even necessary for the applicant to fill out a separate form. The driver simply checks off a box on the license application or renewal form, indicating that he or she wishes to be enlisted as a qualified voter. In its first year motor-voter was credited with adding 140,000 new voters to Colorado's rolls, increasing the number of registered voters by 11 percent. Elsewhere Human-SERVE has sought to promote postcard registration (now in effect in 23 states) and election day registration, long established in Wisconsin, Maine, and Minnesota.

California Senator Alan Cranston has proposed legislation to establish minimal federal standards for state election systems, which would include public agency registration programs such as Motor-Voter, mail-in registration, and election day registration. The proposed federal law would also prohibit certain practices, such as automatically purging citizens from the rolls when they skip an election.

Though working-class voters, especially white voters, have not seemed especially liberal in recent years, it turns out that the perceived "liberalism" or "conservatism" of lower-income voters depends largely on the issue. Survey data and focus group research generally confirm that even socially conservative white working-class voters (when they vote) are reliably liberal on economic issues, in the sense that they welcome activist government interventions on their behalf. Historically, the Democratic Party has been ascendant when its ability to deliver economic benefits to a working- and middle-class base stimulated broad voting turnout, built secure political loyalties, and purchased some running room for the party's more cosmopolitan views on social questions, which otherwise alienate many working-class voters.

Exit polls on Election Day 1986 (asking voters of different backgrounds how they voted) generally revealed that the historic correlation between class and party persists. Richer people still generally support Republicans, poorer ones Democrats. In Georgia, for example, the incumbent Republican senator, Mack Mattingly, swept the white upper-income vote, by a margin of 72 to 28. But Democratic challenger Wyche Fowler was able to gain the votes of 46 percent of whites from households earning $25,000 or less, plus a healthy majority of blacks, and to win the election. The tendency to vote for the progressive candidate goes up as income goes down—but the tendency to vote at all goes down.

Three factors explain low American voter turnouts. The first is the characteristically American fear of the State. In other democracies, where the state routinely keeps a roster of citizens, their addresses, occupations, and so on, there is no such thing as "registration" to vote. Despite the fact that several federal agencies keep rosters of citizens, including the IRS, the Social Security Administration, Selective Service, and the Census Bureau, the idea of a federal responsibility for a universal registry of voters seems to frighten libertarian Americans, or to evoke more ghosts of Tammany. This is ironic, of course, since it would be the surest remedy to concerns about hoodlums and voter fraud that are ostensibly the reason behind the archaic registration systems.

The second reason has to do with social class and political party. It is a staple of political science literature that parties are essential mechanisms for mobilizing lower-status citizens to participate politically. Parties deliver benefits and identities to voters, and deliver voters to polls. The American version of this tradition departs dramatically from the European. The United States, in the famous phrase of the historian Louis Hartz, was "born free," with democratic institutions and relatively scant differences of social class. Much of Europe, on the other hand, fought for basic republican principles and greater class equality almost simultaneously. It understandably developed stronger institutions of class representation, such as trade unions and labor parties, which do a more systematic job of mobilizing lower status voters.

Finally, most of the other democracies have some form of proportional representation in their parliaments. Proportional representation has many variations, but the common idea is to divide parliamentary representation according to the total nationwide vote. One effect is to assure all voters that their vote will "count," even if they happen to live in jurisdictions dominated by another party. Many Americans live in virtually one-party states, or are represented by hopelessly safe incumbents. If you happen to live in such a place, voting can seem futile. Even so, elimination of registration barriers could probably increase our voting turnout to the 75 percent range typical of the United States in the 19th century, and of Britain and Canada today.

The decay of civic participation is a circular problem. People stop voting because they feel they can't make a difference, and then the entire political system seems somebody else's property. Frustrations build up outside the system, and the system needn't respond to them because they are not being articulated politically. Though it seems just as well that the ill-informed and the poorly motivated stay home, in fact a better informed citizenry is probably as much the product of a more active electorate as a precondition. A narrow base of political participation, by definition, corrodes democracy itself. The idea that everybody, credentialed or not, gets to participate is the most wonderful and audacious thing about democracy.

The populist aspect of America's heritage is often only latent, but it can ignite in surprising ways. The revival of tax reform produced the deathbed conversion of one special interest politician after another, and the collapse of the special interests themselves. Taxpayers vote. Anyway, some of them do, and it would be very salutary for American democracy if more of us did.

NO

6.6 In Praise of Low Voter Turnout

Charles Krauthammer

Washington, it seems, is a city in decline. History has taken up residence in Budapest and Tokyo, Brussels and Seoul. After a brief spurt of prominence and wealth owed to the Depression, Hitler and the cold war, Washington, we are told, has lapsed into a somnambular state.

This is an exaggeration, but not too far from the truth. Government has grown huge, and a presidential hiccup can still panic the stock market, but Washington has far less impact on the direction of America and the world than it did a generation ago.

The marginalization of Washington is sometimes taken as proof of American decline. Nonsense. With the implosion of its only superpower rival, America stands alone in the world, its relative power—which the decline theorists insist is the only relevant measure—unsurpassed. (One reason, for example, that hostages are being released is that the thug regimes of the world realize that suddenly there is only one superpower left and they had better warm up to it.)

The marginalization of Washington reflects not the decline of America but the decline of politics. In the West—and it is soon to be true in the East, now that they've got the easy part, revolution, out of the way—history is not made by politics. It is made by economics, by demographics and, above all, by science and technology. Politics lubricates, corrupts mildly and takes a slice of the action. But it does not create new worlds as it did, horribly, in 1917 and 1933 and, blessedly, in 1946–49 when the U.S. established the structures of the postwar world. Politics has become, like much of life, maintenance. The house is built; Republicans and Democrats argue now over who is to repair the roof and how to pay for it.

Moreover, the great political debates are over. The romance with isms, with the secular religions of socialism, egalitarianism and totalitarianism, is dead. The fierce battles over whether, for example, the U.S. should lead the crusade against communism are finished too. American politics is no longer about bearing any burden in defense of liberty. American politics is about the Clean Air Act.

This is not to deride clean air. Clean air is important, and the clean air bill now working its way through Congress is a quite satisfying triumph of democratic compromise, smog-producing Detroit working out with smog-ingesting Los Angeles a political arrangement that the whole country can live with. But the great dichotomies of war and peace, left and right, good and evil are gone. Politicians still try to use these categories to carry the fight, but no one believes them.

This triumph of apolitical bourgeois democracy has been a source of dismay to some. They pine for the heroic age when great ideologies clashed and the life of nations turned on a vote in Congress. On the contrary, I couldn't be happier that the political century is over, and that all that's left is to shuffle cards on the cruise ship. The great disease of the 20th century was the politicization of life. The totalitarians, left and right, showed the way, politicizing everything: economics, education, art, religion, family life. Not even genetics could escape politics. One remembers with disbelief not just Hitler's eugenic lunacies but also Stalin's designation of Lysenko's crackpot genetics as official truth, enforced by secret police.

After such a century, it is a form of salvation, of social health, for politics to be in acute and precipitous decline. As a Portuguese ex-leftist said of his country's recent renaissance, "Portugal's success is that its politics no longer dominate everything."

At its headiest, the aim of 20th century politics was the transformation of man and society by means of power. This great project—politics as redemption—has ended in failure on a breathtaking scale: not just economic and political but also ecological, spiritual and, not surprising for an enterprise of such overweening hubris, moral. The deeper meaning of the overthrow of communism is the realization that man can shape neither history nor society by Five-Year Plans, and that attempts to contradict this truth must end in the grotesque. The revulsion with politics reflects the view that when politicians go about tinkering with something as organic as a poor family or a rural community by means of a federal welfare program or an enormous dam, the law of unintended consequences prevails.

George Bush's great good fortune is that he is a man utterly incapable of vision at a time when the people do not want vision and do not need it. Vision is for Khomeini and Castro, for Jesse Jackson and Pat Robertson. Happily, if only for now, Americans will have none of it.

Which is why when almost every pundit wrings his hands in despair at low voter turnout—some even feel obliged to propose creative schemes to induce people to vote—I am left totally unmoved. Low voter turnout means that people see politics as quite marginal to their lives, as neither salvation nor ruin. That is healthy. Low voter turnout is a leading indicator of contentment. For a country founded on the notion that that government is best that governs least, it seems entirely proper that Americans should in large numbers register a preference against politics by staying home on Election Day.

A few weeks ago, a producer from public television came to ask my advice about planning coverage for the 1992 elections. Toward the end, she raised a special problem: how to get young adults interested in political coverage. I offered the opinion that 19-year-olds who sit in front of a television watching politics could use professional help. At that age they should be playing ball and looking for a date. They'll have time enough at my age to worry about the mortgage and choosing a candidate on the basis of his views on monetary policy.

To say that, of course, is to violate current League of Women Voters standards of good citizenship. Let others struggle valiantly to raise the political awareness of all citizens. Let them rage against the tides of indifference. They will fail, and when they do, relax. Remember that indifference to politics leaves all the more room for the things that really count: science, art, religion, family and play.

_____Chapter 7

Political Parties

C *entral to any discussion of American political parties in the 1990s is the concept of realignment. For nearly two centuries, American politics has been characterized by a party system in which two major political parties contested for power. For most of that time, one of the two parties has been clearly predominant. For example, from 1896 until 1932, the Republican party controlled the White House for twenty-eight out of thirty-six years; during that same period, the Republicans controlled the House of Representatives for twenty-six years and the Senate for thirty years. In 1932, however, in the midst of the Great Depression, voters rebelled against the Republicans. The resulting realignment of the party system left the Democrats clearly in control. From 1932 until 1968, the Democrats' domination of the national government was even greater than the Republicans' had been: the Democrats controlled the presidency for twenty-eight years and the House and the Senate for thirty-two. A realignment like that of the 1930s is marked by clear shifts in party identification by the voters and results in dramatic shifts in federal public policy.*

Realignments were a staple feature of American politics for most of our history and indeed seemed to occur each generation or so. No clear realignment has occurred, however, since the New Deal. As the readings in this chapter suggest, the modern American political system is marked not by a clear majority party but by a split in partisan control of the national government—with Republicans usually controlling the White House and Democrats the House and Senate. This new development is the result of many factors, including the tendency of voters to split their vote among candidates of both parties, depending on the offices and personalities involved, and is the subject, one way or another, of all the readings in this chapter.

Although scholars agree that the modern period has not seen a realignment in the classic sense, there does seem to be a widespread belief that the Reagan presidency marked a watershed in American political history. The Reagan years were characterized by a conservative shift in both domestic and foreign policy, encompassing tax cuts and deregulation at home and a more assertive and interventionist stance abroad. The "Reagan revolution" or "Reagan realignment" may not have been a traditional one or a complete one, but its significance should not be underestimated. Like the New Deal, the Reagan years have placed their stamp on the relationship between the major parties and on the shape and nature of American government itself.

Chapter Questions

1. What is meant by the phrase *party system*? What is a realignment of the party system, in classic terms?

2. In what sense does the modern era—especially since the election of Reagan in 1980—seem like a realignment? In what sense does it seem clearly different? What is meant by the terms *incomplete* and *split-level* realignment?

3. What is the connection between parties, realignments, and public policy? Does the modern party system provide American voters with the opportunity to make sure that the federal government does what they want it to do?

I THE CLASSIC TEXTS

Political parties are among the most important political institutions in the United States, or indeed in any other democracy. Yet the term political party *cannot be defined in a brief, all-inclusive statement because the nature, history, role, and importance of political parties differ from country to country.*

In the following selection, the political scientist V. O. Key provides a brief overview of political parties in the United States. He discusses their history, functions, and purpose and the concept of a party system, in which two or more parties compete for political offices and for control of public policy. Finally, he examines the American two-party system, a characteristic feature of American politics since the beginning of the Republic.

This brief excerpt from his much larger study of political parties amply demonstrates why V. O. Key was regarded as perhaps the leading political scientist of his day. Although his highly regarded book was written nearly thirty years ago, Key's careful, nondogmatic, and painstaking style provides a model of academic scholarship. These few pages present an excellent introduction to the role of parties in American political life.

Questions

1. What is a political party? What roles does it play in a political system? What is meant by the term *party system*?

2. What factors have contributed to the existence in America of a two-party system? Why have third parties had so much difficulty playing an effective role in the system? Notice that Key presents not one but several answers to these questions.

7.1 The Nature and Function of Political Parties

V. O. Key

A salient characteristic of the American party system is its dual form. During most of our history power has alternated between two major parties. While minor parties have arisen from time to time and exerted influence on governmental policy, the two major parties have been the only serious contenders for the Presidency. On occasion a major party has disintegrated, but in due course the biparty division has reasserted itself. For relatively long periods, single parties have dominated the national scene, yet even during these eras the opposition has retained the loyalty of a substantial proportion of the electorate. Most voters consistently place their faith in one or the other of two parties; and neither party has been able to wipe out the other's following.

Concept of Party System

Since many of the peculiarities of American politics are associated with the duality of the party system, the significant features of that system need to be set out concretely. An identification of its main operating characteristics will supplement the insights gained about the role of party in the governing process from our excursion into the genesis of party. To speak of a party *system* is to imply a patterned relationship among elements of a larger whole. A pattern or system of relationships exists between, for example, two football teams. Each team has a role to play in the game, a role that changes from time to time. Within each team a subsystem of relationships ties together the roles of each player. Or, if one prefers mechanical figures, the components of an internal combustion engine combine and perform in specified relation to each other to produce the total engine, or system.

Similarly, a party system consists of interrelated components, each of which has an assigned role. The American party system consists of two major elements, each of which performs in specified ways or follows customary behavior patterns in the total system. To remove or alter the role of one element would destroy the system or create a new one. If one ignores for the moment the internal complexities of parties, the broad features of the system as a whole are simple. The major parties compete for electoral favor by presenting alternate slates of candidates and differing programs of projected action. It is a basic characteristic of the system that each party campaigns with hope of victory, if not in this election perhaps at the next.

In their relations to the electorate, another element of the system, the parties confront the voters with an either-or choice. Commonly the electoral decision either continues a party in power or replaces the executive and a legislative majority by the slate of the outs. The system, thus, differs fundamentally from a multiparty system which ordinarily presents the electorate with no such clear-cut choice; an election may be followed by only a mild modification of the majority coalition. The dual arrangement assigns to its parties a radically different role from that played by parties of a multiparty system. The voters may throw the old crowd out of power and install a completely new management even if they do not set an entirely new policy orientation. The differences in the roles that their respective systems assign to them make a party of a multiparty system by no means the equivalent of a party of a two-party system. A party that may expect to gain complete control of the government must act far differently from one that may expect, at most, to become a component of a parliamentary coalition.

To be distinguished from the roles of parties in electoral competition are the functions of party in the operation of government. The candidates of the victorious party assume public office. As public officers they may become more than partisans: they are cast in public rather than party roles. Yet the party role remains, for the government is operated under the expectation that the party may be held accountable at the next election for its stewardship. To the minority falls the role of criticism, of opposition, and of preparation for the day when it may become the government itself. These functions belong mainly to the minority members in the representative body, but they may also be shared by the party organization outside the government. The minority role constitutes a critical element of the system. The minority may assail governmental ineptitude, serve as a point for the coalescence of discontent, propose alternative governmental policies, and influence the behavior of the majority as well as lay plans to throw it out of power.

In addition to the elements described, the party system includes customary rules which prescribe, often imprecisely, the manner in which the elements of the system shall interact. Of these, the most basic rule is that the government that loses the election shall surrender office to the candidates of the victorious party, a commonplace expectation which becomes significant only by contemplation of the relative infrequency of adherence to such a custom in the history of the government of man. Other rules and customs place limits on the conduct of party warfare. For example, the niceties of the etiquette of parliamentary conflict compel the attribution of good faith, patriotism, and even intelligence to the most despised enemy. Similar limitations, more poorly defined and less effectively sanctioned, apply to party warfare outside the legislative chambers. Multiparty systems are able to accommodate parties opposed to the fundamental principles of the political order. The maintenance of a two-party competition—a winner-take-all system—must, over the long run, rest on a mutual recognition of equal loyalty to the political order.

Such are the rough outlines of the American two-party system described in terms similar to those employed by social theorists in their conception of social systems generally. Real party life does not precisely fit any such pattern of relations among sets of actors. Yet the conception of system alerts the observer to the interrelations of the elements of party institutions.

Why Two Parties?

Foreign observers manifest the utmost bewilderment as they contemplate the American two-party system, and native scholars are not overwhelmingly persuasive in their explanations of it. The pervasive effects on American political life of the dual form make the quest for the causes of this arrangement a favorite topic of speculation. Given the diversity of interests in American society one might expect numerous parties to be formed to represent groups with conflicting aims and objectives. Yet that does not occur. In the less sophisticated explanations of why, the system is attributed to a single "cause." A more tenable assumption would be that several factors drive toward dualism on the American scene.

Persistence of Initial Form

Human institutions have an impressive capacity to perpetuate themselves or at least to preserve their form. The circumstances that happened to mold the American party system into a dual form at its inception must bear a degree of responsibility for its present existence. They included the confrontation of the country with a great issue that could divide it only into the ayes and the nays: the debate over the adoption of the Constitution. As party life began to emerge under the Constitution, again the issues split the country into two camps.

The initial lines of cleavage built also on a dualism of interest in a nation with a far less intricate economic and social structure than that of today. Arthur Macmahon concludes that, in addition to other influences, the two-party division was "induced by the existence of two major complexes of interest in the country." A cleavage between agriculture and the interests of the mercantile and financial community antedated even the adoption of the Constitution. This conflict, with a growing industry allying itself with trade and finance, was fundamental in the debate on the adoption of the Constitution and remained an issue in national politics afterward. The great issues changed from time to time but each party managed to renew itself as it found new followers to replace those it lost. The Civil War, thus, brought a realignment in national politics, yet it re-enforced the dual division. For decades southern Democrats recalled the heroes of the Confederacy and the Republicans waved the "bloody shirt" to rally their followers. As memories of the war faded new alignments gradually took shape within the matrix of the preexisting structure, with each party hierarchy struggling to maintain its position in the system.

Institutional Factors

A recurring question in political analysis is whether formal institutional structure and procedure influence the nature of party groupings. Though it is doubtful that formal governmental structures cause dualism, certain features of American institutions are congenial to two-partyism and certainly over the short run obstruct the growth of splinter parties.

Some commentators, in seeking the influences that lead to two-partyism, attribute great weight to the practice of choosing representatives from single-member districts by a plurality vote in contrast with systems of proportional representation which are based on multimember districts. In a single-member district only two parties can contend for electoral victory with any hope of success; a third party is doomed to perpetual defeat unless it can manage to absorb the following of one of the major parties and thereby become one of them. Parties do not thrive on the certainty of defeat. That prospect tends to drive adherents of minor parties to one or the other of the two major parties. The single-member district thus re-enforces the bipartisan pattern. Each of the contending groups in such a district must formulate its appeals with an eye to attracting a majority of the electors to its banner.

An essential element of the theory is its plurality-election feature. If, so the hypothesis goes, a plurality—be it only 25 per cent of the total vote—is sufficient for victory in a single-member district, the leaders of a group consisting of, say, 15 per cent of the electorate, will join with other such groups before the voting to maximize their chance of being on the winning side. They assume that if they do not form such coalitions, others will. Moreover, concessions will be made to attract the support of smaller groups. If a majority, instead of a plurality, is required to elect, a second election to choose between the two high candidates in the first polling becomes necessary. Such a situation may encourage several parties to enter candidates at the first election, each on the chance that its candidate may be one of the two leaders. Of course, under systems of proportional representation the incentive to form two coalitions, each approaching a majority, is destroyed by the opportunity to elect candidates in proportion to popular strength whatever the number of parties.

The validity of the single-member-district theory has not been adequately tested against the evidence. Obviously, in those states of the United States in which third parties have developed fairly durable strength, the institutional situation has stimulated moves toward coalitions and mergers with one or another of the major parties. Yet the single-member-district

"Political Parties"—A Term with Many Meanings

In this excerpt from Politics, Parties, and Pressure Groups, *V. O. Key discusses the different meanings of the term "political party."*

$\mathcal{A}$ political party, at least on the American scene, tends to be a "group" of a peculiar sort. Perhaps only by courtesy may a party be designated as a group. Among many of its members the sense of belonging, the awareness of shared concern, and the impulse to action in the same direction may be scarcely discernible.

A fundamental difficulty about the term "political party" is that it is applied without discrimination to many types of groups and near-groups. Discussion may be facilitated by some preliminary differentiations of the usages of the word "party." Within the body of voters as a whole, groups are formed of persons who regard themselves as party members. The Democratic group and the Republican group are mobilized only on election day, but in the intervals between elections the members of each group—or many of them—react in characteristic ways to public issues. Party in this sense of the "party-in-the-electorate" is an amorphous group, yet it has a social reality.

In another sense the term "party" may refer to the group of more or less professional political workers. The Republican national committeemen, the Republican state central committees, the Republican county chairmen, and all the men and women who do the work of the political organization constitute a "group" more or less separate and apart from the party-in-the-electorate, but not necessarily independent of it.

At times party denotes groups within the government. Thus, all Democratic Representatives form a group within the House that acts with high solidarity on many matters. Similarly, Republican Senators form a party group. At times there may be a "party-in-the-government" including the President, groups of his party in both House and Senate, and the heads of executive departments. We tend always to speak as if there were such a group which could be held accountable for the conduct of the government.

There are other senses in which the term "party" is used. Often it refers to an entity which rolls into one the party-in-the-electorate, the professional political group, the party-in-the-legislature, and the party-in-the-government. "The Democrats (or the Republicans) are to blame for the parlous state of the country." In truth, this all-encompassing usage has its legitimate application, for all the types of groups called "party" interact more or less closely and at times may be as one. Yet both analytically and operationally the term "party" most of the time must refer to several types of group; and it is useful to keep relatively clear the meaning in which the term is used.

—*V. O. Key*

---

and plurality election can at most encourage a dual division—or discourage a multiparty division—only within each representative district. Other influences must account for the federation of the district units of the principal party groups into two competing national organizations.

The popular election of the Chief Executive is commonly said to exert a centripetal influence upon party organization and to encourage a dualism. The supposed effect of the mode of choice of the President resembles that of the single-member constituency. The winner takes all. The Presidency, unlike a multiparty cabinet, cannot be parceled out among minuscule parties. The circumstances stimulate coalition within the electorate before the election rather than within the parliament after the popular vote. Since no more than two parties can for long compete effectively for the Presidency, two contending groups tend to develop, each built on its constituent units in each of the 50 states.

The president is, in effect, chosen by the voters in 50 single-member constituencies which designate their electors by a plurality vote. The necessity of uniting to have a chance of sharing in a victory in a presidential campaign pulls the state party organizations together.

Systems of Beliefs and Attitudes

Certain patterns of popular political beliefs and attitudes mightily facilitate the existence of a dualism of parties. These patterns of political faith consist in part simply of the absence of groups irreconcilably attached to divisive or parochial beliefs that in other countries provide bases for multiparty systems. Although there are racial minorities in the United States, either they have been politically repressed, as has the Negro, or they have been, as in most instances, able to earn a niche for themselves in the nation's social system. Nor do national minorities form irredentist parties. For example, the Germans of Milwaukee do not form a separatist party to return Milwaukee to the Fatherland. Nor has any church had memories of earlier secular power and the habit of political action that would lead to the formation of religious political parties. Class consciousness among workers has been weak in comparison with that in European countries, and labor parties have made little headway. When one group places the restoration of the monarchy above all other values, another regards the prerogatives of its church as the highest good, still another places its faith in the trade unions, and perhaps a fourth group ranks the allocation of estates among the peasants as the greatest good, then the foundations exist for a multiparty politics.

The attitudes underlying a political dualism do not consist solely in the absence of blocks of people with irreconcilable parochial faiths. A pattern of attitudes exists that favors, or at least permits, a political dualism. Its precise nature must remain elusive, but it is often described as a popular consensus on fundamentals. Powerful mechanisms of education and indoctrination, along with the accidents of history, maintain broad agreement, if not a universal conformity, upon political essentials. At times, it can be said, with a color of truth, that we are all liberals; at another time, it may be equally true that we are all conservatives. Given this tendency for most people to cluster fairly closely together in their attitudes, a dual division becomes possible on the issue of just how conservative or how liberal we are at the moment. Extremists exist, to be sure, who stand far removed from the central mode of opinion, but they never seem to be numerous enough or intransigent enough to form the bases for durable minor parties.

Explanations of the factors determinative of so complex a social structure as a party system must remain unsatisfactory. The safest explanation is that several factors conspired toward the development of the American dual party pattern. These included the accidents of history that produced dual divisions on great issues at critical points in our history, the consequences of our institutional forms, the clustering of popular opinions around a point of central consensus rather than their bipolarization, and perhaps others. The assignment of weights to each of these is an enterprise too uncertain to be hazarded.

II  TRENDS

Political scientists have been fascinated by the concept of party realignment in the United States. Realignments are fundamental shifts in the relative strengths of the political parties among the electorate and are associated with a particular party's control of the institutions of governmental policymaking. Realignments occurred in the

1850s, leading up to the election of Abraham Lincoln; in the 1890s, with the rise of populism; and in the 1930s, with the election of Franklin D. Roosevelt. These episodes seemed to establish a long-term pattern in American politics: one party would hold power for a long period of time, perhaps thirty to forty years; then, under conditions of general crisis, a realignment would occur, leading to a new dominant party at the national level and a repetition of the cycle.

Because the last clear realignment of the party system occurred in the 1930s, political scientists (and politicians) have been waiting since the 1960s for the next realignment. But no such realignment, at least in the classic sense, has taken place. Instead, some scholars have suggested that we are in a period of dealignment, characterized by weak party ties, a proliferation of independent voters, and control of the institutions of the national government split between the two major parties. Other scholars posit that the elections of 1964, 1968, and 1980 showed at least some of the signs of a critical election.

In the following selection, the political scientist Everett Carll Ladd analyzes the election of 1988 and concludes that, irrespective of political scientists' debates on the subject, we are now in a "post–New Deal system" that "has no historic counterpart."

Questions

1. What is a realignment? What is a dealignment? What is meant by the phrase "cognitive Madisonianism"?
2. What are the major characteristics of the post–New Deal system, according to Ladd? How does the current system differ from its historic predecessors?

7.2 The 1988 Elections: Continuation of the Post–New Deal System

Everett Carll Ladd

Predictability was the most striking feature of the 1988 election. It had two separate bases. First, 1988 was an incumbents' election. Conditions prevailing throughout the year strongly encouraged a "no" response to the question, "is it time for a change?" A second basis for its predictability is that the election took place well into the latest of our country's great partisan transformations—this one having begun in the late 1960s. When major change is first evident in the parties and elections system, its central features—shifts in group ties to the political parties, issues cutting in novel directions, etc.—

often startle us. But after we have seen them over a series of elections we take them as givens. That's what happened in 1988. The election told us little we didn't already know. Instead, it was confirming, or reaffirming. The New Deal era now seems as remote as the age of McKinley.

The Immediate Setting

From its beginning the 1988 presidential contest was waged against a backdrop that favored the Republicans. One element of this setting involved the status of the two-term incumbent president. During the last months of his presidency, Ronald Reagan was more popular than when he first took office. In the twelve months or so following the Iran-contra revelations, which broke with such political fury in November 1986, Reagan's popular standing clearly suffered. But by the end of 1987 he had largely recovered. The *Los Angeles Times* Election Day poll on 8 November 1988 found 60 percent of all voters approving Reagan's presidential performance. Such popularity is partly transferable to the party—as Franklin D. Roosevelt proved half a century ago. Under Reagan, Republicans have drawn close to the Democrats in party identification and have pulled ahead among young voters. And no American president ever committed himself as fully to the election of his successor as Reagan did to George Bush.

A second facet of the setting for the 1988 election was the public's response to current conditions in the economy, foreign affairs, and the like. Presidential elections are always in part referendums on national performance. In 1988, most voters thought things were going fairly well and were thus inclined to give the "ins" another chance.

Time for a Change?

To be sure, many analysts had thought that after eight years of Reagan conservatism the public was ready to try something new. The persistence of a clear majority in opinion polls saying that they wanted the next president to change direction in dealing with the nation's problems, rather than follow "the same policies as the Reagan administration," helped form these expectations. In fact, this poll finding was highly misleading. Virtually every time a variant of the question has been asked, going back to the presidency of Franklin Roosevelt, a majority has endorsed a shift from the incumbent's policies. This has not meant, however, support for *some specific alternative* to the incumbent— only that all possible "something elses" are preferred to him.

Testing specific alternatives yields a very different picture. In early August 1988, for example, the CBS News/*New York Times* poll asked whether "you think the Reagan administration has been too conservative, or not conservative enough?" Of those with an opinion, 17 percent volunteered that the administrations's approach was about right. Forty-three percent said it had been too conservative—but 42 percent found it insufficiently so. In the context of a Bush-Dukakis race, the latter were simply not "voters for change."

Views on the economy always influence the electorate's conclusions on whether it's time to change; and in the final months of Campaign '88 these views were both positive and becoming more so. The University of Michigan's Index of Consumer Sentiment was 97.4 in August 1988—not the highest figure in the last 35 years but near the high end of modern experience and the highest it had been in more than two years.

Assessing the Economy

By a margin of 69–26 percent, respondents to an early August 1988 CBS News/*New York Times* poll said they considered themselves better off than they had been "eight years" earlier. By 40–16 percent in an early September Roper Organization survey, respondents declared themselves better off than they had been "four years" previously. Fifty-seven percent in this latter poll expected to be better off four years hence than they are now, just 6 percent worse off. A survey taken 8–11 September by CBS News and the *New York Times* found 68 percent describing the nation's economy as good, 31 percent as bad. Seventy-four percent said their family's financial position was good, just 15 percent bad.

In a question favored by many analysts, respondents are asked whether they think things in general are moving in the "right direction" or are off on the "wrong track." Surveys showed the former response increasing over the summer and fall of 1988. Stanley Greenberg, who polls for many Democratic candidates, told the presidential campaign *Hotline* in early September that "in every statewide and every congressional poll that we've done in the last two weeks, more people thought the country was moving in the right direction than off on the wrong track, whereas two months ago we barely had a district or state—including ones with low unemployment like Delaware and Connecticut—where the right direction exceeded the wrong track." Greenberg concluded that the shift "is part of a general mood in which people are reevaluating where the economy is— beginning to believe that the Reagan years brought positive gains at the economic level that are real. . . ." The type of assessment of the economy that Greenberg described in the late summer persisted throughout the fall campaign.

Democrats are again debating the lessons of the 1988 presidential balloting. "Did we just run a bad campaign, or is our problem deeper?" Part of the answer is that a third alternative has to be factored in to explain what happened in 1988: when an out-of-power party must contend for the presidency in a period of peace and relative prosperity, it is likely to lose. That was the Democrats' problem in 1988. The election results were not inevitable, but they were both likely and predictable. Bush's final margin of roughly 8 percentage points seems to me to be at the low end of the likely range, given the setting in which the contest was waged. Polls in fact suggest that a higher turnout would have resulted in a bigger Republican margin. The CBS News/ *New York Times* post-election survey showed Bush preferred over Dukakis by 12 points among all registered nonvoters interviewed, by 16 points among unregistered nonvoters.

The Context for the Congressional Voting

The United States had, of course, another set of elections on 8 November 1988 that came out very differently than did the presidential contest. The Democrats made net gains of one seat in the Senate, two in the House, and one gov-

ernorship; and they maintained their commanding position in the state legislatures. Thus continued the two-tier electoral system evident for the last quarter century: one partisan outcome for the presidency and another elsewhere. 1988 was a good year for incumbents—not just for the incumbent party seeking four more years in the White House. The lack of any strong sense across the electorate that it was time for a change presumably aided congressional incumbents as well.

Cognitive Madisonianism

Much more is at work, however, accounting for the extraordinary, historically unprecedented divergence of presidential and congressional voting. Some observers speculate on how much the contemporary electorate is being guided by a kind of cognitive Madisonianism. The many variants of this interpretation all start from the fact that with two centuries of experience with a political philosophy and attendant institutions that raise checked-and-divided governmental authority to a lofty status as an instrument for preserving individual liberty, Americans are less likely than their counterparts in other democracies to be troubled by a Republican White House and a Democratic Congress. Never before the last quarter century had Americans regularly experienced sustained divided party control of their national executive and legislative institutions, but their entire history had prepared them for the underlying idea of divided government.

Has a new ideological element been added to the historic mix? Are Americans now seeking a new form of divided power—a Republican executive and Democratic legislature—to express some new set of perspectives or objectives? Certainly the public is saying that they like the idea of divided party control. For example, in a survey taken 23–26 October 1988, NBC News and the *Wall Street Journal* asked: "In general, do you think it is better for the same political party to control both the Congress and the presidency, or do you think it is better to have different political parties controlling the Congress and the presidency?" Only 32 percent opted for unified party control, 54 percent for divided authority. In a survey taken in Connecticut from 29 November through 6 December 1988, the University of Connecticut's Institute for Social Inquiry asked: "The way the election came out, the Republicans control the White House but the Democrats control both Houses of Congress. Do you think this is good for the country, or would it be better if one party had both the presidency and the Congress?" Sixty-seven percent of those interviewed said the prevailing divided arrangements were desirable. By a margin of 55 to 36 percent, those who had voted for George Bush on 8 November and who declared themselves pleased with his victory endorsed as "good for the country" a Democratic congressional majority.

I have often noted that contemporary public opinion research in the United States shows a public highly ambivalent on many major questions of public policy. For example, Americans endorse high levels of governmental protections and services, and at the same time they describe government as too big, expensive, and intrusive. The public wants somewhat contradictory things of the modern state. And we know it sees the Democrats and Republicans differing significantly on the issue of government's role. Would it be surprising, then, if a kind of cognitive Madisonianism in modern guise emerged: Let's set the two parties' views of government's proper role more actively in (hopefully) creative tension, with a Republican executive pushing one way and a Democratic legislature the other.

S. M. Lipset argues that it is by no means chance that leaves the Republicans advantaged in the White House and the Democrats on Capitol Hill. "The Republicans are assisted on the national level by the fact that the presidency is perceived as an elected monarch, as a symbol as well as a leadership position for the entire country, which ideally is above narrow interest conflicts and is heavily involved with domestic moral values and foreign and defense policies. The office is inherently linked to nationalism. . . . Democratic liberals look weak in this context. Reagan and Bush appear strong. Congress, on the other hand, is the place where cleavages get fought out. Members perform services, act as ombudspeople, and represent interests. They appeal narrowly, rather than broadly. And the Democrats, with their links to mass groups and popularly-based interest organizations, are in a better position to fullfill these functions."

Incumbency, et al.

Even those most inclined to see cognitive Madisonianism in the two-tier voting must acknowledge, however, that much else is now at work. The fact is that virtually all incumbents of both parties who seek to win reelection to the U.S. House of Representatives now typically do so by overwhelming margins. A main source of this result and the burgeoning uncompetitiveness is the virtually complete separation of House voting from judgments about the proper course of public policy. While I will not discuss it here, much the same thing seems to be happening in state legislatures, for the same basic reasons.

Political scientist David Mayhew was one of the first to call attention to the "vanishing marginals"—House seats where the winner's margin was small enough that the contest could be seen as competitive. In 1960, while both parties had plenty of safe seats, 203 of the 435 contests were at least marginally competitive, with the winner being held to less than 60 percent of the vote. By 1980, though, only 140 House races saw the winner under 60 percent.

House voting in 1988 was the most uncompetitive in U.S. history. The winner was either unopposed or beat his opponent by 70 to 30 percent or more in 242 districts. A respectable showing for a challenger has become holding the victor to just 60 to 69 percent of the vote, a result obtained in 128 districts in 1988. The losing candidate got as much as 40 percent of the vote in just 65 contests, and he came within 10 percentage points of the winner—that is, losing by 55–45 or less—in only 29 of the 435 House races.

Open seats—those where no incumbent is running—are often quite competitive, but in 1988 there were just twenty-six of them. Only six incumbents seeking reelection lost, and five of them had been tinged by some form of scandal.

What accounts for the virtual disappearance of competitiveness in U.S. House elections? One big part of the story is the enormous advantage incumbents typically enjoy in resources for promoting their candidacies. Staff provided to House members was tripled in the 1960s and 1970s, and members of Congress have put many of their new assistants to work on matters back home in their districts. They have found this useful in serving constituents' needs, of course—but, not incidentally, useful in a narrowly self-serving sense as a little electoral machine made available to them year-round at public expense. Few challengers can match this resource for self-publicizing.

Incumbents generally enjoy a large advantage as well in campaign contributions. Knowing that current office-holders are likely to be reelected and that they will have to deal with them in advancing their legislative objectives, the political action committees (PACs) of the various interest groups heavily back them, regardless of party. In the 1985–1986 election cycle, PAC dollars went to congressional incumbents over their challengers by about $96 to $20 million; and incomplete tabulations for 1987–1988 suggest an even greater margin. Even challengers in races targeted by their political parties for special effort usually have less financial support than the members of Congress they seek to unseat.

In races for governor and U.S. senator—as well, of course, as that for president—many voters know something substantial about the candidates' policy stands or records. In these contests, even well-funded incumbents who are better known than their opponents may readily be defeated when the electorate is in the mood for policy change. But members of Congress simply don't have the policy visibility of governors and senators. Most voters know next to nothing about their representative's voting record. They are, though, more likely to have some vaguely favorable image of him or her than they are of his or her opponent.

Decline of Party Voting

Political party ties are the one thing that could upset this dynamic. That is, a voter might not know anything about a member of Congress's voting record but still vote against him or her in favor of a less-well-known challenger because the voter preferred the challenger's party. This is, of course, exactly what happened historically. But over the last quarter century, as incumbents have accumulated election resources greater than ever before, the proportion of the electorate bound by strong party ties has declined precipitously. Better educated and drawing their political information largely from the communications media, today's voters feel they need parties less than did their counterparts of times past.

In highly visible races like those for president, senator, and governor, voters typically acquire enough information to make up for the decline of the guidance that party ties long provided. At the other end of the spectrum, in elections of school board members, aldermen, etc., voters often have enough close-up, personal knowledge of the candidates to reach informed judgments. House races are where we have our problem. Party voting is no longer decisive, but substantive knowledge of the candidates' records is usually insufficient to furnish a substitute base for substantive choice. Enjoying huge advantages in resources for self-promotion, incumbents in such contests are now winning reelection routinely by escalating margins.

The Republican Presidency

A complex structure is at work producing the outcomes that distinguish the contemporary parties and elections system. Returning to the presidential component, the Republicans won the presidency in 1988 in substantial part because they were the incumbent party in a time of peace and relative prosperity. But clearly more than that was at work. Just as the Democrats' ascendancy in the Congress has persisted over an extended span, so has the GOP's presidential dominance. In the last six presidential elections—1968–1988—the Republicans garnered 53 percent of all the ballots cast, the Democrats just 43 percent. Only one previous extended set of elections was decided more decisively: the five from 1932 through 1948, when the Democrats won 55 percent of the vote to the Republicans' 43 percent.

All manner of short-term factors enter into presidential election outcomes. But margins of the magnitude piled up in the New Deal and in the contemporary cycle show something more than an accumulation of short-term forces. The Democrats' 12 point lead in the Roosevelt era occurred in part because their approach to governing was more popular than the GOP's. Likewise the Republicans' 10 point margin over the last six contests reflects an edge grounded in voters' decisions on the broad reach of public policy.

The Role of Government

Analysts differ as to the precise mix of developments in public policy that has given the Republicans their presidential majority of the modern period. I would identify three components. One results from the tremendous real growth of government over the 1960s and 1970s. In response to this growth, governmental actions came increasingly to be seen as problems, not just as solutions to problems. "Government causes inflation" is one part of this. "Government taxes too much" is another part. The actual tax burden on most citizens increased dramatically after the 1950s. In 1953, families with incomes around the national average paid 11.8 percent of their income in taxes; in 1966 they paid 17.8 percent, and 1980, 22.7 percent. Incomes rose, but the proportion paid out in taxes rose much faster. Taxes claimed about twice as much of the average family's earnings in 1980 as they had twenty-five years earlier.

This ushered in an era of populist protests against big government quite different from anything that occurred in the New Deal era. A substantial segment of the lower-middle and working classes came to resent the amount they had to pay and to be receptive to appeals from conservative politicians on the plank of tax reduction. A similar development occurred in the United Kingdom. In his brilliant account of the rise of Thatcherism, Peter Jenkins describes how in the late 1970s Labour Prime Minister James Callaghan perceived the threat to his party's standing. He told the Labour party's national executive committee: "If you want to retain power you have got to listen to what people—our people—say and what they want. If you talk to people in the factories and in the clubs, they all want to pay less tax. They are more interested in that than the Government giving money away in other directions." Unfortunately for the party, not many of its leaders were prepared to act on this insight. Jenkins stresses Margaret Thatcher's economic appeal to broad segments of British working class.

Social Issues

A second set of issues that challenged the Democratic Party nationally involved a diverse array of social questions. The New Deal coalition, Christopher Jencks has observed, was held together by economic interests. Rural white southerners and the northern working class could unite on greater governmental intervention in the marketplace.

> Neither group had "liberal" views on issues like race, patriotism, capital punishment, or abortion. Once these issues became politically

salient, as they did in the 1960s, Democratic presidential candidates faced, and still face an almost insoluble problem. If they took liberal positions on such issues they estrange the white South and part of the white working class. If they took conservative positions they risked estranging the educated liberals who ran their campaigns and raised their money. Democratic candidates for Congress can often sidestep this problem because most congressional districts are relatively homogenous. . . . This strategy does not work as well in statewide elections, especially if the state is socially diverse. . . . It doesn't seem to work at all in national elections.

Foreign Policy

The third set of issues is in foreign and defense policy. It is easy to forget these days that the Democrats were in the New Deal era the party of the more assertive foreign policy. Indeed, the charge made the rounds in some Republican circles that the United States "got wars" when the Democrats were in office. Certainly the United States got in the 1930s and 1940s from the Democrats a kind of foreign policy nationalism that was the intellectual equivalent of the "new nationalism" that the party pushed in domestic economic affairs—in both cases, following the earlier lead of Franklin's Republican cousin, Theodore Roosevelt. The United States, Democratic leaders insisted, had broad responsibilities for advancing both specific national interests and the cause of democracy through a major assertion of American power into world affairs.

Important segments of the Democratic party would probably have modified this New Deal–era approach in any case, but the Vietnam war served at once to quicken and heighten the reassessment. The Republicans were thus given an enormous opportunity to establish themselves as the more tough-minded of the two parties on foreign policy issues, the one more prepared to maintain a strong national defense and to resist Communist expansion.

The Democrats continued to bring important assets to their policy confrontations with the Republicans, including the widespread perception across middle-class America that they were better than the Republicans in responding to claims for needed protections and services. But the combined disadvantages that accrued to the party from the developments noted in foreign policy, social issues, and taxes and related big government issues were more than their New Deal majority could withstand.

The Generational Component of Party Change

The new policy cleavages made themselves felt in partisan attachments. But the impact was hardly a bolt from the blue. We need to see how changes in the mix of party ties have gradually emerged. In forming party attachments, individuals gain a frame of reference from the decisive events of the period when they first came to political consciousness—usually in their late teens or early twenties—which then shape their subsequent values and actions. Some political leaders are decidedly more respected and popular than others—and sometimes these ascendent politicians are Republicans and sometimes they are Democrats. In the last decade, the Carter-Reagan comparison has been very helpful to the GOP—especially among new voters without a lot of past political experience. Similarly, a distinctive mix of issues dominates political argument as these new voters come of age politically. If the mix generally favors one party over the other—as it did the Democrats in the 1930s and the Republicans in the 1970s and 1980s—the impact of persons without much previous personal political experience is apt to be substantial. This makes young people a key early-warning indicator of major partisan change. As the group ages, it begins to have new and sometimes conflicting political experiences, but these are filtered through an established pattern of party loyalties that are likely to persist, unless and until the mix of new experiences produces a sustained break.

Do available data support this general interpretation? Let's begin by looking at the party preferences of different age groups in the

United States as shown by Gallup surveys taken in 1952 and 1985 (Table 1). The first thing we see is a striking difference in the party preferences of the age groups in the two periods. In 1952 the Democrats' best groups were the young and middle-aged, while the Republicans had large leads among elderly voters. In 1985, however, the Republicans were strongest among the young and the very old, while the Democrats had their greatest strength among people in their fifties, sixties, and early seventies. . . .

The relative standing of the major parties varies substantially across generational groups in a fashion that corresponds in rough terms to what we know of decisive political experiences. For example, both the 1952 and the 1985 Gallup polls show the Democrats' margin over the Republicans' greatest among those who came of age politically at the height of the Democrats' New Deal ascendancy. Since static enters into polling and poll responses, it is especially impressive that the picture provided by the two batches of surveys separated by thirty-three years is so consistent.

People who reached political maturity in the late 1930s and early 1940s were in 1952 unusually pro-Democratic—and they are so today. Republicans had a big edge in the 1890s, but they began to lose this among new voters coming of age in the early twentieth century—reflecting in part the impact of immigration on the makeup of the population. In the 1930s the Democrats began achieving an overwhelming generational advantage over the Republicans; this was not interrupted until the 1950s, when various developments, among them Dwight Eisenhower's personal popularity, cut signifi-

TABLE 1
Party Identification of Americans by Age, in 1952 and 1985

| | 1952 | | | 1985 | | | Democratic Percentage (−) Republican Percentage | |
	D	R	Ind.	D	R	Ind.	1952	1985
18–21 yrs. old	40%	25%	35%	30%	40%	30%	+15%	−10%
22–25 yrs. old	42	27	31	31	35	34	+15	−4
26–29 yrs. old	43	26	31	31	35	33	+17	−4
30–33 yrs. old	45	26	29	34	31	35	+19	+3
34–37 yrs. old	43	29	28	37	30	33	+14	+7
38–41 yrs. old	45	30	26	38	32	30	+15	+6
42–45 yrs. old	38	36	25	37	32	31	+2	+5
46–49 yrs. old	39	36	25	37	33	30	+3	+4
50–53 yrs. old	42	32	25	35	36	28	+10	−1
54–57 yrs. old	39	38	24	41	32	27	+1	+9
58–61 yrs. old	41	37	21	42	35	23	+4	+7
62–65 yrs. old	39	39	22	48	32	21	0	+16
66–69 yrs. old	37	45	18	46	35	19	−8	+11
70–73 yrs. old	40	43	17	47	35	17	−3	+12
74–77 yrs. old	36	49	14	41	41	18	−13	0
78–81 yrs. old	34	50	16	40	41	19	−16	−1
82 yrs. and over	31	57	12	40	42	18	−26	−2
ALL AGES	41	33	26	37	34	29	+8	+3

Source: Gallup polls conducted April through July 1952 (seven in number) and January through July 1985 (eight in number).

Everett Carll Ladd   227

cantly into the Democrats' edge among new voters. The heyday of John Kennedy's New Frontier and Lyndon Johnson's Great Society saw the Democrats recover among new entrants, but over the last decade the GOP has, for the first time in a long while, taken the lead among those just coming into the electorate. This new Republican margin widened during the Reagan presidency.

Surveys taken in 1988 show the pattern . . . continuing. For example, the combined results of four national surveys taken for the Americans Talk Security project (ATS) between February and June 1988 found the Democrats' best age cohort people between 60 and 75 years of age, who had come of age politically in the 1930s and 1940s. The Republicans' best group was those 18–29, the children of the Carter and Reagan years. The Gallup Youth Surveys taken in 1988 showed Republicans doing well in the 13–17 age cohort. These surveys ask: "When you are old enough to vote, do you think you will be more likely to vote for candidates of the Republican party or for candidates of the Democratic party?" Forty-four percent of those interviewed in the three 1988 surveys said the Republicans, 36 percent the Democrats.

These data help us understand why in recent years no dramatic overall swing to the Republicans has occurred in party identification, though the Democrats' lead has been diminished. The Democrats put together a long string where they bested the Republicans among new voters, and they continue to reap the benefits: People who came of age politically from the 1930s through the 1960s remain a large part of the electorate, and the impressive Democratic base among these age groups has by no means been obliterated. The Democrats are down from their once clear ascendancy, but they still have a lot of generational capital. In recent years, the Republicans have reversed the trend among new entrants; should they continue to have this success, they will in time shift the underlying partisan base decisively in their favor.

The Exceptional Case of the White South

On occasion, amidst the many cases of gradual change in the partisan preferences of social groups, there is a really dramatic shift. White southerners are the prime example of such a dramatic change in the contemporary partisan experience. The new issue mix, with a racial component more powerful than elsewhere, has had an explosive impact on this group.

The swing-over in professed party identification was especially sharp in the mid-1980s. According to Gallup data, the percentage of white southerners identifying as Republicans in the January–July 1985 span was 10 points higher than it had been in the spring of 1984, and 18 points higher than in 1979, an unprecedentedly rapid swing. Other polls confirm the picture Gallup provides: The partisan balance was tipped significantly in favor of the Republicans during the 1984 campaign. We don't know precisely why this shift occurred when it did. We can hypothesize, however, that Ronald Reagan's popularity had much to do with it, coming after various events over the past quarter century had already eroded Democratic loyalties.

Groups and the 1988 Balloting

The presidential voting on 8 November further testified to the dramatic shift that has occurred in the partisanship and electoral behavior of white southerners. According to the election day polls of NBS News and the *Wall Street Journal,* for example, Bush received 57 percent of the white vote nationally; but his margins in the South ranged from a low of 63 percent in Florida to a high of 80 percent in Mississippi (Table 2). According to the *Los Angeles Times* exit poll, an extraordinary 74 percent of southern white Protestants voted for George Bush, just 25 percent for Michael Dukakis. In the New Deal era, white southerners' overwhelming support for the national Democratic Party had two main sources: racial tension and memories reaching back to

TABLE 2
Vote in 1988 of Whites, Blacks, and Hispanics

	Whites		Blacks		Hispanics	
	% Bush	% Dukakis	% Bush	% Dukakis	% Bush	% Dukakis
U.S.	57	43	11	89	31	69
Alabama	76	24	7	93	NA	NA
Florida	63	37	8	92	68	32
No. Carolina	67	33	8	97	NA	NA
Texas	65	35	10	90	21	79
Arkansas	63	37	10	90	NA	NA
Louisiana	75	25	10	90	NA	NA
Mississippi	80	20	13	87	NA	NA
So. Carolina	78	22	10	90	NA	NA
Tennessee	67	33	13	87	NA	NA
Georgia	74	26	10	90	NA	NA

Source: The 1988 election day surveys taken by NBC News and the *Wall Street Journal*. The national sample included 11,703 voters, and large independent samples were polled in each of the states shown.

the Civil War, and the fact that white southerners were the most liberal—that is, New Deal policy supporting—regional group in the country. In the contemporary alignment, things have become almost exactly reversed. White southerners have become the most Republican regional group in presidential voting, because of the racial division that finds blacks overwhelmingly Democratic and because they are now generally the most conservative regional group.

Elsewhere, looking at key groups, the changes that have occurred from the New Deal era to the present are surely far less dramatic. Taken together, though, many of these other changes are impressive and together define an electoral universe vastly different from that of the 1930s through the 1950s. Table 3 (p. 230) document[s] this by comparing the presidential and congressional vote in 1988 of ten key groups. . . .

In the New Deal years, men and women had voted almost identically. In 1988, however, according to the CBS News/*New York Times* exit poll, the gender gap was 15 percentage points: Men favored Bush over Dukakis by a 16 point margin, women by just 1 percentage point. The NBC News/*Wall Street Journal* poll put the gap

at 14 points. Analysis of the exit poll data shows that the gap between men and women was especially great among those of high socioeconomic status. The *Los Angeles Times* exit poll found, for example, high status males (college grads, family incomes of $50,000 a year and higher) went for Bush over Dukakis by 2 to 1, while high status women split evenly between the two candidates. High status men are also more likely than their female counterparts to identify as Republicans and to describe themselves as conservatives.

Election day poll data show that the pattern of voting among Hispanics evident in recent past elections persisted almost entirely unchanged in 1988. Nationally, the GOP is the minority party among the nation's Hispanic voters, but it gets a healthy minority share. One group of Hispanics, those of Cuban background concentrated in Florida, is heavily Republican. The GOP's position overall within the rapidly-growing Hispanic population is roughly equivalent to its position among the nation's black voters in the New Deal era. The present overwhelming black support for the Democrats is, of course, yet another product of the shifts of the past quarter century.

TABLE 3
1988 Vote for Selected Social Groups

	Presidential Vote		Congressional Vote	
	Bush	Dukakis	Republican	Democrat
So. White Protestants	74%	25%	52%	40%
High Status Males	66	33	55	36
WASPs	62	36	58	36
Born-Again Christians	60	38	49	43
Young Affluents	57	41	45	44
Everyone	53	45	46	46
White Ethnics	52	47	45	48
High Status Females	50	49	42	52
Blue-Collar White Catholics	45	55	37	55
Hispanics	37	62	42	52
Blacks	11	86	9	78

Note: 6,043 voters were interviewed as they were leaving polling stations around the country.

Source: *Los Angeles Times* Election Day Poll, 8 November 1988.

Northern white Protestants of British ancestry, of high social status—the storied WASP—remain today, as in the past, heavily Republican and conservative. But rivaling the WASPs on both counts are members of another group of a quite different social position: those who say they have had a "born-again experience—a turning point in your life when you committed yourself to Jesus Christ." Born-again Christians are a far larger segment of the contemporary Republican electorate than are WASPs.

In noting these and other elements of change in group voting that help define the contemporary alignment, I should stress that many things have not changed. Every major change in group alignments incorporates important features of its predecessor. The relative voting patterns of various white ethnic groups have, for example, remained remarkably constant. The ABC News exit poll this year showed, for example, Protestants of German ancestry 15 percentage points more Republican in their presidential vote than were German Catholics; Irish Protestants 14 points more Republican than Irish Catholics. Nonetheless, the overall group alignment of the contemporary system differs substantially from that of the New Deal era.

The Contemporary Parties/Elections System

Our present-day electoral alignment, the product of a quarter-century of change, has five principal components: The group basis of the present system has shifted markedly from that of the New Deal years; the new voting alignments reflect profound changes in the mix and cut of issues, which cumulatively have worked to the Democrats' disadvantage in national contests; the Republicans have emerged as the majority party in presidential electioneering; the new alignment displays a split personality—one face evident in presidential balloting, another in state and local contests (where the Democrats predominate); dealignment—the weakening of voters' ties to the parties—is evident throughout the current system, as party-less voting now occurs to an historically unprecedented degree.

Do these features, and changes from the previous system to which they point, constitute a realignment? I remain inclined to say they do. But argument over the term's meaning is simply not worth the candle. For over three decades, political scientists have been engaged in an exceptionally unproductive debate over just what criteria must be met before a proper realignment may be officially declared. As this debate has dragged on, the world of American political parties has been transformed. Let's bury the concept and get on with a precise charting of the new arrangements and their implications. A transformed parties and election system is firmly in place in the United States. It has no historic counterpart, and it seems to this observer to impart as much of consequence to contemporary politics as any of its predecessor systems did to theirs.

III  INTERCONNECTIONS

A realignment—whether in its traditional form or in the modern, "incomplete" sense—involves more than a simple change in party support among the electorate or party control of government institutions. Realignments have their roots in fundamental questions about the proper role of government in society and result in basic changes in the role of government and in the shape of policy. In the following selection, the political scientist William Schneider explores the causes and consequences of the Reagan realignment.

Although the causes of the Reagan realignment are fairly clear, the consequences remain enigmatic. American voters seem to reject the ideology of the Democratic party and find it difficult to cast their ballot for a Democratic candidate. Yet they also seem to accept many of the policies espoused by the Democrats and appear leary of Republican control of social policy. The result, Schneider suggests, is that the parties have realigned around ideological issues, while the electorate remains divided and uncertain.

Questions

1. What are the causes and circumstances that led to the "Reagan revolution"? (*Hint:* Schneider identifies two: the "New Politics" and the rise of "antiestablishment populism." What does he mean by these terms?)

2. What may be the long-term consequences of the Reagan revolution for American politics?

3. Are you among the many American voters who are uncomfortable with either political party? What policies or ideas of the two parties make you uncomfortable?

7.3 The Political Legacy of the Reagan Years

William Schneider

What difference has Ronald Reagan made in American politics? Not much, according to the polls. Public opinion hasn't shifted to the right. If anything, the voters have moved to the left since Reagan took office—there is less support for military spending; more support for domestic social programs: increased concern about arms control, hunger, and poverty. It has long been the conventional wisdom that the president's personal popularity does not translate into public support for his policies. But it does translate into something.

"There has been a profound change in the agenda," said Senator Daniel Patrick Moynihan. "The Stockman strategy of disabling the finances of the federal government worked. It worked disastrously," the New York Democrat hastened to add, "but it worked."

Moynihan reached into his desk. "I have a wonderful document here from Senator [Daniel J.] Evans of Washington. He has a bill he calls 'the Federalism Act of 1986—FACT.' It would expand the coverage of Medicaid and work-training programs to poor pregnant women and to poor children whether they're on welfare or not.

"It's the kind of thing we should have done twenty years ago," the senator added. "It's incremental, sensible, and sane. First you establish Medicaid for indigent, dependent families on welfare. Then you come along and say, 'What about families that are poor but not on welfare? Can't we give a pregnant mother Medicaid attention? Can't we give poor children Medicaid attention?'

"*But,*" the senator rejoined, finger in the air, "Senator Evans says we will have to pay for this by abolishing the Economic Development Administration, the Appalachian Regional Commission, community services block grants, ur-

Danziger in *The Christian Science Monitor* © 1990 The Christian Science Publishing Society.

ban development action grants, community development block grants, mass transit operating assistance, mass transit research, waste water treatment grants, rural waste water disposal grants, federal impact aid, social services block grants, new low-income housing, and vocational education.

"I know something about those programs," Moynihan continued. "They aren't just the social agenda of the last twenty years. Vocational education was begun by the federal government in 1917. You would be abolishing the first entry of the United States government into education. But those are the terms. In order to go forward, you have to go back."

• • •

The Long Run: Institutional Changes

Democrats and Republicans agree that Reagan has transformed the agenda, but in a peculiar way. We want to do the same things as before—fight drug abuse, stabilize the economy, protect the poor and the elderly—only with less government. The impact of the Reagan revolution is more likely to be felt in the long run than in the short run. The president did not, after all, dismantle the New Deal welfare state. As Hugh Heclo has written, "Much as F.D.R. and the New Deal had the effect of conserving capitalism, so Reaganism will eventually be seen to have helped conserve a predominantly status-quo, middle-class welfare state."

Fair enough, but in the same volume on the Reagan legacy, Jack A. Meyer offered what he called "a long-term perspective." "The Administration seems to highlight its *social philosophy* toward federal programs, an area where most of its accomplishments seem rather marginal. By contrast, it downplays and is defensive about its *fiscal policies* which, while incomplete, herald a major accomplishment for the Administration." That accomplishment was to "pull the revenue plug" on the federal government. First came the 1981 tax cut, then year after year of record budget deficits. Now and for the foreseeable future, everything the federal government does must accommodate to one central fact: there is less money.

"I suggest that the United States is entering a new phase of expenditure control policy," Meyer wrote, "in which it is recognized that the safety net for the poor cannot be cut much further; that the social insurance and retirement functions must at least be on the table for discussion . . . ; and that there will not be too much room in the future for all other federal government social expenditures." That, in sum and substance, is the Reagan revolution.

The country bought the administration's economic program as a short-run response to a national calamity. Just before Reagan took office, he was being urged by some of his advisers to declare a national economic emergency. He didn't have to. Everyone knew the country was in an economic crisis. The president sold his tax and budget policies as a means to an end, which was to curb inflation and restore the nation's economic stability. In the public's view, the policies worked. But tax cuts, budget deficits, and tax reform are no longer passing items on the political agenda. They are the basis of a new institutional order, one that will set the terms of political debate far beyond the Reagan years.

Five long-term changes can be identified:

1. The federal budget *deficit* makes it impossible for Democrats to talk about any major new domestic spending programs unless they also talk about raising taxes. Which is exactly what the Republicans want them to talk about. For instance, having taken control of both houses of Congress after the 1986 midterm election, the Democrats proposed "a new agenda for social progress." But they had to face the challenge of financing their new agenda without resorting to a general tax increase. Hence the pressure for "new ideas" in the Democratic Party.

2. *Tax reform* did more than simplify the nation's tax code and curb the influence of special interests. It also weakened the principle of progressive taxation and challenged the notion that the tax system should be used as an instrument of social policy. By reverting to the old idea of "taxes for purposes of revenue only," tax reform has made it harder for the Democrats to legislate through tax policy. And that, President Reagan has said, is exactly what he set out to achieve.

3. A significantly higher level of *defense spending* has become the norm. While there is little public support for the sharp increases President Reagan requests from Congress every year, most Americans still do not want to make substantial cuts in the military budget. Cutting defense has come to mean going back to the perceived military weakness of the 1970s. Thus, as defense spending has risen year after year, the public's response has essentially been, "This far, but no farther." Moreover, arms control does not undermine the president's military program; it helps to institutionalize it. An arms-control agreement represents the long-

awaited payoff for the Reagan administration's defense buildup.

4. By the time he leaves office, President Reagan will have appointed about half of the nation's federal judges. While not all of those appointees can be described as ideologues, the administration paid special attention to their views on key social issues such as affirmative action, abortion, and criminal rights. Throughout the Reagan presidency, the religious right has complained that the administration has done little to fight for its social agenda in the legislative arena. That is correct, and the explanation is that it would have been politically unwise. Instead, President Reagan is relying on the federal *courts* to reverse the judicial activism of the last three decades. Which they may well do—after he leaves office, when he will not have to suffer the political consequences.

5. Finally, the Reagan administration has changed the *political consensus* in both parties. The withdrawal of Howard H. Baker, Jr., from the 1988 presidential race removed the only prospective candidate who represented the traditional moderate Republican establishment. Instead, Baker chose to become White House chief of staff and shore up his Reaganite credentials. All the candidates in the GOP race were conservatives of one sort or another. Representative Jack Kemp was an aggressive leader of the New Right. The Reverend Marion G. (Pat) Robertson tried to muster a Christian army to fight for the religious right. Former Delaware Governor Pierre S. du Pont, despite his high establishment origins, was a born-again populist and supply-sider. Vice President George Bush shed his moderate skin in 1980 and converted to Reaganism. Senate Minority Leader Bob Dole assiduously courted the right during his two years as Senate majority leader. Although he differed with the right on some important issues, Dole established his credentials as someone who could deliver. Dole's message to the right was, "I may not be one of you, but I can deal for you."

Compare the situation in the Democratic Party. With Senator Edward M. Kennedy out of the race and Governor Mario M. Cuomo stepping back, there seemed to be no one to fight for the Old Politics—free-spending, high-taxing, big-government liberalism. To traditional Democrats, the 1988 field looked like Jesse Jackson and a crowd of yuppies (at least until they took a good look at Senator Paul Simon and projected him as a substitute for Cuomo). All the other Democrats were "pragmatists" who wanted to try "new ideas." In the Democratic Party, pragmatism means giving up the burden of defending big government. Government cannot be the solution to every social problem, pragmatists say; instead, it should be the source of new ideas. Thus, the primary role of government is not to redistribute income but to stimulate economic growth. Most Democrats remain committed to the principles of sharing, compassion, mutuality, and help for the disadvantaged. But these days, that message sounds too much like the old politics. It is a message many Democrats fear they can't sell anymore.

The Reagan revolution changed the coalition structure of American politics. Reagan brought together a variety of interests united by a distaste for big government. That coalition is larger than the traditional Republican Party. Consequently, it is more diverse. It includes business interests and middle-class voters who dislike taxes and regulation. It includes racial and religious conservatives who dislike the federal government's reformist social agenda. It includes neoconservatives who want a tougher and more assertive foreign policy. These interests disagree on many things, but they will stick together as long as they see a common enemy, namely, the liberal establishment with its interventionist domestic policies and its noninterventionist foreign policies.

The quarter century from 1964 through 1988 was a distinctive cycle in American politics, an era of ideological change and party realignment. The Reagan revolution was as much a consequence as a cause of those developments. Thus, the changes now visible in American politics have deep roots and cannot be destroyed by the shortcomings of one presidency. [Two changes were particularly important.]

The first was the rise of the New Politics, which brought about the ideological realignment of the Democratic and Republican parties. Beginning in the 1960s, the Republicans moved to the right and began to attract a new conservative coalition. At the same time, the Democrats started moving to the left, with the result that the party gained a new liberal constituency and alienated its old-line conservative wing. These changes occurred mostly at the elite level, among political activists coming out of the New Right and the New Politics left. These activists eventually gained influence over, if not total control of, the two major parties.

The second change, the rise of antiestablishment populism, occurred at the mass level and had little to do with ideology. It was stimulated by two decades of failure and frustration. Populism is neither liberal nor conservative, but antielitist. The last two presidents, one a Democrat and the other a Republican, were both anti-Washington candidates who appealed to this neopopulist sentiment. As a result of the Great Inflation of the 1970s, antiestablishment populism turned into a revolt against government, the ultimate symbol of the establishment and the status quo. The first stirrings were visible in the tax revolt of 1978, two years before Ronald Reagan won the presidency. It was the antigovernment revolt that brought the conservative coalition, and the Reagan revolution, to power.

• • •

This realignment occurred in two stages. First came the social realignment of 1968 and 1972. In 1968, the Democrats lost the support of racial conservatives, mostly southern whites. Then in 1972, they lost a smaller but influential group of foreign-policy conservatives, or neoconservatives. The party was still competitive, however, as demonstrated by its comeback in the 1974 and 1976 elections. All the Democrats needed was a bad economy and a good scandal.

The second stage of realignment, 1980–84, was more damaging because the Democrats were in danger of losing their economic base. What held the Democratic Party together for fifty years was economic populism—the belief that the party would protect people against economic adversity. That belief kept the party going during the years when it was tearing itself apart over civil rights and Vietnam. Under Jimmy Carter, however, the Democrats failed to offer economic protection. Under Reagan, the Republicans succeeded. Without the economic issue, the Democrats risk becoming a liberal party rather than a populist party, that is, a party of upper-middle-class liberals and minority groups who share the same social philosophy.

The realignment has been in the direction of ideological consistency, with the Republican party becoming socially as well as economically conservative and the Democratic party endorsing social as well as economic liberalism. Lower-status voters tend to be liberal on economic issues and conservative on social issues, while higher-status voters are just the reverse. Thus, the typical voter is ideologically inconsistent. Many working-class voters look to the Democratic Party for economic protection but do not trust its social liberalism. Middle-class suburbanites favor Reagan's fiscal conservatism but are disturbed by the messages of religious fundamentalism, antienvironmentalism, and foreign interventionism that sometimes emanate from the White House.

• • •

That is one reason why several moderate Republican senators refused to support Robert Bork's nomination to the U.S. Supreme Court. A conservativized Supreme Court threatened to reopen the agenda on abortion and religious issues, thereby exacerbating class tensions in the Republican Party. These days, religion is to the Republican Party as race is to the Democratic Party: whenever the issue comes up, it tears the party apart. In many ways, the New Deal party system with its ideologically inconsistent parties fit the electorate better. As Walter Dean Burnham has argued, realignment has narrowed the parties' bases and left many voters with no comfortable home.

IV ✇ FOCUS: DEMOCRATS AND REPUBLICANS

As the readings in this chapter indicate, the modern party system provides a mixed bag of blessings and problems for the two major parties. The Republicans have established firm control over the presidency, at least in general, and have dramatically altered the shape of both domestic and foreign policy. Yet they have been unable to extend their success to Congress or to the states. The Democrats, by contrast, seem to be in hopeless disarray at the level of public philosophy but are in firm command of both houses of Congress and seem completely unshakable in the House of Representatives.

The following brief selections survey the hopes and fears of the two major parties in the wake of the 1988 presidential election and examine the current pattern of split-ticket voting.

Question

1. If you were hired as a consultant by the Democratic party, what suggestions might you make to improve the party's chances in the 1990s? What suggestions might you give the Republican party?

7.4 Non-Realignment: Republicans Dream On

Fred Barnes

No snickering please, but Republicans have yet another scheme for seizing control of Congress and dominating American politics. It's the Bush realignment. The 1990 election is unimportant, except for the part it plays in "positioning" ([the late] Republican national chairman Lee Atwater's word) the GOP for 1992. That's the year when lots of big things will happen at once.

One is reapportionment. Another is the retirement of old congressional bulls eager to pocket campaign funds, which won't be allowed after 1992. Still another is the bigger, more conservative turnout in a presidential year with a popular incumbent, President Bush, at the top of the Republican ticket. (OK, Bush's popularity may have faded by then, but this is just a plan, after all.) "If 1992 isn't the last chance [for re-alignment this century], it's at least the best," insists Mark Nuttle of the National Republican Congressional Committee (NRCC).

It's the only chance. Republicans have been plotting to take over Congress for two decades, and they're no closer than when they started. The Reagan era was supposed to bring realignment. It brought only six years of Senate control (1980–86). In the House, Republicans held seventeen more seats when President Reagan arrived in 1981 than when he left eight years later. The Bush era's been no better. Republicans used to gain seats in special House elections to fill vacancies, but in 1989 they were defeated in six of eight, with a net loss of one seat. Today the Democratic edge is 55–45 in the Senate, 257–175 (with three vacancies) in the House. Overturning that won't be easy in 1992, but it's the last opportunity before the millennium.

In 1992, for the first time in twenty years, the congressional election following reapportionment occurs in a presidential year. That means voter turnout will be higher in the most unsettled political year of the decade. There may be as many as eighty open House seats—that is, ones without an incumbent or with an incumbent running in a substantially new district because of reapportionment. Republicans figure to benefit. The old saw about Republicans praying for rain and a low turnout isn't true anymore. Now strategists believe that the higher the turnout, the better for Republican candidates. Why? Because casual voters who go to the polls only every four years tend to be middle-class and lower-middle-class whites aged eighteen to thirty with faint Republican leanings. These voters were pivotal in electing Republican senators in Georgia, Florida, Alabama, North Carolina, and Washington in 1980. Their absence was a major factor in the defeat of all five in 1986, a non-presidential year. In 1992 they'll vote again, giving Republicans a fair chance of capturing the Senate again.

Republican officials insist that polls, focus groups, and close analysis of voting patterns substantiate that casual voters are GOP-inclined by as much as two-to-one. But their evidence isn't overwhelming. The data come from polls in congressional districts and involve a sliver of voters, only twenty percent in some samples. One Republican cites the case of Democratic Representative David Bonior of Michigan. Bonior got sixty-five percent of the vote in 1986, fifty-four percent in 1988. Tom Hofeller, the reapportionment chief for the NRCC, maintains that GOP House candidates do roughly five percent better in presidential years. Democratic Representative Vic Fazio of California, the chairman of the House Democratic group overseeing reapportionment, disputes this. He says Democrats are as likely as not to get a higher percentage in presidential years. He cited himself—a bad example. Fazio got sixty-four percent in 1982, sixty-one percent in 1984, seventy percent in 1986. True, he got ninety-nine percent in 1988, but he ran unopposed.

Reapportionment, based on the 1990 census, is what really intoxicates Republicans. Seventeen or eighteen House seats will shift from the North and Midwest to the Sunbelt, the region of growing Republican strength. Even in states that don't gain or lose seats, lines must be redrawn to ensure districts of equal population. In other words, political uncertainty will reign. This makes the folks who draw the new lines—governors and state legislators—crucial in Republican plans (in Democratic plans too, obviously). For 1990 the Republican National Committee is concentrating its resources on state races. It has formed a strike force to make sure Republicans control the governorship or at least one house of the legislature in most large states. That's enough to give them "a seat at the table" when redistricting begins, says Atwater's deputy Mary Matalin.

The chief task in 1990 is holding the governorships of California, Texas, and Florida. California will gain six or seven House seats, Texas three, Florida three or four. So who participates in line drawing in these states makes an enormous difference. As it stands now, Republicans have the edge in winning the governor's race in Texas, Democrats are favored in Florida, and California's a toss-up. Republicans are desperate to hold their narrow majorities in the state senates of New York, Michigan, Ohio, and Pennsylvania, all states where Democrats have a lock on the state assembly and governor's office. There's a chance the GOP might win the Florida Senate this year, even while losing the governor's race, but that's less than fifty-fifty. At best, Republicans will have a toe-hold in the most populous states, which is more than they had a decade ago in the last reapportionment.

Republicans have another reapportionment tool, the Voting Rights Act. They plan to rely on it to press (in federal court, if necessary) for as many new black and Hispanic seats as possible. These seats would be Democratic, but that's the paradoxical point. To assure the election of a black or Hispanic, new districts will have to be overloaded with minorities, reliable Democrats all. This will make adjacent districts far less Democratic and thus vulnerable to Republican takeover. Sound cynical? It is. Fazio concedes that in Texas, for instance, new Hispanic seats must be created in Houston and the Rio Grande Valley and another black district in Dallas–Ft. Worth. Unless Texas elects a Democratic governor, he says, the new lines will put several Democratic House members in jeopardy. Republicans certainly hope so. They'll also demand black seats in Virginia, North Carolina, South Carolina, Georgia, Alabama, and other states, new Hispanic seats in Illinois, Arizona, and California. Benjamin Ginsberg, the RNC's chief counsel, says the number of black seats, now twenty-four, should double in 1992. If anything like that happens, Republicans will gain too.

Republicans are also poised to benefit from campaign reform. Congress voted last year to bar House members from inheriting unspent campaign funds at retirement, unless they quit in 1992. Republicans are counting on twenty or thirty retirements. They're recruiting candidates to run in 1990 against potential retirees so they'll be positioned to win open seats in 1992. For example, they've recruited a state legislator to challenge Democratic Representative Doug Barnard of Georgia this year. Barnard, who had $527,726 left over after his 1988 race, then announced he will retire in 1992, just what Republicans wanted. They've recruited candidates to run in 1990 against Democrats Jack Brooks of Texas and Frank Annunzio and William Lipinski of Illinois, figuring a strong challenge this year may produce victory the second time around in 1992.

The problem with this part of the Republican scheme is that few members are likely to retire. Being in the House is too cushy and ego-gratifying. Fazio claims that no more than a dozen will take the money and run. The retirees will include Republicans as well as Democrats. If reapportionment produces eighty open seats in 1992, these won't be all Democratic. Nuttle says two-thirds will be, but other Republican officials think the percentage will be considerably lower. In any case, it's not a pool from which a thirty- to forty-seat Republican pick-up in 1992 (Nuttle's target) is going to emerge. Still, it's a far bigger pool of open seats than Republicans will see later in the 1990s, which is why 1992 is the GOP's last chance.

Republicans have abandoned their 1980s game plan of imposing national issues on House races. It only helped Republicans in 1980 when they ran against President Carter and added thirty-three seats. In 1982, during a recession, Democrats ran against Reagan and won twenty-six seats. That dashed GOP dreams of a reapportionment-led realignment in the 1980s. Edward Rollins, the NRCC's executive director, says Republican challengers will have to run individualized, localized campaigns. The problem is that Democratic candidates, ordinarily recruited from state legislatures or local governments, are better at this. To capture Congress, Republicans need an enemy to run against. President Dukakis would have been perfect. Without him to demonize, Republicans will be doing well to match their high-water mark of the last three decades, 192 seats. That would represent a nice pickup, but not realignment.

7.5 Defining Democrats: Party or Coalition?

Ronald D. Elving

We could all be spared the recurrent fuss over the state and fate of the Democrats if we could just get over thinking of them as a party.

In a practical sense, Democrats are better appreciated as a coalition. They come together as needed to organize the House and Senate and most of the state legislatures. But after the ceremonies, they tend to go their separate ways.

Democrats are, if you like, bigger than a party. They encompass multiple mini-parties that coalesce and divide, depending on the issue at hand. Their theme might well be Walt Whitman's line: "Do I contradict myself? Very well, I am large, I contain multitudes."

Democrats came in for a new round of diagnosis and prescription in September [1989] when their House leadership got flattened resisting a cut in capital gains taxes.

Nearly three Democrats out of four voted with the leadership, but it was the 64 lost lambs who kept the reporter-shepherds busy through the night.

Truth is, the Democratic leadership had to work hard to hold the "defectors" to 64. The House was being asked to choose between a fat, juicy tax cut and a cold tax increase (the public seemed unfazed about who would get which).

Moreover, the cut had been proposed by a Democrat, Ed Jenkins of Georgia, runner-up in the vote for majority leader in June.

Jenkins' plan had escaped intact from the Ways and Means Committee because the committee's conservative Democrats voted for it and the committee's liberal Democrats turned down a compromise offered by the chairman.

Democrats have always been like this. Eleven years ago they rolled their own president, Jimmy Carter, on this same issue. The last president they had before Carter was Lyndon B. Johnson, and they drove him out of office.

Of course, Johnson got grief from different Democrats depending on whether he was desegregating the South or defoliating Southeast Asia. But then that's just the point. Even Franklin D. Roosevelt, whose Democratic majorities in Congress beggared those of today, vetoed more bills than any other president.

And yet we cannot resist dissecting the Democrats whenever they seem at odds. After they boot one like capital gains we grill their Hill leaders on the Sunday talk shows, ignoring their Republican counterparts (who, after all, won the vote).

At the same time, Congress is something of a showcase of Democratic unity compared to presidential politics.

Earlier in September, a conference of Democrats was held at the Mayflower Hotel in Washington. Here a score of staffers from failed presidential campaigns met with former chairmen who had left the party in debt to talk about continuing the party's tradition of success.

Ironically, Democrats always seem to expect to be back in the White House soon. They sense deeply that they should be running the country. More than an article of faith, this may be their defining characteristic.

Many Democratic officeholders entered politics in a time or a place where this notion of natural right had some root in reality. They still see "Democratic majority" as redundant; Democrats govern, Republicans vote no.

But at the national level, at least, this attitude seems increasingly anachronistic. The Democrats can elect majorities, even comfortable ones, in the House and Senate. But when an issue of significance arises, a GOP president can pick off Democratic votes by the handful.

Democrats will probably never achieve the ideological consistency of the contemporary GOP. Their pluralistic history—not to mention

oalition of discordant economic,
ltural elements—forbids it.

the coherence for which Democrats
uld hardly guarantee their return to
e House. Nor will the lack of it neces-
ar their return.

rties out of favor, or coalitions out of
er, do not find salvation by their works.
They are reborn in crisis or recreated by the
unifying force of a new issue or leader.

The tacit realization of this has spawned
competing Democratic schools of patience. One
says wait until the next recession, secretly hop-

ing it will be a doozy. Another says wait for
another Jack Kennedy (and features a long-running audition for the part). A third says wait
until the country falls out of love with Ronald
Reagan (the "Jane Wyman School").

But if any lesson stands out from both the
capital gains vote and the 1988 presidential campaign, it is that the new GOP can flourish without Reagan. It need only be strong enough to
exploit the Democrats' traditional divisions. All
that seems necessary for Republicans to triumph is for Democrats to do their thing.

7.6 Key to Survival for Democrats Lies in Split-Ticket Voting

Rhodes Cook

If Republican candidates had won every
congressional district last November [1988] that
George Bush did, their party would hold a
better than 2-to-1 advantage in the House of
Representatives.

The fact that the GOP is on the downside
of a 3-to-2 House deficit illustrates the cross-cut
nature of American politics. In nearly one of
three congressional districts across the country
last fall—and in roughly half the Southern districts—voters elected a Democrat to the House
while supporting Bush for president.

That so many districts produced a split result illustrates the remarkable disconnection between presidential and House voting in this
country, and the success of large numbers of
House Democrats in maintaining an aura of political independence that enables them not only
to survive, but even thrive, in terrain hostile to
their national party.

While they would seem to be the most obvious of targets for Republican strategists, these
split-ticket Democrats have proved difficult to
defeat. Knowing they are potentially vulner-

able, they are unusually attentive to their
districts.

Last year, only one Democratic House incumbent lost in a district that Bush carried. Bill
Chappell Jr. of Florida lost by fewer than 1,000
votes in a district that Bush was carrying by
nearly 70,000 votes, even though Chappell was
badly battered by public questions about his
links to the defense-procurement scandal.

There is another side to the cross-cut coin.
In 13 districts in 1988, voters went Democratic
for president while electing a Republican to the
House.

"It's stunning," says Thomas E. Mann, director of governmental studies at the Brookings
Institution, "how weak the relationship is between the presidential and congressional vote."

Who Are These Democrats?

Altogether, more than half of all House Democrats elected last November (135 out of 260) won
in districts that Bush also carried. Their numbers have been depleted slightly since then with
the resignations of Jim Wright of Texas and

Figure 1

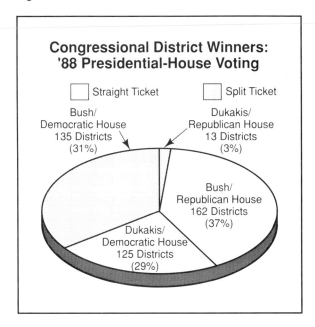

Congressional District Winners: '88 Presidential-House Voting

☐ Straight Ticket ☐ Split Ticket

Bush/
Democratic House
135 Districts
(31%)

Dukakis/
Republican House
13 Districts
(3%)

Bush/
Republican House
162 Districts
(37%)

Dukakis/
Democratic House
125 Districts
(29%)

Tony Coelho of California, the switch to the GOP by Bill Grant of Florida, and the deaths of Bill Nichols of Alabama and Claude Pepper of Florida [Figure 1].

Still, it is a large and varied group—a mix of powerful veterans and raw rookies. House Speaker Thomas S. Foley of Washington, Majority Leader Richard A. Gephardt of Missouri, Chief Deputy Whip David E. Bonior of Michigan and Democratic Congressional Campaign Committee Chairman Beryl Anthony Jr. of Arkansas all were re-elected in districts Bush won. So were former Speaker Wright and former Majority Whip Coelho, and the House's most senior member, Jamie L. Whitten of Mississippi.

But there are also more than two dozen junior House Democrats—members first elected in either 1986 or 1988—who bucked a GOP presidential tide in their districts last November.

The largest concentration of split-ticket Democrats is in the South, where Republicans now dominate in presidential voting but where Democrats continue to hold two-thirds of the House seats. Yet there are also large numbers of split-ticket Democrats in every other region, especially in the East and Midwest.

What virtually all these Democrats have in common is personal vote-getting ability. Well over four-fifths of them won with at least 55 percent of the vote in 1988, even though Bush carried more than three-fifths of their districts by at least that margin.

Many Republicans contend that the success of these House Democrats is closely linked to the perquisites of incumbency, such as free constituent mailings, district offices and access to generous political action committee (PAC) contributions that their challengers do not have. To a degree, the Republicans are correct. More than half of the top 50 recipients of PAC largess in 1988 were Democratic incumbents in Bush districts, according to a preliminary year-end report by the Federal Election Commission.

But Democrats argue that if incumbent perquisites were the prime reason for their candidates' success, then the Republicans should be winning a large share of these seats when they come open, especially in presidential election years when GOP congressional candidates can usually count on top-of-the-ticket help.

That, however, has not been happening. In 1988, Democrats won four of five races for open Democratic seats in districts that Bush carried in presidential voting. And the lone Republican open-seat pickup in this group, by Cliff Stearns in Florida, was offset by the open-seat victories of Democrats Peter Hoagland in Nebraska and Bill Sarpalius in Texas. Each of them bucked a strong Bush tide in his district to win a House seat that a Republican had previously held.

How Do They Do It?

If there is a word that might describe the split-ticket Democrats, it is independent. They often do not run for office as political partisans and much of the time they do not act like partisans in Washington.

One such House Democrat, Ed Jenkins of Georgia's 9th District, describes his legislative record as combining conservatism with a bit of populism. "But above all things," he says, "I'm extremely independent. . . . I would vote the way I do whether the Republican presidential nominee got 70 percent or 40 percent in my district." Bush swept Jenkins' district last fall with 71 percent of the vote.

Jenkins represents a northeast Georgia constituency that extends from the fast-growing suburbs of Atlanta to Republican mountain counties near the Tennessee–North Carolina border. The district, he says, has been politically independent since the Civil War, and "I'm a product of that independence."

In addition to Jenkins, there are a number of other Southern House Democrats who must regularly buck big Republican presidential tides. Nationally in 1988, there were 34 split-ticket Democrats elected in districts that Bush won with at least 60 percent of the vote. Roughly two-thirds of these Democrats were from the South, including Earl Hutto and Bill Nelson of Florida and George "Buddy" Darden and Jenkins of Georgia, who had to overcome Bush tidal waves in their districts that reached 70 percent.

But for Jenkins and other Southern House Democrats, the large Bush vote was not an insurmountable problem, since there are strong Democratic roots to tap in Dixie just below the presidential level.

The voters "recognize I'm in a conservative-to-moderate mold," Jenkins says. "They vote for a Republican presidential nominee based on the same criteria."

But Jenkins sees the changing demographics of the district posing some headaches for him. Many of the newcomers in the Atlanta suburbs tend to vote a straight Republican ticket in presidential election years. Last year, Jenkins' 63 percent share of the vote was his lowest tally in his seven House elections.

Almost invariably, Jenkins and other split-ticket Democrats across the country find it easier to run in midterm elections, when the party ticket is often headed by a popular governor or senator rather than a less appealing presidential candidate. In Georgia, three-term Sen. Sam Nunn will be atop the Democratic ballot in 1990.

In midterm elections, Jenkins says, "I don't have to ignore or disavow the ticket."

"Small D" Democrats

In presidential election years, though, split-ticket Democrats often run as "small 'd'" Democrats. "I don't walk away from the party," says Democratic Rep. Jim Jontz of Indiana. "But at the same time I must have an independent appeal. The biggest point on my literature is not that I'm a Democrat."

Jontz had to overcome a 65 percent vote for Bush last fall in the Indiana 5th to win a second term. He attributes his re-election to extensive person-to-person politicking (especially among normally Republican voters), a devotion to constituency casework and an emphasis on an array of populist economic issues that Jontz sees as having bipartisan voter appeal.

That combination works in seemingly hostile terrain, he believes, because of the small-town nature of his northwest Indiana district. "My belief is that rural areas are very prone to ticket splitting," Jontz says. "Rural voters tend to get more personal contact with the candidates."

Jontz could have a point. A look at the list of split-ticket districts in 1988 shows that many of them in the South and Midwest, in particular, are geographically large, with a significant rural and small-town element.

But basic aspects of Jontz' formula seem to be central to the success of split-ticket Democrats everywhere: Stay on political alert, remain highly visible in the district and keep focused on local concerns.

Congressional Quarterly ratings showed in 1988 that Jontz voted against Reagan more than any other House member. But Jontz maintains that it did not hurt him politically, because even in his overwhelmingly Republican district there was a disparity between Reagan's personal popularity and the support for his programs.

"My [GOP] opponents have asked how the district can elect a Republican president and a Democratic congressman," Jontz says. "I say, 'Name one issue where I haven't voted to represent the district?'" He was reelected in 1988 with 56 percent of the vote, a showing 5 percentage points better than his first time out in 1986.

Keeping a Distance

The disconnected nature of presidential and congressional voting was no more visible than in the trio of special House elections this spring. All three elections were conducted during the "honeymoon" phase of Bush's presidency and in districts that he had carried easily last fall. Bush did not make a personal appearance in any of the districts.

In fact, after a flap involving the National Republican Congressional Committee (NRCC) had embarrassed the GOP candidate in Wyoming, Bush was careful to stay at arm's length. "All I want to do is stand on the sidelines," he said in addressing a rally of Wyoming Republicans by phone.

It is problematic what difference Bush's involvement would have made. Democrats won two of the three special elections in large part because they had better candidates. Republicans realize they will not be able to oust many of the split-ticket Democrats until they offer stronger candidates of their own. "One of the things the Republican Party has a high priority to do is to push Republican realignment at the presidential level to the congressional and local level," says NRCC spokesman John Buckley. "It means coming up with first-rate candidates."

That has been a particular problem for the GOP in the South, where split-ticket Democrats are most prevalent. Many districts that Democrats represent are still overwhelmingly Democratic below the presidential level. As a result, Republicans have little or no "farm team" of local elected officials who could move up to run for Congress.

Also, Democratic House candidates in Dixie usually can inoculate themselves against conservative GOP attacks by emphasizing a hard line on visceral issues such as defense spending, crime and punishment, and gun control. Glen Browder basically did that earlier this year to repel Republican charges that he was a labor-backed, "Michael Dukakis liberal"; he easily won the special election for Nichols' vacated seat in Alabama's 3rd District.

To Browder, Republicans face long odds in trying to win Democratic House seats in rural Dixie. "They must . . . establish a clear distinction between a conservative [Republican] and a liberal [Democrat]." But that is not easy to do in his part of the South, says Browder, because "about any Alabama elected official is conservative on national concerns."

Not Always This Way

A *Congressional Quarterly* tally of last year's presidential vote found that Bush carried 297 House districts and Democrat Michael S. Dukakis won 138. At the same time, 148 districts split their tickets between a presidential candidate of one party and a House candidate of the other party. Besides the 135 districts that went for Bush and a Democratic representative, 13 went the other way, voting for Dukakis and a GOP House member.

Ticket splitting has not always been in vogue. Congressional results used to be tied closely to the presidential vote, so much so that in 1920, when the Republicans launched their last 12-year run in the White House, there were split presidential-House results in only 11 of the 344 districts that could be surveyed.

The number of split-ticket districts rose gradually in the years after that. But the total did not exceed 100 until 1956, a time when the "Solid South" was abandoning the Democrats at the presidential level and the advent of media campaigning most everywhere meant less reliance by House candidates on political party organizations.

Since 1956, the number of split-ticket districts has consistently stayed above 100, and it approached 200 in 1972 and 1984, both years when scores of House Democrats retained their seats despite GOP presidential landslides.

The vast majority of split-ticket districts in recent years have been of the Republican presidential/Democratic House variety. But in each

Toward a Stupidness-Ugliness Theory of National Elections

Political pundits have been trying for years to explain the Republicans' success in modern presidential elections. In the wake of the 1988 elections, the political scientist Lee Sigelman offers this tongue-in-cheek analysis.

For the fifth time in its last six tries, the Democratic Party has managed to parlay its massive lead in party identifiers into another presidential election debacle. One shameless Democratic apologist, groping for a face-saving excuse, has hit upon the bizarre idea that the Democrats lose presidential elections time after time because, being rational political calculators, they find it in their partisan self-interest to do so. This tortured theory overlooks the obvious: Democrats are too stupid to calculate their self-interest.

Although this conclusion may seem unduly harsh, science has proven that Democrats are significantly dumber than Republicans, even when the differing social bases of the two parties are held constant. This intellectual deficit helps explain why, time and time again, the Democrats find themselves hopelessly out-organized, out-strategized and out-maneuvered—in short, out-thought—by the wilier Republicans.

Still, Democrats may have more than a shortage of gray matter to blame for their electoral misadventures. In the television age, what really matters is not what candidates have to say about the great issues of the day, which makes remarkably little difference to anyone, but how they look when they are saying it. In the sage words of Thackeray: "A clever, ugly man every now and then is successful . . . but a handsome fool is irresistible." Is it possible, then, that in addition to being intellectually overshadowed, the Democrats have been aesthetically outflanked? In plain English, are the Democrats ugly as well as stupid?

Data and Methods

Any natural-born citizen who has lived in the United States for 14 years and is at least 35 years old is formally eligible to become president. In practice, however, those without experience in high public office need not apply. Of the 61 active candidates in the last five presidential campaigns, only Alexander Haig, Jesse Jackson, Pat Robertson and Sargent Shriver failed to list on their resumes at least one term as governor or member of Congress.

The issue, then, is whether the Democrats are at a disadvantage because the Republicans have a more eye-pleasing pool of potential presidential candidates from which to choose. In order to find out, the 50 governors, 100 senators and 435 House members pictured in "The Almanac of American Politics 1988" were rated on an Ugliness Scale ranging from +5 ("Yummie") to −5 ("Yecch").[1]

Findings

Very few high officeholders in either party are downright repulsive. Even so, these data contain some worrisome portents. Of the five most hideous officials, four hail from California. So if, as is so widely assumed, it is in the Golden State that the future of American politics takes shape, we seem to be in for a long ugly spell.

Now, what about the inter-party ugliness differential? . . . It is the extremely rare Democrat (only three of 338) who scores above +3 on the ugli-

election, there are always a few that go the other way.

When Democrats last won the White House in 1976, there were 26 districts that voted for Jimmy Carter and a GOP House member. That number declined to 14 in 1980. And in 1984, there was just one district that voted for Walter F. Mondale and a GOP congressman—Bill Green's New York 15th on Manhattan's East Side. It is a mix of the extremely rich and the

ness scale; but more than 10 percent of the Republicans (28 of 247) do so. Meanwhile, 25 of the 26 most unsightly officials are Democrats. Overall, the Republican mean of 1.2 falls significantly above the Democratic mean of −.5. . . .

A regression-based investigation of these possibilities reveals that older office-holders are indeed significantly uglier than their younger colleagues. Also as expected, there is significantly greater per capita pulchritude in governors' mansions and the Senate chambers than can be found on the floor of the House. But the crucial question is whether the inter-party ugliness differential remains when age and position are held constant. The answer is that it does: Controlling for these factors lowers the gap only by one-tenth of a point, from 1.7 to 1.6.

Discussion

In spite of the profusion of gleaming pates, sloping foreheads, crossed eyes, flapping ears, prominent proboscises and cascading chins among them, it would be incorrect to conclude that the Democrats have cornered the market in grotesquerie. There are ugly Republicans, too. Still, the Democrats possess, in truly awesome abundance, physical attributes that torment the eyes of the beholder. Compared to the ugly duckling Democrats, the Republicans are comely Quayles.

Since looks matter so much in modern electoral politics, the Democrats enter each election year at a severe competitive disadvantage. In order to meet the Republicans head to head, so to speak, the Democrats would have to choose their candidates with consummate care. But it is here that cruel reality intercedes, for stupidity and ugliness actually impose a triple burden:

(1) Because there are so few intelligent Democratic contenders to choose from, the Democrats nominate mental lightweights who conduct silly campaigns.

(2) Because there are so many ugly Democratic contenders to choose from, the Democrats select standard bearers who are not only dumb but ugly.

(3) And because the Democrats are so dense, they have no inkling of how much better off they would be if they deliberately nominated someone the voters could bear to look at and listen to. Having chosen a candidate who spends the fall saying stupid things and looking stupid saying them, the Democrats are then invariably shocked when, in November, the Republicans register yet another handsome victory.

Note

1. The rating was done by a middle-aged woman who has an inordinate fondness for pictures of men. She is a known sympathizer of "L-word" causes, and her knee jerked uncontrollably throughout the exercise. This information should allay any suspicion that the ratings may have been "cooked" to support the research hypothesis, a strategy that, I hasten to assure the reader, never even occurred to me.

—Lee Sigelman

extremely poor and the place where the term "limousine liberal" was born.

In 1988, Green was one of 13 split-ticket Republicans. There was at least one elected in each region, with small concentrations in Du-

kakis' New England back yard (where there are three), and the upper Midwest (where there are four).

There seem to be two schools of thought among these Republican House members as to whether Dukakis' success in their districts represents a harbinger of shifting political opinion or was an aberration due to the circumstances of 1988.

Tom Tauke, who represents the 2nd District in northeast Iowa, sees Dukakis' victory in his district as an aberration caused by the state's economic turmoil in the 1980s; the Reagan military buildup, which clashed with Iowa's pacifist mind-set; and a lack of attention to the state from the Bush forces during the 1988 presidential campaign. "That era is essentially behind us," says Tauke. "Bush should benefit from the ongoing economic upturn in the upper Midwest and his foreign policy should be much more in tune" with Iowa.

But Steve Gunderson of Wisconsin, whose district lies just across the Mississippi River from Tauke's, believes that GOP officeholders in his part of the country may still be at risk. There still is enough economic distress, he says, that "whichever party is in the White House will have trouble in rural America."

Gunderson had little trouble winning reelection last year in the Wisconsin 3rd, in spite of Dukakis' victory in his district. But he is not sure how his recent elevation to the GOP House leadership (he is one of two chief deputy whips) will play in a district he considers to be politically marginal.

Gunderson feels his political future rests on being vigilantly attuned to local concerns. To that end, he is promoting a project called "Wisconsin 2000," which he describes as a comprehensive rural-development plan for his district. He believes that his local involvement is helping to inoculate him against any voter dissatisfaction with the Republican White House.

Gunderson's reading of his political situation is much like that of many split-ticket Democrats, and his response to it is much the same—even to the point of projecting a sense of independence. "In a district like mine, you never run as a Republican," he says, "You run as an independent."

_____Chapter 8

Elections and Campaigns

$\mathcal{N}$o other area of American politics has been changing as rapidly as that of campaigns and elections. The impact of television, high technology, campaign finance reforms, and party nomination rules has combined to transform the face of American electoral politics over the past three decades. The electoral process reflects all of the fundamental transformations in the United States and the rest of the world that have taken place since the 1950s: changes in the status of women and minorities, in America's role in the world, and in the state of the world economy.

The process of change has not yet come to an end. Electoral politics has not moved into a new, stable phase; it is, instead, in the midst of a volatile and unstable period, which will keep political scientists and political pundits busy sorting things out for some time to come.

The selections in this chapter revolve around the fundamental theme of change in the American electoral process. The first selection, by political scientists Francis Rourke and John Tierney, compares the 1960 and 1988 presidential elections and provides a sense of how much the system has changed over the past three decades. The other selections focus on particular aspects of this transformation. M. Margaret Conway examines the rise of political action committees, which in a few years have become major forces in campaign finance; Kathleen Hall Jamieson discusses the importance of television, and especially of paid campaign advertisements, in modern elections. Finally, an issue and debate is presented on changes in the nominations process, which have opened up the system and limited the influence of party bosses but have also (some say) made the process irrational, irresponsible, and unrepresentative.

Chapter Questions

1. How has American electoral politics changed over the past several decades? Consider the impact of television, changes in campaign finance laws, and changes in candidate selection rules.

2. Consider the changes in American electoral politics in the light of changes in the party system (see chapter 7). How has the overall weakening of the party system contributed to the trends discussed in the previous question?

I  TRENDS

How much difference has a generation made in American electoral politics? We can get a good idea by comparing the 1960 and 1988 presidential election campaigns. On the surface, these two elections seemed quite similar; beneath the surface, however, they reveal the tremendous changes that have occurred in American electoral politics over the past thirty years.

The similarities between 1960 and 1988 are well known: the Boston-Austin connection in the Democratic party (a presidential candidate from Massachusetts and a vice-presidential candidate from Texas); a sitting vice-president heading up the Republican ticket; a Republican president who, having served two terms, was required to retire from office. Yet the differences between the two campaigns, as Rourke and Tierney point out in this selection, are far more significant.

Questions

1. What were the key differences between 1960 and 1988 in terms of issues? in terms of support for the two parties? in terms of voter turnout?

2. Why did the Republicans win in 1988 but lose in 1960? Or, to ask the same question from the other side, what happened to the Democratic party between 1960 and 1988 that caused it to lose so much support?

3. How can we explain the "split verdict" in 1988—Republican control of the White House, Democratic control of the Congress? What does this tell us about the differences in the two campaigns?

8.1 Changing Patterns of Presidential Politics, 1960 and 1988

Francis E. Rourke and John T. Tierney

Both before and while it was in progress, the presidential campaign of 1988 frequently was compared with the campaign of 1960, which matched Democrat John F. Kennedy against Republican Richard Nixon. The similarities are obvious. In 1988, as in 1960, a Republican vice president was facing a Democratic challenger from Massachusetts, and the Democrat sought to win the election by forging a Boston-to-Austin alliance through the selection of a Texan (Sen. Lyndon B. Johnson in 1960, Sen. Lloyd Bentsen in 1988) as his vice-presidential running mate. The Democratic candidate in 1988, Gov. Michael S. Dukakis, tried to capitalize on the resemblance between the two elections by invoking memories of Kennedy on the campaign trail.

Dukakis's Republican opponent, George Bush, had less reason for such nostalgia—Nixon, after all, lost the 1960 election. But Bush's selection of Dan Quayle, the forty-one-year-old senator from Indiana, as his running mate (regarded among Republicans as well as Democrats as one of the great mysteries of modern American politics), may perhaps be understood as an effort to give his campaign the image of youthful vigor that Kennedy's candidacy had brought to the Democratic ticket.

The similarities between 1960 and 1988 on matters of age and geography lie on the surface of politics. A more fundamental resemblance between the two elections is that in both cases voters faced the certainty of change in national leadership no matter which candidate was victorious. A venerable and generally well-liked Republican incumbent was leaving the presidency after eight years in office: Dwight D. Eisenhower in 1960 and Ronald Reagan in 1988. Each departure was required by the terms of the Constitution's Twenty-second Amendment,

which stipulates that no one can be elected president more than twice. Eisenhower was the first president to feel the effect of this amendment, and Reagan was the second. Since the two-term limit became part of the Constitution in 1951, voters have been unable to escape the necessity of change in the White House after a president has served two terms in office, even if they are sufficiently satisfied with the performance of the incumbent to prefer continuity. In 1989, as in 1961, a new president would take office, either the Republican vice president or his Democratic adversary.

• • •

Why was Kennedy able in 1960, while Dukakis failed in 1988, to convince the voters that he rather than his opponent best represented the change the Twenty-second Amendment demanded? The answer seems to lie mainly in differences between the times in which the two elections occurred.

In 1960 the United States was just emerging from a severe economic recession that already had given the Democrats an overwhelming victory in the congressional elections of 1958. The economic discontent that so often has fueled Democratic campaigns since the days of the New Deal worked very much in Kennedy's favor in 1960. Equally important, Soviet sputniks were circling the globe in 1960, while the American space program was still struggling—literally—to get off the ground. The 1960 election gave the Democrats an opportunity to do something they have not been able to do since—run a campaign based on strong nationalistic appeals to the pride of Americans in their country and to their enduring belief that the United States is destined to be first in all things, celestial as well as terrestrial. This appeal was buttressed by the argument, spurious as it eventually proved to be, that a "missile gap" between the United States and the Soviet Union seriously endangered American national security.

In short, what Kennedy had going for him in 1960 were what are often described as "gut" issues—issues so viscerally powerful that a political newcomer can use them to overcome whatever reluctance voters may have to risk change. A campaign run, as Kennedy's was, on the theme of getting the country moving again was highly credible when the United States was suffering from economic strains and was seemingly being outstripped in space and in national defense by the Soviet Union.

In 1988 Dukakis carried the Democratic banner at a time when the nation was enjoying an extended period of economic prosperity, something for which the incumbent Republican administration claimed much credit. Moreover, the Soviet Union no longer seemed to be outstripping the United States. Instead, the chief goal of Soviet policy was to catch up with the United States and other advanced industrial societies.

If there was a gut issue available for Dukakis, it was the extent to which the United States had fallen behind, not the Soviet "evil empire" of Reagan's legendary rhetoric, but Japan and the capitalist powers of the West. A case could be made for the proposition that the United States had been fighting in the wrong trenches for the past three decades. If nothing else, this approach would have given Dukakis a nationalist appeal equal in its emotional potency to the flag and Pledge of Allegiance issues that Bush used so effectively against him. As he fell behind in the polls, the Massachusetts governor did begin to sound the theme of economic nationalism. But by then it was too late for nationalism to be for him what it had been for Kennedy—the driving force behind an ultimately victorious campaign.

The Changing
Presidential Campaign

As we have seen, Kennedy had advantages in 1960 that were denied to Dukakis in 1988. These advantages illustrate how much American politics had changed in the intervening years. In 1960 the Republican party was still haunted by its image as the party of the Great Depression of the early 1930s. The Democrats, in contrast, basked in the reputation of being the party that had presided over both the recovery from that depression and the American triumph in World War II. To be sure, they had lost the 1952 and 1956 presidential elections. But they had done so under the leadership of Adlai Stevenson II, perhaps the most widely respected loser of presidential elections in modern American history and a candidate who had energized many active supporters for future work within the party.

It is suggestive of the different political settings in which Kennedy and Dukakis ran that in 1960 the two most recent Democratic presidents to whom voters could look to forecast the kind of leadership Kennedy would bring to the country were Franklin Roosevelt and Harry S. Truman. When the Massachusetts governor ran in 1988, the two most recent Democratic presidents were Johnson and Carter. Although history may treat them more kindly than their contemporaries did, today Johnson is best remembered for America's ill-fated involvement in Vietnam and Carter for the humiliating seizure of the American Embassy in Tehran by Iranian militants and a domestic economy beset by inflation.

The Democrats also were hurt by changes that had taken place since 1960 in the conduct of presidential campaigns. One striking feature of the Kennedy-Nixon race was that in 1960 traditional party organizations at the local level were still viewed as largely controlling the outcome. A major player in the Kennedy victory was Mayor Richard J. Daley of Chicago. He headed one of the most formidable of the old-style political machines and was widely credited with putting his state in the Democratic column—whether by fair means or foul was a matter of continuing dispute between partisans of Nixon and Kennedy.

The Republican party came to believe that the Democrats' superior grass-roots organizations had played a significant role in Nixon's defeat. Not long after the election, it appointed a committee headed by Ray Bliss, the Republican party chair in Ohio, to probe the causes of the election failure. The committee's principal conclusion was that the Republicans had lost the presidency in 1960 because their party's organization lagged behind the Democrats in the major cities of the country.

The Republican Edge: White House Experience

By 1988 the political parties' view of what it took to win a presidential election had changed quite radically. Not grass-roots machinery but skill at using the media was regarded as the first requirement for success at the polls in a national campaign. The Republicans were widely credited with being far more talented in this regard than the Democrats. With only a month to go before election day, a neutral observer outlined some of the ways the Republicans had demonstrated their superiority in media strategies during the 1988 campaign.

> Political professionals in both parties generally believe that Mr. Bush's camp has been more adept in using television advertising, more disciplined at finding effective issues and sticking with them for several days at a time, more skillful at controlling damage and more creative in coming up with new speeches and new lines. The Dukakis campaign has paid a backhanded compliment to the skills of the Bush staff by running a series of television advertisements that attack not Mr. Bush, but the professionals who are managing his campaign.

One indication of the change that had taken place in the nature of the presidential campaigning between 1960 and 1988 was that the individuals who were credited with having political savvy in 1988 were not the local party leaders like Daley, but the political advisers skilled at identifying and molding the opinions of a national electorate in a media age. The chief architect of the Bush campaign in 1988, for example, was James A. Baker III, who had honed his skills in media manipulation in three earlier presidential contests.

More important than his campaign experience, however, was that Baker also had played a major role during the Reagan administration in designing strategies to ensure that the president's policies were treated favorably by the news media. For Baker and others in the Bush campaign, the 1988 election was simply a continuation of what they had been doing at the White House for eight years. Samuel Kernell and others have described the importance modern presidents attach to the task of winning public support to ensure the success of their policies—"going public," Kernell calls it. One consequence of going public as a strategy to maintain presidential power is that it gives White House aides considerable practice at hand-to-hand combat with the media, experience that proves extremely useful in a presidential campaign.

• • •

The Character of the Campaign

In retrospect the changes in the style of partisan political combat that took place between the 1960 and 1988 presidential campaigns can be best described in military terms, as a shift from ground war to air war. The media, particularly television, became the principal instrument through which each side sought victory at the polls. The ground forces—namely, grass-roots party organizations—still played an important role in getting out the vote on election day, but the attitudes that voters took with them to the polls already had been shaped largely by what had appeared on television.

As in previous campaigns, television came under severe criticism for its role in the 1988 election. Among other charges, it was accused of trivializing the contest for the presidency by featuring thirty-second "sound bites"—snapshots of the candidates attacking each other on the campaign trail—rather than discussions of the issues that were of most serious consequence to the voters. In their defense, the television networks could well argue that their coverage reflected the campaign the candidates were conducting, a campaign in which little was said about the issues.

The 1988 campaign may be best remembered for its negative character. At the outset, Bush's strategists recognized that their candidate drew a highly negative rating from voters, while Dukakis was viewed quite favorably. Their solution to this problem was to attack the Democrat's competence and character, a strategy that succeeded perhaps beyond their wildest dreams. By late October, Dukakis' negative ratings among voters had climbed dramatically. Even Reagan was drawn into this strategic design, referring to Dukakis at one point in the campaign as an "invalid."

To be sure, Bush's strategy of accentuating the negative forfeited the opportunity to win the sort of mandate for his administration that more positive appeals might have engendered. It also ran the risk of antagonizing Democrats in Congress, who strengthened their majorities in the House and the Senate, and whose support Bush surely would need to put some of his policies and programs into effect. But these disadvantages aside, negative campaigning had one essential virtue in the eyes of Bush campaign aides—it worked. Since rewarded behavior tends to be repeated, the strategy may well become a model for future presidential campaigns.

The Electoral Connection

When John Kennedy mounted his successful campaign for the White House in 1960, the Democratic coalition that Franklin Roosevelt had cemented together almost three decades earlier was still largely intact. Unionized workers, southerners, northern blacks, urban ethnics, and middle-class liberals formed the principal building blocks of Roosevelt's New Deal coalition. What held these disparate constituencies together was a shared set of attitudes: belief in the desirability of an active central government, faith in the ability of government to understand and solve social and economic prob-

lems, and approval of the robust power that such a government must have.

Kennedy carried all the populous Democratic strongholds in the North and East, but lost Ohio. With the help of his running mate, Lyndon Johnson, Kennedy carried seven southern states, including Johnson's home state, Texas. The Democratic ticket also was victorious in two western states—Nevada and New Mexico. Even so, cracks were beginning to appear in the Democrats' traditional coalition. Richard Nixon carried four states from the traditionally Democratic South and almost all of the West.

The cracks evident in 1960 have since become chasms. The South has been virtually realigned into a Republican monolith, as has the Rocky Mountain region. By 1988 the Republican base in presidential elections—defined as those states the party's presidential candidates had carried in every election since 1968—was more than two hundred electoral votes.

What has happened since 1960 to give the Republicans the distinct advantage they now seem to have in presidential elections? The changes can best be understood in terms of the shifting support of broad constituencies, activated by or reacting against sweeping new social movements that emerged in American society.

Civil Rights and the Democrats

The Democrats' potent electoral coalition, which had brought it victory in almost all of the presidential and congressional elections from 1932 to 1964, began to crumble in the mid-1960s on the shoals of civil rights for blacks. Although committed to eliminate from American democracy the stigma of racial discrimination, Kennedy had decided early in his presidency not to push immediately for the passage of civil rights legislation, preferring to advance the cause through assorted executive actions until he felt that the time was ripe politically for legislative initiatives. Not until 1964 did the power and the will coincide to produce the landmark Civil Rights Act, which aimed principally to eliminate racial discrimination in public accommodations and employment. The Voting Rights Act, passed in 1965, greatly enhanced the legal protection for blacks to participate in elections.

Although public opinion polls showed that most Americans favored these legislative efforts to secure the constitutional rights of blacks in the South, popular support for civil rights began to erode after 1964. One reason was that each summer from 1965 to 1968 television screens in living rooms across America carried pictures of ghetto riots by blacks in New York, Los Angeles, Chicago, Cleveland, and many other major cities. Although arising from several sources, urban violence was a manifestation—to whites—of a disturbing change that had occurred in the civil rights movement: the nonviolence that had characterized Martin Luther King's leadership had begun to give way to the more revolutionary impulses of militant blacks such as Stokely Carmichael and H. Rap Brown. The peaceful litigation strategies pursued by the National Association for the Advancement of Colored People (NAACP) were increasingly overshadowed by the more violent confrontational tactics of organizations like the Black Panthers.

By 1966 the cause of civil rights was losing momentum for another reason. The Johnson administration's efforts to secure cultural equality for blacks—embodied chiefly in ambitious inner-city programs created by the Economic Opportunity Act of 1964—did not sit well with many working-class and lower-middle-class ethnic whites, who believed that they would bear the costs of these redistributive programs to help blacks. Equally jarring to some elements of the traditional Democratic coalition were the administration's attempts to bar racial discrimination in the sale or rental of private housing (a practice widespread in the North) and to use "affirmative action" programs to correct past injustices by treating blacks preferentially.

All these policies had a profoundly divisive effect on the Democratic coalition, alienating the white South (once solidly Democratic) and leading to massive defections among working-class Democrats in the North. The Johnson administration's programmatic response to the civil rights movement—namely, policies aimed at promoting racial equality and participatory democracy—disturbed many Democrats, who saw them as threatening to take away gains they had won under the New Deal. The federal government, which under the New Deal had been seen as a source of assistance for the average American, now came to be looked upon by many as the cause of deprivations.

The political harm to the Democratic party first became evident in the 1966 congressional elections, when the Republicans added forty-seven seats to their minority in the House. Polls indicated that many northern white voters thought the Johnson administration was moving too far and too fast in its efforts to help blacks. Moreover, the violence in the inner cities each summer increased the demand for "law and order" and lowered voters' willingness to expend tax dollars for any program that seemed to be rewarding black rioters. The presidential campaign of Republican Richard Nixon in 1968 and that of the independent candidate, Alabama governor George Wallace, successfully exploited these social issues, driving wedges into the traditional Democratic coalition.

Vietnam's Political Legacy

Issues of civil rights and civil disorder were by no means alone in producing new cleavages within the Democratic party. At least as important in that regard was the Vietnam War. Although the Johnson administration's conduct of the war triggered prolonged and acrimonious controversy among the foreign policy elites, the public at large gave the administration firm and even enthusiastic support during the war's early years. But public support began to erode when an American victory seemed elusive and the costs escalated in terms of casualties abroad and disruption at home, including the mobilization of some reserve units, tougher policies on draft deferments, a surtax on incomes, and a decided tilt toward guns in the federal budget's ratio of guns to butter. By 1968 nearly half of the public regarded American military intervention in South Vietnam as a mistake, doubling the number holding that opinion three years earlier.

As with so many other controversies in American political life, however, the fight over Vietnam took place not between the two parties but within the majority party. It was mainly among Democrats that the antiwar movement found candidates to carry its banner. Senators Eugene McCarthy and, later, Robert F. Kennedy led the challenge against President Johnson on the war issue—not just on the floor of the Senate but in presidential primaries as well. McCarthy, waging a campaign supported largely by antiwar activists, ran almost even with Johnson in the hard-fought New Hampshire primary in 1968. The senator's showing was widely interpreted as a moral victory and was credited with dissuading the president from continuing his fight for renomination. When antiwar activists withheld their support from the eventual Democratic nominee, Hubert H. Humphrey, it increased the likelihood that Nixon would defeat the divided opposition without bearing the onus of having to attack the president.

In terms of longer lasting effects, the antiwar demonstrations of the late 1960s and early 1970s and the antiwar candidacy of Democratic senator George McGovern in 1972 also produced a backlash of nationalist sentiment from which the Republicans eventually profited. The Democrats began to be seen as lacking in patriotism and as weak on national defense, a perception that, as noted earlier, has hurt them ever since in presidential politics.

Religion and Politics

Issues of civil rights, war and peace, and national defense were not solely responsible for reshaping the political behavior of the electorate in the late 1960s and early 1970s. The almost simultaneous rise of new social issues had at least as powerful an effect, cutting across all constituency groups but having a particularly strong effect on white evangelical Protestants in the South. Social issues helped to give rise to one of the most powerful movements in modern American politics, the religious Right.

When Kennedy ran for president in 1960, white evangelical Protestants, who comprised about 20 percent of the national electorate, tended to be politically passive but supportive of the Democratic party, especially in the South. By the time Dukakis ran almost thirty years later, Democratic strategists knew that white evangelicals would be among their stiffest opponents, having realigned solidly in support of Reagan and the Republican party.

As A. James Reichley has shown, the transformation of white evangelicals from a passive component of the Democratic coalition to one of the driving forces of the Republican Right has been slow but steady. After supporting Jimmy Carter (a born-again Baptist) in 1976, they became disenchanted over what they considered to be his abandonment of their social agenda. A wide variety of modern trends contributed to their growing uneasiness. As Reichley notes:

> [E]vangelicals in the 1970s felt that their entire way of life, which they tended to identify as the American way of life, was threatened by such by-products of modernity as increase in divorce, rising crime, rapid increase in the percentage of children born out of wedlock, widespread use of recreational drugs, and virtually unrestricted availability of pornography. These symptoms of social decay, they were told by their preachers, were caused by the dominance of a philosophy called "secular humanism" in major universities, the national media, the federal government, and the federal courts.

Particularly threatening to traditional moral values, in the view of evangelicals, were policies such as the prohibition of officially sponsored prayer in public schools, abortion on demand, the proposed Equal Rights Amendment, and demands for gay rights.

During the late 1970s, popular television preachers like Jerry Falwell and Pat Robertson began calling for political action by evangelicals. In 1979 Falwell founded the Moral Majority, an organization that, like other New Right groups, built a strong financial base through sophisticated direct mail fund-raising operations and well-developed grass-roots political organization. The religious Right played an important role in helping Reagan win the White House in 1980. Four years later, the movement was even more active. Evangelical churches engineered ambitious voter registration drives that brought hundreds of thousands of new voters into the electorate in 1984; on election day white evangelicals gave Reagan an astonishing 80 percent of their vote.

Although not nearly as monolithic in their voting as evangelicals, Roman Catholics also have moved to the right since 1960. Catholics never gave a majority of their votes to a Republican presidential candidate until 1972, but they have done so in every election since then, save for 1976. In 1988, 52 percent of Catholic voters chose Bush. The abortion issue accounts for only a small part of the changing Catholic vote; polls show it to be decisive with about one Catholic voter in ten. But the consequence of the decline in Catholics' longstanding loyalty to the Democratic party has been the loss of a solid bloc of reliable support the party once enjoyed in the major industrial states of the Northeast and Midwest. Even the Hispanic vote in Texas is increasingly up for grabs, making it more and more difficult for the Democrats to win the third most populous state.

"New Politics" and the Business Community

Another important element in reshaping the Democratic party's identity—and in inspiring opposition forces to mobilize—was the emergence in the late 1960s and early 1970s of a broad constellation of citizens' organizations. Most of these organizations were committed either to securing the rights of particular groups in society (such as women, the handicapped, and nursing home patients) or to advancing broad public interests (such as consumer rights, environmental protection, and occupational health and safety) against what typically were depicted as the narrow, self-interested claims of powerful corporate interests.

Adopting the tactics of older, more established interest groups, citizens' organizations and public interest groups used every political weapon available. They lobbied legislators, monitored and participated in the administrative process, pursued strategies of litigation, and brought their message to the public, often as dramatically as possible, through finely tuned direct mail campaigns and the skillful use of other new technologies of persuasion. The combination of zeal and practical political skills brought these "new politics" organizations success along two principal avenues, one involving efforts to advance or protect rights (for example, freeing women from credit discrimination and from discrimination in educational institutions), the other involving federal regulations that affect the conditions under which goods and services are produced, the physical characteristics of consumer products, and the disposition of waste from the manufacturing process.

The success of these citizens' groups came to be identified primarily with the Democratic party, which was the principal source of their support in Congress. Yet that association rebounded somewhat to the party's disadvantage in presidential elections. As had been true of earlier social movements, the efforts of the new politics organizations generated a backlash from which the Republican party benefited.

The reaction was nowhere more apparent than in the business community. The antagonism between business and labor that traditionally has been fundamental to the politics of industrial democracies was overshadowed in the 1970s by an even more bitter struggle between business and the axis of interests grouped under the public interest umbrella. Part of the explanation for the hardened antagonism between business and citizens' groups was the changing nature of governmental regulation in the early 1970s. Unlike earlier attempts to regulate railroad freight rates or drug safety, regulatory innovations in the fields of occupational health and safety and environmental preservation were not industry-specific. Rather, they affected business as a whole, thus generating antagonism from all sectors of the business community.

With abundant incentive to protect its interests, American business countermobilized in the late 1970s. Corporations created their own lobbying operations in Washington or hired lawyers and lobbyists to represent their interests. Seduced by Reagan's pledge in 1980 to lift the regulatory crown of thorns that (at least in the eyes of business organizations) had been pressed onto the corporate brow by Democrats, the business community firmly reunited under the Republican banner in 1980. As never before, Republicans had access to seemingly limitless campaign funds and thus to the technological means of victory in modern presidential politics: computers, high-speed printers, opinion and tracking polls, television advertising, and telephone banks.

Business was not alone in reacting negatively to the efforts of citizens' groups. Less easily traced, but probably no less important in its electoral consequences, was a reaction among working-class Democrats, who came to regard "public interest" activism as adverse to their welfare. Many such workers believed that the costs of federal requirements to clean up the air and water and make workplaces and consumer products safer fell disproportionately on their shoulders in the form of lost jobs and income and higher taxes and prices. Moreover, the new politics organizations came to be identified (not always correctly) in the minds of many Americans with the encroaching power of the government into matters of personal behavior or preference, through policies ranging from the proposed saccharin ban at the national level to state-level "bottle-return" regulations, antismoking statutes, and laws to require the use of seat belts or motorcycle crash helmets.

Even as the Democratic party was hurt in presidential elections by its association with the new politics groups, it did not often receive offsetting support from them. Most of these organizations are not particularly effective at delivering large blocs of voters on election day. But this did not prevent them from insisting that the party platform reflect their interests. In 1984, for example, the list of organizations that sought to have their concerns incorporated into the Democratic party platform included environmental groups, gay rights advocates, feminists, peace activists, blacks, senior citizens, Hispanics, and Asian-Americans. As the party tried to accommodate all these demands, its message got muddled and its 1984 candidate, Walter Mondale, was branded a captive of "special interests."

Finally, these new politics organizations, simply by adding to the heterogeneity of interests in the Democratic party, have made it more difficult for Democrats to achieve unity in presidential campaigns. Their disunity provides Republicans with increased opportunities to promote and exploit divisions within the Democratic coalition, especially on social issues.

Epilogue: Perspectives on 1988

The millions of Americans (half the electorate) who failed to vote on November 8, 1988, were wrong if they believed that elections do not matter. Every presidential election opens or closes the door to change in American society in a variety of ways. Elections are the engines that drive the political process, advancing some ideas, retarding others, and sometimes providing mandates for significant social or economic change.

In recent years, one of the principal questions that observers of American politics have asked is whether the nation is undergoing a major shift from Democratic to Republican dominance of its political life. From the 1930s to the 1960s, the Democrats were preeminent, controlling the principal elective institutions in Washington and the states most of the time. Moreover, the Democratic party enjoyed almost a two-to-one edge over the Republicans among voters who were willing to state an allegiance to one party or the other.

But in 1980 the Democrats' seemingly commanding posture in Washington fell before a new Republican juggernaut. Reagan won the presidency, and the Republican party captured control of the Senate and took thirty-three seats away from the Democrats in the House (more than either party had lost in any other presidential election since 1948). Reagan was reelected in 1984, carrying every state but Minnesota. With the 1988 victory, the Republicans had won seven of the last ten presidential elections.

But the Republicans' impressive strength in the presidential arena was not replicated elsewhere in the political system. Even after its defeat in the 1988 presidential election, the Democratic party still held twenty-eight of the nation's fifty governorships, controlled a majority of state legislatures, and, even more important, had secure majorities in both houses of Congress. The Democrats actually gained seats in Congress in 1988 (five in the House, one in the Senate), dealing Bush a setback of the sort normally reserved for midterm elections. Assessing the results during the week following the election, Kevin Phillips, one of the nation's leading Republican political analysts, described the Republican house as a facade with nothing of substance behind it: "The truth is that, for Bush-era Republicanism, the White House is not just a President's mansion; it is becoming the GOP's only major fort on the battlefield of politics."

It is not altogether clear why the American electorate has delivered such a split verdict. At a minimum, the voters have a less than total trust in either political party. Therefore, some suggest, they have added what one observer has called "a new ad hoc element to the Founding Fathers' system of checks and balances." A better explanation is that each party has political advantages and disadvantages that result in Democratic victories in congressional races and the election of Republicans to the White House.

Voters seem to rely on the Democratic party in Congress to defend government benefits or services on which they are particularly dependent. The Democrats excel at serving a variety of local interests through the time-honored device of providing casework and other services to individual constituents. Even more impor-

tant, the Democratic party provides a political umbrella under which a wide range of programmatic groups can gather, including blacks, women, environmentalists, consumers, and senior citizens. Faithfully delivering on its commitments to these interests, the Democratic party has become the institutional embodiment of "interest group liberalism" in American society.

But the same heterogeneity of organized constituencies that is a source of strength for the Democratic party in Congress also weakens the party in the presidential arena, where diversity generates considerable friction between groups with conflicting views on particular issues. During the 1988 Democratic nominating contest, New York mayor Ed Koch said it would be "crazy" for any Jew to vote for the black candidate, Jesse Jackson, in the state's presidential primary. (Jackson was widely regarded in the Jewish community as unsympathetic to Israel in its struggle with the Palestinians.) Other conflicts have erupted in the Democratic party between trade unions that represent workers in defense plants and peace groups anxious to limit military spending, or between "right-to-lifers" who oppose abortion and "prochoice" groups that support the right of women to elect such a procedure.

While constantly struggling to accommodate such diverse interests within its ranks, the Democratic party finds that its heterogeneity renders it vulnerable to external attack from Republicans eager to drive wedges between Democratic constituencies. Nowhere is the Republicans' success at this more evident than with respect to abortion, school prayer, and other social issues, which Republican candidates have skillfully used to separate evangelical Protestants and traditional Catholics from their Democratic moorings.

In trying to handle their internal divisions, the Democrats face difficulties not unlike those encountered long ago by the Austro-Hungarian empire. Acceptance of heterogeneity is useful for territorial expansion because it permits a variety of diverse constituencies to be encompassed within a single sovereign unit. But heterogeneity also becomes a source of internal tension, division, and possible insurrection—as disadvantageous for a political organization like the Democratic party as it has been for empires in the past.

The Republican party, much more homogeneous than its rival, faces no similar balkanization by interests. The internal fault lines within the Republican party tend to be ideological. For example, in the 1950s conservative Republicans complained that the party was dominated at the national level by liberals whose policy preferences were scarcely distinguishable from those of the Democrats. Decades later, conservatives still were complaining, in the wake of the 1988 election, that the "moderate" Bush would bear careful watching. Still, despite the recurring tensions between its two ideological camps, the Republican party has managed to keep its divisions from tearing it asunder in every presidential election except 1964.

The Republican party's strength in presidential politics also has been increased by the lock it seems to have acquired on nationalist fervor in the United States. If there is one issue that can give a party the edge in the presidential electoral arena, nationalism is that issue; it carries a strong emotional appeal that cuts through a variety of constituencies and often transcends the more particular concerns that members of those constituencies may have. In recent presidential elections, Republican campaign strategists have been more successful than the Democrats at manipulating symbols like the flag and at using gauzy rhetoric ("morning in America," for example) to inspire and capitalize on nationalist sentiments.

The Republican edge on nationalism has been reinforced by their most recent exercises of national power abroad, such as the invasion of Grenada in 1983 and the air raid on Libya in 1986. These produced much flag-waving and a large resurgence of national pride, at very little political cost. The Democrats, by contrast, seem to specialize in high-cost exercises abroad—wars in Korea and Vietnam and President Carter's highly controversial grain embargo. Such ventures may have projected an image of American strength abroad, but at home they imposed considerable costs on the president and his party.

Will control over national policy making divided between a Democratic Congress and a Republican president prevent the United States from dealing with its most serious social and economic problems during the Bush presidency? Historically, divided government in the United States has not made political deadlock inevitable. In fact, in the two most recent periods when the nation had a Republican president and a Democratic Congress, there have been significant policy breakthroughs. The collaboration between President Nixon and the Democratic 91st and 92d Congresses between 1969 and 1972 produced landmark legislation in environmental and consumer protection, occupational safety and health, and general revenue sharing. During the final two years of the Reagan presidency, there were major policy achievements, such as welfare reform and arms control, even though the Democrats controlled both houses of Congress.

Even as divided or "coalition" government does not ensure policy deadlock, having the same party in control of both branches provides no guarantee against it. Indeed, the most recent period of interbranch control by one party—the Carter administration—was one of frequent stalemate. Carter failed to secure passage of most of the major domestic legislation he proposed, including welfare reform, energy reform, and hospital cost containment.

Still, even if the partisan cleavage that now separates the president from Congress does not lead to stalemate, the particular issues and policy problems that await action in the wake of the 1988 election may make their own contribution to political paralysis. The budget deficit is the most troublesome of the many issues that face the president and Congress; many observers are convinced that it can be solved only by some combination of tax increases and spending cuts, the very things that elected officials least like to do. Equally formidable are policy problems such as acid rain that will continue to divide Congress internally, not so much by party or ideology as along geographic and regional lines.

For George Bush, as for other presidents, the challenge will be to find support for his policy initiatives in the ranks of both parties. The Democratic 101st Congress faces a task no less formidable—to defend the interests and welfare of its constituents without prejudicing the country's ability to find solutions for its most pressing problems. The ability of the White House and Congress to shape national policy effectively through some mix of combat and compromise will go a long way toward determining the fate of the political parties in the presidential election of 1992, an event that was already on the minds of both Democratic and Republican politicians even before Bush was inaugurated as president January 20, 1989.

II INTERCONNECTIONS: POLITICAL ACTION COMMITTEES

Of all the changes in American electoral politics over the past twenty years, few have caused as much controversy as the emergence of the political action committee (PAC) as a major force in campaign fund raising. Although PACs have existed for a long time, they took on a new prominence after the passage of federal campaign finance legislation in 1974.

The 1974 legislation strictly limited the amount of money that individuals could contribute to political campaigns, but it allowed political action committees—groups sponsored by corporations, labor unions, or other associations—also to contribute to candidates. In fact, although individuals could contribute only $1,000 to each campaign, PACs could contribute $5,000—provided they consisted of at least fifty members and gave to at least five candidates.

Since 1974, PACs have become a major source of campaign funds, especially for congressional incumbents. They have also been the source of considerable controversy. PACs are charged, in effect, with a form of legal "vote buying," in which, allegedly, they trade money for influence. Many incumbents pad their campaign war chests with PAC contributions, but others have avoided PAC contributions altogether, either on principle or from fear of their opponents' attacks.

With all the heat coming from the PAC issue, there has been relatively little light. The following selection takes a careful look at PAC activities and concludes that no easy solution to the problem is in sight.

Questions

1. What roles do PACs play in the American political process? Are they a problem in the American political system? Why or why not? If they are, what are the possible solutions to that problem?

2. What factors influence the strategy and effectiveness of individual PACs? Which factors appear to be most significant in helping us to understand why different PACs act differently?

8.2 PACs in the Political Process

M. Margaret Conway

In the less than two decades since federal laws and Supreme Court decisions conveyed legitimacy on political action committees, their numbers have increased by 600 percent, growing from 608 in 1974 to 4,178 in 1989. While the rate of growth in the number of PACs declined during the 1980s (and their absolute numbers even declined from 1988 to 1989), their role in the funding of congressional elections remained significant. During the 1987–1988 election cycle, PACs provided 40 percent of the funds received by House candidates and 22 percent of Senate candidates' receipts.

Many questions about the role of PACs in American politics are addressed [here] . . . , including: What laws govern the activities of political action committees? Have these laws been effective in achieving their intended aims? What has been the role of PACs in financing congressional campaigns? What types of candidates are favored and what types are disadvantaged by the existing laws? How do PACs make decisions about which candidates should receive PAC contributions and how much to give? What strategies govern contribution decisions by PACs? Do the internal needs of the organization giving the money influence patterns of PAC contributions to congressional candidates?

Two types of political action committees operate at the federal level: independent and affiliated. Independent PACs are officially independent of any existing organization and usually focus on a particular issue or advocate a particular ideology. Affiliated PACs are created by existing organizations such as labor unions, corporations, cooperatives, or trade and professional associations. They serve as a separate, segregated fund to collect money from people affiliated with the organization for contribution to candidates' political campaigns or

for use as independent expenditures for or against a particular candidate.

Federal Law and the Growth of PACs

Political action committees are governed primarily by the Federal Election Campaign Act of 1971 (FECA) and amendments enacted to it in 1974, 1976, and 1979, as well as the Revenue Act of 1971. Also important are regulations and advisory opinions issued by the Federal Election Commission (FEC) which administers and enforces federal campaign finance laws, as well as several court decisions interpreting federal laws.

To limit the influence of any one group or individual in the funding of campaigns for federal office, individuals and most organizations are restricted in the amount of money that they can give directly to a candidate in any one year. The current limits are $1,000 per election to a candidate for federal office, $20,000 per year to the national political party committees, and $5,000 per election to a campaign committee. No individual may contribute more than $25,000 to candidates for federal office in any one year. Federal campaign finance laws, however, give a distinct advantage to multicandidate committees—those contributing to five or more candidates for federal office—whether they are independent or affiliated. A multicandidate committee may contribute as much money as it is able to raise, yet it is restricted to giving no more than $5,000 per candidate in each election. That permits a PAC to give a candidate up to $5,000 for a primary election and $5,000 for a general election contest. There is no limit on how much a political action committee may spend in independent expenditures in behalf of a candidate as long as it does not coordinate its campaign efforts in any way with the candidate, representatives of the candidate,

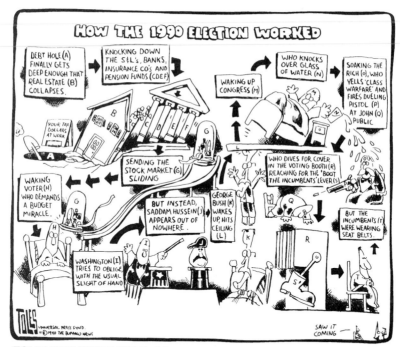

or the candidate's campaign committee. Because PACs are able to raise and funnel large amounts to campaigns for federal office, their numbers have grown; public concern about their influence on members of Congress has grown as well.

The 1974 amendments to the Federal Election Campaign Act permitted government contractors to establish political action committees, thus greatly expanding the universe of businesses and labor unions eligible to create PACs. The decision by the Federal Election Commission in April 1975 to permit corporations and labor unions to use their treasury funds to create political action committees and to administer their activities, including solicitation of funds from employees and stockholders, facilitated the establishment and operation of political action committees. Authorization of the use of payroll deductions to channel funds to PACs also stimulated the creation and continuing operations of PACs.

Supreme Court decisions as well played a major role in stimulating the creation of additional PACs. In *Buckley v. Valeo*, the Supreme Court in January 1976 indicated that the 1974 FECA amendments did not limit the number of local or regional PACs that unions or corporations and their subsidiaries could establish. That decision also clarified the right of PACs to make independent expenditures (those not authorized by nor coordinated with a candidate's campaign) on behalf of a candidate. In 1976 further amendments to FECA restricted labor union and corporation PAC contributions to one $5,000 contribution per election, regardless of the number of PACs created by a corporation's divisions or subsidiaries or a labor union's locals. The process of clarifying what is permissible continues, with the Federal Election Commission and other interested parties proposing amendments to existing laws and a number of advisory opinions being issued by the FEC.

While political action committees had existed prior to 1974, their numbers were limited, most often among labor unions. Between 1974 and 1989 the number of labor union PACs increased by 83 percent, while the number of corporate PACs increased by 1,900 percent. Thus, the first notable effect of changed laws and the FEC's interpretation of the laws was the explosive growth in the number of corporate PACs. Although the number of labor union and corporate PACs has increased significantly, most do not raise and contribute large amounts of money. During the 1987–1988 campaign cycle, only thirty-seven corporate PACs raised more then $350,000 each, but only fourteen contributed to candidates that much from funds raised. Thirty-nine labor union PACs raised $350,000 or more, and twenty-eight contributed at least $350,000 to candidates. More than fifty nonconnected PACs raised $350,000 or more, but only six contributed that much to candidates. Finally, forty-seven trade/membership/health PACs raised at least $350,000, but less than half (twenty-one) contributed at least that much.

After clarification of the laws, other types of PACs were created. The most prominent was the independent or nonconnected PAC. Its numbers increased from 110 in 1977 to 1,060 in 1989.

Affiliated PACs obtain funds through donations for use for political purposes made by individuals associated with the group. Corporations and labor unions are not allowed to make direct campaign contributions from their treasuries, but treasury funds may be used to establish and administer a PAC and to communicate with people associated with the organization—such as corporate employees or shareholders and their families or labor union members and their families—for voter registration and get-out-the-vote drives.

Scholars, journalists, and many political leaders have expressed increasing concern about the role of political action committees in federal campaign funding. PACs may have enormous influence, affecting who is viewed as a viable candidate, the outcomes of elections, access to the policy-making process, and the content of policy. Because PACs have become a major source of campaign funds for congressional candidates, an inability to obtain PAC support may mean a candidate cannot afford to run an effective campaign. If elected, the successful candidate must be ever mindful of campaign funding sources, both past and future. The escalating costs of congressional and senatorial campaigns force incumbent members of Congress to be watchful of how policy positions taken and votes cast on legislation may affect future fund-raising.

Not all aid from PACs, however, is always welcome. The entry of independent PACs into a contest may be unwelcome, even by the candidate the PACs favor. Moreover, a backlash may develop against independent PACs, particularly those that engage in negative campaigning, and that backlash can extend to the candidate supported by the independent PACs. Some candidates believe that identification with a particular PAC's issue positions, the negative campaign tactics often used by independent PACs, or the fact that a PAC is based outside the constituency hurts rather than helps the candidate's chances for electoral success.

PAC Decision Making

A number of variables influence PAC decision making on campaign contributions. These include the goals of the organization, the expectations of contributors to the PAC, the official positions within the organization of those making the decisions, the strategic premises employed by the PAC, and the PAC's competitive position versus those of other organizations.

An organization may follow a "maintaining strategy," simply seeking to continue access to those members of Congress to whom the sponsoring organization already has access. Or, it may follow an "expanding strategy," attempting to gain access to additional representatives or senators who would not normally be attuned to the PAC's interests because of the limited presence of the represented interest within the member's electoral constituency. The results of the limited amount of research done on this topic suggest that PACs generally emphasize a maintaining strategy, with only a third of the contributions representing an expanding strategy. PACs also tend to be more responsive to the needs of vulnerable representatives and senators who have befriended the PAC's interests.

PAC decision-making patterns vary with the structure of the PAC. If the PAC has staff based in Washington, that staff tends to play a greater role in deciding to whom to contribute and how much to contribute. Contributions are also more likely to occur through the mechanism of a Washington-based fund-raising event. PACs in which substantial funds are raised by local affiliates tend to follow the locals' more parochial concerns. That may not be the most rational allocation strategy to pursue, however. Rationality would require that the PAC allocate funds either to strengthen or broaden access or to replace opponents, but parochialism may require that an already supportive member of Congress receive substantial amounts of locally raised funds. The degree of parochialism appears to vary by type of PAC interest—for example, defense interest PACs are more locally oriented than labor interest PACs.

Partisanship and ideology also may influence PAC decision making—for example, defense PACs tend to be less ideological in their contribution decisions than labor, oil, and auto PACs. Business PACs vary in the extent to which they pursue a partisan support strategy; usually this is associated with the vulnerability of a political party's incumbents. When political tides appear to be favoring Republicans, they may contribute more to Republican challengers than when the political climate is less favorable to that party.

Incumbents' voting records on key votes may be a major factor as well in influencing contribution decisions. An incumbent, for example, who voted against legislation the PAC considered of vital importance would be highly unlikely to receive a campaign contribution. One study of PACs affiliated with Fortune 500 companies found voting records on key legislation to be the second most frequently cited

criterion used in making contribution decisions (the most frequently cited was the candidate's attitudes toward business).

Some PACs also must be concerned about competition for supporters, and that concern influences contribution patterns. Contributions that would leave the PAC open to criticism sufficiently severe to cost it future support from donors must be avoided. This is a particular problem for nonconnected PACs that raise funds through mass mail solicitations.

Another factor that influences patterns of PAC contributions is concern about relative influence with key holders of power. If other PACs give to a member of Congress and PAC X does not, will that have an impact on relative access? While some PACs act as though it would, others may pursue a different strategy, gaining the member's attention by giving to his or her challenger. The member of Congress will therefore become more attentive to gain support from the PAC. The effectiveness of that strategy, however, is limited by the extent to which the PAC's preferred policy outcomes conflict with the strength of a contrary ideology held by the member of Congress or the intensity of support for a different policy position present in that member's constituency.

Role of PACs in Campaign Finance

PAC receipts, expenditures, and contributions to congressional candidates have increased significantly since the early 1970s. PAC receipts grew from $19.2 million in 1972 to $369 million in 1988, while PAC expenditures increased from $19 million to $349 million. PAC contributions to congressional candidates increased from $8.5 million for the 1972 elections to $147 million for the 1988 elections. Congressional candidates' dependence on PAC contributions increased by approximately 25 percent between 1982 and 1988.

The changing technology of campaigns stimulates candidates' perceived needs for PAC funds. Extensive use of professional campaign management firms, surveys, television advertising, and the other requirements of modern campaigns have greatly increased campaign costs. Total spending in contests for the Senate increased by 568 percent between 1974 and 1988, with Senate candidates spending a total of $189 million in 1988 compared with $28 million in the 1973–1974 election cycle. Candidates for the House of Representatives spent $221 million in 1987–1988, compared with $44 million in 1973–1974. The average campaign cost for a House incumbent seeking reelection in 1988 was $378,000, while the average campaign cost for Senate incumbents was almost $4 million. In 1974 no candidate for the House spent more than $500,000 in a campaign, but in 1988, 140 House candidates spent more than that.

The dependence on PAC funds to meet the large and ever-increasing costs of campaigns for Congress varies greatly by legislative chamber, incumbent status, and party. In 1988 Democratic House incumbents received 52 percent of their total campaign receipts from PACs, while Republican incumbents in the House obtained 39 percent of their funds from that source. Challengers and candidates for open seats received less, with, for example, Republican challengers receiving 10 percent of their funds from PACs and Democratic challengers receiving 32 percent. Senate candidates are less dependent on PAC money; in 1988 Democratic incumbents obtained 29 percent of their funds from PACS, and Republican incumbents received 26 percent from that source. Challengers and open seat candidates in both parties in the Senate received even less from PACs; neither averaged more than 16 percent.

If candidates obtained a greater share of their funds from other sources, public concern about the role of PACs in American politics would probably lessen. The federal campaign finance laws, however, limit how much political parties may contribute to congressional candidates and spend on their behalf. While those limits are not met in all contests, they may be met in open seat contests or in Senate contests, especially by the Republican campaign finance committees. Permitting parties to give more to

their candidates and changing the campaign finance laws to permit citizens to give more to political parties would encourage reduced dependence on PAC funding.

To overcome the limits on party funding of congressional campaigns contained within the federal laws, two practices have developed whose effects can only be estimated. In the first practice the political party organizations guide individual or PAC contributions to particular candidates, and especially to those whom the parties believe have a good chance of winning if adequate funding were available. The second practice is to guide money—particularly money that may not be given under federal law but is permissible in some states, such as campaign contributions from corporate treasury monies—to state political party organizations to be used for various campaign purposes. The estimated value of these funds in the 1988 election was $30 million. These contributions can be used, of course, for a variety of campaign activities that promote the presidential ticket as well as congressional candidates.

In the 1987–1988 election cycle 65.4 percent of PAC contributions went to candidates for the House of Representatives. Senate campaigns are much more expensive than House contests, and the $5,000 per election restriction limits the impact of PAC contributions on Senate contests. Generally, only a finite number of PACs are interested in any one contest, and most PACs do not give to any one candidate the maximum amount of money allowed under the law. Among the factors considered by PACs when determining whether and how much to give are the nature of the state or district and the interests of the PAC within that constituency and, for incumbents, committee assignments, past voting patterns, and help previously provided by the candidate to the PAC in support of its interests. Affiliated PACs tend to be associated with a particular business, industry, or other economic or social entity and may focus on contests in states where the sponsoring interest group is particularly strong. Independent PACs have tended to focus more on Senate than on

House contests, particularly in making independent expenditures.

Some members of Congress have established their own PACs. Leadership PACs have been created by party leaders within each chamber, and those who have presidential ambitions have formed PACs as well. These member PACs are used not only to fund research on public issues, speaking trips, and other support-building activity among the general public, but also to make campaign contributions to other candidates for Congress. Contributing to other congressional candidates builds support for the attainment and maintenance of formal positions of power within Congress and may accumulate support for a future presidential campaign. Candidate PACs have been used by former representative Jack Kemp, R-N.Y.; Sen. Robert Dole, R-Kan.; and Sen. Edward Kennedy, D-Mass. Candidate PACs also have been used by eventually nominated presidential candidates such as Ronald Reagan, Walter Mondale, and George Bush.

Strategies: Access and Replacement

Two types of strategies are used by PACs to obtain results from their contributions. One emphasizes contributing to obtain access to members of Congress who are positioned to be most helpful in advancing the policy interests of the PAC. The other focuses on electing people to Congress who will be more helpful to the PAC—that is, the goal is to replace members who are not supportive of the PAC's interests or ideology and to elect people to open seats who are viewed as supportive of the PAC's policy objectives.

The access strategy utilizes contributions to obtain access to members who can be of particular help to the PAC in obtaining its legislative goals. The consequence of this strategy is a disproportionate allocation of funds to incumbents. Those members serving on legislative committees whose subject matter jurisdiction includes areas of interest to the PAC are favored in PAC allocations. Also of importance are members who influence budgets for policies relevant to the PAC or who serve on major procedural committees such as the House Rules Committee. PACs also contribute to leaders of the House and Senate whose influence extends over the entire range of legislative policy. PACs are quite aware of a congressional member's voting record on legislation of interest to them, and many PACs make an effort to reward friends in Congress with campaign contributions.

Many kinds of PACs appear to pursue an access strategy; indeed, incumbent support is the strategy generally pursued by most types of PACs. In the 1987–1988 election cycle, 92 percent of corporate contributions went to incumbents. The percentage given to incumbents in the past, however, has varied with the situation, with corporate PACs giving to challengers when the electoral tides indicate that incumbents who have been less supportive of corporate interests may be vulnerable. Thus in 1980, 57 percent of corporate contributions went to incumbents, and 28 percent were given to Republican challengers to incumbent Democrats and to open seat candidates. Other types of business PACs are also highly likely to support incumbents. In contrast, labor union PACs tend to be highly supportive both of incumbent Democrats and of Democratic open seat and challenger candidates. When Democratic incumbents are more vulnerable, a greater share of labor PAC funds goes to incumbents.

The second strategy of trying to replace members of Congress whose ideology and voting records do not coincide with those preferred by the PAC is more likely to be pursued by nonconnected PACs. The proportion of their contributions going to challengers and open seat candidates ranged from 72 percent in 1978 to 33 percent in 1988. Incumbents who are perceived as unlikely to be defeated usually have only limited amounts directed against them.

Sometimes, however, other criteria are involved in targeting. In 1982 Sen. Paul Sarbanes, D-Md., was selected by the National Conservative Political Action Committee (NCPAC) to serve as an object lesson to other members of Congress. NCPAC assumed that other senators and representatives would see the ads run against Sarbanes on the Washington, D.C.–area television stations. The implied threat was that those whose voting records were not sufficiently in accord with NCPAC's preferences also would be the target of negative advertising campaigns. The negative advertising campaign against Sarbanes was not successful, however, and, indeed, the ads were withdrawn before the general election campaign. While not effective in the Sarbanes campaign, other independent expenditure efforts have been perceived as successful. In 1984, for example, more than $1.1 million was spent to influence Illinois voters to cast their votes against Sen. Charles Percy, R-Ill., who lost his reelection bid by 1 percent of the vote. Independent expenditures also can be important in electing candidates; for example, Sen. Phil Gramm, R-Texas, benefited from more than $500,000 spent on his behalf in the 1984 Senate contest.

Although nonconnected PACs ranked first in the amount of funds collected in 1987–1988, raising $97.4 million, they contributed only 20.8 percent of that amount to candidates. In contrast, corporate PACs contributed 58.3 percent of the $96.4 million they collected, and labor PACs contributed 46.7 percent of the $75 million they raised. Nonconnected PACs find it necessary to spend far more to raise money than do affiliated PACs, who have the support of their sponsoring organizations. Nonconnected PACs also allocate more money for direct expenditures in support of or opposition to particular candidates. In 1987–1988, for example, they spent 16 percent of funds raised on expenditures for or against candidates, with three-fourths of that allotted to the presidential campaign.

Partisan Allocation of PAC Contributions

In 1988 Democratic candidates as a group received 62 percent of campaign contributions made by PACs. The division of PAC money between the two parties' candidates, however, differed greatly by PAC, with 47 percent of corporate PAC contributions and 92 percent of labor union PAC contributions going to Democrats. Corporate PACs largely pursued an access strategy, allocating 90 percent of their contributions to incumbents; trade, membership, and health PACs pursued a similar course of action, granting 82 percent of their contributions to incumbents. Labor split its contributions differently; 67 percent to incumbents, 19 percent to challengers, and 13 percent to open seat candidates. Nonconnected PACs also divided their contributions, giving 64 percent to incumbents, 18 percent to challengers, and 16 percent to open seat candidates. In terms of actual amounts, Democratic Senate candidates received more from PACs than did Republicans ($28 million versus $23 million). Democratic House candidates received substantially more from PACs than did Republicans ($68 million versus $35 million).

PACs and the Policy Process

One way in which PACs affect policy is by influencing who wins House and Senate elections. PAC contributions can affect electoral outcomes in several ways. The first is to help incumbents by inciting reluctance among highly qualified potential candidates to enter the contest. Large sums of money in the incumbent's campaign coffers will intimidate many potential candidates and, in effect, act as a preemptive strike against potential candidates. The potential challenger, knowing the incumbent starts with a significant advantage in name recognition and usually with a favorable image with the voters, often concludes that the chance of defeating the incumbent is quite small and thus does not enter the contest.

Large accumulations of campaign funds also permit early campaigning by the incumbent. The objective is to discourage potential opposition, or, if opposition does develop, to control the issue agenda of the campaign. Other goals of early spending include further increasing the incumbent's fund-raising and enhancing the popularity of potentially weak incumbents.

After the campaign has begun, do challengers and incumbents benefit equally from campaign expenditures? One point of view is that the challenger benefits more, as higher levels of funding enable the challenger to establish name recognition and create awareness of his or her candidacy. Thus, substantial benefit accrues from initial expenditures. As more potential voters become aware of the challenger, however, the effectiveness of expenditures decreases. Whether incumbents, who already have greater name recognition, benefit as much as challengers from their expenditures is the subject of considerable debate among scholars. Incumbents may through their expenditures increase turnout, or they may prevent loss of support among those previously committed to them. Those incumbents who spend the most may be the most vulnerable, or they may be aiming for "overkill" to discourage future opposition or to gain public acclaim which will help them seek another office such as the governor's office, a U.S. Senate seat, or even the presidency.

The effectiveness of the challenger's expenditures may depend on whether political trends are favorable or unfavorable to the challenger's party. If the challenger is a Democrat and noncandidate factors that influence congressional election outcomes—such as the level of approval of presidential job performance and economic conditions—favor the Republicans, the challenger's expenditures will buy less support than if these noncandidate factors were less favorable to the opposition.

In addition to influencing electoral outcomes, PAC contributions can influence public policy in other ways. For most PACs a primary objective of campaign contributions is to gain access to the member of Congress in order to present policy views and have them heard in the legislative setting. When an issue is not one of primary concern to a senator's or represen-

tative's constituency and not in conflict with a strongly held party position or the member's ideology, the recipient of campaign contributions from a particular source may be willing to vote in support of that interest group's issue position.

Do campaign contributions generally influence legislative outcomes? Unfortunately, insufficient research exists to permit a definitive answer to the question. Studies that examined the relationship between campaign contributions and legislative roll-call votes reached conflicting conclusions. Some concluded that PAC money affects recipients' support in roll-call votes for legislation. Studies supporting this conclusion analyzed votes on minimum wage legislation; the B-1 bomber; the debt limit, the windfall profits tax, and wage and price controls; trucking deregulation; and legislation of interest to doctors and to auto dealers. A study examining the effects of labor's contributions on both general issues and urban issues concluded that their contributions had a significant impact on five of nine issues relating to urban problems and five of eight general issues, but business contributions were significant in only one issue conflict of each type. Other research confirmed the influence of contributions in support for labor's preferred legislation. Still other research, however, suggested that campaign contributions were not important on roll-call votes on such issues as the Chrysler Corporation's loan guarantee and the windfall profits tax and dairy price supports. One study examined a number of PACs and congressional voting behavior over an eight-year period and concluded that contributions rarely are related to congressional voting patterns. When they are, contributions are a surrogate for other support for the member from the interest group. In summary, the evidence on the importance of PAC contributions in influencing congressional voting behavior is conflicting, and obviously further research on this topic is needed.

Campaign contributions may be given to those who were supportive in the past rather than in an effort to gain future roll-call support. Furthermore, the most important effects of campaign contributions may not be on roll-call votes but on the various earlier stages of the legislative process such as the introduction and sponsorship of bills, the behind-the-scenes negotiations on legislative provisions, the drafting and proposing of amendments, and the markup of bills in subcommittees and committees.

Finally, factors such as constituency interests and ideology and party ties may determine whether campaign contributions influence legislative outcomes. If the issue is important to a significant part of the constituency, for example, constituency interests will likely prevail over PAC policy preferences. Thus, PAC money and the interest group concerns it represents may prevail only on less visible issues where the influences of party, ideology, or constituency are not important.

Criticisms of Interest Group Activity in Campaign Finance

The increased role of PACs since the early 1970s in funding campaigns for Congress has generated substantial criticism. Certainly PAC funding plays a role in who is elected to Congress, even if the evidence about the impact of PAC contributions on roll-call voting is mixed and the research is too limited to draw firm conclusions about its influence on other stages of the congressional decision-making process.

Organization simplifies the representation of interests in a large and complex society, and PACs are one manifestation of the organized representation of interests. Criticism of the campaign finance system, however, has resulted in a number of suggestions for changes in federal law. One issue underlying the suggested changes is whether the total amount of PAC money a candidate may receive should be limited. Proponents argue that such a limitation will limit PAC influence; opponents point out that limiting PAC contributions will make it more difficult for nonincumbents to seek office.

Two ways to overcome this problem are (1) to permit individuals to make larger contributions to candidates and to political parties and (2) to permit political parties both to give more to candidates of the party and to spend more on behalf of party candidates. Generally, the Democrats have opposed these suggestions as being more likely to favor Republicans, who could both raise more money from larger contributions and have more money to give to the party's candidates.

Another criticism of PACs is that they weaken the role of the individual citizen in politics. This criticism is based on the disparity between the amount an individual may contribute ($1,000) and the amount a PAC may contribute ($5,000). To increase the role of individuals the limit on individual contributions could be increased or the limit on PAC contributions reduced. Increasing the maximum an individual may give, however, increases the influence of those more affluent.

Another proposal is to encourage more individuals to give small contributions by permitting them to write off part of the contribution as a deduction from gross income in figuring income taxes or as a deduction from taxes owed. Some proposals would permit the deduction only for contributions to candidates or parties within the state the contributor resides.

Yet another idea is to reduce dependence on PAC money by suggesting limits on the amounts that candidates may spend in their campaigns. Those who accepted the limits would receive partial campaign funding from a government-funded campaign fund. If a candidate accepted the limits but the opponent did not, the candidate would receive more from the fund. But finding the money for such a fund in a very tight federal budget and convincing candidates to limit voluntarily how much they spend are highly unlikely in the present political climate. Other suggestions include establishing firm limits on how much may be spent on congressional campaigns (thereby benefiting the better-known incumbent and disadvantaging lesser-known challengers) and financing campaigns with public funds (again probably benefiting incumbents).

President George Bush proposed a number of campaign finance reforms to Congress in 1989. These included abolishing most types of PACs, retaining only nonconnected PACs (all PACs would, in effect, become nonconnected), increasing how much political parties may spend on behalf of candidates, prohibiting leadership PACs from transferring funds to the campaign committees of other members, permitting each congressional candidate to take only $75,000 from PACs, and establishing voluntary limits on how much a candidate may raise ($200,000 for the primary and $200,000 for the general election) with the candidate in return receiving discounted television and radio time and postage costs. Bundling of funds by PACs also would be prohibited, and fuller disclosure of the sponsorship of independent expenditure campaigns would be required. A number of other reform proposals were being considered by Congress as well, as the nation entered its third century.

A potential problem that the proposals do not address is the imbalance in the representation of interests through PACs. For example, the rapid increase in the number of business-related PACs and the considerable potential for their future growth, compared to the much more limited potential for the growth of labor-related PACs, suggests that an imbalance in this kind of access/influence mechanism between these two types of interests exists and could become much larger. While it could be argued that business PAC activities are merely formalizing that which occurred previously—free services, for example—the amounts being contributed to candidates are larger than in earlier elections. Of course, it also can be pointed out that labor PACs do much more than contribute money; they are very active in the mobilization of other types of resources as well. Other types of interests—those less affluent—are not represented through money-based mechanisms of representation such as PACs.

In summary, the politics of PACs and PAC reform in the funding of campaigns for Congress present many problems. PACs are here and are not likely to be abolished, and their role in the political process will continue, as will the controversies about their role.

III  FOCUS: CAMPAIGN ADVERTISING

No other change in the conduct of American electoral politics has been more fundamental than the emergence of television. As early as 1952, politicians discovered that paid television advertisements were effective in getting their messages across to potential voters. Since then, political advertising has become increasingly sophisticated, and it has become the major expense in most political campaigns. And while at one time political advertisements looked substantially different from ordinary commercial messages, since at least 1968, candidates have been packaged and sold, as the saying goes, like soap.

In the following selection, Kathleen Hall Jamieson, a leading expert on political rhetoric and communication, summarizes the results of her research on the evolution of political campaign advertising over the course of eight campaigns, from 1952 to 1980. Perhaps surprisingly, she concludes that campaign ads do not subvert democratic politics but actually strengthen it.

Questions

1. What functions does political advertising serve to candidates? To voters? In what sense can 30-second TV spots contribute to candidates' "consistent, coherent messages about themselves and the future as they envision it"?

2. How has political advertising changed over the past forty years? Have these changes in form, in Jamieson's view, altered the essential purpose or effect of campaign advertising?

8.3 *Packaging the Presidency*

Kathleen Hall Jamieson

Political advertising is now the major means by which candidates for the presidency communicate their messages to voters. As a conduit of this advertising, television attracts both more candidate dollars and more audience attention than radio or print. Unsurprisingly, the spot ad is the most used and the most viewed of the available forms of advertising. By 1980 the half hour broadcast speech—the norm in 1952—had been replaced by the 60 second spot.

Ads enable candidates to build name recognition, frame the questions they view as central to the election, and expose their temperaments, talents, and agendas for the future in a favorable light. In part because more voters attend to spot ads than to network news and in part because reporters are fixated with who's winning and losing instead of what the candidates are proposing, some scholars believe that ads provide the electorate with more information than network news. Still, ads more often successfully reinforce existing dispositions than create new ones.

Ads also argue the relevance of issues to our lives. In the 1950s the public at large did not find political matters salient to it. From the late 1950s to the early 1970s the perception of the relevance of political matters to one's day-to-day life increased at all educational levels. Citizens saw a greater connection between what

occurred in the political world and what occurred in their lives.

TV ads' ability to personalize and the tendency of TV news to reduce issues to personal impact have, in my judgment, facilitated that change. Ads argued, for example, that a vote against nonproliferation could increase the Strontium 90 in children's ice cream. As the salience of political issues increased so too did the consistency of the beliefs of individual voters. Dissonant views are less likely to be simultaneously held now than before. This tendency is also reinforced by political advertising, for politicians have increasingly argued the interconnection of issues of importance to them. In 1980 Reagan predicated a strong defense on a strong economy. In 1968 Nixon tied crime, lawlessness, and the war in Vietnam into a single bundle and laid it on Humphrey's doorstep.

Ads also define the nature of the presidency by stipulating the attributes a president should have. In the process they legitimize certain occupations. Ike polished the assumption that being a general was a suitable qualification. Carter argued that being an outsider plus an engineer, a farmer, a businessman but not a lawyer qualified him. Reagan contended that being the governor of a large state as well as a union leader were stronger qualifications than being an incumbent president. Eisenhower,

Nixon, Johnson, Ford, and Carter argued that being the incumbent qualified one for the presidency.

. . . Advertising provides an optic through which presidential campaigns can be productively viewed. In the eight campaigns [between 1952 and 1980, we see] for example, various styles of leadership reflected in the candidates' treatment of their advertisers and advertising. Where Nixon maintained tight control over advertising decisions in 1960, Kennedy delegated all responsibility for advertising to others. At the same time, ad campaigns that lurched uncertainly from one message form to another, from one set of strategists to another, as Ford's did in the Republican primaries of 1976, suggested perhaps that the candidate and his advisers were unable to provide a clear sense of the direction in which they wanted to take the country, an observation consistent with that of Ford's admen in the general election who tried and failed to divine the administration's vision of the future under Ford.

Occasionally, a candidate's response to the requirements of advertising raises troublesome questions about his suitability for the office or, perhaps, about the intensity of his desire to hold it. Adlai Stevenson's perpetual quest for the perfect word or perfectly phrased argument and his apparent need to continue to perfect texts even as he was walking to the stage invite doubts about his ability to act decisively.

When the acceptance speech and the election eve telecasts are taken as the brackets bounding advertising, a focus on paid messages can reveal a campaign's fundamental coherence or incoherence. In a coherent campaign, the acceptance speech at the convention synopsizes and polishes the message the candidate has communicated in the primaries as a means of forecasting both the themes of the general election campaign and of this person's presidency. The message is then systematically developed in the advertising of the general election and placed in its final form on election eve where the candidate tries on the presidency by indicating for the country his vision of the next four years under his leadership. When from the first campaign advertising of January through the last on election eve in November, candidates offer consistent, coherent messages about themselves and the future as they envision it, they minimize the likelihood that their record or plans will be distorted effectively by opponents, and create a clear set of expectations to govern their conduct in office, expectations that may haunt them when they seek reelection.

Viewing campaign advertising as an extended message rather than a series of discrete message units also enables us to see how a candidate's response to attacks in the primaries can either strengthen or strangle the candidate's chances in the general election. When attacks are raised in the primaries and effectively neutralized, as were questions about Kennedy's age and religion in 1960, the issues can be effectively dispatched in the general election. Kennedy's widely aired speech to the Houston ministers builds on a structure of belief first cemented in Kennedy's speeches and ads in the West Virginia primary. Accordingly, those including NCPAC [National Conservative Political Action Committee], [John] Glenn, and [Gary] Hart, whose ads in 1984 exploited Mondale's vulnerability to the charge that he was the captive of special interests, may have done Mondale a favor since the charges forced him to demonstrate that he had called and would continue to call for sacrifices from every segment of the electorate including those whose endorsements fueled his candidacy. At the same time, these charges against Mondale forced his natural constituencies to accept a fact they might otherwise have rejected—that if they demanded Mondale's public and total embrace of their agendas, that embrace would enfeeble his candidacy and the credibility of their endorsements.

Preventing candidates from using advertising to create a sense of themselves discrepant from who they are and what they have done is the vigilant presence of opponents and the increasingly vigilant presence of the press. [There are numerous] . . . instances in which candidate's words and actions in settings they did not control undermined the crafted images of their ads. So, for example, the image of the sweating, gaunt, pale Nixon of the first debate in 1960 clashed with the polished presence in his ads. Although ads can and have lied, the vigilance of press and opponents makes that increasingly unlikely.

In many ways televised political advertising is the direct descendant of the advertised messages carried in song and on banners, torches, bandannas, and broadsides. Ads continue to ally the candidate with the people, only now that takes the form of showing the candidate pressing the flesh or answering questions from groups of citizens. Candidates continue to digest their messages into slogans, yet these now appear at the end of broadcast ads rather than on banners and torches. Candidates continue to overstate their accomplishments and understate their failures. So, for example, as governor, despite his claims to the contrary, Ronald Reagan did not increase welfare benefits 43%, although he did increase them just as, contrary to his advertising, Andy Jackson had served in one, not two wars.

What differentiates the claims of Jackson's time from those aired today is the role the press has now assumed as monitor of presidential advertising. While the partisan papers controlled by his opponent revealed Jackson's actual war record and noted that his was not the hand that guided the plow, those papers were not a credible source of information for Jackson's likely supporters. By contrast, in the 1980 campaign, credible newspaper articles and network news stories—bearing the imprint of neither party—publicly scrutinized the adequacy of Reagan's claims. The difficulty in relying on news to correct distortions in advertising is, of course, that comparatively few people consume news while many are exposed to ads.

One of the argumentative ploys born in the political and product advertising of the nineteenth century was refined by politicians in the

age of television and then shunted aside by Watergate. By visually associating the favored candidate with pictures of well-fed cattle, happy families, large bundles of grain, and bulging factories, banners and broadsides argued to literate and illiterate alike that this candidate stood for prosperity. The opponent, on the other hand, was visually tied to drawings of starving cattle, poverty-ravished families, empty grain bins, and fireless factories. Some of the associations seemed to have no direct bearing on what sort of president the candidate would make.

Political argument by visual association flowered for the same reason it appeared in product advertising. Initially, advertising for products simply identified the existence, cost, function, and way to obtain the product. As success bred success, products performing the same function proliferated. Distinguishing attributes—some real, some fictional—were sought to persuade customers that one product rather than its twin should be purchased. Van Buren and Harrison were parity products, differentiated by the associations sculpted by their respective campaigns. Since the advertising of the early nineteenth century relied on drawings rather than photographs the range of possible associations was limited only by the artist's imagination.

The wizardry of videotape and film editing did not change the nature of argument from visual association—it simply increased its subtlety. In the process, the evidentiary burden that candidates should assume dropped. So, for example, Goldwater's ads juxtaposed a picture of Billie Sol Estes with scenes of street riots and then intercut a picture of Bobby Baker. Goldwater then appeared on screen to indict the Democrats for their disregard of law, order, and morality. Estes' relation to Baker, the relation of either to the street riots, or the relation among the three and Lyndon Johnson are not explicitly argued.

In 1968 this type of argument reached a new level of complexity in the Republican ad that intercut scenes from the Vietnam War and from the riots outside the Democratic convention with pictures of Hubert Humphrey, including one in which he appears to be smiling. The juxtaposition of highly evocative images invites the audience to impute causality.

The form of argument embodied in this ad is as powerful as it is irrational. It solicits a visceral and not an intellectual response. As a vehicle of attack, this type of ad was vanquished by Watergate because Watergate forced politicians and public to consider what is and is not fair attack in a political campaign. Lurking in [George] McGovern's campaign are the forms of attack ad that will replace it: the personal witness ad and the neutral reporter ad. Both of these mimic some of the features of news. The personal testimony ads consist of actual individuals reporting their opinions of the opposing candidate's performance. They resembled person-in-the-street interviews and are almost a survey; the opinions expressed are not scripted—indeed, their ungrammatical nature underscores their spontaneity. They do not appear to be unfair because, first, we are taught that everyone is entitled to express his or her opinion and, second, these people are voicing opinions that the electorate presumably is disposed to share. In 1976 Ford used this form against Carter; in 1980 Reagan briefly used it against Carter; in both the primaries and general election of 1980 Carter employed it against his rivals. In the early primaries of 1984 Glenn used it against Mondale.

In the neutral reporter spot, an announcer whose delivery is deliberately low key details facts about the opponent. The ad itself rarely draws any conclusion from the data. That task is left to the audience. Ford did this in a 1976 ad comparing Carter's statements in the campaign with his actual record as governor of Georgia. An ad by Carter did the same to Reagan in 1980.

As strange as it may seem since the independent PACs have been roundly criticized for their advertising against Democratic senators, the PAC presidential ads also fall, in the main, in 1980, into the neutral reporter category. A typical one simply quotes a promise by Carter and demonstrates that he had not kept it. The most cogent are those by the National Conservative Political Action Committee that edit from the Carter-Ford debates specific promises by Carter, show him making them, freeze the frame, and print across the screen the evidence establishing that the promise has been broken.

By replacing attack ads that use visual not verbal means to prompt sweeping inferences with attack ads that verbally and visually invite judgments based on verifiable facts, Watergate temporarily transformed a form of presidential attack advertising from an exercise in the prompting of false inferences to an exercise in traditional argument.

Just as political attack advertising survives, but in a circumscribed form, so too the political speech survives, albeit in shortened form, in televised advertising. Contrary to popular belief, the speech remains the staple of paid political broadcasting. There is not a presidential general election campaign in the televised age in which each candidate did not deliver at least two nationally broadcast speeches. In most campaigns far more are given and the candidates deliver short speeches in spot ads as well. Speeches and segments of speeches also recur in telecast campaign biographies.

The reason we mistakenly think the broadcast speech is an object of antiquity is that half hour speeches tend to draw smaller, more highly partisan audiences than spots. Additionally, when a candidate such as Nixon or Ford delivers addresses by radio, he is speaking on a medium to which many of us do not routinely attend. Moreover, we tend not to think of five minute or 60 second statements by the candidate as speeches. Finally, a televised speech by a presidential candidate was more novel in the 1950s than it is now and so we are more likely to have noted and to long remember its occurrence then than now. Still, if judged by number

Two Famous Campaign Ads

Over forty years, many campaign commercials have achieved a certain degree of fame (or infamy). Here are two.

*I*n 1964, President Lyndon Johnson's campaign wanted a message that would reinforce his image as the candidate of peace, and cement in viewers' minds the picture of his opponent, Barry Goldwater, as the candidate of war. As Johnson's aide Bill Myers describes it, Johnson was worried that "Goldwater the radical was becoming Goldwater the respectable as the campaign progressed, and Johnson wanted to remind people of the earlier Goldwater, the man who talked about lobbing nuclear bombs in the men's room of the Kremlin." The result was "Daisy"—a little girl whose image ran only once, but who has earned a permanent place in the annals of American campaign history.

Video	Audio
Camera up on little girl in field, picking petals off a daisy.	Little girl: "One, two, three, four, five, seven, six, six, eight, nine, nine—"
Girl looks up startled; freeze frame on girl; move into extreme close-up of her eye, until screen is black.	Man's voice, very loud as if heard over a loudspeaker at a test site: "Ten, nine, eight, seven, six, five, four, three, two, one—"
Cut to atom bomb exploding. Move into close-up of explosion	Sound of explosion.
	Johnson [voice-over, VO]: "These are the stakes—to make a world in which all of God's children can live, or to go into the dark. We must either love each other, or we must die."
Cut to white letters on black background: Vote for President Johnson on November 3."	Announcer: "Vote for President Johnson on November 3. The stakes are too high for you to stay home."

of minutes on the air in which the candidate is speaking directly to the audience, Reagan's total exceeds Eisenhower's from either 1952 or 1956. If judged by the total number of televised appearances each made speaking directly to the audience, Reagan leads by a substantial margin.

The widespread perception that being able to present broadcast messages persuasively to a mass public would emerge as a criterion governing selection of presidential candidates is not convincingly confirmed from 1952 to 1980. Of the candidates to receive their party's nomina-

Television's ability to influence voters through pictures and emotions, rather than words and ideas, was fully exploited by Richard Nixon's 1972 campaign against George McGovern. The Nixon campaign sought to depict McGovern—whose opposition to the Vietnam War was a major part of his candidacy—as naive in foreign policy, and weak on defense. This campaign ad fit the bill. Note the use of toy soldiers, ships, and planes, which created both a clear visual image and the subtle implication that McGovern was like a child playing with toys; and the dramatic shift at the end to the presidential Nixon aboard a *real* navy vessel.

Video	**Audio**
Camera up on toy soldiers.	Military drumbeat underneath. Announcer [VO]: "The McGovern defense plan. He would cut the Marines by one-third.
Hand sweeps several away.	The Air Force by one-third.
Cut to another group of toy soldiers; again, hand sweeps several away.	
Cut to another group of toy soldiers; again, hand sweeps several away.	He would cut the Navy personnel by one-fourth.
Cut to toy planes; hand removes several.	He would cut interceptor planes by one-half,
Cut to toy ships; hand removes several.	the Navy fleet by one-half, and
Cut to toy carriers. Hand removes several.	carriers from sixteen to six.
Cut to toys in jumble. Camera pans across.	"Senator Hubert Humphrey has this to say about the McGovern proposal: 'It isn't just cutting into the fat. It isn't just cutting into manpower. It's cutting into the very security of this country.' [Music comes in: "Hail to the Chief."]
Cut to Nixon aboard naval ship.	"President Nixon doesn't believe we should play games with our national security. He believes in a strong America to negotiate for peace from strength."
Fade to slide, white letters on black background: "Democrats for Nixon."	

tion since 1952, Kennedy was an adequate speaker, Goldwater and Nixon often excellent, and only Reagan a master. In short, the ability to deliver televised messages artfully, while certainly an asset for those who possess it, has not become so central a qualification for the presidency that it has exiled candidates who lack it.

Another misconception about political advertising holds that spots and paid programming are somehow alien to the political speech, a thing apart, a bad dream, an aberration. An analysis of both the stock campaign speeches and the acceptance addresses of the presidential candidates suggests instead that the advertising is rarely anything but a digest of the speeches being delivered throughout the country. Occasionally, but not often, the candidate will say something important in a stump speech that does not appear in the paid broadcasting. But these things are usually strategic blunders such as Carter's assertion that Reagan will rend the country North from South.

. . . Convention acceptance speeches are a highly reliable predictor of the content of the candidate's ads in the general election. For those who read the campaign's position papers, examine its brochures, and listen to its stump speeches, the ads function as reinforcement. Those who ignore the other campaign-produced materials receive a digest of them in the ads. This is true both of the advertising against the opponent and the advertising supporting the candidate.

The cost of reaching voters through broadcast advertising poses other problems. Since spot advertising is both costly and often the most cost efficient means of reaching a mass of voters, the contemporary reliance on spots means that those who cannot afford to purchase them, with rare exceptions, are denied the ability to have their ideas either heard or taken seriously in presidential primaries.

For these and related reasons, . . . public concern over the nature and influence of political advertising has been rising. Responding to this escalating public concern, legislators drafted or considered drafting bills that can be grouped into three broad categories. The first would have either the public or the radio and TV stations assume the burden of financing some or all of candidate advertising; the second would give candidates attacked by PACs free response time or—regardless of the origin of attack—would give the attacked candidate free response time; the third, still in the talking stage, . . . would promote changes in the form by offering free time to those agreeing to certain formats (e.g., mandate talking head ads) or lengths (e.g., specify a minimum length or make available free time in no less than five minute and half hour blocks).

Underlying the debate over these and like proposals is widening consensus that the electoral process would benefit if the candidates' cost of reaching a mass audience could be reduced; if all bona-fide candidates could be provided with sufficient access to communicate their basic ideas; if politicians made greater use of longer forms of communication and the electorate as a whole attended more readily to such forms; if candidates assumed or could be enticed to assume the obligation of being viewed by the public in forms such as debates that they do not control; if the advantage PACs can bring to a presidential candidate could be countered or muted.

Still, if political advertising did not exist we would have to invent it. Political advertising legitimizes our political institutions by affirming that change is possible within the political system, that the president can effect change, that votes can make a difference. As a result, advertising channels discontent into the avenues provided by the government and acts as a safety valve for pressures that might otherwise turn against the system to demand its substantial modification or overthrow.

Political advertising does this, in part, by underscoring the power of the ballot. Your vote makes a difference, it says, at the same time as its carefully targeted messages imply that the votes that would go to the opponent are best left uncast.

Political ads affirm that the country is great, has a future, is respected. The contest they reflect is over who should be elected, not over whether there should be an election. The very existence of the contest suggests that there is a choice, that the voters' selection of one candidate over the other will make a difference. Ads also define the problems we face and assure us that there are solutions. If there are no solutions, a candidate would speak that truth at great risk.

IV ▌█ ISSUE AND DEBATE: HAS PARTY REFORM BEEN WORTH IT?

In the aftermath of the 1968 election, the Democratic party instituted new rules designed to wrest control of the process from party bosses meeting in the proverbial smoke-filled rooms and open up the nominating process. The new guidelines, proposed by a Democratic task force known as the McGovern-Fraser commission and adopted by the 1972 convention, abolished the winner-take-all system in delegate selection procedures, required proportional representation of women and minorities, and in a variety of other ways encouraged more direct participation of the rank and file in presidential nominations. One clear result of the 1972 reforms was an explosion in the number of states that chose their delegates by direct primary—in theory the most democratic process of delegate selection available.

The first selection, by Kenneth A. Bode and Carol F. Casey, presents a defense of the various reforms enacted by the Democratic party since the late 1960s. Bode and Casey defend the reforms by debunking several myths frequently presented by opponents of the reforms. The second selection, by the political scientist James W. Ceaser, takes a less enthusiastic position toward the reforms.

Questions

1. What are the arguments in favor of party reform? in favor of the direct primary system?

2. Have the reforms of the Democratic party gone too far? Is the party system truly democratic? What reforms might be useful in forming a proper balance between too much control by party elites and too much participation by party rank and file?

YES

8.4 *Party Reform: Revisionism Revised*

Viewed within the context of the time, the eighteen guidelines adopted by the McGovern-Fraser Commission were a moderate response to very real problems within the Democratic party's nominating process. Generally, they sought to apply the routine standards of fairness, due process, and equal protection enjoyed by voters in general elections to the internal decision-making processes of the party. Over time, the reforms have been adopted, codified, and implemented. They have also attracted a not inconsiderable body of critics, many of whom do not know or remember the genuine procedural abuses and abridgement of the democratic process that characterized the party of Lyndon Johnson in 1968. Like every other political reform in this century, party reform involved a certain redistribution of power. It became an extension of the partisan split of 1968 and prolonged the divisiveness of that year.

Kenneth A. Bode and Carol F. Casey   **277**

Among those who were "distributed" out of power, those who argued backwards from outcomes they did not like, and those whose political theories were offended, certain myths about party reform have become conventional wisdom.

Myth No. 1: The reforms were devised by Senator McGovern for his own benefit and for that of the liberal-activist wing of the Democratic party.

A look at the composition of the commission is enough to defuse this myth. Senator McGovern was chosen to chair the commission by Senator Humphrey, who viewed Senator Harold Hughes of Iowa as too liberal and too closely identified with the McCarthy/Kennedy forces. Humphrey directed Senator Fred Harris, then National Democratic Chairman, to appoint McGovern. All appointments to the commission were made by Harris, a Humphrey backer, whose presidential ambitions were then tied to the Humphrey wing of the party. Commission members included three U.S. senators, one U.S. representative, four persons who were serving or had served as state party chairmen or vice-chairmen, one governor, one former governor, three current or past members of the Democratic National Committee, one state senator, one state treasurer, three labor union leaders, and two professors of political science. Overall, the majority of commission members were party regulars; most had supported Humphrey's 1968 presidential candidacy. As for McGovern, he knew no more about the presidential nominating process in fifty different states than did any other U.S. senator and proved to be an independent though somewhat tentative chairman, committed to democracy and fairness in party procedures, but dispositionally prone to compromise if the other side really dug in its heels.

It is conventional wisdom in some quarters that McGovern rigged the rules to his own benefit—some commentators even conjure a more elaborate scenario wherein the ouster of Mayor [Richard] Daley [of Chicago] from the 1972 convention was contrived years in advance—but they offer only their own phantoms for evidence. McGovern won the nomination not because the reforms gave him an edge but because in a span of less than a month he won primaries in New York, South Dakota, Oregon, California, Rhode Island, and New Jersey—all essentially unreformed, winner-take-all primaries conducted under the same rules as in 1968—and won thereby nearly half the votes he carried with him into the convention.

Myth No. 2: The membership of the commission is irrelevant: The important decisions were made by the commission staff—a staff dominated by young McCarthy/Kennedy political activists who had little regard for the Democratic party as an institution.

Consider for a moment what that says about senators like Birch Bayh, Harold Hughes, and George McGovern, about Governor Calvin Rampton of Utah and former Governor LeRoy Collins of Florida, or about politicians as good as Louis Martin, Warren Christopher, Will Davis, Fred Dutton, and George Mitchell, not to mention Adlai Stevenson of Illinois, and about professors as astute as Sam Beer of Harvard and Austin Ranney of Wisconsin. This group was led around by a couple of thirty-year-old political activists and a band of college interns? Although the staff and consultants did formulate the first draft of the guidelines based upon the information collected from seventeen regional hearings and additional research into each state's 1968 delegate selection system, few of the original guidelines remained intact after the commission had finished its deliberations. The staff proposals were debated at the commission's September 1969 meeting. Then the commission's revised guidelines were circulated to more than 3,000 Democrats, drawn from every list then available, for their comments before the final decisions were made in November 1969—after an additional two days of deliberation.

In the main, the commission had a pragmatic bent and a penchant for fairness. Confronted with a mountain of evidence that revealed flaws in the democratic process, they absorbed an overwhelming amount of detail in a short time about the ways fifty-four jurisdictions chose and mandated delegates. They fashioned practical, straightforward remedies.

The commission's most controversial guidelines were those requiring state parties to encourage the representation of women, blacks, and young people on the national convention delegation in reasonable relationship to their presence in the population—otherwise known as the quota system. These were purely the product of the commission itself. The staff draft contained no such guarantees, merely requiring affirmative steps to overcome the effects of past discrimination. The "quota" language grew out of a motion by Professor Austin Ranney, as expanded by Senator Birch Bayh, and adopted by the full commission.

Myth No. 3: The guidelines eliminated party leaders from the national convention delegations, thereby depriving the convention of their judgment and experience.

There is some truth to this charge: The commission did prohibit party committees or party leaders elected before the year of the national presidential nominating convention from selecting delegates, and it did limit selection of delegates by any party committee to not more than 10 percent of the national convention delegation. However, the ban on national convention delegates' being chosen by officials elected in an "untimely" fashion was merely a direct method of implementing the 1968 national convention's mandate; that mandate did not leave much leeway for interpretation. The 1968 convention said that delegates to the next convention had to be selected through "party primary, convention, or committee procedures open to public participation within the calendar year of the National Convention."

Those who argue that the new rules produced a lower-than-usual ratio of party and public officials in convention delegations tend to forget that politicians may have political reasons for avoiding party conventions. The list of those who did not show up at the 1968 convention contains many Democratic luminaries, including nearly all southern House Democrats who wanted to avoid any association with the national ticket. The list was long in 1972, too, in part because big-name Democrats in 1972 made an early swarm to the candidacy of Edmund Muskie. Not only were the big handicappers wrong, but so were the thousands of middle-level party regulars who went along with them and found themselves sidelined for the convention. In other words, the party's establishment was not at Miami Beach because they had backed the wrong horse.

Even so, data from the 1972 CBS convention survey indicate that the notion of the party convention without party leaders is largely the creation of the propagandists. Exactly one quarter of the delegates had held public office at one time or another, 38 percent had held party office, and 50 percent had been party officials at some time in their lives. Again, as evidence that the rules were not the problem, those same rules produced plenty of party leaders at the convention that nominated Governor Jimmy Carter in 1976.

The ignominy visited upon party leaders by the McGovern Commission guidelines was not that they were barred from participation, only that they were required to compete under the same rules as anyone else.

Myth No. 4: Reforms turned the nominating process over to activist elites whose views are unrepresentative of the total electorate, especially in states without primaries.

One of the fundamental objectives of the guidelines was to open the nominating process to broader participation. Particularly in convention states, the reformers were successful. Participation has jumped in every presidential nominating year so that caucus turnout now nearly rivals the average primary vote. Early results from the 1980 contest showed this trend: the Iowa Democratic precinct caucuses attracted nearly three times as many voters as they had in 1976. In Maine, turnout at the 1980 town caucuses was seven times as great as it was in 1976. Turnout has increased because Democrats have become more familiar with caucus procedures and because state Democratic parties have fulfilled their obligations of having published party rules, setting uniform times and dates for the first stage of the delegate selection process, and giving publicity to those events.

Critics, of course, contend that caucus participants are elites who do not represent the broader base of the Democratic party. Studies have shown, however, that those who attend caucuses are no more "elite" than those who vote in primaries. In both cases, persons with higher income and greater education are more likely to turn out. The same, in fact, is true in general elections. The reform rules are not to blame for the fact that participants in the presidential nominating process do not mirror the socioeconomic characteristics of the electorate as a whole. That is and has been true in every election held in the United States. The reform rules were designed merely to remove barriers to participation and give everyone equal access, not to guarantee advantages to any segment of the Democratic electorate.

Oddly enough, many of the persons who cry "elitism" also denigrate the party's affirmative action requirements as a quota system. The purpose of the outreach efforts imposed on state parties is to bring those groups that traditionally have low rates of political participation—blacks, Hispanics, and youth—into the active party ranks. Affirmative action (if it works) can only make the nominating process less elite.

What alternative do the "antielitists" offer? Basically, they suggest replacing one elite with another. Rather than permitting too much rank-and-file influence, they propose that elected Democratic party and public officials do a larger

Reprinted by permission of UFS, Inc.

measure of the choosing. The professional functionaries of a party, notes Professor Bickel, maintain its continuity and play a role in its identity. Bickel goes on:

> The party's professional cadres should, no doubt, have a voice. The professionals are, if nothing else, a faction that deserves representation. Surely it is also sound institutional policy to reward their services with a measure of influence. Their greatest interest is the party's own institutional interest in winning—at least it is vouchsafed to them to see that interest over the long term. But if they lend the party its character of an "organized appetite" as Felix Frankfurter once wrote, their appetite is sometimes keener for power in the organization than for organizing to secure the power of government.

It is also said the party professionals make well-informed and sophisticated judgments, tending to choose the abler rather than the more popular or glamorous candidate. When party leaders substitute their judgment for the popular view registered in primaries, however, they do not always produce winners. Stevenson was the leaders' choice over Kefauver, the primaries' choice, in 1952, as was Humphrey in 1968. Both lost.

Myth No. 5: Reforms spawned primaries.

Some even argue more specifically that "the controversial rules changes that required a state's delegation to include minorities, young people, and women in proportion to their respective numbers in the state led directly to this proliferation of primaries. State party leaders fearing challenges to the makeup of their delegations, opted for primaries whose results conventions have traditionally been reluctant to upset."

It is true that after the guidelines were adopted, many states enacted presidential primary laws. It is simplistic and inaccurate, however, to say that primaries were adopted *because* of the guidelines. Historically, the result of public dissatisfaction with acrimonious, divisive nominating contests has been the adoption of new primaries. Like it or not, primaries draw a favorable response from the general public. After the bitter Taft-Roosevelt battle in 1912, fourteen states instituted presidential primaries, bringing the total to twenty-six—a record that was not matched until 1976. After the Stevenson-Kefauver contest in 1952, states once again looked toward presidential primaries as a means of giving greater public legitimacy to the selection of delegates. Thus, the adoption of new primaries after 1968 is in keeping with the flux of American political history. By the time the McGovern Commission met for its first deliberative session in 1969, new presidential primaries had been introduced in nine state legislatures. Before the guidelines had been adopted, the number grew to thirteen.

The number of primaries has fluctuated in the past and is likely to do so again. The primaries adopted during the Progressive period were in response to a public desire to wrest control of nominations from the party bosses. Often the primary laws did just the opposite—maintaining control in the hands of party leaders, while providing the illusion of popular participation. In time, dissatisfaction with the way the primaries worked led to their abandonment.

There were a number of reasons why states opted for presidential primaries in 1972 and thereafter. In Maryland, for example, it was merely a case of returning to their usual system. Dismayed that George Wallace had won 43 percent of the 1964 presidential primary vote against LBJ stand-in Senator Daniel Brewster, and fearful that the Alabama governor could equal or better his showing in 1968, the Maryland Democratic party leadership abandoned the primary in favor of a committee selection system for 1968; they reinstituted the primary for 1972. In some instances, primaries are enacted to benefit a potential presidential candidate. The Texas legislature adopted a primary law when Senator Bentsen threw his hat in the presidential ring. This primary was so obviously a vehicle for Bentsen that it carried a self-destruct clause after 1976. The North Carolina primary was to provide a vehicle for Terry Sanford. Georgia became a primary state when Jimmy Carter sought the nomination. In other instances, income and attention are motivating factors: The candidates, their campaigns, and the press who cover them are known to spend a great deal of money in "crucial" primary states. Vermont adopted a primary in the hope of a financial "spillover" from New Hampshire and Massachusetts. States established primaries in cooperation with each other to set up mini-regional primaries that would focus media and candidate attention more sharply on their regional problems. Because New Hampshire would not yield its "first-in-the-nation" status, the New England regional primary never became a reality. In 1976, a de facto western primary occurred when Idaho, Nevada, and Oregon all held their primaries on the same day. In 1980, the Southern regional primary occurred on March 11 when Alabama, Florida, and Georgia Democrats all went to the polls.

In 1972, New Mexico designed a presidential primary—distributing its convention delegates between the top two vote-getters—and scheduled it for the same day as the California primary, hoping for some attention. Most of the state's leading Democrats lined up behind Senator Humphrey. By primary day, the Democratic contests in California had boiled down to a Humphrey versus McGovern shoot-out for that state's winner-take-all lode of 271 delegates. Neither the candidates nor the press bothered with New Mexico. McGovern came in first and Wallace second in the voting; most of the party's leaders stayed home, and the next time around the state abandoned its primary.

Aware that many new primaries were resting in legislative hoppers around the country, the McGovern Commission went out of its way to stress that it had no preference between primary and convention systems, and that, run properly, either system could provide an open, democratic selection contest. It was no easier to comply with the guidelines by adopting a presidential primary law than it was to amend a party constitution to bring a state convention process into conformity with the rules. Using state law as an excuse for noncompliance did not protect a state, as Mayor Daley learned at the 1972 Democratic National Convention. The 9–0 Supreme Court decision in *Cousins* v. *Wigoda* underscores both the national convention's willingness to overturn primary results supported by state law and its right to do so.

In 1980, for the first time in more than a decade, caucus procedures are beginning to get a good press. Voters have discovered that the process is not intimidating and caucus states—at least the early ones—have begun to attract the kind of attention that once made primaries so appealing to party leaders who wanted a larger spot on the national tote board. There is no guarantee of it, of course, but we may be on the verge of another period when the appeal of primaries begins to wane and a more even balance with caucus systems is established.

In any case, the new, post-1968 primaries have assimilated reform requirements that make them more representative of primary voters and of Democratic party members. Presidential candidates now receive national convention delegates in proportion to the votes they win in the primary. Now, only Democrats can vote in Democratic presidential primaries. When voters cast their ballots for candidates seeking to be convention delegates, they know which presidential aspirant the candidate supports. These are significant accomplishments when measured against the type of primaries that were held in 1968 and before.

Myth No. 6: Proportional representation is a notion of European origin that will fragment the American party system, exacerbate divisions, prolong the nominating contest, and make unity more difficult.

The early winnowing of the field in 1976 and the subsequent unity behind Jimmy Carter's nomination took much of the air out of this balloon. Common sense suggests that those who lose a fight fairly will be more likely to rally around the eventual winner than those who lose because they think the deck was stacked against them. Contrast 1976 with 1968.

Myths such as these have clouded a thoughtful evaluation of what party reform did, in fact, accomplish. The rules provided a convenient battleground for a spirited factional dispute within the party. The debate seemed to encourage exaggerations like the current notion that the reforms have made the contest so long and exhausting that only candidates without jobs can compete—witness Jimmy Carter and Ronald Reagan in 1976; George Bush, John Connally, and Reagan again in 1980. Candidates with a lot of time on their hands could do well under the old system, too, as Richard Nixon proved in the two years before 1968. And, as far back as 1959–1960, John Kennedy's attendance record in the Senate got no gold stars.

It is also said that the addition of twenty new presidential primaries has weakened the party system and that primaries are a bypass mechanism that saps the parties' vitality. If this is true (which it may not be), then the place to look to remedy the weakness is at the base of the pyramid where tens of thousands of municipal, county, district, and state primaries determine nearly every nomination of every party in the country.

Parties are getting weaker. Anyone would concede as much. But they have been eroding over the course of the past century, as David Broder points out in his perceptive study, *The Party's Over*. Public financing of elections, the movement of candidates away from political parties as organizing mechanisms to garner support in the electorate, the influence of television on our politics and its use in supplanting party organizations in get-out-the-vote drives—

these, much more than the addition of a few presidential primaries, have been responsible for the weakening of the party system over the past decade.

After the revisionist bombast is cleared away, a few things become clear. First, the original McGovern reforms have undergone two lengthy, thoughtful reviews by follow-up party commissions not predisposed to accept the reforms as gospel. There have been some modifications, some tinkering, but the basic concepts that guided the original reform proposals have been endorsed by both commissions. Ninety percent of the original guidelines have been accepted and codified into party rules around the country. In 1980 we may see the second consecutive hard-fought presidential nomination conferred without procedural bitterness—not a bad accomplishment after 1968 and 1972. In other words, the basic principles of the reform movement have been accepted, and they are with us to stay.

Second, the people seem to be going for the reforms. Participation is up in both parties. In an era of cynicism about parties, a *Los Angeles Times* poll (December 16–18, 1979) found that 70 percent of Americans nationwide said the nominating system was "basically sound," compared with 62 percent for the political system as a whole and only 49 percent for the judicial system.

Finally, those who condemn the party reforms as too radical must at least concede that they headed off worse possibilities. Public opinion polls throughout the late 1960s and 1970s showed whopping majorities of Americans cynical about political parties, politicians, and institutions, and strongly in favor of a national primary, abolition of the electoral college, and establishing a binding national initiative.

The survival of political institutions lies in their adaptability. Party reform is the latest evidence of that.

Kenneth A. Bode and Carol F. Casey   **283**

NO

8.5 Reforming the Reforms _____

James W. Ceaser

Proponents of direct democracy, from Progressives to the New Politics advocates, never accepted . . . [the idea of] moderation. They have been committed to just the opposite: where defenders of the convention and mixed systems have spoken of imposing restraints on new movements, proponents of direct democracy have spoken of stimulating them. Their bias has been toward progress and new ideas. As James Sundquist has written:

> The reforms of the twentieth century have gone a long way toward ensuring that whenever the country polarizes on an issue, the polarization will be quickly and faithfully reflected by the parties. . . . This prospect will encourage more politicians to take their chances with extremism, giving it even greater potential. This is the hazard of an open party system.

The modern reform movement was predicated on the assumption that the major parties alone bore the responsibility for promoting change and that third-party activity was ineffectual and suspect. The great battles over policy and direction, in this view, must take place within the major parties, and the major parties, therefore, have a quasi-public obligation to represent fairly all elements within the electorate. (This notion seems to conflict, however, with the Democratic party's goal of limiting primary and caucus participants to party members.)

The reformers' case against the efficacy of minor parties rested on two dissimilar concerns. First, in 1968, minor parties faced tremendous legal hurdles in securing access to the ballot in many states. These hurdles consisted of inordinately high petition requirements—in some instances over 10 percent of a state's voters—and early filing deadlines. Ironically, these hurdles were an indirect consequence of the re-

forms of the late nineteenth century, which, to prevent corruption and fraud in voting, gave to the states the power not simply for the administrative purpose of running effective elections but also for the promotion of the "public" function of protecting two-party competition. The norm of two-party competition that Van Buren favored was converted into a *legal* doctrine, as states attempted to limit minor party access to the ballots. Since 1968, however, this situation has changed dramatically through intervention by the federal courts. George Wallace successfully challenged an Ohio law that protected two-party competition, and in 1980, John Anderson managed to lower further the legal barriers to entrance of minor parties or independent candidates.

Today, the influence of the legal system on third parties is, therefore, very different than it was in 1968. Minor parties, including those like John Anderson's that form at the very last moment, enjoy much greater access to the electoral process. Minor parties perhaps suffer a slight disadvantage in fundraising in comparison to their situation before the last decade [the 1970s], in that they must now raise funds under stringent campaign contributions laws without receiving any public assistance. If, however, a minor party obtains over 5 percent of the nationwide vote, as John Anderson's independent campaign did in 1980, it receives a pro-rata share of public funding after the election and automatically is given the same share in the next election. The curious effect of this legal intervention in the regulation of parties may be to provide artificial support for certain minor parties after they have served their immediate purpose of registering discontent.

The reformers' second point of attack on the efficacy of minor parties rests on the observation that they have not managed to win the presidency, or even threaten seriously to do so, since the formation of the Republican party before the Civil War. Dismissing third parties on this ground, however, may well be a case of confusing cause with effect. Third parties may have been "incapable" of mounting a serious threat, not because it has been impossible for them to do so but rather because the major parties have managed to remain responsive to the major currents of American politics. Indeed, the development or threat of development of minor parties has helped to force the major parties to remain responsive to public issues. Under this understanding of the electoral system, therefore, the success of the major parties in maintaining their duopoly has been the result of their own efforts. Had both these parties become rigid or unresponsive, they could have been—or could still be—replaced, even as the new Social Democratic party in Great Britain now threatens to replace the Labour party. To be sure, third parties begin at a disadvantage because of their organizational resources and the absence of an existing pool of partisan adherents, but these need not be insuperable obstacles. In fact, conditions today make it much easier in both of these respects for third parties because organization in an age of the mass media counts for less than it did in the past and because there are many more self-described independents in the electorate.

The reformers' insistence, therefore, that the burden of handling the function of choice and change rests exclusively with the major parties is an exaggeration. To the extent that it constituted a valid claim in 1968, because of existing legal barriers, it is much less so today after the Court decisions of the past decade; and further changes in the law could easily remove any unfair disadvantages for minor parties. In short, an open and democratic electoral process—that is, a process open to third parties—can serve as an alternative to direct democracy within the parties as a means of promoting the broad objective of maintaining a capacity for choice and change in the electoral system.

There seems to be little question, however, that the reform movement has opened the major political parties and thereby the political system as a whole to a *more* rapid penetration of new movements. At a minimum, the primary path to the nomination has provided greater access to candidates who seek to redefine what the parties stand for, and in recent nomination contests, many aspirants have run on programs that allegedly have been designed to build fundamentally new coalitions. Although such attempts may have reflected in part the condition of electoral instability caused by the decline of the once solid New Deal coalition, they probably also follow from the very nature of the new system. To justify their quest for the office, candidates frequently must present themselves as offering a new formula for American politics that will bring together previously unconnected elements of the populace. Offering oneself merely as the traditional standard-bearer for the party may not be sufficient. This incentive to attempt to form new coalitions can, of course, be destabilizing, eroding the very stability of a party that enables it to *sustain* change over the course of several elections. The result could be a greater appearance of change with less capacity in the political system to effectuate it.

Yet the experience since the reforms were initiated is sufficient to demonstrate that these "new" movements need not always be issue-directed or ideological. In 1976, Jimmy Carter won the nomination by blurring many of the issues and by emphasizing broad themes like efficiency and honesty in government. The success of his appeal not only surprised ideological liberals within the Democratic party but also caused them to reconsider whether "openness" in the nominating process actually does support more choice and change. The limited number of cases to analyze makes generalization very hazardous, but the logic of the system seems clear: The new system is indeed more open to new movements or moods, which, depending on the nature of the times, may or may not be ideological; in some years, therefore, there may be more ideological choice than the previous system tended to promote, but in other years, perhaps, much less.

Finally, the quality of "moderation" associated with the previous nominating systems was a result not only of a representative decision-making process but also of the particular characteristics of American party organizations since the 1830s. Although by no means devoid of ideological commitment, the organizations were often dominated by persons concerned with victory and with maintaining jobs and patronage for the local party. This incentive gave the leaders of these organizations a certain pragmatic cast of mind, known in the literature of political science by the term "professionalism." Yet party organizations need not be led by professionals in this sense. In many other countries, the most ideological individuals are often the ones who join the parties and dominate their internal organizations. In Britain, for example, the current leaders of the local organizations of the Labour party are decidedly more left of center than either the members of the party in Parliament or their voters; and as they struggle to gain more influence in the leadership selection process, they show every indication of attempting to force their ideology on the British people.

Much the same concern has been voiced about the possible character of American parties in the future. Indeed, as we have seen, there are some today who favor the primaries, not because they stimulate more choice and change, but rather because they moderate the kind of choice in comparison with what it would be if modern party organizations select the nominees in a representative decisionmaking process. In this view, modern party organizations in America, like some of their counterparts in Europe, are likely to be dominated by ideological amateurs, and the people are needed to "save" the parties from their own organization leaders.

Accordingly, legislators today must be certain not just to establish certain institutional forms based on past performance but to ask what goals or ends those forms will promote under present circumstances. Judgments of a practical sort must be made. While the evidence

today clearly suggests that American parties will never again be dominated by the kind of professionals who dominated them in past years, there is no reason yet to think that future representative processes must inevitably be dominated by ideological amateurs. Contrary to the situation in some European systems, there is less of a tradition of ideological politics in America; and the large number of electoral offices at the state and local levels almost certainly will ensure a more pragmatic point of view among the ranks of the party members. If they are ever given the responsibility for making the nominating decisions, so-called amateurs might quickly begin to behave more like professionals.

Influence on the Governing Process

The emphasis that the reformers placed on the functions of legitimacy, choice, and change led them to ignore a connection that past legislators considered fundamental—the influence of the nominating system on the character of presidential leadership and on the relationship between the presidency and the Congress. The nominating system does not, of course, have as direct or as profound an influence on these matters as the constitutional provisions and laws that set forth the basic outlines of presidential and congressional power; but the nominating system can have a significant effect on these institutions, complementing or undoing institutional tendencies that have been established to govern their operation. One of the legislators' goals, accordingly, should be to devise a nominating system that promotes—or at any rate does not detract from—these objectives.

For the Founding Fathers, this goal took precedence over all the others. They viewed the selection process as the means and governing as the end. Each aspect of the selection process was designed to complement a governmental objective. To ensure the president's independence from Congress, the Founding Fathers provided the executive with a base of electoral support apart from the legislature; to maintain the president's partial distance from the immediate pressure of public opinion as well as to remove the possibility of an extraordinary claim for enhanced extraconstitutional power, they devised an indirect electoral scheme of selection by special representatives; and to keep the president above factions or preexisting electoral cleavages, they sought to prevent the formation of political parties and establish a nonpartisan electoral system. As events turned out, some of these planned influences of the selection process proved to be the least durable of all the institutional tendencies that the Founders tried to establish, but they serve nonetheless to illustrate a method by which legislators can approach institutional reform in this area.

For those who established the doctrine of party competition in the 1820s and the 1830s, the influence of the nominating system on the governing process was perhaps not as important a question as was regulating the pace of choice and change and controlling candidate ambition. Yet these legislators were still concerned with such problems in the governing process as the decline of party competition along with nomination by the congressional caucus, which threatened the president's base of electoral independence. The combination of renewed party competition and nomination by convention removed that threat. These legislators were also looking for a mechanism that could provide a connective link between the president and Congress at the level of policymaking without undermining the essential constitutional prerogatives of either institution. The political party could perform this function by serving as an extraconstitutional instrument for assembling authority in a system in which separation of powers made coordination a difficult problem. Indeed, not only did parties provide a link between the president and Congress, but they also linked both to an organizational network that operated throughout the nation. This network provided a potential source of support for national leaders, even while it sometimes limited their discretion. Curiously, it was Woodrow Wilson who best articulated this contribution of the parties:

[Power] can be solidified and drawn to the system only by the external authority of party, an organization outside the government and independent of it, . . . a body that has no constitutional cleavages and is free to tip itself into legislative and executive functions alike by its systematic control of the personnel of all branches of the government.

Despite this praise for parties, Wilson, along with the Progressives, sought to destroy the parties, at least in their existing form, in order to raise the presidency to a new and higher plane in the American political system. Whatever the benefits of the parties, the Progressives believed that they extracted far too high a price in terms of corruption, localism, and weak presidential candidates. Like the Founding Fathers, Wilson and many of the Progressives saw clearly the relationship between the selection system and the governing process, although they appeared to go much further than the Founders in thinking that the presidency could be *changed* in large measure through the influence of the selection process. In the Progressives' view, a stronger presidency would emerge—and one less tied to pluralistic interests—by eliminating the traditional party and allowing presidential aspirants to appeal directly to the people. The president's new base of support would be public opinion, a force that would either allow a president to "compel" congressional acquiescence without a party (the nonpartisan Progressive vision) or else enable the president to control his party (the partisan Progressive vision). Under this system, presidential leadership would be the force that would replace parties and combine the various power centers in a separation-of-powers system.

Modern reformers, who began their call for institutional change at the very moment when doubts were surfacing about an imperial presidency, were obviously in no position to assert that the nominating process should be used to strengthen the president's power. Indeed, as observed, the reform movement offered little systematic analysis of their proposed changes on the governing process. The effects were implicit. At least for the early New Politics adherents of 1968, the overriding purpose of the selection system as it influenced the governing process was to empower leadership that would be responsive to public opinion, which at the time was conceived of as on the verge of being radical and change-oriented. The electoral system, in other words, was designed to promote populistic leadership, a tendency foreshadowed by the Progressives but advocated with less restraint by modern democratic enthusiasts.

Evaluation of the Influence of the Governing Process

The function of the nominating system's influence on the governing process was "rediscovered" by political scientists during the administration of President Carter. Because of this recent rediscovery and the limited time frame in which analysis was conducted, political scientists faced the problem of disentangling the influences of the nominating system from other influences that operated during the same period. Some, unfortunately, may have overinterpreted the effects of reform, attributing virtually every failure of the Carter administration to the institutional decline of parties and ignoring personality and ideological factors, such as President Carter's clearly "non-political" approach to governing and the lack of consensus in the Democratic party. To avoid this error here, it is only necessary to recall that this discussion refers to institutional tendencies and, in the case of the effects of the nominating process, to second-order or indirect consequences.

The absence of a representative decision-making process has weakened one source of the president's support from other political leaders, including members of Congress. Because these leaders have no direct say in choosing their nominee, they are less likely to feel a bond of commitment or the need to cooperate. They are in no sense accountable for the choice of the nominee, as they had no voice in his selection. Yet it is precisely the support from these leaders

that a president needs to govern effectively. Public opinion is no substitute for this support. Quite the contrary, public opinion as a resource of extraconstitutional presidential authority has often proven to be a weak and fickle reed on which to rest political power. As Richard Rose, a well-known political scientist, has written:

> To become a party standard-bearer, an American politician must first of all *divide* his party by contesting primaries against fellow partisans. . . . Presidential candidates may spend years in building a political following, but it is first and foremost a *personal* following. . . . Rootless candidates risk becoming rootless in government. Insofar as a politician concentrates his attention upon the relatively contentless concerns of campaigning, distancing himself from any organization besides his own personal following, he loses a stable commitment of party loyalty to invoke against the sub-governments of Washington.

The current method of pursuing presidential nominations encourages a form of campaigning and leadership that emphasizes divisions, since it is often only by dividing that candidates can activate a popular following and differentiate themselves from their opponents. In comparison to previous selection systems, the current system creates more incentives to promote the differences among factions and fewer incentives to weld these factions together into broad and relatively harmonious coalitions. If the great challenge of governing in American politics requires a curbing of the "mischiefs of faction," then the new system has made the president's task only that much more difficult. Coalitions today, when they form, are created in spite of, and not because of, the current nominating system.

The long and exposed presidential campaign also tends to encourage a kind of popular leadership that promises too much to too many groups and that relies on slogans to excite popular constituencies. These practices may have something to do with the rise of expectations that have been engendered by presidential campaigns, a rise that is perhaps inevitable where so much weight is placed on courting popular favor. Paradoxically, the need to court public favor, especially on a state-by-state basis, may lead to even greater pluralistic pressures and concessions to various interest groups. According to one political scientist, Jeffrey Fischel, the number of specific promises that candidates make over the course of the campaign has increased dramatically over the past two decades. These special appeals are often made in a particular speech or a specialized advertisement, whereas the general appeals made in higher visibility communication media tend to be more image-conscious or ideological. The very problems of demagogic leadership and purely image appeals that Van Buren identified in 1824 may now be endemic to the modern selection process and may in turn have created problematic models of political leadership that influence the public's conception of the presidency.

Finally, there is the effect of the length of the campaign on the governing process. While an election campaign is in progress, and while the public begins to focus its attention on the prospect of a change in power, "normal" politics is put into a state of suspension. Power is partially drained of its steady constitutional basis, as everyone begins to think of the possibility of a new administration with new programs. The nominating process does not, of course, change the date of the election itself, but by intruding the active campaign for the presidency much earlier into the final year of a president's term, it changes the climate in which a president must attempt to govern. For an incumbent seeking renomination, the problem is even greater. The same adverse side effects of "incumbent politics" in presidential campaigns that were identified by Alexis de Tocqueville long ago are now pushed back earlier into the term of each president who is challenged for his party's nomination:

[During the campaign] the President, for his part, is absorbed in the task of defending himself. He no longer rules in the interest of the state, but in that of his own reelection; he prostrates himself before the majority, and often, instead of resisting their passions as duty requires, he hastens to anticipate their caprices.

The length of the current process also poses a serious problem in the case of a president who is popular within his own party, but who, for personal reasons, might wish to retire after one term. To respect the "spirit" of the process as it now exists, the president would be obliged to declare his intention not to run at least nine months before his term expires, in order to allow candidates to engage in primaries and caucuses. Such a step, however, might not be in the interest either of the president or the presidency, for the president would forfeit an important source of his authority—the belief on the part of others that he might be in office for the next term. This problem is one that has never been discussed, perhaps because the chance of its occurring seems so unlikely. Yet it represents more than a hypothetical possibility, and it would leave a president with the uncomfortable choice either of sacrificing needlessly part of his authority or engaging deliberately in an act of dissimulation by insisting, up to the time just before the convention, that he intended to run again.

Many have defended the reforms in the nominating process on the grounds of their greater fairness and openness, but few who have studied their effects on the governing process have rendered a favorable verdict. Whatever modest gains the new system may have brought us in legitimacy, they do not seem to have been worth the price that has been paid in effective governing.

_____*Chapter 9*

Interest Groups

*I*nterest groups play a vital role in American politics. Along with political parties, they are the most important way that Americans organize to express their views to and make their demands on government. Interest groups play vital roles in the electoral arena and in government policymaking. They are active in all three branches of the federal government and in the states.

Interest groups are by no means free of controversy. Government responsiveness to interest groups, if carried too far, can lead to the triumph of special interests at the expense of the public interest. Group involvement in support of particular candidates can be a legitimate way for citizens to advance their interests, but such activity can all too easily cross the line into influence peddling and vote buying.

Above all, the controversy over interest groups rests on a critical debate in modern political science: whether the clash of group interests, if fought on a level playing field where all groups are represented fairly and equitably, will inevitably or even generally result in the victory of the public interest. Those who believe that the public interest is, in effect, the sum of the private interests advocate a large number of effective interest groups. Those on the other side look for ways to limit the power and influence of interest groups in order to allow the public interest to emerge.

This chapter examines the roles played by interest groups in American politics, with particular attention to the dramatic changes in interest group activity over recent decades. It also probes a deeper question: What role should interest groups play in American politics, and should their role be expanded or diminished in order to serve the public interest?

Chapter Questions

1. Is a system of interest group politics consistent with the idea of democracy? Reread Madison's *Federalist No. 10* and *Federalist No. 51* (selections 2.1 and 2.4) as you consider your answer.

2. Why are interest groups important in the American political system? What roles do they play? How have the roles of interest groups changed in the past several decades?

I THE CLASSIC TEXTS

What exactly is an interest group? What is a public interest group, and what distinguishes it from a special interest group? Before examining interest groups in any detail, it is essential to have an accurate understanding of the meaning of these terms and the nature of interest group politics.

The following selection presents a classic explanation and description of interest group politics. Central to Schattschneider's understanding of interest groups are their size and their narrow focus. Interest groups, by definition, are small and specialized. As such, they can be distinguished from political parties, which, to be effective, must be both large and broad based. A political system that encourages the formation of interest groups, and responds to their arguments, demands, and pressures, will of necessity differ from one in which citizens express their views and make their demands felt through the political parties.

Since Schattschneider's book was published in the early 1960s, American politics has, if anything, become even more focused around interest groups (see selection 9.2). The role of parties as effective mechanisms for transmitting the demands of citizens to their elected representatives has correspondingly diminished.

Schattschneider's analysis, though a generation old, remains an excellent introduction to the theoretical underpinnings of interest group politics.

Questions

1. What characteristics distinguish a special interest group from a public interest group? Is this distinction meaningful, in Schattschneider's view?

2. What would one expect to be the logical result of a political system in which small interest groups dominate? What are the implications of such a system for the role of political parties? for the structure of government institutions? for the nature of public policy?

9.1 The Scope and Bias of the Pressure System

E. E. Schattschneider

Pressure groups have played a remarkable role in American politics, but they have played an even more remarkable role in American political theory. Considering the political condition of the country in the first third of the twentieth century, it was probably inevitable that the discussion of special-interest pressure groups should lead to development of "group" theories of politics in which an attempt is made to explain everything in terms of group activity, i.e., an attempt to formulate a universal group theory. Since one of the best ways to test an idea is to ride it into the ground, political theory has unquestionably been improved by the heroic attempt to create a political universe revolving about the group. Now that we have a number of drastic statements of the group theory of politics pushed to a great extreme, we ought to be able to see what the limitations of the idea are.

Political conditions in the first third of the present century were extremely hospitable to the idea. The role of business in the strongly sectional Republican system from 1896 to 1932 made the dictatorship of business seem to be a part of the eternal order of things. Moreover, the regime as a whole seemed to be so stable that questions about the survival of the American community did not arise. The general interests of the community were easily overlooked under these circumstances.

Nevertheless, in spite of the excellent and provocative scholarly work done by Beard, Latham, Truman, Leiserson, Dahl, Lindblom, Laski, and others, the group theory of politics is beset with difficulties. The difficulties are theoretical, growing in part out of sheer overstatements of the idea and in part out of some confusion about the nature of modern government.

One difficulty running through the literature of the subject results from the attempt to explain *everything* in terms of the group theory. On general grounds it would be remarkable indeed if a single hypothesis explained everything about so complex a subject as American politics. Other difficulties have grown out of the fact that group concepts have been stated in terms so universal that the subject seems to have no shape or form.

The question is: Are pressure groups the universal basic ingredient of all political situations, and do they explain everything? To answer this question it is necessary to review a bit of rudimentary political theory.

Two modest reservations might be made merely to test the group dogma. We might clarify our ideas if (1) we explore more fully the possibility of making a distinction between public-interest groups and special-interest groups and (2) if we distinguished between organized and unorganized groups. These reservations do not disturb the main body of group theory, but they may be useful when we attempt to define general propositions more precisely. If both of these distinctions can be validated, we may get hold of something that has scope and limits and is capable of being defined. The awkwardness of a discussion of political phenomena in terms of universals is that the subject has no beginning or end; it is impossible to distinguish one subject from another or to detect the bias of the forces involved because scope and bias are aspects of limitations of the subject. It cannot really be said that we have seen a subject until we have seen its outer limits and thus are able to draw a line between one subject and another.

We might begin to break the problem into its component parts by exploring the distinction between public and private interests. If we can validate this distinction, we shall have established one of the boundaries of the subject.

As a matter of fact, the distinction between *public* and *private* interests is a thoroughly respectable one; it is one of the oldest known to political theory. In the literature of the subject, the public interest refers to general or common interests shared by all or by substantially all members of the community. Presumably no community exists unless there is some kind of community of interests, just as there is no nation without some notion of national interests. If it is really impossible to distinguish between private and public interests, the group theorists have produced a revolution in political thought so great that it is impossible to foresee its consequences. For this reason the distinction ought to be explored with great care.

At a time when nationalism is described as one of the most dynamic forces in the world, it should not be difficult to understand that national interests actually do exist. It is necessary only to consider the proportion of the American budget devoted to national defense to realize that the common interest in national survival is a great one. Measured in dollars this interest is one of the biggest things in the world. Moreover, it is difficult to describe this interest as special. The diet on which the American leviathan feeds is something more than a jungle of disparate special interests. In the literature of democratic theory the body of common agreement found in the community is known as the "consensus," without which it is believed that no democratic system can survive.

The reality of the common interest is suggested by demonstrated capacity of the community to survive. There must be something that holds people together.

In contrast with the common interests are the special interests. The implication of this term is that these are interests shared by only a few people or a fraction of the community; they *exclude* others and may be *adverse* to them. A special interest is exclusive in about the same way as private property is exclusive. In a complex society it is not surprising that there are some interests that are shared by all or substantially all members of the community and some interests that are not shared so widely. The distinction is useful precisely because conflicting claims are made by people about the nature of their interests in controversial matters.

Perfect agreement within the community is not always possible, but an interest may be said to have become public when it is shared so widely as to be substantially universal. Thus, the difference between 99 percent agreement and perfect agreement is not so great that it becomes necessary to argue that all interests are special, that the interests of the 99 percent are as special as the interests of the 1 percent. For example, the law is probably doing an adequate job of defining the public interest in domestic tranquility despite the fact that there is nearly always one dissenter at every hanging. That is, the law defines the public interest in spite of the fact that there may be some outlaws.

Since one function of theory is to explain reality, it is reasonable to add that it is a good deal easier to explain what is going on in politics by making a distinction between public and private interests than it is to attempt to explain *everything* in terms of special interests. The attempt to prove that all interests are special forces us into circumlocutions such as those involved in the argument that people have special interests in the common good. The argument can be made, but it seems a long way around to avoid a useful distinction.

What is to be said about the argument that the distinction between public and special interests is "subjective" and is therefore "unscientific"?

All discussion of interests, special as well as general, refers to the motives, desires, and intentions of people. In this sense the whole discussion of interests is subjective. We have made progress in the study of politics because people have observed some kind of relation between the political behavior of people and certain wholly impersonal data concerning their ownership of property, income, economic status, professions, and the like. All that we know about interests, private as well as public, is based on inferences of this sort. Whether the distinction in any given case is valid depends on the evidence and on the kinds of inferences drawn from the evidence.

The only meaningful way we can speak of

the interests of an association like the National Association of Manufacturers is to draw inferences from the fact that the membership is a select group to which only manufacturers may belong and to try to relate that datum to what the association does. The implications, logic, and deductions are persuasive only if they furnish reasonable explanations of the facts. That is all that any theory about interests can do. It has seemed persuasive to students of politics to suppose that manufacturers do not join an association to which only manufacturers may belong merely to promote philanthropic or cultural or religious interests, for example. The basis of selection of the membership creates an inference about the organization's concerns. The conclusions drawn from this datum seem to fit what we know about the policies promoted by the association; i.e., the policies seem to reflect the exclusive interests of manufacturers. The method is not foolproof, but it works better than many other kinds of analysis and is useful precisely because special-interest groups often tend to rationalize their special interests as public interests.

Is it possible to distinguish between the "interests" of the members of the National Association of Manufacturers and the members of the American League to Abolish Capital Punishment? The facts in the two cases are not identical. First, *the members of the A.L.A.C.P. obviously do not expect to be hanged.* The membership of the A.L.A.C.P. is not restricted to persons under indictment for murder or in jeopardy of the extreme penalty. *Anybody* can join A.L.A.C.P. Its members oppose capital punishment, although they are not personally likely to benefit by the policy they advocate. The inference is therefore that the interest of the A.L.A.C.P. is not adverse, exclusive, or special. It is not like the interest of the Petroleum Institute in depletion allowances.

Take some other cases. The members of the National Child Labor Committee are not children in need of legislative protection against exploitation by employers. The members of the World Peace Foundation apparently want peace, but in the nature of things they must want peace for everyone because no group can be at peace while the rest of the community is at war. Similarly, even if the members of the National Defense League wanted defense only for themselves, they would necessarily have to work for defense for the whole country because national security is indivisible. Only a naive person is likely to imagine that the political involvements of the members of the American Bankers Association and members of the Foreign Policy Association are identical. In other words, we may draw inferences from the exclusive or the nonexclusive nature of benefits sought by organizations as well as we can from the composition of groups. The positions of these groups can be distinguished not on the basis of some subjective process, but by making reasonable inferences from verifiable facts.

On the other hand, because some special-interest groups attempt to identify themselves with the public interest it does not follow that the whole idea of the public interest is a fraud. Mr. Wilson's famous remark that what is good for General Motors is good for the country assumes that people generally do in fact desire the common good. Presumably, Mr. Wilson attempted to explain the special interest of General Motors in terms of the common interest because that was the only way he could talk to people who do not belong to the General Motors organization. *Within* the General Motors organization, discussions might be carried on in terms of naked self-interest, but a *public discussion must be carried on in public terms.*

All public discussion is addressed to the general community. To describe the conflict of special interest groups as a form of politics means that the conflict has become generalized, has become a matter involving the broader public. In the nature of things *a political conflict among special interests is never restricted to the group most immediately interested.* Instead, it is an appeal (initiated by relatively small numbers of people) for the support of vast numbers of people who are sufficiently remote to have a somewhat different perspective on the controversy.

It follows that Mr. Wilson's comment, far from demonstrating that the public interest is a fraud, proves that he thinks that the public interest is so important that even a great private corporation must make obeisance to it.

The distinction between public and special interests is an indispensable tool for the study of politics. To abolish the distinction is to make a shambles of political science by treating things that are different as if they were alike. The kind of distinction made here is a commonplace of all literature dealing with human society, but *if we accept it, we have established one of the outer limits of the subject;* we have split the world of interests in half and have taken one step toward defining the scope of this kind of political conflict.

We can now examine the second distinction, the distinction between organized and unorganized groups. The question here is not whether the distinction can be made but whether or not it is worth making. Organization has been described as "merely a stage or degree of interaction" in the development of a group.

The proposition is a good one, but what conclusions do we draw from it? We do not dispose of the matter by calling the distinction between organized and unorganized groups a "mere" difference of degree because some of the greatest differences in the world are differences of degree. As far as special-interest politics is concerned the implication to be avoided is that a few workmen who habitually stop at a corner saloon for a glass of beer are essentially the same as the United States Army because the difference between them is merely one of degree. At this point we have distinction that makes a difference. The distinction between organized and unorganized groups is worth making because it ought to alert us against an analysis which begins as a general group theory of politics but ends with a defense of pressure politics as inherent, universal, permanent, and inevitable. This kind of confusion comes from the loosening of categories involved in the universalization of group concepts.

Since the beginning of intellectual history, scholars have sought to make progress in their work by distinguishing between things that are unlike and by dividing their subject matter into categories to examine them more intelligently. It is something of a novelty, therefore, when group theorists reverse this process by discussing their subject in terms so universal that they wipe out all categories, because this is the dimension in which it is least possible to understand anything.

If we are able, therefore, to distinguish between public and private interests and between organized and unorganized groups we have marked out the major boundaries of the subject; *we have given the subject shape and scope.* We are now in a position to attempt to define the area we want to explore. Having cut the pie into four pieces, we can now appropriate the piece we want and leave the rest to someone else. For a multitude of reasons *the most likely field of study is that of the organized, special-interest groups.* The advantage of concentrating on organized groups is that they are known, identifiable, and recognizable. The advantage of concentrating on special-interest groups is that they have one important characteristic in common; they are all exclusive. This piece of the pie (the organized special-interest groups) we shall call the *pressure system.* The pressure system has boundaries we can define; we can fix its scope and make an attempt to estimate its bias.

It may be assumed at the outset that all organized special-interest groups have some kind of impact on politics. A sample survey of organizations made by the Trade Associations Division of the United States Department of Commerce in 1942 concluded that "From 70 to 100 percent (of these associations) are planning activities in the field of government relations, trade promotion, trade practices, public relations, annual conventions, cooperation with other organizations, and information services."

The subject of our analysis can be reduced to manageable proportions and brought under control if we restrict ourselves to the groups whose interests in politics are sufficient to have led them to unite in formal organizations having memberships, bylaws, and officers. A further advantage of this kind of definition is, we may assume, that the organized special-interest groups are the most self-conscious, best developed, most intense and active groups. Whatever claims can be made for a group theory of politics ought to be sustained by the evidence concerning these groups, if the claims have any validity at all.

The organized groups listed in the various directories (such as *National Associations of the United States,* published at intervals by the United States Department of Commerce) and specialty yearbooks, registers, etc. and the *Lobby Index,* published by the United States House of Representatives, probably include the bulk of the organizations in the pressure system. All compilations are incomplete, but these are extensive enough to provide us with some basis for estimating the scope of the system.

By the time a group has developed the kind of interest that leads it to organize, it may be assumed that it has also developed some kind of political bias because *organization is itself a mobilization of bias in preparation for action.* Since these groups can be identified and since they have memberships (i.e., they include and exclude people), it is possible to think of the *scope* of the system.

When lists of these organizations are examined, the fact that strikes the student most forcibly is that *the system is very small.* The range of organized, identifiable, known groups is amazingly narrow; there is nothing remotely universal about it. There is a tendency on the part of the publishers of directories of associations to place an undue emphasis on business organizations, an emphasis that is almost inevitable because the business community is by a wide margin the most highly organized segment of society. Publishers doubtless tend also to reflect public demand for information. Nevertheless the dominance of business groups in the pressure system is so marked that it probably cannot be explained away as an accident of the publishing industry.

The business character of the pressure system is shown by almost every list available. *National Associations of the United States* lists 1,860 business associations out of a total of 4,000 in the volume, though it refers without listing to 16,000 organizations of businessmen. One cannot be certain what the total content of the unknown associational universe may be, but, taken with the evidence found in other compilations, it is obvious that business is remarkably well represented. Some evidence of the over-all scope of the system is to be seen in the estimate that 15,000 national trade associations have a gross membership of about one million business firms. The data are incomplete, but even if we do not have a detailed map this is the shore dimly seen.

Much more directly related to pressure politics is the *Lobby Index, 1946–1949* (an index of organizations and individuals registering or filing quarterly reports under the Federal Lobbying Act), published as a report of the House Select Committee on Lobbying Activities. In this compilation, 825 out of a total of 1,247 entries (exclusive of individuals and Indian tribes) represented business. A selected list of the most important of the groups listed in the *Index* (the groups spending the largest sums of money on lobbying) published in the *Congressional Quarterly Log* shows 149 business organizations in a total of 265 listed.

The business or upper-class bias of the pressure system shows up everywhere. Businessmen are four or five times as likely to write to their congressmen as manual laborers are. College graduates are far more apt to write to their congressmen than people in the lowest educational category are.

The limited scope of the business pressure system is indicated by all available statistics. Among business organizations, the National Association of Manufacturers (with about 20,000 corporate members) and the Chamber of Commerce of the United States (about as large as the N.A.M.) are giants. Usually business associations are much smaller. Of 421 trade associations in the metal-products industry listed in

National Associations of the United States, 153 have a membership of less than 20. The median membership was somewhere between 24 and 50. Approximately the same scale of memberships is to be found in the lumber, furniture, and paper industries where 37.3 percent of the associations listed had a membership of less than 20 and the median membership was in the 25 to 50 range.

The statistics in these cases are representative of nearly all other classifications of industry.

Data drawn from other sources support this thesis. Broadly, the pressure system has an upper-class bias. There is overwhelming evidence that participation in voluntary organizations is related to upper social and economic status; the rate of participation is much higher in the upper strata than it is elsewhere. The general proposition is well stated by Lazarsfeld:

> People on the lower SES levels are less likely to belong to any organizations than the people on high SES (Social and Economic Status) levels. (On an A and B level, we find 72 percent of these respondents who belong to one or more organizations. The proportion of respondents who are members of formal organizations decreases steadily as SES level descends until, on the D level only 35 percent of the respondents belong to any associations).

The bias of the system is shown by the fact that *even nonbusiness organizations reflect an upper-class tendency.*

Lazarsfeld's generalization seems to apply equally well to urban and rural populations. The obverse side of the coin is that large areas of the population appear to be wholly outside the system of private organization. A study made by Ira Reid of a Philadelphia area showed that in a sample of 963 persons, 85 percent belonged to no civic or charitable organization and 74 percent belonged to no occupational, business, or professional associations, while another Philadelphia study of 1,154 women showed that 55 percent belonged to no associations of any kind.

A *Fortune* farm poll taken some years ago found that 70.5 percent of farmers belonged to no agricultural organizations. A similar conclusion was reached by two Gallup polls showing that perhaps no more than one third of the farmers of the country belonged to farm organizations, while another *Fortune* poll showed that 86.8 percent of the low-income farmers belonged to no farm organizations. All available data support the generalization that the farmers who do not participate in rural organizations are largely the poorer ones.

A substantial amount of research done by other rural sociologists points to the same conclusion. Mangus and Cottam say, on the basis of a study of 556 heads of Ohio farm families and their wives:

> The present study indicates that comparatively few of those who ranked low on the scale of living took any active part in community organizations as members, attendants, contributors, or leaders. On the other hand, those families that ranked high on the scale of living comprised the vast majority of the highly active participants in formal group activities. . . . Fully two-thirds of those in the lower class as defined in this study were non-participants as compared with only one-tenth of those in the upper class and one-fourth of those in the middle class. . . . When families were classified by the general level-of-living index, 16 times as large a proportion of those in the upper classes as of those in the lower class were active participants. . . .

Along the same line Richardson and Bauder observe, "Socio-economic status was directly related to participation." In still another study it was found that "a highly significant relationship existed between income and formal participation." It was found that persons with more than four years of college education held twenty times as many memberships (per one hundred persons) as did those with less than a fourth-grade education and were forty times as likely to hold office in nonchurch organizations, while persons with an income over $5,000 hold ninety-four times as many offices as persons with incomes less than $250.

D.E. Lindstrom found that 72 percent of farm laborers belonged to no organizations whatever.

There is a great wealth of data supporting the proposition that participation in private associations exhibits a class bias.

The class bias of associational activity gives meaning to the limited scope of the pressure system, because *scope and bias are aspects of the same tendency.* The data raise a serious question about the validity of the proposition that special-interest groups are a universal form of political organization reflecting *all* interests. As a matter of fact, to suppose that everyone participates in pressure-group activity and that all interests get themselves organized in the pressure system is to destroy the meaning of this form of politics. The pressure system makes sense only as the political instrument of a segment of the community. It gets results by being selective and biased; *if everybody got into the act, the unique advantages of this form of organization would be destroyed, for it is possible that if all interests could be mobilized the result would be a stalemate.*

Special-interest organizations are most easily formed when they deal with small numbers of individuals who are acutely aware of their exclusive interests. To describe the conditions of presssure-group organization in this way is, however, to say that it is primarily a business phenomenon. Aside from a few very large organizations (the churches, organized labor, farm organizations, and veterans' organizations) the residue is a small segment of the population. *Pressure politics is essentially the politics of small groups.*

The vice of the groupist theory is that it conceals the most significant aspects of the system. The flaw in the pluralist heaven is that the heavenly chorus sings with a strong upper-class accent. Probably about 90 percent of the people cannot get into the pressure system.

The notion that the pressure system is automatically representative of the whole community is a myth fostered by the universalizing tendency of modern group theories. *Pressure politics is a selective process* ill designed to serve diffuse interests. The system is skewed, loaded, and unbalanced in favor of a fraction of a minority.

On the other hand, pressure tactics are not remarkably successful in mobilizing general interests. When pressure-group organizations attempt to represent the interests of large numbers of people, they are usually able to reach only a small segment of their constituencies. Only a chemical trace of the fifteen million Negroes in the United States belong to the National Association for the Advancement of Colored People. Only one five hundredths of 1 percent of American women belong to the League of Women Voters, only one sixteen hundredths of 1 percent of the consumers belong to the National Consumers' League, and only 6 percent of American automobile drivers belong to the American Automobile Association, while about 15 percent of the veterans belong to the American Legion.

The competing claims of pressure groups and political parties for the loyalty of the American public revolve about the difference between the results likely to be achieved by small-scale and large-scale political organization. Inevitably, the outcome of pressure politics and party politics will be vastly different.

II ◫ TRENDS

Interest groups have long been a part of American politics; "Americans of all ages, all stations in life, and all types of dispositions," Alexis de Tocqueville wrote, "are forever forming associations." In recent years, however, the nature, role, and influence of interest groups has been changing dramatically. In the following selection, political scientists Allan J. Cigler and Burdett A. Loomis discuss these changes, with particular emphasis on how changes in the broader nature of American politics have affected the role of interest groups.

Questions

1. Loomis and Cigler suggest that "the government itself has encouraged many interests to organize and articulate their demands." How has government done this? Why?

2. The authors argue that, in part at least, interest groups have moved in to play roles that used to be played by the political parties. How does this argument accord with the discussions on the modern party system in chapter 7?

9.2 *The Changing Nature of Interest Group Politics*

Allen J. Cigler and Burdett A. Loomis

From James Madison to Madison Avenue, political interests have played a central role in American politics. But this great continuity in our political experience has been matched by the ambivalence with which citizens, politicians, and scholars have approached interest groups. James Madison's warnings on the dangers of faction echo in the rhetoric of reformers ranging from Populists and Progressives near the turn of the century to contemporary so-called public interest advocates.

If organized special interests are nothing new in American politics, can today's group politics be seen as having undergone some fundamental changes? Acknowledging that many important, continuing trends do exist, we seek to place in perspective a broad series of changes

in the modern nature of interest group politics. Among the most substantial of these developments are:

1. a great proliferation of interest groups since the early 1960s;

2. a centralization of group headquarters in Washington, D.C., rather than in New York City or elsewhere;

3. major technological developments in information processing that promote more sophisticated, timelier, and more specialized grass-roots lobbying;

4. the rise of single-issue groups;

5. changes in campaign finance laws (1971, 1974) and the ensuing growth of political action committees (PACs);

6. the increased formal penetration of political and economic interests into the bureaucracy (advisory committees), the presidency (White House group representatives), and the Congress (caucuses of members);

7. the continuing decline of political parties' abilities to perform key electoral and policy-related activities;

8. the increased number, activity, and visibility of public interest groups, such as Common Cause, and the Ralph Nader–inspired public interest research organizations;

9. the growth of activity and impact by institutions, including corporations, universities, state and local governments, and foreign interests; and

10. a continuing rise in the amount and sophistication of group activity in state capitals.

All these developments have their antecedents in previous eras of American political life; there is little genuinely new under the interest group sun. Political action committees have replaced (or complemented) other forms of special interest campaign financing. Group-generated mail directed at Congress has existed as a tactic since at least the early 1900s. And many organizations have long been centered in Washington, members of Congress traditionally have represented local interests, and so on.

At the same time, however, the level of group activity, coupled with growing numbers of organized interests, distinguishes contemporary group politics from the politics of earlier eras. Current trends of group involvement lend credence to the fears of such scholars as political scientist Theodore Lowi and economist Mancur Olson, who view interest-based politics as contributing to governmental stalemate and reduced accountability. If accurate, these analyses point to a fundamentally different role for interest groups than those suggested by Madison and later group theorists.

Several contemporary studies, such as those by Olson and political scientists Robert Salisbury and Terry Moe, illustrate the weakness of much interest group analysis that does not account adequately for the reasons groups form and persist. Only during the last twenty-five years, in the wake of Olson's path-breaking research, have scholars begun to examine realistically why people join and become active in groups. It is by no means self-evident that citizens should naturally become group members—quite the contrary in most instances. We are faced, then, with the paradoxical and complex question of why groups have proliferated, as they certainly have, when usually it is economically unwise for individuals to join them.

Interest Groups in American Politics

Practical politicians and scholars alike generally have concurred that interest groups (also known as factions, pressure groups, and special interests) are natural phenomena in a democratic regime—that is, individuals will band together to protect their interests. In Madison's words, "the causes of faction . . . are sown in the nature of man," but controversy continues as to whether groups and group politics are benign or malignant forces in American politics. "By a faction," Madison wrote, "I understand a number of citizens, whether amounting to a majority or minority of the whole, who are united and actuated by some common impulse of passion, or of interest, adverse to the rights of other citizens, or to the permanent and aggregate interests of the community."

Although Madison rejected the remedy of direct controls over factions as "worse than the disease," he saw the need to limit their negative effects by promoting competition among them and by devising an elaborate system of procedural "checks and balances" to reduce the potential power of any single, strong group, whether representing a majority or minority position.

Hostility toward interest groups became more virulent in an industrialized America, where the great concentrations of power that developed far outstripped anything Madison might have imagined. After the turn of the century many Progressives railed at various monopolistic "trusts" and intimate connections between interests and corrupt politicians. Later, in 1935, Hugo Black, then a senator (and later a Supreme Court justice), painted a grim picture of group malevolence: "Contrary to tradition, against the public morals, and hostile to good government, the lobby has reached such a position of power that it threatens government itself. Its size, its power, its capacity for evil, its greed, trickery, deception and fraud condemn it to the death it deserves."

Similar suspicions are expressed today, especially in light of the substantial growth of PACs since 1974. PAC contributions to congressional candidates rose from almost $23 million in 1976 to $148 million in 1988, which amounted to almost a third of all their funds. Still, the number of PACs has leveled off at just over 4,000, and only a fraction of these are major players in electoral politics. Reformers in and out of Congress have sought to limit purported PAC influence, but as of 1990 legislators could not agree on major changes in laws regulating campaign spending or group activity. PACs continue to be an attractive target for reformers. One typical expression of dismay came from Common Cause, the self-styled public interest lobby: "The Special Interest State is a system in which interest groups dominate the making of government policy. These interests legitimately concentrate on pursuing their own immediate—usually economic—agendas, but in so doing they pay little attention to the impact of their agendas on the nation as a whole."

Despite the considerable popular distrust of interest group politics, political scientists and other observers often have viewed groups in a much more positive light. This perspective also draws upon Madison's *Federalist* writings, but it is tied more closely to the growth of the modern state. Political science scholars such as Arthur Bentley, circa 1910, and David Truman, forty years later, placed groups at the heart of politics and policy making in a complex, large, and increasingly specialized governmental system. The interest group becomes an element of con-

tinuity in a changing political world. Truman noted the "multiplicity of co-ordinate or nearly co-ordinate points of access to governmental decisions," and concluded that "the significance of these many points of access and of the complicated texture of relationships among them is great. This diversity assures various ways for interest groups to participate in the formation of policy, and this variety is a flexible, stabilizing element."

Derived from Truman's work, and that of other group-oriented scholars, is the notion of the pluralist state in which competition among interests, in and out of government, will produce policies roughly responsive to public desires, and no single set of interests will dominate. As one student of group politics summarized,

> Pluralist theory assumes that within the public arena there will be countervailing centers of power within governmental institutions and among outsiders. Competition is implicit in the notion that groups, as surrogates for individuals, will produce products representing the diversity of opinions that might have been possible in the individual decision days of democratic Athens.

In many ways the pluralist vision of American politics corresponds to the basic realities of policy making and the distribution of policy outcomes, but a host of scholars, politicians, and other observers have roundly criticized this perspective. Two broad (although sometimes contradictory) critiques have special merit.

The first critique argues that some interests systematically lose in the policy process; others habitually win. Without making any elite theory contentions that a small number of interests and individuals conspire together to dominate societal policies, one can make a strong case that those interests with more resources (money, access, information, and so forth) usually will obtain better results than those who possess fewer assets and employ them less effectively. The numerically small, cohesive, well-heeled tobacco industry, for example, does well year in

Catastrophic Follies

Interest groups, as we have seen, have become increasingly professionalized and concentrated in Washington, D.C. Although these trends have in many ways made interest groups more effective, they carry with them a major price tag. Paradoxically, interest groups sometimes pursue policies that put them at odds with their own rank-and-file membership.

The following selection, written in 1989, describes the debacle that ensued when the American Association of Retired Persons pushed Congress into passing the Medicare Catastrophic Coverage Act of 1988, a program that provided major benefits to elderly Americans facing serious or long-term medical problems. Congress agreed to pass the bill only if the costs of the program were entirely borne by the elderly themselves. The AARP, ostensibly representing the nation's elderly, agreed.

The AARP's membership was incensed. In effect, the new law required affluent senior citizens to buy catastrophic care coverage from the government instead of from private insurers, and it forced them not only to pay for themselves but also to subsidize coverage for their less affluent counterparts. For the more affluent senior citizens, therefore, the new program was neither a benefit nor a bargain. The membership of the AARP—generally, middle-class or above—rebelled.

What's wrong with this picture? One day this summer, busloads of outraged old people—most of them from Sarasota and other affluent Florida retirement communities—pulled up at the state headquarters of the American Association of Retired Persons in dowdy St. Petersburg and proceeded to picket the building with signs reading "Down with the AARP." They had come to de-nounce the nation's largest senior citizen group (28 million members) for one reason alone: its role in securing the first major expansion of health care benefits for the elderly in a generation.

The Medicare Catastrophic Coverage Act—also the first major social welfare legislation of any sort in more than a decade—passed the House and Senate by overwhelming margins in June 1988 and was signed with a flourish by President Reagan. Now there's talk of even repealing it. What went wrong?

The story begins when Otis Bowen arrived in Washington in late 1985 as Reagan's new secretary of health and human services. When he took charge at HHS, Bowen was still grieving for his wife, who had spent three months in a hospital fighting a losing battle with bone cancer. That experience, he told his staff, had taught him what a raw deal Medicare was when you really needed it.

Medicare, at the time, covered all sorts of routine medical expenses, such as doctor visits and X-rays, but would pay for only the first 60 days of an elderly patient's hospital stay. The affluent elderly could, and usually did, solve this problem with so-called "Medigap" insurance policies from private insurers. But the industry was rife with fraud and spent enormous sums on marketing devices such as hiring Lorne Greene and Art Linkletter. And adequate Medigap policies were beyond the reach of the elderly poor. Even to a conservative Indiana Republican, the private sector seemed to be failing where government could succeed.

Since only a few of the elderly (approximately 0.3 percent) actually require more than 60 continuous days of hospital care per year, Bowen reasoned that government could cheaply insure

and year out in the policy-making process; marginal farmers and the urban poor produce a much less successful track record. Based on the continuing unequal results, critics of the pluralist model argue that interests are still represented unevenly and unfairly.

A second important line of criticism generally agrees that inequality of results remains an

against this risk on an actuarially sound basis. As long as the program was mandatory, government would avoid the problem of adverse selection, which is the tendency of people to buy insurance only when they think they are likely to collect a benefit. . . .

The Gray Lobby had misgivings from the beginning. They were appalled by the White House's insistence that the elderly finance the new program themselves. Some also feared that "catastrophic" hospital coverage would pre-empt a new benefit more sorely coveted by the elderly, long-term nursing-home care. As the nation's third-largest originator of Medigap insurance, the AARP had strong commercial reasons to oppose the Bowen plan. Most of its predominantly middle-class members already had catastrophic coverage, from AARP or somebody else. But the AARP decided in the end that it couldn't very well oppose a major new benefit for the elderly. . . .

By the time it was all over, the bill offered not only free hospital and physician care after $2,000 a year but also, beginning in 1991: 80 percent of the cost of prescription drugs for a $600 deductible; up to 150 days of free skilled nursing-home care; and 38 days plus 80 hours a year of free home health care. The bill also changes the Medicaid (health care for the poor) rules to allow people to qualify for free nursing-home care without using up all the financial resources of a spouse. The prescription-drug benefit alone will easily cost $6.8 million a year, and probably a lot more.

To pay for all this, Congress kept the proposed Medicare premium increase at four dollars a month but added a special 15 percent income tax surtax on Medicare participants who earn enough money to owe at least $150 a year in federal income taxes. That is only about 44 percent of el-derly households. The tax is capped at $800 a year per person, a threshold that is reached at an income of about $50,000 a year.

The surtax was the problem. Because it reflected a cross-subsidy of the elderly poor by the elderly affluent, many would have to pay more for the new benefit than they were paying for the Medigap insurance it replaced. But the rage of the elderly was mostly not that specific. It was against the very idea that they should be expected to pay themselves for any new government benefit they might obtain.

Congressional Democrats campaigning in their districts as early as the 1987 Christmas recess were appalled to find that even among the majority of elderly voters who would be exempt from the surtax, support for the program was far from universal. Many of the elderly had assumed that all the talk about catastrophic health care meant that Congress was getting ready to pass an entitlement to long-term nursing-home care, and were bitterly disappointed when they found out otherwise. . . .

Congress and the AARP have been besieged. The abuse heaped on the AARP by its members this summer has been so unrelenting that its Washington policy staff—most of them idealistic, liberal-minded baby boomers—have begun to talk back like unrepentant granny-bashers. Some congressional offices have been receiving up to 1,000 letters a week from mostly middle- and upper-income retirees demanding that the bill should be repealed or its cost should be shifted onto someone else. . . . [In 1990, Congress agreed to repeal the program.]

—*Phillip Longman*

important aspect of group politics. But this perspective, most forcefully set out by Theodore Lowi, sees interests as generally succeeding in their goals of influencing government—to the point that the government itself, in one form or another, provides a measure of protection to almost all societal interests. Everyone thus retains some vested interest in the ongoing structure of government and array of public policies. This does not mean that all interests obtain just what they desire from governmental policies; rather, all interests get at least some rewards. From this point of view the tobacco industry surely wishes to see its crop subsidies maintained, but the small farmer and the urban poor also have pet programs, such as guaranteed loans and food stamps, which they seek to protect.

Lowi labels the proliferation of groups and their growing access to government "interest-group liberalism," and he sees this phenomenon as pathological for a democratic government: "Interest-group liberal solutions to the problem of power [who will exercise it] provide the system with stability by spreading a *sense* of representation at the expense of genuine flexibility, at the expense of democratic forms, and ultimately at the expense of legitimacy." Interest group liberalism is pluralism, but it is *sponsored* pluralism, and the government is the chief sponsor.

On the surface, it appears that the "unequal results" and "interest-group liberalism" critiques of pluralism are at odds. Reconciliation, however, is relatively straightforward. Lowi does not suggest that all interests are effectively represented. Rather, there exists in many instances only the appearance of representation. Political scientist Murray Edelman pointed out that a single set of policies can provide two related types of rewards: tangible benefits for the few and symbolic reassurances for the many. Such a combination encourages groups to form, become active, and claim success.

Climate for Group Proliferation

Substantial cleavages among a society's citizens are essential for interest group development. American culture and the constitutional arrangements of the U.S. government have encouraged the emergence of multiple political interests. In the pre-Revolutionary period, sharp conflicts existed between commercial and landed interests, debtor and creditor classes,

coastal residents and those in the hinterlands, and citizens with either Tory or Whig political preferences. As the new nation developed, its vastness, characterized by geographical regions varying in climate, economic potential, culture, and tradition, contributed to a great heterogeneity. Open immigration policies further led to a diverse cultural mix with a wide variety of racial, ethnic, and religious backgrounds represented among the populace. Symbolically, the notion of the United States as a "melting pot," emphasizing group assimilation, has received much attention, but a more appropriate image may be a "tossed salad."

The Constitution also contributes to a favorable environment for group development. Guarantees of free speech, association, and the right to petition the government for redress of grievances are basic to group formation. Because political organization often parallels government structure, federalism and the separation of powers principles embodied in the Constitution have greatly influenced the existence of large numbers of interest groups in the United States.

The decentralized political power structure in the United States allows important decisions to be made at the national, state, or local levels. Even within governmental levels, there are multiple points of access. For example, business-related policies such as taxes are acted upon at each level, and interest groups may affect these policies in the legislative, executive, or judicial arenas. Because several organizations such as the U.S. Chamber of Commerce are federations, their state and local affiliates often act independently of the national organization. Numerous business organizations thus focus on the varied channels for access.

In addition, the decentralized political parties found in the United States are less unified and disciplined than parties in many other nations. The resulting power vacuum in the decision-making process offers great potential for alternative political organizations such as interest groups to influence policy.

Finally, American cultural values may well encourage group development. As Alexis de Tocqueville observed in the 1830s, values such as individualism and the need for personal achievement underlie the propensity of citizens to join groups. Moreover, the number of access points—local, state, and national—contributes to Americans' strong sense of political efficacy when compared to that expressed by citizens of other nations. Not only do Americans see themselves as joiners, but they actually tend to belong to more political groups than do people of other countries.

• • •

Contemporary Interest Group Politics

Several notable developments mark the modern age of interest group politics. Of primary importance is the large and growing number of active groups and other interests. The data here are sketchy, but one major study found that most current groups came into existence after World War II and that group formation has accelerated substantially since the early 1960s. Also since the 1960s groups have increasingly directed their attention toward the center of power in Washington, D.C., as the scope of federal policy making has grown, and groups seeking influence have determined to "hunt where the ducks are." As a result, the 1960s and 1970s marked a veritable explosion in the number of groups lobbying in Washington.

A second key change is evident in the composition of the interest group universe. Beginning in the late 1950s political participation patterns underwent some significant transformations. Conventional activities such as voting declined, and political parties, the traditional aggregators and articulators of mass interests, became weaker. Yet at all levels of government, evidence of citizen involvement has been apparent, often in the form of new or revived groups. Particularly impressive has been the growth of citizens' groups—those organized around an idea or cause (at times a

single issue) with no occupational basis for membership. Fully 30 percent of such groups have formed since 1975, and in 1980 they made up more than one-fifth of all groups represented in Washington.

In fact a participation revolution has occurred in the country as large numbers of citizens have become active in an ever-increasing number of protest groups, citizens' organizations, and special interest groups. These groups often comprise issue-oriented activists or individuals who seek collective material benefits. The free-rider problem has proven not to be an insurmountable barrier to group formation, and many new interest groups do not use selective material benefits to gain support.

Third, government itself has had a profound effect on the growth and activity of interest groups. Early in this century, workers found organizing difficult because business and industry used government-backed injunctions to prevent strikes. By the 1930s, however, with the prohibition of injunctions in private labor disputes and the rights of collective bargaining established, most governmental actions directly promoted labor union growth. In recent years changes in the campaign finance laws have led to an explosion in the number of political action committees, especially among business, industry, and issue-oriented groups. Laws facilitating group formation certainly have contributed to group proliferation, but government policy in a broader sense has been equally responsible.

Fourth, not only has the number of membership groups grown in recent decades, but a similar expansion has occurred in the political activity of many other interests such as individual corporations, universities, churches, governmental units, foundations, and think tanks. Historically, most of these interests have been satisfied with representation by trade or professional associations. Since the mid-1960s, however, many of these institutions have chosen to employ their own Washington representatives. Between 1961 and 1982, for example, the number of corporations with Washington offices increased tenfold. The chief beneficiaries of this trend are Washington-based lawyers, lobbyists, and public relations firms. The number of attorneys in the nation's capital, taken as a rough indicator of lobbyist strength, tripled between 1973 and 1983, and the growth of public relations firms was dramatic. The lobbying community of the 1990s is large, increasingly diverse, and part of the expansion of policy domain participation, whether in agriculture, the environment, or industrial development.

Governmental Growth

Since the 1930s the federal government has become an increasingly active and important spur to group formation. A major aim of the New Deal was to use government as an agent in balancing the relationship between contending forces in society, particularly industry and labor. One goal was to create greater equality of opportunity, including the "guarantee of identical liberties to all individuals, especially with regard to their pursuit of economic success." For example, the Wagner Act, which established collective bargaining rights, attempted to equalize workers' rights with those of their employers. Some New Deal programs did have real redistributive qualities, but most, even Social Security, sought only to ensure minimum standards of citizen welfare. Workers were clearly better off, but "the kind of redistribution that took priority in the public philosophy of the New Deal was not of wealth, but a redistribution of power."

The expansion of federal programs has accelerated since 1960. In what political scientist Hugh Heclo termed an "Age of Improvement," the federal budget has grown rapidly (from nearly $100 billion in 1961 to well over a trillion dollars in 1991) and has widened the sweep of federal regulations. Lyndon Johnson's Great Society—a multitude of federal initiatives in education, welfare, health care, civil rights, housing, and urban affairs—created a new array of federal responsibilities and program beneficiaries. The growth of many of these programs has

continued, although it was slowed markedly by the Reagan administration. In the 1970s the federal government further expanded its activities in the areas of consumer affairs, environmental protection, and energy regulation, as well as redefined some policies, such as affirmative action, to seek greater equality of results.

Many of the government policies adopted early in the Age of Improvement did not result from interest group activity by potential beneficiaries. Several targeted groups, such as the poor, were not effectively organized in the period of policy development. Initiatives typically came from elected officials responding to a variety of private and public sources, such as task forces composed of academics and policy professionals.

The proliferation of government activities led to a mushrooming of groups around the affected policy areas. Newly enacted programs provided benefit packages that served to encourage interest group formation. Consider group activity in the field of policy toward the aging. The radical Townsend Movement, based on age grievances, received much attention during the 1930s, but organized political activity focused on age-based concerns had virtually no influence in national politics. Social Security legislation won approval without the involvement of age-based interest groups. Four decades later, by 1978, roughly $112 billion (approximately 24 percent of total federal expenditures) went to the elderly, and it is projected that in fifty years the outlay will be 40 percent of the total budget. The development of such massive benefits has spawned a variety of special interest groups and has encouraged others (often those formed for nonpolitical reasons) to redirect their attention to the politics of the aging.

Across policy areas two types of groups develop in response to governmental policy initiatives: *recipients* and *service deliverers*. In the elderly policy sector, recipient groups are mass-based organizations concerned with protecting—and if possible expanding—old-age benefits. The largest of these groups—indeed, the largest voluntary association represented in Washington—is the American Association of Retired Persons (AARP).

The AARP is twice the size of the AFL-CIO and, after the Roman Catholic church, is the nation's largest organization. In 1988 the AARP counted 28 million members, up from 10 million a decade earlier. Almost half (48 percent) of all Americans over fifty, or one-fifth of all voters, belong to the group. Membership is quite inexpensive—$5 per year; much of the organization's revenues is derived from advertising in its bimonthly magazine, *Modern Maturity.* The organization's headquarters in Washington has its own ZIP Code, a legislative/policy staff of 125, and 18 registered lobbyists. Charles Peters, *Washington Monthly* editor and certified curmudgeon, acidly observed that the "AARP is becoming the most dangerous lobby in America," given its vigorous defense of the elderly's interests.

Federal program growth also has generated substantial growth among service delivery groups. In the health care sector, for example, these range from professional associations of doctors and nurses to hospital groups to the insurance industry to suppliers of drugs and medical equipment. Not only is there enhanced group activity, but many individual corporations (Johnson and Johnson, Prudential, Humana, among many others) have strengthened their lobbying capacities by opening Washington offices or hiring professional representatives from the capital's unending number of lobbying firms.

Federal government policy toward the aging is probably typical of the tendency to "greatly increase the incentives for groups to form around the differential effects of these policies, each refusing to allow any other group to speak in its name." The complexity of government decision making increases under such conditions, and priorities are hard to set. Particularly troublesome for decision makers concerned with national policy is the role played by service delivery groups. In the area of the aging, some groups are largely organizational middlemen concerned with their status as vendors for the elderly. The trade associations, for example, are most interested in the conditions surrounding the payment of funds to the elderly. For example, the major concern of the Gerontological Society, an organization of professionals, is to obtain funds for research on problems of the aged. Middleman organizations do not usually evaluate government programs according to the criteria used by recipient groups; rather, what is important to them is the relationship between the program and the well-being of their organizations. Because many service delivery groups offer their members vitally important selective material incentives (financial advantages and job opportunities), they are usually far better organized than most recipient groups (the elderly in this case, the AARP not withstanding). As a result, they sometimes speak for the recipients. This is particularly true when recipient groups represent disadvantaged people, such as the poor or the mentally ill.

Middleman groups have accounted for a large share of total group growth since 1960, and many of them are state and local government organizations. Since the late 1950s the federal government has grown in expenditures and regulations, not in personnel and bureaucracy. Employment in the federal government has risen only 20 percent since 1955, while that of states and localities has climbed more than 250 percent. Contemporary federal activism largely involves overseeing and regulating state and local governmental units, which seek funding for a wide range of purposes. The intergovernmental lobby, composed of such groups as the National League of Cities, the International City Manager Association, the National Association of Counties, the National Governors' Association, and the U.S. Conference of Mayors, has grown to become one of the most important in Washington. In addition, many local officials such as transportation or public works directors are represented by groups, and even single cities and state boards of regents have established Washington offices.

Not only do public policies contribute to group proliferation, but government often directly intervenes in group creation. This is not an entirely new activity. In the early twentieth century, relevant governmental officials in the Agriculture and Commerce Departments encouraged the formation of the American Farm Bureau Federation and the U.S. Chamber of Commerce, respectively. Since the 1960s the federal government has been especially active in providing start-up funds and sponsoring groups. One study found that government agencies have concentrated on sponsoring organizations of public service professions:

> Federal agencies have an interest in encouraging coordination among the elements of these complex service delivery systems and in improving the diffusion of new ideas and techniques. Groups like the American Public Transit Association or the American Council on Education . . . serve as centers of professional development and informal channels for administrative coordination in an otherwise unwieldy governmental system.

Government sponsorship also helps explain the recent rise of citizens' groups. Most federal domestic legislation has included provisions requiring some citizen participation, which have spurred the development of various citizen action groups, including grass-roots neighborhood associations, environmental action councils, legal defense coalitions, health care organizations, and senior citizens' groups. Such group sponsorship evolved for two reasons:

> First, there is the ever-present danger that administrative agencies may exceed or abuse their discretionary power. In this sense, the regulators need regulating. Although legislatures have responsibility for doing this . . . the administrative bureaucracy has grown too large for them to monitor. Therefore, citizen participation has developed as an alternative means of monitoring government agencies. Second, government agencies are not entirely comfortable with their discretionary power. . . . [T]o

reduce the potential of unpopular or questionable decisions, agencies frequently use citizen participation as a means for improving, justifying, and developing support for their decisions.

Citizen participation thus has two often inconsistent missions: to act as a watchdog over an agency and to act as an advocate for its programs.

Government funding of citizens' groups takes numerous forms. Several federal agencies—including the Federal Trade Commission (FTC), Food and Drug Administration (FDA), and Environmental Protection Agency (EPA)—have reimbursed groups for participation in agency proceedings. At other times the government makes available seed money or outright grants. Interest group scholar Jack Walker found that nine citizens' groups in ten (89 percent) received outside funding in their initial stages of development. Not all the money was from federal sources, but much did come from government grants or contracts. Government can take away as well as give, however, and the Reagan administration made a major effort to "defund" interests on the political Left, especially citizens' groups. But once established, groups have strong instincts for survival. Indeed, the Reagan administration provided an attractive target for many citizens' groups in their recruiting efforts.

Citizens' groups, numbering in the thousands, continually confront the free-rider problem since they are largely concerned with collective goods and rarely can offer the selective material incentives so important for expanding and maintaining membership. With government funding, however, the development of a stable group membership is not crucial. Increasingly, groups have appeared that are essentially staff organizations with little or no membership base.

Government policies contribute to group formation in many *unintended* ways as well. Policy failures can impel groups to form, as happened with the rise of the American Agriculture

Movement in the wake of the Nixon administration's grain export policies. An important factor in the establishment of the Moral Majority was the perceived harassment of church-run schools by government officials. And, as for abortion, the 1973 Supreme Court *Roe v. Wade* decision played a major role in right-to-life group mobilization, as did the 1989 *Webster* decision in the creation of pro-choice groups.

• • •

Decline of Political Parties

In a diverse political culture characterized by divided power, political parties emerged early in our history as instruments to structure conflict and facilitate mass participation. Parties function as intermediaries between the public and formal government institutions, as they reduce and combine citizen demands into a manageable number of issues, enabling the system to focus upon the society's most important problems.

The party performs its mediating function primarily through coalition building—"the process of constructing majorities from the broad sentiments and interests that can be found to bridge the narrower needs and hopes of separate individuals and communities." The New Deal coalition, forged in the 1930s, illustrates how this works. Generally speaking, socioeconomic divisions dominated politics from the 1930s through the 1960s. Less affluent citizens tended to support government provisions for social and economic security and the regulation of private enterprise. Those better off economically usually took the opposite position. The Democratic coalition, by and large, represented disadvantaged urban workers, Catholics, Jews, Italians, eastern Europeans, and blacks. On a variety of issues, southerners joined the coalition along with smatterings of academics and urban liberals. The Republicans were concentrated in the rural and suburban areas outside the South; the party was made up of established ethnic groups, businessmen, and farmers, and was largely Protestant. Party organizations

dominated electoral politics through the New Deal period, and interest group influence was felt primarily through the party apparatus.

Patterns of partisan conflict are never permanent, however, and since the 1940s various social forces have contributed to the creation of new interests and the redefinition of older ones. This has had the effect of destroying the New Deal coalition without putting a new partisan structure in its place and has provided opportunities for the creation of large numbers of political groups—many that are narrowly focused and opposed to the bargaining and compromise patterns of coalition politics.

Taken as a whole, the changes of recent decades reflect the societal transformation that scholars have labeled "postindustrial society," centering on

> several interrelated developments: affluence, advanced technological development, the central importance of knowledge, national communication processes, the growing prominence and independence of the culture, new occupational structures, and with them new life styles and expectations, which is to say new social classes and new centers of power.

At the base is the role of affluence. Between 1947 and 1972 median family income doubled, even after controlling for the effects of inflation. During that same period the percentage of families earning $10,000 and more, in constant dollars, grew from 15 percent to 60 percent of the population. A large proportion of the population thus enjoys substantial discretionary income and has moved beyond subsistence concerns.

The consequences of spreading abundance did not reduce conflict, as some observers had predicted. Instead, conflict heightened, as affluence increased dissatisfaction by contributing to a "mentality of demand, a vastly expanded set of expectations concerning what is one's due, a diminished tolerance of conditions less than ideal." By the 1960s the democratizing impact of affluence had become apparent, as an extraordinary number of people enrolled in institutions of higher education. Not surprisingly, the government was under tremendous pressure to satisfy expectations, and it too contributed to increasing demands both in rhetoric and through many of its own Age of Improvement initiatives.

With the rise in individual expectations, class divisions and conflicts did not disappear, but they were drastically transformed. Political parties scholar Walter Dean Burnham noted that the New Deal's class structure changed and that by the late 1960s the industrial class pattern of upper, middle, and working class had been "supplanted by one which is relevant to a system dominated by advanced postindustrial technology." At the top of the new class structure was a "professional-managerial-technical elite . . . closely connected with the university and research centers and significant parts of it have been drawn—both out of ideology and interest—to the federal government's social activism." This growing group tended to be cosmopolitan and more socially permissive than the rest of society. The spread of affluence in postindustrial society was uneven, however, and certain groups were disadvantaged by the changes. At the bottom of the new class structure were the victims of changes, those "whose economic functions had been undermined or terminated by the technical revolution of the past generation . . . people, black and white, who tend to be in hard core poverty areas." The focus of the War on Poverty was to be on this class.

The traditional political party system found it difficult to deal effectively with citizens' high expectations and a changing class structure. The economic, ethnic, and ideological positions that had developed during the New Deal became less relevant to parties, elections, and voter preferences. The strains were particularly evident among working-class Democrats. New Deal policies had been particularly beneficial to the white working class, enabling that group to earn incomes and adopt lifestyles that resem-

bled those of the middle class. And although Age of Improvement policies initiated by Democratic politicians often benefited minorities, many white workers viewed these policies as attempts to aid lower-class blacks at whites' expense. By the late 1960s the white working class had taken on trappings of the middle class and conservatism, both economically and culturally.

At the same time, such New Deal divisions as ethnicity also had lost their cutting edge because of social and geographic mobility. One analyst observed in 1973 that

> it does not seem inaccurate to portray the current situation as one in which the basic coalitions and many of the political symbols and relationships, which were developed around one set of political issues and problems, are confronted with new issues and new cleavages for which these traditional relationships and associations are not particularly relevant. Given these conditions, the widespread confusion, frustration, and mistrust are not surprising.

Various conditions led to the party system's inability to adapt to the changing societal divisions by "realigning"—building coalitions of groups to address new concerns. For example, consider the difficulty of coalition building around the kinds of issues that have emerged over the past fifteen or twenty years.

"Valence" issues—general evaluations of the goodness or badness of the times—have become important, especially when related to the cost of living. Yet most such issues do not divide the country politically. Everyone is against inflation and crime. A second set of increasingly important issues are those that are highly emotional/cultural/moral in character such as abortion, the "right to die," AIDS, the death penalty, drug laws, and a nuclear freeze. These issues divide the electorate but elicit intense feelings from only a relatively few citizens. Opinion on such issues often is unrelated to traditional group identifications. Moreover, public opinion is generally disorganized or in disarray—that is, opinions often are unrelated or weakly related to one another on major issues, further retarding efforts to build coalitions.

There is some question about whether parties retain the capacity to shape political debate even on issues that lend themselves to coalition building. Although the decline of political parties began well before the 1960s, the weakening of the party organization has accelerated in the postindustrial age. The emergence of a highly educated electorate, less dependent upon party as an electoral cue, has produced a body of citizens that seeks out independent sources of information. Technological developments—such as television, computer-based direct mail, and political polling—have enabled candidates to virtually bypass political parties in their quest for public office. The rise of political consultants has reduced even further the need for party expertise in running for office. The recruitment function of parties also has been largely lost to the mass media, as journalists now "act out the part of talent scouts, conveying the judgment that some contenders are promising, while dismissing others as of no real talent."

Evidence does suggest that parties are finally starting to adapt to this new political environment, but party organizations no longer dominate the electoral process. The weakness of political parties has helped to create a vacuum in electoral politics since 1960, and in recent years interest groups have moved aggressively to fill it.

• • •

Group Impact on Policy and Process

Assessing the policy impact of interest group actions has never been an easy task. We may, however, gain some insights by looking at two different levels of analysis: a broad, societal overview and a middle-range search for relatively specific patterns of influence (for example, the role of direct mail or PAC funding). Considering impact at the level of individual lobbying efforts is also possible, but even the best work relies heavily on nuance and individualistic explanations.

Although the public at large often views lobbying and special interest campaigning with distrust, political scientists have not produced much evidence to support this perspective. Academic studies of interest groups have demonstrated few conclusive links between campaign or lobbying efforts and actual patterns of influence. This does not mean, we emphasize, that such patterns or individual instances do not exist. Rather, the question of determining impact is exceedingly difficult to answer. The difficulty is, in fact, compounded by groups' claims of impact and decision makers' equally vociferous claims of freedom from any outside influence.

The major studies of lobbying in the 1960s generated a most benign view of this activity. Lester Milbrath, in his portrait of Washington lobbyists, painted a Boy Scout–like picture, depicting them as patient contributors to the policy-making process. Rarely stepping over the limits of propriety, lobbyists had only a marginal impact at best. Similarly, Raymond Bauer, Ithiel de Sola Pool, and Lewis Dexter's lengthy analysis of foreign trade policy, published in 1963, found the business community to be largely incapable of influencing Congress in its lobbying attempts. Given the many internal divisions within the private sector over trade matters, this was not an ideal issue to illustrate business cooperation, but the research stood as the central work on lobbying for more than a decade—ironically, in the very period when groups proliferated and became more sophisticated in their tactics. Lewis Dexter, in his 1969 treatment of Washington representatives as an emerging professional group, suggested that lobbyists will play an increasingly important role in complex policy making, but he provided few details.

The pictures of benevolent lobbyists who seek to engender trust and convey information, although accurate in a limited way, does not provide a complete account of the options open to any interest group that seeks to exert influence. Lyndon Johnson's long-term relationship with the Texas-based construction firm of Brown & Root illustrates the depth of some ties between private interests and public officeholders. The Washington representative for Brown & Root claimed that he never went to Capitol Hill for any legislative help because "people would resent political influence." But Johnson, first as a representative and later as a senator, systematically dealt directly with the top management (the Brown family) and aided the firm by passing along crucial information and watching over key government-sponsored construction projects.

> [The Johnson-Brown & Root link] was, indeed, a partnership, the campaign contributions, the congressional look-out, the contracts, the appropriations, the telegrams, the investment advice, the gifts and the hunts and the free airplane rides—it was an alliance of mutual reinforcement between a politician and a corporation. If Lyndon was Brown & Root's kept politician, Brown & Root was Lyndon's kept corporation. Whether he concluded that they were public-spirited partners or corrupt ones, "political allies" or cooperating predators, in its dimensions and its implications for the structure of society, their arrangement was a new phenomenon on its way to becoming the new pattern for American society.

Subsequent events, such as the savings and loan scandal, demonstrate that legislators can be easily approached with unethical and illegal propositions; such access is one price of an open system. More broadly, the growth of interest representation in the late 1980s has raised long-term questions about the ethics of ex-government officials acting as lobbyists.

Contemporary Practices

Modern lobbying emphasizes information, often on complex and difficult subjects. Determining actual influence is, as one lobbyist noted, "like finding a black cat in the coal bin at midnight," but we can make some assess-ments about the overall impact of group proliferation and increased activity.

First, more groups are engaged in more forms of lobbying than ever before—both classic forms, such as offering legislative testimony, and newer forms, such as mounting computer-based direct mail campaigns to stir up grass-roots support. As the number of new groups rises and existing groups become more active, the pressure on decision makers—especially legislators—mounts at a corresponding rate. Thus, a second general point can be made: congressional reforms that opened up the legislative process during the 1970s have provided a much larger number of access points for today's lobbyists. Most committee (and subcommittee) sessions, including the markups or writing of legislation, remain open to the public, as do many conference committee meetings. More roll-call votes are taken, and congressional floor action is televised. Thus, interests can monitor the performance of individual members of Congress as never before. This does nothing, however, to facilitate disinterested decision making or foster statesmanlike compromises on most issues.

In fact, monitoring the legions of Washington policy actors has become the central activity of many groups. As Robert Salisbury recently observed, "Before [organized interests] can advocate a policy, they must determine what position they wish to embrace. Before they do this, they must find out not only what technical policy analysis can tell them but what relevant others, inside and outside the government, are thinking and planning." Given the volume of policy making, just keeping up can represent a major undertaking.

The government itself has encouraged many interests to organize and articulate their demands. The rise of group activity thus leads us to another level of analysis: the impact of contemporary interest group politics on society. Harking back to Lowi's description of interest group liberalism, we see the eventual result to be an immobilized society, trapped by its willingness to allow interests to help fashion self-serving policies that embody no firm criteria of success or failure. For example, even in the midst of the savings and loan debacle, the government continues to offer guarantees to various sectors, based not on future promise but on past bargains and continuing pressures.

The notion advanced by Olson that some such group-related stagnation affects all stable democracies makes the prognosis all the more serious. In summary form, Olson argued, "The longer societies are politically stable, the more interest groups they develop; the more interest groups they develop, the worse they work economically." The United Automobile Workers' protectionist leanings, the American Medical Association's fight against FTC intervention into physicians' business affairs, and the insurance industry's successful prevention of FTC investigations all illustrate the possible linkage between self-centered group action and poor economic performance—that is, higher automobile prices, doctors' fees, and insurance premiums for no better product or service.

Conclusion

The ultimate consequences of the growing number of groups, their expanding activities both in Washington and in state capitals, and the growth of citizens' groups remain unclear. From one perspective, such changes have made politics more representative than ever before. While most occupation-based groups traditionally have been well organized in American politics, many other interests have not. Population groupings such as blacks, Hispanics, and women have mobilized since the 1950s and 1960s; even animals and the unborn are well represented in the interest group arena, as is the broader "public interest," however defined.

Broadening the base of interest group participation may have truly opened up the political process, thus curbing the influence of special interests. For example, agricultural policy making in the postwar era was almost exclusively the prerogative of a tight "iron triangle" composed of congressional committee and subcommittee members from farm states, government officials representing the agriculture bureaucracy, and major agriculture groups such as the American Farm Bureau. Activity in the 1970s by consumer and environmental interest groups changed agricultural politics, making it more visible and lengthening the agenda to consider such questions as how farm subsidies affect consumer purchasing power and how various fertilizers, herbicides, and pesticides affect public health.

From another perspective, more interest groups and more openness do not necessarily mean better policies or ones that genuinely represent the national interest. "Sunshine" and more participants may generate greater complexity and too many demands for decision makers to process effectively. Moreover, the content of demands may be ambiguous and priorities difficult to set. Finally, elected leaders may find it practically impossible to build the kinds of political coalitions necessary to govern effectively, especially in an era of divided government.

This second perspective suggests that the American constitutional system is extraordinarily susceptible to the excesses of minority faction—in an ironic way a potential victim of the Madisonian solution of dealing with the tyranny of the majority. Decentralized government, especially one that wields considerable power, provides no adequate controls over the excessive demands of special interest politics. Decision makers feel obliged to respond to many of these demands, and "the cumulative effect of this pressure has been the relentless and extraordinary rise of government spending and inflationary deficits, as well as the frustration of efforts to enact effective national policies on most major issues."

In sum, the problem of contemporary interest group politics is one of representation. For particular interests, especially those that are well defined and adequately funded, the government is responsive to the issues of their greatest concern. But representation is not just a matter of responding to specific interests or citizens; the government also must respond to the collective needs of a society, and here the success of individual interests reduces the possibility of overall responsiveness. The very vibrancy and success of contemporary groups help contribute to a society that finds it increasingly difficult to formulate solutions to complex policy questions.

III  INTERCONNECTIONS

Lobbying, as Cigler and Loomis pointed out in selection 9.2, has changed fundamentally over the past few decades. In the following selection, the journalist Hedrick Smith contrasts "Old Breed Lobbying"—symbolized by images of secret deals in smoke-filled rooms—with "New Breed Lobbying"—which conjures up images of desktop publishing, direct mail advertising, and computerized phone banks.

Questions

1. What factors have contributed to the rise of new breed lobbying and to the demise of old breed lobbying? Consider selection 9.2 as you answer.

2. What were the advantages and disadvantages of old breed lobbying? of new breed lobbying? Which is more conducive to democratic government? Neither? Both?

9.3 Old-Breed and New-Breed Lobbying _____

Hedrick Smith

Old-Breed Lobbying

In the abstract, lobbying kindles an image of wickedness only barely less disreputable than the skullduggery of the Mafia. It conjures up Upton Sinclair's exposés of the beef and sugar trusts or Thomas Nast oils of robber barons closeted in back rooms, their corpulent figures framed in thick black strokes against a backdrop in red. It has the illicit aroma of cigar smoke, booze, and money delivered in brown envelopes. Or it smacks of big labor muscling congressional minions. But that is a caricature, for lobbying has changed immensely with the rise of mass citizen protests in the 1960s over civil rights and the Vietnam War. It changed further with the breakup of the old power baronies, the arrival of new-breed politicians, and the intrusion of campaign techniques.

Of course, plenty of lobbyists still practice old-fashioned lobbying. At heart, the old-breed game is inside politics. That is why so many lobbyists are former members of Congress, former White House officials, former legislative staff aides, former cabinet officers. Their game thrives on the clubbiness of the old-boy network. It turns on the camaraderie of personal friendships, on expertise born of experience. It taps old loyalties and well-practiced access. It draws on the common bond of old battles and the certain knowledge that you may lose on this year's tax bill, but you'll be back to revise it next year, and that yesterday's foe may be tomorrow's ally. It depends on relationships for the long haul.

The superlobbyists of the old-breed game are people such as Clark Clifford, a courtly, genteel former White House counsel to Harry Truman and secretary of Defense to Lyndon Johnson; Robert Strauss, the wisecracking former Democratic party chairman and Mr. Everything for Jimmy Carter; and Howard Baker, between stints as Senate majority leader and White House chief of staff. Close behind are Tommy Boggs, the able, likable, paunchy son of Representative Lindy Boggs and the late House Democratic Majority Leader Hale Boggs; Charls Walker, an astute, drawling Texas-born tax attorney with high Treasury experience in the Nixon years; and Robert Gray, secretary to the Eisenhower cabinet, who got to know the Reagans in California. These inside fixers cannot do what was possible a generation ago. Yet in a game where access and reputation are the coin of the marketplace, king rainmakers still have influence.

For the essence of the old-breed game is *retail* lobbying: the one-one-one pitch. It is Bob Strauss's note to Treasury Secretary Jim Baker to help a friend seek appointment to the World Bank. It is Howard Baker's contact with an old Senate colleague to see that some client gets a break on the "transition rules" of a tax bill. It is Bob Gray's phone call to the While House to ask the president to address some convention or to wangle an invitation to a state dinner for an industrial big shot. It is breakfast with a committee staff director who is drafting intricate legislation. It is little favors such as tickets to a Washington Redskins football game or helping Ed Meese's wife get a job. It is knowing which buttons to push.

"The best lobbyists' work is basically just socializing," former Speaker O'Neill's spokesman, Chris Matthews, advised me. "They know members of Congress are here three nights a week, alone, without their families. So they say, 'Let's have dinner. Let's go see a ballgame.' Shmooze with them. Make friends. And they don't lean on it all the time. Every once in a while, they call up—maybe once or twice a year—ask a few questions. Call you up and say, 'Say, what's Danny going to do on this tax-reform bill?' Anne Wexler [a former Carter White House official, now a lobbyist] will call up and spend half an hour talking about left-wing politics, and suddenly she'll pop a question, pick up something. They want that little bit of access. That's what does it. You can hear it. It clicks home. They'll call their chief executive officer, and they've delivered. That's how it works. It's not illegal. They work on a personal basis."

An inside tip can be gold. Right after Reagan's inauguration in 1981, John Gunther, executive director of the U.S. Conference of Mayors, got a tip from a cabinet staff aide that the Reagan administration was planning to kill the revenue-sharing program which funneled billions to states, counties, and cities. The timing was serendipitous. The next day a mayor's delegation was scheduled to lunch with the president. Over lunch, the mayors of Peoria, Indianapolis, Denver, and Columbus lobbied Reagan and top aides. The program escaped the guillotine for several years, though it was ultimately reduced.

In another case, a former Reagan White House official turned lobbyist told me that a Washington lawyer telephoned him on behalf of a businessman who had a $497,000 cost overrun on a contract with the Department of Housing and Urban Development. In one telephone call, my lobbyist source learned that HUD had already decided to pay the contractor $350,000 and would tell him in about two weeks. My friend phoned the lawyer back, but before he could speak, the lawyer said his client was willing to pay the lobbyist ten percent of whatever he got. My source stopped in mid-sentence and replied, "Well, let me see what I can do." With some misgivings, but rationalizing that the contractor or the lawyer could have made the same phone call, my source waited a couple of days and then called back to report that the contractor would get $350,000. He never claimed to have fixed the deal, but he got a check for $35,000—for simply knowing whom to ask.

"A lot of it is direct contact," Christopher Matthews commented. "You see Tip, he'll be out at a country club playing golf [usually Burning Tree Country Club], and some lobbyist will walk up to him just as he's about ready to tee up his ball and say, 'Tip, you know, I got to tell you one thing. Do me one favor. Just don't push that state-and-local tax thing through on the tax bill.' You don't think that has an impression? Of course it does. They know what they're doing. Tip's mood can be affected by who the heck he's seen over the weekend. And these guys do their homework. They know right where these members socialize. You think it's an accident some guy walks up and talks to Tip on the golf tee? No. It's smart. It's natural. It's easy."

That is classic old-breed lobbying, and as an old-breed politician, Tip O'Neill was particularly susceptible. Indeed, practically no politician is immune to the flattery and personal attention that are the essence of old-breed lobbying. I remember an article in 1978 about Tongsun Park, a Korean lobbyist who had been close to O'Neill and who wound up getting several other congressmen indicted for taking illegal campaign contributions from a foreigner. But the article, by William Greider in *The Washington Post,* was emphasizing something else: Park's simple but shrewd understanding that politicians need to feel loved.

"Park exploited this weakness with his Georgetown parties and gifts, but that hardly makes him unique," Greider wrote.

> The most effective lobbies on Capitol Hill, whether it is the Pentagon or the Farm Bureau, have always been the ones that played most skillfully to the Congressmen's egos. The military treats them like generals, flies them around in big airplanes and fires off rocket shows to entertain them. The Farm Bureau

awards them plaques and holds banquets in their honor. Politicians are not different in this respect from the rest of us, except that many of them have a stronger personal need for ego gratification. It's what drew them into politics in the first place, the roar of the crowd and all that.

> Now, picture a scrambling politician who works his way up the local ladder, who finally wins a coveted seat in Congress and comes to Washington to collect his glory. The first thing he discovers is that glory gets spread pretty thin in this town. . . . He hardly ever sees his name in the daily newspaper unless he gets into trouble or creates an outrageous media stunt which the press can't resist. When he opens the mail from home, it is a hot blast of complaints, demands, threats. In the last decade, his status has declined considerably, displaced by the new celebrities who dominate Washington's glitter: movie stars, cause advocates, rock musicians, even members of the news media. In this environment, politicians, some of them anyway, will behave like the rest of us—they will devote their attention to people who appreciate them. Lobbyists appreciate congressmen. They thank them constantly for their hard work. They provide them with the trappings, however phony, of exalted status. They protect a congressman, with small favors, while the rest of the world beats up on him.

Old-breed lobbying also thrives on an aura of influence, a promise of the inside track, the hint of priceless contacts. A certain amount of this promise of influence is hokum. There is no year-in, year-out boxscore, but even the big-name lobbyist "rainmakers" lose major battles or settle for much less than they had hoped for. "One of the great myths around is that wheelers and dealers can come in there and write policy and have their way in whatever they want—it's simply not the case," asserts Norm Ornstein, one of the best-known scholars on Congress, who is at the American Enterprise Institute for Public Policy Research. "You pick any big shot, and you're dealing with *some* wins and losses. Any sophisticated person is going to know that you hire a Tommy Boggs, and that doesn't mean you buy victory. What you buy with a

Bruce Plante. *The Chattanooga Times.*

Tommy Boggs is access. Very few people are gonna say they won't see him. You buy acumen. This is somebody who understands how the process works."

Ornstein's skepticism is well taken, for lobbyists are prone to oversell their influence; but his assertion that lobbyists do not write policy is too sweeping. Their effectiveness, suggested David Cohen, codirector of the Advocacy Institute, depends largely on the public visibility of issues. Large issues like the MX missile, environmental legislation, the Voting Rights Act, or broad provisions of tax law are "less susceptible to the superlobbyists because they are highly visible," Cohen argues—correctly, I think. "But when you're dealing with invisible issues and the narrower details of legislation, you can still use the superlawyers and the superlobbyists."

Access is the first arrow in any lobbyist's quiver, especially lobbyists of the old breed. Scores of times I have been told that votes are won simply by gaining an audience with a time-harassed congressman, so he could hear your case. In this access game, the lobbyist's first rule is to make his own services so reliable and indispensable that officeholders become dependent on him—for his information, his contacts, his policy advice, not to mention his money. "A good lobbyist is simply an extension of a congressional member's staff," I was told by Terry Lierman, an energetic health lobbyist and former staff aide for the Senate Appropriations Committee. "If you're a good lobbyist and you're working something, all the members know where you're coming from," Lierman said. "So if they want information and they trust you, they'll call *you* for that information."

That takes expertise. For instance, Representative Tony Coelho, a California Democrat, pointed out how lobbyists work hand in glove with the members and staffs of the highly specialized subcommittees of the House Agriculture Committee. They help craft legislation that covers their own sector. "There are lobbyists who are extremely influential in the subcommittees," Coelho asserted. "They know more about the subject than the staff or the committee members. The Cotton Council will be writing legislation for the cotton industry in the cotton subcommittee."

A top real estate lobbyist explained the premium value of expertise in the final stages of writing a tax bill and why lobbyists gather by the score outside the committee room. "There are very arcane, very turgid, complicated sections of the tax code, and members and their staffs often are not as familiar with how they apply to the industry as we are," explained Wayne Thevnot, president of the National Realty Committee. "So if you've got entrée there and you understand the process and you're present, you can influence the specific drafting of these proposals. Staff and others will come out and seek you out in the halls and say, 'We're on the passive-loss provision, and this is the material-participation test that the staff is proposing. Does that work? Does that solve your problem? And, if not, how can we correct it?' "

AIPAC has institutionalized its influence through this technique. Tom Dine and other staffers draft speeches and legislation for many members of both House and Senate, offering detailed rundowns on the Arab-Israeli military balance, or doing spot checks on Middle Eastern visitors. "We'll get a call from a congressional staffer, say at nine in the morning, and they want a speech on an issue," one midlevel AIPAC legislative assistant disclosed. "By ten-thirty, they'll have a speech." AIPAC has a research staff of fifteen people, well-stocked with papers on many topical issues. Practically every senator or House member known as a spokesman on Israeli issues and scores of lesser lights have leaned on this service or gotten AIPAC's staff to ghostwrite or edit op-ed articles on Middle East issues.

Charles Peters, in his slim and knowing handbook, *How Washington Really Works,* argues that the name of the game for politicians and administration officials is survival, and lobbyists work to become an integral part of the survival networks of people in power. "The smart lobbyist knows he must build networks not only for himself, but for those officials he tries to influence," Peters wrote. "Each time the lobbyist meets an official whose help he needs, he tries to let that official know—in the most subtle

ways possible—that he can be an important part of that official's survival network."

Ultimately that urge to prove a vital part of an officeholder's network gets into campaign money and demonstrating clout with the voters. And that begins to bridge from the old inside game of lobbying to the new outside game.

New-Breed Lobbying

The new-breed game reflects the organic changes in American politics and the institutional changes in Congress. Its medium is mass marketing; its style is packaging issues; its hallmark is wholesale lobbying. New-breed lobbying borrows heavily from the techniques of political campaigns, with their slick P.R., television advertising, orchestrated coalitions, targeted mass mailings, and their crowds of activists. It is the National Rifle Association generating three million telegrams in seventy-two hours and blanketing Capitol Hill with so many phone calls that members cannot make outgoing calls. It is the "gray lobby" dumping up to fifteen million postcards and letters on Jim Wright in one day to warn Congress not to tamper with Social Security cost-of-living adjustments. It is legions of insurance or real estate lobby agents swarming Capitol Hill as a tax markup nears a climax. It is political consultants and campaign strategists elbowing superlawyers aside, to generate grass-roots support for their lobbying clients or to do public-relations campaigns.

For example, when Jonas Savimbi, the Angolan rebel leader, wanted to push his cause in Washington in late 1985 and to bring pressure on Congress and the administration to supply him with missiles to combat Soviet tanks and jets, he paid a fancy $600,000 fee to Back, Manafort, Stone, and Kelly, a hot-shot lobbying firm set up by a group of young political campaign managers and consultants. The firm, whose campaign work gave it ties to the Reagan White House and influential Republican senators, not only arranged entrée at the highest levels of the administration and Congress, but it orchestrated a massive public-relations blitz for Savimbi. In his two-week visit, the jaunty, bearded anti-Communist rebel had scores of press interviews and television appearances. Suddenly Savimbi became a cause célèbre, which helped him get the weapons.

There are literally hundreds of deals like these, tapping the ranks of political campaign specialists for lobbying. That is an important shift away from reliance on lawyers and former government officials for lobbying—a shift symptomatic of how the new politics have altered the Washington power game.

The essence of the new-breed game is grass-roots lobbying. It developed in the 1960s with the advent of citizen protest. The civil rights movement, mass marches against the Vietnam War, and then Ralph Nader and public-interest groups such as Common Cause opened up mass lobbying. Those movements spawned a new generation, a new cadre of players trained in grass-roots activism, many of whom settled into the Washington power game. Business was initially slow to react, but it arrived with a vengeance to play on the new terrain in the late 1970s and gained the upper hand in the 1980s. Now old-breed and new-breed lobbyists jostle, borrowing techniques from each other.

The new game has made lobbying a boom industry. It takes a lot more money and manpower than it did in the old days to touch all the power bases in Congress, and the campaign techniques of working the grass roots shoot costs up exponentially. The swarm of lobbyists in Washington seems to reach new highs every year: from 5,662 registered with the secretary of the Senate in 1981 to 23,011 in mid-1987 (registration is required to work the halls of Congress legally), plus another fifty or sixty thousand more lobbyists and workers in law firms and trade association offices. In the new Washington, practically no big client will settle these days for a single lobbying firm. The style now is "team lobbying" to make all the necessary contacts and to handle all aspects of the influence game: a law firm, a public-relations outfit, a lobbying firm, plus grass-roots political specialists.

One hallmark of new-breed lobbying is its strange political bedfellows. With Congress split for six of the past eight years between a Democratic-controlled House and a Republican-dominated Senate, bipartisan lobbying coalitions became a necessity. Even in 1978, when the Chrysler Corporation was looking for a government bailout loan, it pulled together a big Democratic law firm (Patton, Boggs and Blow) and a big Republican lobbying firm (Timmons and Company). The latest pattern is for each firm to have its own in-house bipartisan coalition. For example, Bill Timmons—who regularly runs Republican national conventions—hired Democratic lobbyists such as Bill Cable from the Carter White House staff and Howard Paster, formerly with the United Auto Workers union.

It is not unusual for lobbying partners to wind up on opposite sides of political campaigns. One striking example is the highly respected firm of Wexler, Reynolds, Harrison & Schule, which principally pairs Anne Wexler, a liberal Democrat from the Carter White House, and Nancy Reynolds, a close confidante and White House aide to Nancy Reagan. In the hot 1986 Senate campaign, their rivalries stretched across the country; Wexler and Reynolds ran fund-raisers for rival candidates in Senate races from Florida and Maryland to Idaho and Nevada. "We don't think anything of it," Anne Wexler told me. "Our having contacts on both sides benefits our clients."

The swarm of lobbyists is so great that members of Congress have grown jaded—quick to challenge Washington lobbyists for evidence that their case has real pull among the voters. Danny Rostenkowski, chairman of the House Ways and Means Committee, told me that while his committee was drafting the 1986 tax bill, he refused to see Washington lobbyists—though he would grant time to constituents from home. And Tom Korologos, an old-breed lobbyist who learned the power game in the 1960s under Utah Senator Wallace Bennett and as congressional liaison in the Nixon White House, concedes: "We have a different breed of congressman who is more active, more publicity prone, more responsive to his district. . . ."

"On the Senate side in the old days you could go talk to two or three committee chairmen," Korologos recalled, "you could talk to John Stennis and Russell Long and Allen Ellender and Warren Magnuson, and you had a policy. You had a defense bill. You had an oil policy. Now, you've got to talk to fifty-one guys. So you fly in the Utah plant manager to see Orrin Hatch and Jake Garn [Utah's two senators], and the Utah plant manager gets in to see 'em. If he doesn't get in, he goes back home and goes to church on Sunday and bowling on Monday and to coffee on Tuesday and says, 'I was in Washington, and the son of a bitch wouldn't see me.' And let that spread around for a while. Political graveyards are filled with statesmen who forgot the folks back home."

"The logistics of trying to persuade Congress have changed enormously," agreed Jim Mooney, for years a top House Democratic staff aide and now chief lobbyist for the cable-television industry. "What's changed is there are so many more groups now and simultaneously a diminution of power in the power centers of Congress. You've got to persuade members one by one."

In the new game, another maxim is that lobbyists must demonstrate that the home folks are with them to prove their political legitimacy. "There's a suspicion on the part of elected officials toward paid lobbyists," acknowledged David Cohen, the public-interest lobbyist. "They often sense a gap between leaders and the rank and file, whether labor unions or other organizations like church groups. I don't think you're a player unless you have a constituency to mobilize."

In an earlier era, labor unions had a near monopoly on lobbying with a mass base. Disgruntled farmers also rolled their tractors onto the Capitol Mall to demonstrate mass anger. Business has now entered that game. Mass-marketing techniques are being used even by people like Charls Walker, a traditional Washington insider whose normal style is lobbying at intimate dinners for selected members of Congress. After serving as an inside tax adviser to the 1980 Reagan campaign, Walker got important tax write-offs for business written into the 1981 tax bill. But more recently he has enlisted help from new-breed lobbyists.

"When a member says to you, 'Go convince my constituents,' then you are thrown into those arenas," Walker explained to me. "You get into targeted mail and all that sort of stuff. The lobbying business is moving toward a full service which will include not just your legislative experts and administration experts, but your public-relations experts, experts in grass-roots communications, targeted communications, cluster-group approaches, grass-roots coalition building." Charls Walker was talking the lingo of the modern political campaign, and in fact, the old-breed lobbyists are turning increasingly to campaign consultants.

IV  FOCUS: INTERESTS IN POLITICAL SCIENCE

Political scientists have long debated the relationship between interests and politics. On the one side are those who argue that the clash of interests (and interest groups) is a natural and desirable part of democracy and that this competition between groups leads to the emergence of the public interest. On the other side are those who believe that the public interest exists independently of this clash of interests; in other words, that the sum total of private interests does not add up to the public interest. The former group believes that good government depends on giving equal play to all interests, by making it easy for interests to organize and by making sure that the government is responsive to those interests; the latter group believes that good government depends on insulating government to some extent from this clash of interests, allowing for dispassionate and unbiased deliberation on what the public interest requires.

Both sides of this debate, suggests the political scientist James Q. Wilson, can trace their intellectual heritage back to James Madison. In an address marking his acceptance of the American Political Science Association's prestigious James Madison award, Wilson argues that Madison's Federalist No. 10 *and* Federalist No. 51 *(selections 2.1 and 2.4) point in opposite directions on this issue and that political science would benefit from the recognition that—like Madison—we should attempt to reconcile rather than choose between these two points of view.*

Questions

1. Are citizens driven by interest, according to Madison? In your view? What kinds of citizen involvement can be explained by interests? What kinds cannot be so explained?

2. How does Madison attempt to resolve the tension between *Federalist No. 10* and *Federalist No. 51*? Do we need to choose between the interest group theory and the deliberation theory of American politics?

9.4 Interests and Deliberation, or Why Madison Would Not Have Received the James Madison Award_____

James Q. Wilson

My deep gratitude for the honor you have given me is in no way diminished by the provocative subtitle I have given to this lecture. I intend no disrespect; I intend only to suggest that so important a moment in the life of a political scientist inevitably leads him to reflect, not only on his own inadequacies (a topic on which I trust you have even stronger views than I), but also on what we mean by "political science."

The case against Madison receiving the Madison Award is easily stated and perhaps compelling: He did not have a Ph.D. degree; he published no articles in refereed journals; he wrote no great books. He is best known for a few dozen op-ed pieces written for a New York

City newspaper and a long set of notes he took during a summer-long conference in Philadelphia, notes that were not published during his lifetime. It would be as if this award were given to some combination of William Safire and a court stenographer. (Some may think that in 1990, it was.)

And yet most of us think of Madison as this nation's first political scientist, and certainly one of its greatest. He importantly shaped the oldest written constitution in the world and, with Alexander Hamilton and John Jay, left behind its most memorable and penetrating explication. The *Federalist Papers* are today the most frequently read works of 18th or 19th century American political thought. Long studied by

Americans, they are now studied as well by newly free Poles, Czechs, and Hungarians.

Madison did not, at least in the *Federalist*, describe his undertaking as "political science"—it was Hamilton who most frequently and enthusiastically referred to his understanding of government as scientific—but it was Madison who gave us, especially in Numbers 10 and 51, the intellectual framework, the ruling paradigm, around which much of contemporary political science is organized.

I should say "frameworks" or "paradigms," for obviously political science today is engaged in a great debate over how best to understand politics. To oversimplify, that debate is between those who take preferences as essentially given and self-serving and those who take them as changeable and to some degree other-regarding. To the former, interests count; to the latter, deliberation matters.

Both sides can find support in James Madison. In that sense he is, indeed, a founder and so, to that degree, we are one discipline; however spirited our debates, we have, should we wish to acknowledge him, a common ancestor.

In *Federalist* Number 51 we find ample Madisonian support for a rational-choice model of politics. The motive of politicians is private interest, in particular, political ambition. Men lack—they suffer from a "defect of"—better motives, and this is as true in public as in private matters. Accordingly, they are likely to use their governmental offices to serve the interests of themselves rather than of their constituents.

Number 51 sets forth what some now call the principal-agent problem. The citizen is the principal: He wishes to advance his interests while preventing others from advancing theirs at his expense. The first aspect of this goal Madison called the problem of faction, the second the problem of liberty. The government official is the agent: He is nominally accountable to his principal, the citizen, but sees opportunities for using his privileged access to power and information in ways that serve his own interest at the expense of his principal's. No "parchment barriers" [Number 48] will prevent this; "auxiliary precautions" are necessary [Number 51].

Madison's solution to the principal-agent problem is well known. We must give "to those who administer each department, the necessary constitutional means, and personal motives, to resist encroachments of the others." We want the legislative, executive, and judicial branches to be able and willing to resist the encroachments of others, not because we want any given branch to be free of constraints, but because we want them all more or less equally constrained so as to minimize each citizen's vulnerability to actions taken either to enhance the power and wealth of government officials or to advance the interests of another citizen.

Though Madison did not do so, one can easily extend the analysis of Number 51 to show how the legislative branch will seek to dominate the bureaucracy; how the bureaucracy will respond by serving the reelection needs of valued legislative allies; how one house of Congress will maneuver against the other; and how each house of Congress will create committees and procedures designed to prevent one faction, by its monopoly of information, from manipulating legislative outcomes in ways that enhance its reelection prospects at the expense of the reelection prospects of less informed members. The late Martin Diamond was, I think, among the first to suggest that reading Number 51 lends support to a geometrical view of politics—governance is a parallelogram of forces in which the following maxim applies: "To the vector belongs the spoils."

Federalist Number 10 strikes a different note. It begins in the same vein as Number 51: citizens are prone to form factions in order to advance their interests and passions. But almost imperceptibly the argument shifts away from the principal-agent problem of Number 51 to a far more difficult problem. That is the specter of a majority faction that always gets its way, whatever justice may require. Madison gives the example of a proposed law governing private debts. Creditors will be on one side, debtors on the other. "Justice ought to hold the balance between them." But instead, "the most numerous party" gets its way. Unlike in Number 51, in Number 10 numerical superiority means political superiority. The government is the supine instrument of the "superior force of an interested and over-bearing majority." No principal-agent problem here. And more: What is this word, "justice," all about? Justice *ought* to decide? What can that mean? Who is to be the instrument of justice, and how can his interest in justice be reconciled with his interest in his interests?

Moreover, the sources of faction turn out to be more complex than one might have suspected from Number 51. To be sure, "the various and unequal distribution of property" is "the most common and durable source of faction," but factions also arise around "passions," "religion," and "opinions." And these opinions in turn reflect not merely circumstances and well-understood wants, but the "fallible" reason of man. But what is fallible is changeable, and if changeable then no longer the stable lodestar, the unmoved first mover, of political action.

In Number 10, long before he gets to the checks and balances of Number 51, Madison proposed a partial solution to the problem of majority faction. His solution was a system of representation set in place in a large or "extended" republic. The effect of a system of representation is not simply to permit checks and balances to operate, but also "to refine and enlarge the public views, by passing them through the medium of a chosen body of citizens, whose wisdom may best discern the true interest of the country, and whose patriotism and love of justice, will be least likely to sacrifice it to temporary or partial considerations."

Of course factious, partial, or even sinister people might become representatives. (Madison was no Pollyanna.) But in a large republic this was less likely to occur than in a small one. If many citizens must vote for a single representative, then "it will be more difficult for unworthy candidates to practice with success the vi-

cious arts, by which elections are too often carried" and elections will be more likely to attract men with "the most attractive merit, and the most diffusive and established character." Having large districts would, of course, worsen the principal-agent problem from the point of view of the citizen, because each representative would now be the agent of many different and perhaps competing principals. The minimum size of a district—thirty thousand people—meant that only two cities, New York and Philadelphia, would have a representative all to themselves. All the other towns and villages, many separated by considerable distances, would share a representative. As a result, most voters would have to rely on reputation as a basis for choosing among candidates, with the effect that the elected representative would have more opportunity to pursue his own interests at the expense of those of his constituents.

The contrast between Number 51 and Number 10 is striking. In the former the goal is to solve the principal-agent problem; in the latter no such problem exists. In the former men rationally pursue their own interests; in the latter they allow their opinions to be refined by the superior judgment of representatives. In the former the separation of powers is proposed as a way of checking the self-serving behavior of representatives; in the latter the prospect of a large republic is embraced as a way of giving effect to the other-regarding tendencies of those representatives.

One can only explain the Founders' willingness to worsen the problem that the separation of powers was meant to solve by understanding the importance that they attached to discussion and deliberation. The Federalists, unlike the Antifederalists, believed that representation should alter and not merely reflect popular views.

This belief in deliberation is implied not only by the argument for an extended republic but also by the contrast Madison draws between opinions and passions, since opinion implies a belief amenable to reason whereas passion implies a disposition beyond reason's reach. By the same token, Madison in Numbers 37 and 39 distinguishes between "partial" and "respectable" opinions and between more or less "fallible" ones. These distinctions imply the existence of a standard, discoverable by reason, by which one can tell a partial or fallible opinion from a respectable one.

Though Madison's view of human nature was certainly sober, it was not bleak. In various places (Numbers 40, 55, 57) Madison suggests that interests alone do not drive citizens. "As there is a degree of depravity in mankind which requires a certain circumspection and distrust: So there are other qualities in human nature, which justify a certain portion of esteem and confidence" [Number 55]. In particular, there seems to be "sufficient virtue" to make republican government possible.

I have exaggerated the difference in emphasis between *Federalist* Numbers 10 and 51; even in the latter, Madison writes of justice being the goal of government. But if you pardon the oversimplifications, the two essays can be read as powerful statements of two different—but in Madison's mind, and in mine—related ways of explaining politics.

The view expressed in Number 51 finds its modern expression in economic or rational-choice models of politics; the view suggested by Number 10 finds its expression among those who are critical of or indifferent to such parsimonious models. That Madison was able to combine both views into a larger synthesis and that we seem unable to do so is one measure of Madison's superior greatness.

Rational-choice models have great advantages. The assumptions on which they are based are generally true and thus generally useful: People do in fact seek their own interests, and we should attend more to how they do it than to how they justify it. These theories direct our attention to the importance of incentives in shaping behavior and put on the defensive those who would explain it largely in terms of attitudes. They render problematic what many

people take for granted—that collective action is easily undertaken. They lead us to examine outcomes: What difference does it make if X as opposed to Y constitutes the condition under which people try to increase their utility? They remind us of the links between the polity and the economy.

But a price is paid for adopting that approach. We may fail to ask how people define their self-interest in those circumstances—and in politics, there are many—where a person's self-interest is ambiguous or the limitations on information make rational choice difficult. Though rational-choice models are in principle as applicable to intangible as to tangible interests, in practice they are more easily applied—and thus more frequently used—to explain behavior on the basis of pecuniary motives. Such theories tend to understate the power of motives, such as duty or fairness, which seem at odds with any conception of immediate self-interest (though one can make a case that they may serve one's long-term self-interest). They rarely give full attention to interdependent utilities, and so cannot provide us with a plausible account of how the well-being of another person (or, conversely, the ill-mannered behavior of another person) limits the extent to which we pursue our own interests (or, conversely, induces us to act even when no interest of ours is at stake).

In short, many contemporary political scientists systematically understate the role of deliberation, the influence of norms, and the power of passion in human affairs, just as many traditional political scientists have overstated the role of deliberation, norms, and attitudes.

Let me offer a few well-known examples. At one time, political scientists took voting for granted—it was, it would seem, an act as natural and unremarkable as reading a newspaper. Regrettably not everyone did it, but more could be induced to do it by persuasion. Today, many political scientists cannot explain why anyone votes. It is irrational, in that casting a vote entails costs for which there are no compensating political benefits except in the absurdly rare case in which one vote can make or break a tie. What once seemed natural now appears weirdly unnatural; what once required no explanation now cannot be explained at all.

If people vote, why do they vote for one candidate rather than another? At one time, political scientists denied that this could be explained by any rational considerations—voters were too poorly informed for that—and so could only be explained by nonrational ones: Voters support parties or candidates with which they "identify." That argument has about the same explanatory power as saying that people eat ice cream because they like it. Today, many political scientists assume that voters seek to maximize their utility by choosing candidates who offer the largest discounted net benefits. (Of course using this assumption creates a problem: if it could not explain why people voted in the first place, how can it be used to explain whom they voted for? But never mind.) Ignoring the question of how the voting booth manages to transform irrational people into calculating ones, we confront another problem: if politicians are preoccupied with election or reelection and voters with the net benefits of government policy and if we make certain reasonable assumptions (for example, that voters' preferences are clustered at the middle of any array of choices), then rival candidates and parties should be as alike as Advil and Tylenol. They would have moved to the center of every discernible preference distribution. As a consequence, we would no longer have liberal and conservative candidates or parties, only indistinguishable ones. But as the briefest glance at any caucus, convention, or party rally shows, parties—or at least the most active elements within them—differ greatly, perhaps fundamentally. Now it is not just the voters who are behaving irrationally, it is the parties as well.

At one time, voters were fools; now they are rational calculators. At one time, people were good enough citizens to vote but not good enough citizens to vote wisely; now citizens are too irrational to realize that voting doesn't pay but rational enough to vote so as to maximize their own interest. At one time the parties were as alike as Tweedledum and Tweedledee, even though many political scientists thought they ought to be as opposed as Tories and Socialists; now they are becoming Tories and Socialists just when many political scientists have concluded that they ought to be Tweedledum and Tweedledee.

Once candidates are elected, their behavior in office must be explained. At one time, legislators were thought to vote for their party's position (though not often enough to please those political scientists who wanted stronger party government). Presumably they voted this way (to the extent that they did) either because of their ideology or because they felt obliged to support the party with whom their constituents identified. But if the reason was ideology, few political scientists wondered where it came from; if the reason was party, few asked why party should matter if, as these same political scientists argued, American parties were so weak that they would not easily control election outcomes. Today, some political scientists assume that legislators are wholly preoccupied with their individual prospects for reelection. Presumably they vote for bills that increase constituent support for them. But in that case it is not obvious why they would trouble to vote at all on bills to which their constituents were indifferent or even why they would not ignore most legislative work (which at best provides general benefits) in favor of individual casework (which supplies highly particular benefits). Moreover, legislators defend their votes or criticize those of others by making arguments about justice, fairness, and the public good. These arguments may be dismissed as rationalizations, as they often are, but they are not mere rationalizations; the fact that they are employed means that people are affected by them, and if they are affected by them, then their behavior can be altered by them. If none of us took seriously an argument about fairness or the common good, we would ignore—or laugh at—all such arguments, and soon they would no longer be employed. But they continue to be employed. In sum: At one time, many political scientists described the actions of legislators without describing the incentives they had to act in that way; today many political scientists analyze the incentives facing legislators without giving an account of behavior that is inconsistent with those incentives.

Some of these legislative outcomes are, of course, influenced by interest groups. On this subject there is more continuity than change. Political scientists throughout this century have been fascinated with interests. But they have had only partial success in accounting for the activities of these interests. At one time, political scientists took for granted that large interest groups would exist (apparently, any "interest" would acquire "group representation"), not pausing to wonder how anyone could persuade large numbers of farmers, workers, blacks, feminists, or conservationists to spend any time, effort, or money on actions which, if they were successful, would benefit the individual whether or not he or she joined in the actions. Today, many political scientists, having discovered the free-rider problem, ask only that question, with the result that they can explain the existence of small interest groups, and interest groups that give material benefits to their members, but they cannot easily explain large, *pro bono* groups. Political scientists who once never asked why large interest groups exist now ask and cannot answer.

Once a bill becomes law, it must be administered. At one time political scientists asked how public administrators could be freed from those particularistic and partisan influences that prevented them from being the selfless agents of public purposes. (They rarely asked whether being freed from such influences would place them more under the sway of ideological or organizational influences.) Once set free they could efficiently adapt organizational means to attain organizational ends. Today, many political scientists argue that bureaucrats will always be agents, not of public purposes, but of private interests, in particular their own interest in pay and promotions. Under these circumstances no efficient public management is possible, because privileged access to information and power will inevitably be used to convert organizational resources into personal gain. Once administrators were nearly selfless, today they are wholly selfish.

Having begun this address with a stylized and simplistic account of Madison's thinking, I have pushed forward with an even more simplistic account (in places, a caricatured one) of two approaches to political science—one that emphasizes norms and deliberation and another that draws attention to interests and calculation. The object has been to discredit neither but to unite both, as they once were united in the writings of the man we truly honor today, James Madison. If I appear to have been more critical of rational choice models, it is only because, among many younger scholars, that is the stronger wind against which one must lean.

• • •

The . . . normative and rationalistic approaches to political science are often warring camps, with the proponents of each relying exclusively on their favored methods and deriding the methods of their rivals. Rationalists charge normativists with being atheoretical and naive; normativists reply that rationalists are bean-counting cynics.

This would have puzzled James Madison, but then he lacked the advantages of highly specialized training and access to refereed journals. The synthesis he achieved in the *Federalist* papers was based on an approach to political science quite different from what some scholars today would deem acceptable. He did not ask, "What theory do I have and how can it be applied here?" He knew, long before the phrase was invented, that to a person holding a hammer the whole world looks like a nail. He asked instead: "What intellectually interesting question do I want to answer, and what are the best ways—not way, ways—in which to answer it?"

The question he tried to answer was this: Can a popular government be designed that will control the mischiefs of faction without endangering essential liberties? To find the answer, his method was to study the history of other attempts at popular rule, to review the theoretical arguments about the meaning of consent and of separated powers, and, most importantly, to reflect deeply on human nature.

His conclusion was that man is sufficiently self-interested and calculating as to make checks and balances necessary but sufficiently virtuous and deliberative as to make it possible to design and operate a constitution that supplies and maintains that system of restraints. As he put it in Number 57, "The aim of every political Constitution is or ought to be first to obtain for rulers, men who possess most wisdom to discern, and most virtue to pursue the common good of the society; and in the next place, to take the most effectual precautions for keeping them virtuous, whilst they continue to hold their public trust." Or to paraphrase a twentieth-century commentator, man is good enough to make republican government possible and bad enough to make it necessary.

Chapter 10

The Media

$\mathcal{A}$ free and unbridled press is one of the safeguards of American liberty. The United States, as Supreme Court justice William Brennan wrote in 1964, has maintained a "profound national commitment to the principle that debate on public issues should be uninhibited, robust, and wide-open." The press plays a critical role in promoting democracy by exposing official mismanagement and corruption, providing vital data on which citizens can make key decisions, and generally providing the people with a window on the activities of their government and the government with feedback on the opinions and viewpoints of the people.

The role of the media in the United States today, however, is not so simple. The media not only reports the news; it also decides what is and what is not news. It not only reports on public opinion; it also plays a vital role in shaping public opinion. In theory, the media may be free and unencumbered, but journalists live and work in a complex environment: their employers are themselves large corporations, which depend on other large corporations for necessary advertising revenue; they have their own agendas to pursue, both professionally and, some would say, ideologically; they must both entertain and inform, especially on television; they are easily manipulated and used by government officials and candidates; they must cope with short deadlines and often with limited information; and they must continually try to fight off boredom, bias, and a pack mentality.

All of this is complicated by television, which has become the dominant medium in the United States. More Americans get their news on television than in any other form; campaigns are waged and the country is governed through media performances, sound bites, and photo opportunities. Understanding television and knowing how to use it can get a candidate elected and help him or her govern; consider, for example, John F. Kennedy and Ronald Reagan. Failing to project the right media image can *ruin both a candidate and a president, as an endless trail of defeated politicians could easily testify.*

This chapter does not deal with the theoretical or constitutional commitment to a free press, themes covered in chapter 16. It deals instead with the day-to-day practical realities of life in the media age, focusing on two major themes. First, how does the press decide what to cover, how to cover it, and in what light to depict it? The journalist's role goes beyond agenda setting to playing an active part in the national debate itself; what motivates and constrains them? Selections 10.1, 10.2, and 10.4 through 10.6 deal in different ways with this question; 10.1 reveals the many factors that led the press to cover a particular campaign incident as they did; 10.2 focuses on day-to-day beat coverage in Washington; 10.4 through 10.6 consider whether the press plays this role in a biased or unbiased way. Second, what special role does television and media politics play in American campaign politics? Television is not only a part of the American press; it is also used by candidates and politicians directly to influence and speak to voters and citizens. This question is dealt with in selection 10.3, which looks at modern "sound bite" politics, and is touched on in selection 10.1 as well.

Chapter Questions

1. What roles do the media play in American politics? How would journalists characterize their role? Has this view changed in recent years?

2. What influences the media's decisions on what news to report and how to report it? To what extent do the media control the agenda in American politics? To what extent are the media manipulated by politicians and government officials?

3. How does television news coverage differ from print coverage? What is the significance of television for campaign politics? for governing?

VIEW FROM THE INSIDE

Never is the role of the press clearer or more critical than in a presidential election campaign. Press coverage can provide the necessary momentum—the "Big Mo," as George Bush called it—that propels a candidate to victory—or, as Gary Hart learned in 1988, press coverage can destroy a viable candidacy.

The following selection, by the political reporter David S. Broder, tells the story of Edmund Muskie's unsuccessful candidacy for president of the United States in 1972. Muskie, a senator from Maine, was the leading contender for the Democratic nomination early that year. Ten days before the critical New Hampshire primary, Muskie went to Manchester, New Hampshire, to take on the conservative newspaper publisher William Loeb, whose paper had made false charges against both the candidate and his wife. Muskie's tearful performance, as it turned out, marked the end of the road for his campaign.

What happened? The press's role in the incident was fourfold. First, they reported the story as it took place, with an emphasis on Muskie's tears. Second, television broadcast the picture of a dejected Muskie, crying, projecting the image of defeat. Third, the handicappers in the press jumped on the incident as an illustration of the disarray that marked Muskie's campaign and—that word again—the momentum that now shifted to George McGovern, his principal rival. Finally, the press played up the Muskie campaign's prediction that their candidate would receive 50 percent of the primary vote; when he won with only 46 percent, they pronounced the election a victory for McGovern. Muskie never recovered.

Evaluating the press's role is no easy task, but it is well worth the effort. The Muskie incident shows the American political press at its best and worst, playing a role that is necessary and valuable but that sometimes exceeds its legitimate scope. As you read this selection, try to evaluate what the press did right, what it could have done differently, why it acted as it did; and whether, as Broder suggests, the press missed the real story altogether.

Questions

1. Why did the press report this story as it did? If you were managing he Muskie campaign, how would you have wanted it reported? How might you have planned the incident differently to elicit a different press response?

2. Was the press justified in playing up the 50 percent prediction? in focusing on what they perceived to be the shifting momentum? Did the press merely report the story, or create it?

10.1 Taken Out of Context: Ed Muskie and the Press in New Hampshire

David S. Broder

The snow was cascading down that Saturday morning in Manchester, New Hampshire, when Senator Edmund S. Muskie headed toward the offices of the *Manchester Union Leader* for the first scheduled event of the day. Like much in modern campaigning, this "event" was designed more for the press and the cameras than for the citizenry. Fewer than a hundred hardy campaign workers and casual passersby, stamping their feet in the snow, would join the newspaper's employees watching from windows.

Ed Muskie was the front-runner in the New Hampshire presidential primary, so when his press aides alerted the reporters living at the Sheraton-Wayfarer in nearby Bedford that Muskie would go to the *Union Leader* Saturday morning to reply to attacks from publisher William Loeb, they were guaranteed that this was one media event that would draw heavy coverage.

As he walked through the snow, hands jammed into his overcoat pockets and his head bent against the snow, Muskie looked as if he might be having second thoughts. But for the reporters trailing him, the setting and the timing were perfect. It was early in the day; we would have plenty of time to file for the early Sunday deadlines. The event would be a natural lead-in to our Sunday wrap-up pieces, summarizing the New Hampshire situation nine days before the primary. In confronting Loeb, who had been giving Muskie the same brutal front-page editorial treatment he had given other moderates and liberals in both parties who appeared to threaten the publisher's favored right-wing candidates, the senator from Maine was symbolically confronting the frustrations which had turned New Hampshire from an expected easy triumph into an exhausting, embittering struggle. The story looked to have some potential.

It proved to have much more than that.

The human factor is always the least predictable element in covering politics. That is why the beat is so fascinating. Under the pressure of campaigns for high office, people react in ways that are always revealing and often unexpected. In this case, Muskie's strategists wanted him to show indignation and righteous wrath and regain the offensive in what they saw as an eroding effort to hold off the challenge of his major rival, Senator George McGovern of South Dakota. The concerns focused on the impact of two *Union Leader* editorials: one concerned an alleged derogatory comment by Muskie about the important French-Canadian voting bloc; the other impugned the behavior and character of the candidate's wife, Jane.

What actually happened there in the snowstorm, as Muskie stood on the flatbed truck drawn up before the *Union Leader* building, was more unexpected and dramatic. By noon, back in the warmth of the Wayfarer, I wrote about it in an unrestrained fashion:

> With tears streaming down his face and his voice choked with emotion, Senator Edmund S. Muskie (D-Maine) stood in the snow outside the *Manchester Union Leader* this morning and accused its publisher of making vicious attacks on him and his wife, Jane.

The Democratic presidential candidate called publisher William Loeb "a gutless coward" for involving Mrs. Muskie in the campaign and said four times that Loeb had lied in charging that Muskie had condoned a slur on Americans of French-Canadian descent.

In defending his wife, Muskie broke down three times in as many minutes—uttering a few words and then standing silent in the near blizzard, rubbing at his face, his shoulders heaving, while he attempted to regain his composure sufficiently to speak.

The story—accompanied by a photo—ran under a four-column headline as the off-lead of the Sunday *Washington Post* and continued for twenty-three paragraphs inside. David Nyhan's story, which described Muskie as "weeping silently," was played even more prominently on the front page of the *Boston Globe*. The *New York Times* ran a photograph on page 1, but relegated the story to page 54, perhaps because reporter James M. Naughton cast his story around Muskie's denunciation of Loeb and mentioned the tears and broken speech only once, in the sixth paragraph. The *Washington Star* used a UPI story on page 2 which noted in the eighth paragraph that Muskie was "visibly shaken" but offered no further details.

That Saturday night, CBS News had an arresting clip of the event, which Roger Mudd introduced by saying that Muskie, after denouncing Loeb, "suddenly became emotional and found it difficult to continue." The screen was filled with Muskie's face, the features contorted.

As Theodore H. White later wrote in *The Making of the President 1972*, "Rarely has the instrument of television been able, without any preconceived political intent, to frame perspectives more strikingly." CBS opened its news show with a brief report on a West Virginia flood, then shifted to a long segment on President Nixon's trip to China, where, as White wrote, "in this context of beauty and majesty there were Richard Nixon and Chou En-lai feeding goldfish from the moon bridge in smiles and amity." Then, with only a commercial break, the scene shifted to Manchester, with "Ed Muskie on the flatbed truck crying, or choking up, but obviously in great distress as his voice broke in a denunciation of the man who had attacked his wife. The contrast between the President's management of great events in Asia and the Democratic candidate's disturbance over an unexplained slander in Manchester, New Hampshire, was sharp."

Watching it on a weekend visit home in Washington, the crack political reporter Jack W. Germond, then with the Gannett newspapers' Washington bureau, instantly decided to fly back to New Hampshire, because, he said, "I knew something was happening."

Indeed it was. Within twenty-four hours, Muskie's weeping became the focus of political talk, not just in New Hampshire, but wherever in America or the world the pattern of the developing presidential race was discussed. His tears would be generally described as one of the contributing causes to his disappointing showing in the March 7 primary. Muskie beat McGovern by a margin of 46 to 37 percent, but his managers had publicized their goal of winning

at least 50 percent of the New Hampshire Democratic vote. Underdog McGovern was able to claim that the results showed Muskie's weakness and his own growing strength. Muskie never recovered from that Saturday in the snow.

At the time, controversy centered on Muskie's insistence he never shed the tears we thought we saw. Melting snow from his hatless head filled his eyes, he said, and had him wiping his face. While admitting that exhaustion and emotion got the better of him that morning, the senator believed that he was damaged more by the press and television coverage of the event than by his own actions.

In retrospect, it is clear that Muskie was victimized neither by himself nor by the press, but by a classic dirty trick that had been engineered by agents of the distant and detached President Nixon. The Loeb editorial that had brought Muskie out in the snowstorm had been based on a letter forged by a White House staff member, intent on destroying Muskie's credibility. But we did not know that.

Drawing by Marc Cullum. Reprinted with permission of Copley News Service.

Does the press make the news or merely report it? Is it an independent watchdog over the American political system or an easily manipulated tool of the Washington establishment? Is it part of the problem or part of the solution?

To Charles Peters, the editor of the liberal, irreverent, and muckraking magazine the Washington Monthly, *the press is part of the problem. Washington politics is one big game of make believe, he suggests, and the news media is "part of the show."*

In the wake of the Watergate scandal and other highly publicized episodes, the press has gained a reputation as the fourth branch of government, dedicated to opposing power-hungry politicians and exposing official corruption. Despite this image, Peters suggests, the press for the most part is simply a part of the Washington crowd. Understanding how Washington reporters really work provides an essential insight into the kind and quality of news we read, see, and hear.

Questions

1. What does Peters mean when he suggests that Washington reporters are often simply "stenographers for government press agents"?

2. What kinds of stories are reporters unlikely to go after, in Peters' view? What kinds of stories are reporters likely to file?

3. Why does the "beat system" contribute to Washington reporters' missing what Peters characterizes as the "real" stories?

10.2 How Washington Really Works: The Press

Charles Peters

• • •

Washington is like the Winter Palace under Nicholas and Alexandra, where there were constant earnest discussions of the lot of the poor, but the discussions were never accompanied by effective action. In Washington bureaucrats confer, the president proclaims, and the Congress legislates, but the impact on reality is negligible if evident at all. The nation's problems don't disappear, and all the activity that supposedly was dedicated to their solution turns out to have been make believe.

The press, instead of exposing the make believe, is part of the show. It dutifully covers the apparent action—the announcement of pro-grams, the enactment of legislation—rather than finding out how the programs are executed and the legislation is implemented or what the government is *not* doing about crucial problems.

One of the reasons for the persistence of make believe is the press's tradition of the beat system. Reporters are regularly assigned to the White House, to the Congress, to the Pentagon, and to the State Department. They cover official pronouncements but only rarely do they find out whether the new weapons system they write about really works or whether the poor are being hired or the drugs are being tested. Tom Wicker of the *New York Times* explains:

"The problem . . . is that the American press

tends to be an institutionalized press. It covers institutions and processes—anything that has official spokesmen and official visible functions.

"When I was a bureau chief in Washington, I had roughly thirty reporters to deploy around town, and I know how hard it is to get away from the 'beat' system. When they are sent out to cover institutions and spokesmen [which is what the beat system is], they inevitably miss a lot of other things that are happening."

The government likes the beat system as much as the reporters do. Every high official has a press secretary or public information officer, who in turn often has his own platoon—and sometimes an army—of assistants. . . .

All these people make it easy for reporters to get news about government officials. They issue press releases almost every day to make sure the reporters are aware of whatever their bosses have said or done that can be made to look good. They coddle reporters in a warm cocoon of perquisites. Here, as described by congressional correspondent Mick Rood, is a typical day for journalists who cover Congress:

"First stop, the Senate press gallery. It's more spacious than the gallery on the House side of the Capitol. There is time to settle into one of the big, old leather chairs to read a copy or two of the ten daily newspapers supplied us by the Congress. Browsing completed, it's back out past the uniformed guard at the gallery door.

"On your way to some morning coffee, you take the 'Press Only' elevator down to one of the Senate cafeterias. Similar to the 'Senators Only' elevator, the 'Press Only' elevator runs about a floor faster than the public elevators. There is a special section reserved to the press in the cafeteria. Around the corner, the public waits in a long line for a chance to eat breakfast in a Senate restaurant. Here, it's time to engage in colloquy with your colleagues, to discuss the issues of the day and what The Leadership is doing. We could linger, but there is a hearing to cover for the newspaper back home.

"Arriving at the hearing room, you are greeted by another uniformed fellow, who

waves you through once you produce your congressional gallery pass. You squeeze by several dozen other people who are standing in line to enter. . . . Once inside, a Senate gallery staff member escorts you to the seat you requested yesterday. Ahead of all others who might be affected by the legislation being considered at the hearing, you are provided copies of testimony by the same gallery staff member. After the hearing, you return to the gallery to bat out a quick story. The typewriter and paper are provided by Congress.

"Lunch hunger calls, but you're out of money. Didn't have time to stop at your bank? No problem. The press gallery superintendent signs off on your personal check. You can cash it downstairs at the Sergeant-at-Arms Bank—along with the legislators and their staffs.

"Off to the House side, where debate has started on the floor on some question or other of great national importance. During debate you may be summoned to the gallery office for telephone calls, which are dutifully logged for you by the gallery staff. The long bank of telephone booths has been provided for in the congressional budget. . . .

"It could be an anniversary, a birthday, or maybe it's Christmas. You've forgotten someone. It's all right. One of the nicest things about serving the people's right to know is the Senate stationery store, where members, staff, *and* reporters can shop at prices below retail.

"As evening falls on Washington, you return to your car, which is parked in the Capitol parking lot. You are among about 180 reporters who share the press slots, bestowed by the House Administration Committee and the Senate Rules Committee." Parking can cost around $70 per month at lots on Capitol Hill, but permit-holding reporters park free.

Reporters assigned to the Defense Department get a lot more than free parking and leather chairs—the Pentagon will fly them across the country and around the world to cover the stories it wants them to print. The White House sometimes even arranges for reporters' families to go along on presidential trips—at one-third to one-half the cost of ordinary fares—to places like Aspen, Key Biscayne, Sea Island, and Santa Barbara. The reporters' part of the bargain is to participate in the make believe that real news is being made in these places rather than just routine statements between rounds of golf.

Because officials are so anxious to get good press, there is often tremendous pressure on the government press agent. Shortly after Robert McKinney became chairman of the Federal Home Loan Bank Board, in the early days of the Carter administration, his public relations officer, Mike Scanlon, arranged a press briefing that put McKinney on the front page of both the *Washington Post* and the *New York Times*. It wasn't long before McKinney came to expect that kind of coverage all the time. When he made a speech in San Francisco that received local publicity but none back East, he fired Scanlon.

Don McClure tells about the time he was serving as public relations officer for the Peace Corps under Sargent Shriver: "One week three magazines—*Newsweek, Look,* and the *Saturday Evening Post*—hit the stands with Peace Corps stories. Shriver wanted to know what had happened with *Time.*"

• • •

People who have reached top levels of government usually have attained their positions at least partly through their skill in handling journalists. They know how to make themselves look good; they also know how to divert attention from the less flattering stories. Reporters who become dependent on these officials, as most do, simply don't get the truth about what's wrong. The most spectacular example of this failure is the case of the White House press corps during the unfolding of the Watergate scandal. Not one of the scores of journalists assigned to full-time coverage of the White House got a major Watergate story. They had been spoon-fed for so long that they lost the habit of independent inquiry. Even when they realized that they had been had, their reaction was not to improve their reporting methods but

simply to be rude to the press secretary and to the president.

This rudeness has become another part of the make believe. It makes the members of the White House press corps feel like tough investigative reporters. But all it usually adds up to is a sardonic gloss on a story that the White House wants them to print or broadcast, a veneer of cynicism the public is supposed to interpret as objectivity.

James Fallows writes of his experience with the press when he was head speechwriter during the Carter administration:

"Within the White House, weekly summaries of the President's schedule were prepared; for each day, they listed what the likely 'news event' would be. Under normal circumstances, that prediction almost always came true; if the President was making an announcement about the U.S. Forest Service, the Forest Service would get one day's news—and would not be in the news again until another announcement was planned.

"But after accepting the government's chosen topic, the reporters treat it in their own way, with reflexive cynicism about the administration's plans. The true lesson of Watergate is the value of hard digging, not only into scandal but everywhere else. The *perceived* lesson of Watergate in the White House press room is the Dan Rather lesson, that a surly attitude can take the place of facts or intelligent analysis. More and more often at the President's press conferences, one sees reporters proving their tough-mindedness by asking insulting questions; in the daily briefings with Jody Powell, open snarling became the norm. TV correspondents feel they've paid homage to the shade of Bob Woodward by ending their reports not with intelligent criticism but with a sophomoric twist: 'The administration says its plans will work but the true result is *still to be seen.* Dan Daring, NBC News, the White House.'"

The men who got the Watergate story, Bob Woodward and Carl Bernstein of the *Washington Post*, did not get it by asking questions of the White House press office. One of their sources,

Deep Throat, is widely suspected to have been David Gergen, who handled publicity for the Reagan administration but was a low-ranking functionary in the Nixon White House. Those whose identities Woodward and Bernstein later revealed were not high-ranking officials. Instead, they were personal secretaries and middle-level executives like Hugh Sloan, the assistant treasurer of the Committee to Re-elect the President. When Bill Moyers was press secretary to Lyndon Johnson, he said the kind of leaker he feared most was not the cabinet member, who could usually be trusted to guard his comments even after infuriatingly disappointing sessions with the president. Rather, Moyers said, the secretary's special assistant, who heard everything about those sessions once the secretary returned to his office, was much more likely to leak.

The Hugh Sloans and the special assistants are more prone to talk because they are several layers removed from personal loyalty to the president and because they are less skilled than their bosses in fending off the inquiries of the press. There is also another factor that sometimes encourages them to be honest: a loyalty to something they see as being more important than the president. This could be the welfare of the country, or it could simply be the welfare of their agency. The reporter who, next to Woodward and Bernstein, did the best job on Watergate, Sandy Smith of *Time*, got most of his material from middle-level bureaucrats at the FBI, who resented Patrick Gray's attempts to make what they regarded as political use of the bureau. And don't forget James McCord's famous letter to Judge Sirica that broke the Watergate dam. It was motivated by McCord's anger at what Nixon had tried to do to the CIA, where McCord had been a middle-level bureaucrat.

It can be argued that Woodward and Bernstein got the Watergate story precisely because they were not White House correspondents but local reporters for the *Washington Post*'s Metro section. If they had been White House correspondents, they would have asked Ziegler and Nixon what was going on and received the usual runaround. Because they weren't, they had to dig down to the lower-level people who knew the story and were willing to talk.

The people who work on the Metro section of the *Post* often try to follow Woodward's and Bernstein's example and make their reputations by uncovering a scandal. But once a Metro reporter has "made it," he or she gets assigned to a prestigious national affairs beat. Unfortunately, the reporter then tends to become a statesman covering other statesmen. This is exactly what happened to Woodward and Bernstein. For all the inside information in their second book, *The Final Days*, they relied heavily on Alexander Haig and Fred Buzhardt, who were high-level officials during the last year of the Nixon administration. Not surprisingly, the book makes both Haig and Buzhardt appear to be fine fellows, if not outright heroes. In fact, both were far from being innocent bystanders in the conspiracy to obstruct justice that was the main activity of the White House during Nixon's last two years as president.

Which brings us to sources. The leaking of information is a Washington art form practiced by bureaucrats and politicians at all levels. As we have seen, many middle-level bureaucrats leak information to the press either because they resent being manipulated by their bosses or because they are loyal to values higher than personal job security. And occasionally people will leak to the press on a touchy subject to make sure their bosses pay attention to warnings they might otherwise choose to ignore: It's easy to bury a folder of unpleasant statistics in a messy office but hard to overlook them on the front page of the *Washington Post* or the *New York Times*.

• • •

Finally, in a quest for exclusive, behind-the-scenes, on-the-spot news, members of the media may find they are helping to create that news instead of merely reporting it. There is a story that in the mid-1960s, CBS bid over $30,000 for the exclusive film rights to an insurrection in Haiti. But when CBS realized this money was helping the rebel army buy guns and ammunition—that, in effect, CBS was subsidizing the invasion, not just covering it—the network withdrew the offer.

A more common failure of investigative reporting is an article about an alleged abuse in which the significance of the abuse is never made clear. Conflicts of interest are reported as evil per se when they are only potentially evil. (When a reporter reveals that some senator owns stock in a company that does business with the government, the reporter too often stops there, with merely finding the conflict of interest, instead of proceeding to determine whether the conflict has ever actually influenced the senator's official behavior, which is the *real* story.) Worst of all for Washington, the investigative reporter looks for scandalous illegality when he should be looking into why the government doesn't work. What's wrong with government today seldom has much to do with illegality. Occasionally it does, such as when a congressman is on the take . . . or when officials in the General Services Administration are taking bribes from government suppliers. But most of the time the explanation of what is wrong lies in the cultures of the bureaucracy, the Congress, the White House, and the judiciary—that is, in the customs and rituals and pressures that govern life in these institutions. The average reporter is remarkably ignorant of these cultures.

Reporters who understand the culture of the bureaucracy would have known, for example, that one or more tragedies such as My Lai were likely to occur in Vietnam as soon as the Pentagon began publishing body counts of enemy casualties to prove America was winning the war. The reporters would have realized that the pressure for more casualties would lead commanders to find those casualties wherever they could. If reporters understood that mentality, they would not have waited for the story to be revealed by a Vietnam veteran a year after the fact. They might even have prevented it by asking questions and writing stories about the dangerous possibility that the numbers game would lead to shooting animals, women, children—anything that could be counted in the casualty totals.

• • •

The influence of the press on government officials cannot be overestimated. This influence can be positive. Think how much chicanery dies on the drawing board when someone says, "We'd better not do that; what if the press finds out?" On the other hand, there are ill effects such as these:

- A public official or a candidate for public office seldom does anything important after 5 P.M. because it won't make the evening news and therefore will not have happened.

- Presidential candidates campaign in the small, out-of-the-way state of New Hampshire because they know reporters are watching.

- Top staff meetings at the White House and in the various agencies and departments are devoted to getting puff pieces written. The puff pieces are then accepted as reality by those who inspired them.

- The transcripts of meetings of the Nuclear Regulatory Commission during the near-disaster of Three-Mile Island indicate that the only time the commissioners devoted sustained attention to one subject was when they debated—sometimes for hours—the wording of a press release. And this during a period when life-and-death decisions affecting hundreds of thousands of people had to be made.

Washington reporters could find out the truth. It doesn't require unusual ability, just the willingness to break free from the conventional beats and go where the *real* action is. But they are too bound up in the make believe system of reporting apparent action, in the ease of being stenographers for government press agents, and in the thrill of rubbing shoulders with the mighty and walking through the White House gate past the admiring eyes of waiting tourists.

William Kovach, the *New York Times*'s [former] bureau chief in Washington, says: "Nothing is more painful than the look on the face of a reporter who has been told that he or she must turn in the White House press pass because someone else needs it more; nor is there any look quite so seraphic as that on the face of one told he or she has just been added to the list of White House press pass holders."

White House reporters will cynically tell you (off the record, of course) all about being spoon-fed by the Jody Powells. They don't say it on the record because they don't want their editors to see it and take them off the White House beat. They know that what they're doing doesn't really count, but the folks back home think it does. It sometimes seems that White House reporters live life for the stories they can tell their friends, stories about Carter and Sadat or Kennedy and his girlfriends. It may be only make believe, but as the press plane takes off for another presidential trip abroad, who cares?

III  TRENDS

Television as a political force was born in the 1950s, but it did not come of age until the 1960s. The decade's first presidential campaign featured the Kennedy-Nixon televised debate, which many commentators believe swung the election to Kennedy; its last campaign, in 1968, is best summed up by the title of Joe McGinnis's book on Nixon's use of paid advertising: The Selling of the President. *By the end of the decade, the common complaint was that presidents were being sold like soap.*

Twenty years later, political observers long with nostalgia for the television politics of the 1960s. Campaigns now reek with negative advertising, 30-second (and even 15-second) commercials, and 10-second sound bites. Candidates and their media advisers sling mud, give (and receive) cheap shots, and avoid issues like the plague. To suggest that presidents are now sold like soap, as one commentator put it, is unfair to soap.

Kiku Adatto, in the following selection, compares the 1988 election to the 1968 election and finds that much has changed in a mere two decades.

Questions

1. What are the main differences between the media politics of 1968 and the media politics of 1988? Why factors have contributed to these changes?

2. What are the disadvantages of the new media politics? Are there any advantages?

10.3 The Incredible Shrinking Sound Bite

Kiku Adatto

Standing before a campaign rally in Pennsylvania, the 1968 Democratic vice presidential candidate, Edmund Muskie, tried to speak, but a group of anti-war protesters drowned him out. Muskie offered the hecklers a deal. He would give the platform to one of their representatives if he could then speak without interruption. Rick Brody, the students' choice, rose to the microphone where, to cheers from the crowd, he denounced the candidates that the 1968 presidential campaign had to offer. "Wallace is no answer. Nixon's no answer. And Humphrey's no answer. Sit out this election!" When Brody finished, Muskie made his case for the Democratic ticket. That night Muskie's confrontation with demonstrators played prominently on the network news. NBC showed fifty-seven seconds of Brody's speech, and more than a minute of Muskie's.

Twenty years later, things had changed. Throughout the entire 1988 campaign, no network allowed either presidential candidate to speak uninterrupted on the evening news for as long as Rick Brody spoke. By 1988 television's tolerance for the languid pace of political discourse, never great, had all but vanished. An analysis of all weekday evening network newscasts (over 280) from Labor Day to Election Day in 1968 and 1988 reveals that the average "sound bite" fell from 42.3 seconds in 1968 to only 9.8 seconds in 1988. Meanwhile the time the networks devoted to visuals of the candidates, unaccompanied by their words, increased by more than 300 percent.

Since the Kennedy-Nixon debates of 1960, television has played a pivotal role in presidential politics. The Nixon campaign of 1968 was the first to be managed and orchestrated to play on the evening news. With the decline of political parties and the direct appeal to voters in the primaries, presidential campaigns became more adept at conveying their messages through visual images, not only in political commercials but also in elaborately staged media events. By the time of Ronald Reagan, the actor turned president, Michael Deaver had perfected the techniques of the video presidency.

For television news, the politicians' mastery of television imagery posed a temptation and a challenge. The temptation was to show the pictures. What network producer could resist the footage of Reagan at Normandy Beach, or of Bush in Boston Harbor? The challenge was to avoid being entangled in the artifice and imagery that the campaigns dispensed. In 1988 the networks tried to have it both ways—to meet the challenge even as they succumbed to the temptation. They showed the images that the campaigns produced—their commercials as well as their media events. But they also sought to retain their objectivity by exposing the artifice of the images, by calling constant attention to their self-conscious design.

The language of political reporting was filled with accounts of staging and backdrops, camera angles and scripts, sound bites and spin control, photo opportunities and media gurus. So attentive was television news to the way the campaigns constructed images for television that political reporters began to sound like theater critics, reporting more on the stagecraft than the substance of politics.

When Bush kicked off his campaign with a Labor Day appearance at Disneyland, the networks covered the event as a performance for television. "In the war of the Labor Day visuals," CBS's Bob Schieffer reported, "George Bush pulled out the heavy artillery. A Disneyland backdrop and lots of pictures with the Disney gang." When Bruce Morton covered Dukakis riding in a tank, the story was the image. "In the trade of politics, it's called a visual," said Morton. "The idea is pictures are symbols that tell the voter important things about the candidate. If your candidate is seen in the polls as weak on defense, put him in a tank."

And when Bush showed up at a military base to observe the destruction of a missile under an arms control treaty, ABC's Brit Hume began his report by telling his viewers that they were watching a media event. "Now, here was a photo opportunity, the vice president watching a Pershing missile burn off its fuel." He went on to describe how the event was staged for television. Standing in front of an open field, Hume reported, "The Army had even gone so far as to bulldoze acres of trees to make sure the vice president and the news media had a clear view."

So familiar is the turn to theater criticism that it is difficult to recall the transformation it represents. Even as they conveyed the first presidential campaign "made for television," TV reporters in 1968 continued to reflect the print journalist tradition from which they had descended. In the marriage of theater and politics, politics remained the focus of reporting. The media events of the day—mostly rallies and press conferences—were covered as political events, not as exercises in impression management.

By 1988 television displaced politics as the focus of coverage. Like a gestalt shift, the images that once formed the background to political events—the setting and the stagecraft—now occupied the foreground. (Only 6 percent of reports in 1968 were devoted to theater criticism, compared with 52 percent in 1988.) And yet, for all their image-conscious coverage in 1988, reporters did not escape their entanglement. They showed the potent visuals even as they attempted to avoid the manipulation by "deconstructing" the imagery and revealing its artifice.

To be sure, theater criticism was not the only kind of political reporting on network newscasts in 1988. Some notable "fact correction" pieces offered admirable exceptions. For example, after each presidential debate, ABC's Jim Wooten compared the candidates' claims with the facts. Not content with the canned images of the politicians, Wooten used television images to document discrepancies between the candidates' rhetoric and their records.

Most coverage simply exposed the contrivances of image-making. But alerting the viewer to the construction of television images proved no substitute for face correction. A superficial "balance" replaced objectivity as the measure of fairness, a balance consisting of equal time for media events, equal time for commercials. But this created a false symmetry, leaving both the press and the public hostage to the play of perceptions the campaigns dispensed.

Even the most critical versions of image-conscious coverage could fail to puncture the pictures they showed. When Bush visited a flag factory in hopes of making patriotism a campaign issue, ABC's Hume reported that Bush was wrapping himself in the flag. "This campaign strives to match its pictures with its points. Today and for much of the past week, the pictures have been of George Bush with the American flag. If the point wasn't to make an issue of patriotism, then the question arises, what was it?" Yet only three days later, in an ABC report on independent voters in New Jersey, the media event that Hume reported with derision was transformed into an innocent visual of Bush. The criticism forgotten, the image played on.

Another striking contrast between the coverage of the 1968 and 1988 campaigns is the increased coverage of political commercials. Although political ads played a prominent role in the 1968 campaign, the networks rarely showed excerpts on the news. During the entire 1968 general election campaign, the evening news programs broadcast only two excerpts from candidates' commercials. By 1988 the number had jumped to 125. In 1968 the only time a negative ad was mentioned on the evening news was when CBS's Walter Cronkite and NBC's Chet Huntley reported that a Nixon campaign ad—showing a smiling Hubert Humphrey superimposed on scenes of war and riot—was withdrawn after the Democrats cried foul. Neither network showed the ad itself.

The networks might argue that in 1988 political ads loomed larger in the campaign, and so required more coverage. But as with their focus on media events, reporters ran the risk of becoming conduits of the television images the campaigns dispensed. Even with a critical narrative, showing commercials on the news gives free time to paid media. And most of the time the narrative was not critical. The networks rarely bothered to correct the distortions or misstatements that the ads contained. Of the 125 excerpts shown on the evening news in 1988, the reporter addressed the veracity of the commercials' claims less than 8 percent of the time. The networks became, in effect, electronic billboards for the candidates, showing political commercials not only as breaking news but as stand-ins for the candidates, and file footage aired interchangeably with news footage of the candidates.

The few cases where reporters corrected the facts illustrate how the networks might have covered political commercials. ABC's Richard Threlkeld ran excerpts from a Bush ad attacking Dukakis's defense stand by freezing the frame and correcting each mistaken or distorted claim. He also pointed out the exaggeration in a Dukakis ad attacking Bush's record on Social Security. CBS's Leslie Stahl corrected a deceptive statistic in Bush's revolving-door furlough ad, noting: "Part of the ad is false. . . . Two hundred sixty-eight murderers did not escape. . . . [T]he truth is only four first-degree murderers escaped while on parole."

Stahl concluded her report by observing, "Dukakis left the Bush attack ads unanswered for six weeks. Today campaign aides are engaged in a round of finger-pointing at who is to blame." But the networks also let the Bush furlough commercial run without challenge or correction. Before and even after her report, CBS ran excerpts of the ad without correction. In all, network newscasts ran excerpts from the revolving-door furlough ad ten times through-

out the campaign, only once correcting the deceptive statistic.

It might be argued that it is up to the candidate to reply to his opponent's charges, not the press. But the networks' frequent use of political ads on the evening news created a strong disincentive for a candidate to challenge his opponent's ads. As Dukakis found, to attack a television ad as unfair or untrue is to invite the networks to run it again. In the final weeks before the election, the Dukakis campaign accused the Republicans of lying about his record on defense, and of using racist tactics in ads featuring Willie Horton, a black convict who raped and killed while on furlough from a Massachusetts prison. In reporting Dukakis's complaint, all three networks ran excerpts of the ads in question, including the highly charged pictures of Horton and the revolving door of convicts. Dukakis's response thus gave Bush's potent visuals another free run on the evening news.

The networks might reply that the ads are news and thus need to be shown, as long as they generate controversy in the campaign. But this rationale leaves them open to manipulation. Oddly enough, the networks were alive to this danger when confronted with the question of whether to air the videos the campaigns produced for their conventions. "I am not into tone poems," Lane Venardos, the executive producer in charge of convention coverage at CBS, told *The New York Times.* "We are not in the business of being propaganda arms of the political parties." But they seemed blind to the same danger during the campaign itself.

So successful was the Bush campaign at getting free time for its ads on the evening news that, after the campaign, commercial advertisers adopted a similar strategy. In 1989 a pharmaceutical company used unauthorized footage of Presidents Bush and Gorbachev to advertise a cold medication. "In the new year," the slogan ran, "may the only cold war in the world be the one being fought by us." Although two of the three networks refused to carry the commercial, dozens of network and local television news programs showed excerpts of the ad, generating millions of dollars of free airtime.

"I realized I started a trend," said Bush media consultant Roger Ailes in *The New York Times*. "Now guys are out there trying to produce commercials for the evening news." When Humphrey and Nixon hired Madison Avenue experts to help in their campaigns, some worried that, in the television age, presidents would be sold like products. Little did they imagine that, twenty years later, products would be sold like presidents.

Along with the attention to commercials and stagecraft in 1988 came an unprecedented focus on the stage managers themselves, the "media gurus," "handlers," and "spin-control artists." Only three reports featured media advisers in 1968, compared with twenty-six in 1988. And the numbers tell only part of the story.

The stance reporters have taken toward media advisers has changed dramatically over the past twenty years. In *The Selling of the President* (1969), Joe McGinniss exposed the growing role of media advisers with a sense of disillusion and outrage. By 1988 television reporters covered image-makers with deference, even admiration. In place of independent fact correction, reporters sought out media advisers as authorities in their own right to analyze the effectiveness and even defend the truthfulness of campaign commercials. They became "media gurus" not only for the candidates but for the networks as well.

For example, in an exchange with CBS anchor Dan Rather on Bush's debate performance, Stahl lavished admiration on the techniques of Bush's media advisers:

> STAHL: "They told him not to look into the camera. [She gestures toward the camera as she speaks.] You know when you look directly into a camera you are cold, apparently they have determined."
>
> RATHER [laughing]: "Bad news for anchormen I'd say."
>
> STAHL: "We have a lot to learn from this. Michael Dukakis kept talking right into the camera. [Stahl talks directly into her own camera to demonstrate.] And according to the Bush people that makes you look programmed, Dan [Stahl laughs]. And they're very adept at these television symbols and television imagery. And according to our poll it worked."
>
> RATHER: "Do you believe it?"
>
> STAHL: "Yes, I think I do, actually."

So hypersensitive were the networks to television image-making in 1988 that minor mishaps—gaffes, slips of the tongue, even faulty microphones—became big news. Politicians were hardly without mishaps in 1968, but these did not count as news. Only once in 1968 did a network even take note of a minor incident unrelated to the content of the campaign. In 1988 some twenty-nine reports highlighted trivial slips.

The emphasis on "failed images" reflected a kind of guerrilla warfare between the networks and the campaigns. The more the campaigns sought to control the images that appeared on the nightly news, the more the reporters tried to beat them at their own game, magnifying a minor mishap into a central feature of the media event.

Early in the 1988 campaign, for example, George Bush delivered a speech to a sympathetic audience of the American Legion, attacking his opponent's defense policies. In a slip, he declared that September 7, rather than December 7, was the anniversary of Pearl Harbor. Murmurs and chuckles from the audience alerted him to his error, and he quickly corrected himself.

The audience was forgiving, but the networks were not. All three network anchors highlighted the slip on the evening news. Dan Rather introduced CBS's report on Bush by declaring solemnly, "Bush's talk to audiences in Louisville was overshadowed by a strange happening." On NBC Tom Brokaw reported, "He departed from his prepared script and left his listeners mystified." Peter Jennings introduced ABC's report by mentioning Bush's attack on Dukakis, adding, "What's more likely to be remembered about today's speech is a slip of the tongue."

Some of the slips the networks highlighted in 1988 were not even verbal gaffes or misstatements, but simply failures on the part of candidates to cater to the cameras. In a report on the travails of the Dukakis campaign, Sam Donaldson seized on Dukakis's failure to play to ABC's television camera as evidence of his campaign's ineffectiveness. Showing Dukakis playing a trumpet with a local marching band, Donaldson chided, "He played the trumpet with his back to the camera." As Dukakis played "Happy Days Are Here Again," Donaldson's voice was heard from off-camera calling, "We're over here, governor."

One way of understanding the turn to image-conscious coverage in 1988 is to see how television news came to partake of the postwar modernist sensibility, particularly the pop art movement of the 1960s. Characteristic of this outlook is a self-conscious attention to art as performance, a focus on the process of image-making rather than on the ideas the images represent.

During the 1960s, when photography and television became potent forces for documentation and entertainment, they also became powerful influences on the work of artists. Photographers began to photograph the television set as part of the social landscape. Newspapers, photographs, and commercial products became part of the collage work of painters such as Robert Rauschenberg. Artists began to explore self-consciously their role in the image-making process.

For example, Lee Friedlander published a book of photography, *Self Portrait*, in which the artist's shadow or reflection was included in every frame. As critic Rod Slemmons notes, "By indicating the photographer is also a performer whose hand is impossible to hide, Friedlander set a precedent for disrupting the normal rules of photography." These "postmodernist" movements in art and photography foreshadowed the form television news would take by the late 1980s.

Andy Warhol once remarked, "The artificial fascinates me." In 1988 network reporters and producers, beguiled by the artifice of the modern presidential campaign, might well have said the same. Reporters alternated between reporting campaign images as if they were facts and exposing their contrived nature. Like Warhol, whose personality was always a presence in his work, reporters became part of the campaign theater they covered—as producers, as performers, and as critics. Like Warhol's reproductions of Campbell's soup cans, the networks' use of candidates' commercials directed our attention away from the content and toward the packaging.

The assumption that the creation of appearances is the essence of political reality pervaded not only the reporting but the candidates' self-understanding and conduct with the press. When Dan Quayle sought to escape his image as a highly managed candidate, he resolved publicly to become his own handler, his own "spin doctor." "The so-called handlers story, part of it's true," he confessed to network reporters. "But there will be no more handlers stories, because I'm the handler and I'll do the spinning." Surrounded by a group of reporters on his campaign plane, Quayle announced, "I'm Doctor Spin, and I want you all to report that."

It may seem a strange way for a politician to talk, but not so strange in a media-conscious environment in which authenticity means being master of your own artificiality. Dukakis too sought to reverse his political fortunes by seeking to be master of his own image. This attempt was best captured in a commercial shown on network news in which Dukakis stood beside a television set and snapped off a Bush commercial attacking his stand on defense. "I'm fed up with it," Dukakis declared. "Never seen anything like it in twenty-five years of public life. George Bush's negative television ads, distorting my record, full of lies, and he knows it." The commercial itself shows an image of an image—a Bush television commercial showing (and ridiculing) the media event where Dukakis rode in a tank. In his commercial, Dukakis complains that Bush's commercial showing the tank ride misstates Dukakis's position on defense.

As it appeared in excerpts on the evening news, Dukakis's commercial displayed a quintessentially modernist image of artifice upon artifice upon artifice: television news covering a Dukakis commercial containing a Bush commercial containing a Dukakis media event. In a political world governed by images of images, it seemed almost natural that the authority of the candidate be depicted by his ability to turn off the television set.

In the 1950s Edward R. Murrow noted that broadcast news was "an incompatible combination of show business, advertising, and news." Still, in its first decades television news continued to reflect a sharp distinction between the news and entertainment divisions of the networks. But by the 1980s network news operations came to be seen as profit centers for the large corporations that owned them, run by people drawn less from journalism than from advertising and entertainment backgrounds. Commercialization led to further emphasis on entertainment values, which heightened the need for dramatic visuals, fast pacing, quick cutting, and short sound bites. Given new technological means to achieve these effects—portable video cameras, satellite hookups, and sophisticated video-editing equipment—the networks were not only disposed but equipped to capture the staged media events of the campaigns.

The search for dramatic visuals and the premium placed on showmanship in the 1980s led to a new complicity between the White House image-makers and the networks. As Susan Zirinsky, a top CBS producer, acknowledged in Martin Schram's *The Great American Video Game*, "In a funny way, the [Reagan White House] advance men and I have the same thing at heart—we want the piece to look as good as [it] possibly can." In 1968 such complicity in stagecraft was scorned. Sanford Socolow, senior producer of the "CBS Evening News with Walter Cronkite," recently observed, "If someone caught you doing that in 1968 you would have been fired."

In a moment of reflection in 1988, CBS's political correspondents expressed their frustration with image-driven campaigns. "It may seem frivolous, even silly at times," said Schieffer. "But setting up pictures that drive home a message has become the No. 1 priority of the modern-day campaign. The problem, of course, is while it is often entertaining, it is seldom enlightening."

Rather shared his colleague's discomfort. But what troubled him about modern campaigns is equally troubling about television's campaign coverage. "With all this emphasis on the image," he asked, "what happens to the issues? What happens to the substance?"

IV  ISSUE AND DEBATE: ARE THE MEDIA BIASED?

Are the media in the United States biased? Ironically, the question has attained importance only in recent years, as journalists have developed a professional ethic that embraces honesty, objectivity, and balance. In years past, newspapers (then the dominant medium) were unabashedly partisan, taking active sides on public issues and presenting their views in an adversarial and contentious manner. In recent years, however, the media's claims to evenhandedness have been called into question, especially by conservative critics.

The question centers primarily on research that shows that reporters and broadcast journalists tend to be more liberal in their personal political views than either the nation at large or other "elite" groups, such as corporate executives. They tend also to be wealthier than the average American and more likely to be less religious and educated at ivy league or other prestigious colleges. These findings are not seriously disputed. The big question, however, is whether these demographic and political findings can be linked to an actual bias in the presentation of the news we read and watch on television. Do reporters and broadcast journalists allow their personal views to creep into their news stories, whether consciously or not? Or does their professional commitment to fairness and balance prevent any such effect? On these questions, the jury is still out.

The following selections present different sides of the story. The first selection, by S. Robert Lichter, Stanley Rothman, and Linda S. Lichter, argues that the media are biased. The second, by Herbert J. Gans, holds that the Lichters-Rothman study is itself the product of bias. In the third selection, communications professor Ted J. Smith calls the debate over whether the press is liberal a "stalemate" and suggests a deeper problem: the press's adversarial nature. The press, he suggests, is "unduly negative and intrusive." The root of the problem, according to Smith, is the changing self-perception of the press. Once journalists thought of themselves as neutral observers; now they see themselves as watchdogs whose function is to "save and perfect" society.

The book from which the first selection is excerpted was published after the Gans critique. The Gans article, however, is based on earlier work by Rothman and the Lichters that made essentially the same points.

Questions

1. What evidence does the Rothman-Lichter-Lichter selection present to suggest that the media are biased? Of the five criticisms Gans makes against their position, which is most convincing?

2. How does the evidence Smith presented concerning the watchdog role of the press help to fuel the liberalism-conservatism debate? Does the press tend to focus its criticisms and negativism on one side or the other? Why?

YES

10.4 The Media Elite

S. Robert Lichter, Stanley Rothman, and Linda S. Lichter

Are the media biased? . . . The question is wrongly phrased. Between overt bias and pristine objectivity exist infinite shadings, subtle colorations, and elective affinities between personal outlook and news product. The trail that leads from journalists' perspectives to the news they report is often poorly marked. It winds through conscious attitudes, unquestioned assumptions, and inner motivations. This [selection] examines the first factor in this complex progression, the actual backgrounds and outlooks of leading journalists.

Who Are the Media Elite?

During 1979 and 1980, we directed hour-long interviews with 238 journalists at America's most influential media outlets: the *New York Times,* the *Washington Post,* the *Wall Street Journal, Time, Newsweek, U.S. News and World Report,* and the news organizations at CBS, NBC, ABC, and PBS. Within each organization, individuals were selected randomly from the news staffs. From print media, we sampled reporters, columnists, department heads, bureau chiefs, editors, and executives. From television, we selected correspondents, anchors, producers, film editors, and news executives. The result is a systematic sample of the men and women who put together the news at America's most important media outlets—the media elite.

To provide comparisons with a more traditional leadership group, we also surveyed 216 executives at six *Fortune*-listed corporations, ranging from a multinational oil company and a major bank to a public utility and a nationwide retail chain. They were chosen randomly from upper and middle management at each company. The focus of our inquiry is the media elite. At appropriate points, however, we will compare their responses to those of the corporate executives.

Origins and Destinations

In some respects, the journalists we interviewed appear typical of leadership groups throughout society. The media elite is composed mainly of white males in their thirties and forties. Only one in twenty is nonwhite, and one in five is female. They are highly educated, well-paid professionals. Ninety-three percent have college degrees, and a majority attended graduate school as well. These figures reveal them to be one of the best-educated groups in America.

Geographically, they are drawn primarily from northern industrial states, especially from the northeast corridor. Forty percent come from three states: New York, New Jersey, and Pennsylvania. Another 10 percent hail from New England, and almost 20 percent were raised in the big industrial states just to the west—Illinois, Indiana, Michigan, and Ohio. Thus, 68 percent of the media elite come from these three clusters of states. By contrast only 3 percent are drawn from the entire Pacific Coast, including California, the nation's most populous state.

Journalism is a profession associated with rapid upward mobility. Yet we found few Horatio Alger stories in the newsroom. On the contrary, many among the media elite enjoyed socially privileged upbringings. Most were raised in upper-middle-class homes. Almost half their fathers were college graduates, and one in four held a graduate degree. Two in five are the children of professionals—doctors, lawyers, teachers, and so on. In fact, one in twelve is following in his or her father's footsteps as a second-generation journalist. Another 40 percent describe their fathers as businessmen. That leaves only one in five whose father was employed in a low-status job. Given these upper-status positions, it is not surprising that their families were relatively well off. Nearly half rate their family's income as above average while they were growing up, compared to one in four who view their early economic status as below average.

A distinctive characteristic of the media elite is its secular outlook. Exactly half eschew any religious affiliation. Another 14 percent are Jewish, and almost one in four (23 percent) was raised in a Jewish household. Only one in five identify as Protestant, and one in eight as Catholic. Very few are regular churchgoers. Only 8 percent go to church or synagogue weekly, and 86 percent seldom or never attend religious services.

In sum, substantial numbers of the media elite grew up at a distance from the social and cultural traditions of small-town middle America. Instead, they came from big cities in the northeast and north central states. Their parents were mostly well off, highly educated members of the upper middle class, especially the educated professions. In short, they are a highly cosmopolitan group, with differentially eastern, urban, ethnic, upper-status, and secular roots.

As in any such group, there are many exceptions to these general tendencies. On the whole, though, they are rather homogeneous. For example, we could find few systematic differences among media outlets or job functions. Even television and print journalists differ mainly in their salaries. The proportions of men and women, whites and blacks, Jews and Gentiles, religious observers and abstainers are all roughly equal at the networks and the major print media. Moreover, the family backgrounds of print and broadcast journalists are similar in terms of national and ethnic heritage, financial status, parents' educational levels, and political preferences.

A New Elite

What do journalists' backgrounds have to do with their work? In general, the way we were brought up and the way we live shape our view of the world. And journalists' perspectives on society have obvious relevance to their work. Indeed, [our research] is devoted to exploring systematically this basic point.

Of particular concern is the impact of leading journalists' rising social and economic status. At the time of our survey, one in three had personal incomes above $50,000, and nearly half (46 percent) said their family incomes exceeded that amount. As salaries continue to rise, these data understate their current income levels. By 1982, the *National Journal* found that well-established reporters at the *Washington Post* and the Washington bureaus of the *New York Times, Newsweek,* and *Time* earned from $55,000 to $60,000. Reporters and editors at the *Washington Post* are now required to file financial disclosure statements detailing holdings in stocks, bonds, and real estate. According to a financial department editor, "it used to be rare that staffers had such investments, but now that annual salaries average in the mid-forties and two-worker families have incomes of $100,000 or more, they are more common."

Moreover, there is sometimes a considerable difference between salaries and overall incomes. Columnists, investigative reporters, and television correspondents are all in demand on the lecture circuit, where they command four- and even five-figure fees. In a 1986 article entitled "The Buckrakers," *The New Republic* reported that television anchors command up to $25,000 for a speech, well-known columnists charge from $12,000 to $18,000, and *Time*'s Washington bureau chief recently raised his fee from $3,000 to $5,000. Thus columnist Jody Powell recently castigated his colleagues for potential conflict of interest over speakers' fees:

> Washington correspondents, anchors, bureau chiefs, columnists and editors are frequent travellers in the lecture circuit too. We speak to groups that have a definite interest in how we make the subjective judgments that are an inherent part of our job. And most of us get paid a good bit more than senators and congressmen who are limited by law to $2,000 for a speech.

This is not to suggest that these journalists do not earn or deserve such incomes. By way of comparison, newly minted law school graduates may earn over $50,000 annually in major New York firms and over $40,000 per year in Washington firms. As this comparison suggests, the figures merely demonstrate that leading journalists are now solidly ensconced in the upper middle class.

• • •

For a modest example of the perspective that worries some journalists, consider a recent magazine article by syndicated columnists Jack Germond and Jules Witcover. The subject is how reporters survive the rigors of the campaign trail. But the underlying theme is the upper-status cosmopolitan's scorn for parochial middle America. The authors' advice: "If you're in some enclave of civilized conduct such as New York . . . have a few belts in the Oak Room at the Plaza . . . if you're in some backwater town like Columbia, South Carolina, your choice is to eat early . . . and then find a decent

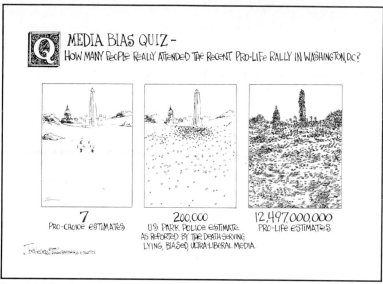

Joseph Heller/*Green Bay Press Gazette*

bar. . . ." They offer survival tips on various "uncivilized" cities. Cleveland: "If you're going to be in a plane crash in Cleveland, it's preferable that it happen going in." Indianapolis: "Pray you don't have to go here. . . ." Birmingham: "Never go there, certainly not overnight. . . ." Such patronizing attitudes can be viewed as following in the great "boobseoisie"-baiting tradition of H. L. Mencken. But it's difficult to imagine many of today's high-flying columnists choosing to live out their lives in Baltimore, like the Sage of Menlo Park, far from the civilized surroundings of the Plaza's Oak Room.

Another alleged result of wealth and celebrity is a sense of self-importance that redefines the role of journalists as newsmakers themselves. For example, the naming of a network anchor is now front-page news in the major dailies. When Roger Mudd was demoted at NBC, the *Wall Street Journal* informed its readers that his "abrupt removal" was one of "two big stories in the national news this week," along with a presidential press conference. The *Washington Post*'s ombudsman responded tartly,

"With highest regard for Mr. Mudd . . . it is respectfully suggested that people paid to convey the news have no business becoming front-page news themselves." He noted, however, a colleague's rationale for the contrary position: "They came into your living room. They set out the complexities of life, like the clergy used to do."

More serious is the question of how journalists' enhanced status has affected their relations with the newsmakers they cover. Some critics maintain that journalists' elite status has undermined their independence or compromised their proper role as public tribune. In Fairlie's words, "The very profession that should be the acid, relentless critic of the affluence and cynicism of Washington is now the most ostentatiously affluent and cynical profession in the city."

Others argue the opposite, that the formerly low status of journalists led them too often to revel in vicarious participation in the halls of power. Bagdikian criticizes old-school journalists for their "habit of close association with formal power which came to be seen as a natural reward of their occupation." By contrast, today's leading journalists may be better paid and better educated than the politicians and bureaucrats they deal with. They may also be even more in demand socially. A publicist for Gray and Company, the influential Washington public relations firm, says matter-of-factly, "When we're putting together a guest list, including a journalist is just as important as including a diplomat or a Cabinet member."

It would not be surprising if many of his colleagues agree with Jack Nelson of the *Los Angeles Times*, "I don't see any reason why we shouldn't consider ourselves on equal footing with those we cover." The extent to which the tables have turned is illustrated by an encounter between Senator (and presidential candidate) Alan Cranston and CBS's Dan Rather during the 1984 New Hampshire primary. The two were having lunch when a CBS aide approached Cranston to say, "Senator, Mr. Rather will only have time for one more question."

If society treats newscasters as more important than senators, it is unrealistic to expect the newscasters to reject society's opinion for long. Nor should we be surprised if journalists make use of their rising status to wrest control of the flow of information from politicians and other newsmakers. In keeping with their newfound status, leading journalists are increasingly likely to see themselves as professionals who translate the news rather than craftsmen who merely transmit it.

Thus, the much-debated adversary relationship between media and government may be partly a function of reporters' changing lifestyles as well as their outlooks. They no longer need defer to the newsmakers they cover. As the late columnist Joseph Kraft wrote in 1981, "those of us in the media enjoyed an enormous surge of status and power in recent years. That surge coincided with the decline of various other groups, to the point where we could perceive ourselves as the only institutional force left on a well-nigh devastated plain . . . increasingly the media are an unrepresentative group—a group that is better educated, more

highly paid, more sure of itself and more hostile to the system than the average."

Kraft's analysis concludes that increases in the social, economic, and educational status of journalists are linked to liberal or anti-establishment attitudes. This is an issue our survey addresses in depth. So let us turn from the demography to the outlook of the media elite.

The View from the Newsroom
Politics and Perspectives

How do the leading journalists describe their own political leanings? A majority see themselves as liberals. Fifty-four percent place themselves to the left of center, compared to only 17 percent who choose the right side of the spectrum. (The remainder pick "middle of the road.") When they rate their fellow workers, an even greater difference emerges. Fifty-six percent say the people they work with are mostly on the Left, and only 8 percent place their co-workers on the Right—a margin of seven to one.

These subjective ratings are consistent with their voting records in presidential elections from 1964 through 1976. Of those who say they voted for major party candidates, the proportion of leading journalists who supported the Democratic candidate never drops below 80 percent. In 1972, when more than 60 percent of all voters chose Nixon, over 80 percent among the media elite voted for McGovern. This does not appear to reflect any unique aversion to Nixon. Despite the well-publicized tensions between the press and his administration, leading journalists in 1976 preferred Carter over Ford by the same margin. In fact, in the Democratic landslide of 1964, journalists picked Johnson over Goldwater by a sixteen-to-one margin, or 94 to 6 percent.

More significant, though, is the long-term trend. Over the entire sixteen-year period, less than 20 percent of the media elite supported any Republican presidential candidate. Across four elections, the Democratic margin among elite journalists was 30 to 50 percent greater than among the entire electorate.

Also consistent with their self-descriptions are the media elite's views on a wide range of social and political issues. In the economic realm, over two-thirds agree that the government should reduce substantially the income gap between the rich and the poor. They are more evenly divided over the issue of guaranteed employment, with a slight majority opposing the entitlement issue. Most are anything but socialists. For example, they overwhelmingly reject the proposition that major corporations should be publicly owned. Only one in eight would agree to public ownership of corporations, and two-thirds declare themselves strongly opposed. Moreover, they overwhelmingly support the idea that people with greater ability should earn higher wages than those with less ability. Most also believe that free enterprise gives workers a fair shake, and that some deregulation of business would serve the national interest.

There is no contradiction between such praise for private enterprise and support for government action to aid the poor and jobless. These attitudes mirror the traditional perspective of American liberals who (unlike many European social democrats) accept an essentially capitalistic economic framework, even as they endorse the welfare state.

In contrast to their acceptance of the economic order, many leading journalists voice discontent with the social system. Almost half agree that "the very structure of our society causes people to feel alienated," and five out of six believe our legal system mainly favors the wealthy. Nonetheless, most would reject calls for a "complete restructuring" of our "basic institutions," and few agree that "all political systems are repressive." But they are united in rejecting social conservatism and traditional norms. Indeed, it is today's divisive "social issues" that bring their liberalism to the fore. Leading journalists emerge from the survey as strong supporters of environmental protection, affirmative action, women's rights, homosexual rights, and sexual freedom in general.

Fewer than one in five agrees that "our environmental problems are not as serious as people have been led to believe." Only 1 percent strongly agree that environmental problems are exaggerated, while a majority of 54 percent strongly disagree. They are nearly as united in supporting affirmative action for minorities. Despite both the heated controversy over this issue and their own predominantly white racial composition, four out of five media leaders endorse the use of strong affirmative action measures to ensure black representation in the workplace.

In their attitudes toward sex and sex roles, members of the media elite are virtually unanimous in opposing both governmental and traditional constraints. A large majority opposes government regulation of sexual activities, upholds a pro-choice position on abortion, and rejects the notion that homosexuality is wrong. In fact, a slight majority would not characterize adultery as wrong.

They overwhelmingly oppose traditional gender-based restrictions. Ninety percent agree that a woman has the right to decide for herself whether to have an abortion; 79 percent agree strongly with this pro-choice position. Only 18 percent believe that working wives whose husbands have jobs should be laid off first, and even fewer, 10 percent, agree that men are emotionally better suited for politics than women.

Only 4 percent agree that government should regulate sexual practices, and 84 percent strongly oppose state control over sexual activities. Seventy-five percent disagree that homosexuality is wrong, and an even larger proportion, 85 percent, uphold the right of homosexuals to teach in public schools. Finally, 54 percent do not regard adultery as wrong, and only 15 percent strongly agree that extramarital affairs are immoral. Thus, members of the media elite emerge as strong supporters of sexual freedom, and as natural opponents of groups like the Moral Majority.

We also inquired about international affairs, focusing on America's relations with Third World countries. The majority agrees that American economic exploitation has contributed to Third World poverty and that America's heavy use of natural resources is "immoral." Precisely half agree that the main goal of our foreign policy has been to protect American business interests.

Two issues dealing more directly with American foreign policy also elicit a nearly even division of opinion. A majority would prohibit the CIA from undermining hostile governments to protect U.S. interests. Just under half would ban foreign arms sales altogether or restrict them to democratic countries. About the same proportion would supply arms to any "friendly" country, regardless of the regime. Only 4 percent would be willing to sell arms to all comers. Thus, in several controversial areas of international relations, the media elite is deeply divided.

In sum, the media elite's perspective is predominantly cosmopolitan and liberal. Their outlook reflects the social (rather than economic) emphasis of what political scientist Everett Ladd calls the "new liberalism" of upper-status groups. Leading journalists criticize traditional social norms and establishment groups; they are very liberal on social issues such as abortion, homosexual rights, affirmative action, and environmental protection. Many endorse an expanded welfare state, but they also emerge as strong supporters of the free enterprise system. Most describe themselves as liberals and most support Democratic presidential candidates.

Not surprisingly, these attitudes place them to the left of business executives, a traditional conservative elite, on virtually every issue the survey addresses. On issues ranging from homosexuality and abortion to income redistribution, the gap between the two groups nears 40 percentage points. For example, 60 percent of the executives agree that homosexuality is wrong, 76 percent call adultery morally wrong, and only 29 percent favor government action to close the income gap between rich and poor. Even journalists' substantial support for free enterprise pales somewhat before businessmen's overwhelming endorsement. For example, 90 percent regard private enterprise as fair to workers, and 86 percent favor less government regulation of business. These figures exceed journalists' support levels by 20 and 25 percent, respectively.

• • •

The New Professionals

Liberal and Democratic sympathies among journalists are not new. What may have changed more over the years is the relevance of journalists' social attitudes to their news product. When Leo Rosten conducted the first systematic survey of the Washington press corps in 1936, he found reporters to be mostly Democrats but very much under the thumb of their superiors. At a time when most newspapers were controlled by Republican publishers, 64 percent of the reporters favored Roosevelt in the coming election, and 6 percent favored Socialist or Communist candidates. Rosten compared these results to a contemporary Gallup poll showing that only 50 percent of the public favored Roosevelt, while 2 percent chose left-wing third parties. At the same time, over 60 percent of reporters agreed with the statement, "My orders are to be objective, but I know how my paper wants stories played." Even more telling, a majority admitted having their stories "played down, cut, or killed for 'policy' reasons."

By 1960, this situation had changed dramatically. In 1961, journalism professor William Rivers again surveyed the Washington press corps. He found that Democrats still outnumbered Republicans among newspaper and broadcast correspondents, by margins exceeding three to one. However, only 7 percent recounted ideological tampering with their work. In fact, Rivers concludes, "of all the changes in the Washington press corps during the past twenty-five years, none is more significant than a new sense of freedom from the prejudices of the home office." He cites one longtime correspondent who recalled the difference from the old days: "the publishers didn't just disagree with the New Deal. They hated it. And the reporters, who liked it, had to write as though they hated it, too."

S. Robert Lichter, Stanley Rothman, and Linda S. Lichter   **351**

Seventeen years after Rivers' study, Hess concludes from his own survey that "writing to fit the editorial positions of publishers [has] simply disappeared as an issue of contention. . . . The near absence of disagreements over political slant is a by-product of higher professional standards as well as the passing of the press 'lords' . . . who view their publications as outlets for their own views." Hess notes further that today's Washington reporters initiate most of their own stories, which usually receive little or no editing. Journalism has come a long way from the days when Henry Luce could defend *Time*'s partisan coverage of the 1952 election with the comment, "it was *Time*'s duty to explain why the country needs Ike. Any other form of journalism would have been unfair and uninvolved."

Our study corroborates the notion of a new era for reporters. We asked subjects how much influence they generally have over the content of news stories with which they are involved. They marked a scale ranging from "very little" to "a great deal" of influence. By far the lowest or least influential scores were recorded by executives of both print and broadcast outlets. So it is not only the press watchers who argue that the influence of reporters has increased relative to that of their bosses. This perception is shared by the journalists themselves.

• • •

None of this proves that media coverage is biased. The whole notion of bias has become a straw man that obscures the far less obvious (and less nefarious) processes that mediate between journalists' perspectives and their product. Psychological tests show how their outlooks can unconsciously operate to shape their conceptions of the news. First, in selecting sources they consider reliable on nuclear energy, welfare reform, consumer protection, and the environment, their choices accord with their own perspectives on business and government.

Second, to a statistically significant degree, leading journalists tend to perceive elements of social controversies in terms that correspond to their own attitudes. The journalists and a business control group were shown specially constructed news stories dealing with topics like affirmative action, bribery in international business practices, and the income gap between blacks and whites. After reading the same stories, the journalists were more likely to recall a rising racial income gap and the businessmen to remember a declining one; the media elite differentially perceived threats to affirmative action where the business group observed reverse discrimination; the newspeople more often stressed business immorality while the executives emphasized unfair standards. The two groups were asked to summarize the stories, not to evaluate the issues involved. But the results show how unconscious evaluation can sometimes help determine perception. Remembering is choosing to remember, though the choice takes us unawares.

This process is not only confined to the political realm. Selective perceptions of controversial cues are emblematic of the many ways we each construct reality for ourselves, projecting yesterday's judgments onto today's events. To show how journalists spontaneously attribute certain characteristics to various social groups and relationships, we probed their apperceptions, the unconscious fantasies they bring to their understanding of the social world. Their responses to the Thematic Apperception Test may show how leading journalists sometimes fill in the gaps between what they know and what they assume when confronting a new situation. When their TAT stories contained socially relevant themes, figures of authority tended to evoke fantasies about the abuse of power in the form of greedy businessmen, deceitful lawyers, conniving politicians, intimidating policemen, and sadistic military superiors. Conversely, socially relevant stories tended to portray the average man as the victim of malevolent higher-ups or an uncaring social system. Once again, these themes and images differed significantly from those produced by corporate executives who saw the same pictures.

In sum, the media elite's conscious opinions seem to be partly reflected in the ways they subconsciously structure social reality. These findings show how pure journalistic objectivity is unattainable, since even the conscious effort to be objective takes place within a mental picture of the world already conditioned, to some degree, by one's beliefs about it. The main question is, are journalists' attitudes and preconceptions consistent with the portrait of social reality that they paint for their audience?

Our study addressed major media coverage of three long-running and controversial stories—nuclear power, busing for racial integration, and the oil industry's role in the energy crisis. After summarizing technical or scholarly knowledge on each topic, we examined its long-term national media coverage. In each instance the coverage diverged from the expert assessments in the direction of the media elite's own perspectives. If journalists' sympathies can sometimes override expert evidence, they presumably also influence coverage on the many topics where such evidence is either missing or irrelevant to the story.

Even according to an arbitrary standard requiring that each side receive equal coverage, the results were consistently one-sided. The media gave greater weight to the anti-nuclear than the pro-nuclear side. They gave greater credence to the advocates of busing than its opponents. They were more sympathetic to the critics of the oil industry than its supporters. In every instance the coverage followed neither the middle path nor the expert evidence. Instead, it veered in the direction one would expect on the basis of the attitude surveys and psychological tests. This is never a case of taking an entirely different path, in the manner of advocacy journalism. But when the road forks, and the signposts are unclear, journalists tend to follow their instincts, those inner road maps that mark our routes of ingrained expectation.

• • •

NO

10.5 U.S. Journalists Are Not Dangerously Liberal

Herbert J. Gans

[Herbert J. Gans identifies five problems with the Rothman-Lichters' analysis. They are:]

First, Rothman and the Lichters hide a political argument behind a seemingly objective study, highlighting the data which support that argument.

The argument is conservative-populist: to show that journalists come from prestigious backgrounds and, holding very liberal views, are therefore out of step with the rest of America. They are described as irreligious, hostile to business, and supportive of homosexuality and adultery, as well as of affirmative action. On economic issues the journalists are somewhat less liberal, the researchers admit, noting that "few are outright socialists." Nonetheless, many are said to favor income redistribution, public ownership of corporations, and other policies that Rothman and the Lichters associate with "welfare capitalism."

The journalists' attitudes are frequently compared to the conservative ones of a sample of corporate managers who were also studied, and occasionally to those of Middle Americans, who are assumed to be even more conservative, even though Rothman and the Lichters never identify who they are or supply research data about their beliefs. Nonetheless, measuring journalists by the standards of corporate managers and conservative Middle Americans enables the authors to justify the conclusion that journalists are "cosmopolitan outsiders" with an "anti-bourgeois social perspective."

In presenting their survey findings, the researchers depart from scientific practice by adding editorial asides to the data to buttress their political argument. Thus, they write that "a *mere* 9 percent feel strongly that homosexuality is wrong"; that "a majority would not characterize *even* adultery as wrong" (emphasis added). At times, Rothman and the Lichters resort to guilt by association, as when they write that "majorities of the media elite voice the same criticisms that are raised in the third world," but more often they damn with faint praise, reporting that "very few sympathize with Marx's doctrine, 'from each according to his ability, to each according to his needs.' " However, the interview schedule included no question about "Marx's doctrine."

Researchers may advance political arguments, of course, but Rothman and the Lichters are less than scientific in their failure to announce their political agenda in advance and to discuss the assumptions that underlie their study. Why, for example, should journalists be compared to corporate managers, when a more apt comparison would be to other employed professionals, like teachers, social workers, and salaried lawyers? Also, what relevance do the journalists' religious affiliations and church- or synagogue-attendance patterns have to do with their performance on the job, particularly in a society that emphasizes the separation of church and state? More important, why should journalists have to share or reflect the attitudes of conservative Middle Americans or any other particular sector of the population when they must serve a much larger and far more diverse audience?

Second, Rothman and the Lichters report findings about journalists which do not accurately reflect the answers they gave to the survey questions they were asked.

The journalists were not asked for their opinions, but were presented with opinion-statements with which they were asked to agree or disagree. This is standard survey technique, but in a number of instances the opinion-statements are only distantly related to the opinions which Rothman and the Lichters then attribute to the journalists—and that is *not* standard survey technique. Take the much-cited finding that 68 percent of the journalists are in favor of income redistribution. The actual opinion-statement read: "The government should work to substantially reduce the income gap between the rich and the poor." This says nothing about income redistribution and could mean such policies as compensatory education, full employment, or better health care, all of which help to reduce the income gap. Indeed, the statement is so vague that the normal journalist, who like any other survey respondent wants to appear as a decent human being to the interviewer, is apt to agree even if he or she is in fact opposed to income redistribution. Incidentally, a massive survey conducted by the *Los Angeles Times* in April 1985 among 3,000 journalists and 3,000 members of the general public included a question closely resembling the above opinion-statement. This time, 50 percent of the "news staff," 37 percent of the editors, but 55 percent of the public responded favorably to the question.

Rothman and the Lichters also claim that "almost 40 percent [of the journalism students] advocate public ownership of corporations," whereas actually they only agreed with a statement that "big corporations should be taken out of private ownership and run in the public interest." The opinion-statement fails to specifically mention public ownership and is limited to big corporations, which are disliked, together with big government and big labor, by many who answer survey questions. In addition, some people, journalists included, may be reluctant to come out against the public interest.

Third, the researchers violate basic survey methodology by first inferring people's opinions from answers to single questions, and then treating their answers as strongly felt opinions in a way that makes the journalists appear militant and radical.

Opinions and values are too complicated to be determined by one opinion-statement that an interviewee can only accept or reject but not discuss. In this instance, the journalists who agreed with the single statement about income-gap reduction are not only wrongly identified as favoring income redistribution but are described as "pressing" for it. Likewise, respondents are reported as being "vehement in their support for affirmative action"; and "many leading journalists" are said to "voice a general discontent with the social system." A "substantial minority" is charged with wanting to "overhaul the entire system."

Fourth, the researchers violate scientific norms by forgetting an explicit promise to their respondents.

Before questioning began, the interviewers read the following statement:

> We realize that some questions in this questionnaire are oversimplified—that is, they do not include all of the possible nuances or qualifications that might occur to a sophisticated person. The investigators are aware of this and will take this into account when analyzing results.

What the investigators did instead when analyzing results has already been suggested. Although their survey data are basically polite reactions to quickly read, overly simple opinion-statements, Rothman and the Lichters have analyzed and reported these data in ways that turn the journalists into opinionated proponents of ideas implied to be unpatriotic. In the process, the researchers have also assumed the journalists' votes in presidential elections to be based solely on ideology; they have treated journalistic tolerance of the rights of women, homosexuals, and others as an almost licentious form of social liberalism; and they have hinted that sizable numbers of their respondents hold some socialist attitudes.

This picture of journalists is sufficiently at odds with other studies of journalistic opinion to suggest that Rothman and the Lichters have let their political argument bias their findings. In contrast, a recent study of CBS and UPI coverage of the 1980 presidential campaign, carried out by Michael J. Robinson and Margaret A. Sheehan, concluded: ". . . in their reporting and in their private interviews, none of our reporters expressed anything approaching antisystem opinion. Most spoke as if they were moderates or 'not very political.' "

The fifth, and perhaps most serious, unscientific practice of the researchers is their presentation of a mass of data on the personal backgrounds and alleged political opinions and values of the journalists without any evidence that these are relevant to how the journalists report the news.

While Rothman and Robert Lichter have recently written—in a letter that appeared in the August 9, 1985, *Wall Street Journal*—that "journalists' personal beliefs matter only if they affect coverage," and that this is "still an open question," they proceed as if the question is closed—as if journalists' beliefs *do* affect the coverage. They do not refute or even discuss a sizable number of studies in which social-science researchers watched and talked with journalists at work, and which found that their personal political beliefs are irrelevant, or virtually so, to the way they covered the news.

These studies, which range across the print and electronic media, generally agree with what working journalists already know: that the news is mainly shaped by the size of the news-hole, news organization budgets, information available from news sources and newsmakers, and by "media considerations"—for example, television's need for dramatic tape or film. Actually, most studies of news content suggest that if any personal beliefs enter the news they are most often the beliefs of the president of the United States and other high federal, state, and local officials, since they dominate the news.

In addition, news is influenced by the audience, notably by its attentiveness to "bad" news. Not only is bad news more dramatic than good news, but it also appears to be necessary for everyday life. Audiences keep up with the news partly for what Harold Lasswell, one of the founders of mass communications research, called *surveillance*—to learn about threatening events, problems, and people in the larger society that could eventually hurt them personally. If, nowadays, conservatives are unhappy about bad news, this may reflect the fact that they are in power and the bad news is likely to be about *their* politicians. But good news does not sell, and is therefore typically reported by news media that do not need to make a profit, including those in communist countries.

I arrived at very similar conclusions about how the news is shaped from my own research, gathered between 1968 and 1978 while observing and interviewing at four news organizations also sampled by Rothman and the Lichters. While I found that journalists, like everyone else, have values, the two that matter most in the newsroom are getting the story and getting it better and faster than their prime competitors—both among their colleagues and at rival news media. Personal political beliefs are left at home, not only because journalists are trained to be objective and detached, but also because their credibility and their paychecks depend on their remaining detached.

Admittedly, some journalists have strong personal beliefs and also the position or power to express them in news stories, but they are most often editors; and editors, like producers in television, have been shown to be more conservative than their news staffs. In local news media with monopolies in their markets, editors and producers sometimes encourage journalists who share their own beliefs to insert these beliefs into the news, but in most national news media the intrusion of personal beliefs is rare.

The beliefs that actually make it into the news are *professional* values that are intrinsic to national journalism and that journalists learn on the job. However, the professional values that particularly antagonize conservatives (and liberals when *they* are in power) are neither liberal nor conservative but *reformist*, reflecting journalism's long adherence to good-government Progressivism. Journalism—and therefore journalists—believes, among other things, in honest, fair, and competent public and private institutions and leaders. While objectivity discourages journalists from advocating this belief in the news, they develop investigative and other kinds of news stories when they find politicians, business people, union officials, and other leaders who are dishonest, unfair, or incompetent. Thus, when the news is about unusually high oil-company profits, or about corruption in antipoverty programs, the journalists are being neither conservative nor liberal in their news judgment but are expressing the reform values of their profession.

These professional values are not imposed by "cosmopolitan outsiders," and while some reflect the do-good impulses of upper-middle class professionals, many are shared by the rest of the audience. They are often called motherhood values, and are defended by the Middle Americans who Rothman and the Lichters feel are being ignored by the journalists. As a result, the general public does not feel that journalists are biased against conservatives. A Roper Organization poll conducted in April 1984 pointedly asked its 2,000 respondents to react to a list of "some people and groups that some have said the press is out to get." Just 12 percent indicated that the press was after conservatives and the same proportion mentioned liberals. In fact, the polls suggest that the public considers the news media to be generally fair and unbiased, although it periodically suspects unfairness on specific stories and may be critical of the news media for other reasons, including reporters' invasions of the privacy of distraught people and journalists' arrogance in asserting their rights and privileges.

• • •

10.6 The Media Bias Debate Misses the Point _____

Ted J. Smith III

Journalism stopped being fun in October 1983. Rudely debarred from the invasion of Grenada, the press exploded with howls of indignation. But this time, the public sided with the government. Worse, a quick check of the polls disclosed a steady decline in popular support for the press since the heady days of Vietnam and Watergate. A "crisis of confidence" was proclaimed, and an outpouring of media criticism swept the land.

Seldom has so much been said and written with so little effect. After six years of debate, it is hard to see any improvement in press performance. And public confidence continues to erode. A 1985 Gallup poll for the Times Mirror Company found 34 percent agreeing that news "stories and reports are often inaccurate." This was especially troubling because the critics tended to be above average in media knowledge, interest, and use. But worse, four followup surveys in 1988 and 1989 found this group had grown to 43 to 50 percent of the population. Similarly, a 1989 Yankelovich poll for *Time* asked in which of five groups "are ethical standards the lowest." Journalists, nominated for this dubious distinction by 21 percent of the respondents, placed second, just behind lawyers, but well ahead of businessmen, congressmen, and members of the Bush administration.

The Bias Stalemate

In short, the crisis of confidence is real, but little has been done to address it. One reason may be that discussion of the problem, while lively and often insightful, has become mired in a sterile subsidiary dispute about political bias in the news. Among conservatives, belief in the liberal bias of the media is almost an article of faith. But critics on the left are equally adamant

in decrying a conservative slant. Meanwhile, journalists insist that coverage is balanced and point to criticism from both sides of the political spectrum as proof of their neutral stance.

The problem is that all parties to the dispute are partly right. Conservatives base their case on the claims that journalists, especially in the prestigious national media, are liberal in their political views, and that those views are reflected in coverage. At least a dozen surveys, several conducted by the press, support the first claim. The second claim is less certain, but it gains plausibility from the proof of the first and is buttressed by a growing body of systematic research.

Critics on the left complain that media coverage is overwhelmingly conservative in the sense that it reinforces the status quo. They attack journalists for being insufficiently critical of mainstream policies, leaders, and institutions, for excluding minority views, and for unreflective repetition of the assumptions and values of capitalist economics and bourgeois democracy. Supported by numerous academic studies, there can be little doubt about the basic validity of this claim.

There is nothing contradictory about these claims. When conservatives say the media are "liberal," they are using the term in its positive sense to denote a particular political outlook. Specifically, most would agree that the media occupy a moderate or mainstream liberal position, perhaps a bit to the left of *The New Republic*. In contrast, when leftists say the media are "conservative," they are using the term in its relative (or generic) sense. Although some would disagree, these critics tend to be located at the fringe of American politics, somewhere in the vicinity of *Mother Jones* or *The Nation*. From this vantage, virtually the entire American political spectrum, including most liberals, can be characterized as conservative. Thus both groups of critics are right.

The assertion that coverage is "balanced" also has some merit. Whatever biases the media may display, they are far from monolithic. Even among the elite national media, there are substantial differences in ideological orientation, and all include at least some voices from across the political spectrum. More important, journalists have shown a marked catholicity of taste in their choice of political targets. Thus leftists can hardly complain that establishment figures such as Dan Quayle and Robert Bork were treated gently by the "conservative" media, and conservatives must acknowledge that a long list of liberals—from Lyndon Johnson to Barney Frank—have been crippled or ruined by the "liberal" press. So while the balance may not be scrupulous, there is a balance of sorts, and in that sense the journalists, too, are right.

Because everyone is partly right, the debate over bias in the media will remain deadlocked. Certainly no one, least of all journalists, can afford to concede defeat. More important, because the bias is only partial, it can only partially explain the widespread disaffection for the press. A deeper problem exists, but its nature is obscure.

Media Changes

The best clue to the nature of that problem is provided by the complaints of the public, for whom political bias has never been a dominant concern. Their most common criticism, endorsed by huge majorities in most polls, is that coverage is unduly negative and intrusive.

Unlike their response to accusations of bias, few journalists bother to dispute this charge. Instead they offer explanations of why coverage *must* be negative. The noblest of these depicts "bad news" as a necessary consequence of the press performing its vital "watchdog" role. This may sound innocuous. After all, there is no question that the framers of the Constitution intended the press to serve a protective function, and all relevant polls show strong public support for the watchdog role and for investi-

gative journalism, its principal modern incarnation. But certain anomalies intrude. Why, if the public supports the watchdog role, does it condemn the negativism it entails? And why has criticism of media negativism surfaced only recently?

One way to sort out these issues is to examine a long-running public-service ad campaign sponsored by the Ad Council and the Society of Professional Journalists. Clearly designed as a response to waning confidence, it seeks to educate the public about the role and value of a free press in a democratic society. Each ad features a news photo (my favorite is the familiar picture of *Challenger* exploding) with the superimposed question: "If the press didn't tell us, who would?" Also included is a toll-free number where the reader can get "printed information on the role of a free press and how it protects your rights."

Rhetorical questions invite reflection, and in this instance the results are illuminating. Consider first the notion that it is "the press" that "protects your rights." Once again, this may sound commonplace, but it is worth recalling that when the First Amendment was drafted, "the press" as we know it did not exist. There were no broadcast media, no wire services, no communication "empires," and above all, no journalists in the modern sense of the term. The press consisted largely of a handful of tiny, local, and often highly partisan newspapers (35 in 1783, only one a daily). Ideals of objectivity, balance, and fairness were not even considered. Instead, it was assumed that each newspaper would attack and defend from a particular position and that truth would emerge from the conflict of all.

The press as we know it began in the 1830s with the appearance of mass-circulation daily newspapers (the "penny press") supported by commercial advertising and intended to turn a profit. Fierce competition and the daily format created a need for a constant flow of "news," and the role of professional journalist emerged in response. Further, profit depended on advertising, advertising depended on circulation, and circulation depended in part on not alienating potential readers. Thus newspapers became markedly less partisan and the ideals of objectivity, balance, and fairness were born. Increasingly, such journals restricted themselves to *reporting* the political debate; in theory, active participation was relegated to the editorial pages.

Today, the press encompasses a profusion of news media, both print and broadcast; foremost among them are the tiny minority that have attained truly national scope. Included in this category are a handful of daily newspapers and weekly newsmagazines, the wire services, network radio news, and above all, the major television networks. Because of their size and prominence, these few set the tone and agenda of coverage for most of the press. In particular, discussion of national and international affairs is conducted largely within their confines, where it is shaped by the ideals of objectivity, balance, and fairness to which nearly all of the news media are now at least nominally committed.

Equally important, the press is now staffed exclusively by a small group of "professional" journalists. A 1983 study estimated that only 112,072 full-time news/editorial workers were employed by all general-interest news media. In comparison, there are about 3.5 million teachers (plus 660,000 professors), 700,000 lawyers, and 515,000 physicians; even architects (135,000) outnumber journalists. Bound together by pronounced similarities in background, training, values, and ideals, these new professionals have transformed the press from an amorphous collection of conflicting individuals and media to a unitary, cohesive, and closed institution. It is also strongly hierarchical, dominated by the elite core of several thousand journalists who operate the national media, to which group most other journalists aspire, and to whose judgments and dictates they often defer.

These developments have wrought profound changes. Press freedom remains an individual right in the sense that anyone may publish a book, and I can write this essay. But a true voice in the debate now requires control of, or unrestricted access to, a national medium, and this is not a realistic possibility for any ordinary citizen. Today, only national journalists enjoy effective freedom of the press because only they have direct and frequent access to the public. Dan Rather can and does address millions of CBS viewers five times each week. In contrast, the president of the United States can directly address the same audience only a few times a year, and even these infrequent appearances require permission from network executives.

There is nothing sinister about these developments. They are merely the unplanned result of countless adjustments to technological, economic, demographic, educational, political, and social change over two centuries. But the inescapable fact is that "the press" has become a far different entity from anything imagined by the Founding Fathers.

Messengers or Messiahs?

Consider next the ads' central question: "If the press didn't tell us, who would?" This invites a response of "No one," followed presumably by a rush of gratitude for the brave lads of the press. But while it is trivially true that most of us get a great deal of our information about contemporary affairs from the news media, it by no means follows that the press is the only or even the principal body engaged in discovering and reporting the truth. If the press didn't tell us, lots of people could, including political leaders and candidates, government agencies, the courts, thousands of organized interest groups, and millions of active and concerned citizens. After all, we do live in a sophisticated constitutional democracy that usually manages to function nicely without the active intervention of the press.

Thus the importance of the question is that it calls attention to a subtle but profound change in the self-conception of the press over the last few decades. That change is grounded in the spread of a sense of special calling among journalists: the role of the press is not merely to serve society by providing an accurate account of the conflict of ideas, but to save and perfect

Why the Sky Is Always Falling

Journalist Gregg Easterbrook illustrates Smith's conception of a negative, adversarial press through a discussion of the press's penchant for bad economic news.

*B*etter sit down and brace yourself: there's an economic trend in progress. It's bad, real bad. What trend? Makes no difference.

Let's take employment. U.S. ECONOMY ADDS 400,000 JOBS IN MONTH: REPORT SPURS FEARS, declaimed the *Washington Post* last February. Some economic naïf might consider job growth to be good news. To the cogniscenti, though, it is a frightening omen: high employment might inspire the Federal Reserve to raise interest rates, the *Post* worried. In March, as unemployment fell to its lowest level since the early 1970s, the *Post* grumped that the Fed would surely have to raise rates now, "since its efforts so far have done little to slow the economy." Talk about a record of shame—failure to slow the economy! CBS, reporting the record employment, warned, "Things may not be as rosy as they seem"—because low joblessness might inspire workers to expect higher wages. You probably thought higher wages for workers was a good thing. Novice! Of course, later when employment expansion slowed somewhat, that was bad too: APRIL JOB GROWTH EASED DECISIVELY, STIRRING CONCERN, the *New York Times* warned. . . .

One force at play in these follies is, of course, the simple desire for bad news. The sentiment that disaster is a great story while normalcy is boring animates not just the media but Congress, where congressional hearings and members' statements enthusiastically embrace that day's sky-is-falling economic line.

The fact that such a line is always available reflects a central truth about economics: almost any economic development is both good *and* bad—good in some ways, bad in others. An expanding economy reduces unemployment, but at some point risks inflation. A strong dollar makes consumer goods cheaper (reducing inflation), but makes American products less competitive. Not only does a change in one direction in any economic variable—interest rates, commodity prices, etc.—create its own pros and cons. It also creates the possibility that policy-makers will throw the machine into reverse, producing exactly the oppo-

it. The watchdog function, once considered remedial and subsidiary, becomes paramount: the primary duty of the journalist is to focus attention on problems and deficiencies, failures and threats. Thus the press has assumed the position of an objective or neutral critic, not *of* the society but somehow *outside* and *above* it. From this vantage, journalists conduct a relentless critique of American policies, leaders, and institutions, sometimes in the form of investigative reports, but more generally through the adversarial structure of routine coverage.

NBC's Irving R. Levine illustrates the new approach in this description of his economic reporting during the Reagan presidency: "I have tried to bring a deep skepticism to the president's politics. My reports on Reagan's economic program focused on their deficiencies and contradictions." Nor is this attitude restricted to the journalistic elite. A 1988 survey conducted by the American Society of Newspaper Editors asked a representative national sample of newspaper journalists how important it is for newspapers to "be an adversary of public officials by being constantly skeptical of their actions." Even given the extreme wording of the question, 52 percent (65 percent at the largest newspapers) rated this function as extremely or quite important.

The most obvious result of this new critical

site pros and cons. (Too-vigorous growth, for example, will lead the Fed to tighten and risk recession.)

If you're determined to concentrate on the cons, there is always a full panoply to choose from. On the other hand, relentless emphasis on the good news in any set of economic statistics—the general approach of whoever happens to be in the White House—can be just as fatuous as relentless emphasis on the bad news, and somewhat more dangerous. It's true that perhaps 95 percent of economic doomsday edicts turn on constructions like "could lead to," "might cause," "analysts warned of possible" (after all, most of the hard economic news has been good for nigh on half a century now). But sometimes it makes sense to risk today's good news to avoid tomorrow's bad news. That unpleasant but necessary job is generally left to the Federal Reserve Board.

However, Fed worship is an additional factor that distinguishes economic coverage from the normal journalists' preference for bad news. The Fed is a big, impressive, mysterious organization with power and the freedom to act, increasingly rare in Washington. A large fraction of economic

gloom stories turns on speculation that this trend or that may cause the Fed to move interest rates this way or the other.

For journalists the Fed provides that useful device, the narrative. Network editors like to imagine that Washington is a sort of master control room of the type found in James Bond movies, where awesomely powerful figures sit before huge panels and radar screens, turning dials that control the course of human events. Few Washington reporters, however sophisticated, can avoid resorting to that sort of imagery every now and then. Thus the president, for example, is sometimes made to appear in control of foreign affairs. . . .

But if the general propensity is to find the cloud for every silver lining, an occasional bizarre shaft of sunlight will pierce the gloom. My nominee for economic headline of 1989 (so far) comes from the *New York Times*: ISRAELIS VIEW A BATTERED ECONOMY AS MOTIVATION FOR A PEACE EFFORT. Seen in that light, may all the world's nations be blessed with economic collapse.

—*Gregg Easterbrook*

---

posture is the cynical, sometimes apocalyptic, negativism that permeates the daily news, especially on network television. Another manifestation is the jealous intrusion of elite journalists into the legitimate operations of other democratic institutions. Almost nothing of importance is permitted to run its natural course. For example, it is now common for government studies to be reported, refuted, and dismissed before they are even released, often on the basis of material leaked by the minority side. Or again, we are now accustomed to media intervention in criminal cases, not as a "court of last resort," but while judicial review is still in progress.

It is sometimes argued that such practices should be seen as benign because they are motivated by lofty altruistic ideals. But this is at best ingenuous. Like all human beings, journalists are driven by a mixture of motives, both noble and base, and the power and commercialism of the press would tend to encourage the latter. Nor is purity of motive a guarantee of positive effect.

Considerations such as these informed the construction of the American government, with its elaborate system of checks and balances. All powerful institutions were included in the conception. In the case of the press, it was assumed that the partisan media would insure against excesses and abuses within their own ranks by mounting attacks against each other. But this constraint disappeared with the transformation of the press into a unitary institution. Indeed, the press is the *only* American institution that is *never* subjected to the full inquisitional rigor of investigative journalism. Combined with the near-absolute protections of the First Amendment—much strengthened of late by sympathetic courts and legislatures—the result is that "the press" has become a unique and uniquely powerful institution. Unfortunately, this also means that journalists have emerged as exactly the kind of powerful, privileged, and active elite that the Constitution sought to preclude. At a minimum, this creates an enormous potential for abuse. But even if the press did manage to function with perfect integrity, there would still be cause for concern. For the sad truth is that the idealized role of the press as an autonomous and neutral critic is inherently and fundamentally flawed.

Thoughtful Critics?

The first problem is grounded in the fact that it is journalists who must serve as the critics. Criticism of the simplest sort involves nothing more than an evaluative response by the critic, a statement of the condition of his glands, as a colleague used to say. At this level, criticism is the easiest of acts. *Thoughtful* criticism, by contrast, centers on a reasoned judgment of worth. At this level, criticism is one of the most difficult of endeavors because it requires the critic to combine four qualities: intellect, special expertise, reflection, and judiciousness.

Journalists are undoubtedly well above average in *intellect*, and some, especially in the more thoughtful of the print media, possess superb minds. On the other hand, some do not, and journalism is seldom seen as an intellectually rigorous field. One reason is that the primary skill required of all journalists is the ability to write or speak interestingly for a general audience—that is, at about a sixth-grade level (which is why the ability to read a daily newspaper can be used as a minimum standard for functional literacy). This is not a requirement

that would tend to attract the best minds to the field. Nor is it clear that those habituated to simplification are particularly well suited to evaluate complex issues.

Similar considerations apply to the question of *expertise*. Compared to the general population, journalists are a highly trained elite; most combine college degrees with years of informal study and practical experience. But in a world marked by the explosive growth of knowledge and extreme intellectual specialization, few journalists qualify as experts. That's one reason why every college freshman is taught that you may not quote *Time* magazine (or any other news medium) as a definitive source in serious writing. Indeed, journalists frequently offer or orchestrate criticism in fields where they lack the credentials even to obtain entry-level employment.

Of the last two prerequisites, *reflection* is needed to ensure that intellect and expertise produce insight. But reflection requires time, and the frenetic pace of journalism makes time a rare commodity. Similarly, an attitude of *judiciousness* is needed to ensure that the positive and negative features of the critical object are properly balanced to produce a fair and reasoned judgment of its overall worth. But for those committed to constant skepticism, judgment is preordained: the object is flawed and criticism is reduced to an enumeration of defects.

All of this suggests that journalists are almost uniquely unsuited to serve as thoughtful critics because the whole structure of their craft militates against successful performance of that role. This in no way diminishes their worth, but it does mean that journalists have set themselves a task that they cannot hope to perform, and their failure could cause incalculable damage to the press and the country.

Accentuate the Negative

The second fundamental problem stems from the negativistic bias that the watchdog stance entails. The most basic tenet of American democracy is that the average citizen, guided by enlightened self-interest, has both the right and the ability to decide the appropriate course of public policy. But to choose wisely, he must be informed about the range and quality of his options. One way to achieve this goal is to encourage the full confrontation of a diversity of competing views by providing virtually unlimited freedom of speech and the press.

The original conception of the press located this conflict of ideas in the debate *among* partisan media, each propounding a particular point of view. In this method, the content of discussion is determined solely by the participants; we would normally expect some voices to argue for continuity, stressing past accomplishments and future opportunities, while others, focusing on present problems and future dangers, would call for reform (and fulfill the watchdog role). Thus debate typically includes a mixture of positive and negative views; in times of peace and prosperity, positive views might even predominate.

With the advent of commercialized mass media, the locus of conflict shifted as each newspaper sought to *reproduce* the debate *within* the confines of its coverage. Here journalists occupy a crucial position, for they decide which views and spokesmen will be heard. But given reporting that is scrupulously accurate, fair, and comprehensive, there is no necessary impact on the course or tone of debate because its content is still determined by the participants. Journalists merely relay their views to the public.

But when journalists adopt the stance of neutral critic, as they have in the last few decades, everything changes. For one thing, they become active participants in the debate, with the power and inclination to modify its agenda. More important, their critical posture is intrinsically reformist in orientation, thereby shifting the balance of discussion. In particular, they are predisposed against positive views and information, which, from a reformist perspective, must be seen as false, flawed, or irrelevant. The result is that the conflict of ideas, as constructed in the press, acquires a predominantly and perpetually negative tone.

This constant emphasis on bad news over good—which most journalists readily acknowledge—denies the public the range of information it needs to guide its decisions. Obviously, effective choice requires knowledge of success as well as failure, of the reasons for a policy or institution in addition to the reasons against. Thus the cost of adopting the role of neutral critic is that the press can no longer adequately discharge its more fundamental task of ensuring an informed electorate. This strikes at the heart of the democratic process.

A recent study provides a particularly clear example of the problem. I analyzed all economic coverage on early evening network television news for three years of the Reagan presidency: July 1 through June 30 of 1982–83, 1984–85, and 1986–87. By most standards, the economy improved in each of the three years, moving from recession and early recovery to strong but slowing growth to renewed expansion. But the tone of economic coverage followed an opposite course. Always overwhelmingly negative, the ratio of predominantly negative to positive stories actually increased from five to one in 1982–83 to about seven to one in 1986–87. This pattern was the result of two reporting practices. First, the steady flow of negative stories was made possible by constant shifts in focus, as journalists moved from sector to sector, searching for new problems. At the same time, coverage of positive economic developments was minimized. As a result, the total number of economic stories dropped from 5,335 in 1982–83 to 3,934 in 1986–87. This decline was especially dramatic in coverage of economic statistics, which are the basis of economic understanding. As the economy improved, reports of the increasingly favorable statistics dropped by 64 percent, from 1,022 to 373. By 1986, the reduction in coverage of basic economic data was so great that it would have been difficult for even the most attentive viewer to form an accurate conception of how the American economy was performing.

Omni-Principled Criticism

The third problem follows from the second. Criticism is inherently tendentious: to say that something is wrong or defective asserts an order of value. But journalistic neutrality demands that no perspective be favored over another. The only way the journalist/critic can meet this demand is to embrace all perspectives simultaneously. Thus universal perfection becomes the standard of critical judgment.

Given this standard, criticism must be comprehensive in scope. Hence the peculiar character of routine coverage, with its continual changes in focus as journalists adopt the perspective of first one group and then another. If a conservative policy is proposed, coverage is dominated by liberal criticisms, but if the policy is liberal, the focus changes to conservative complaints; moderate proposals, especially compromises, are disparaged from all sides. This is why claims of biased reporting are ultimately not compelling. While there may be some tendency for journalists to emphasize liberal concerns, coverage as a whole is more accurately described as "omni-principled."

Unfortunately, omni-principled criticism is also unanswerable, and anyone who tries to stand against it must fail. For example, whenever a political leader or government official advocates a policy, he incurs certain positional commitments and obligations that limit his scope of response. The journalist/critic, in contrast, is subject to no such constraints. He is free to flit from position to position, adopting and discarding attacks until he finds one that draws blood. And if this process fails, he can always change the subject.

This is a neat trick, and one that allows journalists to appear superior to all other social leaders, especially politicians. Whatever is proposed or enacted, journalists are there to show us its flaws. They can get away with this for two reasons. First, by claiming to be neutral, journalists avoid the requirement of consistency that limits the options of committed participants in the conflict of ideas. Thus some politicians can be condemned for seeking to "impose" traditional morality, while at the same time others are driven from office for failing to meet its demands.

Second, and more important, the autonomy of the press allows journalists the luxury of being *irresponsible*. While other participants in the debate are forced to consider issues of possibility and practical efficacy, journalists are not. Their role is merely to identify imperfections; someone else can worry about devising solutions. Thus, to name only a few possibilities, journalists are free to raise unresolvable problems, demand integration of contradictory positions, and enforce standards of conduct that neither they nor anyone else can meet.

In short, the press has emerged as a sort of permanent parliamentary opposition, but without the need to defend a position or offer any reasonable alternatives to the policies it attacks. This shift has already transformed American politics by making traditional sources of opposition subsidiary or redundant. Driven by television's demand for personification and simplification, the status of the presidency has been greatly enhanced, and political debate at the national level now generally takes the form of a continuing conflict between administration officials and watchdog journalists. Partisan opponents still have a role, but only as bit players in a larger spectacle directed by the press. This may explain why the Democrats have had such difficulty of late developing credible national leaders.

Perhaps more important, there are indications that journalists are seeking to expand their influence by imposing new constraints on the course of political discussion. Compare, for example, the bored, cynical, and almost openly dismissive coverage of the 1988 party conventions with the breathless enthusiasm and hyperbole lavished on the televised debates. The latter, of course, are creatures of the press, and offer the purest possible examples of journalists performing as neutral and perfectionist critics. Similarly, the growing media criticism of political advertising undoubtedly reflects a genuine concern for the integrity of the political process. But it is worth noting as well that these ads constitute one of the last remaining ways for a candidate to address the electorate without the active intercession of journalists. If that link is broken or diminished, the power of the press expands. Finally, there is the exceedingly strange press outcry over "negative" campaigning. The situation has now evolved to the point where if a political candidate offers any criticism of an opponent's character, record, or policies, he risks press censure. Yet criticism is essential in testing political leaders and ideas. And as many politicians will affirm, journalists certainly have no qualms about leveling such attacks. Regardless of specific intent, the effect of proscribing negative campaigning is to reserve for journalists the exclusive right to initiate political criticism. And in this scheme, the candidates—who used to be the principal contenders in the conflict of ideas—are reduced to the status of stationary targets, fit only to articulate "positive" proposals and submit to the inquisitions of the press.

Other consequences of the perfectionistic stance of the press are more disturbing. First, and obviously, universal perfection is an *unrealistic* standard for judging mere human accomplishments. Its application in the realm of political and social affairs means that all policies, leaders, and institutions must be seen as deficient, and every accomplishment must always be rated a failure. No longer may we look back with satisfaction on how far we have come, only forward with impatience on how far we have yet to go. And because the goal of universal perfection is unattainable, the remaining distance is always indefinitely long.

Further, perfectionistic criticism requires that any consensus reached through the political process must be attacked, and in that sense the press has become *subversive* of all established order. This leads to a fascinating paradox. In the American form of democracy, political success is based on building the widest possible consensus by integrating diverse perspectives into a single order of value. Thus the more successful the political process, the wider the consensus, but the more the journalist/critic is driven to the margins of debate to find a position outside the consensus from which to attack. This means that supposedly neutral criticism has an inherently *radical* tendency. But worse, positions at the margins of debate are those most likely to be inassimilable. Thus the more successful the political process is in building consensus, the more likely it is that criticisms will be not only extreme but also impossible to meet.

What the Press Must Do

Journalists have taken a false turn, and through their idealistic efforts to perfect American democracy, they may seriously weaken it. The solution is straightforward. The press must abandon its hopelessly flawed role of autonomous and neutral critic, withdraw from direction of the political debate, and rededicate itself to the infinitely difficult and important task of constructing the kind of full and forceful confrontation of ideas that is the essential prerequisite of democratic government. This does not mean that the press must forgo its watchdog role. It does mean that the informative role of the press should be restored to a position of primacy.

This solution asks journalists to relinquish a great deal of power, a prospect that few can find attractive. But the most likely alternatives are even less palatable. For all their good intentions, journalists have assumed a role that is not only beyond their abilities, but also destructive in design. The American public has sensed the change and responded with disapproval. Already, solid majorities support substantial restrictions on the power and autonomy of the press. Journalists may ignore these warnings only at their peril.

Part Three

Institutions of Government

Chapter 11

The Congress

O*ver the long term of American history, it is fair to conclude that Congress has lost political power to the executive branch. Since the New Deal, it has been forced to delegate more and more power to the federal bureaucracy, which has the expertise and resources to deal with increasingly complex and diverse roles of the federal government. Since America's rise to power in international affairs after World War II, Congress has lost power to what some observers have called the "imperial presidency."*

Congress nevertheless remains the focal point of the American national government. Its power in domestic affairs remains paramount, and in recent years it has struggled to regain some of its lost power in foreign policy as well. No president can afford to ignore or slight Congress, especially its leadership, and no agency can afford to ignore or slight a congressional committee or subcommittee with jurisdiction over its affairs. Interest groups direct the lion's share of their energies toward Congress, and the media often take their cues from Congress as to what issues are worth considering. The federal courts, whatever else they do, must focus their energies principally on interpreting congressional statutes. Presidents may propose, as the saying goes, but Congress disposes; and Congress retains the power to investigate wrongdoing in the executive branch, has final budgetary and taxing authority, has the power to confirm executive and judicial appointments, and, as Richard Nixon nearly learned, has the power of impeachment as well.

Three themes dominate the diverse readings in this chapter. The first, and oldest, is the ongoing struggle for power between the legislative and executive branches. Presidents must deal with Congress to accomplish their own objectives (selection 11.4), Congress supervises the federal bureaucracy (selection 11.3), and members of Congress must take the president's wishes into account even if they mean to override them. The separation of powers as conceived in 1787 did not resolve the division of authority between the two branches. In fact, the Framers deliberately created a system in which the two "political branches" would continually joust with each other for power (see chapter 2). Congress and the executive branch have been fighting ever since.

Second, this chapter examines the most important recent trend within the legislative branch: the ongoing decentralization of power. Power in Congress has flowed from the top down over the past thirty or more years—from the leadership to the members, from the committee chair to the individual member, from committees to subcommittees, from individual members to their personal and legislative staff. Congress is no longer a small body of individuals who come together to deliberate on public issues. It is a crazy quilt of overlapping powers and jurisdictions in which power is ever dispersed and parceled out in smaller and smaller pieces. Selection 11.7 deals with this issue directly, although the theme of decentralization runs through every reading in this chapter.

Finally, at the heart of this chapter is a question about the nature of representative government in the United States. Although the Framers clearly wanted congressmen to "refine and filter" the public's views (see the discussion of Federalist 10 [selection 2.1]), members of Congress have always considered themselves "local men, locally minded, whose business began and ended with the interests of their constituency."* This tension between the local interest and the national interest, and between the will of their constituents and their own view of the public interest, remains a problem for members of Congress even today. The Federalists' thoughts on these matters are presented in selections 11.1 and 11.2, the problem of representation as it relates to proposed limitations on congressional terms is treated in selections 11.8 through 11.10, and the problem of balancing the different roles of members of Congress (in this case a congresswoman, Patricia Schroeder, and her colleague Timothy J. Penny) is the subject of selections 11.5 and 11.6.

Chapter Questions

1. Review the Federalists' conception of the separation of powers (selections 2.2 through 2.4). In what ways does the operation of the modern Congress underscore the Framers' belief that "ambition must be made to counteract ambition"? What evidence is there in the readings in this chapter to suggest that Congress plays an active role in the administrative process and that the president plays an active role in the legislative process? The readings in the chapters on the presidency (chapter 12) and the bureaucracy (chapter 13) may cast light on these questions as well.

2. What is meant by the phrase "decentralization of Congress"? What are the causes of this process of decentralization? What problems does decentralization pose for representative government? for democracy in America?

3. What roles do members of Congress play? How do these roles conflict with one another? How do members of Congress seek to balance their own goals, their constituents' interests, and the public or national interest?

* Bernard Bailyn, *The Ideological Origins of the American Revolution* (Cambridge: Belknap Press of Harvard University Press, 1967), p. 162.

The Federalists' view of representation was twofold. Representatives were expected to represent their constituents' interests but also to "refine and enlarge the public views, by passing them through the medium of a chosen body of citizens, whose wisdom may best discern the true interest of their country and whose patriotism and love of justice will be least likely to sacrifice it to temporary or partial considerations" (Federalist No. 10; see selection 2.1). Congress was expected to be a deliberative body that would think about and consider public questions and resolve them in the public interest. Thus, the Framers made the connection between congressmen and their constituents close but not too close: elections were to be held every two years, not every year, despite the popular eighteenth-century slogan that "when annual election end, tyranny begins." Senators were to be elected every six years, and by the state legislatures, not by the people directly.

The Framers' views on representation and on Congress's role as the primary decision-making body, at least in matters of domestic policy, form the background for this chapter. Federalist No. 55, written by James Madison, defends the small size of the original Congress (only sixty-five members) as a way of securing "the benefits of free consultation and discussion." Moreover, the Framers thought, a small House would encourage representatives to think of the national interest instead of the local interest when they voted on public questions (you may want to reflect on this point when you read, in selection 11.7, about the modern Congress, which has more than 500 members and over 20,000 staff members). On the other hand, as Federalist No. 57 points out, the framers believed the members of Congress would still be close to their constituents and would still faithfully represent their interests in the federal capital.

Questions

1. 1. What does Madison mean when he writes, "Had every Athenian citizen been a Socrates, every Athenian assembly would still have been a mob"?

2. How might a member of Congress seek to balance his or her role as the representative of a local district with the sometimes conflicting role of acting in the interest of the entire nation?

11.1 Federalist No. 55

James Madison

The number of which the House of Representatives is to consist forms another and a very interesting point of view under which this branch of the federal legislature may be contemplated. Scarce any article, indeed, in the whole Constitution seems to be rendered more worthy of attention by the weight of character and the apparent force of argument with which it has been assailed. The charges exhibited against it are, first, that so small a number of representatives will be an unsafe depository of the public interests; second, that they will not possess a proper knowledge of the local circumstances of their numerous constituents; third, that they will be taken from that class of citizens which will sympathize least with the feelings of the mass of the people and be most likely to aim at a permanent elevation of the few on the depression of the many; fourth, that defective as the number will be in the first instance, it will be more and more disproportionate, by the increase of the people and the obstacles which will prevent a correspondent increase of the representatives.

In general it may be remarked on this subject that no political problem is less susceptible of a precise solution than that which relates to the number most convenient for a representative legislature; nor is there any point on which the policy of the several States is more at variance, whether we compare their legislative assemblies directly with each other, or consider the proportions which they respectively bear to the number of their constituents. Passing over the difference between the smallest and largest States, as Delaware, whose most numerous branch consists of twenty-one representatives, and Massachusetts, where it amounts to between three and four hundred, a very considerable difference is observable among States nearly equal in population. The number of representatives in Pennsylvania is not more than one fifth of that in the State last mentioned. New York, whose population is to that of South Carolina as six to five, has little more than one third of the number of representatives. As great a disparity prevails between the States of Georgia and Delaware or Rhode Island. In Pennsylvania, the representatives do not bear a greater proportion to their constituents than of one for every four or five thousand. In Rhode Island, they bear a proportion of at least one for every thousand. And according to the constitution of Georgia, the proportion may be carried to one to every ten electors; and must unavoidably far exceed the proportion in any of the other states.

Another general remark to be made is that the ratio between the representatives and the people ought not to be the same where the latter are very numerous as where they are very few. Were the representatives in Virginia to be regulated by the standard in Rhode Island, they would, at this time, amount to between four and five hundred; and twenty or thirty years hence, to a thousand. On the other hand, the ratio of Pennsylvania, if applied to the State of Delaware, would reduce the representative assembly of the latter to seven or eight members. Nothing can be more fallacious than to found our political calculations on arithmetical principles. Sixty or seventy men may be more properly trusted with a given degree of power than six or seven. But it does not follow that six or seven hundred would be proportionably a better depositary. And if we carry on the supposition to six or seven thousand, the whole reasoning ought to be reversed. The truth is that in all cases a certain number at least seems to be necessary to secure the benefits of free consultation and discussion, and to guard against too easy a combination for improper purposes; as, on the other hand, the number ought at most to be kept within a certain limit, in order to avoid the confusion and intemperance of a multitude. In all very numerous assemblies, of whatever characters composed, passion never fails to wrest the scepter from reason. Had every Athenian citizen been a Socrates, every Athenian assembly would still have been a mob.

It is necessary also to recollect here the observations which were applied to the case of biennial elections. For the same reason that the limited powers of the Congress, and the control of the State legislatures, justify less frequent election than the public safety might otherwise require, the members of the Congress need be less numerous than if they possessed the whole power of legislation, and were under no other than the ordinary restraints of other legislative bodies.

With these general ideas in our minds, let us weigh the objections which have been stated against the number of members proposed for

By permission of Doug Marlette and Creators Syndicate.

the House of Representatives. It is said, in the first place, that so small a number cannot be safely trusted with so much power.

The number of which this branch of the legislature is to consist, at the outset of the government, will be sixty-five. Within three years a census is to be taken, when the number may be augmented to one for every thirty thousand inhabitants; and within every successive period of ten years the census is to be renewed, and augmentations may continue to be made under the above limitations. It will not be thought an extravagant conjecture that the first census will, at the rate of one for every thirty thousand, raise the number of representatives to at least one hundred. Estimating the Negroes in the proportion of three fifths, it can scarcely be doubted that the population of the United States will by that time, if it does not already, amount to three millions. At the expiration of twenty-five years, according to the computed rate of increase, the number of representatives will amount to two hundred; and of fifty years, to four hundred. This is a number which, I presume will put an end to all fears arising from the smallness of the body. I take for granted here what I shall, in answering the fourth objection, hereafter show, that the number of representatives will be augmented from time to time in the manner provided by the Constitution. On a contrary supposition, I should admit the objection to have very great weight indeed.

The true question to be decided, then, is whether the smallness of the number, as a temporary regulation, be dangerous to the public liberty? Whether sixty-five members for a few years, and a hundred or two hundred for a few more, be a safe depositary for a limited and well-guarded power of legislating for the United States? I must own that I could not give a negative answer to this question, without first obliterating every impression which I have received with regard to the present genius of the people of America, the spirit which actuates the State legislatures, and the principles which are incorporated with the political character of every class of citizens. I am unable to conceive that the people of America, in their present temper, or under any circumstances which can speedily happen, will choose, and every second year repeat the choice of, sixty-five or a hundred men who would be disposed to form and pursue a scheme of tyranny or treachery. I am unable to conceive that the State legislatures, which must feel so many motives to watch and which possess so many means of counteracting the federal legislature, would fail either to detect or to defeat a conspiracy of the latter against the liberties of their common constituents. I am equally unable to conceive that there are at this time, or can be in any short time, in the United States, any sixty-five or a hundred men capable of recommending themselves to the choice of the people at large, who would either desire or dare, within the short space of two years, to betray the solemn trust committed to them. What change of circumstances time, and a fuller population of our country may produce requires a prophetic spirit to declare, which makes no part of my pretensions. But judging from the circumstances now before us, and from the probable state of them within a moderate period of time, I must pronounce that the liberties of America cannot be unsafe in the number of hands proposed by the federal Constitution. . . .

As there is a degree of depravity in mankind which requires a certain degree of circumspection and distrust, so there are other qualities in human nature which justify a certain portion of esteem and confidence. Republican government presupposes the existence of these qualities in a higher degree than any other form. Were the pictures which have been drawn by the political jealousy of some among us faithful likenesses of the human character, the inference would be that there is not sufficient virtue among men for self-government; and that nothing less than the chains of despotism can restrain them from destroying and devouring one another.

11.2 Federalist No. 57

James Madison

The *third* charge against the House of Representatives is that it will be taken from that class of citizens which will have least sympathy with the mass of the people, and be most likely to aim at an ambitious sacrifice of the many to the aggrandizement of the few.

Of all the objections which have been framed against the federal Constitution, this is perhaps the most extraordinary. Whilst the objection itself is leveled against a pretended oligarchy, the principle of it strikes at the very root of republican government.

The aim of every political constitution is, or ought to be, first to obtain for rulers men who possess most wisdom to discern, and most virtue to pursue, the common good of the society; and in the next place, to take the most effectual precautions for keeping them virtuous whilst they continue to hold their public trust. The elective mode of obtaining rulers is the characteristic policy of republican government. The means relied on in this form of government for preventing their degeneracy are numerous and various. The most effectual one is such a limitation of the term of appointments as will maintain a proper responsibility to the people.

Let me now ask what circumstance there is in the constitution of the House of Representatives that violates the principles of republican government, or favors the elevation of the few on the ruins of the many? Let me ask whether every circumstance is not, on the contrary, strictly comfortable to these principles, and scrupulously impartial to the rights and pretensions of every class and description of citizens?

Who are to be the electors of the federal representatives? Not the rich, more than the poor; not the learned, more than the ignorant; not the haughty heirs of distinguished names, more than the humble sons of obscure and unpropitious fortune. The electors are to be the great body of the people of the United States.

They are to be the same who exercise the right in every State of electing the corresponding branch of the legislature of the State.

Who are to be the objects of popular choice? Every citizen whose merit may recommend him to the esteem and confidence of his country. No qualification of wealth, of birth, of religious faith, or of civil profession is permitted to fetter the judgment or disappoint the inclination of the people.

If we consider the situation of the men on whom the free suffrages of their fellow-citizens may confer the representative trust, we shall find it involving every security which can be devised or desired for their fidelity to their constituents.

In the first place, as they will have been distinguished by the preference of their fellow-citizens, we are to presume that in general they will be somewhat distinguished also by those qualities which entitle them to it, and which promise a sincere and scrupulous regard to the nature of their engagements.

In the second place, they will enter into the public service under circumstances which cannot fail to produce a temporary affection at least to their constituents. There is in every breast a sensibility to marks of honor, of favor, of esteem, and of confidence, which, apart from all considerations of interests, is some pledge for grateful and benevolent returns. Ingratitude is a common topic of declamation against human nature; and it must be confessed that instances of it are but too frequent and flagrant, both in public and in private life. But the universal and extreme indignation which it inspires is itself a proof of the energy and prevalence of the contrary sentiment.

In the third place, those ties which bind the representative to his constituents are strengthened by motives of a more selfish nature. His pride and vanity attach him to a form of government which favors his pretensions and gives him a share in its honors and distinctions. Whatever hopes or projects might be entertained by a few aspiring characters, it must generally happen that a great proportion of the men deriving their advancement from their influence with the people would have more to hope from a preservation of the favor than from innovations in the government subversive of the authority of the people.

All these securities, however, would be found very insufficient without the restraint of frequent elections. Hence, in the fourth place, the House of Representatives is so constituted as to support in the members an habitual recollection of their dependence on the people. Before the sentiments impressed on their minds by the mode of their elevation can be effaced by the exercise of power, they will be compelled to anticipate the moment when their power is to cease, when their exercise of it is to be reviewed, and when they must descend to the level from which they were raised; there forever to remain unless a faithful discharge of their trust shall have established their title to a renewal of it.

I will add, as a fifth circumstance in the situation of the House of Representatives, restraining them from oppressive measures, that they can make no law which will not have its full operation on themselves and their friends, as well as on the great mass of the society. This has always been deemed one of the strongest bonds by which human policy can connect the rulers and the people together. It creates between them that communion of interests and sympathy of sentiments of which few governments have furnished examples; but without which every government degenerates into tyranny. If it be asked, what is to restrain the House of Representatives from making legal discriminations in favor of themselves and a particular class of society? I answer: the genius of the whole system; the nature of just and constitutional laws; and, above all, the vigilant and manly spirit which actuates the people of America—a spirit which nourishes freedom, and in return is nourished by it.

If this spirit shall ever be so far debased as to tolerate a law not obligatory on the legislature, as well as on the people, the people will be prepared to tolerate anything but liberty.

Such will be the relation between the House of Representatives and their constituents. Duty, gratitude, interest, ambition itself, are the cords by which they will be bound to fidelity and sympathy with the great mass of the people. It is possible that these may all be insufficient to control the caprice and wickedness of men. But are they not all that government will admit, and that human prudence can devise? Are they not the genuine and the characteristic means by which republican government provides for the liberty and happiness of the people? . . .

II   INTERCONNECTIONS

Congress is the legislative branch of the federal government, but its role, as Louis Fisher points out, extends to oversight of the administrative process. When Congress supervises the executive branch, Fisher writes, it is exercising a "legitimate role and responsibility." The separation of powers not only does not prohibit Congress from taking an active role in the administrative process, Fisher argues; it requires Congress to do so.

Questions

1. Compare Fisher's view of Congress's role in the administrative process to Madison's view of the separation of powers in *Federalist* No. 47, No. 48, and No. 51 (selections 2.1 through 2.3).

11.3 *Congress as Administrator* _____

Louis Fisher

Constitutional Basis

Administration is not a monopoly of the executive. Congress has a legitimate role and responsibility in supervising the efforts of federal agencies. Little was said at the Philadelphia Convention concerning the president's power as administrator. Certainly the framers were keenly aware of the failings of the Continental Congress, especially its lack of administrative accountability and efficiency. Moreover, Madison discovered in the state legislatures an appetite for usurpation: "The Executives of the States are in general little more than Cyphers; the legislatures omnipotent." James Wilson, Gouverneur Morris, and John Mercer were among the delegates at the Convention who warned against legislative aggrandizement. The delegates rejected the idea of a plural executive, preferring to anchor that responsibility in a single individual. Said John Rutledge: "A single man would feel the greatest responsibility and administer the public affairs best."

It can be argued that congressional participation in administrative matters creates a divided executive, something the framers explicitly rejected. Nevertheless, at the Convention, Roger Sherman considered the executive "nothing more than an institution for carrying the will of the Legislature into effect," and although Alexander Hamilton, Thomas Jefferson, and others had criticized the Continental Congress for meddling in administrative details, the framers were never able to distinguish clearly between legislative and executive duties.

Agencies have a direct responsibility to Congress, which created them. In 1854 Attorney General Caleb Cushing admitted that departmental heads are created by law and "most of their duties are prescribed by law." Congress "may at all times call on them for information or explanation in matters of official duty; and it may, if it see fit, interpose by legislation concerning them, when required by the interests of the Government." The extent to which Congress could direct officials prompted Cushing to warn that Congress might by statute so divide the executive power as to subvert the government "and to change it into a parliamentary despotism, like that of Venice or Great Britain, with a nominal executive chief utterly powerless—whether under the name of Doge, or King, or President."

Not only is the administrative process today open to congressional intervention, but parties from the private sector are invited to participate in agency operations. The Administrative Procedure Act of 1946 requires public notice and comment in rulemaking and provides for group representation in adjudicatory proceedings. The statutory requirement for boards, committees, and task forces allows interested parties from the private sector to advise federal agencies on the implementation of laws. Programs from the Johnson administration called for participation by citizens in antipoverty and urban programs. The Freedom of Information Act, the Sunshine Act of 1976, and funding of public participation in agency proceedings have given citizens and interest groups greater access to the administrative process.

The judiciary is another important participant in the administrative process, reviewing agency decisions to see that they conform to legislative intent, satisfy standards of procedural fairness, and meet the test of constitutionality. Courts are routinely criticized for intervening so deeply in the administrative process that they usurp the policy-making functions of Congress and the agencies.

With participation of this breadth in the administrative process, it seems anomalous to ask Congress to stay out. When members of Congress believe that an agency has departed from its statutory purpose, they are entitled, if not obligated, to express their views through individual statements on the floor, questions at committee hearings, or direct contact with agency officials. The legislative function does not cease with a bill that creates an agency. Only by monitoring the operation of a law can members uncover statutory defects and correct agency misinterpretations.

In a study basically sympathetic to congressional supervision of agencies, Frank Neuman and Harry Keaton concluded: "One point seems obvious. Congress goes too far if it spends so much time supervising that not enough time is left for legislating." This attitude presumes that supervision and legislation are distinct duties, whereas it is impossible to legislate intelligently and effectively without close supervision. Only through regular feedback from administrators can laws be perfected. How much time to allocate for supervision is a judgment left solely to Congress.

Instruments of Legislative Control

A number of express or implied constitutional powers allow Congress to direct administrative matters. Congress has the power to create an office, define its powers and durations, and determine the compensation for officials. Additional legislative guidance comes from the process of confirming presidential appointees, advisory participation in the administrative process, the investigatory and appropriation powers, private bills, casework, and nonstatutory controls. . . .

Personnel Policy

The U.S. Code contains extraordinarily detailed instructions from Congress to cover personnel policy for agencies: examination, selection, and placement of employees; training, performance ratings, and incentive awards; classification of positions, pay rates, and travel expenses; hours of work, leave, and holidays; rights of employees; preferential points in hiring veterans; medical plans and life insurance; and restrictions on political activities by federal employees.

In creating departments, Congress may require that the appointment of certain executive officials be subject to the advice and consent of the Senate. It may stipulate the qualifications of appointees, itemizing in great detail the characteristics a president must consider before submitting a name for Senate action. Congress has the power to delegate the appointment of officers to departmental heads; it may also specify grounds for removal and impose procedural safeguards before administrators suspend or dismiss employees.

During confirmation hearings, senators have an opportunity to explore a nominee's depth of knowledge and policy commitments. Promises may be extracted at that time with regard to keeping the committees informed of proposed actions and even requiring prior approval from the committees on specific issues. In 1972 President Nixon invoked executive privilege to prevent White House aide Peter Flanigan from testifying before the Senate Judiciary Committee. In an adroit countermove, Senator Sam Ervin, Democrat of North Carolina, asked the committee to delay the consideration of Richard Kleindienst's nomination as attorney general until Nixon let Flanigan testify. The tactic worked. Flanigan was permitted to appear before the committee under special ground rules.

Participating as Advisers

The Constitution specifically prohibits persons from simultaneously holding federal office and serving as members of Congress. This Incompatibility Clause is one of the supporting structures of the separation of powers doctrine. Nevertheless, some statutes allow members of Congress to take part in the implementation of laws. The Trade Expansion Act of 1962 directed

the president, before each negotiation, to select four representatives from the congressional tax committees to be accredited as members of the U.S. delegation. Under the Trade Act of 1974, ten members of Congress are accredited by the president as official advisers to U.S. delegations at international conferences, meetings, and negotiation sessions relating to trade agreements. In assigning Secret Service protection for major presidential or vice presidential candidates, the secretary of the treasury consults with an advisory committee consisting of the Speaker of the House, the House minority leader, the Senate majority leader, the Senate minority leader, and a fifth member selected by those four officers.

Congress appoints members of various commissions to oversee the implementation of federal policy. In 1976 Congress established a Commission on Security and Cooperation in Europe to monitor compliance with the Helsinki Agreement on human rights. Congress appoints twelve of its members to the commission. The president appoints three, drawing from the departments of State, Defense, and Commerce. The Speaker of the House designates the chair from among the House members. As if to underscore the mixed executive-legislative nature of this commission, it is funded not from the legislative branch appropriation bill but from the State-Justice appropriation bill. The commission was reconstituted in 1985, retaining the mixed legislative-executive membership but rotating the leadership between the House and the Senate.

An unusual body was created by Congress in 1986 when it established a board of trustees to govern Gallaudet University, which had been set up years before as a school for the deaf. Of the twenty-one-member board, the Speaker of the House appoints two representatives, and the president pro tempore of the Senate appoints one senator. The board governs the university, including hiring its professors and administering the funds appropriated for the school by Congress. President Reagan signed the bill, although he said it raised questions under the Appointments Clause and the Incompatibility Clause of the Constitution.

Investigations

Congress uses the investigative power to scrutinize the administration of programs. The power of Congress to conduct investigations, the Supreme Court noted in 1957, "comprehends probes into departments of the Federal Government to expose corruption, inefficiency or waste." Even Joseph Harris, the author of a 1965 study critical of congressional involvement in administration, recognized that it is not enough for Congress to enact policies and programs into law. Members of Congress "must check to see how those policies are being executed, whether they are accomplishing the desired results, and, if not, what corrective action the legislature may appropriately prescribe."

The House of Representatives sharpens its investigative power through the use of "resolutions of inquiry." A member may introduce a resolution authorizing a committee to request information from the heads of executive departments. All resolutions of inquiry must be reported to the House within one week after presentation. Resolutions of inquiry are answered by departmental officials, either directly or through the president. If the executive branch resists the call for certain papers, congressional committees can issue subpoenas for documents or force individuals to testify. The Court has held that the issuance of a subpoena pursuant to an authorized investigation is "an indispensable ingredient of lawmaking." If a subpoena fails to get the attention of the executive branch, Congress can invoke its contempt power to protect legislative privileges and prerogatives. Contempt proceedings produced material from Secretary of Commerce Rogers Morton, during the Ford administration, and from Secretary of Energy Charles W. Duncan, Jr., during the Carter administration. Similarly, the contempt power was instrumental in prying loose documents from the Reagan administration. . . .

Restrictions on the investigative power generally protect private citizens rather than agency officials. Citizens are entitled to First Amendment rights of free speech and association, the Fourth Amendment right to be free of unreasonable searches and seizures, the Fifth Amendment right that protects witnesses against self-incrimination, and certain Sixth Amendment rights of due process. Committee hearings must be properly authorized; the judiciary insists that committee questions be pertinent and directed toward a legislative purpose.

These limitations do not apply to committee inquiries into agency activities. Agencies are expected to cooperate with legislative efforts to determine the expenditure of taxpayer funds. Presidents may raise the barrier of executive privilege, claiming a constitutional right to withhold information from Congress, but such defenses are rarely employed. President Reagan invoked executive privilege in 1986 to keep from the Senate certain memoranda that Justice William Rehnquist had written while in the Justice Department during the Nixon years, but when it looked as if this action might delay Rehnquist's nomination to be chief justice and therefore prevent the confirmation of Antonin Scalia to be associate justice, the documents were released to the Senate.

The courts have added a few restrictions on congressional investigations into agency affairs. Committees may not intervene in a pending adjudicatory proceeding by focusing on the process used by agency officials to reach a decision; here the congressional interference is not in an agency's "*legislative* function, but rather, in its *judicial* function." The legislative (rulemaking) function of an agency is more open to congressional inquiries than adjudicatory proceedings, but a member may not force an executive official to take into account considerations that Congress had not intended.

For the most part, however, the courts assume that agency officials possess the necessary "backbone" to withstand searching inquiries by congressional committees. Even when pressure during a congressional hearing is the direct impetus for a change in agency policy, the courts treat such influence as "part of the give and take of democratic government."

Appropriations

The power of the purse allows Congress to monitor closely and to control the administration of programs. At the end of each appropriation bill lies a "General Provisions" section that contains dozens of limitations, riders, and restrictions on agency operations. Within each appropriation account are additional restrictions that take the form of "provisos." When Congress felt that the Legal Services Corporation had abused its powers, it resorted to an increasing number of restrictions. For example, the appropriation for fiscal 1986 provided $305.5 million subject to a long list of conditions, prohibiting the corporation from using appropriated funds to lobby the national, state, or local governments; to provide legal assistance for an alien unless certain conditions are met; to support or conduct training programs for the purpose of advocating particular public policies or encouraging political activities; or to take certain other actions proscribed by the appropriation.

Audits by the General Accounting Office (GAO) permit Congress to hold executive officers accountable for the use of public funds. The GAO has the power to "disallow" an expenditure, thereby making the disbursing officer liable for the funds involved in an illegal transaction. For example, in 1974 GAO used this power to stop the expenditure of funds for Secret Service protection to Spiro Agnew after he had resigned as vice president.

The power of the purse cannot be protected merely through the authorization and appropriation process. Congress must monitor the *expenditure* of funds to prevent the abuse of discretionary authority by executive officials. Members of Congress find it necessary to exercise statutory and nonstatutory controls over administrative operations such as transfer of funds, reprogramming of funds, year-end buying, deficiency spending, impoundment, carryover balances, and contractor expenses.

Very few constitutional limits operate on the appropriations power. While the flow of federal money is not "the final arbiter of constitutionally protected rights," only rarely has the judiciary placed restrictions on the power of purse. For example, Congress may not diminish the compensation of members of the federal judiciary, since this is specifically proscribed by the Constitution. In addition, the Supreme Court, in *United States v. Lovett* (1946), declared invalid a section of an appropriation act that prohibited the payment of federal salaries to three named "subversives." The language in the statute was struck down because it represented a bill of attainder which Article II, Section 3 of the Constitution forbids.

Private Bills

Members of Congress introduce private bills to overcome injustices and inadequacies in the administrative process. The flood of private bills after the Civil War to assist constituents turned down by the Pension Bureau was particularly flagrant. President Grover Cleveland declared open season on such measures, often employing sarcastic language in his veto messages to rebuke these legislative efforts. During the 49th Congress (1885–1887) there were over twice as many private laws as public laws: 1,031 to 434. The ratio climbed to 3-to-1 by the 56th Congress (1899–1901)—1,498 private laws and 443 public laws. Private bills introduced in the 59th Congress (1905–1907) topped 6,000.

In an effort to reduce the private bill workload, the Legislative Reorganization Act of 1946 prohibited the consideration of any private bill or resolution (including omnibus claims or pension bills) or an amendment to any bill or resolution authorizing or directing (1) the payment of money for property damages, for personal injuries or death for suits that could be instituted under the Federal Tort Claims Act (Title IV of the 1946 act), or for a pension (other than to carry out a provision of law or treaty stipulation); (2) the construction of a bridge across a navigable stream (Title V of the act); or (3) the correction of a military or naval record.

Due to a surge in legislative activity regarding immigration from 1949 through 1955, private laws averaged more than one thousand in each Congress, but from 1971 to 1986 they were reduced sharply, averaging about one hundred a Congress. Private bills need not be *enacted* to affect the administrative process. Whenever a senator or representative introduces an immigration bill and the judiciary committees request a report from the Immigration and Naturalization Service, a deportation is delayed until action is taken on the bill. This procedure continues to exist even after the Supreme Court declared the legislative veto unconstitutional in 1983. Although private bills are subject to abuse, they allow Congress to correct mistakes in past legislation or current administration.

Casework

Members of Congress often become aware of administrative deficiencies by attending to "casework"—assisting a constituent's contact with the bureaucracy. Much of the literature on Congress refers disparagingly to casework because it supposedly diverts members from more significant matters, making them "errand runners" instead of legislators. But casework, aside from its importance for reelection, helps educate legislators on the actual workings of a law. It forces them to descend from the lofty and often abstract universe of statutes to the mundane world of administration. By responding to constituent requests, legislators obtain information that allows them to perfect laws and improve agency procedures. One member of Congress advised his colleagues:

> You should not underestimate the value of constituent work on the legislative process. Don't you get a lot of your ideas about needed changes in the laws from the problems of your constituents? In processing a problem before the VA or a draft problem you gain your best

insight into how laws operate, and you discover where they might be changed.

Some studies conclude that casework reinforces the "institutionalized suspicion" that administrators and legislators have about each other. To bureaucrats, legislators and their staffs "appear as special pleaders for the narrow interests of their constituents even when these conflict with the 'national welfare,' which bureaucrats tend to equate with the over-all rules and programs of their agency or department to which the senators so often seek exception." Members, in turn, are said to characterize bureaucrats as arbitrary, patronizing, and compulsively attached to their procedures.

These attitudes, while they do exist, are atypical. Most bureaucrats believe that members of Congress should intervene on behalf of constituents. Casework is accepted as a legitimate and healthy input into the administrative process. Administrators find that casework helps them watch over their subordinates, uncover program flaws, and generate improvements in rules and regulations. Much of the congressional liaison apparatus established in agencies and departments is designed to assist members with casework. Departments that are heavily involved in casework—such as the Veterans Administration, the Office of Personnel Management, and the military services—maintain offices in the Senate and House office buildings.

Nonstatutory Controls

Simple resolutions (adopted by either house) and concurrent resolutions (adopted by both houses) are used to direct administrative action. Although these resolutions are not presented to the president, and therefore escape the veto power, they can be effective means of control. Some statutes allow committees, acting by resolutions, to direct an agency to investigate. Most resolutions are advisory only, to be accepted by agencies as a recommended course of action. They express the "sense of Congress" (or of either house) on some aspect of public policy.

Congress directs administrative action through the use of other nonstatutory controls: language placed in committee reports, instructions issued by members during committee hearings, correspondence from committee and subcommittee heads to agency officials, and various types of "gentlemen's agreements." Under a philosophy of good-faith efforts by administrators, this system makes sense for both branches. Instead of locking legislative policy into a rigid statutory mold, agency officials are given substantial leeway to adjust programs throughout the year in response to changing circumstances. In return for this latitude, administrators are expected to follow the legislative policy expressed in nonstatutory directives.

In some cases the system fails. In 1975 a conference report adopted by the House and Senate directed the Navy to produce as its air combat fighter a derivative of an aircraft to be selected by the Air Force. Instead of following the directive in the conference report (usually of high priority as legislative history), the Navy picked a different type of aircraft. The comptroller general decided that nonstatutory controls are not legally binding on agencies unless there is some ambiguity in a statute that requires recourse to the legislative history. Agencies follow nonstatutory controls for practical, not legal, reasons. To ignore such controls invites Congress to cut agency budgets and add restrictive statutory language.

Two other recent disputes highlight the risk of relying on nonstatutory controls to check delegated power. In 1978 the Supreme Court had to decide whether the Tennessee Valley Authority should complete a dam that threatened the existence of a tiny fish called the snail darter. Opponents of the dam claimed that its operation would violate the Endangered Species Act. The Court declined to allow language in the reports of the appropriations committees, urging completion of the dam, to have precedence over a statute, particularly in the circumstances presented by the case. In another dispute two

years later, a lower court reviewed language in a conference report stating that Congress did not contemplate the use of authority given in the bill. The court ruled that the report language could not in any way alter the fact that Congress had granted the authority and had done so with unambiguous language in the bill.

Intervention by the GAO and the judiciary generally is not necessary. Most agencies prefer to adhere as best they can to nonstatutory controls rather than risk new limitations placed in a public law. Nonstatutory controls are especially binding in the case of secret budgets for the U.S. intelligence community, composed of the Central Intelligence Agency and several other federal units. The classified nature of U.S. intelligence activities prevents the disclosure of budgetary recommendations. Instead, the intelligence committees prepare a classified "Schedule of Authorizations," listing the amounts of dollars and personnel ceilings for all the intelligence and intelligence-related programs authorized by Congress. The intelligence community is expected to "comply fully with the limitations, guidelines, directions, and recommendations" in the classified schedule, which is "incorporated" into the bill.

Limitations on Congress

Members of Congress have many legitimate reasons for participating in the administrative process. In some cases, however, the representative function oversteps the legal boundaries and takes on the color of "influence peddling," leading to indictments in the courts against members who use their legislative and oversight positions for personal gain.

This kind of activity is controlled largely by two statutes. The bribery statute (18 U.S.C. 201) is directed against public officials—including members of Congress—who seek or accept anything of value in return for an official act. The conflict-of-interest statute (18 U.S.C. 203) makes it a criminal offense for members of Congress to receive or seek compensation for services relating to any proceeding, contract, claim, or other activities of the federal government. Depending on the circumstances, members may seek immunity under the Speech or Debate Clause of the Constitution, which prohibits questioning a senator or representative for any legislative act.

The Supreme Court has repeatedly held that members of Congress may not use the Speech or Debate Clause as a shield for contacts with the executive branch. Representative Thomas Johnson, Democrat of Maryland, who tried to influence the Justice Department to drop a pending investigation of a savings and loan institution, was accused of receiving more than $20,000 for his efforts. He was found guilty of violating the conflict-of-interest statute. Representative Bertram Podell, Democrat of New York, pleaded guilty in 1974 to conspiracy and conflict-of-interest charges after he had intervened in several federal agency actions to help an airline company obtain a route between Florida and the Bahamas. His family law firm in Manhattan had been collecting monthly legal fees from the airline's parent company. In another action marking the limits of legislative intervention in agency activities, Representative Frank Brasco, Democrat of New York, was found guilty of bribery and conspiracy in a scheme to obtain Post Office contracts for a trucking firm. In a more recent action, Representative Joshua Eilberg, Democrat of Pennsylvania, was indicted for receiving compensation for helping a Philadelphia hospital win a $14.5 million federal grant. After a federal court held in 1979 that his contacts with the executive branch were not protected by the Speech or Debate Clause, Eilberg pleaded guilty to a conflict-of-interest charge.

As part of FBI's Abscam operation during the Carter administration, Representative Michael J. Myers, Democrat of Pennsylvania, was charged with conspiracy, bribery, and traveling in interstate commerce to carry on an unlawful act. In defense, Myers argued that congressional independence would be undermined if government agents could entice members with manufactured opportunities to accept bribes.

His charge of entrapment was rejected by an appellate court, which pointed out that Congress may at any time protect itself by redefining the statutory meaning of bribery to exclude a legislator's acceptance of bribes offered by government undercover agents.

Aside from criminal prosecutions, members who interfere in agency proceedings are subject to other limitations. Members immune under the Speech or Debate Clause may face disciplinary action by the House or the Senate. As a result of a Supreme Court decision in 1979, members of Congress who publicize agency waste or abuse by issuing press releases and newsletters to their constituents are not protected by the Speech or Debate Clause. The case arose from a "Golden Fleece Award" announced by Senator William Proxmire, Democrat of Wisconsin, in 1975. After more than forty hours of staff research and a hearing by the Senate Appropriations Committee, Proxmire gave the award to the National Science Foundation (NSF), the National Aeronautics and Space Administration (NASA), and the Office of Naval Research for grants they had made to Dr. Ronald Hutchinson for his studies on animal aggression. Proxmire was in a key position to judge agency waste and abuse. He chaired the Senate appropriations subcommittee that funds NSF and NASA and was also a member of the defense and HEW [Department of Health, Education and Welfare] appropriations subcommittees. Hutchinson sued Proxmire, claiming that he had been libeled by Proxmire's press release and newsletter publicizing the award and by Proxmire's appearance on the Mike Douglas television show, where he mentioned the award.

Lower courts decided that the press release (almost identical to Proxmire's floor speech) was protected by the Speech or Debate Clause. The newsletter was considered part of the informing function of Congress and therefore immune, while the television appearance was protected by the First Amendment. However, the Supreme Court held that Proxmire's press release and newsletter were not protected by his constitutional function as a legislator. The curious result of this decision is that a member of Congress may disclose the results of agency waste, fraud, and abuse only in official remarks in the *Congressional Record* or in committee hearings. Once the member seeks to publicize the issue, by informing constituents or the press, there is risk of a lawsuit.

III  THE INTERNATIONAL CONTEXT

Unlike prime ministers, who are by definition in command of a parliamentary majority, the president cannot count on the support of Congress. As Richard Rose points out in the following selection, "The federal government operates according to a doctrine of concurring majorities: The White House and Congress must agree in order to sustain most major programs." Every president knows or soon discovers that Congress must be courted—persuaded to go along with the president's program. Under what Rose calls the "no-party American system," however, presidents cannot rely on party ties to persuade Congress but must cope with the fact that "individual politicians are on their own."

The ongoing love/hate relationship between the White House and Congress—each dependent on the other yet in constant competition—is exacerbated by the modern trend toward Republican presidents and Democratic Congresses (see, in particular, selection 7.2).

The backdrop of European parliamentary systems forms a sharp contrast to Rose's description of American legislative-executive relations.

Questions

1. What can a president do to convince members of Congress to vote a particular way on a given issue? Why are these measures so often ineffective in dealing with Congress?

2. How does Rose's view of presidential influence compare and contrast with the views of Hedrick Smith and Richard Neustadt in selections 12.5 and 12.6?

11.4 *Courting Congress*

Richard Rose

The President is compelled to court Congress in order to achieve his goals. Without the approval of Congress, the legislative requests in the State of the Union message remain a dead letter. Without the approval of Congress, the President's budget has no legal authority. Without the consent of the Senate, the President's ap-pointees to executive agencies and the Supreme Court cannot hold office. Moreover, congressional oversight of executive agencies gives it influence with bureaucrats who are nominally supposed to take their direction from the White House. After two years in the White House, ex-Congressman John F. Kennedy reflected:

I think the Congress looks more powerful sitting here than it did when I was there in the Congress. But that is because when you are in Congress you are one of a hundred in the Senate or one of 435 in the House, so that the power is divided. But from here I look at a Congress, and I look at the collective power of the Congress, particularly the bloc action, and it is a substantial power.

Changes since that time have made Congress even harder for the White House to deal with. Instead of power being concentrated among a small number of congressional barons who chair key committees and could deliver on agreements made with the White House, it is now dispersed among hundreds of peasants concerned with district interests that are difficult to aggregate and deliver as a package in a deal with the White House.

Congress is a fundamental and continuing influence on what the President can do. The federal government operates according to a doctrine of concurring majorities: The White House *and* Congress must agree in order to sustain most major programs. When a President goes to Washington, his object is to win the concurrence of Congress for what he wants to do. But what the President wants to do is not only a matter of deciding what policies he would like. The White House must also worry about whether Congress will buy what the President wants to produce. Even an expert wheeler-dealer such as David Stockman, Ronald Reagan's director of OMB [Office of Management and Budget], recognized that it was the end of the line for budget changes when congressmen asked privately: *"When is the White House going to learn something about the political facts of life? You're not going to get a consensus for anything very big or meaningful."*

In a parliamentary system, the Prime Minister and Cabinet can think first about adopting policies that they believe best for the party in government. Parliament *must* endorse the legislative program offered by the Cabinet; MPs [members of Parliament] agree to do so as a condition of securing nomination. A Prime Minister can threaten a member of Parliament who persistently votes against the party with expulsion and virtually certain electoral defeat because of the loss of the party's endorsement. A former British Labour Prime Minister, Harold Wilson, compared a dissident MP with a barking dog, adding that if an MP steps out of line often, "he may not get his dog license renewed when it falls due." As a party leader, the Prime Minister must manage Parliament, retaining the confidence of the majority of MPs there. This is a far less difficult task than bargaining with an independent assembly of barons and peasants.

Differences in Political Self-Interest

In the no-party American system, individual politicians are on their own; this is true of members of Congress as well as the President.

> Senators and Representatives are in business for themselves. From the initial decision to seek the nomination and the rigors of the first primary and general election campaigns all the way to eventual retirement or defeat, they are political entrepreneurs in their states and districts. . . . They are all likely to view themselves first and foremost as individuals, not as members of a party or as part of a President's team.

The self that a congressman seeks to advance is much more narrowly defined than the President's sense of political self. A member of the House of Representatives represents a district that is 1/435th of the nation, and a senator, 1/50th of America. By contrast, a President must try to appeal to all congressional districts and to all the states. A member of the House of Representatives must run for reelection every other year, and prepare for running in the alternate years. A member of Congress perceiving a clash between district and White House interests will normally vote his district, for it is to the district that he owes his place in Congress. The strength of congressional individualism means that there is "a limited capacity of national elections to impose a programmatic vision on a constituency-minded Congress."

A congressman's day involves concern with subgovernment issues; it also tends to insulate him from broader concerns of government. A member of Congress has no responsibility for America's relations with foreign nations, as the President does. Nor does a congressman have a responsibility for the national or international economy; what concerns him is employment in his district, and the prosperity of local factories and businesses. A member of Congress defends a district of about half a million people; the turf that the President defends is the United States in an uncertain world.

Although all the institutions of American government derive from a common Constitution, the view of how the system works differs from one end of Pennsylvania Avenue to the other. Gerald Ford, a congressman for two decades before becoming President, reflected:

> When I was in the Congress myself, I thought it fulfilled its constitutional obligations in a very responsible way, but after I became President my perspective changed. It seemed to me that Congress was beginning to disintegrate as an organized legislative body. It wasn't answering the nation's challenges domestically because it was too fragmented. It responded too often to single-issue special interest groups, and it therefore wound up dealing with minutiae instead of attacking serious problems in a coherent way.

While Congressman Ford accepted the world of district interests and subgovernments, President Ford wanted a legislature that could be disciplined like Parliament to support the President's national perspective.

Alternatives in Approaching Congress

Ironically, the chief constitutional power that the President has in dealing with Congress is the right to ignore it under certain very limited circumstances, for example, when acting as commander-in-chief of the armed forces. The veto is a second formal power, but it is an indication of failure to win support on the Hill. A bill that the President vetoes will not become law unless his veto is overridden by a two-thirds vote in each house of Congress. A veto is usually not overridden by Congress, for a President expects to have the backing of a third of Washington and of much of the public before acting so controversially. While vetoes are often threatened by a President in dispute with Congress, they are not often used.

Whereas the traditional President was committed to ask little from Congress, modern and postmodern Presidents are expected to lead Congress. White House leadership requires cooperation with leaders in Congress. Everyone in the White House is expected to be sensitive to congressional opinion. The White House Office of Congressional Relations is continuously looking after the concerns of individual members of Congress with their district, their policy priorities, and their egos. When important votes come up on the Hill, White House staff alert the President of the need for action to secure the support of individual congressmen on the committee having jurisdiction on a measure and to influence waverers who could be decisive in votes on the floor of the House or the Senate.

The President is the senior White House person dealing with Congress. A President will telephone or meet with congressmen at the White House in efforts to win their support on the merits of the issue, by flattery, and by appeals to self-interest. If a congressman wants something from the White House (a federal judgeship for a friend or a contract for his district), then the White House can offer to trade patronage for votes. For example, in return for Senator Albert Ellender of Louisiana providing support for the administration on a crucial civil rights bill, President Johnson saw that a nuclear frigate the navy did not want was built in a Baton Rouge shipyard. Later, he taxed an aide: "Which do your liberal friends think is more important, voting rights or a nuclear frigate?"

A President's relations with Congress are affected by whether or not he belongs to the party with a majority in the House and Senate. *Everything else being equal,* members of Congress will be inclined to vote along party lines. Since the Democrats are usually in control of Congress, each Democratic President starts with an advantage in dealing with the Hill. But since the Democratic party is a coalition of many disparate groups and there is often disagreement among Democrats about what should be done, a Republican President can play on these divisions to secure support for his measures. For example, Ronald Reagan secured vital support for 1981 budget measures from southern congressmen known as boll weevils, who had more in common with his views of the economy than with those of liberal Democrats. Party indiscipline can benefit a Republican President, whereas a Democratic President tries to discipline an often undisciplined Democratic majority.

The relations of Presidents with Congress are also affected by their view of the Hill. Lyndon Johnson and Gerald Ford had spent most of their adult life as congressmen before entering the Oval Office. Johnson could view the Hill as a former Senate majority leader, and Ford had many years as a leader of the Republicans, the House minority party. By contrast, neither Ronald Reagan nor Jimmy Carter had ever served in Congress, and neither Richard Nixon nor John F. Kennedy had ever sought to be accepted as an insider by the senior congressmen who exercised leadership while they served there.

Presidential styles in dealing with Congress can be classified according to whether or not the President's party has a majority in Congress and whether or not the President sees himself as a partner of Congress or an outsider. Presidents Johnson [a majority leader] and Ford [a minority leader] each saw Congress as a partner, but they differed in their ability to use party loyalty as an argument for support. The 1964 election not only gave Johnson a landslide presidential majority but also a big Democratic majority in Congress. By contrast, the 1974 post-Watergate congressional election was a disaster for the Republicans, reducing further the Republican minority in Congress. Hence, President Ford often turned to vetoes to assert his policy views against Congress.

Both Jimmy Carter and Richard Nixon saw themselves as outsiders in relation to Congress. Carter's sense of estrangement was so great that he had bad relations with a Congress in which his party was a majority. Carter's successor, Republican Ronald Reagan, won good marks from Democrats by treating them with more respect than his Democratic predecessor. As a partner of Congress, President Ford knew how to appeal to the vanity of congressmen. The significance of the President's personal touch is illustrated by an anecdote contrasting Ford and Carter.

> When Gerry Ford would sign a bill, he'd use nice metal pens with his name on them, and then he'd pass them out to the members who had worked on the bill. But Carter signs bills with a felt-tip pen and then he puts the pen back into his pocket.

President Nixon was a fugitive from Congress. As a Republican, he could not appeal for votes on grounds of party loyalty. As a lone wolf by temperament, he was ill at ease in the camaraderie of the Senate cloakroom. The policies that most interested Nixon were international measures, such as the Vietnam war, and negotiations with the Soviet Union. In these international fields, the Oval Office enjoys a substantial measure of discretion. On domestic issues, Nixon took administrative actions to prevent the spending of funds voted by Congress, rather than negotiate with the Hill.

It is not possible to classify Prime Ministers as we do Presidents, for a Prime Minister necessarily commands the confidence of Parliament. Except for France, a Prime Minister will normally have spent years or decades in Parliament; Prime Ministers differ only in the time

Richard Rose   387

spent learning the ropes of Parliament before going government. Each Prime Minister can normally be placed in the same category; he or she is an insider with the support of the majority party in Parliament.

Winning (and Not Winning) Support

While the White House proposes, Congress disposes. A simple index of the President's success in dealing with Congress is the reaction of the Hill to legislative proposals put forward from the White House. On average Congress refuses to approve more than half the measures that the President recommends (see table 1). In the period from Eisenhower through Ford, for which the most complete data are available, the best record was compiled in President Eisenhower's first term, when 66 percent of legislation was approved, and the worst in the abbreviated Presidency of Gerald Ford, when only 31 percent was approved. One reason why the President fails to secure his aims is that one or both houses do not even vote on what is proposed; the President thus loses by default. While Congress more often than not supports a presidential recommendation if it comes to a vote, like the vote itself, such support cannot be taken for granted. Every President can be sure of having some successes to boast about in

Congress, but he will also suffer some defeats. In anticipation of defeat, the White House will avoid putting forward proposals for which the time is not ripe, and trim others in hopes of making them more acceptable to Congress. In a parliamentary system, by contrast, the Prime Minister and Cabinet are certain that their proposals will be brought to a vote, and reasonably certain that they will be approved.

Party control of Congress has a limited impact on what happens to presidential proposals. When Congress and the President are of the same party, a President is likely to see Congress reject a majority of measures that he puts forward. This is also true when Congress is in the hands of the opposing party. The difference in success is only 8 percent; Presidents working with a Congress of their own party can get through only 49 percent of their legislative proposals. A President making recommendations to a Congress of the opposing party on average gets through 41 percent of his measures (see table 1).

The President must rely on party indiscipline in order to secure the enactment of his proposals because a substantial fraction of members of his own party will vote against what the White House proposes. From 1953 to 1983, Democratic Presidents had an average of 31 percent of House Democrats vote against

TABLE 1
Congressional Response to Presidential Proposals

	Submitted N	Approved N	Approved %
President, Congress same party			
Dwight Eisenhower, 1953–54	276	182	66
John F. Kennedy, 1961–63	1054	413	39
Lyndon B. Johnson, 1964–68	1902	991	52
Total	3232	1586	49
President, Congress opposing parties			
Dwight Eisenhower, 1955–60	1283	610	48
Richard Nixon, 1968–74	979	333	34
Gerald Ford, 1974–75	220	68	31
Total	2482	1011	41
(Overall total)	(5714)	(2597)	(45%)

their proposals, and 39 percent of Senate Democrats. Similarly, Republican Presidents have suffered the opposition of 35 percent of House Republicans, and 32 percent of Senate Republicans. Given defections of this magnitude, a Republican President must secure a substantial portion of Democratic votes to get a measure through, and even a Democratic President with a nominal majority in Congress needs some support from the Republican minority to offset the consequence of Democratic defections.

Congressmen do not see themselves as defecting when they vote against a President of their own party. The view from the Hill is that each member of Congress should vote on the basis of an individual calculation, reflecting the views of the district, personal political beliefs, and commitments to other congressmen and pressure groups, as well as on party inclinations, and White House views. The President is always sure to have some support, and some opposition. The White House problem is that it cannot predict how much support it will have on a given measure until after a proposal has gone forward. The actual outcome of a vote in Congress reflects forces "largely beyond the President's control."

By comparison with Prime Ministers, a President's legislative record places him in the second division. When courting Congress, Presidents usually finish below .500, losing more proposals than they win. By contrast, a Prime Minister expects to finish over .800, winning four out of five or better of the government's legislative proposals. In a parliamentary system with strict party discipline such as the British House of Commons, a government can have a .990 record on its bills. A British Prime Minister can rely on the party whip to drive measures through the Commons with majority support by his parliamentary colleagues. As a Cabinet minister once commented, "It's carrying democracy too far if you don't know the result of the vote before the meeting."

In order for a President to be sure of placing his vision of the national interest on the statute book, a fundamental change would be necessary in Washington. Ex-congressman and Reagan budget director, David Stockman concludes: "The world's so-called greatest deliberative body would have to be reduced to the status of a ministerial arm of the White House," giving "rubber stamp approval, nothing less." What Stockman is complaining about is that the national leader that he served is a President rather than a Prime Minister in a parliamentary system.

IV  VIEW FROM THE INSIDE

Members of Congress play many roles, as illustrated by the following two portraits of current members of Congress.

Colorado's Pat Schroeder plays more roles than most other members of Congress. She represents Colorado's 1st District, is a leading voice on a variety of national issues, is a role model for women politicians and would-be politicians, and has been a candidate for president of the United States. Schroeder may not be a typical member of Congress (the House is, after all, more than 90 percent male), but her struggle to balance her many roles and responsibilities is not at all unusual.

The second portrait is of Timothy J. Penny, who represents Minnesota's 1st District. In this selection, he goes home just after the beginning of the Persian Gulf War in January 1991 to keep in touch with his constituents. Penny's attention to the needs and concerns of the voters illustrates the complex relationship between a representative and the people.

Questions

1. Do the many different roles played by Congresswoman Schroeder sometimes conflict with one another? Did her role as a spokesperson for equal rights for women interfere with her presidential campaign, for example?

2. How do the nonlegislative roles of members of Congress relate to their legislative concerns? Consider in particular the relationship between Congressman Penny's votes on the Hill and his role in constituency service.

11.5 The Prime of Pat Schroeder

Susan Ferraro

At the assembly point for Denver's 1990 St. Patrick's Day Parade, a tall, slim woman resplendent in a Kelly-green coat and a glittery, green top hat darted through the genial confusion of skirling bagpipes, Irish wolfhounds, green balloons and teen-age beauty queens showing more goose bumps than cleavage.

"Top o' the mornin' to ya!" she called to onlookers, her face stretched tight in a wide grin.

"Hey, Mrs. Schroeder!" a man shouted.

Heads swiveled and Patricia Schroeder, Denver's nine-term Congresswoman known for her witty one-liners, her fierce dedication to family issues and her brief 1987 exploratory campaign for President, which ended in a flood of tears, stepped eagerly toward the crowd.

"You came to my class to judge Halloween costumes—it must have been in '74," a young father told her. Schroeder grinned. "We thought you'd be wearing a green bunny suit," an official teased, alluding to the Easter bunny suit she may or may not have worn in 1979 to the Great Wall of China. "Well, I thought of it," she replied mildly.

Perched on the back seat of a convertible for the parade, Schroeder waved to the crowd, amid shouts of "Hey, Pat!" and "Pro-choice!" Blinky the Clown, a local children's show celeb-

rity, introduced her to the television audience and, off camera, asked Schroeder to autograph her new book, "Champion of the Great American Family."

As the parade came to an end and Schroeder headed for a small gray sedan, a passer-by shouted, "When are you going to run for President?" Schroeder's stride didn't falter.

"Hey, great to see ya," she said, flashing the grin.

Schroeder had reason to duck the question. Once before, she had been caught unawares. In 1987, she was running to catch a flight from Washington to Denver when an Associated Press reporter asked her if she was considering a Presidential race now that Gary Hart had dropped out. "I feel I have to look at it seriously," she said. By the time her plane landed, reporters were waiting. Her husband, Jim—one of her principal advisers—in Bangkok on business at the time, found out about his wife's plans in *The International Herald Tribune*.

Moreover, after 18 years in Congress, she has a lot to lose. Now the most senior woman in Congress, an incumbent who won her last election with 70 percent of the vote, Schroeder has become part of the Establishment without sacrificing either the family issues she stands for or her independent style, both of which have always set her at odds with it. Long a darling of liberals, she is increasingly welcome within the business community, as was evident when she spoke to Du Pont Company employees in December [1989]. The audience of mostly middle-level managers listened raptly as she talked about the country's military budget: "Power issues are things like—in the post-I.N.F. [intermediate nuclear forces treaty] environment, should the United States have the D-5 missile, the cruise missile, the MX missile, the rail garrison, or all of the above, some of the above, none of the above?" And about the struggles parents face: "Toddlers don't have political action committees, they don't pay you honorariums if you drop by their child-care center, and they don't vote." And about changing our national priorities: the real issues are the national debt, more equitable allocation of defense costs with allies, and "getting our educational resources in place so we are ready to compete."

In Congress, Schroeder sits on the House Armed Services Committee (where she is the fifth-ranking Democrat), and eight other committees and subcommittees; she is chairwoman of the House Armed Services Subcommittee on Military Installations and Facilities. She heads a task force on how tax policies affect families and she is a deputy whip. She is co-head of both the Democratic Caucus's Task Force on National Security and the Congressional Caucus for Women's Issues, a group that has grown, largely by her design, to number 150 members of Congress—a sizable lobbying force.

That kind of influence is useful to a woman who has made a career out of changing systems she doesn't like. Since her election to Congress in 1972, Schroeder has almost single-handedly wrenched family issues—child care and education, pension reform for widows and former spouses, flextime in the work place for parents and women's economic equity—out of the dim peripheries of campaign rhetoric and into the political mainstream.

Given the sudden surge of women in politics, the time may be right for a Schroeder Presidential campaign, though it would presumably take party pols by surprise: few mention Schroeder when the subject of the 1992 campaign comes up. Nationally, 10 women, including Ann Richards of Texas and Dianne Feinstein of California, are running for governor in 1990. Five women, one an incumbent, are running for the United States Senate. Three of the five are members of the House, where 24 women are running for reelection and another 20 or so are running for seats now held by men. Women are seeking office in unprecedented numbers at the local level as well, according to the National Organization for Women.

Many are answering what Schroeder calls the "wake-up call" of the Supreme Court's 1989 Webster decision [see selection 16.5] which gave states the right to restrict abortions. . . . [In Pennsylvania, for example, where abortion regulations are particularly strict and] the number of women seeking election to the . . . State Legislature has historically been almost nonexistent, some 90 women announced candidacies . . . [in 1990], and about 70 made it past primaries. The influx of women into the permanent work force means that so-called women's issues, like child care and health services for the elderly, have an impact on the national economy. Political pioneers like Schroeder, Feinstein and Lynn Martin (R.-Ill.) . . . have been in politics for some time. They can take aim at higher office and talk about, for instance, fiscal policy without encountering sexist condescension.

Schroeder is often rebuked for "running as a woman." Her reply, complete with practiced, elaborate shrug, is: "Do I have a choice?"

At a podium or on the House floor, her searing wit can vaporize an opponent in the 15 seconds suitable for a sound byte: it was she who labeled Reagan "the Teflon President," she who called defense contractors "the welfare queens of the 80's." Behind the scenes she does a surprising amount of homework and displays a shrewd, even lethal political savvy. Over the years she has helped bump not one, but two, chairmen of the House Armed Services Committee.

Off the campaign trail, in committee hearings, she seems to revel in complexity and detail. She serves as head of the Armed Services Committee's panel on Defense Burden Sharing, a term that is Washingtonese for the policy that results in billions of dollars the United States spends defending financially secure allies, and that, she says, has helped Japan, Canada and Germany to become powerful trade competitors. Relieved of the financial drain in their own defense, she points out, these countries have invested in their work force—with programs for education, health care, and even, in some parts of Europe, mandated "spa leave" for workers.

Schroeder proposes alternatives: other developed nations should contribute amounts of their gross national products proportionately equal to what the United States contributes, to help alleviate nonmilitary work threats like the destruction of the environment and overpopulation. (The Japanese, she suggests, would do an "excellent" job on family planning in Asia.)

The woman who manages all this—who seems to inhabit a blur of energy punctuated by a toothy smile—is a curious blend of effusive friendliness and private reserve, a Harvard-trained lawyer who relies on instinct and common sense. On the hustings, she is personal, spontaneous and direct; she delights in cooing babies and seems genuinely moved by the stories people tell her.

Ask about her own struggles, however, and she retreats behind a relentless cheerfulness. "She's not introspective publicly," says Dan Buck, her top staffer in Washington, who has known Schroeder 18 years. "A lot of it is hidden. You let personal things out and people are gonna grab 'em. . . ."

That wariness may be due in part to the extreme reactions Schroeder evokes. To admirers, she has the angularity of Katharine Hepburn, an Irish grin reminiscent of the Kennedys, a passionate speaking style and laughing eyes; her occasional silliness—celebrating the "little holidays" like Valentine's Day, signing notes with a smile face drawn inside the "P"—proves her lack of pretension. They think of her as a woman warrior, a leader.

To critics, she has a "hard" look, a grin that is really a grimace, a nasal-voiced delivery through clenched jaws and eyes that disappear behind a squint; her signature is too cute, her girlish celebrations ridiculous. They think of her as a lightweight.

The reality is that Schroeder is a driven politician who smiles too hard. She makes the complicated ideas behind inventive legislation look easy, maybe too easy. Her preference for simple crowd-pleasing sentences—the one-liners that spin so well into the 11 o'clock news—belies and often undercuts Schroeder's seriousness in a job that, for her, is as much about changing national priorities as representing Colorado's First Congressional District.

At a recent hearing of Schroeder's Subcommittee on Military Installations and Facilities, she wore a tomato-red dress and a wide-shouldered royal-blue sweater; her bright, insouciant style seemed to dominate a room full of military uniforms and dark business suits. But it was obvious that she'd absorbed the implications, political and otherwise, of the material to be discussed that day.

Brig. Gen. Wayne T. Adams, of the Marine Corps, began his comments with pleasantries: "We all thank you for your past support, especially regarding the quality of life and importance of taking care of our troops," he said, addressing Schroeder directly. "Only the accomplishment of the mission is more important." He was flanked by a rear admiral, two major generals, a brigadier general and a spokesman from the office of the Secretary of Defense; under the witness table, some highly polished shoes danced nervously. Schroeder's questions about the 1991 military construction budget were brief but to the point:

Given growing civilian intolerance for training maneuvers in the German countryside, "Why are we there?" Could the committee have a list of such maneuvers from five years ago? "We would like to go through it, specifically thing by thing, so that will help us as we make some decisions."

Why is the United States building a new base for the F-16 bomber in Crotone, "a few miles from Italy's kidnap capital?"

About money set aside to build chapels and family centers on foreign bases: "Why? That's outrageous, I would think! You haven't requested it, but you're going to . . . ?"

("Yessir—uh, ma'am," Rear Adm. David E. Bottorff gulped in reply, glancing too late at the sign he'd taped in front of him that said "Madame Chairwoman.")

"Let me also note why we are putting the first follow-on MX rail garrison in Speaker Foley's district," Schroeder said, referring to one of the controversial installations housing the rail-borne MX missile, which is scheduled for House Speaker Thomas S. Foley's Washington state district, "There wouldn't be any politics involved, would there? You're not trying to solicit more support for rail garrisons?"

Yet for all her military expertise, Schroeder is best known for family issues. Two years ago she put together the "Great American Family Tour," a series of presentations on child care issues with the pediatrician T. Berry Brazelton and Gary David Goldberg, the executive producer of "Family Ties," who once ran a daycare center. She credits the interest the tour generated with getting candidates in the 1988 Presidential election to take child care seriously. She was a primary sponsor of the House's companion bill to the Senate's Act for Better Child Care Services (the A.B.C. bill) and lobbied personally for it. In March [1990], House Speaker Foley guided the bill to passage in the House, 265–145.

Another bill she pushed for with increasing fervor in 1989 and early 1990 was her Family and Medical Leave Act, which gives both male and female workers a minimum amount of job-protection, unpaid leave at the birth or adoption of a child, or for serious but temporary family illness. She first proposed it in 1985, after developing "issues sheets" on the subject with her staff. Not everyone was pleased: "To hear the

Chamber of Commerce talk about it, you'd think we were Communists," says Dan Buck. "In Washington the politicians say, 'There go the people—let's get out in front of 'em!' " Schroeder says. She operates on the assumption that, after a while, the message will trickle up to the politicians.

As she had with the child-care bill, she lobbied for the family-leave bill in Congress and took it directly to the voters in dozens of speeches. When President Bush said he would veto "any kind of maternity leave bill," she accused him of "coming out against motherhood." The bill passed the House on May 10 [1990], 287–187. The companion bill passed the Senate by a voice vote on June 14. Within hours after the vote, White House officials reaffirmed the President's intention to veto the measure "as soon as it reaches his desk."

Long adept at linking domestic issues to foreign policy, Schroeder doubts the "peace dividend" will materialize: "It's now you see it— blink, blink—now you don't," she says. But if it does, she thinks the budget for defense should be "more broadly defined," to include the Department of Energy (where much of the budget goes into nuclear weapons) and the Central Intelligence Agency.

"We've got so much in the intelligence budget it makes you gag—who are we going to spy on, Albania?" she snorts. She believes a $300 billion cut in defense spending is possible over the next five years. Half of that amount should go toward the deficit, the rest into education. "I think it's absolute garbage that young people who have the ability of passing the tests can't go to school because their dad doesn't have the money," she argues vehemently. "How are we going to compete in the 21st century?"

Schroeder's voting record is as independent as her style. In 1989 she voted against positions taken by President Bush more than any other member of the House (79 percent of the time), but among the Colorado delegation, she is also known for not voting with fellow Democrats on "party unity" votes, in which a majority of Democrats oppose a majority of Republicans.

Though a liberal, she is also one of the most fiscally conservative members of the House, according to the National Taxpayers' Union—"Jack Kemp just hates it when I mention that," she says, giggling. Not surprisingly, she is known in the Congress as a "lone wolf," not a compliment.

Partly because of this independence, Schroeder relies heavily on her staff members in Denver and Washington, some of whom have worked for her for their entire careers. She also relies, less formally, on Jim Schroeder, the amiable, low-key man she married almost 28 years ago when the two were students at Harvard Law School. He was the one who first urged her to run for Congress in 1972 in what was supposed to be a hopeless but honorable race. When she won, he abandoned his partnership in a Denver law firm and his own political ambitions (a liberal Democrat, he once ran for office in Denver) to go to Washington: "I had no alternative," he says simply. Often "the first line of defense" at home, as he says, when their children were small, he eventually became a partner at Kaplan, Russin & Vecchi, a Washington law firm with a sizable international practice.

Jim Schroeder, a founder of the Denis Thatcher Society, for men married to powerful women (their motto is "Yes, dear"), plays down his influence on his wife's career today: "When I go home at night I don't want to discuss my cases, she doesn't discuss what happened in committee." But when asked to name her boss's "most trusted adviser," Andrea Camp, Pat Schroeder's Washington press secretary, instantly names him.

In 1987 Jim flew home from Bangkok to manage his wife's unexpected exploratory bid for President. In a campaign in which the eventual victor talked about the "vision thing" but settled for television visuals—Schroeder had vision to spare. Fueled by junk food ("I'm turning my body into a hazardous waste dump"), sometimes catching only a few hours of sleep at night, her theme was "Rendezvous With Reality."

She talked about the environment, arms control, the need for more jobs and defense burden sharing. Her team, made up mostly of volunteers, worked enthusiastically to raise money. The press loved her: she was called Snow White and the other Democratic contenders the Seven Dwarfs, she said the Reagan Administration thought arms control was "deodorant." In a September 1987 *Time* magazine poll, Schroeder led the other Democratic contenders on matters of who would best manage the economy, which candidate people would be "proud" to have as President, and whom they would trust.

Yet the same poll found that only 9 percent of respondents named Schroeder their "first choice" (26 percent named Jesse Jackson; 11 percent, Michael S. Dukakis). And a poll sponsored by the National Women's Political Caucus showed that roughly 30 percent of the population felt that a woman, any woman, would be a "worse" President than a man. By September Schroeder had raised only about $850,000 of the $2 million she said she would need by that point to run. She would decide whether to continue by the end of the month.

Two days before her scheduled announcement, Jim Schroeder wrote his wife a "neutral" memo, listing pros and cons. Then he got three phone calls. He says an executive of a Texas oil and gas organization told him, "We're ready to go, we need a Westerner, we need somebody like your wife: let me know what we can do." The pollster Lou Harris said: "You're wife's already No. 3 and I can promise that by Iowa . . . New Hampshire, she'll be No. 2." Bill Dunfey, the ex-Democratic chairman of New Hampshire, told him: "We're ready up here, let me know what you want us to do."

But the decision, ultimately, was hers. On Sept. 28, she announced her withdrawal. Her late start was a major difficulty, she said; many key people had already pledged support to other candidates. And she cited the dehumanizing process of campaigning on the national level: "I could not figure out how to run and not be separated from those I serve."

But her words were largely ignored, because when her listeners grasped her intent and groaned, she cried. In an astonishingly intimate public moment, she leaned back toward Jim and choked. He gave her a handkerchief. She cried some more. She finished her speech and threw herself into his arms.

"When Reagan left town, the reporters following him were in hip-waders—he was bawling all the time," says Dan Buck. "Bush says he cries at movies—he probably gave 'Who Framed Roger Rabbit' three hankies." John Sununu ended by crying and embracing his wife during his farewell speech as governor to the New Hampshire legislature. "He bawled his head off," Buck adds. Still, conservatives felt she had displayed a dangerous emotionalism, and liberals were embarrassed.

Schroeder herself did not apologize, and explained only that she was "human." But she cracked jokes: that she could make a fortune advertising Kleenex. And she continues to bring it up—for example, in a skit before the Washington Press Club Foundation last January—if only to shrug it off as unimportant.

Patricia Nell Scott was born in Portland, Ore., in the summer of 1940, the first child of Lee and Bernice Scott. He was a licensed pilot, she a first grade teacher; the hospital bill came to $53.35 and the Scotts, who had grown up on farms in Nebraska during the Depression, paid it in two installments.

They were Democrats, with populism in their blood: Lee's father was an Irish immigrant who had served with the three-time Democratic Presidential candidate William Jennings Bryan in the Nebraska State Legislature. They taught Pat and her younger brother, Mike—now a Denver attorney—to be independent and responsible and to manage their own allowance for clothes and trinkets; both children became licensed pilots, Pat by the age of 16. Her early years were not always easy. Pat had crossed eyes, a result of amblyopia. She outgrew it, but the taunts of other children hurt: "With a patch over one eye, I wasn't exactly the No. 1 choice for kickball." The woman known for her brilliant smile often quotes the advice her father gave her: "Never frown at your enemies. Smile—it scares the hell out of them."

Harder still, the family moved often. By the age of 3 Pat learned how to make friends: she lined up her toys on the sidewalk and told her mother, "This ought to get 'em." "I was always the one that was trying to get in," she says. "But in a way, it's one of the things people struggle with all their lives—to define themselves. If you move a lot, then you define yourself."

She graduated from the University of Minnesota in three years, magna cum laude and Phi Beta Kappa, with a major in history and minors in philosophy and political science. At Harvard Law School, which she entered in 1961, she was one of 19 women in a class of 554. A male classmate told her she ought to be ashamed of taking a man's place. She found friends anyway—on her terms: "They were all guys who had been in the service for three years—y'know, I was a pilot, they were pilots," she recalls. "When you find the real people, it's ten times more fun."

One of the ex-servicemen was Jim Schroeder, who had gone into the Navy after graduating from Princeton. "We hit it off pretty well," he recalls laconically. They were married in 1962.

Pat Schroeder wanted children, but pregnancies were difficult. "Some people think of it as a nine-month cruise," she says. "It isn't." While she was pregnant with her first child, a gas leak in the house almost killed the couple, and it was months before they were sure that the baby was not affected. (Scott Schroeder, a 1988 graduate of Georgetown University, now works in Washington.)

A second pregnancy ended grievously at seven months when Schroeder lost twins. She had felt something was wrong all along and had suffered bleeding, but her doctor dismissed her concerns and told her she was "high-strung." "Most of all I was angry at myself," the woman who would later become a champion of underdog issues wrote. "Here I was, a trained lawyer, letting a doctor convince me I had no right to question his judgment about *my* pregnancy and *my* baby. He intimidated me and made me feel powerless." In 1970 she delivered her daughter, Jamie, now a junior at Princeton, without complications, but was rushed back to the hospital with life-threatening bleeding that lasted six weeks.

Jim juggled child care for a 4-year-old and a newborn, went to the office, and worried about Pat; Pat recalls him having a recurring nightmare of driving to work but being unable to go into the office because Jamie was in the back seat. Schroeder tells audiences today that was when "he got it"—when he understood the stress working mothers experience every day.

Two years later she ran for Congress, and Denver was ready for her anti-Vietnam-War stance. Pat Schroeder was sworn into office with diapers in her purse. Her greatest fear as a freshman in Congress, she told reporters, was "losing my housekeeper."

When asked how she could be both a mother and a Congresswoman she snapped, "I have a brain and a uterus, and I use both."

"Her assets are her liabilities, her liabilities are her assets," says Dan Buck and Andrea Camp, speaking in unison.

Schroeder's quick wit grabs headlines, but Republicans claim she is superficial, and even sympathetic audiences can be confused by a wisecrack in the middle of a speech on foreign policy. She is smart (a recent article in *Roll Call*, the Congressional newspaper, named her one of the 20 smartest members of Congress), but as she admits, "I don't think anyone likes a smart aleck."

Jim Schroeder is a strong defender of his wife's controversial style. "Over the years it has really annoyed me that she is called scatter-brained or flip," he says, almost sounding testy. "She has a commendable ability to simplify."

To a certain extent he is right: Schroeder's grasp of military spending and its ramifications on domestic policy, her long battles to turn ideas into statutes, are impressive. But the wide array of causes she embraces can bewilder: an antiwar activist, she supports women in the military; a supporter of abortion rights, she also calls herself pro-life because she favors increased research on infertility.

Her "prepared text" is usually a hastily scribbled list of talking points, and she can be superb. But the freewheeling oratory can be uneven, her endings chopped, as if she has suddenly run out of time or interest. Her debating style (if not her thinking) is scattered: on a recent "Firing Line" program, the subject was free-market competition; Schroeder's one-liners fizzled next to Jeane J. Kirkpatrick's grave pronouncements. At one point she spoke inexplicably about the plight of the Japanese consumer.

For now, Schroeder is running for re-election to the House, her 10th term. Her announced challenger is Gloria Gonzales Roemer, a 37-year-old Republican businesswoman and mother of four. Roemer says she's in the race to win [in the end Schroeder won, with 64 percent of the vote], but political pundits suspect that she wants to establish name recognition before the 1992 race, should Schroeder run for President.

But will she?

Schroeder's serious answer is: "My life would be easier if I find a candidate I can back. If I don't see one, then I would have to seriously consider it." Louis X. (Kip) Cheroutes, her press secretary in the Denver office, says, "I don't think she knows herself" what she will do.

There are signs and portents. Her 1989 book, *Champion of the Great American Family*, outlines a national family policy and is full of personal and political anecdotes.

Some $400,000 left over from the 1987 Presidential bid is available, should Schroeder try again, according to Pam Solo, a top aide in 1987 and until recently co-director of the Institute for Peace and International Security in Cambridge, Mass. (Still, the amount is nowhere near the estimated $20 million a Presidential campaign now costs for a full primary run.)

Her wardrobe, criticized three years ago for a certain haphazardness—she tended toward schoolmarmish ruffles and once Scotch-taped a carnation to her lapel—now features plain collars and sleek, wide-shouldered suits and dresses in strong, bold colors. An image adviser she consulted told her to wear thinner bangs and earrings; most of the time these days, she does both.

In addition to bimonthly visits to Denver, she crisscrosses the country on dozens of trips. In February, a few days after appearing in Hershey, Pa., she flew to Boston; the day's schedule ended in Salem, Mass., and included a luncheon, three press interviews, two major speeches, a cocktail party, a photo session, dinner and a reception.

Back in her hotel room at 10 P.M., she sagged against a couch, legs stretched out. Andrea Camp, who was traveling with her, got some sodas. For the first time all day, Schroeder looked tired; as she relaxed, her angular face softened and her eyes, obscured earlier by the well-known squint, looked large and blue.

"People say that the first woman President will be tough, a man in women's clothing, a conservative," she said. "I don't think so. Sandra Day O'Connor has so disappointed them, so let them down on *Roe* v. *Wade* with this [*Webster*] decision." She made an odd sound, half "no," half growl. "It's a powder-puff decision, a little of this, a little of that.

"Margaret Thatcher can be Prime Minister because she comes from a country raised by strong women. She puts on her pearls, points her finger, and people do it. In this country we don't take that." Schroeder stirred restlessly, searching for a conclusion. "But if we're just going to have a man in woman's clothing? Is that what this is all about? I've got better things to do with my life than spending it in Hershey and Salem and all the places. . . ."

The next morning she was the first one down to the lobby, smile fresh, ready for an interview on WCVB-TV, an ABC affiliate in Needham, Mass.

11.6 *Penny Talks to Folks at Home*

Pamela Fessler

In subzero temperatures early Jan. 25, [1991,] 120 peace activists [in Rochester, Minnesota,] boarded buses to begin the long ride to Washington for the nation's largest rally yet to protest the Persian Gulf War.

The political establishment "can overlook San Francisco, Seattle and New York, but this is the heartland of America," said Mark Frederickson, a leader of the local group, Operation Peace and Justice.

Across town, owners of the Animal Friends kennel were doing what they could to send a message of support to U.S. troops overseas. They adorned each newly groomed dog with red, white and blue bows and, by popular demand, gave the pet's owner a similar ribbon to pin on a shirt or jacket.

Not far away, the next day, a Rochester couple invited about 40 Jewish friends and neighbors to their home to hear and question their congressman, Democratic Rep. Timothy J. Penny, about events in the Middle East. These constituents clearly were worried about the fate of Israel and about how strong an ally Penny would be.

Like much of America, Minnesota's 1st District displays an amalgamation of emotions and beliefs about war with Iraq. Some oppose hostilities at any cost; others have favored military action from the start. Most seem to rest uneasily in the ambiguous middle—uncertain beforehand that war was the correct course to take but resigned now to seeing it through and hoping for the best.

As the district's fifth-term representative, Penny is trying to reflect, understand and perhaps shape opinion in this mostly rural corner of southeastern Minnesota. Like others in Congress, he finds himself searching for a role in what is probably the most important U.S. policy initiative of his career.

It's not easy. Congress' impact on the war, which has consumed the institution and the nation in recent months, is strangely limited. Since both chambers on Jan. 12 endorsed the use of force against Iraq, day-to-day decisions have rested mainly with the military commanders and their boss, President Bush.

For now, most members are confined to influencing at the margins—having hearings, introducing nonbinding resolutions, issuing news releases, offering advice and trying to help constituents cope with the anxieties and problems of armed conflict.

With little opportunity to shape the conduct of war, Penny attends to concerns either closer to home or beyond the horizon.

As in most congressional offices, he and his staff are trying to do what they can to assist district residents with war-related problems— getting mail to relatives in the gulf, fielding complaints from reservists who don't want to be sent overseas and trying to help those who want to enlist.

Penny also serves as a kind of counselor— listening to constituent concerns about the war and trying to let district residents know what he has learned in Washington about its progress. In a sense, his congressional office is an outlet, another place to call, for those who need to talk about and understand the war.

But on a broader level, Penny wants to help shape the 1st District as well as the national debate. He says he tries in all of his appearances and speeches to "take people beyond the present, which is to say that things are going well now, and ultimately we will win, but be prepared that it may be more costly than we expect."

He tells constituents to gird themselves for a longer, rather than a shorter war—months, rather than weeks. And he asks them to start thinking about the future, an area in which legislators likely will play a more critical role. Who will pay for the war? How will long-term regional security be ensured? What about the Palestinian question? And veterans' benefits?

"Our job is not so much to be involved in the day-to-day decisions," Penny says. "It's to think about where this country is going and what our policy toward that region of the world is going to be after the war concludes."

To the consternation of peace activists such as Frederickson, Penny strongly believes that the debate over whether the nation should be at war is finished.

Day in the District

During a recent visit to his chilly, snow-covered district, Penny tried to turn his constituents' sights to the future. To his surprise, the gulf war was not the dominant theme as he moved from event to event, although the subject seldom was ignored.

At a legislative breakfast Jan. 26 sponsored by the Faribault Chamber of Commerce, the No. 1 topic was $194 million in state budget cuts approved two days earlier by the Minnesota House. Residents clearly were more interested in how those cuts would affect Faribault's social services than in asking Penny for his thoughts on the Persian Gulf.

Nonetheless, he took the opportunity to tell the 40 or so participants that the war "might not be as easy and quick as we'd like it to be." He said he thought Iraqi President Saddam Hussein was willing to fight to the very last man. He also asked them to start thinking about future U.S. policy in the region and to prepare themselves for paying the bill.

Afterward, Faribault resident Steve O'Malley thanked Penny for his Jan. 12 vote against the use of force in the Middle East. It's a vote for which Penny has largely won constituent praise, even from those now backing the war effort.

"I wish you had prevailed," O'Malley said. "We can't pay for what we have now. Now, we're going to have to borrow from the Germans and the Japanese to pay for this."

At the Happy Chef restaurant in nearby Owatonna, Penny next met for coffee with the former chancellor of the University of Minnesota's Waseca branch to discuss a rural development project.

But in place of small talk, the two eased into their scheduled topic with a few exchanges about the gulf.

"I think we're looking at a few months," Penny said.

"If it's just a few months, we'll still be OK," the former chancellor replied. "But if it lasts much longer . . . you can just feel the tension building around here."

Next, a quick stop at KRFO, Owatonna's country/pop radio station, to tape an interview. Penny told news director Randy Sobrack that he was surprised people weren't asking him more about the war. But, he said, residents were getting almost as much information from television news as he was receiving in Washington in daily briefings by Pentagon officials.

Again, Penny gave his cautionary message. Listeners should not get carried away with the early successes of the 10-day-old war. "For our own sake, it's better for us to expect the worst than to anticipate an early victory," he said.

From there he went to Bailey's Country Cafe, a tiny roadside restaurant at an isolated intersection on the road to Rochester. Inside, owner Rod Bailey greeted Penny from behind the counter. Pinned to Bailey's apron was a small wooden heart with "Support Our Troops" written across it and red, white, blue and yellow ribbons hanging below. (The pins are the newest rage in the area; one Rochester store reported selling 3,000 the week after the war began.)

But in Bailey's, customers talked with Penny about a range of subjects. As the congressman gulped down milk and a pastry, he listened to opinions on everything from a constitutional amendment against flag burning to the accountability of government employees, and answered questions about farm legislation and his recent trip to the Soviet Union.

But Bryce Tracy of Dodge Center took a moment to thank Penny for his Jan. 12 vote.

"Essentially, I think nobody wanted to see war," he said after Penny had moved on to greet other diners. "But since it began, they're supporting it. You have to have that loyalty."

The subject didn't come up at a reception that followed in Rochester for high school students who had been nominated by Penny for openings in the nation's military academies.

"I think folks have kind of internalized their thoughts about the war," Penny said later. "I think there's just a feeling we have to see it through and go on with life. . . . People are just kind of waiting and watching."

But at the next stop, the talk was of nothing else.

Here, Penny met with the 40 Jewish residents of Rochester and the surrounding area who had gathered in Elaine White's living room. For most, the war came too close to home. One woman told of talking by phone less than an hour earlier with a friend in Haifa, Israel, who had to cut the conversation short because of a Scud missile attack from Iraq.

Penny had no trouble directing his audience's thoughts to the aftermath of war. The residents wanted to know if he would support additional U.S. aid to Israel (probably, but he would have to see the specifics), future U.S. arms sales to Arab nations (he hoped the nation had learned its lesson from past aid to Iraq) and linkage of the Palestinian issue to the war (it shouldn't be, but he warned there would be a lot of pressure to settle the issue).

As Penny left, his hostess thanked him and said, "As you can tell, we're all very worried about what's going to happen. It's good to be able to talk about it."

Constituent Requests

Talking and listening seem to be a big part of the congressional role at this stage of the Persian Gulf War.

In Penny's two district offices, in Rochester and Mankato, and in his congressional office in Washington, staff members spend much of their time fielding calls about the gulf.

Before hostilities began Jan. 16, they heard mostly from those attempting to influence Penny's vote on whether the president should be authorized to use military force against Iraq. Of the 1,000 calls and letters on the subject, more than 90 percent opposed going to war.

The day before hostilities started, Penny's Rochester office received a 40-foot scroll from Operation Peace and Justice with dozens of messages calling for peace and thanking Penny for his Jan. 12 vote.

But when the bombing began, the nature of the messages suddenly changed, as it did in other congressional offices. Now, say aides, almost all calls are from constituents who want help for family members or friends deployed in the Persian Gulf. Only half a dozen or so calls each week express views on the wisdom of war; those are now evenly divided.

Instead, at least six constituent requests are received or directed each day to Penny's district caseworker on military issues, Christopher Cluff. Cluff says the largest number of calls are from those he calls "outers," reservists or their relatives who want the congressman to do something to delay the Pentagon from calling someone up for duty. Others are from "inners," constituents who want to go to the Persian Gulf but for one reason or another have not been accepted.

For the most part, says Cluff, there is little he can do except try to be sympathetic to individual problems and explain that the law is the law.

"A lot of it is just therapeutic," he says. "Knowing that somebody has actually listened to them relieves a lot of the pain, even if we aren't able to give them what they want."

But in one extreme case, the office did intervene. Penny aides received a call from a female Army reservist who had an ill 2-month-old baby and had been called up for active duty. Her husband was in the same unit, and the couple had no close relatives to turn to for help. Cluff says the office persuaded reluctant military authorities to transfer the woman to another unit.

Office aides also spend a great deal of time directing callers to phone numbers and other services available to those worried about loved ones overseas. And one staff member is occupied filling the growing number of constituent requests for U.S. flags—600 in the first six weeks of this year, far more than in all of 1990.

Steve Kingsley, Penny's administrative assistant in Washington, says the office is used to a large volume of calls when big issues emerge. But this round is unusual, he says, because of the great amount of emotionalism attached to the war.

"People who call want to keep you on the phone, they want to get into a passionate discussion with you," he says. "It's not like most issues we're lobbied on, whether the caller just wants to know how the congressman is going to vote and then hangs up."

For instance, he says, the office might get a call from a mother "wild with worry" because she can't get mail through to her son in the gulf. "That puts a lot of pressure on us in dealing with it," he says, "because you know how important this is to her."

The office is under other pressures, as well. Like most Americans, Penny's aides have been glued to the television to keep up with the latest war news.

The news has taken on a special sense of urgency, says Kingsley, because one of the office's workers in Rochester has a 22-year-old son in Saudi Arabia.

"It's made it very personal for all of us," he says. "When you hear about casualties, you can't help worrying if Ellen's son is involved."

Like other congressional offices, Penny's is concerned about security. Staff members have taken political stickers off their cars and are subject to more intense searches when they enter congressional office buildings.

The congressman, who calls himself a fatalist, says he has had to make few changes because of security concerns. However, plane tickets for trips to Minnesota no longer identify him as a member of Congress, but merely as Tim Penny. The two district offices also have been directed not to accept suspicious-looking packages and to arrange extra security precautions with the managers of the buildings in which they are located.

State of the Union

Meanwhile, Penny continues to attend regular Pentagon briefings on the gulf and to try to shape his own opinions about U.S. policy on the war.

"I think most members of Congress are like the American public," he says. "Right now, we're sorting it out and kind of taking it day by day and watching and waiting. But I think you'll see a lot of activity in the not-too-distant future."

Legislatively, Penny says there's little he can do now. He introduced a nonbinding resolution Jan. 15 calling for the costs of Desert Storm to be shared by U.S. allies and for any uncovered expenses to be covered by a surtax on high-income taxpayers and by cuts in military spending. But such resolutions generally serve as little more than political statements.

Possibly more influential could be Penny's brief exchange on the House floor Jan. 29 with the Joint Chiefs of Staff chairman, Gen. Colin L. Powell Jr., as the two awaited President Bush's annual State of the Union address.

Penny says he told Powell that the overwhelming sentiment expressed in the afternoon's congressional briefing was that members could be patient about the length of the air war. He said few were anxious to get into a potentially bloody ground battle with Iraqi troops.

"I told him most members of Congress aren't going to pressure you to bring this to a conclusion if you feel that that risks lives unnecessarily. He said he was glad to hear that because he'd been getting mixed messages," Penny says.

"I suppose they're nervous because of the Vietnam experience about how long the public will support the war. But I think most members are prepared to convey to their electorates that this is the way it has to be, and you can't expect every day to go well and you can't expect it to be over quickly."

But as Penny listened to Bush's speech, he began to worry that the president was not preparing the public for the costs of war.

"He didn't tell us that we had to pay any taxes. He didn't tell us we had to rebuild Kuwait and Israel and other nations. He didn't indicate to us that there's any kind of sacrifice we have to pay to win this war and to secure the peace," he says. "Somehow I expected more. . . . I couldn't help but think, if he can't ask the American public to sacrifice at a time when our young men and women are risking their lives, when will he?"

Penny says he decided then to write an editorial expressing these concerns and send it to district newspapers. He did and as of Feb. 7, aides said at least two papers planned to print it.

V ❓ THE UNWRITTEN CONSTITUTION

The tremendous growth in the role and responsibility of the federal government is reflected in every branch of government, and Congress is no exception. As the government has taken on more and more responsibility, Congress has found it necessary to delegate more power to the president and the bureaucracy. As members of Congress are required to deal with more information and with more technical information, power has also shifted within the legislative branch—to congressional staff, America's "unelected representatives." Michael J. Malbin explores the causes and consequences of the increasing role of congressional staff in the following article, from his 1980 book on the subject.

The changing role of congressional staff, as Malbin points out, tracks changes in the legislative branch as a whole. The themes of this chapter—especially the decentralization of power within Congress and Congress's efforts to maintain and increase its power relative to the president and the bureaucracy—should be evident in the reading. These trends, as Malbin suggests, raise questions about the future role of Congress as a representative and deliberate body.

Questions

1. What factors have led to the growth in congressional staff?

2. In what way does the increasing size and expertise of congressional staff help Congress maintain its power in the face of the president and the bureaucracy?

3. Does the increased role of congressional staff mean that your representative or senator is better able to represent your interests? less able?

11.7 Delegation, Deliberation, and the New Role of Congressional Staff

Michael J. Malbin

The United States Congress in 1979 was an institution made up of 539 senators, representatives, and nonvoting delegates and 23,528 staff (see table 1). By way of comparison, the second most heavily staffed legislature in the world is the Canadian Parliament, with a staff of approximately 3,300.

It was not always this way. Until only a few decades ago, most congressional committees did not have permanent professional staffs, personal staffs were minuscule, and support agency staffs were not much larger. The elected representatives of the people debated, compromised, and reached decisions about the nation's legislative business on their own. The new era began, roughly, with the Legislative Reorganization Act of 1946. At that time, Congress was housed comfortably in six buildings, members worked directly with their colleagues, and people had reason to believe that their opinions, expressed in letters, would be read by the people they voted to put in office. This has all changed. Congress is now a vast enterprise crowded into fifteen buildings, with one more under construction and others in the planning stages.

Of course, many of the 23,528 people do not work directly on legislation. Most of the 10,000 or so on personal staffs work on press releases and constituency related casework, while many in the Library of Congress, General Accounting Office, and various service staffs do work that relates even less directly to the legislative process. The four kinds of staff with the greatest influence over legislation are committee staffs, legislative aides on personal staffs, some support agency staffs, and the staffs serving the leadership and ad hoc groups. All have grown over recent decades. Just as important, all have been hiring a different type of person than the Capitol Hill staffer of decades past, and all have tended to increase the workload while strength-

TABLE 1
Congressional Staffs, 1979

Branch	Employees
House	
Committee staff[a]	2,073
Personal staff	7,067
Leadership staff[b]	160
Officers of the House, staff[c]	1,487
Subtotal, House	10,787
Senate	
Committee staff[a]	1,217
Personal staff	3,612
Leadership staff[b]	170
Officers of the Senate, staff[c]	1,351
Subtotal, Senate	6,350
Joint Committee Staffs	138
Support Agencies	
General Accounting Office [GAO]	5,303
(30 percent of total GAO staff)	(1,591)
Library of Congress	5,390
(Congressional Research [CRS] only)	(847)
Congressional Budget Office	207
Office of Technology Assessment	145
Subtotal, Support Agencies	11,045
(Subtotal, including only CRS in Library of Congress and 30 percent of GAO)	(2,790)
Miscellaneous	
Architect	2,296
Capitol Police Force	1,167
Subtotal	3,463
Total	31,783
(Total, including only CRS in Library of Congress and 30 percent of GAO)	(23,528)

[a] Includes select and special committee staff.
[b] Includes legislative counsels' offices, House Republican Conference, Democratic Steering Committee, Majority and Minority Policy Committees, Office of the Vice-President.
[c] Doorkeepers, parliamentarians, sergeants at arms, clerk of the House, Senate majority and minority secretaries, and postmasters.

ening the forces of institutional decentralization in Congress.

Committee Staffs

Congressional committees began hiring part-time, temporary clerks in the 1840s. In 1856, the Senate Finance and House Ways and Means committees started receiving regular appropriations for full-time clerks, and the remaining committees all had full-time clerks by the end of the century. According to one count, committee staff in 1891 numbered sixty-two in the House and forty-one in the Senate. But until well into the twentieth century these positions were treated as patronage appointments for po-litical cronies. Personal and committee staffs were thoroughly intermingled in practice in the House and by law in the Senate. For example, legislation during the 1920s specified that the three top clerks of the committee from a new Senate chairman's personal staff were to become clerks of the committee and that committee staff was to help the chairman with the work of his personal office.

Nonpartisan professional committee staffs began to be developed at about this time on the House and Senate appropriations committees and on the newly formed (1926) Joint Committee on Internal Revenue Taxation. It was the money committees' successful experience with

The Modern Congress' Smoke-Filled Room

In the fall of 1990, selected members of Congress and key representatives of the Bush administration met to resolve their differences over the federal budget. The meetings—held, in part, in seclusion at Andrews Air Force Base—became known as the Budget Summit.

The summit was a deliberate attempt by the congressional leadership to circumvent the decentralized, cumbersome committee system and thus reach a clear decision. Precisely for that reason, however, the summit came under intense congressional criticism. But according to the **Congressional Quarterly's** *Janet Hook, the summit was only the most obvious example of what is a routine business on the Hill: behind-the-scenes negotiations and compromises that, she argues, represent Congress's modern smoke-filled rooms.*

One legacy of last year's [1990] revolt against the budget summit is a rallying cry for the 102nd Congress among rank-and-file lawmakers: No more summits. The exclusive, secretive talks didn't sit well with a generation of politicians who in the 1970s helped smash the seniority system and institute government-in-the-sunshine reforms.

On its face, the summit seemed like an anachronism, a throwback to an era when major legislation was drafted in smoke-filled rooms by a handful of septuagenarians.

But the fact is, the reforms of the last two decades never did rid Congress of its back rooms. There may be less smoke these days and a younger breed of politician in the room, but major legislative decisions are still routinely made by elite groups in private settings. Indeed, the more important the decision, the more likely it is to be made in a contemporary version of Speaker Sam Rayburn's Board of Education.

The conference committees that write final language of laws are among the most inaccessible, exclusive parts of the legislative process. The final decisions on the big 1986 tax overhaul were made by a conference committee of two—House Ways and Means Chairman Dan Rostenkowski, D-Ill., and Senate Finance Chairman Bob Packwood, R-Ore.

The laws most central to the U.S. budget are routinely written behind closed doors. The Ways and Means Committee almost never writes its tax bills in public. Many House Appropriations subcommittees, which make dozens of spending decisions that subsequently remain untouched, haven't met in the light of day for years.

The critical decisions on last year's [1990] clean air bill were made largely out of public view. In the Senate, congressional and administration negotiators wired a comprehensive deal in Majority Leader George J. Mitchell's Capitol office. In the House, the haggling took place in Energy and Commerce Committee anterooms.

professional staffs that led Congress to institutionalize the practice in the Legislative Reorganization Act of 1946. As part of a general realignment and reduction in the number of congressional committees, the act permitted all committees to hire up to four professional and six clerical workers each. (Exceptions were made for the two appropriations committees, which were allowed to determine their own staffing needs.) The permanent professionals authorized by this act (who have since been designated as "statutory staff") were expected to be nonpartisan. Additional people for specific investigations were to be hired as needed, supposedly on a temporary basis. But as early as the act's first years, committees began to hire such additional people on a quasi-permanent basis, so that ultimately the distinction between statutory and investigative staffs has become one that is honored rather in technical job descriptions than in on-the-job responsibilities.

The aim of nonpartisan professionalism apparently was maintained during the first six years after reorganization. Kenneth Kofmehl's

Sometimes these closely held deals ruffle feathers, but generally they generate little opposition. Remarkably few people make a fuss about closed meetings anymore, and some even conclude that better laws are written when members of Congress are shielded from the glare of special-interest lobbyists.

But what matters most to members of Congress is not whether the door is open or closed but who is in the room. The problem for today's power brokers is that, unlike a generation ago, even the most junior members now expect to have access to the inner circles.

That's why, when the House Democratic leadership has a weekly strategy meeting with its whip organization, it isn't unusual for a third of the caucus to show up to air the party's internal issues.

That's why usually exclusive House-Senate conference committees can turn into sprawling affairs. Competing claims to be on a negotiating team are often resolved by expanding the team.

Still, no one thinks that Congress can be run like a Swiss canton. On most issues, decision-making power is concentrated and authority delegated. But to work, the back room has to be carefully constructed: The right people have to be inside, and others can't feel wholly shut out.

The summit caused a ruckus, it seems, largely because lawmakers thought a deal would be set in concrete by the few in the room, while the many wouldn't even be able to fiddle with details.

Thus, the objections to the budget summit had more to do with power than with secrecy. The summit's legitimacy was questioned because it did violence to the institution's established tool for delegating authority: the committee system. In response, the House Democrats passed a new rule for the 102nd Congress intended to make it harder for the leadership to circumvent the committee system by writing legislation in a task force, summit or other ad hoc group.

But while members themselves were preoccupied with the question of involvement—who was in and who was out—the secrecy of the summit also raised another, more significant issue. It undercut the institution's system of political accountability.

The bipartisan budget talks were expressly designed to produce a deficit-reduction plan for which neither party would be directly responsible. In the privacy of Andrews Air Force Base outside Washington, it was thought, painful policies of austerity could emerge by immaculate political conception. In the process, then, the summit may have represented another, perhaps somewhat more disturbing use for the secrecy of the back room: Not to cloak dirty deeds, but to obscure responsibility for difficult decisions.

—*Janet Hook*

Professional Staffs of Congress, the first book-length treatment of staffs, was based on research done in the three Congresses between 1947 and 1952 (eightieth through eighty-second). It described "the prevailing nonpartisan operation of most committees" with minority party subcommittee chairmen on many committees and the whole staff accessible to every committee member on two-thirds of the committees Kofmehl studied. However, even as Kofmehl did his research, the system was already beginning to break down. By the end of his six years, several committees were beginning to designate some staff members as majority and others as minority. Still, the prevailing conception of staff permitted Kofmehl to describe such party designation as "erroneous":

> It is not the function of the committee aides to promote particular policies but rather to facilitate the work of the entire committee by procuring information, by arranging for the services of other elements of the legislative and executive branch staffs, by pointing up relevant factors the committee should take into account

when considering certain problems, by incorporating the committee's decisions in bills and reports and by discharging the manifold other staff duties that conserve the committee members' time and render less difficult the performance of their vital office. The members of a committee themselves, not the staff, should take care of the majority and minority interests and presumably, as politicians, should be well-qualified to do so.

Today, very few committee staffs even try to meet Kofmehl's standard. Most had already moved decisively away from the nonpartisan even-handedness by the time the first edition of Kofmehl's book came out in 1962. By then, Congressman Clem Miller's published letters to his constituents described committee staffs in terms that showed that he for one regarded them as employees of the chairmen of the full committees and, through them, of the committees' majorities. In the Senate, Randall Ripley's 1965 research led him to conclude:

> On most of the committees, most of the professional staff members are directly responsible only to the chairman. He appoints them and they retain their jobs only so long as they please him with their efforts. They tend to share his political coloration as well as his formal party affiliation. A few of the staff members may not have this special relationship with the chairman; but they are likely to have a similar relationship with the ranking minority member or, in a few cases, another senior member of the committee, probably a member of the majority party.

This control of staff by chairmen led Republicans in the late 1960s to agitate for professional minority staff on every committee. The Legislative Reorganization Act of 1970 appeared to give the Republicans what they wanted. It increased each committee's statutory professional staff from four to six, required that two of the six professionals and one of the six statutory clerical staff be selected by the minority, and said that no less than one-third of each committee's remaining funds should be used for minority staff.

But Democrats in both the Senate and House decided to ignore the one-third minority staff requirement in 1971 and in subsequent years. The provision was revived in House committee reforms adopted in 1974 (H. Res. 988), but the House Democratic Caucus trimmed the proposal back again in 1975 by dropping the one-third guarantee for investigative staff while granting the minority one-third of each committee's increased allotment of eighteen statutory professionals and twelve clerical staff. However, as part of its 1977 reform resolution (S. Res. 4), the Senate required committees to give the minority a full one-third of all statutory and investigative staff within four years, and it is well on its way toward achieving this goal.

At the time the Legislative Reorganization Act of 1970 was passed, House committee staffs were about four times as large as they had been in 1947 (702 versus 167), and Senate committee staffs were about three times as large (635 versus 232). These numbers kept going up during the 1970s. Senate committee staffs nearly doubled again between 1970 and 1979 (to 1,098) while those in the House increased more than two and a half times (to 1,959).

The growth of Senate committee staffs between the 1950s and mid-1970s was a direct result of the dispersal of power to junior senators, a process that began under the majority leadership of Lyndon B. Johnson. The so-called Johnson Rule of the 1950s assured every Democratic senator of at least one good committee assignment. Over the years, as this worked itself out, most Democratic senators were able to become chairmen of subcommittees, each with its own staff.

In the House, too, staff growth and internal democratization have gone hand in hand. The staff increases on House committees in the 1970s resulted largely from the 1973 House Democratic Caucus's "Subcommittee Bill of Rights" that liberated subcommittee chairmen from the control of the chairmen of full committees. As a result, most of the committee staff increases in the House during the 1970s have been at the subcommittee level, and many subcommittee staffs of the late 1970s were as large as full committee staffs of the 1960s.

Thus, in both the House and the Senate, the increases in staffing of the 1950s and early 1960s were accompanied by a shift away from nonpartisan professional staffs serving whole committees to a system of staffs working primarily for individual members, generally chairmen. Since then, the principle of individual control has not changed, but the distribution of staff resources has become more widespread. This broader distribution both results from and reinforces internal democratization as more members have the staff resources to pursue their own legislative ends.

Personal Staffs

Other forms of staff growth also have tended to support the growing decentralization of Congress. In this connection the increased number of legislative aides on personal staffs is an obvious case in point.

Although members who were not chairmen were first allowed to hire staffs of their own in 1893 most of the growth has taken place since 1947. Since 1947, personal staffs have increased from 1,440 to 7,067 in the House and from 590 to 3,612 in the Senate.

Since most personal staff aides do not work on legislation, the growth in personal staff does not by itself say anything about the growth of legislative assistance. Unfortunately, it is impossible to know how many legislative aides there were in the House and Senate before 1970, when the Legislative Reorganization Act introduced formal professional titles for people on personal staffs. But it is possible to talk about growth in the 1970s. The increase in the number of legislative aides in both the House and the Senate has been fairly modest, going up from an average of 1.3 per House member in 1972 to 2.2 in 1979 and from an average of 3.9 per senator in 1973 to 5.5 in 1979.

From the numbers, it seems obvious that most of the members' new personal staff aides do constituency-related work that may help an incumbent win reelection but has little to do with the legislative process. Still, an increase of even one legislative aide per member is enough to produce a large number of amendments for the floor—particularly since the increase in both chambers is greatest among Republicans and Southern Democrats, who are most likely to be opposed to the thrust of committee reported legislation. (Thus, for example, we saw junior Republicans such as David Stockman of Michigan and Richard Cheney of Wyoming having the resources to lead the unsuccessful 1979 floor fight against federal loan guarantees for the Chrysler Corporation even though neither was on the committee that reported the bill.) The increases in personal legislative aides among Republicans and Southern Democrats in turn reflect changing conservative attitudes toward the use of staff. Liberal Northern Democrats were far more likely than Republicans or Southern Democrats to rely heavily on staff during the early 1970s, but the situation was evening up in the late 1970s as some media-conscious, new-style conservatives began using staffs to develop national issues in a manner similar to that pioneered by the liberal Democrats of previous years.

Support Agencies

The support agencies have also grown in the 1970s. Although the connection between this and internal democratization may not be clear at first glance, the link comes through the growth of policy analysis and the way analysis is used by the members.

In 1970, the 332 people who worked for the Library of Congress's Legislative Reference Service performed largely bibliographic, speechwriting, and factual research chores. The role of the service was expanded significantly by the Legislative Reorganization Act of 1970 (Sec. 321), which changed its name to the Congressional Research Service (CRS) and gave it the job of analyzing and evaluating legislative proposals upon request from a committee. Between 1970 and 1976, CRS's staff grew rapidly—from 332 to 806. With the increased staff has come more policy analysis and research. By the end of fiscal 1975, one study estimated that 63 percent of CRS's staff and 71 percent of its budget were devoted to these activities, although "quick and dirty" research done on a fast deadline still seems to outweigh more thoughtful analysis.

The General Accounting Office (GAO), established by the Budget and Accounting Act of 1921, is seven years younger than CRS's forebear, the Legislative Reference Service. During the 1960s it began expanding its traditional auditing functions to include reviews designed to "measure the effectiveness of a wide variety of government programs." Congress affirmed its support of this new emphasis in the 1970 Legislative Reorganization Act, which explicitly directed the GAO to do "cost benefit studies of government programs" (Sec. 204). In response to this mandate, the GAO began hiring a more diverse group of professionals. True, the GAO still considers itself the watchdog of the federal treasury and stations accountants and auditors in every executive branch agency. However, by 1975, only 2,701 of its 4,142 professionals (or 65 percent) were members of the two traditionally dominant professions, accountants and auditors. And, a study of the GAO in 1976 reported that 35 percent of the GAO's workload and more than half of its self-initiated work can be described as program evaluation. Most of these are retrospective analyses of programs already in existence, but a fair number are prospective evaluations of legislation under consideration.

The two small remaining support agencies, the Office of Technology Assessment (OTA) and Congressional Budget Office (CBO), were created by statutes passed in 1972 and 1974, respectively, and began operations in 1974 and 1975. Staff levels at the CBO have been around 200 since its first year, while OTA has grown steadily to a complement of 145 staff in 1979. About one-third of the staff at CBO and all at OTA directly or indirectly analyze and evaluate the implications of policy choices for Congress. (The rest of the staff at CBO works on budget estimating and scorekeeping.)

All four support agencies are organized along bureaucratic lines and are much more akin to the traditional nonpartisan staffs than the recently ascendant individualistic staffs of most committees. Despite this, the growth in support agency policy analysis helps reinforce the same internal decentralizing forces that were responsible for the growth of personalized subcommittee staffs. While most support agency analysis is produced at the request of chairmen or ranking minority members, overlaps in subcommittee jurisdiction as well as the virtual autonomy of most subcommittee chairmen mean that requests for analysis can be placed on just about any controversial issue. Since support agency reports become available to all senators and representatives upon release, the net result is to destroy the monopoly of information once enjoyed by committee chairmen. Anyone willing to let a subcommittee staff member or legislative aide take the time to study these reports is in a position to challenge the judgments of committee chairmen, and often will.

Leadership Staffs and Ad Hoc Groups

The 1970s have seen increases not only in the staffs that introduce, negotiate, and analyze bills and amendments for committee members and other specialists, but also in the staffs that process information so as to help build coalitions among nonspecialists in the last stages before floor votes. These staffs generally do little more than react to materials developed elsewhere.

We already have encountered two other kinds of reactive staff that intervene between committees and the floor: legislative aides and support agency staff. Most legislative assistants in the House and Senate spend their time preparing their members for floor votes on issues that do not vitally concern them. They ride the elevators with their boss before the vote and, in the rush, their nuanced phrases may, unintentionally or intentionally, influence how a member votes. These quick briefings, always important in the Senate, have lately become a factor in the House as well, as the introduction of electronic voting in 1975 has cut the time allowed per roll call from thirty to fifteen minutes, thereby reducing the time available for conversation among members. CRS also helps inform nonspecialist members by nonpartisan "issue briefs" prepared for the House and Senate computer system. However, these briefs tend to be read not by the members but by legislative assistants who then brief the members verbally.

Two remaining kinds of staffs are important at this stage of the process: leadership staffs and the staffs of ad hoc issue and regional caucuses. In general, they are in competition with each other, and their role is very different in the House and in the Senate. As has often been observed, the Senate, with only 100 members, has much less need than the House for formal coordination and a highly structured leadership. The staffs reflect this. Thus, in 1978 the Senate majority leader and majority whip had a combined total staff of only nine while the role of formal issue groups and regional caucuses was virtually nil. In the House, the leadership and caucus staffs are both more significant. In 1978, the Democratic leadership had a staff of forty-six and the Republicans forty-three. Most of these aides help with whip counts, scheduling, press relations, and other tasks related to the leaders' verbal communications with members, but a few in each party add to the written information flow with whip notices and (on the Republican side only) summaries of major bills and amendments.

The Republicans got the idea for doing bill summaries from the oldest of the ad hoc groups in the House, the liberal Democratic Study Group (DSG), which was founded in 1959 and had a staff of fifteen in 1978. Although best known outside Congress for its work on congressional reform, the DSG's summaries of bills and amendments—generally presenting arguments for and against divisive proposals—

are probably read more widely than any other single collection of congressionally produced written material about pending legislation. The small Democratic Research Organization (with a staff of three) and the Republican Study Committee (with a staff of ten) both were formed in the early 1970s to provide conservative alternatives to the written material produced by the DSG and Republican Conference.

The 1970s was a period of explosive growth for ad hoc groups. DSG was the only such group in existence before 1960. Two others were formed during the 1960s, seven between 1970 and 1974, and thirty from 1975 to 1979. While several of the new groups are little more than excuses for occasional press releases (such as the Congressional Roller and Ball Bearing Coalition), most permit a pooling of personal staff resources to create alternative sources of information for members. As such, they compete with committees and with the leadership. Their growth, in other words, has fed the same decentralizing forces that produced the personalization of committee staffs.

Has the staff explosion of the past three decades helped or hurt Congress? We grant without question that senators and representatives are better able to do their own jobs as individuals by having professional legislative staffs accountable directly to them. But our question really is an institutional one: How well does the system that helps the members as individuals serve the legislative branch as a whole?

The answer to this question is not the same at every point of the legislative process. If we take Congress's workload as given and focus on negotiations, we see that the staffs, acting as surrogates for their "bosses," do as creditable a job of representing their interests as any attorney would for a client in a parallel situation outside Congress. With loyal surrogate-lawyers carrying out their wishes, the members are able to follow more issues than they could if they had to attend all meetings personally. Institutionally, this means that both the members as individuals and Congress as a whole are able to manage a heavier workload with the staffs than would be possible without them. To some extent, therefore, the staffs do seem to help Congress do its work.

But . . . the surrogate-lawyers are generally expected to be more than just passive representatives of their clients: they are also expected to go out and drum up new business. The increased use of personalized, entrepreneurial staffs has helped Congress retain its position as key initiator of federal policy, despite the growing power of the executive branch. The relationship between this use of entrepreneurial staff and Congress's power seems almost obvious. Most other national legislatures do not give individual members similar staff resources; most legislatures depend on their cabinets for almost all policy initiatives. Congress is not so passive today, thanks largely to its staff.

The system of individualized staff control seems also to be responsible for much of the oversight that gets accomplished outside of the General Accounting Office. Having a substantial number of staff people with appropriate investigative authority seems a necessary condition for congressional oversight of the executive branch and the independent regulatory commissions. But it is not a sufficient condition. Oversight also depends on chairmen and staffs who consider the effort worthwhile. For some reason, collegial nonpartisan committee staffs have not provided much oversight. Perhaps it is because their accessibility to all members of a committee leaves them with little time for anything else; perhaps because committees that are willing to retain nonpartisan staffs try to restrain their partisanship and maintain close relationships with their counterparts in the executive branch. Thus, the movement away from a system of collegial nonpartisan committee staffing to a more personalized one has been associated with an increase in congressional oversight activity, largely because a personalized system lets chairmen have activist staff entrepreneurs, and chairmen who use entrepreneurial staffs tend to be more interested in maintaining their independence from the executive branch.

Yet, while the growth and use of staff has produced these beneficial results, there is a gloomier side: the effect of staffs on Congress's ability to act as a deliberative body. To see the importance of this issue, we need to consider some of the basic functions Congress was meant to perform in our constitutional scheme of government. Congress, we learn from *Federalist* No. 52, was meant to serve as a substitute for direct meetings of the citizens. Representation was likely to produce not only a more manageable process than direct democracy, but better results. A representative system would require elected members from one district, with one set of needs and interests, to talk to members from districts with different needs and interests, if the members hoped to achieve anything. Indirect communication, such as we see today, was not what was envisioned: direct communication among elected members was considered essential to informed deliberation.

Why are direct conversations important? Why is it not adequate for members to rely on staff mediation and communication by memorandum? The reason is that while indirect communication can convey a great deal of information, it cannot help a member *feel* or *sense* his colleagues' reactions to his own or each other's arguments.

Direct conversations among the members are so important to the legislative process that facilitating them was, until recent years, a primary objective behind many of Congress's otherwise incomprehensible procedures. Most people are inclined to avoid conversing or debating with those with whom they disagree. One of the most important strengths of Congress over the years has been the way its structure has encouraged people to engage in a process that most people naturally prefer to avoid. While party discipline has tended to stifle this process in other countries, Congress's procedures have been designed to encourage, inform, and structure communication among the members in ways that would both promote deliberation and discourage longstanding resentments. That was the real reason for allowing closed committee meetings and for the elaborate rules of personal courtesy governing debate. In recent years, however, the members have weakened the procedures designed to protect their ability to debate and deliberate freely. Debate and discussion have lost their central place in the legislative process, and that loss has had serious consequences. The growing importance of staff is but one reflection of the new situation.

For a process of legislative deliberation to function reasonably well, at least three distinct requirements must be satisfied. The members need accurate information, they need time to think about that information, and they need to talk to each other about the factual, political, and moral implications of the policies they are considering. The new use of staff undercuts each of these requirements. The first, and simplest, relates to the flow of information. We saw from our examples that the growing dominance of large "chairmen's staffs" has produced management problems that result in uncertainties in the flow of information from staffs to chairmen and from chairmen to others in the Senate or House. Most of the information reaching members may well be reliable, but it would take an expert to sort out the reliable from the unreliable, and even an expert cannot know about material that has been stifled to serve a staff's or chairman's own interests.

This problem is probably the easiest of the three major problems associated with the growing role of staff to resolve in principle. If every committee had a nonpartisan staff core, there would be fewer occasions on which Congress would receive intentionally partial or distorted information from its staff. To the extent that nonpartisan professional staffs are inadequate in providing all the Congress asks of its staff, Representative Ullman's solution on the House Ways and Means Committee would seem to have much to recommend it. Let every committee have a dual staff: a nonpartisan professional core to do the kind of work done by the staff of the Joint Committee on Taxation and a personalized chairman's (or ranking minority member's or junior member's) staff to be more entrepreneurial, investigative, or political.

Still, this does not seem to get at the heart of the issue. Improving the accuracy of the information flow would not, for example, have created more time for the members to wade through the kind of complex material they were given on natural gas deregulation. The reason members rely on staffs to do their negotiating, and the reason they are not able to be critical consumers of the information they receive, is that they have more to do than time in which to do it. The second problem with the use of staff, therefore, is that it has not left the members with more time to concentrate on their legislative work. If anything, the use of entrepreneurial staffs has meant an increase in the numbers of hearings and amendments considered every year. About the only way Congress could improve this part of its present condition would be to reduce its agenda systematically and substantially. However, this solution raises further problems. While it is true that reducing the legislative agenda would probably improve deliberations on the items that remain, it hardly would improve the representative character of the government as a whole. If one accepts the present role of government, reducing Congress's agenda would simply let more of what happens in the other branches go without congressional review. As an answer to a problem of democratic representation, that cure seems worse than the disease. But whether desirable or not, it may not even be possible to reduce Congress's agenda substantially, given the present role of government. The bureaucracy finds itself compelled repeatedly to come back to Congress to clarify vague delegations of authority from the legislative branch—delegations that generally are vague because specificity might have endangered the chances for getting anything through Congress. But even if Congress managed to delegate with perfect clarity, the bureaucracy would have an interest in coming back repeatedly to protect or expand its role.

Congress, in other words, would have a hard time ducking out of much of its workload without taking the unlikely step of dealing with that workload's root sources. About the only way to reduce Congress's workload without vastly increasing the discretionary power of the less representative branches of the government would seem to be to reduce the size and complexity of government as a whole. However, the size of the bureaucracy is itself only an intermediate reason for the size of Congress's agenda. The growth of government has come about partly because the nation has become more complex, but even more, as James Q. Wilson has pointed out, because people have changed their ideas about what government should do. People in government have *chosen* to respond to more of the demands being made upon them, and these responses in turn have generated more demands. In fact, elected officials, their staffs, and bureaucrats often do not even wait for someone to articulate a demand before they get to work on the response: given the chance, they look for problems to solve, encouraging demand as much as responding to it.

Thus, there is a connection between the world of ideas, the size of the government's agenda, and the way Congress does its work. That connection helps us understand the third, and most basic, problem with the new role of congressional staff—the use of staff negotiations as a substitute for direct conversation and deliberation among the members. Direct conversations and deliberation still do take place, of course. But there can be no question that in recent decades there has been an increase in indirect negotiation and decrease in direct deliberation. That should come as no surprise. After all, negotiating is precisely what members expect most of the committee staffs and legislative aides to be doing.

We have been talking so far about the ways in which the use of staff has affected Congress procedurally. Has there also been a discernible effect on the substance of public policy? Staffs clearly do influence policy in thousands of little ways in any given year, but has the dependence on staff had any *systematic* impacts on policy? Our answers here must be more tentative than they were for procedural matters, but at least two kinds of effects suggest themselves—one relating to the role of the Washington issue networks and a second relating to the naturally narrow focus and inertia of staff negotiations.

The most direct impact of the role of staff has to do with the reception Congress gives the ideas put forward by groups or individuals that have no identifiable constituency, such as some of the smaller issue groups on the right and left, academicians, and issue specialists in think tanks and consulting firms. Senators and representatives are too busy to see every lobbyist who comes their way and must depend on their staffs to screen them. Organizations and individuals with real political or economic power have little difficulty getting in the door to make their case, but people who have nothing to offer but their ideas have a tougher time. However, since the staff's future careers in the Washington community often depend on their gaining reputations as innovators, it is in their interest to spend time listening to people whose ideas may help them put something new on the oversight or legislative agenda, even if those people have no political constituencies of their own. The interwoven interests of the participants in the various issue networks lead them to work together to identify problems they can then use their expertise to solve. The future interests of the staff flow directly from the changes in career patterns . . . in which staff jobs are stepping stones for ambitious young lawyers instead of places where mid-level bureaucrats and political cronies end their careers.

The tendency of the staffs' career interests to enhance the power of experts without constituencies is reinforced by the staffers' backgrounds. The new staffs tend to be young lawyers who came to Washington because they had been political activists and wanted to "make a mark" on "the system." In addition, their undergraduate and law school training has tended to make them more sympathetic to arguments based on general ideological principles (from the left for Democratic aides and from the right for Republicans) than either their classmates with "real jobs" or the elected members. The technocratic and ideological staffers may be different people, or the same staff person may embrace both attitudes. Moreover, both may work side by side with other staff people whose legal specialization and ambitions, experience, and background lead them to act as interest group advocates. But major corporate, trade association, and labor union interests would have little difficulty being heard in a Washington that had no staffs, nor would an issue-based organization that had developed a deliverable political constituency. Where the staffs make a difference, therefore, is in their openness to, career interest in, and institutional need for ideas and slogans whose political power initially lies only in the fact that staff people and journalists are willing to listen to them.

While the first systematic substantive impact of staff on policy comes out of its entrepreneurial role, the second comes from its role in negotiations. Both have the net effect of increasing the amount of legislation that gets passed and broadening the range of interests served by that legislation. The job of a staff negotiator is to help move the process toward a resolution. While a member may pull him back, it almost always is in the interest of the staff negotiator to see a set of negotiations through to a successful conclusion. This is particularly true if the program contains some section that the staff member can think of as his own. The program— or the planned hearing, if the person is an investigator—may represent a major investment of time for a staff person whose future may depend on gaining recognition in Washington for having made a difference. As a result, the process of staff negotiation tends to lend practical weight to the view that the purpose of the legislative process is to fashion agreements behind which the greatest number of self-appointed interested parties can unite. The impetus of staff, in other words, is to build coalitions by having programs respond, at least

symbolically, to more demands, rather than let them die their natural death. The result is increasingly inclusive, increasingly complex legislation that can only be understood by an expert. Needless to say, this increases the power of permanent Washingtonians with the necessary expertise, such as former staffers.

In the course of building the coalitions described above, staffs consider programs in isolation from each other. It is not normally in their interest to question how a program affects the budget, the overall structure of government, or the ability of citizens to understand what their government is doing. Of course, members themselves have the same inclination to see programs in isolation from each other. If they did not, they would scarcely tolerate the way staffs negotiate in their name. But a member who serves on several different committees, directly communicates with constituents, and sits down with other members to share the results of their composite experiences, is far more likely than an aide to have some basis for getting beyond this narrow focus to think about the relationships between policies in ways that cross lines of issue specialization.

It should be obvious by now that one cannot fully discuss the growth and use of congressional staff without confronting fundamental questions about the nature of representation in an era of governmental complexity. On the one hand, dependence on congressional staff has, as we have seen, increased the relative power of technocratic issue specialists and of groups with no economic or political constituency. This both reflects and reinforces the complexity of government. On the other hand, Congress has reacted to the governmental complexity it has created by building up its staffs defensively to preserve an important role for itself. But the size of those staffs and the way they are used has reinforced the situation in which the deliberative aspect of representation gets short shrift on all but the broad outlines of a few issues.

The weakening of deliberation is serious for a Congress that works best when it responds to constituents' needs and interests in a setting that encourages the members to think more broadly. The process no longer forces members to talk to each other to resolve the tough issues; the agenda keeps them busy with other things. The trouble Congress had in leading the country toward a national consensus on energy policy during the 1970s was but one side effect of this, and the complexifying role of staff must bear part of the blame. If Congress is to play its crucial representative role on whatever replaces energy as the key issue of coming decades, it must find some way to limit its agenda and reinforce the role of direct deliberation. While it is hard to imagine what that might be, the future of representative government may depend on it.

VI  ISSUE AND DEBATE: SHOULD CONGRESSMEN BE LIMITED TO SIX TWO-YEAR TERMS?

In recent years, voters and political commentators have looked at the idea of limiting the amount of time a congressman can serve in the House. The most popular plan would limit congressional service to twelve years, or six two-year terms. Such a plan would be the most direct way to deal with the so-called incumbency effect, which describes the extraordinary job security now enjoyed by most congressional representatives.

Critics of the proposal suggest that the term-limitation cure would be worse than the disease and remind advocates of the idea that the voters can institute their own term limitation plan any time they want—by voting incumbents out of office.

Here are three points of view.

YES

11.8 Twelve Years and Out

Irving Kristol

The opinion polls suggest that the majority of the American public looks favorably on the idea of limiting the terms of congressmen to a total of 12 years—two terms for senators, six terms for members of the House. Congressmen, obviously, are much less enthusiastic about the idea. So, interestingly enough, are most independent political scientists who can claim some expertise on the subject of Congress.

I myself have tended to defer to the opinion of these knowledgeable political scientists. But more recently I have become uneasy. Can it be that the popular intuition, regardless of the simplemindedness with which it is expressed, is the superior wisdom?

There are basically two arguments in favor of the status quo. The first is that it makes no sense to deprive ourselves of the services of congressmen who, over a period of time, demonstrate great ability, achieve the respect of their peers as well as of the media, and reveal exceptional skills at making the legislative process work effectively.

The second argument hangs upon the ever increasing complexity of congressional work, and the long period it takes for a member to acquire a proper expertise with regard, say, to the budget, or military expenditures, or Social Security. Even a first-class social scientist, with far more leisure than a congressman has, cannot hope to master the intricacies of these matters in less than three or four years. Does it make sense to entrust such programs to congressional committees dominated by newly elected novices?

Both arguments have considerable force, which is why so many intelligent and disinterested people are persuaded by them. But I have to say that, after spending the past three years in Washington and observing Congress at close hand, I no longer find them all that persuasive.

To begin with, there is the fact that a limitation on years in office would deprive us of the services not only of many good congressmen but also of many who are less than good, as well as some who are positively awful. The ability to be reelected again and again is not always—alas!—an endorsement of congressional merit. We are all well aware, by now, of the immense advantages of incumbency that congressmen have quite deliberately acquired.

If one were to make four lists of long-serving congressmen who are (a) good, (b) nondescript, (c) poor and (d) awful, where would the balance lie? I really do not know enough about all our congressmen to compile such lists, but my strong impression is that the (a) list would be very much in the minority.

It may be said, by way of rejoinder, that the (a) list would consist of more influential congressmen than the others. Perhaps so—but is it not the case that their influence derives from being clever and experienced enough to satisfy the views and appetites of the (b), (c), and (d) lists? If this is the case, as I suspect it is, then their presence is not nearly so crucial to good government as one might think.

Reprinted with special permission of North American Syndicate, Inc.

As for the time needed to achieve a mastery of complex legislative issues—well, then the question arises: Why are they so complex? Need they be so complex? Is it not possible that veteran congressmen, addressing such issues term after term, have an interest in making them so complex? Does their "mastery" then not add to their prestige and assist in their electability?

It would be perfectly natural if some such process were at work. And it would be naive to deny that it is at work. To be "master" of a complex issue is to be in a very strong position vis-à-vis lobbyists of all kinds, potential financial contributors, and those "public interest" groups that have to learn to negotiate with you. It gives you power and prominence, whether at the national or regional or local level, that helps ensure your reelection.

It is my impression that the American people sense all this and are more than a little disgusted with it. They would like a Congress which, if more "amateurish," nevertheless had less of a stake in the existing system. Above all, they would like a Congress that is in "closer touch" with the American people—and nothing can guarantee that more firmly than the certainty that after 12 years, a congressman would return to the "real world." If that's the world he is going to inhabit, he is likely to regard it more respectfully and be less manipulative in his relations with it.

Congress, today, is not in good repute with the American public. A 12-year limitation may be the price we have to pay for reviving its reputation. And, all in all, it may not be much of a price.

NO

11.9 Limits on Congressional Terms: A Cure Worse Than the Disease

Hodding Carter III

It can be safely said that politics, politicians and governance in general are not in good odor in America today. The cobbled-up budget compromise will do little to change the public's opinion and may instead reinforce it, the elephant having labored so ostentatiously to produce a singularly unappealing mouse. There is a pervasive feeling in the land that those who claim to be laboring in the public interest are traveling under false pretenses.

As one result, there is a small boomlet, if not yet a groundswell, of popular demand in favor of a new constitutional limit on legislative and congressional terms of office. For various reasons, arcane as well as obvious, 12 years seems to be the preferred duration. In Congress, that translates into two terms for senators and six for members of the House.

The argument for limitation is deceptively straightforward. Statistics reveal that in today's Congress an incumbent has close to a mortal lock on his seat. Less than 10% of those who seek re-election are denied it. As an inevitable consequence, goes the theory, Congress is filled with arrogant, unresponsive legislators who ignore the public good while serving the narrow special interests who subsidize their year-in, year-out re-election campaigns.

Another result, say some proponents, is that while presidents come and go, the same old congressmen and senators serve forever. Predictably, this means that Congress steadily accretes power and influence while each president must petition anew to establish his own. The constitutional balance is upset, the general welfare is sacrificed on the altar of particularity, and the Republic suffers.

Hidden agendas abound. The right and the left having switched position over the past 20 years or so, many conservatives place their trust in the executive branch while liberals swear allegiance to the greater democracy of Congress. Thirty years ago it went the other way. If you are looking for principle at the bottom of the role reversal, look no further. There isn't any. What is involved is the Republican "lock" on the presidency post-Kennedy and the continuing Democratic lock on Congress, now 60 years old and growing. If you can't win under the old rules, change them. That's what led the Republicans to lead the fight to limit presidents to two terms, a victory they now regret, and it explains their interest in limiting congressional terms today. If the Constitution is a political annoyance, change it.

That's the cynical agenda. A less blatantly political one is based on an appeal to the restoration of a true balance of powers, supposedly lost. Congress is supposed to have taken on functions and powers severely hampering the efficient functioning of government. Men and women with permanent seats become mini-power centers of executive as well as legislative authority. They form alliances with the permanent bureaucracy, where those who must deal with them over the decades and depend on them to protect their budgets are more responsive to their wishes than to those of the more short-term political appointees they purportedly serve. It is power without responsibility, bad from a civics textbook point of view and bad from a practical one as well.

Finally, there is the desire of the outs of all stripes to become ins. The young want the old to make way. Minorities grow tired of waiting for "their" seats to be vacated by holdovers from different demographic realities in their districts. Money rules the political game today, and flows disproportionately to incumbents without regard to party affiliation. That means truly competitive politics exists more in theory than in practice, which means newcomers are discouraged and the system atrophies.

All the arguments make sense to a degree. The figures on retention speak for themselves. If incumbents don't quit, they don't get beat, and only an idiot believes that proves a majority of the potential voters in all those districts really believe they have the best possible representation. While people as distinguished as Speaker of the House Tom Foley regularly produce figures showing over the past 25 years an enormous turnover in both houses, what those figures ignore is the basic truth that the turnover has had everything to do with death and retirement and virtually nothing to do with electoral defeat. When you get a seat, particularly in the House, you have it until you give it up and everyone knows it. That way lies corruption.

Nevertheless, the suggested cure is worse than the disease. Limiting terms without other substantive changes would make the federal government less, rather than more, responsive. About 50% of the House and Senate would at all times be filled with trainees, just beginning to learn the ropes. Capitol Hill is already too much the domain of congressional staffers. Limit congressional terms, and staffers alone would be the repositories of institutional memory and the architects of enduring coalitions with the permanent government.

Further, to curtail congressional terms while the federal government continues to grow in numbers, cost and complexity is to give the executive branch more power than the Constitution intends. Just about the time certain congressmen had finally mastered the ways and wiles of the CIA, for instance, they would be forced to depart. Few congressmen would ever be able to achieve personal mastery of the details of how the Pentagon uses and abuses its billions, or of how Health and Human Services serves as the lobbying conduit for its far-flung constituencies.

Put another way, to demand that Congress become the home of short-term amateurs while the rest of the government is the province of long-term professionals is to guarantee the irrelevancy of Congress. For an institution already stricken by what sometimes appears to be terminal gridlock, that would be the final blow.

It would also be a way of saying that because the system lacks the will to do the right thing, it must do the wrong thing just so it can say it is doing something. The right thing, of course, is to level the playing field so contenders have at least a fighting chance against incumbents. That means radical reform of the campaign finance laws, the mandated opening of broadcast media for political debate and strict oversight of the laws as enacted.

As usual, money is the root of evil, the evil in this being a Congress whose members can't be beat because their incumbency opens checkbooks while closing them to potential challengers all over the country. This year Capitol Hill has come closer than anyone expected to passing campaign finance reform legislation, but the two houses and the president are on the verge of proving they put partisan advantage above that imperative goal. Assuming it is not reached this year, that should be the target of opportunity for those concerned about making Congress less a final stopping place for professional politicians and more the apex of a fiercely competitive political system.

Tinkering with the Constitution should be a last resort in any case. Tinkering with the Constitution when it is obvious the results will be anemic on the one hand and destructive on the other makes no sense at all. Rather than making the government more responsive, limiting congressional terms would simply be one more proof that the system is irredeemably irresponsible.

ANOTHER VIEW

11.10 The Sudden Security of New Incumbents

Ronald D. Elving

Everyone has heard about the entrenched Congress. The phrase conjures big-bottomed old pols settling slowly into office, thickening their impervious incumbent hides with each re-election.

This sort of imagery fuels the term-limit movement currently building steam as one perceived solution to the nation's ills. But, like all caricatures, this one twists the truth it captures.

No one doubts incumbency has its charms and privileges. But the "entrenchment" paradigm currently in vogue lays so much emphasis on mere longevity as to miss the point.

Consider this fact: During the 101st Congress, 11 House members gained their seats in special elections, replacing incumbents who died, resigned or moved on to other offices.

They are the most junior of members, those who have had the least chance to use their entrenching tools, having barely begun the franking privileges and constituent services widely supposed to be an incumbent's best friends. Not one of them serves on Ways and Means or Appropriations or Rules or any other panel that guarantees a high profile and campaign contributions. They are little-known even in Congress.

And yet, after an average of less than a year on the Hill, all 11 are likely to win in November and return for full terms in the 102nd Congress. Only one of the 11 had a serious primary opponent, and only one other has a real race this fall.

The latter is Jill Long, D-Ind., who was elected by the narrowest of margins in 1989 in the solidly GOP precincts once walked by Vice President Dan Quayle and Dan Coats (who vacated the seat when appointed to succeed Quayle in the Senate).

Many Republicans attributed Long's election to the weakness of their candidate in that race, whose best asset might have been his first name: Dan. But 18 months later, Long is running ahead of the Republicans' new champion, a fundamentalist TV minister named Rick (Hawks).

Two other Democrats, Gene Taylor of Mississippi and Patsy T. Mink of Hawaii, can almost count on re-election, even if their opponents cannot yet be quite counted out.

The other five Democrats—Glen Browder of Alabama, Gary Condit of California, Pete Geren and Craig Washington of Texas, and Jose E. Serrano of New York—are either unopposed or sailing through a "no brainer" contest.

The phenomenon is fully bipartisan. The three special-election freshmen on the Republican side—Susan Molinari of New York, Ileana Ros-Lehtinen of Florida and Craig Thomas of Wyoming—have all reached the sucker-bet level just as fast as their Democratic counterparts.

Why was neither party able to recruit candidates against these, the other party's newest and presumably least ensconced incumbents?

Certainly one answer is money. Members of the special-election class benefited from heavy commitments from their respective parties. Most have also proved formidable fundraisers in their own right, averaging more than $750,000 during their special-election and first re-election cycle (a few could rely on their personal resources for a head start).

Another element often mentioned is the political design of the districts in question. But only a few of these 11 districts are really safe for one party or the other, and only a few of these 11 candidates enjoyed the 60 percent vote share that marks such security. Five of the 11 were elected with 53 percent of the vote or less.

Long, Taylor and Ros-Lehtinen all snatched their districts away from the other party. And four others won in special elections that had been targeted as winnable by both parties (Geren, Condit, Browder and Thomas). And most of the districts won by Democrats in 1989–90 special elections had been carried by George Bush in 1988.

But in a larger sense, these 11 candidates were never going to be soft spots in their respective party lineups. They are strong in the fundamental political assets that get people elected and re-elected, and that have little to do with longevity in office.

Each in his or her way represented the positioning, timing and campaign energy right for their respective races. Long, in particular, has won the admiration of political operatives for her shrewd handling of issues (one GOP operative this fall has proudly described one of his party's candidates as "our Jill Long").

The special-election class of 1989–90 may be said to carry the power of incumbency to the point of absurdity: "You, too, can be an instant powerhouse."

But if these individuals seem so secure after so little time, there must be something more at work than franked mail, constituent service and a long string of years with one's name on the ballot.

Whatever it is, those who would "cure" Congress with a limit on terms are missing it.

[All eleven candidates discussed in this selection did in fact win reelection in November, 1990.]

Chapter 12

The Presidency

*T*he American presidency is the most powerful office in the world. To the president's vast formal powers are added extraordinary informal powers: to lead Congress, to cope with emergency situations, to take charge of world affairs. The president's constitutional authority, broad and expansive, is supplemented by huge delegations of power from Congress and by the power that comes from the prestige of the office itself.

Yet for all his powers, the president is boxed in by limitations of every kind. He must share his constitutional authority with Congress, with which he must continually negotiate and bargain, and with the federal courts, which he can influence only uncertainly and, usually, only in the long run. His own cabinet officials often have their own political bases and their own agendas, and even his personal staff may become ambitious and unreliable. He must spend much of his first term preparing for reelection and all of his second term, if he has one, with the knowledge that the Constitution forbids him from running again.

In the 1990s, the American president faces restraints from abroad. Major U.S. allies—Great Britain, France, Germany, Japan—wield extraordinary economic muscle, and although they look to Washington for guidance, they need not follow where the president leads. U.S. relations with the Soviet Union have improved dramatically, but the United States still faces difficult challenges across the globe—all of which must be faced most directly by the president.

The readings in this chapter share a common theme: they present the paradox of a president whose immense resources are not always sufficient to perform the tasks expected of him by the American people and by the rest of the world. Whether in foreign or domestic affairs, whether dealing with Congress or the Soviet premier, the president always seems to be stretching and straining at the limits of his power.

Chapter Questions

1. What are the sources of the president's formal authority? his informal authority?

2. Consider Richard Neustadt's argument (in selection 12.5) that a president's real power comes from his ability to bargain and persuade effectively. What examples of bargaining and persuading can be found in this chapter? Consider the president's foreign affairs power, his dealings with Congress, and his relationship with his own staff, for starters.

3. The presidency, some suggest, is an eighteenth-century office forced to function in a twentieth-century world. How has the presidency adjusted to the extraordinary political, social, and technological changes of the past 200 years? Has this adaptation been successful?

I THE CONSTITUTIONAL CONTEXT

The Framers of the Constitution recognized the importance of a unitary executive. Legislative bodies could deliberate and plan policy in the long run perhaps, but only a unitary executive could act with the speed, decisiveness, and, when appropriate, secretiveness necessary for effective leadership. These qualities were especially important, the Framers believed, in matters of foreign and military policy.

Americans are so used to a strong presidency that it is easy to forget how much opposition there was in the beginning to such an office. The opponents of the Constitution feared that the presidency would quickly be transformed into an oppressive monarchy (the Articles of Confederation, remember, had no federal executive). They feared broad grants of legislative power to the president (especially the veto power, and the power to make treaties), the commander-in-chief clause, and the president's power to appoint the federal judiciary.

Alexander Hamilton's strong defense of presidential power in the Federalist No. 70 *is a clear indication that the Framers favored both efficiency and liberty and indeed believed that one was impossible without the other. It follows* Federalist No. 68, *in which Hamilton defends the mode of appointment of the president; he suggests that the indirect scheme the Framers designed would ensure to a "moral certainty" that "the office of President will seldom fall to the lot of any man who is not in an eminent degree endowed with the requisite qualifications."*

Yet the Antifederalists' fears were not wholly unfounded. Maintaining the balance between a presidency strong enough to do what is required yet weak enough to be controlled by the people remains a difficult, and daunting, task.

Questions

1. Why is a unitary executive necessary, according to Hamilton? What characteristics does a single individual possess that a body of individuals—Congress, for example—lacks?

2. Have Hamilton's arguments become stronger or weaker over the past 200 years? Has the modern presidency borne out his views or those of his opponents?

3. Consider the argument of James Bryce (see pp. 426–427) on why "great men do not become presidents." How can Bryce's conclusion be reconciled with Hamilton's?

12.1 Federalist No. 68

Alexander Hamilton

The mode of appointment of the Chief Magistrate of the United States is almost the only part of the system, of any consequence, which has escaped without severe censure or which has received the slightest mark of approbation from its opponents. The most plausible of these, who has appeared in print, has even deigned to admit that the election of the President is pretty well guarded. [Hamilton refers to the *Letters of a Federal Farmer*, written by an Antifederalist critic of the Constitution.] I venture somewhat further, and hesitate not to affirm that if the manner of it be not perfect, it is at least excellent. It unites in an eminent degree all the advantages the union of which was to be desired.

It was desirable that the sense of the people should operate in the choice of the person to whom so important a trust was to be confided. This end will be answered by committing the right of making it, not to any pre-established body, but to men chosen by the people for the special purpose, and at the particular conjuncture.

It was equally desirable that the immediate election should be made by men most capable of analyzing the qualities adapted to the station and acting under circumstances favorable to deliberation, and to a judicious combination of all the reasons and inducements which were proper to govern their choice. A small number of persons, selected by their fellow-citizens from the general mass, will be most likely to possess the information and discernment requisite to so complicated an investigation.

It was also peculiarly desirable to afford as little opportunity as possible to tumult and disorder. This evil was not least to be dreaded in the election of a magistrate who was to have so important an agency in the administration of the government as the President of the United States. But the precautions which have been so happily concerted in the system under consideration promise an effectual security against this mischief. The choice of *several* to form an intermediate body of electors will be much less apt to convulse the community with any extraordinary or violent movements than the choice of *one* who was himself to be the final object of the public wishes. And as the electors, chosen in each State, are to assemble and vote in the State in which they are chosen, this detached and divided situation will expose them much less to heats and ferments, which might be communicated from them to the people, than if they were all to be convened at one time, in one place.

Nothing was more to be desired than that every practicable obstacle should be opposed to cabal, intrigue, and corruption. These most deadly adversaries of republican government might naturally have been expected to make their approaches from more than one quarter, but chiefly from the desire in foreign powers to gain an improper ascendant in our councils. How could they better gratify this than by raising a creature of their own to the chief magistracy of the Union? But the convention have guarded against all danger of this sort with the most provident and judicious attention. They have not made the appointment of the President to depend on any preexisting bodies of men who might be tampered with beforehand to prostitute their votes; but they have referred it in the first instance to an immediate act of the people of America, to be exerted in the choice of persons for the temporary and sole purpose of making the appointment. And they have excluded from eligibility to this trust all those who from situation might be suspected of too great devotion to the President in office. No senator, representative, or other person holding a place of trust or profit under the United States can be of the number of the electors. Thus without corrupting the body of the people, the immediate agents in the election will at least enter upon the task free from any sinister bias. Their transient existence and their detached situation, already taken notice of, afford a satisfactory prospect of their continuing so, to the conclusion of it. The business of corruption, when it is to embrace so considerable a number of men, requires time as well as means. Nor would it be found easy suddenly to embark them, dispersed as they would be over thirteen States, in any combinations founded upon motives which, though they could not properly be denominated corrupt, might yet be of a nature to mislead them from their duty.

Another and less important desideratum was that the executive should be independent for his continuance in office on all but the people themselves. He might otherwise be tempted to sacrifice his duty to his complaisance for those whose favor was necessary to the duration of his official consequence. This advantage will also be secured, by making his re-election to depend on a special body of representatives, deputed by the society for the single purpose of making the important choice.

All these advantages will be happily combined in the plan devised by the convention; which is, that the people of each State shall choose a number of persons as electors, equal to the number of senators and representatives of such State in the national government who shall assemble within the State, and vote for some fit person as President. Their votes, thus given, are to be transmitted to the seat of the national government, and the person who may happen to have a majority of the whole number of votes will be the President. But as a majority of the votes might not always happen to center on one man, and as it might be unsafe to permit less than a majority to be conclusive it is provided that, in such a contingency, the House of Representatives shall elect out of the candidates who shall have the five highest number of votes the man who in their opinion may be best qualified for the office.

This process of election affords a moral certainty that the office of President will seldom fall to the lot of any man who is not in an eminent degree endowed with the requisite qualifications. Talents for low intrigue, and the little arts of popularity, may alone suffice to elevate a man to the first honors in a single State; but it will require other talents, and a different kind of merit, to establish him in the esteem and confidence of the whole Union, or of so considerable a portion of it as would be necessary to make him a successful candidate for the distinguished office of President of the United States. It will not be too strong to say that there will be a constant probability of seeing the station filled by characters pre-eminent for ability and virtue. And this will be thought no inconsiderable recommendation of the Constitution by those who are able to estimate the share which the executive in every government must necessarily have in its good or ill administration. Though we cannot acquiesce in the political heresy of the poet who says:

> For forms of government let fools contest—
> That which is best administered is best,—

yet we may safely pronounce that the true test of a good government is its aptitude and tendency to produce a good administration.

The Vice-President is to be chosen in the same manner with the President; with this difference, that the Senate is to do, in respect to the former, what is to be done by the House of Representatives, in respect to the latter.

The appointment of an extraordinary person, as Vice-President, has been objected to as superfluous, if not mischievous. It has been alleged that it would have been preferable to have authorized the Senate to elect out of their own body an officer answering to that description. But two considerations seem to justify the ideas of the convention in this respect. One is that to secure at all times the possibility of a definitive resolution of the body, it is necessary that the President should have only a casting vote. And to take the senator of any State from his seat as senator, to place him in that of President of the Senate, would be to exchange, in regard to the State from which he came, a constant for a contingent vote. The other consideration is that as the Vice-President may occasionally become a substitute for the President, in the supreme executive magistracy, all the reasons which recommend the mode of election prescribed for the one apply with great if not with equal force to the manner of appointing the other. It is remarkable that in this, as in most other instances, the objection which is made would lie against the constitution of this State [New York]. We have a Lieutenant-Governor, chosen by the people at large, who presides in the Senate, and is the constitutional substitute for the Governor, in casualties similar to those which would authorize the Vice-President to exercise the authorities and discharge the duties of the President.

12.2 Federalist No. 70

Alexander Hamilton

There is an idea, which is not without it advocates, that a vigorous executive is inconsistent with the genius of republican government. The enlightened well-wishers to this species of government must at least hope that the supposition is destitute of foundation; since they can never admit its truth, without at the same time admitting the condemnation of their own principles. Energy in the executive is a leading character in the definition of good government. It is essential to the protection of the community against foreign attacks; it is not less essential to the steady administration of the laws; to the protection of property against those irregular and high-handed combinations which sometimes interrupt the ordinary course of justice; to the security of liberty against the enterprises and assaults of ambition, of faction, and of anarchy. Every man the least conversant in Roman history knows how often that republic was obliged to take refuge in the absolute power of a single man, under the formidable title of dictator, as well against the intrigues of ambitious individuals who aspired to the tyranny, and the seditions of whole classes of the community whose conduct threatened the existence of all government, as against the invasions of external enemies who menaced the conquest and destruction of Rome.

There can be no need, however, to multiply arguments or examples on this head. A feeble executive implies a feeble execution of the government. A feeble execution is but another phrase for a bad execution; and a government ill executed, whatever it may be in theory, must be, in practice, a bad government.

Taking it for granted, therefore, that all men of sense will agree in the necessity of an energetic executive, it will only remain to inquire, what are the ingredients which constitute this energy? How far can they be combined with those other ingredients which constitute safety in the republican sense? And how far does this combination characterize the plan which has been reported by the convention?

The ingredients which constitute energy in the executive are unity; duration; an adequate provision for its support; and competent powers.

The ingredients which constitute safety in the republican sense are a due dependence on the people and a due responsibility.

Those politicians and statesmen who have been the most celebrated for the soundness of their principles and for the justness of their views have declared in favor of a single executive and a numerous legislature. They have, with great propriety, considered energy as the most necessary qualification of the former, and have regarded this as most applicable to power in a single hand; while they have, with equal propriety, considered the latter as best adapted to deliberation and wisdom, and best calculated to conciliate the confidence of the people and to secure their privileges and interests.

That unity is conducive to energy will not be disputed. Decision, activity, secrecy, and dispatch will generally characterize the proceedings of one man in a much more eminent degree than the proceedings of any greater number; and in proportion as the number is increased, these qualities will be diminished.

• • •

Whenever two or more persons are engaged in any common enterprise or pursuit, there is always danger of difference of opinion. If it be a public trust or office in which they are clothed with equal dignity and authority, there is peculiar danger of personal emulation and even animosity. From either, and especially from all these causes, the most bitter dissensions are apt to spring. Whenever these happen, they lessen the respectability, weaken the authority, and distract the plans and operations of those whom they divide. If they should unfortunately assail the supreme executive magistracy of a country, consisting of a plurality of persons, they might impede or frustrate the most important measures of the government in the most critical emergencies of the state. And what is still worse, they might split the community into the most violent and irreconcilable factions, adhering differently to the different individuals who composed the magistracy.

Men often oppose a thing merely because they have had no agency in planning it, or because it may have been planned by those whom they dislike. But if they have been consulted, and have happened to disapprove, opposition then becomes, in their estimation, an indispensable duty of self-love. They seem to think themselves bound in honor, and by all the motives of personal infallibility, to defeat the success of what has been resolved upon contrary to their sentiments. Men of upright, benevolent tempers have too many opportunities of remarking, with horror, to what desperate lengths this disposition is sometimes carried, and how often the great interests of society are sacrificed to the vanity, to the conceit, and to the obstinacy of individuals, who have credit enough to make their passions and their caprices interesting to mankind. Perhaps the question now before the public may, in its consequences, afford melancholy proofs of the effects of this despicable frailty, or rather detestable vice, in the human character.

Upon the principles of a free government, inconveniences from the source just mentioned must necessarily be submitted to in the formation of the legislature; but it is unnecessary, and therefore unwise, to introduce them into the constitution of the executive. It is here too that they may be most pernicious. In the legislature, promptitude of decision is oftener an evil than a benefit. The differences of opinion, and the jarring of parties in that department of the government, though they may sometimes obstruct salutary plans, yet often promote deliberation and circumspection, and serve to check excesses in the majority. When a resolution too is once taken, the opposition must be at an end. That resolution is a law, and resistance to it punishable. But no favorable circumstances palliate or atone for the disadvantages of dissension in the executive department. Here they are pure and unmixed. There is no point at which they cease to operate. They serve to embarrass and weaken the execution of the plan or measure to which they relate, from the first step to the final conclusion of it. They constantly counteract those

Why Great Men Are Not Chosen Presidents

Even in the nineteenth century, Alexander Hamilton's prediction in Federalist No. 68 *that the presidency would "seldom fall to the lot of any man who is not in an eminent degree endowed with the requisite qualifications" seemed belied by the facts (especially presidents like Polk, Hayes, Garfield, and Arthur). Many would add some twentieth-century presidents to this list of nonnotables. James Bryce, a British nobleman who wrote* The American Commonwealth *in the late 1800s, explains in this excerpt "why great men are not chosen presidents."*

*E*uropeans often ask, and Americans do not always explain, how it happens that this great office [the presidency], the greatest in the world, unless we except the Papacy, to which any man can rise by his own merits, is not more frequently filled by great and striking men? In America, which is beyond all other countries the country of a "career open to talents," a country, moreover, in which political life is unusually keen and political ambition widely diffused, it might be expected that the highest place would always be won by a man of brilliant gifts. But since the heroes of the Revolution died out with Jefferson and Adams and Madison some sixty years ago, no person except General Grant has reached the chair whose name would have been remembered had he not been President, and no President except Abraham Lincoln has displayed rare or striking qualities in the chair.

Who now knows or cares to know anything about the personality of James K. Polk or Franklin Pierce? The only thing remarkable about them is that being so commonplace they should have climbed so high.

Several reasons may be suggested for the fact, which Americans are themselves the first to admit.

One is that the proportion of first-rate ability drawn into politics is smaller in America than in most European countries. This is a phenomenon whose causes must be elucidated later: in the meantime it is enough to say that in France and Italy, where half-revolutionary conditions have made public life exciting and accessible; in Germany, where an admirably-organized civil service cultivates and develops statecraft with unusual success; in England, where many persons of wealth and leisure seek to enter the political arena, while burning questions touch the interests of all classes and make men eager observers of the combatants, the total quantity of talent devoted to parliamentary or administrative work is far larger, relatively to the population, than in America, where much of the best ability, both for thought and for action, for planning and for executing, rushes into a field which is comparatively narrow in Europe, the business of developing the material resources of the country.

Another is that the methods and habits of Congress, and indeed of political life generally, seem to give fewer opportunities for personal distinction,

qualities in the executive which are the most necessary ingredients in its composition—vigor and expedition, and this without any counterbalancing good. In the conduct of war, in which the energy of the executive is the bulwark of the national security, everything would be to be apprehended from its plurality.

It must be confessed that these observations apply with principal weight to the first case supposed—that is, to a plurality of magistrates of equal dignity and authority, a scheme, the

advocates for which are not likely to form a numerous sect; but they apply, though not with equal yet with considerable weight to the project of a council, whose concurrence is made constitutionally necessary to the operations of the ostensible executive. An artful cabal in that council would be able to distract and to enervate the whole system of administration. If no such cabal should exist, the mere diversity of views and opinions would alone be sufficient to tincture the exercise of the executive author-

fewer modes in which a man may commend himself to his countrymen by eminent capacity in thought, in speech, or in administration, than is the case in the free countries of Europe. . . .

A third reason is that eminent men make more enemies, and give those enemies more assailable points, than obscure men do. They are therefore in so far less desirable candidates. It is true that the eminent man has also made more friends, that his name is more widely known, and may be greeted with louder cheers. Other things being equal, the famous man is preferable. But other things never are equal. The famous man has probably attacked some leaders in his own party, has supplanted others, has expressed his dislike to the crotchet of some active section, has perhaps committed errors which are capable of being magnified into offences. No man stands long before the public and bears a part in great affairs without giving openings to censorious criticism. Fiercer far than the light which beats upon a throne is the light which beats upon a presidential candidate, searching out all the recesses of his past life. Hence, when the choice lies between a brilliant man and a safe man, the safe man is preferred. Party feeling, strong enough to carry in on its back a man without conspicuous positive merits, is not always strong enough to procure forgiveness for a man with positive faults. . . .

It must also be remembered that the merits of a President are one thing and those of a candidate another thing. An eminent American is reported to have said to friends who wished to put him forward, "Gentlemen, let there be no mistake. I should make a good President, but a very bad candidate." Now to a party it is more important that its nominee should be a good candidate than that he should turn out a good President. A nearer danger is a greater danger. As Saladin says in *The Talisman,* "A wild cat in a chamber is more dangerous than a lion in a distant desert." It will be a misfortune to the party, as well as to the country, if the candidate elected should prove a bad President. But it is a greater misfortune to the party that it should be beaten in the impending election, for the evil of losing national patronage will have come four years sooner. "B" (so reason the leaders), "who is one of our possible candidates, may be an abler man than A, who is the other. But we have a better chance of winning with A than with B, while X, the candidate of our opponents, is anyhow no better than A. We must therefore run A." This reasoning is all the more forcible because the previous career of the possible candidates has generally made it easier to say who will succeed as a candidate than who will succeed as a President; and because the wire-pullers with whom the choice rests are better judges of the former question than of the latter.

—*James Bryce*

ity with a spirit of habitual feebleness and dilatoriness.

But one of the weightiest objections to a plurality in the executive, and which lies as much against the last as the first plan is that it tends to conceal faults and destroy responsibility. Responsibility is of two kinds—to censure and to punishment. The first is the more important of the two, especially in an elective office. Men in public trust will much oftener act in such a manner as to render them unworthy of being any longer trusted, than in such a manner as to make them obnoxious to legal punishment. But the multiplication of the executive adds to the difficulty of detection in either case. It often becomes impossible, amidst mutual accusations, to determine on whom the blame or the punishment of a pernicious measure, or series of pernicious measures, ought really to fall. It is shifted from one to another with so much dexterity, and under such plausible appearances, that the public opinion is left in suspense about the real author. The circumstances which may have led to any national miscarriage or misfortune are sometimes so complicated that where there are a number of actors who may have had different degrees and kinds of agency, though we may clearly see upon the whole that there has been mismanagement, yet it may be impracticable to pronounce to whose account the evil which may have been incurred is truly chargeable. . . .

Prior to the appearance of the Constitution, I rarely met with an intelligent man from any of the States who did not admit, as the result of experience, that the UNITY of the executive of this State was one of the best of the distinguishing features of our Constitution.

II THE PERSPECTIVE OF HISTORY

The Framers of the U.S. Constitution made it clear that the federal government would have the exclusive power to make war. Exactly how that authority was to be shared between the executive and legislative branches, however, was not so readily apparent; Congress has the power to "declare war," but the president is designated the "Commander in Chief." This constitutional ambiguity set the stage for dramatic conflicts between the two branches, conflicts that became serious in the twentieth century. Since World War II, the United States has fought three major wars without an official declaration of war, although in the 1991 Persian Gulf War, Congress did pass a resolution of support that was nearly equivalent. As presidents have sought to expand their war-making authority, they have claimed the support of the constitutional text and of the intent of the Framers, based on a broad reading of the commander-in-chief clause and other provisions of the Constitution.

In the following excerpt, David Gray Adler examines the historical background underlying the Constitution's multifarious pronouncements on the war power. History, he concludes, provides little support for presidential exercise of the war power.

Questions

1. What arguments can be advanced to support the presidential view of the war-making power? Consider especially the arguments in *Federalist* No. 70 (selection 12.1)

2. Even if Adler is correct in his analysis, is the constitutional distribution of powers as he describes it realistic for the twentieth century?

12.3 *The President's War-Making Power*

David Gray Adler

The War Clause

The debate on the proper location of the authority to make war occurred at the outset of the Constitutional Convention. On May 29, 1787, Governor Edmund Randolph of Virginia proposed a constitution which included a provision "that a national Executive be instituted." The seventh paragraph stated that the executive "ought to enjoy the Executive rights vested in Congress of the Confederation." The Randolph Plan was taken up by the convention on June 1. In considering the proposal to give to the national executive the executive powers of the Continental Congress, Charles Pinckney objected that "the Executive powers of [the existing] Congress might extend to peace and war which would render the Executive a Monarchy, of the worst kind, towit an elective one." His fellow South Carolinian, John Rutledge, said that "he was for vesting the Executive power in a single person, tho' he was not for giving him the power of war and peace." James Wilson of Pennsylvania sought to reassure them: "Making peace and war are generally determined by writers on the Laws of Nations to be legislative powers." Wilson added: "The prerogatives of the British Monarchy [are not] a proper guide in defining the Executive powers. Some of the prerogatives were of a Legislative nature. Among others that of war & peace." James Madison of Virginia agreed that the war power was legislative in character. Rufus King of Massachusetts noted: "Mad: agrees with Wilson in his definition of executive powers—executive powers ex vi termini [by the force of the term itself], do not include the Rights of war & peace . . . but the powers should be confined and defined—if large we shall have the Evils of elective Monarchies." There was no vote on Randolph's resolution, yet the discussion appears to reflect an understanding that the power of "war & peace"—the power to initiate war—belonged not to the executive but to the legislature.

On August 6 the Committee of Detail circulated a draft constitution which provided: "The legislature of the United States shall have the power . . . To make war." This bore a sharp resemblance to the Articles of Confederation, which vested the "sole and exclusive right and power of determining on peace and war" to the Continental Congress. When the "war clause" was considered in debate on August 17, Charles Pinckney opposed placing the power in Congress. "Its proceedings were too slow. . . . The Senate would be the best depository, being more acquainted with foreign affairs, and most capable of proper resolutions." Pierce Butler of South Carolina "was for vesting the power in the President, who will have all the requisite qualities, and will not make war but when the nation will support it." Butler's opinion shocked Elbridge Gerry of Massachusetts, who said he "never expected to hear in a republic a motion to empower the Executive alone to declare war." Butler stood alone in the convention; there was no support for his opinion and no second to his motion.

The proposal of the Committee of Detail to vest the legislature with the power to "make war" proved unsatisfactory to Madison and Gerry. In a joint resolution, they moved to substitute "declare" for "make," "leaving to the Executive the power to repel sudden attacks." The meaning of the motion is unmistakable: Congress was granted the power to make—that is, to initiate—war; the president, for obvious reasons, could act immediately to repel sudden attacks without authorization from Congress. There was no quarrel whatever with respect to the sudden-attack provision, but there was some question as to whether the substitution of "declare" for "make" would effect the intention of Madison and Gerry. Roger Sherman of Connecticut thought the joint motion stood very well. The executive should be able to repel, but not to commence, war. "'Make' better than 'declare' the latter narrowing the power [of the legislature] too much." Virginia's George Mason reportedly "was agst. giving the power of war to the Executive, because not [safely] to be trusted with it; or to the Senate, because not so constructed as to be entitled to it. He was for clogging rather than facilitating war; but for facilitating peace. He preferred 'declare' to 'make.'" The Madison-Gerry proposal was adopted by a vote of 7 to 2. When Rufus King explained that the word "make" might be understood to authorize Congress to initiate as well as conduct war, Connecticut changed its vote so that the word "declare" was approved, eight states to one.

David Gray Adler   **429**

The debates and the vote on the war clause make it clear Congress alone possesses the authority to initiate war. The war-making power was specifically withheld from the president; a president was given only the authority to repel sudden attacks. Confirmation of this understanding was provided by remarks of ratifiers in various state conventions, as well as by the early practice and contemporaneous statements of political actors.

James Wilson, who was perhaps only slightly less influential than James Madison in the Constitutional Convention, told the Pennsylvania Ratifying Convention: "This system will not hurry us into war; it is calculated to guard against it. It will not be in the power of a single man, or a single body of men, to involve us in such distress; for the important power of declaring war is vested in the legislature at large: this declaration must be made with the concurrence of the House of Representatives: from this circumstance we may draw a certain conclusion that nothing but our national interest can draw us into a war."

Similar assurance was provided in other state ratifying conventions. In North Carolina, James Iredell said, "The President has not the power of declaring war by his own authority. . . . Those powers are vested in other hands. The power of declaring war is expressly given to Congress." And Charles Pinckney, a delegate in Philadelphia, told the South Carolina Ratifying Convention that "the President's powers did not permit him to declare war." Likewise, in New York, Chancellor Robert R. Livingston responded to objections that the Continental Congress did not have "the same powers" as the proposed Congress: "They have the very same. . . . Congress have the power of making war and peace . . . they may involve us in a war at their pleasure."

In spite of the illuminating debate and the vote on the war clause, the shift from "make" to "declare" has induced revisionists to find in the presidency a power to initiate war. Senator Barry Goldwater, for example, has said when the convention deleted from the working draft of the Constitution the authorization of Congress to make war, "the Framers intended to leave the 'making of war' with the President." The scholar Leonard Ratner has explained that the "declare" clause recognized "the warmaking authority of the president, implied by his role as executive and commander-in-chief and by congressional power to declare, but not make, war." John Norton Moore and others have suggested that acts of military force, short of war, might be committed by the president.

For the moment I shall defer consideration of the executive-power and commander-in-chief clauses, but these views ignore that at the time of the framing, the word "declare" enjoyed a settled understanding and an established usage. Simply stated, as early as 1552, the verb "declare" had become synonymous with the verb "commence"; they both meant the initiation of hostilities. This was the established usage of international law as well as in England, where the terms to declare war and to make war were used interchangeably. This practice was familiar to the framers. Chancellor James Kent of New York, one of the leading jurists of the founding period, stated: "As war cannot lawfully be commenced on the part of the United States without an act of Congress, such an act is, of course, a formal official notice to all the world, and equivalent to the most solemn declaration." While Kent interpreted "declare" to mean "commence," he did not assert that the Constitution required a congressional declaration of war before hostilities could be lawfully commenced; he merely asserted that such a declaration is initiated by Congress.

Given the equivalence of "commence" and "declare," it is clear that a congressional declaration of war would initiate military hostilities. According to commentators on international law a declaration of war was desirable because it announced the institution of a state of war, as well as the legal consequences that war entails, to the adversary, to neutral nations, and to citizens of the sovereign who initiated the war. Indeed, this is the essence of a declaration of war—notice by the proper authority of intent to convert a state of peace into a state of war. But all that is required under American law is a joint resolution or an explicit congressional authorization of the use of military force against a named adversary. This can come in the form of a "declaration pure and simple" or in a "conditional declaration of war." There are also two kinds of war, those that United States courts have termed "perfect," or general, and those that are labeled "imperfect," or limited, wars.

At the dawn of the Republic, in three important Supreme Court cases, it was decided that the power of determining perfect and imperfect war lay with Congress. Thus, Chief Justice John Marshall, on behalf of the Court, held in 1801 in *Talbot v. Seeman*, that the power of Congress comprises the power to "declare a general war" and also to "wage a limited war." The power of Congress to authorize limited war is, of course, a necessary concomitant of its power to declare general war. If, as John Bassett Moore has suggested, a president might authorize relatively minor acts of war, or perhaps covert military operations, in circumstances that did not demand a full-blown war, that power could be wielded in a way that would easily eviscerate the Constitution's placement of the war power in Congress. Moore, an eminent scholar of international law, has rebuked that proposition: "There can hardly be room for doubt that the framers of the Constitution, when they vested in Congress the power to declare war, they never imagined that they were leaving it to the executive to use the military and naval forces of the United States all over the world for the purpose of actually coercing other nations, occupying their territory, and killing their soldiers and citizens, all according to his own notion of the fitness of things, as long as he refrained from calling his action war or persisted in calling it peace."

In fact, the framers withheld from the president the power to work such mischief. As we have observed, he was granted only the authority to respond defensively to the initiation of war through sudden attack upon the United States. In 1806, in *United States v. Smith*, Justice William Paterson of the Supreme Court, who had been a delegate to the convention, explained the rationale for a presidential response:

> If, indeed, a foreign nation should invade the territories of the United States, it would, I apprehend, be not only lawful for the president to resist such invasion, but also to carry hostilities into the enemy's own country; and for this plain reason, that a state of complete and absolute war exists between the two nations. In the case of invasive hostilities, there cannot be war on the one side and peace on the other. . . . There is a manifest distinction between our going to war with a nation at peace, and a war being made against us by an actual invasion, or a formal declaration. In the former case, it is the exclusive province of Congress to change a state of peace into a state of war.

As Justice Paterson observed, the reason for vesting the president with authority to repel sudden attacks was that an invasion instituted a state of war, thus rendering a declaration of war by Congress superfluous. In such an event, the president was authorized to initiate offensive action against the attacking enemy. But the president's power of self-defense does not extend to foreign lands. The framers did not give the president the right to intervene in foreign wars or to choose between war and peace or to identify and commence hostilities against an enemy of the American people. Nor did the framers empower a president to initiate force abroad on the basis of his own assessments of the security interests of the United States. These circumstances involve choices that belong to Congress. The president's power is defensive and is limited to attacks against the United States.

All of the offensive powers of the nation, then, were located in Congress. Consistent with this constitutional theory, the convention gave to Congress the power to issue "letters of marque and reprisal." Dating back to the Middle Ages, when sovereigns employed private forces in retaliation for an injury caused by the sovereign of another state or his subjects, the practice of issuing reprisals gradually evolved into the use of public armies. By the time of the convention, the framers considered the power to issue letters of marque and reprisal sufficient to authorize a broad spectrum of armed hostilities short of declared war. In other words, it was regarded as a species of imperfect war. Thus, James Madison, Alexander Hamilton, and Thomas Jefferson, among others, agreed that the authorization of reprisals was an act of war that belonged to Congress. As a direct reply to the revisionists' claim of a presidential power to order acts of war, we may consider what Jefferson said in 1793 about the authority necessary to issue a reprisal: "Congress must be called upon to take it; the right of reprisal being expressly lodged with them by the Constitution, and not with the executive."

In short, it may be said that when the framers granted to Congress the power "to declare war," they were vesting in that body the sole and exclusive prerogative to initiate military hostilities on behalf of the American people. The record reveals that no member of the Philadelphia convention and no member of any state ratifying convention held a different understanding of the meaning of the war clause. Thus, if the revisionists are to find textual authority for a president's power to make war, it must derive from another source.

The Commander-in-Chief Clause

The commander-in-chief clause, in the words of Justice Robert H. Jackson, has been invoked for the "power to do anything, anywhere, that can be done with an army or navy." While he said this in the context of reviewing President Truman's invocation of the clause to support his seizure of the steel mills, Justice Jackson's observations certainly foreshadowed the claims of recent executives who have seized the provision as justification for their military adventures. Presidents Johnson, Nixon, Ford, Carter, and Reagan fall into this category. The clause has also become the principal pillar for those who would vest in the president the constitutional power of war and peace. As we shall see, however, the title of commander in chief conferred

no war-making power whatever; it vested in the president only the authority to repel sudden attacks on the United States and to direct war, "when authorized or begun." In this capacity, presidents would direct the forces Congress placed at their command.

As Francis D. Wormuth has observed, the "office of commander in chief has never carried the power of war and peace, nor was it invented by the framers of the Constitution." In fact, the office was introduced by King Charles I in 1639 when he named the earl of Arundel commander in chief of an army to battle the Scots in the First Bishops' War. In historical usage the title of commander in chief has been a generic term referring to the highest officer in a particular chain of command. The ranking commander in chief, purely a military post, always was under the command of a political superior.

The government of England also transplanted the title to America in the eighteenth century by appointing a number of commanders in chief and by the practice of entitling governors of royal, proprietary, and chartered colonies as commanders in chief, or occasionally as vice-admirals or captains general. The appointment of General Thomas Gage as commander in chief from 1763 to 1776 caused grave concerns for the colonists, for he proceeded to interfere in civil affairs and to acquire considerable influence over Indian relations, trade, and transportation. The bitter memories of his decision to quarter troops in the homes of civilians spawned the Third Amendment to the Constitution. These activities, as well as others, prompted the colonists to complain in the Declaration of Independence that King George III had "affected to render the Military independent of and superior to the Civil Power."

But colonists had no reason to fear the governors as commanders in chief, even though they controlled the provincial forces. After all, the assemblies claimed and asserted the rights to vote funds for the militia and to call it into service. The historian Ernest May has correctly noted that "under one or the other of these principles, they neutralized whatever pernicious power the executive might have had." In fact, the grievances came from the governors; like the duke of Wellington, they complained about the relative impotence of their positions.

The colonial assemblies (and, later, the states) asserted the power of the purse as a check on the commander in chief; this undoubtedly stemmed from the English practice, which extended at least as far back as the middle of the seventeenth century. By 1665, as a means of maintaining political control of the military establishment, Parliament had inaugurated the policy of making annual military appropriations with a lifetime of only one year. This practice, or strategy, sharply emphasized Parliament's power to determine the size of the army to be placed under the direction of the commander in chief.

This practice had a long-term influence. Under the Constitution, the colonial and state assemblies' rights of voting funds for the armed forces were granted to Congress, under its powers to "raise and support armies" and to "provide and maintain a navy." Additionally, "no appropriation of money to that use shall be for a longer term than two years." With the framing of the Constitution, the requirement of legislative approval for the allocation of funds to raise troops—a requirement that had existed in England since the middle of the seventeenth century—underscored the principle of political superiority over military command. It also constitutes a sharp reminder that a commander in chief is dependent upon the legislature for an army to command.

Most of the early state constitutions followed the colonial practice of making the governor "commander in chief" under the authority of state legislatures. For example, Article VII of the Massachusetts Constitution of 1780 provided that the governor shall be "commander-in-chief of the army and navy." But it carefully circumscribed his power—the governor was to "repel, resist [and] expel" attempts to invade the Commonwealth—and it vested him "with all these and other powers incident to the offices of captain general . . . to be exercised agreeably

to the rules and regulations of the Constitution and the laws of the land, and not otherwise."

The Continental Congress continued to use the title when on June 15, 1775, it unanimously decided to appoint George Washington as "general." Dated June 17, his commission named him General and Commander in Chief, of the Army of the United Colonies. The instructions of the Congress, drafted by John Adams, Richard Henry Lee, and Edward Rutledge, kept Washington on a short leash. He was ordered "punctually to observe and follow such orders and directions, from time to time, as you shall receive from this, or a future Congress of these United Colonies, or Committee of Congress." Congress did not hesitate to instruct the commander in chief on military and policy matters.

The practice of entitling the office at the apex of the military hierarchy as commander in chief and of subordinating him to a political superior, whether a king, parliament, or congress, had thus been firmly established for a century and a half and was thoroughly familiar to the framers when they met in Philadelphia. Perhaps this understanding, as well as the consequent absence of concerns about the nature of the post, was the reason there was no debate on the commander-in-chief clause at the convention.

The South Carolinian Charles Pinckney, in the plan he read to the convention on May 29, 1787, introduced the title of president and proposed: "He shall, by Virtue of his Office, be Commander in Chief of the Land Forces of U.S. and Admiral of their Navy." Presumably, Pinckney had drawn on the traditional usage of the title, employed in the South Carolina Constitution of 1776, which provided for a "president and commander-in-chief," and that of 1778, which included a provision for a "governor and commander in chief." There was no such provision in the Randolph, or Virginia, Plan, which was read to the convention on the same day. On June 15, William Paterson submitted the New Jersey Plan, which called for a plural executive and stipulated that the executives ought "to direct all military operations; provided that none of the persons composing the federal executive shall at any time take command of any troops, so as personally to conduct any enterprise as General, or in other capacity." The qualifying clause was meant to discourage a military takeover of the government. When Alexander Hamilton submitted a plan to the convention on June 18, he probably did not propose the title of commander in chief, but he undoubtedly had it in mind when he said the president was "to have the direction of war when authorized or begun."

It was Hamilton's speech, then, that summarized the essence of the president's power as commander in chief: when war is "authorized or begun," the president is to command the military operations of American forces. There was no fear of the legal authority granted by the commander-in-chief clause, and in fact, the clause seemed to excite little dispute. The lone concern was that conveyed by the New Jersey Plan—namely, that a president who personally assumed command of army and naval forces might use them to institute a military coup. In the Virginia Ratifying Convention, George Mason, who had been a delegate to the Constitutional Convention, echoed the concerns of his fellow ratifiers when he said that although it was proper for a president to give overall orders, he thought it dangerous for a president to take command in person. The consent of Congress should be required before a president would be permitted to take command.

But this concern was allayed in the North Carolina Ratifying Convention. Richard Dobbs Spaight, who also had been a delegate to the Constitutional Convention, said that the commander in chief could be controlled by Congress because it had the exclusive authority to raise and support armies, which, indeed, it has. Similar assurance was offered by James Iredell, later an associate justice of the Supreme Court, who delineated the authority of the commander in chief and drew a sharp distinction between the powers of that post and those of the king of England:

In almost every country, the executive has command of the military forces. From the nature of the thing, the command of armies ought to be delegated to one person only. The secrecy, dispatch, and decision, which are necessary in military operations, can only be expected from one person. The President, therefore, is to command the military forces of the United States, and this power I think a proper one; at the same time it will be found to be sufficiently guarded. A very material difference may be observed between this power, and the authority of the king of Great Britain under similar circumstances. The king of Great Britain is not only the commander-in-chief of the land and naval forces, but has power, in time of war, to raise fleets and armies. He also has the power to declare war. The President has not the power of declaring war by his own authority, nor that of raising fleets and armies. The powers are vested in other hands. The power of declaring war is expressly given to Congress, that is, to the two branches of the legislature. . . . They have also expressly delegated to them the powers of raising and supporting armies, and of providing and maintaining a navy.

Iredell's speech reflected *Federalist* number 69, in which Hamilton sought to calm fears surrounding the commander-in-chief clause by noting that although the president's authority as commander in chief would be nominally the same as that of the English king, it would "in substance be much inferior to it." Hamilton added: "It would amount to nothing more than the supreme command and direction of the military and naval forces, as first general and admiral of the Confederacy; while that of the British king extends to the *declaring* of war and to the *raising* and *regulating* of fleets and armies,—all which, by the Constitution under consideration, would appertain to the legislature."

In sum, the president, as commander in chief, was to be "first General and Admiral" in "the direction of war when authorized or begun." Political authority remained in Congress, as it had under the Articles of Confederation. The political scientist Louis Henkin has observed that "generals and admirals, even when they are 'first,' do not determine the political purposes for which troops are to be used; they command them in the execution of policy made by others." The commander in chief, then, according to the tradition of a century and a half, was made subordinate to a political superior. The office carried with it no power to declare war. As Hamilton and Iredell explained, that power was the exclusive prerogative of Congress.

The Executive-Power Clause

In recent years, various presidents and commentators have sought to squeeze from the executive-power clause a presidential authority to make war. In 1966, for example, the State Department cited the president's role as "chief executive" to adduce constitutional support for Lyndon Johnson's entry into the Vietnam War. Richard Nixon's legal advisors similarly invoked the clause to justify his wars in Southeast Asia. In 1975, Gerald Ford found constitutional authority in the "President's Constitutional executive power" for the military activities he ordered in Cambodia. On April 26, 1980, Jimmy Carter authorized an attempt to rescue American citizens who were being held hostage in Iran. He justified the attempt as being "pursuant to the President's powers under the Constitution as Chief Executive and as Commander in Chief."

The very claim asserted by Presidents Johnson, Nixon, Ford, and Carter—that the grant of executive power includes the authority to initiate hostilities—was considered and rejected in the Constitutional Convention; indeed, it caused much alarm. As we have seen, the Randolph Plan provided for a "national executive," which would have "authority to execute the national laws . . . and enjoy the executive rights vested in Congress by the Confederation." In response to concerns that "executive rights" might include the power of war and peace, James Wilson pointed out that the preroga-

tives of the British monarchy were not a proper guide to defining executive powers in the United States. As Madison put it, executive powers "do not include the Rights of war and peace."

No delegate to the convention ever suggested that "executive power" was a fountainhead of power to make war. For the framers, the phrase "executive power" was limited, as Wilson said, to "executing the laws, and appointing officers." Roger Sherman "considered the Executive magistracy as nothing more than an institution for carrying the will of the Legislature into effect." Madison, who agreed with Wilson's definition of executive power, thought it necessary "to fix the extent of Executive authority . . . as certain powers were in their nature Executive, and must be given to that department"; he added that "a definition of their extent would assist the judgment in determining how far they might be safely entrusted to a single officer." The definition of the executive's power should be precise, thought Madison; the executive power should "be confined and defined." And so it was. In a draft reported by James Wilson, the phrase "The Executive Power of the United States should be vested in a single person" first appeared. His draft included an enumeration of the president's powers to grant reprieves and pardons and to serve as commander in chief; it also included the charge that "it shall be his duty to provide for the due and faithful execution of the Laws." The report of the Committee of Detail altered the "faithful execution" phrase to "he shall take care that the laws of the United States be duly and faithfully executed." This form was referred to the Committee of Style, which drafted the version that appears in the Constitution: "The executive power shall be vested in a president of the United States of America. . . . He shall take care that the laws be faithfully executed."

The debate, to the extent that there was one, centered almost entirely on whether there should be a single or a plural presidency. The first sentence of Article II, section 2, "The Executive Power shall be vested in a President," depicts the conclusion reached. Aside from this, there was no argument. There was no challenge to the definition of executive power held by Wilson and Madison; nor was an alternative understanding even advanced. And there was no argument about the scope of "executive power"; indeed, any latent fears were quickly arrested by assurances from Madison and Wilson that the power of "peace and war" was a legislative not an executive function. Given the framers' conception of the chief executive as little more than an institution to carry out the "will of the legislature"—that is, to execute the laws and to appoint officers—there was little about the office to fear. As legal historian Raoul Berger has observed "the 'executive power' was hardly a cornucopia from which could pour undreamed of powers."

Of course, the widespread "aversion of the people to monarchy," the "unhappy memories of the royal prerogative; fear of tyranny, and distrust of any one man, kept the Framers from giving the President too much head." That the framers did not vest the president with "too much" authority is evidenced by the relative calm with which the state ratifying conventions discussed the presidency. No doubt this is attributable to the careful and specific enumeration of the president's full powers. In South Carolina, Charles Pinckney reported that "we have defined his powers, and bound him to such limits, as will effectually prevent his usurping authority." That view was echoed by James Iredell in North Carolina and by James Bowdoin in Massachusetts, who said the president's powers were "precisely those of the governors."

And the powers of the governors were strictly limited. The Virginia Constitution of 1776, for example, stated that the governor shall "exercise the executive powers of government, according to the laws of the Commonwealth; and shall not, under any pretense, exercise any power or prerogative, by virtue of any law, statute, or custom of England." Thomas Jefferson, in his "Draft of a Fundamental Constitution for Virginia," written in 1783 and partially inspired by the excesses of the Virginia legislature, explained: "By Executive powers, we mean no reference to those powers exercised under our former government by the Crown as of its prerogatives. . . . We give to them these powers only, which are necessary to execute the laws (and administer the government)." In short, as James Madison said, state executives across the land were "little more than Cyphers."

It was in this context that the framers designed the office of the presidency. Executive powers amounted to little more than the duty to execute the laws and the right to appoint various officers. There is no intimation in the records of the Constitutional Convention or of the state ratifying conventions that executive power includes the right to make war.

A review of the proceedings in the Constitutional Convention and in the ratifying conventions leads to the conclusion that the war-making power, including the authority to initiate both limited and general war, was vested in Congress. The record establishes that neither the commander-in-chief clause nor the executive-power clause affords support for the claim that the president is empowered to commence hostilities. Indeed, such authority was specifically withheld from the president. That this was the settled understanding of the war power is suggested by the statements of the founding generation, by the views of eminent writers, by early judicial decisions, and by nineteenth-century practice.

The president is generally considered the leader of not only the United States but of the entire noncommunist world. The political scientist Richard Rose shows that recent changes in world politics make it clear that a president neglects or misjudges the rest of the world—friend and enemy alike—at his and his country's peril.

Questions

1. What are the characteristics of the "postmodern" presidency? How does the postmodern presidency differ from the so-called "modern" presidency? How does it differ from the "traditional" presidency?

2. "A postmodern President cannot ignore foreigners when making foreign policy," Rose concludes. Why not?

12.4 The Future of the Postmodern Presidency _____

Richard Rose

As the world closes in on the White House, it is not surprising that some people want to turn their backs on what is happening and be isolated from the world, as in the days of President Ulysses S. Grant. Even so cosmopolitan a policymaker as Henry Kissinger once evoked the language of romantic isolationism:

> Americans admire the cowboy leading the caravan alone astride his horse, the cowboy entering a village or city alone on his horse. Without even a pistol, maybe, because he doesn't go in for shooting. He acts, that's all, aiming at the right spot at the right time. . . . I've always acted alone.

The heroism of a cowboy, whether riding the western plains or the situation room of the White House, has little effect on a world in which the cowboy's enemies can use their political radar to track him riding into their line of sight. A contemporary President can no more escape the implications of interdependence than European Prime Ministers could do so after the end of World War II. In an open international system, the White House *must* learn to get along with other elephants.

Misperceiving the World about Us

Because foreign policy begins at home, each national government perceives the world differently. What it sees—and what it tries to ignore—reflects its institutions, culture, and international commitments. As long as America existed in splendid isolation, it mattered little what America thought. When America could dominate the international system, other nations had to attend to Washington first. As America's influence on other nations becomes less certain, it is more important for Washingtonians to heed Neustadt's dictum: "Influential action turns on accurate perception."

Changes within the United States are making it harder to perceive accurately America's place in the world. For most of American history, the East Coast was politically central, and American foreign policy was oriented toward Europe. The bulk of America's population was in the Northeast, and New York was the home of the foreign policy elite. The shift from the traditional to the modern Presidency was accompanied by a reversal of roles. Instead of America needing defense from Europe, America became central to the defense of Europe. The transition to the postmodern Presidency has been contemporaneous with a dramatic shift in the balance of the American electorate from the Frostbelt to the Sunbelt. In the Sunbelt, Caribbean and Latin American nations are closest in every sense; in the Southwest, Mexico and Mexicans are near at hand; and the Pacific Coast faces toward Japan and the rest of Asia. Immigration and trade give the Sunbelt a very different outlook on the world. A President who seeks to speak for America can do so by turning to Europe, to Latin America, or to Japan and Asia. In each instance, he can be speaking for a different part of America.

In the past quarter-century, tens of millions of Americans have traveled to all corners of the earth. But just as George Bernard Shaw once described America and Britain as two countries separated by a common language, so Americans and citizens of other nations can easily misperceive what they see. We would not want Europeans to judge America by cowboy films or *Rambo*, or citizens of Soviet or Third World nations to draw conclusions about this country from viewing "Dallas" or *The Grapes of Wrath*. So we should hesitate before judging other countries on the basis of package tours designed to provide all the comforts of home. Understanding foreign countries requires empathy, the psychological ability to put yourself in other people's shoes. Now that America cannot rely on hegemonic power, White House representatives need more empathy with foreigners.

Most people close to the President lack experience in dealing with foreign nations. White House jobs are held because of campaign credentials or skills in going Washington. The first test of a national security assistant to the President is who he knows; the confidence of the President is essential in doing the job. The frequent use of military personnel as National Security Council staff ensures that the White House has people who understand the Pentagon well. Nothing in the Naval Academy education of Vice Admiral John Poindexter and Lieutenant Colonel Oliver North prepared them for conducting negotiations with Iran. No one

in the United States thinks it unusual that ambassadors to many foreign countries are ignorant of the country to which they are going. To argue that such ambassadors teach foreigners to understand how American politics works does not encourage foreign confidence in Washington.

Lack of knowledge of foreign countries does not mean lack of intelligence; it reflects a lack of experience outside the Beltway or outside the United States. People rise high in Washington because they are good at something, whether it is playing games with the federal budget, attracting favorable media publicity, or attending to very important persons. The typical high-ranking government official sees his job as knowing Washington inside out. Any travel, whether it involves going public or going international, is related to promoting policies and positions held within the Beltway. If it will help the President to see the Pope or the Emperor of Japan, then many people will volunteer to take their first trip to Rome or Tokyo to make advance plans for a meeting. If it won't, they don't.

The White House is not the only American institution that looks inward when making decisions about the rest of the world. Although America has many multinational corporations, boards of directors are usually not multinational. Ford, General Motors, IBM, and Mobil Oil are four of the world's largest corporations, selling from a third to one-half their output abroad. Yet, none of these companies has had a non-American on its board of directors. When such firms send senior officials abroad, the impression often left with foreign colleagues is that they do not understand how other cultures work: "They are like snails; they carry their house with them wherever they go." Other countries understand how America works; for example, it is the basis of their success in boosting imports to the United States.

To paraphrase the late Andy Warhol, any country can be famous in Washington for fifteen minutes; all that is required is to attack Americans violently and dramatically. This will gain instant attention in the White House and in the national media. A British journalist in Washington notes:

> There always seems to be one story in America; it may be the Middle East, or Central America, or the economy. When one disappears, another pops up. People run out of interest very quickly. Suddenly something else becomes the story. Radio-TV news bulletins concentrate on one or two topics; the rest of the world is ignored.

If knowledge is power, then ignorance is a source of weakness. Fred Bergsten describes the consequences for international economic policy: "Each administration either fails to learn the lessons of its predecessors or consciously chooses to ignore these lessons. Each thus has to proceed through a disruptive shift from one policy extreme to another." Learning from failure is an increasingly expensive form of education for everyone involved, and especially for the United States.

The World Watches Washington

Politicians in other countries are experienced watchers of America, for they have grown up in an era in which American hegemony was a fact of their existence. For example, Japanese Prime Minister Noboru Takeshita and German Chancellor Helmut Kohl each entered politics after their country was under American occupation. European Prime Ministers often find that the only language that they have in common is English. Leaders in other nations watch Washington to see what actions they can or should take in their own national interest. A cosmopolitan American journalist concludes:

> The result is an astonishing asymmetry: The minutiae of American politics and society are followed compulsively by others as a critical component of life in the real world, while the U.S. government and individual American citizens seem to show an ever declining knowledge of and interest in everyone else.

Although a President may consider himself too busy to pay attention to what other nations do in the international economy, foreigners never cease watching the American economy. At every hour of the day and night, foreign exchange dealers somewhere—in Zurich or London, in Tokyo or Hong Kong—are trying to make a quick profit by speculating on the fluctuating value of the dollar against other currencies. Oil-rich nations that invest their surplus capital in dollar accounts in American banks are watching to see what happens to their wealth, and Third World countries that have borrowed more money from American banks than they can repay are watching to see if there is anything that the American government will or can do to help them.

The foreign media cover Washington intensively, but not as Washington hands expect. When Stephen Hess conducted an analysis of foreign press reporting, he assumed that foreigners would normally not be interested in American events for their own sake. Hess thought foreigners would seek what Americans often seek abroad, a local angle, that is, stories that directly linked their country with the United States, for example, "Greek Immigrant's Son Runs for President." This is not the case. Foreign papers report the stories that are big inside Washington, for such is the global significance of American politics that anything important in Washington, such as a change in the budget deficit, is also news abroad.

Foreign nations that follow Washington closely can act as political arbitrageurs, profiting from the difference between their knowledge of Washington and White House attention to them. Because of America's trade deficit with Japan, the Japanese Prime Minister must try to appease American critics of its trade policy, and this requires keeping informed about what is going on at both ends of Pennsylvania Avenue. The Japanese media maintain far more English-speaking journalists in Washington than the American media has Japanese-speaking journalists in Tokyo. By understanding American politics, the Japanese government can time statements in Tokyo and trips to Washington to influence trade protection measures being debated inside the Beltway. A Japanese politician can trade on the asymmetry of understanding by delivering more substance in Tokyo and more symbolic reassurances in Washington.

The Iran-*contra* affair is a textbook example of how actions of the White House are followed carefully abroad, and how foreign arbitrageurs profit, both politically and financially. The arms that Iran obtained for use in its war against Iraq were acquired because Teheran understood the White House, weaknesses and all. Accounts of the Iran-*contra* affair were read carefully in the Middle East. One photograph symbolized this, showing a guerrilla fighter in Beirut momentarily resting, his weapon at hand, reading *Time* magazine's cover story about the testimony of Lieutenant Colonel Oliver North. In Europe, straightforward reporting of what was said at congressional hearings inevitably showed American foreign policy in an unfavorable light. A middle-of-the-road London paper, *The Independent* (3 August 1987), simply quoted the judgment of Senator Daniel Inouye, chairman of the special investigating committee on the Iran-*contra* affair: "This was a rather sordid chapter in our history, a chapter of lies and deceit and deception. I just hope that it will not happen again. But I suppose it will."

Foreign allies of the United States see these faults but take no pleasure in evidence of blunders and weakness in the White House. Former British Prime Minister James Callaghan commented on the Iran-*contra* affair: "A disabled President is as much a weakness and danger to Europe as to his own country. And although there will be occasions and policies on which we shall differ, Europe needs him to be effective while he holds his great office."

Nations long accustomed to living with interdependence want the White House to recognize that interdependence is a two-way street. The White House risks rebuffs if it does not consult with allies. The ability of other nations not to accept direction from a postmodern President is illustrated by the Reagan administration's failure to prevent Europeans from importing natural gas from the Soviet Union via a lengthy pipeline from Siberia. In the wake of the 1973 and 1979 oil price shocks, a group of European nations, including Germany, France, and Italy, negotiated an agreement to import gas from Siberia in order to reduce their dependence on the Middle East, and as a potential contribution to improved East-West relations. By the test of the market, a favorite catchword in Ronald Reagan's Washington, the agreement made sense. The Reagan administration, however, tended to view such trade as a boost to the Soviets—except for grain exports, which Reagan endorsed as a candidate when bidding for the farm vote in 1980.

The White House decided it would punish the Soviet Union by opposing the construction of the natural gas pipeline to Western Europe. When the Siberian gas pipeline was treated as a test case of America's power to control European allies, the White House failed the test. The administration unilaterally extended restrictions imposed on American firms exporting equipment for the pipeline and on foreign companies holding licenses from American firms. European governments ordered their firms to continue supplying the goods, on the grounds that contractual commitments of traders should be honored. European governments continued to believe that the trade made sense, and did not want to bow to unilateral White House action. A European Community statement rejected Washington's opposition thus:

> This action, taken without any consultation with the Community, implies an extra-territorial extension of the U.S. jurisdiction which, in the circumstances, is contrary to the principles of international law, unacceptable to the Community and unlikely to be recognized in courts in the European Economic Community.

In November 1982, President Reagan lifted sanctions that had never been observed. A detailed study of the frustration of the White House concluded:

> A fact of life in the Western alliance is that no one member can issue marching orders to the others. To do so would be to make the alliance

indistinguishable from the Warsaw Pact, which is based on a relationship of intimidation and domination decreed by the Soviet doctrine of limited sovereignty. Alliance policy, in short, must be the product of compromise, not coercion.

For the Soviet Union, a crisis of confidence in Washington is an opportunity for action. In a period of *glasnost,* Mikhail Gorbachev can approach Western European leaders with proposals that appear attractive—if they can be believed. Concurrently, the United States is seen in a less favorable light. For example, in autumn 1987, a four-nation survey found that 62 percent of Americans trusted President Reagan more than Mikhail Gorbachev to reduce cold-war tensions. By contrast, less than one-quarter of Britons, French, and Germans trusted President Reagan more. Consistent with the growth in self-confidence among European leaders, the largest group in Britain, France, and Germany trusted neither foreign leader.

A postmodern President cannot ignore foreigners when making foreign policy, for other nations are checks and balances on America's actions in the international system, and can send shocks through the system, impelling the President to react to problems he would prefer to ignore. Just because a presidential representative may be ignorant or inexperienced does not mean that foreign representatives are similarly uninformed. For example, a presidential appointee negotiating with the Soviet Union about technology learned that it was unusual for the Russians to meet the same American official at the negotiating table for two successive years, whereas Russian officials had continuity. The moral was clear: "They know everything about us, and we are learning about them. That puts us at a terrible disadvantage, however good our people are."

The Future of the Postmodern President

At the signing of the Declaration of Independence, Benjamin Franklin recognized the interdependence of thirteen separate colonies, saying: "We must indeed all hang together, or most assuredly we shall all hang separately." Today, the question is not whether nations will hang together, but how.

There is plenty of goodwill between Washington and leaders of other major nations, for Prime Ministers are as aware as Presidents that their nation's fate is greatly influenced by what happens in the international system. Between the United States, Germany, and Japan, relations are particularly close. In national security, Germany and Japan are each front-line nations, only a few miles from Soviet troops in East Germany or in Siberia, and American troops provide front-line defense to Germany and Japan. The economic interdependence of America, Germany, and Japan is great too, but the terms of the relationship are reversed. Japan and Germany are major exporters, whereas the United States now runs a very large trade deficit. Germany and Japan have currencies that are strong, inflation is low, and savings and investment are high. The American economy is in the opposite shape; the dollar is weak, savings and investment are very low, and the trade and budget deficits increase the risk of inflation. Given interdependence, political decisions affecting the American economy can now be taken in Bonn and Tokyo, as well as in Washington.

Interdependence need not mean cooperation. There are politicians, such as former President Richard M. Nixon, who still believe that the White House enjoys the powers of two decades ago.

> Some say we are entering a period of collective leadership in the West, that because the United States has lagged in economic growth and lost its military supremacy, we are going to have to consult our more prosperous allies and defer to them in the search for a Western consensus. This is nonsense. Consult, of course. But unless the United States leads, nobody will. And unless the President leads, nobody will.

While Ronald Reagan is a postmodern President, he often has not recognized the need for cooperation with other countries financing his deficits. President Reagan has seen the American economy purely in domestic terms, and his domestic political line is "Tax increases will only occur over my dead body."

Noncooperation can cut both ways. British Prime Minister Margaret Thatcher and French President François Mitterrand have each had to take politically unpopular steps to resolve economic problems created by their fiscal mistakes. Each can ask the question: Why should we have sympathy with an American President who claims to be too weak to take unpopular decisions that we have had to take? There is little sympathy abroad when the United States appears to be calling for expansionary policies in Japan and Europe simply to help solve its own problems. The Japanese and Europeans are inclined to respond that since American policies have caused international monetary instability, the solution to the problem must be found in Washington. Nor does any nation want to sacrifice its export markets or export-led growth simply to enable the next President to look good by a reduction in the United States trade deficit.

"If you can't beat them, join them" is an old American adage. Since 1985 Treasury Secretary Baker has been meeting with his counterparts of other major nations in an effort to resolve worldwide economic problems. But financial leaders in other nations have learned that an agreement with the secretary of the U.S. Treasury is not an agreement with the government of the United States. Treasury reflects the position of only one subgovernment in an open market for policy. The White House and Congress have continued to demonstrate the difficulty of agreeing to a coherent economic policy, as can be done in a parliamentary system. Moreover, economists themselves disagree about what the government should do, and about how certain their advice is to produce benefits from international economic policy coordination.

Writing two decades ago, Richard Neustadt described a modern President as enjoying a "wide latitude for ignorance; it scarcely seemed to matter whether we guessed right or wrong." The hegemonic power of the United States meant that allies would have to accept whatever the White House chose to do. For a postmodern President, ignorance is a luxury. Just as going Washington and going public have become increasingly linked, so the line between what was once considered domestic politics (e.g., grain prices in Iowa) and foreign policy (negotiations with the Soviet Union) has dissolved. Increasing pressure from the international system on the United States makes the White House even more the focal point for the linkage of international and domestic politics.

As the world closes in on the White House, the scope and range of the President's concerns widen, while the influence of the White House in the international system is not so certain as before. To make interdependence work on behalf of the United States does not require novel policies. The measures needed to deal with deficits in the economy and adapt national security to the 1990s are in principle similar to those taken by other major nations. Nor is a radical transformation of American society required. As Calleo emphasizes: "Solutions that call for heroic changes in American character and practice seem less promising than solutions proposing that America adapt itself to the real world."

When John F. Kennedy spoke a quarter-century ago of America paying any price to assure the survival of liberty, the price was measured both in dollars and in military force. The United States was then the banker of the world. Dollars went abroad for profitable investments, as foreign aid to underdeveloped countries, and to support military alliances. The United States was also the supreme military force in the world.

The price that a postmodern President must pay is different: It is the price of abandoning illusions. The biggest illusion is the belief that we can turn the clock back to the era when Franklin D. Roosevelt created the modern Presidency, and Dwight D. Eisenhower could rely on American wealth and military force to sustain a global *Pax Americana*. All the rhetoric of a

Kennedy, the wheeling and dealing of a Johnson, and the imperial ambitions of a Nixon, could not maintain American dominance indefinitely. The modern Presidency was an institution of the American century, an era that lasted only a few decades after 1945.

A new century has now commenced, based on global interdependence. America's hegemonic influence is not sufficient to last to the year 2000. In this new era, the postmodern President is even more important, for the Oval Office is the best place to see the links between the international system and America's domestic concerns. While responsibilities are larger, resources are fewer, for the White House is now palpably subject to checks and balances on every continent. In this new world of interdependence, there is much less latitude for ignorance and luck. The postmodern President depends on power armed by an understanding of how the world now works.

IV  INTERCONNECTIONS

In his influential book Presidential Power, *the political scientist Richard Neustadt concluded that the essence of presidential power is "the power to persuade," which, as he put it, "is the power to bargain." All of the president's formal powers, Neustadt wrote, are useless if he cannot convince others, including his own subordinates, that "what the White House wants of them is what they ought to do for their sake and on their authority to do his will." Obviously, as Neustadt suggested, "a President's authority and status give him great advantages in dealing with the men he would persuade"—most important, because those whom the president must persuade are likely both to need and fear him. But presidential bargaining and persuasion is a two-way street; presidents do not have unlimited power and often must convince Congress and their own subordinates to do their bidding.*

In selection 12.4, Neustadt explains his theory. In selection 12.5, veteran Washington reporter Hedrick Smith advises presidents on how they can maximize their advantage when bargaining with and trying to persuade the Congress.

Questions

1. What advantages does a president have in the bargaining process? Does he have any significant disadvantages when dealing with Congress? with the bureaucracy?

2. What circumstances increase a president's ability to build coalitions in Congress? What circumstances hurt the president's attempts to build such coalitions?

12.5 Presidential Power

Richard Neustadt

The separateness of institutions and the sharing of authority prescribe the terms on which a President persuades. When one man shares authority with another, but does not gain or lose his job upon the other's whim, his willingness to act upon the urging of the other turns on whether he conceives the action right for him. The essence of a President's persuasive task is to convince such men that what the White House wants of them is what they ought to do for their sake and on their authority.

Persuasive power, thus defined, amounts to more than charm or reasoned argument. These have their uses for a President, but these are not the whole of his resources. For the men he would induce to do what he wants done on their own responsibility will need or fear some acts by him on his responsibility. If they share his authority, he has some share in theirs. Presidential "powers" may be inconclusive when a President commands, but always remain relevant as he persuades. The status and authority inherent in his office reinforce his logic and his charm.

Status adds something to persuasiveness; authority adds still more. When Truman urged wage changes on his Secretary of Commerce while the latter was administering the steel mills, he and Secretary [Charles] Sawyer were not just two men reasoning with one another. Had they been so, Sawyer probably would never have agreed to act. Truman's status gave him special claims to Sawyer's loyalty, or at least attention. In Walter Bagehot's charming phrase "no man can *argue* on his knees." Although there is no kneeling in this country, few men—and exceedingly few Cabinet officers—are immune to the impulse to say "yes" to the President of the United States. It grows harder to say "no" when they are seated in his oval office at the White House, or in his study on the second floor, where almost tangibly he partakes of the aura of his physical surroundings. In Sawyer's case, moreover, the President possessed formal authority to intervene in many matters of concern to the Secretary of Commerce. These matters ranged from jurisdictional disputes among the defense agencies to legislation pending before Congress and, ultimately, to the tenure of the Secretary, himself. There is nothing in the record to suggest that Truman voiced specific threats when they negotiated over wage increases. But given his *formal* powers and their relevance to Sawyer's other interests, it is safe to assume that Truman's very advocacy of wage action conveyed an implicit threat.

A President's authority and status give him great advantages in dealing with the men he would persuade. Each "power" is a vantage point for him in the degree that other men have use for his authority. From the veto to appointments, from publicity to budgeting, and so down a long list, the White House now controls the most encompassing array of vantage points in the American political system. With hardly an exception, the men who share in governing this country are aware that at some time, in some degree, the doing of *their* jobs, the furthering of *their* ambitions, may depend upon the President of the United States. Their need for presidential action, or their fear of it, is bound to be recurrent if not actually continuous. Their need or fear is his advantage.

A President's advantages are greater than mere listing of his "powers" might suggest. The men with whom he deals must deal with him until the last day of his term. Because they have continuing relationships with him, his future, while it lasts, supports his present influence. Even though there is no need or fear of him today, what he could do tomorrow may supply today's advantage. Continuing relationships may convert any "power," any aspect of his status, into vantage points in almost any case. When he induces other men to do what he wants done, a President can trade on their dependence now *and* later.

The President's advantages are checked by the advantages of others. Continuing relationships will pull in both directions. These are relationships of mutual dependence. A President depends upon the men he would persuade; he has to reckon with his need or fear of them. They too will possess status, or authority, or both, else they would be of little use to him. Their vantage points confront his own; their power tempers his.

Persuasion is a two-way street. Saywer, it will be recalled, did not respond at once to Truman's plan for wage increases at the steel mills. On the contrary, the Secretary hesitated and delayed and only acquiesced when he was satisfied that publicly he would not bear the onus of decision. Sawyer had some points of vantage all his own from which to resist presidential pressure. If he had to reckon with coercive implications in the President's "situations of strength," so had Truman to be mindful of the implications underlying Sawyer's place as a department head, as steel administrator, and as a Cabinet spokesman for business. Loyalty is reciprocal. Having taken on a dirty job in the steel crisis, Sawyer had strong claims to loyal support. Besides, he had authority to do some things that the White House could ill afford. Emulating Wilson, he might have resigned in a huff (the removal power also works two ways).

Or . . . he might have declined to sign necessary orders. Or, he might have let it be known publicly that he deplored what he was told to do and protested its doing. By following any of these courses Sawyer almost surely would have strengthened the position of management, weakened the position of the White House, and embittered the union. But the whole purpose of a wage increase was to enhance White House persuasiveness in urging settlement upon union and companies alike. Although Sawyer's status and authority did not give him the power to prevent an increase outright, they gave him capability to undermine its purpose. If his authority over wage rates had been vested by a statute, not by revocable presidential order, his power of prevention might have been complete. . . .

The power to persuade is the power to bargain. Status and authority yield bargaining advantages. But in a government of "separated institutions sharing powers," they yield them to all sides. With the array of vantage points at his disposal, a President may be far more persuasive than his logic or his charm could make him. But outcomes are not guaranteed by his advantages. There remain the counter pressures those whom he would influence can bring to bear on him from vantage points at their disposal. Command has limited utility; persuasion becomes give-and-take. It is well that the White House holds the vantage points it does. In such a business any President may need them all—and more.

12.6 *The Coalition Game*

Hedrick Smith

The coalition game—building coalitions and making coalitions work—is the heart of our system of government. Although the coalition game is usually ignored during the passions of American election campaigns, no president can succeed unless he can build a governing coalition. For limited periods, presidents can act on their own: devaluing the dollar as Nixon did, negotiating an arms treaty with Moscow as Carter did, sending American Marines into Lebanon or working secret arms deals with Iran as Reagan did. But eventually a president must come to Congress to fund his programs, approve his treaties, finance his wars, or sanction his secret diplomacy. If he cannot bring Congress along—cannot form a governing coalition—his programs founder, his treaty must be shelved, the Marines must come home, his diplomacy must halt. Coalitions are the necessary engines for sustaining policies.

• • •

[*Ronald Reagan, in his first year in office, tried to convince Congress to pass two key measures: a major package of budget reductions and a large tax cut. The coalition he sought to build consisted of conservative Republicans, conservative southern Democrats ("Boll Weevils"), and liberal northern Republicans ("Gypsy Moths").*]

Reagan, in his first, most triumphant year, chose to build his coalition with partisan hardball, not with Eisenhower-style bipartisan compromise. In 1981, Reagan did woo conservative southern Democrats and get some to vote with him against their own congressional party leadership. But Republican unity was Reagan's Gibraltar. This is the primary lesson of American politics—rule number one of the coalition game: *Secure your political base first.* Much was required for Reagan's first-year coalition: the president's wide popular appeal, his knack for lobbying Congress, some tough grass-roots politicking, and of course a winning idea to rally a coalition. But Republican unity was the anchor. With unity forged by Howard Baker and House Republican Leader Bob Michel of Illinois, Reagan made his legislative mark. Without that unity, he would have been destined to one-term mediocrity.

Republican solidarity was far from preordained, nor did it endure. In 1980, Reagan had run against Washington; he had been the populist candidate attacking the system, the radical western Republican overthrowing his party's mainstream eastern establishment, the citizen outsider mocking the inside political game. Now inside this den of power, he needed allies.

Historically, American presidents have turned to their political parties to rally support. But years of revolt and reform in the late 1960s and 1970s had weakened the cohesion of the American party system. Congress had been torn asunder, faction by faction, region by region, interest by interest. Congressional leaders had little patronage to bind followers to them. Many members ran almost independent of party. As Reagan came to power, few people prized the vital cohesion offered by parties, which for so long had served as crucibles of compromise and pulled together coalitions.

• • •

Rule number two in forming a functioning coalition: *Inculcate the mind-set of governing.* It is a subtle, intangible notion—one that comes naturally to parties long in power, but not to parties long out of power. Without that governing mind-set, little can be accomplished in our system; parties clash, factions stalemate each other, individual members of Congress push their agendas, selfish interests overwhelm the common interest, and the machinery of government is immobilized.

Fortunately, politics is like sports: There are electric moments which transform group psychology, dramatically altering the dynamics of the game. When the lead suddenly changes hands, emotions swing from one team to another. Elan soars; partisan juices flow; the other side is thrown off balance. A team or a party, once faltering, gains inspiration; it is suddenly energized. Riding a collective high, individual players pick up tempo and confidence. Shrewd leaders keep the roll going. Winning generates its own momentum.

• • •

It takes more than enthusiasm to consolidate power. In the king of the hill game, rule number three is: *Strike quickly for a win, during the early rush of power.* That helps establish momentum and an aura of success. Lyndon Johnson had a colorful maxim for such moments. "Johnson operated under the philosophy with Congress—if you're not doing it to them, they're doing it to you. And frequently, he used a more vivid word than *doing*," recalled Douglass Cater, one of Johnson's White House advisers.

Copyright, 1990, *Boston Globe*. Distributed by Los Angeles Times Syndicate.
Reprinted by permission.

Winning is power, was the gut summation given me by Jim Baker. "I've always felt that it is extremely important in terms of a president's power—power as opposed to popularity—that presidents succeed on the Hill with what they undertake up there," Baker asserted. "And I really believe that one reason that Ronald Reagan has been so successful is that he succeeded in the high-profile issues that he jumped on in the first term. The way presidents govern is to translate their philosophy into policy by working with Congress. That's why Carter failed in my view. Because he never learned that lesson."

• • •

Success in the coalition game depends enormously on presidential influence with the individual members of Congress; a president can pull enough reluctant votes his way if he has the right political touch. It is an old maxim of politics that an effective leader, mayor, governor, and above all, president, must be both loved and feared. That is how a president marshals support from his natural followers and deters attack from his natural enemies. Issues

matter, of course, but so does human chemistry. A president has to make clear there are benefits for supporting him and consequences for opposing him.

No one understood this better than Lyndon Johnson, who was masterful at ferreting out the weak points and deepest hungers of other politicians. Yet Johnson was so blatantly Machiavellian that it hampered him. He made it hard for people to go along and still retain their dignity and independence. Carter had the opposite problem. Arm-twisting and deal-making were not his forte. When he tried to act strong, he often came across as mean and willful because exaggerated forcefulness was out of character.

At bottom, Carter seemed ill at ease with power, and ill at ease hobnobbing with other politicians. He immersed himself in substance but despised wheeling and dealing with Congress. Many a senator or House member told me that Carter was awkward or hesitant about asking directly for his or her vote. He frowned on horse-trading. Only from painful experience did he learn the value of doing little favors for other politicians. Both his intellect and his engineer's training at Annapolis made him impatient with that vital lubrication of the wheels of legislation: making other politicians feel important.

• • •

Rule number four in the coalition game: *Lavish attention on the Washington power structure.* Democrats were flattered to be courted. Republicans were tickled to walk away with a Reagan story to retell, or some Reagan cuff links, or tickets to the presidential box at the Kennedy Center.

For a man who, like Carter, had run his campaign against Washington, Reagan did a quick 180-degree turn in catering to the Washington establishment. He mounted a mellow social and political campaign that set a Dale Carnegie (*How to Win Friends and Influence People*) standard. Shelving his campaign rhetoric, Reagan played the gracious outsider eager to win acceptance inside the beltway.

• • •

In sum, Reagan's confection of charm and deference seduced the citadels of power before the political battles began. He not only demonstrated that the presidency was now in the hands of an experienced politician, he also calmed the animal instincts of other politicians that his campaign had aroused. His charm treatment disarmed skeptics who had conjured him as a warmonger and a rabid ideologue.

• • •

In the making of a majority coalition, a new president has the great advantage of casting his first major legislative proposal as a personal test of confidence in his presidency. The key to this strategy is rule number five of the coalition game: *Make the president himself the issue, as much as the substance of his proposals.* That strategy immediately puts the congressional opposition on the defensive. It makes voting against the new president almost like repudiating the results of the election just finished, which many politicians are loath to do.

Reagan was doubly armed for this strategy by his election victory and by surging public

sympathy after the attempt on his life. Communications Director David Gergen shrewdly proposed that Reagan capitalize on the outpouring of public goodwill to make what amounted to a second Inaugural Address in 1981, to a joint session of Congress on April 28. It was a very powerful gambit. I remember Reagan that evening, striding confidently into the House, the picture of manly vigor and purpose, bathed in applause, acknowledging it with a frisky toss of his head. Democrats as well as Republicans were cheered by his recovery, warmed by his ruddy good humor. The country was so pro-Reagan then that it was easy for Reagan's lieutenants to frame virtually every vote for another hundred days on Reagan personally: Are you with Reagan or against him?

• • •

Rule number six: *Building a governing coalition hinges on a close working link between the president's top strategist and his party's congressional leaders.* The failures of Carter's aides, Hamilton Jordan and Frank Moore, demonstrated the cost of ignoring this link. In 1985, Reagan paid a high price for touchy relations between his new chief of staff, Don Regan, and Bob Dole, the new Senate majority leader. In his first term, Reagan has superb legislative liaisons led by Max Friedersdorf, a smooth diplomat from the Ford White House, and Ken Duberstein, an amiable, voluble political persuader, who worked the House. Reagan had a warm personal relationship with Howard Baker. But the crucial working alliance was between the two Bakers, Howard and Jim, who were constantly in touch. . . .

Both Jim and Howard Baker—no relation to each other—are mainstream Republicans, temperamentally disposed to compromise and to making the legislative system work. Both Bakers have that vital sense of what was politically doable and what was not. They loyally carried Reagan's water in public, but they argued with him in private, trying to save him from lost causes. Their pragmatic cast of mind made them natural allies and natural coalition makers. Neither was a true Reaganite; both had worked for

Gerald Ford against Reagan in 1976 and had initially opposed Reagan in 1980. They had ties with other Republicans and could widen the circle of Reagan's support. Indeed, if it had been left to hard-core Reaganite ideologues such as Edwin Meese, William Clark, Lyn Nofziger, or Pat Buchanan to pass the first Reagan program, it probably would have been defeated. For ideological rigidity can derail even a partisan coalition, and both Bakers were masterful at bending at the margins and helping Reagan corral the final few votes needed for victory.

• • •

Rule number seven of the coalition game is: *Use the muscle of the president's nationwide political apparatus to swing votes into line for his legislative coalition.* . . . In the game of political persuasion, the Reagan White House took no chances. It played outside as well as inside politics, and it played hardball. . . .

The Reagan team, working like a presidential campaign, generated direct mail, phone banks, radio and television ads, and sent out top speakers to put heat on targeted congressmen. They mobilized the Republican National Committee, Republican Congressional Campaign Committee, National Conservative Political Action Committee, Moral Majority, Fund for a Conservative Majority, and political action committees linked to the U.S. Chamber of Commerce, National Association of Manufacturers, Business Roundtable, American Medical Association, and scores of groups interested in cutting federal spending and taxes.

"The premise of the whole operation is that political reforms and the impact of media have made it so that a congressman's behavior on legislation can be affected more by pressure from within his own district than by lobbying here in Washington," Atwater told me during the operation. "The way we operate, within forty-eight hours any congressman will know he has had a major strike in his district. All of a sudden, Vice President Bush is in your district; Congressman Jack Kemp is in your district. Ten of your top contributors are calling you, the head of the local AMA, the head of the local

realtors' group, local officials. Twenty letters come in. Within forty-eight hours, you're hit by paid media, free media, mail, phone calls, all asking you to support the president."

• • •

Forming the coalition is only the first step; sustaining it long enough to lock up final legislative victory is much harder. In the American system, victory rarely ends the fight—it marks the start of the next battle. This time, it was not Reagan's charm treatment or the grass-roots blitz that rescued the Reagan coalition. It was old-fashioned, Lyndon Johnson–style barter politics: buying votes by doling out favors— what some call "running the soup kitchen." Rule number eight: *Bend at the margins and wheedle votes where you can; don't get hung up on ideological purity.*

Reagan's battle was not over because entrenched committees of Congress resorted to intricate, arcane maneuvers to undo the effects of that first budget vote. The reconciliation measure passed required implementing by regular committees, and they had a field day with the fine print of the legislation, molding it their way. The White House was shocked to see conservative Republicans and Boll Weevils engaging in legislative chicanery along with liberal Democrats, all protecting their favorite programs. Many of the "cuts" enacted were empty numbers that reduced spending only in theory.

"Sabotage!" shouted David Stockman, himself no slouch at fudging budget numbers and tilting estimates when it suited him. In June 1981, he accused the committees of shady bookkeeping, false arithmetic, and phony cutbacks. Pro-Reagan Republicans and the Congressional Budget Office estimated that House committees cut $55 billion for the year 1984, but Stockman reckoned only $25 billion was valid.

In alarm, Stockman persuaded the president that he had to send another whole budget to Congress. "The committees have broken faith with the first budget resolution." Stockman told Reagan in mid-June. "It could jeopardize your entire economic program. We have to make a major fight to restore the provisions in your first budget. If you want to balance the budget in '84, you can't live with the cuts they've made."

Stockman secretly prepared a massive new reconciliation measure, a line-by-line substitute for the congressional bill. It was a high-handed tactic, because Congress—not the budget bureau—is supposed to draft money bills. It meant rejecting the congressional bills and making a fresh effort. Reagan went along with the plan, still counting on one up-or-down vote and the pull of his own popularity to preserve his coalition.

But it was now summer and the Reagan coalition had begun to fray. Moral appeals were not enough to restore it. The White House was short of votes. Gypsy Moths were threatening to bolt unless some modest programs favored in the urban East and Midwest were restored. New York's Bill Green wanted $50 million more for the National Endowment for the Arts, a higher cap on Medicaid for the poor, and guaranteed student loans provided to more families; Jim Leach of Iowa sought $100 million in family planning; Carl Pursell of Michigan wanted $30 million for nurses' training. Others wanted $100 million more for Amtrak and Conrail, another $400 million in energy subsidies for the poor, restoration of economic development grants, and so on. The White House paid their price to get their votes for the final budget package.

The Boll Weevils were demanding sweeteners, too. Georgia Democrats got state-owned cotton warehouses exempted from a new user fee. Some $400 million in cuts of veterans' programs were restored to satisfy Mississippi's Sonny Montgomery, a powerhouse for veterans. Louisiana's John Breaux was lured aboard with a promise to revive sugar import quotas to protect his home state.

"I went for the best deal," Breaux crassly admitted afterward. He maintained his vote had not been bought but—he confessed—"I was rented."

The bargaining was like stock-market bidding, right to the wire. Ironically, to get votes, Stockman had to trade back to Congress things he had objected to in mid-June. The final budget was such a rush job that it reached the floor *after the debate began*, and it mistakenly listed the name and phone number of a congressional staffer—"Rita Seymour, 555-4844"—which someone had scribbled in the margin of a draft copy. Clearly, no one had proofread the retyped version.

The critical test vote came on procedure, not substance. House Democratic leaders tried to outmaneuver the power of Reagan's single up-or-down vote. They figured Reagan's budget would be tougher to pass if it were broken into five packages, forcing Gypsy Moth Republicans and Boll Weevil Democrats to be counted on separate votes—and some of those votes were bound to be unpopular back home. Hoping to break up the Reagan coalition that way, Democratic leaders fashioned a procedural rule which divided the budget into five separate packages.

It was an ingenious tactic, but it backfired, because members wanted to avoid the wrath of constituents who were telling them: Cut the budget, but save our programs. One big vote spared House members that dilemma; it was politically easier to handle. (Rule number nine of the coalition game: *Make votes politically easy.*) Once the big package of cuts was fixed, members could not both cut the budget and save local programs; they had only one choice: yes or no. Since budget cutting was generally popular, they could justify swallowing some distasteful cuts. The Democratic tactic would expose members to cross-pressures to both cut and save programs; so it rankled many House members. As a result, the Gypsy Moths backed Reagan and just enough Boll Weevils defected to beat the Democratic procedural rule by the perilous margin of 217–210. A shift of four votes would have beaten Reagan and radically altered the outcome.

That procedural vote on June 25 was little understood by the public, but it demonstrated the power of technicalities: The vote on the "rule" (for handling the budget bill) framed the ultimate vote on the substance of the budget (one vote or five separate packages).

Defeat of the Democratic rule, moreover, solidified Reagan's coalition and shattered the Democratic leadership's control of the House. It cleared the way for Reagan, on the very next day, to win a similarly close victory on the biggest budget cuts ever enacted at one time.

• • •

August 1981 was the high tide of Reaganism. In just eight months Reagan had pushed through Congress the most massive tax cut in American history and budget cuts far larger than anyone had imagined. Given the monumental deficits that ensured, it was a pyrrhic victory. But that August, political Washington was not heeding economics; it was stunned by Reagan's triumphant coalition making. His was a performance to match Woodrow Wilson's after his first election, FDR's at the start of the New Deal, and Lyndon Johnson's in 1965.

"The system works well at only one time— right after a landslide election," James Sundquist, a presidential scholar at the Brookings Institution, observed. "This is one of those brief periods in our history when a president comes riding a great tide of personal popularity."

V   VIEW FROM THE INSIDE

One of the most difficult realities a president must accept is the limits of his own power. In the following excerpt from his autobiography, President Jimmy Carter tells the very personal story of the Iranian hostage mission and its failure. (In December 1979, Iranian extremists had stormed the American embassy in Tehran and took more than fifty American hostages. In April 1980, President Carter decided on a military rescue mission.)

Questions

1. Compare Jimmy Carter's experiences in the Iranian hostage crisis with the argument of Richard Rose (selection 12.4) that a post-modern president's "responsibilities" are larger but his "resources are fewer" than they were a few decades ago. What advice might Rose have given Carter?

2. What lesson might be drawn from Carter's experience? If you were advising a future president during a similar international incident, what would you say?

12.7 *Keeping Faith: Memoirs of a President* _____

Jimmy Carter

We could no longer afford to depend on diplomacy. I decided to act. On April 11, I called together my top advisers, and we went over the rescue plans again. Because the militants in the compound had threatened to "destroy all the hostages immediately" if any additional moves against them should be launched, we had to plan any action with the utmost care. In the Cabinet Room with me were Vice President Mondale, Secretary Brown, Dr. Brzezinski, Deputy Secretary of State Christopher, Central Intelligence Director Stansfield Turner, General David Jones, Hamilton [Jordan] and Jody [Powell]. (Secretary Vance was on a brief and much needed vacation.) Earlier, I had developed a long list of questions for the military leaders.

Their answers had become much more satisfactory as the training and preparations for the rescue operation had progressed. David Jones said that the earliest date everything could be ready was April 24. I told everyone that it was time for us to bring our hostages home; their safety and our national honor were at stake. When the meeting adjourned, everyone understood that our plans had to be kept a carefully guarded secret. Not wanting anything written in my diary that might somehow be revealing, I made this cryptic entry:

> At the NSC, [National Security Council] meeting we discussed all the options available to us on Iran. There are a few more economic measures we can take before we move to the military options. These involve such things as interruptions of air travel to and from Tehran and the interruption of telecommunications, including news broadcasts. At this meeting we made the basic decisions about the order of priority of our options.
>
> Diary, April 11, 1980

When Vance returned, he objected to my decision to rescue the hostages and wanted to present his own views to the NSC group. His primary argument was that we should be patient and not do anything which might endanger their safety. I held the meeting on April 15, but no one changed his mind.

On Monday, before the rescue mission was to be launched, Secretary Vance, in effect, resigned.

> Our Iranian plans are going on as scheduled. I had Cy, Zbig, and Harold come by to talk about the question of consulting with Congress, and also how to handle the postoperative time.
>
> The Methodists at General Conference in Indianapolis passed an embarrassing resolution [about Iran], mentioning Western imperialism, and so forth. It went to [Iran's] Khomeini, Bani-Sadr, and others. Bishop [William R.] Cannon, D. W. Brooks, and three others want to come in and see me sometime this week, to

encourage us not to take military action. I told Cy I wanted him to meet with them. He said he could not do it.

> I stood up, and the three men left.
>
> Diary, April 21, 1980

Not another word was said. Although simply stated in my diary, this was a very serious moment—the first time I, as President, had ever had anyone directly refuse to obey an official order of mine. My heart went out to Cy Vance, who was deeply troubled and heavily burdened. He was alone in his opposition to the rescue mission among all my advisers, and he knew it.

Cy came back to see me late in the afternoon and submitted his letter of resignation, since he could no longer support my policy toward Iran. I took his letter and said I would keep it. We discussed the fact that my general views and political philosophy were very close to his, and that there was no serious difference between us on major issues of American foreign policy. We agreed that I would speak with him later about whether he should leave, but I said I would not try to talk him out of it. We both knew he had made an irrevocable decision—the only decision possible.

On Wednesday, April 23, I received a last-minute intelligence briefing about Iran, encapsulating information received from all available sources. The substance was that there was little prospect of the hostages' release within the next five or six months, and that everything was favorable for the rescue mission. Our agents in and around Tehran were very optimistic.

That evening, I met with Senator Robert Byrd to discuss the Iranian question, primarily to receive his opinion about necessary notifications to Congress on any possible military action in Iran.

> I told him that before we took any of the military acts that had been prominently mentioned in the press—mining, blockade, and so forth—I would indeed consult with Congress. And that at this time I had no plans to initiate this kind of action.

He drew a sharp distinction between the need to consult on a military plan, and the need to inform Congress at the last minute of any kind of covert operation.

Diary, April 23, 1980

Byrd and I went over a short list of senior senators of both parties who should be notified of any secret operation of this type. I had planned to let him know about the impending rescue mission at the end of this conversation, but now I decided to brief him and the others during the following night, after our team was actually in place and ready to enter Tehran. I therefore told him that such an operation was imminent, but not when it would be launched. Senator Byrd was completely trustworthy, but it was my impression that he would prefer to be informed at the same time as other top congressional leaders. After he left the White House I wondered if it would have been better to involve him more directly in our exact plans for the mission. His advice would have been valuable to me then—and also twenty-four hours later.

The next day was one of the worst of my life. I wanted to spend every moment monitoring the progress of the rescue mission, but had to stick to my regular schedule and act as though nothing of the kind was going on. I asked Zbig to keep notes for me, while I tried to keep my mind on such routine duties as meeting with representatives about legislation, a private session with Israeli Labor party leader Shimon Peres, and a briefing for Hispanic leaders about our anti-inflation program.

Here are some of Brzezinski's notes, using Washington time, with my own clarifying comments in brackets added later.

10:35 A.M. President briefed by ZB on latest intelligence and on the initial stage of the operation. Take-off as planned.

12:00 P.M. Lunch, President, Vice President, Vance, Brown, Brzezinski, Jordan, Powell. First indication that two helicopters may be down short of landing site. [Although the weather forecast had been good, the helicopters ran into severe localized dust storms. One returned to the carrier, and another was left in the southern desert. We never knew until the final personnel count when it was all over that this helicopter crew had been picked up. It was a major worry for me right through the mission.] Iranian post noted two aircraft flying low, without lights. [Our intelligence services were monitoring radio broadcasts throughout Iran.].

3:15 P.M. Two helicopters down; naval task force thinks rest have landed and picked up crews, and thus six are on the way. Should know about Desert One in about half an hour. No upgrading of gendarmerie alert. [The Iranians had small police stations scattered around in the villages and towns. We successfully avoided them. There were no alerts until after our entire rescue team was completely out of Iran.]

All C-130's have landed. Initial problem: three [Iranian motor] vehicles observed. One got away. One of the above, a bus with some 40 [44] people, presumably detained. Brown/Brzezinski consult and agree that no basis for abortion [of mission]; will consult further as information comes in, and Brzezinski will brief the President and obtain his guidance. [This was unexpected bad luck. We had observed this site for several weeks, and vehicular traffic near it was rare. Almost immediately after our landing, though, there was a busload of people, and then a fuel truck followed closely by a pickup truck. The two latter appeared to be driven by smugglers of gasoline, who took off across the desert in the pickup. It was highly unlikely that they would go to the police. In fact, Colonel Beckwith believed they thought our team was Iranian police. But the bus passengers would have to be prevented from sounding an alarm. I approved the removal of all of them to Egypt by C-130 until the rescue itself was concluded, when they would be returned to Iran. We were very careful to avoid any casualties.]

4:21 P.M. General Jones has heard from General Vaught [who was in Egypt and in overall charge of the operation] that everything is under control at Desert One. No one hurt or eliminated. Escaped vehicle proceeded south-west to town 15 miles away, which has gendarmerie post, unmanned at night. Four helicopters refueled at 4:00 P.M. EST; two being refueled. [One had been forced down temporarily in the sand storm, then pressed forward to join the others. This put us somewhat behind schedule, but in itself was no problem.] One that went down has gone back to the carrier. Vaught expects everything to be over in 40 minutes. Has report that everything "green" at drop off, and transport is ready.

4:45 P.M. Brown to Brzezinski: "I think we have an abort situation. One helicopter at Desert One has hydraulic problem. We thus have less than the minimum six to go." C-130's to be used to extract. Request decision on mission termination from the President literally within minutes [because of the importance of completing the operation during nighttime].

4:50 P.M. The President, after obtaining a full report from Brzezinski, requests full information from Brown and Jones and specifically the recommendation from the ground commander. [Ground commander Beckwith, and Vaught in Egypt, both recommended termination, complying with the previous plan which required a minimum of six helicopters.]

4:56 P.M. The President to Brown: "Let's go with his recommendation," and the mission is aborted.

At this point, the Vice President, Christopher, Powell, and Jordan joined me and Zbig in my small study, later followed by Vance, and then Brown. Although despondent about the failure of the mission, we felt we had the situation well under control. Careful plans had been made to abort the operation at any time there might be unforeseen problems or a chance of detection. I was grievously disappointed, but thanked God that there had been no casualties.

5:18 P.M. Brown informs the President that we don't know whereabouts of one helicopter and don't know the crew loss.

5:32 P.M. President calls Jones on secure phone and learns all crews not accounted for. President instructs that needless military action be

avoided; air cover if needed for extraction, but an engagement should be avoided. Show of force first before shooting down any Iranian planes. [All of this referred to the helicopter crew we believed to be on the ground in southern Iran. If necessary, I was ready to send in military forces from the aircraft carriers to protect the crew. At one point, intelligence sources reported a beeper signal from the downed helicopter.]

Discussion of what communication to make to the Iranians and of the needed report to the American people. [After our rescue team departed, I needed to calm the Iranians, who would find our abandoned helicopters. I planned to tell them the truth, and hoped they would believe it.]

5:58 P.M. President on secure phone informed by Jones that helicopter smashed into C-130; some casualties; may be very serious; team transferring into another C-130. [I was sickened with concern about our men. Brief delays seemed like hours as I waited to obtain accurate reports about casualties. All of us sat quietly, very tense. I prayed.]

6:21 P.M. President informed by Jones that a number dead in the crash—helicopter crew, pilot of C-130, and some passengers [members of the rescue team]. The rest are being extricated by C-130. [In taking off to move away from the loaded transport planes, the helicopters had kicked up clouds of dust with their swirling blades. In the poor visibility, one of the helicopters had flown into the nose of the airplane, which itself was preparing to take off. The two aircraft were engulfed in flames, and it was impossible to extract the bodies of the dead Americans. All others were loaded in the other five C-130's and left Desert One, en route to Masirah, a small island off the coast of Oman. Our men had been on the ground for about three hours.]

7:05 P.M. President informed by Jones that at least six probably dead; the team will be back on the ground [in Masirah] around 10:00 P.M.

7:45 P.M. The group without the President convenes in the Cabinet Room to work on necessary notifications and statements. [I sat alone in my small office, listing everything I needed to do to prevent any harm to our hostages, to protect our agents in Tehran, to notify leaders of other nations in the area, and to inform some American leaders and later the general public. First, we had to get our rescue team out of Iran, undetected if possible.]

8:05 P.M. The President joins group in Cabinet Room. [I sent for CIA Director Stan Turner to determine how much time our agents deployed in Tehran for the rescue mission would need to leave the country or to protect themselves from discovery.]

9:05 P.M. Turner joins the group. Discussion of the situation in Iran and implications for public statement. [We had a long discussion about the timing of a public announcement. It was necessary to delay any acknowledgment of our presence in Iran until all our team was out of the country. As soon as it was safe to do so, we wanted to anticipate the Iranians with our announcement of the operation, so as to prevent their exaggeration of the rescue mission into an all-out invasion—a version that might cause them to harm the hostages. We had a number of people stationed in Tehran with trucks, radio equipment, and other compromising materials, who had to be notified and given a chance to protect themselves.]

11:05 P.M. Brown provides fuller debrief on the situation: all helicopter crews accounted for; eight dead, and three burned. [I directed that once the dead men's identities were known, Harold Brown and Fritz Mondale would be responsible for notifying their families.]

11:55 P.M. The President decides public announcement at 2:00 A.M.—changes that to 1:00 A.M., with congressional calls to begin immediately. [We had picked up a few gendarmerie radio broadcasts, although no official alarm had been raised in Iran even three hours after our planes had cleared Iranian airspace.]

The next morning, I dictated a final diary entry.

The cancellation of our mission was caused by a strange series of mishaps—almost completely unpredictable. The operation itself was well planned. The men were well trained. We had every possibility of success, because no Iranian alarm was raised until two or three hours after our people had all left Iran.

I was exhausted when I finally got to bed, after calling Rosalynn in Texas to tell her to cancel her campaigning for tomorrow and to come on home. She was most disturbed, because she didn't have any way to know what had happened. She knew from my guarded comments that we had had serious problems, but I did not want to give her any reports on the telephone.

I had planned on calling in a few members of the House and Senate early Friday morning, before the rescue team began its move into Tehran, in accordance with Bob Byrd's suggestion and Lloyd Cutler's advice. But I never got around to that.

Diary, April 24–25, 1980

I am still haunted by memories of that day— our high hopes for success, the incredible series of mishaps, the bravery of our rescue team, the embarrassment of failure, and above all, the tragic deaths in the lonely desert. I actually slept a couple of hours, and then got up early to prepare my television broadcast, which would explain to the American people what had occurred.

In my brief statement, I took full responsibility for the mission, outlined what had happened, and gave my reasons for the effort. I reminded the world of the continuing Iranian crime and praised the courageous volunteers who had given their lives for the freedom of others.

I will always remember the people who gave me their support that day. The first one who called after my early-morning announcement was Henry Kissinger, full of praise and approval of our attempt and offering to help me in any possible way. I asked him to call the networks and wire services and make a statement. He did so right away. Sadat also offered his immediate help, as did Prime Minister Ohira and most of our European allies. Among the American people, we had overwhelming support, for which I was particularly grateful.

VI ? THE UNWRITTEN CONSTITUTION

With the great expansion of the federal bureaucracy in the 1930s, President Franklin Roosevelt asked political scientist Louis Brownlow to chair a commission that would explore and propose changes in the organization of the executive branch to facilitate effective presidential management. The Brownlow commission, as it was called, concluded among other things that the time had come for the creation of a formal White House staff to advise and support the president. "The President needs help," the commission declared. "He should be given a small number of executive assistants who would be his direct aides in dealing with the managerial agencies and administrative departments of Government." These presidential aides, in the commission's view, "would remain in the background, issue no orders, make no decisions, emit no public statements. . . . They should be men in whom the President has personal confidence and whose character and attitude is such that they would not attempt to exercise power on their own account. They should be possessed of high competence, great physical vigor, and a passion for anonymity."*

More than half a century later, the White House staff has become a permanent fixture of American government, expanded both in size and influence far beyond what the Brownlow commission imagined. Presidents now find it necessary to hire a chief of staff—a White House adviser whose job is to manage and direct the White House staff. The power and influence of the chief of staff vary depending on the style of the individual president but are never insignificant. The following excerpts from a panel discussion among eight men who served as chief of staff for different presidents reveal the wide variety of problems and challenges facing the staff director in the modern White House.

Questions

1. What roles are played by presidential staff? Why are presidential assistants necessary? What advantages do they provide? What disadvantages do they create?

2. Do Presidential staff pose a threat to democracy? If so, what can presidents do to ensure that their staff do not usurp essential powers of the presidency?

---

* President's Committee on Administrative Management, *Administrative Management in the Government of the United States* (Washington, D.C.: Government Printing Office, 1937), p. 5.

12.8 Chief of Staff: Twenty-five Years of Managing the Presidency

Samuel Kernell and Samuel L. Popkin

[John] *Chancellor* [NBC News]: Presidents are human. Presidents make mistakes. Sometimes presidents want to do damn fool things they have to be talked out of, and so my question to all of you to begin this panel today is: How do you talk a president out of a damn fool idea?

Harry McPherson: [special assistant and counsel to President Lyndon B. Johnson, 1964–1965; special counsel, 1965–1969]: Well, very gingerly—*(laughter)*—if your president is Lyndon Johnson.

One morning in 1968, I was at home, and President Johnson called me, outraged because I had sent in a list of cities where I thought we might meet with the North Vietnamese. He didn't want to meet at any of those cities, and he said he was about to announce that he would not meet at any of those cities; if they wanted to meet with him, they could meet—I don't know—San Diego or someplace like that. *(Laughter)*

And I was very tired. I had been up late the night before and had been working with [former Truman adviser and Washington insider] Clark Clifford on this list. Well, I let go and yelled at the president on the phone as loud as I could and for a long time. I called him a lot of rough names. My wife ran down the stairs in dismay because she thought I was talking to the plumber. That's true, and she thought I was going to drive the guy away. *(Laughter)*

When I hung up, I called Clark Clifford to warn him that the president had just called me and had raised hell about this, and he said to his long-time secretary, Miss Wiler—he asked me what time I'd finished talking, and I said, "Exactly 8:30, he called"—and he said, "Miss Wiler, what time did I finish with the President?" Back came the word, "8:29."

So you do it very carefully. You do it with a conviction that what you are doing is in the national interest and very much in the president's political interest.

Donald Rumsfeld [chief of staff for President Gerald R. Ford, 1974–1975]: I think it depends on the president, how you argue or discuss an issue like that.

I can recall President Ford meeting privately with one of his senior officials in the administration and, in effect, coming away with an agreement that he would put forward to the Congress a proposal which had not been staffed out at all and which, in my view, was not very wise—and that is a massive understatement. The way it was finally accomplished was simply by staffing it out. In other words, taking this idea and putting it into the staff system—the people that he had hired and brought aboard, who in some cases had statutory authority over that area of government—and letting them then provide their advice and allowing some time so that he could have the benefit of their views.

Chancellor: Isn't that called stalling? *(Laughter)*

Rumsfeld: No. I would call it professional staff work. But sometimes it takes very, very long. *(Laughter)*

Richard Cheney [chief of staff for President Ford, 1975–1977]: President Ford, of course, because of his personality and his service in Congress, welcomed the debate and the dialogue. You were free at any time to go into the Oval Office and argue with him about something, and he would agree or disagree, and then you could come back two hours later and do it again. He never denied you access because you argued with him.

The biggest problem was the decision that didn't receive attention. It wasn't so much a matter of his making a damn fool decision, as you said, John, as it was his making some kind of offhand decision that hadn't been carefully thought about, and then people took it and ran with it. It's what I called an "Oh, by the way" decision.

It was the kind of thing that would happen when somebody was cleared to go into the Oval Office, a cabinet member, to talk about a subject; the president was prepared. They had their discussion, and as the cabinet member was leaving, he'd turn around and he'd say, "Oh, by the way, Mr. President," and then bring up a totally unrelated subject, get a decision on it, and run with it. That's when you really got into big trouble.

Chancellor: Mr. Haldeman, it has been written that when President Nixon would give you certain kinds of instructions, you'd say "Yes, sir," and then go off and start a process which didn't always result in that action being taken. Can you tell us about that?

H. R. Haldeman [chief of staff for President Richard M. Nixon, 1969–1973]: I don't think I'm unique among this group. *(Laughter)* I suspect that we all shared that kind of activity fairly frequently. But that, I think, is essential; however, it depends on the relationship between the staff person who's making that kind of move and the president himself, because the president has got to feel that there are some people with whom he can explore rather than command, and that in exploring, he's going to raise some things that don't, to him, at the moment he's raising them, seem like damn fool things but could very well turn out to be that or seem so after second thought.

It's the obligation of the staff and the function of the staff to pose the alternatives.

Carrying that a step further, I think, it's the obligation of the senior staff person dealing with any such kind of a situation not to carry out the order until it has been at least reviewed once and then reordered by the president on the basis of making the right decision for the right reasons instead of for the wrong reasons.

• • •

Chancellor: Aren't there crises that are class C, class B, as well as big class A crises, and getting the president involved tends to escalate it? Any thoughts on that?

Cheney: It does, and the one power the president has, probably that's more important than maybe any other power, is his ability to set the national agenda, to decide what is important by focusing on it, by talking about it, by focusing the attention of the press corps on it.

When you bring something to the presidential level, it automatically will—take something like the *Mayaguez* crisis, for example, one I'm familiar with.* All of a sudden, the president, his administration, is evaluated in terms of how he deals with that, although in the broad scheme of things, it's relatively insignificant compared to how you manage the economy or how you deal with your defense budget longterm.

But as Al [Haig] says, the technology now makes it possible for the president to make a decision in a case involving military force that really ought to be made maybe by the

---

* On May 12, 1975, the Khmer Rouge government of Cambodia fired on the U.S. merchant ship *Mayaguez* and forced it into the port of Sihanoukville. President Ford immediately convened the National Security Council and subsequently decided to capture the ship by force. On May 14, an hour before the Cambodian government planned to release the crew, U.S. military planes raided the Cambodian coast while marine units captured the vacant *Mayaguez*. The release of the thirty-nine-man crew proceeded, but the raid continued until the crew had boarded a U.S. naval vessel. Fifteen U.S. servicemen died in the fighting; another twenty-three were killed in a helicopter accident. The decisive nature of the operation was popular with the American people and evoked hearty public support for the president.

commander of the aircraft carrier in the Tonkin Gulf or, in the case of the *Mayaguez*, off Cambodia, and the decision actually goes all the way up the chain, not only to CINCPAC [Commander-in-chief, Pacific] in Hawaii and the secretary of defense and the NSC [National Security Council] but ultimately ends up on the president's desk, and he makes a relatively small decision that can have an enormous impact upon how he's perceived, and really should have been done by somebody else.

Haldeman: John? I think for this question and the general discussion, it's worth looking at the point you made, Isn't there a danger of escalating it by involving the president? That's an outsider's viewpoint. What we are talking about here with this group is really from the inside viewpoint. You aren't necessarily escalating something by bringing it to the president's attention *internally*, without involving the press and the world in the fact of the president's involvement. There can be a real value to the president's ongoing knowledge of the development of a crisis—but without the president running out and making a statement about it or issuing anything through a spokesman even, but simply keeping him involved as the thing progresses.

It depends on the nature of the crisis, as you were saying, the A, B, and C crises. You can make your A, B, and C classification on a lot of different bases. One of them is the immediacy basis. Some crises can't be resolved for a while and can't even be considered, even though you know they've happened. When the North Koreans shot down a plane early in our administration, we knew the plane was shot down but that was *all* we knew at that instant. There wasn't anything you could do about it then, but you had to start developing a plan for what you were going to do, and it was terribly important what that was, right from the earliest reaction. Therefore you brought

the president in at the right time, but you didn't necessarily show the world that he was involved until he was ready to take a presidential position on it.

[*Chancellor:*] Mr. Watson, President Carter organized the White House around his own very good brain, his own dedication to homework and detail. Looking back on that now—and I ask this not in a critical sense—would that be a factor if you were changing how the White House worked under the Carter administration?

[Jack H.] *Watson* [Jr.] [chief of staff for President Jimmy Carter, 1980–1981]: It would, but one thing that you cannot get away from is that the way the White House is organized and the way that it functions are both very much reflections of the man. You take your president as you find him. So to some extent, my sitting here and saying how I would redesign the Carter White House more or less in my own image misses the point. A White House staff has as its function the duty to serve the president in the way that he wishes to be served, to sort of play to his long suits.

Having said that, let me also express a very personal opinion. When we went in [to the office], I had a fear and said so to the president in a private memorandum. I said to him that I thought he was one of the brightest, most well-read, most well-educated persons to assume the presidency in the history of the republic; that he was a student of government. He was a voracious reader, a man who wished to know the pros and the cons and the ins and the outs of every issue before him. I said to him, "That's a danger. There's a danger of your over involvement. There's a danger of pulling too many things into the White House, and you'll be held accountable for things that you ought not to be held accountable for." As a general observation about our administration, I think we made that mistake. I think the president was involved to

Presidential Staff and the "Passion for Anonymity"

How can we reconcile the Brownlow commission's ideal of a "passion for anonymity" with the modern norm of high-visibility, celebrity chiefs of staff? Samuel Kernell and Samuel L. Popkin, who edited the accompanying discussion among the chiefs of staff, commented as follows.

H. R. Haldeman, who because of Watergate remains among the most well-known former chiefs, lets us know early on that we are in for surprises when he emphatically endorses Brownlow's "passion for anonymity" as a vital virtue for staff: "I completely agree with the Brownlow plan, that the White House staff should be an operational unit, not a policy-making or policy-executing unit. It should be there to assist the president in the management of the executive branch and in the office of the president." Toward this end "virtually all the staff members," Haldeman insists, must be "people with Brownlow's passion for anonymity." When [John] Chancellor canvasses the participants [in the discussion] about their public appearances, none reports having ventured more than once or twice onto a network public affairs program.

Desiring anonymity and having it are the difference between ambition and success. Events inevitably make those close to the president newsworthy, and a strong chief of staff like Haldeman will attract news despite his best efforts to remain out of the public limelight. When Brownlow first used the phrase "passion for anonymity" during a briefing, Franklin Roosevelt laughed and exclaimed that whoever came up with that idea "doesn't know his American press."

But the visibility, even notoriety, of senior staff today appears to be fueled by more than the natural desire of the press to report on the foibles of people in power. One contributing factor is that presidential aides conduct so much of their business in public, a tendency exemplified by recent controversies involving President Reagan's past and present aides. In early March 1986, for example, the administration lost a close budget vote in the House of Representatives. When asked to explain the president's defeat, Republican House leaders carped that Chief of Staff Donald Regan had acted as though Congress were his board of directors and he the government's "chief executive officer"—which is precisely how Regan had recently described his job to a reporter. Less than a month later President Reagan lost another close vote in the House, this time on military aid to the Contra forces in Nicaragua. Many Democrats claimed they had been disposed to support the legislation until White House Director of Communications Patrick Buchanan launched a public campaign besmirching congressional opponents with charges of abetting communist expansion. Perhaps Buchanan is correct in arguing that he

too great an extent in too many things. I think we put too many things on the agenda.

In 1977, when he came in, there were simply too many initiatives of too high a level of controversy and complexity that he wanted to do all at once. "Let's pass a national urban policy. Let's pass a comprehensive national energy policy. Let's reorganize the executive branch of government," and so on. "Let's do away with the major boondoggle projects in the West involving water projects and dams and such." Those were things involving huge political capital expenditures, and we did too many things at once.

In terms of organization, if I had to change one thing—and this seems to be a problem that almost every president, though not President Eisenhower, suffers from. They go in with an idea that they are going to have a spokes-of-the-wheel staff. There's going to be equal access.

Chancellor: The president is the hub.

merely provided these congressmen with a convenient foil, which enabled them to oppose the military aid program without picking a fight with a popular president. The fact, however, that an aide had gained sufficient visibility to make him a suitable target distinguishes the contemporary staff from its predecessors.

The theme of the Buchanan squabble recalls for Washington observers the widely publicized and controversial reassignment of Health and Human Services Secretary Margaret Heckler as ambassador to Ireland. She resisted, publicly charging that she was being sacked by Chief of Staff Regan for failing to be a "team player"—another instance of an antagonist attacking the president's aide to skirt a costly fight with the president. Eventually, Heckler succumbed to the call to diplomatic service, but not before Washington correspondents had filed numerous stories reporting gossip from anonymous White House sources and expressions of sympathy from her friends on Capitol Hill.

In late April 1986 two of Reagan's former aides returned to the Washington limelight in ways that added to the administration's embarrassment. With great fanfare former budget director David Stockman held a series of well-staged press conferences and television interviews to promote his "tell-all" book, for which he had earned a $2 million advance. Michael Deaver, a member of the "troika" that ran the White House during Reagan's first term, should have had more modest aspirations for publicity when he returned as a lobbyist representing the interests of his new clients to his former associates in the administration. Unfortunately, the need for discretion escaped him. An early March 1986 issue of *Time* had on its cover a posed photo of Deaver making the lobbying rounds in his limousine. As conflict-of-interest charges mounted in Congress and the press, Deaver garnered the Reagan White House more adverse publicity than had Stockman. Recent events have thus borne out Bob Haldeman's comparison of senior White House aides with movie stars.

As the modern White House has accumulated the resources and mandate necessary to make it a key player in Washington's institutional politics, the job of the senior assistant has been transformed. The anonymous go-between of yesteryear is sometimes today asked to be a "point man," or as in the case of Haldeman's single television appearance, a provocateur. The discreet aide steeped in neutral competence and honest brokerage has (necessarily) been succeeded by celebrity politicians who actively pursue the president's policy goals with other politicians in the executive branch and beyond.

—*Samuel Kernell and Samuel L. Popkin*

Watson: The president is the hub, and he's going to have *x* number of advisors, six or eight or ten. And because they are all important to him and his friends and counselors and people whose judgment and loyalty he trusts and values, he wants all of them reporting directly to him. He's the hub. That is a fatal mistake. The White House can't operate that way. It pulls the president into too much; he's involved in too many things.

It also results in a lack of cohesion, a lack of organization and cutting in on decision making before it reaches the Oval Office, the presidential level. That was, in my judgment, a mistake that President Carter made in the first two years of his administration. He didn't actually appoint a chief of staff until late in the summer of 1979. I think that many of our problems on the Hill, many of our congressional relationships, difficulties, who's speaking for the president, would have been solved had we started from the very beginning with a strong chief of staff.

[Harry C.] *McPherson:* Really? You mean you would have had a Don Regan [President Reagan's chief of staff, 1985–1987] in the Carter White House? That kind of an operation?

Watson: No. It's a fair question, Harry, and I'm not necessarily saying that. We were reacting—with all due respect to my good friend, Bob Haldeman—we were reacting to at least a public perception that there had been a kind of palace guard, to quote a colleague of yours, and that there hadn't been a free flow of diverse ideas and information to the president, that it had been too rigidly controlled, too tight a ship. So part of what we were doing was a reaction against that. As is true of so many things, our pendulum swung too far in the other direction.

The way a White House chief of staff performs his or her function is in itself going to depend on the individual. I think that the way that Jim Baker, to use recent history, performed his role as White House chief of staff for Mr. Reagan, under an organization which was exactly as I'm describing, was very different than the way that Don Regan performs the same role with the same structure. You cannot eliminate or ignore the personal touch of how a particular individual performs a particular job.

But, Harry, my answer to your question is yes, I am suggesting a strong, trusted, even-handed White House chief of staff.

• • •

Bradley Patterson [Brookings Institution]: My question is a question about the size of the White House staff. Every White House staff group, as you go through history, looks to the one that came after it and shakes its head in dismay and says "My God, that's just too many people." The people in the Truman White House look at what came after them and they say "This is just terrible"; the Eisenhower folks look at what came after them and they say "This is just out of control."

Rumsfeld: They were all right. *(Laughter)*

Patterson: What should be, if any, the limits on White House staff size? Does one get to the point where a chief of staff would say, "Hey, this is too big"?

Rumsfeld: There's a natural tendency for staffs to grow. When I was chief of staff for the White House, we did, in fact, reduce it. In my judgment, presidents have different needs, and to the extent that you can move more things out from the departments, just as in a corporation or any other activity, you are better off. At G. D. Searle, I reduced the staff from 850, when I arrived, to 147. And it worked better.

It takes someone who decides that it's important that you not bring every problem into the White House but, in fact, push them out.

To give an example. The Press Secretary in the White House is asked a question by a member of the White House press corps about agriculture. He's got a choice: either he answers it or he says that's a question that should be directed to the Department of Agriculture. Now, the person asking the question doesn't want to go to the department because his paper already has someone covering the Agriculture Department. He wants the story, and so he presses and presses. Finally the press secretary caves in, and pretty soon every question in the world is being answered by the White House press secretary, which is goofy, and then you need a giant White House press staff. Whereas basically, a lot of that should be shoved out. That's true of issue after issue. It's true of substantive jurisdiction.

[Alexander M.] *Haig* [chief of staff for President Nixon, 1973–1974] The simple facts are that this horrendous growth in the White House staff has been paralleled by an even more horrendous growth in the congressional staffs, where today I think you are looking at a figure of about twenty thousand.* A White House has to respond to that behemoth, and therefore it's a natural contributor to this growth.

The other gimmick, which Bob Haldeman will remember, is that administrations that want to show they are lean and mean merely keep the fellows they have but charge them to the departments. It's nicer anyway, because the department has to pay and those fellows are counted on the department's books and not counted by the White House press who are looking for this growth.

I share Don Rumsfeld's view very, very vigorously. Cutting down the staff—and I

know Bob tried to cut it down, I know Don did, I know I did—is the best way. The leaner and meaner you are, the more effective your White House will be.

Watson: Another point, as a matter of clarification. There are about fifteen hundred people in the Office of Management and Budget, which is part of the Executive Office of the President. The White House staff is about 350 or less, generally speaking, and is just one of the components of the executive office.

What runs the numbers of presidential staffers up higher are the Council of Economic Advisors, the Council on Environmental Quality, and other such groups that are in the executive office.

Haig: What's material is who gets in the White House Mess, who gets a parking place. *(Laughter)* If you have been involved in the bureaucratic in-fighting, try to decide that.

---

* Between the mid-1950s and the early 1980s, the growth of staff in Congress and its committees more than matched that of the White House. The staff of the members' offices increased from 3,556 in 1957 to 11,432 in 1981; the number of committee staffers rose from 715 in 1955 to 2,865 in 1981.

VII ISSUE AND DEBATE: SHOULD THE CONSTITUTION BE REFORMED?

Critics of American politics can point to many problems—government corruption, an out-of-control budget deficit, lack of leadership on issues ranging from education to economic development, and others. Some see these problems as essentially structural and therefore argue for fundamental constitutional reforms. Others discount the importance of such structural issues and point instead to different causes. The problems lie not in the Constitution, they suggest, but in ourselves—or in our political leadership.

One of the most hotly debated areas of concern is the separation of powers. Charles Hardin, for one, believes that the separation of powers makes effective government difficult and looks to changes that would make the executive and legislative branches more interdependent. Arthur Schlesinger, Jr., in contrast, sees constitutional reform as irrelevant and even dangerous.

Question

1. Review *Federalist* Nos. 47, 48, and 50 (selections 2.2 through 2.4). How might James Madison weigh in on the questions of constitutional reform debated here?

12.9 The Crisis and Its Cure

Charles Hardin

In 1973 America was gripped by its gravest political crisis since the Civil War. The president all too often was out of control. Unbridled bureaucracies acted with the arrogance befitting their autonomy. Many pressure groups exercised appalling political leverage. Increasingly disorganized, the public felt deceived and disillusioned. The threat of an inquisitorial government's espionage—and even of armed attacks by its minions, regardless of constitutional guarantees—was in the air. A former high official of the Nixon White House, asked by a Senate Watergate Committee member what advice he would give young people inquiring about careers in government, replied—"Stay away!" The audience rocked with cynical laughter. The heritage of Washington, Jefferson, and Lincoln—so long miraculously intact—was crumbling to dust.

A sense of the need for fundamental changes was abroad. Recent presidents—Eisenhower, Kennedy, and Lyndon B. Johnson—had considered and some had urged basic constitutional reforms. In 1973 Richard M. Nixon endorsed a single six-year term for presidents coupled with a four-year term for congressmen. Ironically, his suggestion coincided with the most serious discussion of presidential impeachment since Andrew Johnson. The thought of impeachment made many persons shudder. And yet there was the haunting nightmare of a discredited president continuing in office for forty months. Senator Edward M. Kennedy and ABC commentator Howard K. Smith pointed out that the parliamentary system would enable the displacement of a politically disabled president by political means and for political reasons—a great improvement over impeachment. Clark Clifford, formerly special counsel to President Truman and secretary of defense under President Johnson, called for the president and vice-president to resign pursuant to the twenty-fifth amendment. Among those who denounced Clifford was Arthur H. Dean, formerly negotiator at Panmunjom for the United States and sixteen other nations, American ambassador to South Korea, and holder of many other distinguished assignments. But all that was in the summer; by November 1973 Vice-President Spiro T. Agnew had resigned, the House of Representatives was inquiring through its committee on the judiciary into the evidence for impeaching the president, and the chorus of voices calling for the president to resign had swelled while those opposing resignation had fallen virtually silent.

In this period a number of people, including CBS commentator Eric Sevareid, urged Congress to reassert itself, forgetting that Congress had repeatedly proven unable to provide the concerted leadership required by the times. Former Senator Eugene McCarthy advocated "depersonalizing" the presidency in order to free the energies, "intellectual, spiritual, and moral," of the people. In reality what emerged from the people was a collective sense of the inevitable and virtually ubiquitous crookedness of politicians.

In this situation, two facts were of first importance. First, the crisis of 1973 had been foreshadowed. Presidential abuse of power, though seriously worsened, had been visible for decades; the inadequacy of Congress to provide an alternative to presidential government had been shown from the close of the Civil War to the end of the nineteenth century and fitfully demonstrated again thereafter; and the malaise of public opinion had appeared in the late 1960s. In other words, the problems were longstanding and were rooted in structural faults;

Mike Marland/*Concord Monitor*

they were not associated with one administration and one series of events. Second, there was—there is—a way out, painful, difficult, and dangerous as it may be. It will require constitutional surgery at least as severe as that of 1787. The end result can be briefly stated as "presidential power and accountability" or, to put it another way, as presidential leadership and party government.

It will be useful to set forth the diagnosis and the prescription in an outline:

1. A foremost requirement of a great power is strong executive leadership. The political demand for it, manifest world-wide, arises from the present condition of international relationships, given the state of the military arts; from the inexorable need to develop and use science to maintain national security; and from the nature of modern economic and social organization especially when coupled with emergent ecological considerations.

2. America met the first requirement by its presidency; but in recent decades the presidency has escaped the political controls essential to constitutional, i.e., *limited,* government. New controls must be found.

3. The search for controls is complicated by the danger that curbs may diminish the effectiveness of the presidency. The executive needs energy today at least as much as in the critical years immediately following 1787 when the framers concluded that it should be wielded by a single pair of hands to achieve the "decision, activity, secrecy [yes, secrecy!], and despatch" essential in safeguarding the republic. How to maintain the full force and effect of the presidency and yet to restrain those presidential excesses so generously demonstrated in this century?

4. The beginning of the answer lies in the relationship between the president and the people. The controlling principle had been *vox populi, vox dei.* The voice of the people is the voice of God. This has been the major premise of our theory of representation; for the people cannot govern, and the president has become their surrogate. Accordingly, he personifies their political authority. When he speaks *ex cathedra* from atop his pyramid of forty million votes, with the bulk of the populace reportedly behind him, he is awe-inspiring. His infallibility especially impresses those closest to him whose approval if not their adulation convinces him that he is larger than life. And yet all this authority may dissolve if the public turns against him. The people's choice becomes the people's curse. We have seen it happen four times in this century. The results of an abrupt decline in presidential power are often unfortunate and may be disastrous.

5. It follows (although the logic may be clear only after further reading and reflection) that a measure of control over the president can be provided by subjecting him to the criticism of an organized, focused opposition with leadership centered in one person who will be continuously visible and vocal as the alternative to the president. As the presidency is unified, so should the opposition be unified. As the president speaks with a single voice, so should he be answered by a single voice instead of a clamor of discordant and little-known voices in a legislative body whose present genius is the dispersion of power. If a focused opposition can be achieved, the crucial relationship between the public and its government will begin to change.

Charles Hardin

6. To establish an opposition we must turn to Congress, and the first step is to contradict the myth that the end of providing greater controls over the president without unduly undermining his power may be accomplished merely by increasing the weight of Congress. When powers are separated they are ordinarily less shared than displaced. Either power resides in the presidency with some congressional criticism and subject to some bargaining, or it shifts to the bureaucracy, defined as comprising a conglomerate of power among agencies, strategic congressmen, and interest groups. It must be understood that the genius of Congress is opposite to that of the presidency. Where the presidency comes to life in the unification of power, Congress disperses power among a hundred leaders each with his own base in seniority and in sectional jurisdiction (over taxation, finance, transportation, military, labor, and judiciary or whatever). It appears to be impossible to organize in Congress a concentration of power sufficient to provide an orchestrated and programmatic opposition—let alone a centralized executive government.

7. The nature of Congress is strongly influenced by the manner of its selection—staggered terms for senators, two-year terms for representatives. As with the president, this situation induces a particular relationship between Congress and the public. Where the president is elected as the nonpareil, the father, the leader, the magic helper, the incarnation of the infallible goodness and wisdom of the people, congressmen and senators tend to be chosen as a means of assuring their constituents' shares of national largesse. Henry Adams cynically wrote, "A congressman is like a hog. You have to kick him in the snout." The grain of truth in his statement exists by virtue of the congressman's expression of the sacred demands of the public. The voter's political obligation in electing congressmen is held to be exhausted when he communicates his wants to government. The voter has no share in the responsibility of government. Indeed, the "responsible electorate" has been authoritatively defined as one that

knows on which side its bread is buttered. The logical outcome for public opinion is that Congress "as a whole" is despised because congressmen are generally seen as serving the interests of others—but individual congressmen are typically admired and appreciated by the active and knowledgeable among their constituents.

8. The first reform then must strike at the relationships not only between president and Congress but also between both and the public. The president and Congress should be elected for simultaneous four-year terms. In addition, the defeated candidate for the presidency should have a seat in the House of Representatives, priority in committees and on the floor, and a staff, offices, and other prerequisites suitable to his position as the leader of the opposition.

9. Candidates for Congress of both parties, including a generous slate of candidates running at large on a national ticket, should constitute the nominating conventions for presidential candidates so that when people vote or otherwise share in nominations of congressmen they know that they are also naming those who will nominate for the presidency. The office of vice-president should be abolished. Other reforms [include] . . . the steps to reduce the political leverage of the Senate; the introduction of national at-large candidates in a manner that will ensure the winning presidential candidate a working majority in the House of Representatives; and the provision that the minority party in Congress may remove the defeated presidential candidate as leader of the opposition but that it must replace him with another leader.

10. These changes should give the voters a new sense of their function and of their relationship to government. They will be able to realize a political responsibility that the present constitution denies them, namely, that they share in the selection of a government—or, equally important, of an opposition. This action is rich in significance. *First,* it will cause a salutary change in a basic premise of American political thought. Implicit in the new electoral system is the realization that government—far from being "the greatest of all reflections on human nature"—is a necessity if people are to dwell, as they must as human beings, in communities. *Second,* these changes will give voters the experience that will vindicate an improved theory of representation. Instead of perpetuating the myth that people in general are in position and sufficiently informed to make all political decisions—the idea of the General Will and of the initiative and referendum dear to the Progressives—the new assumption will be in accordance with a sensible division of political labor: the people will elect a government—and an opposition—and hold them accountable, the one for governing, the other for systematically criticizing government during its term in office. A workable theory of representative democracy should emerge. *Third,* an extremely significant step will be taken to restore political controls over the president without diminishing his essential power. He would be seen as the necessary and legitimate leader for a given period rather than as the personification of the deity domiciled in the collective breast of the populace. Instead of governmental decisions resting on the ultimate sanction of the popular will, they would rest on a majority, a sufficiently legitimizing concept, but one that takes into account the fact that nearly half the people will consider the president to be politically fallible—and one that will prevail merely for the good and democratic reason that in a civilized community there must be some way other than violence to settle disputes. Control over the president derived from these propositions will be enhanced by the presence of the leader of the opposition and the alternative government that he heads. The tendency for the instincts, the whims, the idiosyncrasies, or the mind-sets of presidents to become manifest in dangerous initiatives should be greatly reduced. *Fourth,* the sovereign right of the majority to choose a government that, on balance, it considers more favorable to its interests would not be denied; but the emphasis would be placed, where it should

be if the public is to have a practicable and active share in the awful responsibility of modern government, on the choice of who shall rule. *Fifth,* the divisions in the campaign should persist during the period of governance, subject, of course, to accretion and erosion of political parties "like a ball of sticky popcorn"; and this quality of persistence, along with previous characteristics of the new public, will further rationalize the relationship of the people to their government.

11. The new framework of government will increase the ability of politicians to bring bureaucracy as it has crystallized in America under control. And the balance of power between public government and private groups, which is unfortunately tipped toward private groups in the traditional polity of America, will be redressed.

12. Beyond these considerations looms the inability of the American system to replace a president who has become politically discredited. Impeachment is inadequate. The fault of impeachment for removing presidents lies essentially in its juridical character, its legal procedures, its indictments and its trial according to the rules of evidence, to ascertain the *individual's* criminal guilt or innocence. But emphasis on the *legal* criminality of *individuals* hides and even denies the *political* responsibility that must be *collective.* In the modern age the intricate and complex problems of government require a collegial approach (as the current political argot recognizes—the White House team, the task forces, the national security council, the domestic council, the presidential game plan). Political adequacy is judged not by weighing individual guilt or innocence according to the rules of evidence but rather by political procedures for testing confidence in the prudence and judgment of government. Legal guilt by association is anathema; political liability by association is essential. The political process should be capable of registering the collective judgment of responsible politicians—who, in turn, are informed by their sense of public opinion—on the prudence and wisdom of governments. The legality of a president's acts may figure in such judgments, but more important are decisions on presidential prudence, grasp of events, will, wisdom, and self-control.

The reforms proposed will not in themselves provide a vote of confidence, but they will create the setting in which such votes should naturally evolve. For an essential assumption would be that a president needs a majority in the House of Representatives to govern. If he loses the majority he will be incapacitated, and it would be logical for him to resign. It will be argued that the experience of parliamentary regimes shows governments to be extremely durable: prime ministers no longer get ousted because they lose majorities. And yet prime ministers do resign because they have to retain the leadership at least of their own party; and there are ways short of defection in which party members can convey to the prime minister their loss of confidence.

13. Replacement of the president by an adverse vote of confidence—or by so obvious a disintegration in the loyalty of his supporters that he feels compelled to resign—should make way for another evolutionary step, namely, dissolving government and holding new elections.

Once this step is taken, it is hoped, it will become the normal way that one government ends and another is chosen. When this happens, the endless nominating and electoral campaigns will be compressed into a few weeks. One benefit will be the reduction of the cost of campaigns and of the leverage of money in politics. Stringent laws on campaign financing will become enforceable.

14. Finally, there is the promise of more honest politics and less corruptible politicians. This result will come from the collegial responsibility of party government toward which all the reforms suggested above will work. The inherited American system puts all stress on the individual. He can keep himself clean, untainted by the sordid acts of the grafters who surround him, each of whom may profit individually from his crimes—but also may be apprehended, convicted, and sentenced. In the new system members of a government will understand that, just as they govern collectively, so they will be judged collectively for the shortcomings of their colleagues. Party government will provide strong incentives for obedience to a code of political ethics.

NO

12.10 Leave the Constitution Alone

Arthur M. Schlesinger, Jr.

There is a revival of interest in fundamental constitutional change. I am not referring to special-interest amendments—proposals, for example, to permit school prayer or to forbid abortion or to require an annually balanced budget. I have in mind rather the rising feeling that we must take a hard fresh look at our government and determine whether its basic structure is adequate to the challenges of the future.

Those calling for such reexamination aren't just academic theoreticians. They include distinguished public servants, persons with long and honorable government experience, like Douglas Dillon and Lloyd Cutler. Without prejudging conclusions, they raise searching questions. In particular, they ask whether the separation of powers hasn't become a crippling disability. The separation, they suggest, leads to legislative stalemate, increases voter frustration and apathy, invites the meddling of single interest groups and makes it impossible for any party or person to be held accountable for policy. The "question transcending all immediate issues," Mr. Dillon writes, "is whether we can continue to afford the luxury of the separation of power in Washington" and whether we shouldn't consider "a change to some form of parliamentary government that would eliminate or sharply reduce the present division of authority between the executive and legislative arms of government."

These are certainly interesting questions. One wishes the new bicentennial Committee on the Constitutional System all luck in exploring them. They aren't new questions. In the 1880's, for example, Sen. George Pendleton and Prof. Woodrow Wilson argued for a movement toward a parliamentary system. After World War II Thomas K. Finletter in his closely reasoned book "Can Representative Government do the Job?"—still perhaps the best book on the subject—and Congressman Estes Kefauver proposed modifications of the Constitution in the parliamentary direction.

A Function of Weakness

The parliamentary system is to be defined by a fusion rather than by a separation of powers. The executive is drawn from the legislative majority and can count on automatic enactment of its program. No one doubts where responsibility lies for success or failure. But while the parliamentary system formally assumes legislative supremacy, in fact it assures the almost unassailable dominance of the executive over the legislature.

Parliament's superiority over Congress in delivering whatever the executive requests is a function of weakness, not of strength. The no-confidence vote is so drastic an alternative that in Britain, for example, it succeeds in forcing a new general election only two or three times a century.

Churchill made the point to Roosevelt in a wartime conversation. "You, Mr. President," Churchill said, "are concerned to what extent you can act without the approval of Congress. You don't worry about your cabinet. On the other hand, I never worry about Parliament, but I continuously have to consult and have the support of my cabinet."

Thus the prime minister appoints people to office without worrying about parliamentary confirmation, concludes treaties without worrying about parliamentary ratification, declares war without worrying about parliamentary authorization, withholds information without worrying about parliamentary subpoenas, is relatively safe from parliamentary investigation and in many respects has inherited the authority that once belonged to absolute monarchy. As Lloyd George told a select committee in 1931, "Parliament has really no control over the executive; it is a pure fiction." The situation has not improved in the half century since. Only the other day the *Economist* spoke of "Whitehall's continuing contempt for Parliament."

Congress is far more independent of the executive, far more responsive to a diversity of ideas, far better staffed, far more able to check, balance, challenge and investigate the executive government. Take Watergate as an example. The best judgment is that such executive malfeasance would not have been exposed under the British system. "Don't think a Watergate couldn't happen here," writes Woodrow Wyatt, a former British MP. "You just wouldn't hear about it."

In a recent issue of the British magazine *Encounter*, Edward Pearce of the *London Daily Telegraph* agrees:

> If only Mr. Nixon had had the blessing of the British system. . . . Woodward and Bernstein would have been drowned in the usual channels, a D-Notice would have been erected over their evidence, and a properly briefed judge, a figure of outstanding integrity, would have found the essential parts of the tapes to be ei-

ther not relevant or prejudicial to national security or both. The British system of protecting the authorities is almost part of the constitution.

While American constitutional reformers muse about the virtues of a fusion of powers, British reformers yearn for separation. They want to set Parliament free. They want to increase executive accountability. They want a written Bill of Rights. They have finally achieved standing parliamentary committees and want to increase the professional staffs and extend the powers of investigation and oversight. They want the right to examine witnesses in committee during the consideration of pending legislation. They want a select committee to monitor the intelligence services. And the government, the *Economist* recently reported, "is faced with an all-party parliamentary coup aimed at seizing from the treasury the appointment and functions of the comptroller and auditor general, and restoring to the House of Commons power over many aspects of government spending."

A former prime minister spoke to me a few months ago with envy about our mid-term elections. "The only means we have between general elections of bringing national opinion to bear on national policies," he said, "is through by-elections, and this depends on a sufficiency of MPs resigning or dying. Luck has been with Mrs. Thatcher, and she has had far less than the average number of by-elections. How much better to give the whole country a chance to express itself every two years!"

Before succumbing to romantic myths of the parliamentary advantage, Americans would be well advised to listen to those who must live with the realities of the parliamentary order. But fortunately, given the nature of the American political tradition, the parliamentary system is an unreal alternative. The thought that in this era of conspicuous and probably irreversible party decay we can make our parties more commanding and cohesive than they have ever been is surely fantasy. Centralized and rigidly disci-

plined parties, the abolition of primaries, the intolerance of mavericks, the absence of free voting—all such things are against the looser genius of American politics.

One must raise a deeper question: Is the difficulty we encounter these days in meeting our problems really the consequence of defects in the structure of our government? After all, we have had the separation of powers from the beginning of the republic. This has not prevented competent presidents from acting with decision and dispatch. The separation of powers did not notably disable Jefferson or Jackson or Lincoln or Wilson or the Roosevelts. The most powerful plea of this century for a strong national authority—Herbert Croly's *The Promise of American Life*—didn't see the separation of powers as an obstacle to effective government. Why are things presumed to be so much worse today?

It cannot be that, nuclear weapons apart, we face tougher problems than our forefathers. Tougher problems than slavery? the Civil War? the Great Depression? World War II? Let us take care to avoid the fallacy of self-pity that leads every generation to suppose that it is peculiarly persecuted by history.

The real difference is that the presidents who operated the system successfully *knew what they thought should be done*—and were able to persuade Congress and the nation to give their remedies a try.

That possibility remains as open today as it ever was. In his first year as president, Mr. Reagan, who knew what he thought should be done, pushed a comprehensive economic program through Congress—and did so with triumphant success in spite of the fact that the program was manifestly incapable of achieving its contradictory objectives. He is in trouble now, not because of a failure of governmental structure, but because of the failure of the remedy. If his program had worked, he would be irresistible.

Our problem is not at all that we know what to do and are impeded from doing it by some structural logjam in the system. Our problem—

let us face it—is that we do not know what to do. We are as analytically impotent before the problem of inflation, for example, as we were half a century ago before the problem of depression. Our leadership has failed to convince a durable majority that one or another course will do the job.

Majority Is Not Strong Enough

If we don't know what ought to be done, efficient enactment of a poor program is a dubious accomplishment—as the experience of 1981 demonstrates. What is the great advantage of acting with decision and dispatch when you don't know what you are doing?

The issues aren't new. A century ago foreign visitors leveled the same criticism against our governmental structure. Lord Bryce in his great work, *The American Commonwealth*, reported the British view that the separation of powers, party indiscipline and the absence of party accountability made it almost impossible for the American political system to settle major national questions. He also reported the response to this criticism by American political leaders. Congress, they said, had not settled major national questions not because of defects in structure "but because the division of opinion in the country regarding them has been faithfully reflected in Congress. The majority has not been strong enough to get its way; and this has happened, not only because abundant opportunities for resistance arise from the methods of doing business, but still more because no distinct impulse of mandate towards any particular settlement of these questions has been received from the country. It is not for Congress to go faster than the people. When the country knows and speaks its mind, Congress will not fail to act."

When the country is not sure what ought to be done, it may be that delay, debate and further consideration are not a bad idea. And if our leadership is sure what to do, it must in our democracy educate the rest—and that is not a bad idea either. An effective leader with a sensible policy, or even (as in the recent Reagan case) with a less than sensible policy, has the resources under the present Constitution to get his way.

I believe that in the main our Constitution has worked pretty well. It has ensured discussion when we have lacked consensus and has permitted action when a majority can be convinced that the action is right. It allowed Franklin Roosevelt, for example, to enact the New Deal but blocked him when he tried to pack the Supreme Court. The court bill couldn't have failed if we had had a parliamentary system in 1937. In short, when the executive has a persuasive remedy, you don't need basic constitutional change. When the executive remedy is not persuasive, you don't want constitutional change.

My concern is that this agitation about constitutional reform is a form of escapism. Constitution-tinkering is a flight from the hard question, which is the search for remedy. Structure is an alibi for analytical failure. As Bryce wisely reminds us, "The student of institutions, as well as the lawyer, is apt to overrate the effect of mechanical contrivances in politics."

Fascinating as constitutional-tinkering may be, like the Rubik cube, let it not divert us from the real task of statecraft. Let us never forget that politics is the high and serious art of solving substantive problems.

Chapter 13

The Bureaucracy

$\mathcal{B}$ureaucracy is a pervasive and inescapable fact of modern existence. Every large organization in society—not just the government—is managed by a bureaucratic system: tasks are divided among particular experts, and decisions are made and administered according to general rules and regulations. No one who has attended a university, worked for a large corporation, served in the military, or dealt with the government is unfamiliar with the nature of bureaucracies.

Bureaucracies, as the sociologist Max Weber observed, are a necessary feature of modern life. When social organizations are small—as in a small business or a small academic department—decisions can be made and programs carried out by a few individuals using informal procedures and with a minimum of red tape and complicated paperwork. As these organizations grow, it becomes increasingly necessary to delegate authority, develop methods of tracking and assessment, and create general rules instead of deciding matters on a case-by-case basis. Suddenly a bureaucracy has arisen.

In the political realm, bureaucracies serve another purpose. Beginning with the Pendleton Act of 1883, civil service reformers sought to insulate routine governmental decisions from the vagaries of partisan politics—to ensure, in other words, that decisions were made on the basis of merit instead of on the basis of party affiliation. The Pendleton Act greatly reduced the number of presidential appointments in such departments as the Customs Service and the Post Office, putting in place an early version of the merit system. As the federal government's responsibilities grew, the need to keep politics out of such functions as tax collection, administration of social security and welfare, and similar programs became even greater.

The bureaucratization of government therefore serves important purposes: increasing efficiency, promoting fairness, ensuring accountability. Yet at the same time, it creates problems of its own. Bureaucracies have a tendency to grow, to become rigid, to become answerable only to themselves, and to create barriers between citizens and the government. These bureaucratic "pathologies" are well known; they are the subject *of frequent editorials and commentaries. Politicians can always count on stories about bureaucratic inefficiency and callousness to strike a chord with the voting public.*

This chapter provides its share of bureaucracy stories, especially in the vignettes in selections 13.4 through 13.7. But it also seeks to present the other side of the story—to show, as James Q. Wilson points out in selection 13.3, that bureaucratic pathologies are essentially of our own making. They are the result of our attempts to solve certain problems even at the expense of creating others.

Keep in mind that the alternative to bureaucratic government in the modern world is not some sort of utopian system in which all decisions are fair, all programs efficient, all children above average. Limiting the power of bureaucracies means increasing the power of other institutions: Congress, the presidency, private business, or the courts. Reducing the power of the bureaucracy may also create a government that is less fair or less accountable.

Also keep in mind that bureaucrats—like baseball umpires—are most noticeable when they make mistakes. Americans tend to take for granted the extraordinary number of government programs that work well: the letters delivered correctly and on time, the meat inspected properly, the airplanes that land safely. Criticism and evaluation of the bureaucracy must be kept in a reasonable perspective.

The federal bureaucracy interacts not only with individuals and private corporations but also with every other institution of government. The White House, Congress, and the courts each has a role in checking and overseeing the bureaucracy. (Chapters 11, 12 and 14 provide material with respect to these interconnections.)

Chapter Questions

1. What role does the bureaucracy in any large social system play? What functions does the bureaucracy perform? What are its most significant characteristics?

2. What is the relationship between the bureaucracy and the other political institutions in the United States? What are the alternatives to bureaucratic power? What are the advantages and disadvantages of these other forms of power? What are the advantages and disadvantages of bureaucratic power?

I THE CLASSIC TEXTS

Any discussion about bureaucracy—in the United States or anywhere else—must begin with Max Weber, who is best known for his work laying the intellectual foundation for the study of modern sociology. Weber wrote extensively on modern social and political organization; his works include the unfinished Wirtschaft und Gesellschaft [Economy and Society] *(1922) and the influential* The Protestant Ethic and the Spirit of Capitalism *(1904–1905).*

Weber was born in Thuringia, in what is now eastern Germany, in 1864; he died in 1920. Although his observations on bureaucracy draw on historical and contemporary European examples, they were heavily informed by his experiences in the United

States. While traveling in the New World, Weber was struck by the role of bureaucracy in a democratic society. The problem, as he saw it, was that a modern democracy required bureaucratic structures of all kinds in the administration of government and even in the conduct of professional party politics. Handing over the reins to a class of unelected "experts," however, threatened to undermine the very basis of democracy itself. He therefore understood opposition to civil service reform but saw such developments as inevitable in a modern society.

The development of a bureaucracy, according to Weber, cannot be avoided. But that is not to say that modern bureaucracies are without problems. Weber stressed two: the unaccountability of unelected civil servants and the bureaucratic tendency toward inflexibility in the application of rules.

Questions

1. What are the characteristics of the bureaucratic form of governmental power? What are bureaucracy's strong points? weak points?

2. What are the alternatives to bureaucracy, if any, in a modern society? How can the ill effects of bureaucracy be combated?

13.1 Bureaucracy

Max Weber

Characteristics of Bureaucracy

Modern officialdom functions in the following specific manner:

I. There is the principle of fixed and official jurisdictional areas, which are generally ordered by rules, that is, by laws or administrative regulations.

1. The regular activities required for the purposes of the bureaucratically governed structure are distributed in a fixed way as official duties.

2. The authority to give the commands required for the discharge of these duties is distributed in a stable way and is strictly delimited by rules concerning the coercive means, physical, sacerdotal, or otherwise, which may be placed at the disposal of officials.

3. Methodical provision is made for the regular and continuous fulfillment of these du-

ties and for the execution of the corresponding rights; only persons who have the generally regulated qualifications to serve are employed.

In public and lawful government these three elements constitute "bureaucratic authority." In private economic domination, they constitute bureaucratic "management." Bureaucracy, thus understood, is fully developed in political and ecclesiastical communities only in the modern state, and, in the private economy, only in the most advanced institutions of capitalism. Permanent and public office authority, with fixed jurisdiction, is not the historical rule but rather the exception. This is so even in large political structures such as those of the ancient Orient, the Germanic and Mongolian empires of conquest, or of many feudal structures of state. In all these cases, the ruler executes the most important measures through personal trustees, table-companions, or court-servants.

Their commissions and authority are not precisely delimited and are temporarily called into being for each case.

II. The principles of office hierarchy and of levels of graded authority mean a firmly ordered system of super- and subordination in which there is a supervision of the lower offices by the higher ones. Such a system offers the governed the possibility of appealing the decision of a lower office to its higher authority, in a definitely regulated manner. With the full development of the bureaucratic type, the office hierarchy is monocratically organized. The principle of hierarchical office authority is found in all bureaucratic structures: in state and ecclesiastical structures as well as in large party organizations and private enterprises. It does not matter for the character of bureaucracy whether its authority is called "private" or "public."

When the principle of jurisdictional "competency" is fully carried through, hierarchical subordination—at least in public office—does not mean that the "higher" authority is simply authorized to take over the business of the "lower." Indeed, the opposite is the rule. Once established and having fulfilled its task, an office tends to continue in existence and be held by another incumbent.

III. The management of the modern office is based upon written documents ("the files"), which are preserved in their original or draught form. There is, therefore, a staff of subaltern officials and scribes of all sorts. The body of officials actively engaged in a "public" office, along with the respective apparatus of material implements and the files, make up a "bureau." In private enterprise, "the bureau" is often called "the office."

In principle, the modern organization of the civil service separates the bureau from the private domicile of the official, and, in general, bureaucracy segregates official activity as something distinct from the sphere of private life. Public monies and equipment are divorced from the private property of the official. This condition is everywhere the product of a long development. Nowadays, it is found in public as well as in private enterprises; in the latter, the principle extends even to the leading entrepreneur. In principle, the executive office is separated from the household, business from private correspondence, and business assets from private fortunes. The more consistently the modern type of business management has been carried through the more are these separations the case. The beginnings of this process are to be found as early as the Middle Ages.

It is the peculiarity of the modern entrepreneur that he conducts himself as the "first official" of his enterprise, in the very same way in which the ruler of a specifically modern bureaucratic state spoke of himself as "the first servant" of the state. The idea that the bureau activities of the state are intrinsically different in character from the management of private economic offices is a continental European notion and, by way of contrast, is totally foreign to the American way.

IV. Office management, at least all specialized office management—and such management is distinctly modern—usually presupposes thorough and expert training. This increasingly holds for the modern executive and employee of private enterprises, in the same manner as it holds for the state official.

V. When the office is fully developed, official activity demands the full working capacity of the official, irrespective of the fact that his obligatory time in the bureau may be firmly delimited. In the normal case, this is only the product of a long development, in the public as well as in the private office. Formerly, in all cases, the normal state of affairs was reversed: official business was discharged as a secondary activity.

VI. The management of the office follows general rules, which are more or less stable, more or less exhaustive, and which can be learned. Knowledge of these rules represents a special technical learning which the officials possess. It involves jurisprudence, or administrative or business management.

What Sort of Despotism Democratic Nations Have to Fear

The increasing importance of the bureaucratic state was predicted 150 years ago by Alexis de Tocqueville. Here he discusses the sort of despotism that democratic nations have to fear: not the unchecked power of the tyrant but the nagging presence of the schoolmaster.

. . . *I*f a despotism should be established among the democratic nations of our day, it would probably have a different character [than a traditional despotism]. It would be more widespread and milder; it would degrade men rather than torment them.

Doubtless, in such an age of education and equality as our own, rulers could more easily bring all public powers into their own hands alone, and they could impinge deeper and more habitually into the sphere of private interests than was ever possible in antiquity. But that same equality which makes despotism easy tempers it. We have seen how, as men become more alike and more nearly equal, public mores becomes more humane and gentle. When there is no citizen with great power or wealth, tyranny in some degree lacks both target and stage. When all fortunes are middling, passions are naturally restrained, imagination limited, and pleasures simple. Such universal moderation tempers the sovereign's own spirit and keeps within certain limits the disorderly urges of desire.

Apart from these reasons, based on the nature of the state of society itself, I could adduce many others which would take me outside the range of my subject, but I prefer to remain within these self-imposed limits.

Democratic governments might become violent and cruel at times of great excitement and danger, but such crises will be rare and brief.

Taking into consideration the trivial nature of men's passions now, the softness of their mores, the extent of their education, the purity of their religion, their steady habits of patient work, and the restraint which they all show in the indulgence of both their vices and their virtues, I do not expect their leaders to be tyrants, but rather schoolmasters.

Thus I think that the type of oppression which threatens democracies is different from anything there has ever been in the world before. Our contemporaries will find no prototype of it in their memories. I have myself vainly searched for a word which will exactly express the whole of the conception I have formed. Such old words as "despotism" and "tyranny" do not fit. The thing is new, and as I cannot find a word for it, I must try to define it.

I am trying to imagine under what novel features despotism may appear in the world. In the first place, I see an innumerable multitude of men,

---

The reduction of modern office management to rules is deeply embedded in its very nature. The theory of modern public administration, for instance, assumes that the authority to order certain matters by decree—which has been legally granted to public authorities—does not entitle the bureau to regulate the matter by commands given for each case, but only to regulate the matter abstractly. This stands in extreme contrast to the regulation of all relationships through individual privileges and bestowals of favor, which is absolutely dominant in patrimonialism, at least in so far as such relationships are not fixed by sacred tradition.

• • •

Technical Advantages of Bureaucratic Organization

The decisive reason for the advance of bureaucratic organization has always been its purely technical superiority over any other form of organization. The fully developed bureaucratic

alike and equal, constantly circling around in pursuit of the petty and banal pleasures with which they glut their souls. Each one of them, withdrawn into himself, is almost unaware of the fate of the rest. Mankind, for him, consists in his children and his personal friends. As for the rest of his fellow citizens, they are near enough, but he does not notice them. He touches them but feels nothing. He exists in and for himself, and though he still may have a family, one can at least say that he has not got a fatherland.

Over this kind of men stands an immense, protective power which is alone responsible for securing their enjoyment and watching over their fate. That power is absolute, thoughtful of detail, orderly, provident, and gentle. It would resemble parental authority if, father-like, it tried to prepare its charges for a man's life, but on the contrary, it only tries to keep them in perpetual childhood. It likes to see the citizens enjoy themselves, provided that they think of nothing but enjoyment. It gladly works for their happiness but wants to be sole agent and judge of it. It provides for their security, foresees and supplies their necessities, facilitates their pleasures, manages their principal concerns, directs their industry, makes rules for their testaments, and divides their inheritances. Why should it not entirely relieve them from the trouble of thinking and all the cares of living?

Thus it daily makes the exercise of free choice less useful and rarer, restricts the activity of free will within a narrower compass, and little by little robs each citizen of the proper use of his own faculties. Equality has prepared men for all this, predisposing them to endure it and often even regard it as beneficial.

Having thus taken each citizen in turn in its powerful grasp and shaped him to its will, government then extends its embrace to include the whole of society. It covers the whole of social life with a network of petty, complicated rules that are both minute and uniform, through which even men of the greatest originality and the most vigorous temperament cannot force their heads above the crowd. It does not break men's will, but softens, bends, and guides it; it seldom enjoins, but often inhibits, action; it does not destroy anything, but prevents much being born; it is not at all tyrannical, but it hinders, restrains, enervates, stifles, and stultifies so much that in the end each nation is no more than a flock of timid and hardworking animals with the government as its shepherd.

—*Alexis de Tocqueville*

mechanism compares with other organizations exactly as does the machine with the non-mechanical modes of production.

Precision, speed, unambiguity, knowledge of the files, continuity, discretion, unity, strict subordination, reduction of friction and of material and personal costs—these are raised to the optimum point in the strictly bureaucratic administration, and especially in its monocratic form. As compared with all collegiate, honorific, and avocational forms of administration, trained bureaucracy is superior on all these points. And as far as complicated tasks are concerned, paid bureaucratic work is not only more precise but, in the last analysis, it is often cheaper than even formally unremunerated honorific service.

Honorific arrangements make administrative work an avocation and, for this reason alone, honorific service normally functions more slowly; being less bound to schemata and being more formless. Hence it is less precise and less unified than bureaucratic work because it is less dependent upon superiors and because the establishment and exploitation of the apparatus of subordinate officials and filing services are almost unavoidably less economical. Honorific service is less continuous than bureaucratic and frequently quite expensive. This is especially the case if one thinks not only of the money costs to the public treasury—costs which bureaucratic administration, in comparison with administration by notables, usually substantially increases—but also of the frequent economic losses of the governed caused by delays and lack of precision. The possibility of administration by notables normally and permanently exists only where official management can be satisfactorily discharged as an avocation. With the qualitative increase of tasks the administration has to face, administration by notables reaches its limits—today, even in England. Work organized by collegiate bodies causes friction and delay and requires compromises between colliding interests and views. The administration, therefore, runs less precisely and is more independent of superiors; hence, it is less unified and slower. All advances of the Prussian administrative organization have been and will in the future be advances of the bureaucratic, and especially of the monocratic, principle.

Today, it is primarily the capitalist market economy which demands that the official business of the administration be discharged precisely, unambiguously, continuously, and with as much speed as possible. Normally, the very large, modern capitalist enterprises are themselves unequalled models of strict bureaucratic organization. Business management throughout rests on increasing precision, steadiness, and, above all, the speed of operations. This, in turn, is determined by the peculiar nature of the modern means of communication, including, among other things, the news service of the press. The extraordinary increase in the speed by which public announcements, as well as economic and political facts, are transmitted exerts a steady and sharp pressure in the direction of speeding up the tempo of administrative reaction towards various situations. The optimum of such reaction time is normally attained only by a strictly bureaucratic organization.

Bureaucratization offers above all the optimum possibility for carrying through the principle of specializing administrative functions according to purely objective considerations. Individual performances are allocated to functionaries who have specialized training and who by constant practice learn more and more. The "objective" discharge of business primarily means a discharge of business according to *calculable rules* and "without regard for persons."

"Without regard for persons" is also the watchword of the "market" and, in general, of all pursuits of naked economic interests. A consistent execution of bureaucratic domination means the leveling of status "honor." Hence, if the principle of the free-market is not . the same time restricted, it means the universal domination of the "class situation." That this consequence of bureaucratic domination has not set in everywhere, parallel to the extent of bureaucratization, is due to the differences among possible principles by which politics may meet their demands.

The second element mentioned, "calculable rules," also is of paramount importance for modern bureaucracy. The peculiarity of modern culture, and specifically of its technical and economic basis, demands this very "calculability" of results. When fully developed, bureaucracy also stands, in a specific sense, under the principle of *sine ira ac studio.* Its specific nature, which is welcomed by capitalism, develops the more perfectly the more the bureaucracy is "dehumanized," the more completely it succeeds in eliminating from official business love, hatred, and all purely personal, irrational, and emotional elements which escape calculation. This is the specific nature of bureaucracy and it is appraised as its special virtue.

The more complicated and specialized modern culture becomes, the more its external supporting apparatus demands the personally detached and strictly "objective" *expert,* in lieu of the master of older social structures, who was moved by personal sympathy and favor, by grace and gratitude. Bureaucracy offers the attitudes demanded by the external apparatus of modern culture in the most favorable combination. As a rule, only bureaucracy has established the foundation for the administration of a rational law conceptually systematized on the basis of such enactments as the latter Roman imperial period first created with a high degree of technical perfection. During the Middle Ages, this law was received along with the bureaucratization of legal administration, that is to say, with the displacement of the old trial procedure which was bound to tradition or to irrational presuppositions, by the rationally trained and specialized expert.

The Power Position of Bureaucracy

Everywhere the modern state is undergoing bureaucratization. But whether the *power* of bureaucracy within the polity is universally increasing must here remain an open question.

The fact that bureaucratic organization is technically the most highly developed means of power in the hands of the man who controls it does not determine the weight that bureaucracy as such is capable of having in a particular social structure. The ever-increasing "indispensability" of the officialdom, swollen to millions, is no more decisive for this question than is the view of some representatives of the proletarian movement that the economic indispensability of the proletarians is decisive for the measure of their social and political power position. If "indispensability" were decisive, then where slave labor prevailed and where freemen usually abhor work as a dishonor, the "indispensable" slaves ought to have held the positions of power, for they were at least as indispensable as officials and proletarians are today. Whether the power of bureaucracy as such increases cannot be decided *a priori* from such reasons. The drawing in of economic interest groups or other non-official experts, or the drawing in of non-expert lay representatives, the establishment of local, inter-local, or central parliamentary or other representative bodies, or of occupational associations—these *seem* to run directly against the bureaucratic tendency. . . .

Under normal conditions, the power position of a fully developed bureaucracy is always overtowering. The "political master" finds himself in the position of the "dilettante" who stands opposite the "expert," facing the trained official who stands within the management of administration. This holds whether the "master" whom the bureaucracy serves is a "people," equipped with the weapons of "legislative initiative," the "referendum," and the right to remove officials, or a parliament, elected on a more aristocratic or more "democratic" basis and equipped with the right to vote a lack of confidence, or with the actual authority to vote it. It holds whether the master is an aristocratic, collegiate body, legally or actually based on self-recruitment, or whether he is a popularly elected president, a hereditary and "absolute" or a "constitutional" monarch.

Every bureaucracy seeks to increase the superiority of the professionally informed by keeping their knowledge and intentions secret. Bureaucratic administration always tends to be an administration of "secret sessions": in so far as it can, it hides its knowledge and action from criticism. Prussian church authorities now threaten to use disciplinary measures against pastors who make reprimands or other admonitory measures in any way accessible to third parties. They do this because the pastor, in making such criticism available, is "guilty" of facilitating a possible criticism of the church authorities. The treasury officials of the Persian shah have made a secret doctrine of their budgetary art and even use secret script. The official statistics of Prussia, in general, make public only what cannot do any harm to the intentions of the power-wielding bureaucracy. The tendency toward secrecy in certain administrative fields follows their material nature: everywhere that the power interests of the domination structure toward *the outside* are at stake, whether it is an economic competitor of a private enterprise, or a foreign, potentially hostile polity, we find secrecy. If it is to be successful, the management of diplomacy can only be publicly controlled to a very limited extent. The military administration must insist on the concealment of its most important measures; with the increasing significance of purely technical aspects, this is all the more the case. Political parties do not proceed differently, in spite of all the ostensible publicity of Catholic congresses and party conventions. With the increasing bureaucratization of party organizations, this secrecy will prevail even more. Commercial policy, in Germany for instance, brings about a concealment of production statistics. Every fighting posture of a social structure toward the outside tends to buttress the position of the group in power.

The pure interest of the bureaucracy in power, however, is efficacious far beyond those areas where purely functional interests make for secrecy. The concept of the "official secret" is the specific invention of bureaucracy, and nothing is so fanatically defended by the bureaucracy as this attitude, which cannot be substantially justified beyond these specifically qualified areas. In facing a parliament, the bureaucracy, out of a sure power instinct, fights every attempt of the parliament to gain knowledge by means of its own experts or from interest groups. The so-called right of parliamentary investigation is one of the means by which parliament seeks such knowledge. Bureaucracy naturally welcomes a poorly informed and hence a powerless parliament—at least in so far as ignorance somehow agrees with the bureaucracy's interests.

The absolute monarch is powerless opposite the superior knowledge of the bureaucratic expert—in a certain sense more powerless than any other political head. All the scornful decrees of Frederick the Great concerning the "abolition of serfdom" were derailed, as it were, in the course of their realization because the official mechanism simply ignored them as the occasional ideas of a dilettante. When a constitutional king agrees with a socially important part of the governed, he very frequently exerts a

greater influence upon the course of administration than does the absolute monarch. The constitutional king can control these experts better because of what is, at least relatively, the public character of criticism, whereas the absolute monarch is dependent for information solely upon the bureaucracy. The Russian czar of the old regime was seldom able to accomplish permanently anything that displeased his bureaucracy and hurt the power interests of the bureaucrats. His ministerial departments, placed directly under him as the autocrat, represented a conglomerate of satrapies. . . . These satrapies constantly fought against one another by all the means of personal intrigue, and, especially, they bombarded one another with voluminous "memorials," in the face of which, the monarch, as a dilettante, was helpless.

With the transition to constitutional government, the concentration of the power of the central bureaucracy in one head became unavoidable. Officialdom was placed under a monocratic head, the prime minister, through whose hands everything had to go before it got to the monarch. This put the latter, to a large extent, under the tutelage of the chief of the bureaucracy. Wilhelm II, in his well-known conflict with Bismarck, fought against this principle, but he had to withdraw his attack very soon. Under the rule of expert knowledge, the actual influence of the monarch can attain steadiness only by a continuous communication with the bureaucratic chiefs; this intercourse must be methodically planned and directed by the head of the bureaucracy.

At the same time, constitutionalism binds the bureaucracy and the ruler into a community of interests against the desires of party chiefs for power in the parliamentary bodies. And if he cannot find support in parliament the constitutional monarch is powerless against the bureaucracy. The desertion of the "Great of the Reich," the Prussian ministers and top officials of the Reich in November 1918, brought a monarch into approximately the same situation as existed in the feudal state in 1056. However, this is an exception, for, on the whole, the power position of a monarch opposite bureaucratic officials is far stronger than it was in any feudal state or in the "stereotyped" patrimonial state. This is because of the constant presence of aspirants for promotion, with whom the monarch can easily replace inconvenient and independent officials. Other circumstances being equal, only economically independent officials, that is, officials who belong to the propertied strata, can permit themselves to risk the loss of their offices. Today as always, the recruitment of officials from among propertyless strata increases the power of the rulers. Only officials who belong to a socially influential stratum, whom the monarch believes he must take into account as personal supporters, . . . can permanently and completely paralyse the substance of his will.

Only the expert knowledge of private economic interest groups in the field of "business" is superior to the expert knowledge of the bureaucracy. This is so because the exact knowledge of facts in their field is vital to the economic existence of businessmen. Errors in official statistics do not have direct economic consequences for the guilty official, but errors in the calculation of a capitalist enterprise are paid for by losses, perhaps by its existence. The "secret," as a means of power, is, after all, more safely hidden in the books of an enterpriser than it is in the files of public authorities. For this reason alone authorities are held within narrow barriers when they seek to influence economic life in the capitalist epoch. Very frequently the measures of the state in the field of capitalism take unforeseen and unintended courses, or they are made illusory by the superior expert knowledge of interest groups.

II THE INTERNATIONAL CONTEXT

Although the American civil service shares many attributes in common with all other bureaucracies, there are nonetheless certain unique features of public administration in the United States. Those differences include matters of structure and function and extend to the way the bureaucracy is viewed by political scientists. Like the bureaucracy it studies, the field of American public administration itself is unique.

The following brief statement of the differences between American and European public administration highlights both the governmental and academic sides of the question. Some of these differences relate to the American constitutional structure; others stem from historical differences between the United States and Europe; still others are a result of differences in political culture.

Questions

1. Break down the ten items mentioned in this selection into the following categories: (a) historical differences (b) constitutional differences, and (c) cultural differences. (Some of these categories may overlap.)

2. Of the ten items mentioned, which seem most fundamental? least consequential?

3. Which items relate specifically to the structure and function of the government bureaucracy? which to the academic study of public administration? which to both?

13.2 *The Distinctive Nature of American Public Administration*

Gerald E. Caiden, Richard A. Lovard, Thomas J. Pavlak, Lynn F. Sipe, and Molly M. Wong

The scope of American public administration is distinct in at least ten ways. First, in contrast to the European tradition, it excludes public law. Public administration is not seen as the exercise of public law. Law is seen as part of the judiciary and the judicial system, and under the American doctrine of the separation of powers it is identified with the judicial branch of government, not the executive branch. Until recently, whenever the two overlapped, public administration gave way to the superior claims of the legal profession. Now, with public and administrative law becoming increasingly important to the practice of government, public administration is reaching out into judicial dimensions which the legal profession has been reluctant to explore. Nonetheless, public administration falls far short of the strong legal inclusion found in other countries where public law and public administration are indistinguishable.

Second, in contrast to the British tradition, it has excluded, until relatively recently, considerations of the ends of government and the uses of public office. Public administration has not been seen as the exercise of power. Public power has been seen as part of the study of political science and in the dichotomy that was propounded by Wilson and Goodnow the study of politics and uses made of public office were separated from the study of administration. Whenever the two overlapped, public administration yielded in this case to political science. With the acceptance of the administrative state and the emergence of Big Government, the processes of government can no longer be separated from the purposes to which they are put. Public administration has come now to include the objectives as well as the practices of public management. It has also been reaching out into

policy and public interest dimensions which political scientists have been reluctant to explore. Nonetheless, there is still much diffidence, if not downright reluctance, to go beyond the dimensions of the management of public organizations. American public administration falls far short of the strong political inclusion found in other countries where public affairs have never distinguished between policy and administration and where the ends of government have never been separated from the means. Only recently in American public administration has it been realized that the two are (and probably always have been) fused and only recently have strong ideological differences emerged over the role of the administrative state in modern society.

Third, the generalist approach to the administration of public affairs has not been embraced in the United States to the extent that it has been elsewhere. The generalist tradition of the British administrative culture and the stress placed on intellectuality among European bureaucratic elites have provided an inclusive administrative profession to which other public management specialists have been subordinate. In contrast, the early emergence of strong professions in this country before the acceptance of a managerial profession (let alone the notion of a superior administrative cadre in the public bureaucracy) has fragmented the public sector into many rival concerns, few of which have accepted the superior imposition of a generalist administrative elite. Consequently, American public administration has been more of a residual than an inclusive entity. The armed forces and the management of defense have always been excluded; so too have the police and the management of justice, fire fighters, social workers, and teachers as well as members of the traditional professions (law, medicine, religion, higher education) employed in the public sector. These independent professions have jealously guarded their territory against intrusions from a generalist profession of public administrator. Since they were on the scene first, public administration has been reluctant to confront them and has tried to devise an amicable modus vivendi for peaceful coexistence. From a strictly logical point of view, the historical and political boundaries drawn between them make little sense. Compared with other countries, American public administration is less inclusory of public sector activities.

Fourth, the business community has been powerful in the United States and its influence over the public sector has probably been stronger than elsewhere. Many activities directly provided by the public bureaucracy in other countries are provided in the United States by the private sector or the significant third sector betwixt business and government, either directly or under contract with public authorities. Although part of the administrative state, they are not considered part of public administration; that is, scholars and practitioners have been reluctant to include them in their domains. On the one hand, this voluntary abstention has left significant gaps in the study of public administration which are now being filled hesitantly and inadequately. On the other hand, the blurred boundaries among the public, private, and third sectors have also opened up opportunities for the study of their interface which have been seized possibly to a greater extent than elsewhere. The same is probably true of intergovernmental administrative arrangements because of the blurred boundaries and jurisdictions among federal, state, regional, local, and community agencies in the United States.

Public administration in this country, fifth, is pragmatic, not ideological. The major concern has been to discover what works best in the public interest, construed in purely American terms in the light of prevailing conditions; rationalizations, justifications, and theoretical underpinnings have come afterwards. Yet this practical emphasis in American public administration should not be allowed to obscure its strong political roots in liberal democracy and the dominance of political principles over administrative practice and convenience. Democratic liberal values are paramount in American public management theory and practice. They are the lifeblood of the public bureaucracy. They are the unwritten premise on which the administrative state is expected to conduct itself. Since this is so well understood, American public administration has not felt the need to articulate its norms as much as other countries where the conduct of the state is subject to strong ideological differences and continuous political bargaining and shifting compromises.

Sixth, there really is no American public administration. It is a theoretical construct. Like Weber's ideal bureaucracy, it exists nowhere. It is a hybrid of common ideas and practices which have been abstracted from what exists. It is not a complete picture of reality, nor is it a photograph of specific circumstances. The United States is too diverse. Administrative arrangements and practices differ from one place to another, sometimes quite remarkably. In dealing with public administration as it really is, one experiences continual culture shock because experience contrasts so much with expectation. There are no common frames of reference: every office seems to be a law to itself, choosing within limits those practices which best suit itself. It is this variety that confuses and forces a level of abstraction that nowhere conforms exactly with reality. As a result, much in the study of public management is what should be rather than what is, and most is analytical not descriptive.

Next, because of constant change in public administration, history has little contemporary meaning. Historical analysis has little relevance to the present. In any case, administrators are so caught up with the present that they have little time for the past and little interest in having the past reconstructed for them. In brief, there is relatively little administrative history and, as the expense of holding archives for purely historical interest is rarely justifiable, the possibility of reconstructing the past diminishes with every passing year. The task is so daunting that there are few volunteers and precious little market. As a result, there is little historical continuity and many things are continually being rediscovered because often the left hand does not know what the right is doing (or has done). Anyway, Americans are not too proud of their administrative past nor of uncovering administrative skeletons that should remain buried. What is done is done. Only the present counts and making the future better counts even more. Public administration in this country looks forward not back.

Eighth, few figures dominate public administration in the United States. Other countries can point to their administrative heroes, those few individuals who dominated the public bureaucracy in their day or revamped it in their own image which lasted for an appreciable period after them. No so here. Americans do not indulge in much historical veneration, least of all public administrators. One of the few exceptions is Robert Moses who dominated New York government for decades, but his legacy has almost vanished and his reputation has not lasted. The same applies for the scholastic domain where no figure has emerged comparable in status to a Max Weber or a Maynard Keynes. Leonard White exercised some authority for a period as did Dwight Waldo, but the only Nobel Prize recipient has been Herbert Simon, much of whose pathfinding work was done in public administration, but since the 1950's he has not been associated with the field. If there have been no giants, there have been many persons of commendable stature who between them have made the development of the field a co-operative venture.

Ninth, the absence of an intellectual colossus, lateness in arriving on the American scene, and the tendency to fragmentation, have all caused public administration to fight for its place in the sun. It is frequently overshadowed by such more powerful disciplines as law, political science, and business administration which primarily serve other constituencies. These rivals claim that public administration does not exist or that if it does, it is a minor part of something else (usually themselves), that to be anything more than a minor or sub-discipline, it will have to demonstrate more than it has a proper intellectual or theoretical base, a clear and unquestionable core, well-defined boundaries, and a logically consistent whole. In brief, it should have a distinct and commonly accepted paradigm in order to be accepted as a fully fledged member of the academic community. Outside the United States, public administration does not suffer such intellectual indignity nor react with such an intellectual inferiority complex. In this nation, public administration is continually forced to reaffirm itself, to justify its existence and to protect itself from takeover bids. It is continually searching for its soul, for its *raison d'etre*, for its paradigm, for its identity. Periodically, it goes through its "identity crisis" and rediscovers itself. Nowhere else does public administration go through such soul-searching or experience such self-doubts.

Finally, nowhere else is public administration so misunderstood. The environment of public administration is decidedly unfriendly to it. Traditional American values exhort all that public administration is not and cannot be. In a country which once believed that "least government is best government," government management represents, rightly or wrongly, Big Government, bureaucracy, restrictions, taxation, dependency, authority, interference, parasitism, waste, spoils. Admittedly American bureaucracy has its shortcomings and failings, but no matter how well it performs—and to its credit it performs in the main most admirably— it never performs well enough. In mass media, it is rarely given the benefit of the doubt. Its motives are suspect; its actions are detrimental; its results are poor. It is almost axiomatic that business is better, that private enterprise is superior, that private organizations are more economic, efficient, and effective, and that the public sector is none of these things. No matter how satisfied and uncomplaining its clients, public administration cannot shake off its adverse images and stereotypes. It has to spend, perhaps justifiably, much effort not only proving that it does and should exist, but that its performance is good and constantly improving.

III INTERCONNECTIONS

Critics of the American bureaucracy frequently attack the public sector as wasteful, inefficient, and unaccountable to the public. Such criticisms, however, are frequently nothing more than cheap shots, for they ignore the very great differences between the public and private sectors. A fair appraisal of the public bureaucracy must begin with a clear view of what we expect from the public sector and of the constraints under which it must operate.

The government, as James Q. Wilson points out in the following selection, does indeed compare badly to the private sector when viewed in terms of economic efficiency. The problem, he suggests, is that government is constrained in ways that the private sector is not. And those constraints, he concludes, come from the people themselves. It is the people—expressing themselves individually, by way of interest groups, or through the legislature—who impose the constraints under which the bureaucracy must operate.

Central to Wilson's argument is his attempt to broaden the concept of efficiency to include more than economic efficiency. If we measure governmental action by the simple standard of economic efficiency—that is, the cost per unit output—government compares badly to the private sector. Once we recognize that a true measure of bureaucratic efficiency must take into account "all of the valued outputs"—including honesty, accountability, and responsiveness to particular constituents—the equation becomes more complicated, and perhaps more favorable to the government.

Wilson's argument is no whitewash for the government bureaucracy. Even allowing for all of this, as he points out, government agencies may still be inefficient. Recognizing the multifaceted and complex constraints on government officials will, in any event, provide a reasonable and realistic way to evaluate the bureaucracy.

Questions

1. Wilson suggests that government officials operate under very different constraints from their counterparts in the private sector. What are these differences, and what is their effect? Put another way, why does Wilson assert that "the government can't say 'yes'"?

2. What values other than economic efficiency do we demand of government? Why is the avoidance of arbitrariness so important?

3. In recent years, the federal government has been plagued by scandals in various departments, including the Department of Housing and Urban Development and the agencies charged with supervising the savings banks. Does Wilson's analysis help us to understand these scandals?

13.3 Bureaucracy: What Government Agencies Do and Why They Do It

James Q. Wilson

On the morning of May 22, 1986, Donald Trump, the New York real estate developer, called one of his executives, Anthony Glied-man, into his office. They discussed the inability of the City of New York, despite six years of effort and the expenditure of nearly $13 million, to rebuild the ice-skating rink in Central Park. On May 28 Trump offered to take over the rink reconstruction, promising to do the job in less than six months. A week later Mayor Edward Koch accepted the offer and shortly thereafter the city appropriated $3 million on the understanding that Trump would have to pay for any cost overruns out of his own pocket. On October 28, the renovation was complete, over a month ahead of schedule and about $750,000 under budget. Two weeks later, skaters were using it.

For many readers it is obvious that private enterprise is more efficient than are public bureaucracies, and so they would file this story away as simply another illustration of what everyone already knows. But for other readers it is not so obvious what this story means; to them, business is greedy and unless watched like a hawk will fob off shoddy or overpriced goods on the American public, as when it sells the government $435 hammers and $3,000 coffeepots. Trump may have done a good job in this instance, but perhaps there is something about skating rinks or New York City government that gave him a comparative advantage; in any event, no larger lessons should be drawn from it.

Some lessons can be drawn, however, if one looks closely at the incentives and constraints facing Trump and the Department of Parks and Recreation. It becomes apparent that there is not one "bureaucracy problem" but several, and the solution to each in some degree is incompatible with the solution to every other. First there is the problem of accountability—getting agencies to serve agreed-upon goals. Second there is the problem of equity—treating all citizens fairly, which usually means treating them alike on the basis of clear rules known in advance. Third there is the problem of responsiveness—reacting reasonably to the special needs and circumstances of particular people. Fourth there is the problem of efficiency—obtaining the greatest output for a given level of resources. Finally there is the problem of fiscal integrity—assuring that public funds are spent prudently for public purposes. Donald Trump and Mayor Koch were situated differently with respect to most of these matters.

Accountability

The Mayor wanted the old skating rink refurbished, but he also wanted to minimize the cost of the fuel needed to operate the rink (the first effort to rebuild it occurred right after the Arab oil embargo and the attendant increase in energy prices). Trying to achieve both goals led city hall to select a new refrigeration system that it turned out would not work properly. Trump came on the scene when only one goal dominated: get the rink rebuilt. He felt free to select the most reliable refrigeration system without worrying too much about energy costs.

Equity

The Parks and Recreation Department was required by law to give every contractor an equal chance to do the job. This meant it had to put every part of the job out to bid and to accept the lowest without much regard to the reputation or prior performance of the lowest bidder. Moreover, state law forbade city agencies from hiring a general contractor and letting him select the subcontractors; in fact, the law forbade the city from even discussing the project in advance with a general contractor who might later bid on it—that would have been collusion. Trump, by contrast, was free to locate the rink builder with the best reputation and give him the job.

Fiscal Integrity

To reduce the chance of corruption or sweetheart deals the law required Parks and Recreation to furnish complete, detailed plans to every contractor bidding on the job; any changes after that would require renegotiating the contract. No such law constrained Trump; he was free to give incomplete plans to his chosen contractor, hold him accountable for building a satisfactory rink, but allow him to work out the details as he went along.

Efficiency

When the Parks and Recreation Department spent over six years and $13 million and still could not reopen the rink, there was public criticism but no city official lost money. When Trump accepted a contract to do it, any cost overruns or delays would have come out of his pocket and any savings could have gone into his pocket (in this case, Trump agreed not to take a profit on the job).

Gliedman summarized the differences neatly: "The problem with government is that government can't say, 'yes' . . . there is nobody in government that can do that. There are fifteen or twenty people who have to agree. Gov-

"Bureaucratic busybodies! They keep tabs on you from the day you're born!"

Drawing by Starke; © 1972 The New Yorker Magazine, Inc.

James Q. Wilson   **487**

ernment has to be slower. It has to safeguard the process."

Inefficiency

The government can't say "yes." In other words, the government is constrained. Where do the constraints come from? From us.

Herbert Kaufman has explained red tape as being of our own making: "Every restraint and requirement originates in somebody's demand for it." Applied to the Central Park skating rink Kaufman's insight reminds us that civil-service reformers demanded that no city official benefit personally from building a project; that contractors demanded that all be given an equal chance to bid on every job; and that fiscal watchdogs demanded that all contract specifications be as detailed as possible. For each demand a procedure was established; viewed from the outside, those procedures are called red tape. To enforce each procedure a manager was appointed; those managers are called bureaucrats. No organized group demanded that all skating rinks be rebuilt as quickly as possible, no procedure existed to enforce that demand, and no manager was appointed to enforce it. The political process can more easily enforce compliance with constraints than the attainment of goals.

When we denounce bureaucracy for being inefficient we are saying something that is half true. Efficiency is a ratio of valued resources used to valued outputs produced. The smaller that ratio the more efficient the production. If the valued output is a rebuilt skating rink, then whatever process uses the fewest dollars or the least time to produce a satisfactory rink is the most efficient process. By this test Trump was more efficient than the Parks and Recreation Department.

But that is too narrow a view of the matter. The economic definition of efficiency (efficiency in the small, so to speak) assumes that there is only one valued output, the new rink. But government has many valued outputs, including a reputation for integrity, the confidence of the people, and the support of important interest groups. When we complain about skating rinks not being built on time we speak as if all we cared about were skating rinks. But when we complain that contracts were awarded without competitive bidding or in a way that allowed bureaucrats to line their pockets we acknowledge that we care about many things besides skating rinks; we care about the contextual goals—the constraints—that we want government to observe. A government that is slow to build rinks but is honest and accountable in its actions and properly responsive to worthy constituencies may be a very efficient government, *if* we measure efficiency in the large by taking into account *all* of the valued outputs.

Calling a government agency efficient when it is slow, cumbersome, and costly may seem perverse. But that is only because we lack any objective way for deciding how much money or time should be devoted to maintaining honest behavior, producing a fair allocation of benefits, and generating popular support as well as to achieving the main goal of the project. If we could measure these things, and if we agreed as to their value, then we would be in a position to judge the true efficiency of a government agency and decide when it is taking too much time or spending too much money achieving all that we expect of it. But we cannot measure these things nor do we agree about their relative importance, and so government always will appear to be inefficient compared to organizations that have fewer goals.

Put simply, the only way to decide whether an agency is truly inefficient is to decide which of the constraints affecting its action ought to be ignored or discounted. In fact that is what most debates about agency behavior are all about. In fighting crime are the police handcuffed? In educating children are teachers tied down by rules? In launching a space shuttle are we too concerned with safety? In building a dam do we worry excessively about endangered species? In running the Postal Service is it important to have many post offices close to where people live? In the case of the skating rink, was the requirement of competitive bidding for each contract on the basis of detailed specifications a reasonable one? Probably not. But if it were abandoned, the gain (the swifter completion of the rink) would have to be balanced against the costs (complaints from contractors who might lose business and the chance of collusion and corruption in some future projects).

Even allowing for all of these constraints, government agencies may still be inefficient. Indeed, given the fact that bureaucrats cannot (for the most part) benefit monetarily from their agencies' achievements, it would be surprising if they were not inefficient. Efficiency, in the large or the small, doesn't pay.

But some critics of government believe that inefficiency is obvious and vast. Many people remember the 1984 claim of the Grace Commission (officially, the President's Private Sector Survey on Cost Control) that it had identified over $400 billion in savings that could be made if only the federal government were managed properly. Though the commission did not say so, many people inferred that careless bureaucrats were wasting that amount of money. But hardly anybody remembers the study issued jointly by the General Accounting Office and the Congressional Budget Office in February 1984, one month after the Grace Commission report. The GAO and CBO reviewed those Grace recommendations that accounted for about 90 percent of the projected savings, and after eliminating double-counting and recommendations for which no savings could be estimated, and other problems, concluded that the true savings would be less than one-third the claimed amount.

Of course, $100 billion is still a lot of money. But wait. It turns out that about 60 percent of this would require not management improvements but policy changes: for example, taxing welfare benefits, ending certain direct loan programs, adopting new rules to restrict Medicare benefits, restricting eligibility for retirement among federal civilian workers and military personnel, and selling the power produced by government-owned hydroelectric plants at the full market price.

That still leaves roughly $40 billion in management savings. But most of this would require either a new congressional policy (for example, hiring more Internal Revenue Service agents to collect delinquent taxes), some unspecified increase in "worker productivity," or buying more services from private suppliers. Setting aside the desirable goal of increasing productivity (for which no procedures were identified), it turns out that almost all of the projected savings would require Congress to alter the goals and constraints of public agencies. If there is a lot of waste (and it is not clear why the failure to tax welfare benefits or to hire more IRS agents should be called waste), it is congressionally directed waste.

Military procurement, of course, is the biggest source of stories about waste, fraud, and mismanagement. There cannot be a reader of this [selection] who has not heard about the navy paying $435 for a hammer or the air force paying $3,000 for a coffeepot, and nobody, I suspect, believes Defense Department estimates of the cost of a new airplane or missile. If ever one needed evidence that bureaucracy is inefficient, the Pentagon supplies it.

Well, yes. But what kind of efficiency? And why does it occur? To answer these questions one must approach the problem just as we approached the problem of fixing up a skating rink in New York City: We want to understand why the bureaucrats, all of whom are rational and most of whom want to do a good job, behave as they do.

To begin, let us forget about $435 hammers. They never existed. A member of Congress who did not understand (or did not want to understand) government accounting rules created a public stir. The $3,000 coffeepot existed, but it is not clear that it was overpriced.* But that does

* This is what happened: The navy ordered a package of maintenance equipment. One of the items was an inexpensive hammer; some of the others were very expensive test devices. Under the accounting rules then in effect, the sup-

not mean there are no problems; in fact, the real problems are far more costly and intractable than inflated price tags on hammers and coffeemakers. They include sticking too long with new weapons of dubious value, taking forever to acquire even good weapons, and not inducing contractors to increase their efficiency. What follows is not a complete explanation of military procurement problems; it is only an analysis of the contribution bureaucratic systems make to those problems.

When the military buys a new weapons system—a bomber, submarine, or tank—it sets in motion a procurement bureaucracy comprised of two key actors, the military program manager and the civilian contract officer, who must cope with the contractor, the Pentagon hierarchy, and Congress. To understand how they behave we must understand how their tasks get defined, what incentives they have, and what constraints they face.

Tasks

The person nominally in charge of buying a major new weapon is the program manager, typically an army or air force colonel or a navy captain. Officially, his job is to design and oversee the acquisition strategy by establishing specifications and schedules and identifying problems and tradeoffs. Unofficially, his task is somewhat different. For one thing he does not have the authority to make many important decisions; those are referred upward to his military superiors, to Defense Department civilians,

and to Congress. For another, the program he oversees must constantly be sold and resold to the people who control the resources (mostly, the key congressional committees). And finally, he is surrounded by inspectors and auditors looking for any evidence of waste, fraud, or abuse and by the advocates of all manner of special interests (contractors' representatives, proponents of small and minority business utilization, and so on). As the Packard Commission observed, the program manager, "far from being the manager of the program . . . is merely one of the participants who can influence it."

Under these circumstances the actual risk of the program manager tends to be defined as selling the program and staying out of trouble. Harvard Business School professor J. Ronald Fox, who has devoted much of his life to studying and participating in weapons procurement, found that a program manager must spend 30 to 50 percent of his time defending his program inside DOD and to Congress. It is entirely rational for him to do this, for a study by the General Accounting Office showed that weapons programs with effective advocates survived (including some that should have been terminated) and systems without such advocates were more likely to be ended (even some that should have been completed). Just as with the New York City skating rink, in the Pentagon there is no one who can say "yes" and make it stick. The only way to keep winning the support of the countless people who must say "yes" over and over again is to forge ahead at full speed, spending money at a rate high enough to prevent it from being taken away.

The program manager's own background and experience reinforce this definition of his task. He is a military officer, which means he cares deeply about having the best possible airplane, tank, or submarine. In recommending any tradeoffs between cost and performance, his natural inclination is to favor performance over savings. After all, someday he may have to fly in that airplane or sail on that ship. This often leads to what is commonly called "gold-plating": seeking the best possible, most so-

plier was allowed to allocate overhead costs in equal percentages to each item. This was simpler than trying to figure out how much overhead should be attributed to each individual item (in which case the difficult-to-make items would, of course, have accounted for more of the overhead than the easy-to-make ones such as a hammer). As a result, the bill showed the hammer as costing several hundred dollars in "overhead," for a total of $435. When a sailor unpacked the box, he found this bill and, not understanding the equal-allocation formula, called his congressman. A myth was born. The "coffeepot" did cost about $3,000, but it was purchased to make coffee for the more than three hundred soldiers who would be carried on a C-5A transport. Commercial airlines often pay that much for coffeemakers on their jumbo jets.

phisticated weapon and making frequent changes in the contract specifications in order to incorporate new features. The program manager, of course, does not make these decisions, but he is an integral part of a user-dominated process that does make them.

The civilian counterpart to the program manager is the contracting officer. What is clear is that he or she, and not the program manager, is the only person legally authorized to sign the contract. In addition, the contracting officer administers the contract and prepares a report on contractor performance. Everything else is unclear. In principle, contracting officers are supposed to be involved in every step of the acquisition process, from issuing an invitation to bid on the contract through the completion of the project. In practice, as Ronald Fox observes, contracting officers often play only a small role in designing the acquisition strategy or in altering the contracts (this tends to be dominated by the program manager) and must share their authority over enforcing the terms of the contract with a small army of auditors and advocates.

What dominates the task of the contract officer are the rules, the more than 1,200 pages of the Federal Acquisition Regulation and Defense Acquisition Regulation in addition to the countless other pages in DOD directives and congressional authorization legislation and the unwritten "guidance" that arrives with every visit to a defense plant where a contracting officer works. Contract officers are there to enforce constraints, and those constraints have grown exponentially in recent years.

Incentives

In theory, military program managers are supposed to win promotions if they have done a good job supervising weapons procurement. In fact, promotions to the rank of general or admiral usually have been made on the basis of their reputation as combat officers and experience as military leaders. According to Fox, being a program manager is often not a useful ticket to get punched if you want to rise to the highest ranks. In 1985, for example, 94 percent of the lieutenant colonels who had commanded a battalion were promoted by the army to the rank of colonel; the promotion rate for lieutenant colonels without that experience was only half as great. The armed services now claim that they do promote procurement officers at a reasonable rate, but Fox, as well as many officers, remain skeptical. The perceived message is clear: Traditional military specialties are a surer route to the top than experience as a program manager.

Reinforcing this bias against acquisition experience is the generalist ethos of the armed services—good officers can do any job; well-rounded officers have done many jobs. As a result, the typical program manager has a brief tenure in a procurement job. In 1986, the GAO found that the average program manager spent twenty-seven months on the job, and many spent less than two years. By contrast, it takes between eleven and twenty years to procure a major new weapons system, from concept to deployment. This means that during the acquisition of a new aircraft or missile, the identity of the program will change five or ten times.

In 1987, the services, under congressional prodding, established career paths for acquisition officers so that they could rise in rank while continuing to develop experience in procurement tasks. It is not yet clear how significant this change will be. If it encourages talented officers to invest ten or twenty years in mastering procurement policies it will be a major gain, one that will enable program managers from DOD to deal more effectively with experienced industry executives and encourage officers to make tough decisions rather than just keeping the program alive.

Civilian contract officers do have a distinct career path, but as yet not one that produces in them much sense of professional pride or organizational mission. Of the more than twenty thousand civilian contract administrators less than half have a college degree and the great majority are in the lower civil-service grades (GS-5 to GS-12). Even the most senior contract officers rarely earn (in 1988) more than $50,000 a year, less than half or even one-third of what their industry counterparts earn. Moreover, all are aware that they work in offices where the top posts usually are held by military officers; in civil-service jargon, the "head room" available for promotions is quite limited.

Of course, low pay has not prevented the development of a strong sense of mission in other government agencies. But in those organizations training and indoctrination are intensive. In the Defense Contract Administration Service they are not. In 1984, the DOD inspector general reported that two-thirds of the senior contract officers had not received the prescribed training.

The best evidence of the weakness of civilian incentives is the high turnover rate. Fox quotes a former commander of the military acquisition program as saying that "good people are leaving in droves" because "there is much less psychic income today" that would make up for the relatively low monetary income. The Packard Commission surveyed civilian procurement personnel and found that over half would leave their jobs if offered comparable jobs elsewhere in the federal government or in private industry.

In short, the incentives facing procurement officials do not reward people for maximizing efficiency. Military officers are rewarded for keeping programs alive and are encouraged to move on to other assignments; civilian personnel have weak inducements to apply a complex array of inconsistent constraints to contract administration.

Constraints

These constraints are not designed to produce efficiency but to reduce costs, avoid waste, fraud, and abuse, achieve a variety of social goals, and maintain the productive capacity of key contractors.

Reducing costs is not the same thing as increasing efficiency. If too little money is spent, the rate of production may be inefficient and the managerial flexibility necessary to cope with unforeseen circumstances may be absent. Congress typically appropriates money one year at a time. If Congress wishes to cut its spending or if DOD is ordered to slash its budget requests, the easiest thing to do is to reduce the number of aircraft, ships, or missiles being purchased in a given year without reducing the total amount purchased. This stretch-out has the effect of increasing the cost of each individual weapon as manufacturers forgo the economies that come from large-scale production. As Fox observes (but as many critics fail to understand), the typical weapons program in any given year is not overfunded, it is *under*funded. Recognizing that, the Packard Commission called for adopting a two-year budget cycle.

Reducing costs and eliminating fraud are not the same as increasing efficiency. There no doubt are excessive costs and there may be fraud in military procurement, but eliminating them makes procurement more efficient only if the costs of eliminating the waste and fraud exceed the savings thereby realized. To my knowledge no one has systematically compared the cost of all the inspectors, rules, and auditors with the savings they have achieved to see if all the checking and reviewing is worth it. Some anecdotal evidence suggests that the checking does not always pay for itself. In one case the army was required to spend $5,400 to obtain fully competitive bids for spare parts that cost $11,000. In exchange for the $5,400 and the 160 days it took to get the bids, the army saved $100. In short, there is an optimal level of "waste" in any organization, public or private: It is that level below which further savings are worth less than the cost of producing them.

The weapons procurement system must serve a number of "social" goals mandated by Congress. It must support small business, provide opportunities for minority-owned businesses, buy American-made products whenever possible, rehabilitate prisoners, provide employment for the handicapped, protect the environment, and maintain "prevailing" wage rates. One could lower the cost of procurement by eliminating some or all of the social goals the process is obliged to honor; that would produce increases in efficiency, narrowly defined. But what interest group is ready to sacrifice its most cherished goal in the name of efficiency? And if none will volunteer, how does one create a congressional majority to compel the sacrifice?

Weapons procurement also is designed to maintain the productive capacity of the major weapons builders. There is no true market in the manufacture of missiles, military aircraft, and naval vessels because typically there is only one buyer (the government) and no alternative uses for the production lines established to supply this buyer. Northrop, Lockheed, Grumman, McDonnell Douglas, the Bath Iron Works, Martin Marietta—these firms and others like them would not exist, or would exist in very different form, if they did not have a continuous flow of military contracts. As a result, each new weapons system becomes a do-or-die proposition for the executives of these firms. Even if the Pentagon cared nothing about their economic well-being it would have to care about the productive capacity that they represent, for if it were ever lost or much diminished the armed services would have nowhere else to turn when the need arose for a new airplane or ship. And if by chance the Pentagon did not care, Congress would; no member believes he or she was elected to preside over the demise of a major employer.

This constraint produces what some scholars have called the "follow-on imperative": the need to give a new contract to each major supplier as work on an old contract winds down. If one understands this it is not necessary to imagine some sinister "military-industrial complex" conspiring to keep new weapons flowing. The armed services want them because they believe, rightly, that their task is to defend the nation against real though hard to define threats; the contractors want them because they believe, rightly, that the nation cannot afford to dismantle its productive capacity; Congress wants them because its members believe, rightly, that they are elected to maintain the prosperity of their states and districts.

When these beliefs encounter the reality of limited resources and the need to make budget choices, almost everyone has an incentive to overstate the benefits and understate the costs of a new weapons system. To do otherwise—to give a cautious estimate of what the weapon will achieve and a candid view of what it will cost—is to invite rejection. And none of the key actors in the process believe they can afford rejection.

The Bottom Line

The incentives and constraints that confront the military procurement bureaucracy push its members to overstate benefits, understate costs, make frequent and detailed changes in specifications, and enforce a bewildering array of rules designed to minimize criticism and stay out of trouble. There are hardly any incentives pushing officials to leave details to manufacturers or delegate authority to strong program managers whose career prospects will depend on their ability to produce good weapons at a reasonable cost.

In view of all this, what is surprising is that the system works as well as it does. In fact, it works better than most people suppose. The Rand Corporation has been studying military procurement for over thirty years. A summary of its findings suggests some encouraging news, most of it ignored amidst the headlines about hammers and coffeepots. There has been steady improvement in the performance of the system. Between the early 1960s and the mid-1980s, cost overruns, schedule slippages, and performance shortfalls have all decreased. Cost overruns of military programs on the average are now no greater than they are for the civil programs of the government such as highway and water projects and public buildings. Moreover, there is evidence that for all its faults the

American system seems to work as well as or better than that in many European nations.

Improvements can be made but they do not require bright new ideas, more regulations, or the reshuffling of boxes on the organizational chart. The necessary ideas exist in abundance, the top-down reorganizations have been tried without much effect, and the system is drowning in regulations. What is needed are changes in the incentives facing the key members. But . . . the conventional response has always been "regulate and reorganize."

Arbitrary Rule

Inefficiency is not the only bureaucratic problem nor is it even the most important. A perfectly efficient agency could be a monstrous one, swiftly denying us our liberties, economically inflicting injustices, and competently expropriating our wealth. People complain about bureaucracy as often because it is unfair or unreasonable as because it is slow or cumbersome.

Arbitrary rule refers to officials acting without legal authority, or with that authority in a way that offends our sense of justice. Justice means, first, that we require the government to treat people equally on the basis of clear rules known in advance: If Becky and Bob both are driving sixty miles per hour in a thirty-mile-per-hour zone and the police give a ticket to Bob, we believe they also should give a ticket to Becky. Second, we believe that justice obliges the government to take into account the special needs and circumstances of individuals: If Becky is speeding because she is on her way to the hospital to give birth to a child and Bob is speeding for the fun of it, we may feel that the police should ticket Bob but not Becky. Justice in the first sense means fairness, in the second it means responsiveness. Obviously, fairness and responsiveness often are in conflict.

The checks and balances of the American constitutional system reflect our desire to reduce the arbitrariness of official rule. That desire is based squarely on the premise that inefficiency is a small price to pay for freedom and responsiveness. Congressional oversight, judi-cial review, interest-group participation, media investigations, and formalized procedures all are intended to check administrative discretion. It is not hyperbole to say that the constitutional order is animated by the desire to make the government "inefficient."

This creates two great tradeoffs. First, adding constraints reduces the efficiency with which the main goal of an agency can be attained but increases the chances that the agency will act in a nonarbitrary manner. Efficient police departments would seek out criminals without reading them their rights, allowing them to call their attorneys, or releasing them in response to a writ of habeas corpus. An efficient building department would issue construction permits on demand without insisting that the applicant first show that the proposed building meets fire, safety, sanitation, geological, and earthquake standards.

The second great tradeoff is between nonarbitrary governance defined as treating people equally and such governance defined as treating each case on its merits. We want the government to be both fair and responsive, but the more rules we impose to insure fairness (that is, to treat all people alike) the harder we make it for the government to be responsive (that is, to take into account the special needs and circumstances of a particular case).

The way our government manages these tradeoffs reflects both our political culture as well as the rivalries of our governing institutions. Both tend toward the same end: We define claims as rights, impose general rules to insure equal treatment, lament (but do nothing about) the resulting inefficiencies, and respond to revelations about unresponsiveness by adopting new rules intended to guarantee that special circumstances will be handled with special care (rarely bothering to reconcile the rules that require responsiveness with those that require equality). And we do all this out of the best of motives: a desire to be both just and benevolent. Justice inclines us to treat people equally, benevolence to treat them differently; both inclinations are expressed in rules, though in fact only justice can be. It is this futile desire to have a rule for every circumstance that led Herbert Kaufman to explain "how compassion spawns red tape."

Discretion at the Street Level

We worry about arbitrary rule at the hands of those street-level bureaucracies that deal with us as individuals rather than as organized groups and that touch the more intimate aspects of our lives: police, schools, prisons, housing inspectors, mental hospitals, welfare offices, and the like. That worry is natural; in these settings we feel helpless and The State seems omnipotent. We want these bureaucracies to treat us fairly but we also want them to be responsive to our particular needs. The proper reconciliation of these competing desires requires a careful understanding of the tasks of these organizations.

There are at least two questions that must be answered: What constitutes in any specific organization the exercise of arbitrary or unjust power? Under what circumstances will the elaboration of rules reduce at an acceptable cost the unjust use of power? Police officers act unjustly when they arrest people without cause. "Equality before the law" is the bedrock principle of our criminal justice system, however imperfectly it may be realized. And so we create rules defining when people can be arrested.

But making an arrest is different for police patrol officers than for FBI agents. When the former go to the scene of a fight they are trying to restore order and ascertain who started the fight and who wielded the knife. An arrest, if any, is often the culmination of a long, subtle, low-visibility process of interviewing victims, observing people, and questioning suspects, all done on the street in the absence of a supervisor and all based on making inferences from incomplete and disputed assertions. The essence of this process is judgment: deciding whose conduct, demeanor, and appearance make it likely that he has committed a crime. In assessing those traits officers are required not to "treat all people alike" but to treat them very differen.. They cannot do their jobs unless they know that young people are more likely to commit assaults than old, males more likely than females, and acquaintances more likely than strangers. These are only probabilities, but they are important ones. It is very difficult to specify by rule in advance who should be stopped, questioned, or searched. When such rules are specified, as they are when officers are told the circumstances under which they can stop, question, and search people, inevitably the rules will be cumbersome, incomplete, and even inconsistent. Some officers determined to do their jobs will evade the rules; others, determined to stay out of trouble, will use the rules as an excuse for doing as little as possible; and still others will give vent to their frustration in trying to comprehend the rules. In many other democratic nations the law defining a legitimate arrest is not very different from that in the United States, but there are far fewer rules defining what an officer may do short of (or in anticipation of) an arrest. We extend rules further back down the chain of inference and discretion than do our counterparts abroad.

FBI agents are in very different circumstances. They are detectives, not patrol officers; they "solve crimes" rather than "handle situations" or "maintain order." Except in special circumstances they do not intervene in barroom or bedroom quarrels. They usually come to the scene of a crime some time after it occurred; when they are ready to make an arrest they almost always are able to obtain an arrest warrant. A warrant means that in the opinion of a third-party—a judge—the rules governing an arrest have been satisfied. Because their tasks are different from those of patrol officers, FBI agents complain much less about the restrictive nature of rules and are less frequently accused of making arbitrary or unjustified arrests.

Prison administrators differ in their understanding of arbitrary rule. For over twenty years the Texas Department of Corrections ran its prisons by issuing to every officer and inmate a slim, simple book of rules that were enforced

er. By contrast, the Michigan Department [Corrections] had three fat volumes of [governing] every aspect of prison life, from [property] (six single-spaced pages) to prisoner organization. But the rules were not consistently enforced, nor were they intended to be so enforced: The rulebook told officers that "there is no requirement that every rule violation" be punished.

John Dilulio explained the reasons for the differences. The Texas officials believed that the overriding imperative of prison life was to insure order and maintain security; to that end the rules had to specify inmate conduct, be few and simple (otherwise they could not be communicated and enforced), and be rigidly applied (otherwise inmates would think they could ignore them). If order were assured, programs and services then could be supplied. The Michigan officials, by contrast, believed that the overriding imperative of prison life was to encourage inmates to take responsibility for their own behavior: to that end the rules had to specify inmate rights, be many and complex (for rights could not briefly be summarized), and be flexibly enforced (because a rule should never stand in the way of achieving the right result). If inmate self-rule were achieved, order would follow automatically. In Texas "arbitrary rule" meant the inconsistent or unfair enforcement of regulations; in Michigan it meant the failure to encourage inmate self-governance. Dilulio's evidence suggests that the Texas officials were right and the Michigan officials wrong. Until the system deteriorated, Texas inmates were treated justly (that is, they were not abused either by the guards or by other inmates) whereas the Michigan prisoners often were treated unjustly (they were abused by other inmates if not by the guards).

Police patrol officers are members of coping organizations: their discretion is not easily limited by imposing rules. An excessive reliance on rules can lead to shirking or to subversion. To solve the problem of arbitrariness one must rely on effective management, especially on the part of first-line supervisors—sergeants and lieutenants. FBI agents are members of craft organizations: Their outputs are relatively easy to assess, and so they can be held accountable for those outcomes even though their daily routine is hard to observe or control. Rules can be used to limit discretion *if* they are linked to the definition of a good outcome. Prison guards are members of procedural organizations: What they do is observable but the results (at least in terms of the long-run behavior of ex-inmates) are not. Managers therefore are powerfully tempted to design procedures (rules) that reflect a theory of human behavior, ignoring (as in the case of Michigan) the evident short-run cost of applying that theory in the untested belief that long-run benefits would follow.

Discretion at the Headquarters Level

Interest groups also complain about arbitrariness, especially when they deal with regulatory agencies that have either no clear rules (and so the groups do not know whether policies in effect today will be in effect tomorrow) or rules so clear and demanding that there is no freedom to adjust their activities to conform to economic or technological imperatives.

The exercise of discretion by regulatory agencies does not occur because their activities are invisible or their clients are powerless but because these agencies and their legislative supporters have certain beliefs about what constitutes good policy. For many decades after the invention of the regulatory agency, Progressives believed that good decisions were the result of empowering neutral experts to decide cases on the basis of scientifically determined facts and widely shared principles. No one took it amiss that these "principles" often were so vague as to lack any meaning at all. The Federal Communications Commission (FCC) was directed to issue broadcast licenses as the "public interest, convenience, and necessity" shall require. A similar "standard" was to govern the awarding of licenses to airline companies by the now-defunct Civil Aeronautics Board (CAB). The

Antitrust Division of the Justice Department was charged with enforcing the Sherman Act that made "combinations in restraint of trade" illegal.

What the statute left vague "experts" were to imbue with meaning. But expert opinion changes and some experts in fact are politicians who bow to the influence of organized interests or ideologues who embrace the enthusiasms of zealous factions. The result was an invitation for interests to seek particular results in the absence of universal standards.

One might suppose that the agencies, noticing the turmoil caused by having to decide hard cases on the basis of vacuous standards, would try to formulate and state clear policies that would supply to their clients the guidance that the legislature was unwilling to provide; but no. For the most part regulatory agencies with ambiguous statutes did not clarify their policies. I conjecture that this is because the agencies realized what Michel Crozier has stated: Uncertainty is power. If one party needs something from another and cannot predict how that second party will behave, the second party has power over the first. In the extreme case we will do almost anything to please a madman with life-or-death power over us because we cannot predict which behavior will produce what reaction.

The FCC is not a madman, but it has realized that a broadcaster uncertain as to how the FCC would react to a controversial broadcast often would cancel the program rather than risk offending the agency. And this would happen despite the clear statutory provision that forbade the FCC from controlling the contents of programs. The FCC had life-or-death power over a broadcaster because every few years it could decide whether its license to broadcast would be renewed. If it left the broadcaster in doubt as to what went into the renewal decision (which is to say, if it did not write down any clear, comprehensive policies), the broadcaster's worries would lead it to conform to even the most subtle hints and cues from the FCC or its staff.

Do not suppose that regulators were unaware of the power that flowed from ambiguity. Abe Fortas, later to be a justice of the Supreme Court, wrote in 1937 about how the Securities and Exchange Commission ought to behave:

> Unless the administrator has effective bargaining power, little can be expected. He must have sanctions or desired favors which he can trade for changes in [business] practices. . . . He may be asked to exercise his discretion, for example, to accelerate the effective date of registration [of a new security]. Then, if the need is sufficiently urgent, a trade may be consummated. In return for the favor of the administrator, the registrant may amend his practices in accordance with the administrator's conception of justice and equity.

If you find nothing wrong with the SEC bargaining with firms trying to sell stock, reread this quotation, substituting the word "police officer" for "administrator," "citizen" for "registrant," and "right to hold a protest meeting" for "effective date of registration."

IV ◉ FOCUS: THE BUREAUCRACY IN ACTION

The popular and political science literature is replete with examples of the bureaucracy in action. Here, for your consideration, are four examples.

13.4 Parkinson's Law or the Rising Pyramid _____

C. Northcote Parkinson

[*Parkinson's law—"Work expands so as to fill the time available for its completion"—is well known by bureaucrats and college students alike. Parkinson's description of the bureaucratic life-style—one part satire, one part shrewd analysis, and one part keen observation—remains a classic.*]

Work expands so as to fill the time available for its completion. General recognition of this fact is shown in the proverbial phrase "It is the busiest man who has time to spare." Thus, an elderly lady of leisure can spend the entire day in writing and dispatching a postcard to her niece at Bognor Regis. An hour will be spent in finding the postcard, another in hunting for spectacles, half an hour in a search for the address, an hour and a quarter in composition, and twenty minutes in deciding whether or not to take the umbrella when going to the mailbox in the next street. The total effort that would occupy a busy man for three minutes all told may in this fashion leave another person prostrate after a day of doubt, anxiety, and toil.

Granted that work (and especially paperwork) is thus elastic in its demands on time, it is manifest that there need be little or no relationship between the work to be done and the size of the staff to which it may be assigned. A lack of real activity does not, of necessity, result in leisure. A lack of occupation is not necessarily revealed by a manifest idleness. The thing to be done swells in importance and complexity in a direct ratio with the time to be spent. This fact is widely recognized, but less attention has been paid to its wider implications, more especially in the field of public administration. Politicians and taxpayers have assumed (with occasional phases of doubt) that a rising total in the number of civil servants must reflect a growing volume of work to be done. Cynics, in questioning this belief, have imagined that the multiplication of officials must have left some of them idle or all of them able to work for shorter hours. But this is a matter in which faith and doubt seem equally misplaced. The fact is that the number of the officials and the quantity of the work are not related to each other at all. The rise in the total of those employed is governed by Parkinson's Law and would be much the same whether the volume of the work were to increase, diminish, or even disappear. The importance of Parkinson's Law lies in the fact that it is a law of growth based upon an analysis of the factors by which that growth is controlled.

The validity of this recently discovered law must rest mainly on statistical proofs. . . . Of more interest to the general reader is the explanation of the factors underlying the general tendency to which this law gives definition. Omitting technicalities (which are numerous) we may distinguish at the outset two motive forces. They can be represented for the present purpose by two almost axiomatic statements, thus: (1) "An official wants to multiply subordinates, not rivals" and (2) "Officials make work for each other."

To comprehend Factor 1, we must picture a civil servant, called A, who finds himself overworked. Whether this overwork is real or ima-

[At this point in a chapter on the bureaucracy, it is customary to present a chart showing the growth of the federal government over time, usually from 1880 or so until the present. Since this information would probably be of little use to the reader, I have chosen to present instead the lifetime batting statistics of Carl Yastrzemski of the Boston Red Sox.]

Carl Yastrzemski

YASTRZEMSKI, CARL MICHAEL (Yaz)
B. Aug. 22, 1939, Southampton, N. Y.
Hall of Fame 1989.

BL TR 5'11" 175 lbs.

Year	Team	Lg	G	BA	SA	AB	H	2B	3B	HR	HR%	R	RBI	BB	SO	SB			PO	A	E	DP		FA	Position
1961	BOS	A	148	.266	.396	583	155	31	6	11	1.9	71	80	50	96	6	1	0	248	12	10	1	1.8	.963	OF-147
1962			160	.296	.469	646	191	43	6	19	2.9	99	94	66	82	7	0	0	329	15	11	3	2.2	.969	OF-160
1963			151	.321	.475	570	183	40	3	14	2.5	91	68	95	72	8	0	0	283	18	6	3	2.0	.980	OF-151
1964			151	.289	.451	567	164	29	9	15	2.6	77	67	75	90	6	0	0	372	24	11	4	2.7	.973	OF-148, 3B-2
1965			133	.312	.536	494	154	45	3	20	4.0	78	72	70	58	7	3	0	222	11	3	2	1.8	.987	OF-130
1966			160	.278	.431	594	165	39	2	16	2.7	81	80	84	60	8	3	1	310	15	5	2	2.1	.985	OF-158
1967			161	.326	.622	579	189	31	4	44	7.6	112	121	91	69	10	0	0	297	13	7	1	2.0	.978	OF-161
1968			157	.301	.495	539	162	32	2	23	4.3	90	74	119	90	13	0	0	315	13	3	4	2.1	.991	OF-155, 1B-3
1969			162	.255	.507	603	154	28	2	40	6.6	96	111	101	91	15	0	0	427	38	6	31	2.9	.987	OF-143, 1B-22
1970			161	.329	.592	566	186	29	0	40	7.1	125	102	128	66	23	1	0	816	64	14	62	5.6	.984	1B-94, OF-69
1971			148	.254	.392	508	129	21	2	15	3.0	75	70	106	60	8	2	2	281	16	2	4	2.0	.993	OF-146
1972			125	.264	.391	455	120	18	2	12	2.6	70	68	67	44	5	1	0	498	43	8	35	4.4	.985	1B-107, 3B-31, OF-14
1973			152	.296	.463	540	160	25	4	19	3.5	82	95	105	58	9	1	0	979	119	18	87	7.3	.984	1B-107, OF-63, DH-4
1974			148	.301	.445	515	155	25	2	15	2.9	93	79	104	48	12	0	0	806	46	6	68	5.8	.993	1B-84, OF-8, DH-4
1975			149	.269	.405	543	146	30	1	14	2.6	91	60	87	67	8	1	0	1217	88	5	103	8.8	.996	1B-140, OF-8, DH-2
1976			155	.267	.432	546	146	23	2	21	3.8	71	102	80	67	5	1	0	922	55	4	78	6.3	.996	1B-94, OF-51, DH-10
1977			150	.296	.505	558	165	27	3	28	5.0	99	102	73	40	11	0	0	344	22	0	5	2.4	1.000	OF-140, 1B-7, DH-6
1978			144	.277	.423	523	145	21	2	17	3.3	70	81	76	44	4	1	0	523	49	5	49	4.0	.991	OF-71, 1B-50, DH-27
1979			147	.270	.450	518	140	28	1	21	4.1	69	87	62	46	3	3	2	529	56	4	42	4.0	.993	DH-56, 1B-51, OF-36
1980			105	.275	.462	364	100	21	1	15	4.1	49	50	44	38	0	6	0	225	13	4	20	2.3	.983	DH-49, OF-39, 1B-16
1981			91	.246	.355	338	83	14	1	7	2.1	36	53	49	28	0	3	0	353	34	3	26	4.3	.992	DH-102, 1B-14, OF-2
1982			131	.275	.431	459	126	22	1	16	3.5	53	72	59	50	0	15	1	119	10	0	12	1.0	1.000	DH-102, 1B-14, OF-2
1983			119	.266	.408	380	101	24	0	10	2.6	38	56	54	29	0	10	2	22	1	0	1	0.2	1.000	DH-107, 1B-2, OF-1
23 yrs.			3308	.285	.462	11988	3419	646	59	452	3.8	1816	1844	1845	1393	168	52	8	10437	775	135	643	3.4	.988	OF-2076, 1B-765, DH-411, 3B-33
			2nd			3rd	6th	6th					9th	4th											

LEAGUE CHAMPIONSHIP SERIES

Year	Team	Lg	G	BA	SA	AB	H	2B	3B	HR	HR%	R	RBI	BB	SO	SB			PO	A	E	DP		FA	Position
1975	BOS	A	3	.455	.818	11	5	1	0	1	9.1	4	2	1	1	0	0	0	7	2	0	0	3.0	1.000	OF-3

WORLD SERIES

Year	Team	Lg	G	BA	SA	AB	H	2B	3B	HR	HR%	R	RBI	BB	SO	SB			PO	A	E	DP		FA	Position
1967	BOS	A	7	.400	.840	25	10	2	0	3	12.0	4	5	4	1	0	0	0	16	2	0	0	2.6	1.000	OF-7
1975			7	.310	.310	29	9	0	0	0	0.0	7	4	4	1	0	0	0	36	1	0	4	5.3	1.000	OF-4, 1B-4
2 yrs.			14	.352	.556	54	19	2	0	3	5.6	11	9	8	2	0	0	0	52	3	0	4	3.9	1.000	OF-11, 1B-4
			10th																						

ginary is immaterial, but we should observe, in passing, that A's sensation (or illusion) might easily result from his own decreasing energy: a normal symptom of middle age. For this real or imagined overwork there are, broadly speaking, three possible remedies. He may resign; he may ask to halve the work with a colleague called B; he may demand the assistance of two subordinates, to be called C and D. There is probably no instance in history, however, of A choosing any but the third alternative. By resignation he would lose his pension rights. By having B appointed, on his own level in the hierarchy, he would merely bring in a rival for promotion to W's vacancy when W (at long last) retires. So A would rather have C and D, junior men, below him. They will add to his consequence and, by dividing the work into two categories, as between C and D, he will have the merit of being the only man who comprehends both. It is essential to realize at this point that C and D are, as it were, inseparable. To appoint C alone would have been impossible. Why? Because C, if by himself, would divide the work with A and so assume almost the equal status that has been refused in the first instance to B; a status the more emphasized if C is A's only possible successor. Subordinates must thus number two or more, each being thus kept in order by fear of the other's promotion. When C complains in turn of being overworked (as he certainly will) A will, with the concurrence of C, advise the appointment of two assistants to help C. But he can then avert internal friction only by advising the appointment of two more assistants to help D, whose position is much the same. With this recruitment of E, F, G, and H the promotion of A is now practically certain.

Seven officials are now doing what one did before. This is where Factor 2 comes into operation. For these seven make so much work for each other that all are fully occupied and A is actually working harder than ever. An incoming document may well come before each of them in turn. Official E decides that it falls within the province of F, who places a draft reply before C, who amends it drastically before consulting D, who asks G to deal with it. But G goes on leave at this point, handing the file over to H, who drafts a minute that is signed by D and returned to C, who revises his draft accordingly and lays the new version before A.

What does A do? He would have every excuse for signing the thing unread, for he has many other matters on his mind. Knowing now that he is to succeed W next year, he has to decide whether C or D should succeed to his own office. He had to agree to G's going on leave even if not yet strictly entitled to it. He is worried whether H should not have gone instead, for reasons of health. He has looked pale recently—partly but not solely because of his domestic troubles. Then there is the business of F's special increment of salary for the period of the conference and E's application for transfer to the Ministry of Pensions. A has heard that D is in love with a married typist and that G and F are no longer on speaking terms—no one seems to know why. So A might be tempted to sign C's draft and have done with it. But A is a conscientious man. Beset as he is with problems created by his colleagues for themselves and for him—created by the mere fact of these officials' existence—he is not the man to shirk his duty. He reads through the draft with care, deletes the fussy paragraphs added by C and H, and restores the thing back to the form preferred in the first instance by the able (if quarrelsome) F. He corrects the English—none of these young men can write grammatically—and finally produces the same reply he would have written if officials C to H had never been born. Far more people have taken far longer to produce the same result. No one has been idle. All have done their best. And it is late in the evening before A finally quits his office and begins the return journey to Ealing. The last of the office lights are being turned off in the gathering dusk that marks the end of another day's administrative toil. Among the last to leave, A reflects with bowed shoulders and a wry smile that late hours, like gray hairs, are among the penalties of success.

From this description of the factors at work the student of political science will recognize that administrators are more or less bound to multiply. Nothing has yet been said, however, about the period of time likely to elapse between the date of A's appointment and the date from which we can calculate the pensionable service of H. Vast masses of statistical evidence have been collected and it is from a study of this data that Parkinson's Law has been deduced. Space will not allow of detailed analysis but the reader will be interested to know that research began in the British Navy Estimates. These were chosen because the Admiralty's responsibilities are more easily measurable than those of, say, the Board of Trade. The question is merely one of numbers and tonnage. Here are some typical figures. The strength of the Navy in 1914 could be shown as 146,000 officers and men, 3249 dockyard officials and clerks, and 57,000 dockyard workmen. By 1928 there were only 100,000 officers and men and only 62,439 workmen, but the dockyard officials and clerks by then numbered 4558. As for warships, the strength in 1928 was a mere fraction of what it had been in 1914—fewer than 20 capital ships in commission as compared with 62. Over the same period the Admiralty officials had increased in number from 2000 to 3569, providing (as was remarked) "a magnificent navy on land."

13.5 Firemen First or How to Beat a Budget Cut

Charles Peters

[Over Columbus Day weekend in October 1990, President George Bush ordered the federal government to come to a complete standstill—except for essential services— when he and Congress could not work out a satisfactory budget agreement. Most of the government was closed for the holiday in any event, so the presidential order hit most directly on the thousands of tourists who had come to Washington, D.C., to see the sights and who now found themselves locked out of such attractions as the National Zoo and the Washington Monument. Perhaps the president hoped the tourists would blame Congress for ruining their vacation, but if so, the ploy backfired; tourists, like most other Americans, seemed to blame the White House and Congress equally.

In an essay written years before the Columbus Day shutdown, the journalist Charles Peter explained why essential services—like fire fighting and elevator service at the Washington Monument—are the first to go when the government cuts the budget.]

Since parsimony is becoming almost as fashionable among politicians today as patriotism was in the 1940s, a wave of budget-cutting seems likely at all levels of government. The results could be salutary, but might be disastrous. To avoid the latter possibility, it is essential to understand how the Clever Bureaucrat reacts to the threat of fiscal deprivation.

The very first thing C.B. does, when threatened with a budget reduction, is to translate it into specific bad news for congressmen powerful enough to restore his budget to its usual plenitude.

Thus Amtrak, threatened in early 1976 with a budget cut, immediately announced, according to Stephen Aug of *The Washington Star*, that it would be compelled to drop the following routes:

San Francisco–Bakersfield, running through Stockton, the home town of Rep. John J. McFall, chairman of the House Appropriations transportation subcommittee.

St. Louis–Laredo, running through Little Rock, Arkansas, the home of Senator John McClellan, chairman of the Senate Appropriations Committee.

Chicago–Seattle, running through the homes of Senator Mike Mansfield, Senate Majority Leader, and Senator Warren Magnuson, chairman of the Senate Commerce Committee.

And in a triumphant stroke that netted four birds with one roadbed, Norfolk–Chicago, running through the home states of Senator Birch Bayh, chairman of the Senate Appropriations Transportation subcommittee, Senator Vance Hartke, chairman of the Commerce Surface Transportation Subcommittee, Rep. Harley Staggers, chairman of the House Commerce Committee, and Senator Robert Byrd, Senate Majority Whip.

The effectiveness of this device is suggested by a story that appeared in the *Charleston* (West Virginia) *Gazette* a few days after Amtrak's announcement:

Continued Rail Service Byrd's Aim

Senator Robert C. Byrd, D-WVa, has announced that he intends to make an effort today to assure continued rail passenger service for West Virginia.

Byrd, a member of the Senate Appropriations Committee, said he will "either introduce an amendment providing sufficient funds to continue the West Virginia route or try to get language adopted which would guarantee funding for the route of Amtrak."

In the Amtrak case, C.B.'s budget-cutting enemy was President Ford. Sometimes it is a frugal superior in his own department. C.B.'s initial response is much the same. If, for example, a Secretary of Defense from Massachusetts insists upon eliminating useless and out-moded bases, the Navy's C.B. will promptly respond with a list of recommended base-closings, led by the Boston Navy Yard.

Another Bay of Pigs

An irate constituency is, of course, a threat to all elected officials and to every other official who dreams of converting his appointive status into one blessed by the voting public. Even a small irritation can suffice. Thus, Mike Causey of *The Washington Post* tells of a National Park Service C.B. who, confronted with a budget cut, quickly restored congressmen to their senses by eliminating elevator service to the top of the Washington Monument. Every constituent whose children insisted on his walking all the way up was sure to place an outraged call to his congressman's office. Similarly, a Social Security Administration C.B. faced with a budget cut is certain to announce that the result will be substantial delays in the mailing of social security checks.

Whenever possible, a C.B. will assert that the budget cut is certain to result in the loss of jobs. The threatened employees are sure to write emotional protests to their congressmen. And, as the National Rifle Association has proven, even a tiny minority, if sufficiently vigorous in its expression of opinion—vigorous meaning that they make clear they will vote against you if you fail to help them—can move a legislator to take the desired action in the absence of an equally energetic lobby on the other side.

C.B.'s concern about loss of others' jobs is a deeply personal one. He knows you can't be a commander unless you have troops to command.

Not long ago Jack Anderson discovered that the Navy, trying to adjust to less money than it had requested, was depriving the fleet of essential maintenance, while continuing to waste billions on useless supercarriers and transforming small Polaris submarines into giant Tridents.

The reason of course is that the more big ships with big crews we have, the more admirals we need. Rank in the civil service is also determined in part by the number of employees one supervises. Thus a threat to reduce the number of one's employees is a threat not merely to one's ego but to one's income as well.

In its first flush of victory after the 1960 election, the Kennedy Administration embarked on two ill-fated missions. One was the Bay of Pigs. The other was an effort to fire 150 AID [Agency for International Development] employees, all of whom wrote their congressman, as did their fathers, mothers, brothers, sisters, and in all probability their creditors and the creditors' relatives. The 150 were, of course, reinstated.

On the other hand, there are public employees we don't want to fire—teachers in the public schools, for example, where teacher-pupil ratios of 1 to 40 are common. These are the ones C.B. always says he will have to fire when he is menaced with a budget cut. This tactic is based on the principle that the public will support C.B.'s valiant fight against the budget reduction only if essential services are endangered. Thus, C.B. always picks on teachers, policemen, firemen first. In the headquarters bureaucracies of the New York City and the Washington, D.C., school systems there are concentrated some of the most prodigious, do-nothing, time-servers of the modern era. No administrator threatens to fire them. If they are "the fat," and if he is to fight the budget cut, it would of course damage his cause to admit their existence. He must concentrate on threatening a loss of muscle.

Similarly, the Army, when faced with a budget cut, never points the finger at desk-bound lieutenant colonels. The victims are invariably combat troops. . . .

If we continue to let the Clever Bureaucrats of this world take charge, we could end up with a government of planning analysts, friends of congressmen, and trains running to Bakersfield via Stockton.

13.6 A Cost-Benefit Blend That's Hard to Swallow

John H. Cushman, Jr.

[*It is an unhappy fact that government bureaucrats, like many private sector decision makers as well, must make difficult choices. A public hospital might be forced to decide whether to expand its bed space or buy a new diagnostic scanner; an airport may have to decide between more snow-fighting equipment or new radar. In virtually every case, the government applies what economists call cost-benefit analysis; it totals up the costs and benefits of each option and tries to achieve the most bang for its buck.*

Many such decisions require the government to place a value on human life, and under such circumstances the decisions can appear particularly cold-blooded. Following is one example.]

To most people, the fine details of the Federal regulatory process are about as appetizing as a tour of a bologna factory. And those who disregard Bismarck's advice to remain ignorant of the manufacture of sausages and laws often discover that regulators have liberally peppered their products.

The spice is called cost-benefit analysis, and in the case of the Federal Aviation Administration's consideration of new rules governing airplane safety seats for infants and toddlers, it seems that pediatricians, consumers, flight attendants and even the airlines are finding it unpalatable.

In several recent air accidents, babies died who might have lived if they had been buckled into safety seats. One example this year was the Avianca Airlines crash on Long Island in January, now the subject of hearings by Federal safety investigators. Another example was the United Airlines crash in Iowa in July 1989. But F.A.A. rule makers argue that it would endanger babies to require that they be buckled into protective seats during flight.

How come? Because, they say, the costs of requiring safety seats would force families to drive instead of fly, and hence negate any safety benefit from the seats, since cars are statistically more dangerous than airliners.

Similar analysis comes into play whenever major rules are considered, though the exact costs and benefits can rarely be calculated scientifically. A more rarefied example can be found in the debate over cutting emissions of carbon dioxide and methane into the air, perhaps (or perhaps not) slowing economic growth, to ward off global warming, which may (or may not) exist.

On infant seats, the analysis begins with the fact that babies under 2 years old are allowed to fly at no charge if they are held on a parent's lap.

The F.A.A. says that if babies were required to ride in safety seats, they would need tickets. The extra tickets would cost an estimated $210 million a year. Discounts might be available for babies; that is not clear. But the rule makers believe that a safety seat requirement would cause a 21 percent reduction in airplane trips by families with babies. Every year, they calculate, 700,000 such families would decide not to travel by air.

Every state requires babies to sit in approved car seats. And nobody considers a lap the safest place for a child to sit in an airplane. The National Transportation Safety Board, an independent agency, recently joined those calling on the F.A.A. to write a rule requiring that babies be fully restrained, even if it means giving up the cherished free rides.

But the aviation agency continues to balk, recently delaying a final decision on its own proposal to make the safety seats optional for babies—or rather, for their parents, some of whom already choose to buy tickets for their babies and put them in safety seats.

The agency's pro-choice position is supported by a few analysts who believe that rational examination does not support a mandatory safety seat rule. Take the Competitive Enterprise Institute, a nonprofit organization that says it promotes "free-market approaches to regulatory issues." It calls a mandatory rule "a totally unwarranted restriction on consumer choice." Like the aviation agency, the institute argues that the mandatory rule would "cause the deaths of far more people than it might save."

There is a logical trap in this reasoning. Nobody knows how the aviation agency decided, many years ago, that 2 years of age was the cutoff point beyond which tickets must be bought and seat belts worn. Suppose the limit were raised to 3 years old: by the agency's logic, more families could then afford to fly instead of drive, carrying their older children on their laps.

The regulators say they are not considering any such thing. But Sam Kazman, a lawyer with Competitive Enterprise, said he would endorse letting older children ride free on parents' laps. That, he says, is no business of the Government.

In principle, he said, airlines should be allowed to sell standing-room-only tickets for adults—as long as this decision was approved by their marketing departments. A cost-benefit analysis, he said, would show this to be in the public interest.

13.7 The Officer of Death

Philip Caputo

[*The military is probably the quintessential bureaucracy. Every detail of military life—even the grisly business of counting casualties—must be recorded, categorized, and quantified. In his best-selling story of the Vietnam War, Philip Caputo tells of his experiences as the "officer of death."*]

My first night at headquarters was noisy. The big guns across the road fired H-and-I missions until dawn. H-and-I stood for "harassment and interdiction," a type of artillery fire directed at road junctions, hilltops, anywhere the enemy was likely to be. It was supposed to fray the Viet Cong's nerves and keep them off balance. I don't know if the artillery achieved its purpose, but by morning my nerves were plenty frazzled. I had been jolted awake a dozen times by the roaring howitzers. Well, the artillery was on our side, when the shells didn't fall short.

Frazzled, I spent the next day breaking in as assistant adjutant. Schwartz and I plowed through what seemed a truckload of paperwork. Documents had to be inventoried and audited, messages, directives, and regimental orders filed. Looking at all the red tape, I decided that the life of a staff officer was going to be even worse than I had feared. Later, Schwartz briefed me on my extra assignments—additional duties, as they were called. Junior staff officers were given a number of them because nobody else would do them. We were therefore known as SLJOs: shitty little jobs officers. Schwartz listed mine. In addition to assistant adjutant, I was to be: Regimental Casualty Reporting Officer, Regimental Secret and Confidential Documents Officer, Regimental Legal Officer, Regimental Mess Officer.

On paper, it looked like a heavy work load. In fact, Schwartz said, it would not amount to more than three or four hours a day. Then why was I there? Couldn't one of the clerks handle it all? No, because regulations called for an officer to handle these duties. All right, why couldn't Captain Anderson handle them? He was an officer. Yes, he was, but that's what the assistant adjutant was there for—so the captain didn't have to handle it.

Schwartz left for 2d Battalion a few days later, and I took over. He had been right about not having more than three or four hours' work a day. Sometimes there was less than that. I spent my ample leisure time looking for things to do or reading the cheap paperbacks donated by the Red Cross—*Fighting Red Devils*, "the true-life story of Britain's guts and glory paratroopers in World War Two," or just sitting at my desk, sweaty and thoroughly bored.

At night, the junior officers took turns standing watch in the operations tent. The more junior you were, the later the watch. Generally I drew 2400 to 0200 (midnight to two A.M.) or 0200 to 0400. That did not amount to much work, either. All we did was monitor the radios, call the operations officer, Major Conlin, when something unusual happened, and log the situation reports in the unit diary. The sitreps came in about once an hour: disembodied voices crackled over the radio or the EE-8 field phones, and spoke in the Captain Midnight code-word gibberish that passes for language in the military. "Crowd Three this is Burke Three. Burke Alpha Six reports Alpha Two Scorpion in position at grid coordinates Alpha Tango Hotel Hotel Echo Yankee Yankee Lima. All units report Alpha Sierra Sierra Romeo Sierra." All secure, situation remains the same.

As fighting increased, the additional duty of casualty reporting officer kept me busiest. It was also a job that gave me a lot of bad dreams, though it had the beneficial effect of cauterizing whatever silly, abstract, romantic ideas I still had about war.

My job was simply to report on casualties, enemy as well as our own; casualties due to hostile action and those due to nonhostile causes—the accidents that inevitably occur where there are large numbers of young men armed with lethal weapons or at the controls of complicated machinery. Artillery shells sometimes fell on friendly troops, tanks ran over people, helicopters crashed, marines shot other marines by mistake.

It was not the simple task it seemed. The military has elaborate procedures for every-thing, and keeping records of the dead and wounded is no exception. The reports were written on mimeographed forms, one for KIAs [killed in action], one for WIAs [wounded in action], and a third for nonhostile casualties. Each form had spaces for the victim's name, age, rank, serial number, and organization (his unit), and for the date, the description of his injuries, and the circumstances under which they occurred. If he had been killed, the circumstances were almost always described in the same way, and the words could have served as an epitaph for thousands of men: "killed in action while on patrol vicinity of Danang, RVN."

The KIA reports were long and complicated. Much information was required about the dead: their religion, the name and address of their next of kin, beneficiaries of their servicemen's life insurance policies, and whether the money was to be paid in a lump sum or in installments. All reports had to be written in that clinical, euphemistic language the military prefers to simple English. If, say, a marine had been shot through the guts, I could not write "shot through the guts" or "shot through the stomach"; no, I had to say "GSW" (gunshot wound) "through and through, abdomen." Shrapnel wounds were called "multiple fragment lacerations," and the phrase for dismemberment, one of my very favorite phrases, was "traumatic amputation." I had to use it a lot when the Viet Cong began to employ high-explosive weapons and booby traps. A device they used frequently was the command-detonated mine, which was set off electrically from ambush. The mines were similar to our Claymore, packed with hundreds of steel pellets and a few pounds of an explosive called C-4. If I recall correctly, the gas-expansion rate of C-4 is 26,000 feet per second. That terrific force, and the hundreds of steel pellets propelled by it, made the explosion of a command-detonated mine equivalent to the simultaneous firing of seventy twelve-gauge shotguns loaded with double-0 buckshot. Naturally, anyone hit by such a weapon was likely to suffer the "traumatic amputation" of something—an arm, a leg, his head—and many did. After I saw some of the victims, I began to question the accuracy of the phrase. *Traumatic* was precise, for losing a limb is definitely traumatic, but *amputation*, it seemed to me, suggested a surgical operation. I observed, however, that the human body does not break apart cleanly in an explosion. It tends to shatter into irregular and often unrecognizable pieces, so "traumatic fragmentation" would have been a more accurate term and would have preserved the euphemistic tone the military favored.

The shattering or fragmenting effect of high explosives occasionally caused semantic difficulties in reporting injuries of men who had undergone extreme mutilation. It was a rare phenomenon, but some marines had been so badly mangled there seemed to be no words to describe what had happened to them. Sometime that year, Lieutenant Colonel Meyers, one of the regiment's battalion commanders, stepped on a booby-trapped 155-mm shell. They did not find enough of him to fill a willy-peter bag, a waterproof sack a little larger than a shopping bag. In effect, Colonel Meyers had been disintegrated, but the official report read something like "traumatic amputation, both feet; traumatic amputation, both legs and arms; multiple lacerations to abdomen; through-and-through fragment wounds, head and chest." Then came the notation "killed in action."

The battalion adjutants phoned in reports of their units' casualties, and I relayed them to the division combat casualty reporting center. That done, I filed copies of the reports in their respective folders, one labeled CASUALTIES: HOSTILE ACTION and the other CASUALTIES: NON HOSTILE. I believe the two were kept separate because men killed or wounded by enemy fire were automatically awarded Purple Hearts, while those hit by friendly fire were not. That was the only real difference. A man killed by friendly fire (another misleading term, because fire is never friendly if it hits you) was just as dead as one killed by the enemy. And there was often an accidental quality even about battle casualties. Stepping on a mine or stumbling over the trip wire of a booby trap is a mishap, really, not unlike walking in front of a car while crossing a busy street.

Once the reports were filed, I brought Colonel Wheeler's scoreboard up to date. Covered with acetate and divided into vertical and horizontal columns, the board hung behind the executive officer's desk, in the wood-framed tent where he and the colonel made their headquarters. The vertical columns were headed, from left to right, KIA, WIA, DOW (died of wounds), NONHOST, VC-KIA, VC-WIA, and VC-POW. The horizontal columns were labeled with the numerical designations of the units belonging to, or attached to, the regiment: ⅓ for 1st Battalion, 3d Marines, ⅔ for 2d Battalion, and so forth. In the first four vertical columns were written the number of casualties a particular unit had suffered, in the last three the number it had inflicted on the enemy. After an action, I went into the colonel's quarters, erased the old figures and wrote in the new with a grease pencil. The colonel, an easygoing man in most instances, was adamant about maintaining an accurate scoreboard: high-ranking visitors from Danang and Saigon often dropped in unannounced to see how the regiment was performing. And the measures of a unit's performance in Vietnam were not the distances it had advanced or the number of victories it had won, but the number of enemy soldiers it had killed (the body count) and the proportion between that number and the number of its own dead (the kill ratio). The scoreboard thus allowed the colonel to keep track of the battalions and companies under his command and, quickly and crisply, to rattle off impressive figures to visiting dignitaries. My unsung task in that statistical war was to do the arithmetic. If I had been an agent of death as a platoon leader, as a staff officer I was death's bookkeeper.

Chapter 14

The Judiciary

Some thirty years ago, the constitutional scholar Robert G. McCloskey surveyed the history of the Supreme Court of the United States and concluded, "Surely the record teaches that no useful purpose is served when the judges seek the hottest political cauldrons of the moment and dive into the middle of them." Instead, "The Court's greatest successes have been achieved when it has operated near the margins of rather than in the center of political controversy, when it has nudged and gently tugged the nation, instead of trying to rule it."* Writing after the Court's 1954 school desegregation decision but before the controversies over reapportionment of state legislatures, abortion, busing, and school prayer, McCloskey feared for the Court's future if it did not learn the lessons of its past.

The Court, of course, did not follow McCloskey's advice. Over the past three decades, the Supreme Court has become an increasingly important force in American politics and the subject of intense, and at times bitter, political controversy. Besides deciding a whole array of questions involving individual rights, the Court has played a vital role in settling political controversies like the Nixon tapes case, and the federal courts' role in the protection of constitutional rights has led them into the virtual management of state prisons and mental hospitals, and local schools (selections 14.4 and 14.5).

All of this judicial activity has created a highly charged political debate over the proper role of the courts in American society. Presidents Reagan and Bush endeavored to reshape the Court along more conservative lines; several of their nominees provoked considerable controversy, and the nomination of Judge Robert Bork was defeated by the

---

* Robert McCloskey, *The American Supreme Court* (Chicago: University of Chicago Press, 1960), p. 229.

Senate. Each new nomination, and each controversial Court decision, has set off a new round of debate.

This chapter surveys the many aspects of the judiciary's role in American politics and society. Related material on questions of civil rights and civil liberties can be found in chapters 16 and 17.

Chapter Questions

1. What are the advantages and disadvantages of leaving political decisions to the courts instead of to the political branches of the federal government or to the states? What qualities do the courts have that make such activism attractive? unattractive or even dangerous?

2. What is the relationship between the federal judiciary and the other branches of the federal government? In what ways do the three branches work together to make policy—for example, in the area of statutory interpretation? In what ways is the relationship competitive or adversarial?

I THE CLASSIC TEXTS

The Supreme Court's power to review acts of Congress and decide whether they are unconstitutional is perhaps the most extraordinary power possessed by any court in the world; the decision of five of nine justices can nullify the expressed will of the people's representatives in Congress. Moreover, the Court can strike down laws passed by state or local officials based on a conflict with federal law. Although Supreme Court decisions striking down major acts of Congress have been relatively infrequent, the Court has acted often to nullify unconstitutional measures passed by the states.

Despite the enormity of the Court's power of judicial review, as it is known, this power was not explicitly granted to the Court by the Constitution. The lack of specific language in the Constitution on this point—probably because the delegates could not agree as to whether the state or the federal courts should have the last word—made it necessary for the Supreme Court to claim and defend its power of judicial review later. The justices who were most influential in this struggle were Chief Justice John Marshall and his ally, Justice Joseph Story.

The following three selections trace the highlights of this struggle. The first is Alexander Hamilton's classic defense of judicial review in the Federalist Papers No. 78. *The second is Marshall's 1803 decision in* Marbury v. Madison, *in which the Supreme Court first claimed the power of judicial review. The third is Justice Story's 1816 decision in* Martin v. Hunter's Lessee, *in which the Court made it clear that it could overrule state courts on matters of federal law. The significance of this last case is often underappreciated, but without it, individual state courts could nullify the application of federal law within their own territory. The decision in* Martin *therefore provoked a great deal of controversy.*

Questions

1. Hamilton begins his argument with a defense of the Constitution's provision for life appointment of justices of the Supreme Court. How does this argument relate to his and John Marshall's defense of judicial review?

2. Considering the other readings in this chapter, how reasonable is Hamilton's observation that the courts possess "neither FORCE nor WILL but merely judgment"?

3. Consider the validity of this statement by Justice Oliver Wendell Holmes: "I do not think the United States would come to an end if we lost our power to declare an Act of Congress void. I do think the Union would be imperiled if we could not make that declaration as to the laws of the several States."*

14.1 Federalist No. 78

Alexander Hamilton

We proceed now to an examination of the judiciary department of the proposed government.

In unfolding the defects of the existing Confederation, the utility and necessity of a federal judicature have been clearly pointed out. It is the less necessary to recapitulate the considerations there urged, as the propriety of the institution in the abstract is not disputed; the only questions which have been raised being relative to the manner of constituting it, and to its extent. To these points, therefore, our observations shall be confined.

The manner of constituting it seems to embrace these several objects: 1st. The mode of appointing the judges. 2d. The tenure by which they are to hold their places. 3d. The partition of the judiciary authority between different courts, and their relations to each other.

First. As to the mode of appointing the judges; this is the same with that of appointing the officers of the Union in general. . . .

Second. As to the tenure by which the judges are to hold their places; this chiefly concerns their duration in office; the provisions for their support; the precautions for their responsibility.

According to the plan of the convention, all judges who may be appointed by the United States are to hold their offices DURING GOOD BEHAVIOR; which is conformable to the most approved of the State constitutions and among the rest, to that of this State. Its propriety having been drawn into question by the adversaries of that plan, is no light symptom of the rage for objection, which disorders their imaginations and judgments. The standard of good behavior for the continuance in office of the judicial magistracy, is certainly one of the most valuable of the modern improvements in the practice of government. In a monarchy it is an excellent barrier to the despotism of the prince; in a republic it is a no less excellent barrier to the encroachments and oppressions of the representative body. And it is the best expedient which can be devised in any government, to secure a steady, upright, and impartial administration of the laws.

Whoever attentively considers the different departments of power must perceive, that, in a government in which they are separated from each other, the judiciary, from the nature of its

* Oliver Wendell Holmes, "Law and the Court," address delivered February 15, 1913, in *Collected Legal Papers* (New York: Peter Smith, 1952), pp. 295–96.

functions, will always be the least dangerous to the political rights of the Constitution; because it will be least in a capacity to annoy or injure them. The Executive not only dispenses the honors, but holds the sword of the community. The legislature not only commands the purse, but prescribes the rules by which the duties and rights of every citizen are to be regulated. The judiciary, on the contrary, has no influence over either the sword or the purse; no direction either of the strength or of the wealth of the society; and can take no active resolution whatever. It may truly be said to have neither FORCE nor WILL, but merely judgment; and must ultimately depend upon the aid of the executive arm even for the efficacy of its judgments.

This simple view of the matter suggests several important consequences. It proves incontestably, that the judiciary is beyond comparison the weakest of the three departments of power; that it can never attack with success either of the other two; and that all possible care is requisite to enable it to defend itself against their attacks. It equally proves, that though individual oppression may now and then proceed from the courts of justice, the general liberty of the people can never be endangered from that quarter; I mean so long as the judiciary remains truly distinct from both the legislature and the Executive. For I agree, that "there is no liberty, if the power of judging be not separated from the legislative and executive powers." And it proves, in the last place, that as liberty can have nothing to fear from the judiciary alone, but would have every thing to fear from its union with either of the other departments; that as all the effects of such a union must ensue from a dependence of the former on the latter, notwithstanding a nominal and apparent separation; that as, from the natural feebleness of the judiciary, it is in continual jeopardy of being overpowered, awed, or influenced by its coordinate branches; and that as nothing can contribute so much to its firmness and independence as permanency in office, this quality may therefore be justly regarded as an indispensable ingredient in its constitution, and, in a great

Danziger in *The Christian Science Monitor* © 1990 The Christian Science Publishing Society.

measure, as the citadel of the public justice and the public security.

The complete independence of the courts of justice is peculiarly essential in a limited Constitution. By a limited Constitution, I understand one which contains certain specified exceptions to the legislative authority; such, for instance, as that it shall pass no bills of attainder, no *ex-post-facto* laws, and the like. Limitations of this kind can be preserved in practice no other way than through the medium of courts of justice, whose duty it must be to declare all acts contrary to the manifest tenor of the Constitution void. Without this, all the reservations of particular rights or privileges would amount to nothing.

Some perplexity respecting the rights of the courts to pronounce legislative acts void, because contrary to the Constitution, has arisen from an imagination that the doctrine would imply a superiority of the judiciary to the legislative power. It is urged that the authority which can declare the acts of another void, must necessarily be superior to the one whose acts may be declared void. As this doctrine is of great importance in all the American constitutions, a brief discussion of the ground on which it rests cannot be unacceptable.

There is no position which depends on clearer principles, than that every act of a delegated authority, contrary to the tenor of the commission under which it is exercised, is void. No legislative act, therefore, contrary to the Constitution, can be valid. To deny this, would be to affirm, that the deputy is greater than his principal; that the servant is above his master; that the representatives of the people are superior to the people themselves; that men acting by virtue of powers, may do not only what their powers do not authorize, but what they forbid.

If it be said that the legislative body are themselves the constitutional judges of their own powers, and that the construction they put upon them is conclusive upon the other departments, it may be answered, that this cannot be the natural presumption, where it is not to be collected from any particular provisions in the Constitution. It is not otherwise to be supposed, that the Constitution could intend to enable the representatives of the people to substitute their WILL to that of their constituents. It is far more rational to suppose, that the courts were designed to be an intermediate body between the people and the legislature, in order, among other things, to keep the latter within the limits assigned to their authority. The interpretation of the laws is the proper and peculiar province of the courts. A constitution is, in fact, and must be regarded by the judges, as a fundamental law. It therefore belongs to them to ascertain its meaning, as well as the meaning of any particular act proceeding from the legislative body. If there should happen to be an irreconcilable variance between the two, that which has the superior obligation and validity ought, of course, to be preferred; or, in other words, the Constitution ought to be preferred to the statute, the intention of the people to the intention of their agents.

Nor does this conclusion by any means suppose a superiority of the judicial to the legislative power. It only supposes that the power of the people is superior to both; and that where the will of the legislature, declared in its statutes, stands in opposition to that of the people, declared in the Constitution, the judges ought to be governed by the latter rather than the former. They ought to regulate their decisions by the fundamental laws, rather than by those which are not fundamental.

This exercise of judicial discretion, in determining between two contradictory laws, is exemplified in a familiar instance. It not uncommonly happens, that there are two statutes existing at one time, clashing in whole or in part with each other, and neither of them containing any repealing clause or expression. In such a case, it is the province of the courts to liquidate and fix their meaning and operation. So far as they can, by any fair construction, be reconciled to each other, reason and law conspire to dictate that this should be done; where this is impracticable, it becomes a matter of necessity to give effect to one, in exclusion of the other. The rule which has obtained in the courts for determining their relative validity is, that the last in order of time shall be preferred to the first. But this is a mere rule of construction, not derived from any positive law, but from the nature and reason of the thing. It is a rule not enjoined upon the courts by legislative provision, but adopted by themselves, as consonant to truth and propriety, for the direction of their conduct as interpreters of the law. They thought it reasonable, that between the interfering acts of an EQUAL authority, that which was the last indication of its will should have the preference.

But in regard to the interfering acts of a superior and subordinate authority, of an original and derivative power, the nature and reason of the thing indicate the converse of that rule as proper to be followed. They teach us that the prior act of a superior ought to be preferred to the subsequent act of an inferior and subordinate authority; and that accordingly, whenever a particular statute contravenes the Constitution, it will be the duty of the judicial tribunals to adhere to the latter and disregard the former.

It can be of no weight to say that the courts, on the pretense of a repugnancy, may substitute their own pleasure to the constitutional intentions of the legislature. This might as well happen in the case of two contradictory statutes; or it might as well happen in every adjudication upon any single statute. The courts must declare the sense of the law; and if they should be disposed to exercise WILL instead of JUDGMENT, the consequence would equally be the substitution of their pleasure to that of the legislative body. The observation, if it prove any thing, would prove that there ought to be no judges distinct from that body.

If, then, the courts of justice are to be considered as the bulwarks of a limited Constitution against legislative encroachments, this consideration will afford a strong argument for the permanent tenure of judicial offices, since nothing will contribute so much as this to that independent spirit in the judges which must be essential to the faithful performance of so arduous a duty.

This independence of the judges is equally requisite to guard the Constitution and the rights of individuals from the effects of those ill humors, which the arts of designing men, or the influence of particular conjunctures, sometimes disseminate among the people themselves, and which, though they speedily give place to better information, and more deliberate reflection, have a tendency, in the meantime, to occasion dangerous innovations in the government, and serious oppressions of the minor party in the community. Though I trust the friends of the proposed Constitution will never concur with its enemies, in questioning that fundamental principle of republican government, which admits the right of the people to alter or abolish the established Constitution, whenever they find it inconsistent with their happiness, yet it is not to be inferred from this principle, that the representatives of the people, whenever a momentary inclination happens to lay hold of a majority of their constituents, incompatible with the provisions in the existing Constitution, would, on that account, be justifiable in a violation of those provisions; or that the courts would be under a greater obligation to connive at infractions in this shape, than when they had proceeded wholly from the cabals of the representative body. Until the people have, by some solemn and authoritative act, annulled or changed the established form, it is binding upon themselves collectively, as well as individually; and no presumption, or even knowledge, of their sentiments, can warrant their representatives in a departure from it, prior to such an act. But it is easy to see, that it would require an uncommon portion of fortitude in the judges to do their duty as faithful guardians of the Constitution, where legislative invasions of it had been instigated by the major voice of the community.

But it is not with a view to infractions of the Constitution only, that the independence of the judges may be an essential safeguard against the effects of occasional ill humors in the society. These sometimes extend no farther than to the injury of the private rights of particular classes of citizens, by unjust and partial laws. Here also the firmness of the judicial magistracy is of vast importance in mitigating the severity and confining the operation of such laws. It not only serves to moderate the immediate mischiefs of those which may have been passed, but it operates as a check upon the legislative body in passing them; who, perceiving that obstacles to the success of iniquitous intention are to be expected from the scruples of the courts, are in a manner compelled, by the very motives of the injustice they meditate, to qualify their attempts. This is a circumstance calculated to have more influence upon the character of our governments, than but few may be aware of. The benefits of the integrity and moderation of the judiciary have already been felt in more States than one; and though they may have displeased those whose sinister expectations they may have disappointed, they must have commanded the esteem and applause of all the virtuous and disinterested. Considerate men, of every description, ought to prize whatever will tend to beget or fortify that temper in the courts: as no man can be sure that he may not be to-morrow the victim of a spirit of injustice, by which he may be a gainer to-day. And every man must now feel, that the inevitable tendency of such a spirit is to sap the foundations of public and private confidence, and to introduce in its stead universal distrust and distress.

That inflexible and uniform adherence to the rights of the Constitution, and of individuals, which we perceive to be indispensable in the courts of justice, can certainly not be expected from judges who hold their offices by a temporary commission. Periodical appointments, however regulated, or by whomsoever made, would, in some way or other, be fatal to their necessary independence. If the power of making them was committed either to the Executive or legislature, there would be danger of an improper complaisance to the branch which possessed it; if to both, there would be an unwillingness to hazard the displeasure of either; if to the people, or the persons chosen by them for the special purpose, there would be too great a disposition to consult popularity, to justify a reliance that nothing would be consulted but the Constitution and the laws.

There is yet a further and a weightier reason for the permanency of the judicial offices, which is deducible from the nature of the qualifications they require. It has been frequently remarked, with great propriety, that a voluminous code of laws is one of the inconveniences necessarily connected with the advantages of a free government. To avoid an arbitrary discretion in the courts, it is indispensable that they should be bound down by strict rules and precedents, which serve to define and point out their duty in every particular case that comes before them; and it will readily be conceived from the variety of controversies which grow out of the folly and wickedness of mankind, that the records of those precedents must unavoidably swell to a very considerable bulk, and must demand long and laborious study to acquire a competent knowledge of them. Hence it is, that there can be but few men in the society who will have sufficient skill in the laws to qualify them for the stations of judges. And making the proper deductions for the ordinary depravity of human nature, the number must be still smaller of those who unite the requisite integrity with the requisite knowledge. These considerations apprise us, that the government can have no great option between fit character; and that a temporary duration in office, which would naturally discourage such characters from quitting a lucrative line of practice to accept a seat on the bench, would have a tendency to throw the administration of justice into hands less able, and less well qualified, to conduct it with utility and dignity. In the present circumstances of this country, and in those in which it is likely to be for a long time to come, the disadvantages on this score would be greater than they may at first sight appear; but it must be confessed, that they are far inferior to those which present themselves under the other aspects of the subject.

Upon the whole, there can be no room to doubt that the convention acted wisely in copying from the models of those constitutions which have established GOOD BEHAVIOR as the tenure of their judicial offices, in point of duration; and that so far from being blamable on this account, their plan would have been inexcusably defective, if it had wanted this important feature of good government. The experience of Great Britain affords an illustrious comment on the excellence of the institution.

14.2 Marbury v. Madison

[In 1801, at the very end of his presidential term, John Adams made a number of last-minute judicial appointments, hoping to install members of his own Federalist party in key positions before the Republican president, Thomas Jefferson, took over. One of these appointments was given to William Marbury, who was appointed to be a justice of the peace of the District of Columbia. In the confusion of the last few days of Adams's term, however, Marbury's commission was never delivered to him. When President Jefferson came into the White House, he held *up Marbury's commission. Marbury sued in the Supreme Court, asking the Court to order the new secretary of state, James Madison, to deliver the commission to him.*

The legal and political aspects of the case are extremely complex. Chief Justice Marshall, a staunch Federalist, did not want to condone Jefferson's actions, but he also did not want to risk ordering the administration to deliver the commission; he would be a laughing stock if Jefferson and Madison simply ignored him. He solved this dilemma by writing a strong opinion condemning Jefferson's acts as illegal but refusing to issue a compliance order. To do so, Marshall concluded, would be unconstitutional.

In one stroke, Marshall embarrassed Jefferson, protected his own position, and claimed for the first time the power to review acts of Congress as unconstitutional. The part of the argument making the last point follows.]

• • •

The question, whether an act, repugnant to the constitution, can become the law of the land, is a question deeply interesting to the United States; but, happily, not of an intricacy proportioned to its interest. It seems only necessary to recognize certain principles, supposed to have been long and well established, to decide it.

That the people have an original right to establish, for their future government, such principles as, in their opinion, shall most conduce to their own happiness, is the basis on which the whole American fabric has been erected. The exercise of this original right is a very great exertion; nor can it, nor ought it, to be frequently repeated. The principles, therefore, so established, are deemed fundamental. And as the authority from which they proceed, is supreme, and can seldom act, they are designed to be permanent.

This original and supreme will organizes the government, and assigns, to different departments, their respective powers. It may either stop here; or establish certain limits not to be transcended by those departments.

The government of the United States is of the latter description. The powers of the legislature are defined, and limited; and that those limits may not be mistaken, or forgotten, the constitution is written. To what purpose are powers limited, and to what purpose is that limitation committed to writing, if these limits may, at any time, be passed by those intended to be restrained? The distinction, between a government with limited and unlimited powers, is abolished, if those limits do not confine the persons on whom they are imposed, and if acts prohibited and acts allowed, are of equal obligation. It is a proposition too plain to be contested, that the constitution controls any legislative act repugnant to it; or, that the legislature may alter the constitution by an ordinary act.

Between these alternatives there is no middle ground. The constitution is either a superior, paramount law, unchangeable by ordinary means, or it is on a level with ordinary legislative acts, and, like other acts, is alterable when the legislature shall please to alter it.

If the former part of the alternative be true, then a legislative act contrary to the constitution is not law: if the latter part be true, then written constitutions are absurd attempts, on the part of the people, to limit a power, in its own nature illimitable.

Certainly all those who have framed written constitutions contemplate them as forming the fundamental and paramount law of the nation, and consequently the theory of every such government must be, that an act of the legislature, repugnant to the constitution, is void.

This theory is essentially attached to a written constitution, and is, consequently to be considered, by this court, as one of the fundamental principles of our society. It is not therefore to be lost sight of in the future consideration of this subject.

If an act of the legislature, repugnant to the constitution, is void, does it, notwithstanding its invalidity, bind the courts, and oblige them to give it effect? Or, in other words, though it be not law, does it constitute a rule as operative as if it was a law? This would be to overthrow in fact what was established in theory; and would seem, at first view, an absurdity too gross to be insisted on. It shall, however, receive a more attentive consideration.

It is emphatically the province and duty of the judicial department to say what the law is. Those who apply the rule to particular cases, must of necessity expound and interpret that rule. If two laws conflict with each other, the courts must decide on the operation of each.

So if a law be in opposition to the constitution; if both the law and the constitution apply to a particular case, so that the court must either decide that case conformably to the law, disregarding the constitution; or conformably to the constitution, disregarding the law; the court must determine which of these conflicting rules governs the case. This is of the very essence of judicial duty.

If, then, the courts are to regard the constitution; and the constitution is superior to any ordinary act of the legislature; the constitution, and not such ordinary act, must govern the case to which they both apply.

Those then who controvert the principle that the constitution is to be considered, in court, as a paramount law, are reduced to the necessity of maintaining that courts must close their eyes on the constitution, and see only the law.

This doctrine would subvert the very foundation of all written constitutions. It would declare that an act which, according to the principles and theory of our government, is entirely void; is yet, in practice, completely obligatory. It would declare, that if the legislature shall do what is expressly forbidden, such act, notwithstanding the express prohibition, is in reality effectual. It would be giving to the legislature a practical and real omnipotence, with the same breath which professes to restrict their powers within narrow limits. It is prescribing limits, and declaring that those limits may be passed at pleasure.

That it thus reduces to nothing what we have deemed the greatest improvement on political institutions—a written constitution—would of itself be sufficient, in America, where written constitutions have been viewed with so much reverence, for rejecting the construction. But the peculiar expressions of the constitution of the United States furnish additional arguments in favour of its rejection.

The judicial power of the United States is extended to all cases arising under the constitution.

Could it be the intention of those who gave this power, to say that, in using it, the constitution should not be looked into? That a case arising under the constitution should be decided without examining the instrument under which it arises?

This is too extravagant to be maintained.

In some cases, then, the constitution must be looked into by the judges. And if they can open it at all, what part of it are they forbidden to read, or to obey?

There are many other parts of the constitution which serve to illustrate this subject. It is declared that "no tax or duty shall be laid on articles exported from any state." Suppose a duty on the export of cotton, of tobacco, or of flour; and a suit instituted to recover it. Ought judgment to be rendered in such a case? ought the judges to close their eyes on the constitution, and only see the law?

The constitution declares that "no bill of attainder or *ex post facto* law shall be passed."

If, however, such a bill should be passed and a person should be prosecuted under it; must the court condemn to death those victims whom the constitution endeavors to preserve?

"No person," says the constitution, "shall be convicted of treason unless on the testimony of two witnesses to the same overt act, or on confession in open court."

Here the language of the constitution is addressed especially to the courts. It prescribes, directly for them, a rule of evidence not to be departed from. If the legislature should change that rule, and declare one witness, or a confession out of court, sufficient for conviction, must the constitutional principle yield to the legislative act?

From these, and many other selections which might be made, it is apparent, that the framers of the constitution contemplated that instrument, as a rule for the government of *courts*, as well as of the legislature.

Why otherwise does it direct the judges to take an oath to support it? This oath certainly applies, in an especial manner, to their conduct in their official character. How immoral to impose it on them, if they were to be used as the instruments, and the knowing instruments, for violating what they swear to support!

The oath of office, too, imposed by the legislature, is completely demonstrative of the legislative opinion on this subject. It is in these words: "I do solemnly swear that I will administer justice without respect to persons, and do equal right to the poor and to the rich; and that I will faithfully and impartially discharge all the duties incumbent on me as according to the best of my abilities and understanding, agreeably to *the constitution*, and laws of the United States."

Why does a judge swear to discharge his duties agreeably to the constitution of the United States, if that constitution forms no rule for his government? If it is closed upon him, and cannot be inspected by him?

If such be the real state of things, this is worse than solemn mockery. To prescribe, or to take this oath, becomes equally a crime.

It is also not entirely unworthy of observation that in declaring what shall be the *supreme* law of the land, the *constitution* itself is first mentioned; and not the laws of the United States generally, but those only which shall be made in *pursuance* of the constitution, have that rank.

Thus, the particular phraseology of the constitution of the United States confirms and strengthens the principle, supposed to be essential to all written constitutions, that a law repugnant to the constitution is void; and that *courts*, as well as other departments, are bound by that instrument. . . .

14.3 Martin *v.* Hunter's Lessee

[*The complex case of* Martin v. Hunter's Lessee *grew out of land claims arising from the treaties of settlement between the United States and Great Britain after the Revolutionary War. The Virginia state courts sided with Hunter, who had been given the land by the state of Virginia. But when the U.S. Supreme Court heard the case for the first time, it ruled in favor of Martin, who had inherited the property from Lord Fairfax. Fairfax's land, the Supreme Court ruled, had been restored to him by the treaty between Great Britain and the United States.*

The dispute in the second case, excerpted here, centered around whether the Supreme Court's decision overturning the Virginia court's ruling should prevail. The Constitution, Justice Story wrote, required that questions of federal law (like the application of a federal treaty) be decided in the end by the federal courts and that, therefore, the Supreme Court had the power to overturn decisions of the state courts on questions of federal law. Chief Justice Marshall, by the way, did not participate in the case because he had a financial interest in the property.

Martin *is an extremely important case. Then, as now, both state and federal courts were routinely called upon to apply and interpret federal law. Without the rule of law established in this case, each state's supreme court would have been free to interpret federal treaties, laws, and even the Constitution as it saw fit—and the Supreme Court of the United States would have been powerless to do anything about it.*

Only that part of the Court's opinion dealing with the supremacy of the federal judiciary over the state courts on matters of federal law is reproduced here.]

• • •

Appellate jurisdiction is given by the constitution to the supreme court, in all cases where it has not original jurisdiction; subject, however, to such exceptions and regulations as congress may prescribe. It is, therefore, capable of embracing every case enumerated in the constitution, which is not exclusively to be decided by way of original jurisdiction. . . .

What is there to restrain its exercise over state tribunals, in the enumerated cases? The appellate power is not limited by the terms of the third article to any particular courts. The words are, "the judicial power (which includes appellate power) shall extend *to all cases*," &c., and "in all other cases before mentioned the supreme court shall have appellate jurisdiction." It is the *case,* then, and not the *court,* that gives the jurisdiction. If the judicial power extends to the case, it will be in vain to search in the letter of the constitution for any qualification as to the tribunal where it depends. It is incumbent, then, upon those who assert such a qualification to show its existence by necessary implication. . . .

[It must] be conceded that the constitution not only contemplated, but meant to provide for cases within the scope of the judicial power of the United States, which might yet depend before state tribunals. It was foreseen that in the exercise of their ordinary jurisdiction, state courts would incidentally take cognisance of cases arising under the constitution, the laws, and treaties of the United States. Yet to all these cases, the judicial power, by the very terms of the constitution, is to extend. It cannot extend by original jurisdiction if that was already rightfully and exclusively attached in the state courts, which (as has been already shown) may occur; it must, therefore, extend by appellate jurisdiction, or not at all. It would seem to follow that the appellate power of the United States must, in such cases, extend to state tribunals; and if in such cases, there is no reason why it should not equally attach upon all others within the purview of the constitution.

It has been argued that such an appellate jurisdiction over state courts is inconsistent with the genius of our governments, and the spirit of the constitution. That the latter was never designed to act upon state sovereignties, but only upon the people, and that if the power exists, it will materially impair the sovereignty of the states, and the independence of their courts. We cannot yield to the force of this reasoning; it assumes principles which we cannot admit, and draws conclusions to which we do not yield our assent.

It is a mistake [to believe] that the constitution was not designed to operate upon states in their corporate capacities. It is crowded with provisions which restrain or annul the sovereignty of the states in some of the highest branches of their prerogatives. The tenth section of the first article contains a long list of disabilities and prohibitions imposed upon the states. Surely, when such essential portions of state sovereignty are taken away, or prohibited to be exercised, it cannot be correctly asserted that the constitution does not act upon the states. . . .

When, therefore, the states are stripped of some of the highest attributes of sovereignty, and the same are given to the United States; when the legislatures of the states are in some respects, under the control of congress, and in every case are, under the constitution, bound by the paramount authority of the United States; it is certainly difficult to support the argument that the appellate power over the decisions of state courts is contrary to the genius of our institutions. The courts of the United States can, without question, revise the proceedings of the executive and legislative authorities of the states, and if they are found to be contrary to the constitution, may declare them to be of no legal validity. Surely, the exercise of the same right over judicial tribunals is not a higher or more dangerous act of sovereign power.

Nor can such a right be deemed to impair the independence of state judges. It is assuming the very ground in controversy to assert that they possess an absolute independence of the United States. In respect to the powers granted to the United States, they are not independent; they are expressly bound to obedience, by the letter of the constitution; and if they should unintentionally transcend their authority, or misconstrue the constitution, there is no more reason for giving their judgments an absolute and irresistible force, than for giving it to the acts of the other co-ordinate departments of state sovereignty.

The argument urged from the possibility of the abuse of the revising power, is equally unsatisfactory. It is always a doubtful course, to argue against the use or existence of a power, from the possibility of its abuse. It is still more difficult, by such an argument, to ingraft upon a general power a restriction which is not to be found in the terms in which it is given. From the very nature of things, the absolute right of decision, in the last resort, must rest somewhere—wherever it may be vested, it is susceptible of abuse. In all questions of jurisdiction, the inferior, or appellate court, must pronounce the final judgment; and common sense, as well as legal reasoning, has conferred it upon the latter . . .

It is further argued, that no great public mischief can result from a construction which shall limit the appellate power of the United States to cases in their own courts: first, because state judges are bound by an oath to support the constitution of the United States, and must be presumed to be men of learning and integrity; and secondly, because congress must have an unquestionable right to remove all cases within the scope of the judicial power from the state courts to the courts of the United States, at any time before final judgment, though not after final judgment. As to the first reason— admitting that the judges of the state courts are, and always will be, of as much learning, integrity and wisdom, as those of the courts of the United States, (which we very cheerfully admit,) it does not aid the argument. It is manifest that the constitution has proceeded upon a theory of its own, and given or withheld powers according to the judgment of the American people, by whom it was adopted. We can only

construe its powers, and cannot inquire into the policy or principles which induced the grant of them. The constitution has presumed (whether rightly or wrongly we do not inquire) that state attachments, state prejudices, state jealousies, and state interests, might sometimes obstruct, or control, or be supposed to obstruct or control, the regular administration of justice. Hence, in controversies between states; between citizens of different states; between citizens claiming grants under different states; between a state and its citizens, or foreigners, and between citizens and foreigners, it enables the parties, under the authority of congress, to have the controversies heard, tried, and determined before the national tribunals. No other reason than that which has been stated can be assigned, why some, at least, of those cases should not have been left to the cognizance of the state courts. In respect to the other enumerated cases—the cases arising under the constitution, laws and treaties of the United States, cases affecting ambassadors and other public ministers, and cases of admiralty and maritime jurisdiction—reasons of a higher and more extensive nature, touching the safety, peace and sovereignty of the nation, might well justify a grant of exclusive jurisdiction.

This is not all. A motive of another kind, perfectly compatible with the most sincere respect for state tribunals, might induce the grant of appellate power over their decisions. That motive is the importance, and even necessity of *uniformity* of decisions throughout the whole United States, upon all subjects within the purview of the constitution. Judges of equal learning and integrity, in different states, might differently interpret a statute, or a treaty of the United States, or even the constitution itself: If there were no revising authority to control these jarring and discordant judgments, and harmonize them into uniformity, the laws, the treaties and the constitution of the United States would be different in different states, and might, perhaps, never have precisely the same construction, obligation, or efficacy, in any two states. The public mischiefs that would attend such a state of things would be truly deplorable; and it cannot be believed that they could have escaped the enlightened convention which formed the constitution. What indeed, might then have been only prophecy, has now become fact; and the appellate jurisdiction must continue to be the only adequate remedy for such evils.

...

II  TRENDS

Over the past thirty years, the federal courts have played an increasingly important role in the shaping of social policy. As former attorney general William French Smith wrote in 1981, "Federal courts have attempted to restructure entire school systems in desegregation cases. . . . They have asserted similar control over entire prison systems and public housing projects. They have restructured the employment criteria to be used by American business and government. . . . At least one federal judge even attempted to administer a local sewer system."* Whether courts should play this role is an important and difficult question, but that they do make important social policy decisions is beyond dispute.

The following selections present two sides of the coin. In selection 14.4, one of the most influential and outspoken members of the federal judiciary—District Judge Frank Johnson of Alabama—speaks out in defense of judicial activism in the shaping of social policy. He discusses his involvement in cases that resulted in judicial intervention in Alabama's penal and mental health care systems. Next, social scientist Donald L. Horowitz cautions that courts are not ideally suited for such an activist role; the peculiar features of the adjudicative process produce both pluses and minuses when courts attempt to tackle social issues.

Questions

1. What factors prompted Judge Johnson to act in the cases he discusses? How might Horowitz critique the courts' capacity to make such decisions wisely?

2. "To reclaim responsibilities passed by default to the judiciary," Judge Johnson writes, "state officials must confront their governmental responsibilities with the diligence and honesty their constituencies deserve." In the light of the materials studied in previous chapters (especially chapters 5, 8, 11, and 13), how realistic is this suggestion?

* *Judges' Journal* 21 (Winter 1982):7.

14.4 The Constitution and the Federal District Judge

Frank M. Johnson

Modern American society depends upon our judicial system to play a critical role in maintaining the balance between governmental powers and individual rights. The increasing concern paid by our courts toward the functioning of government and its agencies has received much comment and some criticism recently. As governmental institutions at all levels have assumed a greater role in providing public services, courts increasingly have been confronted with the unavoidable duty of determining whether those services meet basic constitutional requirements. Time and again citizens have brought to the federal courts, and those courts reluctantly have decided, such basic questions as how and when to make available equal quality public education to all our children; how to guarantee all citizens an opportunity to serve on juries, to vote, and to have their votes counted equally; under what minimal living conditions criminal offenders may be incarcerated; and what minimum standards of care and treatment state institutions must provide the mentally ill and mentally retarded who have been involuntarily committed to the custody of the state.

The reluctance with which courts and judges have undertaken the complex task of deciding such questions has at least three important sources. First, one of the founding principles of our Government, a principle derived from the French philosophers of the eighteenth century, is that the powers of government should be separate and distinct, lest all the awesome power of government unite as one force unchecked in its exercise. The drafters of our Constitution formulated the doctrine of separation of powers to promote the independence of each branch of government in its sphere of operation. To the extent that courts respond to requests to look to the future and to change existing conditions by making new rules, however, they become subject to the charge of usurping authority from the legislative or executive branch.

Second, our Constitution and laws have strictly limited the power of the federal judiciary to participate in what are essentially political affairs. The tenth amendment reserves any power not delegated to the United States to the individual states or to the people. Reflecting the distrust of centralized government expressed by this amendment, courts and citizens alike since the Nation's beginning have regarded certain governmental functions as primarily, if not exclusively, state responsibilities. Among these are public education; maintenance of state and local penal institutions; domestic relations; and provision for the poor, homeless, aged, and infirm. A further limitation on the role of federal courts with respect to other governmental bodies lies in the creation and maintenance of these courts as courts of limited jurisdiction.

Last, federal judges properly hesitate to make decisions either that require the exercise of political judgment or that necessitate expertise they lack. Judges are professionally trained in the law—not in sociology, education, medicine, penology, or public administration. In an ideal society, elected officials would make all decisions relating to the allocation of resources; experts trained in corrections would make all penological decisions; physicians would make all medical decisions; scientists would make all technological decisions; and educators would make all educational decisions. Too often, however, we have failed to achieve this ideal system. Many times, those persons to whom we have entrusted these responsibilities have acted or failed to act in ways that do not fall within the bounds of discretion permitted by the Constitution and the laws. When such transgressions are properly and formally brought before a court—and increasingly before federal courts—it becomes the responsibility of the judiciary to ensure that the Constitution and laws of the United States remain, in fact as well as in theory, the supreme law of the land.

On far too many occasions the intransigent and unremitting opposition of state officials who have neglected or refused to correct unconstitutional or unlawful state policies and practices has necessitated federal intervention to enforce the law. Courts in all sections of the Nation have expended and continue to expend untold resources in repeated litigation brought to compel local school officials to follow a rule of law first announced by the Supreme Court almost twenty-two years ago. In addition to deciding scores of school cases, federal courts in Alabama alone have ordered the desegregation of mental institutions, penal facilities, public parks, city buses, interstate and intrastate buses and bus terminals, airport terminals, and public libraries and museums. Although I refer to Alabama and specific cases litigated in the federal courts of Alabama, I do not intend to suggest that similar problems do not exist in many of our other states.

The history of public school desegregation has been a story of repeated intervention by the courts to overcome not only the threats and violence of extremists attempting to block school desegregation but also the numerous attempts by local and state officials to thwart the orderly, efficient, and lawful resolution of this complicated social problem. Desegregation is not the only area of state responsibility in which Alabama officials have forfeited their decision-making powers by such a dereliction of duty as to require judicial intervention. Having found Alabama's legislative apportionment plan unconstitutional, the District Court for the Middle District of Alabama waited ten years for State officials to carry out the duty properly imposed upon them by the Constitution and expressly set out in the court's order. The continued refusal of those officials to comply left the court no choice but to assume that duty itself and to impose its own reapportionment plan. State officers by their inaction have also handed over to the courts property tax assessment plans, standards for the care and treatment of mentally ill and mentally retarded persons committed to the State's custody, and the procedures by which such persons are committed.

Some of these cases are extremely troublesome and time consuming for all concerned. I speak in particular of those lawsuits challenging the operation of state institutions for the custody and control of citizens who cannot or will not function at a safe and self-sustaining capacity in a free society. Ordinarily these cases proceed as class actions seeking to determine the rights of large numbers of people. As a result, the courts' decisions necessarily have wide-ranging effect and momentous importance, whether they grant or deny the relief sought.

A shocking example of a failure of state officials to discharge their duty was forcefully presented in a lawsuit tried before me in 1972, *Newman v. Alabama*, which challenged the constitutional sufficiency of medical care available to prisoners in the Alabama penal system. The evidence in that case convincingly demonstrated that correctional officers on occasion intentionally denied inmates the right to examination by a physician or to treatment by trained medical personnel, and that they routinely withheld medicine and other treatments prescribed by physicians. Further evidence showed that untrained inmates served as ward attendants and X-ray, laboratory, and dental technicians; rags were used as bandages; ambulance oxygen tanks remained empty for long periods of time; and unsupervised inmates without formal training pulled teeth, gave injections, sutured, and performed minor surgery. In fact, death resulting from gross neglect and totally inadequate treatment was not unusual.

A nineteen-year-old with an extremely high fever who was diagnosed as having acute pneumonia was left unsupervised and allowed to take cold showers at will for two days before his death. A quadriplegic with bedsores infested with maggots was bathed and had his bandages changed only once in the month before his death. An inmate who could not eat

received no nourishment for the three days prior to his death even though intravenous feeding had been ordered by a doctor. A geriatric inmate who had suffered a stroke was made to sit each day on a wooden bench so that he would not soil his bed; he frequently fell onto the floor; his legs became swollen from a lack of circulation, necessitating the amputation of a leg the day before his death.

Based on the virtually uncontradicted evidence presented at trial, the district court entered a comprehensive order designed to remedy each specific abuse proved at trial and to establish additional safeguards so that the medical program in Alabama prisons would never again regress to its past level of inadequacy. The State was ordered to bring the general hospital at the Medical and Diagnostic Center (now Kilby Corrections Facility) up to the minimum standards required of hospitals by the United States Department of Health, Education, and Welfare for participation in the medicare program. The court also directed the Alabama State Board of Health to inspect regularly for general sanitation all the medical and food processing facilities in the prison system. Finally, the court decreed that all inmates receive physical examinations by physicians at regular intervals of not more than two years.

One of the most comprehensive orders that I have entered concerning the operation and management of state institutions relates to the facilities maintained by the Alabama Department of Mental Health for the mentally ill and mentally retarded. Plaintiffs in *Wyatt v. Stickney* brought a class action on behalf of all patients involuntarily confined at Bryce Hospital, the State's largest mental hospital, to establish the minimum standards of care and treatment to which the civilly committed are entitled under the Constitution. Patients at Searcy Hospital in southern Alabama and residents at the Partlow State School and Hospital in Tuscaloosa joined the action as plaintiffs, thereby compelling a comprehensive inquiry into the entire Alabama mental health and retardation treatment and habilitation program.

At trial plaintiffs produced evidence showing that Bryce Hospital, built in the 1850's, was grossly overcrowded, housing more than 5000 patients. Of these 5000 people ostensibly committed to Bryce for treatment of mental illness, about 1600—almost one-third—were geriatrics neither needing nor receiving any treatment for mental illness. Another 1000 or more of the patients at Bryce were mentally retarded rather than mentally ill. A totally inadequate staff, only a small percentage professionally trained, served these 5000 patients. The hospital employed only six staff members qualified to deal with mental patients—three medical doctors with psychiatric training, one Ph.D. psychologist, and two social workers with master's degrees in social work. The evidence indicated that the general living conditions and lack of individualized treatment programs were as intolerable and deplorable as Alabama's rank of fiftieth among the states in per patient expenditures would suggest. For example, the hospital spent less than fifty cents per patient each day for food.

The evidence concerning Partlow State School and Hospital for the retarded proved even more shocking than the evidence relating to the mental hospitals. The extremely dangerous conditions compelled the court to issue an interim emergency order requiring Partlow officials to take immediate steps to protect the lives and safety of the residents. The Associate Commissioner for Mental Retardation for the Alabama Department of Mental Health testified that Partlow was sixty percent overcrowded; that the school, although it had not, could immediately discharge at least 300 residents; *and that seventy percent of the residents should never have been committed at all.* The conclusion that there was no opportunity for habilitation for its residents was inescapable. Indeed, the evidence reflected that one resident was scalded to death when a fellow resident hosed water from one of the bath facilities on him; another died as a result of the insertion of a running water hose into his rectum by a working resident who was cleaning him; one died when soapy water was forced into his mouth; another died of a self-administered overdose of inadequately stored drugs; and authorities restrained another resident in a straitjacket for *nine years* to prevent

him from sucking his hands and fingers. Witnesses described the Partlow facilities as barbaric and primitive; some residents had no place to sit to eat meals, and coffee cans served as toilets in some areas of the institution.

With the exception of the interim emergency order designed to eliminate hazardous conditions at Partlow, the court at first declined to devise specific steps to improve existing conditions in Alabama's mental health and retardation facilities. Instead, it directed the Department of Mental Health to design its own plan for upgrading the system to meet constitutional standards. Only after two deadlines had passed without any signs of acceptable progress did the court itself, relying upon the proposals of counsel for all parties and amici curiae, define the minimal constitutional standards of care, treatment, and habilitation for which the case of *Wyatt v. Stickney* has become generally known.

During the past several years conditions at the Partlow State School for the retarded have improved markedly. It was pleasing to read in a Montgomery newspaper that members of the State Mental Health Board (the *Wyatt* defendants) recently met at Partlow and agreed that "what they saw was a different world" compared to four years ago; that "things are now unbelievably better," with most students "out in the sunshine on playground swings or tossing softballs [,] . . . responding to a kind word or touch with smiles and squeals of delight"; and that "enrollment has been nearly cut in half, down from 2,300 to just under 1,300 while the staff has tripled from 600 to 1,800."

• • •

The fourteenth amendment, which generates much of the litigation discussed above, forbids a state to "deprive any person of life, liberty or property, without due process of law" or to "deny to any person within its jurisdiction the equal protection of the laws." The Supreme Court has interpreted the due process clause to require that the states fulfill most of the obligations toward citizens that the Bill of Rights imposes on the federal government. Each state in all its dealings with its people must recognize and preserve their guaranteed freedoms.

Nevertheless, state officials have frequently raised the tenth amendment's reservation of powers to the states as a defense to the exercise of federal jurisdiction over actions alleging state violations of constitutional rights. While the tenth amendment clearly preserves for the states a wide and important sphere of power, it does not permit any state to frustrate or to ignore the mandates of the Constitution. *The tenth amendment does not relieve the states of a single obligation imposed upon them by the Constitution of the United States.* Surely the concept of states' rights has never purported to allow states to abdicate their responsibility to protect their citizens from criminal acts and inhumane conditions. I find it sad and ironic that citizens of Alabama held in "protective custody" by Alabama had to obtain federal court orders to protect themselves from violent crimes and barbaric conditions.

The cornerstone of our American legal system rests on recognition of the Constitution as the supreme law of the land, and the paramount duty of the federal judiciary is to uphold that law. Thus, when a state fails to meet constitutionally mandated requirements, it is the solemn duty of the courts to assure compliance with the Constitution. One writer has termed the habit adopted by some states of neglecting their responsibilities until faced with a federal court order "the Alabama Federal Intervention Syndrome," characterizing it as

> the tendency of many state officials to punt their problems with constituencies to the federal courts. Many federal judges have grown accustomed to allowing state officials to make political speeches as a prelude to receiving the order of the district court. This role requires the federal courts to serve as a buffer between the state officials and their constituencies, raising the familiar criticism that state officials rely upon the federal courts to impose needed reforms rather than accomplishing them themselves.

As long as those state officials entrusted with the responsibility for fair and equitable governance completely disregard that responsibility, the judiciary must and will stand ready to intervene on behalf of the deprived. Judge Richard T. Rives of the Court of Appeals for the Fifth Circuit, in joining a three-judge panel that struck down attempts by state officials to frustrate the registration of black voters, eloquently expressed the reluctance with which the vast majority of federal judges approach intervention in state affairs:

> I look forward to the day when the State and its political subdivisions will again take up their mantle of responsibility, treating all of their citizens equally, and thereby relieve the federal Government of the necessity of intervening in their affairs. Until that day arrives, the responsibility for this intervention must rest with those who through their ineptitude and public disservice have forced it.

We in the judiciary await the day when the Alabama Federal Intervention Syndrome, in that State and elsewhere, will become a relic of the past. To reclaim responsibilities passed by default to the judiciary—most often the federal judiciary—and to find solutions for ever-changing challenges, the states must preserve their ability to respond flexibly, creatively, and with due regard for the rights of all. State officials must confront their governmental responsibilities with the diligence and honesty that their constituencies deserve. When lawful rights are being denied, only the exercise of conscientious, responsible leadership, which is usually long on work and short on complimentary news headlines, can avoid judicial intervention. The most fitting Bicentennial observance I can conceive would be for all government officials to take up the constitutional mantle and diligently strive to protect the basic human rights recognized by the founders of our Republic two hundred years ago.

14.5 The Courts and Social Policy_____

Donald L. Horowitz

Each decision process leaves its distinctive mark on the issues it touches. Each of them snatches a few transactions from the flow of events, brings them to the foreground and blurs others into the background. Each applies its own mode of analysis to these magnified phenomena. Each has its own set of tools that it uses to devise solutions to problems it has analyzed. No one tool kit is exactly the same as any other. Equally important, each decision process decides some things and leaves other things undecided. There are significant and characteristic patterns of non-decision, as there are patterns of decision.

Adjudication, of course, has its own devices for choosing problems, its own habits of analysis, its own criteria of the relevance of phenomena to issues, its own repertoire of solutions. These hallmarks of adjudication have . . . a common origin: judicial preoccupation with the unique case. This admirable preoccupation imparts to the judicial process many of the characteristics that differentiate it in degree or in kind from the legislative and administrative processes, both of which accord greater explicitness and legitimacy to their general policymaking functions.

In what follows, I attempt to elicit some of these distinctive characteristics of adjudication. Adjudication is naturally a large subject, and it will be necessary to speak in rather sweeping, often unqualified, terms. Some of the enumerated consequences of these characteristics for social policymaking amount to propositions that can be stated with a high level of confidence; others are simply inferences from the structure of litigation. There are often explicit comparisons to the legislative and administrative process . . .

1. *Adjudication is focused.* The usual question before the judge is simply: Does one party have a *right?* Does another party have a *duty?* This should be contrasted with the question before a "planner," whether legislative or bureaucratic: What are the *alternatives?* These are quite different ways of casting problems for decision. For the judge, alternatives may be relevant, but they are relevant primarily to the subsequent issue of what "remedies" are appropriate to redress "wrongs" done to those who possess "rights." In other words, the initial focus on rights tends to defer the question of alternatives to a later stage of the inquiry and to consider it a purely technical question.

As this suggests, the initial focus on rights is also a serious impediment to the analysis of costs, for, in principle at least, if rights exist they are not bounded by considerations of cost. If a person possesses a right, he possesses it whatever the cost.

Costing may, to be sure, creep into litigation through the back door, in a variety of disguises. One of the masks it wears is the "balancing of convenience" that occurs in deciding whether an injunction will issue and to what activities it will extend. Judges, confronted with a plaintiff's assertion that he has a right to a hearing before a governmental body acts in a matter affecting his interests, have been known to inquire how many such additional hearings would be required if the plaintiff's right to one were recognized and how much disruption that might inflict on the work of the governmental body. But they tend to regard such questions as tangential and, if pressed on this front, are likely to recoil from a judgment that would make rights stand or fall on considerations of such an order.

Adjudication, then, is narrow in a double sense. The format of decision inhibits the presentation of an array of alternatives and the explicit matching of benefits to costs.

The contrast between rights and alternatives suggests the much broader framework in which non-adjudicative policymakers function. This is best seen in what the lawyers and judges call remedies. As indicated above, there is some flexibility in tailoring a remedy to the nature of the wrong it is designed to correct, but for the most part this flexibility extends only to the terms and timing of the injunction to be issued. For, paradoxically enough, though they have the fewest coercive resources at their command, the courts have only the option of issuing coercive orders: injunctions that direct parties to do or refrain from doing something.

Legislators and administrators, on the other hand, have a wider range of tools in their kit. They may resort to the same kinds of sanctions judges invoke, or they may use taxation, incentives and subsidies of various kinds, interventions in the marketplace, the establishment of new organizations or the takeover of old ones, or a number of other ways of seeking to attain their goals. The judiciary, having no budget (save for administrative expenses), no power to tax or to create new institutions, has much less ability to experiment or to adjust its techniques to the problems it confronts. The courts can forbid, require, or permit activity, but in general they cannot permit activity conditionally (for example, by taxing something so as to discourage it). Many of the tools that are favored by economists in particular are missing from the judicial black bag.

There is a caveat that must be added, however. Although judges do not have the power to tax or spend, sometimes the decrees they issue have the effect of requiring expenditure. Their decisions can therefore get caught up in the budgetary process, and may stimulate exercises of the appropriation power. Whether a decree will be complied with by spending or not spending and, if by spending, by reallocating a fixed sum or by expanding the total sum available, affects in a fundamental way the outcome of judicial action. Significantly, however, the choice of this response remains outside the control of the court.

2. *Adjudication is piecemeal.* The lawsuit is the supreme example of incremental decisionmak-ing. As such, it shares the advantages and the defects of the species. The outcome of litigation may give the illusion of a decisive victory, but the victory is often on a very limited point. The judge's power to decide extends, in principle, only to those issues that are before him. Related issues, not raised by the instant dispute, must generally await later litigation. So it is at least in traditional conception.

Incrementalism may be entirely appropriate for some kinds of policy. For others, it may be simply too slow or too disjointed.

Incrementalism is, of course, well suited to decisionmaking when information is scarce. Since adequate information is so often scarce when decisions must be confronted, many decisions are of an incremental character, regardless of where they are made. The less the change imposed by the decision, the less the potential error. With courts, this is an especially important consideration. Judges do not choose their cases and so may often have to act in matters in which they lack complete confidence in their information base. Step-by-step adjustment can thus be viewed as a protective measure responding to the limited control courts have over the choice of issues they decide . . .

Related to limited information is the enhanced ability to backtrack when just a few steps have been taken: "at the heart of incrementalism lies the notion of reversibility."

In the case of courts, however, reversibility presents some very special problems. Courts do sometimes alter a course they have recently embarked on, but the change is not generally in response to new information about the consequences of the course chosen. Courts are not possessed of great ability to detect the need for backtracking. . . .

Moreover, there are special inhibitions on changing judicial course. These derive principally from the doctrine of precedent. However innovative or experimental it is in fact, adjudicative policymaking is sanctified as law, which is in principle permanent. The courts, therefore, have only limited ability to admit candidly the tentative nature of conclusions they have reached. To say that a person or group "has a right" is to take a position difficult to reverse. Courts are on this account loath to give the appearance of fickleness that might attend unrestrained willingness to change course whenever circumstances seem to require change. In constitutional cases, these inhibitions are less prominent, but they do not disappear altogether, so that when change comes it often takes the form of engrafting qualifications onto old decisions rather than starting fresh. Even judicial backtracking tends to be decremental.

The net result of these special limitations both of doctrine and of lack of information is that the theoretical advantages of reversibility on the basis of new factual material are not usually realized in judicial practice. Changes of direction do, of course, occur, but only rarely do they occur when a court has both the information and the ability to admit in retrospect the failure of a given course of policy to affect behavior as intended.

At the same time, the piecemeal quality of judicial decisions has a number of important negative effects. Piecemeal decisions unsettle old patterns without providing unambiguous new patterns to which expectations can conform. Time and again, public and private decisionmakers have both underread and underreacted to and overread and overreacted to the implications of a new trend of Supreme Court decisions—only to find later that their adaptations had been, respectively, insufficient or excessive.

• • •

3. *Courts must act when litigants call.* The passivity of the judicial process is one of its most prominent characteristics. Judges sit to hear disputes brought to them by parties; they do not initiate action. This makes the sequencing of judicially ordered change dependent on the capricious timing of litigants rather than the planning of a public body. It also makes it difficult to ascertain the extent to which the situation of the litigants faithfully represents or illustrates the dimensions of the problem they bring to court.

So central is this aspect of the judicial process that some writers have viewed it as a definitional property of adjudication: "a judge of an organized body is a man appointed by that body to determine duties and the corresponding rights upon application of persons claiming those rights. It is the fact that such application must be made to him, which distinguishes a judge from an administrative officer." Courts, a critic has said, "are like defective clocks; they have to be shaken to set them going."

It is, of course, the impartiality of the judges that restricts them to a passive, responsive role. If a judge were to play a part in initiating proceedings, that might imply that he had "a certain commitment and often a theory of what occurred." With such preconceptions, how could he sit in judgment?

In addition, courts do not purport to possess the administrative machinery to know when "something is wrong"—indeed, wrong enough to require their intervention. For this reason, it is frequently said that courts are "poorly equipped to perform early warning functions since there are no motivated parties to clearly present the issue" before the harm is certain to occur. Litigation generally occurs after the grievance has crystallized, when the harm is about to be inflicted and it is too late to plan to avert the unwanted occurrence. Because litigation is often a last resort, much may already have transpired. Every so often, however, a grievance triggers a lawsuit very early, before the shape of the conflict between the parties is clear. For such cases, the federal courts devised a cautionary rule, now much diluted, against entertaining controversies that have not yet "ripened." Either way, adjudication proceeds by fits and starts, now too early, now too late, only occasionally well timed.

The sequence of judicial decisions also depends on the chance order in which grievances find their way to court. Theorists of social change have noted the importance of having some changes precede others. The stability of the British polity has often been attributed in part to sequencing: England became a nation before she had a state; on the Continent the reverse was more common. The decisions of the Warren Court on the rights of criminal suspects have perhaps made easier police acceptance of the rights of political demonstrators; it seems doubtful that decisions on the rights of demonstrators would have had much effect on the police view of the rights of criminal suspects. Some changes, in other words, may pave the way for others, and the resulting social amalgam may depend heavily on the order in which issues are faced. The point here is simply that courts control their calendar but not their agenda. Accordingly, the sequencing of innovation is to a large extent left to the vagaries of private initiative.

To be sure, courts do occasionally signal their readiness to entertain an issue. But although the entry of the courts into new fields may stimulate the filing of new cases or new appeals, it does not necessarily generate cases in any particular order. Lawyers, of course, can be acutely aware of this and sometimes try to insure that the most favorable case in the most favorable court reaches its destination ahead of less favorable cases in less favorable courts, pushing in the former, stalling in the latter. The most favorable case, of course, is not just the one that has the most attractive factual setting; it may also be the one that seems to require the least innovation, the smallest doctrinal jump, to achieve the desired result. It is much easier to build a bridge over a stream than over a river.

But if lawyers know this—and the incremental, precedential character of the judicial process gives them ample reason to know it—it does not follow that they can generally do anything much about it. Although judges are dependent on parties and their lawyers to bring lawsuits, parties and lawyers are dependent on judges to decide them. The tempo of decision may be affected by efforts of counsel to speed it up, but in the end there is no hurrying a judge determined to reflect long and hard on his problem and no stalling a judge determined to act on a sense of urgency.

Quite apart from this lack of control, there is typically a lack of coordination among cases as well. Lawyers see their cases as essentially individual matters, and they are generally unwilling to collaborate to the point of subordinating their cases for the sake of insuring that a better case is brought or appealed. Where organizations are involved, there is the added problem of gaining constituency authorization to coordinate in this manner. There have, of course, been exceptions, but these generally occur where one organization is in control of litigation in a whole field. Otherwise, communication becomes too difficult, discipline is impossible to impose, and targets of opportunity are hard to resist.

• • •

The passive role of the courts in choosing and deciding cases has another important consequence. Judicial decision becomes a chance occurrence, with no guarantee that the litigants are representative of the universe of problems their case purports to present. In fact, the guarantees are all the other way. As a matter of litigation strategy, plaintiffs' lawyers are likely to bring not the most representative case but the most extreme case of discrimination, of fraud, of violation of statute, of abuse of discretion, and so on.

• • •

There is, in [addition], no assurance that litigants constitute a random sample of the class of cases that might be affected by a decree. Because courts respond only to the cases that come their way, they make general law from what may be very special situations. Courts see the tip of the iceberg as well as the bottom of the barrel. The law they make may be law for the worst case or for the best, but it is not necessarily law for the mean or modal case.

The unrepresentative character of litigants raises another problem. Unlike legislation, litigation is not a finely tuned device for registering intensities of preference. Bargaining and compromise—at least bargaining and compromise beyond the confines of the individual case—are more difficult because of the adversary setting and the limited number of interested participants. Dependent as it is on an uncompromisingly partisan presentation, the adversary process is not conducive to the ordering of preferences. It compels the litigants to argue favorable positions with a vigor that may be out of proportion to their actual preferences and that may therefore mislead the judge; in any case, their preferences may have little support in the wider social group the litigants ostensibly represent. In ascertaining the configuration and intensity of public preferences, the judge is, for the most part, left to roam at large.

This problem is naturally exacerbated by the deliberately imposed isolation of judges from their communities. The prohibition on judges discussing pending cases with individuals or groups interested in the outcome is obviously designed to insure the independence and impartiality of the judiciary. But what fosters the detachment of judges is necessarily at odds with their sensitivity to social forces.

4. *Fact-finding in adjudication is ill-adapted to the ascertainment of social facts.* The fact that judges function at some distance from the social milieu from which their cases spring puts them at an initial disadvantage in understanding the dimensions of social policy problems. The focused, piecemeal quality of adjudication implies that judicial decisions tend to be abstracted from social contexts broader than the immediate setting in which the litigation arises, and, as already indicated, the potentially unrepresentative character of the litigants makes it hazardous to generalize from their situation to the wider context.

The judicial fact-finding process carries forward this abstraction of the case from its more general social context. To make this clear, it is necessary to distinguish between two kinds of facts: historical facts and social facts. *Historical facts* are the events that have transpired between the parties to a lawsuit. *Social facts* are the recurrent patterns of behavior on which policy must be based. Historical facts, as I use the term, have occasionally been called "adjudicative facts" by lawyers, and social facts have also been called "legislative facts." I avoid these terms because of the preconceptions they carry and the division of labor they imply. Nonetheless, by whatever designation they are known, these are two distinct kinds of facts, and a process set up to establish the one is not necessarily adequate to ascertain the other.

Social facts are nothing new in litigation. Courts have always had to make assumptions or inferences about general conditions that would guide their decisions. The broader the issue, the more such imponderables there are. The breadth of the issues in constitutional law has always made it a fertile field for empirical speculation. Does a civil service law barring alleged subversives from public employment have a "chilling effect" on free speech? Is the use of third-degree methods by the police sufficiently widespread to justify a prophylactic rule that would exclude from evidence even some confessions that are not coerced? Does pornography stimulate the commission of sex crimes, or does it provide cathartic release for those who might otherwise commit such crimes?

Constitutional law is a fertile field, but it is not the only field in which such questions arise. If a court refuses to enforce against a bankrupt corporation an "unconscionable contract" for the repayment of borrowed money, will that make it more difficult for firms needing credit to obtain it and perhaps precipitate more such bankruptcies? Does it encourage carelessness and thus undercut a prime purpose of the law of negligence if an automobile driver, a shopkeeper, or a theater owner is permitted to insure himself against liability inflicted as a result of his own fault?

These are, all of them, behavioral questions. They share an important characteristic: no amount of proof about the conduct of the individual litigants involved in a civil service, confession, obscenity, bankruptcy, or negligence case can provide answers to these probabilistic questions about the behavior of whole categories of people. As a matter of fact, proof of one kind of fact can be misleading about the other. What is true in the individual case may be false in the generality of cases, and vice versa. The judicial process, however, makes it much easier to learn reliably about the individual case than about the run of cases.

The increasing involvement of the courts in social policy questions has increased the number and importance of social fact questions in litigation. As the courts move into new, specialized, unfamiliar policy areas, they are confronted by a plethora of questions about human behavior that are beyond their ability to answer on the basis of common experience or the usual modicum of expert testimony. A few examples, drawn from a social science manual for lawyers, will make the point:

> Do the attrition rates for different racial groups applying for admission to a union apprenticeship program suggest a pattern of racial discrimination?
> How would the elimination of a local bus system through bankruptcy affect low income people and the elderly poor in particular?
> How are different income groups and communities of varying sizes differentially affected by the formula allocation of General Revenue Sharing funds?

Obtaining answers to such behavioral questions has become exigent, and not only because the interstices in which courts make fresh policy keep expanding. If a judge or a jury makes a mistake of fact relating only to the case before it, "the effects of the mistake are quarantined." But if the factual materials form the foundation for a general policy, the consequences cannot be so confined.

Traditionally, the courts have been modest about their competence to ascertain social facts and have tried to leave this function primarily to other agencies. They have shielded themselves by applying doctrines that have the effect of deferring to the fact-finding abilities of legislatures and administrative bodies, to avoid having to establish social facts in the course of litigation.

The reasons for this general modesty are well grounded. There is tension between two different judicial responsibilities: deciding the particular case and formulating a general policy. Two different kinds of fact-finding processes are required for these two different functions. The adversary system of presentation and the rules of evidence were both developed for the former, and they leave much to be desired for the latter.

In general, the parties can be depended upon to elicit all of the relevant historical facts, through the ordinary use of testimony and documentary evidence, and the judge or jury can be presumed competent to evaluate that evidence. Social facts, on the other hand, may not be elicited at all by the parties, almost surely not fully, and the competence of the decision-maker in this field cannot be taken for granted.

• • •

How have social fact issues been handled by the courts in practice? They have been handled in much the same way that the rules of evidence and the adversary system have been adapted to accommodate social facts: by neglect or by improvisation.

A first, quite common way is to ignore them or to assume, sometimes rightly, sometimes wrongly, that the litigants' case is representative. This is patently inadequate.

A second way, more sophisticated but not always adequate, is to derive behavioral expectations from what might be called the logical structure of incentives. That is, courts may consciously formulate rules of law calculated to appeal to the interests of "legal man" in rather the same way as the marketplace is thought to appeal to the interests of "economic man." A rule is designed to shape (more than follow) the behavior of all those calculative creatures who wish to gain its benefits and avoid its penalties. The problem with this, of course, is that it is deductive rather than empirical. There is no assurance that the judge has correctly formulated the structure of incentives: his logic and the logic of the actors affected by rules of law may begin from different premises. The problem of ascertaining existing behavior is then compounded by the problem of forecasting future behavior.

A third way of dealing with social facts is to go outside the record of the case in search of information. This is what Mr. Justice Murphy did when he sent questionnaires to police forces in thirty-eight cities in order to determine the relationship between the admissibility of illegally obtained evidence and police training in the law of search and seizure. The same impulse has sometimes moved other judges, restless in their ignorance of behavioral fact, to consult experts of their acquaintance, as Judge Charles Clark, then former Dean of the Yale Law School, consulted the Yale University organist about a music copyright case that was pending before him. These attempts, primitive as they are, show the existence of a deeply felt need rather than a method of satisfying it.

• • •

5. *Adjudication makes no provision for policy review.* As the judicial process neglects social facts in favor of historical facts, so, too, does it slight what might be called *consequential facts.* Judges base their decisions on *antecedent facts,* on behavior that antedates the litigation. Consequential facts—those that relate to the impact of a decision on behavior—are equally important but much neglected.

This, of course, is a result of the focus on rights and duties rather than alternatives. Litigation is geared to rectifying the injustices of the past and present rather than to planning for some change to occur in the future. The very notion of planning is alien to adjudication.

In the judicial process, the modification of behavior still tends to be treated as a question of compliance or enforcement. Difficulties of adjusting behavior to new rules of law are mainly regarded as being relevant to the nature of the remedy that is appropriate, as I indicated earlier. In the simpler world of the common law—in which the adjudicative process is still firmly rooted—compliance was merely a question of obedience. Ability to comply could be taken for granted. The judicial process has not really faced up to the issue of compliance costs in social policy cases. Still less has it considered the problem of unintended consequences of decisions.

Now it might be said with considerable justification that all decisionmaking processes are unduly based on what has happened in the past and insufficiently attuned to what might happen in the future, even to what might happen as a result of their action. Furthermore, there is nothing particularly unusual about the character of the unanticipated consequences produced by judicial decisions. A court decision may eliminate one obstacle to eligibility for welfare, only to cause welfare officials to tighten their enforcement of other eligibility requirements, thereby reducing the total number of beneficiaries. A new building code that upgrades housing requirements in the interests of health and safety may have similar effects. It may contract the supply of decent housing, just as strict code enforcement by administrative authorities may induce landlords to abandon their properties. The courts have no monopoly on unintended consequences.

There is no need to take issue with these points as general propositions, for what is at issue is not the propensity of decisions to have untoward effects. The point is rather that the courts suffer from an unusual poverty of resources to minimize the incidence of unintended consequences in advance and especially to detect and correct them once they occur.

The inability of courts to prevent unintended consequences flows in part from the allocation of work discussed earlier. The assignment of cases on a rotational basis impedes the growth of a pool of experience in particular kinds of problems that might sensitize a judge to difficulties he might face in later cases having similar characteristics. The experience is there, of course, but it is widely distributed among all the judges rather than concentrated along functional lines. Experience distributed so widely is hard to tap when decisions must be made by a single judge, as they generally are in the federal district courts, or by a panel of three judges, as they are in the federal courts of appeals.

Beyond this, it has been argued that lawyers (and presumably judges) have inordinate faith in the power of the written word to shape behavior and a concomitant tendency to minimize the likelihood of behavior that deviates from the requirements of properly drafted regulations. There has indeed been a propensity, as I have said, to assume that properly framed court orders would be more or less self-executing. This tendency detracts from what might otherwise be a more frequently perceived need to improve the judicial capacity for forecasting, as well as for follow-up.

It may be, however, that the judicial insensitivity to unanticipated consequences in advance of their occurrence is only marginally greater than that of other decisionmakers. All decisionmakers like to think that the choices they make will be translated into action, and they prefer not to think of the forces that may deflect their policies from their intended course. So it is just possible that the focus on rights rather than alternatives, the apportionment of work among judges, and the faith of lawyers and judges in the ability of a proper verbal formulation to induce action in accordance with it—it is possible that these characteristics simply exaggerate a uniform human tendency.

Perhaps so, but there is no mistaking the singular lack of judicial machinery to detect and correct unintended consequences after they have occurred. Here the deficiencies of adjudication are formidable.

If a party subject to an injunction does not comply with it, or if his compliance creates unforeseen difficulties for him or for other parties to the suit, the court that issued the decree may subsequently be advised that this is the case. Either the party subject to the decree or another party to the suit may return to court seeking enforcement, amendment, or dissolution of the injunction. The court is then informed of the consequences of its former action and may begin the consideration of alternatives. The key to this consideration is private initiative. Parties to the suit have an investment in its outcome and a reason to provide the court with an updating of results.

Private initiative breaks down, however, when the non-compliance is not that of a party but of one who may be only similarly situated. If courts make law rather than merely decide individual cases, then their decisions are expected to have ramifications that often extend beyond the parties, at least to all those who share the same characteristics. If decisions do not have those expected ramifications, or if the compliance of non-parties creates unforeseen consequences, the court is unlikely to be advised of such developments.

This is because courts have no self-starting mechanisms. They are dependent on litigants to ignite their processes. If litigants fail to take the initiative, because they do not have the resources or the energy or because they have moved on to other matters, then the effects of judicial action will probably pass unnoticed.

• • •

The courts, then, depend on the vagaries of litigants and litigation for their feedback about the effects of earlier decisions. Slowly, through a line of cases—always interspersed in a large pool of cases of many other kinds—the realization that there are problems stemming from earlier decisions may strike the judges. If so, they may turn to corrective action, doubtless long after the initial decisions and long after people have adjusted their behavior to them. And all of this is, needless to say, very much a matter of chance.

• • •

The courts are mainly dependent for their impact information on a single feedback mechanism: the follow-up lawsuit. This mechanism tends to be slow, erratic, unsystematic. Courts have no inspectors who move out into the field to ascertain what has happened. They receive no regular reports on the implementation of their policies. (It is, however, a mark of the increasing overlap between courts and administrators that some decrees now require periodic compliance reports, but only to monitor compliance by the parties.) The judges have no grapevine extending into the organizations and groups whose behavior they affect. Judicial proprieties foster isolation rather than contact. Neither do the courts learn about the effects of their decisions by conducting investigations or planning exercises; as I have said, they do not have these self-starting mechanisms.

In all of these respects, the information-gathering resources of administrators are vastly superior; those of legislators, modestly superior. Neither labors under the same disabilities as the courts do: neither is passive, and neither is dependent on a single channel of information.

As the courts have no policy review process that would enable them to gather or utilize impact information, they also have no way of sensitizing lawyers and judges to the empirically questionable inferences courts draw in the course of making decisions. The absence of policy review means that the courts miss an opportunity for general learning about the relation of their decisions to their environment. The neglect of social facts and the neglect of impact facts are therefore mutually reinforcing. Without policy review, judicial decisions possess a finality that legislative and administrative decisions do not necessarily have. This finality, buttressed by the doctrine of precedent, amounts to an immunity from amendment in the light of impact facts. This means that the courts have very limited ability to monitor and control unintended consequences.

• • •

III  FOCUS: STATUTORY INTERPRETATION

One of the most important roles of the federal courts is to interpret the laws passed by Congress. In the end, congressional statutes mean only what the judges say they mean.

Some congressional statutes, of course, are clear and straightforward and allow little room for judicial creativity in interpretation. Many congressional enactments, however, are vague and unclear and allow room for considerable judicial latitude.

Some of this ambiguity in the statutes is unavoidable. In many cases, it is entirely appropriate for Congress to leave statutes vague and open-ended in order to ensure that the law will remain flexible and adaptable to changing conditions. A law, for example, might prohibit the carrying of a "concealed weapon." Rather than listing every possible device that could be used as a weapon, Congress leaves it to the courts to determine what is and what is not a concealed weapon under the law. Congress also may choose to write broad, unspecific statutes because it lacks the time and expertise to fill in the blanks. It might mandate that airlines perform "reasonable and appropriate safety checks" on airplanes, leaving the Department of Transportation to write specific rules and regulations. After such rules are written, it is up to the courts to determine if they are consistent with the law passed by Congress.

Still other laws are left vague for political reasons. Congress may be unable to agree on specific wording in a bill and might write ambiguous language that all sides agree to but that, in the end, is practically meaningless. The Clean Air Act of 1970, for example, required the Environmental Protection Agency to regulate automobile exhaust emissions that "will endanger the public health or welfare." Again it is up to the executive branch, and the courts, to supply specific content.

In interpreting acts of Congress, courts are guided by a number of traditional practices. Laws are always presumed to be constitutional, and courts will interpret a statute so as to make it constitutional in preference to striking it down as unconstitutional. Courts also attempt to judge Congress's intent using evidence from committee reports and floor debates. Because congressmen are aware of this practice, however, they often make comments on the floor or write committee reports with the specific purpose of influencing later judicial decisions.

In the end, judges have considerable leeway in interpreting congressional statutes. The following cases are exceptional, but they demonstrate that, in the end, the courts (especially the Supreme Court) can greatly determine what the law means.

In these cases from 1965 and 1970, the Supreme Court dealt with the law exempting conscientious objectors from military service. The law as written exempted from military duty those who by virtue of "religious training and belief" are opposed to participation in war in any form. "Religious training and belief" is defined in the statute as "an individual's belief in relation to a Supreme Being" and excludes "essentially political, sociological, or philosophical views or a merely personal moral code." Nevertheless, in two cases, the Court decided that, under the statute, a belief in God was not necessary to quality for conscientious objector status and that, in fact, even a religious belief was unnecessary. Thus, a congressional statute that on its face required a belief in a supreme being to qualify for conscientious objector status was interpreted to require only that the individual in question hold his beliefs "with the strength of more traditional religious convictions."

In these cases, notice the Court's reliance on statutory language and statements of congressional intent.

Questions

1. Is the Court's interpretation of Section 6(j) a reasonable one? In what sense did Congress "intend" to permit exemptions in cases like *Seeger* or *Welch*?

2. Is the evidence of congressional intent as presented by the Court persuasive?

14.6 United States *v.* Seeger

Mr. Justice Clark delivered the opinion of the Court.

These cases involve claims of conscientious objectors under §6(j) of the Universal Military Training and Service Act, 50 U. S. C. App. §456(j) (1958 ed.), which exempts from combatant training and service in the armed forces of the United States those persons who by reason of their religious training and belief are consci-entiously opposed to participation in war in any form. The cases were consolidated for argument and we consider them together although each involves different facts and circumstances. The parties raise the basic question of the constitutionality of the section which defines the term "religious training and belief," as used in the Act, as "an individual's belief in a relation to a Supreme Being involving duties superior to those arising from any human relation, but [not including] essentially political, sociological, or philosophical views or a merely personal moral code." The constitutional attack is launched under the First Amendment's Establishment and Free Exercise Clauses and is twofold: (1) The section does not exempt nonreligious conscientious objectors; and (2) it discriminates between different forms of religious expression in violation of the Due Process Clause of the Fifth Amendment.

• • •

We have concluded that Congress, in using the expression "Supreme Being" rather than the designation "God," was merely clarifying the meaning of religious training and belief so as to embrace all religions and to exclude essentially political, sociological, or philosophical views. We believe that under this construction, the test of belief "in a relation to a Supreme Being" is whether a given belief that is sincere and meaningful occupies a place in the life of its possessor parallel to that filled by the orthodox belief in God of one who clearly qualifies for the exemption. Where such beliefs have parallel positions in the lives of their respective holders we cannot say that one is "in a relation to a Supreme Being" and the other is not. We have concluded that the beliefs of the objectors in these cases meet these criteria, and, accordingly, we affirm the [lower court's decision in *Seeger*].

The Facts in the Cases

Seeger was convicted in the District Court for the Southern District of New York of having refused to submit to induction in the armed forces. He was originally classified 1-A in 1953 by his local board, but this classification was changed in 1955 to 2-S (student) and he remained in this status until 1958 when he was reclassified 1-A. He first claimed exemption as a conscientious objector in 1957 after successive annual renewals of his student classification. Although he did not adopt verbatim the printed Selective Service System form, he declared that he was conscientiously opposed to participation in war in any form by reason of his "religious"

belief; that he preferred to leave the question as to his belief in a Supreme Being open, "rather than answer 'yes' or 'no' "; that his "skepticism or disbelief in the existence of God" did "not necessarily mean lack of faith in anything whatsoever"; that his was a "belief in and devotion to goodness and virtue for their own sakes, and a religious faith in a purely ethical creed." He cited such personages as Plato, Aristotle and Spinoza for support of his ethical belief in intellectual and moral integrity "without belief in God, except in the remotest sense." His belief was found to be sincere, honest, and made in good faith; and his conscientious objection to be based upon individual training and belief, both of which included research in religious and cultural fields. Seeger's claim, however, was denied solely because it was not based upon a "belief in a relation to a Supreme Being" as required by §6(j) of the Act. At trial Seeger's counsel admitted that Seeger's belief was not in relation to a Supreme Being as commonly understood, but contended that he was entitled to the exemption because "under the present law Mr. Seeger's position would also include definitions of religion which have been stated more recently," and could be "accommodated" under the definition of religious training and belief in the Act. He was convicted and the Court of Appeals reversed, holding that the Supreme Being requirement of the section distinguished "between internally derived and externally compelled beliefs" and was, therefore, an "impermissible classification" under the Due Process Clause of the Fifth Amendment.

Interpretation of §6(j)

1. The crux of the problem lies in the phrase "religious training and belief" which Congress has defined as "belief in a relation to a Supreme Being involving duties superior to those arising from any human relation." In assigning meaning to this statutory language we may narrow the inquiry by noting briefly those scruples expressly excepted from the definition. The section excludes those persons who, disavowing religious belief, decide on the basis of essentially political, sociological or economic considerations that war is wrong and that they will have no part of it. These judgments have historically been reserved for the Government, and in matters which can be said to fall within these areas the conviction of the individual has never been permitted to override that of the state. The statute further excludes those whose opposition to war stems from a "merely personal moral code," a phrase to which we shall have occasion to turn later in discussing the application of §6(j) to these cases. We also pause to take note of what is not involved in this litigation. No party claims to be an atheist or attacks the statute on this ground. The question is not, therefore, one between theistic and atheistic beliefs. We do not deal with or intimate any decision on that situation in these cases. Nor do the parties claim the monotheistic belief that there is but one God; what they claim (with the possible exception of Seeger who bases his position here not on factual but on purely constitutional grounds) is that they adhere to theism, which is the "Belief in the existence of a god or gods; . . . Belief in superhuman powers or spiritual agencies in one or many gods," as opposed to atheism. Our question, therefore, is the narrow one: Does the term "Supreme Being" as used in §6(j) mean the orthodox God or the broader concept of a power or being, or a faith, "to which all else is subordinate or upon which all else is ultimately dependent"? In considering this question we resolve it solely in relation to the language of §6(j) and not otherwise.

2. Few would quarrel, we think, with the proposition that in no field of human endeavor has the tool of language proved so inadequate in the communication of ideas as it has in dealing with the fundamental questions of man's predicament in life, in death or in final judgment and retribution. This fact makes the task of discerning the intent of Congress in using the phrase "Supreme Being" a complex one. Nor is it made the easier by the richness and variety of spiritual life in our country. Over 250 sects inhabit our land. Some believe in a purely personal God, some in a supernatural deity;

others think of religion as a way of life envisioning as its ultimate goal the day when all men can live together in perfect understanding and peace. There are those who think of God as the depth of our being; others, such as the Buddhists, strive for a state of lasting rest through self-denial and inner purification; in Hindu philosophy, the Supreme Being is the transcendental reality which is truth, knowledge and bliss. Even those religious groups which have traditionally opposed war in every form have splintered into various denominations: from 1940 to 1947 there were four denominations using the name "Friends"; the "Church of the Brethren" was the official name of the oldest and largest church body of four denominations composed of those commonly called Brethren; and the "Mennonite Church" was the largest of 17 denominations, including the Amish and Hutterites, grouped as "Mennonite bodies" in the 1936 report on the Census of Religious Bodies. This vast panoply of beliefs reveals the magnitude of the problem which faced the Congress when it set about providing an exemption from armed service. It also emphasizes the care that Congress realized was necessary in the fashioning of an exemption which would be in keeping with its long-established policy of not picking and choosing among religious beliefs.

In spite of the elusive nature of the inquiry, we are not without certain guidelines. In amending the 1940 Act, Congress adopted almost intact the language of Chief Justice Hughes in *United States* v. *Macintosh*: "The essence of religion is belief in a relation to *God* involving duties superior to those arising from any human relation." By comparing the statutory definition with those words, however, it becomes readily apparent that the Congress deliberately broadened them by substituting the phrase "Supreme Being" for the appellation "God." And in so doing it is also significant that Congress did not elaborate on the form or nature of this higher authority which it chose to designate as "Supreme Being." By so refraining it must have had in mind the admonitions of the Chief Justice when he said in the same opinion that even the word "God" had myriad meanings for men of faith:

> [P]utting aside dogmas with their particular conceptions of deity, freedom of conscience itself implies respect for an innate conviction of paramount duty. The battle for religious liberty has been fought and won with respect to religious beliefs and practices, which are not in conflict with good order, upon the very ground of the supremacy of conscience within its proper field.

Moreover, the Senate Report on the bill specifically states that §6(j) was intended to re-enact "substantially the same provisions as were found" in the 1940 Act. That statute, of course, refers to "religious training and belief" without more. Admittedly, all of the parties here purport to base their objection on religious belief. It appears, therefore, that we need only look to this clear statement of congressional intent as set out in the report. Under the 1940 Act it was necessary only to have a conviction based upon religious training and belief; we believe that is all that is required here. Within that phrase would come all sincere religious beliefs which are based upon a power or being, or upon a faith, to which all else is subordinate or upon which all else is ultimately dependent. The test might be stated in these words: A sincere and meaningful belief which occupies in the life of its possessor a place parallel to that filled by the God of those admittedly qualifying for the exemption comes within the statutory definition. This construction avoids imputing to Congress an intent to classify different religious beliefs, exempting some and excluding others, and is in accord with the well-established congressional policy of equal treatment for those whose opposition to service is grounded in their religious tenets.

• • •

We recognize the difficulties that have always faced the trier of fact in these cases. We hope that the test that we lay down proves less onerous. The examiner is furnished a standard that permits consideration of criteria with which he has had considerable experience. While the applicant's words may differ, the test is simple of application. It is essentially an objective one, namely, does the claimed belief occupy the same place in the life of the objector as an orthodox belief in God holds in the life of one clearly qualified for exemption?

Application of §6(j) to the Instant Cases

As we noted earlier, the statutory definition excepts those registrants whose beliefs are based on a "merely personal moral code." The records in these cases, however, show that at no time did any one of the applicants suggest that his objection was based on a "merely personal moral code." Indeed at the outset each of them claimed in his application that his objection was based on a religious belief. We have construed the statutory definition broadly and it follows that any exception to it must be interpreted narrowly. The use by Congress of the words "merely personal" seems to us to restrict the exception to a moral code which is not only personal but which is the sole basis for the registrant's belief and is in no way related to a Supreme Being. It follows, therefore, that if the claimed religious beliefs of the respective registrants in these cases meet the test that we lay down then their objections cannot be based on a "merely personal" moral code.

In *Seeger*, the Court of Appeals failed to find sufficient "externally compelled beliefs." However, it did find that "it would seem impossible to say with assurance that [Seeger] is not bowing to 'external commands' in virtually the same sense as is the objector who defers to the will of a supernatural power." . . . Of course, as we have said, the statute does not distinguish between externally and internally derived beliefs. Such a determination would, as the Court of Appeals observed, prove impossible as a practical matter, and we have found that Congress intended no such distinction.

The Court of Appeals also found that there was no question of the applicant's sincerity. He was a product of a devout Roman Catholic home; he was a close student of Quaker beliefs from which he said "much of [his] thought is derived"; he approved of their opposition to war in any form; he devoted his spare hours to the American Friends Service Committee and was assigned to hospital duty.

In summary, Seeger professed "religious belief" and "religious faith." He did not disavow any belief "in a relation to a Supreme Being"; indeed he stated that "the cosmic order does, perhaps, suggest a creative intelligence." He decried the tremendous "spiritual" price man must pay for his willingness to destroy human life. In light of his beliefs and the unquestioned sincerity with which he held them, we think the Board, had it applied the test we propose today, would have granted him the exemption. We think it clear that the beliefs which prompted his objection occupy the same place in his life as the belief in a traditional deity holds in the lives of his friends, the Quakers. We are reminded once more of Dr. Tillich's thoughts:

> And if that word [God] has not much meaning for you, translate it, and speak of the depths of your life, of the source of your being, of your ultimate concern, *of what you take seriously without any reservation.* Perhaps, in order to do so, you must forget everything traditional that you have learned about God. . . . Tillich, The Shaking of the Foundations 57 (1948). (Emphasis supplied.)

It may be that Seeger did not clearly demonstrate what his beliefs were with regard to the usual understanding of the term "Supreme Being." But as we have said Congress did not intend that to be the test. We therefore affirm the judgment in [*Seeger*].

14.7 Welsh *v.* United States

Mr. Justice Black announced the judgment of the Court. . . .

The petitioner, Elliott Ashton Welsh II, was convicted by a United States District Judge of refusing to submit to induction into the Armed Forces in violation of 50 U. S. C. App. §462(a), and was on June 1, 1966, sentenced to imprisonment for three years. One of petitioner's defenses to the prosecution was that §6(j) of the Universal Military Training and Service Act exempted him from combat and noncombat service because he was "by reason of religious training and belief . . . conscientiously opposed to participation in war in any form." After finding that there was no religious basis for petitioner's conscientious objector claim, the Court of Appeals, Judge Hamley dissenting, affirmed the conviction. We granted certiorari chiefly to review the contention that Welsh's conviction should be set aside on the basis of this Court's decision in *United States* v. *Seeger*. For the reasons to be stated, and without passing upon the constitutional arguments that have been raised, we vote to reverse this conviction because of its fundamental inconsistency with *United States* v. *Seeger*.

The controlling facts in this case are strikingly similar to those in *Seeger*. Both Seeger and Welsh were brought up in religious homes and attended church in their childhood, but in neither case was this church one which taught its members not to engage in war at any time for any reason. Neither Seeger nor Welsh continued his childhood religious ties into his young manhood, and neither belonged to any religious group or adhered to the teachings of any organized religion during the period of his involvement with the Selective Service System. At the time of registration for the draft, neither had yet come to accept pacifist principles. Their views on war developed only in subsequent years, but when their ideas did fully mature both made application to their local draft boards for conscientious objector exemptions from military service under §6(j) of the Universal Military Training and Service Act. That section then provided, in part:*

> Nothing contained in this title shall be construed to require any person to be subject to combatant training and service in the armed forces of the United States who, by reason of religious training and belief, is conscientiously opposed to participation in war in any form. Religious training and belief in this connection means an individual's belief in a relation to a Supreme Being involving duties superior to those arising from any human relation, but does not include essentially political, sociological, or philosophical views or a merely personal moral code.

In filling out their exemption applications both Seeger and Welsh were unable to sign the statement that, as printed in the Selective Service form, stated "I am, by reason of my religious training and belief, conscientiously opposed to participation in war in any form." Seeger could sign only after striking the words "training and" and putting quotation marks around the word "religious." Welsh could sign only after striking the words "my religious training and." On those same applications, neither could definitely affirm or deny that he believed in a "Supreme Being," both stating that they preferred to leave the question open. But both Seeger and Welsh affirmed on those applications that they held deep conscientious scruples against taking part in wars where people were killed. Both strongly believed that killing in war was wrong, unethical, and immoral, and their consciences forbade them to take part in such an evil practice. Their objection to participating in war in any form could not be said to come from a "still, small voice of conscience"; rather, for them that

---

* 62 Stat. 612. An amendment to the Act in 1967, subsequent to the Court's decision in the Seeger case, deleted the reference to a "Supreme Being" but continued to provide that "religious training and belief" does not include "essentially political, sociological, or philosophical views, or a merely personal moral code." [Footnote by the Court.]

voice was so loud and insistent that both men preferred to go to jail rather than serve in the Armed Forces. There was never any question about the sincerity and depth of Seeger's convictions as a conscientious objector, and the same is true of Welsh. In this regard the Court of Appeals noted, "[t]he government concedes that [Welsh's] beliefs are held with the strength of more traditional religious convictions." But in both cases the Selective Service System concluded that the beliefs of these men were in some sense insufficiently "religious" to qualify them for conscientious objector exemptions under the terms of §6(j). Seeger's conscientious objector claim was denied "solely because it was not based upon a 'belief in a relation to a Supreme Being' as required by §6(j) of the Act," while Welsh was denied the exemption because his Appeal Board and the Department of Justice hearing officer "could find no religious basis for the registrant's beliefs, opinions and convictions." Both Seeger and Welsh subsequently refused to submit to induction into the military and both were convicted of that offense.

In *Seeger* the Court was confronted, first, with the problem that §6(j) defined "religious training and belief" in terms of a "belief in a relation to a Supreme Being . . . ," a definition that arguably gave a preference to those who believed in a conventional God as opposed to those who did not. Noting the "vast panoply of beliefs" prevalent in our country, the Court construed the congressional intent as being in keeping with its long-established policy of not picking and choosing among religious beliefs," and accordingly interpreted "the meaning of religious training and belief so as to embrace *all* religions. . . ." But, having decided that all religious conscientious objectors were entitled to the exemption, we faced the more serious problem of determining which beliefs were "religious" within the meaning of the statute. This question was particularly difficult in the case of Seeger himself. Seeger stated that his was a "belief in and devotion to goodness and virtue for their own sakes, and a religious faith in a purely ethical creed." In a letter to his draft board, he wrote:

> My decision arises from what I believe to be considerations of validity from the standpoint of the welfare of humanity and the preservation of the democratic values which we in the United States are struggling to maintain. I have concluded that war, from the practical standpoint, is futile and self-defeating, and that from the more important moral standpoint, it is unethical.

On the basis of these and similar assertions, the Government argued that Seeger's conscientious objection to war was not "religious" but stemmed from "essentially political, sociological, or philosophical views or a merely personal moral code."

In resolving the question whether Seeger and the other registrants in that case qualified for the exemption, the Court stated that "[the] task is to decide whether the beliefs professed by a registrant are sincerely held and whether they are, *in his own scheme of things,* religious." (Emphasis added.) The reference to the registrant's "own scheme of things" was intended to indicate that the central consideration in determining whether the registrant's beliefs are religious is whether these beliefs play the role of a religion and function as a religion in the registrant's life. The Court's principal statement of its test for determining whether a conscientious objector's beliefs are religious within the meaning of §6(j) was as follows:

> The test might be stated in these words: A sincere and meaningful belief which occupies in the life of its possessor a place parallel to that filled by the God of those admittedly qualifying for the exemption comes within the statutory definition.

The Court made it clear that these sincere and meaningful beliefs that prompt the registrant's objection to all wars need not be confined in either source or content to traditional or parochial concepts of religion. It held that §6(j) "does not distinguish between externally and internally derived beliefs," and also held that "intensely personal" convictions which some might find "incomprehensible" or "incorrect" come within the meaning of "religious belief" in the Act. What is necessary under *Seeger* for a registrant's conscientious objection to all war to be "religious" within the meaning of §6(j) is that this opposition to war stem from the registrant's moral, ethical, or religious beliefs about what is right and wrong and that these beliefs be held with the strength of traditional religious convictions.

• • •

In the case before us the Government seeks to distinguish our holding in *Seeger* on basically two grounds, both of which were relied upon by the Court of Appeals in affirming Welsh's conviction. First, it is stressed that Welsh was far more insistent and explicit than Seeger in denying that his views were religious. For example, in filling out their conscientious objector applications, Seeger put quotation marks around the word "religious," but Welsh struck the word "religious" entirely and later characterized his beliefs as having been formed "by reading in the fields of history and sociology." The Court of Appeals found that Welsh had "denied that his objection to war was premised on religious belief" and concluded that "[t]he Appeal Board was entitled to take him at his word." We think this attempt to distinguish *Seeger* fails for the reason that it places undue emphasis on the registrant's interpretation of his own beliefs. The Court's statement in *Seeger* that a registrant's characterization of his own belief as "religious" should carry great weight does not imply that his declaration that his views are nonreligious should be treated similarly. When a registrant states that his objections to war are "religious," that information is highly relevant to the question of the function his beliefs have in his life. But very few registrants are fully aware of the broad scope of the word "religious" as used in §6(j), and accordingly a registrant's statement that his beliefs are nonreligious is a highly unreliable guide for those charged with administering the exemption. Welsh himself presents a case in point. Although he originally characterized his beliefs as nonreligious, he later upon reflection wrote a long and thoughtful letter to his Appeal Board in which he declared that his beliefs were "certainly religious in the ethical sense of the word." He explained:

> I believe I mentioned taking of life as not being, for me, a religious wrong. Again, I assumed Mr. [Brady (the Department of Justice hearing officer)] was using the word "religious" in the conventional sense, and, in order to be perfectly honest did not characterize my belief as "religious."

The Government also seeks to distinguish *Seeger* on the ground that Welsh's views, unlike Seeger's, were "essentially political, sociological, or philosophical views or a merely personal moral code." As previously noted, the Government made the same argument about *Seeger*, and not without reason, for Seeger's views had a substantial political dimension. In this case, Welsh's conscientious objection to war was undeniably based in part on his perception of world politics. In a letter to his local board, he wrote:

> I can only act according to what I am and what I see. And I see that the military complex wastes both human and material resources, that it fosters disregard for (what I consider a paramount concern) human needs and ends; I see that the means we employ to "defend" our "way of life" profoundly change that way of life. I see that in our failure to recognize the political, social, and economic realities of the world, we, *as a nation*, fail our responsibility *as a nation*.

We certainly do not think that §6(j)'s exclusion of those persons with "essentially political, sociological, or philosophical views or a merely personal moral code" should be read to exclude those who hold strong beliefs about our domestic and foreign affairs or even those whose conscientious objection to participation in all wars is founded to a substantial extent upon considerations of public policy. The two groups of registrants that obviously do fall within these exclusions from the exemption are those whose beliefs are not deeply held and those whose objection to war does not rest at all upon moral, ethical, or religious principle but instead rests solely upon considerations of policy, pragmatism, or expediency. In applying §6(j)'s exclusion of those whose views are "essentially political, sociological, or philosophical" or of those who have a "merely personal moral code," it should be remembered that these exclusions are definitional and do not therefore restrict the category of persons who are conscientious objectors by "religious training and belief." Once the Selective Service System has taken the first step and determined under the standards set out here and in *Seeger* that the registrant is a "religious" conscientious objector, it follows that his views cannot be "essentially political, sociological, or philosophical." Nor can they be a "merely personal moral code."

Welsh stated that he "believe[d] the taking of life—anyone's life—to be morally wrong." In his original conscientious objector application he wrote the following:

> I believe that human life is valuable in and of itself; in its living; therefore I will not injure or kill another human being. This belief (and the corresponding "duty" to abstain from violence toward another person) is not "superior to those arising from any human relation." On the contrary: *it is essential to every human relation.* I cannot, therefore, conscientiously comply with the Government's insistence that I assume duties which I feel are immoral and totally repugnant.

Welsh elaborated his beliefs in later communications with Selective Service officials. On the basis of these beliefs and the conclusion of the Court of Appeals that he held them "with the strength of more traditional religious convictions," we think Welsh was clearly entitled to a conscientious objector exemption. Section 6(j) requires no more. That section exempts from military service all those whose consciences, spurred by deeply held moral, ethical, or religious beliefs, would give them no rest or peace if they allowed themselves to become a part of an instrument of war.

The judgment is

Reversed.

IV  THE UNWRITTEN CONSTITUTION

The justices of the Supreme Court, like the president and members of Congress, rely on professional staff to assist them in their work. At the Court, the most important staff members are the law clerks—typically recent graduates who were at the top of the class of the best law schools—who help the justices do legal research, write opinions, and review cases brought before the Court for possible action. Much has changed since the days when Oliver Wendell Holmes could proudly declare, "We do our own work here"; today, the law clerks are an integral part of the way the Court does business.

Most of the time, the law clerks remain in the shadows and draw little public attention. Once in a while, they find themselves before the public eye. When two Washington Post reporters, Bob Woodward and Scott Armstrong, wrote The Brethren, *giving an inside look at the Court, they relied heavily on the testimony of unnamed law clerks—and produced considerable controversy. Legal scholars have also raised questions as to the potential problems created by having recent law school graduates performing some of the delicate tasks that most Americans assume are left to the justices themselves.*

In the following selection, David O'Brien surveys the role and responsibilities of the law clerks and discusses how the clerking system has evolved over the past century.

Question

1. What measures can a justice take to ensure that the law clerk's role remains subordinate and advisory and does not encroach on the responsibilities of the justice whom he or she serves?

14.8 Law Clerks in the Chambers

David M. O'Brien

Law clerks have been in the [Supreme] Court just over a century. As the Court's caseload increased, the justices acquired more clerks and delegated more of their work. But in addition to relieving some of the justices' workload pres-sures, clerks bring fresh perspectives to the Court. For young lawyers one or two years out of law school, the opportunity of clerking is invaluable for their later careers. After their year at the Court, clerks go on to teach at leading law schools or to work for prestigious law firms.

On his appointment in 1882, Horace Gray initiated (at first at his own expense) the practice of hiring each year a graduate of Harvard Law School as "secretary" or law clerk. When Oliver Wendell Holmes succeeded Gray, he continued the practice, and other justices gradually followed him. Most justices have had clerks serve for only one year. There are some notable exceptions: one clerk for Pierce Butler served sixteen years; McKenna's first clerk worked for twelve; Frank Murphy kept Eugene Gressman for six; and Owen Roberts had a husband-and-wife team as his permanent clerk and secretary. Chief Justices Stone and Vinson had overlapping terms for one of their two clerks each year; and Burger had his special legal assistant sign on for three to four years.

The selection of clerks is entirely a personal matter and may be one of the most important decisions that a justice makes in any given year. The selection process varies with each justice. But four considerations appear to enter into everyone's selection process: the justice's preference for (1) certain law schools, (2) special geographic regions, (3) prior clerking experience on certain courts or with particular judges, and (4) personal compatibility.

Following Gray and Holmes, Brandeis, Frankfurter, and Brennan, in their early years on the bench, chose graduates of Harvard Law School. Taft and Vinson selected graduates from Yale and Northwestern, respectively. Other justices likewise tend to draw on their alma maters. Though graduates from Ivy League schools still continue to be selected in disproportionately large numbers, there is now a greater diversity. Of the thirty-six clerks in the 1988–1989 term (including one for retired Chief Justice Burger and Justice Powell), for example, sixteen graduated from Harvard or Yale Law School; four from the University of Chicago; three each from Columbia and Stanford; two each from Michigan, Virginia, and Northwestern; and one each from Iowa, New York University, Emory, and the University of Miami.

Several justices have favored particular geographic regions when selecting clerks. Douglas and Warren tended to select individuals from the West, Charles Whittaker those from the Midwest, and Black those from the South and, in particular, from Alabama. As one former clerk remarked, "The perfect clerk for Justice Black was an Alabama boy who went to Alabama Law School. If that wasn't possible, then someone from the south who went to a leading law school."

As the Court's caseload and involvement with constitutional and statutory interpretation grew, the justices started drawing clerks from lower federal or state courts. Consequently, formal legal education may carry no more weight than clerking for a respected judge or on a leading court in the country. Of the new clerks during 1988–1989, more than half (seventeen of the thirty-six) had previously clerked for judges on the Court of Appeals for the District of Columbia Circuit; five came from the second circuit; and four from federal district courts; the remainder were from other federal appellate courts. Most justices choose clerks for their legal training and experience and not because of ideological affinity with particular federal judges. However, Scalia tends to favor those who in law school belonged to the Federalist Society, a national conservative legal fraternity which he helped found in 1979 while teaching at the University of Chicago Law School.

The position and duties of clerks naturally vary with the justice. Oliver Wendell Holmes initially had little casual contact with his clerks, but when his eyesight began to fade in his later years, they served as companions and often read aloud to him. According to Walter Gellhorn, Stone "made one feel a co-worker—a very junior and subordinate co-worker, to be sure, but nevertheless one whose opinions counted and whose assistance was valued." Likewise, Harold Burton told his law clerks that he wanted each "to feel a keen personal interest in our joint product," and he encouraged "the most complete possible exchange of views and the utmost freedom of expression of opinion on all matters to the end that the best possible product may result." Earl Warren's law clerks communicated with him almost always by memorandum. Some justices prefer to work more or less alone, and some like Douglas and Burger simply do not establish relationships easily. By contrast, Brennan, Blackmun, Powell, Rehnquist, and Stevens set up rather warm working relationships with their clerks. The level of work and responsibility depends on the capabilities and the number of the clerks and varies from justice to justice and over the course of the clerkship year.

At one extreme, perhaps, is Dean Acheson, who said of his working with Brandeis, "He wrote the opinion; I wrote the footnotes." At the other are clerks like Butler's, Byrnes's, and Murphy's who draft almost all of a justice's written work. Indeed, within the Court, Murphy's law clerks were snidely referred to as "Mr. Justice Huddleson" and "Mr. Justice Gressman." In one instance, Rutledge wrote to the chief justice, "After discussion with Justices Black and Douglas and Justice Murphy's clerk, Mr. Gressman, it has been agreed that I should inform you that the four of us" agree that the petition should be granted review and that "the case should be set for argument forthwith." On another occasion, Gressman wrote Rutledge, "I have tried in vain to reach Justice Murphy. But I know that he would want to join Black's statement if he files it. It certainly expresses his sentiments. I feel it perfectly O.K. to put his name on it—he would want it that way, especially since you are putting your name on it."

Most clerks' roles falls somewhere between these two extremes. Stone let his clerks craft footnotes that often announced novel principles of law. Stone's technique, in the view of his clerk Herbert Wechsler, was like that of "a squirrel storing nuts to be pulled out at some later time." Frankfurter had his clerks prepare lengthy memoranda, such as the ninety-one-page examination of segregation prepared by Alexander Bickel in 1954, as well as some of his better-known opinions, such as his dissent in the landmark reapportionment case, *Baker* v.

Carr (1962). From the perspective of other justices, Frankfurter also "used his law clerks as flying squadrons against the law clerks of other Justices and even against the Justices themselves. Frankfurter, a proselytizer, never missed a chance to line up a vote."

A justice's background, facility in writing, dedication, and age affect his style of work and his reliance on law clerks. Few are academic lawyers like Stone, "a New England wood carver" devoted to craftsmanship. Most come from an administrative-political background, where they learned law in government law offices and were accustomed to the assistance of large staffs. As two of his former clerks observed. "The fact that [Chief Justice Vinson] wasn't going to sit down with a blank yellow pad and start from scratch was characteristic of an administrator." Moreover, unlike someone like Frankfurter, he "was not a legal scholar who took great delight in the intellectual approach to the law for its own sake." Exceptional are justices who have the ability of a Douglas or a Jackson to write quickly and with flair. Reed, for one, struggled to write what he wanted to say. "Wouldn't it be nice if we could write the way we think," he once lamented. Like many of his successors, Reed for the most part relied on the clerks for first drafts—"the clerk had the first word and he had the last word."

Most justices now delegate the preliminary writing of opinions to their clerks. Earl Warren's practice, for instance, was to have one of his clerks do a first draft of an opinion. Warren would meet with the clerk and sketch an outline of the main points to be included in the opinion. Later he would give the clerk's draft a "word for word edit" in order to get his own style down. Chief Justice Rehnquist follows a similar pattern. He usually has one of his clerks do a first draft, without bothering about style, and gives him about ten days to prepare it. Before having a clerk begin work on an opinion, Rehnquist goes over the conference discussion with the clerk and explains how he thinks "an opinion can be written supporting the result reached by the majority." It is not "a very sweeping original type of assignment," he emphasizes. "It is not telling the clerk just figure out how you'd like to decide this case and write something about. It's not that at all." Once the clerk has finished a preliminary draft, Rehnquist reworks the opinion—using some, none, or all of the draft—to get his own style down. The draft opinion then typically circulates three or four times among the clerks in his chambers, before Rehnquist sends it to the other justices for their comments.

Even though they delegate the preliminary opinion writing, justices differ in their approach when revising first drafts. If a clerk's draft is "in the ball park," they often edit rather than rewrite. But some, like Burton, virtually rewrite their clerks' drafts, while others, like Reed, tend to insert paragraphs in the draft opinions prepared by their clerks. As one former clerk recalled, Reed simply "didn't like to start from the beginning and go to the ending." Consequently, his opinions tend to read like a dialogue with "a change of voice from paragraph to paragraph." Reed's patchwork opinions did not stem from excessive delegation of responsibility or lack of dedication. At least in his early years on the Court, he took opinion writing seriously but found that words did not flow easily for him. "The problem with Stanley," Frankfurter once said, "is that he doesn't let his law clerks do enough of the work. The trouble with Murphy is that he lets them do too much of the work." In time, as Reed grew older and the pressures of the caseload increased, he, like others on the Court, found it necessary to delegate more and more opinion writing to law clerks.

Though there are differences in the duties and manner in which clerks function, certain responsibilities are now commonly assigned in all chambers. Clerks play an indispensable role in the justices' deciding what to decide. As the number of filings each year rose, justices delegated the responsibility of initially reading all filings: appeals, which require mandatory review, and petitions for certiorari—"pets for cert.," as Justice Holmes referred to them—

which seek review but may be denied or granted at the Court's own discretion. Clerks then write a one- to two-page summary of the facts, the questions presented, and the recommended course of action—that is, whether the case should be denied, dismissed, or granted full briefing and plenary consideration.

This practice originated with the handling of indigents' petitions—in forma pauperis petitions, or "Ifp's"—by Chief Justice Hughes and his clerks. Unlike paid petitions and appeals, which are filed in multiple copies, petitions of indigents are typically filed without the assistance of an attorney in a single, handwritten copy. From the time of Hughes through that of Warren, these petitions were solely the responsibility of the chief justice and his law clerks (and this also explains why the chief justice had one more law clerk than the other justices). Except when an Ifp raised important legal issues or involved a capital case, Chief Justice Hughes as a matter of course neither circulated the petition to the other justices nor placed it on the conference list for discussion. Stone, Vinson, and Warren had their law clerks' certiorari memos routinely circulated to the other chambers. Chief justices, of course, differ in how carefully they study Ifp's. Hughes and Warren were especially conscientious and scrupulous about Ifp's; the latter told his clerks, "[I]t is necessary for you to be their counsel, in a sense." As the number of Ifp's and other filings grew, they became too much for the chief's chambers to handle alone. They were thus distributed along with other paid petitions and jurisdictional statements to all chambers for each justice's consideration. Accordingly, almost all filings, with the exception of those handled by the Legal Office, are now circulated to the chambers, where clerks draft short memos on most.

With the mounting workload in the 1970s, the role of law clerks in the screening process changed again. In 1972, at the suggestion of Lewis Powell, a majority of the Court's members began to pool their clerks, dividing up all filings and having a single clerk's certiorari memo then circulate to all those participating in the "cert. pool." Six justices—Rehnquist, White, Blackmun, O'Connor, Scalia, and Kennedy—now share the memos prepared by their pool of clerks. When the memos from the cert. pool are circulated, each justice typically has one of his or her clerks go over each memo and make a recommendation on whether the case should be granted or denied.

Those justices who objected to the establishment of the cert. pool and who refuse to join nevertheless find it necessary to have their clerks prepare memos on the most important of those one hundred or more filings that come in each week. Brennan has described his use of clerks this way: Although "I try not to delegate any of the screening function to my law clerks and to do the complete task myself," he reports,

> I make exceptions during the summer recess when their initial screening of petitions is invaluable training for next Term's new law clerks. And I also must make some few exceptions during the Term on occasions when opinion work must take precedence. When law clerks do screening, they prepare a memorandum of not more than a page or two in each case, noting whether the case is properly before the Court, what federal issues are presented, how they were decided by the courts below, and summarizing the positions of the parties pro and con the grant of the case.

Stevens, who does not participate in the cert. pool either, has a somewhat different practice. "I have found it necessary to delegate a great deal of responsibility in the review of certiorari petitions to my clerks," Stevens has said. "They examine them all and select a small minority that they believe I should read myself. As a result, I do not even look at the papers in over 80 percent of the cases that are filed." Stevens's two clerks write memos on only those petitions they deem important. He reviews those and reads the lower-court opinions on all cases to be discussed at conference. For Stevens, the preliminary screening of cases consumes about a day and a half per week.

After the justices vote in conference to hear a case, each usually assigns that case to a clerk. The clerk then researches the background and prepares a "bench memo." Bench memos outline pertinent facts and issues, propose possible questions to be put to participating attorneys during oral arguments, and address the merits of the cases. The clerk stays with the case as long as the justice does, helping with research and draft opinions. The nature of the work at this stage varies with the justice and the case, but it includes research, a hand in drafting the opinion and in commenting on other justices' responses to it, and the subsequent checking of citations and proofreading of the final version. Justices may also tell their clerks to draft concurring and dissenting opinions, while they themselves concentrate on the opinions they are assigned to write for the Court. As each term draws to a close and the justices feel the pressure of completing their opinions by the end of June or the first week of July, clerks perhaps inevitably assume an even greater role in the opinion-writing process.

Has too much responsibility been delegated to law clerks? Do they substantively influence the justices' voting and the final disposition of cases? After thirty-six years on the bench, Douglas claimed that circumstances were such that "many law clerks did much of the work of the justices." Rehnquist has provided one perspective on the function of law clerks: "I don't think people are shocked any longer to learn that an appellate judge receives a draft of a proposed opinion from a law clerk." He adds, however:

> I think they would be shocked, and properly shocked, to learn that an appellate judge simply "signed off" on such a draft without fully understanding its import and in all probability making some changes in it. The line between having law clerks help one with one's work, and supervising subordinates in the performance of *their* work, may be a hazy one, but it is at the heart . . . [of] the fundamental concept of "judging."

Some twenty-five years earlier, Rehnquist, who clerked for two years with Robert Jackson, had charged that law clerks—who he also claimed tend to be more "liberal" than the justices for whom they work—have a substantive influence on the justices when preparing both certiorari memos and first drafts of opinions. The degree to which law clerks substantively influence justices' voting and opinion writing is difficult to gauge, and it certainly varies from justice to justice. With the increasing caseload, justices have perhaps inevitably come to rely more heavily on their law clerks' recommendations when voting in conference. Yet even when Rehnquist served as a clerk and when the caseload was less than a third of its present size, justices no doubt voted overwhelmingly along the lines recommended by their law clerks. Vinson, for one, tallied the number of times he differed from his law clerks. There were differences in less than 5 percent of the cases. . . .

Clerks would look very powerful indeed if they were not transients in the Court. Clerks, as Alexander Bickel once noted, "are in no respect any kind of a powerful kitchen cabinet." As a clerk, Rehnquist, for instance, was unable to dissuade Justice Jackson from eventually going along with the decision in the landmark school desegregation ruling in *Brown* v. *Board of Education* (1954). In a memorandum entitled "A Random Thought on the Segregation Cases," Rehnquist charged that if the Court struck down segregated schools, it would do so by reading "its own sociological views into the Constitution," just as a majority of the Court had read its own economic philosophy into the Constitution when it struck down most of the early New Deal legislation. Later, at his confirmation hearing in 1971, Rehnquist claimed that the memo was written at Jackson's request and reflected the justice's views rather than his own. And he maintained that position during his 1986 confirmation hearings on being elevated to chief justice. But the content and the style of the memo (as well as the fact that there are several other similar memos written by Rehnquist in Justice Jackson's private papers) indicate that it was Rehnquist's own handiwork. . . . Rehnquist remains a staunch strict constructionist, maintaining that the Court goes awry when it ventures beyond what he considers to be the meaning of the language and historical context of constitutional provisions.

As part of the institutionalization of the Court, law clerks have assumed a greater role in conducting the business of the Court. Their role in the justices' screening process is now considerably greater than it was in the past. At the stage of opinion writing, the substantive influence of law clerks varies from justice to justice, and from time to time in each chamber, as well as from case to case. No less important, the greater numbers of law clerks and of delegated responsibilities contribute to the steady increase in the volume of concurring and dissenting opinions written each year and to the justices' production of longer and more heavily footnoted opinions.

V  ISSUE AND DEBATE: SHOULD JUDICIAL ACTIVISM BE DISCOURAGED?

Should the federal courts play an activist role in the American political system, or should they restrain themselves from interfering with the decisions made by elected state or federal officials? This question came to a head in the 1980s when Attorney General Edwin Meese and Justice William Brennan squared off in what became known as the Meese-Brennan debate.

Meese opened the argument with a speech before the American Bar Association in July 1985; Brennan responded three months later with a blistering attack on the attorney general's opinion. The key dispute was whether the courts should interpret the Constitution according to the Framers' "original intent" or whether they should interpret the Constitution as a living, evolving document.

The argument is by no means a simple one. The Court's constitutional decisions may turn not on the simple application of Meese's or Brennan's theory but on a complex set of variables, including our knowledge of the Framers' views, the impact of later constitutional amendments, and existing court precedents. Nevertheless, the Meese-Brennan debate provides a sharp focus for one of the most vexing issues of our time.

Questions

1. How might Brennan respond to Meese's charge that "to allow the courts to govern simply by what it views at the time as fair and decent, is a scheme of government no longer popular"? How might Meese respond to Brennan's argument that "the genius of the Constitution rests not in any static meaning it might have had in a world that is dead and gone, but in the adaptability of its great principles to cope with current problems and current needs"?

2. What should a court do, in Meese's view, when faced with a constitutional provision the original intent of which is unclear or unknown? What might Brennan suggest?

YES

14.9 End Judicial Activism

Edwin Meese III

It is important to take a moment and reflect upon the proper role of the Supreme Court in our constitutional system. The intended role of the judiciary generally and the Supreme Court in particular was to serve as the "bulwarks of a limited constitution." The judges, the Founders believed, would not fail to regard the Constitution as "fundamental law" and would "regulate their decisions" by it. As the "faithful guardians of the Constitution," the judges were expected to resist any political effort to depart from the literal provisions of the Constitution. The text of the document and the original intention of those who framed it would be the judicial standard in giving effect to the Constitution.

You will recall that Alexander Hamilton, defending the federal courts to be created by the new Constitution, remarked that the want of a judicial power under the Articles of Confederation had been the crowning defect of that first effort at a national constitution. Ever the consummate lawyer, Hamilton pointed out that "laws are a dead letter without courts to expound and define their true meaning."

The Anti-Federalist *Brutus* took him to task in the New York press for what the critics of the Constitution considered his naiveté. That prompted Hamilton to write his classic defense of judicial power in *The Federalist*, No. 78. An independent judiciary under the Constitution, he said, would prove to be the "citadel of public justice and the public security." Courts were "peculiarly essential in a limited constitution." Without them, there would be no security against "the encroachments and oppressions of the representative body," no protection against "unjust and partial" laws.

Hamilton, like his colleague Madison, knew that all political power is "of an encroaching nature." In order to keep the powers created by the Constitution within the boundaries marked out by the Constitution, an independent—but constitutionally bound—judiciary was essential. The purpose of the Constitution, after all, was the creation of limited but also energetic government, institutions with the power to govern, but also with structures to keep the power in check. As Madison put it, the Constitution enabled the government to control the governed, but also obliged it to control itself.

But even beyond the institutional role, the Court serves the American republic in yet another, more subtle way. The problem of any popular government, of course, is seeing to it that the people obey the laws. There are but two ways: either by physical force or by moral force. In many ways the Court remains the primary moral force in American politics. Tocqueville put it best:

> The great object of justice is to substitute the idea of right for that of violence, to put intermediaries between the government and the use of its physical force. . . .
>
> It is something astonishing what authority is accorded to the intervention of a court of justice by the general opinion of mankind. . . .
>
> The moral force in which tribunals are clothed

makes the use of physical force infinitely rarer, for in most cases it takes its place; and when finally physical force is required, its power is doubled by his moral authority.

By fulfilling its proper function, the Supreme Court contributes both to institutional checks and balances and to the moral undergirding of the entire constitutional edifice. For the Supreme Court is the only national institution that daily grapples with the most fundamental political questions—and defends them with written expositions. Nothing less would serve to perpetuate the sanctity of the rule of law so effectively.

But that is not to suggest that the justices are a body of Platonic guardians. Far from it. The Court is what it was understood to be when the Constitution was framed—a political body. The judicial process is, at its most fundamental level, a political process. While not a partisan political process, it is political in the truest sense of that word. It is a process wherein public deliberations occur over what constitutes the common good under the terms of a written constitution.

As a result, as Benjamin Cardozo pointed out, "the greatest tides and currents which engulf the rest of men do not turn aside in their course and pass the judges by." Granting that, Tocqueville knew what was required. As he wrote:

> The federal judges therefore must not only be good citizens and men of education and integrity, . . . [they] must also be statesmen; they must know how to understand the spirit of the age, to confront those obstacles that can be overcome, and to steer out of the current when the tide threatens to carry them away, and with them the sovereignty of the union and obedience to its laws.

On that confident note, let's consider the Court's work this past year [1984–1985]. As has been generally true in recent years, the 1984 term did not yield a coherent set of decisions. Rather, it seemed to produce what one commentator has called a "jurisprudence of idiosyncrasy." Taken as a whole, the work of the term defies analysis by any strict standard. It is neither simply liberal nor simply conservative; neither simply activist nor simply restrained; neither simply principled nor simply partisan. The Court this term continued to roam at large in a veritable constitutional forest.

I believe, however, that there are at least three general arenas that merit close scrutiny: Federalism, Criminal Law, and Freedom of Religion.

Federalism

In *Garcia* v. *San Antonio Metropolitan Transit Authority* (1985), the Court displayed what was in the view of this Administration an inaccurate reading of the text of the Constitution and a disregard for the Framers' intention that state and local governments be a buffer against the centralizing tendencies of the national Leviathan. Specifically, five Justices denied that the Tenth Amendment protects States from federal laws regulating the wages and hours of state or local employees. Thus the Court overruled—but barely—a contrary holding in *National League of Cities* v. *Usery* (1976). We hope for a day when the Court returns to the basic principles of the Constitution as expressed in *Usery;* such instability in decisions concerning the fundamental principle of federalism does our Constitution no service.

Meanwhile, the constitutional status of the States further suffered as the Court curbed state power to regulate the economy, notably the professions. In *Metropolitan Life Insurance Co.* v. *Ward* (1985), the Court used the Equal Protection Clause to spear an Alabama insurance tax on gross premiums preferring in-state companies over out-of-state rivals. In *Supreme Court of New Hampshire* v. *Piper* (1985), the Court held that the Privileges and Immunities Clause of Article IV barred New Hampshire from completely excluding a nonresident from admission to its bar. With the apparent policy objective of creating unfettered national markets for occupations before its eyes, the Court unleashed

Article IV against any State preference for residents involving the professions or service industries. *Hicklin* v. *Orbeck* (1978) and *Baldwin* v. *Montana Fish and Game Commission* (1978) are illustrative.

On the other hand, we gratefully acknowledge the respect shown by the Court for state and local sovereignty in a number of cases, including *Atascadero State Hospital* v. *Scanlon* (1985).

In *Atascadero,* a case involving violations of §504 of the Rehabilitation Act of 1973, the Court honored the Eleventh Amendment in limiting private damage suits against States. Congress, it said, must express its intent to expose States to liability affirmatively and clearly.

In *Haille* v. *Eau Claire* (1985), the Court found that active state supervision of municipal activity was not required to cloak municipalities with immunity under the Sherman Act. And, States were judged able to confer Sherman Act immunity upon private parties in *Southern Motor Carrier Rate Conference, Inc.* v. *United States* (1985). They must, said the Court, clearly articulate and affirmatively express a policy to displace competition with compelling anticompetitive action so long as the private action is actively supervised by the State.

And, in *Oklahoma City* v. *Tuttle* (1985), the Court held that a single incident of unconstitutional and egregious police misconduct is insufficient to support a Section 1983 [42 U.S.C. §1983] action against municipalities for allegedly inadequate police training or supervision.

Our view is that federalism is one of the most basic principles of our Constitution. By allowing the States sovereignty sufficient to govern, we better secure our ultimate goal of political liberty through decentralized government. We do not advocate States' rights; we advocate States' responsibilities. We need to remember that state and local governments are not inevitably abusive of rights. It was, after all, at the turn of the century the States that were the laboratories of social and economic progress—and the federal courts that blocked their way. We believe that there is a proper constitutional sphere for state governance under our scheme of limited, popular government.

Criminal Law

Recognizing, perhaps, that the nation is in the throes of a drug epidemic which has severely increased the burden borne by law enforcement officers, the Court took a more progressive stance on the Fourth Amendment, undoing some of the damage previously done by its piecemeal incorporation through the Fourteenth Amendment. Advancing from its landmark [decision in] *United States* v. *Leon* (1984). . . . which created a good-faith exception to the Exclusionary Rule when a flawed warrant is obtained by police, the Court permitted warrantless searches under certain limited circumstances.

The most prominent among these Fourth Amendment cases were:

- *New Jersey* v. *T.L.O.* (1985), which upheld warrantless searches of public school students based on reasonable suspicion that a law or school rule has been violated; this also restored a clear local authority over another problem in our society, school discipline;

- *California* v. *Carney* (1985), which upheld the warrantless search of a mobile home;

- *United States* v. *Sharpe* (1985), which approved on-the-spot detention of a suspect for preliminary questioning and investigation;

- *United States* v. *Johns* (1985), upholding the warrantless search of sealed packages in a car several days after their removal by police who possessed probable cause to believe the vehicle contained contraband;

- *United States* v. *Hensley* (1985), which permitted a warrantless investigatory stop based on an unsworn flyer from a neighboring police department which possessed reasonable suspicion that the detainee was a felon;

- *Hayes* v. *Florida* (1985), which tacitly endorsed warrantless seizures in the field for the purpose of finger-printing based on reasonable suspicion of criminal activity;

Similarly, the Court took steps this term to place the *Miranda* v. *Arizona* (1966) ruling in proper perspective stressing its origin in the Court rather than in the Constitution. In *Oregon* v. *Elstad* (1985), the Court held that failure to administer *Miranda* warnings and the consequent receipt of a confession ordinarily will not taint a second confession after *Miranda* warnings are received.

The enforcement of criminal law remains one of our most important efforts. It is crucial that the state and local authorities—from the police to the prosecutors—be able to combat the growing tide of crime effectively. Toward that end we advocate a due regard for the rights of the accused—but also a due regard for the keeping of the public peace and the safety and happiness of the people. We will continue to press for a proper scope for the rules of exclusion, lest truth in the fact finding process be allowed to suffer.

I have mentioned the areas of Federalism and Criminal Law, now I will turn to the Religion cases.

Most probably, this term will be best remembered for the decisions concerning the Establishment Clause of the First Amendment. The Court continued to apply its standard three-pronged test. Four cases merit mention.

In the first, *City of Grand Rapids* v. *Ball* (1985), the Court nullified Shared Time and Community Education programs offered within parochial schools. Although the programs provided instruction in non-sectarian subjects, and were taught by full-time or part-time public school teachers, the Court nonetheless found that they promoted religion in three ways: the state-paid instructors might wittingly or unwittingly indoctrinate students; the symbolic union of church and state interest in state-provided instruction signaled support for religion; and, the programs in effect subsidized the religious functions of parochial schools by relieving them of responsibility for teaching some secular subjects. The symbolism test proposed in *Ball* precludes virtually any state assistance offered to parochial schools.

In *Aguilor* v. *Felton* (1985), the Court invalidated a program of secular instruction for low-income students in sectarian schools, provided by public school teachers who were supervised to safeguard students against efforts of indoctrination. With a bewildering Catch-22 logic, the Court declared that the supervisory safeguards at issue in the statute constituted unconstitutional government entanglement: "The religious school, which has as a primary purpose the advancement and preservation of a particular religion, must endure the ongoing presence of state personnel whose primary purpose is to monitor teachers and students in an attempt to guard against the infiltration of religious thought."

In *Wallace* v. *Jaffree* (1985), the Court said in essence that states may set aside time in public schools for meditation or reflection so long as the legislation does not stipulate that it be used for voluntary prayer. Of course, what the Court gave with one hand, it took back with the other; the Alabama moment of silence statute failed to pass muster.

In *Thornton* v. *Caldor* (1985), a 7-2 majority overturned a state law prohibiting private employers from discharging an employee for refusing to work on his Sabbath. We hope that this does not mean that the Court is abandoning last term's first but tentative steps toward state accommodation of religion in the Creche case.

In trying to make sense of the religion cases—from whichever side—it is important to remember how this body of tangled case law came about. Most Americans forget that it was not until 1925, in *Gitlow* v. *New York* (1925), that *any* provision of the Bill of Rights was applied to the states. Nor was it until 1947 that the Establishment Clause was made applicable to the states through the 14th Amendment. This is striking because the Bill of Rights, as debated, created and ratified was designed to apply *only* to the national government.

The Bill of Rights came about largely as the result of the demands of the critics of the new Constitution, the unfortunately misnamed Anti-Federalists. They feared, as George Mason of Virginia put it, that in time the national authority would "devour" the states. Since each state had a bill of rights, it was only appropriate that so powerful a national government as that created by the Constitution have one as well. Though Hamilton insisted a Bill of Rights was not necessary and even destructive, and Madison (at least at first) thought a Bill of Rights to be but a "parchment barrier" to political power, the Federalists agreed to add a Bill of Rights.

Though the first ten amendments that were ultimately ratified fell far short of what the Anti-Federalists desired, both Federalists and Anti-Federalists agreed that the amendments were a curb on national power. When this view was questioned before the Supreme Court in *Barron* v. *Baltimore* (1833), Chief Justice Marshall wholeheartedly agreed. The Constitution said what it meant and meant what is said. Neither political expediency nor judicial desire was sufficient to change the clear import of the language of the Constitution. The Bill of Rights did not apply to the states—and, he said, that was that.

Until 1925, that is.

Since then a good portion of constitutional adjudication has been aimed at extending the scope of the doctrine of incorporation. But the most that can be done is to expand the scope; nothing can be done to shore up the intellectually shaky foundation upon which the doctrine rests. And nowhere else has the principle of federalism been dealt so politically violent and constitutionally suspect a blow as by the theory of incorporation.

In thinking particularly of the use to which the First Amendment has been put in the area of religion, one finds much merit in Justice Rehnquist's recent dissent in *Jaffree*. "It is impossible," Justice Rehnquist argued, "to build sound constitutional doctrine upon a mistaken understanding of constitutional history." His conclusion was bluntly to the point: "If a constitutional theory has no basis in the history of the amendment it seeks to interpret, it is difficult to apply and yields unprincipled results."

The point, of course, is that the Establishment Clause of the First Amendment was designed to prohibit Congress from establishing a national church. The belief was that the Constitution should not allow Congress to designate a particular faith or sect as politically above the rest. But to have argued, as is popular today, that the Amendment demands a strict neutrality between religion and irreligion would have struck the founding generation as bizarre. The purpose was to prohibit religious tyranny, not to undermine religion generally.

In considering these areas of adjudication— Federalism, Criminal Law, and Religion—it seems fair to conclude that far too many of the Court's opinions were, on the whole, more policy choices than articulations of constitutional principle. The voting blocs, the arguments, all reveal a greater allegiance to what the Court thinks constitutes sound public policy than a deference to what the Constitution—its text and intention—may demand. It is also safe to say that until there emerges a coherent jurisprudential stance, the work of the Court will continue in this ad hoc fashion. But that is not to argue for *any* jurisprudence. In my opinion a drift back toward the radical egalitarianism and expansive civil libertarianism of the Warren Court would once again be a threat to the notion of limited but energetic government.

What, then, should a constitutional jurisprudence actually be? It should be a Jurisprudence of Original Intention. By seeking to judge policies in light of principles, rather than remold principles in light of policies, the Court could avoid both the charge of incoherence *and* the charge of being either too conservative or too liberal.

A jurisprudence seriously aimed at the explication of original intention would produce defensible principles of government that would not be tainted by ideological predilection. This belief in a Jurisprudence of Original Intention

also reflects a deeply rooted commitment to the idea of democracy. The Constitution is the fundamental will of the people; that is why it is the fundamental law. To allow the courts to govern simply by what it views at the time as fair and decent, is a scheme of government no longer popular; the idea of democracy has suffered. The permanence of the Constitution has been weakened. A constitution that is viewed as only what the judges say it is, is no longer a constitution in the true sense.

Those who framed the Constitution chose their words carefully; they debated at great length the most minute points. The language they chose meant something. It is incumbent upon the Court to determine what that meaning was. This is not a shockingly new theory; nor is it arcane or archaic.

Joseph Story, who was in a way a lawyer's Everyman—lawyer, justice, and teacher of law—had a theory of judging that merits reconsideration. Though speaking specifically of the Constitution, his logic reaches to statutory construction as well.

> In construing the Constitution of the United States, we are in the first instance to consider, what are its nature and objects, its scope and design, as apparent from the structure of the instrument, viewed as a whole and also viewed in its component parts. Where its words are plain, clear and determinate, they require no interpretation. . . . Where the words admit of two senses, each of which is conformable to general usage, that sense is to be adopted, which without departing from the literal import of the words, best harmonizes with the nature and objects, the scope and design of the instrument.

A Jurisprudence of Original Intention would take seriously the admonition of Justice Story's friend and colleague, John Marshall, in *Marbury* that the Constitution is a limitation of judicial power as well as executive and legislative. That is what Chief Justice Marshall meant in *McCulloch* when he cautioned judges never to forget it is a constitution they are expounding.

It has been and will continue to be the policy of this administration to press for a Jurisprudence of Original Intention. In the cases we file and those we join as *amicus,* we will endeavor to resurrect the original meaning of constitutional provisions and statutes as the only reliable guide for judgement.

We will pursue our agenda within the context of our written Constitution of limited yet energetic powers. Our guide in every case will be the sanctity of the rule of law and the proper limits of governmental power.

It is our belief that only "the sense in which the Constitution was accepted and ratified by the nation," and only the sense in which laws were drafted and passed provide a solid foundation for adjudication. Any other standard suffers the defect of pouring new meaning into old words, thus creating new powers and new rights totally at odds with the logic of our Constitution and its commitment to the rule of law.

NO

14.10 A Defense of Judicial Activism

William Brennan

. . . The text I have chosen for exploration is the amended Constitution of the United States, which, of course, entrenches the Bill of Rights and the Civil War amendments, and draws sustenance from the bedrock principles of another great text, the Magna Carta. So fashioned, the Constitution embodies the aspiration to social justice, brotherhood, and human dignity that brought this nation into being. The Declaration of Independence, the Constitution and the Bill of Rights solemnly committed the United States to be a country where the dignity and rights of all persons were equal before all authority. In all candor we must concede that part of this egalitarianism in America has been more pretension than realized fact. But we are an aspiring people, a people with faith in progress. Our amended Constitution is the lodestar for our aspirations. Like every text worth reading, it is not crystalline. The phrasing is broad and the limitations of its provisions are not clearly marked. Its majestic generalities and ennobling pronouncements are both luminous and obscure. This ambiguity of course calls forth interpretation, the interaction of reader and text. The encounter with the Constitutional text has been, in many senses, my life's work. . . .

. . . My encounters with the constitutional text are not purely or even primarily introspective; the Constitution cannot be for me simply a contemplative haven for private moral reflection. My relation to this great text is inescapably public. That is not to say that my reading of the text is not a personal reading, only that the personal reading perforce occurs in a public context, and is open to critical scrutiny from all quarters.

The Constitution is fundamentally a public text—the monumental charter of a government and a people—and a Justice of the Supreme Court must apply it to resolve public controversies. For, from our beginnings, a most important consequence of the constitutionally created separation of powers has been the American habit, extraordinary to other democracies, of casting social, economic, philosophical and political questions in the form of law suits, in an attempt to secure ultimate resolution by the Supreme Court. In this way, important aspects of

Judicial Activism: Even on the Right, It's Wrong

One of the ironies of the debate over judicial activism has been the emergence of a school of defenders of judicial activism from the right. These conservatives, frustrated that their political goals have been stymied in the legislatures, urge newly appointed conservative judges not to abandon judicial activism but, rather, to use activism to implement conservative rather than liberal policies. Lino A. Graglia, however, cautions that judicial activism, whether on the left or the right, is wrong. Here is a brief excerpt from his argument.

*T*he best hope for conservatives, some believe, is not to fight but to seek to capture or rechannel judicial power. This is surely the best hope for libertarians, who like liberals have a well-defined political agenda that most Americans reject. Although the liberals' objective—the powerful government necessary to impose and enforce equality—and the libertarians' objective—the least powerful government necessary to protect individual liberty—could hardly be more opposed, their arguments for judicial activism are identical. Because the Constitution no more places American government in a libertarian straitjacket than in a liberal one, the libertarian agenda, like the liberal one, requires that the Constitution be ignored in favor of something more conducive to judicial legislation.

• • •

Many texts are indeed difficult to understand, but the Constitution is not among them. We almost always know all that we need to know about the Constitution to decide actual cases; it is almost always entirely clear that nothing in the Constitution forbids the challenged policy choice. The Court's controversial constitutional decisions are not controversial because of disagreements about the meaning of constitutional provisions, but because it is clear that those decisions are not required by *any* constitutional provision. No one really believes, for example, that the states lost the power to prohibit abortion because Supreme Court justices decided to take one more look at the Constitution in 1973 to see what it had to say on the subject and discovered in the Fourteenth Amendment—which was then 105 years old—what had never been noticed before. Similarly, the states did not lose the right to make policy regarding prayer and Bible reading in public schools because a majority of the justices noticed for the first time in 1962 and 1963 that the First Amendment, supposedly applicable to the states by reason of the Fourteenth, deprives them of that right; the states lost this authority not because of but despite the First Amendment, which was clearly intended to prevent exactly that kind of federal interference.

Furthermore, if the meaning of a constitutional provision is in fact so obscure as to defy interpretation, it cannot provide a basis for holding a law unconstitutional. An indecipherable constitutional provision is a nullity—not . . . a grant of unlimited authority to judges to invalidate laws in the name of "moral philosophy" or the "principles of justice and natural rights." It is incredible that the Framers meant to make such a grant; if they did, our first order of business would be to rescind it as inconsistent with self-government. Such a grant would, in any event, deprive the Constitution of further relevance to judicial review; constitutional interpretation would play no further role in the judicial process—except that the decisions would still be called constitutional decisions and invalidated laws would still be described as unconstitutional.

—*Lino A. Graglia*

the most fundamental issues confronting our democracy may finally arrive in the Supreme Court for judicial determination. Not infrequently, these are the issues upon which contemporary society is most deeply divided. They arouse our deepest emotions. The main burden of my twenty-nine Terms on the Supreme Court has thus been to wrestle with the Constitution in this heightened public context, to draw meaning from the text in order to resolve public controversies.

Two other aspects of my relation to this text warrant mention. First, constitutional interpretation for a federal judge is, for the most part, obligatory. When litigants approach the bar of court to adjudicate a constitutional dispute, they may justifiably demand an answer. Judges cannot avoid a definitive interpretation because they feel unable to, or would prefer not to, penetrate to the full meaning of the Constitution's provisions. Unlike literary critics, judges cannot merely savor the tensions or revel in the ambiguities inhering in the text—judges must resolve them.

Second, consequences flow from a Justice's interpretation in a direct and immediate way. A judicial decision respecting the incompatibility of Jim Crow with a constitutional guarantee of equality is not simply a contemplative exercise in defining the shape of a just society. It is an order—supported by the full coercive power of the State—that the present society change in a fundamental aspect. Under such circumstances the process of deciding can be a lonely, troubling experience for fallible human beings conscious that their best may not be adequate to the challenge. We Justices are certainly aware that we are not final because we are infallible; we know that we are infallible only because we are final. One does not forget how much may depend on the decision. More than the litigants may be affected. The course of vital social, economic and political currents may be directed.

These three defining characteristics of my relation to the constitutional text—its public nature, obligatory character, and consequentialist aspect—cannot help but influence the way I read that text. When Justices interpret the Constitution they speak for their community, not for themselves alone. The act of interpretation must be undertaken with full consciousness that it is, in a very real sense, the community's interpretation that is sought. Justices are not platonic guardians appointed to wield authority according to their personal moral predelictions. Precisely because coercive force must attend any judicial decision to countermand the will of a contemporary majority, the Justices must render constitutional interpretations that are received as legitimate. The source of legitimacy is, of course, a wellspring of controversy in legal and political circles. At the core of the debate is what the late Yale Law School professor Alexander Bickel labeled "the counter-majoritarian difficulty." Our commitment to self-governance in a representative democracy must be reconciled with vesting in electorally unaccountable Justices the power to invalidate the expressed desires of representative bodies on the ground of inconsistency with higher law. Because judicial power resides in the authority to give meaning to the Constitution, the debate is really a debate about how to read the text, about constraints on what is legitimate interpretation.

There are those who find legitimacy in fidelity to what they call "the intentions of the Framers." In its most doctrinaire incarnation, this view demands that Justices discern exactly what the Framers thought about the question under consideration and simply follow that intention in resolving the case before them. It is a view that feigns self-effacing deference to the specific judgments of those who forged our original social compact. But in truth it is little more than arrogance cloaked as humility. It is arrogant to pretend that from our vantage we can gauge accurately the intent of the Framers on application of principle to specific, contemporary questions. All too often, sources of potential enlightenment such as records of the ratification debates provide sparse or ambiguous evidence of the original intention. Typically, all that can be gleaned is that the Framers themselves did not agree about the application or meaning of particular constitutional provisions, and hid their differences in cloaks of generality. Indeed, it is far from clear whose intention is relevant—that of the drafters, the congressional disputants, or the ratifiers in the states?—or even whether the idea of an original intention is a coherent way of thinking about a jointly drafted document drawing its authority from a general assent of the states. And apart from the problematic nature of the sources, our distance of two centuries cannot but work as a prism refracting all we perceive. One cannot help but speculate that the chorus of lamentations calling for interpretation faithful to "original intention"—and proposing nullification of interpretations that fail this quick litmus test—must inevitably come from persons who have no familiarity with the historical record.

Perhaps most importantly, while proponents of this facile historicism justify it as a depoliticization of the judiciary, the political underpinnings of such a choice should not escape notice. A position that upholds constitutional claims only if they were within the specific contemplation of the Framers in effect establishes a presumption of resolving textual ambiguities against the claim of constitutional right. It is far from clear what justifies such a presumption against claims of right. Nothing intrinsic in the nature of interpretation—if there is such a thing as the "nature" of interpretation—commands such a passive approach to ambiguity. This is a choice no less political than any other; it expresses antipathy to claims of the minority to rights against the majority. Those who would restrict claims of right to the values of 1789 specifically articulated in the Constitution turn a blind eye to social progress and eschew adaptation of overarching principles to changes of social circumstance.

Another, perhaps more sophisticated, response to the potential power of judicial interpretation stresses democratic theory: because ours is a government of the people's elected representatives, substantive value choices should by and large be left to them. This view emphasizes not the transcendent historical authority of the Framers but the predominant contemporary authority of the elected branches of government. Yet it has similar consequences for the nature of proper judicial interpretation. Faith in the majoritarian process counsels re-

straint. Even under more expansive formulations of this approach, judicial review is appropriate only to the extent of ensuring that our democratic process functions smoothly. Thus, for example, we would protect freedom of speech merely to ensure that the people are heard by their representatives, rather than as a separate, substantive value. When, by contrast, society tosses up to the Supreme Court a dispute that would require invalidation of a legislature's substantive policy choice, the Court generally would stay its hand because the Constitution was meant as a plan of government and not as an embodiment of fundamental substantive values.

The view that all matters of substantive policy should be resolved through the majoritarian process has appeal under some circumstances, but I think it ultimately will not do. Unabashed enshrinement of majority will would permit the imposition of a social caste system or wholesale confiscation of property so long as a majority of the authorized legislative body, fairly elected, approved. Our Constitution could not abide such a situation. It is the very purpose of a Constitution—and particularly of the Bill of Rights—to declare certain values transcendent, beyond the reach of temporary political majorities. The majoritarian process cannot be expected to rectify claims of minority right that arise as a response to the outcomes of that very majoritarian process. As James Madison put it:

> The prescriptions in favor of liberty ought to be levelled against that quarter where the greatest danger lies, namely, that which possesses the highest prerogative of power. But this is not found in either the Executive or Legislative departments of Government, but in the body of the people, operating by the majority against the minority.

Faith in democracy is one thing, blind faith quite another. Those who drafted our Constitution understood the difference. One cannot read the text without admitting that it embodies substantive value choices; it places certain values beyond the power of any legislature. Obvious are the separation of powers; the privilege of the Writ of Habeas Corpus; prohibition of Bills of Attainder and ex post facto laws; prohibition of cruel and unusual punishments; the requirement of just compensation for official taking of property; the prohibition of laws tending to establish religion or enjoining the free exercise of religion; and since the Civil War, the banishment of slavery and official race discrimination. With respect to at least such principles, we simply have not constituted ourselves as strict utilitarians. While the Constitution may be amended, such amendments require an immense effort by the People as a whole.

To remain faithful to the content of the Constitution, therefore, an approach to interpreting the text must account for the existence of these substantive value choices, and must accept the ambiguity inherent in the effort to apply them to modern circumstances. The Framers discerned fundamental principles through struggles against particular malefactions of the Crown; the struggle shapes the particular contours of the articulated principles. But our acceptance of the fundamental principles has not and should not bind us to those precise, at times anachronistic, contours. Successive generations of Americans have continued to respect these fundamental choices and adopt them as their own guide to evaluating quite different historical practices. Each generation has the choice to overrule or add to the fundamental principles enunciated by the Framers; the Constitution can be amended or it can be ignored. Yet with respect to its fundamental principles, the text has suffered neither fate. Thus, if I may borrow the words of an esteemed predecessor, Justice Robert Jackson, the burden of judicial interpretation is to translate "the majestic generalities of the Bill of Rights, conceived as part of the pattern of liberal government in the eighteenth century, into concrete restraints on officials dealing with the problems of the twentieth century."

We current Justices read the Constitution in the only way that we can: as Twentieth Century Americans. We look to the history of the time of framing and to the intervening history of interpretation. But the ultimate question must be, What do the words of the text mean in our time? For the genius of the Constitution rests not in any static meaning it might have had in a world that is dead and gone, but in the adaptability of its great principles to cope with current problems and current needs. What the constitutional fundamentals meant to the wisdom of other times cannot be their measure to the vision of our time. Similarly, what those fundamentals mean for us, our descendants will learn, cannot be the measure to the vision of their time. This realization is not, I assure you, a novel one of my own creation. Permit me to quote from one of the opinions of our Court, *Weems* v. *United States*, written nearly a century ago:

> Time works changes, brings into existence new conditions and purposes. Therefore, a principle to be vital must be capable of wider application than the mischief which gave it birth. This is peculiarly true of constitutions. They are not ephemeral enactments, designed to meet passing occasions. They are, to use the words of Chief Justice John Marshall, "designed to approach immortality as nearly as human institutions can approach it." The future is their care and provision for events of good and bad tendencies of which no prophesy can be made. In the application of a constitution, therefore, our contemplation cannot be only of what has been, but of what may be.

Interpretation must account for the transformative purpose of the text. Our Constitution was not intended to preserve a preexisting society but to make a new one, to put in place new principles that the prior political community had not sufficiently recognized. Thus, for example, when we interpret the Civil War Amendments to the charter—abolishing slavery, guaranteeing blacks equality under law, and guaranteeing blacks the right to vote—we must remember that those who put them in place had no desire to enshrine the status quo. Their goal was to make over their world, to eliminate all vestige of slave caste.

Having discussed at some length how I, as a Supreme Court Justice, interact with this text, I think it time to turn to the fruits of this discourse. For the Constitution is a sublime oration on the dignity of man, a bold commitment by a people to the ideal of libertarian dignity protected through law. Some reflection is perhaps required before this can be seen.

The Constitution on its face is, in large measure, a structuring text, a blueprint for government. And when the text is not prescribing the form of government it is limiting the powers of that government. The original document, before addition of any of the amendments, does not speak primarily of the rights of man, but of the abilities and disabilities of government. When one reflects upon the text's preoccupation with the scope of government as well as its shape, however, one comes to understand that what this text is about is the relationship of the individual and the state. The text marks the metes and bounds of official authority and individual autonomy. When one studies the boundary that the text marks out, one gets a sense of the vision of the individual embodied in the Constitution.

As augmented by the Bill of Rights and the Civil War Amendments, this text is a sparkling vision of the supremacy of the human dignity of every individual. This vision is reflected in the very choice of democratic self-governance: the supreme value of a democracy is the presumed worth of each individual. And this vision manifests itself most dramatically in the specific prohibitions of the Bill of Rights, a term which I . . . apply to describe not only the original first eight amendments, but the Civil War amendments as well. It is a vision that has guided us as a people throughout our history, although the precise rules by which we have protected fundamental human dignity have been transformed over time in response to both transformations of social condition and evolution of our concepts of human dignity.

• • •

Part Four

The Politics of Public Policy

Chapter 15

Domestic
Policymaking

$\mathcal{T}$*he purpose and function of government is to make policy—that is, to create and implement the rules and programs by which society is to be governed. In a sense, all of the previous chapters have been examining the policymaking process: the institutions that interact to create it and the constitutional basis under which they operate; its relationship to public opinion and the electoral process; and the role of nongovernmental actors—like the media and interest groups—in its development. In this and the final chapters, we turn to examining the total picture, first as it relates to domestic policy and then as it relates to foreign and military affairs.*

Domestic policymaking in the United States has undergone several transformations in this century. The New Deal greatly expanded the federal government's role in economic regulation and social policymaking. In the 1960s, Lyndon Johnson's Great Society widened the scope of federal welfare programs, a trend continued under President Richard Nixon. In the 1980s, the election of Ronald Reagan initiated a period of struggle—still ongoing—for control over the scope and direction of federal social policy.

This chapter examines domestic policymaking from three points of view. In selection 15.1, the overall shape of public policy in the United States is examined from a comparative perspective. In selections 15.2 and 15.3, we look at the policymaking process, with particular attention to the decentralized, fragmented nature of much federal policymaking and to the ongoing conflict between the White House and Congress over the nature of the federal government's proper role. Selections 15.4, 15.5 and 15.6, follow trends in domestic policy over the past three decades, looking at the future of the American economy and examining whether Lyndon Johnson's war on poverty was in fact a victory or a defeat.

Chapter Questions

1. How have the larger trends and currents in American politics over the past thirty years affected domestic policy? Consider the impact of divided government (that is, the separation of powers), increased federal budget deficits, and the ascendancy of conservatism at the presidential level.

2. How does the president and the congressional leadership help to set public policy? What is the impact, by contrast, of smaller "subgovernments," made up of congressional subcommittees, executive agencies, and particular interest groups?

3. Do the factors discussed in questions 1 and 2 help explain the apparent lack of rationality and coherence in many government policies? the apparent lack of long-range planning?

I THE INTERNATIONAL CONTEXT

In the first two parts of a three-part article, the political scientist Anthony King surveyed five Western democracies—the United States, Canada, Great Britain, France, and West Germany—in an attempt to describe and understand the role played by the state in a number of public policy areas. In the first two parts, King concluded that "the part played by the State [the government] in the United States is certainly greater than it used to be—hence the talk in America of 'big government'—but, with the major exception of education, it is still, for better or worse, much smaller than elsewhere." Public ownership of major industrial enterprises in the United States, King suggested, is a "non-story—of proposals that were not made and of things that did not happen."* Governments in the United States play a larger role in the provision of social services, but their role is still small when compared to governments in the other four countries studied. (The only exception King noted is in the field of education, where the role of state and local governments is quite large. The government's large role in education, King concludes, is possible only because Americans understand that "if the State did not supply education, no one else would" and that "education was a field—almost the only field—in which the State could expand without competing, except in a very small way, with private institutions.")†

King sets out five possible explanations for the smaller role of government in the United States and concludes that only the last—ideas—can provide a satisfactory explanation.

Without a comparative basis of analysis, it is easy to overstate the concept of big government in America. This is especially true because government's role today is quite large by historical standards. King's argument reminds us that, in comparative

---

* Anthony King, "Ideas, Institutions, and the Policies of Governments: A Comparative Analysis: Parts I and II," *British Journal of Political Science* 3 (1973): 302.
† Anthony King, "Ideas, Institutions, and the Policies of Governments: A Comparative Analysis: Part III," *British Journal of Political Science* 3 (1973): 420.

perspective, the role of government in the domestic public policy of the United States remains quite low.

Questions

1. What are some of the ideas that have contributed to Americans' reluctance to allow the role of the state to expand to the levels seen in other Western democracies? Consider in particular the readings in chapter 4 on American political culture.

2. King notes that education is the one major exception to his analysis. Are there other, perhaps lesser, exceptions? How are these exceptions defended or explained in the American context?

15.1 Ideas, Institutions, and the Policies of Governments: A Comparative Analysis

Anthony King

[Earlier in this paper,] we noticed that the countries have pursued policies that diverge widely, at least with respect to the size of the direct operating role of the State in the provision of public services. We also noticed that the United States differs from the four other countries far more than they do from each other. These findings will not have come as a great surprise to anybody, although some readers may have been surprised—in view of the common assumption that all major western countries are "welfare states"—to discover just how much the countries differ and what different histories they have had.

In any event, it is time now to turn directly to the problem of explanation. Obviously any explanation, were it to account for all of the phenomena we have referred to, would have to be exceedingly elaborate. It would have to encompass a large number of particular events within the five countries as well as the variations amongst them. All we will attempt here is a general explanation of why the United States is so strikingly different. We shall assume that the explanation we need is indeed general:

in other words, that the pattern we have observed is not simply the chance outcome of a series of more or less random occurrences. We shall also assume that it is the American pattern, in particular, that needs to be accounted for.

Much of the most important work in the field of public policy in recent years has, of course, been concerned with a very similar problem: accounting for variations in the expenditure policies of the American states. The writers on this subject have singled out two types of (mainly quantifiable) variable: "political" (e.g. extent of party competition, relationship between governor and legislature, apportionment of legislative districts), and "socio-economic" (e.g. *per capita* income, degree of urbanization, degree of industrialization). They have then gone on, using correlation techniques, to relate these variables to one another and to the variations in policy to be explained. Unfortunately this approach is denied us here, given the problem we have set ourselves. Quite apart from the fact that we are dealing with five units instead of fifty, there is no reason to suppose that any of the expenditures-in-the-states variables is significantly related to any of the differences between the United States and the other four countries. All five are, or have been during much of their recent history, rich, urban, industrial and politically competitive; to the extent that there have been variations in, for example, their constitutions, these variations have not had any discernible bearing on their policies. It is, in effect, as though we were trying to account for the differences, not amongst all fifty states, but only amongst (say) New York, New Jersey, Connecticut, Massachusetts and Pennsylvania.

We must therefore look elsewhere. We shall consider explanations in terms of five possible variables: elites, demands, interest groups, institutions, and ideas. These variables obviously interact with one another, or at least they could. Some examples of such interaction will be noted below, but for simplicity's sake the five variables will mostly be treated separately. . . .

Elites

It could be maintained, first, that government plays a smaller role in the US because *the US,* *unlike the other four countries, is dominated by an* *elite which wishes to inhibit the expansion of State* *activity and succeeds in doing so.* For this proposition to be true, at least one of the following propositions would also have to be true: either America is dominated by an elite whereas the other four countries are not; or the American elite is alone in wishing to limit the sphere of the State; or the American elite is not alone in wishing to limit the sphere of the State but is alone in actually succeeding in doing so. It would also have to be the case that there were in the US factors making for the expansion of State activity, which would have their effect but for the elite's intervention.

Much in this line of argument is not very plausible. America may or may not be dominated by an elite, but, if it is, then so are Canada, Britain, France and West Germany; there is hardly an industrial country anywhere whose power structure has not been interpreted . . . There is similarly no reason to suppose—on the assumption that all five countries are dominated by elites—that the American elite is somehow more successful than the others in imposing its will, or in thwarting the wills of others; indeed

Copyright, 1990, Boston Globe. Distributed by Los Angeles Times Syndicate. Reprinted with permission.

it would be paradoxical to say of an elite that it was an elite but yet could not get its way in matters that were important to it. Nevertheless, there is one element in the elitist explanation—the possibility that the American elite, if it exists, is alone in wishing to limit the sphere of the State—which cannot be dismissed out of hand. We shall come back to it at the end.

Demands

A second possible explanation of the relatively limited role played by government in the US is that, *whereas the mass publics in the other countries have demanded expansions of State activity, the American mass public has not.* In other words, irrespective of whether the United States is dominated by an elite, it may be that little has happened because little has been called for. An alternative rendering of this hypothesis would be that, whereas in any or all of the other countries governments do things whether or not they are demanded, in the US governments act only on demand and, since little has been demanded, little has been done; in other words, public opinion may play a more important part in American political life than elsewhere.

These possibilities raise all sorts of questions, as yet unanswered, in the empirical theory of representation. They also pose a very real problem of evidence: who is to say what the Canadian people wanted in 1917 or the French in the 1920s? All the same, there are a number of points which can be made with some confidence, and, while they should not lead anyone to reject the demands hypothesis outright, they make one wonder whether it can provide more than a very small part of the general explanation we are looking for.

It is hard to think of any act of nationalization in Canada or Europe that took place as the result of widespread public demand for it. The British case is probably typical. Many historians believe that, if anything, Labour won the 1945 general election despite its commitments to nationalization not because of them, and that most voters remained pretty indifferent to the Labour Government's subsequent nationalization measures. Butler and Stokes found in the 1960s that,

of a panel of electors interviewed twice at an interval of approximately sixteen months, 61 per cent either had no opinion at all on nationalization or no stable opinion; of the minority with definite opinions, the great majority wanted either no more nationalization or even the denationalization of industries already in the public sector. Yet in 1967 the Wilson Government nationalized the great bulk of the British iron and steel industry.

The only exception to this pattern of indifference/hostility is probably France in 1944–6, where the overwhelming need for national reconstruction and the anti-patriotic aura that private business had acquired during the Occupation seem to have created a climate of public opinion favourable to State ownership. It has been claimed by a French historian that in 1944 "the great majority of Frenchmen were convinced of the economic, social and political superiority of nationalised industry over private industry."

• • •

The explanation in terms of a dominant elite and the explanation in terms of demands are not perhaps very convincing, even on the face of it. Certainly, although much has been written about both elites and demands, neither has often been used for the purpose of explaining variations in policy. The next three lines of argument are, however, frequently advanced, sometimes by different writers, sometimes in combination by the same writer.

Interest Groups

The first of these holds that government plays a more limited role in America because, *whereas in other countries interest groups have not prevented the role of government from expanding, in the US they have.* This argument looks straightforward enough, but it could in fact mean one or more of at least three quite different things. It could mean that interest groups are in possession of more politically usable resources in the United States than in other countries; or it could mean that, although interest groups in most countries are almost equally well endowed with resources, interest groups in America, unlike those elsewhere, have used their resources to keep the State within relatively narrow confines; or it could mean that, although American interest groups have no more resources than other interest groups and do not use their resources for different purposes from other interest groups, they do have the good fortune to work within a framework of institutions that affords them the maximum opportunity to use their resources successfully.

The first of these propositions—that interest groups have more resources in the US than elsewhere—would probably at one time have been widely accepted as true; but the work of Beer and others has made it clear that the conditions under which interest groups can be expected to be strong are to be found in most industrial democracies. The interest groups of Britain, West Germany and Canada have the same sorts of resources at their disposal as those of the United States: leadership skills, knowledge, numbers, access to the media of communication, in some cases, ultimately, the sanction of withdrawing their co-operation. In Britain at least, the major interests are less fragmented organizationally than their American counterparts and succeed in organizing a larger proportion of their potential memberships. In Britain and West Germany, groups benefit from being regarded as having a legitimate right to participate actively in governmental decision making. Only in France do interest groups appear to have considerable difficulty in mobilizing themselves effectively. Since, France apart, American interest groups are not stronger, in this sense, than interest groups in other countries, it follows that the strength of the American groups cannot be used to explain the idiosyncratic pattern of American policy.

The second of the three propositions mentioned above—that interest groups in the United States are more concerned than those in other countries with keeping the State within narrow confines—is worth saying something about, even though there is no comparative literature on the aims of interest groups—indeed precisely for that reason.

Up till now, academic research on interest groups has tended to take groups' perceptions of their own interests as given: a group's beliefs about its interests *are* its interests. On this interpretation, questions about where a group's true interests lie arise only when they are actually raised within the group, by contending factions or by dissident minorities. Even then, the observer usually merely notes the existence of the differences of opinion and does not adjudicate among them; he does not "second guess" the group's leadership or take sides in its quarrels.

This approach may be the only one that can be adopted most of the time; but the attempt to comprehend the behaviour of comparable interest groups across national frontiers exposes a latent weakness in it. Suppose that two interest groups, one in one country, one in another, seem, as regards their material interests, to be in very similar situations: both are faced with a piece of new legislation that may reasonably be expected to affect (say) their incomes or hours of work. Suppose further, however, that the group in one country generally accepts the legislation and tries only to modify it in detail, while the group in the other rejects it out of hand and expends enormous resources campaigning against it. One possible explanation for the groups' discrepant behaviour may be that they possess different information or are making different predictions about the future. Another may be that they find themselves in different tactical situations such that, if either were in the other's position, it would behave similarly. But another possible explanation is that the two groups perceive their interests differently. And they may perceive their interests differently because they have absorbed the values, beliefs and expectations characteristic of the different polities within which they operate. This is too large a theme to be pursued here, but anyone comparing the rhetoric of American interest groups with that of groups in other countries is bound to be struck by what seems to be the American groups' much greater disposition to state their positions in abstract terms and, in particular, to raise, continually, large questions about the role of the State. This tendency probably tells us something about the considerations that American groups have in mind in determining where their interests lie. It undoubtedly tells us a great deal also about the sorts of considerations which the groups believe will appeal to the American mass public and to American decision makers.

The third of the three propositions relating to interest groups suggests that, whatever their resources and their aims, American groups have the great good fortune to work within a framework of institutions that affords them the maximum opportunities for using their resources effectively, especially when what they want to do is prevent things from happening. Since this proposition has more to do with the institutions than with the interest groups themselves, we will consider it in the next section.

Institutions

The classic explanation of the limited role played by the State in the United States as compared with other countries is one having to do with the structure and functioning of American institutions. The contention here is that *the American political system has a number of unusual institutional features, which have the effect of maximizing the probability that any given proposal for a change in policy will be rejected or deferred.* These features include: federalism, the separation of powers between executive and legislature, the constitutional position of the Supreme Court, the part played by committees in Congress, the seniority system in Congress, the malapportionment (until quite recently) of congressional districts, and the absence of disciplined political parties.

To do full justice to this explanation would require a paper much longer than this one. It would also require a great deal of imagination, since this explanation, in an even more demanding way than the others, forces us to try to conceive of what the gross pattern of public policy in the United States would be like were American institutions radically other than they are: it is rather like trying to imagine which of two grand masters would win a tournament if

they played not chess or even checkers but croquet. This explanation also differs completely from the others discussed so far in that, whereas in the case of elites, demands and interest groups we were arguing that the US does not differ in most material respects from the other four countries, in this case there can be no doubt that political realities as well as constitutional forms in the US are quite unlike those in Canada and western Europe.

The question, then, is not whether America's institutions differ from the other countries' but whether these differences can account for the observed differences in their patterns of policy. There would seem to be three reasons for supposing that they cannot—at least not on their own.

First . . . it has never seriously been suggested in the US that certain tasks undertaken by governments in Canada and Europe—for instance, the operation of railways and airlines—should also be undertaken by government in America. Suggestions of this kind have occasionally been made but almost never by major national leaders or parties. And this fact seems hard to attribute to institutional resistances. Of course politicians often refrain from putting forward proposals because they know they have no chance of success; possible courses of action may not even cross their minds for the same reason. But it is very hard to believe that American political leaders have consistently, over a period of nearly a hundred years, failed to advance proposals which they might otherwise have advanced simply or even mainly because they feared defeat as the result of obstruction in the House Rules Committee or an adverse ruling by the Supreme Court. It seems much more probable that politicians in the US have not advanced such proposals either because they did not believe in them themselves, or because they believed that other politicians did not believe in them, i.e. that they could obtain majorities in the various governmental arenas.

Second, in comparative perspective, even reformist Congresses and Administrations, like those of Franklin Roosevelt and Lyndon Johnson, appear as remarkable for what they have not done as for what they have. Only small excursions have been made into the field of public enterprise; and, among the social services, Medicare is only the most conspicuous instance of State provision having been introduced in the United States on a relatively limited basis although substantially more developed programmes had already been in existence, sometimes for many years, in other countries. This apparent reluctance on the part of even reformist majorities to expand the role of the State very far cannot be accounted for in institutional terms.

Third, the institutional obstacles, although they undoubtedly exist, can be surmounted. One of the striking things about the American experience is that almost all of the major innovations in the policy fields we have been discussing have been concentrated in a small number of Congresses: Roosevelt's first three, and the 89th elected with Johnson in 1964. And what distinguished these Congresses was not the absence of procedural obstacles (although minor procedural changes were made) but the presence of determined reformist majorities. In 1935 the Social Security Act passed both houses of Congress in under six months; in 1965 Medicare, having been debated in one form or another for nearly twenty years, was enacted in under seven months. The Social Security Act passed the House of Representatives by 371 votes to 33, Medicare by 315 votes to 115. When the will to surmount them is there, the institutional obstacles do not seem so formidable after all.

These points need to be qualified. For one thing, although the obstacles usually referred to—federalism, the separation of powers, and so forth—are not insuperable, it may be that other institutional factors—for example, the structure of American political parties or the expensiveness of political campaigns—result in the election of Congresses and Administrations (especially the former) that are less willing than the electorate to envisage the State's playing an expanded role. For instance, as late as 1961 the congressional liaison staff of the Department of Health, Education and Welfare reckoned that Medicare still could not command a simple majority in the House of Representatives even though the evidence suggested that public opinion had supported Medicare or something like it for many years. For another, it would be wrong wholly to discount the role played by the Supreme Court prior to 1937. Although not entirely consistent in its judgements, the Court repeatedly struck down legislation that offended against the canons of *laissez-faire*: in 1905, a New York statute regulating working hours in bakeshops; in 1908, a federal law prohibiting "yellow dog" labour contracts (in which workers bound themselves not to join trade unions); in 1918 and 1922, two federal Child Labor Acts; in 1923, a District of Columbia minimum wage law; and so on. The belief that the Court would strike down other similar pieces of legislation undoubtedly prevented many of them from being considered in the first place.

These qualifications are important. Nevertheless, it seems pretty clear that, for the three reasons given, the institutional explanation by itself is not enough. To the extent that institutional factors operate, they must, it seems, operate in conjunction with others.

Ideas

The time has come to let the cat out of the bag—especially since most readers will have noticed that it has already been squirming for a long time. If the argument so far is correct, it follows that the most satisfactory single solution to our problem is also the simplest: *the State plays a more limited role in America than elsewhere because Americans, more than other people, want it to play a limited role.* In other words, the most satisfactory explanation is one in terms of Americans' beliefs and assumptions, especially their beliefs and assumptions about government.

There is no need to go into detail here about what these beliefs and assumptions are. They can be summarized in a series of catch phrases: free enterprise is more efficient than government; governments should concentrate on encouraging private initiative and free competition; government is wasteful; governments should not provide people with things they can provide for themselves; too much government endangers liberty; and so on.

Obviously many Americans' political beliefs are much more elaborate and subtle than such phrases imply. Obviously, too, not all Americans believe all of these things. The central point is that almost every American takes it for granted that the State has very few—and should have very few—direct operating responsibilities: that the State should opt "for the role of referee rather than that of manager." If a proposal is made in the United States that the State should not merely supervise the doing of something by somebody else but should actually do it itself, the onus is on the proposer to demonstrate that the case in favour of State action is simply overwhelming. It has to be overwhelming since Americans, unlike Europeans, are not accustomed to a high level of governmental activity and since it will simply be assumed, probably even by the proposer himself, that the *a priori* objections to State action are exceedingly powerful. It is against this background that organizations like the AMA practically always bring forward highly general anti-State arguments against the most specific proposals entailing an expansion of the government's role.

• • •

The contrast between the United States and our other four countries is not complete: most Canadians probably make the same sorts of assumptions as Americans about the role of the State, and the Conservative Party in Britain has a strong bias in favour of the private sector. But the contrast is very great nonetheless. Certainly it is more than great enough to account for the policy divergences we have observed. Not only are social democrats in Canada and Europe committed to making extensive use of the machinery of the State: equally important, conservatives in the other four countries, as we have seen, are also not consistently anti-Statist in attitude; on the contrary, they often express a highly exalted view of the role of the State in economic and social life. It was not a socialist but a British Conservative MP who said: "In many respects . . . the individual is as much derived from the State as the State is from the individual." It was not a socialist but de Gaulle who said: "It is to the State that it falls to build the nation's power, which, henceforth, depends on the economy."

• • •

There is nothing new, of course, in our assertion that a limited conception of the role of government is a central element in American political thinking: every textbook has a paragraph on the subject. There is nothing new either in our saying that Europeans and even Canadians do not share this conception to anything like the same degree—if they share it at all. What probably is new in this paper is the contention that these differences in beliefs and assumptions are crucial to an understanding of the distinctive pattern of American policy. It is our contention that the pattern of American policy is what it is, not because America is dominated by an elite (though it may be); not because the demands made on government are different from those made on governments in other countries; not because American interest groups have greater resources than those in other countries; not because American institutions are more resistant to change than those in other countries (though they probably are); but rather because Americans believe things that other people do not believe and make assumptions that other people do not make. More precisely, elites, demands, interest groups and institutions constitute neither necessary nor sufficient conditions of the American policy pattern; ideas, we contend, constitute both a necessary condition and a sufficient one.

II ⬙ INTERCONNECTIONS

Government policy is made by all three branches and is heavily influenced and constrained by public opinion and by the electoral process. The Framers designed a system that prevents any one branch from making policy on its own, and to a great extent the system in fact works just that way. Policymaking, in general, involves cooperation, negotiation, and at times conflict among many different players. Nor is that process completed once a policy is enacted into law; the law must be implemented by the executive branch, under congressional and judicial supervision; when necessary, the program must be modified to fit new or unexpected circumstances. Each year the program must be funded through the congressional budget process; periodically it must be reauthorized by Congress as well.

Political scientists have categorized public policymaking along several dimensions; for example, one can look at the various stages of the process, at the different types of policy, or at the different political actors involved. The following selection, by two political scientists, examines public policymaking from a variety of perspectives.

Questions

1. "Policies all too often mirror Congress's scattered and decentralized structure," Davidson and Oleszek write. Explain. (Consider the selections in chapter 11, as well as this one.)

2. Define these terms: *distributive policies, regulatory policies,* and *redistributive policies.* What are the defining characteristics of each?

15.2 *Congress and Domestic Policymaking*———————

Roger H. Davidson and Walter J. Oleszek

Definitions of Policy

Because policies ultimately are what government is about, it is not surprising that definitions of policy and policy making are diverse and influenced by the beholder's eye. David Easton's celebrated definition of public policy as society's "authoritative allocations" of values or resources is one approach to the question. To put it another way, policies can be regarded as reflecting "who gets what, when, and how" in a society. A more serviceable definition of policy is offered by Randall Ripley and Grace Franklin:

policy is what the government says and does about perceived problems.

How do we recognize policies when we see them? The answer is not as simple as it may seem. Many policies, of course are explicitly labeled and recognized as authoritative statements of what the government is doing, or intends to do, about a given matter. The measures may be far-reaching, like financing the Social Security system; they may be trivial, like proclaiming a "Smokey Bear Week," "National Goat Awareness Week," or "National Ice Cream

Month." Nonetheless, they are obvious statements of policy. They are written down, often in painfully precise legal language. They boast documented life histories in committee hearings, reports, or floor deliberations that indicate what legislators had in mind as they hammered out the policy's final provisions.

Not all policies, however, are formal enough to be considered "the law of the land." Some are articulated by officials but, for one reason or another, never set down in laws or rules. The "Monroe Doctrine," which declared U.S. resistance to European intervention in the Western Hemisphere, was developed by Secretary of State John Quincy Adams in the second decade of the nineteenth century and has been adhered to ever since by successive generations of policy makers. Other policies, especially of a symbolic or exhorting nature, gain currency in the eyes of elites or the public without formal or legal elaboration.

Some policies stress substance—programs designed to build the nation's defense, for example. Others stress procedure, such as those requiring contractor insurance for military weapons, imposing personnel ceilings on federal agencies, or mandating program management standards. Still other policies are amalgams of rules or practices meeting specific demands but not perceived as comprising a whole.

It was not until the 1970s that people began to talk about "energy policy," but in truth the nation had such a policy for several generations—a something-for-everyone mixture of producers' tax advantages, artificially low consumer costs, and gasoline-powered transportation (highways, for example). This hodgepodge of programs, which encouraged inefficient use of energy and guaranteed dependence upon foreign oil, haunts the nation's energy policy even today.

Finally, there are policies that are made by negation. Doing nothing about a problem often has results that are as profound as passing a law about it. The nation had no general immigration law prior to 1924 and no medical care program before 1965, but its policies on those matters—favoring unregulated private activity—were unmistakable.

The process of arriving at these policies is *policy making.* The process may be simple or complex, highly publicized or nearly invisible, concentrated or diffuse. It may happen virtually overnight, as when President Ronald Reagan decided in 1983 to dispatch U.S. troops to the Caribbean island of Grenada. Or it may require years or even decades to formulate, as in the case of Medicare or civil rights.

Stages of Policy Making

Whatever the time frame, policy making normally has several distinct stages or phases: setting the agenda, formulating policy, adopting policy, and implementing policy.

Setting the Agenda

At the initial stage public problems are spotted and moved onto the *national agenda*, which can be defined as "the list of subjects to which government officials and those around them are paying serious attention." In a large, complex country like the United States, this agenda at any given moment is extensive and strenuously debated.

How do problems get placed on the agenda? Some are heralded by a crisis or some other prominent event—the hijacking of a plane by terrorists, the demise of savings and loan associations, or a campaign funding scandal. Others are occasioned by the gradual accumulation of knowledge—for example, growing awareness of an environmental hazard like acid rain or new technologies that make the telecommunications laws dating from the 1930s obsolete. Still other agenda items represent the accumulation of past problems that can no longer be avoided or ignored. Finally, agendas may be triggered by political processes—election results, turnover in Congress, or shifts in public opinion.

Agenda items are pushed by *policy entrepreneurs,* people willing to invest time and energy to promote a particular issue. Numerous Washington "think tanks" and interest groups, especially at the start of a new president's term, issue reports that seek to influence the economic, social, or foreign policy agenda of the nation. Usually, however, elected officials and their staffs or appointees are more apt to shape agendas than career bureaucrats or nongovernmental actors. Notable policy entrepreneurs on Capitol Hill are congressional leaders who push their party's policy initiatives. "We'll develop our proposals, [Bush] will submit his and then we'll try to mesh them," said Senate Majority Leader George Mitchell, D-Maine. "I don't think we have any obligation . . . just simply to sit and wait for him to make a proposal. There may be some areas in which he makes no proposal at all."

Lawmakers are frequent policy entrepreneurs because they are expected to voice the concerns of constituents and organized groups and to promote legislative solutions. Generally speaking, politicians gravitate toward issues that are visible, salient, and solvable. Tough, arcane, or conflictual problems may be shunned because they offer few payoffs and little hope of success. Sometimes only a crisis—like the 1973 and 1979 oil price increases that triggered long gasoline lines and shortages—can force lawmakers to address such questions. Yet despite enactment of legislation designed to ameliorate future energy problems, Americans today are as dependent on imported oil as they were before. Forecasters predict another energy crisis unless steps are taken to reduce the demand for oil, especially from the volatile Middle East, and to develop alternative fuels. This type of "creeping crisis" is often difficult for members of Congress to grapple with in part because of the "two Congresses." As conscientious lawmakers, they may want to forge long-term solutions. But as representatives of their constituents, they are deterred from acting when most citizens don't see any problems with the immediate situation.

Formulating Policy

In the second stage of policy making, items on the political agenda are discussed and po-

tential solutions explored. At this stage members of Congress and their staffs play crucial roles by conducting hearings and writing committee reports. They are aided by policy experts in executive agencies, interest groups, and the private sector.

Another term for this stage is *policy incubation*, which entails "keeping a proposal alive while it picks up support, or waits for a better climate, or while a consensus begins to form that the problem to which it is addressed exists." Sometimes this process takes only a few months; more often it requires years. During the Eisenhower administration (1953–1961), for example, congressional Democrats explored and refined policy options that, while not immediately accepted, were ripe for adoption by the time their party's nominee, John F. Kennedy, was elected president.

Although policy incubation occurs in both chambers, it is especially promoted in the Senate because of that body's flexible rules, more varied constituent pressures, and greater media coverage. The policy-generating role is particularly characteristic of senators with presidential ambitions who need to capture the attention of both the press and the public.

The incubation process not only brings policies to maturity but also refines solutions to the problems. The process may break down if workable solutions are not available. The seeming intractability of many modern issues complicates problem solving. Speaker Thomas S. Foley, D-Wash., finds issues today far more complicated than when he came to Congress in 1965. At that time

> the civil rights issue facing the legislators was whether the right to vote should be federally guaranteed for blacks and Hispanics. Now members are called on to deal with more ambiguous policies like affirmative action and racial quotas.

Solutions to problems normally involve "some fairly simple routines emphasizing the tried and true (or at least not discredited)." There exists a repertoire of responses—for example, blue-ribbon commissions, trust funds, or pilot projects—that can be applied to a variety of unsolved problems.

Adopting Policy

Laws are ideas whose time has come. The right time for a policy is what scholar John Kingdon calls the *policy window:* the opportunity presented by circumstances and attitudes to enact a policy into law. Policy entrepreneurs must seize the opportunity for the policy window may close and the idea's time pass.

Once policies are ripe for adoption, they must gain popular acceptance. This is the function of *legitimation,* the process through which policies come to be viewed by the public as right or proper. Inasmuch as citizens are expected to comply with laws or regulations—pay taxes, observe rules, or make sacrifices of one sort or another—the policies themselves must appear to have been properly considered and enacted. A nation whose policies lack legitimacy is in deep trouble.

Symbolic acts, such as voting on the House or Senate floor or bill signing by the president, signal to everyone that policies have been duly adopted according to traditional forms. Hearings and debates, moreover, serve not only to fine-tune policies but also to cultivate support among affected interests. Answering critics of Congress's slowness in adopting energy legislation, Sen. Ted Stevens, R-Alaska, asked:

> Would you want an energy bill to flow through the Senate and not have anyone consider the impacts on housing or on the automotive industry or on the energy industries that provide our light and power? Should we ignore the problems of the miner or the producer or the distributor? Our legislative process must reflect all of those problems if the public is to have confidence in the government.

Legitimating, in other words, often demands a measured pace and attention to procedural details.

Implementing Policy

In the final stage policies shaped by the legislature and the highest executive levels are put into effect, usually by a federal agency. Policies are not self-executing: they must be promulgated and enforced. A law or executive order rarely tells exactly how a particular policy will be implemented. Congress and the president usually delegate most decisions about implementation to the responsible agencies under broad but stated guidelines. Implementation then determines the ultimate impact of policies. Officials of the executive branch can thwart a policy by foot dragging or sheer inefficiency. By the same token, overzealous administrators can push a policy far beyond its creators' intent.

Therefore, Congress then must exercise its oversight role. It may require executive agencies to report or consult with congressional committees or to follow certain formal procedures. Members of Congress get feedback on the operation of federal programs through a variety of channels: media coverage, group protests, and even constituent casework. With such information Congress can and often does pass judgment by adjusting funding, introducing amendments, or recasting the basic legislation governing the policy.

Types of Domestic Policies

One way to understand public policies is to analyze the nature of the policies themselves. Scholars have classified policies in many different ways. The typology we will use identifies three types of domestic policies: distributive, regulatory, and redistributive.

Distributive Policies

Distributive policies or programs are government actions that convey tangible benefits to private individuals, groups, or firms. Invariably there are subsidies to favored individuals or groups. The benefits are often dubbed *pork* (special-interest spending for projects in members' states or districts), although the appellation is sometimes difficult to define. After all, "one person's pork is another person's steak." The projects also come in several different varieties.

> Dams, roads and bridges, known as "green pork," are old hat. These days, there is also

"academic pork" in the form of research grants to colleges, "defense pork" in the form of geographically specific military expenditures and lately "high-tech pork," for example the intense fight to authorize research into super computers and high-definition television (HDTV).

Distributive politics—which make many interests better off and few, if any, visibly worse off—are natural in Congress, which as a non-hierarchical institution must build coalitions in order to function. A textbook example was the $1-billion-plus National Parks and Recreation Act of 1978. Dubbed the "park barrel" bill, it created so many parks, historical sites, seashores, wilderness areas, wild and scenic rivers, and national trails that it sailed through the Interior Committee and passed the House by a 341-to-61 vote. "Notice how quiet we are. We all got something in there," said one House member, after the Rules Committee cleared the bill in five minutes flat. Another member explained: "If it had a blade of grass and a squirrel, it got in the bill." Distributive politics of this kind throws into sharp relief the "two Congresses" notion: national policy as a mosaic of local interests.

The politics of distribution works best when tax revenues are expanding, fueled by high productivity and economic growth—characteristics of the U.S. economy from the end of World War II through the mid-1970s. When productivity declines or zealous tax cutting squeezes revenues, it becomes difficult to add new benefits or expand old ones. Such was the plight of lawmakers in the 1980s. Yet distributive impulses remained strong, adding pressure to wring distributive elements out of tight budgets and to hand out more noneconomic, symbolic benefits (commemorative legislation, for example).

Regulatory Policies

Regulatory policies are designed to protect the public against harm or abuse that might result from unbridled private activity. Thus, the Food and Drug Administration (FDA) monitors standards for foodstuffs and tests drugs for purity, safety, and effectiveness. The Federal Trade Commission (FTC) guards against illegal business practices such as deceptive advertising. The National Labor Relations Board (NLRB) combats unfair labor practices by business firms.

Federal regulation against certain abuses dates from the late nineteenth century when the Interstate Commerce Act and the Sherman Antitrust Act were enacted to protect against transport and monopoly abuses. As the present century dawned, scandalous practices in slaughterhouses and food processing plants, colorfully reported by reform-minded muckraking reporters, led to meatpacking, food, and drug regulations. The 1929 stock market collapse and the Great Depression paved the way for the New Deal legislation regulating the banking and securities industries and labor-management relations. Consumer rights and environmental protection came of age in the 1960s and 1970s. Dramatic attacks on unsafe automobiles by Ralph Nader and others led to new laws mandating tougher safety standards. Concern about smog produced by auto exhausts led to the Clean Air Act of 1970. And concern about airline delay, congestion, and safety during the 1980s prompted Congress to consider new regulatory controls for the nation's air traffic system.

In these cases and many similar ones Congress responded to reformist pressure and passed laws to protect the public. Theorists refer to such policies as *protective regulation* because their purpose is to protect the public and prevent anticipated abuses. In most cases industries stoutly oppose protective regulation, arguing that the public would be better off with self-regulation or mild guidelines than with tough, detailed standards and cumbersome reporting and enforcement procedures. Faced with stiff competition from efficient foreign cars, for example, the auto industry blamed its plight on the plethora of government regulations—safety, low pollution, and fuel economy—and sought relief in quotas.

Competitive regulation is regulatory policy that grants firms or organizations a favored place in the market and helps protect that place by limiting the entry of newcomers to the field. Only occasionally are protective and competitive regulatory policies clearly differentiated. Most regulations serve the dual purpose of protecting the public while at the same time guarding the competitive position of firms within the regulated industry. The policy thus serves distributive as well as regulatory functions, and for this reason the line between distribution and regulation is hard to draw. Many policies, at least in their inception, contain regulatory elements. Potential confusion on the airwaves demands licensing for the public's convenience as well as broadcasters'. Certifying aircraft protects competitors but also guards against unsafe equipment. Many regulations serve the industry's convenience, which underscores the pervasiveness of distributive policies and the tendency of policies to slip into the distributive mode even though they originated for other purposes.

Conflicts about deregulation began in the late 1970s. The trucking, airline, banking, and broadcasting industries were deregulated because economists and consumer groups concluded that federal regulations wasted resources and ultimately hurt consumers. Initially, the industries and their allies, including the regulators and the relevant congressional committees, resisted deregulation. The predictable world of governmental protection seemed more comfortable than the unpredictable world of competition. In these cases the mounting costs of compliance, not to mention the consumers' benefits from competition, overcame the fears of the more conservative sectors of the industry, and Congress authorized relaxation of earlier regulation. By the late 1980s, however, there was growing public and congressional interest in reregulating areas such as public health and safety and industries such as savings and loans and the airlines. "I don't think you can ask the free market to make sure that airplanes are working or that the cockpit crew is rested," said Rep. Dan Glickman, D-Kan.

Redistributive Policies

Redistribution is the most difficult of all political feats insofar as it shifts resources visibly from one group to another. Because it is controversial, redistributive policy engages a broad spectrum of political actors—not only in the House and Senate chambers, but in the executive branch, interest groups, and even the public at large. Redistributive issues tend to be ideological. They often separate liberals and conservatives because they upset relationships between social and economic classes. Theodore R. Marmor described the thirty-year fight over medical care for the aged as "cast in terms of class conflict."

> The leading adversaries . . . brought into the opposing camps a large number of groups whose interests were not directly affected by the Medicare outcome. . . . [I]deological charges and countercharges dominated public discussion, and each side seemed to regard compromise as unacceptable.

Of all public issues, redistribution is the most visible because it involves the most conspicuous allocations of values and resources. Most of the diverse socioeconomic issues of the past generation—civil rights, affirmative action, school busing, aid to education, homelessness, abortion, tax reform—were redistributive problems. Fiscal policy making has taken on a redistributive character as federal expenditures run ahead of revenues and lawmakers are forced to find ways to close the gap. Cutting the federal benefits and opening up new revenue sources both involve redistribution because they turn "haves" into "have nots." That is why politicians today find budget and revenue issues so burdensome. "I wasn't here in the glory days, when a guy with a bright idea of a scholarship program or whatever could get a few hundred million dollars to pursue it," lamented Rep. Richard Durbin, D-Ill. "Now you've got to take from one to give to the other."

Roger H. Davidson and Walter J. Oleszek 577

Federal budgeting is marked not only by extreme conflict, but also by techniques to disguise the redistributions or make them more palatable. For example, omnibus packages permit legislators to approve cuts *en bloc* rather than one by one, and across-the-board formulas (like "freezes") give the appearance of spreading the misery equally to affected clienteles. In all such vehicles distributive elements are added to placate the more vocal opponents of change. Such is the unhappy lot of politicians consigned to a redistributive mode.

Characteristics of Congressional Policy Making

As a policy-making machine, Congress displayed the traits and biases of its membership and structure. Congress is bicameral with divergent electoral and procedural traditions. It is representative, especially where geographic interests are concerned. It is decentralized, having few mechanisms for integrating or coordinating its policy decisions. And it is reactive, mirroring conventional public or elite perceptions of problems.

Bicameralism

Several differences between the House and Senate—terms of office, size and character of their constituencies, and size of their legislative bodies—powerfully influence the policies they make. Six-year terms, it is argued, allow senators to play the "statesman" for at least part of each term before they are forced by oncoming elections to concentrate on fence mending. This distinction may be more apparent than real, but empirical studies of senators' voting habits lend some support to it.

The different constituencies unquestionably pull in divergent directions, as already noted. The more homogeneous House districts often promote clear and unambiguous positions on a narrower range of questions than those considered by senators who must weigh the claims of many competing interests on a broad range of matters. The size of the chambers, moreover,

dictates procedural characteristics. House rules are designed to allow majorities to have their way, as restless Republicans have found to their dismay. In contrast, Senate rules give individual senators great latitude to influence action. "One person can tie this place into a knot," said Senate GOP whip Alan K. Simpson. "And two can do it even more beautifully."

Are the biases of the two bodies consistent? Probably not. For years the Senate appeared more "liberal" than the House because of the presence of urban configurations in most of the states and the lingering effects of malapportionment favoring rural areas in drawing House districts. Today that generalization would be hard to sustain. During the 1980s, Republicans controlled the Senate for six years, while Democrats retained majorities in the House. The two chambers thus differed in outlook, constituency, and strategy. Viewing the mixed long-term policy results, Benjamin Page concludes that bicameralism is less important in promoting or discouraging particular kinds of policies than in "the furtherance of deliberation, the production of evidence, and the revealing of error." In recent years commentators have been struck by the convergence of the two chambers. Senators, like House members, are constantly engaged in reelection activities.

Localism

Congressional policies respond to constituents' needs, particularly those that can be mapped geographically. Sometimes these needs are pinpointed with startling directness. For example, an aviation noise control bill required construction of a control tower "at latitude 40 degrees, 43 minutes, 45 seconds north and at longitude 73 degrees, 24 minutes, 50 seconds west"—the exact location of a Farmingdale, New York, airport in the district of the Democratic representative who requested the provision.

Usually, however, programs are directed toward states, municipalities, counties, or geographic regions. Funds are often transferred directly to local government agencies, which in turn deliver the aid or services to citizens. Or local agencies may act, individually or in consortiums, as "prime sponsors" for a bundle of closely related services—in community development or worker training, for example—that can be tailored to local needs.

Although national and local policies are necessarily intertwined, the level of government making a policy is important for several reasons. First, interest groups wield different degrees of influence at various governmental levels. Racial, ethnic, and labor groups, for example, traditionally prefer national legislation; business and industry groups tend to prefer local action, which they feel more confident of bending to their purposes. Second, policy makers are sensitive to local traditions, some of which may be far ahead of the "nationwide consensus" and others of which may lag behind. Members of Congress represent localities and often share local policy makers' views.

Finally, national policies can be advanced by state and local governments, or states and localities can develop innovations that can spur national action. "I can't think of a time when they [state governments] have been so involved in helping to shape federal legislation," stated Rep. Thomas Downey, D-N.Y. With shrinking fiscal assistance from the federal government, states and localities are fashioning creative solutions to many problems that the national government has been unable or unwilling to address. Some states have been so active in passing laws and issuing regulations that original advocates of local controls, such as business executives, "have found themselves running back to the arms of the federal government, asking Washington to preempt [legal and regulatory] action taken by the states."

Many policy debates therefore revolve around the governmental level at which they should be resolved. Ideology makes little difference: liberals seek to enforce national standards in civil rights or environmental protection, but conservatives are equally eager to override local preferences in drunk driving or drug trafficking standards, "equal access" of religious groups to school facilities, and other policies. Preference for a given level of government is invariably overridden by one's zeal for the policy itself.

Piecemeal Policy Making

Policies all too often mirror Congress's scattered and decentralized structure. Policies are typically considered piecemeal, reflecting the patchwork of committee and subcommittee jurisdictions. Sometimes policies are duplicative or even contradictory; committees may sponsor price supports and agricultural research promoting tobacco production at the same time they fund research on lung cancer. Congress's segmented decision making is typified by authorizing and appropriating processes in which separate committees consider the same programs often without consulting each other.

The structure of a given policy often depends on which committees have reported it. Working from varying jurisdictions, committees can take different approaches to the same problem. A program from the taxing committees will feature tax provisions, from the appropriations committees a fiscal approach, from the commerce panels a regulatory approach, and so forth. The approach may be well or ill suited to the policy objective—it all depends on which committee was the best positioned to promote the bill.

Symbolic Policy Making

Despite its reputation for uncontrolled spending binges, Congress is actually addicted to solutions to problems that are inexpensive and often symbolic. Not infrequently a bold national policy is coupled with funds limited to a few pilot projects or scattered too widely for maximum effect. Underfunding of programs is at least as common as overfunding. Sometimes this happens because of unforeseen consequences (for example, the number of eligible citizens rises); just as often it flows from political wishful thinking.

A wide repertoire of low-cost options exist for any given policy goal. Rather than finance a new standard, Congress can mandate the standard and pass on the cost of compliance to manufacturers or consumers. In selecting policy targets, Congress can choose low-ticket items over really tough, expensive ones. Rather than finance a program completely, Congress can offer a pilot program or loan guarantees, with repayment expected. Finally, lawmakers can hold out the prospect of recovering funds by eliminating "fraud, waste, and abuse."

At heart, congressional policy making deals with appearances as much or more than with substantive results. Symbolic actions are important to all politicians. This is not the same thing as saying that politicians are merely cynical manipulators of symbols. Words and concepts— *equal opportunity, affirmative action, cost of living, parity*—are contested earnestly in committee rooms and on the House and Senate floor. The result, however, is that federal goals frequently are stated in vague, optimistic language, not spelled out in terms of specific measures of success or failure.

Often measures are passed to give the impression that action is being taken when the impact or efficacy of the measure is wholly unknown. Groups outside of Congress continually demand: "Don't just stand there, do something." Doing "something" is often the only politically feasible alternative, even when no one really knows what to do or when inaction might be just as effective.

Reactive Policy Making

At any given moment elected officials are seldom far ahead or far behind the collective views of the citizenry. Hence, it would be misguided to expect the national legislature to express "radical" solutions to problems. Members know that radical views are unlikely to attract widespread public support.

Congress is essentially a reactive institution, as one House member explained:

> When decision rests on the consent of the governed, it comes slowly, only after consensus has built or crisis has focused public opinion in some unusual way, the representatives in the meantime hanging back until the signs are unmistakable. Government decision, then, is not generally the cutting edge of change but a belated reaction to change.

The reactive character of Congress's policy making is evident in its budget process. Under pressures to reform, Congress reacted in 1974, 1985, and again in 1987 with changes in how it makes budget decisions. The annual budget passed by Congress reflects the policy priorities of the nation. Today's budget process, dating from the mid-1970s, was designed to bring coherence to the way standing committees handle the president's budget. Since then it has decisively shaped both Congress's internal decision making and legislative-executive relations.

III  FOCUS: THE FEDERAL BUDGET

Once upon a time, the federal budget process was a relatively straightforward affair. The president would propose a budget, Congress would make a variety of relatively minor changes, and the budget would be enacted into law.

All that changed beginning in the late 1960s and early 1970s. One reason is that the election of Richard Nixon in 1968 inaugurated the modern era of divided government in which (for the most part) Congress and the White House are controlled by different parties, with different policy goals, political philosophies, and budget priori-

ties. Congress also wanted a voice in setting the nation's fiscal policy (that is, using the overall size of the federal revenues and expenditures—and hence the surplus or deficit—as a tool for managing the national economy). Congress's response was the Budget Control and Impoundment Act of 1974, which sought to centralize the budget process in Congress and create a real opportunity for a congressional, rather than presidential, budget.

The budget equation was transformed in the 1980s by the era of high deficits. With less and less money to go around for social spending (that is, less as compared to inflation and to the growing demands on the federal government), Congress needed a way to set budget priorities and to prevent even larger deficits. The result was the Gramm-Rudman-Hollings Act of 1985, which set overall deficit reduction targets and initiated (in theory) a process of automatic budget reductions if those targets were not met.

Most political scientist and Washington watchers would agree that neither budget act has been very successful. The budget process remains decentralized, and the federal deficit remains high. In this selection, James A. Thurber examines the impact of the budget reforms on congressional-presidential relations and assesses their efficacy in making the process more rational and more controllable.

Question

1. Examine the budget process from Congress's point of view. What were the purposes of the 1974 and 1985 budget reforms? Did they work? How might Congress assess the current budget process? Now look at the process from the president's point of view. What were the problems with the 1974 and 1985 reforms? How might the White House assess the current process?

15.3 The Impact of Budget Reform on Presidential and Congressional Governance

James A. Thurber

Decisions about the federal budget are at the heart of American politics. The Constitution gives Congress the power of the purse: the authority to establish revenue policy and to authorize and appropriate funds for the president and the executive branch of government. The president can tax and spend only to the extent allowed by Congress. Budgets reveal the degree of cooperation and conflict between the president and Congress over public policy priorities. The give and take between Congress and the president over federal spending, revenues, deficits, and debt affects the economy, national security, and many other crucial issues that are addressed by government.

Although the Constitution granted Congress the power of the purse, it did not prescribe the budgetary system to be used. Consequently, the system Congress has developed for itself and the president is based on its own rules, statutes, and legislative traditions. Over the past two hundred years, Congress has alternatively delegated significant budgetary powers to the president and tried to control the president's spending authority. This oscillation between budgetary delegation and control, between cooperation and conflict, has led to major changes in the way budgets are formulated.

Congress enacted the Budget and Accounting Act of 1921 to control presidential spending power. This act required the president to submit an annual budget for the federal government, but it also gave him the power to control and coordinate agency budget requests and to monitor spending through the Bureau of the Budget (renamed the Office of Management and Budget in 1970). From the Great Depression of the 1930s through the Vietnam War and Great Society legislation of the 1960s, there was an unprecedented escalation of program growth and federal spending. By the late 1960s the deficit had begun to increase, and a variety of seemingly uncontrollable deficit budgetary problems besieged Congress. Delayed action on appropriations bills caused alarm inside and outside the legislative branch. President Richard Nixon criticized members of Congress as being irresponsible big spenders, and he impounded appropriated funds for popular programs.

To regain from the president some of its budgetary power and to improve the way it made spending and revenue decisions, Congress passed the Budget and Impoundment Control Act of 1974 (Public Law 93-344, Titles I-IX). The act required Congress to adopt two budget resolutions setting spending and revenue levels and estimating deficits each year. In practice, however, Congress has adopted only a single budget resolution every year since 1983, and often late at that. Moreover, since the early 1980s, legislative-executive "gridlock" over the deficit has further disrupted the budget process and revealed serious problems in presidential-congressional relations.

In late 1985, in response to widespread frustration over the budget deficit, Congress passed the Balanced Budget and Emergency Deficit Control Act (Public Law 99-177). This act is usually referred to by the names of its sponsors:

Senators Phil Gramm, R-Texas; Warren B. Rudman, R-N.H.; and Ernest F. Hollings, D-S.C. The GRH legislation mandates a set of deficit targets for each fiscal year. If the president and Congress cannot agree on a budget that comes within $10 billion of the annual deficit target, a mechanism is triggered that reduces expenditures automatically to meet the deficit target. The original act called for a balanced budget in 1991. It set out to eliminate the deficit by imposing limits that shrank every year. A revision of the original act, the Balanced Budget and Emergency Deficit Control Reaffirmation Act of 1987, calls for a balanced budget in 1993. The strain of deficit reduction has led to further proposals to reform the congressional budget process, but no clear consensus has been reached within Congress or between Congress and the president on what should be done.

With the Budget and Impoundment Control Act of 1974 and the GRH legislation, Congress sought to recapture power over the budget process. But by failing to achieve annual deficit targets, thus triggering the GRH automatic budget-cutting mechanism, Congress effectively limited its own power. . . .

The Origins of Congressional Budget Reform

Before 1974 Congress considered the president's annual budget in a decentralized, piecemeal manner. Authorizations for federal agencies and programs were considered separately by congressional authorizing committees. Appropriations of funds for these agencies and programs were considered by the House and Senate appropriations committees working through subcommittees.

Revenue policies were handled in the House by the Ways and Means Committee and in the Senate by the Finance Committee. Congress never evaluated the relation between total expenditures and total revenues or the economic consequences of these disconnected budgetary decisions.

Moreover, interest groups and agencies strongly influenced the legislative process. The president's budget reflected the power of these interests more than a central fiscal policy. At no point was there an orderly review of the total budget by a single congressional committee or by the House and Senate as a whole. The budget was not even visible until all of the appropriations subcommittees' bills were passed, and frequently they were not passed before the beginning of the fiscal year. To compound the problem, supplemental appropriations bills were often passed in the middle of a fiscal year, making the size of the budget a moving target. Congress had neither budget committees nor skilled budget experts nor a comprehensive system to bring discipline to the budget-making process and to challenge the president's budget.

The Budget and Impoundment Control Act of 1974 established several major institutions and procedures that changed congressional-presidential relations. The act created separate House and Senate Budget committees, responsible for setting overall tax and spending levels. Most important, it required Congress each year to establish levels of expenditures and revenues, and it prescribed procedures for arriving at those spending and income totals. The procedures, later revised by GRH, included three important elements: (1) a timetable for action on budget-related legislation to ensure completion of the budget plan before the start of each fiscal year; (2) a requirement to adopt concurrent budget resolutions (which do not require presidential approval) for total budget authority, budget outlays, and revenues for the upcoming fiscal year; and (3) a reconciliation process to conform revenue, spending, and debt legislation to the levels specified in the budget resolution. The 1974 legislation also created the Congressional Budget Office, which provides Congress with independent information and analysis on the budget. Title X of the act limited presidential use of two kinds of impoundments: deferrals and rescissions. *Deferrals* are presidential requests to Congress to postpone or delay spending for a particular program for up to twelve months. *Rescissions* are presidential requests to abolish funding permanently for a program.

The GRH legislation, as noted earlier, established a procedure to reduce deficits to annual maximum levels through mandatory sequestration of funds when Congress did not reduce the deficit through legislation. If the deficit limits are not met, the Office of Management and Budget (OMB) will make automatic spending cuts, using a congressionally mandated formula.

In summary, the budget legislation passed in 1974, 1985, and 1987 has greatly influenced congressional-presidential cooperation and conflict over budgetary decisions.

• • •

Congressional and Presidential Influence over Budget Priorities

Advocates of the 1974 budget act argued for "an improved congressional system for determining relative funding priorities." Many felt reform was needed to unify the disaggregated budgetary process in Congress and to create a mechanism for challenging and changing the president's budget priorities. The first chairman of the House Budget Committee, Rep. Brock Adams, D-Wash., stated it simply: "Perhaps the most important aspect of the budget resolution is the fact that it contains the budget of Congress and that of the president."

Congressional-presidential spending priorities are often driven by a highly representative and decentralized system that makes distributive decisions in favor of strong interest groups, agencies, and congressional committees. The budget process is both pluralistic and incremental, with each agency and interest group zealously guarding its part of the budget. Past budgetary outlays are given preference over new spending requests. Congress has had to learn to "just say no" to major increases and new programs and to say it to presidents, interest groups, and constituents, an often distasteful and politically risky task. Indeed, GRH forces Congress to reaffirm existing budget priorities, thereby leaving few resources and little congressional energy to tackle new programs. Automatic across-the-board cuts in a sequester under

GRH do not, by definition, change budget priorities; they simply set existing program preferences permanently in place. Change in budget priorities has come increment by increment or by exception, not through radical reordering of budget priorities based on new-found congressional budgetary power.

From 1974 to 1990, federal budget outlays grew dramatically—from $538.7 billion to an estimated $1.2 trillion (in constant dollars). As a percentage of gross national product spent by the federal government, this represented an increase from 19 percent to more than 21 percent. During the same period, outlays for various budget functions changed only slightly. For example, from 1974 to 1988, expenditures for national defense dropped from 29.5 percent to 29.0 percent of outlays, and those for human resources dropped from 50.4 to 50.0 percent. The most dramatic shift in spending preferences was caused by the government's borrowing to pay interest on the federal debt. From 1974 to 1989, the interest increased from $21.4 billion to $165.7 billion, or from 8 percent to more than 14 percent of the budget.

The real growth in government spending happened almost automatically through pluralistic incrementalism. Interest groups, agencies, and committees have been as successful under the 1974 budget process in protecting their base funding and securing their fair share of increase as they were before Congress centralized budgetary decision making. No major groups have been significantly disadvantaged by budget reform. No major programs have been cut. No congressional committees have tried to abolish programs under their jurisdiction. Spending priorities have not greatly changed as a direct result of the 1974 budget process or GRH.

The budget act of 1974 and the GRH legislation have given Congress some means to compete with the president's policy agenda; however, the complexity of the process (including entrenchment of its principal participants and the size of the federal debt) has led to evenly distributed spending cuts and budget accounting tricks by Congress rather than to dramatic changes in presidential spending priorities. Although the reforms potentially gave Congress more budgetary power, the power as exercised checked how much the president spent; it did not change what he spent it on. Ironically, the reforms gave the president the same power: the power to block but not to initiate major changes in spending outlays. Thus, whether the reforms have increased congressional influence over presidential budget priorities is still an open question.

•••

Centralization of the Budget Process

Before the budget act was passed, the stable roles, relationships, and routines of the president, OMB [Office of Management and Budget], executive branch agencies, congressional party leaders, congressional committees, and interest groups led to few surprises in the federal budget process. Predictable pluralistic incrementalism with a narrow scope and low level of political conflict predominated over distributive budgetary processes. Since 1974, when the reforms were passed, however, two oil crises, stagflation, high interest rates, and Reaganomics have changed the economy and destabilized the budget process. Reagan era tax cuts forced Congress to make redistributive budget decisions that widened the number of participants in the conflict over the budget and increased the conflict's visibility. President Reagan achieved his purpose "to limit the growth of . . . government by limiting the revenues available to be spent." The 1974 budget reform and GRH placed restraints on spending by openly relating outlays to revenues and calling for a balanced budget. A latent consequence of both acts has been increased budgetary conflict, confusion, and stalemate between Congress and the president.

The budget reforms centralized budget decisions and caused some jockeying for jurisdictional turf between the budget committees and the other standing committees, especially the appropriations and taxing committees. The authorization committees have lost power because of the appropriations committees' right to cap new backdoor spending. There are three kinds of backdoor spending techniques: "*Contract authority* permits agencies to enter into contracts that subsequently must be liquidated by appropriations. *Borrowing authority* allows agencies to spend money they have borrowed from the public or the Treasury. And *mandatory entitlements* grant eligible individuals and governments the right to receive payments from the national government. . . . Entitlements, for Medicare, for example, establish judicially enforceable rights without reference to dollar amounts." The 1974 budget reforms restricted the authorization committees' use of contract authority and borrowing authority. But pre-1974 entitlement programs and net interest payments continue to reduce the ability of both Congress and the president to control the budget.

The 1974 budget act requires all standing committees to estimate the cost of programs within their jurisdiction early in the budget cycle. These estimates of authorizations tend to limit the committees' freedom and that of executive agencies and interest groups, which have a natural tendency to push for new programs and high authorizations. The committees are forced to state priorities and to make difficult choices among programs very early in the process; they are much less vulnerable to twelfth-hour lobbying by agencies and strong, well-organized interest groups. Before the 1974 reform program, authorization levels were commonly double and even triple the final appropriations. The authorization committees would often approve programs at very high levels to placate strong pressures from outside Congress, knowing full well that the appropriations committees would decrease the funding to more reasonable levels. After 1974 and GRH, the authorization committees could no longer play this game. The requirement to estimate program costs reduces the gap between authorizations and appropriations and puts a cap on

the political pressures from agencies and interest groups.

White House staff now find it necessary to work the Hill continually in order to win spending battles. The process is relatively open and thus more burdensome for the president and executive branch officials, forcing them to bargain more openly with members of Congress and to monitor the budget process carefully. OMB staff attend budget hearings and mark-ups, and the director often sits at the bargaining table with budget committee leaders to negotiate the final budget resolutions.

House-Senate Comparisons

Budgetary power in the Senate has generally been firmly in the hands of the committee chairs. House party leaders have played a stronger role in the budget process than have their Senate counterparts. House leaders set budget figures and offer refining amendments in order to marshal support for the budget resolutions. One of the consequences of the budget reform on the House majority leadership is that it has forced centralization, coordination, and the construction of a Democratic coalition behind congressional budgets. The Senate budget is more bipartisan, and the Senate has less conflict than the House in building budget resolutions.

House and Senate leaders from both parties, however, have helped give the budget process an independence from the president but not always from the power and expertise of committee and subcommittee chairs, who put pressure on the budget committees for higher spending for their favorite programs. When constituency interests and budget-committee priorities confront each other, the substantive committees with strong support from interest groups and agencies usually win in the battle over the budget.

A major challenge to the independence of the congressional budget process came during President Reagan's first year in office. OMB director David Stockman, a former representative who had an excellent understanding of the congressional budget reforms, used the reconciliation process to make severe cuts in spending by congressional committees. Interest groups and their friends on committees and in agencies were taken by surprise when Stockman and his allies on Capitol Hill locked in spending ceilings in the first concurrent resolution, thus changing the focus of the budget debate from line items to the highly centralized reconciliation resolution. In support of President Reagan, Republicans and conservative Democrats joined to increase defense spending and worked through the reconciliation process to reduce nondefense expenditures over the 1981–1983 period. The cuts totaled $100 billion. Democratic opponents were unable to stop the massive cuts until they weakened the conservative coalition in the House and eventually recaptured the Senate. The budget confrontations in 1981 and 1982 showed that the president can use the budget process to his advantage. Since 1983 interest groups, committees, and executive branch agencies have regained their protectionist power over the budget.

The reconciliation process was President Reagan's way of achieving reductions in expenditures within the protected jurisdiction of the tax committees and the sacred turf of the appropriations committees. Louis Fisher estimates that more than half the spending reductions in the reconciliation acts were within the jurisdiction of the House Ways and Means and Senate Finance committees. After 1983 Congress used the reconciliation process to challenge several presidential budgetary priorities.

In conclusion, budget reforms have the potential to limit the power of policy subsystems—that is, interest groups, committees, and agencies with jurisdiction over specific programs—by giving presidents and congressional leaders tools to coordinate and centralize budgeting on Capitol Hill. Yet strong interests continue to win and weak interests continue to lose in the battle of the budget, no matter how centralized and well coordinated the budget process has become.

Budget Control: Congress versus the President

Have the 1974 reforms tightened control of the federal budget? In 1974 approximately 70 percent of the budget was considered relatively uncontrollable, coming primarily from interest payments on the debt and indexed permanently authorized entitlements (such as Social Security, which is 21 percent of the budget). These areas cannot be directly controlled by the president and the appropriations committees on an annual basis. In 1988 OMB considered 77.5 percent of the budget uncontrollable, a 7.5 percent increase since 1974. This lack of budgetary control comes from payments for individuals (43.5 percent), fixed program costs (15.1 percent), and prior-year contracts and obligations (18.9 percent). If interest payments of 14.1 percent are added to the OMB estimates, more than 90 percent of the budget is relatively uncontrollable.

Levels of benefit are normally established in authorizing law rather than through appropriations of budget authority. Efforts by Congress or the president to reduce spending on these entitlement programs require changing the authorizing legislation, which is politically very difficult. In the absence of such legislative changes, the payments are made automatically, and in many cases they are made from the budget authority that is available without appropriations action to finance the program. The rise in permanent budget authority—resulting largely from these various forms of pre-1974 backdoor spending—has diminished the connection between congressional budgetary decisions in any given year and the actual outlays for that year. In short, the budget reforms have not significantly improved the capacity of Congress to control the budget.

GRH has put increased pressure on Congress and the president to focus on the uncontrollables; however, there is little evidence that members of Congress and the president have the political will to reduce spending for popular entitlement programs such as Social Security.

As Stockman's successor at OMB, James C. Miller III, explains: "Deficits create many winners and few losers. . . . Every legislator is in a position to try to confer benefits on his or her favorite constituencies, and the incentive for any individual legislator to refrain from such behavior is virtually nonexistent." As a representative assembly, Congress finds it difficult to oppose well-organized national interest groups, such as those protecting the interests of Social Security recipients. Once a relatively closed process for financing government agencies, congressional-presidential budgeting has been transformed into an open process for providing benefits and contracts to Americans. The more open the congressional budget process has become, the more Congress and the president have increased the flow of benefits to outsiders.

The deficit could be reduced by changing entitlements, by cutting defense spending rapidly, or by raising taxes. All of these solutions, however, require tighter budget control and spell political, if not electoral, suicide for members of Congress and the president. There is little evidence that the reforms have created greater control over the budget; thus the hypothesis that Congress has greater control over federal spending than it did before 1974 cannot be confirmed. Congress does not have greater control of the budget, and neither does the president.

Conclusion

The Budget and Impoundment Control Act of 1974 and the 1985 and 1987 GRH legislation are some of the most important structural and procedural budgetary reforms adopted by Congress in the past fifty years. Their consequences for presidential and congressional governance, cooperation, and conflict are far-reaching. The reforms:

- created an environment in which budget votes dominate roll-call voting in Congress;
- created a congressional budget process more independent of the president;
- opened up the budget process and required

the president and executive staff to work more closely with Congress;

- established a coherent and constitutional method of congressional review over presidential impoundments;
- centralized congressional budget decision making and limited the power of authorization committees—and, potentially the power of interest groups and agencies—in the budget process; and
- focused public attention on macroeconomics and microeconomic trade-offs, but with little effect on the controllability of the budget.

Budgeting by the president and Congress has become more democratic yet more conflicted. Frequently, the result is policymaking gridlock. Congress is fundamentally a representative institution. Because it responds to political pressures and public preferences, any effort to make the budget process more efficient is in direct conflict with its constitutional design and natural state. The struggle inside Congress vacillates between centralization and decentralization of authority, and it will continue to cause delay, deadlock, and even a breakdown in congressional-presidential budgeting until the American people wish something different. New budget reforms—such as a balanced budget amendment, a biennial budget, combined appropriations and authorizations committees, or the line-item veto—will be problematic and unlikely to work unless there is a clear public consensus for change.

A major objective of the budget reforms was to force consensus where none had existed. Budgeting rules, however, have not changed the desire of presidents and members of Congress to represent and to be reelected. It is clear that the executive-legislative divisions over budget policy remain as entrenched as ever. Increased budgetary discipline by Congress and the president is not a simple matter of legislation. Congress and the president will continue to bargain and compromise over incremental spending changes no matter what new budget reforms are adopted.

IV  TRENDS

The appropriate role for government in managing, encouraging, and regulating the national economy has been a major source of contention between the Democrats and Republicans throughout their history. In recent years, as the economist Robert B. Reich argues below, Republicans have pushed forward the idea that "everyone benefits when the rich are allowed to keep more of their income for themselves." Democrats have countered with the opposite idea: "taxes on the wealthy should be raised, and government should spread the wealth directly, through a myriad of social programs."

According to Reich, however, the two political parties are both missing the point. In the new world economy of the twenty-first century, he suggests, the key to national wealth will be the skills of the work force and the quality of the social and economic infrastructure that supports them. The answer is not for government to do nothing or for it to redistribute the wealth but for it to adopt a fundamentally new approach to economic problem solving.

Questions

1. The American economy in the twenty-first century, Reich argues, will be fundamentally different from the economy of the past. What will be the key differences, in Reich's view? What are the implications of these differences for the government's role?

2. Consider Reich's proposed agenda in view of the argument of Anthony King (selection 15.1). Would Reich's ideas sell in the American marketplace of ideas? If you were advising a political candidate who sought to implement Reich's program, how might you advise him or her in presenting the idea to the electorate? Do you think your candidate would have a good chance of success on this basis?

15.4 *The REAL Economy*

Robert B. Reich

The central tenet of Republican economics is that everyone benefits when the rich are allowed to keep more of their income for themselves. Ronald Reagan believed that the benefits of the 1981 tax cut for wealthy Americans would "trickle down" to everyone else. For most of his presidency thus far George Bush has claimed that a lower tax on capital gains (which would benefit the wealthy, who own most of the nation's capital assets) would give a surge of momentum to the economy, and thus help all of us. In contrast, the central tenet of Democratic economics is that this allocation of the tax burden isn't fair. Taxes on the wealthy should be raised, and government should spread the wealth directly, through a myriad of social programs.

The two sides were at a stalemate throughout the 1980s. Taxes on the wealthy stayed low *and* entitlements stayed high (while military expenditures grew), with the result that the federal budget ballooned. In last year's [1990] budget agreement both sides conceded a bit: taxes on the rich will rise somewhat (but not anywhere near as high as they were in the late 1970s), and entitlement programs will grow when there is money to finance them. But underlying the compromise—which is more like a truce in an ongoing war—the same choice remains: growth or fairness, private investment or public spending, tax cuts for the rich or entitlements for everyone else. In this contest Republicans continue to represent the brute force of American capitalism, Democrats the softer and more generous side of our natures.

But this isn't the real choice facing Americans as we approach the twenty first century, and it creates a false picture of where the economy is heading and what must be done. Republican economics is wrong: The success of American capitalism no longer depends on the private investments of highly motivated American capitalists. Our nation's future economic success depends instead on our unique attributes—the skills and insights of our work force, and how well we link those skills and insights to the world economy. The Democratic rejoinder is equally wrongheaded: The government's role is not just to spread the wealth. It is to build our human capital and infrastructure, and to bargain with global capital on our behalf. To prepare us for twenty-first-century capitalism, American economic policy must be adapted to the new realities of the world economy.

Global Capital

Again, Republicans have it wrong. The investments of wealthier Americans (who have the wherewithal to save and invest) no longer trickle down to the rest of the American population. Instead, they trickle out to wherever on the globe the best returns can be had. The savings of foreigners, meanwhile, trickle in to find promising projects within the United States. Foreign investments in America rose to a record $2 trillion in 1989, up 12 percent from the year before. Since 1980 foreign capital investment in the United States has increased fourfold. Capital—in the form of loans, shares of stock, and corporate factories, equipment, and research laboratories—moves around the world with scant respect for national boundaries.

Global stock trading is now commonplace. In 1989 Americans poured $13.7 billion into foreign stocks, up 813 percent from 1988. All told, net cross-border equity investments soared to a record $92.3 billion—nearly triple the previous high of $31.7 billion, set in 1986. Such cross-border investments are undertaken quietly; the American investor, assigning his or her savings to a mutual fund, an insurance fund, or a pension plan, may often be unaware of lending to or buying into companies with foreign-sounding names, headquartered in exotic places. But the people who manage the funds, and who compete furiously to achieve higher returns than other fund managers, now scour the globe for investment prospects. There's a good reason: during the 1980s overseas stocks gained an average of 22 percent a year, calculated in U.S. dollars; U.S. stocks gained 17 percent a year. In a recent survey conducted by Louis Harris & Associates, money managers, traders, and corporate finance officers predicted that nearly a quarter of their trading volume would involve foreign securities by 1995, up from 14 percent today. More than half of the 198 corporate treasurers interviewed predicted that in five years they would be selling bonds, stocks, and commercial paper in overseas markets.

American capital also leaves the United States in the form of factories, equipment, and laboratories placed in foreign lands by American-owned corporations. Here, too, the reason is that higher profits are often available abroad. Europe is booming in anticipation of 1992's integrated European market. Many East Asian economies continue to expand at a breakneck

Robert B. Reich   **589**

Ronald Reagan's Legacy: Two Views

Depending on whom you ask, Ronald Reagan's domestic policies were either a great success or a great failure. Either way, they set the terms of the debate over domestic policy, probably for years to come. Here are two assessments of the Reagan presidency from different points of view, both written just after the end of Reagan's second term, in early 1989.

Reagan's Legacy Needs No Slogan

I have never liked the term *Reaganomics*. It symbolizes what's wrong with our economic debates. Sloganeering substitutes for clear thinking.

Reaganomics was a catchword of President Reagan's friends and foes alike to mean whatever they pleased. For both, it signified something new—either wonderful or terrifying. This was always hype. Reagan had no new theory. His economic success rested on an old truth: Private enterprise works. As he leaves office, it's important to get this straight.

Reagan understood (as many economists do not) that private enterprise is the economy's central engine of growth. The quest for bigger markets and profits spurs expansion, innovation, efficiency. This being so, Reagan strove to create a climate in which private enterprise could flourish. Ending double-digit inflation was essential because it subverted growth; people and business couldn't plan for the future. Quite naturally, Reagan supported the Federal Reserve Board's tough anti-inflation policies that led to the deep 1981–82 recession. . . .

He demonstrated that less is more. It's not that the government's main economic tools—changes in interest rates, taxes or government spending—are irrelevant. They can help prevent great depressions (of the 1929–39 variety) or runaway inflation. But trying to use these tools to avert every recession or squeeze a little extra growth from the economy is excessively ambitious. The

economy can't be manipulated so exactly. Two decades of activist policies did more harm than good.

Sadly, this message may be obscured by Reagan's major failure: the budget deficits. They've been so huge that they're often seen as the essence of Reagan's policies, as if nothing else mattered. Yes, the federal debt (the total of all past deficits) has nearly tripled since 1980 to more than $2.6 trillion. Some of Reagan's prosperity was borrowed from the future. People were a little better off, temporarily, because the country went into debt.

But Reagan's critics are wrong when they argue that this failure discredits his entire performance. It's not true, for example, that the budget deficits created the strong Reagan recovery. The budget deficits contributed mostly to big trade deficits. As a nation, Americans were overspending. Most of the extra demand was satisfied by imports; they covered the gap between our production and our purchases. Nor will the budget deficits inevitably cause a future economic crisis. Predictions of catastrophe have repeatedly proved to be overblown.

If Reagan's critics exaggerate, so do his supporters. They're already bragging that the country's recovery vindicates "supply-side economics." Reagan did cut the top personal tax rate from 70% to 33%, as the supply-side approach urged. Although this move was sensible, it didn't unleash a burst of economic growth. During the current recovery, the growth rate of the economy has been about equal to the average of previous postwar recoveries. One reason the economic recovery has lasted so long is that it came after the worst recession since World War II. With unemployment nearly 11% in 1982, there was ample room for expansion. . . .

So forget Reaganomics. Reagan's years are best understood without slogans. Mostly he taught us about economic growth. Government doesn't create it. Private enterprise still has plenty of vitality. Government policies permit, distort or discourage growth. Especially discouraging are high levels of inflation. It will be a pity if these basic lessons aren't learned.

—*Robert J. Samuelson*

I Had a Dream

The last eight years have given us FAX machines, car phones, compact disks, and laptops, but maybe it's just as well nobody has invented a time machine. Because if somebody had, my 1981 self might have received a visit from my 1989 self, and I'm not sure my 1981 self could have stood the aggravation.

"Here's what's happening," the '89 me might tell the '81 me. "We never had that nuclear war you were so worried about. Ditto any new Vietnams. Unemployment's way down. Inflation's almost invisible. There's a woman on the Supreme Court. A movie glorifying Gandhi won the Oscar. The Russians lost in Afghanistan. They'll be out of there in a couple of weeks. Also, they're taking half a million troops plus all their missiles out of Eastern Europe, they published *Darkness at Noon, 1984,* and *Dr. Zhivago,* and Sakharov's back in Moscow troubleshooting for the new Party boss. Martin Luther King's birthday is a national holiday. Jeff Greenfield is a TV star. They've got democracy in Argentina, the Philippines, Pakistan, and South Korea. The national security adviser is a black guy. The PLO swore off terrorism. The Chileans voted to kick out Pinochet—"

"Wait a minute," the '81 me would interrupt. "What is all this? Did they invalidate the results of the 1980 election? Did Reagan and Bush resign and let Tip O'Neill take over? Did benevolent aliens conquer the planet?"

Of course, now-me would be putting then-me

on a bit, not by saying anything untrue, exactly, but by leaving a few things out—things about the Reagan era that haven't been so attractive, like sleaze, homelessness, Lebanon, yuppie scum, the deliberate fostering of extremes of poverty and wealth, environmental negligence, Rambo movies, the selling off of the country's assets to foreigners, Iran-*contra,* staggering sums poured down Pentagon ratholes, and skinhead political TV game shows like "The McLaughlin Group," Morton Downey Jr., the Willie Horton commercial, etc.

Without exception, moreover, these nasty developments can be laid at the doorstep of Reagan and Reaganism. Allotting credit for the plus side is harder. Yes, you have to hand it to Reagan for Madame Justice O'Connor and for sticking to the bipartisan policy of aid to the Afghan resistance. But the advent of a Soviet leader willing to say yes to American arms control proposals that were offered only in the belief that they were too outlandish to be accepted was pure dumb luck. The economic boom, an orgy of consumption financed largely by foreign borrowing, did less than nothing to bolster the productive strength of the economy. If popular and congressional pressure had not deflected the Reagan administration from its original trajectory, the civil rights and environmental enforcement machinery of the government would have been destroyed, abortion would now be a crime, Falwellian Christian piety would be the state religion, the United States would have stuck with "friendly authoritarians" to the end, and American troops would in all likelihood be bogged down in a bloody war in Central America. The checks and balances, fortunately, checked and balanced.

—*Hendrik Hertzberg*

rate (although not quite so fast as they did). Thus, although profits earned in the United States by American multinational corporations dropped by 19 percent in 1989, the overseas profits of these firms surged by 14 percent. Small wonder that American firms, having increased their capital investments abroad by 13 percent in 1989, expected to increase them still more—by a whopping 17 percent—last year, while increasing their American investments by slightly more than six percent. Hewlett-Packard now designs and makes personal computers in France; Texas Instruments makes a large percentage of its semiconductor chips in Japan; more and more of the automobiles produced by the Big Three are designed and engineered in Germany, Italy, or Japan.

Wealthy Americans may reap high returns from their worldwide investments, but the rest of us enjoy few of the beneficial consequences. With the connections between American capitalists and the American economy thus unraveling, all that remains rooted within our borders is the American *people*.

National Assets

The answer isn't simply to take money from the wealthy and spread it around, however, as Democrats often want to do. Even though the investments of individual Americans are becoming disconnected from the American economy, there is a growing connection between the amount and kind of investments we make together as a nation and the capacity of America to attract global capital. Herein the new logic of economic nationalism: the skills and insights of a nation's work force, and the quality of its transportation and communication links to the world (its infrastructure), are what make it unique, and uniquely attractive, in the new world economy. Increasingly, educated brainpower—along with roads, airports, computers, and fiber-optic cables connecting it up—determines a nation's standard of living.

To understand why, it's first necessary to grasp what is happening to the global economy. The highest earnings in most worldwide indus-

tries are to be found in locations where specialized knowledge is brought to bear on problems whose solutions define new horizons of possibility. Whether the industry is old or new, mature or high-tech, specialized knowledge is accounting for a larger and larger portion of its revenues. The hottest sector of the tool-and-die-casting industry, for example, produces precision castings out of aluminum and zinc for computer parts. The leading textile businesses depend on the knowledge needed to produce specially coated and finished fabrics for automobiles, office furniture, rain gear, and wall coverings, among a great many other products. The fastest-growing semiconductor firms make microprocessors and customized chips that are tailored to the particular needs of buyers. As computers with standard operating systems become virtually identical, the high profits come from devising software to meet particular user needs.

Traditional services are experiencing the same rapid transformation. The fastest-growing telecommunications services involve specialized knowledge: voice, video, and information processing; the development of "smart buildings," to connect office telephones, computers, and facsimile machines; and running specialized communications networks that link employees in different locations. The fastest-growing trucking, rail, and air-freight businesses meet shippers' needs for specialized pickups and deliveries, unique containers, and worldwide integration of different modes of transportation. The leading financial businesses offer a wide range of interconnected services, including banking, insurance, and investment, tailored to the unique needs of individuals and companies.

These businesses are highly profitable both because customers are willing to pay a premium for goods and services that exactly meet their needs and, more important, because they are knowledge-intensive businesses that cannot easily be duplicated by low-cost competitors elsewhere in the world. Worldwide competition continues to compress profits on anything that is uniform, routine, and standard—that is, on anything that can be made, reproduced, or extracted in volume almost anywhere on the globe. The evidence shows that successful businesses in advanced nations respond to this dynamic by moving toward the higher ground of specialized products and services.

To be sure, successful companies have not entirely jettisoned high-volume, standardized production. Japanese companies, for example, continue to improve their synchronized systems for mass-producing automobiles, video-cassette recorders, and semiconductor chips. And there will always be a lucrative worldwide market for Coca-Cola, blue jeans, and other staples of modern society. But to maintain competitiveness even in mass-produced commodities requires continuous improvement. Japanese cars, VCRs, and computer chips appear in ever greater variety and at ever higher quality; Coca-Cola develops new formulas and products and marketing techniques. Here, as elsewhere, the barrier to entry is not volume or price; it is skill in finding new and ever-more-valuable connections between particular ideas and particular markets.

The Core Skills

Look closely at these high-value businesses and you see three different but related skills that drive them forward. First are the *problem-solving* skills required to put things together in unique ways (be they alloys, molecules, semiconductor chips, software codes, movie scripts, or pension portfolios). Next are the *problem-identifying* skills required to help customers understand their needs and how those needs can best be met by customized products. In contrast to marketing and selling standard commodities—which requires persuading many customers of the virtues of one particular product, taking lots of orders for it, and meeting sales quotas—the key here is to identify new problems to which customized products might be applicable. The art of persuasion is replaced by the identification of opportunity.

Third are the skills needed to link problem-solvers and problem-identifiers. Those with

such skills must understand enough about specific technologies and markets to see the potential for a new product, raise whatever money is necessary to launch the project, and assemble the right personnel to solve and identify problems. They play the role of *strategic brokers*.

In the high-value businesses, profits derive not from scale and volume but from an ongoing discovery of connections between the solutions to problems and the identification of new needs. The idea of "goods" as something distinct from "services" has become meaningless, because so much of the value provided by a successful enterprise—in fact, the only value that cannot be easily replicated worldwide—entails services: the specialized research, engineering, design, and production services necessary to solve problems; the specialized sales, marketing, and consulting services necessary to identify problems; and the specialized strategic, financial, and management services necessary to broker the first two. High-value enterprises are in the business of providing such services.

Steelmaking, for example, is becoming a service business. When alloys are molded to a specific weight and tolerance, services account for a significant part of the value of the resulting product. Steel service centers help customers choose the steels and alloys they need, and then inspect, slit, coat, store, and deliver the materials. Computer manufacturers are likewise in the service business, because a larger and larger portion of every consumer dollar goes toward customizing software and then integrating and installing systems around it. The immensely successful IBM personal computer comprised a collection of services—research, design, engineering, sales, maintenance; only about 10 or 15 percent of its purchase price reflects the actual cost of manufacture.

America's arcane system of national accounting still has separate categories for manufacturing and services—classifying, for example, computer software as a service (although it is reproduced like a manufactured item), and a computer as manufactured goods (although an ever-larger portion of its cost lies in services).

The pharmaceutical industry is classified under "manufacturing" although production costs represent a tiny fraction of the price of a drug; most costs derive from research and development, clinical trials, patent applications and regulatory clearances, drug marketing, and distribution. Ninety-one percent of the increase in the number of jobs since the 1982 recession was in services, and, remarkably, 73 percent of private-sector employees now work in service businesses. But as the line between services and goods blurs, such numbers are increasingly meaningless—they do not tell us what is actually going on in the economy, and where the real value lies.

A Nation's Key Exports

It follows that the value a nation's work force adds to the world economy is no longer measurable in terms of products shipped across borders. Increasingly a nation's key exports are the skills involved in solving, identifying, and brokering new problems. Products are becoming composites of global services from many different nations. Consider: A London department-store buyer of high-fashion apparel orders a line of dresses devised by a New York fashion designer. Within an hour of the order the designer sends via satellite the drawings and specifications for making the dresses to a fiber-optic link in Hong Kong, where they appear on a high-resolution computer monitor, ready for a manufacturing engineer to transform them into prototype garments. The prototypes are then reproduced in a Chinese factory. The designer, the engineer, and the factory supervisor conduct a video teleconference to work out details, and the finished garments arrive in London less than six weeks after the order was placed. Here, America "exported" a fashion design and some management services linking the design with the London buyer and the Hong Kong and Chinese technicians.

This sort of trade is hard to pin down. When, as now, traders deal repeatedly with one another across borders—exchanging services that are priced not on an open market but by agreement among divisions of the same global corporation or according to complex employment contracts, profit-sharing agreements, or long-term supply arrangements—determinations about what it is that one nation has paid out to another nation can be no better than fair approximations. Thus trade statistics are notoriously imprecise, subject to wide swings and seemingly inexplicable corrections. The truth is that these days no one knows exactly at any given time whether America's (or any other nation's) international trade is in or out of balance, by how much, or what the significance of an imbalance might be. For the same reason, it's becoming impossible for governments seeking to levy corporate taxes to tell exactly how much of a given product is made where. Peter J. Sprague, the chairman of the American-owned National Semiconductor Corporation, says, "We are using Russian engineers living in Israel to design chips that are made in America and then assembled in Asia." Is it an American product? Who can tell?

The notion that products have national origins is so deeply ingrained that governments, and the publics they represent, are often preoccupied with such things as calibrating trade imbalances and determining corporate taxes—both predicated on subtle measurements and elaborate legal definitions—when they should be concerned about a far more relevant issue: what portion of the value of any given product derives from the ability of the nation's workers to conceptualize problems and solutions?

Why Ownership Matters Less

The key industrial struggle of the late nineteenth and the first half of the twentieth century was between those who owned the machines and those who ran them. Each side wanted a larger share of the resulting revenues. American politics reflected this tug-of-war: the Republican Party emerged as the voice of the American industrialist, the Democratic Party as that of the American blue-collar worker. The dominant images of the two parties even today owe much to this struggle.

In the emerging global economy, however, the interests both of laborers and of investors are increasingly subordinated to the interests of those who solve, identify, and broker new problems. This trend has been gathering momentum for several decades. Through the postwar era the wages of U.S. workers engaged in routine production have steadily declined as a percentage of the gross national product, from 11.6 percent in 1949 to approximately 4.6 percent in 1990. During the same interval corporate profits have also diminished as a percentage of the gross national product. In the mid-1960s corporate profits reached 10.98 percent of GNP, and then fell, to 7.48 percent in 1970. Subsequent percentages have been lower at both expansionary heights and recessionary lows. By the end of the 1980s profits claimed only 6.29 percent of GNP.

As the portions of GNP going to routine laborers and to investors have steadily dwindled, the portion going to those who solve or identify problems and those who broker solutions has steadily grown. In 1915 the wages of routine production workers in the typical American manufacturing firm accounted for about 45 percent of the cost of making the product. By 1975 they made up only 25 percent, with most of the remainder going to designers, technicians, researchers, manufacturing engineers, industrial engineers, planners, strategists, financial specialists, accountants, executive officers, lawyers, advertisers, and marketers. Almost 80 percent of the cost of a high-technology item such as a computer is attributable to conceptualizers like these.

The increasing subordination of financial capital to intellectual capital has confused investors. "Owning" a company no longer means what it once did. Members of the accounting profession, not known for public displays of emotion, have fretted openly about the difficulties of informing potential investors about the true worth of enterprises whose value rests in the brains of employees. As intellectual capital continues to displace plant and equipment as the key asset of corporations, shareholders find themselves in an ever more tenuous position, for much of the value of an enterprise can disappear with the departure of key employees. In 1986 General Electric assumed that it had acquired Kidder, Peabody, the financial-services firm. But when GE tried to exert control over its new acquisition, many of Kidder's most highly skilled employees departed for more congenial surroundings.

Certain intellectual assets will remain even after talented employees depart, of course— among them patents and copyrights. But in the emerging economy such distilled intellectual capital often loses its value quickly. After all, patents and copyrights only guard discoveries made at a particular point in time; they do not protect the identification of a specific problem that consumers are eager to solve (for example, how to record television programs for viewing at a more convenient time) or insights gained after the patenting of a given solution (such as that consumers might like a video-cassette recorder to double as a lightweight camcorder). Yet these sorts of discoveries—that a market exists, and that there are various ways to serve it—are often even more valuable than the original patented or copyrighted invention. Problem-solvers, problem-identifiers, and brokers who may have had no part in developing the original product race to exploit the new markets that have been uncovered and stimulated by the discovery. Often, greater rewards flow to quick and clever followers than to brilliant and original inventors. Although legally protected, inventions are rapidly outmoded and replaced.

The steady subordination of financial capital to intellectual capital has confused Americans who worry that foreigners are "buying up" the nation's technological assets. Such worries are usually unfounded. In fact it is often the case that without the foreign money, the intellectual capital that has already accumulated in the United States would not develop further.

Consider two typical American firms that were acquired by foreigners in 1989: Materials Research, a semiconductor-equipment manufacturer whose American owners sold it to Sony after the firm found it impossible to raise money from American investors or to borrow it from American banks; and Arco Solar, sold to Germany's Siemens by Atlantic Richfield, the giant American oil company, which was no longer willing to finance Arco's effort to become the world leader in photovoltaic technology. Superficially it appears that foreigners are running off with two of America's leading-edge technology companies. But look closely at these two firms and you find groups of American problem-solvers and problem-identifiers who have accumulated potentially valuable insights about how to produce highly efficient semiconductor equipment and solar energy, respectively. In acquiring them, the foreign firms have not destroyed this cumulative learning, nor have they enslaved these Americans and shipped them back to Japan and Germany; the American problem-solvers and problem-identifiers have no intention of leaving the United States. That some of the profits now go to investors outside the United States is no cause for great alarm; the assets with the greatest value, commanding the highest return, remain within our borders.

Such cumulative skills and insights, upon which future innovations are based, make up the nation's key technological assets. They will be lost only if insufficiently nurtured and developed, as they might have been in these cases had foreign capital not come to the rescue.

The Virtuous Cycle

In the emerging economy of the twenty-first century only one asset is growing more valuable as it is used: the problem-solving, problem-identifying, and strategic-brokering skills of a nation's citizens. Unlike machinery that gradually wears out, raw materials that become depleted, and patents and copyrights that grow obsolete, the skills and insights that come from discovering new linkages between technologies and needs increase with practice.

The more complex the task, the better preparation it provides for the next, even more complex task. One puzzle leads to another. Assembling just the right combination of technical and marketing skills to develop software for assisting mechanical engineers can help strategic brokers gain insight into what's needed to develop more complex software for aerospace engineers. Developing and marketing specialty chemicals can lead to developing and marketing high-performance ceramics and single-crystal silicon. And so forth.

Conventional economic theory assumes that a resource gets used up when it is put to work. As it becomes scarce, its price increases; the price rise in turn encourages buyers to conserve the resource and find cheaper substitutes, which ultimately brings the price down again. One of the great advantages of a price system, as all economists will quickly attest, is that it tends to balance itself automatically. But human capital operates according to a different principle. Because people learn through practice, the value of what they do tends to increase as they gain experience. This system is not self-correcting, in the sense that workers who first gain knowledge and insights do not eventually lose whatever premium in price they have commanded in world markets when others catch up with them. Rather, a work force can become steadily more valuable over time as insights lead to other insights.

Thus a virtuous cycle can be set in motion: A work force possessing a good basic education, which can efficiently bring the fruits of its labors to the global economy, can attract global capital for its performance of moderately complex tasks. The experience gained by performing these tasks generates additional on-the-job training and experience, which serve to lure global capital for more-complex activities. As skills build and experience accumulates, the nation's citizens receive more and more from the rest of the world in exchange for their services—which permits them to invest in better schools, transportation, research, and communications systems. As their problem-solving, problem-identifying, and brokering skills grow, and their links with the world steadily improve, their income rises.

But without adequate skills and infrastructure, the relationship can be the opposite—a vicious cycle in which global money and technology are lured only by low wages and low taxes. These enticements in turn make it more difficult to finance adequate education and infrastructure; the jobs available under these conditions provide little on-the-job training or experience pertinent to more-complex jobs in the future. Such a vicious cycle has no natural stopping place. Theoretically it can continue to push wages downward until the citizens of the nation (or region, or city) have a standard of living like that typical of the Third World.

The choice is rarely as stark as this, of course. Virtuous or vicious cycles gather momentum gradually, and often imperceptibly. No one would intentionally choose the vicious cycle, but in the contest for global capital such a choice is sometimes made implicitly. Politicians are everywhere trying to lure the world's capital, like traveling salesmen hawking their wares or carnival barkers pitching their special attractions. Mikhail Gorbachev tells business leaders in Minneapolis about the benefits of investing in the Soviet Union; President Gnassingbe Eyadema, of Togo, courts executives in Atlanta; Governor Bill Clinton sells Japanese business executives on the wonders of Arkansas; Mayor David Dinkins touts New York to European investors. Similar pitches must be made even to hometown investors, lest they take their savings elsewhere. "There is the greatest competition in the last forty-five years for financial capital," William T. Archey, the international vice-president of the U.S. Chamber of Commerce, told *The Washington Post.* The U.S. Chamber of Commerce is visited every eight to ten days by some foreign delegation seeking investments by American companies.

Some carnival barkers promise skilled workers and world-class infrastructure; others promise low wages. If they want to improve the standard of living of their citizens, they will make the former kind of promise, and they will bargain for the sort of jobs that will give their workers on-the-job training in conceptualizing problems and solutions.

In virtuous cycles low wages are not the central attraction. The average worker in the former West Germany earns a higher hourly wage than the average American, but global capital is nonetheless attracted to Germany by the nation's pool of skilled workers and its first-class transportation and communications facilities. There most non-college-bound young people enter apprenticeship programs, in which they learn technical skills. Germany is already on the way to transforming its modern system of autobahns into "smart" superhighways that can regulate traffic flow by computer. France, another high-wage nation, has provided a videotext system free of charge to all telephone subscribers, has recently launched a computerized library and information bank designed to be accessible from every home, and is aggressively training scientists and engineers. Japan is building a $250 billion fiber-optic network that by the year 2000 will carry video, voice, and data around the nation up to 1,000 times faster than existing networks can. All three of these nations are spending significant sums of money on education, training, and research and development.

The National Bargain

It is easier to form a virtuous relationship with global capital if you are a nation strongly committed to economic development—ruled by a benevolent dictator like Singapore's Lee Kuan Yew, dominated by a single political party and an "old boy" oligarchy, as in Japan, or habituated to a form of corporatist planning orchestrated by big banks and major industrial firms, as in Germany. In such countries political power is sufficiently concentrated that substantial resources can be mobilized for education, training, research, and infrastructure—and sacrifices can be elicited from the public in order to make these investments. Moreover, deals can be cut with global corporations—offering subsidies, tax breaks, or access to the national market in exchange for good jobs.

But what of a decentralized and contentious democracy like the United States, which deeply distrusts concentrated power? Apart from war emergencies, are we able to make large public investments and demand sacrifices of ourselves in order to pay for them? Are we capable of bargaining with global corporations?

Much of the responsibility for America's national economic development has fallen by default to states and cities. America bids for global capital through fifty state governments that compete against one another, and thousands of cities and townships, which also compete. Who successfully lures the jobs becomes a matter of state and local pride as well as employment; it may also bear significantly on the future careers of politicians who have pledged to win them. The possibility of establishing a factory in the region sets off a furious auction; a threat to remove one initiates equally impassioned negotiations. All too often these jurisdictions bargain for routine jobs that will be automated out of existence in years to come or else will drift to the Third World. Lacking educated workers and up-to-date infrastructure, many of our governors and mayors have little to offer except what is euphemistically known as a "good business environment"—meaning low wages, few regulations, low taxes, and generous subsidies.

Forty-three states maintain offices in foreign capitals for the express purpose of bargaining for global capital, according to the National Association of State Development Agencies. Unlike most nations, which have a unified international economic strategy, the United States has dozens—emanating from such places as Little Rock, Arkansas, and Lansing, Michigan. When Chrysler-Mitsubishi's Diamond-Star Motors announced, in 1985, that it would begin assembling automobiles in America, four states (Illinois, Indiana, Michigan, and Ohio) entered the competition. The winner was Illinois, which offered a ten-year package of direct aid and incentives worth $276 million—or about $25,000 for every new job that Mitsubishi planned to create in the state. As the bidding has intensified during the past fifteen years, the incentives

have become more generous. In 1977 the state of Ohio induced Honda to build an auto plant there by promising $22 million in subsidies and tax breaks; by 1986 it took a $100 million package from Kentucky for Toyota to create about the same number of jobs there.

The total amount of subsidies and tax breaks flowing to global firms of whatever nationality is much higher than it would be if the United States did its bargaining as a whole, through the federal government. Nations whose constituent parts refrain from internecine battles end up paying far less to lure jobs their way. Although direct comparisons between the United States and other nations are hard to come by, an analogous situation suggests the magnitude of the difference. In seeking the rights to televise the 1988 Olympic Games in Calgary, the Western European nations bid as a whole. In the United States, in contrast, each television network made its own separate bid. The Western European market contains even more people than the U.S. market, with buying power that is at least as great. Nevertheless, because Western Europe negotiated as a whole, it got the rights to televise the Olympics in Europe for $5.7 million. The winning network in the United States paid $309 million to televise the Olympics here.

Disinvestment

Even if America bargained for global capital as a nation, it would still have difficulty attracting good jobs unless it could offer an educated work force and first-class transportation and communication systems. And here lies a more serious problem. For even as other nations have been increasing their public investments in people and infrastructure, the United States as a *nation* has been cutting back. . . . Federal spending on infrastructure, nondefense research and development, and education has steadily dropped as a proportion of the gross national product from 1980 onward. By 1990 federal investment as a proportion of GNP was lower in each of these categories than it was in 1970. States and cities with large populations of poorer Americans have been hard pressed to make up the difference.

Consider infrastructure. David Aschauer, an economist at Bates College and formerly a researcher at the Federal Reserve Bank of Chicago, has shown a direct link between America's investments in infrastructure and the productivity of the nation's work force: a one-dollar increase in the stock of public infrastructure adds as much to the productivity of Americans as a four-dollar increase in the stock of business capital. His calculations imply that a one-time increase of $10 billion in the stock of public infrastructure would result in a *permanent* increase of $7 billion in the annual GNP. Aschauer's study has been criticized for being too optimistic; after all, he demonstrates only that public investment and national productivity growth have increased and decreased together, over the same interval of time—not that the one necessarily caused the other. But even accepting the possibility of other explanations for why American productivity growth has slowed, the correlation is striking. The United States began to cut back on public investments just when public investments became uniquely important in the new global economy.

In the early 1960s the United States began building a modern transportation system. Spending on infrastructure at all levels of government then absorbed almost four percent of the nation's GNP; it held that position through the 1960s. That's when we began to build the interstate highway system, for example. The productivity of the American work force soared. But the growth of public spending on the nation's transportation system declined throughout the 1970s, just as our productivity growth declined. Infrastructure spending declined even more sharply in the 1980s, to the point where the nation was spending only two percent of GNP on building and maintaining infrastructure. Hence the specter of collapsing bridges, crumbling highways, and rush-hour traffic jams extending for miles.

Although part of the decline in spending represents a failure to maintain existing infrastructure, spending on new infrastructure has fallen even more dramatically, from 2.3 percent of GNP in 1963 to only one percent in 1989. As Western Europe and Japan lay plans for "smart" roads, high-speed trains, and national information networks, America lies dormant; the nation has not even built a new airport since 1974. As of the beginning of [1990] Washington was annually investing about the same amount of money in infrastructure (in constant dollars) as it had invested thirty years before, although the gross national product had grown 144 percent in the interim. It is projected that physical capital investment, which accounted for 24 percent of total federal outlays in 1960, will account for less than 11 percent in 1991.

Expenditures on public elementary and secondary education have shown a similarly perverse pattern—falling short just as intellectual capital has become a uniquely important national asset. Many politicians and business leaders (and many ordinary citizens) are quick to claim that the current crisis in public education is unrelated to a lack of public funding. One premise of their argument—that there are many means of improving American schools that do not require large public outlays—is surely correct. Yes, responsibility for teaching needs to be transferred from educational bureaucracies to classroom teachers; and yes, the inculcation of basic skills must be the primary mission of the schools.

Researchers have, however, found that schools with smaller classes and better-paid teachers produce young people who command higher salaries once they join the work force. David Card and Alan Krueger, researchers at Princeton University, studied the education and incomes of a million men born from 1920 to 1949 who attended public schools. They found that even within the same socio-economic group, higher lifetime earnings correlate with smaller class size and better-paid teachers (for every year of schooling above eighth grade, students' subsequent earnings increased 0.4 percent for every five fewer students per teacher, and for every 10 percent hike in teacher salaries, subsequent earnings increased 0.1 percent). The extra tax revenues generated by these higher lifetime incomes alone would finance the smaller classes and better-paid teachers.

Controlled for inflation, public spending on primary and secondary education per student increased during the 1980s, when the nation began to fret openly about the quality of its public schools, but not appreciably faster than it did during the 1970s. From 1970 to 1980 annual spending per student grew 36 percent in real terms; since 1980 it has grown 38 percent.

Yet there are several reasons for believing that the more recent increases have been inadequate. First is the comparative measure of what other nations are spending. By the late 1980s America's per-pupil expenditures were below per-pupil expenditures (converted to dollars using 1988 exchange rates) in eight other nations—namely, Sweden, Norway, Japan, Denmark, Austria, West Germany, Canada, and Switzerland. (Even using the exchange rate from 1985, when the dollar was at its height relative to other currencies, the United States is still behind—but in fourth place rather than ninth.)

International comparisons aside, it is true that the demands on public education in the United States have grown significantly during the past fifteen years. Increasing numbers of broken homes, single-parent households, and immigrants (both legal and illegal) have placed great strains on our schools, particularly in poor inner-city and rural areas. And with one out of five American children now falling below the poverty line—a significantly higher proportion than obtained fifteen years ago—the challenges are magnified. As for today's teachers, their wages have barely risen in real terms since the early 1970s—and yet talented women today have many more lucrative career options than teaching, and we also want to attract talented men to the profession.

Ironically, the schools facing the biggest social problems have been getting the least help. The averaging of figures on per-pupil expendi-

tures in the United States disguises growing disparities among states and school districts. As federal support for elementary and secondary education has waned and states and localities have been forced to pick up the bill, the burden has fallen especially heavily on the poorest jurisdictions with the most limited tax bases. New Trier High School, in one of Chicago's most affluent suburbs, pays its teachers 34 percent more than the average teacher in Chicago's public high schools, whose pedagogic challenges are substantially greater. Public schools in White Plains and Great Neck, two of the richest suburbs of New York, spend twice as much per pupil as schools in the Bronx. (The first set of students in each of these comparisons is on the way to a virtuous relationship with global capital, the second set to a vicious one.)

In 1965 the nation decided that all students who qualified to attend college should have access to higher education. Here again, public investment ranked high on the nation's agenda. The resulting Higher Education Act established a system of grants and loan guarantees for low-income students, thus increasing their proportion even at private universities, from 22 to 26 percent by the mid-1970s. But by 1988, with grants and loan guarantees drying up, the proportion of low-income students at private universities had fallen below 20 percent. The high costs of higher education have helped to push them out and set them on their way toward a vicious relationship with global capital. (In the compromise 1991 budget federal funds for student aid will increase 10 percent for the academic year 1991–1992, but the prospect for the following year looks grim.) Meanwhile, in an equally ominous development, the federal retreat from higher education is being replicated at the state level. The rate of increase in state support for higher education dropped to a thirty-year low in 1990, representing the smallest increment since data on this subject have been collected. State universities have long promoted mobility among children of less affluent families. These data suggest that in the future there will be less mobility. Even high schoolers safely in the middle class are being squeezed out of college. From 1982 to 1989, while the proportion of American middle-income families ($40,000 to $60,000) dropped five percent, the proportion of middle-income students in public universities dropped 10 percent.

Federal support for research and development (excluding defense and space) has also languished; it now accounts for 0.31 percent of GNP, the smallest proportion in twenty years. Corporate America hasn't filled the gap. All told, nondefense R&D accounts for two percent of GNP in the United States, compared with almost three percent in Japan and 2.6 percent in the former West Germany. We have sacrificed, as a consequence, not breakthrough discoveries (which, after all, are almost immediately shared in by the scientific community and corporations worldwide) but the know-how and experience that come from *doing* current research.

While Western Europe, Japan, and many developing nations are ensuring that their scientists and engineers are ready to embrace the microelectronic and molecular technologies of the future, America is squandering its scientific and engineering brainpower. Federal funding of university research dropped 18 percent in real terms from 1967 to 1990. The National Science Foundation's 1990 budget for most small research projects in mathematics, physics, chemistry, engineering, biology, and computer science—the seed corn of science—fell below even that for 1988. Steven Younger, of the Los Alamos National Laboratory, told *The New York Times*, "The foundation of university science is dying."

Federal funding to train and retrain workers, meanwhile, dropped by more than 50 percent during the 1980s, from $13.2 billion to $5.6 billion. Most other industrialized nations—including Germany, France, Britain, and Japan—devote a much higher percentage of their GNP to workplace training. Private training, the costs of which corporations deduct from their taxable

incomes, has hardly made up the difference. American companies claim to spend some $30 billion a year training their employees, but most of these funds have been used on what is euphemistically termed "executive training." College graduates are 50 percent more likely to be trained by their corporations than are high school graduates, and employees with postgraduate degrees are 30 percent more likely than college graduates. Those who lack a rudimentary educational background receive little compensatory training from the private sector.

Can We Afford It?

The official reason given for why America cannot invest more money in infrastructure, education, research, and training is that we cannot afford it. In his inaugural address George Bush noted regretfully, "We have more will than wallet." It has become a frequent lament. But only excessive politeness constrains one from inquiring, Whose will? Whose wallet?

The claim that America cannot afford to invest any more money than it does in the future productivity of its citizens is a curious one, to say the least. Americans are not overtaxed. In 1989 we paid less in taxes as a percentage of GNP (about 30 percent) than the citizens of any other industrialized country. Wealthy Americans, in particular, are not overtaxed. Their marginal income-tax rate is the lowest top rate in any industrialized nation. Nor does the U.S. government overspend. If defense is excluded from the calculation, the combined spending of state, local, and federal government accounts for a smaller share of GNP in America than in any other industrialized country, including Japan.

This nation was willing to dig deep into its wallet to rebuild Western Europe and Japan after the Second World War. Now, with an economy four times as large as it was then, we should be able to rebuild America. Bush has it backward: We have the wallet. What we lack is the will. Republicans do not want taxes on the wealthy raised; Democrats do not want entitlement programs diminished for the middle class. As a result, less and less is left over for public investment.

The current debate between Republicans and Democrats over economic growth or fairness obscures the real issue, which is how much we are willing to invest in the future productivity of Americans. Each year the American economy generates about $5 trillion worth of goods and services. If we dedicated only four percent of this sum—about $200 billion a year—to public investment during the 1990s, the nation could get ready for the twenty-first century.

Where would the money come from? First: a more progressive income tax. During each of the past few years American citizens have had about $3,500 billion to spend, after taxes. About half this sum has gone to the lower four fifths of wage earners, the other half to the top fifth. Were the personal income tax as progressive as it was even as late as 1977, in 1989 the top tenth would have paid $93 billion more in taxes than they did. At that rate, from 1991 to 2000 they would contribute close to a trillion dollars more, even if their incomes failed to rise.

Second: limiting entitlements to those who need them. If there were no cap on the income on which the pension and disability portions of Social Security payroll taxes are levied, and if all Social Security benefits were treated as taxable income, another $600 billion would be freed during the decade.

Third: defense cuts. If defense spending were to fall during the decade by 15 percent (a fairly modest, and by most accounts realistic, decrease, even considering the cost of policing regional conflicts in the Middle East and elsewhere), we would have an additional $450 billion. A strong national economy is more important to our national security than troops and weapons.

The grand total: more than $2 trillion for the 1990s—to say nothing of all the savings that could be achieved by bargaining with global capital through the federal government instead of the states and cities. This sum would constitute a significant down payment on the future productivity of *all* Americans. The $2 trillion should be spent on education (at all levels), training, research, and infrastructure. It should *not* be used to reduce the budget deficit. Contrary to what many in government and much of the public assumes, there is nothing wrong with being indebted so long as the borrowings are invested in means of enhancing our future wealth. In fact, taking on debt for this purpose is preferable to maintaining a balanced budget by deferring or cutting back on such investments. Debt is a problem only if the borrowings are squandered on consumption. Any competent business person understands the soundness of this principle: If necessary, you borrow in order to invest in the greater future productivity of your enterprise. Once the new levels of productivity are achieved, they enable you to pay back the debt and enjoy higher returns thereafter.

To be sure, we have already engaged in a consumption frenzy, in the 1980s; can we afford to embark on a new era of investment off this base of indebtedness? The question should be reversed: Can we afford not to? Our future capacity both to pay off the debt and to assure our children and grandchildren a high standard of living depends largely on the public investments we make today—a principle that we have irresponsibly neglected over the past decade. The long-term case is compelling. But even as a short-term anti-recession strategy, increasing public investment makes sense.

Politicians and business leaders are quick to concede the central importance of national economic strength, but they fail to comprehend the new basis of that strength, which is to an ever greater extent public investments in work-force skills and infrastructure. "Increased economic strength is . . . fundamental to success in the global competition with rising economic superpowers," the Bush Administration noted, correctly, in its 1991 budget submission to Congress. "Thus, there is a first-order issue for the budget (and the economic policy it represents): How can it best preserve and build upon America's strengths, while advancing the American economy toward even greater capacities for leadership and growth?" Having asked the right question, Bush's budget wizards got the answer wrong. They advocated public parsimony—sometimes outright cuts—in infrastructure, education, training, and related public endeavors, accompanied by reductions in the tax rate for capital gains. "National economic strength" was tacitly equated with the savings and investments of individual Americans. Further, the Administration has signaled that whatever savings result from smaller defense outlays should be used to cut the budget deficit and, if possible, reduce taxes, rather than be invested in good schools, roads, and other forms of public capital.

Yet the national wealth no longer depends, as it once did, on the accumulation of financial capital in American hands. It depends on the development of the skills and insights of our citizens, and on the infrastructure necessary to link them to the new world economy. The Democrats have displayed almost as little insight on this point as have the Republicans. In the final budget compromise of last October [1990] the Democrats carefully insulated Social Security benefits from future cuts by removing the entire program from budget calculations, and barely touched Medicare. As a result, these programs for the elderly will account for the only real growth in domestic spending to occur between now and the year 2000. But what about the nation's future productivity? As part of the same compromise, the total of public investments in education, training, research and development, and infrastructure will be frozen at the 1991 level, adjusted for inflation. (Slight increases for several of these programs in 1991 will be offset by cuts in 1992.) It was further agreed that any additional revenues from tax increases would be used only to expand entitlements or to reduce the budget deficit.

A message for Republicans and Democrats alike: Stop fighting over how much money government is taking from the wealthy and redistributing to everyone else. Start worrying about the capacity of Americans to add value to the emerging global economy. What we own is coming to be far less important than what we are able to do.

V ■ ISSUE AND DEBATE: DID WE WIN THE WAR ON POVERTY?

The War on Poverty was the most ambitious set of social programs—with the exception of the New Deal—in American history. The attempt to wipe out poverty in America was conceived by the Kennedy administration and implemented by the Johnson administration, part of the larger set of social policy initiatives that came to be known as the Great Society. President Johnson revealed the program in his first State of the Union address, in January 1964. "This administration today, here and now, declares unconditional war on poverty in America," he told the nation. "It will not be a short or easy struggle," he warned; but it was a war "we cannot afford to lose."

No one would disagree with the statement that Johnson's war on poverty, combined with all the other welfare policy initiatives of the 1960s and early 1970s, fundamentally changed the federal government's role in assisting lower-income Americans. Whether the war was actually won, however, is another question. The following two selections present two views on that question. John E. Schwartz argues that America did win the war on poverty; Charles Murray charges that those who most needed help—particularly poor blacks and members of other minority groups—actually suffered as a result of these federal programs. He also suggests why the programs failed:

they did not provide the poor with appropriate or realistic incentives to encourage them to climb their way out of poverty.

Both Murray and Schwartz wrote during the Reagan era. Murray's book became a favorite of conservatives who sought to downplay the federal government's role in the welfare state; Schwartz's book became a favorite source for liberals seeking to defend that role. In both style and in substance, these two books capture the ongoing debate over welfare policy in the United States.

Questions

1. Is there any way to reconcile the arguments by Schwartz and Murray? Might it be argued that the war was won in one sense but was lost in another? Did Americans win certain battles on poverty but lose the war? lose certain battles but win the war?

2. After any war, one can ask not only whether the war was won but whether it was worth the cost. What were the costs of the war on poverty? Were they worth paying?

YES

15.5 America's Hidden Success

John Schwartz

[Schwartz begins with a snapshot of American poverty in 1960–1961 and then argues that the War on Poverty was a success and that it was won not by private economic growth but by the programs of the federal government.]

Poverty in America

Scenes from the winter of 1960–61:

A 33-year-old man . . . was found hanged in his apartment just seven hours ago. He was apparently despondent over not being able to find a job, and unemployment compensation had been exhausted. His wife and four children had left him and had returned to Mississippi where they had immigrated from seven years ago. The family had been several months [in] arrears in rent, and there was not proper food and clothing for the family during the harsh Chicago winter months.

A man over the age of forty has been in search of a job for eighteen months: "When I come to the hiring window, the man just looks at me: he doesn't even ask questions: he says. 'You're too old.'"

She gently wept as she told me of her small daughter: "I can remember just like it was yesterday at the hospital with my Lisa. We didn't eat much in those days. Maybe we'd have potatoes and bread is all, or beans. We had one room and it was always cold and damp. A lot of sickness, too. This time Lisa was sick, so sick I didn't know what to do her fever was so high. Scared is what I was. I went down to the hospital carrying her in my arms. I had no doctor, no money. I sat the whole day through in the hospital rocking her. The whole day just waiting to see a doctor until my Lisa died right in my arms.

Because the percentage of people living below the poverty line in the United States remained substantial even at the end of the 1950s, the attempt to reduce poverty in America was no small undertaking at the start of the post-Eisenhower years. In the wealthiest nation ever at the beginning of the 1960s about one in every five of us lived in a condition of poverty. Flagrant malnutrition, substandard housing, and pitifully inadequate medical care were common.

Consider this. Imagine all the people living today in the industrial states of Massachusetts and Michigan, with such cities as Boston and Detroit. Then add all the people living in the states of Minnesota, Colorado, Oregon, Arizona, Maryland, and Kentucky. These states contain Minneapolis, St. Paul, Denver, Portland, Phoenix, Tucson, Baltimore, and Louisville. To complete the picture, include some of the more rural states such as New Hampshire, South Carolina, and Iowa. Then imagine every person in every one of these states living in poverty. That describes the number of people and the breadth of the poverty existing in America in 1960 at the end of the Eisenhower era.

Another point must be understood. Many Americans living in poverty either had jobs or had worked for their entire adult life. During the early 1960s, the heads of about half the families living in poverty held jobs, and one out of every four impoverished family heads had full-time employment all year long. Even in the last half of the 1970s, about 1 million heads of poor families in America who were employed full time were still living below the poverty line. They and their dependents numbered almost 5 million Americans. The size of the problem is made real enough by these figures. As head of a family of four, could a worker earn his or her way out of poverty? Possibly, but for many Americans—bookkeepers, laborers, janitors, secretaries, household workers, library aides, small farmers, cashiers, receptionists, nurse's aides—not easily.

With poverty facing from 30 million to 40 million Americans in 1960, and near-poverty facing millions more, the government created or greatly enlarged many programs during the ensuing Kennedy, Johnson, and Nixon years. These programs can be divided into at least three general categories. First, some programs gave direct aid in the form of income, which recipients could use for any purpose. Among the well-known examples are Aid to Families with Dependent Children, supplemental income programs for the impoverished elderly, social security, and unemployment compensation. A second kind of program worked toward a more specific end. It was intended to assure that certain basic needs would be met, particularly the nutritional, medical, and housing needs of impoverished persons as well as other categories of persons covered under the programs. The best known among these programs are Medicare and Medicaid, food stamps, and the public housing and rent supplement programs. The third type of program had quite a different objective. It sought to improve the skills of impoverished or near-impoverished persons to enable them to become independent, and thus to compete and earn a secure living in the private economy. Examples of these programs are Head Start and the job training and job creation programs.

Toward the end of the 1960s, a view emerged that suggested that these social programs had been expanded far more than Americans wanted and that the programs had become more creatures of the government than the expression of the public. This idea took many forms. Most memorable were the repeated references to the existence of a "silent majority" of Americans whose attitudes were very different from those expressed in the domestic goals and programs of the government. However, evidence from a succession of public-opinion polls indicates that a solid majority of Americans backed the government's effort to reduce poverty from the start and continued to do so throughout and even beyond the period during which the programs had become fully established. In acting to eliminate poverty and

"Here is the way it works: We take from the rich and give to the poor—keeping only enough for salaries, travel, equipment, depreciation, and so on, and so on."

Drawing by Ross; © 1968 The New Yorker Magazine, Inc.

in greatly enlarging the programs, the government traveled down paths that virtually all segments of the American public warmly approved.

The Results of the Attack on Poverty

Perhaps the best overall indicator of the substantial progress made by the nation in the battle against poverty after 1960 is that by the second half of the 1970s only 4 to 8 percent of the American public remained beneath the poverty level compared with about 18 percent in 1960. These figures take into account the income Americans received from every source, including income from all private economic activities and the private sector as well as from governmental programs. In the space of one generation, the economic growth of the times combined with the government's programs had reduced poverty among Americans by about 60 percent.

To what extent did this accomplishment owe itself to the government's programs as contrasted to the extraordinary expansion of the

nation's economy over much of the period? To many, the answer is obvious. Probably most would agree with Martin Anderson, formerly President Reagan's chief domestic aide, who emphasizes the growing economy. In his view the most important single force was "the strong, sustained economic growth of the private sector." This answer is so obvious to Anderson that he feels little need to offer much evidence in its defense. He simply points to the vigorous economic growth that took place in the nation during the 1960s and early 1970s; the enormous expansion of real national income as well as of wages and salaries and the spectacular growth in new jobs that occurred over these years. From this it follows, presumably, that poverty would also be greatly reduced. True, the private sector provided 83 percent of all employment during the post-Eisenhower years. Considering the sheer magnitude of the private sector, perhaps it is only natural to infer that the economic growth of the private sector was a prime factor in the reduction of poverty in America.

This common presumption, however, is in error. Rather, the reduction of poverty was accomplished primarily through the government's programs. Anderson is correct in stating that real economic growth mushroomed from 1960 to 1980. To appreciate the government's contribution to the reduction of poverty, we can look at the decline in poverty during a period of vigorous economic expansion at the midpoint of the post-Eisenhower years. From 1965 through 1972, the real, disposable income per American rose, on an average, about 3 percent per year, or 24 percent over the seven years. Because I am speaking of real, disposable income, this 24 percent growth is what remained in our pockets *after* subtracting for inflation and most taxes that we paid to the government. More growth in real, disposable income per American occurred in the seven years from 1965 to the end of 1972 than took place during the entire decade of the glorious 1950s, when income per person climbed by about 13 percent. The gross national product also rose at a faster annual rate between 1965 and 1972 than it had during the 1950s.

Surely one would anticipate that a period of such robust economic growth—growth that was very strong after inflation and taxes— would lower the percentage of impoverished Americans. The validity of this presumption can be examined by considering what the private economy accomplished in reducing poverty. Let us compare 1965 and 1972. When one takes all income except that transferred to individuals through governmental programs, census evidence for 1965 indicates that about 21.3 percent of the public would have been living in poverty; in 1972, again considering all sources of income except that received from governmental programs, census figures show that about 19.2 percent of the public would have been living in poverty, about one-tenth less than in 1965. Thus, the private sector, in these times of substantial economic growth, reduced the percentage of Americans living in poverty by about one in every ten Americans; and exclusive of governmental programs, even by 1972 almost one in five Americans would still have been living in poverty.

Obviously, the economy's growth during these highly prosperous years alleviated poverty only marginally. In contrast to private economic performance, consider the performance of the programs of government. As a result of the government's programs, more than half of the remaining 19 percent of impoverished Americans rose above the poverty line, leaving about 9 percent of the American people below the poverty line by 1972; and by the late 1970s that figure was further reduced to between 7 and 8 percent, and possibly even lower.

But how could this be? Why did vigorous economic growth on its own make such little headway in reducing poverty among Americans? Why were governmental programs necessary? The experience of the 1960s and early 1970s reveals fissures in the theory that poverty will necessarily be reduced by a robustly growing economy. For in certain crucial circumstances, economic growth does not help the very weak. Several major groups of Americans—groups that comprised millions upon millions of people across the nation—were almost completely excluded from the benefits of the private economic growth that occurred over these years.

The expanding economy did not directly touch, at least not very much, the impoverished elderly, for example. Most of our elderly are retired. Senior citizens who try to find jobs after retirement soon learn—if they can locate new employment at all—that the private sector is often unwilling to pay more than a marginal wage to people over 65 who reenter the labor market. This reality becomes ever more omnipresent when the labor markets are overcrowded with job seekers and the competition for jobs is intense, a circumstance that prevailed during the entire 1965–80 period with the maturation of the children of the postwar "baby boom" and the increased number of women taking up employment due to a change in attitude about entering the work force and necessity engendered by the rising incidence of marital separation and divorce. Although the private economy grew markedly in the second half of the 1960s and early 1970s, it hardly touched the poverty level of the elderly at all, male or female. Real, disposable income per person rose by about 24 percent during the 1965–72 period in the nation as a whole; yet, outside the effects of the government's programs, the percentage of male-headed elderly families below the poverty line declined by only 6 percent, from 57 to 51 percent. For female-headed elderly families, the percentage remained at 45 both in 1965 and 1972, amounting to no reduction in poverty at all among these families outside the functioning of the government's programs. Thus, a prosperously growing economy in the nation at large did little, directly, for the impoverished elderly.

A second important group of Americans bypassed by the expanding economy included white and nonwhite families headed by women under the age of 65. Although more than one in seven families are headed by women, the average earnings of women in the private economy are about 60 percent that of males. In addition, the jobs available to women are often dead end, with little possibility for advancement. Again, when the labor markets teem and the competition for jobs is severe, opportunities for women are particularly limited. In this light, consider the plight of white female family heads under the age of 65. The period from 1965 through 1972 produced a remarkable result with respect to this group. Exclusive of the government's programs, a slightly *higher* proportion of these female-headed families found themselves in poverty in 1972 than in 1965: Forty percent of these families lived in poverty in 1972, an increase of 4 percent over 1965. And the figures for nonwhite female family heads under the age of 65 are no more encouraging. The nation's substantial economic growth made little dent in the levels of poverty experienced by these families, for, aside from the government's programs, poverty within this group dropped only 3 percent, from 69 percent in 1965 to 66 percent in 1972.

The situation encountered by women in the private sector of the economy has always been difficult. Even after very high rates of growth, the private economy left millions of women and their families in poverty, as great a percentage after the economic expansion as before. Traditionally, the job opportunities available to women have been more marginal than those available to men, and in the crowded labor markets of the post-Eisenhower years, the competition women faced in getting better jobs only increased in intensity as compared with earlier years. In addition, as family separations grew in numbers, more and more single women were required to assume the role of family head. Employment opportunities for women with very young children to care for are indeed scarce. This combination of very difficult circumstances helps explain what the census figures on poverty show: Had it not been for the government's presence, hardly any change in the rate of poverty facing this very large group of Americans would have been realized over the whole of this prosperous period.

The plight of a third group, really a subgroup of females, the families headed by females under the age of 25, is similarly desperate. For the young, who are just beginning their work careers, are highly vulnerable in a labor market full to overflowing and an economy undergoing change. The rate of poverty among these families in 1965 was 62 percent; by 1972, although personal income growth in real terms had risen by more than one-fifth per American in the nation at large, the percentage of these families living beneath the poverty level remained the same. Seven years of vigorous economic growth had not alleviated their situation by even one percentage point.

On its own, above-average economic expansion reduced the overall rate of poverty among American people marginally, from 21.3 percent (exclusive of governmental programs) in 1965 to 19.2 percent in 1972. Whereas economic growth reduced the poverty of one in ten Americans, governmental intervention reduced that of more than one in two Americans over the same period, a rate five to six times greater than that of the private economy. Economic growth did help some segments of the population, particularly families headed by males (white and nonwhite) under the age of 65. Among these families, rates of poverty declined sharply, by one-third or more, exclusive of governmental intervention. Yet, these were the strongest and most competitive economic groups, groups that entered the era of economic expansion already with, comparatively, the lowest rates of poverty. By way of contrast, economic expansion made little or no difference to the poverty rates of many other groups, particularly the elderly, white and minority women, and the youngest of the economically weak. In light of this experience, it would be nothing less than blind faith to argue that vigorous economic growth alone would have effectively reduced poverty in America within a reasonable time span. The circumstances of the 1960s and early 1970s demonstrate that while a prosperous economy may benefit the stronger economic groups, its impact on weaker groups can equally be nonexistent, reducing some to even more dire situations. *The government's programs were vital in fighting poverty precisely because the private sector was itself incapable of making more than a marginal dent in poverty among the many millions of Americans who remained trapped within the weaker economic groups*, either too old to get work or channeled into dead-end jobs that often paid little more than half-time wages for full-time work. Including their dependents, more than 30 million Americans lived in such families.

The economic experience of the 1960s and 1970s equally belies a second familiar belief, that is, that welfare programs substantially reduce the incentive to work. True, some effect is possible; it is most likely to be experienced by those Americans who remain at or near the poverty level even when holding down full-time jobs. Nevertheless, neither the expansion of the poverty programs in the 1960s and 1970s, nor the decisive contribution they made to reducing poverty, seems to have come at the cost of much reduction in the incentive of Americans to become a part of the work force and earn a living. To help set the context, consider that the numbers of people seeking work and taking jobs increased at historically high rates during these years, by 35 percent in 1965–80 alone. Employment climbed at a far faster pace during and after the great acceleration of the poverty and welfare programs in 1965–80 than during the preceding fifteen-year period (employment during 1950–65 rose by 21 percent). How much more might employment have climbed had there been less spending on welfare? One estimate of the impact of welfare programs on employment brings together the results of a host of other studies. It suggests that had all the main public-assistance programs for persons under the age of 65 been completely eliminated, including Aid to Families with Dependent Children, Medicaid, food stamps, and veterans' benefits, the numbers of hours worked by Americans would have risen by about 1 percent. Another point, too, helps place matters in perspective: Following 1965, even as the government's poverty and welfare programs experienced their most rapid enlargement, the rate of increase in unemployment in the United States rose *less* than it did in most other major Western nations. The vast expansion in the number of employed people after 1965, an increase diminished hardly at all by the welfare programs, and the comparatively slow rate of growth in the nation's unemployment make it apparent that the expansion of the government's attempts to attack poverty had very little effect on the number of Americans with the desire and incentive to work.

If so many filled jobs, who then were the families living on welfare? The single, largest federal welfare program giving direct cash assistance to low-income Americans is Aid to Families with Dependent Children (AFDC). The AFDC population is distinguished by three main characteristics: the male- and the female-headed families are entirely different, the female-headed families are in the large majority, and most families remain on AFDC only a few years.

At the end of the 1970s, for example, the male-headed families constituted only about 14 percent of all families on the AFDC welfare rolls. Of these, about half the family heads were incapacitated by injuries, black or brown lung disease, and other disabling physical handicaps and conditions. Of the remaining male heads, most had no skills and had not completed high school. By law, these able-bodied persons were required to participate in either a work-training program . . . or the Work Incentive Program, a job location and placement service. Failure to cooperate in job placement under the Work Incentive Program could lead to the total loss of welfare assistance, a requirement that was likely used as much as a threat to gain compliance as in the final enforcement.

Throughout 1960–80, the large majority of AFDC families were headed by females. Many of these family heads with very young children turned to AFDC when they were widowed or otherwise separated from their husbands. Critics contend that long-term welfare dependency frequently develops in these families. However, because having very young children to care for is so often a crucial factor, and because the total number of children in AFDC families is small (just over two children per family on average), AFDC actually experiences a high turnover. One study reports that 75 percent of all AFDC cases close within three years; another puts the figure at 60 percent. Since participation in AFDC is commonly a relatively transitional experience, it becomes plausible that the most extensive exploration of family situations in America during the late 1960s and the 1970s would find *no* significant evidence that children from welfare families, compared with children from low-income families not on welfare, have themselves been disproportionately likely to go on welfare when they subsequently set up their own households.

The work ethic continues to prevail in the United States. For the majority of AFDC recipients, the use of the federal government's major welfare program has been transitory, except when family heads are disabled. There exist few better indicators of the survival of the work ethic than to note the special kinds of situations that have commonly led families to turn to AFDC assistance and the relatively high turnover of the majority of families on welfare. Moreover, as a way of placing all this in context, it is relevant that even as such assistance became more widely available, the number of Americans who became employed grew at an unprecedented rate, one barely diminished by the programs' existence, and the rate of unemployment grew comparatively little. Even among the families living in poverty, the percentage of family heads who were employed in the late 1970s was almost as high as in the early 1960s, before the programs' rapid expansion. The most powerful and widely cited critique of welfare, Charles Murray's *Losing Ground*, itself shows that welfare had little effect on unemployment. Something else was going on in America; it was not a denial of the work ethic.

Instead, the economy's growth, combined with the sizable expansion of income after inflation that accompanied it, simply failed on its own to reach large numbers of people. As indicated earlier, this was due partly to the intensely crowded labor markets after 1965. . . . The intense competition for jobs meant that, even though economic growth ran apace, an employer's market still prevailed, at times fabulously so, with the result that job seekers from the weaker economic groups were rendered even weaker. Despite these circumstances, the government programs of the post-Eisenhower era reduced the percentage of Americans living in poverty by more than half, greatly surpassing the impact of even a substantial expansion of the private economy, which itself reduced poverty by about 10 percent. Moreover, the private economy concentrated its smaller contribution on helping those Americans who were in the strongest economic position. The government's programs made their far larger contribution by reaching, and reducing poverty within, the economically less-competitive groups of American people, groups of Americans whose situations had generally been ignored by the vigorous expansion of the private sector.

NO

15.6 Losing Ground

Charles Murray

[Murray begins with a thought experiment to demonstrate his contention that the War on Poverty was a failure; then, by focusing on the individual incentives facing a hypothetical poor couple in 1960 as compared to 1970, he suggests why.]

Let us imagine that it is June 1966. I am a policy analyst in the Johnson White House. My task is to help design the next phase of the War on Poverty. To this end I have been asked to project the progress of the disadvantaged some years out—to, say, 1980. I am told to use as my test population for this purpose the most disadvantaged group of all, black Americans. The analytic question is this: Based on what we know now—through 1965—what can we expect the future to hold? The purpose of the analysis is to separate the problems that will more or less solve themselves in the natural course of events from those that will continue to plague the disadvantaged unless special remedial steps are taken.

As analysts often do in such cases, I begin by defining an "optimistic" scenario and a "pessimistic" scenario. If I project on this basis for each of the scenarios independently, an envelope is formed within which the true future is likely to fall.

As the basis for the optimistic scenario, I am inclined to take the years since John Kennedy came to office to the present—that is, 1961 to 1965. The year 1961 is a natural breakpoint, dividing the Eisenhower from the post-Eisenhower period. Also, I reason, 1961–65 has been a period of steady economic growth, reductions in poverty, stabilization of black unemployment among the young, and reductions of black unemployment among older workers. As the basis for the pessimistic scenario, I take the years 1954–61—the post-Korea Eisenhower years. I

choose 1954 in part out of necessity—it is the first year for which detailed annual information about the black population is available—but it also has a symbolic appropriateness as well, marking the *Brown v. Board of Education* decision, the first of the great civil rights victories in the courts.

I call the scenarios "optimistic" and "pessimistic," but in reality I consider both of them to be biased toward the pessimistic side. Even the optimistic one says, "This is what 1980 will look like if the rate of progress is no better and no worse than it was from 1961 to 1965," and, from my perspective in 1966, that is not an ambitious objective. I do not consider that the period 1961–65 has been an exceptionally good one for blacks. Black voices have been raised, but black economic and social progress has been slow. The civil rights movement has not yet brought about the necessary rates of improvement. It has finally produced the instruments—legislation, court rulings, regulations—that are indispensable to adequate improvement, but the effects of these steps have barely begun to be felt. The economic and social action programs of the Great Society are just getting off the ground. It must be presumed that the implementation of these laws and programs will accelerate the bootstrap progress that blacks have made to date. And there is no telling what additional social legislation will be passed in future, especially given Johnson's continuing legislative hegemony. On all these counts, a straight-line projection of black progress in either 1954–61 *or* 1961–65 should tend to underestimate the real rate of improvement from 1965 to 1980.

As I proceed with my analysis, I choose indicators of two types. First I choose five indicators to assess the progress of the poorest blacks who have survived on the fringes of American society. Two of the indicators represent the problems that have been much worse for these blacks than for other groups:

- black victims of homicide, and
- black illegitimate births.

I want to see both of them go down. The other three of the indicators represent paths for getting off the bottom and up the socioeconomic ladder:

- labor force participation of black males aged 20–24 (it should go up);
- jobs for young black males (I use the unemployment ratio of black males aged 20–24 to white males of the same age, and hope to see it diminish); and
- two-parent families (which, aside from their noneconomic merits, are a mechanism whereby poor people accumulate resources, and are hoped to increase).

The second set of indicators that I choose for my analysis for the White House is primarily for assessing the progress of blacks who are already within the economic mainstream—seldom rich, but regularly employed, making a decent living. They have been held down by discrimination. How will they fare in 1980? I select four measures:

- income ratio of full-time, year-round black workers to comparable white workers (it should rise);
- unemployment ratio of black males aged 45–54 (an age group representing the mature male, with a family to support, who is almost always in the labor force unless physically incapacitated) to comparable white workers (it should come down);
- percentage of black workers employed in white-collar jobs (it should go up); and
- percentage of black persons of college and graduate school age (20–24) enrolled in school (it should go up).

Upon calculating my upper and lower bounds for each indicator, I soon discover that my "optimistic" and "pessimistic" scenarios do not altogether square with what has happened as of 1966. On six out of my nine indicators (unemployment ratio among young males, two-parent families, illegitimate births, arrests for violent crimes, income ratio of full-time workers, and persons of college age enrolled in school), a linear projection from the period of 1954–61 yields a more positive projection for 1980 than the one based on 1961–65.

I attribute this to extremely low baselines for some of the indicators. For the others, it seems plausible (*ex post facto* thinking at work) that the ferment of change in the black community might have short-term dislocating effects, causing such things as a higher illegitimacy rate and lower proportion of two-parent families. These are presumably only temporary phenomena. But I do re-label my trendlines, putting the "optimistic" label on whichever line is more positive, regardless of whether it came from the 1954–61 period or the 1961–65 period. I prepare my graphs, give them to my supervisor, and they show up in someone's briefing book a few weeks later. By 1980, I have forgotten that I ever made such foolish guesses.

Had anyone in 1966 actually been given the task of projecting these indicators to 1980 (analogous exercises were actually conducted), the projections would have been of the same order as the ones in the graphs we are about to examine—not because people were naive then, not because the techniques are inherently inappropriate, but because, in the absence of some strange and powerful intervening factor, they are roughly the ranges within which reasonable people would have expected these indicators to fall. With that in mind, let us examine the mocked-up 1966 projections, adding to them the true value of each indicator as of 1980. I begin with a sample of the general format, a projection of real per capita GNP (see fig. 1).

The other graphs follow this model, with abbreviated notation. Before leaving the sam-

FIGURE 15.1 A Projection of Per Capita GNP from 1965 to 1980

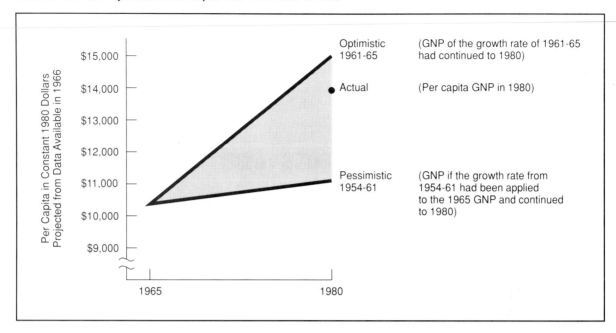

ple, take note that real per capita GNP was just about where it was supposed to be by 1980, a bit toward the optimistic side of the envelope.

Figure 2 (p. 614) shows the indicators pertaining especially to the black poor. The graphs convey in summary form, and perhaps more vividly than any of the individual discussions could, . . . how far outside the "normal course of events" the black poor have moved. Nor are these indicators unrepresentative. One may choose virtually any measure concerning the black poor for which data are available and come up with the same finding. In 1966, we were very far off the mark when we tried to imagine what "pessimistic" might mean when it came to projecting the future of the most disadvantaged of black Americans.

• • •

Dramatis Personae

Our guides [for explaining this failure of the War on Poverty] are a young couple—call them Harold and Phyllis. I deliberately make them unremarkable except for the bare fact of being poor. They are not of a special lower-class cul-

ture. They have no socialized propensities for "serial monogamy." They are not people we think of as "the type who are on welfare." They have just graduated from an average public school in an average American city. Neither of them is particularly industrious or indolent, intelligent or dull. They are the children of low-income parents, are not motivated to go to college, and have no special vocational skills. Harold and Phyllis went together during their last year in high school and find themselves in a familiar predicament. She is pregnant.

They will have a child together. They will face the kinds of painful decisions that many young people have had to face. What will they decide? What will seem to them to be "rational" behavior?

We shall examine the options twice—first, as they were in 1960, then as they were only ten years later, in 1970. We shall ignore the turbulent social history of the intervening decade. We shall ignore our couple's whiteness or blackness. We simply shall ask: Given the extant system of rewards and punishments, what course of action makes sense?

FIGURE 2   The View from 1966, Part II: Black Prospects on Indicators Especially Pertinent to the Not-Poor.

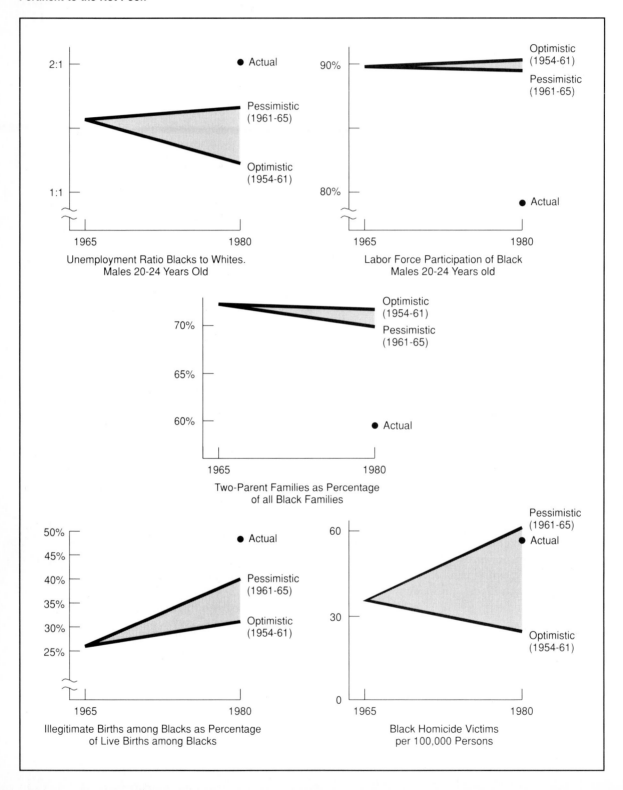

Options in 1960

Harold's Calculations, Pre-Reform

Harold's parents have no money. Phyllis has no money. If Harold remains within the law, he has two choices: He can get a job, or he can try to get Phyllis to help support him.

Getting Phyllis to support him is intrinsically more attractive, but the possibilities are not promising. If Phyllis has the baby, she will qualify for $23 a week in AFDC [Aid to Families with Dependent Children] ($63 in 1980 purchasing power). This is not enough to support the three of them. And, under the rules of AFDC, Phyllis will not be able to contribute more to the budget. If she gets a job, she will lose benefits on a dollar-for-dollar basis. There is in 1960 no way to make the AFDC payment part of a larger package.

Also, Harold and Phyllis will not be able to live together. AFDC regulations in 1960 prohibit benefits if there is "a man in the house." Apart from its psychic and sexual disadvantages, this regulation also means that Harold cannot benefit from Phyllis's weekly check. The amount cannot possibly be stretched across two households.

It follows that, completely apart from the moral stance of Harold, his parents, or society, it is not possible to use Phyllis for support. Whether or not he decides to stay with her, he will have to find a job.

The only job he can find is working the presses in a dry cleaning shop. It pays the rock-bottom minimum wage—$40 for a forty-hour week, or about $111 in the purchasing power of the 1980 dollar. It is not much of a living, not much of a job. There is no future in it, no career path. But it pays for food and shelter. And Harold has no choice.

The job turns out to be as tedious as he expected. It is hot in the laundry, and Harold is on his feet all day; he would much rather not stay there. But the consequences of leaving the job are intolerable. Unemployment Insurance will pay him only $20 ($56 in 1980 purchasing power). He stays at the laundry and vaguely hopes that something better will come along.

Phyllis's Calculations, Pre-Reform

Phyllis has three (legal) options: to support herself (either keeping the baby or giving it up for adoption); to go on AFDC (which means keeping the baby); or to marry Harold.

Other things being equal, supporting herself is the least attractive of these options. Like Harold, she can expect to find only menial minimum-wage employment. There is no intrinsic reason to take such a job.

The AFDC option is worth considering. The advantage is that it will enable her to keep the baby without having to work. The disadvantages are the ones that Harold perceives. The money is too little, and she is not permitted to supplement it. And Harold would not be permitted to be a live-in husband or father. If she tries to circumvent the rules and gets caught, she faces being cut off from any benefits for the foreseeable future.

If Phyllis thinks ahead, the economic attraction of AFDC might appear more enticing. The total benefits she will receive if she has several children may seem fairly large. If she were already on AFDC it might make sense to have more children. But, right now, setting up a household with Harold is by far the most sensible choice, even given the miserable wage he is making at the laundry.

Being married (as opposed to just living together) has no short-term economic implications. This is shown in the following table:

		Living Together	
		Unmarried	Married
Harold employed?	Yes	$111	$111
	No	0	0

The choice of whether to get married is dependent primarily on noneconomic motivations, plus the economic advantages to Phyllis of having Harold legally responsible for the support of her and the baby.

Once the decision not to go on AFDC is made, a new option opens up. As long as Phyllis is not on AFDC, no penalty is attached to getting a part-time or full-time job.

Options in 1970

Harold's and Phyllis's namesakes just ten years later find themselves in the identical situation. Their parents have no money; he doesn't want to go to school any longer; she is pregnant; the only job he can get is in the back room of a dry cleaners. That much is unchanged from 1960.

Harold's Calculations, Post-Reform

Harold's options have changed considerably. If he were more clever or less honest (or, perhaps, just more aggressive), he would have even more new options. But since he is none of those things, the major changes in his calculations are limited to these:

First, the AFDC option. In 1960, he had three objections to letting Phyllis go on welfare: too little money, no way to supplement it, and having to live separately from his family. By 1970, all three objections have been removed.

Economically, the total package of AFDC and other welfare benefits has become comparable to working. Phyllis will get about $50 a week in cash ($106 in 1980 dollars) and another $11 in Food Stamps ($23 in 1980 dollars). She is eligible for substantial rent subsidies under the many federal housing programs, but only a minority of AFDC recipients use them, so we will omit housing from the package. She will get Medicaid. We assume that a year's worth of doctor's bills and medication for a mother and infant is likely to be more than $250 (many times that if there is even one major illness), and we therefore add $5 a week (1980 dollars) onto the package. Without bending or even being imaginative about the new regulations, without tapping nearly all the possible sources of public support, and using conservative estimates in reaching a dollar total, the package of benefits

available to Phyllis in a typical northern state has a purchasing power of about $134. This minimal package adds up to $23 more than the purchasing power of forty hours of work at a minimum-wage job ten years earlier, in 1960.

Also, the money can be supplemented. If Phyllis works, she can keep the first thirty dollars she makes. After that, her benefits are reduced by two dollars for every three additional dollars of income.

Harold has even greater flexibility. *As long as he is not legally responsible for the care of the child*—a crucial proviso—his income will not count against her eligibility for benefits. He is free to work when they need a little extra money to supplement their basic (welfare) income.

The third objection, being separated from Phyllis, has become irrelevant. By Supreme Court ruling, the presence of a man in the house of a single woman cannot be used as a reason to deny her benefits.

The old-fashioned solution of getting married and living off their earned income has become markedly inferior. Working a full forty-hour week in the dry-cleaning shop will pay Harold $64 ($136 in 1980 dollars) *before* Social Security and taxes are taken out. The bottom line is this: Harold can get married and work forty hours a week in a hot, tiresome job; or he can live with Phyllis and their baby without getting married, not work, and have more disposable income. From an economic point of view, getting married is dumb. From a non-economic point of view, it involves him in a legal relationship that has no payoff for him. If he thinks he may sometime tire of Phyllis and fatherhood, the 1970 rules thus provide a further incentive for keeping the relationship off the books.

Phyllis's Calculations, Post-Reform

To keep the baby or give it up? To get married or not? What are the pros and cons?

Phyllis comes from a poor family. They want her out of the house, just as she wants to get out of the house. If she gives up the baby for adoption (or, in some states by 1970, has a legal abortion), she will be expected to support herself; and, as in 1960, the only job she will be able to find is likely to be unattractive, with no security and a paycheck no larger than her baby would provide. *The only circumstance under which giving up the baby is rational is if she prefers any sort of job to having and caring for a baby.* It is commonly written that poor teenaged girls have babies so they will have someone to love them. This may be true for some. But one *need* not look for psychological explanations. Under the rules of 1970, it was rational on grounds of dollars and cents for a poor, unmarried woman who found herself to be pregnant to have and keep the baby even if she did not particularly want a child.

In Phyllis's case, the balance favors having the baby. What about getting married?

If Phyllis and Harold marry and he is employed, she will lose her AFDC benefits. His minimum wage job at the laundry will produce no more income than she can make, and, not insignificantly, he, not she, will have control of the check. In exchange for giving up this degree of independence, she gains no real security. Harold's job is not nearly as stable as the welfare system. And, should her marriage break up, she will not be able to count on residual benefits. Enforcement of payment of child support has fallen to near-zero in poor communities. In sum, marriage buys Phyllis nothing—not companionship she couldn't have otherwise, not financial security, not even increased income. In 1970, her child provides her with the economic insurance that a husband used to represent.

Against these penalties for getting married is the powerful positive inducement to remain single: Any money that Harold makes is added to their income without affecting her benefits as long as they remain unmarried. It is difficult to think of a good economic reason from Phyllis's viewpoint why marriage might be attractive.

Let us pause and update the table of economic choices, plugging in the values for 1970. Again, we assume that the two want to live together. Their maximum weekly incomes (ignoring payroll deductions and Harold's means-tested benefits) are:

		Living Together	
		Unmarried	Married
Harold employed?	Yes	$270	$136
	No	$134	$134

The dominant cell for maximizing income is clearly "living together unmarried, Harold employed." If they for some reason do decide to get married and they live in a state that permits AFDC for families with unemployed fathers (as most of the industrial states do), they are about equally well off whether or not Harold is employed. Or, more precisely, they are about equally well off, in the short run, if Harold moves in and out of the labor market to conform to whatever local rules apply to maintaining eligibility. This is a distinction worth emphasizing . . . the changed rules do not encourage permanent unemployment so much as they encourage periodic unemployment.

Harold and Phyllis take the economically logical step—she has the baby, they live together without getting married, and Harold looks for a job to make some extra money. He finds the job at the laundry. It is just as unpleasant a job as it was in 1960, but the implications of persevering are different. In 1970, unlike 1960, Harold's job is *not* his basic source of income. Thus, when the back room of the laundry has been too hot for too long, it becomes economically feasible and indeed reasonable to move in and out of the labor market. In 1980 dollars, Unemployment Insurance pays him $68 per week. As the sole means of support it is not an attractive sum. But added to Phyllis's package, the total is $202, which beats the heat of the presses. And, if it comes to it, Harold can survive even without the Unemployment payment. In 1970, Phyllis's welfare package is bringing in more real income than did a minimum-wage job in 1960.

Such is the story of Harold and Phyllis. They were put in a characteristically working-class situation. In 1960, the logic of their world led them to behave in traditional working-class ways. Ten years later, the logic of their world had changed and, lo and behold, they behaved indistinguishably from "welfare types." What if we had hypothesized a more typical example—or at least one that fits the stereotype? What if we had posited the lower-class and black cultural influences that are said to foster high illegitimacy rates and welfare dependency? The answer is that the same general logic would apply, but with even more power. When economic incentives are buttressed by social norms, the effects on behavior are multiplied. But the main point is that the social factors are not necessary to explain behavior. There is no "breakdown of the work ethic" in this account of rational choices among alternatives. There is no shiftless irresponsibility. It makes no difference whether Harold is white or black. There is no need to invoke the spectres of cultural pathologies or inferior upbringing. The choices may be seen much more simply, much more naturally, as the behavior of people responding to the reality of the world around them and making the decisions—the legal, approved, and even encouraged decisions—that maximize their quality of life.

_____Chapter 16

Civil Liberties

$\mathcal{T}$he American commitment to individual rights and liberties is one of the distinguishing characteristics of our political system. Even more striking is the fact that we have a written Bill of Rights and that we rely to a great extent on the judicial system to define and defend the rights enumerated there.

Originally the Bill of Rights applied only to the federal government. The First Amendment, for example, states explicitly that "Congress shall make no law . . . abridging the freedom of speech." An 1833 case, Barron v. Baltimore, made it clear that the restrictions of the first eight amendments were not intended to interfere with laws passed by the states. Over the course of the twentieth century, however, the Supreme Court has applied the various provisions of the Bill of Rights, one by one, to the states.

The emphasis in American politics on individual rights raises two sorts of problems. The first involves balancing competing rights. The publication of the name of a rape victim, for example, might violate the victim's right to privacy; punishing such publication, on the other hand, might interfere with a newspaper's right to free speech. Such problems can be extremely vexing, but even more serious are problems that pit the interests of an individual against society itself. The Flag Salute Case (selection 16.6) is an example. How far can society go in promoting citizenship and loyalty before its interests are outweighed by the individual's rights to free speech and free exercise of religion? To a great extent, the abortion cases (selections 16.3 through 16.5) also fit in this category as the courts balance society's right to protect unborn life against a woman's right to privacy.

The other readings in this chapter provide essential background for understanding these and other civil liberties issues. Selection 16.1, from John Stuart Mill's On Liberty, presents the classic liberal argument for individuality. Selection 16.2 provides a

619

brief history of the American Civil Liberties Union, an often controversial interest group dedicated to protecting individual freedoms.

You may note that there is no "Issue and Debate" section in this chapter. The reason should be clear. To paraphrase Justice Oliver Wendell Holmes, Jr., every issue in the area of civil liberties is, it seems, an incitement to debate and controversy.

Chapter Questions

1. What are "civil liberties"? Why are they important in a society that values freedom? Why is freedom of thought and expression particularly important?

2. How are individual rights defined and balanced against the rights of other citizens and against the interests of society at large? What factors work to tip such a balancing process in favor of society? in favor of individual rights?

3. Why are the courts so heavily involved in determining civil liberties questions? What impact does the legal process have on the determination of such questions? What is the role of legal precedent? of the American Civil Liberties Union?

I THE CLASSIC TEXTS

One of the greatest advocates of civil liberties was the English philosopher John Stuart Mill. Published in 1859, Mill's On Liberty *is perhaps the most important statement of the "importance of freedom for the discovery of truth and for the full development of individuality."* Although written in England, Mill's argument found a more receptive audience in the United States; his ideas greatly influenced the U.S. Supreme Court in later years, especially the opinions of Justices Oliver Wendell Holmes, who served on the Court from 1902 to 1932, and Louis Brandeis, who served from 1916 to 1939.*

Mill was a utilitarian; he believed that all arguments had to be grounded in practical reasons and justified with reference to the social good that would be brought about or the social evils that would be prevented. Therefore, his argument for allowing the individual the maximum freedom to decide how to live stresses the reasons that such freedom ultimately is good for society, even if the opinions expressed are clearly wrong. Note that his argument—unlike American constitutional arguments—is not based on claims of individual rights. Still, Mill's reasoning lies behind American liberal arguments as to the importance of protecting liberty under the Bill of Rights.

Questions

1. How does Mill justify the protection of individuality even when an individual's actions are clearly detrimental to that person's well-being?

* David Spitz, Preface to John Stuart Mill, *On Liberty* (New York: W. W. Norton & Co., 1975), p. vii.

16.1 On Liberty

John Stuart Mill

We have now recognised the necessity to the mental well-being of mankind (on which all their other well-being depends) of freedom of opinion, and freedom of the expression of opinion, on four distinct grounds; which we will now briefly recapitulate.

First, if any opinion is compelled to silence, that opinion may, for aught we can certainly know, be true. To deny this is to assume our own infallibility.

Secondly, though the silenced opinion be an error, it may, and very commonly does, contain a portion of truth; and since the general or prevailing opinion on any subject is rarely or never the whole truth, it is only by the collision of adverse opinions that the remainder of the truth has any chance of being supplied.

Thirdly, even if the received opinion be not only true, but the whole truth; unless it is suffered to be, and actually is, vigorously and earnestly contested, it will, by most of those who receive it, be held in the manner of a prejudice, with little comprehension or feeling of its rational grounds. And not only this, but, fourthly, the meaning of the doctrine itself will be in danger of being lost, or enfeebled, and deprived of its vital effect on the character and conduct; the dogma becoming a mere formal profession, inefficacious for good, but cumbering the ground, and preventing the growth of any real and heartfelt conviction from reason or personal experience.

• • •

Such being the reasons which make it imperative that human beings should be free to form opinions, and to express their opinions without reserve; and such the baneful consequences to the intellectual, and through that to the moral nature of man, unless this liberty is either conceded, or asserted in spite of prohibition; let us next examine whether the same reasons do not require that men should be free to act upon their opinions—to carry these out in their lives, without hindrance, either physical or moral, from their fellow-men, so long as it is at their own risk and peril. This last proviso is of course indispensable. No one pretends that actions should be as free as opinions. On the contrary, even opinions lose their immunity when the circumstances in which they are expressed are such as to constitute their expression a positive instigation to some mischievous act. An opinion that corn-dealers are starvers of the poor, or that private property is robbery, ought to be unmolested when simply circulated through the press, but may justly incur punishment when delivered orally to an excited mob assembled before the house of a corn-dealer, or when handed about among the same mob in the form of a placard. Acts, of whatever kind, which, without justifiable cause, do harm to others, may be, and in the more important cases absolutely require to be, controlled by the unfavourable sentiments, and, when needful, by the active interference of mankind. The liberty of the individual must be thus far limited; he must not make himself a nuisance to other people. But if he refrains from molesting others in what concerns them, and merely acts according to his own inclination and judgment in things which concern himself, the same reasons which show that opinion should be free, prove also that he should be allowed, without molestation, to carry his opinions into practice at his own cost. That mankind are not infallible; that their truths, for the most part, are only half-truths; that unity of opinion, unless resulting from the fullest and freest comparison of opposite opinions, is not desirable, and diversity not an evil, but a good, until mankind are much more capable than at present of recognising all sides of the truth, are principles applicable to men's modes of action, not less than to their opinions. As it is useful that while mankind are imperfect there should be different opinions, so it is that there should be different experiments of living; that free scope should be given to varieties of character, short of injury to others; and that the worth of different modes of life should be proved practically, when any one thinks fit to try them. It is desirable, in short, that in things which do not primarily concern others, individuality should assert itself. Where, not the person's own character, but the traditions or customs of other people are the rule of conduct, there is wanting one of the principal ingredients of human happiness, and quite the chief ingredient of individual and social progress.

In maintaining this principle, the greatest difficulty to be encountered does not lie in the appreciation of means towards an acknowledged end, but in the indifference of persons in general to the end itself. If it were felt that the free development of individuality is one of the leading essentials of well-being; that it is not only a coordinate element with all that is designated by the terms civilisation, instruction, education, culture, but is itself a necessary part and condition of all those things; there would be no danger that liberty should be undervalued, and the adjustment of the boundaries between it and social control would present no extraordinary difficulty. But the evil is, that individual spontaneity is hardly recognised by the common modes of thinking as having any intrinsic worth, or deserving any regard on its own account. The majority, being satisfied with the ways of mankind as they now are (for it is they who make them what they are), cannot comprehend why those ways should not be good enough for everybody; and what is more, spontaneity forms no part of the ideal of the majority of moral and social reformers, but is rather looked on with jealousy, as a troublesome and perhaps rebellious obstruction to the general acceptance of what these reformers, in their own judgment, think would be best for mankind. Few persons, out of Germany, even comprehend the meaning of the doctrine which Wilhelm von Humboldt, so eminent both as a *savant* and as a politician, made the text of a treatise—that "the end of man, or that which is prescribed by the eternal or immutable dictates of reason, and not suggested by vague and transient desires, is the highest and most harmonious development of his powers to a complete and consistent whole;" that, therefore, the object "towards which every human being must ceaselessly direct his efforts, and on which especially those who design to influence their fellow-men must ever keep their eyes, is the individuality of power and development;" that for this there are two requisites, "freedom, and variety of situations;" and that from the union of these arise "individual vigour and manifold diversity," which combine themselves in "originality."

Little, however, as people are accustomed to a doctrine like that of Von Humboldt, and surprising as it may be to them to find so high a value attached to individuality, the question, one must nevertheless think, can only be one of degree. No one's idea of excellence in conduct is that people should do absolutely nothing but copy one another. No one would assert that people ought not to put into their mode of life, and into the conduct of their concerns, any impress whatever of their own judgment, or of their own individual character. On the other hand, it would be absurd to pretend that people ought to live as if nothing whatever had been known in the world before they came into it; as if experience had as yet done nothing towards showing that one mode of existence, or of conduct, is preferable to another. Nobody denies that people should be so taught and trained in youth as to know and benefit by the ascertained results of human experience. But it is the privilege and proper condition of a human being, arrived at the maturity of his faculties, to use and interpret experience in his own way. It is for him to find out what part of recorded experience is properly applicable to his own circumstances and character. The traditions and customs of other people are, to a certain extent, evidence of what their experience has taught *them*; presumptive evidence, and as such, have a claim to his deference: but, in the first place, their experience may be too narrow; or they may not have interpreted it rightly. Secondly, their interpretation of experience may be correct, but unsuitable to him. Customs are made for customary circumstances and customary characters; and his circumstances or his character may be uncustomary. Thirdly, though the customs be both good as customs, and suitable to him, yet to conform to custom, merely *as* custom, does not educate or develop in him any of the qualities which are the distinctive endowment of a human being. The human faculties of perception, judgment, discriminative feeling, mental activity, and even moral preference, are exercised only in making a choice. He who does anything because it is the custom makes no choice. He gains no practice either in discerning or in desiring what is best. The mental and moral, like the muscular powers, are improved only by being used. The faculties are called into no exercise by doing a thing merely because others do it, no more than by believing a thing only because others believe it. If the grounds of an opinion are not conclusive to the person's own reason, his reason cannot be strengthened, but is likely to be weakened, by his adopting it: and if the inducements to an act are not such as are consentaneous to his own feelings and character (where affection, or the rights of others, are not concerned) it is so much done towards rendering his feelings and character inert and torpid, instead of active and energetic.

He who lets the world, or his own portion of it, choose his plan of life for him, has no need of any other faculty than the ape-like one of imitation. He who chooses his plan for himself, employs all his faculties. He must use observation to see, reasoning and judgment to foresee, activity to gather materials for decision, discrimination to decide, and when he has decided, firmness and self-control to hold to his deliberate decision. And these qualities he requires and exercises exactly in proportion as the part of his conduct which he determines according to his own judgment and feelings is a large one. It is possible that he might be guided in some good path, and kept out of harm's way, without any of these things. But what will be his comparative worth as a human being? It really is of importance, not only what men do, but also what manner of men they are that do it. Among the works of man, which human life is rightly employed in perfecting and beautifying, the first in importance surely is man himself. Supposing it were possible to get houses built, corn grown, battles fought, causes tried, and even churches erected and prayers said, by machinery—by automatons in human form—it would be a considerable loss to exchange for these automatons even the men and women who at present inhabit the more civilised parts of the world, and who assuredly are but starved specimens of what nature can and will produce. Human nature is not a machine to be built after a model, and set to do exactly the work prescribed for it, but a tree, which requires to grow and develop itself on all sides, according to the tendency of the inward forces which make it a living thing.

It will probably be conceded that it is desirable people should exercise their understandings, and that an intelligent following of custom, or even occasionally an intelligent deviation from custom, is better than a blind and simply mechanical adhesion to it. To a certain extent it is admitted that our understanding should be our own: but there is not the same willingness to admit that our desires and impulses should be our own likewise; or that to possess impulses of our own, and of any strength, is anything but a peril and a snare. Yet desires and impulses are as much a part of

Federalist No. 84

*When the Constitution was ratified, it contained no
Bill of Rights; the Bill of Rights, which comprises
the first ten amendments to the Constitution, was
added in 1791. In this selection from the* Federalist
Papers, *Alexander Hamilton defends the Constitution's lack of a Bill of Rights, which, he suggested,
would be unnecessary and even dangerous. Hamilton's colleague, James Madison, originally took the
same position, but eventually he led the effort to
push the Bill of Rights through Congress.*

*I*t has been several times truly remarked that
bills of rights are, in their origin, stipulations between kings and their subjects, abridgments of
prerogative in favor of privilege, reservations of
rights not surrendered to the prince. . . .

But a minute detail of particular rights is certainly far less applicable to a Constitution like that
under consideration, which is merely intended to
regulate the general political interests of the nation, than to a constitution which has the regulation of every species of personal and private concerns. If, therefore, the loud clamors against the
plan of the convention, on this score, are well
founded, no epithets of reprobation will be too
strong for the constitution of this State. But the
truth is that both of them contain all which, in relation to their objects, is reasonably to be desired.

I go further and affirm that bills of rights, in the
sense and to the extent in which they are contended for, are not only unnecessary in the proposed Constitution but would even be dangerous.
They would contain various exceptions to powers
which are not granted; and, on this very account,
would afford a colorable pretext to claim more
than were granted. For why declare that things
shall not be done which there is no power to do?
Why, for instance, should it be said that the liberty
of the press shall not be restrained, when no
power is given by which restrictions may be imposed? I will not contend that such a provision
would confer a regulating power; but it is evident
that it would furnish, to men disposed to usurp, a
plausible pretense for claiming that power. They
might urge with a semblance of reason that the
Constitution ought not to be charged with the absurdity of providing against the abuse of an authority which was not given, and that the provision
against restraining the liberty of the press afforded
a clear implication that a power to prescribe
proper regulations concerning it was intended to
be vested in the national government. This may
serve as a specimen of the numerous handles
which would be given to the doctrine of constructive powers, by the indulgence of an injudicious
zeal for bills of rights.

On the subject of the liberty of the press, as
much as has been said, I cannot forbear adding a
remark or two: in the first place, I observe, that
there is not a syllable concerning it in the constitu-

a perfect human being as beliefs and restraints:
and strong impulses are only perilous when not
properly balanced; when one set of aims and
inclinations is developed into strength, while
others, which ought to co-exist with them, remain weak and inactive. It is not because men's
desires are strong that they act ill; it is because
their consciences are weak. There is no natural
connection between strong impulses and a
weak conscience. The natural connection is the
other way. To say that one person's desires and
feelings are stronger and more various than

those of another, is merely to say that he has
more of the raw material of human nature, and
is therefore capable, perhaps of more evil, but
certainly of more good. Strong impulses are but
another name for energy. Energy may be turned
to bad uses; but more good may always be made
of an energetic nature, than of an indolent and
impassive one. Those who have most natural
feeling, are always those whose cultivated feelings may be made the strongest. The same
strong susceptibilities which make the personal
impulses vivid and powerful, are also the

tion of this State; in the next, I contend that whatever has been said about it in that of any other State amounts to nothing. What signifies a declaration that "the liberty of the press shall be inviolably preserved?" What is the liberty of the press? Who can give it any definition which would not leave the utmost latitude for evasion? I hold it to be impracticable; and from this I infer that its security, whatever fine declarations may be inserted in any constitution respecting it, must altogether depend on public opinion, and on the general spirit of the people and of the government. And here, after all, as is intimated upon another occasion, must we seek for the only solid basis of all our rights.

There remains but one other view of this matter to conclude the point. The truth is, after all the declamations we have heard, that the Constitution is itself, in every rational sense, and to every useful purpose, A BILL OF RIGHTS. The several bills of rights in Great Britain form its Constitution, and conversely the constitution of each State is its bill of rights. And the proposed Constitution, if adopted, will be the bill of rights of the Union. Is it one object of a bill of rights to declare and specify the political privileges of the citizens in the structure and administration of the government? This is done in the most ample and precise manner in the plan of the convention; comprehending various precautions for the public security which are not to be found in any of the State constitutions. Is another object of a bill of rights to define certain immunities and modes of proceeding, which are relative to personal and private concerns? This we have seen has also been attended to in a variety of cases in the same plan. Adverting therefore to the substantial meaning of a bill of rights, it is absurd to allege that it is not to be found in the work of the convention. It may be said that it does not go far enough though it will not be easy to make this appear; but it can with no propriety be contended that there is no such thing. It certainly must be immaterial what mode is observed as to the order of declaring the rights of the citizens if they are to be found in any part of the instrument which establishes the government. And hence it must be apparent that much of what has been said on this subject rests merely on verbal and nominal distinctions, entirely foreign from the substance of the thing.

• • •

—*Alexander Hamilton*

source from whence are generated the most passionate love of virtue, and the sternest self-control. It is through the cultivation of these that society both does its duty and protects its interests: not by rejecting the stuff of which heroes are made, because it knows not how to make them. A person whose desires and impulses are his own—are the expression of his own nature, as it has been developed and modified by his own culture—is said to have a character. One whose desires and impulses are not his own, has no character, no more than a steam-engine has a character. If, in addition to being his own, his impulses are strong, and are under the government of a strong will, he has an energetic character. Whoever thinks that individuality of desires and impulses should not be encouraged to unfold itself, must maintain that society has no need of strong natures—is not the better for containing many persons who have much character—and that a high general average of energy is not desirable.

In some early states of society, these forces might be, and were, too much ahead of the power which society then possessed of disciplining and controlling them. There has been a time when the element of spontaneity and individuality was in excess, and the social principle had a hard struggle with it. The difficulty then was to induce men of strong bodies or minds to pay obedience to any rules which required them to control their impulses. To overcome this difficulty, law and discipline, like the Popes struggling against the Emperors, asserted a power over the whole man, claiming to control all his life in order to control his character—which society had not found any other sufficient means of binding. But society has now fairly got the better of individuality; and the danger which threatens human nature is not the excess, but the deficiency, of personal impulses and preferences. Things are vastly changed since the passions of those who were strong by station or by personal endowment were in a state of habitual rebellion against laws and ordinances, and required to be rigorously chained up to enable the persons within their reach to enjoy any particle of security. In our times, from the highest class of society down to the lowest, every one lives as under the eye of a hostile and dreaded censorship. Not only in what concerns others, but in what concerns only themselves, the individual or the family do not ask themselves—what do I prefer? or, what would suit my character an disposition? or, what would allow the best and highest in me to have fair play, and enable it to grow and thrive? They ask themselves, what is suitable to my position? what is usually done by persons of my station and pecuniary circumstances? or (worse still) what is usually done by persons of a station and circumstances superior to mine? I do not mean that they choose what is customary in preference to what suits their own inclination. It does not occur to them to have any inclination, except for what is customary. Thus the mind itself is bowed to the yoke: even in what people do for pleasure, conformity is the first thing thought of; they like in crowds; they exercise choice only among things commonly done: peculiarity of taste, eccentricity of conduct, are shunned equally with crimes: until by dint of not following their own nature they have no nature to follow: their human capacities are withered and starved: they become incapable of any strong wishes or native pleasures, and are generally without either opinions or feelings of home growth, or properly their own.

• • •

It is not by wearing down into uniformity all that is individual in themselves, but by cultivating it, and calling it forth, within the limits imposed by the rights and interests of others, that human beings become a noble and beautiful object of contemplation; and as the works partake the character of those who do them, by the same process human life also becomes rich, diversified, and animating, furnishing more abundant aliment to high thoughts and elevating feelings, and strengthening the tie which binds every individual to the race, by making the race infinitely better worth belonging to. In proportion to the development of his individuality, each person becomes more valuable to himself, and is therefore capable of being more valuable to others. There is a greater fulness of life about his own existence, and when there is more life in the units there is more in the mass which is composed of them. As much compression as is necessary to prevent the stronger specimens of human nature from encroaching on the rights of others, cannot be dispensed with; but for this there is ample compensation even in the point of view of human development. The means of development which the individual loses by being prevented from gratifying his inclinations to the injury of others, are chiefly obtained at the expense of the development of other people. And even to himself there is a full equivalent in the better development of the social part of his nature, rendered possible by the restraint put upon the selfish part. To be held to rigid rules of justice for the sake of others, develops the feelings and capacities which have the good of others for their object. But to be restrained in things not affecting their good, by their mere displeasure, develops nothing valuable, except such force of character as may unfold itself in resisting the restraint. If acquiesced in, it dulls and blunts the whole nature. To give any fair play to the nature of each, it is essential that different persons should be allowed to lead different lives. In proportion as this latitude has been exercised in any age, has that age been noteworthy to posterity. Even despotism does not produce its worst effects, so long as individuality exists under it; and whatever crushes individuality is despotism, by whatever name it may be called, and whether it professes to be enforcing the will of God or the unjunctions of men.

Having said that the individuality is the same thing with development, and that it is only the cultivation of individuality which produces, or can produce, well-developed human beings, I might here close the argument: for what more or better can be said of any condition of human affairs than that it brings human beings themselves nearer to the best things they can be? or what worse can be said of any obstruction to good than that it prevents this? Doubtless, however, these considerations will not suffice to convince those who most need convincing; and it is necessary further to show, that these developed human beings are of some use to the undeveloped—to point out to those who do not desire liberty, and would not avail themselves of it, that they may be in some intelligible manner rewarded for allowing other people to make use of it without hindrance.

In the first place, then, I would suggest that they might possibly learn something from them. It will not be denied by anybody, that originality is a valuable element in human affairs. There is always need of persons not only to discover new truths, and point out when what were once truths are true no longer, but also to commence new practices, and set the example of more enlightened conduct, and better taste and sense in human life. This cannot well be gainsaid by anybody who does not believe that the world has already attained perfection in all its ways and practices. It is true that this benefit is not capable of being rendered by everybody alike: there are but few persons, in comparison with the whole of mankind, whose experiments, if adopted by others, would be likely to be any improvement on established practice. But these few are the salt of the earth; without them, human life would become a stagnant pool. Not only is it they who introduce good things which did not before exist; it is they who keep the life in those which already exist. If there were nothing new to be done, would human intellect cease to be necessary? Would it be a reason why those who do the old things should forget why they are done, and do them like cattle, not like human beings? There is only too great a tendency in the best beliefs and practices to degenerate into the mechanical; and unless there were a succession of persons whose ever-recurring originality prevents the grounds of those beliefs and practices from becoming merely traditional, such dead matter would not resist the smaller shock from anything really alive, and there would be no reason why civilisation should not die out, as in the Byzantine Empire. Persons of genius, it is true, are, and are always likely to be, a small minority; but in order to have them, it is necessary to preserve the soil in which they grow. Genius can only breathe freely in an *atmosphere* of freedom. Persons of genius are, *ex vi termini*, more individual than any other people—less capable, consequently, of fitting themselves, without hurtful compression, into any of the small number of moulds which society provides in order to save its members the trouble of forming their own character. If from timidity they consent to be forced into one of these moulds, and to let all that part of themselves which cannot expand under the pressure remain unexpanded, society will be little the better for their genius. If they are of a strong character, and break their fetters, they become a mark for the society which has not succeeded in reducing them to commonplace, to point out with solemn warning as "wild," "erratic," and the like; much as if one should complain of the Niagara river for not flowing smoothly between its banks like a Dutch canal.

I insist thus emphatically on the importance of genius, and the necessity of allowing it to unfold itself freely both in thought and in practice, being well aware that no one will deny the position in theory, but knowing also that almost every one, in reality, is totally indifferent to it. People think genius a fine thing if it enables a man to write an exciting poem, or paint a picture. But in its true sense, that of originality in thought and action, though no one says that it is not a thing to be admired, nearly all, at heart, think that they can do very well without it. Unhappily this is too natural to be wondered at. Originality is the one thing which unoriginal minds cannot feel the use of. They cannot see what it is to do for them: how should they? If they could see what it would do for them, it would not be originality. The first service which originality has to render them, is that of opening their eyes: which being once fully done, they would have a chance of being themselves original. Meanwhile, recollecting that nothing was ever yet done which some one was not the first to do, and that all good things which exist are the fruits of originality, let them be modest enough to believe that there is something still left for it to accomplish, and assure themselves that they are more in need of originality, the less they are conscious of the want.

In sober truth, whatever homage may be professed, or even paid, to real or supposed mental superiority, the general tendency of things throughout the world is to render mediocrity the ascendant power among mankind. In ancient history, in the Middle Ages, and in a diminishing degree through the long transition from feudality to the present time, the individual was a power in himself; and if he had either great talents or a high social position, he was a considerable power. At present individuals are lost in the crowd. In politics it is almost a triviality to say that public opinion now rules the world. The only power deserving the name is that of masses, and of governments while

they make themselves the organ of the tendencies and instincts of masses. This is as true in the moral and social relations of private life as in public transactions. Those whose opinions go by the name of public opinion are not always the same sort of public: in America they are the whole white population; in England chiefly the middle class. But they are always a mass, that is to say, collective mediocrity. And what is a still greater novelty, the mass do not now take their opinions from dignitaries in Church or State, from ostensible leaders, or from books. Their thinking is done for them by men much like themselves, addressing them or speaking in their name, on the spur of the moment, through the newspapers. I am not complaining of all this. I do not assert that anything better is compatible, as a general rule, with the present low state of the human mind. But that does not hinder the government of mediocrity from being mediocre government. No government by a democracy or a numerous aristocracy, either in its political acts or in the opinions, qualities, and tone of mind which it fosters, ever did or could rise above mediocrity, except in so far as the sovereign. Many have let themselves be guided (which in their best times they always have done) by the counsels and influence of a more highly gifted and instructed One or Few. The initiation of all wise or noble things comes and must come from individuals; generally at first from some one individual. The honour and glory of the average man is that he is capable of following that initiative; that he can respond internally to wise and noble things, and be led to them with his eyes open. I am not countenancing the sort of "hero-worship" which applauds the strong man of genius for forcibly seizing on the government of the world and making it do his bidding in spite of itself. All he can claim is, freedom to point out the way. The power of compelling others into it is not only inconsistent with the freedom and development of all the rest, but corrupting to the strong man himself. It does seem, however, that when the opinions of masses of merely average men are everywhere become or becoming the dominant power, the counterpoise and corrective to that tendency would be the more and more pronounced individuality of those who stand on the higher eminences of thought. It is in these circumstances most especially, that exceptional individuals, instead of being deterred, should be encouraged in acting differently from the mass. In other times there was no advantage in their doing so, unless they acted not only differently but better. In this age, the mere example of non-conformity, the mere refusal to bend the knee to custom, is itself a service. Precisely because the tyranny of opinion is such as to make eccentricity a reproach, it is desirable, in order to break through that tyranny, that people should be eccentric. Eccentricity has always abounded when and where strength of character has abounded; and the amount of eccentricity in a society has generally been proportional to the amount of genius, mental vigour, and moral courage it contained. That so few now dare to be eccentric marks the chief danger of the time.

I have said that it is important to give the freest scope possible to uncustomary things, in order that it may in time appear which of these are fit to be converted into customs. But independence of action, and disregard of custom, are not solely deserving of encouragement for the chance they afford that better modes of action, and customs more worthy of general adoption, may be struck out; nor is it only persons of decided mental superiority who have a just claim to carry on their lives in their own way. There is no reason that all human existence should be constructed on some one or some small number of patterns. If a person possesses any tolerable amount of common sense and experience, his own mode of laying out his existence is the best, not because it is the best in itself, but because it is his own mode. Human beings are not like sheep; and even sheep are not undistinguishably alike. A man cannot get a coat or a pair of boots to fit him unless they are either made to his measure, or he has a whole warehouseful to choose from: and is it easier to fit him with a life than with a coat, or

are human beings more like one another in their whole physical and spiritual conformation than in the shape of their feet? If it were only that people have diversities of taste, that is reason enough for not attempting to shape them all after one model. But different persons also require different conditions for their spiritual development; and can no more exist healthily in the same moral, than all the variety of plants can in the same physical, atmosphere and climate. The same things which are helps to one person towards the cultivation of higher nature are hindrances to another. The same mode of life is a healthy excitement to one, keeping all his faculties of action and enjoyment in their best order, while to another it is a distracting burthen, which suspends or crushes all internal life. Such are the differences among human beings in their sources of pleasure, their susceptibilities of pain, and the operation on them of different physical and moral agencies, that unless there is a corresponding diversity in their modes of life, they neither obtain their fair share of happiness, nor grow up to the mental, moral, and aesthetic stature of which their nature is capable. Why then should tolerance, as far as the public sentiment is concerned, extend only to tastes and modes of life which extort acquiescence by the multitude of their adherents? Nowhere (except in some monastic institutions) is diversity of taste entirely unrecognised; a person may, without blame, either like or dislike rowing, or smoking, or music, or athletic exercises, or chess, or cards, or study, because both those who like each of these things, and those who dislike them, are too numerous to be put down. But the man, and still more the woman, who can be accused either of doing "what nobody does," or of not doing "what everybody does," is the subject of as much depreciatory remark as if he or she had committed some grave moral delinquency. Persons require to possess a title, or some other badge of rank, or of the consideration of people of rank, to be able to indulge somewhat in the luxury of doing as they like without detriment to their estimation. To indulge somewhat, I repeat: for whoever allow themselves much of that indulgence, incur the risk of something worse than disparaging speeches—they are in peril of a commission *de lunatico*,* and of having their property taken from them and given to their relations.

There is one characteristic of the present direction of public opinion peculiarly calculated to make it intolerant of any marked demonstration of individuality. The general average of mankind are not only moderate in intellect, but also moderate in inclinations: they have no tastes or wishes strong enough to incline them to do anything unusual, and they consequently do not understand those who have, and class all such with the wild and intemperate whom they are accustomed to look down upon. Now, in addition to this fact which is general, we have only to suppose that a strong movement has set in towards the improvement of morals, and it is evident what we have to expect. In these days such a movement has set in; much has actually been effected in the way of increased regularity of conduct and discouragement of excesses; and there is a philanthropic spirit abroad, for the exercise of which there is no more inviting field than the moral and prudential improvement of our fellow-creatures. These tendencies of the times cause the public to be more disposed than at most former periods to prescribe general rules of conduct, and endeavour to make every one conform to the approved standard. And that standard, express or tacit, is to desire nothing strongly. Its ideal of character is to be without any marked character; to maim by compression, like a Chinese lady's foot, every part of human nature which stands out prominently, and tends to make the person markedly dissimilar in outline to commonplace humanity.

As is usually the case with ideals which exclude one-half of what is desirable, the present standard of approbation produces only an inferior imitation of the other half. Instead of great energies guided by vigorous reason, and strong feelings strongly controlled by a conscientious will, its result is weak feelings and weak

energies, which therefore can be kept in outward conformity to rule without any strength either of will or of reason. Already energetic characters on any large scale are becoming merely traditional. There is now scarcely any outlet for energy in this country except business. The energy expended in this may still be regarded as considerable. What little is left from that employment is expended on some hobby; which may be a useful, even a philanthropic hobby, but is always some one thing, and generally a thing of small dimensions. The greatness of England is now all collective; individually small, we only appear capable of anything great by our habit of combining; and with this our moral and religious philanthropists are perfectly contented. But it was men of another stamp than this that made England what it has been; and men of another stamp will be needed to prevent its decline.

The despotism of custom is everywhere the standing hindrance to human advancement, being in unceasing antagonism to that disposition to aim at something better than customary, which is called, according to circumstances, the spirit of liberty, or that of progress or improvement. The spirit of improvement is not always a spirit of liberty, for it may aim at forcing improvements on an unwilling people; and the spirit of liberty, in so far as it resists such attempts, may ally itself locally and temporarily with the opponents of improvement; but the only unfailing and permanent source of improvement is liberty, since by it there are as many possible independent centres of improvement as there are individuals. The progressive principle, however, in either shape, whether as the love of liberty or of improvement, is antagonistic to the sway of Custom, involving at least emancipation from that yoke; and the contest between the two constitutes the chief interest of the history of mankind. The greater part of the world has, properly speaking, no history, because the despotism of Custom is complete. This is the case over the whole East. Custom is there, in all things, the final appeal; justice and right mean conformity to custom; the argument of custom no one, unless some tyrant intoxi-

* A commission to ascertain the presence of insanity.

cated with power, thinks of resisting. And we see the result. Those nations must once have had originality; they did not start out of the ground populous, lettered, and versed in many of the arts of life; they made themselves all this, and were then the greatest and most powerful nations of the world. What are they now? The subjects or dependents of tribes whose forefathers wandered in the forests when theirs had magnificent palaces and gorgeous temples, but over whom custom exercised only a divided rule with liberty and progress. A people, it appears, may be progressive for a certain length of time, and then stop: when does it stop? When it ceases to possess individuality. If a similar change should befall the nations of Europe, it will not be in exactly the same shape: the despotism of custom with which these nations are threatened is not precisely stationariness. It proscribes singularity, but it does not preclude change, provided all change together. We have discarded the fixed costumes of our forefathers; every one must still dress like other people, but the fashion may change once or twice a year. We thus take care that when there is a change, it shall be for change's sake, and not from any idea of beauty or convenience; for the same idea of beauty or convenience would not strike all the world at the same moment, and be simultaneously thrown aside by all at another moment. But we are progressive as well as changeable: we continually make new inventions in mechanical things, and keep them until they are again superseded by better; we are eager for improvement in politics, in education, even in morals, though in this last our idea of improvement chiefly consists in persuading or forcing other people to be as good as ourselves. It is not progress that we object to; on the contrary, we flatter ourselves that we are the most progressive people who ever lived. It is individuality that we war against: we should think we had done wonders if we had made ourselves all alike; forgetting that the unlikeness of one person to another is generally the first thing which draws the attention of either to the imperfection of his own type, and the superiority of another, or the possibility, by combining the advantages of both, of producing something better than either. We have a warning example in China—a nation of much talent, and, in some respects, even wisdom, owing to the rare good fortune of having been provided at an early period with a particularly good set of customs, the work, in some measure, of men to whom even the most enlightened European must accord, under certain limitations, the title of sages and philosophers. They are remarkable, too, in the excellence of their apparatus for impressing, as far as possible, the best wisdom they possess upon every mind in the community, and securing that those who have appropriated most of it shall occupy the posts of honour and power. Surely the people who did this have discovered the secret of human progressiveness, and must have kept themselves steadily at the head of the movement of the world. On the contrary, they have become stationary—have remained so for thousands of years; and if they are ever to be farther improved, it must be by foreigners. They have succeeded beyond all hope in what English philanthropists are so industriously working at—in making a people all alike, all governing their thoughts and conduct by the same maxims and rules; and these are the fruits. The modern *régime* of public opinion is, in an unorganised form, what the Chinese educational and political systems are in an organised; and unless individuality shall be able successfully to assert itself against this yoke, Europe, notwithstanding its noble antecedents and its professed Christianity, will tend to become another China.

What is it that has hitherto preserved Europe from this lot? What has made the European family of nations an improving, instead of a stationary portion of mankind? Not any superior excellence in them, which, when it exists, exists as the effect, not as the cause; but their remarkable diversity of character and culture. Individuals, classes, nations, have been extremely unlike one another: they have struck out a great variety of paths, each leading to something valuable; and although at every period those who travelled in different paths have been intolerant of one another, and each would have thought it an excellent thing if all the rest could have been compelled to travel his road, their attempts to thwart each other's development have rarely had any permanent success, and each has in time endured to receive the good which the others have offered. Europe is, in my judgment, wholly indebted to this plurality of paths for its progressive and many-sided development. But it already begins to possess this benefit in a considerably less degree. It is decidedly advancing towards the Chinese ideal of making all people alike. M. de Tocqueville . . . remarks how much more the Frenchmen of the present day resemble one another than did those even of the last generation. The same remark might be made of Englishmen in a far greater degree. In a passage already quoted from Wilhelm von Humboldt, he points out two things as necessary conditions of human development, because necessary to render people unlike one another; namely, freedom, and variety of situations. The second of these two conditions is in this country every day diminishing. The circumstances which surround different classes and individuals, and shape their characters, are daily becoming more assimilated. Formerly, different ranks, different neighbourhoods, different trades and professions, lived in what might be called different worlds; at present to a great degree in the same. Comparatively speaking, they now read the same things, listen to the same things, see the same things, go to the same places, have their hopes and fears directed to the same objects, have the same rights and liberties, and the same means of asserting them. Great as are the differences of position which remain, they are nothing to those which have ceased. And the assimilation is still proceeding. All the political changes of the age promote it, since they all tend to raise the low and to lower the high. Every extension of education promotes it, because education brings people under common influences, and gives them access to the general stock of facts and sentiments. Improvement in the means of communication promotes it, by bringing the inhabitants of distant places into personal contact, and keeping up a rapid flow of changes of res-

idence between one place and another. The increase of commerce and manufactures promotes it, by diffusing more widely the advantages of easy circumstances, and opening all objects of ambition, even the highest, to general competition, whereby the desire of rising becomes no longer the character of a particular class, but of all classes. A more powerful agency than even all these, in bringing about a general similarity among mankind, is the complete establishment, in this and other free countries, of the ascendancy of public opinion in the State. As the various social eminences which enabled persons entrenched on them to disregard the opinion of the multitude gradually become levelled; as the very idea of resisting the will of the public, when it is positively known that they have a will, disappears more and more from the minds of practical politicians; there ceases to be any social support for nonconformity—any substantive power in society which, itself opposed to the ascendancy of numbers, is interested in taking under its protection opinions and tendencies at variance with those of the public.

The combination of all these causes forms so great a mass of influences hostile to Individuality, that it is not easy to see how it can stand its ground. It will do so with increasing difficulty, unless the intelligent part of the public can be made to feel its value—to see that it is good there should be differences, even though not for the better, even though, as it may appear to them, some should be for the worse. If the claims of individuality are ever to be asserted, the time is now, while much is still wanting to complete the enforced assimilation. It is only in the earlier stages that any stand can be successfully made against the encroachment. The demand that all other people shall resemble ourselves grows by what it feeds on. If resistance waits till life is reduced *nearly* to one uniform type, all deviations from that type will come to be considered impious, immoral, even monstrous and contrary to nature. Mankind speedily become unable to conceive diversity, when they have been for some time unaccustomed to see it.

II ? THE UNWRITTEN CONSTITUTION

The American Civil Liberties Union (ACLU) is the nation's leading exponent of civil liberties and individual freedom. To its supporters, it is the nation's first line of defense against tyranny; to its opponents, it is an ultraliberal organization dedicated to undermining American life and values; former Attorney General Edwin Meese went so far as to call it the "criminals' lobby." That the ACLU is controversial should come as no surprise; it is passionately committed to the defense of free speech, the separation of church and state, the protection of privacy rights, and the preservation and extension of the rights of criminal defendants to due process of law. Its clients are rarely popular and have included the American Nazi party, the Ku Klux Klan, communists, atheists, and convicted murderers. The common denominator is that in every case, the ACLU has been on the side of freedom—as it has defined freedom. Sometimes, its own supporters disagree with the ACLU's definition of freedom, as when it defended the right of the Nazis to march in the predominantly Jewish suburb of Skokie, Illinois, in 1977. At other times, it has confused both supporters and critics—for example, when it argued in favor of the right of the conservative hero Oliver North to a fair trial.

Whatever one's view of the ACLU, it is impossible to deny that it has played a critical role in American politics over the past seventy-five years. The following excerpt is a brief look at this extraordinary organization.

Question

1. "In the 1988 presidential campaign," Walker writes in the following selection, "George Bush invoked the ACLU as a symbol. But a symbol of what? Why does the very mention of its name arouse such intense passion?" Answer Walker's question. Recall selection 8.1.

16.2 The ACLU, Civil Liberties, and American Life

Samuel Walker

A Revolution in American Life

The history of the American Civil Liberties Union is the story of America in this century. Born out of the fight to defend free speech during World War I, the ACLU has been at the storm center of controversy ever since then. Its part in some of the most famous events in American history—the Scopes "monkey trial," the internment of the Japanese-Americans in World War II, the cold war anti-Communist witch hunt, the fight for abortion rights, and many others—has made it one of the most important and, at times, unpopular organizations in the country.

In the 1988 presidential election campaign, Republican candidate George Bush attacked his opponent, Michael Dukakis, for being a "card-carrying member of the ACLU." Citing the organization's stand on pornography and the separation of church and state, Bush accused the ACLU of being out of the "mainstream" of

American life. But as well as casting aspersions on Dukakis, Bush's attack raised more fundamental questions about the nature of American values and the place of the Bill of Rights in American society.

With some justification, the ACLU can claim to have shaped contemporary values. Principles of individual freedom, protection against arbitrary government action, equal protection, and privacy have pervaded our society. When the ACLU was founded in 1920, the promises of the Bill of Rights had little practical meaning for ordinary people. Today, there is a substantial body of law in all the major areas of civil liberties: freedom of speech and press, separation of church and state, free exercise of religion, due process of law, equal protection, and privacy. The growth of civil liberties since World War I represents one of the most important long-term developments in modern American history, a revolution in the law and public attitudes toward individual liberty. Some have called it the "rights revolution"; we prefer to call it the civil liberties revolution. This change forms one of the great themes in twentieth-century American history. Although scarcely mentioned in standard history textbooks, it equals in significance the commonly cited themes of industrialization, urbanization, and American involvement in the world economy.

The ACLU can legitimately claim much of the credit—or be assigned the blame, if you prefer—for the growth of modern constitutional law. Consult a standard constitutional law textbook and note the cases deemed important enough to be listed in the table of contents—the proverbial "landmark" cases. The ACLU was involved in over 80 percent of them; in several critical cases, the Supreme Court's opinion was drawn directly from the ACLU brief. As even its critics have charged, the ACLU has exerted "an influence out of all proportion to its size."

Despite the evident acceptance of many once-unpopular concepts, such as the right to criticize the government during wartime, the ACLU itself remains controversial. Americans have always had a curiously ambivalent attitude

Reprinted with special permission of King Features Syndicate, Inc

toward the Constitution and the Bill of Rights. It has often been a self-centered approach: my freedom, yes; your freedom, no. The majority has not hesitated to impose its views on the minority and to suppress ideas it did not like. The history of the ACLU lays bare some of the least attractive aspects of American society: ugly strands of religious intolerance and racism and a habit of falling prey to hysteria over alleged threats from foreigners or "foreign ideas." But that same history illuminates a parallel counter-theme: the growth of tolerance for different, even obnoxious ideas; the end of some of the worst forms of racial discrimination; and a new sense of privacy that, in myriad ways, limits government intrusion into our lives. These more hopeful changes, rooted in the Bill of Rights, comprise the civil liberties revolution.

What Is the ACLU?

Although its name is widely known, the ACLU is little understood. In the 1988 presidential campaign, George Bush invoked the ACLU as a symbol. But a symbol of what? Why does the very mention of its name arouse such intense passion? Who are the civil libertarians, and what drives them?

In a formal sense, the ACLU is a private voluntary organization dedicated to defending the Bill of Rights. Officially established in 1920, the ACLU now claims over 270,000 members. In addition to a national office in New York and a large legislative office in Washington, D.C., it maintains staffed affiliates in forty-six states. The often feisty and independent affiliates handle 80 percent of the ACLU's legal cases. With some justification, the ACLU calls itself "the nation's largest law firm." At any given moment it is involved in an estimated one thousand cases, and it appears before the Supreme Court more often than does any other organization except the federal government. The four thousand to five thousand volunteer "cooperating attorneys," the traditional backbone of ACLU litigation, are joined by over sixty paid staff attorneys—in the national office, the eleven "special projects," and the larger affiliates. The ACLU Washington office, with eleven full-time lobbyists, dwarfs other civil rights groups.

The essential feature of the ACLU is its professed commitment to the nonpartisan defense of the Bill of Rights. This means defending the civil liberties of everyone, including the free speech rights of Communists, Nazis, and Ku Klux Klan members. It means defending the due process rights of even the most despicable criminals. Defense of the unpopular has always been the ACLU's touchstone, its proudest principle, and the cause of the most bitter attacks on it. The ACLU's "absolutist" position on freedom from censorship and separation of church and state has led it to oppose censorship of pornography and, every winter at holiday time, to fight religious displays on government property.

It is precisely this absolutist approach that arouses the hatred of its opponents, causes despair among many would-be friends, and inspires its members. The powerless and the despised have been the ACLU's most frequent clients, for the simple reason that they have been the most frequent victims of intolerance and repression. As a result, most ACLU members have historically been liberals or people with leftist sympathies. What distinguishes ACLU members from mainstream liberals, however, is their skepticism of government power and a willingness to challenge extensions of that

power justified in the name of social betterment. What distinguishes the ACLU from the left has been its running war with Marxists over their habit of denying that their opponents (Fascists, racists, and such) are entitled to the same freedoms they claim for themselves. And finally, the ACLU differs from most professed conservatives by its commitment to give flesh and blood to traditional Fourth of July rhetoric about liberty, to afford the protections of the Bill of Rights to everyone.

The ACLU is a unique organization, without parallel in other democratic countries. True, there are civil liberties organizations elsewhere—for instance, the National Council on Civil Liberties (NCCL) in England and the Japanese Civil Liberties Union (JCLU) in Japan. None of them, however, plays such a large and controversial role in its country as the ACLU does in the United States. The NCCL, for example, has long taken an explicitly partisan stance on behalf of labor and has neglected to defend the rights of employers or racists. The JCLU has a grand total of seven hundred members and few court cases: Even most of the affiliates of the ACLU are larger and more active.

The uniqueness of the ACLU is a consequence of several important features of American life: a written Constitution with a Bill of Rights, a cultural heritage that places a premium on individual liberty, and a legal and political tradition in which the Supreme Court plays a prominent role in resolving conflict in terms of constitutional law. Thus, understanding the ACLU's history provides important insight into these basic aspects of American history and culture. Critics who accuse the ACLU of taking the Bill of Rights to extremes are, in effect, voicing a more fundamental complaint about the Constitution, the courts, and some of the deepest impulses in American society.

Yet to say that the ACLU defends civil liberties only raises another question: What is a civil liberty?

What Is a Civil Liberty?

The Encyclopedia of the Constitution defines civil liberties as those rights that individual citizens may assert against the government. In the United States, such liberties are enumerated in the Bill of Rights. The encyclopedia definition, however, begs all the important questions. What does freedom of speech encompass? Is picketing or wearing an armband a form of speech? What exactly does the phrase "due process of law" mean? What is an unreasonable search? What constitutes cruel and unusual punishment? Is there a constitutional right of privacy? More fundamentally, what standard should we use in trying to answer these questions?

The text of the Bill of Rights provides no definitive answers to these questions. Although advocates of the "original intent" school of constitutional law argue that we should adhere strictly to the specific language of the Bill of Rights, our history suggests that the genius of the Constitution is its flexibility and capacity to adapt to changing circumstances. Seventy years ago, in one of his most famous opinions, Justice Oliver Wendell Holmes wrote that our constitutional form of government is "an experiment, as all life is an experiment." The history of civil liberties is the story of that experiment. It is the story of an ongoing effort to redefine the nature of freedom within the framework of the Bill of Rights.

The ACLU is itself an ongoing experiment, with an agenda that constantly changes. Many ACLU members will be surprised to learn that the organization did not always take an "absolutist" position on censorship or the separation of church and state. They will be equally surprised to learn that for a time the ACLU took a strong stand against corporate monopolies in the field of communications. . . .

The ACLU has generally been not just an agent but also a symptom of change—an avenue through which emerging ideas about liberty have been able to express themselves and gain force in the marketplace of ideas.

Critics often charge the ACLU with arrogance. Who, they ask, gave it license to say what a civil liberty is? Who gave it authority to impose its will on the rest of the country? The answers to these questions are, respectively, that no one gave the ACLU any special license and that it has not imposed its will on the country. The ACLU has had no greater authority than any other advocacy group has had. It has argued its point of view in the courts and the arena of public opinion along with every other group. And finally, the remarkable fact is that it has succeeded in persuading many courts, including the U.S. Supreme Court, and a broad spectrum of the public that its views are right.

The ACLU's very success in this regard illuminates some of the most important developments in American history: the changing public attitudes toward individual liberty and the role of the Constitution as a framework for achieving individual freedom in the context of a pluralistic and bureaucratic society. The great controversies over ACLU policies—pornography, separation of church and state, the rights of suspected criminals—go to the heart of the matter: What is the nature of freedom in a democratic society? Where should the lines be drawn in determining the boundaries of individual rights? . . . [The ACLU,] a small but remarkable organization[,] . . . has contributed much to answering these questions.

III ⚞📊⚟ TRENDS

Surely the most controversial decision the Supreme Court has made in recent years is that a woman's right to obtain an abortion is protected by the U.S. Constitution. The original decision, handed down in 1973 in Roe v. Wade *(selection 16.3) sparked extraordinary controversy and inflamed an issue that remains divisive and contentious. "Pro-life" groups sprung up to attack the decision; "pro-choice" groups rose to its defense. The battle has raged ever since.*

The Court's decision in Roe v. Wade *made essentially four points. First, the right to terminate a pregnancy is included within the constitutional right to privacy. Second, the Fourteenth Amendment (which protects the right to life, liberty, and property) is not applicable to an unborn fetus. Third, a state cannot arbitrarily decide that life begins at conception and thereby block the woman's right to obtain an abortion. Finally, the woman's right of privacy is not absolute; the state's interest in protecting the potential life of the fetus grows as the fetus grows and eventually outweighs the woman's right. In the first trimester of pregnancy, therefore, the state cannot interfere at all with her choice; during the second, it can regulate the abortion procedure but not prohibit abortion altogether; in the third, the state can completely ban all abortions.*

A major strategy of the campaign against abortion has been the attempt to replace pro-choice justices on the Supreme Court with justices willing or eager to overturn Roe v. Wade. *Jimmy Carter had no opportunity to appoint a Court justice, but Republican presidents since Carter have had the opportunity to reshape the Court, and abortion has played at least some role in several of the recent appointments. Beginning in 1983, the slim majority in favor of* Roe *began to weaken. In that year, Justice Sandra Day O'Connor, appointed by President Reagan in 1981, wrote an important dissent in* Akron v. Akron Center for Reproductive Health *(selection 16.4). O'Connor attacked the validity of* Roe v. Wade's *trimester schema, setting the stage for further attacks on the abortion right itself.*

In 1989, the Court took an even bigger step toward reversing Roe. *In* Webster v. Reproductive Health Services *(selection 16.5), a majority of the justices revealed themselves willing either to overturn* Roe *or to restrict its scope. Although the opinions of the justices were deeply divided, most commentators believe* Webster *signaled another step in the direction of undermining* Roe *and thus sending the abortion decision back to the states. As of mid-1991, the Court has not overturned* Roe, *but Court-watchers expect new developments within the next few years.*

Selections 5.3 and 6.4 contain related material.

Questions

1. What is the constitutional basis for the right to privacy elaborated in *Roe* v. *Wade?* What provisions of the Constitution and the Bill of Rights support the idea that the Constitution protects privacy?

2. Why does Justice O'Connor dispute the Court's trimester scheme for regulating abortion? What alternative does she propose?

3. Evaluate *Roe* v. *Wade* in terms of the debate over judicial activism and restraint, as presented in chapter 14.

16.3 Roe *v.* Wade

Mr. Justice Blackmun delivered the opinion of the Court.

This [case] . . . present[s] constitutional challenges to state criminal abortion legislation. . . .

We forthwith acknowledge our awareness of the sensitive and emotional nature of the abortion controversy, of the vigorous opposing views, even among physicians, and of the deep and seemingly absolute convictions that the subject inspires. One's philosophy, one's experiences, one's exposure to the raw edges of human existence, one's religious training, one's attitudes toward life and family and their values, and the moral standards one establishes and seeks to observe, are all likely to influence and to color one's thinking and conclusions about abortion.

In addition, population growth, pollution, poverty, and racial overtones tend to complicate and not to simplify the problem.

Our task, of course, is to resolve the issue by constitutional measurement, free of emotion and of predilection. We seek earnestly to do this, and, because we do, we have inquired into, and in this opinion place some emphasis upon, medical and medical-legal history and what that history reveals about man's attitudes toward the abortion procedure over the centuries. We bear in mind, too, Mr. Justice Holmes' admonition in his now-vindicated dissent in *Lochner* v. *New York* (1905):

[The Constitution] is made for people of fundamentally differing views, and the accident of our finding certain opinions natural and familiar or novel and even shocking ought not to conclude our judgment upon the question whether statutes embodying them conflict with the Constitution of the United States.

I

The Texas statutes that concern us here are Arts. 1191–1194 and 1196 of the State's Penal Code. These make it a crime to "procure an abortion," as therein defined, or to attempt one, except with respect to "an abortion procured or attempted by medical advice for the purpose of saving the life of the mother." Similar statutes are in existence in a majority of the States.

Texas first enacted a criminal abortion statute in 1854. This was soon modified into language that has remained substantially unchanged to the present time. [The Texas statute provides an] . . . exception for an abortion by "medical advice for the purpose of saving the life of the mother."

• • •

II

The principal thrust of appellant's attack on the Texas statutes is that they improperly invade a right, said to be possessed by the pregnant woman, to choose to terminate her pregnancy. Appellant would discover this right in the concept of personal "liberty" embodied in the Fourteenth Amendment's Due Process Clause; or in personal, marital, familial, and sexual privacy said to be protected by the Bill of Rights or its penumbras; or among those rights reserved to the people by the Ninth Amendment. Before addressing this claim, we feel it desirable briefly to survey, in several aspects, the history of abortion, for such insight as that history may afford us, and then to examine the state purposes and interests behind the criminal abortion laws.

III

It perhaps is not generally appreciated that the restrictive criminal abortion laws in effect in a majority of States today are of relatively recent vintage. Those laws, generally proscribing abortion or its attempt at any time during pregnancy except when necessary to preserve the pregnant woman's life, are not of ancient or even of common-law origin. Instead, they derive from statutory changes effected, for the most part, in the latter half of the 19th century.

• • •

The law in effect in all but a few States until mid-19th century was the pre-existing English common law. Connecticut, the first State to enact abortion legislation, adopted in 1821 that part of Lord Ellenborough's Act that related to a woman "quick with child." The death penalty was not imposed. Abortion before quickening was made a crime in that State only in 1860. In 1828, New York enacted legislation that, in two respects, was to serve as a model for early anti-abortion statutes. First, while barring destruction of an unquickened fetus as well as a quick fetus, it made the former only a misdemeanor, but the latter second-degree manslaughter. Second, it incorporated a concept of therapeutic abortion by providing that an abortion was excused if it "shall have been necessary to preserve the life of such mother, or shall have been advised by two physicians to be necessary for such purpose." By 1840, when Texans had received the common law, only eight American States had statutes dealing with abortion. It was not until after the War Between the States that legislation began generally to replace the common law. Most of these initial statutes dealt severely with abortion after quickening but were lenient with it before quickening. Most punished attempts equally with completed abortions. While many statutes included the exception for an abortion thought by one or more physicians to be necessary to save the mother's life, that provision soon disappeared and the typical law required that the procedure actually be necessary for that purpose.

Gradually, in the middle and late 19th century the quickening distinction disappeared from the statutory law of most States and the degree of the offense and the penalties were increased. By the end of the 1950's, a large majority of the jurisdictions banned abortion, however and whenever performed, unless done to save or preserve the life of the mother. The exceptions, Alabama and the District of Columbia, permitted abortion to preserve the mother's health. Three States permitted abortions that were not "unlawfully" performed or that were not "without lawful justification," leaving interpretations of those standards to the courts. In the past several years, however, a trend toward liberalization of abortion statutes has resulted in adoption, by about one-third of the States, of less stringent laws.

• • •

[IV]

Three reasons have been advanced to explain historically the enactment of criminal abortion laws in the 19th century and to justify their continued existence.

It has been argued occasionally that these laws were the product of a Victorian social concern to discourage illicit sexual conduct. Texas, however, does not advance this justification in the present case, and it appears that no court or commentator has taken the argument seriously. . . .

A second reason is concerned with abortion as a medical procedure. When most criminal abortion laws were first enacted, the procedure was a hazardous one for the woman. This was particularly true prior to the development of antisepsis. Antiseptic techniques, of course, were based on discoveries by Lister, Pasteur, and others first announced in 1867, but were not generally accepted and employed until about the turn of the century. Abortion mortality was high. Even after 1900, and perhaps until as late as the development of antibiotics in the 1940's, standard modern techniques such as dilation and curettage were not nearly so safe as they are today. Thus, it has been argued that a

State's real concern in enacting a criminal abortion law was to protect the pregnant woman, that is, to restrain her from submitting to a procedure that placed her life in serious jeopardy.

Modern medical techniques have altered this situation. Appellants and various *amici* refer to medical data indicating that abortion in early pregnancy, that is, prior to the end of the first trimester, although not without its risk, is now relatively safe. Mortality rates for women undergoing early abortions, where the procedure is legal, appear to be as low as or lower than the rates for normal childbirth. Consequently, any interest of the State in protecting the woman from an inherently hazardous procedure, except when it would be equally dangerous for her to forgo it, has largely disappeared. Of course, important state interests in the areas of health and medical standards do remain. The state has a legitimate interest in seeing to it that abortion, like any other medical procedure, is performed under circumstances that insure maximum safety for the patient. This interest obviously extends at least to the performing physician and his staff, to the facilities involved, to the availability of after-care, and to adequate provision for any complication or emergency that might arise. The prevalence of high mortality rates at illegal "abortion mills" strengthens, rather than weakens, the State's interest in regulating the conditions under which abortions are performed. Moreover, the risk to the woman increases as her pregnancy continues. Thus, the State retains a definite interest in protecting the woman's own health and safety when an abortion is proposed at a late stage of pregnancy.

The third reason is the State's interest—some phrase it in terms of duty—in protecting prenatal life. Some of the argument for this justification rests on the theory that a new human life is present from the moment of conception. The State's interest and general obligation to protect life then extends, it is argued, to prenatal life. Only when the life of the pregnant mother herself is at stake, balanced against the life she carries within her, should the interest of the embryo or fetus not prevail. Logically, of course, a legitimate state interest in this area need not stand or fall on acceptance of the belief that life begins at conception or at some other point prior to live birth. In assessing the State's interest, recognition may be given to the less rigid claim that as long as at least *potential* life is involved, the State may assert interests beyond the protection of the pregnant woman alone.

• • •

It is with these interests, and the weight to be attached to them, that this case is concerned.

[V]

The Constitution does not explicitly mention any right of privacy. In a line of decisions, however, going back perhaps as far as *Union Pacific R. Co. v. Botsford* (1891), the Court has recognized that a right of personal privacy, or a guarantee of certain areas of zones of privacy, does exist under the Constitution. In varying contexts, the Court or individual Justices have, indeed, found at least the roots of that right in the First Amendment; in the Fourth and Fifth Amendments; in the penumbras of the Bill of Rights; in the Ninth Amendment; or in the concept of liberty guaranteed by the first section of the Fourteenth Amendment. These decisions make it clear that only personal rights that can be deemed "fundamental" or "implicit in the concept of ordered liberty" are included in this guarantee of personal privacy. They also make it clear that the right has some extension to activities relating to marriage, procreation, contraception, family relationships, and child rearing and education.

This right of privacy, whether it be founded in the Fourteenth Amendment's concept of personal liberty and restrictions upon state action, as we feel it is, or, as the District Court determined, in the Ninth Amendment's reservation of rights to the people, is broad enough to encompass a woman's decision whether or not to terminate her pregnancy. The detriment that the State would impose upon the pregnant woman by denying this choice altogether is apparent. Specific and direct harm medically diagnosable even in early pregnancy may be involved. Maternity, or additional offspring, may force upon the woman a distressful life and future. Psychological harm may be imminent. Mental and physical health may be taxed by child care. There is also the distress, for all concerned, associated with the unwanted child, and there is the problem of bringing a child into a family already unable, psychologically and otherwise, to care for it. In other cases, as in this one, the additional difficulties and continuing stigma of unwed motherhood may be involved. All these are factors the woman and her responsible physician necessarily will consider in consultation.

On the basis of elements such as these, appellant and some *amici* argue that the woman's right is absolute and that she is entitled to terminate her pregnancy at whatever time, in whatever way, and for whatever reason she alone chooses. With this we do not agree. Appellant's arguments that Texas either has no valid interest at all in regulating the abortion decision, or no interest strong enough to support any limitation upon the woman's sole determination, are unpersuasive. The Court's decisions recognizing a right of privacy also acknowledge that some state regulation in areas protected by that right is appropriate. As noted above, a State may properly assert important interests in safeguarding health, in maintaining medical standards, and in protecting potential life. At some point in pregnancy, these respective interests become sufficiently compelling to sustain regulation of the factors that govern the abortion decision. The privacy right involved, therefore, cannot be said to be absolute. In fact, it is not clear to us that the claim asserted by some *amici* that one has an unlimited right to do with one's body as one pleases bears a close relationship to the right of privacy previously articulated in the Court's decisions. The Court has refused to recognize an unlimited right of this kind in the past.

We, therefore, conclude that the right of personal privacy includes the abortion decision,

but that this right is not unqualified and must be considered against important state interests in regulation.

• • •

Where certain "fundamental rights" are involved, the Court has held that regulation limiting these rights may be justified only by a "compelling state interest," and that legislative enactments must be narrowly drawn to express only the legitimate state interests at stake.

In the recent abortion cases, . . . courts have recognized these principles. Those striking down state laws have generally scrutinized the State's interests in protecting health and potential life, and have concluded that neither interest justified broad limitations on the reasons for which a physician and his pregnant patient might decide that she should have an abortion in the early stages of pregnancy. Courts sustaining state laws have held that the State's determinations to protect health or prenatal life are dominant and constitutionally justifiable.

The . . . [State] argue[s] that the fetus is a "person" within the language and meaning of the Fourteenth Amendment. In support of this, they outline at length and in detail the well-known facts of fetal development. If this suggestion of personhood is established, the appellant's case, of course, collapses, for the fetus' right to life would then be guaranteed specifically by the Amendment. The appellant conceded as much on reargument. On the other hand, the appellee conceded on reargument that no case could be cited that holds that a fetus is a person within the meaning of the Fourteenth Amendment.

The Constitution does not define "person" in so many words. Section 1 of the Fourteenth Amendment contains three references to "person." The first, in defining "citizens," speaks of "persons born or naturalized in the United States." The word also appears both in the Due Process Clause and in the Equal Protection Clause. "Person" is used in other places in the Constitution: in the listing of qualifications for Representatives and Senators, in the Apportionment Clause, in the Migration and Importation provision, in the Emolument Clause, in the Electors provisions, in the provision outlining qualifications for the office of President, in the Extradition provisions, and in the Fifth, Twelfth, and Twenty-second Amendments, as well as in §§2 and 3 of the Fourteenth Amendment. But in nearly all these instances, the use of the word is such that it has application only postnatally. None indicates, with any assurance, that it has any possible pre-natal application.

All this, together with our observation, that throughout the major portion of the 19th century prevailing legal abortion practices were far freer than they are today, persuades us that the word "person," as used in the Fourteenth Amendment, does not include the unborn. . . .

This conclusion, however, does not of itself fully answer the contentions raised by Texas, and we pass on to other considerations.

B. The pregnant woman cannot be isolated in her privacy. She carries an embryo and, later, a fetus, if one accepts the medical definitions of the developing young in the human uterus. The situation therefore is inherently different from marital intimacy, or bedroom possession of obscene material, or marriage, or procreation, or education. . . . As we have intimated above, it is reasonable and appropriate for a State to decide that at some point in time another interest, that of health of the mother or that of potential human life, becomes significantly involved. The woman's privacy is no longer sole and any right of privacy she possesses must be measured accordingly.

Texas urges that, apart from the Fourteenth Amendment, life begins at conception and is present throughout pregnancy, and that, therefore, the State has a compelling interest in protecting that life from and after conception. We need not resolve the difficult question of when life begins. When those trained in the respective disciplines of medicine, philosophy, and theology are unable to arrive at any consensus, the judiciary, at this point in the development of man's knowledge, is not in a position to speculate as to the answer.

It should be sufficient to note briefly the wide divergence of thinking on this most sensitive and difficult question. There has always been strong support for the view that life does not begin until live birth. This was the belief of the Stoics. It appears to be the predominant, though not the unanimous, attitude of the Jewish faith. It may be taken to represent also the position of a large segment of the Protestant community, insofar as that can be ascertained; organized groups that have taken a formal position on the abortion issue have generally regarded abortion as a matter for the conscience of the individual and her family. As we have noted, the common law found greater significance in quickening. Physicians and their scientific colleagues have regarded that event with less interest and have tended to focus either upon conception, upon live birth, or upon the interim point at which the fetus becomes "viable," that is, potentially able to live outside the mother's womb, albeit with artificial aid. Viability is usually placed at about seven months (28 weeks) but may occur earlier, even at 24 weeks. The Aristotelian theory of "mediate animation," that held sway throughout the Middle Ages and the Renaissance in Europe, continued to be official Roman Catholic dogma until the 19th century, despite opposition to this "ensoulment" theory from those in the Church who would recognize the existence of life from the moment of conception. The latter is now, of course, the official belief of the Catholic Church. As one brief *amicus* discloses, this is a view strongly held by many non-Catholics as well, and by many physicians. Substantial problems for precise definition of this view are posed, however, by new embryological data that purport to indicate that conception is a "process" over time, rather than an event, and by new medical techniques such as menstrual extraction, the "morning-after" pill, implantation of embryos, artificial insemination, and even artificial wombs.

In areas other than criminal abortion, the law has been reluctant to endorse any theory that life, as we recognize it, begins before live birth or to accord legal rights to the unborn except in narrowly defined situations and except when the rights are contingent upon live birth. For example, the traditional rule of tort law denied recovery for prenatal injuries even though the child was born alive. That rule has been changed in almost every jurisdiction. In most States, recovery is said to be permitted only if the fetus was viable, or at least quick, when the injuries were sustained, though few courts have squarely so held. In a recent development, generally opposed by the commentators, some States permit the parents of a stillborn child to maintain an action for wrongful death because of prenatal injuries. Such an action, however, would appear to be one to vindicate the parents' interest and is thus consistent with the view that the fetus, at most, represents only the potentiality of life. Similarly, unborn children have been recognized as acquiring rights or interests by way of inheritance or other devolution of property, and have been represented by guardians *ad litem*. Perfection of the interests involved, again, has generally been contingent upon live birth. In short, the unborn have never been recognized in the law as persons in the whole sense.

[VI]

In view of all this, we do not agree that, by adopting one theory of life, Texas may override the rights of the pregnant woman that are at stake. We repeat, however, that the State does have an important and legitimate interest in preserving and protecting the health of the pregnant woman, whether she be a resident of the State or a nonresident who seeks medical consultation and treatment there, and that it has still *another* important and legitimate interest in protecting the potentiality of human life. These interests are separate and distinct. Each grows in substantiality as the woman approaches term and, at a point during pregnancy, each becomes "compelling."

With respect to the State's important and legitimate interest in the health of the mother, the "compelling" point, in the light of present medical knowledge, is at approximately the end of the first trimester. This is so because of the now-established medical fact, . . . that until the end of the first trimester mortality in abortion may be less than mortality in normal childbirth. It follows that, from and after this point, a State may regulate the abortion procedure to the extent that the regulation reasonably relates to the preservation and protection of maternal health. Examples of permissible state regulation in this area are requirements as to the qualifications of the person who is to perform the abortion; as to the licensure of that person; as to the facility in which the procedure is to be performed, that is, whether it must be a hospital or may be a clinic or some other place of less-than-hospital status; as to the licensing of the facility; and the like.

This means, on the other hand, that, for the period of pregnancy prior to this "compelling" point, the attending physician, in consultation with his patient, is free to determine, without regulation by the State, that, in his medical judgment, the patient's pregnancy should be terminated. If that decision is reached, the judgment may be effectuated by an abortion free of interference by the State.

With respect to the State's important and legitimate interest in potential life, the "compelling" point is at viability. This is so because the fetus then presumably has the capability of meaningful life outside the mother's womb. State regulation protective of fetal life after viability thus has both logical and biological justifications. If the State is interested in protecting fetal life after viability, it may go so far as to proscribe abortion during that period, except when it is necessary to preserve the life or health of the mother.

Measured against these standards, [Texas] in restricting legal abortions to those "procured or attempted by medical advice for the purpose of saving the life of the mother," sweeps too broadly. The statute makes no distinction between abortions performed early in pregnancy and those performed later, and it limits to a single reason, "saving" the mother's life, the legal justification for the procedure. The statute, therefore, cannot survive the constitutional attack made upon it here.

• • •

16.4 Akron v. Akron Center for Reproductive Health

[*An Akron, Ohio, law required all abortions after the first trimester to be performed in a hospital, prohibited a physician from performing an abortion on an unmarried minor without the consent of her parents or of a court, required the attending physician to inform his or her patient of the status of the pregnancy and the viability of the fetus, and required a twenty-four-hour waiting period after the woman signed a consent form before an abortion could be performed. The Supreme Court, affirming* Roe v. Wade, *struck down all these regulations. Justice Sandra Day O'Connor's dissenting opinion follows.*]

In *Roe* v. *Wade*, the Court held that the "right of privacy . . . founded in the Fourteenth Amendment's concept of personal liberty and restrictions upon state action . . . is broad enough to encompass a woman's decision whether or not to terminate her pregnancy." The parties in these cases have not asked the Court to re-examine the validity of that holding and the court below did not address it. Accordingly, the Court does not re-examine its previous holding. Nonetheless, it is apparent from the Court's opinion that neither sound constitutional theory nor our need to decide cases based on the application of neutral principles can accommodate an analytical framework that varies according to the "stages" of pregnancy, where those stages, and their concomitant standards of review, differ according to the level of medical technology available when a particular challenge to state regulation occurs. The Court's analysis of the Akron regulations is inconsistent both with the methods of analysis employed in previous cases dealing with abortion, and with the Court's approach to fundamental rights in other areas.

Our recent cases indicate that a regulation imposed on "a lawful abortion 'is not unconstitutional unless it unduly burdens the right to seek an abortion.'" In my view, this "unduly burdensome" standard should be applied to the challenged regulations throughout the entire pregnancy without reference to the particular "stage" of pregnancy involved. If the particular regulation does not "unduly burde[n]" the fundamental right, then our evaluation of that regulation is limited to our determination that the regulation rationally relates to a legitimate state purpose. Irrespective of what we may believe is wise or prudent policy in this difficult area, "the Constitution does not constitute us as 'Platonic Guardians' nor does it vest in this Court the authority to strike down laws because they do not meet our standards of desirable social policy, 'wisdom,' or 'common sense.'"

I

The trimester or "three-stage" approach adopted by the Court in *Roe*, and, in a modified form, employed by the Court to analyze the regulations in these cases, cannot be supported as a legitimate or useful framework for accommodating the woman's right and the State's interests. The decision of the Court today graphically illustrates why the trimester approach is a completely unworkable method of accommodating the conflicting personal rights and compelling state interests that are involved in the abortion context.

As the Court indicates today, the State's compelling interest in maternal health changes as medical technology changes, and any health regulation must not "depart from accepted medical practice." In applying this standard, the Court holds that "the safety of second-trimester abortions has increased dramatically" since 1973, when *Roe* was decided. Although a regulation such as one requiring that all second-trimester abortions be performed in hospitals "had strong support" in 1973 "as a reasonable health regulation," this regulation can no longer stand because, according to the Court's diligent research into medical and scientific literature, the dilation and evacuation (D&E) procedure, used in 1973 only for first-trimester abortions, "is now widely and successfully used for second-trimester abortions." Further, the medical literature relied on by the Court indicates that the D&E procedure may be performed in an appropriate nonhospital setting for "at least . . . the early weeks of the second trimester. . . ." The Court then chooses the period of 16 weeks of gestation as that point at which D&E procedures may be performed safely in a nonhospital setting, and thereby invalidates the Akron hospitalization regulation.

It is not difficult to see that despite the Court's purported adherence to the trimester approach adopted in *Roe*, the lines drawn in that decision have now been "blurred" because of what the Court accepts as technological advancement in the safety of abortion procedure. The State may no longer rely on a "bright line" that separates permissible from impermissible regulation, and it is no longer free to consider the second trimester as a unit and weigh the risks posed by all abortion procedures throughout that trimester. Rather, the State must continuously and conscientiously study contemporary medical and scientific literature in order to determine whether the effect of a particular regulation is to "depart from accepted medical practice" insofar as particular procedures and particular periods within the trimester are concerned. Assuming that legislative bodies are able to engage in this exacting task, it is difficult to believe that our Constitution *requires* that they do it as a prelude to protecting the health of their citizens. It is even more difficult to believe that this Court, without the resources available to those bodies entrusted with making legislative choices, believes itself competent to make these inquiries and to revise these standards every time the American College of Obstetricians and Gynecologists (ACOG) or similar group revises its views about what is and what is not appropriate medical procedure in this area. Indeed, the ACOG Standards on which the Court relies were changed in 1982 after trial in the present cases. Before ACOG changed its Standards in 1982, it recommended that all midtrimester abortions be performed in a hospital.

As today's decision indicates, medical technology is changing, and this change will necessitate our continued functioning as the Nation's "*ex officio* medical board with powers to approve or disapprove medical and operative practices and standards throughout the United States."

Just as improvements in medical technology inevitably will move *forward* the point at which the State may regulate for reasons for maternal health, different technological improvements will move *backward* the point of viability at which the State may proscribe abortions except when necessary to preserve the life and health of the mother.

In 1973, viability before 28 weeks was considered unusual. The 14th edition of L. Hellman & J. Pritchard, Williams Obstetrics (1971), on which the Court relied in *Roe* for its understanding of viability, stated that "[a]ttainment of a [fetal] weight of 1,000 g [or a fetal age of approximately 28 weeks' gestation] is . . . widely used as the criterion of viability." However, recent studies have demonstrated increasingly earlier fetal viability. It is certainly reasonable to believe that fetal viability in the first trimester of pregnancy may be possible in the not too distant future. Indeed, the Court has explicitly acknowledged that *Roe* left the point of viability "flexible for anticipated advancements in medical skill." "[W]e recognized in *Roe* that viability was a matter of medical judgment, skill, and technical ability, and we preserved the flexibility of the term."

The *Roe* framework, then, is clearly on a collision course with itself. As the medical risks of various abortion procedures decrease, the point at which the State may regulate for reasons of maternal health is moved further forward to actual childbirth. As medical science becomes better able to provide for the separate existence of the fetus, the point of viability is moved further back toward conception. Moreover, it is clear that the trimester approach violates the fundamental aspiration of judicial decisionmaking through the application of neutral principles "sufficiently absolute to give them roots throughout the community and continuity over significant periods of time. . . ." The *Roe* framework is inherently tied to the state of medical technology that exists whenever particular litigation ensues. Although legislatures are better suited to make the necessary factual judgments in this area, the Court's framework forces legislatures, as a matter of constitutional law, to speculate about what constitutes "accepted medical practice" at any given time. Without the necessary expertise or ability, courts must then pretend to act as science review boards and examine those legislative judgments.

The Court adheres to the *Roe* framework because the doctrine of *stare decisis* "demands respect in a society governed by the rule of law."* Although respect for *stare decisis* cannot be challenged, "this Court's considered practice [is] not to apply *stare decisis* as rigidly in constitutional as in nonconstitutional cases." Although we must be mindful of the "desirability of continuity of decision in constitutional questions . . . when convinced of former error, this Court has never felt constrained to follow precedent. In constitutional questions, where correction depends upon amendment and not upon legislative action this Court throughout its history has freely exercised its power to reexamine the basis of its constitutional decisions."

Even assuming that there is a fundamental right to terminate pregnancy in some situations, there is no justification in law or logic for the trimester framework adopted in *Roe* and employed by the Court today on the basis of *stare decisis*. For the reasons stated above, that framework is clearly an unworkable means of balancing the fundamental right and the compelling state interests that are indisputably implicated.

II

The Court in *Roe* correctly realized that the State has important interests "in the areas of health and medical standards" and that "[t]he State has a legitimate interest in seeing to it that abor-

---

* *Stare decisis* ("to stand by decisions") refers to the policy of the courts to abide by settled decisions, or precedents.

tion, like any other medical procedure, is performed under circumstances that insure maximum safety for the patient." The Court also recognized that the State has "*another* important and legitimate interest in protecting the potentiality of human life." I agree completely that the State has these interests, but in my view, the point at which these interests become compelling does not depend on the trimester of pregnancy. Rather, these interests are present *throughout* pregnancy.

This Court has never failed to recognize that "a State may properly assert important interests in safeguarding health [and] in maintaining medical standards." It cannot be doubted that as long as a state statute is within "the bounds of reason and [does not] assum[e] the character of a merely arbitrary fiat . . . [then] [t]he State . . . must decide upon measures that are needful for the protection of its people. . . ." "There is nothing in the United States Constitution which limits the State's power to require that medical procedures be done safely. . . ." "The mode and procedure of medical diagnostic procedures is not the business of judges." Under the *Roe* framework, however, the state interest in maternal health cannot become compelling until the onset of the second trimester of pregnancy because "until the end of the first trimester mortality in abortion may be less than mortality in normal childbirth." Before the second trimester, the decision to perform an abortion "must be left to the medical judgment of the pregnant woman's attending physician."

The fallacy inherent in the *Roe* framework is apparent: just because the State has a compelling interest in ensuring maternal safety once an abortion may be more dangerous than childbirth, it simply does not follow that the State has *no* interest before that point that justifies state regulation to ensure that first-trimester abortions are performed as safely as possible.

The state interest in potential human life is likewise extant throughout pregnancy. In *Roe*, the Court held that although the State had an important and legitimate interest in protecting potential life, that interest could not become compelling until the point at which the fetus was viable. The difficulty with this analysis is clear: *potential* life is no less potential in the first weeks of pregnancy than it is at viability or afterward. At any stage in pregnancy, there is the *potential* for human life. Although the Court refused to "resolve the difficult question of when life begins," the Court chose the point of viability—when the fetus is *capable* of life independent of its mother—to permit the complete proscription of abortion. The choice of viability as the point at which the state interest in *potential* life becomes compelling is no less arbitrary than choosing any point before viability or any point afterward. Accordingly, I believe that the State's interest in protecting potential human life exists throughout the pregnancy.

[*Justice O'Connor concluded that the Supreme Court should scrap the trimester framework and strike down abortion regulations only when those regulations impose an "undue burden" on the privacy rights recognized in* Roe v. Wade.]

16.5 Webster *v.* Reproductive Health Services_____

[*The Supreme Court sustained a Missouri law containing several restrictions on abortion. Justice William Rehnquist's discussion of the most important provision of that law follows.*]

Section 188.029 of the Missouri Act provides:

Before a physician performs an abortion on a woman he has reason to believe is carrying an unborn child of twenty or more weeks gestational age, the physician shall first determine if the unborn child is viable by using and exercising that degree of care, skill, and proficiency commonly exercised by the ordinarily skillful, careful, and prudent physician engaged in similar practice under the same or similar conditions. In making this determination of viability, the physician shall perform or cause to be performed such medical examinations and tests as are necessary to make a finding of the gestational age, weight, and lung maturity of the unborn child and shall enter such findings and determination of viability in the medical record of the mother.

. . . The parties disagree over the meaning of this statutory provision. The State emphasizes the language of the first sentence, which speaks in terms of the physician's determination of viability being made by the standards of ordinary skill in the medical profession. Appellees stress the language of the second sentence, which prescribes such "tests as are necessary" to make a finding of gestational age, fetal weight, and lung maturity.

The Court of Appeals read §188.029 as requiring that after 20 weeks "doctors *must* perform tests to find gestational age, fetal weight and lung maturity." The court indicated that the tests needed to determine fetal weight at 20 weeks are "unreliable and inaccurate" and would add $125 to $250 to the cost of an abortion. It also stated that "amniocentesis, the only method available to determine lung maturity, is contrary to accepted medical practice until 28–30 weeks of gestation, expensive, and imposes significant health risks for both the pregnant woman and the fetus."

We must first determine the meaning of §188.029 under Missouri law. Our usual practice is to defer to the lower court's construction of a state statute, but we believe the Court of Appeals has "fallen into plain error" in this case. "'In expounding a statute, we must not be guided by a single sentence or member of a sentence, but look to the provisions of the whole law, and to its object and policy.'" The Court of Appeals' interpretation also runs "afoul of the well-established principle that statutes will be interpreted to avoid constitutional difficulties."

We think the viability-testing provision makes sense only if the second sentence is read to require only those tests that are useful to making subsidiary findings as to viability. If we construe this provision to require a physician to perform those tests needed to make the three specified findings *in all circumstances,* including when the physician's reasonable professional judgment indicates that the tests would be irrelevant to determining viability or even dangerous to the mother and the fetus, the second sentence of §188.029 would conflict with the first sentence's *requirement* that a physician apply his reasonable professional skill and judgment. It would also be incongruous to read this provision, especially the word "necessary," to require the performance of tests irrelevant to the expressed statutory purpose of determining viability. It thus seems clear to us that the Court of Appeals' construction of §188.029 violates well-accepted canons of statutory interpretation used in the Missouri courts. . . .

The viability-testing provision of the Missouri Act is concerned with promoting the State's interest in potential human life rather than in maternal health. Section 188.029 creates what is essentially a presumption of viability at 20 weeks, which the physician must rebut with tests indicating that the fetus is not viable prior to performing an abortion. It also directs the physician's determination as to viability by specifying consideration, if feasible, of gestational age, fetal weight, and lung capacity. The District Court found that "the medical evidence is uncontradicted that a 20-week fetus is *not* viable," and that "23½ to 24 weeks gestation is the earliest point in pregnancy where a reasonable possibility of viability exists." But it also found that there may be a 4-week error in estimating gestational age, which supports testing at 20 weeks.

In *Roe* v. *Wade,* the Court recognized that the State has "important and legitimate" interests in protecting maternal health and in the potentiality of human life. During the second trimester, the State "may, if it chooses, regulate the abortion procedure in ways that are reasonably related to maternal health." After viability, when the State's interest in potential human life was held to become compelling, the State "may, if it chooses, regulate, and even proscribe, abortion except where it is necessary, in appropriate medical judgment, for the preservation of the life or health of the mother."

In *Colautti* v. *Franklin,* . . . the Court held that a Pennsylvania statute regulating the standard of care to be used by a physician performing an abortion of a possibly viable fetus was void for vagueness. But in the course of reaching that conclusion, the Court reaffirmed its earlier statement in *Planned Parenthood of Central Missouri* v. *Danforth,* that "'the determination of whether a particular fetus is viable is, and must be, a matter for the judgement of the responsible attending physician.'" . . . To the extent that §188.029 regulates the method for determining viability, it undoubtedly does superimpose state regulation on the medical determination of whether a particular fetus is viable. The Court of Appeals and the District Court thought it unconstitutional for this reason. To the extent that the viability tests increase the cost of what are in fact second-trimester abortions, their validity may also be questioned under *Akron,* where the Court held that a requirement that second trimester abortions must be performed in hospitals was invalid because it substantially increased the expense of those procedures.

We think that the doubt cast upon the Missouri statute by these cases is not so much a flaw in the statute as it is a reflection of the fact that the rigid trimester analysis of the course of a pregnancy enunciated in *Roe* has resulted in subsequent cases . . . making constitutional law in this area a virtual Procrustean bed. Statutes specifying elements of informed consent to be provided abortion patients, for example, were invalidated if they were thought to "structur[e] . . . the dialogue between the woman and her physician." . . . Such a statute would have been sustained under any traditional standard of judicial review, or for any other surgical procedure except abortion.

Stare decisis is a cornerstone of our legal system, but it has less power in constitutional cases, where, save for constitutional amendments, this Court is the only body able to make needed changes. We have not refrained from reconsideration of a prior construction of the Constitution that has proved "unsound in principle and unworkable in practice." We think the *Roe* trimester framework falls into that category.

In the first place, the rigid *Roe* framework is hardly consistent with the notion of a Constitution cast in general terms, as ours is, and usually speaking in general principles, as ours does. The key elements of the *Roe* framework—trimesters and viability—are not found in the text of the Constitution or in any place else one would expect to find a constitutional principle. Since the bounds of the inquiry are essentially indeterminate, the result has been a web of legal rules that have become increasingly intricate, resembling a code of regulations rather than a body of constitutional doctrine. As Justice White has put it, the trimester framework has left this Court to serve as the country's *"ex officio* medical board with powers to approve or disapprove medical and operative practices and standards throughout the United States."

In the second place, we do not see why the State's interest in protecting potential human life should come into existence only at the point of viability, and that there should therefore be a rigid line allowing state regulation after viability but prohibiting it before viability. The dissenters in *Thornburgh* [v. *American College of Obstetricians and Gynecologists* (1986)],* writing in the context of the *Roe* trimester analysis, would have recognized this fact by positing against the "fundamental right" recognized in *Roe* the State's "compelling interest" in protecting potential human life throughout pregnancy.

"[T]he State's interest, if compelling after viability, is equally compelling before viability."

The tests that §188.029 requires the physician to perform are designed to determine viability. The State here has chosen viability as the point at which its interest in potential human life must be safeguarded. It is true that the tests in question increase the expense of abortion, and regulate the discretion of the physician in determining the viability of the fetus. Since the tests will undoubtedly show in many cases that the fetus is not viable, the tests will have been performed for what were in fact second-trimester abortions. But we are satisfied that the requirement of these tests permissibly furthers the State's interest in protecting potential human life, and we therefore believe §188.029 to be constitutional.

The dissent takes us to task for our failure to join in a "great issues" debate as to whether the Constitution includes an "unenumerated" general right to privacy as recognized in cases such as *Griswold* v. *Connecticut*† and *Roe*. But *Griswold* v. *Connecticut*, unlike *Roe*, did not purport to adopt a whole framework, complete with detailed rules and distinctions, to govern the cases in which the asserted liberty interest would apply. As such, it was far different from the opinion, if not the holding, of *Roe* v. *Wade*, which sought to establish a constitutional framework for judging state regulation of abortion during the entire term of pregnancy. That framework sought to deal with areas of medical practice traditionally subject to state regulation, and it sought to balance once and for all by reference only to the calendar the claims of the State to protect the fetus as a form of human life against the claims of a woman to decide for herself whether or not to abort a fetus she was carrying. The experience of the Court in applying *Roe* v. *Wade* in later cases suggests to us that there is wisdom in not unnecessarily attempting to elaborate the abstract differences between a

---

* In *Thornburgh,* the Court invalidated a number of restrictions on a woman's right to abortion.

† In *Griswold* (1965), the Supreme Court struck down state laws banning the use of contraceptives by married couples. The right to use contraceptives was extended to unmarried persons in *Eisenstadt* v. *Baird* (1972).

"fundamental right" to abortion, as the Court described it in *Akron,* which Justice Blackmun's dissent today treats *Roe* as having established, or a liberty interest protected by the Due Process Clause, which we believe it to be. The Missouri testing requirement here is reasonably designed to ensure that abortions are not performed where the fetus is viable—an end which all concede is legitimate—and that is sufficient to sustain its constitutionality.

The dissent also accuses us, *inter alia,* of cowardice and illegitimacy in dealing with "the most politically divisive domestic legal issue of our time." There is no doubt that our holding today will allow some governmental regulation of abortion that would have been prohibited under the language of [earlier] cases. . . . But the goal of constitutional adjudication is surely not to remove inexorably "politically divisive" issues from the ambit of the legislative process, whereby the people through their elected representatives deal with matters of concern to them. The goal of constitutional adjudication is to hold true the balance between that which the Constitution puts beyond the reach of the democratic process and that which it does not. We think we have done that today. . . .

Both appellants and the United States as *Amicus Curiae* have urged that we overrule our decision in *Roe* v. *Wade.* The facts of the present case, however, differ from those at issue in *Roe.* Here, Missouri has determined that viability is the point at which its interest in potential human life must be safeguarded. In *Roe,* on the other hand, the Texas statute criminalized the performance of *all* abortions, except when the mother's life was at stake. This case therefore affords us no occasion to revisit the holding of *Roe,* which was that the Texas statute unconstitutionally infringed the right to an abortion derived from the Due Process Clause, and we leave it undisturbed. To the extent indicated in our opinion, we would modify and narrow *Roe* and succeeding cases.

Because none of the challenged provisions of the Missouri Act properly before us conflict with the Constitution, the judgment of the Court of Appeals is

Reversed.

IV  FOCUS: THE FLAG SALUTE CASE

The American flag has recently been the subject of political controversy, largely because of the use of the pledge of allegiance issue in the 1988 presidential campaign against Michael Dukakis and because of Supreme Court decisions in 1989 and 1990 striking down laws prohibiting burning or otherwise desecrating the flag. Political and legal controversy surrounding the flag, however, goes back to at least World War II. The following case presents a slightly different question from the flag burning cases: whether an individual (in this case, a student in a public school) can be compelled to salute the American flag. The basic principles at issue remain the same in the 1990s as in 1943, and the Flag Salute Case represents a classic statement of the contending points of view.

Questions

1. What are the state's reasons for requiring a flag salute? What methods, in Justice Robert Jackson's view, would be legitimate ways of trying to accomplish the state's objectives?

2. Is Justice Jackson correct in asserting that "there is no doubt that . . . the flag salute is a 'form of utterance'"? Is burning the flag a form of utterance as well?

16.6 West Virginia *v.* Barnette

[A West Virginia statute adopted in 1942 required that all teachers and pupils in the public schools participate in a salute honoring the American flag and provided that "refusal to salute the Flag . . . [shall] be regarded as an act of insubordination, and shall be dealt with accordingly." The penalties for refusal included expulsion of the child and subsequent treatment as a delinquent and fines and/or a jail sentence for his or her parents. The flag salute requirement was challenged by a member of the Jehovah's Witnesses sect, who refused to obey the law because of their literal belief in the biblical commandment, "Thou shalt not make unto thee a graven image. . . . Thou shalt not bow down thyself to them nor serve them" (Exodus 20:4–5).

The Barnettes's challenge to the flag salute law provided the Supreme Court with the opportunity to review its decision in Minersville v. Gobitis, *decided only three years earlier.* Gobitis *had upheld a similar statute; now, the Court reversed itself.*

Although the challenge to the flag salute law was made on religious grounds—the Barnettes claimed that the statute could not constitutionally be applied to them because of their religious beliefs—the Court's opinion was far broader. No one, the Court held, could be forced to salute the American flag—whether that objection was based on religious, political, philosophical, or personal views. Thus, Barnette *is properly regarded as a free speech case rather than as a free exercise of religion case.*

Justice Robert H. Jackson delivered the opinion of the court.]

The freedom asserted by these appellees does not bring them into collision with rights asserted by any other individual. It is such conflicts which most frequently require intervention of the State to determine where the rights of one end and those of another begin. But the refusal of these persons to participate in the ceremony does not interfere with or deny rights of others to do so. Nor is there any question in this case that their behavior is peaceable and orderly. The sole conflict is between authority and rights of the individual. The State asserts power to condition access to public education on making a prescribed sign and profession and at the same time to coerce attendance by punishing both parent and child. The latter stand on a right of self-determination in matters that touch individual opinion and personal attitude.

As the present Chief Justice said in dissent in the *Gobitis* case, the State may "require teaching by instruction and study of all in our history and in the structure and organization of our government, including the guaranties of civil liberty, which tend to inspire patriotism and love of country." Here, however, we are dealing with a compulsion of students to declare a belief. They are not merely made acquainted with the flag salute so that they may be informed as to what it is or even what it means. The issue here is whether this slow and easily neglected route to aroused loyalties constitutionally may be short-cut by substituting a compulsory salute and slogan.

• • •

There is no doubt that, in connection with the pledges, the flag salute is a form of utterance. Symbolism is a primitive but effective way of communicating ideas. The use of an emblem or flag to symbolize some system, idea, institution, or personality, is a short cut from mind to mind. Causes and nations, political parties, lodges and ecclesiastical groups seek to knit the loyalty of their followings to a flag or banner, a color or design. The State announces rank, function, and authority through crowns and maces, uniforms and black robes; the church speaks through the Cross, the Crucifix, the altar and shrine, and clerical raiment. Symbols of State often convey political ideas just as religious symbols come to convey theological ones. Associated with many of these symbols are appropriate gestures of acceptance or respect: a salute, a bowed or bared head, a bended knee. A person gets from a symbol the meaning he puts into it, and what is one man's comfort and inspiration is another's jest and scorn.

Over a decade ago Chief Justice Hughes led this Court in holding that the display of a red flag as a symbol of opposition by peaceful and legal means to organized government was protected by the free speech guaranties of the Constitution. Here it is the State that employs a flag as a symbol of adherence to government as presently organized. It requires the individual to communicate by word and sign his acceptance of the political ideas it thus bespeaks. Objection to this form of communication when coerced is an old one, well known to the framers of the Bill of Rights.

It is also to be noted that the compulsory flag salute and pledge requires affirmation of a belief and an attitude of mind. It is not clear whether the regulation contemplates that pupils forego any contrary convictions of their own and become unwilling converts to the prescribed ceremony or whether it will be acceptable if they simulate assent by words without belief and by a gesture barren of meaning. It is now a commonplace that censorship or suppression of expression of opinion is tolerated by our Constitution only when the expression presents a clear and present danger of action of a kind the State is empowered to prevent and punish. It would seem that involuntary affirmation could be commanded only on even more immediate and urgent grounds than silence. But here the power of compulsion is

invoked without any allegation that remaining passive during a flag salute ritual creates a clear and present danger that would justify an effort even to muffle expression. To sustain the compulsory flag salute we are required to say that a Bill of Rights which guards the individual's right to speak his own mind, left it open to public authorities to compel him to utter what is not in his mind.

Whether the First Amendment to the Constitution will permit officials to order observance of ritual of this nature does not depend upon whether as a voluntary exercise we would think it to be good, bad or merely innocuous. Any credo of nationalism is likely to include what some disapprove or to omit what others think essential, and to give off different overtones as it takes on different accents or interpretations. If official power exists to coerce acceptance of any patriotic creed, what it shall contain cannot be decided by courts, but must be largely discretionary with the ordaining authority, whose power to prescribe would no doubt include power to amend. Hence validity of the asserted power to force an American citizen publicly to profess any statement of belief or to engage in any ceremony of assent to one, presents questions of power that must be considered independently of any idea we may have as to the utility of the ceremony in question.

Nor does the issue as we see it turn on one's possession of particular religious views or the sincerity with which they are held. While religion supplies appellees' motive for enduring the discomforts of making the issue in this case, many citizens who do not share these religious views hold such a compulsory rite to infringe constitutional liberty of the individual. It is not necessary to inquire whether non-conformist beliefs will exempt from the duty to salute unless we first find power to make the salute a legal duty.

The *Gobitis* decision, however, *assumed*, as did the argument in that case and in this, that power exists in the State to impose the flag salute discipline upon school children in general. The Court only examined and rejected a

Reprinted with special permission of North America Syndicate, Inc.

claim based on religious beliefs of immunity from an unquestioned general rule. The question which underlies the flag salute controversy is whether such a ceremony so touching matters of opinion and political attitude may be imposed upon the individual by official authority under powers committed to any political organization under our Constitution . . .

1. It was said that the flag-salute controversy confronted the Court with "the problem which Lincoln cast in memorable dilemma: 'Must a government of necessity be too *strong* for the liberties of its people, or too *weak* to maintain its own existence?' " and that the answer must be in favor of strength.

We think these issues may be examined free of pressure or restraint growing out of such considerations.

It may be doubted whether Mr. Lincoln would have thought that the strength of government to maintain itself would be impressively vindicated by our confirming power of the State to expel a handful of children from school. Such oversimplification, so handy in political debate, often lacks the precision necessary to postulates of judicial reasoning. If validly applied to this problem, the utterance cited would

resolve every issue of power in favor of those in authority and would require us to override every liberty thought to weaken or delay execution of their policies.

Government of limited power need not be anemic government. Assurance that rights are secure tends to diminish fear and jealousy of strong government, and by making us feel safe to live under it makes for its better support. Without promise of a limiting Bill of Rights it is doubtful if our Constitution could have mustered enough strength to enable its ratification. To enforce those rights today is not to choose weak government over strong government. It is only to adhere as a means of strength to individual freedom of mind in preference to officially disciplined uniformity for which history indicates a disappointing and disastrous end.

The subject now before us exemplifies this principle. Free public education, if faithful to the ideal of secular instruction and political neutrality, will not be partisan or enemy of any class, creed, party, or faction. If it is to impose any ideological discipline, however, each party or denomination must seek to control, or failing that, to weaken the influence of the educational system. Observance of the limitations of the

Constitution will not weaken government in the field appropriate for its exercise.

• • •

[2]. The *Gobitis* opinion reasoned that this is a field "where courts possess no marked and certainly no controlling competence," that it is committed to the legislatures as well as the courts to guard cherished liberties and that it is constitutionally appropriate to "fight out the wise use of legislative authority in the forum of public opinion and before legislative assemblies rather than to transfer such a contest to the judicial arena," since all the "effective means of inducing political changes are left free."

The very purpose of a Bill of Rights was to withdraw certain subjects from the vicissitudes of political controversy, to place them beyond the reach of majorities and officials and to establish them as legal principles to be applied by the courts. One's right to life, liberty, and property, to free speech, a free press, freedom of worship and assembly, and other fundamental rights may not be submitted to vote; they depend on the outcome of no elections.

• • •

[3]. Lastly, and this is the very heart of the *Gobitis* opinion, it reasons that "National unity is the basis of national security," that the authorities have "the right to select appropriate means for its attainment," and hence reaches the conclusion that such compulsory measures toward "national unity" are constitutional. Upon the verity of this assumption depends our answer in this case.

National unity as an end which officials may foster by persuasion and example is not in question. The problem is whether under our Constitution compulsion as here employed is a permissible means for its achievement.

Struggles to coerce uniformity of sentiment in support of some end thought essential to their time and country have been waged by many good as well as by evil men. Nationalism is a relatively recent phenomenon but at other times and places the ends have been racial or territorial security, support of a dynasty or re-

gime, and particular plans for saving souls. As first and moderate methods to attain unity have failed, those bent on its accomplishments must resort to an ever-increasing severity. As governmental pressure toward unity becomes greater, so strife becomes more bitter as to whose unity it shall be. Probably no deeper division of our people could proceed from any provocation than from finding it necessary to choose what doctrine and whose program public educational officials shall compel youth to unite in embracing. Ultimate futility of such attempts to compel coherence is the lesson of every such effort from the Roman drive to stamp out Christianity as a disturber of its pagan unity, the Inquisition, as a means to religious and dynastic unity, the Siberian exiles as a means to Russian unity, down to the fast failing efforts of our present totalitarian enemies. Those who begin coercive elimination of dissent soon find themselves exterminating dissenters. Compulsory unification of opinion achieves only the unanimity of the graveyard.

It seems trite but necessary to say that the First Amendment to our Constitution was designed to avoid these ends by avoiding these beginnings. There is no mysticism in the American concept of the State or of the nature or origin of its authority. We set up government by consent of the governed, and the Bill of Rights denies those in power any legal opportunity to coerce that consent. Authority here is to be controlled by public opinion, not public opinion by authority.

The case is made difficult not because the principles of its decision are obscure but because the flag involved is our own. Nevertheless, we apply the limitations of the Constitution with no fear that freedom to be intellectually and spiritually diverse or even contrary will disintegrate the social organization. To believe that patriotism will not flourish if patriotic ceremonies are voluntary and spontaneous instead of a compulsory routine is to make an unflattering estimate of the appeal of our institutions to free minds. We can have intellectual individualism and the rich cultural diversities that we owe to exceptional minds only at the price of occasional eccentricity and abnormal attitudes. When they are so harmless to others or to the State as those we deal with here, the price is not too great. But freedom to differ is not limited to things that do not matter much. That would be a mere shadow of freedom. The test of its substance is the right to differ as to things that touch the heart of the existing order.

If there is any fixed star in our constitutional constellation, it is that no official, high or petty, can prescribe what shall be orthodox in politics, nationalism, religion, or other matters of opinion or force citizens to confess by word or act their faith therein. If there are any circumstances which permit an exception, they do not now occur to us.

We think the action of the local authorities in compelling the flag salute and pledge transcends constitutional limitations on their power and invades the sphere of intellect and spirit which it is the purpose of the First Amendment to our Constitution to reserve from all official control.

The decision of this Court in *Minersville School District* v. *Gobitis* . . . [is] overruled, and the judgment enjoining enforcement of the West Virginia Regulation is

Affirmed.

Mr. Justice Black and Mr. Justice Douglas, concurring:

We are substantially in agreement with the opinion just read, but since we originally joined with the Court in the *Gobitis* case, it is appropriate that we make a brief statement of reasons for our change of view.

Reluctance to make the Federal Constitution a rigid bar against state regulation of conduct thought inimical to the public welfare was the controlling influence which moved us to consent to the *Gobitis* decision. Long reflection convinced us that although the principle is sound,

its application in the particular case was wrong. We believe that the statute before us fails to accord full scope to the freedom of religion secured to the appellees by the First and Fourteenth Amendments.

The statute requires the appellees to participate in a ceremony aimed at inculcating respect for the flag and for this country. The Jehovah's Witnesses, without any desire to show disrespect for either the flag or the country, interpret the Bible as commanding, at the risk of God's displeasure, that they not go through the form of a pledge of allegiance to any flag. The devoutness of their belief is evidenced by their willingness to suffer persecution and punishment, rather than make the pledge.

No well-ordered society can leave to the individuals an absolute right to make final decisions, unassailable by the State, as to everything they will or will not do. The First Amendment does not go so far. Religious faiths, honestly held, do not free individuals from responsibility to conduct themselves obediently to laws which are either imperatively necessary to protect society as a whole from grave and pressingly imminent dangers or which, without any general prohibition, merely regulate time, place or manner of religious activity. Decision as to the constitutionality of particular laws which strike at the substance of religious tenets and practices must be made by this Court. The duty is a solemn one, and in meeting it we cannot say that a failure, because of religious scruples, to assume a particular physical position and to repeat the words of a patriotic formula creates a grave danger to the nation. Such a statutory exaction is a form of test oath, and the test oath has always been abhorrent in the United States.

Words uttered under coercion are proof of loyalty to nothing but self-interest. Love of country must spring from willing hearts and free minds, inspired by a fair administration of wise laws enacted by the people's elected representatives within the bounds of express constitutional prohibitions. These laws must, to be consistent with the First Amendment, permit the widest toleration of conflicting viewpoints consistent with a society of free men.

Neither our domestic tranquillity in peace nor our martial effort in war depend on compelling little children to participate in a ceremony which ends in nothing for them but a fear of spiritual condemnation. If, as we think, their fears are groundless, time and reason are the proper antidotes for their errors. The ceremonial, when enforced against conscientious objectors, more likely to defeat than to serve its high purpose, is a handy implement for disguised religious persecution. As such, it is inconsistent with our Constitution's plan and purpose.

Mr. Justice Frankfurter, dissenting:

One who belongs to the most vilified and persecuted minority in history is not likely to be insensible in the freedoms guaranteed by our Constitution [Frankfurter, born in Vienna in 1882, was Jewish.] Were my purely personal attitude relevant I should wholeheartedly associate myself with the general libertarian views in the Court's opinion, representing as they do the thought and action of a lifetime. But as judges we are neither Jew nor Gentile, neither Catholic nor agnostic. We owe equal attachment to the Constitution and are equally bound by our judicial obligations whether we derive our citizenship from the earliest or the latest immigrants to these shores. As a member of this Court I am not justified in writing my private notions of policy into the Constitution, no matter how deeply I may cherish them or how mischievous I may deem their disregard. The duty of a judge who must decide which of two claims before the Court shall prevail, that of a State to enact and enforce laws within its general competence or that of an individual to refuse obedience because of the demands of his conscience, is not that of the ordinary person. It can never be emphasized too much that one's own opinion about the wisdom or evil of a law should be excluded altogether when one is doing one's duty on the bench. The only opinion of our own even looking in that direction that is material is our opinion whether legislators could in reason have enacted such a law. In the light of all the circumstances, including the history of this question in this Court, it would require more daring than I possess to deny that reasonable legislators could have taken the action which is before us for review. Most unwillingly, therefore, I must differ from my brethren with regard to legislation like this. I cannot bring my mind to believe that the "liberty" secured by the Due Process Clause gives this Court authority to deny to the State of West Virginia the attainment of that which we all recognize as a legitimate legislative end, namely, the promotion of good citizenship, by employment of the means here chosen.

• • •

We are told that a flag salute is a doubtful substitute for adequate understanding of our institutions. The states that require such a school exercise do not have to justify it as the only means for promoting good citizenship in children, but merely as one of diverse means for accomplishing a worthy end. We may deem it a foolish measure, but the point is that this Court is not the organ of government to resolve doubts as to whether it will fulfill its purpose. Only if there be no doubt that any reasonable mind could entertain can we deny to the states the right to resolve doubts their way and not ours.

That which to the majority may seem essential for the welfare of the state may offend the consciences of a minority. But, so long as no inroads are made upon the actual exercise of religion by the minority, to deny the political power of the majority to enact laws concerned with civil matters, simply because they may offend the consciences of a minority, really means that the consciences of a minority are more sacred and more enshrined in the Constitution than the consciences of a majority.

We are told that symbolism is a dramatic but primitive way of communicating ideas. Symbolism is inescapable. Even the most sophisticated live by symbols. But it is not for this

Court to make psychological judgments as to the effectiveness of a particular symbol in inculcating concededly indispensable feelings, particularly if the state happens to see fit to utilize the symbol that represents our heritage and our hopes. And surely only flippancy could be responsible for the suggestion that constitutional validity of a requirement to salute our flag implies equal validity of a requirement to salute a dictator. The significance of a symbol lies in what it represents. To reject the swastika does not imply rejection of the Cross. And so it bears repetition to say that it mocks reason and denies our whole history to find in the allowance of a requirement to salute our flag on fitting occasions the seeds of sanction for obeisance to a leader. To deny the power to employ educational symbols is to say that the state's educational system may not stimulate the imagination because this may lead to unwise stimulation.

• • •

Saluting the flag suppresses no belief nor curbs it. Children and their parents may believe what they please, avow their belief and practice it. It is not even remotely suggested that the requirement for saluting the flag involves the slightest restriction against the fullest opportunity on the part both of the children and of their parents to disavow as publicly as they choose to do so the meaning that others attach to the gesture of salute. All channels of affirmative free expression are open to both children and parents. Had we before us any act of the state putting the slightest curbs upon such free expression, I should not lag behind any member of this Court in striking down such an invasion of the right to freedom of thought and freedom of speech protected by the Constitution.

• • •

Of course patriotism can not be enforced by the flag salute. But neither can the liberal spirit be enforced by judicial invalidation of illiberal legislation. Our constant preoccupation with the constitutionality of legislation rather than with its wisdom tends to preoccupation of the American mind with a false value. The tendency of focussing attention on constitutionality is to make constitutionality synonymous with wisdom, to regard a law as all right if it is constitutional. Such an attitude is a great enemy of liberalism. Particularly in legislation affecting freedom of thought and freedom of speech much which should offend a free-spirited society is constitutional. Reliance for the most precious interests of civilization, therefore, must be found outside of their vindication in courts of law. Only a persistent positive translation of the faith of a free society into the convictions and habits and actions of a community is the ultimate reliance against unabated temptations to fetter the human spirit.

Chapter 17

Civil Rights

$\mathcal{T}$he civil rights movement was one of the central forces in American politics in the second half of the twentieth century. Nearly a hundred years after Lincoln's Emancipation Proclamation freed the slaves, the United States began to address the gross disparities between the promise of racial equality and the reality of racial discrimination.

The modern civil rights movement began in the 1930s with legal challenges to segregation in higher education. The legal battles continued in the 1940s and led ultimately to the landmark school desegregation case, Brown v. Board of Education, decided in 1954. Brown overturned the Supreme Court's 1896 decision in Plessy v. Ferguson, which had upheld "separate but equal" facilities as constitutional (selections 17.1 through 17.3).

At the same time, the struggle for racial equality moved to the political arena. The adoption of a civil rights plank in the Democratic party's 1948 platform led thirty-five southern delegates to walk out of the convention, and later 6,000 southerners met in a separate convention to nominate J. Strom Thurmond of South Carolina on the so-called Dixiecrat ticket. Also in 1948, President Harry Truman ordered the desegregation of the U.S. armed forces.

The political branches did not really move forward on civil rights, however, until the 1960s. In 1963, President John F. Kennedy proposed major civil rights legislation, although Congress did not act. Pressure was building, however; a series of events in 1963, including police violence in Birmingham, Alabama, and a major march on Washington, D.C., greatly raised the visibility of the movement. The following year, after Kennedy's assassination, President Lyndon B. Johnson pushed through the most important civil rights legislation since the 1860s, the Civil Rights Act of 1964. A year later Congress added the Voting Rights Act of 1965, which secured to blacks, at last, a meaningful right to vote (selection 17.5).

Recent years have seen controversy and divisiveness in the civil rights area. One major area of controversy is affirmative action, which involves race-conscious and race-

specific remedies to problems of past and present discrimination. The merits of affirmative action (called "reverse discrimination" by its critics) are debated in selections 17.7 and 17.8. The 1980s and 1990s have also produced major shifts in the leadership style and political agendas of black politicians, as selection 17.6 suggests.

The civil rights movement gave rise to a number of other similar attempts to secure equality to other victims of legal and societal discrimination. One offshoot was the women's movement, which successfully persuaded the Supreme Court to extend the equal protection of the law to women. Although attempts to amend the Constitution to secure sex equality failed in the 1970s and 1980s, a series of court decisions and congressional legislation helped bring about substantial legal equality for women (selection 17.4).

For women, blacks, and members of other minority groups, the civil rights movement is an ongoing struggle. This chapter traces the historical background and current context of civil rights in America.

Chapter Questions

1. At the heart of any discussion of civil rights is the meaning of equality. What alternative views on equality are illustrated in the readings in this chapter? How has the meaning of equality changed over the past 200 years?

2. How have legal conceptions of civil rights changed over the past century? Consider *Plessy, Brown,* and *Bakke.*

3. Consider the new questions and problems faced by advocates of civil rights in the 1980s and 1990s, among them the extension of civil rights to previously unprotected groups, including women, and new splits and tensions both inside and outside the civil rights movement. How are these tensions related to the goals and purposes of the original civil rights movement?

I THE CLASSIC TEXTS

Any discussion of civil rights in the modern era must start with Brown v. Board of Education, *the 1954 school desegregation case. The impact of* Brown *on race and politics in the United States has been immense. Although* Brown *itself had little effect on school segregation in the Deep South, it set in motion a process that would lead to the civil rights movement, the Civil Rights Act of 1964, and a host of federal and state programs designed to eliminate and address the effects of racial discrimination.*

Brown *reversed* Plessy v. Ferguson *(selection 17.1), an 1896 case that upheld segregation of railroad cars in Louisiana.* Brown *based its rejection of* Plessy *on narrow grounds relating to the dangers of segregation in the educational process. In practice, however, the elimination of segregation in public schools led quickly to judicial determinations that all state-sponsored segregation was unconstitutional.*

Chief Justice Earl Warren, who wrote the Brown *opinion, carefully avoided a direct attack on segregation in general; note specifically how his 1954 argument differs from the 1896 dissent of Justice John Harlan. Warren's concern was twofold: he sought to ensure that the Court would speak with one voice, and believed that an approach such as Harlan's might alienate one or more members of the Court; and he wanted to avoid giving potential critics of the decision a broad target to aim at. His opinion, though criticized by some liberals as insufficiently high-minded, got the job done.*

The decision in Brown *was accompanied by a parallel decision in* Bolling v. Sharpe *(selection 17.3), which dealt with segregation in the District of Columbia. Because the equal protection clause applies to the states and not to the federal government, the Court used the due process clause to strike down segregation in the district.*

The first Brown *decision (selection 17.2) simply announced that segregated schools were unconstitutional. Implementation of that decision was postponed one year, until 1955, when the Court ordered the federal district courts to implement* Brown *"with all deliberate speed."*

Questions

1. Why, in Earl Warren's view, are "separate educational facilities inherently unequal"?

2. Does Justice Harlan's dissent in *Plessy* provide an alternative approach to deciding *Brown*? What are the advantages and disadvantages of this approach?

3. As you read the arguments on affirmative action in selections 17.7 and 17.8, consider the implications of Justice Harlan's declaration that the Constitution is "color-blind"—an opinion never adopted by the Court—for the affirmative action issue.

17.1 Plessy *v.* Ferguson

This case turns upon the constitutionality of an act of the General Assembly of the State of Louisiana, passed in 1890, providing for separate railway carriages for the white and colored races.

• • •

The constitutionality of this act is attacked upon the ground that it conflicts with the Thirteenth Amendment of the Constitution, abolishing slavery, and the Fourteenth Amendment, which prohibits certain restrictive legislation on the part of the States.

1. That it does not conflict with the Thirteenth Amendment, which abolished slavery and involuntary servitude, except as a punishment for crime, is too clear for argument. Slavery implies involuntary servitude—a state of bondage; the ownership of mankind as a chattel, or at least the control of the labor and services of one man for the benefit of another, and the absence of a legal right to the disposal of his own person, property and services. This amendment was said in the *Slaughter-house cases* to have been intended primarily to abolish slav-

ery, as it had been previously known in this country, and that it equally forbade Mexican peonage or the Chinese coolie trade, when they amounted to slavery or involuntary servitude, and that the use of the word "servitude" was intended to prohibit the use of all forms of involuntary slavery, of whatever class or nature. It was intimated, however, in that case that this amendment was regarded by the statesmen of that day as insufficient to protect the colored race from certain laws which had been enacted in the Southern States, imposing upon the colored race onerous disabilities and burdens, and curtailing their rights in the pursuit of life, liberty and property to such an extent that their freedom was of little value; and that the Fourteenth Amendment was devised to meet this exigency.

So, too, in the *Civil Rights cases* it was said that the act of a mere individual, the owner of an inn, a public conveyance or place of amusement, refusing accommodations to colored people, cannot be justly regarded as imposing any badge of slavery or servitude upon the applicant, but only as involving an ordinary civil injury, properly cognizable by the laws of the State, and presumably subject to redress by those laws until the contrary appears. "It would be running the slavery argument into the ground," said Mr. Justice Bradley, "to make it apply to every act of discrimination which a person may see fit to make as to the guests he will entertain, or as to the people he will take into his coach or cab or car, or admit to his concert or theatre, or deal with in other matters of intercourse or business."

A statute which implies merely a legal distinction between the white and colored races— a distinction which is founded in the color of the two races, and which must always exist so long as white men are distinguished from the other race by color—has no tendency to destroy the legal equality of the two races, or reestablish a state of involuntary servitude. Indeed, we do not understand that the Thirteenth Amendment is strenuously relied upon by the plaintiff in error in this connection.

2. By the Fourteenth Amendment, all persons born or naturalized in the United States, and subject to the jurisdiction thereof, are made citizens of the United States and of the State wherein they reside; and the States are forbidden from making or enforcing any law which shall abridge the privileges or immunities of citizens of the United States, or shall deprive any person of life, liberty or property without due process of law, or deny to any person within their jurisdiction the equal protection of the laws.

The proper construction of this amendment was first called to the attention of this court in the *Slaughter-house cases,* which involved, however, not a question of race, but one of exclusive privileges. The case did not call for any expression of opinion as to the exact rights it was intended to secure to the colored race, but it was said generally that its main purpose was to establish the citizenship of the negro; to give definitions of citizenship of the United States and of the States, and to protect from the hostile legislation of the States the privileges and immunities of citizens of the United States, as distinguished from those of citizens of the States.

The object of the amendment was undoubtedly to enforce the absolute equality of the two races before the law but in the nature of things it could not have been intended to abolish distinctions based upon color, or to enforce social, as distinguished from political equality, or a commingling of the two races upon terms unsatisfactory to either. Laws permitting, and even requiring, their separation in places where they are liable to be brought into contact do not necessarily imply the inferiority of either race to the other, and have been generally, if not universally, recognized as within the competency of the state legislatures in the exercise of their police power. The most common instance of this is connected with the establishment of separate schools for white and colored children, which has been held to be a valid exercise of the legislative power even by courts of States where the political rights of the colored race have been longest and most earnestly enforced.

***

So far, then, as a conflict with the Fourteenth Amendment is concerned, the case reduces itself to the question whether the statute of Louisiana is a reasonable regulation, and with respect to this there must necessarily be a large discretion on the part of the legislature. In determining the question of reasonableness it is at liberty to act with reference to the established usages, customs and traditions of the people, and with a view to the promotion of their comfort, and the preservation of the public peace and good order. Gauged by this standard, we cannot say that a law which authorizes or even requires the separation of the two races in public conveyances is unreasonable, or more obnoxious to the Fourteenth Amendment than the acts of Congress requiring separate schools for colored children in the District of Columbia, the constitutionality of which does not seem to have been questioned, or the corresponding acts of state legislatures.

We consider the underlying fallacy of the plaintiff's argument to consist in the assumption that the enforced separation of the two races stamps the colored race with a badge of inferiority. If this be so, it is not by reason of anything found in the act, but solely because the colored race chooses to put that construction upon it. The argument necessarily assumes that if, as has been more than once the case, and is not unlikely to be so again, the colored race should become the dominant power in the state legislature, and should enact a law in precisely similar terms, it would thereby relegate the white race to an inferior position. We imagine that the white race, at least, would not acquiesce in this assumption. The argument also assumes that social prejudices may be overcome by legislation, and that equal rights cannot be secured to the negro except by an enforced commingling of the two races. We cannot accept this proposition. If the two races are to meet upon terms of social equality, it must be the result of natural affinities, a mutual appreciation of each other's merits and a voluntary consent of individuals. As was said by the Court of

Appeals of New York in *People* v. *Gallagher*, "this end can neither be accomplished nor promoted by laws which conflict with the general sentiment of the community upon whom they are designed to operate. When the government, therefore, has secured to each of its citizens equal rights before the law and equal opportunities for improvement and progress, it has accomplished the end for which it was organized and performed all of the functions respecting social advantages with which it is endowed." Legislation is powerless to eradicate racial instincts or to abolish distinctions based upon physical differences, and the attempt to do so can only result in accentuating the difficulties of the present situation. If the civil and political rights of both races be equal one cannot be inferior to the other civilly or politically. If one race be inferior to the other socially, the Constitution of the United States cannot put them upon the same place.

***

Mr. Justice Harlan dissenting.

By the Louisiana statute, the validity of which is here involved, all railway companies (other than street railroad companies) carrying passengers in that State are required to have separate but equal accommodations for white and colored persons, "by providing two or more passenger coaches for each passenger train, *or* by dividing the passenger coaches by a *partition* so as to secure separate accommodations." Under this statute, no colored person is permitted to occupy a seat in a coach assigned to white persons; nor any white person, to occupy a seat in a coach assigned to colored persons. The managers of the railroad are not allowed to exercise any discretion in the premises, but are required to assign each passenger to some coach or compartment set apart for the exclusive use of his race. If a passenger insists upon going into a coach or compartment not set apart for persons of his race, he is subject to be fined, or to be imprisoned in the parish jail. Penalties are prescribed for the refusal or neglect of the officers, directors, conductors and employes of railroad companies to comply with the provisions of the act.

• • •

In respect of civil rights, common to all citizens, the Constitution of the United Sates does not, I think, permit any public authority to know the race of those entitled to be protected in the enjoyment of such rights. Every true man has pride of race, and under appropriate circumstances when the rights of others, his equals before the law, are not to be affected, it is his privilege to express such pride and to take such action based upon it as to him seems proper. But I deny that any legislative body or judicial tribunal may have regard to the race of citizens when the civil rights of those citizens are involved. Indeed, such legislation, as that here in question, is inconsistent not only with that equality of rights which pertains to citizenship, National and State, but with the personal liberty enjoyed by every one within the United States.

• • •

The white race deems itself to be the dominant race in this country. And so it is, in prestige, in achievements, in education, in wealth and power. So, I doubt not, it will continue to be for all time, if it remains true to its great heritage and holds fast in the principles of constitutional liberty. But in view of the Constitution, in the eye of the law, there is in this country no superior, dominant, ruling class of citizens. There is no caste here. Our Constitution is color-blind, and neither knows nor tolerates classes among citizens. In respect of civil rights, all citizens are equal before the law. The humblest is the peer of the most powerful. The law regards man as man, and takes no account of his surroundings or of his color when his civil rights as guaranteed by the supreme law of the land are involved. It is, therefore, to be regretted that this high tribunal, the final expositor of the fundamental law of the land, has reached the conclusion that it is competent for a State to regulate the enjoyment by citizens of their civil rights solely upon the basis of race.

• • •

17.2 Brown v. Board of Education ⸻

Mr. Chief Justice Warren delivered the opinion of the Court.

These cases come to us from the States of Kansas, South Carolina, Virginia, and Delaware. They are premised on different facts and different local conditions, but a common legal question justifies their consideration together in this consolidated opinion.

In each of the cases, minors of the Negro race, through their legal representatives, seek the aid of the courts in obtaining admission to the public schools of the community on a nonsegregated basis. In each instance, they had been denied admission to schools attended by white children under laws requiring or permitting segregation according to race. This segregation was alleged to deprive the plaintiffs of the equal protection of the laws under the Fourteenth Amendment. In each of the cases other than the Delaware case, a three-judge federal district court denied relief to the plaintiffs on the so-called "separate but equal" doctrine announced by this Court in Plessy v. Ferguson. Under that doctrine, equality of treatment is accorded when the races are provided substantially equal facilities, even though these facilities be separate. In the Delaware case, the Supreme Court of Delaware adhered to that doctrine, but ordered that the plaintiffs be admitted to the white schools because of their superiority to the Negro schools.

The plaintiffs contend that segregated public schools are not "equal" and cannot be made "equal," and that hence they are deprived of the equal protection of the laws. Because of the obvious importance of the question presented, the Court took jurisdiction. Argument was heard in the 1952 Term, and reargument was heard this Term on certain questions propounded by the Court.

Reargument was largely devoted to the circumstances surrounding the adoption of the Fourteenth Amendment in 1868. It covered exhaustively consideration of the Amendment in Congress, ratification by the states, then existing practices in racial segregation, and the views of proponents and opponents of the Amendment. This discussion and our own investigation convince us that, although these sources cast some light, it is not enough to resolve the problem with which we are faced. At best, they are inconclusive. The most avid proponents of the post-War Amendments undoubtedly intended them to remove all legal distinctions among "all persons born or naturalized in the United States." Their opponents, just as certainly, were antagonistic to both the letter and the spirit of the Amendments and wished them to have the most limited effect. What others in Congress and the state legislatures had in mind cannot be determined with any degree of certainty.

An additional reason for the inconclusive nature of the Amendment's history, with respect to segregated schools, is the status of public education at that time. In the South, the movement toward free common schools, supported by general taxation, had not yet taken hold. Education of white children was largely in the hands of private groups. Education of Negroes was almost nonexistent, and practically all of the race were illiterate. In fact, any education of Negroes was forbidden by law in some states. Today, in contrast, many Negroes have achieved outstanding success in the arts and sciences as well as in the business and professional world. It is true that public school education at the time of the Amendment had advanced further in the North, but the effect of the Amendment on Northern States was generally ignored in the congressional debates.

Even in the North, the conditions of public education did not approximate those existing today. The curriculum was usually rudimentary; ungraded schools were common in rural areas; the school term was but three months a year in many states; and compulsory school attendance was virtually unknown. As a consequence, it is not surprising that there should be so little in the history of the Fourteenth Amendment relating to its intended effect on public education.

In the first cases in this Court construing the Fourteenth Amendment, decided shortly after its adoption, the Court interpreted it as proscribing all state-imposed discriminations against the Negro race. The doctrine of "separate but equal" did not make its appearance in this Court until 1896 in the case of *Plessy* v. *Ferguson*, involving not education but transportation. American courts have since labored with the doctrine for over half a century. In this Court, there have been six cases involving the "separate but equal" doctrine in the field of public education. In *Cumming* v. *County Board of Education* and *Gong Lum* v. *Rice* the validity of the doctrine itself was not challenged. In more recent cases, all on the graduate school level, inequality was found in that specific benefits enjoyed by white students were denied to Negro students of the same educational qualifications. In none of these cases was it necessary to re-examine the doctrine to grant relief to the Negro plaintiff. And in *Sweatt* v. *Painter*, the Court expressly reserved decision on the question whether *Plessy* v. *Ferguson* should be held inapplicable to public education.

In the instant cases, that question is directly presented. Here, unlike *Sweatt* v. *Painter*, there are findings below that the Negro and white schools involved have been equalized, or are being equalized, with respect to buildings, curricula, qualifications and salaries of teachers, and other "tangible" factors. Our decision, therefore, cannot turn on merely a comparison of these tangible factors in the Negro and white schools involved in each of the cases. We must look instead to the effect of segregation itself on public education.

In approaching this problem, we cannot turn the clock back to 1868 when the Amendment was adopted, or even to 1896 when *Plessy* v. *Ferguson* was written. We must consider public education in the light of its full development and its present place in American life throughout the Nation. Only in this way can it be determined if segregation in public schools deprives these plaintiffs of the equal protection of the laws.

Today, education is perhaps the most important function of state and local governments. Compulsory school attendance laws and the great expenditures for education both demonstrate our recognition of the importance of education to our democratic society. It is required in the performance of our most basic public responsibilities, even service in the armed forces. It is the very foundation of good citizenship. Today it is a principal instrument in awakening the child to cultural values, in preparing him for later professional training, and in helping him to adjust normally to his environment. In these days, it is doubtful that any child may reasonably be expected to succeed in life if he is denied the opportunity of an education. Such an opportunity, where the state has undertaken to provide it, is a right which must be made available to all on equal terms.

We come then to the question presented: Does segregation of children in public schools solely on the basis of race, even though the physical facilities and other "tangible" factors may be equal, deprive the children of the minority group of equal educational opportunities? We believe that it does.

In *Sweatt* v. *Painter*, in finding that a segregated law school for Negroes could not provide them equal educational opportunities, this Court relied in large part on "those qualities which are incapable of objective measurement but which make for greatness in a law school." In *McLaurin* v. *Oklahoma State Regents*, the Court, in requiring that a Negro admitted to a white graduate school be treated like all other students, again resorted to intangible considerations: ". . . his ability to study, to engage in discussions and exchange views with other students, and, in general, to learn his profession." Such considerations apply with added force to children in grade and high schools. To separate them from others of similar age and qualifications solely because of their race generates a feeling of inferiority as to their status in the community that may affect their hearts and minds in a way unlikely ever to be undone. The effect of this separation on their educational opportunities was well stated by a finding in the Kansas case by a court which nevertheless felt compelled to rule against the Negro plaintiffs:

> Segregation of white and colored children in public schools has a detrimental effect upon the colored children. The impact is greater when it has the sanction of the law; for the policy of separating the races is usually interpreted as denoting the inferiority of the negro group. A sense of inferiority affects the motivation of a child to learn. Segregation with the sanction of law, therefore, has a tendency to [retard] the educational and mental development of negro children and to deprive them of some of the benefits they would receive in a racial[ly] integrated school system.

Whatever may have been the extent of psychological knowledge at the time of *Plessy* v. *Ferguson*, this finding is amply supported by modern authority.* Any language in *Plessy* v. *Ferguson* contrary to this finding is rejected.

We conclude that in the field of public education the doctrine of "separate but equal" has no place. Separate educational facilities are inherently unequal. Therefore, we hold that the

* [This footnote, number 11 in the original, has become famous. It is frequently referred to simply as "footnote 11."] K. B. Clark, Effect of Prejudice and Discrimination on Personality Development (Midcentury White House Conference on Children and Youth, 1950); Witmer and Kotinsky, Personality in the Making (1952), c. VI; Deutscher and Chein, The Psychological Effects of Enforced Segregation: A Survey of Social Science Opinion, 26 J. Psychol. 259 (1948); Chein, What are the Psychological Effects of Segregation Under Conditions of Equal Facilities?, 3 Int. J. Opinion and Attitude Res. 229 (1949); Brameld, Educational Costs, in Discrimination and National Welfare (MacIver, ed., 1949), 44–48; Frazier, The Negro in the United States (1949), 674–681. And see generally Myrdal, An American Dilemma (1944).

plaintiffs and others similarly situated for whom the actions have been brought are, by reason of the segregation complained of, deprived of the equal protection of the laws guaranteed by the Fourteenth Amendment. This disposition makes unnecessary any discussion whether such segregation also violates the Due Process Clause of the Fourteenth Amendment.

Because these are class actions, because of the wide applicability of this decision, and because of the great variety of local conditions, the formulation of decrees in these cases presents problems of considerable complexity. On reargument, the consideration of appropriate relief was necessarily subordinated to the primary question—the constitutionality of segre-gation in public education. We have now announced that such segregation is a denial of the equal protection of the laws. In order that we may have the full assistance of the parties in formulating decrees, the cases will be restored to the docket, and the parties are requested to present further argument on Questions 4 and 5 previously propounded by the Court for the reargument this Term. The Attorney General of the United States is again invited to participate. The Attorneys General of the states requiring or permitting segregation in public education will also be permitted to appear as *amici curiae* upon request to do so by September 15, 1954, and submission of briefs by October 1, 1954.

It is so ordered.

17.3 Bolling *v.* Sharpe

Mr. Chief Justice Warren delivered the opinion of the Court.

This case challenges the validity of segregation in the public schools of the District of Columbia. The petitioners, minors of the Negro race, allege that such segregation deprives them of due process of law under the Fifth Amendment. They were refused admission to a public school attended by white children solely because of their race. They sought the aid of the District Court for the District of Columbia in obtaining admission. That court dismissed their complaint. The Court granted a writ of certiorari before judgment in the Court of Appeals because of the importance of the constitutional question presented.

We have this day held that the Equal Protection Clause of the Fourteenth Amendment prohibits the states from maintaining racially segregated public schools. The legal problem in the District of Columbia is somewhat different, however. The Fifth Amendment, which is applicable in the District of Columbia, does not contain an equal protection clause as does the Fourteenth Amendment which applies only to the states. But the concepts of equal protection and due process, both stemming from our American ideal of fairness, are not mutually exclusive. The "equal protection of the laws" is a more explicit safeguard of prohibited unfairness than "due process of law," and, therefore, we do not imply that the two are always interchangeable phrases. But, as this Court has recognized, discrimination may be so unjustifiable as to be violative of due process.

Classifications based solely upon race must be scrutinized with particular care, since they are contrary to our traditions and hence constitutionally suspect. As long ago as 1896, this Court declared the principle "that the Constitution of the United States, in its present form, forbids, so far as civil and political rights are concerned, discrimination by the General Government, or by the States, against any citizen because of his race." And in *Buchanan* v. *Warley,* the Court held that a statute which limited the right of a property owner to convey his property to a person of another race was, as an unreasonable discrimination, a denial of due process of law.

Although the Court has not assumed to define "liberty" with any great precision, that term is not confined to mere freedom from bodily restraint. Liberty under law extends to the full range of conduct which the individual is free to pursue, and it cannot be restricted except for a proper governmental objective. Segregation in public education is not reasonably related to any proper governmental objective, and thus it imposes on Negro children of the District of Columbia a burden that constitutes an arbitrary deprivation of their liberty in violation of the Due Process Clause.

In view of our decision that the Constitution prohibits the states from maintaining racially segregated public schools, it would be unthinkable that the same Constitution would impose a lesser duty on the Federal Government. We hold that racial segregation in the public schools of the District of Columbia is a denial of the due process of law guaranteed by the Fifth Amendment to the Constitution.

II FOCUS: GENDER EQUALITY

The Supreme Court did not specifically extend to women the guarantees of the equal protection clause ("No State shall . . . deny to any person within its jurisdiction the equal protection of the laws") until 1971, when it held that states could not discriminate against women merely for administrative convenience. Five years later, the Court held that states could make classifications based on gender only if such classifications served "important" governmental interests and if they were "substantially related" to those interests. Although these tests are somewhat vague, in practice the Court has upheld only those laws discriminating on the basis of gender that are carefully drawn to serve remedial or other important purposes and has generally struck down those based on outmoded or thoughtless sexual stereotypes. Among the laws the Court has struck down are those that permitted women to drink alcohol at an earlier age than men and those giving preferential treatment to the dependents of male, as opposed to female, members of the armed forces. Among the relatively few laws the Court has upheld are the all-male military draft and a statutory rape statute that punishes males but not females who engage in sexual relations with persons under 18.

The following case, from 1982, involves the constitutionality of an all-female university. It is of particular importance because it was Justice Sandra Day O'Connor's first gender discrimination case and because it nicely lays out the Court's test to determine whether a particular state law or program violates the equal protection clause.

Chief Justice Warren Burger and Justices William Rehnquist and Lewis Powell dissented from the opinion of the Court, arguing that the decision "frustrates the liberating spirit of the Equal Protection Clause" by forbidding the states "from providing women with an opportunity to choose the type of university they prefer."

Questions

1. The Supreme Court requires that states show an "important" interest in order to justify a gender classification. What interests does the state of Mississippi advance to justify the all-female college?

2. Under what circumstances is Justice O'Connor inclined to strike down gender classifications? What factors might influence her to uphold such classifications?

17.4 Mississippi University for Women *v.* Hogan _____

Justice O'Connor delivered the opinion of the Court. . . .

In 1884, the Mississippi Legislature created the Mississippi Industrial Institute and College for the Education of White Girls of the State of Mississippi, now the oldest state-supported all-female college in the United States. The school, known today as Mississippi University for Women (MUW), has from its inception limited its enrollment to women.

[*Joe Hogan, a registered nurse who did not hold a baccalaureate degree, applied to MUW's nursing program. He was denied admission to the degree program solely because of his sex.*]

We begin our analysis aided by several firmly established principles. Because the challenged policy expressly discriminates among applicants on the basis of gender, it is subject to scrutiny under the Equal Protection Clause of the Fourteenth Amendment. That this statutory policy discriminates against males rather than against females does not exempt it from scrutiny or reduce the standard of review. Our decisions also establish that the party seeking to uphold a statute that classifies individuals on the basis of their gender must carry the burden of showing an "exceedingly persuasive justification" for the classification. The burden is met only by showing at least that the classification serves "important governmental objectives and that the discriminatory means employed" are "substantially related to the achievement of those objectives."

Although the test for determining the validity of a gender-based classification is straightforward, it must be applied free of fixed notions concerning the roles and abilities of males and females. Care must be taken in ascertaining whether the statutory objective itself reflects archaic and stereotypic notions. Thus, if the statutory objective is to exclude or "protect" members of one gender because they are presumed to suffer from an inherent handicap or to be innately inferior, the object itself is illegitimate.

If the State's objective is legitimate and important, we next determine whether the requisite direct, substantial relationship between objective and means is present. The purpose of requiring that close relationship is to assure that the validity of a classification is determined through reasoned analysis rather than through the mechanical application of traditional, often inaccurate, assumptions about the proper roles of men and women. The need for the requirement is amply revealed by reference to the broad range of statutes already invalidated by this Court, statutes that relied upon the simplistic, outdated assumption that gender could be used as a "proxy for other, more germane bases of classification" to establish a link between objective and classification.

Applying this framework, we now analyze the arguments advanced by the State to justify its refusal to allow males to enroll for credit in MUW's School of Nursing.

• • •

The State's primary justification for maintaining the single-sex admissions policy of MUW's School of Nursing is that it compensates for discrimination against women and, therefore, constitutes educational affirmative action. As applied to the School of Nursing, we find the State's argument unpersuasive.

In limited circumstances, a gender-based classification favoring one sex can be justified if it intentionally and directly assists members of the sex that is disproportionately burdened. However, we consistently have emphasized that "the mere recitation of a benign, compensatory purpose is not an automatic shield which protects against any inquiry into the actual purposes underlying a statutory scheme." The same searching analysis must be made, regardless of whether the State's objective is to eliminate family controversy, to achieve administrative efficiency, or to balance the burdens borne by males and females.

It is readily apparent that a State can evoke a compensatory purpose to justify an otherwise discriminatory classification only if members of the gender benefited by the classification actually suffer a disadvantage related to the classification. We considered such a situation in *Califano* v. *Webster* (1977), which involved a challenge to a statutory classification that allowed women to eliminate more low-earning years than men for purposes of computing Social Security retirement benefits. Although the effect of the classification was to allow women higher monthly benefits than were available to men with the same earning history, we upheld the statutory scheme, noting that it took into account that women "as such have been unfairly hindered from earning as much as men" and "work[ed] directly to remedy" the resulting economic disparity.

The retirement of Justice William Brennan in 1990 raised fears and hopes that the Supreme Court would reverse its previous decisions on women's rights, especially *Roe* v. *Wade*, the abortion case.

A similar pattern of discrimination against women influenced our decision in *Schlesinger* v. *Ballard* [1975]. There, we considered a federal statute that granted female Naval officers a 13-year tenure of commissioned service before mandatory discharge, but accorded male officers only a 9-year tenure. We recognized that, because women were barred from combat duty, they had had fewer opportunities for promotion than had their male counterparts. By allowing women an additional four years to reach a particular rank before subjecting them to mandatory discharge, the statute directly compensated for other statutory barriers to advancement.

In sharp contrast, Mississippi has made no showing that women lacked opportunities to obtain training in the field of nursing or to attain positions of leadership in that field when the MUW School of Nursing opened its door or that women currently are deprived of such opportunities. In fact, in 1970, the year before the School of Nursing's first class enrolled, women earned 94 percent of the nursing baccalaureate degrees conferred in Mississippi and 98.6 percent of the degrees earned nationwide. That year was not an aberration; one decade earlier, women had earned all the nursing degrees conferred in Mississippi and 98.9 percent of the degrees conferred nationwide. As one would expect, the labor force reflects the same predominance of women in nursing. When MUW's School of Nursing began operation, nearly 98 percent of all employed registered nurses were female.

Rather than compensate for discriminatory barriers faced by women, MUW's policy of excluding males from admission to the School of Nursing tends to perpetuate the stereotyped view of nursing as an exclusively woman's job. By assuring that Mississippi allots more openings in its state-supported nursing schools to women than it does to men, MUW's admissions policy lends credibility to the old view that women, not men, should become nurses, and makes the assumption that nursing is a field for women a self-fulfilling prophecy. Thus, we conclude that, although the State recited a "benign, compensatory purpose," it failed to establish that the alleged objective is the actual purpose underlying the discriminatory classification.

The policy is invalid also because it fails the second part of the equal protection test, for the State has made no showing that the gender-based classification is substantially and directly related to its proposed compensatory objective. To the contrary, MUW's policy of permitting men to attend classes as auditors fatally undermines its claim that women, at least those in the School of Nursing, are adversely affected by the presence of men.

MUW permits men who audit to participate fully in classes. Additionally, both men and women take part in continuing education courses offered by the School of Nursing, in which regular nursing students also can enroll. The uncontroverted record reveals that admitting men to nursing classes does not affect teaching style, that the presence of men in the classroom would not affect the performance of the female nursing students, and that men in coeducational nursing schools do not dominate the classroom. In sum, the record in this case is flatly inconsistent with the claim that excluding men from the School of Nursing is necessary to reach any of MUW's educational goals.

Thus, considering both the asserted interest and the relationship between the interest and the methods used by the State, we conclude that the State has fallen far short of establishing the "exceedingly persuasive justification" needed to sustain the gender-based classification. Accordingly, we hold that MUW's policy of denying males the right to enroll for credit in its School of Nursing violates the Equal Protection Clause of the Fourteenth Amendment.

• • •

In an additional attempt to justify its exclusion of men from MUW's School of Nursing, the State contends that MUW is the direct beneficiary "of specific congressional legislation which, on its face, permits the institution to exist as it has in the past." The argument is based upon the language of §901(a) in Title IX of the Education Amendments of 1972. Although §901(a) prohibits gender discrimination in education programs that receive federal financial assistance, subsection 5 exempts the admissions policies of undergraduate institutions "that traditionally and continually from [their] establishment [have] had a policy of admitting only students of one sex" from the general prohibition. Arguing that Congress enacted Title IX in furtherance of its power to enforce the Fourteenth Amendment, a power granted by §5 of that Amendment, the State would have us conclude that §901(a)(5) is but "a congressional limitation upon the broad prohibitions of the Equal Protection Clause of the Fourteenth Amendment."

The argument requires little comment. Initially, it is far from clear that Congress intended, through §901(a)(5), to exempt MUW from any constitutional obligation. Rather, Congress apparently intended, at most, to exempt MUW from the requirements of Title IX.

Even if Congress envisioned a constitutional exemption, the State's argument would fail. Section 5 of the Fourteenth Amendment gives Congress broad power indeed to enforce the command of the Amendment and "to secure to all persons the enjoyment of perfect equality of civil rights and the equal protection of the laws against State denial or invasion. . . ." Congress' power under §5, however, "is limited to adopting measures to enforce the guarantees of the Amendment; §5 grants Congress no power to restrict, abrogate, or dilute these guarantees." Although we give deference to congressional decisions and classifications, neither Congress nor a State can validate a law that denies the rights guaranteed by the Fourteenth Amendment.

The fact that the language of §901(a)(5) applies to MUW provides the State no solace: "[A] statute apparently governing a dispute cannot be applied by judges, consistently with their obligations under the Supremacy Clause, when such an application of the statute would conflict with the Constitution."

• • •

Because we conclude that the State's policy of excluding males from MUW's School of Nursing violates the Equal Protection Clause of the Fourteenth Amendment, we affirm the judgment of the Court of Appeals.

It is so ordered.

• • •

III  THE PERSPECTIVE OF HISTORY

In the 1960s, the focus of the civil rights movement shifted from litigation to politics. Despite the Supreme Court's landmark decision in Brown, *progress on civil rights remained glacially slow. Congress had passed minor civil rights laws in 1957 and 1960, but the South remained largely segregated, and blacks were still denied the right to vote and other basic liberties.*

A series of protests, sit-ins, and boycotts at last brought action from Washington. President John F. Kennedy, initially reluctant to jeopardize his political fortunes by pushing forward on civil rights, proposed a sweeping civil rights law in 1963. He was assassinated before the bill could become law, but his crusade was continued by his successor, Lyndon Baines Johnson, and the legislation was finally passed in 1964.

That law, known as the Civil Rights Act of 1964, was perhaps the most important piece of civil rights legislation ever passed. It banned segregation in all public places, including hotels, restaurants, and theaters, and prohibited discrimination in employment and education. Combined with the 1965 Voting Rights Act, which gave effect to

Donald G. Nieman **671**

the Fifteenth Amendment's guarantee of voting rights, the Civil Rights Act began the transformation of race relations in the United States.

In the following selection, historian Donald Nieman traces the political history of the civil rights movement in the early 1960s and ends with a discussion of the Supreme Court cases that upheld the constitutionality of the Civil Rights Act and the Voting Rights Act.

Questions

1. What strategies did the civil rights movement pursue in the early 1960s to convince the government to act? Why was the strategy successful?

2. How would you rate John F. Kennedy's performance on civil rights during his three-year presidency: positive for ultimately pushing forward with the civil rights bill or negative for taking so long to do so?

17.5 Promises to Keep

Donald G. Nieman

On February 1, 1960, four neatly dressed black freshmen at North Carolina Agricultural and Technical College in Greensboro, walked into the local Woolworth store, sat down at its segregated lunch counter, and politely asked to be served. When the waitress refused, the young men remained at the counter, studying quietly, until the store closed. During the weeks that followed, more than 1,000 students joined these 4 pioneers, as the sit-ins spread to other Greensboro lunch counters, and local blacks closed ranks with the students, picketing and boycotting Woolworth and other variety stores that discriminated against blacks. The Greensboro sit-ins sparked a direct action campaign that spread across the South like wildfire. In dozens of towns and cities, in every southern state, black youths defied segregation at lunch counters, restaurants, motels, swimming pools, beaches, libraries, and theaters and staged massive demonstrations. Using the tactics of nonviolent resistance, the demonstrators politely asserted their moral right to equal treatment and turned the other cheek when whites verbally and physically abused them. Thousands of demonstrators were arrested and chose jail over bail (or payment of fines) in order to highlight the repressiveness of the caste system. In Orangeburg, South Carolina, for example, police filled the city and county jails and incarcerated 300 more black student protesters in a hastily improvised stockade.

The sit-ins marked a turning point in the civil rights struggle. In response to the new militance, more than 200 cities began desegregation of public accommodations. Although most towns and small cities in the Deep South refused to budge, students boasted that in six months they had moved the South closer to integration than the federal courts had done in the six years following *Brown* [v. *Board of Education*]. Even more important, the students demonstrated a new sense of urgency, indicating that they were tired of gradualism and were no longer willing to wait until judges and politicians decided the time was ripe for them to enjoy their rights. "[W]e cannot tolerate, in a nation professing democracy and among people professing Christianity, the discriminatory conditions under which the Negro is living today," Atlanta sit-in leaders proclaimed. "We do not intend to wait placidly for those rights which are already legally and morally ours to be meted out to us one at a time."

This impatience and militance was not a flash in the pan. It was institutionalized in April 1960, when black student leaders formed the Student Non-Violent Coordinating Committee (SNCC, pronounced "snick") to perpetuate and expand the direct action campaign. Just as the young radicals were influenced by older civil rights leaders, their actions affected established civil rights groups. The Congress of Racial Equality (CORE), a small northern interracial group that had brought nonviolent resistance to the civil rights effort in the 1940s, sent representatives to the conference that gave birth to SNCC and advised the young activists on the tactics of direct action. CORE was itself invigorated by the success of the students and, in the year following the sit-ins, grew steadily and expanded its activities into the South. Martin Luther King's philosophy and tactics of nonviolent resistance, developed during the Montgomery bus boycott, had inspired the students, and King himself had participated in the sit-ins. At the same time, the students reaffirmed the potential of direct action for King and his colleagues in the Southern Christian Leadership Conference (SCLC), prompting them to place greater emphasis on civil disobedience.

When John F. Kennedy came to the White House in January 1961, black leaders were becoming increasingly bold and impatient. Despite his youthful vigor and personal dislike for segregation, the new president spoke the language of gradualism and moved cautiously on civil rights. Blacks had played a crucial role in his razor thin victory in 1960 and would be taken care of. But they would have to settle for more federal appointments (Thurgood Marshall, for example, was appointed to the U.S. Court of Appeals for the Second Circuit in 1961), vigorous enforcement of the voting rights laws, and an economic policy that promised higher wages to all working-class Americans. Kennedy refused to ask Congress for comprehensive civil rights legislation. It had no chance of passing, he believed, and, besides, it carried too high a price tag. A bold civil rights initiative on Capitol Hill would cost support among southern whites, who would be crucial to a 1964 reelection bid, and alienate southern Democrats in Congress, whose backing on other issues was crucial.

The administration also resisted federal intervention in the South to protect civil rights activists. Attorney General Robert Kennedy resolutely maintained that the federal system gave the states responsibility for general law enforcement; the federal government had neither the constitutional authority nor the personnel to take responsibility for maintaining law and order. He pointed out that the Supreme Court's venerable state action interpretation of the Fourteenth Amendment denied the government authority to prosecute private individuals who used violence and intimidation to deny blacks equal rights and due process. The attorney general also pleaded that the federal government did not possess a police force capable of preserving the peace. Both the United States Marshals Service and the Federal Bureau of Investigation had far too few officers to take responsibility for general law enforcement in the South. Moreover, he maintained that the creation of a national police force was a threat to liberty because it could afford a ruthless president the means to suppress dissent.

Although these objections had some merit, they also "accord[ed] nicely with the political needs of the Kennedy brothers," according to historian Michal Belknap. The state action restriction made successful prosecution of anti–civil rights violence problematical, but the Supreme Court might be convinced to reverse itself, as it had in *Brown*. While there were too few federal officers to police the South, there were enough of them to handle selected cases, and a small number of prosecutions might deter future violence. Federal intervention was neither impossible nor a potential threat to liberty.

It was, however, calculated to raise the hackles of white southerners and therefore politically risky.

The administration's response to the freedom rides of 1961 illustrate its reluctance to intervene in the South. In December 1960, the Supreme Court ruled that the Interstate Commerce Act forbade discrimination in bus terminals serving interstate carriers. The following May, CORE and SNCC activists left Washington, D.C. for a bus trip into the Deep South to test compliance with the Court's decision. On May 14, in Anniston and Birmingham and on May 20, in Montgomery, three separate groups of freedom riders were attacked and beaten by mobs of Alabama whites wielding chains, pipes, and baseball bats. Although local police refused to protect the protesters, Robert Kennedy resisted calls for federal intervention, choosing to work behind the scenes to defuse the crisis. He pressed the Interstate Commerce Commission to issue regulations compelling obedience to the Court's decision. (In November, the commission barred interstate carriers from using segregated terminals, forcing most southern terminals to capitulate.) He also prodded state officials to preserve order, repeatedly urging Governor John Patterson of Alabama to protect the riders and sending aides to Montgomery to confer with Patterson and to monitor the situation.

The Justice Department intervened only when state officials proved beyond all doubt that they would not act. On the evening of May 21—after a week of pleading and cajoling—the attorney general finally gave up on state officials when Montgomery police refused to respond as a mob threatened to overrun a church where Martin Luther King, Jr., spoke at a ceremony honoring the freedom riders. Fearing bloodshed, department officials deployed 100 U.S. marshals to hold the angry crowd at bay. Yet this limited intervention was the exception. As the freedom riders moved into Mississippi, the attorney general, fearing a repetition of events in Alabama, negotiated a deal with state officials. The state agreed to guarantee the safety of the riders on the condition that the Justice Department would not interfere with local prosecution of persons who violated state segregation laws. The riders were protected from Mississippi mobs, but by the end of the summer more than 300 of them were in Mississippi jails. During the ensuing months, when mobs threatened freedom riders in three other cities, the attorney general urged state officials to preserve order but rejected calls for federal intervention.

While unsympathetic to direct action, the Kennedys were not oblivious to the demands of blacks. They believed that equality could be achieved gradually and with a minimum of confrontation if barriers to black voting were destroyed. Like Reconstruction-era Republicans, they contended that once blacks possessed the ballot, state officials would become responsive to their demands for justice. Thus the rights of blacks could be protected without major alterations in the federal system and without the need for politically embarrassing federal confrontations with state officials. In the bargain, most new black voters would join the Democratic party, helping reverse the steady erosion of Democratic strength that had occurred during the post-World War II years.

During late 1961 and 1962, administration officials urged civil rights activists to refocus their efforts from direct action to voter registration. Justice Department officials participated in a series of meetings that led to the creation of the Voter Education Project, a two-and-one-half year campaign to register southern blacks which was financed by $870,000 from northern foundations. SCLC, CORE, and NAACP [National Association for the Advancement of Colored People] all readily agreed to participate. SNCC leaders were suspicious of being coopted by the administration but ultimately agreed to go along. The voter registration campaign, they believed, could help raise the consciousness of rural southern blacks and encourage them to challenge white supremacy.

As the campaign began, the Justice Department itself devoted greater attention to disfranchisement. Especially in the rural black belt, whites had developed a variety of techniques to keep blacks politically inactive. Although the literacy rate among blacks had increased dramatically, local officials manipulated literacy tests to deny literate blacks the right to vote. Often going beyond the letter of state law, they asked blacks difficult questions about the Constitution and state and local government—questions they never put to whites. In addition, officials developed complex voter registration forms and refused to register blacks (but not whites) who made even slight errors in completing them. Registration boards also foiled blacks' efforts to register by meeting infrequently and irregularly and by not publicizing the hours they were open for business. Officials were only part of the problem. In small towns and rural areas blacks who attempted to register might be fired, turned off the land they farmed, denied credit by local merchants, or worse. In this climate, many blacks did not attempt to register. In 1962, only one-fourth of voting age southern blacks were registered; in Mississippi the figure stood at five percent and in Alabama, thirteen percent.

Intent on rooting out these practices, Robert Kennedy dramatically increased the size of the Civil Rights Division staff and directed it to begin wholesale prosecution of voting rights cases. The primary weapons in the campaign were the provisions of the Civil Rights Act of 1957 permitting the Justice Department to seek injunctions against attempting to prevent citizens from registering or voting. Government lawyers won injunctions barring officials from refusing to register blacks who made minor mistakes on their applications and from imposing more stringent literacy tests on blacks than on whites. They also challenged private intimidation of blacks by securing injunctions against economic coercion directed at blacks who challenged discriminatory registration practices or who were active in voter registration drives.

The campaign's results were mixed. In tandem with the Voter Education Project, Justice Department litigation helped increase the proportion of southern black adults who were registered from twenty-six to forty percent between 1962 and 1964. Nevertheless, department officials had to proceed county by county, conducting in-depth investigations to establish proof of discrimination or economic coercion. The process was time-consuming and limited the number of localities in which cases could be initiated. Furthermore, the injunctions department lawyers won ordered persons to stop a certain type of discriminatory or coercive behavior. Local whites were generally resourceful enough to devise other means to hinder black registration, forcing department lawyers to conduct further investigations and return to court. By the end of 1964, only seven percent of the black adults residing in the 46 counties in which the government had initiated suits were registered, and black registration was below 10 percent in 100 southern counties.

The administration's hope that voter registration would cool off tensions produced by the sit-ins and the freedom rides, was soon disappointed. SNCC took its voter registration campaign into black belt counties in Georgia and Mississippi, where whites viewed black political empowerment as a dire threat. Predictably, whites launched a campaign of terror designed to drive out SNCC workers and to intimidate local blacks. Although state officials failed to punish the perpetrators of this violence, the Justice Department refused to make arrests or initiate prosecutions, clinging to its position that responsibility for law enforcement lay primarily with state officials. Only in October 1962, when Mississippi officials and an armed mob prevented enforcement of a court order admitting James Meredith to the University of Mississippi, did the administration act forcefully to curb racist violence. As Eisenhower had done in the Little Rock crisis, Kennedy dispatched U.S. marshals and troops to the campus to break resistance to federal authority and to enable Meredith to enroll.

Events in Birmingham during the spring of 1963, however, finally forced President Kennedy to abandon his cautious approach to civil rights. During the winter of 1962–1963, Martin Luther King, Jr., and his closest advisors devised a bold plan for massive demonstrations in Birmingham, the toughest, most segregated city in the South. King knew that he would meet bitter resistance from the police commissioner, Eugene "Bull" Connor, a hard-line segregationist with a short fuse. Connor, who had earned his spurs during the 1930s in a brutal campaign to keep the unions out of Birmingham's steel mills, ruled the city with an iron fist and could be counted on to respond with violence. Consequently, the city offered King an opportunity to focus the nation's attention on the brutality of segregation, to precipitate a crisis that would force the administration off dead-center, and to win a stunning victory that would reinvigorate a sagging civil rights movement. Wyatt Tee Walker, the SCLC staff member who drafted the Birmingham plan, called it "Project C"—for confrontation.

The Birmingham campaign began in early April with a boycott of downtown merchants, sit-ins at segregated lunch counters, and marches on city hall. Connor responded by arresting protesters and obtaining an injunction against further demonstrations, but the protest continued and grew larger after King himself was arrested on April 12. During the remainder of the month, white leaders refused to negotiate, demonstrations and arrests continued, and police brutality increased. Having won the attention of the administration and the national media, King turned up the pressure. During the first week in May, he brought thousands of black children into the demonstrations, filling the city's jail and pushing Connor over the edge. The police commissioner responded to the "children's crusade" by unleashing club swinging patrolmen, snarling police dogs, and high pressure water hoses on peaceful demonstrators and bystanders, cracking their heads, breaking their bones, tearing their flesh, and bruising their bodies.

King's strategy worked. As pictures of police brutality appeared on the front pages of newspapers and on TV screens in living rooms across the nation, civil rights again took centerstage, and northern support for national action mounted. The president sent Justice Department mediators to Birmingham to arrange a settlement and pressured the city's business elite to compromise. Negotiations began promptly and were successfully concluded on May 10, when King announced that whites had agreed to desegregate lunch counters, drinking fountains, rest rooms, and department store fitting rooms and had pledged to implement a nondiscriminatory hiring program in the city's industries. The victory over Bull Connor emboldened blacks across the South, touching off more than 800 boycotts and demonstrations in 200 southern towns and cities during the summer of 1963. Birmingham kindled a new assertiveness among blacks, leading them to reject tokenism and to demand fundamental change—and to demand it without delay.

Birmingham also forced John Kennedy to make civil rights a top priority—something that no president since Ulysses Grant had done. He realized that blacks were no longer willing to wait patiently and feared that unless sweeping changes were initiated, racial confrontation would tear the nation apart. Indeed, while King continued to espouse nonviolence, there were indications that blacks were growing tired of turning the other cheek. On May 11, in response to a wave of racist bombings, Birmingham blacks took to the streets, pelting police with rocks and bottles and burning several white-owned businesses located in the ghetto. Elsewhere black writer James Baldwin wrote of *The Fire Next Time*, and Malcolm X, the militant black nationalist who appeared on television more than any other black leader in 1963, insisted that "the day of nonviolent resistance is over." Faced with a growing racial crisis and sensing greater support for action, Kennedy went on national television on June 11 to announce that he was sending sweeping civil rights legislation to Congress. He appealed to principle, arguing that the nation confronted a moral issue "as old as the scriptures and . . . as clear as the American Constitution." But he also warned that the issue could no longer be avoided. "The events in Birmingham and elsewhere," he suggested, meant that legislation was essential "if we are to move this problem from the streets to the courts."

Having committed himself, the president moved quickly. He submitted legislation strengthening the voting rights laws, authorizing the attorney general to file school desegregation suits, empowering the president to end federal financial assistance to discriminatory state and local programs, and banning discrimination in places of public accommodation such as motels, restaurants, theaters, retail stores, and gas stations. Kennedy could count on support from many labor leaders, the major national Jewish organizations, and liberal groups such as Americans for Democratic Action as well as the votes of northern Democrats, but he needed support from Republican leaders to offset opposition by southern Democrats and to overcome the inevitable Senate filibuster. The president worked hard to line up Republican support, and when liberal Democrats jeopardized his efforts by attempting to broaden the bill, he intervened, convincing liberals to keep amendments to a minimum and preserving bipartisan support. When an assassin's bullet felled Kennedy in November 1963, his successor, Lyndon Johnson, made the civil rights bill his top legislative priority. Strengthening the bipartisan alliance Kennedy had forged, President Johnson secured congressional approval for the bill in June 1964.

The Civil Rights Act of 1964 translated most of the objectives of the early civil rights movement into law, harnessing the principle of equal rights to the engine of federal power. At the heart of the bill lay the goal of banishing segregation from American life, thereby realizing the principle announced ten years earlier in *Brown*. Titles III and IV authorized the attorney general to institute lawsuits challenging discrimination in public schools and other facilities "owned, operated, or managed by or on behalf of any State or subdivision thereof," thus removing from private individuals the entire burden of desegregation. Title VI used the power of the purse to attack discrimination. It directed federal agencies to adopt regulations banning discrimination in all programs receiving federal funds and to cut the flow of federal dollars if they failed to comply. With many state and local governments becoming increasingly dependent on federal largesse, especially to finance public education, this offered a potent weapon against discrimination.

The law also set its sights on discrimination in privately owned and operated businesses that served the public. Relying on an expanded commerce power that was the legacy of the New Deal, Title II prohibited discrimination on account of race, color, religion, or national origin by restaurants, hotels, motels, gas stations, theaters, stadiums, concert halls, or other places of entertainment that "affected" interstate commerce. Although victims of discrimination might institute lawsuits and recover monetary damages, the act's sponsors realized that private citizens might be reluctant to sue. Consequently, they authorized the attorney general to initiate suits against businesses that violated the act.

Finally, the law attacked employment discrimination, a target of black leaders and congressional liberals since the 1930s. Title VII prohibited discrimination on account of race, color, religion, national origin, or sex by employers and labor unions with more than twenty-five employees or members and by employment agencies. Liberals pressed for establishment of an administrative agency to investigate complaints of employment discrimination and to issue cease-and-desist orders against violators. This afforded a far more effective remedy, they argued, than going to court. In order to maintain Republican support, however, the bill's sponsors were forced to accept watered down enforcement provisions. They established a five-member Equal Employment Opportunity Commission (EEOC) and authorized it to investigate complaints of employment discrimination. When it found evidence of discrimination, the commission was to persuade the employer

The March on Washington, 1963

The March on Washington in August 1963 was one of the central moments in the decades-long civil rights movement. It brought 250,000 Americans to the nation's capital to demonstrate for "jobs and freedom." Millions more watched on television as Martin Luther King, Jr., proclaimed his dream of racial equality (p. 8). The following selection provides three personal accounts of the march and helps give a feeling for the magnitude and importance of the event.

Burke Marshall [Assistant Attorney General for Civil Rights]

The politicians in Washington—I'm not speaking of the president or the attorney general at the moment, I'm speaking of Congress—were scared to death of the march, just totally irrational. I don't know what they thought a march on Washington was going to be. I guess they thought people were going to march down Constitution Avenue throwing stones at them or something like that. There were congressmen who would call up the White House and say, We'd better have troops all over the place. No troops, we said.

We were in constant touch with the organizers of the march, especially Mr. [Bayard] Rustin. We wanted it to be a success. The president was as interested in having it a success as the organizers of the march were, because of the effect it would have politically, on the movement, on momentum in the House of Representatives, particularly on the civil rights bill. I remember that Dick Gregory came into my office and he said to me, "I know these senators and congressmen are scared of what's going to happen. I'll tell you what's going to happen. It's going to be a great big Sunday school picnic."

• • •

Bayard Rustin [Deputy Directory of the March on Washington]

It wasn't the Harry Belafontes and the greats from Hollywood that made the march. What made the march was that black people voted that day with their feet. They came from every state, they came in jalopies, on trains, buses, anything they could get—some walked. There were about three hundred congressmen there, but none of them said a word. We

or union to end its discriminatory practices. If conciliation failed, the victim of discrimination could go to court or the commission could ask the attorney general to initiate a lawsuit.

With the Civil Rights Act on the books, President Johnson turned to the problem of disfranchisement. As the administration consulted civil rights leaders and prepared new legislation, events in Selma, Alabama, lent greater urgency to the issue. Despite several years of voter registration efforts and Justice Department lawsuits, only two percent of the black adults in Dallas County were registered. In January and February 1965, SNCC and SCLC staged massive demonstrations at the county courthouse in Selma to focus attention to the

problem. Local officials responded by arresting more than 3,000 protesters. On March 7, as 500 protesters defied a state court injunction and began a march from Selma to the state capitol in Montgomery, some sixty miles away, state police and a mounted posse led by the sheriff moved against them. As the panic-stricken demonstrators fled, they were trampled by horsemen, shocked with electric cattle prods, and beaten with clubs and chains. That evening the television networks interrupted programs—ABC was airing *Judgment at Nuremberg*—to show the attack, and the next morning Selma was page-one news throughout the country. Lyndon Johnson seized the moment, promptly submitting a sweeping voting rights bill to Con-

had told them to come, but we wanted to talk with them, they were not to talk to us. And after they came and saw that it was very orderly, that there was fantastic determination, that there were all kinds of people there other than black people, they knew there was a consensus in this country for the civil rights bill. After the March on Washington, when Kennedy called into the White House the leaders who had been resistant before the march, he made it very clear to them now he was prepared to put his weight behind the bill.

The march ended for me when we had finally made sure we had not left one piece of paper, not a cup, nothing. We had a five-hundred-man cleanup squad. I went back to the hotel and said to Mr. Randolph, "Chief, I want you to see that there is not a piece of paper or any dirt or filth or anything left here." And Mr. Randolph went to thank me and tears began to come down his cheeks.

I think it was the greatest moment in my life. A. Philip Randolph in my view was the greatest leader of the twentieth century, in terms of the basic analysis and program for blacks. He is a man that history does not record so well as many others. But to me, he was a giant. And to see this giant with tears in his eyes moved me to want to do everything I humanly could to bring about justice, not only for black people but for whoever is in trouble.

Ralph Abernathy [Civil Rights Leader]

The March on Washington established visibility in this nation. It showed the struggle was nearing a close, that people were coming together, that all the organizations could stand together. It demonstrated that there was a unity in the black community for the cause of freedom and justice. It made it clear that we did not have to use violence to achieve the goals which we were seeking.

I went back to the grounds about six or seven o'clock that evening. There was nothing but the wind blowing across the reflection pool, moving and blowing and keeping music. We were so proud that no violence had taken place that day. We were so pleased. This beautiful scene of the wind dancing on the sands of the Lincoln Memorial I will never forget. This was the greatest day of my life.

—Henry Hampton and Steve Fayer

gress and making a nationally televised speech to demand speedy passage. Lawmakers quickly fell into line, completing action on the bill in less than five months.

Cutting through state registration requirements and procedures that purported to be racially neutral, the Voting Rights Act of 1965 established formulas to identify an effective means to end discrimination. The act set its sights on the literacy test, historically the most notorious disfranchising device. In any state or county where fewer than fifty percent of the adults were registered to vote, it automatically suspended the operation of any "test or device" that was a prerequisite for voting. Congress also provided a remedy for other types of discrimination. In counties in which there was substantial evidence of racial discrimination—as indicated by complaints filed by twenty residents or a voting discrimination suit instituted by the attorney general—federal examiners would be appointed to register voters. Moreover, lawmakers attempted to prevent southern officials from developing new techniques of discrimination. States and localities covered by the act would be required to obtain clearance from the attorney general of a three-judge district court in Washington, D.C., before implementing any new voting requirements or procedures.

After years of temporizing, the president and Congress had finally taken the lead in civil rights, drawing on the deep reservoirs of federal power to promote equality. The Supreme Court quickly gave its blessing. In two 1964 cases, *Heart of Atlanta Motel* v. *United States* and *Katzenbach* v. *McClung,* the Court considered the Civil Rights Act's ban on discrimination by motels and restaurants. Drawing on a long line of cases that gave Congress broad authority to regulate businesses affecting interstate commerce, the Court unanimously upheld the statute. The *McClung* case emphasized the breadth of Congress's authority. The business involved, Ollie's Barbeque, was a small Birmingham restaurant that served a local clientele. The Court noted that Ollie's came within the scope of the law because it was open to interstate customers and because part of the food it sold had moved in interstate commerce. Moreover, it ruled that Congress had "a rational basis" for believing that such businesses affected interstate commerce and for subjecting them to regulation. They not only purchased food and other goods from interstate suppliers, but their discriminatory policies made interstate travel by blacks difficult.

Concurring opinions by Justices William Douglas and Arthur Goldberg offered a more direct way of upholding the act. Congress's authority to enforce the equal protection clause, they maintained, authorized it to ban discrimination in businesses open to the public. Their analysis abandoned the hoary principle, established in the *Civil Rights Cases* of 1883, that the amendment authorized Congress to ban discriminatory action by states but not by private individuals or businesses. Although the majority rejected this approach, its willingness to accept a prohibition against discrimination by private businesses enacted under the commerce power gave Congress the authority to reach most private discrimination and suggested the demise of the old distinction between state and private action that had long crippled effective civil rights legislation.

Two years later, in *South Carolina* v. *Katzenbach* (1966), the Court gave its blessing to the Voting Rights Act. Chief Justice Warren emphasized that in enforcing the Fifteenth Amend-

ment, Congress was free to choose the means best suited to eliminate racial discrimination in voting. Surveying the provisions adopted by Congress—suspension of literacy tests, appointment of federal examiners, and judicial supervision of changes in voting procedures—he concluded that they were clearly designed to meet problems that Congress had encountered in its long struggle to overcome state and local officials' ingenious and persistent efforts to deny blacks the right to vote. Consequently, while the act represented an unprecedented exercise of federal power, it was clearly within Congress's authority to adopt legislation necessary and proper to enforce the Fifteenth Amendment.

The Court not only sustained the Voting Rights Act but went where Congress had feared to tread, striking down the poll tax. This device was a far less serious obstacle to black voting than discriminatory administration of literacy tests; by 1960, all but four states—Virginia, Alabama, Mississippi, and Texas—had repealed it. Nevertheless, in those states it deterred the very poor from voting and had a disproportionate effect on blacks. Anti-poll tax legislation had long received strong support on Capitol Hill, and in 1962 Congress had passed the Twenty-fourth Amendment (which was ratified two years later) banning the poll tax as a requirement for voting in *federal* elections. Although liberals made a strong effort to extend the prohibition to state elections in the Voting Rights Act, doubts about the constitutionality of a poll tax repealer torpedoed their effort. Opponents argued that, unlike literacy tests, which were administered in a discriminatory fashion, the poll tax was applied to whites and blacks alike and therefore did not violate the Fifteenth Amendment. One year later, however, the Supreme Court gave opponents of the poll tax the outright victory that had eluded them for decades. In *Harper* v. *Virginia Board of Elections* (1966), the Court ruled the tax unconstitutional, resting its decision on the Fourteenth rather than the Fifteenth Amendment. Writing for the majority, Justice Douglas asserted that the poll tax discriminated against the poor and thus violated the amendment's guarantee of equal protection.

The Court also expanded the government's authority to punish anti–civil rights violence. By early 1965, growing northern outrage over violence against civil rights workers convinced the Justice Department to initiate prosecutions in several highly publicized cases of racist violence. Because the federal system gave states primary responsibility for criminal justice, crimes such as assault and murder were state, not federal, offenses. There were, however, federal statutes that punished persons who deprived others of their civil rights, and it was these which federal prosecutors employed. Principally, Justice Department officials relied on Title 18, section 241 of the *United States Code*, which punished persons who conspired to use force or intimidation to prevent anyone from exercising rights secured by the Constitution or laws of the United States.

Although the law appeared adequate to the task, many questioned whether it could be used to prosecute perpetrators of racist violence. First, many lawyers and scholars doubted whether the rights protected by section 241 included Fourteenth Amendment rights of equal protection and due process. In 1951, the Court had divided 4–4 on the question, with Justice Frankfurter maintaining that rights mentioned in section 241 were limited to those created by the Constitution (such as the right to vote in *federal* elections), not rights that government was prohibited from violating (such as the Fourteenth Amendment rights of equal protection and due process and the rights mentioned in the Bill of Rights). Otherwise, Frankfurter believed, the federal government would have carte blanche to usurp law enforcement activities that properly belonged to the states. Although Frankfurter's opinion did not represent a majority and was not binding, it cast a shadow over the government's authority to prosecute perpetrators of racist violence on grounds that they denied their victims equal protection or due process. In addition, many observers believed that the state action rule precluded prosecution of private citizens under section 241. Given the long line of Supreme Court rulings holding that the Fourteenth Amendment authorized Congress to provide remedies against state, but not private, denials of equal protection and due process, it was doubtful whether section 241 could be employed against private citizens, even if it were interpreted to protect Fourteenth Amendment rights. Although the Court had whittled away at the state action limitation on the Fourteenth Amendment, it had not abandoned it, as *Heart of Atlanta Motel* and *McClung* had suggested.

Two 1966 rulings swept these doubts aside. In *United States* v. *Price*, which involved the prosecution of eighteen whites implicated in the cold-blooded murder of three civil rights workers in Neshoba County, Mississippi, the Court ruled that Fourteenth Amendment rights were protected by section 241. Justice Abe Fortas pointed out that section 241 had its origins in Reconstruction legislation (the 1870 Enforcement Act) designed to enforce the guarantees of the Fourteenth and Fifteenth Amendments. "In this context," he concluded, "it is hardly conceivable that Congress intended [it] . . . to apply only to a narrow and relatively unimportant category of rights." Unquestionably, its "purpose and effect" was "to reach assaults upon rights under the entire Constitution . . . not merely under part of it."

In a companion case, *United States* v. *Guest*, the Supreme Court considered whether Congress could punish private as well as state interference with Fourteenth Amendment rights. Although Justice Potter Stewart's opinion for the Court ducked the issue, concurring opinions by Justices William Brennan and Tom Clark (which were joined by six justices) were much bolder. Challenging the limitations imposed on Congress in the *Civil Rights Cases* (1883), Justice Brennan insisted that Congress enjoyed broad power to enforce the amendment's guarantees. "Section 5 [of the Fourteenth Amendment] authorizes Congress to make laws that it concludes are reasonably necessary to protect a right created by . . . that Amendment," he wrote, "and Congress is thus fully empowered to determine that punishment of private conspiracies interfering with the exercise of such a right is necessary to its full protection." In short, Brennan concluded, Congress is authorized "to exercise its discretion in fashioning remedies to achieve civil and political equality for all citizens."

The *Price* and *Guest* cases did not bury the state action rule. They suggested that Congress's authority to enforce the amendment (expressly conferred in section 5) gave it broad discretion to strike at state and private action. Yet the justices did not claim such authority for themselves. When the Court enforced the equal protection clause (rather than congressional legislation enforcing it), it would still require the presence of state action in order to prohibit discrimination. Nevertheless, *Guest* and *Price* gave the government the authority necessary to prosecute anti-civil rights violence. In 1966 and 1967 government lawyers used the newly reinvigorated section 241 to win convictions in several of the most outrageous instances of violence against blacks and civil rights workers. More important, the decisions unshackled Congress from the state action theory, offering it greater authority to protect individual rights. Lawmakers promptly took advantage of the Court's largesse. In Title I of the Civil Rights Act of 1968 they established a much clearer definition of federally protected civil rights than did the maddeningly vague section 241. Additionally, they gave the attorney general broad authority to prosecute anyone who used force or intimidation to interfere with these rights.

IV  TRENDS

At a time of considerable racial tension and a tendency toward polarization in racial politics, some politicians are moving the other way: toward a "new politics," as Rob Gurwitt describes it, of "inclusion and racial unity." A leading example, Gurwitt reports, is Cleveland's Mayor Michael White, elected in a close race in 1989.

Gurwitt's portrait of White depicts a member of the new generation of black leadership: those who grew up in a world shaped by the victories—and disappointments— of the civil rights movement. Their concerns are less with overt issues of discrimination and more with the difficult problems now facing blacks—and whites. Their approach is based on the idea that, having secured access to the system in the 1950s and 1960s, blacks can now use the system to their political and economic advantage.

Questions

1. What factors help explain the different perspectives of the new generation of black leaders and their elders? Consider differences in personal backgrounds and in the changing nature of race relations, and racial politics, in the United States.

2. Gurwitt describes the new-style politics as "coalition politics." Who makes up the new coalitions? How have black politicians like those described in this reading been able to appeal successfully to white voters as well as blacks?

17.6 A Younger Generation of Black Politicians Challenges Its Elders

Rob Gurwitt

On the day last November [1989] that Douglas Wilder and David Dinkins became two of the country's best-known black elected officials, a relatively obscure black candidate named Michael White was scratching out a hard-fought runoff victory for mayor of Cleveland. His achievement drew scarce notice beyond the plain-spun precincts of his own city; in all the lines of newspaper ink and long minutes of television coverage trumpeting the elections in Virginia and New York City, White barely rated a mention.

For anyone interested in the course of racial politics in this country, that was unfortunate. There is no doubt that the wins scored by Wilder and Dinkins that day were historic: Dinkins was chosen the first black mayor of New York, and Wilder became the first black man in the country's history to be elected governor. But the to-do over their victories obscured a notable development in the political world.

White's election marked the first time that a black politician had successfully blended two currents that have begun to nudge the course of black politics in new directions. In defeating City Council President George Forbes, Cleveland's premiere black politician, White abandoned the race-conscious politics that had marked both Cleveland and Forbes in the past, campaigning on the more quietly potent theme of inclusion and racial unity. At the same time, he laid down a challenge to Forbes and other established black political leaders, arguing that they had failed to deliver economically for poor and working-class neighborhoods both black and white, and had concentrated instead on downtown business development and their own political careers.

White was by no means last year's only practitioner of a moderate, inclusive style that could appeal to voters of any race: Wilder and Dinkins based their campaigns on it, and John Daniels and Norm Rice likewise rode it to victory in their mayoral campaigns in New Haven and Seattle. Nor was White the first insurgent black politician to reach the mayoralty by criticizing an entrenched black leader for ignoring neighborhood economic development; Sharpe James used the same argument to defeat Kenneth Gibson in Newark in 1986.

But where Dinkins, Wilder, Daniels and Rice were leaders of their local black establishments, White was attacking his. And where Newark's overwhelmingly black population allowed James to concentrate his appeal on the black electorate, White won on the basis of support from white voters. At 38, he is now the second of the younger generation of black politicians to reach the pinnacle of big-city politics, after Kurt Schmoke of Baltimore. His success in Cleveland seems to be clear evidence that cross-racial politics and a somewhat populist critique of the black political establishment have the potential to be more than local oddities.

White is one of a growing number of younger black politicians who have been brought to coalition politics by inclination, education and background, not just circumstances. Moreover, in cities such as Los Angeles and New Haven, as well as in Cleveland, there are signs among younger black activists and professionals of a developing challenge to entrenched black politicians based on the notion that the older generation has been content to reign as symbols of black political power without adequately using it to address the black community's needs.

Neither of these developments is strong enough yet to justify a conclusion that black politics has entered a new era, but there is little doubt that this is a time of transition. White and his allies in Cleveland are members of a new generation that is just starting to flex its muscles, and there is little question that it holds the potential for radically altering the black political landscape.

White's victory was a revolution of sorts in Cleveland politics. Forbes was one of the leading political presences in the city, a veteran who had risen with and eventually outlasted such contemporaries as two-term Mayor Carl Stokes to become Cleveland's most powerful black politician.

White, a one-time Forbes protégé on the city council, owes his place in the mayor's office in part to Forbes' record on the council. In his years on the council, Forbes had used a confrontational, sometimes abusive style to subdue his opponents and consolidate his power. He had also used race and charges of racism as a political cudgel, a ploy that had a particular resonance in racially divided Cleveland. None of that endeared him to white voters—or to some black voters. "There were people who had

been waiting 20 years to vote against George Forbes," says Bob Nece, chairman of the United Auto Workers' Community Action Program in Cleveland, which backed White in the general election.

Even so, White's emergence from the primary (which also included three well-known white candidates) as Forbes' runoff opponent rested squarely on his ability to appeal to voters' longing for a candidate who preached racial healing and talked about how issues such as job creation and crime prevention united the city's racially divided east and west sides. Even in the general election, Nece says, "Mike had to show he was an acceptable candidate. Then the anti-Forbes factor came into play." In the end, White pulled in a full 80 percent of the votes from Cleveland's white community, compared with 30 percent from the city's black voters.

If White's nonconfrontational, inclusionary approach made for good campaign tactics, it also stemmed from a more fundamental development taking place within the black community in Cleveland and elsewhere. Marvin

McMickle, a Baptist minister who heads the NAACP [National Association for the Advancement of Colored People] in Cleveland, says the generational struggle among black politicians "is between the old and aging leaders of the civil rights movement and this new group of baby boomers, who might not have been veterans of Birmingham, but have been shaped and groomed in political science and with law degrees and MBAs. With this group will come a new style of politics that reflects their own ability to live and move in a multicultural environment."

Jeff Johnson agrees. A practitioner of this new politics who had been in line to be majority leader on Cleveland's city council until he was tapped to replace White in the state Senate, he says, "The difference is based not only on perspective but on style. We try to be professional, not disrespectful, in public, and to be well-mannered but tough."

As the white-haired Dinkins and Wilder demonstrated last year, the ability to maneuver without reference to color is not just a function of age, and there is little doubt that the future holds more of the moderate, racially inclusive campaigning that marked last year's elections. That is a matter, in part, of simple hard-headed politics.

"The available political jurisdictions that are majority black are drying up," says Ron Walters, a political scientist at Howard University. "So to increase the number of black elected officials, they will have to come from majority white districts. You cannot run there in the same way as in a majority black district and be successful." Dinkins and Wilder, two established black leaders, responded to that simple reality.

But it is equally true that younger black politicians and professionals have grown up in an environment very different from their elders'. "The out-and-out, flagrant racism that my father's generation dealt with was far more serious than what we've encountered," says Pete Taylor, a former staffer in the California Legislature who now works for GTE in Los Angeles.

"We grew up in a different kind of environment that taught us to be more sophisticated at this age in dealing with nonblack people and nonblack issues."

Although there are still only a few new-style black mayors of large cities, there are others of this stripe who have begun to win city council seats, local administrative positions and state legislative posts in cities such as Atlanta, Chicago and Oakland, as well as in Cleveland.

None of this is to say that any of this younger generation sees racism as having disappeared or discounts the race-consciousness that their elders preached. But many of them argue that times have changed, and that what is demanded of them has to change with it. "The civil rights movement was much more about confronting the system," says Elihu Harris, a California state Assembly member who represents Oakland. "People now think about working within the system."

Inevitably, that new thinking about style and tactics has been accompanied by a reassessment of the black community's agenda.

Daniel Tabor, a member of the city council in Inglewood, a heavily black city next to Los Angeles, argues that established black political leaders have not helped their communities learn to hold them accountable and so have been able to avoid dealing with a variety of difficult problems. "There has been a true failure on the part of elected officials to lead in any direction," he says. "Why should it take black elected officials a longer period of time to respond to the issue of gangs in their community than it took white officials? Why should it take them a longer period of time to respond to the failings of education?"

In some ways, the rhetoric that for decades has brought success within the black community has lost its hold on politicians like Tabor and White. "During the black power movement, a lot of the electoral success of black candidates stemmed from symbolism—the 'Vote for me, I'll set you free' sort of thing," says Mark Harris, a vice president of the California Bar Association. "Now, there's a fight to solve all the problems that have been ignored, and we're finding that the tune has not changed from those black politicians."

In Cleveland, White set out to challenge Forbes on precisely that score, arguing that in an old Rust Belt city with a struggling working class and some 40 percent of the population living below the poverty level, the city's downtown building boom had to include some payoff for its neighborhoods, white and black. Forbes was especially vulnerable on the point, since his strength on the city council had rested on a close alliance with downtown business interests. It was also an argument that could be expected to have a certain resonance in a white community made up of large numbers of blue-collar workers feeling left behind by downtown office development.

It is unclear to what degree White scored with that point, but it's worth noting that three black city council members also lost their seats. Although in two cases the defeated councilmen were involved in minor scandals, McMickle, the NAACP leader, argues that they had more going against them than that.

"They were part of a political machine orchestrated out of City Hall that was not being productive for the neighborhoods," he says. "It was productive for downtown development, but the fruits did not reach into public housing or inner-city neighborhoods, and had no impact at all on the quality of public education. People could see that their investment in those persons was without any return."

Around the country, says Tom Cavanaugh, director of the Center for the Study of American Government at Johns Hopkins University, "one of the fault lines that run through city politics is a conflict between downtown and the neighborhoods." Many black mayors and political leaders in large cities, he notes, have cemented their political bases by working closely with the downtown business establishment—the real estate industry, developers, banks and downtown retailers. Although the leaders have often insisted that minority-owned businesses and black workers be included in the development activity, black neighborhoods as a whole have often gone without seeing any tangible benefits.

That is certainly the case in Los Angeles, where the south central part of the city around Watts continues to be an emblem of inner-city troubles. Along with several black city council members, longtime Mayor Tom Bradley, who in many ways established the model for today's cross-racial black politicians, has come under fire recently from within the black community for failing to steer resources to poor black neighborhoods.

"We understand things had to get into place, that the harbor and the airport and building downtown bring resources," says Juanita Tate, vice president of the leading community organization in Watts, Concerned Citizens of South Central Los Angeles. "But those resources could have been more fairly and evenly distributed." Tate serves on a commission Bradley recently established, in part as a response to pressure from within the black community, to suggest ways to develop the south central area.

In Los Angeles' case, the development of a cadre of younger black politicians openly critical of the establishment has been slow, mostly because there has been almost no movement among established black politicians in Los Angeles for the last several years, and as a consequence, few opportunities for these younger activists and professionals to win their own offices. Even so, there is a growing cluster of establishment critics in some community organizations and in business or the professions, and a few with political experience are eyeing challenges to incumbent black city council members [in 1991] based on the argument that they have not paid enough attention to their communities.

Simply in terms of political office, similar stagnation has existed in New Haven. But there, John Daniels' campaign for mayor has brought sudden legitimacy to a small group of young black politicians-in-the-making who have set out to challenge the black establishment.

For several decades, New Haven has mostly been run by a group of politicians, many of them Italian-American, based in City Hall and at the head of the Democratic Party. Many of the black aldermen and party officials who were able to secure positions of stature did so in large part by remaining loyal to the party machinery—at the expense, the young black activists charge, of standing up for the needs of their community, which is among the poorest in the nation.

Brought together initially by a somewhat quixotic primary challenge to incumbent Mayor Biagio DiLieto in 1987, the young activists used the intervening two years to build their own political base by organizing among inner-city voters in their late teens and early 20s, and in the city's housing project. "The majority of working black folks are registered Democrats and are plugged into Democratic machine politicians," says Lisa Sullivan, a black political science graduate student at Yale who is actively involved in the "Kiddie Korner," as the older politicians called them. "But there are people in public housing and younger folks who are not plugged in, who are restless and fed up with politics as usual." They were the young activists' target.

The route that Sullivan and her allies followed was essentially to build an operation that could bring those alienated voters to the polls. "We realized that on a technical level we had to be different from what we call the 'Old Heads,'" says Steve White, who would eventually run Daniels' campaign staff. "We knew that the only way to have an impact was to be organizationally sound, to be able to do effective canvassing, both door to door and by phone." They demonstrated their proficiency by delivering a large bloc of votes to Daniels in his primary against a DiLieto aide and repeated the performance in his victory over Republican Robie Pooley.

With Daniels in office, they will concentrate on pushing for programs aimed at inner-city youth, particularly on issues of drugs and violence. "We understand that Daniels has to continue a commitment to downtown development, but we're offering him a way to deliver to the black community through youth services," says Sullivan.

As advocates of the new coalition politics and upstart challengers of the black establishment grow in numbers, they are certain to find that attaining political power, difficult as it may be, is a cakewalk compared with using it.

If there are any lessons to be looked for from last year's mayoral contests, they almost certainly lie in the troublesome nature of keeping coalition politics alive. In New York, for example, the grouping of blacks, Hispanics, organized labor, white liberals and business leaders that Dinkins used to put himself in office is at its best a shaky one. "Some people call it a 'no-sneeze' coalition—you better not sneeze, because it might fall apart," says James Jennings, a political scientist at the University of Massachusetts in Boston.

On the one hand, a general sense of both physical erosion, as parts of the city's infrastructure deteriorate, and social erosion, as race relations and the reach of poverty worsen, already may be straining the willingness of the white middle class and businesses to put up with the city. Any move Dinkins makes that is seen by them as a threat will only make things worse.

On the other hand, Dinkins will clearly be faced with a challenge from the black community to shift the city's limited resources to meet its demands. "Black people are saying, 'We don't want sanitation to go to white neighborhoods and not come to ours,'" says Assemblywoman Cynthia Jenkins, who represents southeast Queens. "When it snows, the white community's snow is plowed, and in the black community, God's sun has to melt it. We want potholes filled, we want storm sewers so we don't have to wear boots when it rains, we want moderate- and low-income housing. We want true affirmative action when it comes to jobs."

Although a spokesman for former Mayor Ed Koch disputes Jenkins' charges of unequal treatment, it may be that for Dinkins' purposes, reality is irrelevant. "It's the perception among black people that is the problem, not whether it's accurate or not," says Andrew Cooper, publisher of the *City Sun*, one of the city's prominent black newspapers. "He's got to demonstrate that the reality is not so by going an extra step and showing that there are changes being made."

Mike White is almost certain to face a similar problem. The leading white candidate in Cleveland's mayoral primary last year, Clerk of Cleveland Municipal Courts Benny Bonanno, had immense popularity among ethnic blue-collar voters on the city's West Side, and although he was bruised by the primary, he may be able to pose a potent challenge in four years' time. Few people in the city are convinced that racial sentiment has advanced to the point that White could hold on to the white vote in the face of a popular white opponent.

But if White is to make it as a coalition politician, he must find ways to cement his support among black voters while holding on to as much of the white electorate as possible. As Dinkins' dilemma makes clear, it is not an easy course. There are some black political thinkers who doubt that can be done by Dinkins, White or anyone else. "The thing that makes it almost impossible to do is the dynamics of racism and racial politics in America," says political scientist Ron Walters. There are almost no issues, he says, that can work to unite white and black voters, other than drugs. To survive politically, he says, a politician almost has to choose which community he will play to, and then "hope there are enough supporters on the other side to put him over the top at election time."

Even Cleveland's Jeff Johnson admits that it has been difficult to convince black voters that they have interests in common with white voters. "It's true that the older generation in particular, which went through the trauma and struggle of the civil rights movement and knows overt discrimination, finds it very hard to accept coalition politics," he says.

White has no models to guide him as he tries to build his base within the black community and still hold onto his white supporters. The only other young black mayor who built a multiracial coalition as his route to power, Bal-

timore's Schmoke, defeated a better-established black candidate using a nonracial campaign that stressed his professional credentials. He has not risked alienating black voters by challenging the black establishment in his city.

It may turn out that White's populist criticism of the political establishment is the key to building a permanent coalition. By concentrating on an issue such as finding a way to spread the resources generated by Cleveland's economic development around to its neighborhoods, he may be in a position to offer a tangible benefit to voters in both black and white areas.

White is likely to have help. The city council's new president is a white liberal named Jay Westbrook, who comes out of the community development–oriented organization Citizen Action, and who, like White, is committed to keeping developers from winning still more of the tax breaks that they have been getting in recent years. Both Westbrook and White may also look at ways of requiring developers who get approval for downtown projects to contribute funds for neighborhood development—a course that has been tried in other cities.

White's ability to steer an admittedly tricky course between encouraging such linkage and driving development away may prove crucial to his success. Should White be able to get from downtown developers more financial resources for Cleveland's schools, housing stock and community centers, Johnson and others argue, he will benefit among both black and white voters.

Moreover, Johnson maintains, the white community will respond to the right rhetorical appeal. "Cleveland is used to having issues defined by race," he says. "But economics has provided an audience of people of both races who are seeking leaders—middle-class residents who are struggling, working-class people who are one paycheck away from poverty." The key to appealing to black voters without alienating whites, he argues, is not to ignore race but to acknowledge the common difficulties faced by both. "You can say, 'Look, I'm concerned about joblessness for both black and white, but particularly black males.' You can talk about both, and home in on one. The white community will accept that. It's when you say that it's only blacks who have troubles that you begin to alienate them."

In the end, it may be that the success of efforts by politicians like White to carve out a new political direction lies outside their control. Redistributing the benefits of economic development works only when development is taking place, and an economic downturn could set different groups at one another's throats over a shrinking financial base. Or it may turn out that White's approach is the kind that works only in older industrial cities that still have a large white working class. Or racial antipathies could well up, despite the best efforts of political leaders to avoid them.

Whatever the case, it is unlikely that the generation represented by White, Johnson and other young Cleveland blacks is going to disappear, and their experiences can be expected to shape the approach of young politicians down the road. "These are people who don't have the baggage of 25 years of previous political involvements and partisanship," says Cleveland's Marvin McMickle. "They really are our hope."

V  ISSUE AND DEBATE: IS AFFIRMATIVE ACTION FAIR?

Although there is now widespread agreement in favor of equal treatment of minority groups under the law, there is anything but agreement on the legal, moral, and practical justification of affirmative action. Whereas early civil rights decisions and legislation aimed at simply erasing all legal distinctions based on race, affirmative action seeks to remedy the effects of historic discrimination through programs aimed at bettering the lot of women and minorities. The problem is that not everyone who is classified as a minority for affirmative action purposes has actually felt the ill effects of discrimination and that many of those who are disadvantaged by such programs were neither at fault nor in any way assisted by such discrimination.

The Supreme Court first upheld affirmative action in the 1978 case of Bakke v. Regents of the University of California. *Racial preferences were appropriate in the case of medical school admissions, the Court reasoned, because of the university's compelling interest in creating a diverse student body. In recent years the Court has split deeply over affirmative action, approving some programs but striking down others.*

The moral and practical sides of the affirmative action question are as intractable as the legal side. In the following selections, two leading scholars stake out opposing sides on this vexing question. Writing shortly before the Bakke *case was decided, the legal philosopher Ronald Dworkin argued that Bakke had no cause for complaint. Dworkin's argument is answered by the economist Thomas Sowell, a leading black conservative known, among other things, for his opposition to affirmative action.*

Question

1. Consider the meaning of equality as expressed in the Declaration of Independence (selection 1.2) and in Martin Luther King's "I Have a Dream" speech (p. 8). How might the ideas expressed in these classic texts affect arguments about affirmative action?

YES

17.7 Bakke's Case: Quotas Are Not Unfair _____

Ronald Dworkin

On October 12, 1977, the Supreme Court heard oral argument in the case of *The Regents of the University of California v. Allan Bakke*. No lawsuit has ever been more widely watched or more thoroughly debated in the national and international press before the Court's decision. Still, some of the most pertinent facts set before the Court have not been clearly summarized.

The medical school of the University of California at Davis has an affirmative action program (called the "task force program") designed to admit more black and other minority students. It sets sixteen places aside for which only members of "educationally and economically disadvantaged minorities" compete. Allan Bakke, white, applied for one of the remaining eighty-four places; he was rejected but, since his test scores were relatively high, the medical school has conceded that it could not prove that he would have been rejected if the sixteen places reserved had been open to him. Bakke sued, arguing that the task force program deprived him of his constitutional rights. The California Supreme Court agreed, and ordered the medical school to admit him. The university appealed to the Supreme Court.

The Davis program for minorities is in certain respects more forthright (some would say cruder) than similar plans now in force in many other American universities and professional schools. Such programs aim to increase the enrollment of black and other minority students by allowing the fact of their race to count affirmatively as part of the case for admitting them. Some schools set a "target" of a particular number of minority places instead of setting aside a flat number of places. But Davis would not fill the number of places set aside unless there were sixteen minority candidates it considered clearly qualified for medical education. The difference

is therefore one of administrative strategy and not of principle.

So the constitutional question raised by *Bakke* is of capital importance for higher education in the United States, and a large number of universities and schools have entered briefs *amicus curiae* urging the Court to reverse the California decision. They believe that if they are not free to use explicit racial criteria in their admissions programs, they will be unable to fulfill what they take to be their responsibilities to the nation.

It is often said that affirmative action programs aim to achieve a racially conscious society divided into racial and ethnic groups, each entitled as a group to some proportionable share of resources, careers, or opportunities. That is a perverse description. American society is currently a racially conscious society; this is the inevitable and evident consequence of a history of slavery, repression, and prejudice. Black men and women, boys and girls, are not free to choose for themselves in what roles—or as members of which social groups—others will characterize them. They are black, and no other feature of personality or allegiance or ambition will so thoroughly influence how they will be perceived and treated by others, and the range and character of the lives that will be open to them.

The tiny number of black doctors and other professionals is both a consequence and a continuing cause of American racial consciousness, one link in a long and self-fueling chain reaction. Affirmative action programs use racially explicit criteria because their immediate goal is to increase the number of members of certain races in these professions. But their long-term goal is to *reduce* the degree to which American society is overall a racially conscious society.

The programs rest on two judgments. The first is a judgment of social theory: that the United States will continue to be pervaded by racial divisions as long as the most lucrative, satisfying, and important careers remain mainly the prerogative of members of the white race, while others feel themselves systematically excluded from a professional and social elite. The second is a calculation of strategy: that increasing the number of blacks who are at work in the professions will, in the long run, reduce the sense of frustration and injustice and racial self-consciousness in the black community to the point at which blacks may begin to think of themselves as individuals who can succeed like others through talent and initiative. At that future point the consequences of nonracial admissions programs, whatever these consequences might be, could be accepted with no sense of racial barriers or injustice.

It is therefore the worst possible misunderstanding to suppose that affirmative action programs are designed to produce a balkanized America, divided into racial and ethnic subnations. They use strong measures because weaker ones will fail; but their ultimate goal is to lessen not to increase the importance of race in American social and professional life.

According to the 1970 census, only 2.1 percent of American doctors were black. Affirmative action programs aim to provide more black doctors to serve black patients. This is not because it is desirable that blacks treat blacks and whites treat whites, but because blacks, through no fault of their own, are now unlikely to be well served by whites, and because a failure to provide the doctors they trust will exacerbate rather than reduce the resentment that now leads them to trust only their own. Affirmative action tries to provide more blacks as classmates for white doctors, not because it is desirable that a medical school class reflect the racial makeup of the community as a whole, but because professional association between blacks and whites will decrease the degree to which whites think of blacks as a race rather than as people, and thus the degree to which blacks think of

themselves that way. It tries to provide "role models" for future black doctors, not because it is desirable for a black boy or girl to find adult models only among blacks, but because our history has made them so conscious of their race that the success of whites, for now, is likely to mean little or nothing for them.

The history of the campaign against racial injustice since 1954, when the Supreme Court decided *Brown v. Board of Education*, is a history in large part of failure. We have not succeeded in reforming the racial consciousness of our society by racially neutral means. We are therefore obliged to look upon the arguments for affirmative action with sympathy and an open mind. Of course, if Bakke is right that such programs, no matter how effective they may be, violate his constitutional rights, then they cannot be permitted to continue. But we must not forbid them in the name of some mindless maxim, like the maxim that it cannot be right to fight fire with fire, or that the end cannot justify the means. If the strategic claims for affirmative action are cogent, they cannot be dismissed on the ground that racially explicit tests are distasteful. If such tests are distasteful, it can only be for reasons that make the underlying social realities the programs attack more distasteful still.

It is said that, in a pluralistic society, membership in a particular group cannot be used as a criterion of inclusion or exclusion from benefits. But group membership is, as a matter of social reality rather than formal admission standards, part of what determines inclusion or exclusion for us now. If we must choose between a society that is in fact liberal and an illiberal society that scrupulously avoids formal racial criteria, we can hardly appeal to the ideals of liberal pluralism to prefer the latter.

Archibald Cox of Harvard Law School, speaking for the University of California in oral argument, told the Supreme Court that this is the choice the United States must make. As things stand, he said, affirmative action programs are the only effective means of increasing the absurdly small number of black doctors. The

California Supreme Court, in approving Bakke's claim, had urged the university to pursue that goal by methods that do not explicitly take race into account. But that is unrealistic. We must distinguish, Cox said, between two interpretations of what the California Court's recommendation means. It might mean that the university should aim at the same immediate goal, of increasing the proportion of black and other minority students in the medical school, by an admissions procedure that on the surface is not racially conscious.

That is a recommendation of hypocrisy. If those who administer the admissions standards, however these are phrased, understand that their immediate goal is to increase the number of blacks in the school, then they will use race as a criterion in making the various subjective judgments the explicit criteria will require, because that will be, given the goal, the only right way to make those judgments. The recommendation might mean, on the other hand, that the school should adopt some non-racially conscious goal, like increasing the number of disadvantaged students of all races, and then hope that that goal will produce an increase in the number of blacks as a by-product. But even if that strategy is less hypocritical (which is far from plain), it will almost certainly fail because no different goal, scrupulously administered in a non-racially conscious way, will significantly increase the number of black medical students.

Cox offered powerful evidence for that conclusion, and it is supported by the recent and comprehensive report of the Carnegie Council on Policy Studies in Higher Education. Suppose, for example, that the medical school sets aside separate places for applicants "disadvantaged" on some racially neutral test, like poverty, allowing only those disadvantaged in that way to compete for these places. If the school selects those from that group who scored best on standard medical school aptitude tests, then it will take almost no blacks, because blacks score relatively low even among the economically disadvantaged. But if the school chooses among the disadvantaged on some basis other than test scores, just so that more blacks will succeed, then it will not be administering the special procedure in a non-racially conscious way.

So Cox was able to put his case in the form of two simple propositions. A racially conscious test for admission, even one that sets aside certain places for qualified minority applicants exclusively, serves goals that are in themselves unobjectionable and even urgent. Such programs are, moreover, the only means that offer any significant promise of achieving these goals. If these programs are halted, then no more than a trickle of black students will enter medical or other professional schools for another generation at least.

If these propositions are sound, then on what ground can it be thought that such programs are either wrong or unconstitutional? We must notice an important distinction between two different sorts of objections that might be made. These programs are intended, as I said, to decrease the importance of race in the United States in the long run. It may be objected, first, that the programs will harm that goal more than they will advance it. There is no way now to prove that that is not so. Cox conceded in his argument that there are costs and risks in these programs.

Affirmative action programs seem to encourage, for example, a popular misunderstanding, which is that they assume that racial or ethnic groups are entitled to proportionate shares of opportunities, so that Italian or Polish ethnic minorities are, in theory, as entitled to their proportionate shares as blacks or Chicanos or American Indians are entitled to the shares the present programs give them. That is a plain mistake: the programs are not based on the idea that those who are aided are entitled to aid, but only on the strategic hypothesis that helping them is now an effective way of attacking a national problem. Some medical schools may well make that judgment, under certain circumstances, about a white ethnic minority. Indeed it seems likely that some medical schools are even now attempting to help white Appalachian applicants, for example, under programs of regional distribution.

So the popular understanding is wrong, but so long as it persists it is a cost of the program because the attitudes it encourages tend to a degree to make people more rather than less conscious of race. There are other possible costs. It is said, for example, that some blacks find affirmative action degrading; they find that it makes them more rather than less conscious of prejudice against their race as such. This attitude is also based on a misperception, I think, but for a small minority of blacks at least it is a genuine cost.

In the view of the many important universities which have such programs, however, the gains will very probably exceed the losses in reducing racial consciousness overall. This view is hardly so implausible that it is wrong for these universities to seek to acquire the experience that will allow us to judge whether they are right. It would be particularly silly to forbid these experiments if we know that the failure to try will mean, as the evidence shows, that the status quo will almost certainly continue. In any case, this first objection could provide no argument that would justify a decision by the Supreme Court holding the programs unconstitutional. The Court has no business substituting its speculative judgment about the probable consequences of educational policies for the judgment of professional educators.

So the acknowledged uncertainties about the long-term results of such programs could not justify a Supreme Court decision making them illegal. But there is a second and very different form of objection. It may be argued that even if the programs *are* effective in making our society less a society dominated by race, they are nevertheless unconstitutional because they violate the individual constitutional rights of those, like Allan Bakke, who lose places in consequence. In the oral argument Reynold H. Colvin of San Francisco, who is Bakke's lawyer, made plain that his objection takes this second form. Mr. Justice White asked him whether he accepted that the goals affirmative action pro-

grams seek are important goals. Colvin acknowledged that they were. Suppose, Justice White continued, that affirmative action programs are, as Cox had argued, the only effective means of seeking such goals. Would Colvin nevertheless maintain that the programs are unconstitutional? Yes, he insisted, they would be, because his client has a constitutional right that the programs be abandoned, no matter what the consequences.

Colvin was wise to put his objections on this second ground; he was wise to claim that his client has rights that do not depend on any judgment about the likely consequences of affirmative action for society as a whole, because if he sustains that claim, then the Court must give him the relief he seeks.

But can he be right? If Allan Bakke has a constitutional right so important that the urgent goals of affirmative action must yield, then this must be because affirmative action violates some fundamental principle of political morality. This is not a case in which what might be called formal or technical law requires a decision one way or the other. There is no language in the Constitution whose plain meaning forbids affirmative action. Only the most naive theories of statutory construction could argue that such a result is required by the language of any earlier Supreme Court decision or of the Civil Rights Act of 1964 or of any other congressional enactment. If Colvin is right, it must be because Allan Bakke has not simply some technical legal right but an important moral right as well.

What could that right be? The popular argument frequently made on editorial pages is that Bakke has a right to be judged on his merit. Or that he has a right to be judged as an individual rather than as a member of a social group. Or that he has a right, as much as any black man, not to be sacrificed or excluded from any opportunity because of his race alone. But these catch phrases are deceptive here, because, as reflection demonstrates, the only genuine principle they describe is the principle that no one should suffer from the prejudice or contempt of others. And that principle is not at stake in this case at all. In spite of popular opinion, the idea that the *Bakke* case presents a conflict between a desirable social goal and important individual rights is a piece of intellectual confusion.

Consider, for example, the claim that individuals applying for places in medical school should be judged on merit, and merit alone. If that slogan means that admissions committees should take nothing into account but scores on some particular intelligence test, then it is arbitrary and, in any case, contradicted by the long-standing practice of every medical school. If it means, on the other hand, that a medical school should choose candidates that it supposes will make the most useful doctors, then everything turns on the judgment of what factors make different doctors useful. The Davis medical school assigned to each regular applicant, as well as to each minority applicant, what it called a "benchmark score." This reflected not only the results of aptitude tests and college grade averages, but a subjective evaluation of the applicant's chances of functioning as an effective doctor, in view of society's present needs for medical service. Presumably the qualities deemed important were different from the qualities that a law school or engineering school or business school would seek, just as the intelligence tests a medical school might use would be different from the tests these other schools would find appropriate.

There is no combination of abilities and skills and traits that constitutes "merit" in the abstract; if quick hands count as "merit" in the case of a prospective surgeon, this is because quick hands will enable him to serve the public better and for no other reason. If a black skin will, as a matter of regrettable fact, enable another doctor to do a different medical job better, then that black skin is by the same token "merit" as well. That argument may strike some as dangerous; but only because they confuse its conclusion—that black skin may be a socially useful trait in particular circumstances—with the very different and despicable idea that one race may be inherently more worthy than another.

Consider the second of the catch phrases I have mentioned. It is said that Bakke has a right to be judged as an "individual," in deciding whether he is to be admitted to medical school and thus to the medical profession, and not as a member of some group that is being judged as a whole. What can that mean? Any admissions procedure must rely on generalizations about groups that are justified only statistically. The regular admissions process at Davis, for example, set a cutoff figure for college grade-point averages. Applicants whose averages fell below that figure were not invited to any interview, and therefore rejected out of hand.

An applicant whose average fell one point below the cutoff might well have had personal qualities of dedication or sympathy that would have been revealed at an interview, and that would have made him or her a better doctor than some applicant whose average rose one point above the line. But the former is excluded from the process on the basis of a decision taken for administrative convenience and grounded in the generalization, unlikely to hold true for every individual, that those with grade averages below the cutoff will not have other qualities sufficiently persuasive. Even the use of standard Medical College Aptitude Tests (MCAT) as part of the admissions procedure requires judging people as part of groups, because it assumes that test scores are a guide to medical intelligence, which is in turn a guide to medical ability. Though this judgment is no doubt true statistically, it hardly holds true for every individual.

Allan Bakke was himself refused admission to two other medical schools, not because of his race but because of his age: these schools thought that a student entering medical school at the age of thirty-three was likely to make less of a contribution to medical care over his career than someone entering at the standard age of twenty-one. Suppose these schools relied, not on any detailed investigation of whether Bakke himself had abilities that would contradict the generalization in his specific case, but on a rule of thumb that allowed only the most cursory look at applicants over (say) the age of thirty.

Did these two medical schools violate his right to be judged as an individual rather than as a member of a group?

The Davis medical school permitted whites to apply for the sixteen places reserved for members of "educationally or economically disadvantaged minorities," a phrase whose meaning might well include white ethnic minorities. In fact several whites have applied, though none has been accepted, and the California Court found that the special committee charged with administering the program had decided, in advance, against admitting any. Suppose that decision had been based on the following administrative theory: it is so unlikely that any white doctor can do as much to counteract racial imbalance in the medical professions as a well-qualified and trained black doctor can do that the committee should for reasons of convenience proceed on the presumption no white doctor could. That presumption is, as a matter of fact, more plausible than the corresponding presumption about medical students over the age of thirty, or even the presumption about applicants whose grade-point averages fall below the cutoff line. If the latter presumptions do not deny the alleged right of individuals to be judged as individuals in an admissions procedure, then neither can the former.

Colvin, in oral argument, argued the third of the catch phrases I mentioned. He said that his client had a right not to be excluded from medical school because of his race alone, and this as a statement of constitutional right sounds more plausible than claims about the right to be judged on merit or as an individual. It sounds plausible, however, because it suggests the following more complex principle. Every citizen has a constitutional right that he not suffer disadvantage, at least in the competition for any public benefit, because the race or religion or sect or region or other natural or artificial group to which he belongs is the object of prejudice or contempt.

That is a fundamentally important constitutional right, and it is that right that was systematically violated for many years by racist exclusions and anti-Semitic quotas. Color bars and Jewish quotas were not unfair just because they made race or religion relevant or because they fixed on qualities beyond individual control. It is true that blacks or Jews do not choose to be blacks or Jews. But it is also true that those who score low in aptitude or admissions tests do not choose their levels of intelligence. Nor do those denied admission because they are too old, or because they do not come from a part of the country underrepresented in the school, or because they cannot play basketball well, choose not to have the qualities that made the difference.

Race seems different because exclusions based on race have historically been motivated not by some instrumental calculation, as in the case of intelligence or age or regional distribution or athletic ability, but because of contempt for the excluded race or religion as such. Exclusion by race was in itself an insult, because it was generated by and signaled contempt.

Bakke's claim, therefore, must be made more specific than it is. He says he was kept out of medical school because of his race. Does he mean that he was kept out because his race is the object of prejudice or contempt? That suggestion is absurd. A very high proportion of those who were accepted (and, presumably, of those who run the admissions program) were members of the same race. He therefore means simply that if he had been black he would have been accepted, with no suggestion that this would have been so because blacks are thought more worthy or honorable than whites.

That is true: no doubt he would have been accepted if he were black. But it is also true, and in exactly the same sense, that he would have been accepted if he had been more intelligent, or made a better impression in his interview, or, in the case of other schools, if he had been younger when he decided to become a doctor. Race is not, in *his* case, a different matter from these other factors equally beyond his control. It is not a different matter because in his case race is not distinguished by the special character of public insult. On the contrary, the program presupposes that his race is still widely if wrongly thought to be superior to others.

In the past it made sense to say that an excluded black or Jewish student was being sacrificed because of his race or religion; that meant that his or her exclusion was treated as desirable in itself, not because it contributed to any goal in which he as well as the rest of society might take pride. Allan Bakke is being "sacrificed" because of his race only in a very artificial sense of the word. He is being "sacrificed" in the same artificial sense because of his level of intelligence, since he would have been accepted if he were more clever than he is. In both cases he is being excluded not by prejudice but because of a rational calculation about the socially most beneficial use of limited resources for medical education.

It may now be said that this distinction is too subtle, and that if racial classifications have been and may still be used for malign purposes, then everyone has a flat right that racial classifications not be used at all. This is the familiar appeal to the lazy virtue of simplicity. It supposes that if a line is difficult to draw, or might be difficult to administer if drawn, then there is wisdom in not making the attempt to draw it. There may be cases in which that is wise, but those would be cases in which nothing of great value would as a consequence be lost. If racially conscious admissions policies now offer the only substantial hope for bringing more qualified black and other minority doctors into the profession, then a great loss is suffered if medical schools are not allowed voluntarily to pursue such programs. We should then be trading away a chance to attack certain and present injustice in order to gain protection we may not need against speculative abuses we have other means to prevent. And such abuses cannot, in any case, be worse than the injustice to which we would then surrender.

We have now considered three familiar slogans, each widely thought to name a constitutional right that enables Allan Bakke to stop programs of affirmative action no matter how effective or necessary these might be. When we inspect these slogans, we find that they can stand for no genuine principle except one. This is the important principle that no one in our society should suffer because he is a member of a group thought less worthy of respect, as a group, than other groups. We have different aspects of that principle in mind when we say that individuals should be judged on merit, that they should be judged as individuals, and that they should not suffer disadvantages because of their race. The spirit of that fundamental principle is the spirit of the goal that affirmative action is intended to serve. The principle furnishes no support for those who find, as Bakke does, that their own interests conflict with that goal.

It is regrettable when any citizen's expectations are defeated by new programs serving some more general concern. It is regrettable, for example, when established small businesses fail because new and superior roads are built: in that case people have invested more than Bakke has. And they have more reason to believe their businesses will continue than Bakke had to suppose he could have entered the Davis medical school at thirty-three, even without a task force program.

There is, of course, no suggestion in that program that Bakke shares in any collective or individual guilt for racial injustice in the United States; or that he is any less entitled to concern or respect than any black student accepted in the program. He has been disappointed, and he must have the sympathy due that disappointment, just as any other disappointed applicant—even one with much worse test scores who would not have been accepted in any event—must have sympathy. Each is disappointed because places in medical schools are scarce resources and must be used to provide what the more general society most needs. It is not Bakke's fault that racial justice is now a special need—but he has no right to prevent the most effective measures of securing that justice from being used.

NO

17.8 *From Equal Opportunity to Affirmative Action*

Thomas Sowell

The very meaning of the phrase "civil rights" has changed greatly since the *Brown* decision in 1954, or since the Civil Rights Act of 1964. Initially, civil rights meant, quite simply, that all individuals should be treated the same under the law, regardless of their race, religion, sex or other such social categories. For blacks, especially, this would have represented a dramatic improvement in those states where law and public policy mandated racially separate institutions and highly discriminatory treatment.

Many Americans who supported the initial thrust of civil rights, as represented by the *Brown* v. *Board of Education* decision and the Civil Rights Act of 1964, later felt betrayed as the original concept of equal individual *opportunity* evolved toward the concept of equal group *results*. The idea that statistical differences in results were weighty presumptive evidence of discriminatory processes was not initially an explicit part of civil rights law. But neither was it merely an inexplicable perversion, as many critics seem to think, for it followed logically from the civil rights *vision*.

If the causes of intergroup differences can be dichotomized into discrimination and innate ability, then non-racists and non-sexists must expect equal results from non-discrimination. Conversely, the persistence of highly disparate results must indicate that discrimination continues to be pervasive among recalcitrant employers, culturally biased tests, hypocritical educational institutions, etc. The early leaders and supporters of the civil rights movement did not advocate such corollaries, and many explicitly repudiated them, especially during the congressional debates that preceded passage of the Civil Rights Act of 1964. But the corollaries were implicit in the vision—and in the long run that proved to be more decisive than the positions taken by the original leaders in the cause of civil rights. In the face of crying injustices, many Americans accepted a vision that promised to further a noble cause, without quibbling over its assumptions or verbal formulations. But visions have a momentum of their own, and those who accept their assumptions have entailed their corollaries, however surprised they may be when these corollaries emerge historically.

From Rights to Quotas

"Equal opportunity" laws and policies require that individuals be judged on their qualifications as individuals, *without regard* to race, sex, age, etc. "Affirmative action" requires that they be judged *with regard* to such group membership, receiving preferential or compensatory treatment in some cases to achieve a more proportional "representation" in various institutions and occupations.

The conflict between equal opportunity and affirmative action developed almost imperceptibly at first, though it later became a heated issue, repeatedly debated by the time the Civil Rights Act of 1964 was being considered by Congress. The term "affirmative action" was first used in a racial discrimination context in President John F. Kennedy's Executive Order No. 10,925 in 1961. But, as initially presented, affirmative action referred to various activities, such as monitoring subordinate decision makers to ensure the fairness of their hiring and promotion decisions, and spreading information about employment or other opportunities so as to encourage previously excluded groups to apply—after which the actual selection could be made *without regard* to group membership. Thus, it was both meaningful and consistent for President Kennedy's Executive Order to say that federal contractors should "take affirmative action to ensure that the applicants are employed, and that employees are treated during employment, without regard to their race, creed, color, or national origin."

Tendencies toward shifting the emphasis from equality of prospective opportunity toward statistical parity of retrospective results were already observed, at both state and federal levels, by the time that the Civil Rights Act of 1964 was under consideration in Congress. Senator Hubert Humphrey, while guiding this bill through the Senate, assured his colleagues that it "does not require an employer to achieve any kind of racial balance in his work force by giving preferential treatment to any individual or group." He pointed out that subsection 703(j) under Title VII of the Civil Rights Act "is added to state this point expressly." That subsection declared that nothing in Title VII required an employer "to grant preferential treatment to any individual or group on account of any imbalance which may exist" with respect to the numbers of employees in such groups "in comparison with the total number or percentage of persons of such race, color, religion, sex, or national origin in any community, State, section or other area."

Virtually all the issues involved in the later controversies over affirmative action, in the specifically numerical sense, were raised in the legislative debates preceding passage of the Civil Rights Act. Under subsection 706(g) of that Act, an employer was held liable only for his own "intentional" discrimination, not for societal patterns reflected in his work force. According to Senator Humphrey, the "express requirement of intent is designed to make it wholly clear that inadvertent or accidental discriminations will not violate the Title or result in the entry of court orders." Vague claims of differential institutional policy impact—"institutional racism"—were not to be countenanced. For example, tests with differential impact on differ-

ent groups were considered by Humphrey to be "legal unless used for the purpose of discrimination." There was no burden of proof placed upon employers to "validate" such tests.

In general there was to be no burden of proof on employers; rather the Equal Employment Opportunity Commission (EEOC) created by the Act "must prove by a preponderance" that an adverse decision was based on race (or, presumably, other forbidden categories), according to Senator Joseph Clark, another leading advocate of the Civil Rights Act. Senator Clark also declared that the Civil Rights Act "will not require an employer to change existing seniority lists," even though such lists might have differential impact on blacks as the last hired and first fired. Still another supporter, Senator Harrison Williams, declared that an employer with an all-white work force could continue to hire "only the best qualified persons even if they were all white."

In short, Congress declared itself in favor of equal opportunity and opposed to affirmative action. So has the American public. Opinion polls show a majority of blacks opposed to preferential treatment, as is an even larger majority of women. Federal administrative agencies and the courts led the change from the prospective concept of individual equal opportunity to the retrospective concept of parity of group "representation" (or "correction" of "imbalances").

The key development in this process was the creation of the Office of Federal Contract Compliance in the U.S. Department of Labor by President Lyndon Johnson's Executive Order No. 11,246 in 1965. In May 1968, this office issued guidelines containing the fateful expression "goals and timetables" and "representation." But as yet these were still not quotas, for 1968 guidelines spoke of "goals and timetables for the prompt achievement of full and equal employment opportunity." By 1970, however, new guidelines referred to "results-oriented procedures," which hinted more strongly at what was to come. In December 1971, the decisive guidelines were issued, which made it clear that "goals and timetables" were meant to "increase materially the utilization of minorities and women," with "under-utilization" being spelled out as "having fewer minorities or women in a particular job classification than would reasonably be expected by their availability . . ." Employers were required to confess to "deficiencies in the utilization" of minorities and women whenever this statistical parity could not be found in all job classifications, as a first step toward correcting this situation. The burden of proof—and remedy—was on the employer. "Affirmative action" was now decisively transformed into a numerical concept, whether called "goals" or "quotas."

Though lacking in either legislative authorization or public support for numerical group preferences, administrative agencies of government were able to enforce such policies with the support of the federal courts in general and the U.S. Supreme Court in particular. In the landmark [*United Steelworkers* v.] *Weber* [1979] case the Supreme Court simply rejected "a literal interpretation" of the words of the Civil Rights Act. Instead, it sought the "spirit" of the Act, its "primary concern" with the economic problems of blacks. According to Justice William Brennan, writing the majority opinion, these words do not bar "temporary, voluntary, affirmative action measures undertaken to eliminate manifest racial imbalance in traditionally segregated job categories." This performance received the sarcastic tribute of Justice Rehnquist that it was "*a tour de force* reminiscent not of jurists such as Hale, Holmes, and Hughes but of escape artists such as Houdini." Rehnquist's dissent inundated the Supreme Court with the legislative history of the Act, and Congress' repeated and emphatic rejection of the whole approach of correcting imbalances or compensating for the past. The spirit of the Act was as contrary to the decision as was the letter.

Equality of Rights and Results

Those who carry the civil rights vision to its ultimate conclusion see no great difference between promoting equality of opportunity and equality of results. If there are not equal results among groups presumed to have equal genetic potential, then some inequality of opportunity must have intervened somewhere, and the question of precisely where is less important than the remedy of restoring the less fortunate to their just position. The fatal flaw in this kind of thinking is that there are many reasons, besides genes and discrimination, why groups differ in their economic performances and rewards. Groups differ by large amounts demographically, culturally, and geographically—and all of these differences have profound effects on incomes and occupations.

Age differences are quite large. Blacks are a decade younger than the Japanese. Jews are a quarter of a century older than Puerto Ricans. Polish Americans are twice as old as American Indians. These represent major differences in the quantity of work experience, in an economy where income differences between age brackets are even greater than black-white income differences. Even if the various racial and ethnic groups were identical in every other respect, their age differences alone would prevent their being equally represented in occupations requiring experience or higher education. Their very different age distributions likewise prevent their being equally represented in colleges, jails, homes for the elderly, the armed forces, sports and numerous other institutions and activities that tend to have more people from one age bracket than from another.

Cultural differences add to the age differences. . . . Half of all Mexican American wives were married in their teens, while only 10 percent of Japanese American wives married that young. Such very different patterns imply not only different values but also very different future opportunities. Those who marry and begin having children earlier face more restricted options for future education and less geographic mobility for seeking their best career opportunities. Even among those young people who go on to colleges and universities, their opportunities to prepare themselves for the better paid professions are severely limited by their previous educational choices and performances, as well as by their selections of fields of study in the colleges and universities. All of these things vary enormously from one group to another.

For example, mathematics preparation and performance differ greatly from one ethnic group to another and between men and women. A study of high school students in northern California showed that four-fifths of Asian youngsters were enrolled in the sequence of mathematics courses that culminate in calculus, while only one-fifth of black youngsters were enrolled in such courses. Moreover, even among those who began this sequence in geometry, the percentage that persisted all the way through to calculus was several times higher among the Asian students. Sex differences in mathematics preparation are comparably large. Among both black and white freshmen at the University of Maryland, the men had had four years of mathematics in high school more than twice as often as the women.

Mathematics is of decisive importance for many more professions than that of mathematician. Whole ranges of fields of study and work are off-limits to those without the necessary mathematical foundation. Physicists, chemists, statisticians, and engineers are only some of the more obvious occupations. In some colleges, one cannot even be an undergraduate economics major without having had calculus, and to go on to graduate school and become a professional economist requires much more mathematics, as well as statistical analysis. Even in fields where mathematics is not an absolute prerequisite, its presence or absence makes a major difference in one's ability to rise in the profession. Mathematics is becoming an important factor in the social sciences and is even beginning to invade some of the humanities. To be mathematically illiterate is to carry an increasing burden into an increasing number of occupations. Even the ability to pass a civil service examination for modest clerical jobs is helped or hindered by one's facility in mathematics.

It is hardly surprising that test scores reflect these group differences in mathematics preparation. Nationwide results on the Scholastic Aptitude Test (SAT) for college applicants show Asians and whites consistently scoring higher on the quantitative test than Hispanics or blacks, and men scoring higher than women. Nor are these differences merely the result of socioeconomic "disadvantage" caused by "society." Black, Mexican American, and American Indian youngsters from families with incomes of $50,000 and up score lower than Asians from families whose incomes are just $6,000 and under. Moreover, Asians as a group score higher than whites as a group on the quantitative portion of the SAT and the Japanese in Japan specialize in mathematics, science and engineering to a far greater extent than do American students in the United States. Cultural differences are real, and cannot be talked away by using pejorative terms such as "stereotypes" or "racism."

The racial, ethnic, and sex differences in mathematics that begin in high school (or earlier) continue on through to the Ph.D. level, affecting career choices and economic rewards. Hispanic Ph.D.'s outnumber Asian Ph.D.'s in the United States by three-to-one in history, but the Asians outnumber the Hispanics by ten-to-one in chemistry. More than half of all Asian Ph.D.'s are in mathematics, science or engineering, and more than half the Asians who teach college teach in those fields. By contrast, more than half of all black doctorates are in the field of education, a notoriously undemanding and less remunerative field. So are half the doctorates received by American Indians, not one of whom received a Ph.D. in either mathematics or physics in 1980. Female Ph.D.'s are in quantitatively-based fields only half as frequently as male Ph.D's.

Important as mathematics is in itself, it is also a symptom of broader and deeper disparities in educational choices and performances in general. Those groups with smaller quantities of education tend also to have lower qualities of education, and these disparities follow them all the way through their educational careers and into the job market. The children of lower income racial and ethnic groups typically score lower on tests all through school and attend lower quality colleges when they go to college at all, as well as majoring in the easier courses in fields with the least economic promise. How much of this is due to the home environment and how much to the deficiencies of the public schools in their neighborhoods is a large question that cannot be answered here. But what is clear is that what is called the "same" education, measured in years of schooling, is not even remotely the same in reality.

The civil rights vision relies heavily on statistical "disparities" in income and employment between members of different groups to support its sweeping claims of rampant discrimination. The U.S. Civil Rights Commission, for example, considers itself to be "controlling for those factors" when it examines people of the same age with the same number of years of schooling—resolutely ignoring the substance of that schooling.

Age and education do not begin to exhaust the differences between groups. They are simply more readily quantifiable than some other differences. The geographic distributions of groups also vary greatly, with Mexican Americans being concentrated in the southwest, Puerto Ricans in the northeast, half of blacks in the South, and most Asians in California and Hawaii. Differences in income between the states are also larger than black-white income differences, so that these distributional differences affect national income differences. A number of past studies, for example, have shown black and Puerto Rican incomes to be very similar nationally, but blacks generally earn higher incomes than Puerto Ricans in New York and other places where Puerto Ricans are concentrated. Their incomes nationally have shown up in these studies as similar, because there are very few Puerto Ricans living in low-income southern states.

One of the most important causes of differences in income and employment is the way people work—some diligently, carefully, persistently, cooperatively, and without requiring much supervision or warnings about absenteeism, tardiness, or drinking, and others requiring much such concern over such matters. Not only are such things inherently difficult to quantify; any suggestion that such differences even exist is sure to bring forth a storm of condemnation. In short, the civil rights vision has been hermetically sealed off from any such evidence. Both historical and contemporary observations on intergroup differences in work habits, discipline, reliability, sobriety, cleanliness, or cooperative attitude—anywhere in the world—are automatically dismissed as evidence only of the bias or bigotry of the observers. "Stereotypes" is the magic word that makes thinking about such things unnecessary. Yet despite this closed circle of reasoning that surrounds the civil rights vision, there is some evidence that cannot be disposed of in that way.

Self-employed farmers, for example, do not depend for their rewards on the biases of employers or the stereotypes of observers. Yet self-employed farmers of different ethnicity have fared very differently on the same land, even in earlier pre-mechanization times, when the principal input was the farmer's own labor. German farmers, for example, had more prosperous farms than other farmers in colonial America—and were more prosperous than Irish farmers in eighteenth-century Ireland, as well as more prosperous than Brazilian farmers in Brazil, Mexican farmers in Mexico, Russian farmers in Russia, and Chilean farmers in Chile. We may ignore the forbidden testimony from all these countries as to how hard the German farmers worked, how frugally they lived, or how sober they were. Still, the results speak for themselves.

That Jews earn far higher incomes than Hispanics in the United States might be taken as evidence that anti-Hispanic bias is stronger than anti-Semitism—if one followed the logic of the civil rights vision. But this explanation is considerably weakened by the greater prosperity of Jews than Hispanics *in Hispanic countries* throughout Latin America. Again, even if one dismisses out of hand all the observers who see great differences in the way these two groups work, study, or save, major tangible differences in economic performance remain that cannot be explained in terms of the civil rights vision.

One of the commonly used indices of intergroup economic differences is family income. Yet families are of different sizes from group to group, reflecting differences in the incidence of broken homes. Female headed households are several times more common among blacks than among whites, and in both groups these are the lowest income families. Moreover, the proportion of people working differs greatly from group to group. More than three-fifths of all Japanese American families have multiple income earners while only about a third of Puerto Rican families do. Nor is this a purely socioeconomic phenomenon, as distinguished from a cultural phenomenon. Blacks have similar incomes to Puerto Ricans, but the proportion of black families with a woman working is nearly three times that among Puerto Ricans.

None of this disproves the existence of discrimination, nor is that its purpose. What is at issue is whether statistical differences mean discrimination, or whether there are innumerable demographic, cultural, and geographic differences that make this crucial automatic inference highly questionable.

Chapter 18

Foreign and Military Policymaking

T_he great expansion of the federal government's role in domestic affairs during the New Deal period was matched during and after World War II by a massive increase in American responsibilities overseas. Within a matter of years, the United States was transformed from a relatively isolationist, minor power into a military and economic giant._

This transition to superpower status was not without cost. In the postwar era, the United States found itself involved in two bloody wars in Asia and in a balance-of-terror cold war with the Soviet Union. The dramatic expansion of American military and foreign responsibilities provided the impetus for a strengthening of the executive branch at the expense of Congress; the communist threat was invoked as a catch-all to limit free speech and other civil liberties.

Now, in the 1990s, the United States seems to be passing into a new phase in its worldwide role. No longer at loggerheads with the Soviet Union and no longer an economic giant among pygmies, the United States is groping to find its place in a new world order. It must face regional threats in the Middle East and Central America, the growing economic might of Japan and a reunified Germany, and the increasing political weight of a more unified Europe.

The field of foreign and military policy is so diverse that this chapter can only touch upon the highlights. Three issues are always at or near the surface, however. The first is American's emerging world role in the 1990s—still important but no longer predominant. The second is the tenuous relationship of public opinion, democracy, and foreign policy—a relationship that, in de Tocqueville's view, bodes ill for foreign policy but in the minds of others needs to be nurtured and strengthened. The third is the foreign policy balance between the White House and Congress, a contest that, for reasons that should become clear, the White House has been winning.

Our thinking about foreign and military policy in the United States has been shaped to a great extent by the great military victories and defeats of the past half-century: World War II, the Korean War, the Vietnam War, and the Persian Gulf War. One or more of these events is never very far from the surface of the selections in this chapter.

Chapter Questions

1. How is America's world role changing in the 1990s? Will Americans be worse off economically than in the post–World War II era? better off? Why?

2. How did the Vietnam experience change American politics? Recall the 1974 reforms in the congressional leadership structure, the Budget Act of 1974, and the War Powers Resolution of 1973. To what extent was each of these affected, directly or indirectly, by the Vietnam experience? Has the success of the 1991 Persian Gulf War truly ended the "Vietnam syndrome" in American politics?

3. Can foreign policy be governed effectively by the people in a democratic system? What are the obstacles to democratic control of foreign policy?

I THE CLASSIC TEXTS

Can foreign policy decisions in a democracy be made intelligently and thoughtfully by the people? Or are such decisions particularly ill suited to the democratic process? The Framers sought to insulate the foreign policymaking process from the people, vesting extraordinary powers in this area in the indirectly elected president and (at that time) Senate. Those who wished to place foreign affairs power in a popular assembly, wrote John Jay, co-author of the **Federalist Papers,** *"seem not to recollect that such a body must necessarily be inadequate to the attainment of those great objects which require to be steadily contemplated in all their relations and circumstances, and which can only be approached and achieved by measures which not only talents, but also exact information, and often much time, are necessary to concert and to execute."* In foreign affairs, above all, the Framers' fears of direct democracy were paramount.*

The Framers' attempt to remove foreign policy from the direct control of the people has been echoed by many presidents, who have sought to reduce Congress's role in the process for the same reasons. Nevertheless, despite all these arrangements, the people still exercise tremendous control over foreign policy, at least in the long run. To Alexis de Tocqueville (see selection 4.1), American foreign policy was still dominated by the characteristic features—he might say flaws—of any democracy. The problem, as he put it, was that "foreign policy does not require any of the good qualities peculiar to democracy but does demand the cultivation of almost all those which it lacks."

* *Federalist Papers No. 64.*

Questions

1. What are the qualities demanded by foreign policy? Why are aristocracies more likely to possess such qualities?

2. Is de Tocqueville too quick to dismiss the good qualities of democracy with respect to foreign policy? Are there aspects of foreign policy to which democracies are well suited?

18.1 How American Democracy Conducts the External Affairs of State

Alexis de Tocqueville

We have noted that the federal Constitution put the permanent control of the nation's foreign interests in the hands of the President and the Senate, which to some extent frees the Union's general policy from direct and daily popular control. One should not therefore assert without qualification that American democracy controls the state's external affairs.

Two men have set a direction for American policy which is still followed today; the first is Washington and the second Jefferson.

Washington, in that admirable letter addressed to his fellow citizens which was that great man's political testament, says:

The great rule of conduct for us, in regard to foreign nations, is, in extending our commercial relations, to have with them as little *political* connection as possible. So far as we have already formed engagements, let them be fulfilled with perfect good faith. Here let us stop.

Europe has a set of primary interests which to us have none, or a very remote relation. Hence she must be engaged in frequent controversies, the causes of which are essentially foreign to our concerns. Hence, therefore, it must be unwise in us to implicate ourselves, by artificial ties, in the ordinary vicissitudes of her politics or in the ordinary combinations and the collisions of her friendships or enmities.

Our detached and distant situation invites and enables us to pursue a different course. If we remain one people, under an efficient government, the period is not far off when we may defy material injury from external annoyance; when we may take such an attitude as will cause the neutrality we may at any time resolve upon to be scrupulously respected; when belligerent nations, under the impossibility of making acquisitions upon us, will not lightly hazard the giving us provocation; when we may choose peace or war, as our interest, guided by justice, shall counsel.

Why forgo the advantages of so peculiar a situation? Why quit our own to stand upon foreign ground? Why, by interweaving our destiny with that of any part of Europe, entangle our peace and prosperity in the toils of European ambition, rivalship, interest, humor, or caprice?

It is our true policy to steer clear of permanent alliances with any portion of the foreign world; so far, I mean, as we are now at liberty to do it; for let me not be understood as capable of patronizing infidelity to existing engagements. I hold the maxim no less applicable to public than to private affairs, that honesty is always the best policy. I repeat it, therefore, let those engagements be observed in their genuine sense; but, in my opinion, it is unnecessary and would be unwise to extend them.

Taking care always to keep ourselves, by suitable establishments, in a respectable defensive posture, we may safely trust to temporary alliances for extraordinary emergencies.

Clausewitz on War

Perhaps the greatest theoretician of war was Carl von Clausewitz, a Prussian soldier and writer who lived from 1780 until 1831. His great work (from which the following is excerpted) was On War, published posthumously in 1832. Clausewitz's philosophy of war has had a profound influence on European (and American) attitudes since the nineteenth century.

Definition

We shall not enter into any of the abstruse definitions of War used by publicists. We shall keep to the element of the thing itself, to a duel. War is nothing but a duel on an extensive scale. If we would conceive as a unit the countless number of duels which make up a War, we shall do so best by supposing to ourselves two wrestlers. Each strives by physical force to compel the other to submit to his will: each endeavours to throw his adversary, and thus render him incapable of further resistance.

War therefore is an act of violence intended to compel our opponent to fulfil our will.

Violence arms itself with the inventions of Art and Science in order to contend against violence. Self-imposed restrictions, almost imperceptible and hardly worth mentioning, termed usages of International Law, accompany it without essentially impairing its power. Violence, that is to say, physical force (for there is no moral force without the conception of States and Law), is therefore the *means*; the compulsory submission of the enemy to our will is the ultimate *object*. In order to attain this object fully, the enemy must be disarmed, and disarmament becomes therefore the immediate object of hostilities in theory. It takes the place of the final object, and puts it aside as something we can eliminate from our calculations.

• • •

The Political Object Now Reappears

Here the question which we had laid aside forces itself again into consideration, viz. *the political object of the War*. The law of the extreme, the view to disarm the adversary, to overthrow him, has hitherto to a certain extent usurped the place of this end or object. Just as this law loses its force, the political object must again come forward. If the whole consideration is a calculation of probability based on definite persons and relations, then the political object, being the original motive, must be an essential factor in the product. The smaller the sacrifice we demand from our opponent, the smaller, it may be expected, will be the means of resistance which he will employ; but the smaller his preparation, the smaller will ours require to be. Further, the smaller our political object, the less value shall we set upon it, and the more easily shall we be induced to give it up altogether.

Thus, therefore, the political object, as the original motive of the War, will be the standard for determining both the aim of the military force and also the amount of effort to be made. This it cannot be in itself, but it is so in relation to both the belligerent States, because we are concerned with realities, not with mere abstractions. One and the same political object may produce totally dif-

---

Earlier Washington had expressed this beautiful and true idea: "The nation which indulges towards another an habitual hatred, or an habitual fondness, is in some degree a slave. It is a slave to its animosity or to its affection. . . ."

Washington's political conduct was always guided by these maxims. He succeeded in keeping his country at peace while all the rest of the world was at war, and he established it as a fundamental doctrine that the true interest of the Americans was never to take part in the internal quarrels of Europe.

Jefferson went still further and introduced another maxim into American politics: "that the Americans should never ask for privileges from

ferent effects upon different people, or even upon the same people at different times; we can, therefore, only admit the political object as the measure, by considering it in its effects upon those masses which it is to move, and consequently the nature of those masses also comes into consideration. It is easy to see that thus the result may be very different according as these masses are animated with a spirit which will infuse vigour into the action or otherwise. It is quite possible for such a state of feeling to exist between two States that a very trifling political motive for War may produce an effect quite disproportionate—in fact, a perfect explosion.

This applies to the efforts which the political object will call forth in the two States, and to the aim which the military action shall prescribe for itself. At times it may itself be that aim, as, for example, the conquest of a province. At other times the political object itself is not suitable for the aim of military action; then such a one must be chosen as will be an equivalent for it, and stand in its place as regards the conclusion of peace. But also, in this, due attention to the peculiar character of the States concerned is always supposed. There are circumstances in which the equivalent must be much greater than the political object, in order to secure the latter. The political object will be so much the more the standard of aim and effort, and have more influence in itself, the more the masses are indifferent, the less that any mutual feeling of hostility prevails in the two States from other causes, and therefore there are cases where the political object almost alone will be decisive.

If the aim of the military action is an equivalent for the political object, that action will in general diminish as the political object diminishes, and in a greater degree the more the political object dominates. Thus it is explained how, without any contradiction in itself, there may be Wars of all degrees of importance and energy, from a War of extermination down to the mere use of an army of observation. This, however, leads to a question of another kind which we have hereafter to develop and answer.

• • •

War is a Mere Continuation of Policy by Other Means

We see, therefore, that War is not merely a political act, but also a real political instrument, a continuation of political commerce, a carrying out of the same by other means. All beyond this which is strictly peculiar to War relates merely to the peculiar nature of the means which it uses. That the tendencies and views of policy shall not be incompatible with these means, the Art of War in general and the Commander in each particular case may demand, and this claim is truly not a trifling one. But however powerfully this may react on political views in particular cases, still it must always be regarded as only a modification of them; for the political view is the object, War is the means, and the means must always include the object in our conception.

—*Carl von Clausewitz*

foreign nations, in order not to be obliged to grant any in return."

These two principles, whose evident truth makes them easily grasped by the multitudes, have greatly simplified the foreign policy of the United States.

As the Union does not meddle in the affairs of Europe, it has, so to say, no external interests at stake, for as yet it has no powerful neighbors in America. Detached by geography as well as by choice from the passions of the Old World, it neither needs to protect itself against them nor to espouse them. As for those of the New World, they are still hidden in the future.

The Union is free from preexisting obligations; it can therefore profit from the experience of Europe without being obliged, as European nations are, to take the past into account and adapt it to the present; nor need it, like them, accept a vast heritage of mixed glory and shame, national friendships and national hatreds, bequeathed by its ancestors. Expectancy is the keynote of American foreign policy; it consists much more in abstaining than in doing.

It is therefore hard as yet to know what talents American democracy might develop in conducting the state's foreign affairs. Both friends and enemies should suspend judgment on that point.

For my part, I have no hesitation in saying that in the control of society's foreign affairs democratic governments do appear decidedly inferior to others. Experience, mores, and education almost always do give a democracy that sort of practical everyday wisdom and understanding of the petty business of life which we call common sense. Common sense is enough for society's current needs, and in a nation whose education has been completed, democratic liberty applied to the state's internal affairs brings blessings greater than the ills resulting from a democratic government's mistakes. But that is not always true of relations between nation and nation.

Foreign policy does not require the use of any of the good qualities peculiar to democracy but does demand the cultivation of almost all those which it lacks. Democracy favors the growth of the state's internal resources; it extends comfort and develops public spirit, strengthens respect for law in the various classes of society, all of which things have no more than an indirect influence on the standing of one nation in respect to another. But a democracy finds it difficult to coordinate the details of a great undertaking and to fix on some plan and carry it through with determination in spite of obstacles. It has little capacity for combining measures in secret and waiting patiently for the result. Such qualities are more likely to belong to a single man or to an aristocracy. But

these are just the qualities which, in the long run, make a nation, and a man too, prevail.

But if you turn your attention to the natural defects of aristocracy, you find that their possible effects are hardly noticeable in the conduct of the state's external affairs. The main vice for which aristocracy is reproached is that of working for itself alone and not for the whole community. However, in foreign policy it very seldom happens that an aristocracy has an interest distinct from that of the people.

In politics the tendency of a democracy to obey its feelings rather than its calculations and to abandon a long-matured plan to satisfy a momentary passion was well seen in America at the time when the French Revolution broke out. The simplest lights of reason were enough then, as they are now, to make the Americans see that they had no interest in joining the struggle which was to lead to such bloodshed in Europe, but from which the United States could suffer no damage.

Nevertheless, the people's sympathies for France declared themselves with such violence that nothing less than the inflexible character of Washington and the immense popularity he enjoyed sufficed to prevent them from declaring war on England. Moreover, the austere arguments used by that great man to combat the generous but ill-considered passions of his fellow citizens came near to depriving him of the only reward he ever claimed, the love of his country. The majority pronounced against his policy; now the whole nation approves it.

If the Constitution and public favor had not given Washington control over the state's foreign policy, it is certain that the nation would then have done exactly what it now condemns.

Almost all the nations that have exercised a powerful influence on the world's destiny by conceiving, following up, and carrying to completion great designs, from the Romans down to the English, were controlled by an aristocracy, and how can one be surprised at that?

Nothing in the world is so fixed in its views as an aristocracy. The mass of the people may be seduced by its ignorance or its passions; a king may be taken off his guard and induced to vacillate in his plans; and moreover, a king is not immortal. But an aristocratic body is too numerous to be caught, and yet so small that it does not easily yield to the intoxication of thoughtless passions. An aristocratic body is a firm and enlightened man who never dies.

II INTERCONNECTIONS

The late 1980s and early 1990s have seen extraordinary changes in the shape of the world balance of power. With the development of glasnost *(openness) and* perestroika *(restructuring) in the Soviet Union, the rapid decline of communism in Eastern Europe, the reunification of Germany, and the solidification of the European Community, it can truly be said that the post–World War II order is no longer with us. The world—and the United States with it—must now adapt to a new set of power relationships.*

Most important among these new relationships, some would argue, are those between the United States and Germany and between the United States and Japan. Japan and Germany's new status as economic superpowers makes it necessary for the United States to reconsider and recast its relationships with these nations, seeking a balance between cooperation and competition, leadership and independence.

The task is complicated by the ambivalent feelings many Americans have for these two nations. Our principal enemies in World War II, Japan and Germany were rebuilt largely with American money, protected from communism by American soldiers, and helped to economic independence with American technology. In the 1990s, the tables seem turned. The United States is now dependent on German and Japanese investment and imports; German and Japanese dependence on American military muscle seems less critical. As with any other relationship, these remarkable changes in little more than a generation have produced great strains and tensions among these three economic superpowers.

Peter Tarnoff, president of the Council on Foreign Relations, examines America's new "special relationships" and suggests that, however awkward America might feel toward its former enemies, it is time to welcome Berlin and Tokyo into a more active role in world affairs.

Questions

1. Why does Tarnoff believe it is so vitally important that Washington "make sure that Germany and Japan are substantively engaged on every major international issue"?

2. Where does the Soviet Union fit into Tarnoff's "triangular diplomacy" scheme? China? A united Europe?

18.2 America's New Special Relationships

Peter Tarnoff

As Americans wonder whether or not to maintain their substantial international commitments, it may seem paradoxical to learn that Bonn and Tokyo consider good relations with Washington to be indispensable even as the Soviet threat recedes. During the present period of transition and uncertainty, and as both move to center stage, Japan and Germany are looking for support and counsel from the most reliable and experienced of their allies, the United States.

Take security matters, which are still more preoccupying in Tokyo, Bonn and Washington than elsewhere in the West. From a German perspective, the United States is by far the most important other participant in the "two plus four" negotiations about unifying Germany.* Most Germans believe that a continuing American military presence in Europe and in Germany, albeit at reduced levels, is essential to the foundation of any new European security structure.

They also know that American nuclear weapons on the continent, preferably in the arsenals of both land and air forces, give credibility to the American deterrent at a time of transformation and instability in Eastern Europe and the Soviet Union. Germans realize that it will take an American conventional and nuclear commitment in Western Europe to reassure the other members of NATO [North Atlantic Treaty Organization], the neutral countries and the governments of Eastern Europe that the new Germany presents no long-term threat. Germany will need the U.S. military less for protection but more for political cover in the coming decade. Thoughts that a European "pillar" of NATO might gradually replace the U.S. military in Europe are less than appealing to many at a time when defense budgets are certain to decrease and an all-German defense force would dominate any West European security organization.

For its part Japan, concerned about the intentions of the Soviet Union, the dangers of chaos in the U.S.S.R., and uncertain transitions in North Korea and perhaps China, also wants the American commitment to endure. While strengthening their technical cooperation with the U.S. military and slowly augmenting the quality of their own armed forces, the Japanese are mindful that substantially increasing their own defenses would frighten the rest of Asia. Nuclear weapons aside, Japan now can field conventional forces superior to any save those of the United States and U.S.S.R.

In most of the countries of Europe and Asia there now seems to be stronger support for an overseas American military presence than at any time since the death of Stalin. The principal reason for the change is the emergence of Germany and Japan as potent international players. Leaders throughout Europe and Asia now understand that even under conditions of a reduced Soviet military and political challenge, a credible Western security system must include a United States that is militarily first among political equals.

America's economic strength, despite uncertainties about its competitiveness and the cumulative effects of its trade and current account deficits, is also important to Japan and Germany. The Japanese still ship almost 40 percent of their exports to the United States. Washington remains Tokyo's principal economic and financial partner, and despite persistent trade problems between the two nations neither is likely to find an alternative to the other in the years to come. Political tensions may grow and the tenor of the dialogue between the United

---

* The "two plus four" talks involved the two Germanies (East and West) and the four powers that occupied Germany in 1945: the United States, the Soviet Union, Great Britain, and France.

States and Japan could deteriorate further, but a rupture of economic ties is unthinkable; U.S.-Japanese trade relations may be strained but they will not break. The recent agreement between Washington and Tokyo, providing for Japan to make sweeping changes in domestic commercial practices, is the latest example of the progress being made in opening Japan to freer trade. Moreover, Japan can be expected to come to the aid of the United States in subtle but significant ways in times of financial hardship, for Tokyo knows the consequences for itself and the world of any major disruptions in the American economy.

Germany's economic relations with the United States are determined in large part by its membership in the European Community and its greater trade with the rest of Europe. Nonetheless, the growing role of the Deutsche mark in the world economy will link it more to the dollar. The German Bundesbank and U.S. Federal Reserve system both enjoy a high degree of autonomy, facilitating close cooperation and setting them apart from the other Western central banks, which are more closely tied to national governments. In addition Germany wants the United States to help carry the investment burdens in Eastern Europe, where the newly independent governments are themselves worried at the prospect of German economic hegemony.

It is also likely that Japan and Germany will become more politically active outside of their own regions. Tokyo has committed substantial funds to international peacekeeping operations, to Eastern Europe and Latin America and has promoted dialogue between the OECD [Organization for Economic Cooperation and Development] countries and newly industrializing Asian economies. The EC's [European Community] framework for European political cooperation will influence Berlin's views, but in areas of special interest to Germany (Southern Africa and the Middle East, for example) the German chancellor will enjoy some freedom of action and be increasingly inclined to play a more active role.

In the early 1970s, Richard Nixon and Henry Kissinger conceived a form of triangular diplomacy to guide Washington's relations with Moscow and Beijing. Because the United States enjoyed better relations with the U.S.S.R. and China than the two major communist powers did with each other, Washington was able to practice a global diplomacy designed to exert maximum leverage on each of its principal foreign adversaries. It was also perceived to be in America's interest for the U.S.S.R. and China to remain estranged from each other, if not in direct conflict.

The triangular diplomacy of the 1970s brought mixed results: it created a favorable climate for significant strategic arms control and normalization with China on terms acceptable to the United States, but it failed to resolve the war in Vietnam or to slow the proliferation of regional disputes involving proxies of the superpowers. This triangular approach to American diplomacy foundered when détente with the U.S.S.R. expired in Angola, Afghanistan, Cambodia and Central America, and the Reagan administration was swept into office on a strong tide of anti-Soviet and pro-defense sentiment.

In the 1990s there will be an opportunity for Washington to practice a quieter but also more constructive form of triangular diplomacy. The potential for American leadership in dealing with Germany and Japan is premised in part on closer American ties to both than either has with the other. Of all their foreign partners, only the United States today enjoys sufficient standing in both Japan and Germany to be in a position to discuss fully with either the essential elements of a common course for the West.

Early in his first year, and before German unification seemed imminent, President Bush demonstrated his understanding that Bonn had become America's most powerful friend in Western Europe and a government worth cultivating assiduously. Despite initial differences with the F.R.G. [Federal Republic of Germany] over the modernization of American Lance missiles on German soil—an issue later resolved during the May 1989 NATO summit in Bonn and now moot—Washington and Bonn remained in close step during the frantic collapse of the East European communist regimes and the rapid rapprochement between East and West Germany. There is greater enthusiasm for German unification in the United States than anywhere in non-German Europe. A recent poll indicates that three-quarters of Americans are favorably disposed to German unification, and a majority of Americans support the maintenance of current levels of U.S. forces in Europe. West German Chancellor Helmut Kohl, whose position was reinforced by the strong electoral showing of the Christian Democratic forces in East Germany last March and who is favored to win the December [1990] general elections in the F.R.G., has every reason to expect that President Bush will be a solid supporter during the course of the multilateral negotiations leading to German unification. At this juncture, and probably for some time to come, neither French President François Mitterrand nor British Prime Minister Margaret Thatcher will be on equally good political terms with the German chancellor.

High-level attention to Japan has been less constant in the Bush administration. Uncertainty over the leadership and future strength of the governing Liberal Democratic Party [LDP] may have been one reason for Washington's restraint—before the LDP won a majority in the February [1990] elections for the lower house of the Diet. It is striking, however, that President Bush met with European Commission President Jacques Delors five times in 1989 but found time to see the Japanese prime minister only once that year. In dealing with Asia, the prolonged but futile attempts by the administration to moderate the course of events in China, as well as lingering expectations that Beijing might develop into an economic and political superpower within a decade or two, may also have distracted Washington from attending to a country whose bilateral importance to the United States is second to none. It now seems clear to Washington that the Japan connection is of consummate long-term importance and must not be neglected even when more dramatic developments in the U.S.S.R. and Eastern Europe dominate the headlines.

The primary objective of a new triangular diplomacy by the Bush administration would be for Washington to make sure that Germany and Japan are substantively engaged on every major international issue so that, wherever possible, positions can be harmonized. In addition, the United States should seek to ensure that channels are opened between Berlin and Tokyo. This bridging operation, initiated by the United States, as delicate as it is desirable, could have a significant impact on the building of a new Western system of understanding. Communication between Western Europe and Japan is still insufficient on most issues of high public policy. Tokyo's absence from the deliberations of the European Community, NATO and the Conference on Security and Cooperation in Europe (CSCE) compounds the problem of its isolation. Moreover Japan's only treaty relationships are its alliance ties to the United States, and the other Western assemblies that do include Japan—the OECD, the Group of Seven and annual economic summits—cannot cope with the volume of consultation now required.

There are, of course, European issues in which Japan need not play a central role—the mechanics of the unification of Germany, or the future structure of NATO, the Warsaw Pact and any Pan-European security system—all of which should be discussed among the Atlantic alliance partners and then decided in the CSCE context. Nonetheless, other pressing matters exist where European-Japanese understanding brokered by the United States could prove critical: policies for dealing with the U.S.S.R. and China, sustaining the new East European regimes, North-South development issues and regional conflict resolution, as well as global environmental, scientific and special issues such as drugs, terrorism, population, health and famine.

Of comparable importance is the need for better communication between Europe and Japan on a wide range of economic and trade issues. These two major trading entities often regard each other with extreme suspicion. With the Uruguay round of the General Agreement on Tariffs and Trade negotiations well under way, and with the increased likelihood of protectionism and the expansion of regional economic blocs, there is a need for the West to reach broader agreements on new configurations for the world economic system. North Americans, Japanese and West Europeans often meet to talk about immediate short-term economic and financial issues, but even during these summits there is rarely any serious discussion of macroeconomic planning involving collective responsibility and guidelines for the management of their economies.

It is also apparent that the leaders of the developed countries pay insufficient attention to the painful issues of widespread poverty, violence and disease in the poorest countries of the world. In an era of unprecedented prosperity and political promise, the industrialized democracies should not neglect the hundreds of millions—principally in Africa—suffering from hunger, disease and despair. The only way to attend to the acute humanitarian needs of the present and gradually build modest hopes for the future is for the new "Big Three" to take the lead and the responsibility. It is argued that voters will not tolerate the use of more public funds for this purpose, but what is political and moral leadership if not to press the case and set an example—especially in the wealthiest country in the world, which manages to find several hundred billion dollars of taxpayers' money to bail out its savings and loan industry?

The challenge of developing approaches to these issues is great, but there is little hope for progress if Germany, Japan and the United States—countries where nine percent of the world's population produces 40 percent of its wealth—are unable to find ways to work cooperatively. Pending the establishment of broader coordination mechanisms, enhanced consultations involving the United States, Japan and Germany are urgently needed. Although some Europeans may be concerned at what they perceive to be an attempt to impose a three-power directorate or "Group of Three" at the apex of the global hierarchy, tripartite contacts consisting of informal two- and three-way conversations should reduce alliance anxieties.

The success of these consultations will ultimately depend, of course, not on their structure but on their content. Such talks will make a contribution if the United States displays leadership in the form of ideas and resources. On matters relating to Eastern Europe, for example, the United States cannot pretend to be a major player if Washington defers primarily to the West Europeans for initiative and financing. On questions of debt relief and development for the poorer countries, the United States should encourage Japan to propose policies at a conceptual level and should recognize Tokyo, in terms of prestige and position, as a leader—not just a primary funder. Why should the next president of the World Bank not be Japanese, and why should Japan not be given greater voting strength than the United States in international financial institutions if Tokyo's contributions exceed those of Washington? There is a better chance that Japan will consent to provide greater assistance from its burgeoning capital surpluses if Tokyo perceives itself to be a senior partner, not merely an automatic teller machine, in the allocation process.

The ability of the United States to help establish a new international agenda with Germany and Japan also will depend on the vitality of America itself. We cannot stand tall in the world on feet of clay or on a mountain of dollars provided to us by the Japanese. It is clear that America's ability to maintain an international leadership role will depend in large measure on the support of the American voter and solutions to challenges Washington faces at home.

As the Soviet threat fades, there is already growing public pressure to reduce America's foreign entanglements. In such a climate the United States can successfully resist an abrupt contraction in American involvement abroad only if its citizens believe they can deal internationally from a position of strength that, in turn, is based on confidence that their domestic economy will adjust to the exigencies of change at home and abroad. If, on the other hand, the United States is consumed by its failure to resolve internal social problems, American leaders will have little political support for an activist international role. America's principal foreign partners also will judge the resiliency of the United States in part on the degree of its domestic consensus, its prosperity and its stability. Moreover, if Americans continue to poormouth themselves, claiming that resources are lacking to innovate or improve conditions here or abroad, they will convince others that the United States is unable to deal capably with the demands of the 21st century.

Recognizing the critical importance of Japan and Germany, and operating diplomatically to engage them profoundly in the reconstruction of the post–Cold War world, presents a formidable opportunity for the United States. Even though it lacks the overwhelming economic and military superiority it had in the late 1940s, the United States occupies a pivotal place in the changing constellation of world politics: its economy remains the largest, its military strength unequaled and its values widely acclaimed. For their part, Japan and Germany would find advantages in working to define their larger international purposes in conjunction with the United States. A primary goal of a revived American diplomacy would be to provide further inducements to Berlin and Tokyo to remain cornerstones of the Western alliance systems. This anchoring to the West is especially important for Japan, which has fewer historical and cultural ties to its developed partners than does Germany. As a consequence, and assuming that the U.S.S.R. no longer presents a military threat to the West, and that the dissolution of communist power in Eastern Europe is irreversible, America's leading international partners will likely be Berlin and Tokyo.

It will be a bitter experience for some in the West to depend heavily on the collaboration of countries that caused so much havoc half a century ago. These sentiments are understandable, but it would be wiser to take heart from ample evidence that Japan and Germany, after paying a high price themselves, have performed extremely well in the span of only two generations, and have successfully built democratic political institutions. Moreover, it is now in the greater interest of the West to have Berlin and Tokyo participate more energetically and creatively in world affairs, because our system and way of life will directly benefit. It is time to take advantage of the fact that Germany and Japan have earned a fair share of power in the world, as well as our support, friendship and respect.

III  THE PERSPECTIVE OF HISTORY

One of the great paradoxes of American foreign policy is that a constitutional and political system designed for a minor nation with little world significance could be adapted, in just a few years, to fit a world superpower with economic, military, and diplomatic commitments on every continent. Recent events leading to the end of the cold war and the decline of communism in Eastern Europe are only the latest example of the constantly changing world to which American foreign policy must adapt and in which it must operate.

All the while, as de Tocqueville pointed out (selection 18.1), foreign policymakers have had to operate within the bounds of the democratic political system. And that—

whatever else it might signify—has meant that American foreign policy has had to take account not only of world events but also of American public opinion. Presidents and secretaries of state have sometimes been able to lead public opinion and at other times have been forced to follow it; never could they ignore it with impunity.

In the following selection, historian Norman Graebner traces the course of American foreign policy in the twentieth century and its relation to public opinion. Right or wrong, he concludes, American foreign policy has always been guided or at least approved of by public opinion. (For related material, see chapter 5.)

Questions

1. How does public opinion influence foreign policy? How do foreign policy elites influence public opinion in the United States? Is it easier or harder for those who govern to influence public opinion in matters of foreign policy or of domestic policy? Why?

2. How have changes in media coverage of foreign affairs affected public opinion on foreign policy? Has it become easier or harder for foreign policy elites to influence public opinion in the United States?

18.3 Public Opinion and Foreign Policy: A Pragmatic View

Norman A. Graebner

The Historic Dominance of the Executive in External Affairs

The idea of democracy rests on the assumption that the public is the ultimate source of political power. Democracy claims superiority as a political system because policies democratically formed will be supported by the combined intelligence and virtue of the masses. Democracy proclaims majority rule, not because the majority possesses the greater power in society, but because with free expressions of opinion it is more apt to be right. Throughout modern times, however, the public's understandable deficiencies in essential knowledge and the difficulties it has faced in judging the costs and benefits of alternative policies have tended to eliminate questions of foreign policy from normal democratic processes. How was a people to know the possible effect of a revolution, a change in gov-

ernment, an act of aggression, or a variety of mundane events in distant lands on its own interests or those of other countries? Of what use, moreover, were public preferences that exceeded the possibilities of successful action abroad? Such opinion, if effective, could drive a nation to disaster. Thus, even in democratic states, external affairs evolved outside the boundaries of legitimate public discourse. Foreign offices determined the world's foreign policies; the masses could judge them but could not control them.

What challenged this elitist control of foreign policy was the tragedy of the Great War of 1914–1918. The failure of Europe's leaders to prevent the outbreak of that war and, thereafter, to curtail its destructiveness discredited the old diplomacy. "After the war," observed one member of the British House of Commons in 1918, "the old diplomacy of Court and upper classes will be in the eyes of most people, obsolete and inadequate." The national and human sacrifices which that war levied on the populace made it clear that future decisions would require public support or fail. As Lord Strang, later undersecretary in the British Foreign Office, observed, "In a world where war is everybody's tragedy and everybody's nightmare, diplomacy is everybody's business." People who would man the barricades and make the sacrifices that would follow any breakdown of the peace had the right to approve or disapprove every policy proposal that involved a national obligation.

•••

The Interwar Years: A Public Misled

Seldom after [World War I ended with the Treaty of] Versailles was the public influential or troublesome. The major foreign policies of the interwar years reflected a broad consensus that included both government officials and the public. Republican and Democratic leaders, sharing the post-Versailles euphoria with its central assumption that the Great War had eliminated power politics from international life, logically denied that conditions abroad necessitated any costly American responsibility for the maintenance of order. Their denial merely reinforced the country's distrust of traditional diplomacy, its assumptions of moral superiority, its lack of interest in foreign commitments (especially toward Europe), and its preference for avoiding rather than confronting the challenges to international stability that were bound to recur. Successive policy proposals, all emanating from the government, assured the public that the nation could achieve a peaceful future without cost, commitment, or responsibility. The universal emphasis on peace encouraged opinion makers inside and outside the government to exaggerate the importance, even the unique morality, of the status quo. It was true

that any serious disturbance of the Versailles treaty structure could endanger regional stability if not world stability. Still the appealing conviction, common in official thought, that only peaceful change could be legitimate burdened diplomacy, not with the traditional management of change, but with its total elimination. The only defense against such varied forms of official overexpectation lay in the nonexistent capacity of the public to recognize and resist them.

Isolationists argued fundamentally that Europe would not involve the United States in another continental conflict. Internationalists insisted not only that the United States would not escape another European war but also that it carried a moral obligation to lead the world toward the further institutionalization of the peace. Both isolationists and internationalists were strangers to the conservative tradition of American diplomacy. Both denied that the United States need be concerned with any specific political or military configuration in Europe or Asia. Whereas isolationists limited the nation's interests to the Western Hemisphere, internationalists assumed that American interests were universal—wherever mankind was oppressed or threatened by aggression. In practice, however, the internationalists would control the world environment, not with the traditional devices of diplomacy or force, but by confronting aggressors with a combination of international law, signed agreements, and world opinion. Behind such undemanding assurances the American foreign policy consensus became almost unshakable. Internationalists offered their four major causes of the 1920s—membership in the League of Nations, membership in the World Court, the Four Power Pact for the Far East, and the Kellogg-Briand Peace Pact—as devices to maintain the status quo without cost or obligation. What mattered in world politics was the limitation of change to peaceful means. In the hands of the internationalists the concepts of peace and peaceful change thus became the bulwark of the status quo, for change limited to general agreement could alter the international order little if at all.

Clearly Franklin D. Roosevelt, after 1933, faced a country addicted to a combination of isolationism and utopian internationalism, either of which would impede the creation of a strategic concept based on interests and power. If his efforts to redirect American policy before the Nazi invasion of Poland in September 1939 were futile, the explanation lies no more in the crippling influence of public opinion than in his adherence to the utopian formula of peaceful change that he inherited from his Republican predecessors. Roosevelt and his advisers did little to counter the isolationism of the decade. A *Christian Century* poll of 1935 revealed that 91 percent of all Americans agreed that they "would regard as an imbecile anyone who might suggest that, in the event of another European war, the United States should again participate in it." This antiwar sentiment fueled the popular support for the neutrality legislation of 1935–1937. But many of the decisions of the Roosevelt years were no measure of either the strength of American isolationism or Roosevelt's concern with public opinion. Isolationist sentiment embraced only the imperative that the United States avoid another European war; it did not curtail Roosevelt's initiatives elsewhere, especially in Latin America and the Far East. Public opinion favored the recognition of Russia in 1933 by a margin of two to one. Still the decision to end Russia's diplomatic isolation from the United States probably evolved within the administration itself, with executive officials and the press succumbing to parallel arguments.

Roosevelt's Quarantine Speech of October 1937 constituted a cautious assault on isolationist opinion. The reaction to the speech was complex, but it was not an isolationist triumph. Actually there was little in Roosevelt's proposal from which the public could demand a retreat. Even the president's mail conveyed an overwhelming expression of approval. Roosevelt's references to a quarantine defined no program of action, nor did they require much of the American people. They did propose some form of action; that was too much for his critics. Roosevelt admitted to newsmen that his speech constituted less a program than an attitude and a search for a program. What remained was the chasm between the suggestion of a quarantine and the negotiation of a firm alliance against Hitler. Nothing in the American experience prepared Roosevelt to embark on that venture. In the 1930s even the study of international relations, Louis J. Halle has written, "applied to the world as the professors thought it ought to be, rather than to the world as it was. In this dream world, power politics was a thing of the past, power no longer counted, international organization sufficed for the maintenance of international security."

Long before the fall of France in June 1940 isolationism was on the wane, the victim of more Nazi aggressions than of Roosevelt's anti-Nazi preachments. Britain, standing alone, became the central object of American opinion. As early as February 1939 some 69 percent of all Americans polled favored aid to Britain short of war; by April, 66 percent were prepared to send arms and ammunition to Britain in case of war. The battle for Britain, the election of 1940, and lend-lease reaffirmed the commitment of the United States to Britain. When on May 27, 1941, Roosevelt declared in a national radio address that the United States faced the task of ensuring the delivery of American goods in Britain, his mail was overwhelming in its approval. But the president informed newsmen that he had no intention of instituting a system of convoys. Already extreme isolationists who opposed aid to Britain had dwindled to a small minority. Some had become vulnerable to charges of un-Americanism. Still, Roosevelt would not defy the country's isolationists by asking Congress for a declaration of war against Germany. He had anchored his appeal for congressional support to the argument that aid to Britain would keep the United States out of war. Those who favored aid to Britain on the president's terms had carried the interventionist legislation. Roosevelt could not ask such congressmen for war until the Japanese attack on Pearl Harbor destroyed what remained of isolationist influence in Congress.

Executive Leadership and the Creation of the Cold War Consensus: The Truman Years

Americans in 1945 shared a deep respect for the Soviet Union because of that country's special contribution to Germany's destruction. Unfortunately the mutual interests that underwrote the wartime cooperation could not survive the disagreements over the postwar reconstruction of Europe. Polish and other Slavic minorities in the United States, supported by the Catholic press, revealed a deep dissatisfaction with the Yalta agreements, but most Americans regarded the Soviet occupation of Eastern Europe with profound detachment. Even amid the burgeoning evidences of conflict, public attitudes toward the Soviet Union remained ambivalent. Indeed, there was a strong current of pro-Soviet sentiment in the United States as late as the autumn of 1945. Facing a divided and largely unconcerned public, President Harry S. Truman and his advisers were in complete control of American policy. The decision to elevate Eastern Europe into a major issue in United States–Soviet relations emanated from the administration itself. Stalin's belligerent speech of February 1, 1946, and the subsequent Iranian crisis produced a sharp increase in anti-Soviet sentiment, although the bitter reaction to Winston Churchill's Iron Curtain speech in March revealed a still divided opinion toward the emergence of a divided Europe. Throughout 1946 public anti-Soviet opinion lagged behind that of the State Department. The doubts regarding Soviet intentions that dominated the pages of the diaries of James Forrestal, George Kennan's "long telegram" of February 1946, and Clark Clifford's report to the president belonged largely to government insiders.

• • •

Within that context the North Korean invasion of South Korea in June 1950 was merely another demonstration of Soviet imperialism in Asia. As Truman explained to the American people in January 1951, "Our men are fighting . . . because they know, as we do, that the aggression in Korea is part of the attempt of the Russian communist dictatorship to take over the world, step by step." John Foster Dulles, in his capacity as State Department adviser, informed a New York audience in May 1951, "By the test of conception, birth, nurture, and obedience, the Mao Tse-tung regime [of China] is a creature of the Moscow Politburo, and it is in behalf of Moscow, not of China, that it is destroying the friendship of the Chinese people toward the United States." It was left for Senator Joseph McCarthy of Wisconsin and other Republican leaders to create the required partisan rationale that the Truman administration had alternative policy choices but rejected them because of internal Communist sympathies. Subsequent Republican campaigning reinforced the twin conclusions that communism in Asia was a danger to Asian and Western security and that a spectrum of anti-Communist policies in Asia, centered largely in U.S. recognition and support of the exiled Nationalist regime on Formosa, would contain Communist power in Asia and eventually send it into retreat. Such assumptions of policy in Asia became an essential element in the American consensus on the Cold War.

By midcentury the American foreign policy elite, almost synonymous with the New York Council on Foreign Relations, came into its own as a group of immense influence, thoroughly united internally and truly representative of the American consensus on the Cold War. Yet the very completeness of the consensus from the beginning was an indication that its spokesmen, in power and out, would tend to eliminate from their considerations questions of real complexity. The assumption that the United States possessed the power to render its policies effective eliminated for them the need to examine with sophistication such matters as Soviet intentions or the nature of communism in Asia. It was enough that American policies of containment recognized the presence of danger and prepared to limit that danger through various forms of military expansion and collective security. The consensus on the Cold War had the effect of identifying American conservatism with anticommunism. This deprived conservatism of its historic emphasis on means and bound it to ends that defied the creation of policy. What was lacking in the spectrum of opinion was an organized opposition that could analyze and criticize American policy in conservative terms. Mainline Democratic liberals, represented by the Americans for Democratic Action, had joined the Cold War consensus. Henry Wallace's more radical strain of American liberalism rejected the consensus, as did a minority of Republican isolationists, led by Robert A. Taft and Herbert Hoover. Those who commanded the consensus managed to discredit the objections of both political factions. What remained in potentially effective opposition was a small group of critics from journalism and the universities, led by George Kennan, Walter Lippmann, and Hans J. Morgenthau.

The Eisenhower Consensus: Executive Power in a Divided Nation

Long before Dwight D. Eisenhower entered the White House in January 1953, the nation's foreign policy elites had formulated two distinct approaches to the challenge of Soviet power and ideology. One group, among them leading public officials, such as Dean Acheson, saw the European situation as one in flux, with the Soviets, having taken possession of Slavic Europe, determined to extend their influence, if not their military power, over portions of Western Europe. Soviet power, alleged to be in control of China and the Communist-led forces of Indochina, had converted these traditionally friendly and nonaggressive regions into enemies of peace and stability in Asia. To meet this global challenge, by definition centered in the Kremlin, the United States sustained its commitment both to NATO [North Atlantic Treaty Organi-

zation] and to the anti-Communist elements in China, Indochina, and Korea. American officials and those who supported them were determined to accept no change in world politics that flowed from the Soviet victory over Germany or from the triumph of Mao Tse-tung in China. The greater their perceptions of danger, the greater was their insistence that the United States eliminate Soviet control from Eastern Europe and the Peking regime from China. For official Washington the achievement of such purposes presented no problem. Successful containment, they predicted, would aggravate the inconsistencies within the Communist world and assure an ultimate victory without war.

Those who questioned this official view of the Cold War—and they were not numerous—argued that Europe, if divided, was stable and that the Soviet intention was less to conquer Western Europe than to legitimize the Russian hegemony in Eastern Europe. Such assumptions dictated two realistic courses of action for the United States and its allies in Europe: the maintenance of NATO at a reduced level of military expenditure and the ultimate diplomatic recognition of the military-political division of Europe as the best settlement available without another war. Such recognition might achieve a reduction in United States–Soviet tensions and permit a broader range of agreements. The critics of official American policy in Asia argued that the power that propelled both Mao Tse-tung and Ho Chi Minh, Indochina's Communist leader, into positions of leadership and established their goals was not a monolithic communism centered in the Kremlin, but a radical, indigenous nationalism that sought above all the creation of two successful, thoroughly independent nations in East Asia. Since the Peking regime, they warned, rested on the foundation of a massive internal revolution, not the power and influence of the Soviet Union, it would survive any American effort to return Chiang Kai-shek to power over the mainland. Ultimately, therefore, the United States had no choice but to recognize Peking. Similarly, this minority argued, the United States would be no more successful in resisting Ho Chi Minh in his crusade to free Indochina of French rule and unite its people into one independent nation. Thus the United States had no realistic alternative to that of coming to terms with the Communist leaders of Indochina.

Whatever the responsibility of John Foster Dulles for the foreign policy decisions of the Eisenhower years, American policy after January 1953 received its tone from the words and personality of the noted secretary of state. His reliance on dramatic phrases such as "liberation," "massive retaliation," "unleashing Chiang Kai-shek," "agonizing reappraisal," and "united action" suggested that his policies were grander in purpose and more successful in performance than were those he inherited from the Truman administration. In every case the words and the intentions reflected the will of the administration, not the public. Still, the specific goals that Dulles sought—the liberation of Eastern Europe, China, and Indochina from Communist rule—appealed to powerful, organized minorities. Unfortunately, Dulles's objectives exceeded the possibilities of American policies and thereby rendered them insolvent. Many questioned the rhetoric and the objectives; the administration, free to maneuver, remained firm. Dulles confronted his critics with a consensus so overwhelming that the goals he advocated remained untouchable long after his death in 1959.

• • •

Following the Korean truce of July 1953, the Committee of One Million, headed by Marvin Liebman of New York, organized and directed the national effort to keep the Peking regime of China out of the United Nations and prevent Washington's recognition of that government. Much of the committee's activity centered on the Congress, where large majorities endorsed its support of Chiang Kai-shek. In many respects the operation of the Committee of One Million was an example of congressional initiative in postwar American foreign policy. When Congress, under periodic prodding from the committee, endorsed the anti-Peking posture of nonrecognition, it generally did so with unanimous votes. From the beginning, however, the committee used Secretary Dulles's uncompromising arguments for nonrecognition to further its cause and saw itself as the necessary source of support for the Eisenhower administration in Far Eastern matters. The progression of events in 1954 and 1955—the formation of the Southeast Asia Treaty Organization (SEATO), the negotiation of the United States–Nationalist China security pact, and the crisis over the offshore islands—enabled the committee, as Liebman phrased it, to strengthen the hand of the Eisenhower administration on China policy.

Whatever the committee's influence on public opinion, it was Dulles himself who led the crusade against mainland China and perfected the rationale for nonrecognition. It was Dulles who assured the country that nonrecognition ultimately would achieve the destruction of the Peking regime. "We can confidently assume," he informed the nation in June 1957, "that international communism's rule of strict conformity is, in China, as elsewhere, a passing and not a perpetual phase. We owe it to ourselves, our allies, and the Chinese people to do all that we can to contribute to that passing." Supported by such predictions of success, the government turned on its critics with a ferocity that suggested grave internal doubts. Few dared dissent from the thesis that China had become part of the Soviet empire and that nonrecognition could determine China's political future. Not even the press chose to offer a more objective and balanced portrayal; it shared responsibility for sustaining the premises that involved the country in China's internal affairs for more than two decades. After 1961 the Committee of One Million accepted the task of holding Congress in line behind the nonrecognition policies of the Kennedy and Johnson administrations. But the committee's influence on Congress and the public never transcended that of the government itself.

Unlike Eastern Europe and China, Indochina had no American constituency at all. Except for the presumption that Ho Chi Minh's North Vietnam had become the Asian spearhead of a Moscow-based international Communist conspiracy, the United States would have avoided its long and humiliating engagement in Indochina. By predicting disaster for the globe should South Vietnam fall, successive administrations transformed a small jungle country into a critical area in the struggle against world communism. Dulles informed the Overseas Press Club of New York on March 29, 1954: "Under the conditions of today the imposition on Southeast Asia of the political system of Communist Russia and its Chinese Communist ally . . . would be a grave threat to the whole free community." After that warning Dulles had no choice but to revise downward the official American estimation of the region's strategic importance or commit the United States to the defense of the province. By escaping this fundamental decision, the Eisenhower administration succeeded in bringing the defense of South Vietnam into the American foreign policy consensus. Whatever the magnitude of the danger, the administration insisted that its support of the new Saigon regime of Ngo Dinh Diem assured Ho's destruction.

Replacing the French in 1954 after the forces of Ho Chi Minh had put them to rout, the administration recognized no lesson in the French defeat at Dienbienphu and ignored the existence of Indochinese nationalism and Ho's relationship to it. Logically, therefore, it would always place too much reliance on Saigon and underestimate the power of Ho Chi Minh. By 1957 American officials spoke freely of Diem's "miracle" in South Vietnam and predicted the unification of that country under free elections. Should the Saigon regime fail to destroy Ho Chi Minh politically, the newly created Southeast Asia Treaty Organization, supported by American air and naval power, would assure Ho's destruction militarily. When after 1961 it was apparent that neither program carried any assurance of success, the Kennedy administration, without any review of the Eisenhower policies, reaffirmed the commitment of the United States to Saigon and began the process of increasing the American presence in Southeast Asia. Determined to avoid a hard decision, Kennedy committed the nation to victory, but with increments of military and economic aid sufficient only to sustain the administration's options, not large enough to require formal national approval. The United States drifted into the war, fought it, and left it without the benefit of a national decision. It was not strange that the involvement ended in disaster.

Kennedy to Kissinger: The Changing Consensus

For more than a decade the Eisenhower-Dulles consensus toward Europe, China, and Indochina was almost complete. The fears of Russian-based communism, combined with the absence of war, rendered the nation's approval even more profound. Right-wing groups, with strong minority support, urged the government to avoid accommodation with Moscow or Peking, convinced that firmness would ultimately produce victory. Senator Barry Goldwater of Arizona emerged as the country's leading spokesman for such foreign policy views. He argued his case for victory in two books, *The Conscience of a Conservative* (1960) and *Why Not Victory?* (1961). Still, the ease with which Eisenhower and his successors defended their anti-Communist foreign policies never eliminated the critics, led by Senator J. William Fulbright of Arkansas and a number of scholars, who argued that the United States lacked both the interests and the means to render its basic policies effective. As early as the Kennedy years, U.S. policy toward China began to waver and with it the influence of the Committee of One Million. State Department official Roger Hilsman's noted speech on China in 1963 suggested no dramatic changes in American policy, but it assumed the persistence of the Peking regime and anticipated the time when the United States would seek accommodation with a less hostile Chinese government. As late as 1965 the committee could still muster majorities in both houses of Congress, but it could no longer maintain much interest outside government or in the United Nations. In December 1966 several senators, including Paul Douglas of Illinois, formally severed their ties with the committee. By 1968 the committee had fewer than one hundred supporters in the House and failed that year in its effort to extract a hard anti-Chinese statement from Republican candidate Richard Nixon. Indeed, by 1968 much of the Congress and the nation's intellectual community demanded a new approach to China.

Still, any changes in policy would come hard and reflect internal conviction far more than external pressure. That power which enabled the government to create policy with little regard for public opinion provided it with ample capacity to resist its critics. The internal impediments to change were prodigious. Once officials have generated the necessary fears and expectations, have perfected their arguments, and have honed their phrases to achieve the desired public response, they have no desire to desert what has required so much time and energy to create. Ongoing policies, whatever their promises of success, encourage bureaucratic inertia by establishing individual interests in those policies. It is not difficult for officials to become convinced that the policies they defend are indeed the best available. Those in power have no desire to admit error; they face no compulsion to change what is merely extravagant or pointless.

Finally, no government cares to downgrade its commitments to allies. For twenty years Washington resisted every pressure to curtail its obligations to Peking, Saigon, and Berlin. To maintain its cordial relations with West Germany, Washington sustained an uncompromising mood within NATO on the question of unification. George Kennan noted the price of such inflexibility in an interview with J. Robert Moskin, which appeared in *Look* on November 19, 1963:

This coalition is incapable of agreeing on any negotiated solutions except unconditional capit-

ulation and the satisfaction of the maximum demands of each of our allies. It is easier for a coalition to agree to ask for everything but the kitchen sink, rather than take a real negotiating position. This worries me because there is not going to be any capitulation. Our adversaries are not weak. If we cannot find any negotiating position, the Cold War will continue, and the dangers will not decrease.

After the mid-1960s, world events increasingly demonstrated the limitations of established policies toward Russia and China. The old assumptions that containment would lead to the disintegration of both powers no longer held any promise. By January 1969, when Nixon entered the White House, the times seemed to call for some significant reversals of policy. Henry A. Kissinger, the new president's national security adviser and, after 1973, the secretary of state, explained:

When I came into office with the Nixon Administration, we were really at the end of a period of American foreign policy in which a redesign would have been necessary to do no matter who took over. . . . First, Western Europe and Japan had regained economic vitality and some political constancy. Secondly, the simplicities of the cold war began to evaporate. The domestic pressures in all countries for putting an end to tension became greater and greater, and within the Communist world it was self-evident that we were no longer confronting a monolith. . . . So our problem was how to orient America in this world and how to do it in such a way that we could avoid these oscillations between excessive moralism and excessive pragmatism, with excessive concern with power and total rejection of power, which have been fairly characteristic of American policy.

During 1969 President Nixon announced the resumption of ambassadorial talks with China in Warsaw; soon thereafter the State Department published a three-phased relaxation of trade restrictions with China. Early that year Liebman moved to London. In his preparations for the Peking and Moscow summits of 1972 Nixon recognized the new circumstances on the world scene and the opportunities afforded by the Sino-Soviet conflict for improved East-West relations. Both the American people and Congress regarded Nixon's summit conferences and the SALT agreements as important achievements in foreign policy. Nixon was the first president in twenty years to recognize the legitimacy of the Peking regime and to exorcise liberation from American purposes in Europe. Kissinger was the first secretary of state in three generations to judge countries and deal with them on the basis of interest and power, not their alleged moral qualities. It was precisely his political approach to diplomacy, and the arrangements that it permitted, that brought such widespread approval of his activities. What was astonishing in this acceptance of Kissinger's basically pragmatic approach was the fact that it won the plaudits of the same groups that had lauded the largely moralistic and legalistic policies of his predecessors from Cordell Hull to Dean Rusk. The public, Kissinger again demonstrated, is inclined to follow the government.

Vietnam, an American concern, ran its separate course. Lyndon Johnson sustained the necessary majorities in Congress and among the people to escalate the American involvement. By 1968 critics of the war dominated the press, the television networks, the colleges and universities, and the public declarations of congressmen. That year, the Vietnam War broke the consensus of the establishment on American Cold War policy for the first time as the administration now faced the opposition of such establishment figures as Clark Clifford and Dean Acheson. What had rendered the struggle for Vietnam critical for Western security was not the expansionism of North Vietnam but the global force of international communism, supposedly centered in Russia and China. The recognition of the Sino-Soviet split and the assumption that both Communist giants either were or could be enticed to become status quo powers eliminated the significance of Vietnam

as a danger to world security. Still, the Nixon administration sustained the direct American involvement another four years with ample public endorsement. By offering the country the alternative of immediate withdrawal, leading, said Nixon, to global disaster, or Vietnamization of the war with its promise of victory and American withdrawal, the president maintained the necessary public and congressional support until the truce of January 1973 enabled him to withdraw all remaining American ground forces. Polls revealed a steady decline in the number of Americans who favored the initial intervention from 61 percent in August 1965 to 35 percent in August 1968 and 28 percent in May 1971. What supported the war to the end was the majority who hoped that the country could still avoid defeat or at least manage a graceful escape. As Saigon fell in April 1975, bringing the American effort to its long-predicted conclusion, the administration assumed no responsibility for what it and its predecessors had done. The time had come, Kissinger informed newsmen, to put Vietnam behind us and to concentrate on the problems of the future.

Conclusion

In the long run foreign policy is self-corrective. Whatever the governmental or bureaucratic resistance to change, the perennial dichotomy between declared purpose and actual performance will take its toll on national decisions. Experience will test the validity of official evaluations of interest and power embodied in national purposes. The political realities of Eastern Europe, China, and Indochina were no less detectable in 1950 than they were twenty years later. Ultimately the United States would come to terms with them. That the American people supported the full spectrum of the country's foreign policies from the Truman Doctrine to the Vietnam War, including those that would never achieve their designated goals, measured the influence of government over public opinion. Throughout the Cold War, no less than during the interwar years, the American people were no more right or wrong than the policies themselves. Every external cause that failed did so because of errors in official judgment.

Unfortunately, when policies fail, it is not always obvious why they do so. The public can learn from experience only to the extent that government leaders evaluate past decisions openly and offer the nation that education which alone can compensate it for the costs of mistaken policy. In practice, even those who preside at moments of change or failure seldom acknowledge the existence of error in previous decisions.

IV  VIEW FROM THE INSIDE

The great hero of the Persian Gulf War in 1991 was "Stormin' Norman" Schwarzkopf, the allied commander. Schwarzkopf's great military victory, combined with his distinctive style before nationally televised press briefings, combined to make him the kind of larger-than-life military figure America had not seen since the days of George Patton, Dwight Eisenhower, and Douglas MacArthur.

Who is Norman Schwarzkopf, and what shaped his attitudes toward war and politics? C. D. B. Bryan, author of **Friendly Fire** *(an account of the tragic events in Vietnam that led to the death by "friendly fire" of an American GI), suggests that the answers lie in his experiences in Vietnam, which present a microcosm of the experiences of the American military—and of the lessons they drew from the conflict. This article was written during the air phase of the Persian Gulf War, just before the brief and highly successful ground campaign that ended the military conflict. (See also selection 18.7.)*

Questions

1. What lessons did Schwarzkopf draw from his experiences in Vietnam? How did he apply those experiences to the Persian Gulf War?

2. What does Schwarzkopf have to say about the relationship between the military and the civilian authorities? How, in his view, should a soldier react to immoral or unconscionable orders? Is his answer persuasive?

18.4 Operation Desert Norm

C. D. B. Bryan

I

I have read the stories about "Stormin' Norman," the terrible-tempered "Bear" who is a "pussycat" to his family. I have read how this general with the 170 genius-level IQ lulls himself to sleep in his Riyadh quarters listening to Pavarotti and Willie Nelson. I have read of his fluency in French and German; his love for the ballet and opera; and his membership in the International Brotherhood of Magicians. And I am sure, as reported, he has studied T. E. Lawrence's *Seven Pillars of Wisdom,* and that he has *The Kingdom,* Robert Lacey's acclaimed history of Saudi Arabia, on his nightstand. I especially enjoyed the account of how, at his Kuwaiti hosts' insistence, Schwarzkopf several years ago donned Arab robes and later said of the experience, "It was just like the scene in *Lawrence of Arabia* when the British officer's clothes are taken away and replaced by robes, and he waltzes into the desert, intrigued by their feel and grace. I stood in front of the mirror and did the same dance. It was wonderful." When we spoke by phone on February 16 [1991], I asked him if that quote had been accurate. "No," he laughed, "I didn't say I did the same dance. I mean, it wasn't exactly a dance. I *will* admit, I stood there and sort of twirled around and let the robes flow."

I can see him doing that. I first met H. Norman Schwarzkopf in October 1971. He was then a 37-year-old lieutenant colonel not long back from completing his second tour of duty in Vietnam. Twice wounded, he had just been released from the Walter Reed Army Medical Center and was recuperating at home in Annandale, Virginia, with his wife, Brenda, and his 2-year-old daughter, Cindy. Schwarzkopf— a large man at six-feet-three-and-a-half inches and, in those days, maybe 225 pounds—looked even more huge in a cast that covered him from his hips to his shoulders.

Seventeen months earlier, on May 28, 1970, Schwarzkopf had been commanding the Americal Division's 1st Battalion of the 6th Infantry Brigade in South Vietnam's Batangan Peninsula when a portion of his battalion's Bravo Company became trapped in a mine field. Bravo's company commander and a lieutenant had both been badly wounded, and a med-evac helicopter had been called for. Schwarzkopf, airborne in his Huey helicopter with Captain Bob Trabbert, his artillery liaison officer, reached the stranded unit first and turned over his Huey to

get the wounded out. Schwarzkopf and Trabbert then stayed behind.

The remainder of the patrol was still frozen in the middle of the mine field. Schwarzkopf said the young soldiers were on the edge of panic. Their commanders had been evacuated; they felt leaderless, abandoned. Schwarzkopf told them calmly that they were going to be all right, to walk back out the way they had walked in: "Watch where you put your feet, keep to your old tracks, stay calm, keep your distance."

They had begun to move again when a young soldier a dozen yards from Schwarzkopf stepped on another mine. The explosion punched the kid up into the air and injured Trabbert and Schwarzkopf slightly. They felt the impact, the pain before the young soldier even hit the ground. The boy's right leg was flapping out to one side. "My leg! MY LEG!" he screamed, and Schwarzkopf sensed the men beginning to panic again. He told them to keep still, and called to Trabbert to radio the med-evac helicopter to hurry. The private who had stepped on the mine was screaming and thrashing about on the ground. The men around him were terrified that his flailing would trigger another explosion. Schwarzkopf began inching across the mine field to reach him. He still had twenty feet to go when the private started panicking again. "I'm going to die! We're all going to die!"

Schwarzkopf's legs began to shake uncontrollably. His knees were suddenly so watery that he had to reach down and grip them until they stilled. Perspiration stung his eyes. The men were watching him, waiting for him to move again. To his astonishment, Schwarzkopf said, he suddenly thought of the sign on Harry Truman's White House desk: "The buck stops here."

The kid was whimpering, "I don't want to die! You've got to get me out of here."

"I'll get you out," Schwarzkopf said. "Just keep still. You're all right."

Five feet . . . three feet . . . Schwarzkopf gently lowered himself across the wounded boy's body to keep him still. "I don't want you to move around," Schwarzkopf told him. "We're going to have to set that leg."

Schwarzkopf needed a splint and spotted a small, waist-high tree back where he had left Trabbert and three other men. Schwarzkopf called to them to cut some splints from the tree. Trabbert pulled out his sheath knife and passed it to one of the men. The soldier took one step toward the tree and triggered another mine.

Schwarzkopf was horrified. Trabbert had taken the full force of the explosion. His left leg was blown off, an arm broken backward so that the bone of the elbow socket showed, and a great hole was gouged in his head. He would survive, but the three other men were killed instantly.

For having crossed the mine field to rescue the wounded private, Schwarzkopf was awarded his third Silver Star. He says he had no other choice. It was his responsibility. And by being there in the mine field taking care of the boy instead of with Trabbert, his life was saved. "But you live with those things," he said. "You become terribly fatalistic in combat."

I was interviewing Schwarzkopf for *Friendly Fire*, the book I was writing about an Iowa family whose 25-year-old son was killed by a howitzer shell fired by his own supporting artillery in Vietnam. Michael Mullen had been a sergeant in Charlie Company, one of the infantry companies in Schwarzkopf's battalion. I had gone to see Schwarzkopf because Michael's parents were wrongly convinced he was responsible for their son's death.

The term "friendly fire" has been in the news a lot lately. What Schwarzkopf said then about Mullen's death holds true for those other young men killed by friendly fire in the Gulf war: "Michael's death was a terrible, terrible tragedy," he told me. "A tragedy typical of a profane thing called war—maybe 'typical' isn't the word. It isn't a daily occurrence. It's a unique thing that happens on a very occasional basis. But it happens!" Schwarzkopf paused and rubbed his brow. "Try to think of it this way: Michael was killed due to an error. It was

a tragedy that Michael was killed. But I don't think it was an error of deliberate negligence."

Mullen's death deeply distressed Schwarzkopf—as did the death of any soldier who served under him. In fact, twenty years ago he was clearly distressed about the entire Vietnam experience. Late that first night he said to me, "I *hate* what Vietnam has done to our country! I *hate* what Vietnam has done to our Army! The government sends you off to fight its war. It's not *your* war, it's the government's war. You go off and fight not only once, but twice, OK? And suddenly, a decision is made, 'Well, look, you guys were all wrong. You're a bunch of dirty bastards! You never should have been there!' Now this is going to make me think long and hard before I go off to war again. This is me, Norm Schwarzkopf, personally. . . . And when they get ready to send me again, I'm going to have to stop and ask myself, 'Is it worth it?'"

It was an extraordinary comment for a young West Point lieutenant colonel with three Silver Stars. Overnight he must have realized it, too. The next morning it was one of the first things he mentioned after we had again sat down. "Let me clarify that," he said. "If I decide to remain in the service and the government orders me to go, I will go. I don't see how I can refuse unless I felt so strongly about it that my only alternative was to resign from the Army." Schwarzkopf paused for a moment. "We can get into a very subtle discussion here of conscience and duty, the Nuremberg trials, the Japanese war criminals, etc. What is moral? What is immoral? Where does duty stop and morality begin? Are we now saying that the military is supposed to question the morality of our government's commitment to war? I don't know. . . . If we allow the military to question whether or not to go, then it seems to me we also have to look at the other side of the coin: What if the government decides *not* to go? Do we allow the military the right to criticize this decision? . . . See, the military is required to follow the orders given it by the government. How they pursue it is another question—and here is where you get into civilian casualties, war crimes, atrocities, ovens, and all that business. . . . If it ever came to a choice between compromising my moral principles and the performance of my duties, I know I'd go with my moral principles. At the same time, however, I would also cease being an Army officer. I would have to resign my commission. But even at that I could be accomplishing my duty as I see it."

Where did this man come from? H. Norman Schwarzkopf was born in Trenton, New Jersey, on August 22, 1934. His father, Herbert Norman Schwarzkopf, was the son of German immigrants who spoke no English in the home. (Schwarzkopf senior so hated "Herbert" that he gave his son the initial, but not the name.) Schwarzkopf senior graduated from West Point and, at his son's birth, was head of the New Jersey State Police, overseeing the conviction and execution of Bruno Hauptman for the kidnap-murder of Charles and Anne Morrow Lindbergh's baby. He later hosted the old radio show "Gangbusters" before returning to active duty with the Army during World War II. It is hard to know how great an influence the father had on the son, but Schwarzkopf told me, "A lot of my love of country stemmed from my father. My dad was a genuine public servant who had a deep and abiding love for his country, and he wanted to serve."

In 1946, 12-year-old H. Norman Schwarzkopf went to Iran to join his father, who was training that country's police. (In 1953 he was instrumental in the coup that overthrew Iran's Prime Minister Mossadegh and restored the Shah to his throne.) The young Schwarzkopf lived in Iran for a year, in Germany for two years, and then in Italy for a year before he was 17. At West Point he wrestled and played tennis and football; he conducted the chapel choir and graduated in the top 10 percent of his class of 1956 both academically (43rd out of 480) and militarily (he was a captain, the highest cadet rank one could attain). Upon graduation he was commissioned a second lieutenant, entered active duty, and soon afterward almost resigned.

"I had an alcoholic commander," he explained. "I had an executive officer who was a coward. I saw terrible things going on around me and I said 'Who needs it? When my three years are up, I'm getting out!' But a very sage guy sat me down and said, 'Young man, you know, if all the guys who see these bad things happening quit, then all the guys who don't think these things are so bad are going to be doing them later on. If you really think it's that bad, why don't you stick around until someday you get into a position to do something about it?"

In 1984, when I next saw H. Norman Schwarzkopf, he was in "a position to do something about it." He was a major general in command of the 24th Infantry Division (Mech) at Fort Stewart, Georgia. Commanding an American combat division is a plum assignment. Only sixteen generals get it. Speaking of the fun of being a general, he said, "Now I can fix all those things out there in my domain that I think are broken." And then he laughed and added, "At the same time, you hope your judgment is good, because there are a lot of other generals that have gone around thinking they were fixing things, and they were just breaking them like crazy!"

We were sitting in his quarters enjoying an after-dinner whiskey, and, not surprisingly, conversation had turned to the Vietnam War. His first tour in Vietnam had been as a young captain/major assigned to the South Vietnamese Airborne battalion as a task force adviser. It was in 1965–66, the very heat of battle, and Schwarzkopf and the Vietnamese Airborne had been in the middle of it. "We fought for almost every day of every month for thirteen months," he said. Schwarzkopf was proud of his unit, and of his own service. "I really thought we had done something good, just like George Washington," he said. "I had gone and fought for Freedom."

Upon completing that tour Schwarzkopf flew out of Vietnam practically non-stop to New York. He was 32 years old and in uniform—"because," he said, "I was this soldier coming home from war." But there were no parades, no crowds to greet him. The terminal was empty. He grabbed his duffel bag, walked out into the early morning fog, and hopped in a helicopter to Newark. He expected the cab driver who was taking him to his mother's home in East Orange to see his uniform and say, "Oh! Are you just back from Vietnam?" But the driver didn't say a thing. And when Schwarzkopf said, "Sure is great to be back in the U.S. again!" the driver didn't even ask, "Where have you been?"

By 1969, when Schwarzkopf was sent to Vietnam a second time, he was married to Brenda. He served as a battalion commander with the Americal Division and returned in 1970. "And this time when I came home," he said, "not only was I not getting greeted and flowers thrown on me and loved—except for Brenda, who was happy to see me—this time, when I came back the uniform was spit upon and people were calling me a baby burner." Schwarzkopf gave several speeches before civic organizations, and people in the audience, he told me, would stand up and ask, "What about the babies you napalmed? What about the villages you burned?" Television was depicting the career military officer as "a Neanderthal," he said, "who with blind, unquestioning obedience burned villages and killed babies. And what made it so difficult was the fact that *I hadn't done any of that!*"

"Everyone who went to Vietnam and came home, after it was over, has had to come to his personal accommodation for that experience," Schwarzkopf said. He compared it to undergoing surgery for cancer. "When it's all over you've got the scar, number one; and number two, you're not really ever sure that you got it all out of your system. You never know when it's going to rear its ugly head again. But if you're going to live your life, you're going to have to learn to live with that. But I have to tell you, I was undergoing tremendous peaks and valleys to arrive at my own accommodation for my life. There were times when I was tempted

to just bail out and go build myself a cabin in the wilderness and commune with nature. . . ."

The critical moment for him, he said, came not long after we had first spoken. It was the spring of 1972, the year before the last American troops left Vietnam; the Schwarzkopfs were still living in their Annandale apartment. "My sister Sally—whom I love dearly, we are very, very close—came over one night with a magnum of excellent wine," he said. "And Sally and Brenda and I were consuming this vast quantity of wonderful wine and the TV was sort of on. It was the worst kind of war picture, totally contrived, with no realism in the whole thing." The soldiers in the movie had come to a mine field and started across; Schwarzkopf was watching it out of the corner of his eye. "You just knew any damn minute some damn mine was going to go off," he said, "something you had been through a thousand times in real life, and all of a sudden the mine went off and people were blowing up in the mine field." Schwarzkopf immediately became drenched with sweat. "It was a terrible experience for me to see that, and my sister started asking me why I was having such an awful response."

"I started trying to explain to her the emotionalism of this thing," he said. "All the—the, my God, what we had gone through. And how we'd come back from the war and it wasn't appreciated. And then Sally, this sister who I truly love, started saying, 'Well, you have to understand the other side of this thing.'" Despite her support for her brother, Sally was opposed to the war and suggested that the protesters demonstrating against the American presence in Vietnam had a point, that perhaps they were right. "And I *burst into tears!*" Schwarzkopf told me. "Here was my own flesh and blood doubting. I was in tears and she could even *dare* take the other side."

He told his sister to get out of his house; and Sally, also in tears, kept asking, "Why are you throwing me out of the house?" And Schwarzkopf was yelling, "Goddamn it! If you can even think that about our service there!"

The next morning Schwarzkopf woke up thinking to himself, "You were wrong, Norm Schwarzkopf, you were dead wrong!" He called his sister and apologized, and she of course said she was sorry too. And he came to the conclusion that this anger, his frustration, his grief, his confusion over his service in Vietnam could consume him. "I recognized that . . . whatever it was eating me away could absolutely destroy me if I didn't get a handle on it. In hindsight, from a personal, emotional standpoint, that was probably a major turning point for me."

Another occurred on Sunday, October 23, 1983.

II

Schwarzkopf had spent that Sunday bass fishing near Fort Stewart. "I had promised a lot of people that I was a magnificent fisherman," he said, "and I hadn't caught very many fish since I'd been here. So I came home and announced to my family, 'Eureka! Tonight I'm cooking dinner. I am going to take these bass and give you a beautiful Southern fried bass dinner with corn meal.' And I had covered all the bass with corn meal, and I had just dunked the first fillets in the frying pan with the telephone rang. It was the Deputy Chief of Staff of Operations from [Army] Forces [of the Atlantic] Command in Atlanta. And he said to me, "What is it you think you're going to be doing for the next three weeks?'"

Schwarzkopf smiled. "Ever been asked a question like that? That really sets your head to spinning very quickly. I told him what I thought I would be doing and he said, 'You're probably not going to be doing that. You've been selected for a special mission.'"

"I said, 'What am I going to be doing?'"

"And he said, 'I can't tell you that.'"

"I said, 'Where am I going to be?'"

"And he said, 'I can't tell you that, but since I now know what your availability is, your selection has to be cleared. I'll call you back in a couple of hours and let you know."

Schwarzkopf said, "Suddenly I had no appetite at all. You've got to remember the day before they had blown up the Marine barracks in Beirut, so every thought in my mind was Lebanon."

Twenty-four hours later he was on the aircraft carrier *Guam*. There had been a bloody coup in Grenada four days earlier, and Maurice Bishop, the popular, charismatic, legitimate prime minister, had been placed under house arrest (and in fact, unknown to us, killed) by General Hudson Austin, the military commander, and Bernard Coard, the radical deputy prime minister.

Schwarzkopf had been told only that he would be engaging in a predominately Navy commanded exercise, and that he had been selected to advise the Navy commander, Vice Admiral Joseph Metcalf III, of the proper utilization of the Army forces. He had also been warned that the Navy didn't really feel there was a need for him, and that he might not be too welcome when he got there.

"We were floating around somewhere out in the middle of the Caribbean and we still didn't know if the Grenada rescue operation was going to take place. It was about 7 P.M. . . . [when] we got the orders to go. We sent messages out to everybody that, OK, it's a go, tomorrow morning at 5 A.M. it's going to happen. And I went out and I was standing on the flight deck and the ship was kind of tossing a little bit, the wind was blowing in my face, and I thought, *Grenada*! The United States of America is about to launch a military operation into Grenada and I'm involved. And, of course, a lot of the Vietnam memories came rushing back: What am I getting into here? Why is the U.S. going into Grenada? What are we doing? What are our strategic interests in Grenada?

"And then I thought, 'Hey, Schwarzkopf'— and you will probably never believe this, but I thought of that conversation we had had years ago about 'immoral wars' and whether an Army officer should stand up and say this is an immoral war and, therefore, I choose not to fight this one. And I thought, this is sort of the bottom line, the very crux of the difference between being an Army officer and being in some other line of work. I took an oath that said I would obey the lawful orders of my commanding officers, one of whom is the president of the United States. After—at that time—twenty-eight years in the U.S. Army, of having my salary paid and my children clothed, of having a roof over my head and rising to the rank of Major General, do I now have an option to say, 'Hey, before I commit myself to this thing, I'd like to talk about it a bit more'?"

I asked Schwarzkopf what he had thought he was getting into. "I didn't really know," he said. "I knew we were going in to free the [American] students. But I didn't know how we were going to be greeted by the Grenadan people. I certainly didn't know how the American people were going to take it. Or Congress. But . . . my orders were very clear to me, and I honestly don't think you have the right as an Army officer to consider that you have an option. Now *don't* misunderstand me," he said, "because the other image that comes back to me is 'I was only doing my duty. They gave me my orders and I went out and mowed down the Jews.' That is obviously an immoral act, and if someone told me to do something like that I would refuse the order fully recognizing that I would be turning in my 'suit' the next day."

The Grenada operation was, he said, "a highly successful military operation by any measure." It clearly was a success for him. He so impressed the Grenada invasion force commander, Vice Admiral Metcalf, that in two days he went from being somewhat of an uninvited guest to Metcalf's deputy task force commander.

"The object was to go in with what really started as a relatively unconventional operation," Schwarzkopf told me. "It was going to be quick in, quick and dirty: we were going to isolate the two airfields, we were going to get in on top of all those critical buildings"—the government buildings, the radio station, the prison where Bishop was believed held, etc.— "take them all and say, 'That's it, it's over with.'

And at the end of Day One, the whole exercise was going to be done. But what started as a highly unconventional, surgical in nature operation went sour right away. And it went sour because of the assumption that the Cubans weren't going to fight. We had 800 Cubans on the island who were well armed and damn sure *were* going to fight."

It was also assumed that the anti-aircraft weapons on the island would be largely ineffective and that, therefore, helicopter movement would be relatively unhampered. And it was believed that the guns were antiquated quad-30mms, that the gunners were untrained, and that their morale was poor. But as the invading American forces—among them the special strike teams—soon discovered, many of the gunners had been trained in Cuba; they were brave and highly disciplined; not only did they remain at their posts in the face of withering fire from U.S. helicopter gunships, they fired back.

"One of the criticisms everybody has is, 'Oh, my God, you ended up with 6,000 Americans in there and only 800 Cubans, it seems to me you should have rolled over them!'" Schwarzkopf said, "If it had been a conventional battle, where we were using artillery, fighting conventional tactics without regard to civilian casualties and collateral damage, we probably would have. . . . I could have rolled into Grenada with my mechanized armor division, my overwhelming division artillery; I could have hit the beach with LSTs, rolled my tanks off, cranked up my artillery, and blown St. George's off the map. . . . 'Sure, a few civilian casualties here and there, what the hell, you know? We're fighting for *freedom*!' I could have had the whole thing tied up in a neat little bundle in an hour, maybe an hour and a half. But that wasn't the nature of the operation, and it obviously would have been a terrible thing to do."

Three other incidents from Schwarzkopf's conversation about Grenada stand out in my mind. First, how fact can follow fantasy: U.S. Army helicopter pilots, influenced by Francis

Ford Coppola's *Apocalypse Now,* strung loudspeakers to their landing struts and invaded the island with Wagner's *Die Walküre* blasting from the amplifiers. Second, that flying toward the island himself, Schwarzkopf, seeing a crudely lettered message painted in red on a soccer field and fully expecting it to say, "Yankees Go Home," was surprised to see that it read, "GOD BLESS AMERICA!" And third, upon his return to Fort Stewart, how moved he was that a small group had gathered at the airfield to welcome him.

The Army band was there; his wife, Brenda, the children, and his black Labrador "Bear" were there; as were his enlisted aide, some of the privates he shot skeet with, some members of his staff, and their wives and children. "Johnny was coming home from war again and I had expected to come home just the same way I came home from war the last two times: no big deal. It was going to be routine. But the airplane landed, the band was out there, and there were big signs saying, "WELCOME HOME," and I walked out of the airplane and everybody started cheering and my wife and kids ran up and hugged me, and I didn't understand what was going on! Isn't that crazy? Do you see what I'm saying? But I've got to tell you, when it finally dawned on me, it was probably one of the greatest thrills I have ever had in my entire life." That night Schwarzkopf told me that if he had returned from Grenada to an American press that had been violently anti-Grenada, an American people that were violently anti-Grenada, he didn't think he could have handled it.

Schwarzkopf's black Labrador came in and lay his big head on the general's lap. He stroked the dog's head idly. Then he took a deep breath and let it out slowly. "When you commit military forces," he said, "you ought to know what you want that force to do. You can't kind of say, 'Go out and pacify the entire countryside.' There has got to be a more specific definition of exactly what you want that force to accomplish. In Grenada the objective was very clear. . . ." He paused for a moment, and then he continued: "But when I hearken back to Vietnam, I have never been able to find anywhere where we have been able to clearly define in precise terms what the ultimate objectives of our military were.

"It is very important," he said, "that if we commit again to any kind of battle that we are sure we understand the ramifications of what happens if we *do* accomplish our objectives. It is conceivable that we could want to demonstrate our resolve in an area, but be unable to arrive at a set of military objectives that would satisfactorily accomplish them. And if that's the case, then you should not commit the military. There may be other ways to do it. . . . We should not just go ahead and throw them in 'to show our resolve' because it could be that we end up losing, failing in our initial objective, which was to show resolve."

III

It is an indication of General H. Norman Schwarzkopf's thoughtfulness and thoroughness that five days before Saddam Hussein invaded Kuwait, he and his U.S. Central Command staff had run an exercise predicated on that very scenario.

When we spoke on February 16 I asked him how the reality of Operation Desert Storm has differed from the war game plan. "At that time," he said, "Iraq had an extremely large military force—some said the fourth largest, others the sixth depending on how you want to count it. And we gave them credit for being ten feet tall and sometimes twenty feet tall in certain areas. The reality that has surprised us probably more than any other is that they're nowhere near as tough as we gave them credit. You know how I feel about military operations: never underestimate your enemy. It goes right back to the mistake we made in Grenada. . . . I never underestimate the enemy after that experience. I look at his capabilities and assume he has them until we find out differently."

Unlike in Vietnam, the military objectives in the Gulf are clearly defined: if the Iraqi forces do not withdraw from Kuwait, the coalition forces are to eject them. "One of the reasons why we are pursuing the battle the way we are is because it's very important we understand that we don't want to win the war and lose the peace. That's why we're in this coalition. That's why the rules of engagement we have are such. That's why what we are trying to accomplish is, I would say, limited in objective rather than unlimited from the standpoint of wreaking mass destruction upon the entire nation of Iraq."

I asked the general about Iraq's Revolutionary Command Council statement of February 15 expressing a willingness to discuss its withdrawal from Kuwait if numerous conditions of its own were met. Schwarzkopf responded, "The only thing new in the offer was that for the first time since, I guess, the third of August, the 'W-word' was mentioned. That, to me, is the only significant thing that happened. I will freely admit, in the hearts of a lot of people around here there was a little bit of hope. A *lot* of hope. But also, based on the continuous series of lies we've heard out of Iraq and Saddam Hussein, there was so much skepticism here that I didn't allow myself to become overjoyed by this whole thing. And it pretty well turned out to be what I thought it would be: there were so many conditions attached that it wasn't any kind of offer at all. That doesn't say that deep in my heart we're not all hoping that this thing can be over and over very quickly. But at the present time we're just continuing to march as we've marched before." He added, "However, I am quite confident that if the Iraqis make an unconditional withdrawal from Kuwait—which is what the U.N. resolution called for, and that's what the president of the United States has said is our objective—I think in a heartbeat the war would stop."

Norm Schwarzkopf has been preparing for Operation Desert Storm command all his life. With him in Saudi Arabia is the 24th Infantry Division he formerly led. It is a mechanized division specifically designed for the sort of open terrain tank warfare it now faces. I asked him whether, if the war ended without him having the opportunity to utilize his ground forces, he would be disappointed.

"Not in the least!" he said vehemently. "I don't want to kill one more American! I don't want to see one more American die—be it from an accident or from battle. There's no bloodlust on the part of myself or anybody else around here. What we want to do is to accomplish the objectives of this whole thing, get it over as quickly as we can, and get back home. And, I tell you, that's the attitude of everybody from the top general down to the lowest private."

His response made me think of the soldiers in that previous war and how often that phrase about getting it over as quickly as possible and getting back home surfaced in their letters from Vietnam. There is one big difference, though: "The troops' morale over here is very, very high," Schwarzkopf told me. "They feel good about what they're doing over here. There's absolutely no question but that the reason why they feel that way is because they know they have the support of the overwhelming majority of the American people. . . . And, of course, feeling good about themselves helps them to do their job better and it helps them to put up with all the suffering they've had to put up with."

After we had hung up I rooted out the parcel Schwarzkopf had sent me after I saw him at Fort Stewart seven years before. Among its contents, I remembered, was a bound series of lectures on generalship given as part of an Art of War Colloquium held at the U.S. Army War College at Carlisle Barracks, Pennsylvania. The collection opened with the following quote from an A. von Bogulawski:

> For what art can surpass that of the general—an art which deals not with dead matter but with living beings, who are subject to every impression of the moment, such as fear, precipitation, exhaustion—in short, to every human passion and excitement. The general not only has to reckon with unknown quantities, such as time, weather, accidents of all kinds, but he has before him one who seeks to disturb

and frustrate his plans and labours in every way; and at the same time this man, upon whom all eyes are directed, feels upon his mind the weight of responsibility not only for the lives and honor of hundreds of thousands, but even for the welfare and existence of his country.

In a recent *Washington Post* interview Schwarzkopf said, "Every waking and sleeping moment, my nightmare is the fact that I will ¦ an order that will cause countless number. human beings to lose their lives. I don't want my troops to die. I don't want my troops to be maimed. It's an intensely personal, emotional thing for me. Any decision you have to make that involves the loss of human life is nothing you do lightly. I agonize over it."

I believe him.

V  FOCUS: VIETNAM AND ITS AFTERMATH

Few other episodes in American history have been as painful, or as divisive, as the Vietnam War. Begun in the early 1960s as a popular police action, the war quickly escalated into a major conflict. At its peak, the war involved over a half-million American soldiers; in the end, it cost the lives of more than 50,000. The war provoked massive protests at home, including the 1969 tragedy at Kent State University, in which four students were killed by National Guardsmen.

Two decades later, Vietnam still casts its spell. Soldiers and civilians alike cannot help but react to events abroad with the Vietnam experience clearly in mind. And although President George Bush suggested after the Persian Gulf War that the nation had at last shaken off the "Vietnam syndrome," the lessons of Vietnam still help to shape our understanding of that conflict as well.

The following three selections present different perspectives on the difficult questions raised by American military intervention around the world. In the first two selections, the journalists Hendrik Hertzberg and Fred Barnes—writing on the tenth anniversary of the end of the war—debate the lessons of Vietnam. Hertzberg presents a classic argument against the war; Barnes, who opposed the war at the time, explains why he changed his mind. In the third selection, written just after the conclusion of the Gulf War, the journalist R. W. Apple draws some new lessons.

Questions

1. What are the lessons of Vietnam? Consider the lessons as applied to military strategy, political responsibility, public opinion and foreign policy, and America's proper role in the world in the 1990s.

2. Does America's experience in the Persian Gulf War confirm or refute the lessons of Vietnam?

18.5 Why the War Was Immoral

Hendrik Hertzberg

Was the war in Vietnam wrong? Not just inadvisable, not just a costly mistake, but morally wrong? How one answers that depends partly, I guess, on how one experienced the war and the opposition to it. A few days ago, at the university where I'm spending a semester, I found myself deep in conversation with a tutor in the philosophy department, an intense, articulate man five or six years younger than I am. (I'm 41.) We were talking about our experiences in the antiwar movement—ten and 15 and nearly 20 years ago—and he said that when he looks back on that time he feels mostly a kind of angry regret. He had been a member of Students for a Democratic Society when SDS dropped its homegrown ideology of participatory democracy in favor of mindless Maoism; he had chanted, "Ho! Ho! Ho Chi Minh! NLF is gonna win!"; he had longed for the triumph of the forces of "liberation" not only in Vietnam but everywhere in the Third World and ultimately at home; he had spelled it Amerika and dismissed its political system—"bourgeois democracy"—as a hoax, a cover for racism and imperialism. When the war ended and Indochina vanished into blood-soaked totalitarianism (instead of the gentle egalitarianism he had expected), he was wrenchingly disillusioned. Gradually he discovered that the "revolutionary socialism" of the Third World is brutal, that the Soviet Union is armed and dangerous, that for all its flaws American democracy is the moral superior of any form of communism. "I was wrong, just totally wrong," he told me. Last year he voted for Reagan.

I was luckier. I happened to have been brought up in a political and moral atmosphere of left-wing anti-communism. Reared on Orwell, Gandhi, and Silone, it was no great trick for me to avoid the more blatant naïvetés of New Leftism, and thus also to avoid the subsequent disillusionments. I took my antiwar arguments from Theodore Draper, not Noam Chomsky; from *Commentary* (yes, *Commentary*) and *The New Republic*, not the *National Guardian* and *Monthly Review*. I was similarly lucky in my encounter with military service. Opposed to what was then still called the "Vietnam policy," yet not so fiercely opposed as to be willing to risk prison, and too straight to dodge the draft, I signed up at the end of 1966 for a three-year hitch in the Navy. I asked to be sent to Vietnam, figuring a desk job in Saigon would be interesting without being unduly risky, but was sent—catch-22—to a sleepy shore billet in New York instead. Two years later I *was* ordered to Vietnam (desk job in Da Nang); but by then my antiwar convictions had grown so strong I preferred jail to further military service, and I announced my intention to refuse the orders. I hoped for antiwar martyrdom; instead, quite by chance, a medical difficulty developed, and I was hastily mustered out. I'd managed to have it both ways: veteran (sort of), and resister (in a way). In the Navy and after, I campaigned for Bobby Kennedy and Allard Lowenstein and other antiwar politicians; went on all the marches; hung around the office of a lively little pacifist weekly, *Win*, whose editor had two stickers on the bumper of his Volkswagen: US OUT OF VIETNAM and RUSSIA OUT OF LATVIA. But I didn't join any of what the inimitable Norman Podhoretz calls (in *Why We Were in Vietnam*) "the three main currents of the 'antiwar' movement": pro-Communist, anti-anti-Communist, and anti-American. I guess that I (along with more prominent opponents of the war, such as Podhoretz himself) must have joined one of the non-main currents. Perhaps it was the current that cheered when Norman Thomas, whom I had been taught to revere and who never disappointed, advised the movement to wash the flag, not burn it.

It's no surprise that the differences over

Vietnam, rooted as they are in such different experiences, persist in the form of different histories remembered, different lessons learned. The war turned my tutor friend into a "communist" and me into a pacifist. A decade later, neither of us is what we were. We are merely a Republican and a Democrat, passing the time in earnest conversation. And I still think the war was immoral. So when my tutor friend told me the story of his days in the movement, I readily agreed with him that he had been wrong. "It could have been worse, though," I added. "You could have *supported* the war."

There were always two main arguments in favor of the war, the geopolitical and the "moral." The war's aftermath has undermined the first argument, but has seemingly strengthened the second. For the aftermath proved to be at once worse than the war's opponents had predicted and better than its supporters had feared—worse for the Indochinese, better for everyone else.

The geopolitical argument took many forms, some of which lay in ruins long before the war ended. The notion that the war was needed to stop Sino-Soviet expansionism, for example, had become an embarrassment well before Nixon arrived in Peking. So had the notion that the war was needed to convince the Chinese to abandon revolution and follow the Soviet example of peaceful coexistence.

The most persistent form of the geopolitical argument was the domino theory. Some of the war's retrospective defenders maintain that the fall of Cambodia and Laos proves that the theory was correct. Not so. Cambodia and Laos were Vietnam battlefields long before the Americans arrived, and by the end the three countries became one domino. Anyway, the domino theory always encompassed more than Indochina. Even in its most ardent version it envisaged the loss of all Southeast Asia, which is to say Thailand, Burma, and Malaysia. And in its more grandiose form it predicted that Indonesia, India, Australia, and Hawaii would topple too. None of this has happened; on the contrary, the American position in Asia and the Pacific is stronger now than it was before 1975. S troubles as do exist there, such as instability the Philippines, cannot remotely be traced to the defeat in Vietnam.

A milder corollary to the domino theory was the argument from will: we needed to go on fighting in Vietnam in order to demonstrate our resolve and reliability. This argument implicitly recognized that the fate of Vietnam was, by itself, peripheral to the national security of the United States; it shifted the ground of discussion from the geopolitics of the map to the geopolitics of the soul. Yes, their will to rid their country of foreigners was stronger than our will to demonstrate our will; but by any reasonable standard, our resolve was strong. We did far, far more than enough to meet our treaty obligations, demonstrate our will, and prove our reliability. We financed a quarter of a century of war in Vietnam. We fought there in strength for ten years—longer than we fought in World War I, in World War II, or in Korea, longer than in all of them put together. Fifty-eight thousand American soldiers were killed. We said we would fight, therefore we must fight: at many a juncture along the way that logic seemed compelling. But it was not a compelling reason to fight forever. Our guarantees were not worthless. It was the war that was worthless.

The importance of the collapse of the domino theory to the debate over the war's morality is that the theory, if correct, could arguably have justified an enormous degree of suffering and death. What if it had really been true that the loss of Vietnam would doom Australia, India, Hawaii, and the rest to war followed by Communist totalitarianism? A firm moral case can be made that preventing the certain devastation and enslavement of many countries can justify the destruction, even the total destruction, of one. "We had to destroy this village in order to save a hundred villages" is a defensible proposition. But "we had to destroy this village in order to save it" is a moral absurdity. When the domino theory fell, so, domino-like, did one of the moral props of the war.

We are left, then, with the "moral case," as

Podhoretz calls it—the view that the war was moral because it was an attempt to save South Vietnam from Communism. My tutor friend, back in his SDS days, did not think this a moral aim, would not have thought it a moral aim even if it could have been achieved without cost. In thinking these things he made a moral error, and he is right to rue it. Even those of us who took the view that it did not make much difference to the South Vietnamese whether they lived under Communism or under the Saigon regime made a moral error. Take away the war and the Saigon regime, with all its noisy corruption and repressiveness, was orally preferable to the totalitarian silence that now rules, with scarcely less corruption, in Ho Chi Minh City. Except that you can't take away the war.

The overwhelming majority of those who opposed the war did not in any case reject the aim of saving South Vietnam from Communism. And to the extent that the war was fought for this aim it was fought for a moral aim. But this says no more than that the war was fought with good intentions rather than evil ones, which is saying very little. If good intentions were enough, there would be no neoconservatives.

In war the moral question is always the same: does the end justify the means? The calculations are necessarily ugly, but they are unavoidable. Ten years ago the choice was not between a Communist South Vietnam and a non-Communist one. It was between a Communist South Vietnam on the one hand, and the terrible cost of keeping South Vietnam non-Communist on the other. The aftermath of the war—the boat people, the "reeducation" camps, above all the unimaginable horror that engulfed Cambodia—has made the "moral case," the argument that the war was worth fighting solely for the sake of the people of Indochina, seem much more plausible than it did at the time. But for the "moral case" to be clinched, the war must be judged to have been winnable—winnable, moreover, at a lower cost

in suffering and death than the cost of the Communist victory.

The retrospective defenders of the war must argue that the war could have been won, and their arguments mostly take the form of "if only." If only the bombers had hit "worthwhile targets" on their 1,000 sorties a day, says the military analyst Edward Luttwak in a current *Harper's* symposium, it "would have ended the war in a day." If only Lyndon Johnson had rallied the country behind the war as a moral imperative, writes Podhoretz in his Vietnam book, then the American people would have remained steadfast. If only the United States had followed a purposeful military strategy, argues Harry G. Summers in *On Strategy: A Critical Analysis of the Vietnam War*, then the conditions for a successful South Vietnamese war against the Vietcong might have been created. If only Congress hadn't voted down supplementary military aid to the Saigon government in 1975, contends Richard Nixon in his new book, *No More Vietnams*, then everything might have turned out fine.

All of these arguments rest on the assumption that there was a point at which North Vietnam, having calculated that the actual costs of war were exceeding the prospective benefits of victory, would have stopped fighting. It seems clearer than ever today that there was no such point. Some people understood this at the time. Ten years ago, [the *New Republic*] published a special issue devoted to the end of the war. Richard Holbrooke, who had resigned in protest from the foreign service, and who later became an assistant secretary of state, began his essay with these words:

> For at least eight years it seemed reasonable to me to assume that sooner or later, no matter what we did in Vietnam, things would end badly for us. This feeling was not based on any desire to see us humiliated, or any feeling that the other side represented the forces of goodness and light; it just seemed that the only way to stave off an eventual Communist victory was with an open-ended, and therefore endless, ap-

plication of American firepower in support of the South Vietnamese regime. No matter how much force we were willing to use, this would not end the war, only prevent Saigon's defeat. And the human suffering would be bottomless. The war would go on until the North Vietnamese achieved their objectives.

Holbrooke's judgment has stood up well. "The essential reality of the struggle," wrote Stanley Karnow in *Vietnam: A History,* published in 1983, "was that the Communists, imbued with an almost fanatical sense of dedication to a reunified Vietnam under their control, saw the war against the United States and its South Vietnamese ally as the continuation of two thousand years of resistance to Chinese and later French rule. They were prepared to accept limitless casualties to attain their sacred objective. Ho Chi Minh, their leader, had made that calculation plain to the French as they braced for war in the late 1940s. 'You can kill ten of my men for every one I kill of yours,' he warned them, 'but even at those odds, you will lose and I will win.'" William Broyles, Jr., who fought in Vietnam 15 years ago as a Marine officer, and who recently went back for a visit during which he talked to hundreds of his former enemies, has a similar assessment. Writing in the April *Atlantic* he concludes, "Whatever the price of winning the war—twenty more years of fighting, another million dead, the destruction of Hanoi—the North Vietnamese were willing to pay it."

If the North Vietnamese were willing to accept limitless casualties, if they were willing to pay any price, then the war could not have been won except by the physical destruction of North Vietnam and the killing of a large proportion of its people. A million? Three million? Six million? The shrill accusation of some in the antiwar movement that the war was "genocidal" was not entirely without justice. Of course no American wanted to kill everybody in North Vietnam. Americans are not monsters. But Americans are not losers, either. Americans are winners. But the logic of winning in Vietnam

was inescapably the logic of genocide. We did not lose in Vietnam. We chose not to win. If our entry into the war had something to do with preserving our values, so did our exit from it.

Even Podhoretz, in his book on Vietnam, admits repeatedly that the war could not have been won. In the end, he writes, "The United Sates demonstrated that saving South Vietnam from Communism was not only beyond its reasonable military, political, and intellectual capabilities but that it was ultimately beyond its moral capabilities as well." Yes, it was beyond our moral capabilities—except that what he understands as a moral failure I understand as a moral success. It wasn't cowardice that finally impelled us to quit. It was conscience.

The old arguments for the war still walk among us, zombielike, in the form of the theory of the Vietnam syndrome, a term calculated to make the American people's desire to avoid another Vietnam sound pathological rather than prudent. Of course, if the war did result in a syndrome, if it did result in a paralysis of American will and so forth, that is hardly an argument that the war was a good idea. Nor do the follies of parts of the antiwar movement somehow vindicate the war. On the contrary, the antiwar movement was created by the war. Is it really so surprising that this unending, unwinnable war became a machine for producing irrationality, hysteria, and rage? The conservatives' anger at the antiwar movement is misplaced.

The actual consequences of this so-called syndrome are highly problematic. We "lost" Iran after Vietnam, but we "lost" Cuba before it. A more precise effect of the war upon the American political psyche was diagnosed in 1971 by Nathan Glazer, who wrote a famous *Commentary* article titled "Vietnam: The Case for Immediate Withdrawal" that "the experience of Vietnam has turned the American people into haters of war." That seems exactly right. By August 1964, 300 Americans had been killed and 1,000 wounded in Vietnam. Yet there were only a half-dozen American correspondents reporting on the war. (Meanwhile President Johnson was running as the peace candidate, with the support of SDS.) Such relative public indifference to a war with American deaths running into the hundreds would be unthinkable today. It took years for any significant movement of protest to develop against the Vietnam War. The premises of U.S. involvement were scarcely questioned for the first 15 years. But if the Reagan administration launches an invasion of Nicaragua today, thousands of church people are ready to commit civil disobedience tomorrow. And before giving its support to the new war, the public would insist on a full and prompt discussion of its aims, purposes, and prospects—not out of cynicism or morbid suspicion, but out of a healthy, skeptical, democratic spirit of self-government. War can sometimes be a necessity, but is always to be abhorred. Yes, we were right to oppose the Vietnam War, all of us. Even my friend the Reagan-voting ex-SDSer. Even Norman Podhoretz.

18.6 My Change of Heart

Fred Barnes

I can't tell you what I was doing when I heard that President John F. Kennedy had been shot, but I remember exactly where I was the day Vietnam fell. Or at least the day after. I was sitting in Kay's coffee shop near the White House reading *The New York Times*. Its coverage of the events in Vietnam was thorough that day, and I read every word. After an hour or so, a thought suddenly occurred to me, namely that the Communist victory in Vietnam was a very, very bad thing—indeed, the worst of all possible fates for Vietnam. And I recalled, from having read *Cold Friday* many years before, the apocalyptic phrase Whittaker Chambers had used to characterize the triumph of communism. "The great nightfall," he called it.

Now, the thought that Vietnam would suffer horrendously under communism was neither profound nor original; people whose views I despised, like George Meany and Joseph Alsop, had been saying this for years. But for me, at any rate, it was new. I had opposed the American effort in Vietnam. My opposition wasn't as passionate as that of the Berrigan brothers or Tom Hayden, but it was strong enough. I participated in the 1967 march on the Pentagon in which Norman Mailer got arrested (I didn't). A year or two later, I arranged for an antiwar group to use my proxy for a few shares of Boeing stock I owned so it could denounce the company at a stockholders' meeting. I voted for the most fervently antiwar candidates, which meant Dick Gregory in 1968 and George McGovern in 1972.

And I bought the conventional wisdom of the day. During a long evening in 1966, I sought to persuade a distant cousin that the whole struggle in Vietnam was a civil war. He was an Army captain, a West Pointer, and he had spent a year as a military adviser in Vietnam. He was unconvinced; I was adamant. They're all Vietnamese, the government troops and the Vietcong, aren't they? That makes it a civil war that the United States has no business getting involved in. I pointed out that preserving the corrupt South Vietnamese government was not worth a single American life. I always cited the supposed suppression of Buddhism, the stifling of dissent and the practice—I must have read about this somewhere—of American troops routinely handing over Vietcong prisoners to South Vietnamese soldiers, who immediately executed the prisoners. But my root argument against the war was one of moral equivalence.

The government of South Vietnam was brutal and undemocratic. And although the Vietcong and its allies weren't pussycats, they surely couldn't be worse.

Well, I was wrong. There was something worse that could happen to Vietnam, to Indochina, than having American troops on the ground or a discredited government that was supported, financially and morally, by the United States. What is worse is what has happened. Why couldn't I foresee this at the time? For one thing, the horror of combat overshadowed everything else—Khe Sanh, Hué, the Tet offensive. As a reporter for *The Washington Star*, I wrote a piece about a young man from my hometown (Arlington, Virginia) who had been killed in Vietnam. His death seemed senseless, all the more so every time I read a newspaper story about corruption in South Vietnam. And various administrations in Washington never offered a compelling principle that justified military intervention. Ward off the Chicoms? That was preposterous. Save an embryonic democracy? Come on.

True, I was not alone in being so mistaken. Nearly everyone I knew thought the American policy in Vietnam was at best misguided. Millions of people opposed to the war voiced the same clichés I did. Yet now that these have proved to be illusory—now that we know about the holocaust in Cambodia and "reeducation" camps in Vietnam and the boat people and the refusal of the North Vietnamese to give the South Vietnamese a role in their own government—only a handful of politicians have second-guessed the antiwar position. It is as if opposing the war was an end in itself, something laudable regardless of what transpired in its aftermath.

No group has been less reflective than the press. When I was on a fellowship at Harvard University in the late seventies, a prominent American reporter, Richard Dudman of the *St. Louis Post-Dispatch*, delivered a talk there on his impressions of Vietnam under communism. He'd just returned from a tour, and he was cautiously enthusiastic. The country was poor but on the move. As I recall it, he said he'd been taken to a reeducation camp, and surprisingly enough the inmates didn't appear too unhappy over their imprisonment. They were coming around, starting to accept the new system.

During the war, American press coverage tended to substantiate antiwar clichés. One reason was access; reporters had access to American officials and soldiers, not to Vietcong or North Vietnamese ones. My Lai, where 170-odd civilians were killed by U.S. troops, became a household word; Hué, where the Vietcong murdered 3,000 civilians, didn't. Repression and corruption and chaos in South Vietnam were well covered; the same among the Vietcong and North Vietnamese wasn't. For all its investigative prowess, the press never uncovered the fundamental nature of the Vietcong as a wholly owned subsidiary of North Vietnam.

But the press's most egregious error was the miscoverage of the 1968 Tet offensive. It was treated as a breathtaking defeat for the South Vietnamese and Americans, an indication of the shocking power of the Vietcong. This, we now know, was not the real story. In truth, the Vietcong suffered a disastrous defeat during Tet, just as General William Westmoreland claimed. One journalist who was in Saigon at the time, Peter Braestrup, has shown in his two-volume study *Big Story* just how the press blew the Tet story.

You don't hear many apologies, though. Certainly not from Walter Cronkite, whose fresh-from-Vietnam report on Tet that the war was unwinnable shocked President Johnson and led him to believe that the American people were fed up with the war. "All that optimism, and here were the Vietcong right in the city of Saigon," Cronkite told *Newsweek* recently. "You know, that was what kind of turned so many of us at that point into saying: 'Come on, now. This is the end. Stop it.'" If Walter Cronkite has learned nothing, neither has his former colleague Harry Reasoner. "I am not a dupe," Reasoner told Stephen Lesher, author of *Media Unbound*. " . . . But to say that this was somehow an American cum South Vietnamese victory that the press concealed, I think is arrant nonsense." It isn't concealment the press has been accused of, but of misreporting the pivotal military engagement of the war. Reasoner said of those who made this charge, "They're wrong."

Reasoner's act of denial is small compared to that of leaders of the antiwar movement. Who among them has acknowledged the torture of American POWs in North Vietnam, which was an early indication of how the North Vietnamese might act once ensconced in Saigon? Who among them has been willing to suggest that the murder of a million or more Cambodians by the Khmer Rouge might have been averted if American military force had not been removed from Indochina? If any of them spoke out this way, I missed it. But I did hear Noam Chomsky seek to prove the Cambodian genocide hadn't happened.

In a forum on Vietnam in the April issue of *Harper's*, Peter Marin, billed as "a novelist and essayist who has written on the moral and cultural issues raised by the Vietnam war," took another tack when conservative George Gilder declared the holocaust in Cambodia is "what happens when a country is lost to communism." Marin objected: "That's much too simple

a view. The effects of Vietnam are more tragic, and less ideological, than that. Many Americans are smart enough to realize that while our withdrawal from Vietnam had certain tragic consequences, our presence, had we remained there, would have led to a different, and equally tragic, set of consequences." Just as tragic as the mountains of corpses in Cambodia and the thousands upon thousands of Vietnamese boat people swallowed by the South China Sea? That is inconceivable, and it is also unknowable.

You know you're a repentant dove when you start agreeing with Ronald Reagan on Vietnam. I was covering his presidential campaign for the Baltimore *Sun* in August 1980 when Reagan told the Veterans of Foreign Wars convention that American involvement in Vietnam had been "a noble cause." Naturally, this prompted reporters covering Reagan to write that he had committed a gaffe. I didn't quite see it that way. If Reagan meant that the United States intervened despite having little to gain except the containment of communist expansion and the protection of countries that might evolve into democracies some day, I'd say he was just about right. But noble or not, the American effort was better than the alternative.

18.7 Done. A Short, Persuasive Lesson in Warfare

R. W. Apple

The 42-day war in the Persian Gulf—Gen. H. Norman Schwarzkopf's hit-hard, hurry-up, high-tech, hyper-successful campaign to savage Iraq's military and oust it from Kuwait—was a study in lessons learned.

In a political, military and especially a psychological sense, it drew a line beneath the hauntingly inconclusive Vietnam tragedy. The United States will not soon forget its sins and

humiliations in Southeast Asia a generation ago, but it has learned from them, and as President Bush exulted . . . , "By God, we've kicked the Vietnam syndrome once and for all."

The list of lessons is long, but start with this trio.

- Never go to war before insuring domestic consensus and establishing international support. Lyndon B. Johnson never managed to do either; George Bush did both, with a master's touch. The President coaxed Congress to the point of backing war—not by much, but by enough to carry him through a few weeks or a few months—and he and his Secretary of State, James A. Baker 3d, built and maintained an international coalition that cut across lines of economic, religious, political, ideological, regional and even personal conflict. They said it couldn't last, but it did.

The First Principle

- Never go to war without a clear objective. Lieut. Gen. Thomas Kelly, the avuncular oracle of the Pentagon these past weeks, called it "the first principle of war"—a target, clearly designated and steadfastly lit by the politicians, that the generals and admirals could take a bead on. Mr. Bush must have said five times a day for six months that Saddam Hussein had to leave Kuwait, without conditions, to satisy the United States. No such goal was ever convincingly articulated for the Vietnam adventure.

- Take no half measures. Mr. Bush gave his commanders the troops they said they needed, right away, instead of feeding them in slowly. He granted no sanctuaries to the enemy. He resisted the inevitable calls for a cease-fire until he judged the job done, lest he give the Iraqis a chance to catch their breath, rearm and fight again. Those three decisions enabled General Schwarzkopf to develop and execute a strategy that placed the heaviest fighting squarely on President Saddam Hussein's own territory, brought American firepower to bear all at once and kept it there to do the job. The result was clearest, perhaps, in the casualty figures— the staggering gap between the 89 Americans known to have been killed and the tens of thousands of Iraqis dead on the battlefield as well as even vaster numbers taken prisoner.

There were old lessons, too, left over from other wars in other decades, other centuries, but no less apt for that. Here are seven:

- Deception can be worth a dozen divisions. General Schwarzkopf assembled all the paraphernalia and manpower for amphibious operations, practiced amphibious operations and talked about amphibious operations. But they were never part of his basic plan. He fooled his foe into wasting thousands of men and guns. On an elaborate battle model of Kuwait City discovered in a school on Thursday, every Iraqi gun and troop unit in the region of the capital faced the sea, like the guns of Singapore during World War II. They were of little use in combating invaders coming from other directions.

- Without air cover, tanks are tin gasoline cans, just waiting to blow up. When the Luftwaffe could no longer protect him, Rommel lost in North Africa; when the clouds that had protected him finally parted, von Rundstedt lost the Battle of the Bulge; with his air force destroyed or dispersed and his attack helicopters—Soviet, French and German—mysteriously uninvolved, Mr. Hussein could do nothing to protect his T-72's and T-62's from American tanks and, especially, the terrifying Hellfire missiles fired by the army's Apache helicopters and the equally deadly Mavericks fired by A-10 Warthog attack planes flown by the Air Force.

- In the desert, supply is everything. Armies can live off the land to a degree, in many parts of the world, but not in the sands of Arabia, where nature is an implacable enemy. Again, air supremacy made the difference. It meant American logistics specialists, under a tough general from Pennsylvania named Gus Pagonis, could move mountains, and allied forces had 10 of everything, thousands of miles from home; it meant many front-line Iraqi troops had so little they ate grass and hoarded cups of rainwater.

Modern weapons become obsolete terrifyingly quickly, which is why maintaining modern armed forces costs so much. For all the oil wealth he squandered on arms, Saddam Hussein went to war against the United States—cruise missiles, Stealth bombers, electronic countermeasures and all—with an air-defense system that was a generation or two out of date.

Men matter as much as machines, and there the Iraqi forces were outclassed in two ways. One was training, skill, sheer ability. "Not everything depends on the quality of the technology," said Nikolai Kutsenko, a ranking military planner in the Soviet Union, which supplied so much of Iraq's best equipment. "More depends on the professional training of those who use and service it, and both, in the Iraqi Army, left much to be desired."

So did the troops' morale, a second key area of deficiency. For that, General Schwarzkopf blamed a leadership "so uncaring that in the end they could keep them there only at the point of a gun."

If you can't communicate, you can't command. Battlefield evidence collected by Marines showed chemical weapons ready for use, but orders never came from the top. And the total lack of coordination between squadrons of tanks and between tanks and artillery in the big battle that ended the war convinced American armored commanders that their adversaries were operating with nothing approaching adequate radio links between units.

- Get around him, if you can, and hit him from the flank or the rear, rather than marching into his strength. Talking military history long before he launched last week's ground offensive, General Schwarzkopf often dwelt on Cannae, the epic battle in the heel of the Italian boot in which Hannibal perfected the double envelopment. The American commander used a single envelopment to equally good effect, forcing the Republican Guards, potential battle-winners, to fight on his ground at a time of his choosing.

In Vietnam, the United States overestimated its own power and prowess and underestimated that of the enemy. Here, it was just the opposite.

Saddam Hussein proved to be as full of folly on the battlefield as in the halls of diplomacy, relying on a Maginot line as easily flankable as the original, making his tanks vulnerable by digging them into the sand and robbing them of their mobility.

It proved impossible for a nation with the population of the Netherlands and the gross domestic product of Portugal even to dent a coalition that included the United States, Europe and two of the main Arab military powers.

On the other side of the line, the new, all-volunteer American military, with its new, smart weapons, proved formidable. Especially the Air Force, Naval air and Army air, which severed the enemy's logistical lifelines, scrambled his communications, blinded his reconnaissance eyes and finally killed his advance tanks, his last best hope of averting disaster.

As Col. Hal Hornburg, a top Air Force pilot, said, it took the grunts to apply the coup de grâce. It always does. But air power decided it.

VI ■ ISSUE AND DEBATE: CAN THE PRESIDENT WAGE WAR ALONE?

Who has the power to make war? The Constitution is unclear: Congress is given the power to declare war and to raise and support the armed forces, but the president is made the commander-in-chief of the armed forces. History is also unclear: the United States has fought in five declared wars, but Korea and Vietnam were never declared, and the Persian Gulf War was approved by Congress but without a formal declaration of war. A host of smaller conflicts, moreover, have been fought without congressional approval.

In 1973, Congress attempted to assert itself in the foreign policy field by passing the War Powers Resolution, which recognized the president's authority to send troops into situations involving hostilities or "imminent hostilities" but also stressed Congress's power to require that the troops be withdrawn within sixty days if the legislature so directed. The War Powers Act was passed over Richard M. Nixon's veto, and every president since has questioned its constitutionality; nevertheless, Presidents Bush and Reagan both sought congressional approval before undertaking major military missions.

In the following selections from the historic January 1991 debate over whether to authorize the use of force in the Persian Gulf, Senators Joseph Biden (Democrat, Delaware) and Jesse Helms (Republican, North Carolina) debate the meaning of the Constitution's ambivalence on the war power.

Question

1. Consider the Helms-Biden debate in terms of the Framers' view of the separation of powers (selections 2.2 through 2.4), and in terms of the historical material presented in selection 12.3. Which side seems to have the better of the historical arguments?

YES

18.8 Remarks on the Crisis in the Persian Gulf

Jesse Helms

Mr. President, there are certain occasions in the history of nations when the people are called upon to reaffirm the integrity of the national interest.

This is one of those occasions.

The President has dispatched over 400,000 American military personnel to the Persian Gulf to protect the national interest. We must support the President in the course he has laid out.

On August 27, 1787, the Constitutional Convention meeting in Philadelphia adopted without debate the words of article II, section

2, clause 1, that the President is "Commander in Chief of the Army and Navy of the United States . . ." He is also the head of the militia of the several States, if federalized.

Thus the Constitution made the President the only Commander in Chief of the Armed Forces of this Nation. The President is therefore obligated to protect the interests of the United States, to defend the rights of its citizenry, and to preserve the national security by whatever means are necessary.

Thirteen years later, at the beginning of the second decade of the Constitutional Republic, Congressman John Marshall, before he was appointed Chief Justice, declared on the floor of the House of Representatives that "the President is the sole organ of the Nation in its external relations, and its sole representative with foreign nations."

There is no historical evidence that Chief Justice Marshall ever changed his mind. The phrase "sole organ of the Nation in its external relations" was emphatically restated by the U.S. Supreme Court in 1936 (U.S. versus Curtiss Wright Corp.). This view has never been repudiated by the Court.

On the other hand the Constitution fails to provide for 535 other Commanders in Chief.

Article III, section 8, clauses 11–16, specifically enumerate the war powers of the Congress in the Constitution. Congress is given the power: First, to declare war; second, to raise and support armies; third, to provide and maintain a navy; fourth, to make laws regulating the Armed Forces; and fifth, to support the militia of the Federal States. These specific powers encompass the sole authority of the U.S. Congress with regard to war.

Thus Congress can in no way limit or authorize the President's constitutional authority as Commander in Chief. Congress has attempted to do that in the War Powers Act, an act which I strongly opposed at the time of its passage in 1973, and which no Chief Executive has ever accepted; but I believe that the War Powers Act is plainly unconstitutional. I have consulted many distinguished constitutional authorities on this point, but most especially our late distinguished colleague, Senator Sam Ervin of North Carolina. There were 18 of us who voted against the War Powers Act, and now only Senator Thurmond and I remain in the Senate. Nor can Congress authorize or restrict the President's war power by any of the resolutions which have been proposed or circulated in the past few days.

In the short time that the Convention spent debating the subject, the Founders made a careful distinction between making war and declaring war. James Madison and Elbridge Gerry were responsible for enlarging the Presidential prerogative to enable the Chief Executive to meet the demands of national security.

As Madison warned in Federalist No. 48, encroachments by one branch upon another branch will upset the delicate balance of the tripartite constitutional system. Thus, it is exceedingly important to hold the branches to their intended functions with respect to the conduct of American foreign relations.

What the Framers originally intended, Mr. President, was to make a careful distinction between declaring war and making war. The Constitution is silent on whether the President is required to make war after Congress declares war; at the same time, it is silent on whether the President is prohibited from making war if Congress has not declared war. Clearly, common sense requires that the President seek the agreement and cooperation of Congress in any endeavor that commits the lives and fortunes of the American people. And the President has done so.

The powers to declare and make war are inherent powers of national sovereignty. The President has welcomed the cooperation of the United Nations and our allies in the United Nations who have supported us with diplomacy and by conducting troops. But the U.S. Constitution is superior to any obligations which we may or may not have undertaken by assenting to the U.N. Charter. No treaty can compel us, either in fact or in intention, to set aside any provision of the U.S. Constitution. The power to declare and make war therefore remains with the United States, and has not been delegated to the United Nations.

The U.N. resolutions, therefore, provide a framework for U.S. diplomacy, ratifying the individual bilateral relationships which the United States has with each of the members separately. They are a sign or symbol of the international support and common agreement which the President has organized through his leadership, merely ratifying the assent of our allies to our broad policy. There is nothing in them which require the President or the U.S. Congress to perform any acts.

So the burden falls upon Congress, and it falls upon this body to demonstrate the solidarity which the Nation needs in time of crisis. The President's leadership has been superb. His toughness and courage have called upon a moral strength in the Nation which skeptics said no longer existed. Unless these virtues are nourished and cherished, this Nation, as a nation, will disappear from the field of history.

There are, of course, practical problems. There are sacrifices that will be required. There will be a price to pay. But there will be overwhelming practical problems, sacrifices not of our choosing, and prices too high to pay if we do not follow the course which the President has outlined.

Of course, there is a role for constructive criticism. But the naysayers who deny our national interest, who speak for delay when they really mean never, and who are more interested in narrow political advantage than in the national advantage—there is no room for these if the inner heart and soul of our Nation is to flourish.

So let us get down to the particulars.

Secretary [of State James] Baker's 7-hour meeting in Geneva made clear that President Bush and Secretary Baker have exhausted every reasonable diplomatic effort to resolve the crisis in Kuwait. The Iraqi refusal even to receive the President's letter in a diplomatic forum demonstrates a complete lack of good faith in the peace process.

It is now time for the American people to rally around the President, and support the 400,000 American troops now poised in the gulf. These 400,000 American troops in the Persian Gulf are in a situation fraught with danger.

For the past 5 months the American people have been subjected to a cacophony of carping criticism and second-guessing that, intentional or not, has persuaded Saddam Hussein that the will of the American people is weak when vital principles are at stake. The only hope for avoiding hostilities—if there is a hope—is for Saddam Hussein to be convinced beyond a doubt that the American people stand behind their President.

Politics must stop at the water's edge. This is no time for posturing politicians to strut across the TV screens, presuming to second-guess the Commander in Chief. I have not agreed with all aspects of the President's program—for example, I felt that more support by our allies should have been nailed down at the outset—but I communicated my concerns to him privately. I have issued no press releases, nor have I consented to go on television to differ with the President. Now that the critical moment has arrived, it is time for all of us to stand united behind him.

On August 8, in response to the request by Saudi Arabia, the President sent United States troops to the gulf. The President stated four goals:

First, the immediate and unconditional withdrawal of Iraqi forces from Kuwait;

Second, the restoration of the legitimate government of Kuwait;

Third, the security and stability of the Persian Gulf; and

Fourth, the protection of the lives of American citizens abroad.

All four of these goals are directly related to the national interest of the United States. The principle of national sovereignty is the very basis of our independence and national survival. It follows from the rule of national sovereignty that legitimate governments have the right not to be disturbed by foreign aggression. These principles are of particular importance to the United States when the victim whose sovereignty is violated is a country such as Kuwait, which has a key role in economic and diplomatic relationships with the United States.

President Bush is to be commended. He has not deviated from his original purposes. His forthright stand has protected American lives in Kuwait and Iraq. Moreover, he has demonstrated that we are willing and able to protect the security and stability of the Persian Gulf.

All Presidents in modern times have made the security and stability of the Persian Gulf a paramount interest of our foreign policy. Our interest is not, in the first place, economic. But the oil supplied by the gulf is indeed a major element in our own national security and stability. If we allow aggression to disrupt our relationships with friendly governments, the strength and independence of the United States is threatened.

The President's action in August was therefore action in the defense of the Nation. Presidents have taken similar actions 216 times, solely on their constitutional authority as Commander in Chief. When U.S. troops are sent abroad in defense of the Nation against specific challenges to our national sovereignty and independence, this Senator believes that the issues involved are too important for public squabbling.

Some have argued that the sanctions imposed upon Iraq must be given time to work. They have already worked. They have demonstrated that the whole world is standing together against the aggression of Saddam Hussein. The world does not turn upon economic issues alone, and it is difficult to imagine that a tyrant who has killed 500,000 of his own people for political reasons will be persuaded ultimately by an an economic squeeze. Besides, Saddam Hussein has stolen almost $7 billion in gold and cash from the Kuwait central bank, and he has the economic cushion to resist the squeeze.

The U.S. Constitution was carefully crafted to allow much room for judgment. And in matters of war, the power to declare war does indeed lie with Congress. Nobody, nobody disputes that. But Congress has used that power only five times. On the other hand, the power to make war clearly belongs to the Commander in Chief, and we do not have but one Commander in Chief at a time.

The President has a duty to seek the support of Congress, and he has done that. I have sat in on endless meetings since this crisis began. But the Congress has a duty to close ranks and abandon partisanship, just as it did 50 years ago when another tyrant threatened the freedom and security of the world.

NO

18.9 Remarks on the Crisis in the Persian Gulf

Joseph Biden

We are here today because our Constitution, a document written by men who shed blood to free this land from tyranny of any one individual, commands the Congress to decide the gravest question any country faces: Should it go to war? Let there be no mistake about it, Mr. President, this is a question which the Congress—and only the Congress—can answer.

On this point the Constitution is as clear as it is plain. While article II of the Constitution gives the President the power to command our troops, article I of the Constitution commits to Congress—and Congress alone—the power to decide if this Nation will go to war. The Framers of our Constitution took great pains to ensure that the Government they established for us would differ from the rule of the British monarchs. They knew first-hand of the consequences of leaving the choice between war and peace to one man.

In England, the king alone could decide to take a nation to war. But in America, the Federalist Papers tell us this power "by the Constitution appertains to the legislature."

As Framer James Wilson assured those who feared the President's military power when they gathered to vote on the Constitution: "It will not be in the power of any single man to invoke us in such distress for the important power of declaring war is vested in the legislature at large."

In light of this, Mr. President, it seems almost impossible to believe we are having a serious argument in this country today about whether, under the Constitution, the President alone can take the Nation to war. The Constitution's language says that the war power rests with the Congress, and from James Madison to John Marshall, the Constitution's fathers all understood this to be a key principle of the Republic.

Lest anyone in this body or anyone listening wonder why I am raising this question—since we will soon vote on a resolution authorizing the use of force—I am raising it because the President continues to insist he does not need the will of the people, spoken through the Congress as envisioned by the Constitution, to decide whether or not to go to war. I assume that means he would believe he had the constitutional authority even if we vote down a resolution authorizing him to use force. Whether he would politically do that or not is another question. But at least it should be somewhere on the record that there is ample evidence, constitutional scholarship to suggest that he has no such authority.

On Tuesday, [January 8, 1991], President Bush asked this Congress to debate and decide whether to take the Nation to war. Unfortunately, the President stopped short of abandoning his previous claim that he has the power, acting alone, to start a war. His Secretary of Defense has said, "We do not believe that the President requires any additional authorization from the Congress before committing U.S. forces to achieve our objectives in the gulf."

And his Secretary of State has said, "The President has the right as a matter of practice and principle to initiate military action."

Just yesterday, as I mentioned earlier, the President himself said that he alone has the constitutional authority to initiate war.

To put it simply, these views are at odds with the Constitution. They may accurately describe the power of leaders of other countries,

© Kirk/*Toledo Blade*/Rothco.

but they do not describe the power of the President of the United States.

As one of the Framers said at the Constitutional Convention in 1787, and as he would say, I suspect, today, if he could hear the Secretaries of State and Defense, "I never expected to hear in a Republic a motion to empower the Executive alone to declare war."

Yes, the President is the Commander in Chief. But in the Framers' view, according to Alexander Hamilton, this amounts to, "nothing more than the supreme command and direction of the military and naval force." In short, the Congress decides whether to make war. And the President decides how to do so.

The meaning of the Constitution in this case is clear, direct, and indisputable.

Before President Bush can launch an offensive action of 400,000 troops—by anybody's standard a war—he must obtain a congressional authorization or declaration. It need not be a formal declaration of war, according to precedents and all the constitutional scholars, but it must be a clear, unambiguous authorization. To do less would be to flagrantly violate the very document that our troops are there sworn to uphold.

This has been my view since the President's first deployment of U.S. troops in early August. It is supported by the language of the Constitution, by the intentions of the Framers, and by the history of our Nation. And, I might add, most importantly, by the spirit of our democracy.

My view on the constitutional issue was strongly reinforced earlier this week when the Senate Judiciary Committee held the first congressional hearings to address the question of the President's authority under our Constitution to initiate military action against Iraq.

At our hearing we heard from distinguished constitutional scholars on the matter. Their testimony, I think, is enormously persuasive. In the words of former Attorney General Nicholas Katzenbach, "Unless the grant of section 8 is to be read out of the Constitution entirely, the President is obliged in the present circumstances to seek congressional approval for an attack to force Iraq out of Kuwait."

As Prof. Louis Henkin, perhaps the Nation's foremost expert in international law and the U.S. Constitution—and a supporter of the U.N. resolution against Iraq—told the committee, "The President has no authority under the

Constitution to take military action that would constitute going to war against Iraq unless he receives authorization from Congress by a clear and unambiguous indication in advance."

Professor Henkin's statements reinforce another important point. Congressional silence in this field cannot be interpreted as an assent to war. Under our Constitution, the President does not possess the power to launch a war unless the Congress stops him. That is not what it says. Rather, it says he has the power to command in a war only if the Congress chooses to launch one.

As Prof. William van Alstyne told the committee, the President "may not loose the dogs of war until the Congress affirmatively authorizes it. It is just that simple." As Prof. Harold Koh of Yale put it, "silence has a sound, and the sound is no."

Of course, I do not think the Congress should remain silent. That is why we are here today. Indeed, since last August [1990] I have been calling for full congressional debate and a vote on this matter, as my friend from Massachusetts and others have since that time as well.

This is not simply a constitutional requirement, but a political necessity. How can we remain silent on a great issue being debated around the country? How can the President contemplate initiating military action of this magnitude without the clearly expressed support of the American people through their elected representatives? Without that support, whatever policy the President chooses, through wisdom or folly, cannot possibly succeed.

The Framers knew this and that is why they delegated to us the power to choose between war and peace. The responsibility is awesome; the decision is difficult; and it is a choice some in Congress may prefer to avoid. But whatever our view on this ultimate decision, this is one point on which all should agree; the decision whether or not to go to war rests with the Congress. The overwhelming opinion of scholars and historians rest on this side; yet the administration and a handful of scholars reject this

constitutional command. I want to briefly address their arguments now.

The arguments for Presidential power fall into two categories: general and specific. The general arguments say that the President has the constitutional power to launch a military attack without congressional authorization under almost every conceivable circumstance, including this one.

The specific arguments rely on particular aspects of this crisis to establish Presidential authority. Let me consider them both in turn.

The most general argument for Presidential authority cites the President's power as Commander in Chief and notes that in our history, military force has been used over 200 times against foreign adversaries, and only five times with a declaration of war. That has been mentioned time and again here.

But upon examination of the record, as I have and I hope others will, of those over 200 instances—the record demonstrates that many of those 200 instances were not attacks against sovereign nations and, thus, war could not have been declared. Others were mostly minor police actions to protect American property or citizens living abroad, or others were sufficiently time urgent to fit under the rubric of the President's constitutional power to repel sudden attacks. Others were authorized by congressional enactments that served as de facto declarations of war, such as the Tonkin Gulf resolution.

To demonstrate the absurdity of this superficially appealing claim, let me give my colleagues one example of these 200 precedents being cited by the President.

In 1824, an American ship sent out a landing party to the Spanish possession of Cuba in pursuit of pirates. There could be no comparing pursuing pirates on the Spanish possession of Cuba by an American ship with what is going on today.

We have now deployed a major portion of our air, naval, and land forces to the region. The gulf standoff has persisted for months without significant military action. American hostages have been released. American diplomats can be evacuated.

Four hundred thousand Americans sit in the desert ready to launch an assault that would be vastly larger than D-day in its size and scope. If the Constitution does not require a declaration of war in this case, it is hard for me to imagine when it ever would apply.

In sum, our constitutional tradition does not support the President's view, but rather just the opposite, and throughout our history, American Presidents have acknowledged the proper division between their role and that of the Congress.

For example, when Thomas Jefferson considered launching a military assault on the Spanish, he wrote: "Considering that Congress alone is constitutionally invested with the power of changing our condition from peace to war, I have thought it my duty to await their authority for using force. The course belongs to Congress exclusively to yield or to deny."

President James Buchanan put it similarly: "Without the authority of Congress," he said, "the President cannot fire a hostile gun in any case except to repel attacks of any enemy."

Perhaps because they knew that history was against them, the President's advisers have also said that the circumstances of modern warfare are such that extensive debate cannot reasonably precede the use of military force, less the enemy be made aware of our intentions.

Thus, early on in this crisis, when I proposed a resolution authorizing the use of force under certain circumstances but requiring the President to return and ask Congress for the authority to initiate offensive action, Secretary of State Baker argued that if the President had to follow this approach, we would lose the element of surprise in our military planning.

That was on October 17, 1990. Yet 1 month later, the administration went to the U.N. Security Council, where an authorization for the use of force was debated and ultimately passed. What happened to the element of surprise? The longstanding claim that we cannot debate war in the modern age has been shown to be a red herring by the U.N. resolution.

This argument that we do not have time to debate this issue clearly, in this case, was specious from the outset. Moreover, the mere fact that submitting this question to the Congress is inconvenient does not in any way lessen the clarity of the constitutional command. As the Supreme Court has written, "The fact that a given procedure is efficient, convenient, and useful in facilitating functions of the Government will not save it if it is contrary to the Constitution. Convenience and efficiency are not the primary objectives—or the hallmarks—of a democratic government."

In sum, the general argument for Presidential authority to initiate war is profoundly misguided and deeply undemocratic. In the words again of Professor Henkin, this view is "without foundation in [constitutional] text, in original intent, or in our constitutional history."

Appendix

The Constitution
of the United States

Preamble

We the People of the United States, in Order to form a more perfect Union, establish Justice, insure domestic Tranquility, provide for the common defence, promote the general Welfare, and secure the Blessings of Liberty to ourselves and our Posterity, do ordain and establish this Constitution for the United States of America.

ARTICLE I.

Bicameral Congress

Section 1. All legislative Powers herein granted shall be vested in a Congress of the United States, which shall consist of a Senate and House of Representatives.

Membership of the House

Section 2. The House of Representatives shall be composed of Members chosen every second Year by the People of the several States, and the Electors in each State shall have the Qualifications requisite for Electors of the most numerous Branch of the State Legislature.

No Person shall be a Representative who shall not have attained to the age of twenty five Years, and been seven Years a Citizen of the United States, and who shall not, when elected, be an Inhabitant of that State in which he shall be chosen.

Representatives and direct Taxes shall be apportioned among the several States which may be included within this Union, according to their respective Numbers, which shall be determined by adding to the whole Number of free Persons, including those bound to Service for a Term of Years, and excluding Indians not taxed, three fifths of all other Persons.[1] The actual Enumeration shall be made within three Years after the first Meeting of the Congress of the United States, and within every subsequent Term of ten Years, in such Manner, as they shall by Law direct. The Number of Representatives shall not exceed one for every thirty Thousand, but each State shall have at Least one Representative; and until such enumeration shall be made, the State of New Hampshire shall be entitled to chuse three, Massachusetts eight, Rhode-Island and Providence Plantations one, Connecticut five, New-York six, New Jersey four,

---

[1] Changed by the Fourteenth Amendment, section 2.

NOTE: The topical headings are not part of the original Constitution. Excluding the Preamble and Closing, those portions set in italic type have been superseded or changed by later amendments.

Pennsylvania eight, Delaware one, Maryland six, Virginia ten, North Carolina five, South Carolina five, and Georgia three.

When vacancies happen in the Representation from any State, the Executive Authority thereof shall issue Writs of Election to fill such Vacancies.

Power to impeach

The House of Representatives shall chuse their Speaker and other Officers; and shall have the sole Power of Impeachment.

Membership of the Senate

Section 3. The Senate of the United States shall be composed of two Senators from each State, *chosen by the Legislature thereof,*[2] for six Years; and each Senator shall have one Vote.

Immediately after they shall be assembled in Consequence of the first Election, they shall be divided as equally as may be into three Classes. The Seats of the Senators of the first class shall be vacated at the Expiration of the second Year, of the second Class at the Expiration of the fourth Year, and of the third Class at the Expiration of the sixth Year, so that one third may be chosen every second Year; *and if Vacancies happen by Resignation, or otherwise, during the Recess of the Legislature of any State, the Executive thereof may make temporary Appointments until the next Meeting of the Legislature, which shall then fill such Vacancies.*[3]

No Person shall be a Senator who shall not have attained to the Age of thirty Years, and been nine Years a Citizen of the United States, and who shall not, when elected, be an Inhabitant of that State for which he shall be chosen.

The Vice President of the United States shall be President of the Senate, but shall have no Vote, unless they be equally divided.

The Senate shall chuse their other Officers, and also a President pro tempore, in the Absence of the Vice President, or when he shall exercise the Office of President of the United States.

Power to try impeachments

The Senate shall have the sole Power to try all Impeachments. When sitting for that Purpose, they shall be on Oath or Affirmation. When the President of the United States is tried the Chief Justice shall preside: And no Person shall be convicted without the Concurrence of two thirds of the Members present.

Judgment in Cases of Impeachment shall not extend further than to removal from Office, and disqualification to hold and enjoy any Office of honor, Trust or Profit under the United States: but the Party convicted shall nevertheless be liable and subject to Indictment, Trial, Judgment and Punishment, according to Law.

Laws governing elections

Section 4. The Times, Places and Manner of holding Elections for Senators and Representatives, shall be prescribed in each State by the Legislature thereof; but the Congress may at any time by Law make or alter such Regulations, except as to the Places of chusing Senators.

The Congress shall assemble at least once in every year, and such Meeting shall be on the *first Monday in December, unless they shall by Law appoint a different Day.*[4]

Rules of Congress

Section 5. Each House shall be the Judge of Elections, Returns and Qualifications of its own Members, and a Majority of each shall constitute a Quorum to do Business; but a smaller Number may adjourn from day to day, and may be

---

[2] Changed by the Seventeenth Amendment.
[3] Changed by the Seventeenth Amendment.
[4] Changed by the Twentieth Amendment, section 2.

authorized to compel the Attendance of absent Members, in such Manner, and under such Penalties as each House may provide.

Each House may determine the Rules of its Proceedings, punish its members for disorderly Behaviour, and, with the Concurrence of two thirds, expel a Member.

Each House shall keep a Journal of its Proceedings, and from time to time publish the same, excepting such Parts as may in their Judgment require Secrecy; and the Yeas and Nays of the Members of either House on any question shall, at the Desire of one fifth of those Present, be entered on the Journal.

Neither House, during the Session of Congress, shall, without the Consent of the other, adjourn for more than three days, nor to any other Place than that in which the two Houses shall be sitting.

Salaries and immunities of members

Section 6. The Senators and Representatives shall receive a Compensation for their Services, to be ascertained by Law, and paid out of the Treasury of the United States. They shall in all Cases, except Treason, Felony and Breach of the Peace, be privileged fom Arrest during their Attendance at the Session of their respective Houses, and in going to and returning from the same; and for any Speech or Debate in either House, they shall not be questioned in any other Place.

Bar on members of Congress holding federal appointive office

No Senator or Representative shall, during the Time for which he was elected, be appointed to any civil Office under the Authority of the United States, which shall have been created, or the Emoluments whereof shall have been encreased during such time; and no Person holding any Office under the United States, shall be a Member of either House during his Continuance in Office.

Money bills originate in House

Section 7. All Bills for raising Revenue shall originate in the House of Representatives; but the Senate may propose or concur with Amendments as on other Bills.

Procedure for enacting laws; veto power

Every Bill which shall have passed the House of Representatives and the Senate, shall, before it become a Law, be presented to the President of the United States; If he approve he shall sign it, but if not he shall return it, with his Objections to that House in which it shall have originated, who shall enter the Objections at large on their Journal, and proceed to reconsider it. If after such Reconsideration two thirds of that House shall agree to pass the Bill, it shall be sent, together with the Objections, to the other House, by which it shall likewise be reconsidered, and if approved by two thirds of that House, it shall become a Law. But in all such Cases the Votes of both Houses shall be determined by yeas and Nays, and the Names of the Persons voting for and against the Bill shall be entered on the Journal of each House respectively. If any Bill shall not be returned by the President within ten Days (Sundays excepted) after it shall have been presented to him, the Same shall be a Law, in like Manner as if he had signed it, unless the Congress by their Adjournment prevent its Return, in which Case it shall not be a Law.

Every Order, Resolution, or Vote to which the Concurrence of the Senate and House of Representatives may be necessary (except on a question of Adjournment) shall be presented to the President of the United States; and before the Same shall take Effect, shall be approved by him, or being disapproved by him, shall be repassed by two thirds of the Senate and House of Representatives, according to the Rules and Limitations prescribed in the Case of a Bill.

Powers of Congress:
—taxing and spending

Section 8. The Congress shall have Power To lay and collect taxes, Duties, Imposts and Excises, to pay the Debts and provide for the common Defence and general Welfare of the United States; but all Duties, Imposts and Excises shall be uniform throughout the United States.

—borrowing	To borrow Money on the credit of the United States;
—regulation of commerce	To regulate Commerce with foreign Nations, and among the several States, and with the Indian Tribes;
—naturalization and bankruptcy	To establish an uniform Rule of Naturalization, and uniform Laws on the subject of Bankruptcies throughout the United States;
—money	To coin Money, regulate the Value thereof, and of foreign Coin, and fix the Standard of Weights and Measures;
—counterfeiting	To provide for the Punishment of counterfeiting the Securities and current Coin of the United States;
—post office	To establish Post Offices and post Roads;
—patents and copyrights	To promote the Progress of Science and useful Arts, by securing for limited Times to Authors and Inventors the exclusive Right to their respective Writings and Discoveries;
—create courts	To constitute Tribunals inferior to the Supreme Court;
—punish piracies	To define and punish Piracies and Felonies committed on the high Seas, and Offences against the Law of Nations;
—declare war	To declare War, grant Letters of Marque and Reprisal, and make Rules concerning Captures on Land and Water;
—create army and navy	To raise and support Armies, but no Appropriation of Money to that Use shall be for a longer Term than two Years;
	To provide and maintain a Navy;
	To make Rules for the Government and Regulation of the land and naval Forces;
—call the militia	To provide for calling forth the Militia to execute the Laws of the Union, suppress Insurrections and repel Invasions;
	To provide for organizing, arming, and disciplining, the Militia, and for governing such Part of them as may be employed in the Service of the United States, reserving to the States respectively, the Appointment of the Officers, and the Authority of training the Militia according to the discipline prescribed by Congress;
—govern District of Columbia	To exercise exclusive Legislation in all Cases whatsoever, over such District (not exceeding ten Miles square) as may, by Cession of Particular States, and the Acceptance of Congress, become the Seat of the Government of the United States, and to exercise like Authority over all Places purchased by the Consent of the Legislature of the State in which the Same shall be, for the Erection of Forts, Magazines, Arsenals, dock-Yards and other needful Buildings;—And
—"necessary-and-proper" clause	To make all Laws which shall be necessary and proper for carrying into Execution the foregoing Powers, and all other Powers vested by this Constitution in the Government of the United States, or in any Department or Officer thereof.
Restrictions on powers of Congress	**Section 9.** The Migration or Importation of such Persons as any of the States now existing shall think proper to admit, shall not be prohibited by the Congress prior to the Year one thousand eight hundred and eight, but a Tax or duty may be imposed on such Importation, not exceeding ten dollars for each Person.
—slave trade	
—habeas corpus	The Privilege of the Writ of Habeas Corpus shall not be suspended, unless when in Cases of Rebellion or Invasion the public Safety may require it.
—no bill of attainder or ex post facto law	No bill of Attainder or ex post facto Law shall be passed.
	No Capitation, or other direct, Tax shall be laid, *unless in Proportion to the Census or Enumeration herein before directed to be taken.*[5]

[5] Changed by the Sixteenth Amendment.

No Tax or Duty shall be laid on Articles exported from any State.

No Preference shall be given by any Regulation of Commerce or Revenue to the Ports of one State over those of another; nor shall Vessels bound to, or from, one State, be obliged to enter, clear or pay Duties in another.

No Money shall be drawn from the Treasury, but in Consequence of Appropriations made by Law; and a regular Statement and Account of the Receipts and Expenditures of all public Money shall be published from time to time.

No Title of Nobility shall be granted by the United States: And no Person holding any Office of Profit or Trust under them, shall, without the Consent of the Congress, accept of any present, Emolument, Office, or Title, of any kind whatever, from any King, Prince, or foreign State.

Section 10. No State shall enter into any Treaty, Alliance, or Confederation; grant Letters of Marque and Reprisal; coin Money; emit Bills of Credit; make any Thing but gold and silver Coin a Tender in Payment of Debts; pass any Bill of Attainder, ex post facto Law, or Law impairing the Obligation of Contracts, or grant any Title of Nobility.

No State shall, without the Consent of Congress, lay any Imposts or Duties on Imports or Exports, except what may be absolutely necessary for executing its inspection Laws: and the net Produce of all Duties and Imposts, laid by any State on Imports or Exports, shall be for the Use of the Treasury of the United States; and all such Laws shall be subject to the Revision and Controul of the Congress.

No State shall, without the Consent of Congress, lay any Duty of Tonnage, keep Troops, or Ships of War in time of Peace, enter into any Agreement or Compact with another State, or with a foreign Power, or engage in War, unless actually invaded, or in such imminent Danger as will not admit of delay.

ARTICLE II.

Section 1. The executive Power shall be vested in a President of the United States of America. He shall hold his Office during the Term of four Years, and, together with the Vice President, chosen for the same Term, be elected, as follows

Each State shall appoint, in such Manner as the Legislature thereof may direct, a Number of Electors, equal to the whole Number of Senators and Representatives to which the State may be entitled in the Congress: but no Senator or Representative, or Person holding an Office of Trust or Profit under the United States, shall be appointed an Elector.

The Electors shall meet in their respective States, and vote by Ballot for two Persons, of whom one at least shall not be an Inhabitant of the same State with themselves. And they shall make a List of all the Persons voted for, and of the Number of Votes for each; which List they shall sign and certify, and transmit sealed to the Seat of the Government of the United States, directed to the President of the Senate. The President of the Senate shall, in the Presence of the Senate and House of Representatives, open all the Certificates, and the Votes shall then be counted. The Person having the greatest Number of Votes shall be the President, if such Number be a Majority of the whole Number of Electors appointed; and if there be more than one who have such Majority, and have an equal Number of Votes, then the House of Representatives shall immediately chuse by Ballot one of them for President; and if no Person have a Majority, then from the five highest on the List the said House shall in like Manner chuse the President. But in chusing the President, the Votes shall be taken by States, the Representation from each State having one Vote; a quorum for this Purpose shall consist of a Member or Members from two thirds of the States, and a

Majority of all the States shall be necessary to a Choice. In every Case, after the Choice of the President, the Person having the greatest Number of Votes of the Electors shall be the Vice President. But if there should remain two or more who have equal Votes, the Senate shall chuse from them by Ballot the Vice President.[6]

The Congress may determine the Time of chusing the Electors, and the Day on which they shall give their Votes; which Day shall be the same throughout the United States.

Qualifications to be president

No Person except a natural born Citizen, or a Citizen of the United States, at the time of the Adoption of this Constitution, shall be eligible to the Office of President; neither shall any person be eligible to that Office who shall not have attained to the Age of thirty five Years, and been fourteen Years a Resident within the United States.

In Case of the Removal of the President from Office, or of his Death, Resignation, or Inability to discharge the Powers and Duties of the said Office, the Same shall devolve on the Vice President, and the Congress may by Law provide for the Case of Removal, Death, Resignation or Inability, both of the President and Vice President, declaring what Officer shall then act as President, and such Officer shall act accordingly, until the Disability be removed, or a President shall be elected.[7]

Pay of president

The President shall, at stated Times, receive for his Services, a Compensation, which shall neither be encreased nor diminished during the Period for which he shall have been elected, and he shall not receive within that Period any other Emolument from the United States, or any of them.

Before he enter on the Execution of his Office, he shall take the following Oath or Affirmation:—"I do solemnly swear (or affirm) that I will faithfully execute the Office of President of the United States, and will to the best of my Ability, preserve, protect and defend the Constitution of the United States."

Powers of president
—commander in chief

Section 2. The President shall be Commander in Chief of the Army and Navy of the United States, and of the Militia of the several States, when called into the actual Service of the United States; he may require the Opinion, in writing, of the principal Officer in each of the executive Departments, upon any Subject relating to the Duties of their respective Offices, and he shall have Power to grant Reprieves

—pardons

and Pardons for Offences against the United States, except in Cases of Impeachment.

—treaties and appointments

He shall have Power, by and with the Advice and Consent of the Senate, to make Treaties, provided two thirds of the Senators present concur; and he shall nominate, and by and with the Advice and Consent of the Senate, shall appoint Ambassadors, other public Ministers and Consuls, Judges of the supreme Court, and all other Officers of the United States, whose Appointments are not herein otherwise provided for, and which shall be established by Law: but the Congress may by Law vest the Appointment of such inferior Officers, as they think proper, in the President alone, in the Courts of Law, or in the Heads of Departments.

The President shall have Power to fill up all Vacancies that may happen during the Recess of the Senate, by granting Commissions which shall expire at the End of their next Session.

[6] Superseded by the Twelfth Amendment.
[7] Modified by the Twenty-fifth Amendment.

Relations of president with Congress	**Section 3.** He shall from time to time give to the Congress Information of the State of the Union, and recommend to their Consideration such Measures as he shall judge necessary and expedient; he may, on extraordinary Occasions, convene both Houses, or either of them, and in Case of Disagreement between them, with Respect to the Time of Adjournment, he may adjourn them to such Time as he shall think proper; he shall receive Ambassadors and other public Ministers; he shall take Care that the Laws be faithfully executed, and shall Commission all the Officers of the United States.
Impeachment	**Section 4.** The President, Vice President and all civil Officers of the United States, shall be removed from Office on Impeachment for, and Conviction of, Treason, Bribery, or other high Crimes and Misdemeanors.

ARTICLE III.

Federal courts	**Section 1.** The judicial Power of the United States, shall be vested in one supreme Court, and in such inferior Courts as the Congress may from time to time ordain and establish. The Judges, both of the supreme and inferior Courts, shall hold their Offices during good Behaviour, and shall, at stated Times, receive for their Services, a Compensation, which shall not be diminished during their Continuance in Office.
Jurisdiction of courts	**Section 2.** The judicial Power shall extend to all Cases, in Law and Equity, arising under this Constitution, the Laws of the United States, and Treaties made, or which shall be made, under their Authority;—to all Cases affecting Ambassadors, other public Ministers and Consuls;—to all Cases of admiralty and maritime Jurisdiction;—to Controversies to which the United States shall be a Party;—to Controversies between two or more States;—*between a State and Citizens of another State;*[8]—between Citizens of different States;—between Citizens of the same State claiming Lands under Grants of different States, and between a State, or the Citizens thereof, and foreign States, Citizens or Subjects.
—*original* —*appellate*	In all Cases affecting Ambassadors, other public Ministers and Consuls, and those in which a State shall be Party, the supreme Court shall have original Jurisdiction. In all the other Cases before mentioned, the supreme Court shall have appellate Jurisdiction, both as to Law and Fact, with such Exceptions, and under such Regulations as the Congress shall make.
	The Trial of all Crimes, except in Cases of Impeachment, shall be by Jury; and such Trial shall be held in the State where the said Crimes shall have been committed; but when not committed within any State, the Trial shall be at such Place or Places as the Congress may by Law have directed.
Treason	**Section 3.** Treason against the United States, shall consist only in levying War against them, or in adhering to their Enemies, giving them Aid and Comfort. No Person shall be convicted of Treason unless on the Testimony of two Witnesses to the same overt Act, or on Confession in open Court.
	The Congress shall have Power to declare the Punishment of Treason, but no Attainder of Treason shall work Corruption of Blood, or Forfeiture except during the Life of the Person attained.

[8] Modified by the Eleventh Amendment.

Full faith and credit

Section 1. Full Faith and Credit shall be given in each State to the public Acts, Records, and judicial Proceedings of every other State. And the Congress may by general Laws prescribe the Manner in which such Acts, Records and Proceedings shall be proved, and the Effect thereof.

Privileges and immunities

Section 2. The Citizens of each State shall be entitled to all Privileges and Immunities of Citizens in the several States.

Extradition

A person charged in any State with Treason, Felony, or other Crime, who shall flee from Justice, and be found in another State, shall on Demand of the executive Authority of the State from which he fled, be delivered up, to be removed to the State having Jurisdiction of the Crime.

No Person held to Service or Labour in one State, under the Laws thereof, escaping into another, shall, in Consequence of any Law or Regulation therein, be discharged from such Service or Labour, but shall be delivered up on Claim of the Party to whom such Service or Labour may be due.[9]

Creation of new states

Section 3. New States may be admitted by the Congress into this Union; but no new State shall be formed or erected within the Jurisdiction of any other State; nor any State be formed by the Junction of two or more States, or Parts of States, without the Consent of the Legislatures of the States concerned as well as of the Congress.

Governing territories

The Congress shall have Power to dispose of and make all needful Rules and Regulations respecting the Territory or other Property belonging to the United States; and nothing in this Constitution shall be so construed as to Prejudice any Claims of the United States, or of any particular State.

Protection of states

Section 4. The United States shall guarantee to every State in this Union, a Republican Form of Government, and shall protect each of them against Invasion; and on Application of the Legislature, or of the Executive (when the Legislature cannot be convened) against domestic Violence.

ARTICLE V.

Amending the Constitution

The Congress, whenever two thirds of both Houses shall deem it necessary, shall propose Amendments to this Constitution, or, on the Application of the Legislatures of two thirds of the several States, shall call a Convention for proposing Amendments, which, in either Case, shall be valid to all Intents and Purposes, as Part of this Constitution, when ratified by the Legislatures of three fourths of the several States, or by Conventions in three fourths thereof, as the one or the other Mode of Ratification may be proposed by the Congress; Provided that no Amendment which may be made prior to the Year One thousand eight hundred and eight shall in any Manner affect the first and fourth Clauses in the Ninth Section of the first Article; and that no State, without its Consent, shall be deprived of its equal Suffrage in the Senate.

[9] Changed by the Thirteenth Amendment.

ARTICLE VI.

Assumption of debts of Confederation

All Debts contracted and Engagements entered into, before the Adoption of this Constitution, shall be as valid against the United States under this Constitution, as under the Confederation.

Supremacy of federal laws and treaties

This Constitution, and the Laws of the United States which shall be made in Pursuance thereof; and all Treaties made, or which shall be made, under the Authority of the United States, shall be the supreme Law of the Land; and the Judges in every State shall be bound thereby, any Thing in the Constitution or Laws of any State to the Contrary notwithstanding.

No religious test

The Senators and Representatives before mentioned, and the Members of the several State Legislatures, and all executive and judicial Officers, both of the United States and of the several States, shall be bound by Oath or Affirmation, to support this Constitution; but no religious Test shall ever be required as a Qualification to any Office or public Trust under the United States.

ARTICLE VII.

Ratification procedure

The Ratification of the Conventions of nine States, shall be sufficient for the Establishment of this Constitution between the States so ratifying the Same.

Done in Convention by the Unanimous Consent of the States present the Seventeenth Day of September in the Year of our Lord one thousand seven hundred and Eighty seven and of the Independence of the United States of America the Twelfth In witness whereof We have hereunto subscribed our Names,

G: WASHINGTON—*Presid*:
and deputy from Virginia

New Hampshire	JOHN LANGDON		
	NICHOLAS GILMAN	*Delaware*	GEO: READ
Massachusetts	NATHANIEL GORHAM		GUNNING BEDFORD jun
	RUFUS KING		JOHN DICKINSON
Connecticut	W:M SAM:L JOHNSON		RICHARD BASSETT
	ROGER SHERMAN		JACO: BROOM
New York	ALEXANDER HAMILTON	*Maryland*	JAMES M:C:HENRY
	WIL: LIVINGSTON		DAN OF S:T THO:S JENIFER
New Jersey	DAVID BREARLEY		DAN:L CARROLL
	W:M PATERSON	*Virginia*	JOHN BLAIR—
	JONA: DAYTON		JAMES MADISON JR.
Pennsylvania	B FRANKLIN	*North Carolina*	W:M BLOUNT
	THOMAS MIFFLIN		RICH:D DOBBS SPAIGHT
	ROB:T MORRIS		HU WILLIAMSON
	GEO. CLYMER	*South Carolina*	J. RUTLEDGE
	THO:S FITZSIMONS		CHARLES COTESWORTH PINCKNEY
	JARED INGERSOLL		CHARLES PINCKNEY
	JAMES WILSON		PIERCE BUTLER
	GOUV MORRIS	*Georgia*	WILLIAM FEW
			ABR BALDWIN

[The first ten amendments, known as the "Bill of rights," were ratified in 1791.]

AMENDMENT I.

Freedom of religion, speech, press, assembly

Congress shall make no law respecting an establishment of religion, or prohibiting the free exercise thereof; or abridging the freedom of speech, or of the press; or the right of the people peaceably to assemble, and to petition the Government for a redress of grievances.

AMENDMENT II.

Right to bear arms

A well regulated Militia, being necessary to the security of a free State, the right of the people to keep and bear Arms, shall not be infringed.

AMENDMENT III.

Quartering troops in private homes

No Soldier shall, in time of peace be quartered in any house, without the consent of the Owner, nor in time of war, but in a manner prescribed by law.

AMENDMENT IV.

Prohibition against unreasonable searches and seizures

The right of the people to be secure in their persons, houses, papers, and effects, against unreasonable searches and seizures, shall not be violated, and no Warrants shall issue, but upon probable cause, supported by Oath or affirmation, and particularly describing the place to be searched, and the persons or things to be seized.

AMENDMENT V.

Rights when accused; "due-process" clause

No person shall be held to answer for a capital, or otherwise infamous crime, unless on a presentment or indictment of a Grand Jury, except in cases arising in the land or naval forces, or in the Militia, when in actual service in time of War or public danger; nor shall any person be subject for the same offence to be twice put in jeopardy of life or limb; nor shall be compelled in any criminal case to be a witness against himself, nor be deprived of life, liberty, or property, without due process of law, nor shall private property be taken for public use, without just compensation.

AMENDMENT VI.

Rights when on trial

In all criminal prosecutions, the accused shall enjoy the right to a speedy and public trial, by an impartial jury of the State and district wherein the crime shall have been committed, which district shall have been previously ascertained by law, and to be informed of the nature and cause of the accusation; to be confronted with the witnesses against him; to have compulsory process for obtaining witnesses in his favor, and to have Assistance of Counsel for his defence.

AMENDMENT VII.

Common-law suits

In Suits at common law, where the value in controversy shall exceed twenty dollars, the right of trial by jury shall be preserved, and no fact tried by a jury, shall be otherwise reexamined in any Court of the United States, than according to the rules of the common law.

Bail; no "cruel and unusual" punishments

Excessive bail shall not be required, nor excessive fines imposed, nor cruel and unusual punishments inflicted.

AMENDMENT IX.

Unenumerated rights protected

The enumeration in the Constitution, of certain rights, shall not be construed to deny or disparage others retained by the people.

AMENDMENT X.

Powers reserved to states or to the people

The powers not delegated to the United States by the Constitution, nor prohibited by it to the States, are reserved to the States respectively, or to the people.

AMENDMENT XI.
[*Ratified in 1795.*]

Limits on suits against states

The Judicial power of the United States shall not be construed to extend to any suit in law or equity, commenced or prosecuted against one of the United States by Citizens of another State, or by Citizens or Subjects of any Foreign State.

AMENDMENT XII.
[*Ratified in 1804.*]

Revision of electoral-college procedure

The Electors shall meet in their respective states and vote by ballot for President and Vice President, one of whom, at least, shall not be an inhabitant of the same state with themselves; they shall name in their ballots the person voted for as President, and in distinct ballots the person voted for as Vice President, and they shall make distinct lists of all persons voted for as President, and of all persons voted for as Vice President, and of the number of votes for each, which lists they shall sign and certify, and transmit sealed to the seat of the government of the United States, directed to the President of the Senate;—The President of the Senate shall, in the presence of the Senate and House of Representatives, open all the certificates and the votes shall then be counted;—The person having the greatest number of votes for President, shall be the President, if such number be a majority of the whole number of Electors appointed; and if no person have such majority, then from the persons having the highest numbers not exceeding three on the list of those voted for as President, the House of Representatives shall choose immediately, by ballot, the President. But in choosing the President, the votes shall be taken by states, the representation from each state having one vote; a quorum for this purpose shall consist of a member or members from two-thirds of the states, and a majority of all the states shall be necessary to a choice. *And if the House of Representatives shall not choose a President whenever the right of choice shall devolve upon them, before the fourth day of March next following, then the Vice President shall act as President, as in the case of the death or other constitutional disability of the President.*—[10] The person having the greatest number of votes as Vice President, shall be the Vice President, if such number be a majority of the whole number of

[10] Changed by the Twentieth Amendment, section 3.

Electors appointed, and if no person have a majority, then from the two highest numbers on the list, the Senate shall choose the Vice President; a quorum for the purpose shall consist of two-thirds of the whole number of Senators, and a majority of the whole number shall be necessary to a choice. But no person constitutionally ineligible to the office of President shall be eligible to that of Vice President of the United States.

AMENDMENT XIII.
[*Ratified in 1865.*]

Slavery prohibited

Section 1. Neither slavery nor involuntary servitude, except as a punishment for crime whereof the party shall have been duly convicted, shall exist within the United States, or any place subject to their jurisdiction.

Section 2. Congress shall have power to enforce this article by appropriate legislation.

AMENDMENT XIV.
[*Ratified in 1868.*]

Citizenship

"Due-process" clause applied to states
"Equal-protection" clause

Section 1. All persons born or naturalized in the United States and subject to the jurisdiction thereof, are citizens of the United States and of the State wherein they reside. No State shall make or enforce any law which shall abridge the privileges or immunities of citizens of the United States; nor shall any State deprive any person of life, liberty, or property, without due process of law; nor deny to any person within its jurisdiction the equal protection of the laws.

Reduction in congressional representation for states denying adult males the right to vote

Section 2. Representatives shall be apportioned among the several States according to their respective numbers, counting the whole number of persons in each State, excluding Indians not taxed. But when the right to vote at any election for the choice of electors for President and Vice President of the United States, Representatives in Congress, the Executive and Judicial officers of a State, or the members of the Legislature thereof, is denied to any of the male inhabitants of such State, being *twenty-one*[11] years of age, and citizens of the United States, or in any way abridged, except for participation in rebellion, or other crime, the basis of representation therein shall be reduced in the proportion which the number of such male citizens shall bear to the whole number of male citizens twenty-one years of age in such State.

Southern rebels denied federal office

Section 3. No person shall be a Senator or Representative in Congress, or elector of President and Vice President, or hold any office, civil or military, under the United States, or under any State, who, having previously taken an oath, as a member of Congress, or as an officer of the United States, or as a member of any State legislature, or as an executive or judicial officer of any State, to support the Constitution of the United States, shall have engaged in insurrection or rebellion against the same, or given aid or comfort to the enemies thereof. But Congress may by a vote of two-thirds of each House, remove such disability.

[11] Changed by the Twenty-sixth Amendment.

Rebel debts repudiated

Section 4. The validity of the public debt of the United States, authorized by law, including debts incurred for payment of pensions and bounties for services in suppressing insurrection or rebellion, shall not be questioned. But neither the United States nor any State shall assume or pay any debt or obligation incurred in aid of insurrection or rebellion against the United States, or any claim for the loss or emancipation of any slave; but all such debts, obligations and claims shall be held illegal and void.

Section 5. The Congress shall have power to enforce, by appropriate legislation, the provisions of this article.

AMENDMENT XV.
[*Ratified in 1870.*]

Blacks given right to vote

Section 1. The right of citizens of the United States to vote shall not be denied or abridged by the United States or by any State on account of race, color, or previous condition of servitude.

Section 2. The Congress shall have power to enforce this article by appropriate legislation.

AMENDMENT XVI.
[*Ratified in 1913.*]

Authorizes federal income tax

The Congress shall have power to lay and collect taxes on incomes, from whatever source derived, without apportionment among the several States, and without regard to any census or enumeration.

AMENDMENT XVII.
[*Ratified in 1913.*]

Requires popular election of senators

The Senate of the United States shall be composed of two Senators from each State, elected by the people thereof, for six years; and each Senator shall have one vote. The electors in each State shall have the qualifications requisite for electors of the most numerous branch of the State legislatures.

When vacancies happen in the representation of any State in the Senate, the executive authority of such State shall issue writs of election to fill such vacancies: Provided, That the legislature of any State may empower the executive thereof to make temporary appointments until the people fill the vacancies by election as the legislation may direct.

This amendment shall not be so construed as to affect the election or term of any Senator chosen before it becomes valid as part of the Constitution.

AMENDMENT XVIII.
[*Ratified in 1919.*]

Prohibits manufacture and sale of liquor

Section 1. *After one year from the ratification of this article the manufacture, sale, or transportation of intoxicating liquors within, the importation thereof into, or the exportation thereof from the United States and all territory subject to the jurisdiction thereof for beverage purposes is hereby prohibited.*

Section 2. *The Congress and the several States shall have concurrent power to enforce this article by appropriate legislation.*

Section 3. *This article shall be inoperative unless it shall have been ratified as an amendment to the Constitution by the legislatures of the several States, as provided in the Constitution, within seven years from the date of the submission hereof to the States by the Congress.*[12]

AMENDMENT XIX.
[*Ratified in 1920.*]

Right to vote for women

The right of citizens of the United States to vote shall not be denied or abridged by the United States or by any State on account of sex.

Congress shall have power to enforce this article by appropriate legislation.

AMENDMENT XX.
[*Ratified in 1933.*]

Federal terms of office to begin in January

Section 1. The terms of the President and Vice President shall end at noon on the 20th day of January, and the terms of Senators and Representatives at noon on the 3d day of January, of the years in which such terms would have ended if this article had not been ratified; and the terms of their successors shall then begin.

Section 2. The Congress shall assemble at least once in every year, and such meeting shall begin at noon on the 3d day of January, unless they shall by law appoint a different day.

Emergency presidential succession

Section 3. If, at the time fixed for the beginning of the term of the President, the President elect shall have died, the Vice President shall become President. If a President shall not have been chosen before the time fixed for the beginning of his term, or if the President elect shall have failed to qualify, then the Vice President elect shall act as President until a President shall have qualified; and the Congress may by law provide for the case wherein neither a President nor a Vice President elect shall have qualified, declaring who shall then act as President, or the manner in which one who is to act shall be selected, and such person shall act accordingly until a President or Vice President shall have qualified.

Section 4. The Congress may by law provide for the case of the death of any of the persons from whom the House of Representatives may choose a President whenever the right of choice shall have devolved upon them, and for the case of the death of any of the persons from whom the Senate may choose a Vice President whenever the right of choice shall have devolved upon them.

Section 5. Sections 1 and 2 shall take effect on the 15th day of October following the ratification of this article.

Section 6. This article shall be inoperative unless it shall have been ratified as an amendment to the Constitution by the legislatures of three-fourths of the several States within seven years from the date of its submission.

---

[12] Repealed by the Twenty-first Amendment.

AMENDMENT XXI.
[*Ratified in 1933.*]

Repeals Prohibition

Section 1. The eighteenth article of amendment to the Constitution of the United States is hereby repealed.

Section 2. The transportation or importation into any State, Territory, or possession of the United States for delivery or use therein of intoxicating liquors, in violation of the laws thereof, is hereby prohibited.

Section 3. This article shall be inoperative unless it shall have been ratified as an amendment to the Constitution by conventions in the several States, as provided in the Constitution, within seven years from the date of the submission hereof to the States by the Congress.

AMENDMENT XXII.
[*Ratified in 1951.*]

Two-term limit for president

Section 1. No person shall be elected to the office of President more than twice, and no person who has held the office of President, or acted as President, for more than two years of a term to which some other person was elected President shall be elected to the office of the President more than once. But this Article shall not apply to any person holding the office of President when this Article was proposed by the Congress, and shall not prevent any person who may be holding the office of President, or acting as President, during the term within which this Article becomes operative from holding the office of President or acting as President during the remainder of such term.

Section 2. This Article shall be inoperative unless it shall have been ratified as an amendment to the Constitution by the legislatures of three-fourths of the several States within seven years from the date of its submission to the States by the Congress.

AMENDMENT XXIII.
[*Ratified in 1961.*]

Right to vote for president in District of Columbia

Section 1. The District constituting the seat of Government of the United States shall appoint in such manner as the Congress may direct:

A number of electors of President and Vice President equal to the whole number of Senators and Representatives in Congress to which the District would be entitled if it were a State, but in no event more than the least populous State; they shall be in addition to those appointed by the States, but they shall be considered, for the purposes of the election of President and Vice President, to be electors appointed by a State; and they shall meet in the District and perform such duties as provided by the twelfth article of amendment.

Section 2. The Congress shall have power to enforce this article by appropriate legislation.

AMENDMENT XXIV.
[*Ratified in 1964.*]

Prohibits poll taxes in federal elections

Section 1. The right of citizens of the United States to vote in any primary or other election for President or Vice President, for electors for President or Vice President, or for Senator or Representative in Congress, shall not be denied or abridged by the United States or any State by reason of failure to pay any poll tax or other tax.

Section 2. The Congress shall have power to enforce this article by appropriate legislation.

AMENDMENT XXV.
[*Ratified in 1967.*]

Presidential disability and succession

Section 1. In case of the removal of the President from office or of his death or resignation, the Vice President shall become President.

Section 2. Whenever there is a vacancy in the office of the Vice President, the President shall nominate a Vice President who shall take office upon confirmation by a majority vote of both Houses of Congress.

Section 3. Whenever the President transmits to the President pro tempore of the Senate and the Speaker of the House of Representatives his written declaration that he is unable to discharge the powers and duties of his office, and until he transmits to them a written declaration to the contrary, such powers and duties shall be discharged by the Vice President as Acting President.

Section 4. Whenever the Vice President and a majority of either the principal officers of the executive departments or of such other body as Congress may by law provide, transmit to the President pro tempore of the Senate and the Speaker of the House of Representatives their written declaration that the President is unable to discharge the powers and duties of his office, the Vice President shall immediately assume the powers and duties of the office as Acting President.

Thereafter, when the President transmits to the President pro tempore of the Senate and the Speaker of the House of Representatives his written declaration that no inability exists, he shall resume the powers and duties of his office unless the Vice President and a majority of either the principal officers of the executive department[s] or of such other body as Congress may by law provide, transmit within four days to the President pro tempore of the Senate and the Speaker of the House of Representatives their written declaration that the President is unable to discharge the powers and duties of his office. Thereupon Congress shall decide the issue, assembling within forty-eight hours for that purpose if not in session. If the Congress, within twenty-one days after receipt of the latter written declaration, or, if Congress is not in session, within twenty-one days after Congress is required to assemble, determines by two-thirds vote of both Houses that the President is unable to discharge the powers and duties of his office, the Vice President shall continue to discharge the same as Acting President; otherwise, the President shall resume the powers and duties of his office.

AMENDMENT XXVI.
[*Ratified in 1971.*]

Voting age lowered to eighteen

Section 1. The right of citizens of the United States, who are eighteen years of age or older, to vote shall not be denied or abridged by the United States or by any State on account of age.

Section 2. The Congress shall have power to enforce this article by appropriate legislation.

Index of Authors and Titles

Acknowledgments

p. 8 "I Have a Dream" Speech by Martin Luther King, Jr. Reprinted by permission of Joan Daves Agency. Copyright © 1963 by Martin Luther King, Jr.

p. 50 "The Founding Fathers: A Reform Caucus in Action" by John P. Roche in *American Political Science Review, 55,* (1961), pp. 799–816. Reprinted by permission of the American Political Science Association.

p. 60 "Democracy and THE FEDERALIST: A Reconsideration of the Framers' Intent" by Martin Diamond in *American Political Science Review, 53,* (1959), pp. 52–68. Reprinted by permission of the American Political Science Association.

p. 67 from *The Creation of the American Republic, 1776–1787,* by Gordon S. Wood, pp. 483–499. Published for the Institute of Early American History and Culture, Williamsburg, Virginia. © 1969 by The University of North Carolina Press. Used by permission of the author and publisher.

p. 76 from *What The Antifederalists Were For* by Herbert Storing, pp. 9–14. Copyright © 1981. Reprinted by permission of The University of Chicago Press.

p. 93 "Federalism in America: An Obituary" by Forrest McDonald and Ellen Shapiro McDonald from *Requiem: Variations on Eighteenth-Century Themes,* pp. 195–206. Copyright © 1988. Reprinted by permission of University Press of Kansas.

p. 94 "States' Rights" by Dennis J. Mahoney. Reprinted with permission of Macmillan Publishing Company from *Encyclopedia of the American Constitution,* Leonard W. Levy, Editor-in-chief. *Vol. 4,* pp. 1755–1757. Copyright © 1986 by Macmillan Publishing Company, A Division of Macmillan, Inc.

p. 100 "The Entrepreneurial States" by Carl E. Van Horn from Carl E. Van Horn, *The State of the States,* pp. 209–221. Copyright © 1989. Reprinted by permission of Congressional Quarterly, Inc.

p. 111 Excerpts from *Democracy in America* by Alexis de Tocqueville. Copyright © 1965 by Harper & Row, Publishers, Inc. Reprinted by permission of HarperCollins Publishers.

p. 112 "Why I Love America" by Henry Fairlie, *The New Republic* (July 1983), p. 12. Reprinted by permission of The New Republic. Copyright © 1983, The New Republic, Inc.

p. 128 from *American Politics: The Promise of Disharmony* by Samuel Huntington, pp. 14–23. Copyright © 1981 by Samuel P. Huntington. Reprinted by permission of the publishers.

p. 135 from *The New Politics of Old Values* by John Kenneth White, pp. 110–121. Copyright © 1988 by University Press of New England. Reprinted by permission of University Press of New England.

p. 146 from *Public Opinion and American Democracy* by V. O. Key (New York: Alfred A. Knopf, 1964), pp. 7–14. Reprinted by permission.

p. 152 excerpts from pp. 77–94 of *Citizen Politics in Western Democracies: Public Opinion and Political Parties in the United States, Great Britain, West Germany, and France* by Russell J. Dalton. Coyright © 1988 by Chatham House Publishers, Inc. Reprinted by permission.

p. 164 "Abortion: the Issue Politicians Wish Would Just Go Away" by Rob Gurwitt, from *Governing* (January 1990), pp. 50–56. Reprinted with permission of Governing Magazine, Copyright 1990.

p. 170 "The Power of the Presidents' Pollsters" by Michael Barone (October 1988), pp. 2–4, 57. Reprinted with the permission of the American Enterprise Institute for Public Policy Research, Washington, D.C.

p. 174 "Why the 1936 Literary Digest Poll Failed" by Peverill Squire *Public Opinion*, 52, (1988), pp. 125–32. Copyright © 1988. Reprinted by permission of The University of Chicago Press.

p. 182 "Voter Turnout: An International Comparison" by David Glass, Peverill Squire, and Raymond Wolfinger, *Public Opinion*, (December/January 1984), pp. 49–55. Reprinted with the permission of the American Enterprise Institute for Public Policy Research, Washington, D.C.

p. 191 from *The Civic Culture: Political Attitudes and Democracy in Five Nations* by Gabriel A. Almond and Sidney Verba, pp. 440–446. Copyright © 1963 by Princeton University Press. Reprinted by permission.

p. 195 "A National Morale Problem," *Washington Post National Weekly Edition*, (May 1990), pp. 6–7, 14–20.

p. 199 "Beyond Legislative Lobbying: Women's Rights Groups and the Supreme Court" by Karen O'Connor and Lee Epstein, *Judicature*, (September 1983), pp. 134–145. Reprinted by permission of the authors.

p. 205 "Why Americans Don't Vote" by Robert Kuttner, *The New Republic* (September 1987), pp. 19–21. Reprinted by permission of The New Republic. Copyright © 1987. The New Republic, Inc.

p. 211 "In Praise of Low Voter Turnout" by Charles Krauthammer, *TIME*, May 21, 1990, p. 88. Copyright 1990 by The Time, Inc. Magazine Company. Reprinted by permission.

p. 215 pages 205–210 from *Politics, Parties, and Pressure Groups*, 5th ed. by V. O. Key. Copyright 1942, 1947, 1952, © 1958, 1964 by Thomas Crowell Co. Reprinted by permission of HarperCollins Publishers.

p. 218 pages 163–165 from *Politics, Parties, and Pressure Groups*, 5th ed. by V. O. Key. Copyright 1942, 1947, 1952, © 1958, 1964 by Thomas Crowell Co. Reprinted by permission of HarperCollins Publishers.

p. 220 "The 1988 Elections: Continuation of the Post-New Deal System" by Everett Carll Ladd. Reprinted with permission from *Political Science Quarterly 104* (Spring 1989): pp. 1–18.

p. 232 excerpts from *The Reagan Legacy* by Sidney Blumenthal and Thomas Byrne Edsall, pp. 51–98. Copyright © 1988 by William Schneider. Reprinted by Permission of Pantheon Books, Inc., a division of Random House, Inc.

p. 236 "Non-Realignment: Republicans Dream On" by Fred Barnes. *The New Republic* (April 1990), pp. 10–12. Reprinted by permission of The New Republic. Copyright © 1990, The New Republic, Inc.

p. 239 "Defining Democrats: Party or Coalition?" by Ronald D. Elving, *Congressional Quarterly Weekly Report*, October 7, 1989, p. 2674. Reprinted with permission of Congressional Quarterly, Inc.

p. 240 "Key to Survival for Democrats Lies in Split-Ticket Voting" *Congressional Quarterly Weekly Report* July 8, 1989, p. 1710–16. Reprinted with permission of Congressional Quarterly, Inc.

p. 244 "Toward a Stupidity-Ugliness Theory of National Elections" by Lee Sigelman, *The Washington Post*, September 16, 1990, p. B5.

p. 249 from "The Setting: Changing Patterns of Presidential Politics, 1960 and 1988" by Francis E. Rourke and John T. Tierney in *The Elections of 1988*, pp. 1–24. Copyright 1989. Reprinted with the permission of the American Enterprise Institute for Public Policy Research, Washington, D.C.

p. 260 "PACs in the Political Process" by M. Margaret Conway from *Interest Group Politics* 3rd ed. by Allan J. Cigler and Burdett A. Loomis, pp. 199–214. Copyright © 1991. Reprinted by permission of Congressional Quarterly, Inc.

p. 270 from *Packaging the Presidency: A History and Criticism of Presidential Campaign Advertising*, by Kathleen Hall Jamieson, pp. 446–453. Copyright © 1984 by Kathleen Hall Jamieson. Reprinted by permission of Oxford University Press, Inc.

p. 274 from *The Spot: The Rise of Political Advertising on Television* by Edwin Diamond and Stephen Bates. Copyright © 1984. Reprinted by permission of MIT Press.

p. 278 "Party Reform: Revisionism Revised" by Kenneth A. Bode and Carol F. Casey from *Political Parties in the Eighties*, ed. Robert A. Goldwin. Copyright 1980. Reprinted with the permission of the American Enterprise Institute for Public Policy Research, Washington, D.C.

p. 284 from *Reforming the Reforms: A Critical Analysis of the Presidential Selection Process* by James W. Ceaser, pp. 99–111. Copyright © 1982 by Princeton University Press. Reprinted by permission of Princeton University Press.

p. 292 from *The Semisovereign People: A Realist's View of Democracy in America*, pp. 21–35. Copyright © 1975 by E. E. Schattschneider. Reprinted by permission of Holt, Rinehart and Winston, Inc.

p. 299 "Introduction: The Changing Nature of Interest Group Politics" by Allan J. Cigler and Burdett A. Loomis from *Interest Group Politics* 3rd ed., pp. 1–32. Copyright © 1991. Reprinted by permission of Congressional Quarterly, Inc.

p. 302 "Catastrophic Follies" by Phillip Longman, *The New Republic* (August 1989), pp. 16–18. Reprinted by permission of The New Republic. Copyright © 1989, The New Republic, Inc.

p. 314 from *The Power Game: How Washington Really Works* by Hendrick Smith, pp. 230–238. Copyright © 1988 by Hendrick Smith. Reprinted by permission of Random House, Inc.

p. 320 "Interests and Deliberation in the American Republic, or, Why James Madison Would Never Have Received the James Madison Award" by James Q. Wilson, *Political Science and Politics, 23*, (December 1990), pp. 558–562. Reprinted by permission of the American Political Science Association.

p. 330 from *Behind the Front Page: A Candid Look at How the News is Made* by David S. Broder, pp. 23–49. Copyright © 1987 by David S. Broder. Reprinted by permission of Simon & Schuster, Inc.

p. 333 "The Press" by Charles Peters from Chapter 2 of *How Washington Really Works*. Copyright © 1983 by Charles Peters. Reprinted by permission of Addison-Wesley Publishing Co., Inc.

p. 339 "The Incredible Shrinking Sound Bite" by Kiku Adatto, *The New Republic*, (May 1990), pp. 20–23. Reprinted by permission of The New Republic. Copyright © 1990, The New Republic, Inc.

p. 345 from *The Media Elite* by S. Robert Lichter, Stanley Rothman, and Linda S. Lichter, pp. 20–44, 294–296. Copyright © 1986 by S. Robert Lichter, Stanley Rothman, and Linda S. Lichter. Reprinted with permission of Adler & Adler Publishers, Inc., Bethesda, MD.

p. 353 "Are US Journalists Dangerously Liberal?" by Herbert J. Gans, *Columbia Journalism Review*, (November/December 1985), pp. 29–33. Reprinted with the permission of the author.

p. 357 "The Watchdog's Bite" by Ted J. Smith, III, *American Enterprise*, (January/February 1990), pp. 63–70. Reprinted with the permission of the American Enterprise Institute for Public Policy Research, Washington, D.C.

p. 360 "Why the Sky is Always Falling" by Gregg Easterbrook, *The New Republic*, August 21, 1989, pp. 21–25. Reprinted by permission of the author.

p. 376 "Congress as Administrator" by Louis Fisher, from *The Politics of Shared Power: Congress and the Executive*, 2nd ed., pp. 74–84. Copyright © 1987. Reprinted by permission of Congressional Quarterly, Inc.

p. 384 "Courting Congress" by Richard Rose from *The Postmodern President: The White House Meets the World*, pp. 132–139. Copyright © 1988 by Chatham House Publishers, Inc. Reprinted by permission.

p. 390 "The Prime of Pat Schroeder" by Susan Ferraro, *The New York Times*, July 1, 1990. Copyright © 1990 by The New York Times Company. Reprinted by permission.

p. 397 "Penny Talks to Folks at Home" by Pamela Fessler, *Congressional Quarterly Weekly Report*, February 9, 1991, pp. 327–329. Reprinted with permission of Congressional Quarterly, Inc.

p. 402 "Delegation, Deliberation, and the New Role of Congressional Staff" by Michael J. Malbin from *The New Congress* ed. by Thomas E. Mann and Norman J. Ornstein, pp. 134–148, 170–77. Copyright 1981. Reprinted with the permission of the American Enterprise Institute for Public Policy Research, Washington, D.C.

p. 404 "The Modern Congress' Smoke-Filled Room" by Janet Hook, *Congressional Quarterly Weekly Report*, January 19, 1991, p. 210. Reprinted with permission of Congressional Quarterly, Inc.

p. 414 "12 Years and Out" by Irving Kristol, *The Washington Post*, June 10, 1990, p. C7.

p. 416 "Limits on Congressional Terms: A Cure Worse Than the Disease" by Hodding Carter III, *The Wall Street Journal*, 4 October 1990, p. A21. Reprinted with permission of The Wall Street Journal. Copyright © 1990 by Dow Jones & Company, Inc. All rights reserved.

p. 418 "The Sudden Security of New Incumbents" by Ronald D. Elving, *Congressional Quarterly Weekly Report*, October 20, 1990, p. 3558. Reprinted with permission of Congressional Quarterly, Inc.

p. 426 "Why Great Men Are Not Chosen Presidents" by James Bryce from *The American Commonwealth* (London: The Macmillan Press Ltd., 1892), pp. 73–76.

p. 428 "The President's War Making Power" by David Gray Adler from *Inventing the American Presidency* ed. by Thomas E. Cronin, pp. 121–132. Copyright © 1989. Reprinted by permission of University Press of Kansas.

p. 437 from *The Postmodern President: The White House Meets the World* by Richard Rose, pp. 296–304. Copyright © 1988 by Chatham House Publishers, Inc. Reprinted by permission.

p. 444 from *Presidential Power: The Politics of Leadership* by Richard Neustadt, pp. 34–36. Published by John Wiley & Sons, Inc. Copyright © 1960 by Richard Neustadt. Reprinted with the permission of the author.

p. 445 from *The Power Game: How Washington Works* by Hendrick Smith, pp. 445–473. Copyright © 1988 by Hendrick Smith. Reprinted by Permission of Random House, Inc.

p. 451 from *Keeping Faith: Memoirs of A President* by Jimmy Carter, pp. 506–507, 513–522. Copyright © 1982 by Jimmy Carter. Used by permission of Bantam Books, a division of Bantam, Doubleday, Dell Publishing Group, Inc.

p. 457 excerpts from *Chief of Staff: Twenty-Five Years of Managing the Presidency* ed. by Samuel Kernell and Samuel L. Popkin, pp. 19–21, 32–34, 70–73, 103–5. Copyright © 1986 by The Regents of the University of California. Reprinted with the permission of the publisher.

p. 460 *Chief of Staff: Twenty-Five Years of Managing the Presidency* ed. by Samuel Kernell and Samuel L. Popkin, pp. 195–198. Copyright © 1986 by The Regents of the University of California. Reprinted with the permission of the publisher.

p. 464 "The Crisis and Its Cure" by Charles Hardin from *Presidential Power and Accountability*, pp. 1–8. Copyright © 1974. Reprinted by permission of The University of Chicago Press.

p. 474 excerpts from *Max Weber: Essays in Sociology*, edited, translated by H. H. Gerth and C. Wright Mills, pp. 196–8, 214–6, 232–5. Copyright © 1946 by Oxford University Press,

Inc.; renewed by Hans H. Gerth. Reprinted by permission of the publisher.

p. 476 excerpts from *Democracy in America* by Alexis de Tocqueville. Copyright © 1965 by Harper & Row, Publishers, Inc. Reprinted by permission of HarperCollins Publishers.

p. 482 from *American Public Administration: A Bibliographical Guide to the Literature* by Gerald E. Caiden, et al., pp. 4–8. Copyright © 1983. Reprinted by permission of Garland Publishing, Inc.

p. 486 from *Bureaucracy: What Government Agencies Do and Why They Do It* by James Q. Wilson, pp. 315–325. Copyright © 1989 by Basic Books, Inc. Reprinted by permission of Basic Books, a division of HarperCollins Publishers.

p. 498 from *Parkinson's Law and Other Studies in Administration* by C. Northcote Parkinson, pp. 2–8. Copyright © 1957, 1960, 1962, 1970, 1979 by C. Northcote Parkinson. Reprinted by permission of Houghton Mifflin Company.

p. 499 Lifetime batting statistics of Carl M. Yastrzemski, reprinted with permission of Macmillan Publishing Company from *The Baseball Encyclopedia* edited by Joseph L. Reichler, p. 1620. Copyright © 1969, 1974, 1976, 1979, 1983, 1985, 1988, 1990 by Macmillan Publishing Company, a Division of Macmillan, Inc.

p. 501 "Firement First or How to Beat a Budget Cut" by Charles Peters from *The Culture of Bureaucracy* ed. by Charles Peters and Michael Nelson, pp. 11–15. Reprinted with permission from The Washington Monthly. Copyright by The Washington Monthly Company, 1611 Connecticut Avenue, N.W., Washington, D.C. 20009.

p. 503 "A Cost-Benefit Blend That's Hard to Swallow" by John H. Cushman, Jr., *The New York Times*, June 21, 1990. Copyright © 1990 by The New York Times Company. Reprinted by permission.

p. 504 from *A Rumor of War* by Philip Caputo, pp. 165–169. Copyright © 1977 by Philip Caputo. Reprinted by permission of Henry Holt and Company, Inc.

p. 520 "Observation: The Constitution and the Federal District Judge" by Frank M. Johnson, pp. 903–916. Published originally in *54 Texas Law Review* (1976). Copyright © 1976 by the Texas Law Review Association. Reprinted by permission.

p. 525 from *The Courts and Social Policy* by Donald L. Horowitz, pp. 33–36. Copyright © 1977. Reprinted by permission of The Brookings Institution.

p. 542 "Law Clerks in the Chambers," reprinted from *Storm Center: The Supreme Court in American Politics*, Second Edition, by David M. O'Brien, pp. 159–170, by permission of W. W. Norton & Company, Inc. Copyright © 1990, 1986 by David M. O'Brien.

p. 555 "Judicial Activism: Even on the Right, It's Wrong" by Lino Graglia, *The Public Interest, No. 95*, (Spring 1989), pp. 57–74. Reprinted with the permission of the author.

p. 565 "Ideas, Institutions, and the Policies of Governments: A Comparative Analysis: Part III" by Anthony King, *British Journal of Political Science 3*, (1973), pp. 409–423. Copyright © 1973. Reprinted with the permission of Cambridge University Press.

p. 572 from *Congress and Its Members* by Roger H. Davidson and Walter J. Oleszek 3rd ed., pp. 365–377. Copyright © 1990. Reprinted by permission of Congressional Quarterly, Inc.

p. 581 "The Impact of Budget Reform on Presidential and Congressional Governance" by James A. Thurber from *Divided Democracy: Cooperation and Conflict Between the President and Congress*, pp. 145–170. Copyright 1991. Reprinted by permission of Congressional Quarterly, Inc.

p. 588 "The REAL Economy" by Robert B. Reich, *Atlantic Monthly*, (February 1991), pp. 35–52. Reprinted by permission of Professor Robert B. Reich, Professor of political economy and management at Harvard University.

p. 590 "Reagan's Legacy Needs No Slogan" by Robert J. Samuelson, *Newsweek*, January 11, 1989. Reprinted with permission of the author.

p. 591 "I Had a Dream" by Hendrik Hertzberg, *The New Republic*, (February 1989), p. 4. Reprinted by permission of The New Republic. Copyright © 1989, The New Republic, Inc.

p. 604 Reprinted from *America's Hidden Success: A Reassessment of Public Policy From Kennedy to Reagan*, revised by John E. Schwarz, pp. 21–36, by permission of W. W. Norton & Company, Inc. Copyright © 1988, 1983 by John E. Schwarz.

p. 611 from *Losing Ground: American Social Policy, 1950–1980* by Charles Murray, pp. 136–142, 157–162. Copyright © 1984 by Charles Murray. Reprinted by permission of Basic Books, a division of HarperCollins Publishers.

p. 621 Reprinted from *On Liberty by John Stuart Mill*, A Norton Critical Edition, edited by David Spitz, pp. 50–69, by permission of W. W. Norton & Company, Inc. Copyright © 1975 by W. W. Norton & Company, Inc.

p. 633 from *In Defense of American Liberties: A History of the ACLU* by Samuel Walker, pp. 3–7. Copyright © 1990 by Samuel Walker. Reprinted by permission of Oxford University Press, Inc.

p. 672 from *Promises To Keep: African-Americans and the Constitutional Order* by Donald G. Nieman, pp. 162–176. Copyright © 1991 by Oxford University Press, Inc. Reprinted by permission.

p. 638 "A Younger Generation of Black Politicians Challenges Its Elders" by Rob Gurwitt, *Governing*, (February 1990), pp. 29–33. Reprinted with permission of Governing Magazine. Copyright © 1990.

p. 690 "Bakke's Case: Are Quotas Really Unfair?" reprinted by permission of the publishers of *A Matter of Principle* by Ronald Dworkin, pp. 293–303. Harvard University Press. Copyright © 1977, 1978 by Ronald Dworkin.

p. 697 "From Equal Opportunity to Affirmative Action" by Thomas Sowell from *Civil Rights: Rhetoric or Reality*, pp. 37–48. Copyright © 1984, reprinted by permission of William Morrow & Co., Inc. Publishers, New York.

p. 677 "The March on Washington, 1963" from *Voices of Freedom* by Henry Hampton and Steve Fayer, pp. 161–170. Copyright © 1990 by Blackside, Inc. Used by permission of Bantam Books, a division of Bantam, Doubleday, Dell Publishing Group, Inc.

p. 705 from *Democracy in America* by Alexis de Tocqueville. Copyright © 1965 by Harper & Row, Publishers, Inc. Reprinted by permission of HarperCollins Publishers.

p. 710 "America's New Special Relationships" by Peter Tarnoff. Reprinted by permission of *Foreign Affairs*, (Summer 1990), pp. 67–80. Copyright © 1990 by the Council on Foreign Relations, Inc.

p. 715 "Public Opinion and Foreign Policy: A Pragmatic View" by Norman A. Graebner, Chapter 1 in Don C. Piper and Ronald J. Terchek, eds., *Interaction: Foreign Policy and Public Policy*. Copyright © 1983. Reprinted with the permission of the American Enterprise Institute for Public Policy Research, Washington, D.C.

p. 724 "Opertion Desert Norm" by C. D. B. Bryan, *The New Republic*, (March 1991), pp. 20–27. Copyright © 1990 by C.

D. B. Bryan. Reprinted by permission of Brandt & Brandt Literary Agents, Inc.

p. 734 "Why the War Was Immoral" by Hendrick Hertzberg, *The New Republic*, (April 1985), pp. 13–16. Reprinted by permission of The New Republic. Copyright © 1985, The New Republic, Inc.

p. 738 "My Change of Heart" by Fred Barnes, *The New Republic*, (April 1985), pp. 11–12. Reprinted by permission of The New Republic. Copyright © 1985, The New Republic, Inc.

p. 740 "Done. A Short, Persuasive Lesson in Warfare" by R. W. Apple, *The New York Times*, March 3, 1991. Copyright © 1991 by The New York Times Company. Reprinted by permission.